HANDBOOK OF RESEARCH ON THE EDUCATION OF YOUNG CHILDREN

The *Handbook of Research on the Education of Young Children* is the essential reference on research on early childhood education throughout the world. This singular resource provides a comprehensive overview of important contemporary issues as well as the information necessary to make informed judgments about these issues. The field has changed significantly since the publication of the second edition, and this third edition of the handbook takes care to address the entirety of vital new developments.

A valuable tool for all those who work and study in the field of early childhood education, this volume addresses critical, cutting edge research on child development, curriculum, policy, and research and evaluation strategies. With a multitude of new and updated chapters, The *Handbook of Research on the Education of Young Children,* third edition, makes the expanding knowledge base related to early childhood education readily available and accessible.

Olivia N. Saracho is Professor of Education in the Department of Teaching and Learning, Policy and Leadership at the University of Maryland.

Bernard Spodek is Professor Emeritus of Early Childhood Education at the University of Illinois.

HANDBOOK OF RESEARCH ON THE EDUCATION OF YOUNG CHILDREN

THIRD EDITION

Edited by

Olivia N. Saracho with Bernard Spodek

Routledge
Taylor & Francis Group

NEW YORK AND LONDON

Third edition published 2013
by Routledge
711 Third Avenue, New York, NY 10017

Simultaneously published in the UK
by Routledge
2 Park Square, Milton Park, Abingdon, Oxon OX14 4RN

Routledge is an imprint of the Taylor & Francis Group, an informa business

First edition published by Macmillan 1993
Second edition published by Routledge 2005

Library of Congress Cataloging in Publication Data
Handbook of research on the education of young children / edited by Olivia N. Saracho & Bernard Spodek. — 3rd ed.
    p. cm.
    Includes bibliographical references and index.
    1. Child development. 2. Early childhood education—Curricula. 3. Early childhood education—Research. 4. Child development—Research. I. Saracho, Olivia N. II. Spodek, Bernard.
    LB1119.H25 2012
    372.21—dc23
    2011049635

ISBN 13: 978-0-415-88434-1 (hbk)
ISBN 13: 978-0-415-88435-8 (pbk)
ISBN13: 978-0-203-84119-8 (ebk)

Typeset in Times
by EvS Communication Networx, Inc.

Contents

Part III. Foundations of Early Childhood Educational Policy

Editorial Advisory Board

Preface

Early childhood education is a field that includes practitioners in nursery schools, elementary schools, child care centers, family homes, and other institutions. Its practitioners are referred to as teachers, child development specialists, early childhood educators, child care givers, and by other names. As a field it serves children whose ages range from birth to approximately eight years old; occasionally parents of these children are also considered as its clients. The purposes of early childhood education include education, child care, and the nurturing of development. Seldom does a single program of early childhood education serve children across this entire age range. Nor do programs for all children in this educational range look alike. Programs for infants and toddlers include activities and physical settings that are different from one another. Some early childhood programs emphasize the caring function, whereas, other programs emphasize the educational function and some engage in what Magda Gerber calls "educaring," which refers to caring and treating infants with respect and trust in their abilities to develop naturally at their own pace. In addition, there are programs for children within the same age range that differ from one another. They may serve children with different characteristics, for example, children with disabling conditions, children who are gifted, children who are at-risk, or children for whom English is not their initial language. Thus, although there is a coherence to the field of early childhood, programs in the field vary by age, by characteristics of their clients, by purpose, and by institutional sponsorship.

In the 1960s early childhood education was a minor field that was still evolving. Public kindergartens for children in the southeast or the central parts of the United States were not available. There were limited teacher preparation programs in colleges or universities at that time. In addition, community colleges had not been established. In 1964, the National Association for Nursery Education (NANE) became the National Association for the Education of Young Children (NAEYC) with less than 1500 members throughout the United States, although there were many more members of local and regional groups that later became affiliates of NAEYC. The Association for Childhood Education International (ACEI) was the other national association that focused its attention in early childhood education. At that time, it had tens of thousands of members, but it only concentrated on the education of children in nursery schools, kindergartens, and elementary schools, with its special focus on kindergarten and primary education. The World Organization for Early Childhood Education (OMEP) was the international organization that had national committees functioning in many of the 70 countries represented in the organization. The OMEP Committee in the United Sates was a small organization at that time and continues to be relatively small.

Although the field of early childhood education has a history of more than 150 years, research specific to early childhood is more recent. The scientific study of education is only about 100 years old, as is the scientific study of the development of children. Much of the early child development research, from the work of G. Stanley Hall through the studies conducted by the illustrious early childhood research centers funded by the Laura Spellman Rockefeller Foundation, focused primarily on understanding young children. The research attempted to establish patterns of development, the range of individual differences in those patterns, as well as the influence of various environmental factors.

As the field continued to evolve in the 1960s, we began to see the creation of a broad range of educational interventions to enhance young children's learning and development through the creation of program "models". The reaction toward these models of early childhood education, and their implementation, especially with children who might risk academic failure in their later school careers, led to research on the short- and long-term outcomes of programs for young children. Much of the early research in early childhood education programs now seems naive. Often the objective of these experimental programs was to increase IQ scores through short periods of attendance in early childhood education programs. However, this research led to a realization that early childhood programs can have serious short- and long-term educational consequences for many populations of young children.

Since the era of the 1960s, the field of early childhood education has expanded greatly. Today, the majority of children entering kindergarten have previously been in some type of early childhood education program, and kindergarten education has become almost universal. With this growth has come increased research in the field of early childhood education. One indication of that increase is the creation of early childhood journals in recent years, the *Early Childhood Research Quarterly*, the *Journal of Research in Childhood Education*, *Early Child Development and Care*, *Early Education and Development*, and *Early Childhood Education Journal*, devoted almost exclusively to reporting research in early childhood education. Not only has the number of studies in the field expanded over the years, but the range of research topics and of research methodologies used has expanded as well.

Research and practice in early childhood education are still closely allied with the field of child development. What children in this age range are capable of learning is determined to a great extent by their level of development. In addition, how children develop at this stage is determined by what they learn and many environmental factors including education and cultural contexts. As a result, practice and research in early childhood education are informed by and related to child development research.

Whereas research in the various domains of early child development has generated significant knowledge related to early childhood education, so has research on young children's learning in the various educational content areas. Early childhood research, however, goes well beyond classroom practices. Increasingly, research is being used as a basis for suggesting new social policies as well as for looking at the consequences of those already established social policies. Setting standards for programs and for personnel requires the establishment of legal requirements that programs must meet. Such standards are found in state school codes, state licensing regulations for child care centers, and state teacher certification requirements. Standards are also set voluntarily, through the accreditation of early childhood programs and of programs that prepare early childhood personnel. Such standards should not be arbitrary; they should enable the profession to improve the quality of the education offered to young children. Therefore, regulatory agencies must continually seek knowledge upon which to base these standards. Increasingly in the last several years, research in early childhood education has been policy oriented.

Just as early childhood educational practice changes, so does early childhood educational research change. Understanding the nature of the research process and the new approaches to educational research that are evolving is important to educators who utilize research as well as to those who produce research. Thus, the chapters in this volume review and critically analyze studies that use different types of research methodologies. For example, since the studies in the children's literature chapter are conducted based on a literary perspective, most of them use literary criticism or critical theories for their methodology.

The development of any book requires that choices be made in what to include and exclude. There is no way that everything that everyone might consider relevant can be addressed in a single volume. Authors who have written specific chapters have been forced to select carefully what to include. As editors, we had to make similar choices. Important areas of research and theory have not been included. Although some of this might be the result of oversight, generally, it is the result of forced choices in the context of what seemed to be of critical importance at this point in the development of the field. If this *Handbook* had been developed at another time, another set of choices might have been made.

This book is designed to be used by students of early childhood education at all levels of professional development and levels of sophistication such as mature scholars seeking research outcomes in areas to be further studied in depth as well as others searching for summary statements of various aspects of the field. It should be of use to administrators and policy makers as a source of information to be consulted in policy development. It should also be a resource to classroom teachers as a way to help them reflect on practice, acquaint them with theories and empirical research to explain classroom circumstances, and provide suggestions for what might become classroom activities.

It is hoped that this *Handbook of Research on the Education of Young Children* will serve the needs of many in the educational community. Scholars seeking the current state of research knowledge in various areas should find this volume useful. Practitioners who are trying to seek knowledge of research and its practical implications should find that this volume serves their needs. Policy makers who shape the early childhood educational enterprise through law and regulation will also find this volume useful. We have tried to make this *Handbook* both informative and accessible, with individual chapters presenting a review and critical analysis of relevant and current research and identifying the implications of this research for practice and policy development.

Bernard Spodek
Olivia N. Saracho

Acknowledgments

The preparation of this volume involved the work of many people. The contributions of the individual chapter authors are evident, and these authors deserve thanks for their careful attention to the domains they surveyed. A special thanks needs to be given to members of the *Handbook's* Editorial Advisory Board. They have provided excellent advice from the very beginning; they reviewed and commented on the basic conception of the book, they made suggestions about topics to be covered and about scholars who might be interested in contributing a chapter. Individual members of the Editorial Advisory Board also served as chapter reviewers; they carefully read drafts of chapter manuscripts and provided suggestions for their improvement. In addition, we sought out several scholars to be reviewers as well. We wish to thank those colleagues who helped us in this review. They read, critically reacted, and provided recommendations for each of the chapters. Both the names of the members of the *Handbook's* Editorial Advisory Board and other reviewers are acknowledged in a separate section of this *Handbook*. The help and support of the editorial staff at Routledge/ Taylor & Francis must also be acknowledged, especially Heather Jarrow who helped to initiate the *Handbook* and Alex Masulis who provided continued support and encouragement toward its completion.

1

Introduction

A Contemporary Researcher's Vade Mecum (Redux)

Olivia N. Saracho and Bernard Spodek

Early childhood education programs have been developed across the world over a period of many decades. Programs for young children in different countries have encountered numerous challenges and concerns. Today, society has acknowledged the importance of young children's learning. This is evident in the increase in enrollments in early childhood education programs. In 2007–2008 state prekindergarten enrollment for children ages 3 to 4 in the United States reached an estimated 1.4 million children whereas state funding for prekindergarten programs was an estimated $4.6 billion (Barnett, Epstein, Friedman, Boyd, & Hustedt, 2008). The largest increase in U.S. enrollment rates in public and private schools between 1970 and 2009 came from children ages 3 to 4 years old. In 2008–2009, approximately 49.3 million U.S. students attended public elementary and secondary schools. Of these students, 34.3 million were enrolled in prekindergarten through grade 8. In the year 2020–2021, it is projected that this population will increase to 37.4 million students (Aud et al., 2011).

The importance of young children's learning is also evident in the increases in early childhood teacher education programs at the community college and university level. Parallel to this growth has been the increase in knowledge generating activities in the field, part of which might be attributed to the general knowledge explosion in our society and throughout the world. Evidence of this can be seen in increased research activities in the field and the growth of research journals and research associations (Spodek & Saracho, 2003) as well as increases in government funding.

During the past decade the importance and the quality of early childhood education has considerably improved, which may be the result of a nationwide demand to improve accountability for schools and also funded government education programs by agencies such as the National Research Council (2008) and the Administration for Children and Families (U.S. Department of Health and Human Services, Administration for Children and Families, 2010). In addition, the Head Start Act (2007) has continued the Head Start program's focus on readying young children for school before they enter kindergarten (Waterman, McDermott, Fantuzzo, & Gadsden, 2011). Throughout the United States, the implementation of standards-based accountability education reforms such as the federal government's No Child Left Behind Act (NCLB) is generating a new set of challenges in early childhood education (Brown, 2011).

Funding increases have served to underscore the need for effective education and care for children at the earliest ages, well before they enroll in elementary school. For example, the Pew Center on the States has been conducting groundbreaking research in early childhood education to provide feedback to policymakers. Pew released a research report indicating that the public education systems in America need to admit children who are below the level of kindergarten. It describes strategies to revamp public education to include preschool children, which refers to children ages 3 to 5. This transformation is supported by rigorous research conducted by leading scholars and institutions that have determined the knowledge and skills that children will need to succeed in school and identified the teaching practices that are most appropriate for them. Pew's report concludes that for more than 40 years, prekindergarten has been one of their most well-researched public education areas. Their results support the view that young children who attend quality prekindergarten programs are more academically and socially prepared when they make their transition to public school and more likely to finish high school and become productive adults in society (Pew Center on the States, 2011).

This explosion of knowledge and the related increase in research results related to early childhood education must be more available and readily accessible to the field. This requirement led earlier to the publication of the first and second editions of the *Handbook of Research on the Education of Young Children* and now to the creation of this third edition. The *Handbook* can be a valuable tool to all who work and study in the field. Thus, the *Handbook* can be referred to as a *vade mecum* (a permanent companion) that focuses on important contemporary issues in early childhood education and that provides the information necessary to make judgments about these issues.

Knowledge of Early Childhood Education

Knowledge of the field of early childhood education is of three kinds: theory, research, and practice. Although these spheres often seem independent of one another, they are interrelated. The process of knowledge generation is *cyclical*, rather than being deductive (top down) or linear (one step always follows another). The forms all overlap. The process usually begins with a problem or issue that needs to be studied through research; this research is driven by theory and practice. The results also contribute to theory and practice, which then provide directions for future research studies. This cyclical process is presented in Figure 1.1.

This *Handbook* focuses on research conducted over the past decade or so. The decision to focus on the most recent research was made so that there would be minimum overlap with the work presented in the first and second editions of the handbook. The editors recognize that this is a limitation. They also acknowledge, as they have noted elsewhere, that our current research is only possible because of the theoretical work and the research studies that have been conducted in the past. We feel very much that we "stand on the shoulders of giants" (Spodek & Saracho, 2003). However, as a field, we have seen a significant amount of new theory building as well as the development and use of new research paradigms to study early childhood education. These are acknowledged here.

Current social and historical conditions have also aroused a more dynamic focus on the potential for practical contributions to the systematic study of early childhood education. These circumstances have led many early childhood education scholars to respond by focusing their research attention on applied problems, such as improving teaching techniques and raising the children's educational and intellectual status. Empirical investigations in these problem areas have contributed to both theoretical and practical underpinnings. By using knowledge generated in the past along with knowledge that is being generated in the contemporary scene, we can best understand early childhood education and serve the teachers and children who engage in it.

History of Early Childhood Education

The field of early childhood education has a history of more than 150 years. The first educational programs in the United States that were specifically designed for young children were *infant schools*. This program was based on the ideas that Robert Owen had developed in Scotland (Owen, 1824). Even before Owen himself came to America, his ideas had crossed the ocean. Infant schools were established in a number of communities in the eastern United States during the first quarter of the 19th century. These programs did not flourish for long. The infant school educated young children separately from their families. The idea of educating young children outside the home was counter to the family ethic of the time (Strickland, 1983).

Later, German immigrants brought the *kindergarten*, created by Friedrich Fröebel in Germany, to the United

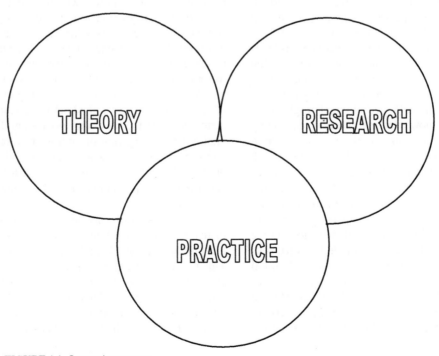

FIGURE 1.1 Interaction process

Froebel opened first kindergarten in 1837

States. Sponsored by various organizations the kindergarten slowly expanded in the United States, and served a number of purposes in addition to educating young children. By the late 19th century, kindergartens began to be incorporated into public school systems (Shapiro, 1983). Today, kindergartens are part of public elementary schools throughout the United States and almost all 5-year-olds go to kindergarten. Recently, some public elementary schools have also begun to admit children ages 3 and 4. *> Pre-K*

Other approaches to early childhood education were imported to the United States in the first quarter of the 20th century. The *nursery school*, which originated in England with Margaret Macmillan at the beginning of the 20th century to serve low-income children and their families, was soon established in America. The Montessori method, which originated in Italy, was brought to the United States after World War I. These schools closed during the Great Depression of the 1930s, but the movement was resurrected in the late 1950s and early 1960s.

The nature of the early childhood programs evolved over the years. Nursery schools and Montessori schools, which were originally designed to serve children of poor families, came to be used by more affluent families in America. Kindergarten, which was originally Froebelian, was influenced by American progressive education and reconstructed to become the American kindergarten we see today. Even now changes are taking place in early childhood education. Kindergartens are essentially part of the elementary school in America, and have consequently been influenced by, and at the same time have influenced the program of the primary grades. Today, American kindergartens are more academically oriented, especially since the NCLB Act (2001) was passed. In addition to the original Montessori method, a modified method was developed in the United States that was supported by the American Montessori Society. Similar changes have taken place in other approaches to early childhood education. The changes that have taken place over the years were the result of many influences, but were little influenced by research until the 1960s. *interesting - from the 60s grp*

The changes in early childhood education programs took place as programs originally developed in other countries were modified to better fit into American society. In addition, as American society has changed, programs for young children have also changed.

Early Childhood Education Research

Research in early childhood education has had a much briefer history than has practice. It seems that research in early childhood education has followed practice and that a strong foundation of practice was needed before research could become established in the field. Until the early 1960s even though the field of early childhood education is older, the only research on young children was research in child development. While universities often established "laboratory nursery schools" on their campuses, these often served to provide "laboratory experiences" for students in child development, home economics, and education or to provide research subjects for studies of child development. Seldom were these laboratory nursery schools used to inquire into the nature and consequences of the educational process for young children or as a way of testing new curriculum ideas in early childhood education.

Only in the late 1950s and early 1960s did we see a movement toward establishing a research base that was specific to early childhood education. The impetus came from several major changes in developmental psychology, in a concern for America's national defense, and in a concern for social justice. *catalyst for beginning to est. research base for early childhood education* *× keep up with Russia*

For years in America, the maturationist theory of Arnold Gesell and his followers was the accepted theory in child development. This theory posited that most human attributes were determined genetically and were therefore fixed at birth. It was believed that one could thwart developmental attributes by not providing a proper environment, but one could not increase a person's intelligence or modify any other attribute—than making her or him taller. Thus, any attempt to increase the intelligence of individuals or change any other attribute was regarded as futile. Academic learning was the domain of the elementary and secondary school. The nursery school and kindergarten were designed to keep children healthy and safe so that their genetic makeup would unfold. Readiness was a naturally occurring maturational process. Real education, it was believed, began in the primary grades when children were taught to read. *unbelievable*

This changed when new English translations of the work of Jean Piaget and Lev Semenovich Vygotsky reached our shore. The arguments regarding the impact of environment were further supported when J. McVicker Hunt (1964), an American psychologist, pulled together a range of studies supporting this notion in a book that had a major impact on psychology and education: *Intelligence and Experience*. Others further argued that preschool experiences could have a greater impact on human development than experiences provided to children later in life (Bloom, 1964). In addition, behavioral psychologists were arguing that environmental conditions could shape human development (Bijou, 1977). It was further found that children growing up in poverty suffered from significant environmental deficiencies that impacted on their learning and development. By offering these children early educational experiences, it was argued, society might be able to ameliorate the consequences of poverty—and ultimately even eliminate poverty. *★ love this*

A second influence was the consequence of the Soviet Union's space efforts, which took place when the Soviets launched orbiting rockets in the 1950s, well before our own space program got underway. There was a concern that we were losing the Cold War and that Soviet technology was overshadowing our own. As a result, there was a push to improve the education of children and youth in our schools. This led to the enactment of the National Defense Education Act (1958) that was designed to improve public education in America. Teachers were provided with additional education to increase their competence. In addition, a series of curriculum development projects were launched to improve elementary and secondary education. These projects were designed to bring the subject matter of the school more closely in line with the knowledge that scholars in the various fields were currently developing.

These projects in science, mathematics, social studies, and language were focused on the education of children from kindergarten to the upper grades. Among the products of the curriculum research projects were materials from the *Elementary Science Study* (Allen, 1970), which consisted of three activity-based programs: Elementary Science Study (ESS), Science—A Process Approach (SAPA), and the Science Curriculum Improvement Study (SCIS). Bredderman (1983) provides the following descriptions for these science programs.

- **The Elementary Science Study** (ESS) was developed at the Educational Development Center, Newton, Massachusetts, between 1961 and 1971. The ESS was the least structured in comparison to the other activity-based programs. It lacked sequenced objectives and detailed instructional procedures. The program included 56 independent units with no fixed sequence across the elementary grades. The ESS included life and physical science units and some units that entailed activities in spatial relations, logic, and perception. Its activities were considered to be motivating and provided children with opportunities for problem solving and understanding natural phenomena. In the activities children were introduced to a challenge, problem, or perplexing situation; then they engaged in open-ended exploration; and concluded with a class discussion. Teachers informally observed the children in order to evaluate them.

- The development of the **Science—A Process Approach** (SAPA) was directed by the Commission on Science Education of the American Association for the Advancement of Science (AAAS), Washington, DC, from 1963 until 1974. SAPA was a very structured program that focused on teaching specific science processes. It had approximately eight basic and six advanced science processes. Each process was broken down into additional small procedures for instructional purposes. All procedures were described using behavioral terms and were hierarchically organized. SAPA's content was drawn from both the life and physical sciences and was considered to be understandable and applicable. The sequenced objectives were used to evaluate individual children or the whole class.

- **The Science Curriculum Improvement Study** (SCIS) was developed at the Lawrence Hall of Science, University of California, Berkeley between 1962 and 1974. The main goal of the program was to develop scientific literacy. It had a combination of basic knowledge about the natural environment and focused on the children's

investigative ability and curiosity. SCIS had 12 units that included one life and one physical science unit at each elementary grade level. Approximately 10 key concepts were developed each year. These concepts were interconnected and were supposed to provide a conceptual framework for the children's thinking. SCIS provided children with opportunities to develop their science processes. The regular instructional pattern encouraged children to explore new materials, learn a new concept, and apply the new concept in a variety of new situations. Children were evaluated through observation during activities, through examination of their work, and through assessment with special evaluation instruments.

These three innovative science programs, which were developed and tested as part of the curriculum reform movement, began at the kindergarten level. The first two programs used Piagetian theory to justify the design of their activities. The third used a behavioral approach. Each of them ran counter to the uses of kindergarten suggested by the maturationist theorists of child development who saw kindergarten primarily as either a place for children to adjust to the rigors of the elementary school or a place that supported the development of children's readiness for school learning.

The third influence was the concern for social justice in America. In many ways, as the history of the kindergarten movement has shown, historically, early childhood education has been linked to a concern for social justice. Kindergartens early on were used as a way to ameliorate the damage to children caused by poverty or to deal with other social ills impacting on children (Shapiro, 1983). This influence was further felt as President Lyndon Johnson established the Head Start program in 1965 as part of his War on Poverty. Even before the creation of Head Start, a number of research projects, funded by educational foundations, had been developed to test the influence of different curriculums on the development of children from low-income families. These various programs were based on different assumptions about what might be considered an effective early education (see Spodek [1973] for a description of these program assumptions).

These early research projects were the basis later for a major national study of Head Start programs called the Planned Variations project—an attempt to compare the outcomes of different approaches to early education in terms of children's intelligence and school success. These outcomes were to show which curriculum was most effective for young children. Unfortunately, the evaluation of the outcomes of these various projects was controversial and no "one best system" prevailed. However, the idea that various early educational curriculums can be tested in practice and that various aspects of early childhood education are worthy of study led to a growth in research relating to early education in the United States. In addition, various research studies were undertaken to test the impact of Head Start on children's learning and development. It can be argued that this was the beginning of early childhood educational research in the United States.

Conditions that Support Early Childhood Education Research

There are a number of conditions that are necessary for research in a field to flourish. There needs to be a place where research will be nurtured or at least allowed to develop. There needs to be a cadre of well-trained researchers who are knowledgeable in their field. There needs to be financial support for research to be conducted. And there needs to be a way for researchers to share their work—to communicate with one another and with practitioners, administrators, and policymakers. These conditions slowly developed in America.

The majority of research in the United States is conducted in universities. After World War II many of the state teachers colleges expanded to become multipurpose colleges and finally full-fledged universities. Thus, a number of venues were created in which research could flourish and there was an increase in the output of research in this era, but not in early childhood education.

However, early childhood education was a small field well into the 1960s. There were no public kindergartens for children in the southeast or central parts of the United States. There were few teacher-training programs in colleges or universities in the 1960s nor were community colleges yet established. Starting in the 1970s there was an expansion of kindergarten education as well as an expansion of the entire field of early childhood education. With that came the establishment and expansion of early childhood education programs in colleges and universities. At the same time, doctoral programs in early childhood education also grew in number as did the number of candidates in early childhood education who were trained in research in the area and went on to produce their dissertations. In addition, most universities require that their faculty engage in research and that the research be published.

While the production of research in early childhood education increased in the United States, the vehicles for disseminating that research were limited. Over the years, American organizations began to sponsor research journals: The *Early Childhood Research Quarterly*, sponsored by the National Association for the Education of Young Children (NAEYC) and published originally by Ablex and currently by Elsevier began publication in 1986. The *Journal of Research in Childhood Education* was published by the Association of Childhood Education International (ACEI) and began publication at the same time. Although it was originally published by ACEI, it is currently published by Taylor and Francis/ Routledge. Additional journals related to research in early childhood education have developed over the years, such as *Early Child Development and Care*, *Early Education and Development*, and *Early Childhood*

Education Journal; these have become more scholarly and research-oriented.

There were two other organizations that have served to disseminate research in early childhood education. One of these is the Society for Research in Child Development (SRCD). This organization focuses primarily on child development research and has paid less attention to early childhood education in recent years, both in its journal and in its conference programs. SRCD publishes *Child Development*, their research journal, and has a biennial research conference. The other organization is the American Educational Research Association (AERA). In addition to sponsoring a number of journals, AERA holds an annual conference. Its divisions and its Special Interest Groups (SIGs) determine the content of that conference. Many early childhood studies are presented in sessions sponsored by Divisions B (Curriculum Studies) and C (Learning and Instruction) of the organization. Most important, there are two special interest groups (SIGs) that are specifically devoted to early childhood education: the Early Education and Child Development SIG and the Critical Perspectives in Early Childhood Education SIG. In addition, the conference of the National Association for the Education of Young Children includes a research track. Thus there have been avenues for the reporting of research and these have increased in the recent past.

While the production and dissemination of research in early childhood education has increased substantially in recent years in the United States, it has also increased substantially in other parts of the world as well. The European Early Childhood Education Research Association with its annual research conference and journal, the *European Journal of Research in Early Childhood Education* as well as the Pacific Early Childhood Education Research Association with its annual research conference and journal, the *Asia-Pacific Journal of Research in Early Childhood Education* give evidence of this.

The *Handbook of Research in Early Childhood Education* (Spodek, 1982) and the two editions of the *Handbook of Research on the Education of Young Children* (Spodek, 1993, Spodek & Saracho, 2006) were developed to bring together in one source the research available at that time in early childhood education. Since the field has changed significantly since 2006, there is a need for an update of these handbooks and one that focuses primarily on studies conducted during the last decade of scholarly activity in the field. Hence, there is a need for this volume.

Organization of the Current Volume

This handbook is organized into three sections: (1) "Early Childhood Education and Child Development," (2) "Early Childhood Educational Curriculum and Instruction," and (3) "Foundations of Early Childhood Educational Policy." This is very similar to the sections of the first and second editions except that we eliminated the fourth section on research and evaluation strategies for early childhood education. Although some of the chapters cover the same areas of research as the previous editions, and in a few cases the authors are the same, all the material in this edition is new. In addition, some areas that were covered in the first and second editions of the *Handbook* are not covered here while new areas are covered.

In the section on "Child Development and Early Childhood Education," we have the same chapters from the second edition but eliminated the one on moral development. We maintained the areas that are taking on increasing importance in our study of early childhood education.

In the section on "Early Childhood Educational Curriculum," we have added chapters on children's literature, digital technologies, science, and social studies—we found that important research had been conducted in these areas in the last few years.

In our final section on "Foundations of Early Childhood Educational Policy," we have included chapters on childhood poverty, children who are at risk, bilingual children, children with disabilities, children who are in child care, families, and the professional development of teachers. Although we no longer include the chapter on creating indoor and outdoor play environments in early childhood education, we have included the chapters on nurturing preschool teachers, early education programs in the public schools, assessing children's learning, and evaluating the quality of early childhood education programs, because we believe that studies in these areas are making an impact in our study of early childhood education.

In this edition of the *Handbook* we included a number of new authors. Among those are scholars in early childhood education and related fields from countries other than the United States including Australia, Canada, and Great Britain. This provides some recognition that the study of early childhood education is not limited to our own country. Rather, it is an international endeavor.

Overview of the Handbook

The chapters included in the three sections of this *Handbook* present current reviews of research and theory within the various areas of early childhood education. The chapters provide critical analyses of the research in important areas that are currently changing theoretical frameworks in early childhood education.

Early Childhood Education and Child Development

Much of the theory and research in early childhood education is derived from the field of child development. Indeed, there are some educators who view the field as one of applied child development. The first section of this *Handbook* presents reviews of research in the areas of child development that are of particular significance to early childhood education. Also included is a discussion of the uses of child development knowledge for early childhood education.

Although early childhood education is allied with cognitive psychology, the social nature of early childhood education means that only certain *parts* of psychology have direct usefulness to teachers. For example, cognitive research related to neuropsychology cannot really give specific advice about how young children learn in classrooms. Areas that focus on cognitive processes (e.g., information processing) can be specific and thus helpful, but only if envisioned within the social ecology of early childhood classroom life. Yet many areas (e.g., joint attention, pretend play, or bilingualism) have direct classroom implications because of the frankly social way they are framed. The social basis of early childhood education needs to be understood more fully so that developmental psychology can focus its support for early childhood education more effectively.

In the chapter titled, "Cognitive Development and the Education of Young Children," Kelvin L. Seifert's chapter has several sections, followed by a conclusion. He begins by assessing the contribution of neuropsychology (sometimes nicknamed "brain research") for understanding and supporting children's cognition. As will be seen, neuropsychology has promise for the future of developmental studies, but its current practical uses for teachers of young children are focused somewhat narrowly, in spite of large amounts of research in the area.

The next section describes several lines of research that look more directly at connections between cognition and social experience, even though in some cases the researchers that were reviewed did not present their work as "social" research. First is information processing theory—traditionally considered a thoroughly cognitive topic, even though it is in fact based on social encounters between and among adults and children. Next are studies of language development, in both its psycholinguistic and sociolinguistic aspects. Finally, Seifert presents studies that show relationships between social experience and cognitive development. After considering these three areas of research, he discusses how cognitive development can be facilitated with appropriate social encounters in the light of the practical, current constraints on the work of early childhood education teachers.

Cultural roots, philosophical perspectives, history, and scientific theories have motivated current members of societies to embrace the premise that early experience plays a critical role in human development. Researchers have become interested in early relationships and their role in children's growth and development. For many years, theory and research on early socialization have focused on parent–child relationships, but it has become increasingly clear that age mates or peers also contribute to young children's development. In the chapter titled, "Young Children's Peer Relations and Social Competence," Gary W. Ladd and Casey M. Sechler consider a number of questions that have motivated research on young children's peer relations and the evidence that has been gathered to address these questions. Chief among these are questions about how children meet peers, form and maintain various types of peer relationships, and are affected by their interactions and relationships with age mates. Ladd and Sechler also take into account evidence that reflects on the enduring question of whether it is possible to improve children's peer relations and social competence. Other central foci include features of children's lives that may facilitate or inhibit their access to the peer culture, their participation in this context, and their ability to profit from interactions and relationships they have with age mates. In particular, Ladd and Sechler focus on the potential contributions of socialization agents, such as parents and teachers, and contextual factors, including the physical and interpersonal features of neighborhoods, communities, childcare settings, and schools. In general, the content of their review makes it apparent that much has been learned about each of these questions and issues and that significant empirical discoveries have been made over the course of the last decade.

The current educational environment focuses on the children's cognitive development, which promotes their preacademic skills. Recent early childhood educational research trends reveal an increasing focus on children's school readiness and predicting their academic success. However, their emotional competence is essential for their social development. The elements of emotional competence help to ensure effective social interactions built upon specific skills such as listening, cooperating, seeking appropriate help, joining interactions, and negotiating. Successful, independent interactions with age mates is a critical predictor for the children's later mental health and well-being, beginning during preschool, continuing during the grade school years when peer reputations solidify. In the chapter titled, "The Emotional Basis of Learning and Development in Early Childhood Education," Susanne A. Denham, Katherine M. Zinsser, and Chavaughn A. Brown provide theoretical underpinnings that demonstrate the importance of children's social-emotional learning (SEL) for such outcomes. They present developmental milestones for the separate components of emotional competence (i.e., experience and expression of emotion, emotion regulation, and other-oriented emotion knowledge), as well as their direct and indirect contributions to both social competence and school success. Then they describe the intra- and interpersonal contributions such as emotional competence, particularly the ways in which parents socialize youngsters' emotional competence via their modeling of expressiveness, reactions to children's emotions, and teaching about emotions. Finally, Denham, Zinsser, and Brown clarify the importance of these issues to early childhood education, the current state of examination of emotional competence and its socialization by teachers, and possible next steps for the classroom and broader policy arena. They trust that their chapter will encourage readers to consider the importance of SEL when examining factors that contribute to later academic success.

Motor development examines the individuals' changes in motor behavior across their lifespan. These changes are a result of experiences rather than age. In 2009 the National Association of Sport and Physical Education (NASPE) revised "Active Start," a set of national physical activity guidelines for children aged zero to 5 years. In "Motor Development in Young Children," Jackie Goodway, John C. Ozmun, and David L. Gallahue provide an overview of the emergence of motor skills in early childhood using a dynamic systems theoretical approach. They discuss a summary of principles of motor development underlying the acquisition of motor skills. Then they present three models of motor development where they emphasize the importance of the early childhood years in the development of fundamental motor skills (FMS), with these FMS being foundational to engagement in future sport and physical activity. Then Goodway, Ozmun, and Gallahue describe the theoretical and empirical support of FMS development along with the variety of factors that affect motor skill development. They also provide a description of the developmental sequences of FMS along with practical applications to early childhood educators. Then they summarize early motor skill interventions using direct instruction, mastery motivational approaches, and parents as teachers. Finally, Goodway et al. conclude with "Active Start" national physical activity guidelines and a brief summary of issues associated with the physical activity of young children.

Creativity is a critical element for young children and their development. Preschoolers' creativity can be observed in their spontaneous comments, songs, play, drawings, and dance. Progressively, school aged children express their creativity in more intentional activities that may lead to works of art or novel solutions to hassles and problems. Researchers are making great progress in developing age-appropriate assessments of childhood creativity and understanding its development. In "The Development of Children's Creativity," Mark A. Runco and Nur Cayirdag review recent research on children's creativity. They identify influences on children's creativity and define it in a manner that allows adults to recognize it. They begin by reviewing two concepts (i.e., stages and domains) which describe how creative children may differ from one another. The creativity of preschool children is, for instance, different from that of school-aged children, which in turn differs from that of adolescents and adults. Next they explore domains of creative performance, for it is impossible to understand creativity without putting it into context. This is especially true at the individual level: A child who has creative potential in the musical domain may be quite dissimilar to the child who has creative potential in some other domain (e.g., verbal). First they describe these two concepts—stages and domains—because very little about creativity applies to everyone; almost everything about creativity must be qualified by taking stages and domains into account. Then Runco and Cayirdag discuss stages and domains and present the influences on creative potential and its fulfillment. They also discuss family and cultural context, for each is a significant influence on creativity and its development. They describe the implicit theories held by parents and teachers after cultural context, and review research on creativity and play, art, and divergent thinking. Because it deemphasizes products and achievements, they describe in some detail the theory of personal creativity and its importance when thinking about children's creativity. Finally, Runco and Cayirdag conclude with a brief elaboration of the concept of optimization. That may be the most general practical principle: Creativity flourishes when developmental experiences and conditions are optimal.

Early Childhood Educational Curriculum and Instruction

Over the past several decades, our understanding of language learning has shifted from a behaviorist and then information processing view toward an increasing awareness and understanding of the social dimensions of language learning and the recognition of how language development is shaped by the social and cultural contexts in which children and their families live. In the chapter titled, "Rethinking Language Education in Early Childhood: Sociocultural Perspectives," Jim Anderson, Lyndsay Moffatt, Marianne McTavish, and Jon Shapiro first articulate a sociocultural perspective of language learning. Then they examine research that demonstrates the social dimension of language learning, noting the shift in recognizing the significant roles played by siblings and peers in addition to parents. They also explore some of the literature on young children learning a second or additional language. Next, they critically examine issues of assessment of children's language in an age of increasing accountability while society at the same time has become increasingly global and diverse. Then, Anderson et al. report current trends that support children's language learning, focusing on a critical examination of research in shared book reading, family literacy, and phonemic awareness. Finally, they conclude by highlighting some persistent issues, suggesting some possible research directions, and offering possibilities as to how educators might continue to reconceptualize language education in early childhood.

During the last century, children's literature has come to be valued and appreciated as an art form for children. Research evidence supports that it provides young children with the foundation for later literary understanding and aesthetic development. The young children's aesthetic experiences assist them in all facets of their lives, including their language and linguistic development. In addition, studies suggest that children's literature has a significant effect on the young children's intellectual and emotional experiences in their wider world (Kiefer, 2004). In the chapter titled, "Views and Issues in Children's Literature," Olivia N. Saracho presents the different scholars' definitions of children's literature, discusses how children's play is reflected in classic literature, and provides an historical

perspective on the development of scholarship in children's literature. She also describes the different theories in children's literature including their controversies and reports research in children's literature from a literary perspective. Saracho concludes by discussing the implications of children's literature in early childhood education.

Research into early literacy has often been of a predictive nature to find discrete elements of literacy that may be precursors of future development. Studies that focus on new literacies in early childhood increasingly explore how the electronic world is changing the way in which alphabetic literacy is used, and how it also places new demands on children as they become literate (Duke & Moses, 2004). Recently, researchers have examined the effects of communication technologies on early literacy development. They have also developed new research methodologies for exploring these phenomena. In the chapter titled, "Early Literacy: Towards a Semiotic Approach," Susan E. Hill and Sue Nichols provide a review of how early literacy begins by considering different theoretical perspectives and their implications. Then they examine a move toward semiotic approaches to early literacy research as literacy is increasingly viewed as multimodal within young children's electronic and digital worlds. The semiotic approach focuses on context and incorporates oral and written language as well as other modes of representing and communicating meaning. Hill and Nichols conclude with a call for early literacy researchers to consider research from a semiotic theoretical position with a close observation of how children are making meaning with new multimodal forms of literacy.

Recent data suggest that young dual-language learners make up a growing percentage of the school age population. Approximately more than 5.5 million—or 10% of all U.S. students lack sufficient proficiency in English to engage academically without support. According to Goldenberg (2008), the enrollment of young dual-language learner students has recently increased 150%. Today, children whose native language differs from English make up more than 20% of children ages 5 to 17 (Planty et al., 2009). The focus of the chapter titled, "The Education of Young Dual-Language Learners: An Overview," by Robert Rueda and David B. Yaden, Jr. is primarily on the education of young dual-language learners (under the age of 5) and the acquisition of early literacy, given the latter's strong relationship to later academic outcomes. Rueda and Yaden synthesize recent national and state reports that have particular importance to this population by providing some recent data on characteristics of and changes in the profiles of young children. They do include some studies of kindergarten and first grade since the outcomes from those grades are often reported in large-scale, national investigations of young children's literacy development after preschool. While they are aware that the majority of research on dual-language learners has been in Spanish, Rueda and Yaden believe that, in many cases, recommendations for increasing access to educational services and developmentally appropriate instructional strategies can be cautiously used with young children who are speaking languages other than English. For this reason, in general, they concur with the recommendations of the National Task Force on Early Childhood Education for Hispanics (2007) to increase access to services and academic outcomes for all children.[1] These recommendations include the following: (1) increasing Latino children's access to high-quality early education; (2) increasing the numbers of teachers and language-acquisition specialists who are proficient in both English and Spanish; (3) increasing the capacity of center-based programs in Latino neighborhoods; and (4) increasing efforts to design, test, and evaluate early childhood education strategies that can strengthen the language and literacy development of Latino children.

There are several preschool mathematics programs that have been found to be reliable and effective (e.g., Clements & Sarama, 2008; Gormley, Phillips, & Gayer, 2008; Klein, Starkey, Clements, Sarama, & Iyer, 2008). These early childhood mathematics programs integrate the best knowledge that young children need to learn about mathematics and identify ways to support their mathematics learning. Continuing mathematics research in early childhood education (e.g., Anthony & Walshaw, 2009; Mulligan & Mitchelmore, 2009) and in developmental psychology (cf., Geary, 2006; Mix, 2010; Sophian, 2007) can contribute to our knowledge about how young children think and learn about mathematics, and about how instruction can contribute to that thinking and learning. In the chapter titled, "Mathematics for Early Childhood Education," Catherine Sophian reviews the research on the development of mathematical knowledge in early childhood and discusses the implications for early childhood mathematics instruction. After reviewing the evidence that children's early mathematical knowledge is an important predictor of subsequent learning, Sophian considers developmental research on the nature of young children's mathematical knowledge because that research has its roots in Piaget's ideas about the operational nature of quantitative understanding. Although research on young children's counting has undermined Piaget's predominantly negative characterization of young children's mathematical knowledge, his emphasis on children's ideas about relations between quantities remains important in understanding the limitations on early mathematical knowledge and correspondingly in identifying ways in which early childhood programs can help children develop a stronger foundation for learning mathematics. Two important limitations on young children's thinking about relations between quantities are that (1) they do not differentiate clearly between different quantitative dimensions and (2) they do not have a good understanding of numerical units. Instruction based on comparisons between quantities has the potential not only to increase children's numerical knowledge but also to build links between numeracy and other important components of early childhood mathematics.

Over the past 20 years, the federal government has been concerned with science education generally and during the past decade the U. S. Department of Education and the National Science Foundation have each provided funding to develop curriculum and assessment tools for science education at the early childhood level. As part of the nationwide move toward establishing educational standards across all grade levels, both the National Research Council (1996) and the American Association for the Advancement of Science (1993/2009) have published standards/benchmarks to guide science educators. In addition, most states have developed science standards for the primary grades and many states have done so at the prekindergarten level. Howe (1993) noted a gap between the approaches to science education in preschool and the elementary grades: the elementary curriculum was based on a view of science as a body of facts to be mastered whereas preschool educators tended to adopt a Piagetian-inspired emphasis on independent exploration of the environment as a means for the child to construct knowledge. This gap has been resolved such that there is a strong consensus among scholars that science education across all grade levels should involve students' active participation in conducting investigations, sharing ideas with peers, using specialized ways of talking and writing, and developing representations of phenomena. In other words, there has been a shift from a perspective that students need to "learn science in order to do science" to a perspective that they must "do science in order to learn science."

At the same time, with respect to science education at the early childhood level, there has been a reaction against assumptions based on the traditional interpretation of Piagetian theory that young children are unable to learn science because of cognitive limitations. Research commencing in the 1970s and continuing along various pathways since that time has shown that young children are much more cognitively capable than the traditional interpretations of Piagetian theory gave them credit for.

In the chapter titled, "Science Education in the Early Years," Lucia A. French and Suzanne D. Woodring review research and other developments in science education during the early childhood years, looking back to the early 1990s. They also discuss young children's curiosity about and natural preparedness to learn about their everyday world; the form science education should take at the early childhood level; ways of capitalizing on children's interest in learning about the everyday world as an authentic context for teaching vocabulary; early literacy and mathematics; and ways of assessing young children's knowledge of science or the opportunities they are provided with to learn science during preschool and the primary grades. They describe materials available to support teachers in science education, including trade books and three preschool science curricula developed with the support from the National Science Foundation. French and Woodring suggest opportunities for parents and teachers to support children's participation in informal science learning and in citizen science activities. Then they briefly describe the efforts of a few scholars to introduce engineering into early childhood classrooms, and also discuss the differences and similarities between literature directed toward practitioners and scholars in early childhood science education. French and Woodring provide a concluding section that notes that very little science education takes place during the early childhood years, in large part because of the imperative that teachers feel to teach literacy. There have been a number of small-scale implementations of science-based early childhood programs that have received positive responses from children, teachers, and parents; but at this point there is no mechanism for their large-scale dissemination and implementation. Recommendations are that state teacher certification requirements and teacher preparation programs be reformed to include courses on teaching science at the early childhood level, that professional development supports teachers in learning to incorporate language, literacy, and mathematics into inquiry-based science activities, and that all adults take responsibility for introducing the children they care for to science inquiry and science content.

During the last decade new technologies have assumed a major role in young children's learning. New technologies are changing the developmental landscape for young people. In the chapter titled, "Techno-Tykes: Digital Technologies in Early Childhood," Marina Umaschi Bers and Elizabeth R. Kazakoff inform and inspire educators, parents, and influential adults in children's lives to use technology with young children in developmentally appropriate ways. While some researchers have written about the negative impact of new technologies in early childhood, Bers and Kazakoff describe how new technologies are having a positive impact on children's learning and development and how young children, ages 2 to 7, are making use of those technologies in different contexts. They discuss the positive use of new digital technologies in early childhood by following the Positive Technological Development framework (Bers, 2006, 2010). Then they discuss digital technologies, usage statistics, interactive fears, and future directions for research.

Contemporary sociocultural theory is based on the work of Vygotsky, Dewey, Boas, and others. It represents the merging of several disciplines including cultural psychology, anthropology, and linguistics (Daniels, Wertsch, & Cole, 2007; Vásquez, 2008). Although the sociocultural perspective embraces a variety of perspectives, the field is unified around its effort to understand the "social formation of mind" (Daniels, 2008, p. 51). The fundamental understanding in sociocultural theory is that human thought is of a social, rather than strictly individual origin. Higher-order mental processes (e.g., memory, attention, reasoning) are considered to be mediated by cultural tools including language, systems for counting, mnemonic strategies, and modes of logic. In the chapter titled, "Social Competence Education in Early Childhood: A Sociocultural Perspective," Stacy DeZutter and Melissa K. Kelly examine research on early childhood educational programs that aim to prepare children for participation in a democratic society. They review and analyze existing research on three prominent approaches: social studies, democratic classrooms, and social skills training. They critique the current research landscape from a sociocultural perspective, emphasizing the importance of multiple foci of analysis within each body of literature, and calling for greater attention to the situation of social competence education within and across contexts. DeZutter and Kelly conclude by noting three emerging lines of study that they find especially promising. These include comparative and cross-national research, life-wide research, and the problem of transfer, which are elaborated in detail in their chapter.

Research on the visual arts in early childhood traditionally focused on issues of development approached within a psychological paradigm that was compatible in many ways with a modernist understanding of the origins and functions of artmaking in human life. In the past 30 years, however, attention has shifted from an emphasis on preservation of the innate creativity of individual children toward recognition of art making, even in its earliest manifestations, as a social and historical activity, undertaken in dialogue with peers, adults, and the surrounding culture. In the chapter titled, "Repositioning the Visual Arts in Early Childhood Education: Continuing Reconsideration," Christine Marmé Thompson reviews literature that presents contemporary research as it extends, critiques, and exists alongside earlier understandings of what child art is, what it means for human functioning, and how it is influenced by formal and informal teaching and learning. She addresses these issues of development, context, and curriculum from the perspective of early childhood art education as a palimpsest in which modernist and postmodernist concepts of childhood, art, and education continue to coexist, often in contradictory relationships, reflecting the complexity of attitudes that shape research, theory, and practice.

Movement may be a form of primary intelligence, because it paves the way for both vocal and verbal language development and uses visual-spatial, auditory, and other sensory development. The children's evolving sense of self and understanding of the world of objects are based on their reflexive, responsive, volitional, interactive, and expressive actions. Therefore, it seems that the complete learning process may be seen as a form of "dancing"—as an increasingly conscious choosing to explore and interact with data that are based in rhythmic and spatial sequences of movements. In the chapter titled, "The Dance of Learning," Karen Bradley provides an overview of research and analysis on the ways in which dance experiences reveal, support, and enhance young children's learning in every domain. She addresses the breadth of vocabulary that is used in creative dance experiences and makes the case for the ways in which movement organizes and prepares young children for learning, reveals aspects of personal expressive style, fosters community and other relationships, reinforces and clarifies knowledge, and promotes creative thinking. In addition, Bradley stresses the need for more comparative and rigorous investigations on ways in which dance specifically does those things.

Until recently early childhood music education research was mostly focused on the preschool years and on the types of activity typical of educational settings. Over the last decade this focus has expanded in two directions. The age phases of focus have expanded to include babies and children under 3 years of age. In addition, the contexts of focus have expanded beyond educational settings to include diverse contexts, including a keen interest in the home and family. Both expansions reflect contemporary social, cultural, and technological changes and how they have impacted on the lives of infants and very young children. In the chapter titled, "Musical Childhoods: A Survey of Contemporary Research," Susan Young presents research within these two directions of expansion. However, these recent developments do not supersede earlier research, which continues and is not diminished in importance and value to the field. The focus on identifying pathways of development in the main areas of musical experience for young children was predominant in earlier research and we continue to benefit from this work and to expand upon it. She also explains this and the main bodies of research. However, there are criticisms from a sociological perspective of attempts to arrive at models of musical development which are considered to be universal. New perspectives on childhood recognize diversity and variation and seek to emphasize this in the accounts of musical experience that are now emerging from research. Young incorporates in her chapter examples of research perspectives from new early childhood studies. She concludes by emphasizing the importance of understanding children's musicality and musical childhoods in designing educational approaches and then provides an account of the relationships between different types of music education, research, and practice, including the relationship between research and some of the recognized, named music pedagogical approaches.

Play in early childhood education is a very broad topic that continues to create much discussion and debate. It is also complex and difficult to define, which threatens the place of play in the field. In the chapter titled, "Play in Early Childhood Education," James E. Johnson, Serap Sevimli-Celik, and Monirah Al-Mansour address the need to explain and support play as a means of learning in early education by focusing on scholarship and recent research relating to three major areas: (1) definition and articulation of educational play; (2) discussion of importance of play during the early years; and (3) presentation of play pedagogy. They refer to recent work that shows the value of play for self-regulation, social and emotional competence, early academic learning, physical development, and creative expression. They conclude with implications for teacher education and research, in particular the need to learn more about teachers and play—how teacher education and professional development presents play knowledge and

application, and the effects on teachers, their classrooms, and the young children served in early education programs.

The contemporary multicultural movement includes children who are not part of the mainstream, middle-class White culture, including children of color, girls, children with disabilities, children with issues of sexual orientation, immigrants, the poor, and non-English speaking children. The 1954 Supreme Court decision, *Brown vs. the Board of Education of Topeka*, provides a good place to begin the history of multicultural education in the United States. In the chapter titled, "U.S. Early Childhood Multicultural Education," Francis Wardle uses various approaches to analyze multicultural education, including postmodern perspectives that help to examine issues of power and privilege. Because the early childhood field covers infants to age 8, and a large diversity of settings and approaches, early childhood multicultural education addresses a diversity of complex issues. Four contemporary influences include the Human Genome Project, increased immigration, multiracial children, and NCLB; also, the almost totally female nature of the field must be considered. Research studies show that young children are aware of differences (especially observable ones) and are beginning to process cultural messages associated with these differences. Wardle reviews several topics including parent involvement, culture and identity, authoritarian discipline approaches, social justice, the impact of NCLB on children's achievement, and the impact of inequalities beyond the school. He concludes with suggestions for future research such as program comparisons that isolate critical variables to determine their influence on the future academic success of underserved, disenfranchised children.

Foundations of Early Childhood Educational Policy

Growing up in poverty can significantly affect young children's readiness to learn upon school entry. In 2009, over one in five children under the age of 6 years in the United States were living below the official poverty threshold. In the chapter titled, "Childhood Poverty: Implications for School Readiness and Early Childhood Education," Rebecca M. Ryan, Rebecca C. Fauth, and Jeanne Brooks-Gunn discuss both how and why growing up in poverty can impact a child's readiness to learn upon school entry, as well as ways public policy can help reduce developmental risks for children living in poor families. Poverty experienced during early childhood—particularly deep and persistent poverty—has a negative impact on children's cognitive and verbal development, as well as on their emotional and behavioral outcomes, although the effect sizes for the latter associations are relatively small. They also discuss two different pathways through which poverty may impact child development, one emphasizing the role of familial relationships and parenting and the other stressing the impact of parental investments in resources to support children's development. In addition, they discuss ways public policy can affect associations among poverty, child development, and school readiness, analyzing the roles of cash assistance programs, in-kind benefit programs, and early interventions for children and their families.

The education of young children who are at risk for school failure due to poverty is widely recognized as an important factor in determining their future success in school and in life. Studies indicate that programs for these children whose ages range between 3 and 5 years, or before they begin kindergarten, demonstrate that early childhood education is a worthwhile investment. In the chapter titled, "Effective Early Childhood Education Programs for Disadvantaged Children: A Systematic Review and Case Studies," Bette Chambers, Oli de Botton, Alan Cheung, and Robert E. Slavin summarize the findings of a current systematic review of studies that compared the research on different types of preschool programs. They present the findings of a systematic review of early childhood programs for children who are at risk that they found to have strong evidence of effectiveness. Then they use their review to systematically apply consistent methodological standards to assess programs that early childhood educators might consider adopting to prepare children for success in elementary school. Thirty-eight studies evaluating 27 different programs met the inclusion criteria. Effective programs had explicit academic content, a balance of teacher-led and child-initiated activity, and significant professional development. They conclude that their findings add to the evidence that early childhood education programs can impact on the school readiness of young children who are at-risk.

Historically, educational policy regarding bilingual students has been marked by a continuing tension between the ideologies of assimilation and multiculturalism. While the education of bilingual children from age 5 years (kindergarten) to age 10 years (third grade) has drawn significant policy attention, their *early* education (ages birth to 5 years) has not (García & Frede, 2010). Key policy "players" in the education of bilingual students have included the federal courts, the U.S. Congress, state related agencies, and state level initiatives. As the United States advances educational policy for students in an ever-diversified population, the continued underachievement of bilingual children poses a particular challenge to educators who look to educational agencies for help in realizing the moral imperatives of equity and social justice. In the chapter titled, "Educational Policy in the United States Regarding Bilinguals in Early Childhood Education," Eugene E. García and Ann-Marie Wiese describe the historical trends of both federal and state policies and at the same time, focus on the emerging trend of restrictive language policies and the resulting responses (Gandara & Hopkins, 2010).

Young children with disabilities are increasingly attending inclusive early childhood programs with their typically developing peers. Within these programs, the development of positive attitudes toward peers with disabilities has been considered an indicator of successful inclusion, a benefit that typically developing children can obtain from partici-

pating in inclusive classrooms, and a foundation for positive peer relationships between children with and without disabilities. Given the importance of developing positive attitudes toward peers with disabilities, and the subsequent potential for the development of positive relationships between children with and without disabilities, in the chapter titled, "Young Children's Understanding of Disabilities: Implications for Attitude Development and Inclusive Education," Seon Yeong Yu and Michaelene M. Ostrosky address young children's understanding of disabilities with a focus on attitude development and inclusive education. They also discuss factors that impact young children's attitude development toward their peers with disabilities, such as child, family, and school characteristics. They conclude their chapter with strategies for promoting positive attitudes toward peers with disabilities and implications for future research.

Early childhood education and care is part of the national discourse. Despite common knowledge regarding the importance of early experiences, child care in the United States is still highly variable in quality and quantity, with those who need it the least likely to receive it. Recent developments in research of child care for young children have continued with nationally representative or multisite childcare studies producing copious amounts of information on prekindergarten children's experiences in early education. Additionally, there is documentation of the effects of early education on the school years and beyond. While much has changed, the importance of teacher–child interaction in terms of emotional and instructional support has not diminished; and the focus on and the definition of quality, as well as the need to include ethnic and cultural diversity in study designs continue to be expanded. In the chapter titled, "Child Care for Young Children," Kay Sanders and Carollee Howes focus on the state of child care by discussing the research pertaining to child care and children's experiences in it. They discuss an important policy movement that focuses on quality in child care: the Quality Rating and Improvement Systems (QRIS). While other initiatives, such as program accreditation by the National Association for the Education of Young Children and director credentialing efforts are also occurring, they only focus on QRIS due to the emphasis that the Office of Child Care has placed on these state-initiated movements at this time. Finally, they conclude the chapter with future directions for child care research.

All children are raised in some form of family. But families take different forms in terms of number of adults in the household, contact with extended kin, and sheer size of the group. Families differ in the beliefs that they hold about trustworthiness of relationships and in their daily practices and routines. Families live in neighborhoods that reflect available resources for healthy foods, physical activity, social support, and quality of education. In the chapter titled, "Family Context in Early Childhood: Connecting Beliefs, Practices, and Ecologies," Barbara H. Fiese describes how families are dynamic systems with shared practices and beliefs that contribute to children's well-being and preparedness to learn. These practices and beliefs are embedded in a socioeconomic context that includes cultural influences as well as neighborhood context. Thus, she proposes an ecological model (Bronfenbrenner & Morris, 1998) to situate the family in a larger developmental context.

In some cases, and at some times, families function in such a way that children's growth is fostered and there is optimal development. In other cases, however, individual and socioeconomic forces compromise the family's ability to provide a supportive environment for their children. Fiese provides examples of the effects of cumulative risk under high risk child-raising conditions such as poverty or parental psychopathology that may derail the positive family process and make children vulnerable to behavioral and learning problems. There is reason for optimism, however, as protective factors may promote positive development through responsive parent–child interactions and structured home environments.

Family life is often marked by transitions. Marriage, the birth of a child, going to school, leaving home, marriage of children, and becoming grandparents are just a few of the transitions that members experience as part of normative changes (Walsh, 2003). Several transitions are apparent during early childhood; gaining autonomy through learning to walk, asserting opinions in learning to talk, and being poised to learn when transitioning from home to school. An important transition where characteristics of the child, family, social institutions, and culture come together is the transition to formal school. The family plays an important role in easing these transitions by establishing partnerships with childcare providers and school personnel. However, this transition is moderated by available resources in the community and the cultural context in which education is provided. In the third section of the chapter, Fiese discusses family partnerships with early childhood care providers and educators and the transition to kindergarten as important settings for early learning. Further, in this section she highlights the importance of establishing partnerships between early childcare settings in light of increasing diversity in family life.

Currently there is considerable interest in professional development (PD) for in-service teachers as a tool for strengthening the impact of early childhood classrooms on children's learning and development. Professional development (PD) for in-service teachers is increasingly used as a tool to strengthen the impact of early childhood classrooms on children's outcomes. PD is a major focus of recent policy and programmatic initiatives aimed at improving the effects of programs for young children across a range of early childhood sectors, including child care, state-supported prekindergarten, and Head Start (Martínez-Beck & Zaslow, 2006). The concept of PD as the pathway to better student outcomes goes beyond the early childhood period. Increasingly, education reform is synonymous with teachers'

professional development. In the chapter titled, "Promising Approaches to Professional Development for Early Childhood Educators," Douglas R. Powell, Karen E. Diamond, and Mary K. Cockburn briefly describe an emerging conceptualization of PD that emphasizes intensity, duration, and linking content to the realities of teachers' classrooms and contexts. They examine characteristics and outcomes from research related to three promising approaches to PD. Then they discuss the approaches that are needed for professional learning communities, coaching and similar forms of individualized work with teachers, and uses of innovative technologies in the delivery of PD. Powell, Diamond, and Cockburn conclude with a discussion of factors associated with variations in the implementation and engagement of PD and identify needed directions in PD research.

Parents and policymakers express rising concern over the quality of preschools—as access continues to expand, public investment climbs, and effects on children's early learning remain uneven. Unfortunately, the quality of preschools remains uneven. Even mediocre programs give millions of parents the opportunity to enter the labor force, which serves to lift household income. But these programs usually fail to appreciably boost children's early learning. In the chapter titled "Lifting Preschool Quality: Nurturing Effective Teachers," Bruce Fuller, Rebecca Anguiano, and John W. Gasko ask, "How can preschool quality best be lifted?" Conventional regulatory approaches, where state governments intensify rules in hopes of boosting quality, show few empirical benefits for young children. They propose new efforts to boost quality. They focus on two promising efforts that aim to enrich social relationships and learning tasks inside preschool classrooms—models that are showing strong benefits for teachers' motivation and young children's growth. Then they address how these promising approaches to mentoring and ongoing reflection on classroom practice are being taken to scale within states, which includes the challenge of maintaining the integrity of teacher-development efforts within early childhood education institutions.

Early childhood education programs operate in a variety of settings, including public schools, Head Start, and childcare centers. Each type of sponsorship offers different capacities related to educational effectiveness. State-funded prekindergarten initiatives, which operate primarily in public school settings, have grown quickly in recent years. As a result, it is critical to understand the current status of such programs. In the chapter titled, "Early Childhood Education Programs in the Public Schools," Jason T. Hustedt, Dale J. Epstein, and W. Steven Barnett employ data from a nationwide survey of state prekindergarten policies to illustrate the wide variability in enrollment policies, quality standards, and spending patterns across different states. While some states serve as models combining broad accessibility, high standards, and adequate funding, this is typically the exception rather than the norm. They conclude with recommendations for promoting a more effective and better integrated system of publicly funded early childhood education in the United States.

Understanding assessment in early childhood education is a complex process. In early childhood education there are diverse contexts in which children learn and develop as well as a multiplicity of reasons for assessing them. In the chapter titled, "Assessing Children's Learning in Early Childhood Education Settings," Dominic F. Gullo discusses the assessment of individual children within early childhood education settings. He examines four areas related to early childhood assessment. First, he explores research related to general assessment concerns. These include issues related to purposeful assessment as well as concerns associated with using standardized assessments with young children. In the second section, Gullo focuses on authentic assessment. In this section, he defines authentic assessment and discusses research related to various forms and uses of authentic assessment. He describes benefits along with cautions. In the third and fourth sections of this chapter, Gullo examines assessment concerns related to special populations of children. He discusses research and issues related to young children who are culturally and linguistically different as well as to children who have been identified as having special educational needs. Finally, he proposes suggestions for school and teacher education reforms.

While preschoolers may soon begin their formal schooling years, approximately 15 years later most of these children will enter the country's work force. The recent extension of public education into the prekindergarten years makes early childhood education settings the first introduction for many children to the world of more formal learning in a group setting. These early experiences are critical for establishing learning and dispositional patterns that may affect children's interactions with classrooms for years to come. Over the years, however, no clear or coherent consensus has emerged for the purpose of early childhood education nor whether there should be different purposes in caring for or educating young children. In the chapter titled, "Evaluating the Quality of Early Childhood Education Programs," Dale C. Farran and Kerry Hofer review efforts to find measures that can be used to evaluate the quality of early childhood education, an effort that has been complicated by the very different histories and missions of programs in this field. They split the types of early childhood education programs in the United States into two types: (1) those with a caring mission (child care) and (2) those with an education mission (prekindergarten and Head Start). The original measures of quality developed to assess child care environments helped to bring attention to the needs of young children and made states aware of their responsibilities to do more than just make sure these settings were healthy and safe. These quality measures have not, however, transferred effectively to programs with a compensatory education mission. For those programs, the clear implication of their mission is that children's academic outcomes must be improved. The academic outcomes found to be most important for later school success are math, reading (language/literacy), and attention. Farran and Hofer believe that none of the quality measures currently in the field have demonstrated much capacity for identifying classrooms that are more effective in helping children learn those skills. They argue that the first step in developing effective measures of classroom quality has to be empirical investigations of the behaviors of teachers and children demonstrated to be linked to gains in those three skill areas.

A Final Note

In the first and second editions we ended the introduction with the following paragraph. We believe it is as valid today as it was several years ago:

> A book such as this is often seen as more theoretical than practical. Although research studies educational practice, it seldom leads to the creation of educational practice. Yet research informs practice. By helping practitioners reflect on practice and assess their ideas about their work, the *Handbook* can suggest new visions or early childhood education. In this way it may be among the most practical of educational endeavors.

Note

1. In this chapter, Rueda and Yaden follow the Census practice of using *Hispanic* and *Latino* as synonyms although they acknowledge that there are differences in the performance of various populations speaking Spanish, some of which they report in their chapter.

References

Allen, L. R. (1970). An evaluation of certain cognitive aspects of the material objects unit of the Science Curriculum Improvement Study elementary science program. *Journal of Research in Science Teaching, 7*(4), 277–281.

American Association for the Advancement of Science. (2009). *Benchmarks for science literacy*. Washington, DC: American Association for the Advancement of Science. (Original work published 1993)

Anthony, G., & Walshaw, M. (2009). Mathematics education in the early years: Building bridges. *Contemporary Issues in Early Childhood, 10*, 107–121.

Aud, S., Hussar, W., Kena, G., Bianco, K., Frohlich, L., Kemp, J., et al. (2011). *The condition of education 2011* (NCES 2011-033). U.S. Department of Education, National Center for Education Statistics. Washington, DC: U.S. Government Printing Office.

Barnett, W., Epstein, D., Friedman, A., Boyd, J., & Hustedt, J. (2008). *The state of preschool 2008: State preschool yearbook*. New Brunswick, NJ: The National Institute for Early Education Research.

Bers, M. (2006). The role of new technologies to foster positive youth development. *Applied Developmental Science, 10*(4), 200–219.

Bers, M (2010) Beyond computer literacy: Supporting youth's positive development through technology. *New Directions for Youth Development: Theory, Practice, and Research, 128*, 13–23.

Bijou, S. W. (1977). Behavior analysis applied to early childhood education. In B. Spodek & H. J. Walberg (Eds.), *Early childhood education: Issues and insights* (pp. 138–156). Berkeley, CA: McCutchan.

Bloom, B. (1964). *Stability and change in human characteristics*. New York: Wiley.

Bredderman, T. (1983). Effects of activity-based elementary science on student outcomes: A quantitative synthesis. *Review of Educational Research, 53*(4), 499–518.

Bronfenbrenner, U., & Morris, P. A. (1998). The ecology of developmental processes. In W. Damon & R. M. Lerner (Eds.), *Handbook of child psychology* (pp. 993–1028). Hoboken, NJ: Wiley.

Brown, C. (2011). Searching for the norm in a system of absolutes: A case study of standards-based accountability reform in pre-kindergarten. *Early Education & Development, 22*(1), 151–177.

Clements, D. H., & Sarama, J. (2008). Experimental evaluation of the effects of a research-based preschool mathematics curriculum. *American Educational Research Journal, 45*, 443–494.

Daniels, H. (2008). *Vygotsky and research*. New York: Routledge.

Daniels, H., Wertsch, J., & Cole, M. (Eds.). (2007). *The Cambridge companion to Vygotsky*. Cambridge, England: Cambridge University Press.

Duke, N., & Moses, A., (2004). Essay book review: On what crosses, and does not cross, our desks in early literacy. *Reading Research Quarterly, 39*(3), 360–366.

Gandara, P., & Hopkins, M. (2010). *Forbidden languages: English learners and restrictive language policies*. New York: Teachers College Press.

García, E. E., & Frede, E. C. (2010). *Young English language learners*. New York: Teachers College Press.

Geary, D. C. (2006). Development of mathematical understanding. In W. Damon & R. M. Lerner (Series Eds.) & D. Kuhn & R. S. Siegler (Vol. Eds.), *Handbook of child psychology: Vol. 2. Cognition, perception, and language* (6th ed., pp. 777–810). New York: Wiley.

Goldenberg, C. (2008). Teaching English language learners: What the research does and does not say. *American Educator, 32*(2), 8–23, 42–44.

Gormley, W. T., Phillips, D., & Gayer, T. (2008). Preschool programs can boost school readiness. *Science, 320*, 1723–1724.

Head Start Act, 42 U.S.C. §9801 (2007). PL 110-134—Dec. 12, 2007 121 STAT. 1363. Retrieved from http://www.gpo.gov/fdsys/pkg/PLAW-110publ134/pdf/PLAW-110publ134.pdf

Howe, A. C. (1993). Science in early childhood education. In B. Spodek (Ed.), *Handbook of research on the education of young children* (pp. 225–235). New York: Macmillan.

Hunt, J. McV. (1964). *Experience and intelligence*. New York: Roland Press.

Kiefer, B. Z. (2004). Children's literature and children's literacy: Preparing early literacy teachers to understand the aesthetic values of children's literature. In O. N. Saracho & B. Spodek (Eds.), *Contemporary perspectives on language policy and literacy instruction in early childhood education* (pp. 161–180). Greenwich, CT: Information Age.

Klein, A., Starkey, P., Clements, D., Sarama, J., & Iyer, R. (2008). Effects of a pre-kindergarten mathematics intervention: A randomized experiment. *Journal of Research on Educational Effectiveness, 1*, 155–178.

Martínez-Beck, I., & Zaslow, M. (2006). The context for critical issues in early childhood professional development. In M. Zaslow & I. Martinez-Beck (Eds.), *Critical issues in early childhood professional development* (pp. 1–16). Baltimore, MD: Brookes.

Mix, K. S. (2010). Early numeracy: The transition from infancy to early childhood. In R. E. Trembley, R. G. Barr, R. DeV. Peters, & M. Boivin (Eds.), *Encyclopedia on early childhood development* (pp. 1–6). Montreal, Quebec: Centre of Excellence for Early Childhood Development. Retrieved from http://www.child-encyclopedia.com/documents/MixANGxp.pdf.

Mulligan, J., & Mitchelmore, M. (2009). Awareness of pattern and structure in early mathematical development. *Mathematics Education Research Journal, 21*, 33–49.

National Association for Sport and Physical Education. (2009). *Active start: A statement of physical activity guidelines for children from birth to age 5*. Reston, VA: Author.

National Research Council. (1996). *National science education standards*. Washington, DC: The National Academies Press.

National Research Council. (2008). *Early childhood assessment: Why, what, and how*. Washington, DC: National Academies Press.

National Task Force on Early Childhood Education for Hispanics. (2007). *Expanding and improving early education for Hispanics Main Report*. Tempe, AZ: National Task Force on Early Childhood Education for Hispanics, Arizona State University.

No Child Left Behind Act (2001). Conference report to accompany H.R. 1[Rep. No. 107-334], 107th Congress, 1st session (2001).

Owen, R. D. (1824). *Outline of the system of education at New Lanark*. Glasgow, Scotland: Wardlaw & Cunningham.

Pew Center on the States. (2011). *Transforming public education: Pathway to a Pre-K-12 future*. Washington, DC: Pew Charitable Trusts. Retrieved from http://www.pewcenteronthestates.org/uploadedFiles/wwwpewcenteronthestatesorg/Initiatives/Pre-K_Education/Pew_PreK_Transforming_Public_Education.pdf

Planty, M., Hussar, W., Snyder, T., Kena, G., Kewal Ramani, A., Kemp, J., et al. (2009). *The condition of education 2009* (NCES 2009-081). Washington, DC: U.S. Department of Education National Center for Education Statistics, Institute of Education Sciences.

Shapiro, M. S. (1983). *Child's garden: The kindergarten movement from Froebel to Dewey*. University Park: Pennsylvania State University Press.

Sophian, C. (2007). *The origins of mathematical knowledge in childhood*. Mahwah, NJ: Erlbaum.

Spodek. B. (1973). *Early childhood education*. Englewood Cliffs, NJ: Prentice-Hall.

Spodek. B. (Ed.). (1982). *Handbook of research in early childhood education*. New York: Free Press.

Spodek. B. (Ed.). (1993). *Handbook of research on the education of young children*. New York: Macmillan.

Spodek, B., & Saracho, O. N. (2003). On the shoulders of giants: Exploring the traditions of early childhood education. *Early Childhood Education Journal, 31*(1), 3–10.

Spodek, B., & Saracho, O. N. (2006). *Handbook of research on the education of young children* (2nd ed.). Mahwah, NJ: Erlbaum.

Strickland (1983). Paths not taken. In B. Spodek (Ed.), *Handbook of research in early childhood education* (pp. 321–340). New York: Free Press.

U.S. Department of Health and Human Services, Administration for Children and Families. (2010, January). *Head Start impact study, final report*. Washington, DC: Administration for Children and Families, Administration on Children, Youth, and Families, & Head Start Bureau.

Vásquez, O. A. (2008). Cross national explorations of sociocultural research on learning. *Review of Research in Education, 30*, 33–64.

Walsh, F. (2003). *Normal Family Processes* (3rd ed.). New York: Guilford.

Waterman, C., McDermott, P. A., Fantuzzo, J. E., & Gadsden, V. L. (2011). The matter of assessor variance in early childhood education—Or whose score is it anyway? *Early Childhood Research Quarterly*, doi:10.1016/j.ecresq.2011.06.003

Part I

Early Childhood Education and Child Development

2

Cognitive Development and the Education of Young Children

Kelvin L. Seifert
University of Manitoba

As was the case in previous editions of this handbook, this chapter is not about cognitive development per se, but about how cognitive development relates to and can be influenced by early childhood educators. As before, the content is therefore selective: in spite of the importance of cognition within developmental psychology, I do not survey "all" of the research here (even if it were possible!). Instead I select and frame material according to its relevance to the work of early childhood educators. Since their work usually takes place in classrooms, homes, and other locations with strongly social features, the chapter also has a markedly social emphasis. As a result, some topics with strong research programs, such as the neuropsychology of cognition, receive less emphasis than might be expected. Others, such as information processing theory, are discussed only for their relevance to how early childhood educators might use the research to influence children's cognition. The converse of this practical idea—that educators might use children's cognition to regulate their social experiences—of course is important as well. It is acknowledged from time to time in this chapter, but is more appropriately discussed elsewhere in this volume (Sokol, Muller, Carpendale, Young, & Iarocci, 2010).

For this particular chapter, my assumption is that early childhood classrooms are busy, social places, and that teachers of the young normally rely on the richness of that social life to nudge or move children toward more mature forms of thinking. From this perspective, social experience is primarily construed as stimulus, independent variable, or cause, and cognition as response, outcome, or effect. Reviews based on other assumptions also exist and are in fact already plentiful in the literature of developmental psychology (e.g., Asamen, Ellis, & Berry, 2008; Barbarin & Wasik, 2009; Haith & Benson, 2008; Kuhn & Siegler, 2006). The alternatives are valuable to read, and I recommend them to interested readers, but their purposes do not speak to the needs of early childhood educators as directly as this chapter does (I hope).

Fortunately, there is ample research about the effects of children's social development on cognitive functioning. Most of it is founded on and continues major traditions of child study dating back 100 years (Dick & Overton, 2010; Lewis & Carpendale, 2009). The original fathers (and mothers) of developmental psychology were very aware that social experiences are likely to influence children's thinking, and they commented at length on the possible relationships. Freud described how cognitive distortions sometimes originate in unfortunate social experiences; William James speculated philosophically about the nature of social/cognitive links; Piaget noted that cooperative games were both cause and effect of taking the perspective of others; Vygotsky emphasized the importance of social mentoring for learning common conventional knowledge. The current research has echoes of all of these ideas.

The chapter has several sections, followed by a conclusion. I begin by assessing the contribution of neuropsychology (sometimes nicknamed "brain research") for understanding and supporting children's cognition. As will be seen, neuropsychology has promise for the future of developmental studies, but its current practical uses for teachers of young children are focused somewhat narrowly, in spite of large amounts of research in the area. The next section describes several lines of research that look more directly at connections between cognition and social experience, even though in some cases the researchers did not present their work as "social" research. First is information processing theory—traditionally considered a thoroughly cognitive topic, even though it is in fact based on social encounters between and among adults and children. Next are studies of language development, in both its psycholinguistic and sociolinguistic aspects. Finally there are studies framed to show relationships between social experience and cognitive development. After considering these three areas of research, I consider again the theme of the chapter—that cognitive development can be facilitated with appropriate social encounters—in the light of the practical, current constraints on early childhood teachers' work.

Neuropsychology: Its Value and Limits

Neuropsychology seeks to explain cognition in terms of the brain structures and functions that animate or make cognition possible (Fusaro & Nelson, 2009). From this point of view, cognitive development has a lot to do with biological development: children may not be able to perform certain cognitive activities because they have not yet developed or "grown" the necessary physical brain structures. Neuropsychologists have pointed out, for example, that the physiological process of *myelination,* or formation of conductive sheaths along nerve fibers, is still incomplete in younger preschool-age children. Since myelination helps in conducting impulses along nerve fibers, it is hypothesized that comparatively limited myelination may limit younger preschoolers' cognitive abilities. This limitation may be part of the reason (though not the only reason) that young preschoolers (age 3) cannot be taught new language skills as efficiently as older children (age 8) can be taught (Pujol et al., 2006; Tsujimoto, 2009).

Neuropsychological research has also highlighted a number of *social* experiences that support the healthy development of brain structures (Kagan & Herskowitz, 2009). The most important of these happen not during the preschool years, but during the first 3 years of life. They include, for example, the nurture of attachment between the infant and caregiver(s), early visual exposure to print materials, and provision of responsive, interactive language environments. Infants benefit from these experiences because their brain physiology "expects" them; except for individuals with certain physical disabilities or biochemical abnormalities, every child's nervous system is especially sensitive and ready for them during infancy and toddlerhood. They can make up for deficits in these experiences later in childhood, or even in adulthood, but remediation is not always complete, and it is never as efficient as when children have had the experiences during the relatively critical period of infancy (Fox, Levitt, & Nelson, 2010; Kagan & Herskowitz, 2009).

Neuropsychological explanations offer important general insights about why young children may be able to perform certain cognitive skills but not others. As such it can be helpful in grounding instruction in developmentally appropriate practices. It should be noted, though, that the field so far has not provided advice or information for early childhood educators that is very specific (Bruer, 1997; Odom, Barbarin, & Wasik, 2009; Varma, McCandliss, & Schwartz, 2008). Even advocates intent on bridging the gap between neuroscience and educators have relied not on evidence-based research, but on teachers' own interpretations or constructions of the relevance of neuroscience (Dubinsky, 2010).

There are two problems with "brain science" from the point of view of early childhood educators. One is its emphasis on studying infants rather than preschool children, and the resulting implication that the most malleable time of life, physiologically speaking, is not early childhood but infancy. A corollary is that interventions on behalf of infants will be more effective than interventions on behalf of preschool children. Much of the value of the field therefore consists of general guidance in understanding what the very young can and cannot do—a sort of broad diagnosis of developmental capacities. Much of it takes the form of cautions about the limits of cognition in the young: if child X is missing brain structure Y at age Z, then teachers should not expect general skill W to be learned at that age, no matter how well it is taught or encouraged.

A second problem relates to the uniqueness of its findings for teachers. Even if neuropsychology eventually can diagnose children's brains precisely, its value to early childhood educators will depend on whether its findings yield insights that are relatively specific and not already available from current, socially based knowledge of children's development. So far educational recommendations based on brain science coincide to a remarkable extent with those already justified on social or cultural grounds (e.g., Bredekamp & Copple, 1997; National Association for the Education of Young Children, 2009; Ritchie, Maxwell, & Bredekamp, 2010). In this sense the field tends simply to add support for preexisting professional knowledge and policy. Such support helps to build public and professional support in early childhood education. But professional early educators in particular need more than general support; to fulfill their mission they also need advice related to classroom theory and practice that is fairly specific. So far specifics are provided by neuropsychology only to a limited extent.

Information Processing: The Interplay of Cognitive Components

Unlike accounts based in neuropsychology, information processing studies of cognitive development do not "reduce" or equate thinking with biological processes. Instead they identify components of cognition, and investigate how the components interact (or fail to do so) to produce children's thinking (e.g., Garon, Bryson, & Smith, 2008; Hrabok & Kerns, 2010; Marti, 2003). Much attention has gone to understanding so-called *executive functions* of thinking, those associated with activity in the frontal cortex, such as reasoning, planning, self-regulation of attention, memory strategies, and the like. The implied research paradigm is that a younger child (or in some cases an infant, not a preschooler) can perform a simple component X, but not a more complex component Y without first developing another relatively simple component Z. Describing the combined activity of X + Z, and perhaps of other components as well, therefore provides an account of cognitive development that is more functional than causal. Suppose, for example, that X refers to the ability to perform one-digit addition (2+3, 5+4, etc.) and Y refers to the ability to perform two-digit addition (23+54, 74+93, etc.). A child who can solve one-digit problems is not able to solve two-digit problems without first learning certain additional, simple component skills (call them Zs). An obvious additional component might be the algorithm for carrying a digit to the next column of figures—though skilled teachers might also feel that there are others as well.

Functional accounts have produced a number of findings useful to educators. Interpreting them, however, requires keeping their intellectual risks clearly in mind. Many information processing accounts of cognition verge on presenting only descriptions of cognitive functioning—simply detailed observations of the components of children's thinking—even when they claim to present explanations (Dick & Overton, 2010). Common measures of executive function—for example, the Wisconsin Card Sort Test (Heaton, 1993)—are published and frequently used as measures of "cognitive flexibility" without evidence of flexibility other than the test result itself.

By the standards of most educators, furthermore, information processing research tends to simplify or even ignore the social and cultural context in which thinking and development occurs—a tendency that Martin and Failows (2010) call "psychologism." Development is sometimes described or explained as if it happens only "inside" the individual child, with external influences that are minimal and under far better control than educators normally experience. These tendencies do not render information processing accounts unusable by early childhood educators, but they do necessitate conceptual work in order to situate and use them in the rather complicated, social atmosphere of classrooms or families.

A general conclusion from information processing research on young children is that most everyday academic skills (e.g., reading or mathematics) activate not one, but many cognitive functions simultaneously (Fusaro & Nelson, 2009). Learning to read, for example, involves at least the following cognitive skills, if not more: (1) knowledge of typical letter–sound correspondences; (2) knowledge of important exceptions to these correspondences; (3) aural pattern recognition of common phonemes and written letter patterns; (4) long-term recognition memory for common words ("sight vocabulary"); and (5) short-term recall memory of the written context of a particular word or phrase.

Another general conclusion from information processing research is that rendering new learning really memorable or permanent takes both practice and time *away* from overt, deliberate instruction (Bauer, 2009). Neither of these conclusions may be news to experienced early childhood teachers, but the detailed documentation of information processing studies can be helpful to educators nonetheless. The principle that memory for learning takes time and repetition, for example, applies to students of any age,

but most especially to those who are the youngest. As a rule of thumb, the younger the child, the longer it takes to insure that memory of new material remains with the child permanently. Infants take longer than preschoolers, and preschoolers take longer than primary-grade students. One way that information processing theory explains the age-related improvement is in terms of increases in the richness of children's associative abilities. Relative to younger ones, older children have more prior knowledge to which new information can be connected, at least if they are *shown* ways to make the connections. They also have acquired more knowledge of which memory strategies are especially helpful in classroom settings, and of when to deploy them—essentially a metamemory or metacognitive skill. The result is that (1) memories consolidate (i.e., become organized and easy to retrieve) more quickly in older, compared to younger children, and (2) there is no way for teachers to avoid dealing with this developmental difference. Older children are more "intelligent" than younger children in the sense that they can often remember things more easily. In recalling a classmate's e-mail address, for example, older children are helped both by greater familiarity with the variety of e-mail formats typical where they live, by knowledge that e-mail addresses can easily be forgotten unless deliberate effort is made to remember them accurately, and by experience with typical ways to make that effort (e.g., by writing down an e-mail address).

But such ideas should not be taken to suggest that deliberate teaching makes no difference. Even infants, it seems, can learn from deliberate instruction. In a series of experiments, Bauer and her associates induced infants 16 to 20 months of age to imitate an experimenter striking a miniature, table-size "gong" (Bauer, 2005, 2007). The babies showed patterns of learning very familiar to parents and teachers of older children. As with older preschoolers, most infants could reproduce at least some of the actions of gong-striking after just a single demonstration, and many could still reproduce the actions even after a two-week interval. Like older children, too, most infants could remember how to strike a gong *better* if they had had more than one demonstration of the correct actions initially. And not surprisingly, older infants' memories were less impaired by a two-week delay than were young infants' memories. Bauer interpreted these findings primarily as showing the importance of cognitive consolidation, a relatively slow process of organizing recent memories and linking them to prior skills and knowledge. Consolidation, she argued, is both inevitable and necessary to form permanent memories (including memories of how to strike a gong). But consolidation takes significant time, repeated exposure to the material to be learned, and slight but deliberate variation of the exposures each time new material is presented.

As noted, these findings also describe what practicing teachers observe in students every day. In writing as a developmental psychologist, Bauer unfortunately does not go on to discuss how to reconcile children's need for consolidation with the practical dilemmas of teaching, such as common pressures to "cover" an overly large curriculum, insufficient instructional time, or diversity in students' background skills—all of which affect individuals' needs and capacity for consolidating material. But the findings do show relatively pure examples of how children, even infants, can develop a cognitive skill (memory for the striking of a gong) as the result of a social experience (the modeling of a behavior by a "teacher-experimenter"). Bauer summarized the findings in two slogans meant as advice for teachers: *"Repeat, with variation on the theme,"* and *"Link early, link often."* To insure that learning is not forgotten, that is, teachers need to provide material more than once, each time in a slightly different way so that students can form new associations with the material during each encounter. The advice is reminiscent of Jerome Bruner's (1960) classic recommendation to follow a "spiral curriculum," one in which ideas are revisited repeatedly, but each time in a new or different form.

Studies of infant memory like these confirm the importance of links between social and cognitive experiences for young children: it appears that the stock-in-trade of teachers, social interaction, can stimulate cognitive development in preschoolers, at least under some conditions. No doubt other factors, including physical brain growth and society-wide cultural practices, also affect children's thinking. Since neither physical growth nor culture are normally under teachers' direct control, however, they are more important to teachers as background knowledge—as reminders to hold expectations for children's learning that are realistic.

Directly or indirectly, many studies in the information processing tradition have supported the importance of talking *to* and *with* children. They also suggest that adults' style of interaction matters a lot. For example, Haden, Ornstein, Eckerman, and Didow (2001) and Ornstein, Haden, and Hedrick (2004) have studied dramatic play "adventures" in which mothers and their 3- and 4-year-old children enacted a make-believe scene using dramatic play materials provided by the researchers. One adventure consisted of a make-believe camping outing; another, of a make-believe bird watching activity; a third, of a reenactment of an ice cream store. In each case appropriate props were provided. The dramatic play experiences were videotaped, and investigators analyzed the tapes for how the mothers' interaction styles affected their preschool children. Children were then interviewed one day after the experience, as well as three weeks later to find out how much they remembered. In general, the children remembered significantly more of the dramatic play experience if the mother had encouraged the child not only to talk jointly with her about the materials as they were used, but also to handle the props jointly with her. Joint discussion without joint handling was somewhat less helpful to a child's later memory, and a lack of both joint discussion and joint handling was least helpful of all.

In another study using the same dramatic play events and children of similar ages, Hendrick and colleagues (Hendrick, Haden, & Ornstein, 2009; Hendrick, Sans Souci, Haden, & Ornstein, 2009) analyzed the verbal interactions between mother and child to identify the specific features of the joint-talk conversations that might account for their effectiveness. They found that in high joint-talk conversations, mothers more often asked open-ended *Wh*-questions (*who, what, where, when, why,* or *how*), and these tended to elicit more elaborate responses from the children. In a related program of research, furthermore, Boland, Haden, and Ornstein (2003) successfully trained mothers to interact more effectively with their preschool children. Specifically, they were trained to use (1) more *wh- questions* to elicit their child's participation; (2) more *associations* of the current activity to what the mothers knew that the child already knew; (3) *follow-ins*, or comments that supported and extended features of the situation in which the child showed interest; and (4) *positive evaluations* or praise for the child's participation. Mothers learned these techniques successfully, and children of trained mothers recalled more of the dramatic play activities than children of untrained mothers.

A follow-up study used a similar training procedure, but instead of training mothers, it trained researchers unfamiliar with the children to use the same interaction techniques (Hendrick, Haden, & Ornstein, 2009). During the later memory interviews, in addition, the researchers were also trained to use "high elaborative event talk," which involved interaction techniques similar to those used during the dramatic play events themselves. The overall results gave clear support for the benefits of the high elaborative event talk both during the dramatic play itself and during later recall conversations. Asking open-end *wh-* questions led to better recall if used during the dramatic play, as in the earlier studies, but so did asking *wh-* questions later, during the recall interview or "test." Most effective of all was to ask *wh-* questions on both occasions.

Put in terms a bit more familiar to educators, the mothers and researchers using high elaborative event talk were *scaffolding* memory strategies for young children, though without actually calling the process by this term. The *wh*-questions and follow-ins stimulated classic mnemonic strategies—elaboration and rehearsal—and modeled them for the child, albeit unconsciously or subliminally. In the short-term the events created examples of a *zone of proximal development* in the Vygotskian sense: the child could do more (i.e., recall more) in the presence of a mentoring adult than she could do alone (Hoskyn, 2010; Stetsenko & Vianna, 2009). The long-term result was a stabilization of the child's new knowledge, along with a richer experience observing and using, but not thinking consciously about, memory strategies.

There is a further education-related inference from these ideas: it seems plausible, as children grow a bit older, that parents, teachers, and other caregivers might wish to transfer some of their scaffolding responsibility more fully to the child. Transferring responsibility would presumably involve making the existence and benefits of metacognitive memory strategies conscious within the child. This cognitive developmental goal would seem especially appropriate for teachers of young children, since metacognitive strategies would serve children well as they moved on into the elementary school years.

These ideas guided a study by Ornstein, Coffman, and Grammer (2009), who observed first-grade teachers in action as they taught lessons in language-arts and mathematics, and who then tested the students' memory with a card sorting task at intervals throughout first- and second grade. Not surprisingly, they found variation in how habitually and explicitly teachers described memory strategies to students, and how often they recommended strategies or urged students to create strategies of their own. After several months, however, the students of the "high-mnemonics" teachers showed greater use of memory strategies, an advantage that continued through the end of second grade. Detailed analysis showed three further points about the individual differences: (1) the students who benefitted the most from high-mnemonics teaching tended to be lower-achieving students; (2) higher-achieving students were relatively unaffected by the teacher's use of mnemonics (perhaps because they already were using effective memory strategies without coaching); and (3) students of high-mnemonics teachers did *not* show better memory performance initially, but required several months of such teaching to begin showing their advantage.

As mentioned earlier, the studies just described are all framed in functional terms: a child (or infant) can do simpler function X, but not harder function Z without first developing at least one other simpler function Y. In Bauer's studies of infants remembering how to hit a gong, for example, the younger infants were shown capable of imitating elements of the action (simpler function X), but not of reproducing the entire sequence reliably (more complex function Z) without first consolidating the simpler elements by associating the elements mentally—on their own time, so to speak—in between practice sessions (simpler function Y). In the dramatic-play recall studies by Ornstein and associates, preschoolers could recall fragments or elements of a make-believe episode (simpler function X), but not the entire experience (complex function Z) without elaborating on elements of the episode while it was happening (simpler function Y). In the studies of first-grade teachers using mnemonics, school-age students could perform an arbitrary memory task to some extent (simpler function X), but they did it without coaching (complex function Z) if they were repeatedly coached not on the task itself, but on memory strategies to apply to the task (a set of simpler functions Y).

Insights like these highlight the relationships among cognitive skills, and they are useful for helping early childhood educators identify and sequence reasonable instructional and developmental goals for children. But they overlook the obviously social elements of "cognitive" tasks as experienced by the children. The cognitive benefits described above develop not *just* because of other cognitive skills, but also because of significant social interactions and positive emotional relationships. To state an obvious but overlooked point: in every case a kindly, reasonable adult arranges a particular kind of conversation or experience with the child, and the child elects to trust the adult's motives in the social situation thus created. The child's trust in turn derives from a history of social encounters that published accounts of child cognition often put in the background because of the constraints of experimental design. A relevant background factor might be the fact that a mother and child (hopefully) love each other, for example, so that her child is willing to follow an experimental procedure simply because she asks him to do so. Another background factor might be that a teacher who recommends metacognitive strategies to students has *already* developed such good rapport with the students that they are willing to give her recommendations a trial sight unseen, so to speak. Still other background factors are the broad cultural regularities that influence behavior during every research experiment, such as whether a child considers it acceptable for any adult in authority to ask "test" questions (ones to which the adult already knows the answer), or whether arbitrary problems framed outside of everyday contexts are really worth thinking about.

In spite of these comments, I should emphasize that these "social" omissions are not the fault either of the researchers or of the information processing framework adopted for their studies; they were not, after all, trying to conduct social or cultural research. I mention them instead in order to place cognitive developmental research in the context of early childhood education, a task for which it is often not directly designed. The latter activity is primarily based on the activities of an adult who enjoys children and who interacts with a number of young children or students. To be useful to early childhood teachers, therefore, strictly cognitive studies often need a degree of reframing, *not* because they are badly conceived or conducted, but to take the obviously social emphasis of early childhood education into account.

Socially Focused Studies of Early Cognition

Notwithstanding the previous comments, many studies of children's thinking have in fact looked relatively directly at relationships between social experiences and the development of cognitive skills. These often require less reframing than studies that are more exclusively cognitive. How well a particular study serves the needs of early childhood teaching, however, depends on how closely it parallels or represents significant features of classroom teaching and learning. Since even "social" studies vary on this dimension, it is still necessary to interpret the educational usefulness of a developmental study carefully.

In this section I attempt to make such interpretations with regard to several programs of research connecting social experiences to cognitive change. Most involve language in some way, though their effects are simultaneously cognitive and social. I begin with an overview (a "grand tour") of development from this perspective, and follow the overview with more detailed discussion of the individual steps in the development. Later sections therefore hark back to the initial overview.

A Grand Tour of Social Influences on Cognition

A lot of cognition is acquired and influenced by the gestures and language witnessed by and directed to a child during social activities (see Wells, 2009). The resulting cognitive changes begin shortly after birth and continue through early childhood and beyond. In this section I begin with a brief "grand tour" of several social influences on cognition, and then explain the key elements of each in more detail.

Arguably, the first social influence on cognition is *joint attention,* in which an infant and adult use gestures or vocalizations to call each other's attention to a commonly experienced event, such as looking at the family cat, or commenting on the arrival or departure of a parent (Eilan, Heal, McCormack, & Roessler, 2005). When the adult includes bits of speech to the exchange—for example, says "cat!" while pointing and looking at the cat—the spoken words become part of the experience for the child (Sabbagh & Baldwin, 2005). Thanks to the child's initial egocentricity, and possibly also to innate human biases facilitating language learning, a child usually assumes that speech labels are *conventional.* She behaves, that is, as if the same word is used for the same object on all occasions and by all people, and that the word is unique and distinctive from words used for other objects or events (Kalish & Sabbagh, 2007). The assumption of conventionality simplifies the learning of vocabulary and thus makes language development much easier. With time and further language development, however, the child also begins noticing variations in the certainty and reliability of other persons' knowledge and beliefs—clues expressed through various *evidentiality markers* (Jeschull & Roeper, 2009; Matsui & Fitneva, 2009). As awareness of such variability dawns on the child, she qualifies or limits the general assumption of conventionality (Callanan, Siegel, & Luce, 2007). There is more than one way, she realizes, to say the "same" thing, and individuals sometimes differ in how they refer to the "same" object or event.

Awareness of the variability of knowledge prompts the child to begin expressing, if not truly reflecting on, the cognitive status of her own knowledge and reasoning—her own degree of certainty. The rudimentary self-awareness implied by evidentiality markers in turn allows for more effective problem solving skills to develop; the child begins to know what she knows and what she may only imagine or suppose—early evidence of an emerging "theory of mind," discussed further below. Continuing dialogues with adults support further improvements in the child's problem solving skills, and features of these dialogues are eventually appropriated by the child in the form of *private speech,* or *self-directed talk* that allows thinking and problem solving to become more autonomous. Using private speech, the child can talk her way through more challenging problems than in the past, and that would otherwise confuse the child or require adult assistance (Winsler, Fernyhough, & Montero, 2009). More or less at the same time, the child's public speech becomes more nuanced: she can begin understanding and using irony and sarcasm, for example, and engage in extended dialogues at social gatherings such as mealtimes or in play activities. The next several sections examine these multifaceted developments, beginning with the earliest—joint attention and the emergence of private speech.

The Educational Significance of Joint Attention and Private Speech

As described above, infants as young as 6 months can follow an adult's gaze or pointing gesture, and by 18 months they have perfected this behavior to a high degree (Butterworth, 1995). Why is such *joint attention*—an eminently social experience—important to early childhood educators? The short answer is that joint attention makes learning possible because adults often pay attention to objects, people, and events that are especially important, interesting, dangerous, or complicated. Adults often also accompany their attention with language, which for the child's purposes initially becomes part of the experience (Woodward, 2005). The challenge for the infant—one that takes months or years to accomplish—is to understand *why* an adult attends to or gazes at an object. Tracing the course of the infant's detective work is the focus of much research about infant cognitive development (Eilan et al., 2005).

Both experimental and correlational studies suggest that the language learned during joint attention encourages a number of cognitive functions, particularly an ability to inhibit one response deliberately in favor of a competing response. This ability is illustrated by the common children's game of "Simon Says." In the game, a child hears a series of commands to perform a motor response ("Touch your head," "Touch the floor," etc.), some of which are prefaced by the words "Simon says…." The child is supposed to perform *only* the actions prefaced by "Simon says…" and inhibit responses to the others. The game can be interpreted either as testing inhibition of one language cue ("Simon says…") against another (no "Simon says…"), or as testing inhibition of a dominant response to act against a nondominant verbal cue not to act. In any case, listening carefully to slight variations in verbal instructions allows a child to be more successful in the game. Ability to direct or focus attention in this way is also a skill that early childhood teachers encourage, and not surprisingly it has been shown to correlate with positive kindergarten outcomes (Ponitz, McClelland, Matthews, & Morrison, 2009).

In a controlled assessment of an analogous skill involving inhibition, Muller, Jacques, Brocki, and Zelazo (2009) devised what they called the "Colored Smarties" task. Preschool children were presented with an array of colored cards, each of which had a candy on it (the Smartie) that did *not* match the color of the card. In order to win a Smartie to eat, a child had to select a card of a particular color *without* being distracted by the color of the Smartie itself. Three-year-olds had considerable difficulty with this task, but 4- and 5-year-olds performed it almost perfectly. A series of experiments with the task suggested that the challenge for 3-year-olds was language-related: if a child *said* the name of the card before selecting it, he or she was less distracted by the color of the Smartie, and performed better. Older preschoolers either used this strategy of their own accord or else discovered it for themselves during the task. Younger children did not usually say the color words on their own initiative, though Muller showed that they could be trained to do so, and that training improved their performance significantly.

The language needed for the colored Smarties task was a simple example of *self-directed* or *private speech,* which Vygotsky and others have argued serves as a transition between problem solving with the assistance of linguistic support from an adult, and fully autonomous problem solving by the child. In the research by Muller and colleagues, for example, the child was in essence encouraged to "talk to himself" as a way of insuring cognitive success. Other studies corroborate the influence of language heard initially in social encounters on the development of private speech. A longitudinal study by Landry, Miller-Loncar, Smith, and Swank (2002), for example, observed verbal interaction between mothers and children during free play when the children were 3 or 4 years old. Two years later, when the children were 6, they observed the children's problem solving abilities. They found significant correlations between the mothers' earlier tendency to *scaffold* the child's actions during free play, and the child's later skill at various problem solving tasks. Scaffolding in this case included expressing explicit links among objects, people, and activities in which the child was engaged. The authors argued that the parents' language style at the earlier age provided children with language-related models for thinking or reasoning, models which children later used without assistance and on their own initiative.

Landry and colleagues did not actually observe the presence or absence of self-directed speech directly, but other research has done so. Fernyhough and Fradley (2005), for example, used a "Tower of London" game, in which a child sorts and transfers a stack of nested rings from one peg to another following a few simple rules. For research purposes, the task has the advantage that its difficulty level can be adjusted easily—there can be many rings to sort or just a few. Using this task with 5- and 6-year-olds, Fernyhough and Fradley found that private speech increased with task difficulty up to intermediate levels of challenge, after which it decreased somewhat. The trend suggested that children used self-directed speech to assist if necessary and helpful, but that when a problem became so difficult that success was unlikely, they gave up using it as a cognitive strategy.

The Educational Significance of Conventionality, Evidentiality, and Theory of Mind

What of the later social influences—the child's assumption of conventionality, learning of evidentiality, and developing a theory of mind? Why might these changes matter to early childhood educators? In general, the answer is that as these three developments evolve, they facilitate success in social situations—including classrooms in particular. Another part of the answer is that social skills, conventionality, evidentiality, and theory of mind are accessible to daily classroom influence. It is important therefore for early educators to understand their nature.

As pointed out earlier, the basic feature of *conventionality* is a belief that when people label objects, they all use the same word, and that the label does not change from one occasion to the next (Sabbagh & Henderson, 2007). When taught an unfamiliar label for an object by one speaker (e.g., "This is a teega"), for example, a young child will later point to the same object even when asked to identify it by a different speaker (e.g., the new person asks, "Which one is the teega?"). Notably for educators' purposes, however, is that conventionality is assumed for objects but *not* for personal preferences or for proper names. Apparently therefore even 2-year-olds do not assume that every person has the same preferences or the same name (Graham, Stock, & Henderson, 2006)—a crucial precursor to social sensitivity and tolerance needed in most classrooms.

By ages 3 and 4, furthermore, children show a consistent preference for learning labels from speakers who express certainty and who have a proven history of accuracy (Koenig & Harris, 2005). When interacting with two adults who label objects, one of whom has consistently made labeling mistakes in the past, preschoolers will attend to and remember the labels primarily from the "accurate labeler." If a child is asked to look for a hidden object, furthermore, the child is more likely to follow the advice of one who says, "I saw it in this box" than one who says, "I think it is in this box." Distinguishing knowledge from belief, and certainty from uncertainty, lays the groundwork for academic commitment: sources of certainty (e.g., the teacher, and later textbooks and the like) begin evolving into preferred sources of learning. The necessary cognitive distinctions develop initially through conversations with parents, though it is probably also supplemented by other adults who have sustained relationships with children—presumably including early childhood teachers (Callanan et al., 2007).

Differentiating knowledge and belief is expressed through lexical, pragmatic, and grammatical features of language—so-called *evidentiality markers* mentioned earlier in this section (Matsui & Fitneva, 2009). As pointed out there, English-language evidentiality markers usually take the form of words or phrases indicating the source, reliability, or certainty of knowledge, as when someone says, "Apparently he ate the cake," as compared to "I saw him eat the cake," or "I think he may have eaten the cake." English speakers also use nonverbal gestures and vocalizations to indicate the status of their knowledge—a well-timed shrug of the shoulders, for example, or a tentative tone of voice. Many non-English languages, in addition, have "built-in" grammatical (syntactic) features that indicate sources and levels of certainty and that provide additional ways to recognize types of evidence and to express the differences. Whether grammatical features are available or not, though, evidentiality markers encourage the idea that individuals have minds of their own: that people vary not only in what they know, but also in their certainty and trustworthiness (Fitneva, 2009; Jaswal & Neeley, 2006).

The conventionality assumption, it should be noted, does not begin as a "belief" in the adult sense of the term, but more as an expression of immature egocentrism or *lack* of thoughtful belief on the part of the young child (Sabbagh & Henderson, 2007). Two-year-olds probably do not hold a conscious principle that everyone uses language in the same way. Instead they simply, and thoughtlessly, behave as if everyone does—and as it happens, the assumption facilitates the learning of common language and the development of social relationships. The evidentiality distinctions that gradually develop in children's social encounters, in turn, facilitate cognitive development in their own way: by initiating glimmers of reflection about the nature and sources of knowledge. Partly because of conventionality and evidentiality, the child begins to wonder about who knows what and why, and therefore also who has a mind of his or her own, so to speak.

All in all, conventionality and evidentiality contribute gradually to developing a *theory of mind,* or attributions about individual mental states (Wellman, 2003). By about age 4, a child comes to act as if other persons perceive objects and events based on beliefs and knowledge unique to each person's experience. Prior to this age, a child is apt to believe that others believe and know whatever the child himself believes and knows. The phenomenon is illustrated clearly in the widely researched "false belief task." In one common version of the task, a child watches while an object is hidden behind one of two boxes in the presence of a third person. Then the object is moved to the other box while the child watches, but without the third party seeing or knowing about the move. Older preschoolers (ages 4 or 5) know that the third person will mistakenly believe that the object is still behind the original (first) box, and that the third person can be expected to search for it there. Younger children will assume instead that the third person

knows whatever the child himself has witnessed; that is, that the person will therefore search behind the *second* box. The ability of the child to differentiate his own knowledge from the other person's false belief is taken as evidence of a "theory of mind." The child has (apparently) developed a belief or assumption that each person experiences the world independently of other persons, based in this case on their individual sources of knowledge.

If all goes well, then, children who are 3 or 4 years old are already able to share attention, reason privately, if not fully logically, to themselves, begin sensing certainty of others' knowledge, and begin sensing that individuals are independent sources of ideas and beliefs. In these ways—at least if all goes well—they are ready for group settings such as are common in early childhood programs. But their development obviously does not end at this point: as they grow toward the age of school entrance, cognition and language improve enough to allow understanding of verbal irony, to participate in extended dialogues, to become more cognitively flexible under certain circumstances, and to participate in forms of group pretense. All of these achievements create the possibility of further, more subtle or "sophisticated" learning at school. The next sections therefore explain these later developments in turn, beginning with the development of a sense of irony.

The Cognitive Benefits of Ambiguity: Irony

Several researchers have argued that social interactions that are ambiguous stimulate cognitive conflict—a sort of Piagetian disequilibrium—that motivates children to develop their interpretive and expressive skills beyond current levels. Ambiguous contacts may actually be relatively plentiful for young children, who are still mastering the nuances of language as well as appropriate uses for nonverbal gestures and social behaviors. One obvious example of such a challenge occurs, for example, when a parent or adult uses *sarcasm* or *verbal irony,* either directed to the child or simply witnessed by her. Sarcasm by nature communicates double meanings; the literal words "say" one thing but the speaker intends something else. Sorting out the two meanings requires metacognitive work: the child must hold the literal meaning of a remark in mind, but simultaneously discern, or at least guess, a different underlying meaning or intention. Studies show that children learn this cognitive skill by about age 5 or 6; at about that age they know when a person is sarcastic—that is, does not mean what he or she says (Pexman, 2008; Pexman, Whalen, & Green, 2010). Note, though, that irony is by nature prone to misunderstanding at any age; there is always a risk that a listener will take the speaker literally and not notice an implied meaning distinct from the words. Perhaps for this reason children are slower to use irony than to recognize it when it occurs (Pexman, Zdrazilova, McConnachie, Deater-Deckard, & Petrill, 2009). Many do not use it at all until well into the elementary school years, though some children do begin making ironic remarks late in the preschool period, especially if they have parents who report using it in their own conversations more than usual (Hala, Pexman, Climie, Rostad, & Glenwright, 2010; Pexman et al., 2009).

In early childhood classrooms, should irony be fostered, merely tolerated, or discouraged? The answer is mixed. In favor of encouraging it is the evidence that learning to use irony is correlated with simulating metacognition—a skill that is generally helpful in academic work. Against encouraging it is the ease with which irony can be misconstrued by children who are not ready to understand its multiple cognitive levels. Perhaps the optimal strategy is a middle road: use irony only sparingly, and only when an individual child offers cues that he or she is already using and understanding it as intended. Such a strategy, of course, requires a teacher to fine tune and individualize her listening and observation skills.

The Cognitive Benefits of Ambiguity: Bilingualism

Another sort of ambiguity that confronts some preschoolers is the learning of a second language. Whether learning a second language or simply using one, a child in a bilingual family has to keep two languages actively in mind at the same time, decide repeatedly which grammar and lexicon to draw on, and inhibit responses using the nonrelevant language. The result is continual linguistic disequilibrium that may stimulate a number of cognitive skills that extend beyond a child's use of language and even influence the people around her (Adescope, Lavin, Thompson, & Ungerleider, 2010). One such skill, for example, is cognitive flexibility—an ability to switch attention easily from one dimension of a situation to another dimension. Suppose both monolingual and bilingual preschoolers are given a set of cards that vary in two ways, such as color and shape. If the children are asked to sort the cards by one of the dimensions (e.g., color), 3- and 4-year-olds succeed to a large extent, whatever their language backgrounds. If they are then asked to switch to sorting the cards by the other dimension (shape), however, monolingual children experience significantly more trouble than bilingual children; the monolinguals tend to perseverate on using the first sorting dimension. Researchers have interpreted the difference as evidence for a cognitive benefit of bilingualism: a skill at shifting attention flexibly from one dimension of language to another, and of dealing with the cognitive conflict resulting from the shift. The flexibility appears to generalize beyond language as such (Bialystok & Craik, 2010).

Mealtimes and Extended Dialogue

Family conversations at mealtimes have been studied extensively since the 1970s, and the results generally show a number of benefits for children's language and cognitive development (Hamilton & Wilson, 2009; Kiser, Medoff, Nurse, Black, & Fiese, 2010). By providing extended dialogue between parent and child, for example, mealtimes give children opportunities to hear unusual words used in context, listen to explanations of the words, and to begin using the words themselves (Snow & Beals, 2006). The extended dialogue of mealtimes includes both extended explanatory talk ("logical" problem solving) and extended narrative talk (story telling), and allows children chances to enhance their own expressive skill with these genres. The discourse skills thus acquired are important for academic success in the elementary grades, and are also therefore important as educational goals for preschool and primary-grade classrooms. Unfortunately, because of issues of administration, class size, and classroom group management, teachers of very young children are not always able to provide extended conversations with individual children, even when their programs literally involve serving meals (Helburn, 1995). Intervention experiments in early childhood programs have shown, however, that teachers are quite capable of engaging in extended dialogue with children—and indeed prefer to do so—when supported with appropriate ideas and materials (Bradley & Reinking, 2010). Observations of lunchtimes at childcare centers, in any case, show that preschool children engage in substantial language play, narrative, and explanatory talk at these times with each other, even when adults are *not* present to participate (Holmes, 2010). From the point of view of an early childhood teacher, therefore, a constructive teaching strategy may simply be to encourage all extended conversations to happen, even those among children. Another may be for teachers to participate in dialogue whenever possible, even if time for longer talks is limited.

Pretense Play and Games as Preparation for Institutional Life

Much has been written about the cognitive functions of play (Berk, Mann, & Ogan, 2006; Linn, 2008; Piaget, 1962). As Piaget emphasized and subsequent research has generally confirmed, make-believe play both stimulates and uses young children's ability to represent objects and activities. It nudges preschoolers beyond the sensorimotor here-and-now of infancy and less organized representations of the preoperational period into more logical, but still rather concrete worlds of concrete operations. More recent writing has further argued that make-believe actually fosters a component of hypothetical thinking, because children use objects "as if" they were something not immediately visible and in this sense treat objects as abstractions—a necessary though not sufficient feature of hypothetical thinking (Seifert, 2006). Abstract, counterfactual thinking is a feature of formal or hypothetical thinking posited by Piagetian psychologists for the period of adolescence, with the obvious difference that adolescents manipulate representations that are both more abstract and more logically coherent.

Games with rules carry this cognitive challenge a step further than the earlier make-believe by challenging children not just to use one object to represent another, but to agree with *others* about how to represent an object or action. Small, round pieces of wood are markers in a board game of checkers, and they can only be moved in certain ways. But this is true only because people who play the game agree to define and use the wood in these ways. People could instead agree to use rocks, bits of paper, or glass. On a community-wide scale—to consider a broader example—slips of paper with certain markings on them become "money" because people conventionally agree to treat the slips as such, even though other objects (lumps of metal or even heads of cattle) could be defined as "money" by convention. On a culture-wide scale, in fact, most human institutions owe their reality to objects and actions with meanings agreed on by convention.

During the preschool years, games with rules provide children with early experiences of conventionally assigned statuses, and in this sense games initiate a journey toward understanding the nature of institutional life that characterizes much of adulthood (Rakoczy, 2007). Young children must understand that a game of hide-and-seek, for example, is a "game" because the players agree that it is, and agree on the rules for playing it. The rules acquire their key properties not because of their intrinsic features, but because of agreements among the participants. If the conventionality is not understood, then hide-and-seek ceases to be "just a game," and players either fail to coordinate their actions or else hurt each other's feelings easily.

As Piaget pointed out, children at first may treat the rules of a game simply as sacred, unchangeable laws governing behavior and needing strict enforcement (Kalish, 2005). They fail to see that rules are also constituted from human agreement, and therefore can in principle be revised by mutual agreement. Such misunderstanding is especially likely for the youngest children, who have the least experience with inventing or negotiating revisions to rules. But repeated experience at games-with-rules helps develop their views toward more mature perspectives about conventions. As it happens, early childhood teachers are well-positioned to provide such experiences, because the group settings that typify early childhood programs lend themselves to play and games (Singer, Golinkoff, & Hirsh-Pasek, 2006).

How Can Cognitive Developmental Research Be Used?

As the preceding sections suggest, cognitive developmental research offers ideas relevant to the teaching of young children. At a minimum the research helps early childhood professionals to hold expectations about children's cognition that are appropriate, and sometimes in addition it suggests ways to intervene on children's behalf actively. From cognitive developmental research we know, for example,

that children can remember aspects of "instructional" experiences almost from birth, and that no matter how young, children benefit from opportunities to consolidate memories of experiences. Consolidation takes time, however, and short cuts may or may not be possible. The research confirms the commonsense notion that younger children do not remember as reliably as older children, but it also suggests that the younger children's memory can be improved significantly when encouraged to use deliberate mnemonic strategies.

There is also ample evidence that children benefit cognitively from extended conversations in a variety of situations—eating meals, reading story books, interacting with a second language, playing at make-believe or games-with-rules. Cognitive developmental research also suggests why extended conversation helps: it exposes the child to new vocabulary and gives chances to practice using complex discourse genres. Conversation also engages the child's attention jointly with that of the adults. The joint attention makes it more likely that a child will learn not only what adults consider to be important, but also ways to talk that recognize universal conventions of meaning as well as diversity in the credibility and reliability of others' knowledge. As a partial result, problem solving becomes more clear-headed and focused.

Yet if history is a guide, ideas such as these will make their way into professional practice only partially and slowly. There are several reasons for this prediction, some of which are easier to remedy than others. One reason is that teachers' may often simply lack knowledge of recent relevant research. An interview study by Deniz (2009), for example, found that many early childhood teachers were not aware of the idea that preschoolers' self-directed private speech during problem solving might serve as a bridge between active verbal support from adults and completely silent thinking by the child. Instead teachers often took private speech as a sign of a child's persistent *immaturity* rather than as a step toward the greater maturity of silent thought. In class, therefore, they sometimes discouraged children from talking to themselves, rather than allowing or respecting this behavior. To deal with such misunderstanding, Deniz recommended professional development education about language development.

Another factor that limits adoption of cognitive developmental research is the extent of cultural diversity and of associated differences in values and behaviors. Culturally based interaction patterns that are comfortable to researchers or even to participants in a study may be inappropriate outside the study context (Sternberg, 2007; Tharp & Dalton, 2007), even including the contexts served by early childhood programs. A frequent finding of child development research, for example, is that lively give-and-take between child and adult is not only beneficial cognitively, but also trainable in parents and children. Yet some families—or even whole communities—may consider lively interaction with adults to be disrespectful on the part of the child, and therefore discourage children from engaging in it (Philips, 2009).

Many cognitive developmental studies also depend on children's willingness to engage with problems or tasks out of their normally expected context. Judging by cross-cultural and other ethnographic research, however, such interactions often pose problems that are social as well as cognitive. In observing mealtimes at child care centers in Asia and the United States, for example, Tobin and his associates found a range of practices, many of which seemed *un*likely to encourage productive dialogue between children and adults (Tobin, Hsueh, & Karasawa, 2009). At one center (in Japan), the youngest children were served not by adults, but by older children. Mealtime conversation presumably did happen during these encounters, but it is reasonable to suspect that their conversation may have been more limited linguistically or more focused on the immediate practicalities of eating. In any case the setting was not really what American educators and psychologists have in mind in recommending mealtimes as a venue for fostering language and cognitive skills (Hamilton & Wilson, 2009; Kiser et al., 2010; Snow & Beals 2006). In another child care center (in the United States) observed by Tobin, staff members were obliged by certification requirements to serve meals "family style," meaning that preschool children were not served by adults, but helped themselves from bowls of food set at group tables. Again, developmentally productive conversations may have happened anyway, but the need to monitor spills, excess helpings, and logistics with a large number of young children suggests that conversations might easily focus more on management than on cognitive stimulation of the children.

An especially important factor limiting adoption of research on cognitive development, however, stems from incommensurability between the goals and conditions of research studies, compared to the goals and conditions typical of early childhood classrooms. I alluded to some of these already in this chapter, and they have been discussed thoroughly elsewhere in the literature on educational research (e.g., Reason & Bradbury, 2006). Whereas developmental psychology research aims for (and often achieves) control over confounding factors, a major purpose of early childhood classroom practice is not to control "extraneous" factors, but to recognize and work with them—that is, work with the entire context of a child's experience. Whereas research aims for conceptual clarity, early childhood practice aims for broad human development and welfare. The differences mean that the factors that can make research "fail" are the very ones that can make practice successful. The confounding factors take many forms: the continual distraction and influence of peers, personal diversity among children, continual revision of lesson plans on the fly, the interplay of ideas, needs, and issues from persons outside the classroom. As has often been pointed out, classrooms are therefore messy, but research studies are comparatively clean, or at least try to be.

As a result, it is hard to "see" the results of research studies in many classroom situations. Of particular relevance to this chapter, classroom tasks and activities that are purely cognitive are rare or nonexistent; all cognitive activities either serve additional social or emotional purposes, or else begin explicitly as a social encounter. Given that early childhood programs tend by definition to be group settings, a pervasive social influence should not be surprising even if the nominal focus of some activities is cognitive.

It should also not surprise us that teachers, parents, and children construe the idea of *intelligence* not as a strictly cognitive talent, but as a quality that integrates social skills with cognition. In interview studies by Sara Harkness and her associates, for example, teachers from five societies (Italy, the Netherlands, Poland, Spain, and the United States) described their "best" or ideal students in terms that were at least as social as they were cognitive (Harkness et al., 2007). The best students were not necessarily the cleverest ones intellectually, nor the highest performing on cognitive tasks. Instead they were the ones who mixed lively personality, creativity, and social and emotional sensitivity to others—qualities that presumably facilitated their ability to learn from others. The teachers' vocabulary for describing these qualities varied, of course, but there was an underlying sense that cognitive development did not happen in a social or emotional vacuum, but was made possible by social interactions and relationships. Parents in these societies echoed these attitudes. Even when some used the term *smart* to describe their own child (a tendency especially of American parents), further questioning suggested that they were talking about cognitive outcomes that were made possible by social skills (Harkness & Super, 2006). Even children themselves seem to regard intelligence in similar terms. In an ethnographic study by Chen (2010), for example, first-grade students described classmates as only *mildly* successful as students if they performed well academically, but as *very* successful if they were popular socially. Academic success, furthermore, was implicitly regarded as a component of social success, not as a separate domain of it.

What actually may be surprising is that political and funding agencies have not recognized these beliefs and attitudes, but instead have promoted the teaching of cognitive skills as if they exist independently of other domains of development (Lewin, 2010; U.S. Department of Education, 2001; see also Zigler & Bishop-Josef, 2006). Partly as a result, assessments of early childhood programs often make this same distinction (e.g., Burger, 2009; Camilli, Vargas, Ryan, & Barnett, 2010; Dee & Jacobson, 2010; Mashburn et al., 2008); the social basis of cognition is either ignored or assessed as if it develops independently of cognition. The long-term result has been to pressure early childhood educators to teach specific cognitive skill behaviors, but to leave them to their own devices when teaching the social skills that make cognition possible, such as ability to self-regulate attention or to learn by watching and listening to others. The pressure, along with recent trends to limit public budgets, has made it difficult for early childhood educators to implement the best possible programs for children. As one program administrator put it, "we are caught between the NCLB and the NAEYC"—between accountability for instilling academic skills and commitment to developmentally appropriate practice (Tobin, Hseuh, & Karasawa, 2009, pp. 185–186). Even if educators can eventually learn to live with this dilemma themselves, it will indirectly limit their effectiveness with children.

But all hope is not lost. A good starting point is the fact, noted above, that teachers often already recognize the importance of social relationships and interactions for developing children's cognitive functions. One logical next step may therefore be to follow Deniz's advice mentioned above: to share the relevant research as widely as possible with early childhood educators—especially any research that offers details of how relationships and interactions affect cognition. In addition to such professional development, however, it would also help to listen more closely to the comments and questions that early childhood educators themselves consider most important for their work, and to adjust or at least reinterpret the cognitive research agenda accordingly. Toward this goal—and more radically—it would help to bridge the research–practice divide by inviting developmental psychologists to take a turn walking in the shoes of practicing early childhood educators. Doing so might vividly clarify to them how the epistemology, the freedom to act or lack thereof, and the priority questions about children differ between the academic and professional worlds. Researchers may or may not want to alter their research agendas in view of this additional knowledge, and in fact may not always be able to so. But at least they would know more clearly what questions educators care about the most, and they would be able to assess more accurately the usefulness of existing developmental research in the landscape of educational and societal needs.

References

Adescope, O., Lavin, T., Thompson, T., & Ungerleider, C. (2010). A systematic review and meta-analysis of the cognitive correlates of bilingualism. *Review of Educational Research, 80*(2), 207–245.

Asamen, J., Ellis, M., & Berry, G. (Eds.). (2008). *The Sage handbook of child development, multiculturalism, and media.* Thousand Oaks, CA: Sage.

Barbarin, O., & Wasik, B. (Eds.). (2009). *Handbook of child development and early education: Research to practice.* New York: Guilford.

Bauer, P. (2005). New developments in the study of infant memory. In D. M. Teti (Ed.), *Blackwell handbook of research methods in developmental science* (pp. 467–488). Oxford, England: Blackwell.

Bauer, P. (2007). *Remembering the times of our lives: Memory in infancy and beyond.* Mahwah, NJ: Erlbaum.

Bauer, P. (2009). Neurodevelopmental changes in infancy and beyond: Implications for learning and memory. In O. Barbarin & B. Wasik (Eds.), *Handbook of child development and early education: Research to practice* (pp. 78–102). New York: Guilford.

Berk, L., Mann, T., & Ogan, A. (2006). Make-believe play: Wellspring for development of self-regulation. In D. Singer, R. Golinkoff, & K. Hirsh-Pasek (Eds.), *Play=learning: How play motivates and enhances children's cognitive and social-emotional growth* (pp. 74–100). New York: Oxford University Press.

Bialystok, E., & Craik, F. (2010). Cognitive and linguistic processing in the bilingual mind. *Current Directions in Psychological Science, 19*(1), 19–23.

Boland, A., Haden, C., & Ornstein, P. (2003). Boosting children's memory by training mothers in the use of an elaborative conversational style as an event unfolds. *Journal of Cognition and Development, 4*(1), 39–65.

Bradley, B. & Reinking, D. (2010). Enhancing research and practice in early childhood through formative and design experiments. *Early Child Development and Care, 180,* 1–15.

Bredekamp, S., & Copple, C. (Eds.). (1997). *Developmentally appropriate practice in early childhood programs* (rev. ed.). Washington, DC: National Association for the Education of Young Children.

Bruer, J. (1997). Education and the brain: A bridge too far. *Educational Researcher, 26*(8), 4–16.

Bruner, J. (1960). *The process of education.* Cambridge, MA: Harvard University Press.

Burger, K. (2009). How does early childhood care and education affect cognitive development? *Early Childhood Research Quarterly, 25,* 140–165.

Butterworth, G. (1995). Origins of mind in perception and action. In C. Moore & P. Dunham (Eds.), *Joint attention: Its origins and role in development* (pp. 29–40). Hillsdale, NJ: Erlbaum.

Callanan, M., Siegel, D., & Luce, M. (2007). Conventionality in family conversations about everyday objects. *New Directions in Child and Adolescent Development, 115,* 83-96.

Camilli, G., Vargas, S., Ryan, S., & Barnett, S. (2010). Meta-analysis of the effects of early education interventions on cognitive and social development. *Teachers' College Record, 112*(3), 579–620.

Chen, R. (2010). *Early childhood identity: Construction, culture, and the self.* New York: Peter Lang.

Dee, T., & Jacob, B. (2009). *The impact of No Child Left Behind on student achievement.* Cambridge, MA: National Bureau of Economic Research.

Deniz, C. (2009). Early childhood teachers' awareness, beliefs, and practices toward children's private speech. In A. Winsler, C. Fernyhough, & I. Montero (Eds.), *Private speech, executive functioning, and the development of verbal self-regulation* (pp. 236–246). New York: Cambridge University Press.

Dick, A., & Overton, W. (2010). Executive function: Description and explanation. In B. Sokol, U. Muller, J. Carpendale, A. Young, & G. Iarocci (Eds.), *Self and social regulation: Social interaction and the development social understanding and executive functions* (pp. 2–34). New York: Oxford University Press.

Dubinsky, J. (2010). Neuroscience education for prekindergarten-12 teachers. *The Journal of Neuroscience, 30*(24), 8057–8060.

Eilan, N., Heal, C., McCormack, T., & Roessler, J. (Eds.). (2005). *Joint attention: Communication and other minds.* New York: Oxford University Press.

Fernyhough, C., & Fradley, E. (2005). Private speech on an executive task: Relations with task difficulty and task performance. *Cognitive Development, 20,* 10–120.

Fitneva, S. (2009). Evidentiality and trust: The effect of informational goals. *New Directions in Child and Adolescent Development, 123,* 49–62.

Fox, S., Levitt, P., & Nelson, C. (2010). How the timing and quality of early experiences influence the development of brain architecture. *Child Development, 8*(1), 28–40.

Fusaro, M., & Nelson, C. (2009). Developmental cognitive neuroscience and educational practice. In O. Barbarin & B. Wasik (Eds.), *Handbook of child development and early education: Research to practice* (pp. 55–77). New York: Guilford.

Garon, N., Bryson, S., & Smith, I. (2008). Executive function in preschoolers: A review using an integrative framework. *Psychological Bulletin, 134*(1), 31–60.

Graham, S., Stock, H., & Henderson, A. (2006). Nineteen-month-olds' understanding of the conventionality of object labels versus desires. *Infancy, 9,* 341–350.

Haden, C., Ornstein, P., Eckerman, C., & Didow, S. (2001). Mother–child conversational interactions as events unfold: Linkages to subsequent remembering. *Child Development, 72,* 1016–1031.

Haith, M., & Benson, J. (2008). *Encyclopedia of infant and early childhood development.* Boston, MA: Elsevier/Academic Press.

Hala, S., Pexman, P., Climie, E., Rostad, K., & Glenwright, M. (2010). A bidirectional view of executive function and social interaction. In B. Sokol, U. Muller, J. Carpendale, A. Young, & G. Iarocci (Eds.), *Self and social regulation: Social interaction and the development social understanding and executive functions* (pp. 293–311). New York: Oxford University Press.

Hamilton, S., & Wilson, J. (2009). Family mealtimes: Worth the effort? *Infant, Child, and Adolescent Nutrition, 1*(6), 346–350.

Harkness, S., Blom, M., Oliva, A., Moscardino, U., Zylicz, P., Bermudez, M., et al. (2007). Teachers' ethnotheories of the "ideal student" in five western cultures. *Comparative Education, 43*(1), 113–135.

Harkness, S., & Super, C. (2006). Themes and variations: Parental ethnotheories in western cultures. In K. Rubin (Ed.), *Parental beliefs, behaviors, and parent-child relations: A cross-cultural perspective* (pp. 61–80). New York: Psychology Press.

Heaton, R. (1993). *The Wisconsin Card Sorting Test* (rev.ed.). Odessa, FL: Psychological Assessment Resources.

Helburn, S. (1995). *Cost, quality, and child outcomes in childcare centers.* Denver, CO: Center for Research in Economics and Social Policy, University of Colorado.

Hendrick, A., Haden, C., & Ornstein, P. (2009). Elaborative talking during and after an event: Conversational style influences children's remembering. *Journal of Cognition and Development, 10*(3), 188–209.

Hendrick, A., San Souci, P., Haden, C., & Ornstein, P. (2009). Mother–child joint conversational exchanges during events: Linkages to children's event memory over time. *Journal of Cognition and Development, 10*(3), 143–161.

Holmes, R. (2010). "Do you like Doritos?": Preschoolers' table talk during lunchtime. *Early Child Development and Care, 180,* 1–12.

Hoskyn, M. (2010). Working memory in infancy and early childhood: What develops? In B. Sokol, U. Muller, J. Carpendale, A. Young, & G. Iarocci (Eds.), *Self and social regulation: Social interaction and the development social understanding and executive functions* (pp. 155–184). New York: Oxford University Press.

Hrabok, M., & Kerns, K. (2010). The development of self-regulation: A neuropsychological perspective. In B. Sokol, U. Muller, J. Carpendale, A. Young, & G. Iarocci (Eds.), *Self and social regulation: Social interaction and the development social understanding and executive functions* (pp. 129–154). New York: Oxford University Press.

Jaswal, V., & Neely, L. (2006). Adults don't always know best: Preschoolers use past reliability over age when judging reliability. *Psychological Science, 17*(9), 757–758.

Jeschull, L., & Roeper, T. (2009). Evidentiality vs. certainty: Do children trust their minds more than their eyes? In J. Crawford, K. Otaki, & M. Takahashi (Eds.). *Proceedings of the 3rd conference on generative approaches to language acquisition North America* (pp. 107–115). Somerville, MA: Cascadilla Proceedings Project. Retrieved from http://www.lingref.com.

Kagan, J., & Herskowitz, N. (2009). *A young mind in a growing brain.* In O. Barbarin & B. Wasik (Eds.), *Handbook of child development and early education: Research to practice* (pp. 579–597). New York: Guilford.

Kalish, C. (2005). Becoming status conscious: Children's appreciation of social reality. *Philosophical explorations, 8*(3), 245–263.

Kalish, C., & Sabbagh, M. (2007). Conventionality and cognitive development: Learning to think the right way. *New Directions in Child and Adolescent Development, 115,* 1–7.

Kiser, L., Medoff, D., Nurse, W., Black, M., & Fiese, B. (2010). Family mealtime Q-sort: A measure of mealtime practices. *Journal of Family Psychology, 24*(1), 92–96.

Koenig, M. & Harris, P. (2005). Preschoolers' mistrust of ignorant and inaccurate speakers. *Child Development, 6,* 1261–1277.

Kuhn, D., & Siegler, R. (Eds.). (2006). *Handbook of child psychology: Vol. 2. Cognition, perception, and language.* Hoboken, NJ: Wiley.

Landry, S., Miller-Loncar, C., Smith, K., & Swank, P. (2002). The role of early parenting in children's development of executive processes. *Developmental Neuropsychology, 21,* 15–41.

Lewin, T. (2010, July 21). Many states adopt national standards for their schools. *New York Times,* p. A1.

Lewis, C., & Carpendale, J. (2009). Introduction: Links between social interaction and executive function. In C. Lewis & J. Carpendale (Eds.), Social interaction and development of executive function. *New Directions in Child and Adolescent Development, 123,* 1–15.

Linn, S. (2008). *The case for make-believe play: Saving play in a commercialized world.* New York: New Press.

Marti, E. (2003). Strengths and weaknesses of cognition over preschool years. In J. Valsiner & K. Connolly (Eds.), *Sage handbook of developmental psychology* (pp. 257–275). Thousand Oaks, CA: Sage.

Martin, J., & Failows, L. (2010). Executive function: Theoretical concerns. In B. Sokol, U. Muller, J. Carpendale, A. Young, & G. Iarocci (Eds.), *Self and social regulation: Social interaction and the development social understanding and executive functions* (pp. 35–55). New York: Oxford University Press.

Mashburn, A., Pianta, R., Hamre, B., Downer, J., Barbarin, O., Bryant, D., et al. (2008). Measures of classroom quality in prekindergarten and children's development academic, language and social skills. *Child Development, 79*(3), 732–749.

Matsui, T., & Fitneva, S. (2009). Knowing how we know: Evidentiality and cognitive development. *New Directions in Child and Adolescent Development, 123,* 1–11.

Muller, U., Jacques, S., Brocki, K., & Zelazo, P. (2009). The executive functions of language in preschool children. In A. Winsler, C. Fernyhough, & I. Montero, *Private speech, executive functioning, and the development of verbal self-regulation* (pp. 53–68). New York: Cambridge University Press.

National Association for the Education of Young Children. (2009). *Position statement on developmentally appropriate practice in early childhood programs.* Washington, DC: Author. Retrieved from http://www.naeyc. org/files/naeyc/file/positions/position%20statement%20Web.pdf.

Odom, S., Barbarin, O., & Wasik, B. (2009). Applying lessons from developmental science to early education. In O. Barbarin & B. Wasik (Eds.), *Handbook of child development and early education: Research to practice* (pp. 579–597). New York: Guilford.

Ornstein, P., Coffman, J., & Grammer, J. (2009). Learning to remember. In O. Barbarin & B. Wasik (Eds.), *Handbook of child development and early education: Research to practice* (pp.103–122). New York: Guilford.

Ornstein, P., Haden, C., & Hedrick, A. (2004). Learning to remember: Social-communicative exchanges and the development of children's memory skills. *Developmental Review, 24,* 374–395.

Pexman, P. (2008). It's fascinating research: The cognition of verbal irony. *Current Directions in Psychological Science, 17,* 286–290.

Pexman, P., Whalen, J., & Green, J. (2010). Understanding verbal irony: Clues from interpretation of direct and indirect ironic remarks. *Discourse Processes, 47,* 237–261.

Pexman, P., Zdrazilova, L., McConnachie, D., Deater-Deckard, K., & Petrill, S. (2009). "That was smooth, Mom": Children's production of verbal and gestural irony. *Metaphor and Symbol, 24*(4), 237–248.

Philips, S. (2009). Participant structures and communicative competence: The Warm Springs children in community and classroom. In A. Duranti (Ed.), *Linguistic anthropology: A reader* (2nd ed., pp. 329–344). Malden, MA: Wiley-Blackwell.

Piaget, J. (1962). *Plays, dreams, and imitation in childhood.* New York: Norton.

Ponitz, C., McClelland, M., Matthews, J., & Morrison, F. (2009). A structured observation of behavioral self-regulation and its contribution to kindergarten outcomes. *Developmental Psychology, 45*(3), 605–619.

Pujol, J., Soriano-Mas, C., Ortiz, H., Sebastian-Galles, N., Losilla, J., & Deus, J. (2006). Myelination of language-related areas in the developing brain. *Neurology, 66*(3), 339–343.

Rakoczy, H. (2007). Play, games, and the development of collective intentionality. *New Directions in Child and Adolescent Development, 115,* 53–67.

Reason, P. & Bradbury, H. (Eds.). (2006). *Handbook of action research.* Thousand Oaks, CA: Sage.

Ritchie, S., Maxwell, K., & Bredekamp, S. (2010). Rethinking early schooling: Using developmental science to transform children's early school experiences. In O. Barbarin, & B. Wasik (Eds.), *Handbook of child development and early education: Research to practice* (pp. 14–37). New York: Guilford.

Sabbagh, M., & Baldwin, D. (2005). Understanding the role of communicative intentions in word learning. In N. Eilan, C. Heal, T. McCormack, & J. Roessler (Eds.), *Joint attention: Communication and other minds* (pp. 165–184). New York: Oxford University Press.

Sabbagh, M., & Henderson, A. (2007). How an appreciation of conventionality shapes early word learning. *New Directions in Child and Adolescent Development, 115,* 25–37.

Seifert, K. (2006). Cognitive development and the education of young children. In B. Spodek & O. Saracho (Eds.), *Handbook of research on the education of young children* (2nd ed., pp. 9–22). Mahwah, NJ: Erlbaum.

Singer, D., Golinkoff, R., & Hirsh-Pasek, K. (Eds.). (2006). *Play=learning: How play motivates and enhances children's cognitive and social-emotional growth.* New York: Oxford University Press.

Snow, C., & Beals, D. (2006). Mealtime talk that supports literacy development. *New Directions in Child and Adolescent Development, 111,* 51–66.

Sokol, B., Muller, U., Carpendale, J., Young, A., & Iarocci, G. (Eds.). (2010). *Self and social regulation: Social interaction and the development of social understanding and executive functions.* New York: Oxford University Press.

Sternberg, R. (2007). Culture, instruction, and assessment. *Comparative Education, 43*(1), 5–22.

Stetsenko, A. & Vianna, E. (2009). Bridging developmental theory and educational practice. In O. Barbarin & B. Wasik (Eds.), *Handbook of child development and early education: Research to practice* (pp. 38–54). New York: Guilford.

Tharp, R., & Dalton, S. (2007). Orthodoxy, cultural compatibility, and universals in education. *Comparative Education, 43*(1), 53–79.

Tobin, J., Hsueh, Y., & Karasawa, M. (2009). *Preschool in three cultures revisited.* Chicago, IL: University of Chicago Press.

Tsujimoto, S. (2009). The prefrontal cortex: Functional neural development during early childhood. *The neuroscientist, 14*(4), 345–358.

U.S. Department of Education. (2001). No Child Left Behind Act of 2001. Retrieved from http://www2.ed.gov/policy/elsec/leg/esea02/index.html .

Varma, S., McCandliss, B., & Schwartz, D. (2008). Scientific and pragmatic challenges for bridging education and neuroscience. *Educational Researcher, 37,* 140–152.

Wellman, H. (2003). Understanding the psychological world: Developing a theory of mind. In U. Goswani (Ed.), *Blackwell handbook of childhood cognitive development* (pp. 167–187). Malden, MA: Blackwell.

Wells, G. (2009). The social context of language and literacy development. In O. Barbarin & B. Wasik (Eds.), *Handbook of child development and early education: Research to practice* (pp. 271–302). New York: Guilford.

Winsler, A., Fernyhough, C., & Montero, I. (2009). *Private speech, executive functioning, and the development of verbal self-regulation.* New York: Cambridge University Press.

Woodward, A. (2005). Infants' joint attention of the actions involved in joint attention. In N. Eilan, C. Heal, T. McCormack, & J. Roessler (Eds.), *Joint attention: Communication and other minds* (pp. 110–128). New York: Oxford University Press.

Zigler, E., & Bishop-Josef, S. (2006). The cognitive child versus the whole child: Lessons from 40 years of Head Start. In D. Singer, R. Golinkoff, & K. Hirsh-Pasek (Eds.), *Play=learning: How play motivates and enhances children's cognitive and social-emotional growth* (pp. 15–35). New York: Oxford University Press.

3

Young Children's Peer Relations and Social Competence

GARY W. LADD AND CASEY M. SECHLER
Arizona State University

Introduction

Cultural roots, philosophical perspectives, history, and scientific theories have encouraged members of today's societies to embrace the premise that early experience plays a critical role in human development (see Kessen, 1979; Sears, 1975). In research communities, this premise has spurred an interest in early relationships and their role in children's growth and development. Although parent–child relationships have long been a focal point for theory and research on early socialization (see Ladd & Pettit, 2002), it has become increasingly clear that age mates, or peers, also contribute to children's development (e.g., see Berndt & Ladd, 1989; Harris, 1995; Ladd, 1999). In fact, some have hypothesized (Bowlby, 1973; Freud & Dann, 1951; Rutter, 1979) that early childhood may be a sensitive period for social development, and that certain types of peer experiences contribute uniquely to children's development during this period.

Perhaps not surprisingly, the "peers-as-socializers" hypothesis has gained stature in recent years among scientists and the lay public alike (see Ladd, 2005; Rubin, Bukowski, & Laursen, 2009). Among investigators, evidence implicating peers as change agents in children's development has encouraged some to elevate the importance of peer relations within theories of socialization and development (see Harris, 1995). Likewise, caregivers and educators have come to see peer relations as important because increasing numbers of parents have joined the workforce (Belsky, 2001) making it necessary for young children to spend large amounts of time with peers in out-of-home contexts (e.g., day care, preschools, family day care). As Edwards (1992) observed, "The increasing use of preschools, organized playgroups, and childcare arrangements has brought the age of access to peer relations down near the beginning of life" (p. 297). In many industrialized nations, families have become increasingly isolated within their communities and separate from larger kin networks. Further, parents who value achievement and economic success enroll their children in preschools and day care programs at early ages so they can be exposed to age mates and develop the skills needed for success in grade school (Edwards, 1992).

Given these scientific and secular trends, it has become increasingly important for parents and child-oriented professionals to understand the nature and impact of children's early experience with peers. Fortunately, over the past 100 years, researchers have spent considerable time and energy learning about young children's social competencies, the types of peer relationships they form during the early childhood years, and the potential consequences that may accrue from children's participation in these relationships (see Ladd, 2005). The purpose of this chapter is to survey extant findings on the development of young children's peer relations and social competence, and examine the extent to which these factors are linked with current and later indicators of children's health, development, and adjustment.

Identifying and Describing Children's Early Peer Relationships

Children's interest in peers and the competencies they possess to relate with them are present very early in life. Infants orient toward peers by 2 months of age, make simple gestures by 3 to 4 months, and direct smiles and vocalizations toward peers by 6 months (Vincze, 1971). Interactions begin early too; in their first year, infants direct actions toward peers, and by the second and third years, toddlers create "games" based on reciprocal gestures and play (see Eckerman, Davis, & Didow, 1989; Vandell & Mueller, 1980). Very young children also form relationships with peers. As early as 2 years, toddlers exhibit strong preferences for particular play partners (Ross & Lollis, 1989; Vandell & Mueller, 1980) and, over time, these early play preferences can develop into complex relationships.

By the preschool years, at least three types of relationships can be discerned in the peer context: *friendships, peer group relations*, and *aggressor–victim relations* (i.e., peer victimization*)*. Whereas friendship refers to a voluntary, *dyadic* relationship that often entails a positive affective bond between participants (Berndt, 1996; Howes, 1988), peer group acceptance/rejection is defined as the degree to which an individual child is liked or disliked by the members of his or her social *group* (Asher, Singleton, Tinsley, Hymel, 1979). In contrast, peer victimization refers to a form of relationship in which individuals are actively maltreated (e.g., frequently harassed or aggressed upon) by one or more members of their peer group (Perry, Kusel, & Perry, 1988).

Most young children simultaneously participate in more than one form of peer relationship (Ladd, Kochenderfer, & Coleman, 1997). A child may, for example, have a friend but be largely disliked (rejected) and mistreated (victimized) by members or his or her peer group (Masters & Furman, 1981; Parker & Asher, 1989). In large part, the effects that peers have on children occur within these relationships, and the nature of these "effects" depends on the types of relationships children have formed and the nature of the experiences they have in each type of relationship. Different types of peer relationships appear to create distinct experiences—ones that may have positive ("benefits") or negative ("costs") effects on children's development and well-being (Furman & Robbins, 1985; Ladd et al., 1997).

It should also be noted that friendship, peer group acceptance/rejection, and victim–aggressor relations are theoretical constructs and that researchers have differing views about how these forms of relationship are best defined and measured. For these reasons, it is essential to consider how researchers have defined and measured friendship, peer status, and victimization at different age levels.

Friendships

Friendship appears to take somewhat different forms, and has been defined and investigated in different ways depending on children's ages. To study early friendships, investigators have relied on parent- and teacher-report measures, self/peer report measures, and observations of children's social interactions (see Ladd, 1988; Price & Ladd, 1986).

Infants and Toddlers.   With infants and toddlers, the criteria that researchers have used to identify friendships include peer familiarity, interaction frequency or consistency, mutual display of positive affect, reciprocity in sharing and play, and so on (Howes, 1988, 1996; Vandell & Mueller, 1980). Howes (1983), for example, considered toddlers to be friends if: (a) at least 50% of their social initiations resulted in social interaction (mutual preference); (b) one or more exchanges of positive affect occurred between partners (mutual enjoyment); and (c) one or more episodes of reciprocal or complementary play occurred between partners (skillful interaction).

Evidence indicates that infants and toddlers form friendships (see Hinde, Titmus, Easton, & Tamplin, 1985; Howes, 1983), and attempts to characterize these relationships show that young children are capable of adapting their behavior to fit their partners', and that friends or frequent associates interact with each other in ways that are different from the ways they treat other children (Ross & Lollis, 1989). Toddlers' friendships, in particular, can be enduring (Howes, 1988; Howes & Phillipsen, 1992; Vandell & Mueller, 1980). Howes and colleagues (1983; Howes & Phillipsen, 1992), for example, found that 60% of toddlers' friendships were sustained over one or more months, and that toddlers' friendships—particularly cross-gender friendships—often lasted well into the preschool years.

Preschoolers and Young Children.   Preschoolers' friendships have been identified using an assortment of criteria, including indicators of companionship, intimacy, affection, reciprocal play, and frequency of interaction (see Berndt, 1989; Howes, 1996; Parker & Gottman, 1989). For example, Hayes, Gershman, and Bolin (1980) considered preschoolers to be "friends" if they spent at least 50% of playtime interacting with each other in either parallel or cooperative play. Similarly, Hinde, Titmus, Easton, and Tamplin (1985) considered preschoolers to be "strong associates" if they were frequently in each other's company (i.e., > 30% of time sampled). Children's self-reports have also been used to identify friendships (see Howes, 1988; Masters & Furman, 1981; Price & Ladd, 1986) because preschoolers are able to name their best friends and articulate reasons for liking them (e.g., common activities, general play; Hayes 1978).

As with toddlers, evidence suggests that preschoolers' friendships can be stable. Park and Waters (1989) found that many preschoolers had friendships that lasted 7 months or more, and about half of these relationships persisted for as long as 18 months. Similar estimates were obtained by Howes (1988) and Gershman and Hayes (1983), although Howes found that nearly 10% of preschoolers' friendships lasted as long as two years. Moreover, it appears that many preschoolers are capable of maintaining their friendships across the transition from preschool into formal schooling (i.e., kindergarten; see Ladd, 1988, 1990).

At these ages, friendship stability is associated with the initial quality of the friendship (Berndt, Hawkins, & Hoyle, 1986; Bukowski, Hoza, & Boivin, 1993; Ladd, Kochenderfer, & Coleman, 1996). Accordingly, it appears that preschoolers' friendships are more likely to withstand the test of time if these relationships possess positive qualities.

Peer Group Relations

The study of young children's peer group relations has a long history (see Ladd, 2005), and the construct of peer group acceptance/rejection has received the most attention. This aspect of young children's peer relations has been studied primarily in early educational and childcare settings, where children tend to be grouped with age mates or near-age mates. Peer acceptance/rejection refers to the degree to which individuals are accepted versus rejected by members of their peer group (Bukowski & Hoza, 1989; Ladd, 1999), and is typically measured by asking peer group members (e.g., preschool classmates) to *rate* or *nominate* individuals with whom they are most or least likely to associate (see Ladd, 1988; Ladd & Coleman, 1993). Whereas children who receive high ratings or many positive nominations from peers are considered accepted, those who receive low ratings or many negative nominations are referred to as low-accepted or rejected (see Poteat, Ironsmith, & Bullock, 1986). Thus, rating methods provide a continuous measure of acceptance/rejection (with high scores denoting acceptance and low scores nonacceptance; see Cassidy & Asher, 1992), and nomination methods enable investigators to classify children into "peer status" categories (i.e., popular, average, controversial, neglected, and rejected; see Hazen & Black, 1989; Ladd, Price, & Hart, 1988; Mize & Ladd, 1990).

Peer Victimization

The study of peer victimization began in Scandinavian countries when researchers became concerned about a specific form of peer aggression that was unprovoked, performed repeatedly over time, and perpetrated by a stronger child (the bully) against a weaker child (the victim; see Olweus, 1993, 1999). In this research, terms such as *whipping boys* were used to identify children who were harassed by *bullies* (Olweus, 1978, 2001). More recently, however, children of both genders who are accosted by peers have been called *victims* (see Graham & Juvonen, 1998; Kochenderfer & Ladd, 1996; Kochenderfer-Ladd & Ladd, 2001; D. G. Perry, Kusel, & Perry, 1988).

Victimization may be conceptualized in relational terms because victims and aggressors often manifest consistent and recurring interaction patterns (see Elicker, Englund, & Sroufe, 1992; Pierce & Cohen, 1995). Unlike friendship and peer acceptance/rejection, however, which imply dyadic- and group-level relationships, respectively, peer victimization refers to relations that occur among a "limited minority of the peer group" (i.e., one or more aggressors and their victims; Perry, Kusel, & Perry, 1988). Victims also differ from children who participate in other types of peer relationships because they are more likely to experience active and frequent forms of abuse (e.g., persistent physical aggression, harassment, exploitation).

To identify children who are victimized by peers, investigators primarily have relied on self- or peer-report questionnaires. However, some evidence suggests that, prior to grade 2, peer reports of victimization tend not to be as reliable as self-reports (see Ladd & Kochenderfer-Ladd, 2002). For these and other reasons, it has become more common for investigators to assess victimization using information from multiple informants (e.g., composite indicators; Ladd &

Kochenderfer-Ladd, 2002). Additionally, researchers have begun to develop and utilize observational methods to identify and study victimized children (see Snyder et al., 2003).

Child Characteristics

Evidence indicating that some children succeed in peer relations while others have difficulties has often been interpreted as support for the social competence hypothesis; that is, the view that children are differentially skilled and therefore bring different levels of competence to social tasks such as making friends or gaining acceptance in peer groups. Essentially, this perspective suggests children are, in part, "the architects of their own social successes and difficulties" (Ladd, 2005) and emphasizes attributes that reside "in the child." Different explanatory foci have been proposed as possible explanations for observed differences in children's social competence. Whereas some perspectives place greater emphasis on genetics or heredity, such as theories of child temperament, others emphasize the role of learning and socialization.

Children's Temperament and Emotion Regulation

Temperament, which refers to individual differences in self-regulation and reactivity, has been of particular interest to those examining young children's peer relations. Temperamental characteristics exhibit wide individual variability and considerable stability (Rothbart & Bates, 2006), making it an important construct to consider when studying young children's socioemotional development.

Temperament is generally considered to refer to a child's behavioral style (Thomas & Chess, 1977), and is viewed as constitutionally based. Despite its biological foundation, it is acknowledged that the nature and expression of temperament is continuously modified by interaction with the environment (Sanson & Rothbart, 1995). Thus, child attributes, such as specific temperament traits, are attenuated or exacerbated via interactions with the environment, including those with peers, to produce differences in child outcomes, such as social adjustment.

Mary Rothbart's model of temperament is currently the most influential for the conceptualization and measurement of the multidimensional construct (Rothbart & Bates, 2006). In this model, temperament is thought to comprise two primary dimensions: regulation and reactivity (Rothbart & Bates, 2006). At the core of temperamental regulation is effortful control (EC), defined as "the efficiency of executive function, including the ability to inhibit a dominant response to activate a subdominant response" (Rothbart & Bates, 2006, p. 129). Effortful control emerges between 6 and 12 months of age and improves substantially in the preschool years (Kochanska, Murray, & Harlan, 2000). It includes skills such as the ability to shift and focus attention as needed, particularly when one does not feel like doing so, as well as integrating information, planning, and perhaps most directly related to socioemotional competence, modulating emotion and behavior (Eisenberg, Vaughn, & Hofer, 2009; Eisenberg, Vidmar et al., 2010).

Several investigators have found that EC is related to and predicts a variety of positive developmental outcomes, including the quality of social functioning. Effortful control is positively associated with peer acceptance, socially competent behavior, friendship quality, and sympathetic and prosocial tendencies (see Eisenberg, Vaughn, & Hofer, 2009; Spinrad et al, 2006). Even as early as preschool, children who are viewed by adults as well regulated (i.e., high in EC and behavioral self-control), are generally well liked rather than rejected by peers (Gunnar, Sebanc, Tout, Donzella, & van Dulmen, 2003). Similarly, David and Murphy (2007) found that EC predicted low levels of problematic peer behaviors (e.g., observed hostility, negative affect, and provocative behavior during peer interactions and teacher-rated low social competence) among preschoolers. Analogous findings have been obtained for elementary-aged children. For instance, Wilson (2003) found that popular and prosocial kindergartners and first graders displayed less difficulty shifting attention from negative to positive affect and were better able to regulate their ability after experiencing social failure. Further, it is likely that EC affects children's aggression, which influences the quality of their interactions and relationships with peers (see Eisenberg, Fabes, Guthrie, & Reiser, 2000, Eisenberg, Spinrad et al., 2004). Overall, children who are high in effortful regulation demonstrate the skills needed to get along with others and to engage in socially constructive behaviors with peers (e.g., prosocial behaviors), which in turn, enhance liking by peers (Eisenberg, Fabes et al., 2000; Spinrad et al., 2006).

The second component of temperament is reactivity, and it refers to an individual's arousability of motor, affective, and sensory response systems (Rothbart, Ahadi, Hershey, & Fisher, 2001). Reactivity also includes one's responsiveness to change in the external and internal environment. These reactive processes are thought to be the result of overcontrol (i.e., behavioral inhibition), undercontrol (i.e., impulsivity), and negative emotionality, such as fear, anger, and sadness (Rothbart & Bates, 2006). The behavioral tendencies associated with over- and undercontrol appear to be detrimental to children's development, and have been linked with poorer social adjustment. For example, children who are overcontrolled exhibit rigidity in their behavior and may withdraw from social environments (Derryberry & Rothbart, 1997; Spinrad et al., 2006). Conversely, children who have a tendency to be undercontrolled display signs of impulsivity, such as aggressive behaviors. It is thought that children may "act out" due to unregulated anger and frustration (Eisenberg et al., 2001).

Based on the literature reviewed, it may be concluded that children who exhibit difficulties with effortful or reactive control may be at greater risk for social maladjustment, and those who are high in EC tend to be viewed as socially competent. Despite the associations between temperament

and adjustment, researchers have found evidence that the relations between temperamental constructs and positive social functioning may not always operate directly. That is, Spinrad et al. (2006) found that EC predicted another personality characteristic (i.e., resiliency), which in turn, predicted children's social competence. Similarly, some studies suggest that the relation differs for boys and girls, such that girls have an advantage (e.g., Spinrad et al., 2006).

Children's Behavioral Orientations and Repertoires

Investigators who work from learning and socialization perspectives tend to construe social competence in terms of behavioral skills and skill deficits that children have accumulated over time through interactions with parents, teachers, siblings, and peers. In studies of this type, one of the principal investigative strategies has been to compare the behaviors of children who were more or less successful at fundamental social tasks. For example, investigators examined the behavioral antecedents of friendship, peer group entry, and peer group status and discovered that, whereas some of children's behavior patterns predicted positive relational outcomes (e.g., formation of a friendship, peer group acceptance), others forecasted negative relational consequences (e.g., failure to make a friend, peer group rejection). On the basis of this evidence, many investigators concluded that social competence could be conceptualized in behavioral terms.

Investigators working from this perspective have tended to study three types of child behavior as antecedents of children's success or difficulty in peer relations. These include *antisocial behaviors* (e.g., aggression), *prosocial behaviors* (e.g., cooperative interaction patterns), and *asocial behaviors*. Investigators have often worked from the premise that antisocial behaviors create high social costs for their interaction partners, and deprive peers of sought-after psychological benefits (e.g., reliable alliance, social support). In contrast, prosocial actions seldom create interpersonal costs and often benefit partners. Children prone to asocial behavior are likely to be a burden for their partners by being unskillful and failing to maintain interactions.

Prosocial Behavior. A substantial body of evidence indicates that prosocial behaviors, such as friendliness, cooperation, and helping, are markers of social competence in young children, and that such behaviors predict children's success at forming positive peer relationships (Ladd, 2005). In studies of peer group acceptance, investigators discovered that preschoolers who exhibit higher levels of cooperative play tended to become better liked by classmates over time (Ladd, Price, Hart (1988, 1990). Even across the transition from preschool to kindergarten, preschooler's prosocial behaviors predicted the extent to which they became liked by new kindergarten classmates (Ladd & Price, 1987). In studies of friendship, researchers have found that prosocial preschoolers are more supportive toward their friends (Sebanc, 2003).

Aggressive Behavior. As early as preschool and kindergarten, some children are more aggressive than others, and this behavioral style is a significant predictor of later misconduct, violence, and school adjustment problems (see Ladd, 2005). For example, Ladd and Burgess (1999, 2001) found that aggressive kindergarteners tended to have social difficulties with peers and teachers throughout the primary grades.

Investigators have also identified and studied different types of aggression, including those that have been conceptualized as direct aggression (i.e., aggression that is directly expressed toward others; also termed confrontational or overt aggression), and indirect aggression (i.e., those manifested indirectly, often termed covert, social, or relational aggression; see Underwood, 2003). Current research suggests that both direct and indirect forms of aggression are predictive of children's adjustment problems (Crick & Grotpeter, 1996).

Based on these findings, many researchers' have concluded that aggression in childhood is a moderately strong predictor of early and later maladjustment (i.e., poor peer relationships, developing conduct disorders, dropping out of school; see Coie, 2004; Ladd, 2005). There is also considerable evidence to suggest that aggressive preschoolers are at risk for poorer school performance and adjustment (e.g., Ladd & Mars, 1986; Ladd & Price, 1987).

Withdrawn Behavior. Children who interact infrequently with peers can be identified as early as the toddler and preschool years (Rubin, Burgess, & Hastings, 2002). Evidence suggests that these children differ from normative samples in that they tend to make fewer requests of peers, comply more during peer interactions, and are often ignored by peers (Rubin, 1982; Rubin & Borwick, 1984).

Many researchers have attempted to identify different types of withdrawn children and ascertain the level of risk associated with each subtype (e.g., see Gazelle & Ladd, 2003; Harrist, Zaia, Bates, Dodge, & Pettit, 1997). Rubin and colleagues (see Rubin, Coplan, & Bowker, 2009) have identified four solitary subtypes (i.e., isolate, solitary-passive, solitary-active, reticent) and differentiated them as follows: isolate preschoolers tend to play alone. Solitary-passive children play alone in a constructive manner, whereas those who are solitary-active engage in repetitive or dramatic play that tends to be disruptive. Lastly, reticent children tend to be wary or seek to maintain distance from peers. Other terms that researchers have used to define solitary children are "anxious-solitary," "active-isolated," "withdrawn-depressed," and "unsociable" or "asocial-withdrawn" and "aggressive-withdrawn" (see Gazelle & Ladd, 2003; Harrist et al., 1997; Ladd & Burgess, 1999).

Children who manifest a combination of withdrawn behaviors and anxiety (e.g., anxious-solitary or reticence) have been shown to be at greater risk for internalizing problems and peer rejection (Coplan, 2000; Coplan, Rubin, Fox, Calkins, & Stewart, 1994; Coplan & Rubin, 1998; Ladd & Troop-Gordon, 2003). Hart et al. (2000) found that reticent solitary behavior was associated with peer rejection as early as preschool, and Gazelle and Ladd (2003) found that kindergartners who had stable patterns of anxious-withdrawal were often excluded by peers. Moreover, children who were both anxious-withdrawn and excluded were more likely to have elevated trajectories of depression well into middle childhood. In contrast, active isolates or aggressive-withdrawn children appear to be at risk for externalizing problems (Coplan, 2000; Coplan, Gavinsky-Molina, Lagace-Seguin, & Wichmann, 2001; Coplan & Rubin, 1998).

Agents and Contexts that Foster Children's Peer Relations

Evidence from numerous studies suggests that young children's peer relations and social competence are socialized in a variety of settings and by many different types of socialization agents. Included among these agents and contexts are parents and teachers, the family milieu, neighborhoods and community settings, and childcare and preschool environments.

Parental Involvement

It has been proposed that the parent–child and child–peer social systems are linked, such that families influence children's peer relationships and vice versa (Ladd, 1992; Ladd & Pettit, 2002; Parke & Ladd, 1992). Some researchers (e.g., Harris, 1995, 1998), however, have challenged these assumptions by arguing that variations in children's behavior and relationships are largely genetically determined and that parents and families have little impact on children's social development (see Harris, 2000; cf., Vandell, 2000). However, if families do influence some aspects of children's social competence, it becomes important to understand how this might occur, and how such effects might be transmitted.

Ladd and Pettit (2002) have distinguished two family processes that may affect children's social competence and peer relations, and they have labeled these *indirect* and *direct* family influences. Indirect influences represent "aspects of family life that may affect children's social competence, but that do not "provide the child with any explicit connection to the world of peers"(p. 270). In contrast, direct influences are defined as "parent's efforts to socialize or manage children's social development, especially as it pertains to the peer context." (p. 270). These distinctions are used to organize relevant research on the links between parent's socialization practices and children's peer relationships.

Indirect Influences. Whether they realize it or not, parents likely affect young children's peer relationships or social competence *indirectly* through their everyday interactions and relations within the family. Substantial differences exist in the quality of family environments and parent–child relations, and variations in these factors may have consequences for children's peer relations. To illustrate: Indirect family processes might affect children's peer relations when children transfer behaviors, beliefs, or relationship patterns that they have learned within the family to the peer context.

Attachment. Some researchers theorize that children obtain emotional resources and relationship schemas (i.e., working models of relationships) from the attachments they form with parents. Once acquired, children transfer these resources and schemas to other, nonparental relationships such as those formed with peers (Bowlby, 1973; Cummings & Cummings, 2002; Elicker et al., 1992).

Studies show that children who were securely, as compared to insecurely attached to their caregivers, tended to exhibit greater social competence among peers in preschool (Waters, Wippman, & Sroufe, 1979). Moreover, secure attachment and associated relationship schemas, have been linked with children's participation in friendships and the quality of these relationships (Cassidy, Kirsh, Scolton, & Parke, 1996; Kerns, Klepac, & Cole, 1996; Lieberman, Doyle, & Markiewicz, 1999). Securely attached children also have larger support networks (Bost, Vaughn, Washington, Cielinski, & Bradbard, 1998), more positive affect displays, and higher levels of peer acceptance (LaFreniere & Sroufe, 1985).

The strength of these findings, however, has been questioned. In a meta-analysis of 63 empirical studies, Schneider, Atkinson, and Tardif (2001) obtained only modest effect sizes, leading them to conclude that attachment is only one of many factors that may contribute to children's social competence.

Parent–Child Relationships. Research on parenting as a potential influence on children's social competence and peer relations began with investigations of global parenting styles (see Baumrind, 1967). Since that time, however, investigation has shifted toward more specific aspects of the parenting process, such as parents' emotions, relationships, and interaction styles with children.

Parents' emotional and linguistic responsiveness (Black & Logan, 1995; Cassidy, Parke, Bukovsky, & Braungart, 1992), connectedness with the child (Clark & Ladd, 2000), support (Pettit, Bates, & Dodge, 1997; Pettit, Clawson, Dodge, & Bates, 1996), and synchrony or balance in parent–child relationships (Pettit & Harrist, 1993) are among the processes that have been linked with children's social competence and success in peer relationships. To illustrate, Clark and Ladd (2000) discovered that parent–child connectedness correlated positively with many features of children's peer relationships, including friendship, friendship quality, and peer group acceptance. Other similar constructs, such as parent–child mutuality (i.e., the degree of balance in parents' and children's rates of initiating play

and complying with others' initiations) have been found to correlate positively with children's peer acceptance (see Ladd & Pettit, 2002).

The way parents play with their children may also be important. Studies show that parents' directiveness and verbal engagement during play are associated with children's peer acceptance (MacDonald & Parke, 1984; Parke, MacDonald, Beitel, & Bhavnagri, 1988; Parke, MacDonald, Burks et al., 1989). Other findings revealed that, whereas mothers' play styles were more strongly linked with their daughters' social competence, fathers' play styles correlated more strongly with their sons' peer competence (Lindsey & Mize, 2000; Pettit, Brown, Mize, & Lindsey, 1998). Among the social skills that parents appear to foster when adopting the playmate role are turn-taking, synchrony in exchanges, mutuality in the determination of the content and direction of play, and matching of emotional states (Russell, Pettit, & Mize, 1998).

Negative qualities of the parent–child relationship have also been examined. Thus far, evidence reveals that intrusiveness, control, and overprotectiveness in parent–child relationships increase children's risk for peer problems, including victimization and peer abuse (Finnegan, Hodges, & Perry, 1998). For example, Ladd and Kochenderfer-Ladd (1998) reported that boys whose parent–child relationships were overly close, or enmeshed, had a greater likelihood of being victimized by their peers. Eisenberg, Fabes, and Murphy (1996) examined mothers' reactions to their children's emotional experiences and found that mothers who minimized their own feelings had children who exhibited lower levels of social competence.

Parent's Discipline Styles. There is evidence to suggest that harsh discipline may teach children (i.e., model for) antisocial behaviors. G. R. Patterson, Reid, and Dishion (1992) found that children who participated in coercive interactions within their families were more likely to use these same behaviors (e.g., aggression and noncompliance) in peer interactions. Other studies suggest that both the parent's power-assertive tactics toward their child and the child's aggressiveness toward their parents were associated with children's use of aggression among peers (Dishion, 1990; Hart, Ladd, & Burleson, 1990; Pettit, Bates, & Dodge, 1997).

Discipline that is administered in unpredictable, overcontrolling, or psychologically manipulative ways also appears to interfere with children's social competence. Such behaviors likely undermine children's autonomy and confidence, making it more difficult for them to assert themselves or take initiative in peer situations. Extreme forms of psychological or emotional control may make children submissive, making them more vulnerable to peer victimization (Finnegan, 1995; Ladd & Kochenderfer-Ladd, 1998).

In sum, findings imply that harsh, coercive, or unpredictable parenting styles impede children's competence at peer relations. Such disciplinary practices may influence children's peer relations through schemas or emotional reactions that children have acquired from these interactions (see Ladd & Pettit, 2002).

The Family Environment. Stress in the family may negatively impact children's peer relationships by limiting or removing effective parenting, models of socially competent behavior, and emotional reactions to distress. To illustrate, DeMulder, Denham, Schmidt, and Mitchell (2000) found that family stress was negatively related to children's competence with peers at school (particularly for boys).

Chronic stressors, such as poverty and sustained loss of income, have been linked with children's interpersonal maladjustment (see Magnuson & Duncan, 2002). In one study, stress, socioeconomic status (SES), and single-parent status were assessed as indexes of adversity as children entered kindergarten, and all were found to predict children's future social difficulties (Pettit, Bates, & Dodge, 1997). Similarly, extreme forms of poverty (e.g., homelessness) have been linked with childhood anxiety and depression which, in turn, have been shown to predict poor peer relations (see Buckner, Bassuk, Weinreb, & Brooks, 1999; Cole, Peeke, Martin, Truglio, & Seroczynski, 1998; Harrist, Zaia et al., 1997). Additionally, children exposed to marital conflict tend to be oppositional toward peers and less successful in friendships (Katz & Gottman, 1993).

Multiple stressors typically operate in families, and larger numbers of stressors tend to have cumulative effects on children. Patterson and colleagues (C. J. Patterson, Vaden, & Kupersmidt, 1991; G. R. Patterson, Reid, & Dishion, 1992) found that children who were exposed to a greater number of stressors were more likely to exhibit interpersonal difficulties such as peer rejection.

In sum, the evidence suggests that a number of indirect parental and family processes are associated with children's social competence and success in peer relations. Considered next are parenting practices that are directly linked to the world of peers.

Direct Influences.   Parents' attempts to manage their children's peer relations can be construed as direct influences (Ladd & Pettit, 2002) because these activities are typically performed with the aim of assisting or preparing children to participate in the peer culture. Examples include parents' attempts to mediate or regulate children's access to particular playmates, and supervise children's interactions with peers (Ladd & Pettit, 2002; Ladd, Profilet, & Hart, 1992).

Parent's Mediation of Children's Peer Contacts and Playgroups. Parents mediate, or help young children transition from the family to the peer culture by initiating and arranging playdates or other types of peer contacts. Some parents initiate peer contacts for children at very early ages, including the toddler and preschool years (Ladd, Hart, Wadsworth, & Golter, 1988). However, parents' roles in this form of mediation appear to vary with the child's age. Bhavnagri (1987) found that parent-initiated peer contacts were more often utilized for toddlers than for preschool children. It would appear that, as children get older, they

become more capable of arranging their own playdates, or need less assistance from parents to accomplish this task.

In studies conducted with preschoolers, researchers found that when parents initiated playdates for preschoolers, children tended to develop better peer relations in school (Ladd & Golter, 1988; Ladd & Hart, 1992). How parents socialized preschoolers to initiate their own playdates was investigated by Ladd and Hart (1992). These investigators found that when parents actively scaffolded the child's skill at initiating playdates, their children tended to become more active and competent at self-initiating these activities. Moreover, when compared to other preschoolers who had not been socialized this way, these children exhibited greater success in their kindergarten peer relations.

Another way that parents mediate young children's peer relations is through the arrangement of larger, group-oriented peer activities, such as weekly playgroups. In larger group settings, children may acquire the communicative and leadership skills that are needed for success in school and other group-oriented settings (Ladd et al., 1992). Lieberman (1977) found that children who had participated in playgroups were more responsive and verbal with playmates. In contrast, Ladd, Hart et al. (1988) reported that playgroup experience correlated positively with classroom adjustment for older preschoolers (ages 41 to 55 months), but not younger preschoolers (ages 23 to 40 months). It would appear that the experiences children have in peer playgroups, which may closely parallel those that occur in childcare settings and preschools, may be more beneficial for older as opposed to younger preschoolers.

Parent's Supervision and Monitoring of Children's Peer Interactions and Relations. Parental supervision has been defined as efforts to oversee and regulate children's ongoing interactions, activities, and relationships with peers. Parental monitoring, in contrast, has been variously defined as observing or knowing about children's whereabouts (e.g., surveillance), and as acquiring information from children about their social activities (see Ladd & Pettit, 2002; Stattin & Kerr, 2000). In research with young children, investigators have identified three basic types of parental supervision: interactive intervention, directive intervention, and monitoring.

Interactive Intervention. Parents engage in interactive intervention when they supervise children's peer interactions as active participants within the play context. Very young children, or social novices, benefit most from this type of supervision because they require the support of a socially skilled partner to maintain interactions with peers (see Lollis, Ross, & Tate, 1992). Bhavnagri and Parke (1991), for example, found that toddlers derived greater benefits from interactive interventions than did preschoolers.

Directive Intervention. This type of supervision tends be reactive rather than proactive, in the sense that parents intervene in children's peer interactions only when conflicts or problems arise (Lollis et al., 1992). Directive interventions tend to be used with older preschoolers, and children who receive this form of supervision tend to exhibit higher levels of peer acceptance in school settings (see Ladd & Pettit, 2002).

Monitoring. Beyond the preschool years, parents rely more on distal forms of supervision to assess children's activities with peers. Evidence reveals that low levels of parental monitoring are associated with social and academic problems in adolescents (Dishion & McMahon, 1998). However, seldom has parental supervision been studied with young children (for an exception, see Ladd & Golter, 1988).

Contextual Antecedents

Peer contexts are the environmental settings that often bring young children into contact with age mates. Examples include neighborhoods, larger community settings, childcare and preschools, and early school environments.

Neighborhoods. Because young children have limited mobility, their social encounters are dictated partly by the physical and socioeconomic characteristics of neighborhoods (Medrich, Roizen, Rubin, & Buckley, 1982). Studies show that friends tend to live near each other (Gallagher, 1958; Segoe, 1939), and that children's contacts with peers are more frequent in neighborhoods that are flat rather than hilly, and that have sidewalks, parks, and playgrounds (Medrich et al., 1982). In contrast, children have fewer peer contacts in rural and dangerous neighborhoods (see Medrich et al., 1982; Ladd, Profilet, & Hart, 1992).

Community Activities and Settings. Organized community activities, such as Brownies, Cub Scouts, and Little League, and community settings such as parks, public libraries, and community pools often serve as contexts where children meet, interact, and form relationships with peers. Young children's participation in these peer contexts appears to vary with age and social class. Older children engage in organized activities more than younger children, and middle-class children appear to be the primary participants in organized activities (Bryant, 1985; O'Donnell & Stueve, 1983). One team of investigators found that preschool children's experiences in settings such as community libraries and pools predicted lower levels of anxiety and school avoidance during their transition to kindergarten (Ladd & Price, 1987).

Childcare. Understanding how childcare affects young children's development has become a national priority. In studies designed to address this aim, researchers have examined the association between childcare participation and changes in children's social competence, peer relations, and school readiness. Thus far, evidence reflecting on this aim has been mixed (Belsky et al., 2007; National Institutes of Child Health and Human Development, Early Child Care Research Network [NICHD ECCRN], 2003; Prodromidis, Lamb, Sternberg, Hwang, & Broberg, 1995), and there have

been controversies about how the effects of childcare should be investigated, and how the resulting evidence should be interpreted. For this reason, a variety of perspectives and findings must be considered.

Members of the NICHD ECCRN have examined a plethora of childcare variables as correlates, antecedents, and predictors of children's development. Of principal interest are the effects of nonmaternal care on children's socioemotional development. One of the Network's findings was that children who spent greater time in childcare exhibited more behavior problems. This finding was corroborated by prior data showing that children's participation in childcare correlated positively with acting out behavior (Youngblade, 2003), and externalizing problems (Egeland & Heister, 1995; Han, Waldfogel, & Brooks-Gunn, 2001).

Investigators who have explored this link more thoroughly have found that while the number of hours in child care serves as a risk factor for young children's socioemotional development, this relation often depends on additional contextual factors. In particular, children who spent more hours in childcare were observed to have more negative interactions with peers (NICHD ECCRN, 2001) and higher externalizing scores (McCartney et al., 2010); however, this association seems to only hold for children who spend substantial hours in childcare (i.e., 45 hours per week) over an extended period (i.e., 3–54 months; Vandell, 2004). Further, the number of hours children spent in care was a stronger predictor of externalizing behavior for those in lower quality care than children in higher quality care (McCartney et al., 2010). Investigators have also explored the possibility of a "dose-response" relation between time spent in childcare and children's externalizing behavior, with the argument being that if a causal relation exists, there should be evidence to support that an increase in childcare hours leads to higher externalizing scores, and conversely, a decrease in childcare hours should lead to lower scores. Although longitudinal analyses do not support such a dose-response relation, McCartney et al. (2010) explored another hypothesis that would explain a causal relation between childcare hours and externalizing scores. Specifically, results indicate that children who spent a greater proportion of time with a large group of peers scored higher on externalizing behavior than other children, and this difference was greater for children who spent more hours in childcare. Finally, studies by Gunnar and colleagues (Dettling, Gunnar, & Donzella, 1999; Tout, de Haan, Campbell, & Gunnar, 1998; Watamura, Donzella, Alwin, & Gunnar, 2003) suggest another potentially gainful avenue for understanding the relations between hours in care and children's adjustment (see Vandell, 2004 for a review). These investigators examined children's cortisol levels and patterns and compared levels when children were at home with when they were at childcare. Salivary cortisol was observed to increase on days that children were in centers but not on days when these same children were at home (Watamura et al., 2003). Further, the largest increases in cortisol levels were evident in children who had difficulty regulating negative emotions and behavior (Dettling et al., 1999) and were less socially competent (Tout et al., 1998). Rises were also manifested to a greater extent in toddlers and preschoolers than in infants and school-aged children (Dettling et al., 1999; Watamura et al., 2003), suggesting that toddlers and preschoolers may experience group settings in which they are learning to negotiate with peers as stressful. An interesting next step will be to determine whether changes in childcare settings (e.g., organization of programs, caregivers' efforts) will affect how children perceive these social environments—that is, whether they see them as more supportive and less stressful (Maccoby & Lewis, 2003).

Even though evidence suggests that children who spend more time in childcare often exhibit more behavior problems, positive links between children's childcare experience and peer relations have also been reported (see Fabes, Hanish, & Martin, 2003; Ladd, Profilet, & Hart, 1992), and support for this contention has increased in recent years (see Field, Masi, Goldstein, Perry, & Park, 1988; Howes, 1988; Prodromidis et al., 1995). For example, Howes (1988) found that, in the context of childcare settings, young children formed friendships at very early ages, and tended to maintain these friendships over considerable periods of time (e.g., up to 2 years). Findings also indicate that the friendships children form in childcare or preschool settings, and the associated interpersonal skills they acquire in these contexts, may function as supports during subsequent developmental transitions, such as entrance into grade school (see Ladd, 1990; Ladd & Price, 1987). Further, when coupled with preventive or compensatory educational programming, childcare has been linked with positive growth in other aspects of children's development. Love et al. (2003), for example, found that children from low income families who were enrolled in Early Head Start programs displayed reductions in aggressive behavior problems and gains in cognitive, language, and socioemotional development. These results suggest that higher quality childcare environments have the potential not only to improve children's social development but also transmit skills that prepare them for subsequent developmental challenges.

Early School Environments.   Many young children participate in preschool programs and, by the time they reach age 5 or 6, nearly all children attend school (Coie, Watt et al., 1993). Classrooms are an important context for children's social development, but some types of classrooms appear more beneficial for this purpose than do others. Kontos, Burchinal, Howes, Wisseh, and Galinsky (2002) found that the provision of creative activities for children (e.g., books, art supplies, creative play, group learning) and teacher involvement (coded as routine, complex, or none) were significant predictors of children's interactions with peers. More specifically, creative activities (e.g., open-ended art projects, fantasy play) and little or no teacher involvement predicted more complex interactions with peers.

Other findings have shown that in high-density classrooms (i.e., those with less physical space per child) there is a higher incidence of children's behavior problems (Campbell & Dill, 1985; see Phyfe-Perkins, 1980; Smith & Connolly, 1980). Higher levels of cooperative peer play and positive talk have been documented in classrooms with individual learning centers (Field et al., 1988). More fighting and nonsocial play (e.g., parallel play) has been observed in classrooms that contain fewer toys. Some types of play materials, such as Play-Doh, sand, water, crayons, or paint appear to elicit primarily nonsocial forms of play (Rubin, 1977; Rubin, Fein, & Vandenberg, 1983).

School playgrounds are another important context for peer interaction (Hart, 1993; Ladd & Price, 1993). Evidence suggests that outdoor playgrounds can stimulate as much or more social play than indoor environments (Frost, 1986; Hart, 1993). Evidence implies that children develop certain behavioral styles on the playground and these styles may affect the way a child is perceived by her or his peers. For example, aggressive children tended to become disliked by peers, whereas cooperative children were favored as play partners (see Ladd et al., 1988; Ladd & Price, 1993).

Out-of-School Care.   Researchers and policymakers have exhibited a growing interest in the role of out-of-school contexts for children and youth. Largely, the impetus for this interest has stemmed from the varied outcomes children seem to experience, depending on the type of out-of-school care they are involved in, and evidence indicating that growing numbers of children are participating in before- and after-school programs and other extracurricular activities. For instance, this type of programming is one of the fastest growing segments of childcare services (Seligson, Gannett, & Cotlin, 1992).

Much of the research to date has compared children who attend programs with those who are involved in other care settings including self-care (time spent without adult supervision), mother care (returning home), formal adult-supervised care (after-school programs), and other supervised arrangements (see NICHD ECCRN, 2004; Vandell, Pierce, & Dadisman, 2005). Thus far, investigators have found that whereas children in self-care arrangements often engaged in antisocial behavior, children in formal, adult-supervised care were less prone toward misconduct (Posner & Vandell, 1994). In fact, Posner and Vandell found that children who participated in formal after-school care spent more time in academic and enrichment activities (e.g., art, music, drama) and less time watching television. These children were better adjusted on a number of developmental criteria, including academic achievement and peer relations. Further corroboration of these findings was obtained by Pettit, Laird, Bates, and Dodge (1997). These investigators studied young school-age children in a variety of after-school care arrangements, and found that the amount of time spent without adult supervision, both before and after school, predicted lower levels of peer competence.

Given that families have increasingly turned to formal care arrangements to assist with the gap between children's school and parents' work schedules, investigators have focused their attention on associations between children's formal program participation and developmental outcomes. Studies addressing this aim have yielded mixed findings. Some investigators have detected no effects or, in some cases, even negative relations between program participation and children's functioning, whereas others have found that involvement in formal programs was linked positively with academic and social outcomes (e.g., NICHD ECCRN 2004; Posner & Vandell, 1994; Pierce, Bolt, & Vandell, 2010). Similar to early research in childcare, these discrepant findings may be a result of differing program quality and children's varied experiences in such programs.

Findings from research conducted by the NICHD ECCRN (2004) indicated that there are important relations between family factors and out-of-school care, such that children with certain family characteristics were more likely to be involved in adult supervised out-of-school arrangements. In particular, participation in before- and after-school programs was more likely if family income was higher, mothers were employed for more hours, and mothers were single parents. Given these characteristics, these findings support the hypothesis that a primary function of such programs is supervision of children of working mothers. Additionally, consistent participation in before- and after-school programs was also related to early childcare, such that children who spent more hours in early childcare were more likely to attend programs in kindergarten and first grade. Accordingly, although programs are promoted as a means to endow children, particularly those of low-income families, with additional educational and enrichment activities (Larner, Zippiroli, & Behrman, 1999), there was little evidence to suggest that programs were serving this function, at least for the children participating in the NICHD childcare study. Similarly, family factors were also related to children's involvement in extracurricular activities. Children were more likely to participate in extracurricular activities if family incomes were higher and mothers were more educated. Unlike participation in before- and after-school programs, however, which was more likely when mothers worked more hours per week and children spent more hours in early childcare, participation in extracurricular activities was *less* likely when mothers worked more hours and when children spent more hours in early childcare. The NICHD ECCRN posited that these findings suggest a key function of extracurricular activities in the early elementary grades is supplemental enrichment.

Finally, given that not all after-school programs are of similar quality, scholars have called for examination of specific program features that may be associated with high-quality care. In particular, three identified setting characteristics have received endorsement as practices consistent with high-quality programming because all appear to have the potential to confer developmental benefits upon participants. A positive staff–child relationship, which has been characterized by staff's positive and supportive behavior with all children in the program, has been related to children's academic and social skills (Pierce et al., 2010). Another feature of high-quality programming is diversity in the array of developmentally appropriate activities that are provided as opportunities for skill building (Pierce et al., 2010). The final setting characteristic associated with positive child outcomes is programming flexibility (Beckett, Hawken, & Jacknowitz, 2001). Surprisingly, Pierce et al. (2010) did not find that supporting children's freedom to choose in the selection of activities was related to academic and social development during the early grade school years. These investigators speculate that support for autonomy within activities, rather than student choice of activities, may be more salient for positive child outcomes.

In sum, research findings are consistent with the hypothesis that physical and organizational features of classrooms and after-school arrangements are associated with children's peer relations and social adjustment. Next, the teacher–child relationship is considered as a determinant of young children's peer relations and competence.

Teacher–Child Relationships

Compared to evidence assembled on other socializing agents and contexts, relatively less is known about children's relationships with teachers, particularly how these relationships are linked with children's social development. Accordingly, investigators have begun to study specific features of the teacher–child relationship, and the association that exists between these features and children's social and scholastic competence (see Birch & Ladd, 1996; Pianta, Hamre, & Stuhlman, 2003).

Features of the Teacher–Child Relationship. Several investigators have theorized that the teacher–child relationship encompasses multiple important relationship features. Howes and colleagues (e.g., Howes & Hamilton, 1992, 1993; Howes & Matheson, 1992) conceptualized the teacher–child relationship from an attachment perspective, and used this framework to demarcate its features (e.g., secure, avoidant, resistant/ambivalent). Other investigators, such as Lynch & Cicchetti (1992), identified similar features but gave them different labels (e.g., optimal, deprived, disengaged, confused, average). Pianta and colleagues have drawn upon attachment theory and related empirical findings to formulate a model of the teacher–child relationship that contains three qualitative features: closeness, conflict, and dependency (Hamre & Pianta, 2001; Pianta & Steinberg, 1992; Pianta, Steinberg, & Rollins, 1995). Most of the research conducted to date has been undertaken to evaluate the tripartite teacher–child relationship model and probe its antecedents and associations with student outcomes. In particular, higher levels of teacher–child closeness predict good work habits and fewer internalizing and externalizing problems in later school years (Baker, 2006; Birch & Ladd, 1997; Hamre & Pianta, 2001). Conversely, negative teacher–child relationships are characterized by high conflict and dependency and low closeness, and appear to operate as risk factors for children's school success. Given the consistent pattern of findings supporting the benefit of a close teacher–child relationship, investigators sought to further examine potential predictors of teacher–child relationships of varying quality.

Antecedents of the Teacher–Child Relationship. A key assumption guiding research on the teacher–child relationship is that the child's typical way of interacting or behaving toward others, or their behavioral orientations, affects the relationships they form with teachers. Ladd and colleagues (e.g., Birch & Ladd, 1998; Ladd, Birch, & Buhs, 1999; Ladd & Burgess, 1999) found that the behavioral orientations that predicted children's success or difficulty in peer relationships also forecast the type of relationships they developed with teachers. To be specific, throughout the early school years, aggressive children were much more likely to develop conflictual rather than close relationships with their teachers. Asocial behavior was also a correlate of children's concurrent and future problems in both relationship domains. Prosocial styles of interacting with peers and teachers were closely tied to children's concurrent closeness with teachers, but were not as predictive of future teacher–child relationship quality as antisocial or asocial behavioral styles.

Additionally, distinctions between boys' and girls' behavior, or at least teachers' perceptions of their behavior, have been found to differentially predict teacher–child relationship quality. For instance, boys are more likely to be rated by teachers as having conflictual teacher–child relationships, while girls are more likely to be perceived as having teacher–child closeness (Hamre & Pianta, 2001; Rudasill & Rimm-Kaufman, 2009). Further, it appears that children's asocial behavior is more deleterious to boys' than girls' adjustment in kindergarten (Coplan, Prakash, O'Niel, & Armer, 2004; Nelson, Rubin, & Fox, 2005). Accordingly, boys may be at greater risk for negative teacher–child interactions than girls.

Research examining differences in children's temperament is beginning to emerge as a potentially fruitful avenue for understanding how child attributes may differentially relate to teacher–child relationship quality. Temperament has been described as an individual's style of responding to environmental stimuli. It is a biologically based, multidimensional construct that emerges during infancy and is shaped by environmental features (Rudasill & Rimm-Kaufman, 2009; Rothbart & Bates, 2006; Thomas & Chess, 1977). Primarily, temperament is studied as a two-system construct comprised of reactivity and regulation dimensions. There tend to be profound differences in these dimensions for young children, which may affect their socioemotional development. Two common measures of temperament include

children's shyness and effortful control. Children's shyness may suppress their ability to form positive teacher–child relationships. To be specific, evidence suggests that high levels of shyness may pose risks to children's relationships because shy children are less likely to initiate interactions with teachers, which may impede their ability to develop closeness (Rudasill & Rimm-Kaufman, 2009). In addition to shyness, researchers are also interested in the internal regulatory system underlying children's social behavior—effortful control. Two dimensions that are thought to work together to contribute to children's effortful control are inhibitory control and attentional focusing. Low effortful control has been associated with children's externalizing behaviors, and consequently, children's difficulty forming positive relationships in school (Fantuzzo, McWayne, Perry, & Childs, 2004; Olson, Sameroff, Kerr, Lopez, & Wellman, 2005). Conversely, high levels of effortful control relate to children's social competence and positive peer relationships (Goldsmith, Aksan, Essex, Smider, & Vandell, 2001). Similarly, effortful control appears to contribute to children's ability to successfully interact with teachers and, in turn, form positive teacher–child relationships (Blair, Denham, Kochanoff, & Whipple, 2004). Rudasill and Rimm-Kaufman (2009) provided additional support for these findings such that children with lower levels of effortful control were more likely to have conflict with teachers, whereas children with higher levels were more likely to exhibit teacher–child closeness. Thus, children with higher levels of effortful control were likely to be perceived more positively by teachers.

While children's attributes that contribute to teacher–child relationships are becoming well documented, identifying teacher characteristics that are related to relationship quality with children remains an understudied area of research. This dearth of information begs for additional research to delineate teachers' individual characteristics and classroom practices that successfully engage children in close, supportive relationships.

The Teacher–Child Relationship and Children's Peer Relations and School Adjustment. Within early classroom environments, the relationships that children form with teachers have been hypothesized to yield various social "provisions" (i.e., supports, stressors) that may operate as risks or protective factors for children's development (see Birch & Ladd, 1996; Ladd et al., 1997). Evidence gathered in a study conducted by Ladd et al. (1999) showed that kindergarten children who exhibited higher levels of antisocial behavior not only developed less close and more conflictual relationships with their teachers, but also lower levels of peer acceptance and friendships with classroom peers. Subsequently, children who developed these adverse relationships with both teachers and peers manifested lower levels of classroom participation and less favorable achievement trajectories.

Beyond these findings, some corroboration was found

for the premise that teacher–child relationships buffer children from maladjustment, especially during periods of challenge or transition. To illustrate, it was discovered that teacher–child closeness at the outset of kindergarten forecast increases in children's participation in classroom peer activities and in their affection toward school, regardless of their tendency to engage in aggressive behaviors (Ladd, Buhs, & Seid, 2000; Ladd & Burgess, 2001). Teacher–child relationship quality has also been found to moderate the relation between temperament and peer play among preschoolers. Young children with more difficult temperaments were found to exhibit more disruptive peer play when teacher–child relationships were characterized by conflict. However, Griggs, Gagnon, Huelsman, Kidder-Ashley, and Ballard (2009) found that in teacher–child relationships with low or even typical levels of conflict, there was no association between easy or difficult temperament and disruptive peer play. Thus, lower levels of conflict in teacher–child relationships may reduce the risk of negative behavioral outcomes generally associated with preschoolers who have difficult temperaments.

Compelling evidence suggests that positive teacher–child relationships may be particularly salient for children who are at increased risk of behavioral and academic maladjustment. In particular, Meehan, Hughes, and Cavell (2003) found that positive teacher–child relationships serve a compensatory function for children with multiple risk factors, such as aggressive children who exhibit additional characteristics commonly associated with poorer outcomes (e.g., minority status). Data suggest that children who are African American or Hispanic and aggressive are at heightened risk because these students are less likely to enjoy positive relationships with teachers (Ladd et al., 1999) and are disproportionately represented in statistics on poor school adjustment (Burchinal, Peisner-Feinberg, Pianta, & Hughes, 2002). In light of these data, Meehan et al. (2003) tested a moderated model of teacher support as a compensatory resource for children under conditions of dual risk, namely, aggression and minority status (i.e., African American and Hispanic). Results indicate that after controlling for initial levels of aggression, teacher ratings of support significantly predicted lower levels of teacher-rated aggression for African American, Hispanic, and Caucasian children 18 months later; however, positive teacher–child relationships were more strongly predictive of lower levels of aggression for aggressive African American and Hispanic children. This evidence may suggest that although aggressive African American and Hispanic children in the early school years may experience less positive relationships with teachers than aggressive Caucasian students, African American and Hispanic children may be more responsive to teachers' efforts to establish warm and supportive relationships than are aggressive Caucasian students for whom positive interactions with teachers are more commonplace. Meehan et al. further suggest that salient, positive interactions with teachers might, in turn, promote aggressive Afri-

can American and Hispanic students' sense of belonging in the classroom and enhance their commitment to academic and social norms.

Overall, closer teacher–child relationships seem to provide young children with resources (e.g., emotional security, guidance, aid) that facilitate an "approach" orientation (as opposed to an "avoidant" or "resistant" stance) toward the interpersonal and scholastic demands of the classroom and school (Birch & Ladd, 1996; Howes, Matheson, & Hamilton, 1994; Pianta et al., 1995).

Features and Functions of Children's Early Peer Relationships

In addition to describing the types of relationships children have with peers, researchers have also investigated how these relationships are formed, the types of experiences that children have in these relationships, and the possible effects that peer relationships have on children's development. Interest in these processes has been the impetus for a large number of investigations.

Formation of Children's Peer Relationships

In order for young children to form friendships, become accepted in their peer group, or extricate themselves from aggressor–victim relations, they must first develop the social skills and competencies that are needed to form, maintain, and terminate peer relationships. For young children, these skills are most likely acquired through peer interactions that occur during playdates, in neighborhoods, childcare, and school.

Friendship Formation. Not all of children's interactions with peers result in the formation of a friendship. Children are selective about the persons they choose as friends, and their choices are guided by demographic (Hartup, 1983), behavioral (Rubin, Lynch, Coplan, Rose-Krasnor, & Booth, 1994), personal (see Aboud & Mendelson, 1996), or psychological considerations (Epstein, 1989). Children typically befriend others who are similar to themselves in age (Hartup, 1970), gender (DeRosier, & Patterson, 1995; Graham & Cohen, 1997; Howes & Phillipsen, 1992; Kupersmidt, Masters, & Furman, 1981; also see Gottman, 1986), and race (Asher, Oden, & Gottman, 1977; Graham & Cohen, 1997; Kupersmidt et al. 1995). In addition, children often choose friends that have similar attitudes, beliefs, personalities, and interactional styles (Epstein, 1989). Rubin et al. (1994) observed the interactions of unfamiliar preschoolers and found that children tended to associate with peers who engaged in similar play behaviors. Similarly, Poulin et al. (1997) found that third graders tended to be friends with peers who displayed similar behavior patterns including aggression, shyness, leadership, and rough-and-tumble play.

Although the degree of similarity between children is an essential ingredient for friendship, it is also important to understand that some aspects of similarity may vary with children's developmental stage or may be "created" out of children's interests and interactions. It is also of note that children need not be similar in all ways to become friends. Rather, only those characteristics or interests that are salient or important to the two partners may matter (Furman, 1982). For example, among toddlers, shared interest in a particular toy could provide the foundation for sustained interaction and, eventually, "friendship," whereas preschoolers or young children may require more complex similarities for a friendship to develop.

Although there is evidence indicating that children are attracted to peers with whom they share similarities, it is also clear that children do not develop friendships with all of the children to whom they are attracted (Parker, 1986). In fact, it is likely that the friendship formation process is complex. As two children interact and become acquainted and aware of each other's social behaviors, skills, and personalities, their interest in each other may wax and wane (Furman, 1982).

To examine the acquaintanceship process, and gain more insight into how children make friends, Gottman (1983) investigated the role of conversational processes in the formation of preschoolers' friendships. In these studies, Gottman set out to determine whether specific conversational processes would predict the extent to which pairs of unacquainted children "hit it off" and progressed toward friendship. After recording the interactions of many pairs of preschoolers, Gottman (1983) evaluated a small number of salient conversational processes to determine their ability to predict friendship formation. Six conversational elements emerged as important predictors of successful friendship formation: (a) connectedness and clarity of information; (b) information exchange; (c) establishment of common ground; (d) conflict resolution; (e) positive reciprocity; and (f) self-disclosure. Children who were successful at making friends were likely to use information exchange as a safe interaction strategy when conversation went astray, and were able to adeptly escalate and deescalate levels of play as necessary. Moreover, individual children differed in their ability to successfully execute many of these conversational processes. Taken together, these findings suggest that some or all of these six conversational processes aided in the development of friendships.

Building upon this work, Parker (1986) designed a novel study in which the same six conversational processes identified by Gottman (1983) were manipulated in order to determine whether they were causally related to friendship formation. To accomplish this task, a "surrogate" preschool child called "Panduit" acted as an experimental confederate. Panduit was a 2-foot-tall green doll that contained a hidden electronic receiver/speaker that enabled it to carry on age-appropriate conversations with preschoolers. A female and male assistant were trained to speak as Panduit in a child-like voice while systematically varying the skillfulness of their conversation. Two experimental condi-

tions were created, one in which Panduit was skilled and one in which Panduit was unskilled. Results showed that preschoolers who interacted with the skilled Panduit were more likely to hit it off than children who were paired with the unskilled Panduit.

The findings from this study, and from Gottman's (1983) longitudinal investigation, illustrate the importance of preschoolers' conversational skills for friendship formation. As young children become acquainted, the clarity and connectedness of communication, information exchange, establishment of common-ground activities, and conflict resolution become increasingly important as determinants of friendship or "hitting it off." Disclosing information about oneself, although of little predictive value during initial encounters, did forecast progress toward friendship as children became better acquainted. Clearly, these investigations offer considerable insight into the means by which young children form friendships.

Becoming Accepted or Rejected in Peer Groups. Joining and becoming an accepted member of a peer group are important social tasks that nearly all children confront as they venture forth into neighborhoods, day care, or school systems. To understand why some children are more successful at these tasks than others, researchers have studied how children enter peer activities, and how they develop social reputations in peer groups (e.g., become accepted or rejected by peers).

Peer Group Entry Research. Investigators relied on observational methods to study how preschoolers attempted to join peers' activities. Corsaro (1981), for example, took extensive field notes detailing children's efforts to enter ongoing playgroups, and peers' responses to children's entry attempts. He discovered that children's entry bids were initially resisted about 50% of the time, and that peers tended to use one of five strategies to exclude potential entrants: claims of ownership, appeals to limitations based on overcrowding, verbal resistance without justification, denial of friendship, and reference to arbitrary rules. Even when children were excluded, however, Corsaro found that some persisted and eventually gained access to peers' activities.

Putallaz and Gottman (1981) extended this line of research by examining how children who were more or less accepted by peers differed in their attempts to enter ongoing peer group activities. Second and third graders who were the most and least accepted by their classmates participated in the study as either an entrant (i.e., the child attempting to enter the group) or as a member of the peer group (dyads were used to represent peer groups). Gaining entry into the dyad's game proved somewhat difficult for all children because the study was designed so that no child was able to join the group without some resistance. The findings showed that popular, more than unpopular children, were more likely to have their entry bids ignored or rejected. This likely occurred because the unpopular children tended to use entry bids that drew attention to themselves (i.e., talked about themselves, stated their feelings and opinions) as opposed to acting in ways that were relevant to the peers' ongoing conversation or activity. Thus, Putallaz and Gottman concluded that well-liked children may be better equipped to negotiate entry into peer groups because they are capable of identifying situational norms or expectations and acting accordingly.

Putallaz (1983) investigated this hypothesis further with preschool boys while simultaneously trying to correct for previous methodological problems such as the entrant's prior familiarity with the peer group and the lack of standardization of responses across children's entry bids. To overcome these limitations, the investigator used two confederates, who were not known by the entrant, to serve as the peer group in the entry situations. The confederates were trained to carry out a scripted conversation while playing different games to ensure that all entrants were exposed to a comparable entry situation. Results corroborated Putallaz and Gottman's (1981) findings in that children who used entry bids that drew attention to themselves were less likely to gain access to the peer activity. Children in the study who made these self-focused, low relevance entry bids were often not well-accepted by their classmates in kindergarten, whereas children who became accepted tended to use more appropriate bids. Putallaz (1983) concluded that the relevance of a child's entry bids in relation to peers' activities was an important factor in determining whether the peer group would accept them.

Dodge, Schlundt, Schocken, and Delugach (1983) found that boys' attempts to enter groups were more often successful when they used a particular sequence of entry behaviors. Successful entrants first gathered information by observing peers' behavior while waiting or hovering on the periphery of their activity. Next, based on information they had gleaned by observing peers and their play, the entrants imitated some of the peer's behaviors. Finally, after completing these steps, the entrants made an effort to join the play by enacting relevant, group-oriented statements or entry behaviors. Results showed that popular and average boys were three times more likely to follow this order of entry behaviors than were rejected or neglected boys. Dodge et al. concluded that children's success at group entry was maximized when they followed this strategy of progressing from lower to higher risk entry behaviors.

In later investigations, researchers investigated how characteristics of both the entrants and the peer group might affect children's success at joining peer groups. Putallaz and Wasserman (1989) observed the entry behaviors of first-, third- and fifth-grade children in a naturalistic setting and found that children were less likely to approach peer dyads and triads than individuals or groups composed of four or more peers. They also found that girls' entry bids, as opposed to boys' bids, were more likely to be rejected or ignored by their peers. Zarbatany and colleagues (Borja-Alvarez, Zarbatany, & Pepper, 1991; Zarbatany & Pepper, 1996; Zarbatany, Van Brunschot, Meadows, & Pepper, 1996) found that, when attempting to join peers, girls were less obtrusive and active than boys, and when in the role of a group member or "host," girls admitted more newcomers and were more attentive to entrants than were boys.

Research on the Antecedents of Children's Peer Group Status. In addition to studies of peer group entry, which focused on the behaviors children utilized to access ongoing peer activities, researchers also investigated other factors that were hypothesized to have an effect on children's acceptance by members of their peer groups (e.g., classmates). Initially, investigators searched for child characteristics that correlated with peer group acceptance versus rejection. However, as the limits of correlational data became apparent (see Moore, 1967), researchers began to study the behavioral antecedents of children's peer status. The most important of these investigations were conducted with school-age boys and were designed as short-term longitudinal studies (see Coie & Kupersmidt, 1983; Dodge, 1983). Dodge (1983) created small playgroups of unacquainted boys and observed their interactions during eight play sessions conducted over a two-week period. Following the final play session, children completed sociometric interviews, and those who had become popular, average, rejected, or controversial with their play partners were identified. Analyses were then conducted to determine how children behaved before they developed their status or reputations with play partners. Dodge found that different patterns of behavior emerged over time for children in each status group. For example, boys who engaged in high rates of social conversation and cooperative play, and seldom acted aggressively, became well-accepted by their playgroup companions. Rejected boys, on the other hand, were prone to display more inappropriate, disruptive play behaviors and made more hostile verbalizations than boys who were later identified as average in status. Compared to children in the other status groups, rejected boys also hit peers more often.

Using a similar methodology, Coie and Kupersmidt (1983) identified boys who were classified as popular, average, rejected, or neglected by their peer groups at school, and then observed them in either unfamiliar or familiar playgroups over a six-week period. Four boys, one from each of the four sociometric categories, were assigned to each group. Videotaped observations and sociometric interviews were used to chart the boys' behavior and their evolving peer status in each type of playgroup. These investigators found that, in both types of playgroups (i.e., familiar and unfamiliar partners), popular boys rarely engaged in aggressive behavior, often reminded others of the rules, and established group norms. Rejected boys, in contrast, were viewed by playmates as troublemakers (e.g., as persons who start fights) and tended to be more hostile and aggressive in their interactions with peers. In addition, it was discovered that boys who were rejected by their classmates in school quickly formed the same reputations in unfamiliar playgroups. In fact, after only three play sessions, the correlation between children's classroom peer status and the reputations they acquired in their playgroups was as high in the unfamiliar condition as it was in groups of familiar peers. Based on these findings, Coie and Kupersmidt concluded that the rejected peer status could be quite stable across peer groups, because boys who are rejected by peers tend to bring aversive behaviors with them into new peer situations.

Similar findings were reported with samples of preschool children in naturalistic contexts (e.g., classrooms and playgrounds). Ladd, Price, and Hart (1988, 1990) found that preschooler's playground behaviors at the outset of school predicted changes in their status among classmates by the middle and end of the school year. Children with higher levels of cooperative play tended to become better liked by classmates over time, whereas children who frequently argued and engaged in physical aggression tended to become disliked and rejected by peers. Likewise, in research on the transition to school (Ladd & Price, 1987), it was discovered that children who utilized prosocial behaviors with a broad range of peers in preschool tended to become more liked and less rejected by their new classmates in kindergarten. In contrast, preschoolers who tended to coerce many of their classmates in preschool were often rejected by peers and perceived by teachers as hostile toward classmates as they entered kindergarten.

In later years, these findings were augmented by innovations in researcher's conceptions of aggression and its function in peer interactions. Instead of defining aggression as a global construct, distinctions were made between qualitatively different forms of aggression (i.e., reactive and proactive aggression) based on their likely social functions (Coie, Dodge, Terry, & Wright, 1991; Dodge & Coie, 1987; Dodge, Coie, Pettit, & Price, 1990). In general, reactive aggression was defined as aversive behaviors, often elicited by children's emotional or defensive reactions to some form of peer provocation. Conversely, proactive aggression involved performing aggressive behaviors in order to achieve a specific goal or consequence. In addition, the concept of proactive aggression was further differentiated into instrumental aggression, which served the purpose of obtaining external, often object-oriented goals (e.g., hitting to gain access to another's toy) and bullying, which was often used to achieve social domination or control over peers.

To better understand how these different forms of aggression affected children's reputations in the peer group, researchers conducted another wave of playgroup studies with children of different ages. For example, Dodge et al. (1990) examined the social interactions of groups of unacquainted first- and third-grade boys. Results demonstrated that instrumental aggression was associated with peer group rejection at all ages whereas reactive aggression and bullying were found to be more closely associated with peer group rejection only in older children.

One limitation of this line of research was that investigators tended to record direct forms of aggression (e.g., physical aggression) and overlook indirect modes that were thought to be typical of girls (indirect, social, or relational aggression; i.e., subtle or covert acts such as gossiping behind a child's back, telling others not to play with a particular child, and revealing another child's secrets; see Cairns, Cairns, Neckerman, Ferguson, Gariepy, 1989; Crick & Grotpeter, 1995; Galen & Underwood; 1997; Lagerspetz, Bjorkqvist, & Peltonen, 1988). Because investigators tended to study physical attacks, they often found that boys were more aggressive than girls (Coie, Dodge, & Coppotelli, 1982; Coie, Dodge, & Kupersmidt, 1990; French, 1988, 1990). Eventually, these findings were challenged by researchers who argued that girls did act aggressively, but unlike boys, they were more likely to express such behavior in indirect and subtle ways (Cairns et al., 1989; Crick & Grotpeter, 1995; Lagerspetz et al., 1988).

After more than a decade of investigation, analyses of the evidence (e.g., meta-analyses were conducted on multiple studies; see Card, Studky, Sawalani, & Little, 2008) provide support for the hypothesis that boys exhibit higher levels of direct aggression than do girls. When hitting, kicking, pushing, and other forms of physical aggression are monitored in peer interactions, the evidence suggests that boys more than girls are the perpetrators. Lesser support has been found, however, for the proposition that girls exceed boys in the use of indirect aggression, or the idea that indirect methods of attack are preferred by females. Based on data from 148 studies, Card et al. concluded that differences in girls' and boys' use of indirect aggression were "negligible." Rather, the two forms of aggression correlated substantially, suggesting that children who tended to use one form of assault were also likely to use the other.

Other aspects of children's social interactions and skills may play a role in the development of peer status as well. As is the case with friendship (cf. Gottman, 1983), recent studies suggest that children's communication skills, particularly those contributing to the connectedness and coherence of their discourse with peers, are related to the emergence and maintenance of social status. Hazen and Black (1989) found that well-liked (i.e., high-status) children were more skilled than disliked children at clearly directing verbal and nonverbal communications toward specific peers, and at responding to peers' communications in a contingent and relevant way. High-status children were also more likely to offer a rationale or alternative idea when rejecting peer's initiations.

In a second study, Black and Hazen (1990) identified high- and low-status preschoolers and then observed their communications with acquainted and unacquainted peers. In both the acquainted and unacquainted groups, low-status children were less likely than their high-status counterparts to respond contingently to the questions and initiations of others. They also initiated more irrelevant turns in the conversation than did more accepted peers. Because disliked children demonstrated these response patterns with acquainted and unacquainted peers, the investigators concluded that communication clarity and connectedness may contribute to both the formation and maintenance of peer status (Black & Hazen, 1990).

Pathways to Peer Victimization

Because it is unethical to experimentally manipulate the possible causes of peer abuse to determine whether children become victimized, researchers have addressed this question by searching for factors that precede or correlate with peer victimization. Of course, this approach to understanding the processes that lead to victimization is limited because it does not allow researchers to fully discern cause and effect (D. G. Perry, Hodges, & Egan, 2001). Thus, caution must be observed when interpreting findings so as not to unfairly blame victims for the maltreatment they experience.

In the last decade or so, the possible determinants of peer victimization that received the most empirical attention were child, interpersonal, and family factors (see Graham & Juvonen, 1998; D. G. Perry et al., 2001). Although each of these potential determinants is reviewed separately, it is likely that young children's risk for peer victimization is affected by a confluence of child, peer, and family factors (see D. G. Perry et al., 2001).

Types of Victims. Evidence suggests that victimized children fall into at least two behavioral subtypes— *nonaggressive victims* and *aggressive or "bully" victims* (victims who are also aggressive or who bully others; see Perren & Alsaker, 2006; Schwartz, Dodge, Pettit, & Bates, 1997). More research attention has been focused on nonaggressive victims than on their aggressive counterparts because fewer of the latter subtype tend to be identified in research samples (Kochenderfer-Ladd & Ladd, 2001; Ladd & Kochenderfer-Ladd, 1998; Olweus, 1978; Schwartz et al., 1997; Schwartz, Proctor, & Chien, 2001).

Antecedents of Victimization and Victimization Trajectories. Both environmental and genetic factors have been examined as potential causes of peer victimization. Thus far, greater empirical support has been found for environmental determinants. Evidence from twin studies, for example, suggests that victimization is better predicted by environmental than genetic determinants (Brendgen et al., 2008).

Child Characteristics. Differences in children's behavior and cognitions have been examined as potential causes of peer victimization. Early studies of victimized children characterized them as emotionally anxious, low in self-esteem, and physically weaker than bullies (Olweus, 1978, 1984). Subsequent studies show that nonaggressive victims differ from other children in a variety of ways. For example, data from a Swiss study of 5- to 7-year-olds (Perren & Alsaker, 2006) showed that victims differed

from nonvictims, bullies, and bully-victims on a number of behavioral (e.g., submissive, lacked leadership skills, less sociable, less cooperative) and relational dimensions (e.g., more isolated, fewer playmates).

In addition, victimized children appear to have thought patterns that differ from nonvictimized children. Like other types of aggressive children, *aggressive victims* appear to assume that peers harbor hostile intentions toward them (Schwartz et al., 1997; Schwartz, Procter, & Chien, 2001). Reactive-aggressive victims, in particular, have been found to have hostile attributional biases, or a tendency to misinterpret peers' motives in ambiguous circumstances as hostile (Schwartz et al., 1997). Low self-regard has been documented in both passive and aggressive victims, with the latter group manifesting the most debilitating self-perceptions (Perry et al., 2001). Findings reported by Egan and Perry (1998) showed that children's sense of social failure not only anteceded peer victimization, but also grew stronger after they had been victimized, suggesting that low self-regard is both a cause and a consequence of peer victimization. Similarly, Graham and Juvonen (1998) compared the responses of victimized and nonvictimized children, and found that victims were significantly more likely to blame themselves for peers' attacks than were nonvictims.

Parenting and Socialization in the Family. The features of children's early rearing environments, and parenting practices in particular, have been implicated as potential determinants of young children's exposure to peer victimization. Barker and colleagues (Barker et al., 2008) followed victimized preschoolers and found that these children tended to traverse one of three trajectories as they matured (i.e., low/increasing, moderate/increasing, or high/chronic victimization). Exposure to harsh parenting emerged as one the best predictors of whether children followed the most severe (high/chronic) of the three victimization trajectories. Other findings indicate that preschoolers with histories of anxious-resistant or anxious-avoidant caregiver attachment tend to be victimized (Troy & Sroufe, 1987), and that kindergartners exposed to higher levels of maternal directiveness are at risk for victimization (Reavis, Keane, & Calkins, 2010).

In studies of passive victims, it has been reported that parents' coercive control and lack of responsiveness correlated positively with girls' status as victims, and that maternal overprotectiveness correlated positively with boys' status as victims (Finnegan, 1995; Olweus, 1993). Among aggressive boys, abusive family conditions were associated with vulnerability to peer victimization (Schwartz et al., 1997).

Peer Relationships and Victimization. Research shows that children who fail to develop allies within their peer groups are more likely to become victimized. In particular, children who are rejected, or highly disliked by most members of their peer groups, appear to be vulnerable to this kind of maltreatment (Gazelle & Ladd, 2002;

Perry et al., 2001) and become increasingly victimized over time (Hodges & Perry, 1999). Results from other investigations indicate that children with a greater number of reciprocated friendships experienced less victimization, even when they exhibited other risk factors that may precipitate peer abuse (physical weakness, poor family relationships; Hodges, Boivin, Vitaro, & Bukowski, 1999; Hodges, Malone, & Perry, 1997; Schwartz, Dodge, Pettit, & Bates, 2000).

The School Context and Victimization. Because victimization is particularly likely to happen when adult supervision is minimal, it has been argued that unmonitored school contexts (e.g., school playgrounds, bathrooms, recess periods) may be especially conducive to victimization. At least one researcher (Olweus, 1993) has shown that lower teacher–student ratios during school recess were associated with higher levels of peer victimization.

Features and Processes of Children's Peer Relationships

After identifying the different forms of children's peer relationships (i.e., friendship, peer group acceptance/ rejection, victimization), investigators turned their attention toward describing the nature of peer relationships in terms of their underlying features and processes (Ladd, 1999). The impetus for identifying and assessing features of children's peer relationships was to better ascertain how those relationships might expose children to different types of social experiences which in turn, could uniquely contribute to their social, emotional, and cognitive development.

Friendship Features and Friendship Quality. To understand the inner workings of children's friendships, researchers have utilized the concepts of friendship features and friendship quality (Berndt, 1996). Friendship features refer to both positive and negative attributes (e.g., companionship, validation, help, power, conflict) and can be differentiated into relationship processes (i.e., observable behaviors and exchanges among friendship dyads such as play styles, conflict, or cooperation) and relationship provisions (i.e., benefits children gain from their friendships such as self-affirmation, companionship, or security; see Ladd & Kochenderfer, 1996). In contrast, friendship quality represents a relationship's worth as estimated from a child's point of view.

Investigators have created multiple measures of friendship features and quality (for a review see Ladd, 2005), many of which can be used with young children (i.e., preschoolers, kindergarteners, and elementary grade-schoolers). There is a moderate amount of agreement on the dimensions that children regard as positive and negative aspects of friendship (see Furman, 1996). In a meta-analysis, Newcomb and Bagwell (1995) found that children's interactions in friendships were characterized by more positive behaviors (i.e., smiling,

laughing, and sharing) and fewer rivalries. Although the incidence of conflict did not differ between friends and nonfriends, friends were more likely to resolve conflicts via disengagement and negotiation strategies as opposed to power assertion. Additional research suggests that young children are more willing to make sacrifices that benefit a friend rather than an acquaintance (Zarbatany et al., 1996), and that preschoolers show greater sympathy toward a distressed friend than a distressed acquaintance (Costin & Jones, 1992).

Friendship processes among young children may also be characterized on the basis of the level, or complexity of interaction that occurs between members of the dyad. For example, Parker and Gottman (1989) theorized that the putative goal of preschool children's play is to maximize enjoyment, entertainment, and satisfaction within the ongoing play activity. Achievement of this goal depends upon the partners' coordination of play. At the lowest level of coordination, children play in parallel—performing the same activity, perhaps side by side—but with little or no social interaction (i.e., "peaceful companionship"; Parker & Gottman, 1989, p. 105). Joint peer activity requires a higher level of coordination, and offers greater potential for conflict as well as for solidarity and amusement. Fantasy play is the most complex form of joint activity, and it typically occurs between friends. In this type of play, the partners immerse themselves in mutually defined symbolic and make-believe activities, and thus reach the highest level of coordination and presumably the highest level of enjoyment (Parker & Gottman, 1989).

Evidence gathered on the quality of children's friendships tends to show that relationship *satisfaction* is related to the positive or negative features that make up the friendship. Friendships with few negative and many positive features are often perceived to be high in quality (Berndt, 1996). Conversely, low quality friendships tend to be characterized by more negative features such as conflict or power imbalance. Ladd et al. (1996) found that kindergarten friends reported greater satisfaction with their friendships if they perceived these relationships to have higher levels of self-affirmation, support, and lower levels of conflict.

Peer Group Status Characteristics and Processes. Research on peer group dynamics indicates that children's experience in the peer group varies as a function of their peer status (Ladd, 1983). Masters and Furman (1981) found that young children interacted more positively with liked peers than with disliked peers. In addition, Ladd et al. (1990) found that, as the school year progressed, preschoolers at all levels of social status interacted with popular classmates most often; thus, the popular children appeared to become the focus of the entire peer group's interactions (Ladd et al., 1990). In contrast, it has been shown that peers often abuse and mistreat disliked children (Buhs & Ladd, 2001).

Once children are rejected by their peer group, they change the nature of their play and contact patterns with peers. Ladd et al. (1990) discovered that, over the course of a school year, popular preschoolers became more selective in their choice of playmates and focused their interactions upon a relatively small number of consistent play partners. In contrast, rejected children maintained an extensive pattern of play contacts, and often "bounced" from one playmate to another. Thus, the patterns of peer contact that emerge after children become rejected appeared to be a consequence of their prior, negative reputations among peers. Once children become disliked, they may be increasingly avoided or excluded by peers, and thus, forced to search out playmates among a broad range of peers (Buhs & Ladd, 2001; Ladd et al., 1990).

The plight of peer-rejected children is especially problematic in light of the pervasiveness of peer group rejection and the relative stability of peer status classifications over time and across peer groups (Ladd & Price, 1987). To estimate the prevalence of peer group rejection, Ladd, Herald, Slutzky, and Andrews (2004) reported the percentages of children who were identified in large community samples as belonging to different peer status categories (as indicated by various sociometric classification systems; see Asher & Dodge, 1986; Coie & Dodge, 1983; Coie et al., 1982; Newcomb & Bukowski, 1983). The resulting prevalence estimates implied that approximately 12% to 16% of children from normative, community samples were designated as rejected by peers.

The stability of peer group rejection is also important because it has been shown that chronic rather than transient rejection is a more powerful predictor of children's later interpersonal and scholastic adjustment (Ladd & Burgess, 2001; Ladd, Herald-Brown, & Reiser, 2008; Ladd & Troop-Gordon, 2003). In studies conducted with young children, Howes (1988) reported that 60% of the popular-, 60% of the rejected-, 65% of the average-, 33% of the neglected-, and 80% of the controversial-status preschoolers in her sample were assigned to the same status classifications one year later. Furthermore, Ladd and Price (1987) found that group acceptance scores (i.e., mean sociometric ratings received from all peer group members) were relatively stable from preschool to the beginning of kindergarten ($r = .48$), and from preschool to the end of kindergarten ($r = .47$). Studies conducted with older samples indicate that peer rejection becomes increasingly stable and difficult to change as children get older (Coie & Dodge, 1983; Poteat et al., 1986).

Children's Participation in Aggressor–Victim Relations. Findings from surveys and epidemiological studies suggest that a substantial number of American children regularly suffer one or more forms of peer abuse, and that this form of victimization is about as prevalent and debilitating as other forms of child maltreatment (e.g., child abuse perpetrated by parents). Surveys conducted in U.S. schools show that peer abuse begins early in children's lives and, for some, may persist over many years (see Kochenderfer-Ladd & Ladd, 2001). It has been shown

that a substantial percentage of children (20%–23%) suffer moderate to severe levels of peer abuse soon after they enter kindergarten (see Kochenderfer & Ladd, 1996), and as many as 5% to 10% of these children are chronically abused well into middle childhood (Kochenderfer & Wardrop, 2001). By the time children reach middle school and high school, evidence suggests that the prevalence of peer abuse is somewhat lower (e.g., 5%–13%; Craig, 1997; Nansel et al., 2001). Similarly, recent cross-national surveys suggest that, depending on children's age and nationality, 6% to 22% report moderate to severe levels of peer abuse while in school or traveling to or from school (see Boulton & Underwood, 1992; Boney-McCoy & Finkelhor, 1995; Kochenderfer & Ladd, 1996; Nansel et al., 2001; Perry et al., 1988). Collectively, these findings show that the probability that children will suffer peer abuse increases as they enter grade school and gradually declines until the mid- to late high school years.

Thus far, stability of peer victimization largely has been estimated using self-report or peer-report measures (see Ladd & Kochenderfer-Ladd, 2002). Estimates based on self-report measures indicate low to moderate stability during children's first year in school (kindergarten; Kochenderfer & Ladd, 1996), and somewhat higher stability during the later elementary grades (e.g., Hawker, 1997). Estimates obtained using peer-report measures depict victimization as being more stable during middle and later childhood (Boivin, Hymel, & Bukowski, 1995; Hawker, 1997; Perry et al., 1988). Longer-term longitudinal findings reported by Kochenderfer-Ladd and Wardop (2001) suggested that, during the early school years, stable or chronic victimization occurs, but such cases are not highly prevalent. In this study, children were followed from kindergarten through third grade, and results showed that less than 4% of the sampled children were chronically victimized over a four-year period.

Contributions of Peer Relationships to Children's Development and Adjustment

Researchers have been particularly interested in determining whether peer relationships contribute to children's development and adjustment and, beyond this, they have sought to isolate the contributions of specific forms of relationship (see Ladd, 2005). The hypothesis that peers contribute to children's development originated in socialization theories, particularly those that have emphasized the role of age mates as socializers (see Asher & Gottman, 1981; Berndt & Ladd, 1989; Hartup, 1970; Harris, 1995; Ladd, 2005; Parker & Asher, 1987).

Historically, two types of investigative strategies have been used to explicate the contributions of peer relationships to children's development. Initially, investigators examined differences in children's participation in peer relationships (e.g., whether or not children had friends, were accepted by peers, were victimized by peers) as correlates and predictors of specific developmental criteria. Later, the predictive contributions of children's peer relationships were examined in the context of differing child attributes, such as children's propensity to engage in aggressive and withdrawn behaviors. The latter paradigm—often termed a "child by environment" or a "child and environment" perspective—gained favor because it provided investigators with a way of estimating the contributions of peer relationships while also taking into account the role of children's behavior (e.g., typical behavior patterns). Child environment models are built on the premise that children's behavior patterns and their participation in relationships (social ties and relational experiences) work together to additively or conjointly influence development (see Ladd, 2003).

Peer Relationships as Predictors of Adjustment. In the initial studies that were undertaken to understand how peer relationships affect children's development, researchers identified children whose participation in particular forms of relationship varied (e.g., those who were accepted vs. those rejected by classmates), and then looked to see whether these relationship differences were associated with (or predictive of) specific developmental outcomes. Although positive ties with peers were examined, much of the evidence gathered was guided by the hypothesis that children's participation in poor or dysfunctional peer relationships impairs their development or adjustment.

Friendship. It has been common for researchers to argue that children benefit from having a friend (Buhrmester & Furman, 1986; Furman & Robbins, 1985), and the converse of this logic is that children without friends are at greater risk for maladjustment. Indeed, friendships, as well as the quality of children's friendships, have been shown to be important predictors of children's emotional health (Bukowski & Hoza, 1989; Bukowski, Newcomb, & Hartup, 1996; Parker & Asher, 1993), and their adjustment during early and middle childhood (Ladd et al., 1996; Ladd & Troop-Gordon, 2003). Children with close friendships view themselves more positively (Berndt & Burgy, 1996; Keefe & Berndt, 1996; Savin-Williams & Berndt, 1990), and children who have one or more close friendships tend to experience greater perceived social support and less loneliness (Ladd, Kochenderfer, & Coleman, 1996; Parker & Asher, 1993). In addition, children who have positive features in their friendships, such as intimacy and support, tend to have higher levels of self-esteem (Berndt, 1996).

In studies conducted with young children, classroom friendships have been linked with indicators of school adjustment. The presence of preestablished friendships in children's kindergarten classrooms (e.g., starting school with a friend established during preschool) was found to predict gains in school adjustment (Ladd, 1990). Further, as children enter school, those who form new friendships tend to develop more favorable perceptions of school and perform better scholastically than those with fewer friends (Ladd, 1990). The processes that typify friends' interactions

have also been implicated in children's school adjustment. Among kindergartners, boys who reported conflict within their friendships were found to have greater adjustment difficulties, including lower levels of classroom engagement and participation (Ladd, Kochenderfer, & Coleman, 1996). Ladd et al. (1996) also found that when children saw their friendships as offering higher levels of validation (support) and aid (assistance) they tended to perceive classrooms as supportive interpersonal environments.

Peer Group Acceptance and Rejection. Like friendship, acceptance or rejection by one's classmates has been shown to be a significant predictor of young children's school adjustment. To illustrate, early peer rejection—at school entry—was found to predict problems such as negative school attitudes, school avoidance, and underachievement during the first year of schooling (Buhs & Ladd, 2001; Ladd, 1990; Ladd et al., 1999). Later, in the elementary years, peer acceptance has been linked with loneliness (Parker & Asher, 1993), peer interaction difficulties, lower emotional well-being, and academic deficits (Ladd et al., 1997; Vandell & Hembree 1994). Evidence from other longitudinal studies suggests that peer rejection predicts absenteeism during the grade school years (e.g., DeRosier, Kupersmidt, & Patterson, 1994; Hymel, Rubin, Rowden, & LeMare, 1990), and grade retention and adjustment difficulties during the transition to middle school (Coie, Lochman, Terry, & Hyman, 1992).

Peer Victimization. Children's participation in relationships in which they are victimized by peers has been linked with a variety of internalizing problems including depression, anxiety, suicide and suicidal ideation, loneliness, low self-esteem, and psychosomatic complaints (see Hawker & Boulton, 2000). Evidence indicates that victimized children, regardless of their behavioral propensities (e.g., passive as well as aggressive victims), suffer higher levels of depression (Austin & Joseph, 1996; Kumpulainen et al., 1998; Rigby, 1998; Schwartz, 2000). In one long-term follow-up study, it was found that boys who were victimized during their school years displayed higher rates of depressive symptoms and low self-esteem at age 23 (Olweus, 1993).

Passive victims tend to report moderate to severe levels of anxiety following bouts of bullying at school (Faust & Forehand, 1994; Rigby, 1998, 2001; Schwartz, 2000; Sharp, 1995). Moreover, peer victimization has been linked with both generalized anxiety (Slee, 1994, 1995) and social anxiety (Boulton & Smith, 1994; Crick & Grotpeter, 1996; Slee, 1994), and various somatic complaints such as headaches, stomach aches, and other minor physical ills (Kumpulainen et al., 1998; Williams, Chambers, Logan, & Robinson, 1996). In contrast, aggressive victims are more likely to develop higher levels of externalizing problems such as misconduct and delinquency (Kumpulainen et al., 1998).

Victimized children also have a higher probability of experiencing mild to severe school adjustment problems.

Research on school transitions has shown that, following children's entrance into kindergarten, the frequency of children's exposure to peer abuse forecasts significant gains in loneliness and school avoidance over their first year in school (Kochenderfer & Ladd, 1996). Moreover, it was discovered that pronounced or prolonged (e.g., chronic) peer abuse predicted more serious or debilitating forms of school maladjustment (Kochenderfer-Ladd & Wardrop, 2001). Researchers have also reported that peer victimization predicts both transient and enduring loneliness in children as early as school entry. Kochenderfer and Ladd (1996) found that the frequency of children's peer victimization experiences as they entered kindergarten forecast significant gains in loneliness over the remainder of the school year.

Differential Contributions of Peer Relationships to Children's Adjustment. After investigating peer relationships individually, researchers began to study children's participation in multiple forms of peer relationship and the relative (differential) "contributions" of these relationships to specific adjustment outcomes (see Ladd, 1989, 1996, 1999; Perry & Weinstein, 1998). Initial efforts to investigate multiple relationships as antecedents of adjustment were primarily focused on friendship and peer acceptance (e.g., see Parker & Asher, 1993; Vandell & Hembree, 1994).

Thus far, most findings suggest that friendship, peer acceptance, and peer victimization make separate contributions to the prediction of both socioemotional adjustment and academic competence (Ladd et al., 1997; Parker & Asher, 1993; Vandell & Hembree, 1994). For young children in particular, it has been shown that friendship, peer acceptance, and peer victimization uniquely predicted changes in kindergartner's school perceptions, avoidance, and performance (Ladd, 1990; Ladd et al., 1997). To be specific, Ladd et al. (1997) examined four forms of peer relationships (i.e., two forms of friendship, peer group acceptance, and peer victimization) as predictors of changes in multiple indices of kindergarten children's school adjustment. Results showed that after adjusting for shared predictive linkages among the four relational predictors, some types of peer relationships better predicted certain adjustment indices than did others. Peer victimization, for example, predicted gains in children's loneliness above and beyond associations that were attributable to the other three forms of peer relationship. In contrast, peer group acceptance uniquely predicted improvements in children's achievement. Such findings are consistent with the hypothesis that the effects of friendship on children's development are unique relative to those conferred by peer acceptance, and that these relationships differ in their adaptive value for specific adjustment outcomes.

Child by Environment Perspectives. Child by environment models, in contrast, are based on the premise that both children's behavioral characteristics (child attributes) and

their participation in peer relationships (experiences in the social environment) codetermine their development and adjustment (see Coie, Watt et al., 1993; Ladd, 2003). Researchers who have relied on this framework tend to study both children's behaviors and their peer relationships as predictors of their development. In peer relations research, child by environment frameworks have been closely aligned with the concepts of risk and protective factors, as derived from epidemiological research (see Garmezy et al., 1984; Rutter, 1990). Risk factors refer to aspects of children's behaviors or relationships that increase the probability of adjustment problems, whereas protective factors (or resources) are defined as features that decrease the likelihood of dysfunction.

Research on the Conjoint Influences of Children's Behavior and Peer Relationships. Much research on the interface between behavioral and relational risk factors has focused on the contributions of aggression and peer rejection to children's maladjustment (see Ladd, 1999; MacDougall, Hymel, Vaillancourt, & Mercer, 2001). In recent reviews of this literature (Ladd, 2003, 2005; MacDougall et al., 2001), investigators have concluded that in addition to behavioral risks such as aggression, exposure to relational risks, such as peer group rejection, raises the probability that children will develop internalizing problems (e.g., anxiety, depression, and loneliness; Coie, Terry, Lenox, Lochman, & Hyman, 1995; Lochman & Wayland, 1994; Renshaw & Brown, 1993). Other findings suggest that the combinations of aggression and peer rejection increase the likelihood of externalizing problems such as misconduct (e.g. Coie, Lochman et al., 1992; Hymel at el., 1990).

With young children, findings from two short-term longitudinal studies (see Ladd et al., 1999) showed that, as children entered kindergarten, their initial behavioral orientations influenced the types of relationships they formed with peers. In particular, young children's use of force or coercive tactics was directly associated with rejection by the peer group. Additional findings showed that, after children were rejected by their classmates, they were less likely to participate in classroom activities, suggesting that this form of relational adversity (e.g., peer rejection) interferes with children's involvement in learning activities and eventually impairs their achievement.

Chronic Behavior Patterns and Stable Participation in Peer Relationships. Another line of inquiry has explored how enduring behavioral styles and chronic peer adversity (e.g., chronic victimization or peer rejection) or support (e.g., friendship or peer acceptance) combine to predict children's psychological and school adjustment. Ladd and Burgess (2001) used prospective longitudinal assessments to assess children's risk status for aggression and exposure to adverse versus supportive peer relationships as they entered kindergarten (initial behavioral and relational status) and progressed through the primary grades. Results revealed that, after adjusting for children's kindergarten aggression scores, the chronicity of their aggressive risk status across grades predicted changes in a host of school adjustment criteria, including increases in attention problems, thought problems, and behavioral misconduct, and decreases in cooperative classroom participation, and academic achievement. However, it was also discovered that the stability of peer group rejection predicted many of the same forms of school maladjustment after controlling for children's aggressive histories. In contrast, however, Ladd and Burgess (2001) also found that social supports such as sustained peer group acceptance predicted positive adjustment trajectories, including decreases in children's attention problems and gains in cooperative classroom participation. These findings implied that a powerful behavioral risk (chronic aggressiveness) can be exacerbated by stable relational risks but buffered by stable relational supports, further illustrating the importance of children's peer relationship histories.

In a follow-up prospective longitudinal investigation conducted from kindergarten to fourth grade, Ladd and Troop-Gordon (2003) examined the hypothesis that children who participate in chronic adverse peer relationships have greater exposure to negative relational processes (e.g., sustained peer exclusion, peer abuse, lack of dyadic emotional support), and that the accumulation of such experiences is a more powerful risk factor than are the adversities present in their contemporary peer relationships. Among other findings, results showed that chronic friendlessness, chronic rejection, and chronic victimization were predictive of later forms of maladjustment, including loneliness and maladaptive behavior. Because these predictive associations were adjusted for children's concurrent peer relationships, the results of this investigation revealed that *chronic* peer relationship adversity, more than the strains of *contemporary* peer relationships, predicted children's later maladjustment.

Intervention Programs Targeting Negative Peer Relationships

Given that early exposure to negative peer relationships, particularly peer group rejection, has been linked with later maladjustment (e.g., see Kupersmidt & Dodge, 2004; MacDougall et al., 2001), researchers have attempted to develop interventions that improve children's peer relations. Often this research has been designed to help children who are already displaying peer relationship difficulties, such as peer group rejection or peer victimization. However, with the emergence of prevention science, investigators have also developed interventions that are designed to prevent or reduce the likelihood that children will develop peer relationship problems (i.e., universal, selective, and indicated prevention interventions; see Ladd, Herald, Slutzky, & Andrews, 2004). Thus, experimental studies have been undertaken not only to ascertain whether children's peer relations are improved when they acquire

specific social competencies, but also to determine whether competence-building procedures prevent children from developing social difficulties with peers.

Given this chapter's focus, the ensuing review is limited to research based on the social skill hypothesis; that is, interventions in which social skill instruction/learning is implemented with young children as a method for improving their peer relationships. Thus, no attempt is made to review programs that: (a) attempt to improve children's peer relations via other means (e.g., redesigning school policies or environments to reduce bullying and victimization; see Smith, Pepler, & Rigby, 2004); (b) address broader educational or socioemotional objectives (e.g., school success skills; see Brigman, Lane, Lane, Lawrence, & Switzer, 1999; Brigman & Webb, 2003); or (c) lack evidence of program effects on children's peer relationships (e.g., evidence that links skill learning with changes in peer relationships).

Social Skills Training Intervention Programs

Most of the interventions that have been designed to help children develop social skills for peer relationships have been based on fundamental social learning principles and aimed at reducing children's skill deficits or overcoming behavioral excesses (see Ladd, Herald, et al., 2004; Ladd & Mize, 1983). The majority of these interventions have been referred to as modeling, coaching, or shaping programs (see Ladd, Buhs, & Troop, 2002). In modeling interventions, children are encouraged to emulate the behaviors of adults or peers who demonstrate exemplary social skills, as shown in training videos and narratives (see Ladd, Herald, et al., 2004). Coaching interventions, in contrast, require children to participate in multiple skill training sessions that provide participants with instruction in skilled behaviors, opportunities to practice the skill behaviors, and ongoing feedback about skill usage in real-life peer interactions (see Ladd & Mize, 1983; Mize & Ladd, 1990). Interventions that are based on shaping principles present children with rewards after they enact targeted skills, or achieve successive approximations of the targeted skills (see Ladd, Herald et al., 2004).

Modeling interventions (e.g., O'Connor, 1969, 1972) have seldom been proven to have lasting effects on young children's social skills (see Ladd & Mize, 1983). However, there is evidence to suggest that coaching programs do help young children acquire social skills and improve their peer relations (see Mize & Ladd, 1990). Finally, when used in conjunction with other treatment methods (i.e., coaching programs), shaping programs show a modest record of success at promoting prosocial behaviors, discouraging antisocial behaviors, and enhancing children's peer relationships (e.g., see Bierman, Miller, & Stabb, 1987).

Exemplary Interventions. Initially, coaching interventions were designed to improve rejected or low-accepted children's success in peer groups. In these early studies, no attempt was made to distinguish between aggressive-rejected or withdrawn-rejected children, or study the effects of intervention on these subtypes. In one of the first coaching programs, Oden and Asher (1977) taught low-accepted third- and fourth graders interpersonal skills related to four specific areas of social interaction: communication, cooperation, participation, and validation-support. Results showed that children who were coached, unlike those in a control condition, made significant gains in peer acceptance that were maintained over one year.

Ladd (1981) investigated the effects of social skills training on unpopular third graders by randomly assigning low-accepted children to one of three conditions: a coaching, a no-treatment control, or an attention-control group. The attention-control group was included in order to rule out the possibility that it was the provision of adult attention and not the skill coaching that led to gains in children's peer acceptance. Whereas coached children exhibited gains in peer group acceptance immediately after the intervention and several weeks later (i.e., in posttest and follow-up assessments), such gains were not evident for children in the two control groups.

In a coaching intervention that was designed for young children, Mize and Ladd (1990) intervened with low-accepted preschool children and coached them on verbal communication skills including leading (e.g., making suggestions about play activities), asking questions, showing support through positive statements, and making comments during play activities with peers. Results showed that the coached children, unlike controls, made gains in their understanding of social interaction principles and classroom peer acceptance after completing the intervention.

After researchers established that there were subtypes of peer group rejection (i.e., aggressive-rejected and withdrawn-rejected children), they began to develop interventions tailored to children's specific behavioral and relational difficulties. For example, Lochman, Coie, Underwood, and Terry (1993) developed a treatment program that was designed to improve aggressive-rejected fourth graders' social problem solving skills, relationship formation skills, and control over their anger and aggressive behavior. To test the effectiveness of deficit-specific training, the treatment was given to an aggressive-rejected as well as a nonaggressive-rejected group of children (i.e., children classified as rejected but not aggressive). Analyses revealed that the aggressive-rejected children, unlike the controls, exhibited a reduction in aggressive behavior and peer group rejection over and above that which was exhibited by nonaggressive-rejected children. The efficacy of deficit specific instruction, as an approach to skill training, has also been documented by other investigators (e.g., Bienert & Schneider, 1995).

Preventive Intervention Programs

Instead of targeting only those children who have already developed poor peer relations, prevention scientists have attempted to develop school- or classroom-wide preventive programs (i.e., universal interventions) that are designed to help all children improve their social skills and peer relationships (see Harrist & Bradley, 2003; Ladd, Herald et al., 2004). Although not yet well researched, early evidence suggests that such programs may help large numbers of children learn pivotal social skills and reduce their chances of developing peer relationship problems.

To illustrate, Harrist and Bradley (2003) conducted a prevention study with young children who were in either treatment or control classrooms. Children in the treatment classrooms listened to a fairy tale (Paley, 1992) that illustrated themes about children's inclusion or exclusion from peer playgroup activities. Upon finishing the fairy tale, children participated in discussions and role-plays that elaborated on these same themes. After children completed 8 to 10 intervention sessions, the experimenters introduced a nonexclusion rule (i.e., "You can't say you can't play") in children's classrooms. Evaluations of this program, which included data from direct observations, teacher reports, child reports, and peer sociometrics, showed that children in the treatment classes liked each other more than did children in the control classes. This effect generalized across all children in the class, not just those who had initially been identified by peers as excluded (i.e., rejected or neglected). Children in the treatment classrooms also reported higher levels of social dissatisfaction at the end of the school year. Based on these results, the investigators concluded that even though the class-wide social intervention improved children's feelings about their classmates, it may have also prompted children to reflect on their own social positions amongst peers' questions as to whether they were satisfied with their peer relationships.

Summary and Conclusions

Sometime after children have formed their first social relationships, typically with adult caregivers, they move beyond this context into the world of peers. Most likely, the peer culture has always been an important force in young children's development. By nature, peers provide children with experiences that expand their conceptions of the social world and encourage adaptation to this context. Moreover, because peers are similar to children in age and developmental status, but are raised in different families, they offer children a form of companionship that cannot be entirely duplicated by parents, teachers, and other adults (Edwards, 1992; Hartup, 1970; Piaget, 1965; Sullivan, 1953).

Modern times have made these speculations into truisms. Secular changes in families, childcare, and schooling have thrust children into the world of peers at earlier and earlier ages. It would no longer be an exaggeration to say that many young children now spend about as much of their time in the company of peers as they do with their parents (see Ladd & Coleman, 1993).

This review was organized around a number of basic questions that have motivated research on children's peer relations for nearly 100 years (see Ladd, 2005). Chief among these were questions about how children meet peers, form and maintain various types of peer relationships, and are affected by their interactions and relationships with age mates. Also considered was the enduring question of whether it is possible to improve children's peer relations (see Chittenden, 1942; Koch, 1935). Other central foci were features of children's lives that may facilitate or inhibit their access to the peer culture, their participation in this context, and their ability to profit from interactions and relationships they have with age mates. In particular, attention was focused on the potential contributions of socialization agents, such as parents and teachers, and contextual factors, including the physical and interpersonal features of neighborhoods, communities, childcare settings, and schools.

The content of this review we hope makes it apparent that much has been learned about each of these questions and issues. But given the substantial corpus of evidence that has been reviewed in this article, what specific inferences and conclusions can be drawn?

Insight into the Formation of Children's Peer Relationships

First, evidence suggests that the processes of relationship formation are complex, and that not all children achieve the same level of success at forming friendships, becoming accepted members of their peer groups, repelling bullies, and so on. Access to age mates does not guarantee that children will develop supportive, high-quality peer relationships. Rather, it appears to be the case that many antecedents, including children's attributes, their social skills, inputs from parents and teachers, and features of their rearing environments play a role in this process (see Ladd, 2005).

Fortunately, progress has been toward mapping some of the factors that appear to operate as precursors of relationship formation. For example, Gottman's (1983) temporal analysis of preschoolers' communications made it possible to describe a sequence of conversational processes that often led to friendship. Similarly, researchers who investigated the antecedents of peer group entry mapped out a sequence of bids that were associated with children's success at this task. Results showed that children who observed a peer group's activities (i.e., waiting and hovering) and then utilized relevant entry bids (i.e., mimicking, group-oriented statements) were more likely to be granted access to the group than children who used disrupting, self-oriented bids. Investigators were also able to highlight how charac-

teristics of the child (i.e., gender, sociometric status; e.g., Borja-Alvarez et al., 1991; Putallaz & Wasserman, 1989; Zarbatany & Pepper, 1996; Zarbatany et al., 1996), the peer group (i.e., relationship with the entrant, sociometric statuses; e.g., Zarbatany et al., 1996), and the entry situation (i.e., peer group size; Putallaz & Wasserman, 1989) affected the types of entry bids children made and their eventual rate of success at gaining inclusion.

Similarly, by isolating behavior patterns that were differentially linked with emergent peer group status, it was possible for researchers to draw inferences about the likely effects of particular behavioral styles (e.g., aggression vs. prosocial behavior) on the status that children developed in their peer groups (e.g., Dodge, 1983; Ladd, Hart et al.. 1988). Moreover, we may also infer from these data that there is substantial continuity in children's social status across school settings and peer groups (Ladd, 2005). Clearly, these findings support the conclusion that children's behaviors are partly responsible for the status they develop among peers.

Although less well understood, it also may be the case that the effects of children's behaviors on their peer relationships partly depend on the nature and norms of their peer groups, and the reputations they form in these groups. To illustrate, Wright, Giammarino, and Parad (1986) found that aggressive grade-school children tended to be more disliked in peer groups composed of nonaggressive peers, and that withdrawn children tended to be more disliked in groups containing larger numbers of aggressive peers. Perhaps, as these investigators suggest, the effect of children's behavior (or other characteristics) on their peer status is mediated by their similarity to the peer group.

In sum, findings from research with preschool and grade-school samples illustrate the importance of children's behavior (i.e., interaction patterns) as a determinant of their status among peers. One general principle that appeared to cut across all of these findings was that children who succeed in forming peer relationships did so by managing their interactions in ways that nurtured and respected the interests of their play companions.

Unfortunately, past accomplishments have not always fueled future discoveries. For example, despite some fairly dramatic successes (e.g., Black & Hazen, 1990; Coie & Kupersmidt, 1983; Dodge, 1983; Gottman 1983; Parker, 1986) in describing some of the processes that underlie the formation of friendship and peer status, investigations of this type (i.e., longitudinal or experimental studies designed to illuminate the antecedents of children's friendships and peer group relations) have not become more prevalent in recent years. This has particularly been the case for research on the antecedents of friendship (although see Parker & Seal, 1996). As a result, knowledge about other types of behavioral processes that may be important precursors to friendship in young children remains limited. Likewise, it has been rare for researchers to investigate whether some types of interaction processes are more central to friendship formation at different ages, or for children of different genders. As such, there is a compelling need to further explore the interpersonal or behavioral processes that lead to friendships in boys and girls as they progress through the early childhood years (e.g., male and female toddlers, preschoolers, and early grade-schoolers).

The Role of Adult Socialization Agents

There has also been progress toward an understanding of the interconnections between family processes and children's peer relations, and the practices that caregivers use to prepare children for the world of peers. On the one hand, extant evidence indicates that parent–child relations are complex and that many aspects of parenting and family relationships are associated with children's peer competence (Ladd & Pettit, 2002). On the other hand, this realization led researchers to revise existing assumptions, and develop new models for investigating the roles that parents and teachers play in children's social development. Movement in this direction has been accompanied by a conceptual shift away from unidirectional perspectives (i.e., child or parent-effects models) and toward more dyadic and transactional investigative frameworks (see Ladd, 2005) and the consideration of genetic effects (Brendgen et al. 2008). This is reflected in researchers' propensities to develop and utilize dyadic measures of parent–child relations, work from paradigms in which the direction(s) of effect within parent–child relations are hypothesized to be bidirectional or transactional, and undertake twin studies. Among the more noteworthy discoveries were findings showing that children who have experienced secure attachment relations tend to form higher quality friendships; that synchronous and emotionally supportive parent–child interactions precede similar forms of competence in children's peer interactions; that harsh disciplinary styles antecede children's risk for peer victimization; and that stressful family environments are predictive of children's peer difficulties.

Although it is possible that parents "mindlessly" arrange, supervise, and monitor young children's playdates and peer contacts, it now appears that many parents perform these functions with specific socialization objectives in mind (see Bhavnagri & Parke, 1991; Ladd & Hart, 1992; Lollis et al., 1992). When children are young, it appears that parents act as mediators in order to initiate peer interactions, find playmates for their children, arrange play opportunities, and maintain relationships with specific children (Ladd & Pettit, 2002). As children mature, it appears that parents' supervision of their peer activities changes; results suggest that, as children get older, parents increasingly resort to less direct methods of supervision, and that these adaptations are beneficial for children. Extant evidence is, for example, consistent with the premise that interactive interventions facilitate young children's (e.g., toddlers) peer competence, but that this form of supervision may actually interfere with older children's (preschoolers) ability to develop autonomous and self-regulated play skills. Quite possibly, parents who mediate, supervise, and monitor children's peer interactions play an important role in the socialization of children's social competence. However, because the existing evidence is correlational in nature, it remains to be seen whether direct parental influences are in fact causes or consequences of children's success and competence in peer relations.

Unfortunately, less is known about how children's relationships with teachers are associated with their peer relations and social adjustment. Thus far, investigators have tended to study two features of the teacher–child relationship—conflict and closeness—and examine how these relationship features are related to children's participation and performance in classrooms (see Birch & Ladd, 1996; Rudasill & Rimm-Kaufman, 2009). In general, evidence has been consistent with the hypothesis that closeness in the teacher–child relationship, a feature characterized by warmth and open communication, operates as a source of emotional support or security that fosters children's participation in classroom activities. Conflictual teacher–child relationships, in contrast, are characterized by discordant, acrimonious, and noncompliant interactions (e.g., causes of anger, resentment, or anxiety), and have been linked with children's classroom disengagement and disruptiveness. Among the more novel contributions of these investigations were findings indicating that even after controlling for the association between kindergartners' peer relations and the quality of their classroom participation, those who formed conflictual teacher–child relationships tended to become less involved in classroom activities (Ladd et al., 1999). Equally important were findings showing that both the features of young children' teacher–child relationships, and their tendencies to engage in risky behaviors (e.g., aggression), predicted early-emerging adjustment (Ladd & Burgess, 2001). Evidence indicated that conflictual teacher–child relationships were linked with increases in maladjustment, regardless of children's propensity to engage in aggression. Thus, conflict in the teacher–child relationship appeared to increase most children's risk for maladjustment. However, for aggressive children, teacher–child conflict appeared to compound (i.e., add to) their adjustment difficulties. In contrast, relational supports such as closeness in the teacher–child relationship predicted decreases in maladjustment independently of aggression, suggesting that this relationship feature reduced maladjustment, regardless of children's risk status for aggression. Further, teacher–child closeness also predicted greater reductions in aggressive behavior for children who experienced conditions of additive risk (i.e., aggression and minority status), suggesting that supportive interactions between teachers and children may be particularly salient for students who do not typically enjoy positive relationships with teachers (Meehan et al., 2003). Despite what has been learned about the features of teacher–child relationships, much less in known about teacher attributes that contribute to relationship quality with children, or the specific mechanisms that affect children's peer relationships. That is, we do not yet have a clear understanding of how teacher–child relationships contribute to differences in children's peer competence.

The Role of Socialization Contexts

It is also clear that child rearing and socialization contexts, such as neighborhoods, community settings, and schools play an important role in young children's social development. It is within these contexts that young children meet familiar and unfamiliar age mates, and are afforded opportunities to establish and maintain peer relationships. It is also in these contexts that children find opportunities to practice social skills, experience the consequences of peers' reactions, and learn new interpersonal behaviors. Further, it would appear that regular exposure to peers in community settings fosters adaptation to novel situations, such as those encountered during school entrance. These settings may even act as a protective factor for school dropout and behavior problems in later years (Mahoney & Cairns, 1997).

Over the past 30 years, childcare has increasingly become an extension of the family's childrearing practices, and a context that is used to promote the socialization of children. Mothers of young children have been a regular part of the workforce for decades now, and the need to understand the potential effects of childcare on children has become a national priority. As has been illustrated, investigative efforts have produced an extensive body of evidence on childcare and its correlates, and some of these findings have raised concerns about the effects of childcare on children's socioemotional development (e.g., McCartney et al., 2010; NICHD ECCRN, 2001; Vandell, 2004). Although these findings remain controversial, it has not been uncommon for investigators and policy makers to characterize childcare as a context that is beneficial for children's peer relations and social competence. Fabes, Hanish, and Martin (2003), for example, have argued that childcare impacts child development because it is a setting in which children learn from peers. Childcare is often children's first extended exposure to peers (especially groups of peers) and, thus, it may play a role in facilitating children's relationships with age mates, social competence, adaptation to school, and future adjustment. This interpretation is consistent with the argument that children enrolled in childcare and preschool programs tend to meet a larger number of unfamiliar peers at an earlier age (Belsky, 1984; Rubenstein & Howes, 1983) and, thus, have greater opportunity to practice social skills and make friends (Howes, 1988).

Similarly, it appears that preschool and grade school classrooms may be an important staging area for children's social competence and peer relations. Evidence suggests that schools and the types of peer interactions children encounter in classrooms vary substantially, and some children may profit more than others depending on the types of experiences they have in this context. However, here again, it can be argued that schools and the social milieu of classrooms require children to come into contact with peers, and negotiate interpersonal challenges such as making friends and establishing themselves within fairly large peer groups (see Ladd, Herald, & Kochel, 2006).

In addition to time in school, there is growing evidence to suggest that the time children spend with peers before or after school may play a role in shaping their social development. Collectively, available evidence suggests that any benefits that children accrue from their participation in out-of-school activities likely depend on the physical and organizational features of these arrangements (Pierce et al., 2010). It appears that, if nonschool or after-school experiences are well supervised and designed to suit children's needs, they can serve as an important arena for skill development (Howes, Olenick, & Der-Kiureghian, 1987; NICHD ECCRN, 2004; Vandell et al., 2005). Thus far, however, the weight of the evidence seems to suggest that adult supervised before- and after-school activities, rather than informal or nonsupervised care, are positively associated with children's peer competence (Pierce et al., 2010; Posner & Vandell, 1994). In contrast, unsupervised or self-care arrangements appear to be linked with children's developmental difficulties, particularly behavioral and social maladjustment (Pettit, Bates, Dodge, & Meece, 1999; Posner & Vandell, 1994).

Explicating the Features and Functions of Children's Early Peer Relationships

In general, extant evidence suggests that young children who become accepted by members of their peer groups, form friendships that have positive, supportive features, avoid becoming victimized by age mates, and tend to manifest fewer and less severe psychological and school adjustment problems. These findings corroborate the hypothesis that certain features of childhood peer relationships increase risk or afford protection from different types of short- and long-term adjustment problems. Further, this evidence is consistent with the view that peer relationships are both specialized in the types of resources or constraints they create for children, but also diverse in the sense that some resources may be found in more than one form of relationship.

However, research guided by "child by environment" frameworks implies that conclusions like those listed above may lack precision. To say that children have experiences in peer relationships that affect their adjustment ignores the fact that they also have certain behavioral attributes (e.g., behavioral styles) that contribute to such outcomes. Moreover, it may be the case that children's behavioral propensities shape how peers' respond to them and affect the types of relationships they form with peers. These relational developments, in turn, might create additional social challenges (e.g., coping with peer rejection or victimization). Thus, it seems likely that development and its course is influenced by a complex array of factors including the nature of the child (e.g., the child's behavior) and features of the child's peer environment (e.g., participation in peer relationships).

Evidence suggests that, over the course of development, children's behavioral styles and their participation in peer relationships essentially codetermine their success in adapting to life- and school-based challenges. In particular, the findings reviewed in this chapter lend themselves to several preliminary conclusions. First, although it can be said that both children's behavioral dispositions and features of their peer relationships are related to their social development, there is accumulating evidence to suggest that the predictive power of either factor alone appears to be less than their combined or conjoint contributions. For example, children's early behavioral dispositions may affect the kind of relationships they develop with peers. But, once peer relationships have formed, the experiences children have in these relationships also may impact on their development (see Ladd, 2006). Second, it would appear that enduring rather than transient relationship experiences (e.g., chronic peer rejection), deprivation (e.g., sustained friendlessness), or support (e.g., stable peer acceptance) are more closely associated with children's development and adjustment. In this sense, research findings not only illustrate the adaptive significance of children's peer relationships, but also suggest that children who suffer sustained adversity in their peer relations are likely to have the largest or most severe adjustment problems (e.g., see Ladd & Burgess, 2001; Ladd, Herald-Brown, & Reiser, 2008; Ladd & Troop-Gordon, 2003). Third, other recent discoveries raise the possibility that enduring peer relationship adversity (e.g., chronic victimization) may worsen children's preexisting behavior problems, and thus make it even more likely that they will act in ways that alter their development (see Gazelle & Ladd, 2003). Conversely, it also appears that sustained relationship advantages (e.g., a history of peer acceptance) may mitigate children's preexisting behavior problems (e.g., see Ladd & Burgess, 2001).

Intervening on Behalf of Young Children Who Have, or Are At Risk for Peer Relationship Difficulties

Finally, the results of experimental prevention and intervention programs provide qualified support for the conclusion that young children can learn social skills that improve peer relationships or prevent relationship difficulties (see Mize & Ladd, 1990). Particularly promising are results indicating that universal prevention programs can alter the social dynamics of entire classrooms and, therefore, benefit substantial numbers of young children. Equally reassuring are findings showing that some types of intervention programs can effect changes in children's interpersonal skills as well as in their acceptance by classroom peers. Unfortunately, too little has been done to develop and evaluate prevention and intervention programs for young children who are

friendless or suffer peer abuse (e.g., bully–victim relations; see Gazelle & Ladd, 2002).

Notes

Preparation of this article was supported in part by grants from the National Institutes of Health (1 & 2-RO1MH-49223; R01HD-045906) and the Institute for Educational Sciences (R305A090386) to Gary W. Ladd.

Correspondence should be addressed to Gary W. Ladd, P.O. Box 852502, Arizona State University, Tempe, AZ, USA 85287-2502.

References

Aboud, F. E., & Mendelson, M. J. (1996). Determinants of friendship selection and quality: Developmental perspectives. In W. M. Bukowski, A. F. Newcomb, & W. W. Hartup (Eds.), *The company they keep: Friendship in childhood and adolescence* (pp. 66–86). New York: Cambridge University Press.

Asher, S. R., & Dodge, K. A. (1986). Identifying children who are rejected by their peers. *Developmental Psychology, 22,* 442–449.

Asher, S. R., & Gottman, J. M. (1981). *The development of children's friendships.* New York: Cambridge University Press.

Asher, S. R., Oden, S. L., & Gottman, J. M. (1977). Children's friendships in school settings. In L. G. Katz (Ed.), *Current topics in early childhood education* (Vol. 1, pp. 33–61). Norwood, NJ: Ablex.

Asher, S. R., & Renshaw, P. D. (1981). Children without friends: Social knowledge and social skills training. In S. R. Asher & J. M. Gottman (Eds.), *The development of children's friendships* (pp. 273–296). New York: Cambridge University Press.

Asher, S. R., Singleton, L. C., Tinsley, B. R., & Hymel, S. (1979). A reliable sociometric measure for preschool children. *Developmental Psychology, 15,* 443–444.

Austin, S., & Joseph, S. (1996). Assessment of bully/victim problems in 8 to 11 year-olds. *British Journal of Educational Psychology, 66,* 447–456.

Baker, J. A. (2006). Contributions of teacher-child relationships to positive school adjustment during elementary school. *Journal of School Psychology, 44,* 211–229.

Barker, E. D., Boivin, M., Brendgen, M., Fontaine, N., Arseneault, L., Vitaro, F. et al. (2008). Predictive validity and early predictors of peer-victimization trajectories in preschool. *Archives of General Psychiatry, 65,* 1185–1192.

Baumrind, D. (1967). Childcare practices anteceding three patterns of preschool behavior. *Genetic Psychology Monographs, 75,* 43–88.

Beckett, M., Hawken, A., & Jacknowitz, A. (2001). *Accountability for after-school care: Devising standards and measuring adherence to them.* Los Angeles, CA: RAND Corporation.

Belsky, J. (1984). Two waves of day care research: Developmental effects and conditions of quality. In R. C. Ainslie (Ed.), *The child and the day care setting: Qualitative variations and development* (pp. 37–53). New York: Praeger.

Belsky, J. (2001). Emmanuel Miller Lecture: Developmental risks (still) associated with early child care. *Journal of Child Psychology and Psychiatry, 42,* 845–859.

Belsky, J. Vandell, D. L., Burchinal, M., Clarke-Stewart, K. A., McCartney, K., & Owen, M. T. (2007). Are there long-term effects of early child care? *Child Development, 78,* 681–701.

Berndt, T. J. (1989). Contributions of peer relationships to children's development. In T. J. Berndt, & G. W. Ladd (Eds.), *Peer relationships in child development* (pp. 407–416). New York: Wiley.

Berndt, T. J. (1996). Exploring the effects of friendship quality on social development. In W. M. Bukowski, A. F. Newcomb, & W. W. Hartup (Eds.), *The company they keep: Friendship in childhood and adolescence* (pp. 346–365). New York: Cambridge University Press.

Berndt, T. J., & Burgy, L. (1996). Social self-concept. In B. A. Bracken (Ed.), *Handbook of self- concept: Developmental, social, and clinical considerations* (pp. 171–209). New York: Wiley.

Berndt, T. J., Hawkins, J. A., & Hoyle, S. G. (1986). Changes in friendship during a school year: Effects of children's and adolescent's impressions of friendship and sharing with friends. *Child Development, 57,* 1284–1297.

Berndt, T. J., & Ladd, G. W. (1989). *Peer relationships in child development*. New York: Wiley.

Bhavnagri, N. (1987). *Parents as facilitators of preschool children's peer relationships*. Unpublished doctoral dissertation, University of Illinois at Urbana-Champaign.

Bhavnagri, N., & Parke, R. D. (1991). Parents as direct facilitators of children's peer relationships: Effects of age of child and sex of parent. *Journal of Social and Personal Relationships, 8,* 423–440.

Bienert, H., & Schneider, B. H. (1995). Deficit-specific social skills training with peer-nominated aggressive-disruptive and sensitive-isolated preadolescents. *Journal of Clinical Child Psychology, 24,* 287–299.

Bierman, K. L., Miller, C. L., & Stabb, S. D. (1987). Improving the social behavior and peer acceptance of rejected boys: Effects of social skill training with instructions and prohibitions. *Journal of Consulting & Clinical Psychology, 55,* 194–200.

Birch, S. H., & Ladd, G. W. (1996). Contributions of teachers and peers to children's early school adjustment. In K. Wentzel & J. Juvonen (Eds.), *Social motivation: Understanding children's school adjustment* (pp. 199–225). New York: Cambridge University Press.

Birch, S. H., & Ladd, G. W. (1997). The teacher–child relationship and children's early school adjustment. *Journal of School Psychology, 35,* 61–79.

Birch, S. H., & Ladd, G. W. (1998). Children's interpersonal behaviors and the teacher–child relationship. *Developmental Psychology, 34,* 934–946.

Black, B., & Hazen, N. L. (1990). Social status and patterns of communication in acquainted and unacquainted preschool children. *Developmental Psychology, 26,* 379–387.

Black, B., & Logan, A. (1995). Links between communication patterns in mother–child, father–child, and child–peer interactions and children's social status. *Child Development, 66,* 255–271.

Blair, K. A., Denham, S. A., Kochanoff, A., & Whipple, B. (2004). Playing it cool: Temperament, emotion regulation, and social behavior in preschoolers. *Journal of School Psychology, 42,* 419–443.

Boivin, M., Hymel, S., & Bukowski, W. M. (1995). The roles of social withdrawal, peer rejection, and victimization by peers in predicting loneliness and depressed mood in childhood. *Development and Psychopathology, 7,* 765–785.

Boney-McCoy, S., & Finkelhor, D. (1995). Special populations: Psychological sequelae of violent victimization in a national youth sample. *Journal of Consulting and Clinical Psychology, 63,* 726–736.

Borja-Alvarez, T., Zarbatany, L., & Pepper, S. (1991). Contributions of male and female guests and hosts to peer group entry. *Child Development, 62,* 1079–1090.

Bost, K. K., Vaughn, B. E., Washington, W. N., Cielinski, K. L., & Bradbard, M. R. (1998). Social competence, social support, and attachment: Demarcation of construct domains, measurement, and paths of influence for preschool children attending Head Start. *Child Development, 69,* 192–218.

Boulton, M. J., & Smith, P. K. (1994). Bully/victim problems in middle-school children: Stability, self-perceived competence, peer perceptions, and peer acceptance. *British Journal of Developmental Psychology, 12,* 315–329.

Boulton, M. J., & Underwood, K. (1992). Bully/victim problems among middle school children. British Journal of Educational Psychology, *62, 73–87.*

Bowlby, J. (1973). *Attachment and loss: Vol. 2. Separation.* New York: Basic Books.

Brendgen, M., Boivin, M., Vitaro, F., Girard, A., Dionne, G., & Perusse, D. (2008). Gene-environment interaction between peer victimization and child aggression. *Development and Psychopathology, 20,* 455–471.

Brigman, G. A., Lane, D., Lane, D., Lawrence, R., & Switzer, D. (1999). Teaching children school success skills. *Journal of Educational Research, 92,* 323–328.

Brigman, G. A., & Webb, L. D. (2003). Teaching kindergarten students school success skills. *Journal of Educational Research, 96,* 286–292.

Bryant, B. (1985). The neighborhood walk: Sources of support in middle childhood. *Monographs of the Society for Research in Child Development, 50*(3, serial No. 210).

Buckner, J. C, Bassuk, E. L., Weinreb, L. F., & Brooks, M. G. (1999). Homelessness and its relation to the mental health and behavior of low-income schoolchildren. *Developmental Psychology, 35,* 246–257.

Buhrmester, D., & Furman, W. (1986). The changing functions of friends in childhood: A Neo-Sullivanian perspective. In V. J. Derlega & B. A. Winstead (Eds.), *Friendship and social interaction* (pp. 41–61). New York: Springer-Verlag.

Buhs, E. S., & Ladd, G. W. (2001). Peer rejection as an antecedent of young children's school adjustment: An examination of mediating processes. *Developmental Psychology, 37,* 550–560.

Bukowski, W. M., & Hoza, B. (1989). Popularity and friendship: Issues in theory, measurement and outcome. In T. J. Berndt & G. W. Ladd (Eds.), *Peer relationships in child development* (pp. 13–45). New York: Wiley.

Bukowski, W. M., Hoza, B., & Boivin, M. (1993). Popularity, friendship, and emotional adjustment during early adolescence. *New Directions for Child Development, 60,* 23–37.

Bukowski, W. M., Newcomb, A. F., & Hartup, W. W. (1996). *The company they keep: Friendship in childhood and adolescence.* New York: Cambridge University Press.

Burchinal, M. R., Peisner-Feinberg, E., Pianta, R., & Howes, C. (2002). Development of academic skills from preschool through second grade: Family and classroom predictors of developmental trajectories. *Journal of School Psychology, 40,* 415–436.

Cairns, R. B., Cairns, B. D., Neckerman, H. J., Ferguson, L. L., & Gariepy, J. L. (1989). Growth and aggression I: Childhood to early adolescence. *Developmental Psychology, 25,* 320–330.

Campbell, S. N., & Dill, N. (1985). The impact of changes in spatial density on children's behaviors in a day care setting. In J. L. Frost & S. Sunderlin (Eds.), *When children play* (pp. 255–264). Wheaton, MD: Association for Childhood Education International.

Card, N. A., Stucky, B. D., Sawalani, G. M., & Little, T. D. (2008). Direct and indirect aggression during childhood and adolescence: A meta-analytic review of gender differences, intercorrelations, and relations to maladjustment. *Child Development, 79,* 1185–1229.

Cassidy, J., & Asher, S. R. (1992). Loneliness and peer relations in young children. *Child Development, 63,* 350–365.

Cassidy, J., Kirsh, S. J., Scolton, K. L., & Parke, R. D. (1996). Attachment and representations of peer relationships. *Developmental Psychology, 32,* 892–904.

Cassidy, J., Parke, R. D., Bukovsky, L., & Braungart, J. M. (1992). Family-peer connections: The roles of emotional expressiveness within the family and children's understanding of emotions. *Child Development, 63,* 603–618.

Chittenden, G. F. (1942). An experimental study in measuring and modifying assertive behavior in young children. *Monographs of the Society for Research in Child Development, 7,* (No. 1, Serial number 31).

Clark, K. E., & Ladd, G. W. (2000). Connectedness and autonomy support in parent–child relationships: Links to children's socio-emotional orientation and peer relationships. *Developmental Psychology, 36,* 485–498.

Coie, J. D. (2004). The impact of negative social experiences on the development of antisocial behavior. In J. B. Kupersmidt & K. A. Dodge (Eds.), *Children's peer relations: From development to intervention* (pp. 243–267). Washington, DC: American Psychological Association.

Coie, J. D., & Dodge, K. A. (1983). Continuities and changes in children's social status: A five-year longitudinal study. *Merrill-Palmer Quarterly, 29,* 261–282.

Coie, J. D., Dodge, K. A., & Coppotelli, H. (1982). Dimensions and types of social status: A cross -age perspective. *Developmental Psychology, 18,* 557–570.

Coie, J. D., Dodge, K. A., Terry, R., & Wright, V. (1991). The role of aggression in peer relations: An analysis of aggression episodes in boys' play groups. *Child Development, 62,* 812–826.

Coie, J. D., & Kupersmidt, J. B. (1983). A behavioral analysis of emerging social status in boys' groups. *Child Development, 54,* 1400–1416.

Coie, J. D., Lochman, J. E., Terry, R., & Hyman, C. (1992). Predicting early adolescent disorder from childhood aggression and peer rejection. *Journal of Consulting and Clinical Psychology, 60,* 783–792.

Coie, J. D., Terry, R., Lenox, K., Lochman, J., & Hyman, C. (1995). Childhood peer rejection and aggression as predictors of stable patterns of adolescent disorder. *Development and Psychopathology, 7,* 697–713.

Coie, J. D., Watt, N. F., West, S. G., Hawkins, D., Asarnow, J. R., Markman, H. J. et al. (1993). The science of prevention: A conceptual framework and some directions for a national research program. *American Psychologist, 48,* 1013–1022.

Cole, D. A., Peeke, L. G., Martin, J. M., Truglio, R., & Seroczynski, A. D. (1998). A longitudinal look at the relation between depression and anxiety in children. *Journal of Consulting & Clinical Psychology, 66,* 451–460.

Coplan, R. J. (2000). Assessing nonsocial play in early childhood: Conceptual and methodological approaches. In K. Gitlin-Weiner, A. Sandgrund, & C. Schaefer (Eds.), *Play diagnosis and assessment* (2nd ed.; pp. 563–598). New York: Wiley.

Coplan, R. J., Gavinski-Molina, M. H., Lagace-Seguin, D. G., & Wichmann, C. (2001). When girls and boys play alone: Nonsocial play and adjustment in kindergarten. *Developmental Psychology, 37,* 464–474.

Coplan, R. J., Prakash, K., O'Neil, K., & Armer, M. (2004). Do you "want" to play? Distinguishing between conflicted-shyness and social disinterest in early childhood. *Developmental Psychology, 40,* 244–258.

Coplan, R. J., & Rubin, K. H. (1998). Exploring and assessing nonsocial play in the preschool: The development and validation of the Preschool Play Behavior Scale. *Social Development, 7,* 73–91.

Coplan, R. J., Rubin, K. H., Fox, N. A., Calkins, S. A., & Stewart, S. L. (1994). Being alone, playing alone, and acting alone: Distinguishing among reticence, and passive- and active-solitude in young children. *Child Development, 65,* 129–137.

Corsaro, W. A. (1981). Friendship in the nursery school: Social organization in a peer environment. In S. R. Asher & J. M. Gottman (Eds.), *The development of children's friendships* (pp. 207–241). New York: Cambridge University Press.

Costin, S. E., & Jones, D. C. (1992). Friendship as a facilitator of emotional responsiveness and prosocial interventions among young children. *Developmental Psychology, 28,* 941–947.

Craig, W. (1997). A comparison among self-, peer-, and teacher-identified victims, bullies, and bully/victims: Are victims an under-identified risk group? In B. Kochenderfer (Chair), *Research on bully/victim problems: Agendas from several cultures.* Symposium conducted at the biennial meetings of the Society for Research in Child Development, Washington, DC.

Crick, N. R., & Grotpeter, J. K. (1995). Relational aggression, gender, and social-psychological adjustment. *Child Development, 66,* 710–722.

Crick, N. R., & Grotpeter, J. K. (1996). Children's treatment by peers: Victims of relational and overt aggression. *Development and Psychopathology, 8,* 367–380.

Cummings, M. E. & Cummings, J. S. (2002). Parenting and attachment. In M. H. Borenstein (Ed.), *Handbook of parenting: Vol. 5. Practical issues in parenting* (2nd ed., pp. 35–58). Mahwah, NJ: Erlbaum.

David, K. M., & Murphy, B. C. (2007). Interparental conflict and preschoolers' peer relations: The moderating roles of temperament and gender. *Social Development, 16,* 1–20.

DeMulder, E. K., Denham, S., Schmidt, M., & Mitchell, J. (2000). Q-sort assessment of attachment security during the preschool years: Link from home to school. *Developmental Psychology, 36,* 274–282.

DeRosier, M. E., Kupersmidt, J. B., & Patterson, C. J. (1994). Children's academic and behavioral adjustment as a function of the chronicity and proximity of peer rejection. *Child Development, 65,* 1799–1813.

Derryberry, D., & Rothbart, M. K. (1997). Reactive and effortful processes in the organization of temperament. *Development and Psychopathology, 9,* 633–652.

Dettling, A. C., Gunnar, M. R., & Donzella, B. (1999). Cortisol levels of young children in full-day childcare centers: Relations with age and temperament. *Psychoneuroendocrinology, 24,* 519–536.

Dishion, T. J. (1990). The family ecology of boys' peer relations in middle childhood. *Child Development, 61,* 874–892.

Dishion, T. J., & McMahon, R. J. (1998). Parental monitoring and the prevention of child and adolescent problem behavior: A conceptual and empirical formulation. *Clinical Child and Family Psychology Review, 1,* 61–75.

Dodge, K. (1983). Behavioral antecedents of peer social status. *Child Development, 54,* 1386–1399.

Dodge, K. A., & Coie, J. D. (1987). Social-information-processing factors in reactive and proactive aggression in children's peer groups. *Journal of Personality and Social Psychology, 53,* 1146–1158.

Dodge, K. A., Coie, J. D., Pettit, G. S., & Price, J. M. (1990). Peer status and aggression in boys' groups: Developmental and contextual analyses. *Child Development, 61,* 1289–1309.

Dodge, K. A., Schlundt, D., Schocken, I., & Delugach, J. (1983). Social competence and children's sociometric status: The role of peer group entry strategies. *Merrill-Palmer Quarterly, 29,* 309–336.

Eckerman, C. O., Davis, C. & Didow, S. (1989). Toddler's emerging ways of achieving social coordination with a peer. *Child Development, 60,* 440–453.

Edwards, C. P. (1992). Cross cultural perspectives on family-peer relations. In R. D. Parke & G. W. Ladd (Eds.), *Family-peer relationships: Modes of linkage* (pp. 285–316). Hillsdale, NJ: Erlbaum.

Egan, S. E., & Perry, D. G. (1998). Does low self-regard invite victimization? *Developmental Psychology, 34,* 299–309.

Egeland, B., & Heister, M. (1995). The long term consequences of infant day care and mother-infant attachment. *Child Development, 66,* 74–85.

Eisenberg, N., Cumberland, A., Spinrad, T. L., Fabes, R. A., Shepard, S. A., Reiser, M., et al. (2001). The relations of regulation and remotionality to children's externalizing and internalizing problem behavior. *Child Development, 72,* 1112–1134.

Eisenberg, N., Fabes, R. A., Guthrie, I. K., & Reiser, M. (2000). Dispositional emotionality and regulation: Their role in predicting quality of social functioning. *Journal of Personality and Social Psychology, 78,* 136–157.

Eisenberg, N., Fabes, R. A., & Murphy, B. C. (1996). Parent's reactions to children's negative emotions: Relations to children's social competence and comforting behaviors. *Child Development, 67,* 2227–2247.

Eisenberg, N., Spinrad, T. L., Fabes, R. A., Reiser, M., Cumberland, A., Shepard, S. A., et al. (2004). The relations of effortful control and impulsivity to children's resiliency and adjustment. *Child Development, 75,* 25–46.

Eisenberg, N., Vaughn, J., & Hofer, C. (2009). Temperament, self-regulation, and peer social competence. In K. Rubin, W. Bukowski, & B. Laursen (Eds.), *Handbook of peer interactions, relationships, and groups* (pp. 473–489). New York: Guilford.

Elicker, J., Englund, M., & Sroufe, L. A. (1992). Predicting peer competence and peer relations in childhood from early parent–child relationships. In R. D. Parke & G. W. Ladd (Eds.), *Family-peer relationships: Modes of linkage* (pp. 77–106). Hillsdale, NJ: Erlbaum.

Epstein, J. L. (1989). The selection of friends: Changes across the grades and in different school environments. In T. J. Berndt & G. W. Ladd (Eds.), *Peer relationships in child development* (pp.158–187). Oxford, England: Wiley.

Fabes, R. A., Hanish, L. A., Martin, C. L. (2003). Children at play: The role of peers in understanding the effects of child care. *Child Development, 74,* 1039–1043.

Fantuzzo, J., McWayne, C., Perry, M.A., & Childs, S. (2004). Multiple dimensions of family involvement and their relations to behavioral and learning competencies for urban, low-income children. *School Psychology Review, 33,* 467–480.

Faust, J., & Forehand, R. (1994). Adolescents' physical complaints as a function of anxiety due to familial and peer stress: A causal model. *Journal of Anxiety Disorders, 8,* 139–153.

Field, T., Masi, W., Goldstein, S., Perry, S., & Parl, S. (1988). Infant day care facilitates preschool behavior. *Early Childhood Research Quarterly, 3,* 341–359.

Finnegan, R. A. (March, 1995). *Aggression and victimization in the peer group: Links with the mother–child relationship.* Poster presented at the biennial meeting of the Society for Research in Child Development, Indianapolis, IN.

Finnegan, R. A., Hodges, E. V. E., & Perry, D. G. (1998). Victimization by peers: Associations with children's reports of mother–child interaction. *Journal of Personality and Social Psychology, 75,* 1076–1086.

French, D. C. (1988). Heterogeneity of peer-rejected boys: Aggressive and nonaggressive subtypes. *Child Development, 59,* 976–985.

French, D. C. (1990). Heterogeneity of peer-rejected girls. *Child Development, 61,* 2028–2031.

Freud, A., & Dann, S. (1951). An experiment in group upbringing. In R. Eisler, A. Freud, H. Hartmann, & E. Kris (Eds.), *Psychoanalytic study of the child* (Vol. 6, pp. 127–168). New York: International Universities Press.

Frost, J. L. (1986). Children's playgrounds: Research and practice. In G. Fein & M. Rivikin (Eds.), *The young child at play* (pp.195–211). Washington, DC: National Association for the Education of Young Children.

Furman, W. (1982). Children's friendships. In T. M. Field, A. Huston, H. C. Quay, L. Troll, & G. E. Finley (Eds.), *Review of human development* (pp. 327–339). New York: Wiley.

Furman, W. (1996). The measurement of friendship perceptions. In W. M. Bukowski, A. F. Newcomb, & W. W. Hartup (Eds.), *The company they keep: Friendship in childhood and adolescence* (pp. 41–65). New York: Cambridge University Press.

Furman, W., & Robbins, P. (1985). What's the point? Issues in the selection of treatment objectives. In B. Schneider, K. H. Rubin, & J. E. Ledingham (Eds.), *Children's peer relations: Issues in assessment and intervention* (pp. 41–54). New York: Springer-Verlag.

Galen, B. R., & Underwood, M. K. (1997). A developmental investigation of social aggression among children. *Developmental Psychology, 33,* 589–600.

Gallagher, J. J. (1958). Social status of children related to intelligence, propinquity, and social perception. *Elementary School Journal, 59,* 225–231.

Garmezy, N., Masten, A. S., & Tellegen, A. (1984). The study of stress and competence in children: A building block for developmental psychopathology. *Child Development, 55,* 97–111.

Gazelle, H., & Ladd, G. W. (2002). Intervention for children who are victims of peer aggression: Conceptualizing intervention at an individual and relationship level. In P. Schewe (Ed.), *Preventing intimate partner violence: Developmentally appropriate interventions across the life span* (pp. 55–78). Washington, DC: American Psychological Association.

Gazelle, H., & Ladd, G. W. (2003). Anxious solitude and peer exclusion: A diathesis-stress model of internalizing trajectories in childhood. *Child Development, 74,* 257–278.

Gershman, E. S., & Hayes, D. S. (1983). Differential stability of reciprocal friendships and unilateral relationships among preschool children. *Merrill-Palmer Quarterly, 29,* 169–177.

Goldsmith, H. H., Aksan, N., Essex, M., Smider, N. A., & Vandell, D. L. (2001). Temperament and socioemotional adjustment to kindergarten: A multi-informant perspective. In T. D. Wachs & G. A. Kohnstamm (Eds.), *Temperament in context* (pp. 103–138). Mahwah, NJ: Erlbaum.

Gottman, J. M. (1983). How children become friends. *Monographs of the Society for Research in Child Development, 48*(3, Serial No. 201).

Gottman, J. M. (1986). The world of coordinated play: Same and cross-sex friendship in young children. In J. M. Gottman & J. G. Parker (Eds.), *Conversations of friends* (pp. 197–253). New York: Cambridge University Press.

Graham, J. A., & Cohen, R. (1997). Race and sex as factors in children's sociometric ratings and friendship choices. *Social Development, 6,* 355–372.

Graham, S., & Juvonen, J. (1998). Self-blame and peer victimization in middle school: An attributional analysis. *Developmental Psychology, 34,* 587–599.

Griggs, M. S., Gagnon, S. G., Huelsman, T. J., Kidder-Ashley, P., & Ballard, M. (2009). Student–teacher relationships matter: Moderating influences between temperament and preschool social competence. *Psychology in the Schools, 46,* 553–567.

Gunnar, M. R., Sebanc, A.M., Tout, K., Donzella, B., & van Dulmen, M. M. (2003). Peer rejection, temperament, and cortisol activity in preschoolers. *Developmental Psychology, 43,* 346–358.

Hamre, B. K., & Pianta, R. C. (2001). Early teacher–child relationships and the trajectory of children's school outcomes through eighth grade. *Child Development, 72,* 625–638.

Han, W., Waldfogel, J., & Brooks-Gunn, J. (2001). The effects of early maternal employment on later cognitive and behavioral outcomes. *Journal of Marriage and the Family, 63,* 336–354.

Harris, J. R. (1995). Where is the child's environment? A group socialization theory of development. *Psychological Review, 102,* 458–489.

Harris, J. R. (1998). *The nurture assumption.* New York: Free Press.

Harris, J. R. (2000). Socialization, personality development, and the child's environment: A comment on Vandell (2000). *Developmental Psychology, 36,* 711–723.

Harrist, A. W., & Bradley, K. D. (2003). "You can't say you can't play": Intervening in the process of social exclusion in the kindergarten classroom. *Early Childhood Research Quarterly, 18,* 185–205.

Harrist, A. W., Zaia, A. F., Bates, J. E., Dodge, K. A., & Pettit, G. S. (1997). Subtypes of social withdrawal in early childhood: Sociometric status and social-cognitive differences across four years. *Child Development, 68,* 278–294.

Hart, C. H. (1993) *Children on playgrounds: Research perspectives and applications.* Albany: State University of New York Press.

Hart, C. H., Ladd, G. W., & Burleson, B. R. (1990). Children's expectations of the outcomes of social strategies: Relations with sociometric status and maternal discipline styles. *Child Development, 61,* 127–137.

Hart, C. H., Yang, C., Nelson, L. J., Robinson, C. C., Olsen, J. A., & Nelson, D. A., et al., (2000). Peer acceptance in early childhood and subtypes of socially withdrawn behavior in China, Russia, and the United States. *International Journal of Behavioral Development, 24,* 73–81.

Hartup, W. (1970). Peer interaction and social organization. In P. H. Mussen (Ed.), *Carmichael's manual of child psychology* (3rd ed., Vol. 2, pp. 360–456). New York: Wiley.

Hartup, W. W. (1983). Peer relations. In P. H. Mussen (Series Ed.) & E. M. Heatherington (Vol. Ed.), *Handbook of child psychology: Vol. 4. Socialization, personality, and social development* (4th ed., pp. 103–196). New York: Wiley.

Hawker, D., & Boulton, M. J. (2000). Twenty years' research on peer victimization and psychosocial maladjustment: A meta-analytic review of cross-sectional studies. *Journal of Child Psychology and Psychiatry and Allied Disciplines, 41,* 441–455.

Hawker, D. S. J. (1997). *Socioemotional maladjustment among victims of different forms of peer aggression.* Unpublished doctoral dissertation, Keele University, Newcastle, U.K.

Hayes, D. (1978). Cognitive bases for liking and disliking among preschool children. *Child Development, 49,* 906–909.

Hayes, D., Gershman, E., & Bolin, T. (1980). Friends and enemies: Cognitive bases for preschool children's unilateral and reciprocal relationships. *Child Development, 51,* 1276–1279.

Hazen, N., & Black, B. (1989). Preschool peer communication skills: The role of social status and interactional context. *Child Development, 60,* 867–876.

Hinde, R. S., Titmus, G., Easton, D., & Tamplin, A. (1985). Incidence of friendship and behavior toward strong associates versus nonassociates in preschoolers. *Child Development, 56,* 234–245.

Hodges, E. V. E., Boivin, M., Vitaro, F., & Bukowski, W. M. (1999). The power of friendship: Protection against an escalating cycle of peer victimization. *Developmental Psychology, 35,* 94–101.

Hodges, E. V. E., Malone, M. J., & Perry, D. G. (1997). Individual risk and social risk as interacting determinants of victimization in the peer group. *Developmental Psychology, 33,* 1032–1039.

Hodges, E. V. E., & Perry, D. G. (1999). Personal and interpersonal antecedents and consequences of victimization by peers. *Journal of Personality and Social Psychology, 76,* 677–685.

Howes, C. (1983). Patterns of friendship. *Child Development, 54,* 1041–1053.

Howes, C. (1988). Peer interaction of young children. *Monographs of the Society for Research in Child Development, 53*(1, Serial No. 217).

Howes, C. (1996). The earliest friendships. In W. M. Bukowski, A. F. Newcomb, & W. W. Hartup (Eds.), *The company they keep: Friendship in childhood and adolescence* (pp. 66–86). New York: Cambridge University Press.

Howes, C., & Hamilton, C. E. (1992). Children's relationships with caregivers: Mothers and child care teachers. *Child Development, 63,* 859–866.

Howes, C., & Hamilton, C. E. (1993). The changing experience of child care: Changes in teachers and in teacher–child relationships and children's social competence with peers. *Early Childhood Research Quarterly, 8,* 15–32.

Howes, C., & Matheson, C. C. (1992). Sequences in the development of competent play with peers: Social and pretend play. *Developmental Psychology, 28,* 961–974.

Howes, C., Matheson, C., & Hamilton, C. E. (1994). Maternal, teacher, and child-care history correlates of children's relationships with peers. *Child Development, 65,* 264–273.

Howes, C., Olenick, M., & Der-Kiureghian, T. (1987). After school child care in an elementary school: Social development and continuity and complementarity of programs. *Elementary School Journal, 88,* 93–103.

Howes, C., & Phillipsen, L. C. (1992). Gender and friendship: Relationships within peer groups of young children. *Social Development, 1,* 231–242.

Hymel, S., Rubin, K. H., Rowden, L., & LeMare, L. (1990). Children's peer relationships: Longitudinal prediction of internalizing and externalizing problems from middle to late childhood. *Child Development, 61,* 2004–2021.

Katz, L. F., & Gottman, J. M. (1993). Patterns of marital conflict predict children's internalizing and externalizing behaviors. *Developmental Psychology, 29,* 940–950.

Keefe, K., & Berndt, T. J. (1996). Relations of friendship quality to self-esteem in early adolescence. *Journal of Early Adolescence, 16,* 110–129.

Kerns, K. A., Klepac, L., & Cole, A. K. (1996). Peer relationships and preadolescents perceptions of security in the child–mother relationship. *Developmental Psychology, 32,* 457–466.

Kessen, W. (1979). The American child and other cultural inventions. *American Psychologist, 34,* 815–820.

Koch, H. L. (1935). The modification of unsocialness in preschool children. Psychology Bulletin, 32, 700–701.

Kochanska, G., Murray, K.T., & Harlan, E.T. (2000). Effortful control in early childhood: Continuity and change, antecedents, and implications for social development. *Developmental Psychology, 36,* 220–232.

Kochenderfer, B. J., & Ladd, G. W. (1996). Peer victimization: Cause or consequence of school maladjustment? *Child Development, 67,* 1305–1317.

Kochenderfer-Ladd, B. J., & Ladd, G. W. (2001). Variations in peer victimization: Relations to children's maladjustment. In J. Juvonen & S. Graham (Eds.), *Peer harassment in school* (pp. 25–48). New York: Guilford.

Kochenderfer-Ladd, B. J., & Wardrop, J. (2001). Chronicity and instability in children's peer victimization experiences as predictors of loneliness and social satisfaction trajectories. *Child Development, 72,* 134–151.

Kontos, S., Burchinal, M., Howes, C., Wisseh, S., & Galinsky, E. (2002). An eco-behavioral approach to examining the contextual effects of early childhood classrooms. *Early Childhood Research Quarterly, 17,* 239–258.

Kumpulainen, K., Rasanen, E., Henttonen, I., Almqvist, F., Kresanov, K., Linna, S. L., et al. (1998). Bullying and psychiatric symptoms among elementary school-age children. *Child Abuse and Neglect, 22,* 705–717.

Kupersmidt, J. B., DeRosier, M. E., & Patterson, C. P. (1995). Similarity as the basis for children's friendships: The roles of sociometric status, aggressive and withdrawn behavior, academic achievement and demographic characteristics. *Journal of Social and Personal Relationships, 12,* 439–452.

Kupersmidt, J. B., & Dodge, K. A. (2004). *Children's peer relations: From development to intervention.* Washington, DC: American Psychological Association.

Ladd, G. W. (1981). Effectiveness of a social learning method for enhancing children's social interaction and peer acceptance. *Child Development, 52,* 171–178.

Ladd, G. W. (1983). Social networks of popular, average, and rejected children in school settings. *Merrill-Palmer Quarterly, 29,* 283–307.

Ladd, G. W. (1988). Friendship patterns and peer status during early and middle childhood. *Journal of Developmental and Behavioral Pediatrics, 9,* 229–238.

Ladd, G. W. (1989). Toward a further understanding of peer relationships and their contributions to child development. In T. J. Berndt & G. W. Ladd (Eds.), *Peer relationships in child development* (pp. 1–15). New York: Wiley.

Ladd, G. W. (1990). Having friends, keeping friends, making friends, and being liked by peers in the classroom: Predictors of children's early school adjustment? *Child Development, 61,* 1081–1100.

Ladd, G. W. (1992). Themes and theories: Perspectives in process in family-peer relationships. In R. D. Parke & G. W. Ladd (Eds.), *Family–peer relationships: Modes of linkage* (pp. 1–34). Hillsdale, NJ: Erlbaum.

Ladd, G. W. (1996). Shifting ecologies during the 5–7 year period: Predicting children's adjustment to grade school. In A. Sameroff & M. Haith (Eds.), *The* five to seven year shift (pp. 363–386). Chicago, IL: University of Chicago Press.

Ladd, G. W. (1999). Peer relationships and social competence during early and middle childhood. *Annual Review of Psychology, 50,* 333–359.

Ladd, G. W. (2003). Probing the adaptive significance of children's behavior and relationships in the school context: A child by environment perspective. In R. Kail (Ed.), *Advances in child behavior and development* (Vol. 31, pp. 43–104). New York: Wiley.

Ladd, G. W. (2005). *Children's peer relationships and social competence.* New Haven, CT: Yale University Press.

Ladd, G. W. (2006). Peer rejection, aggressive or withdrawn behavior, and psychological maladjustment from ages 5 to 12: An examination of four predictive models. *Child Development, 77,* 822–846.

Ladd, G. W., Birch, S. H., & Buhs, E. S. (1999). Children's social and scholastic lives in kindergarten: Related spheres of influence? *Child Development, 70,* 1373–1400.

Ladd, G. W., Buhs, E., & Seid, M. (2000). Children's initial sentiments about kindergarten: Is school liking an antecedent of early classroom participation and achievement? *Merrill-Palmer Quarterly, 46,* 255–279.

Ladd, G. W., Buhs, E. & Troop, W. (2002). Children's interpersonal skills and relationships in school settings: Adaptive significance and implications for school-based prevention and intervention programs. In P. K. Smith & C. H. Hart (Eds.), *Blackwell's handbook of childhood social development* (pp. 394–415). London: Blackwell.

Ladd, G. W., & Burgess, K. B. (1999). Charting the relationship trajectories of aggressive, withdrawn, and aggressive/withdrawn children during early grade school. *Child Development, 70,* 910–929.

Ladd, G. W., & Burgess, K. B. (2001). Do relational risks and protective factors moderate the linkages between childhood aggression and early psychological and school adjustment? Child Development, 72, 1579–1601.

Ladd, G. W., & Coleman, C. C. (1993). Young children's peer relationships: Forms, features, and functions. In B. Spodek (Ed.), *Handbook of research on the education of young children* (pp. 57–76). New York: Macmillan.

Ladd, G. W., & Golter, B. (1988). Parents' management of preschoolers peer relationships: Is it related to children's social competence? *Developmental Psychology, 24,* 109–117.

Ladd, G. W., & Hart, C. H. (1992). Creating informal play opportunities: Are parents' and preschoolers' initiations related to children's competence with peers? *Developmental Psychology, 28,* 1179–1187.

Ladd, G. W., Hart, C. H., Wadsworth, E. M., & Golter, B. S. (1988). Preschoolers' peer networks in nonschool settings: Relationship to family characteristics and school adjustment. In S. Salzinger, J. Antrobus, & M. Hammer (Eds.), *Social networks of children, adolescents, and college students* (pp. 61–92). Hillsdale, NJ: Erlbaum.

Ladd, G. W., Herald, S. L., & Kochel, K. P. (2006). School readiness: Are there social prerequisites? *Early Education and Development, 17,* 115–150.

Ladd, G. W., Herald-Brown, S. L., & Reiser, M. (2008). Does chronic classroom peer rejection predict the development of children's classroom participation during the grade school years? *Child Development, 79,* 1001–1015.

Ladd, G. W., Herald, S., Slutzky, C., & Andrews, K. (2004). Preventive interventions for peer group rejection. In L. Rapp-Paglicci, C. N., Dulmus, & J. S. Wodarski (Eds.), *Handbook of prevention interventions for children and adolescents* (pp. 15–48). New York: Wiley.

Ladd, G. W., & Kochenderfer, B. J. (1996). Linkages between friendship and adjustment during early school transitions. In W. M. Bukowski, A. F. Newcomb, & W. W. Hartup (Eds.), *The company they keep: Friendship in childhood and adolescence* (pp. 322–345). New York: Cambridge University Press.

Ladd, G. W., & Kochenderfer, B. J., & Coleman, C. C. (1997). Classroom peer acceptance, friendship, and victimization: Distinct relational systems that contribute uniquely to children's school adjustment? *Child Development, 68,* 1181–1197.

Ladd, G. W., Kochenderfer, B. J., & Coleman, C. C. (1996). Friendship quality as a predictor of young children's early school adjustment. *Child Development, 67,* 1103–1118.

Ladd, G. W., & Kochenderfer-Ladd, B. J. (1998). Parenting behaviors and the parent–child relationship: Correlates of peer victimization in kindergarten? *Developmental Psychology, 34,* 1450–1458.

Ladd, G. W., & Kochenderfer-Ladd, B. J. (2002). Identifying victims of peer aggression from early to middle childhood: Analysis of cross-informant data for concordance, estimation of relational adjustment, prevalence of victimization, and characteristics of identified victims. *Psychological Assessment, 14,* 74–96.

Ladd, G. W., & Mars, K. T. (1986). Reliability and validity of preschoolers' perceptions of peer behavior. *Journal of Clinical Child Psychology, 15,* 16–25.

Ladd, G. W., & Mize, J. (1983). A cognitive-social learning model of social-skill training. *Psychological Review, 90,* 127–157.

Ladd, G. W., & Pettit, G. S. (2002). Parenting and the development of children's peer relationships. In M. H. Borenstein (Ed.), *Handbook of parenting* (2nd ed., Vol 5, pp. 269–310). Mahwah, NJ: Erlbaum.

Ladd, G. W., & Price, J. M. (1987). Predicting children's social and school adjustment following the transition from preschool to kindergarten. *Child Development, 58,* 1168–1189.

Ladd, G. W., & Price, J. M. (1993). Playstyles of peer-accepted and peer-rejected children on the playground. In C. H. Hart (Eds.), *Children on playgrounds: Research perspectives and applications* (pp. 130–183). Albany: State University of New York Press.

Ladd, G. W., Price, J. M., & Hart, C. H. (1988). Predicting children's peer status from their playground behaviors. *Child Development, 59,* 986–992.

Ladd, G. W., Price, J. M., & Hart, C. H. (1990). Preschoolers' behavioral orientations and patterns of peer contact: Predictive of social status? In S. R. Asher & J. D. Coie (Eds.), *Peer rejection in childhood* (pp. 90–118). New York: Cambridge University Press.

Ladd, G. W., Profilet, S., & Hart, C. H. (1992). Parents' management of children's peer relations: Facilitating and supervising children's activities in the peer culture. In R. D. Parke & G. W. Ladd (Eds.), *Family-peer relationships: Modes of linkage* (pp. 215–254). Hillsdale, NJ: Erlbaum.

Ladd, G. W., & Troop-Gordon, W. P. (2003). The role of chronic peer difficulties in the development of children's psychological adjustment problems. *Child Development, 74,* 1325–1348.

LaFreniere, P. J., & Sroufe, L. A. (1985). Profiles of peer competence in the preschool: Interrelations between measures, influences of social ecology, and relation to attachment history. *Developmental Psychology, 21,* 56–69.

Lagerspetz, K. M. J., Bjorkqvist, K., & Peltonen, T. (1988). Is indirect aggression typical of females? Gender differences in aggressiveness in 11- to 12-year-old children. *Aggressive Behavior, 14,* 403–414.

Larner, M. B., Zippiroli, L., & Behrman, R.E. (1999). When school is out: Analysis and recommendations. *The Future of Children, 9,* 4–20.

Lieberman, A.F. (1977). Preschoolers' competence with peers: Relations with attachment and peer experience. *Child Development, 48,* 1277–1287.

Lieberman, A. F., Doyle, A. B., & Markiewicz, D. (1999). Developmental patterns in security of attachment to mother and father in late childhood and early adolescence: Associations with peer relations. *Child Development, 70,* 202–213.

Lindsey, E. W., & Mize, J. (2000). Parent–child physical and pretence play: Links to children's social competence. *Merrill-Palmer Quarterly, 46,* 565–591.

Lochman, J. E., Coie, J. D., Underwood, M. K., & Terry, R. (1993). Effectiveness of a social relations intervention program for aggressive and nonaggressive, rejected children. *Journal of Consulting and Clinical Psychology, 61,* 1053–1058.

Lochman, J. E., & Wayland, K. K. (1994). Aggression, social acceptance and race as predictors of negative adolescent outcomes. *Journal of the American Academy of Child and Adolescent Psychiatry, 33,* 1026–1035.

Lollis, S. P., Ross, H. S., & Tate, E. (1992). Parents' regulation of children's peer interactions: Direct influence. In R. D. Parke & G. W. Ladd (Eds.), *Family-peer relationships: Modes of lineage* (pp. 255–294). Hillsdale, NJ: Erlbaum.

Love, J. M., Harrison, L., Sagi-Schwartz, A., van Ijzendoorn, M. H., Ross, C., Ungerer, J. A., et al. (2003). Child care quality matters: How conclusions may vary with context. *Child Development, 74,* 1021–1033.

Lynch, M., & Cicchetti, D. (1992). Maltreated children's reports of relatedness to their teachers. In R. C. Pianta (Ed.), *Beyond the parent: The role of other adults in children's lives* (New Directions for Child Development, No. 57; pp. 81–107). San Francisco, CA: Jossey-Bass.

Maccoby, E. E., & Lewis, C. C. (2003). Less day care or different day care? *Child Development, 74,* 1069–1075.

MacDonald, K. B., & Parke, R. D. (1984). Bridging the gap: Parent–child play interaction and interactive competence. *Child Development, 55,* 1265–1277.

MacDougall, P., Hymel, S., Vaillancourt, T., & Mercer, L. (2001). The consequences of childhood peer rejection. In M. R. Leary (Ed.), *Interpersonal rejection* (pp. 213–237). Oxford, England: Oxford University Press.

Magnuson, K., & Duncan, G. (2002). Parents in poverty. In M. H. Bornstein (Ed.), *Handbook of parenting: Vol. 4. Social conditions and applied parenting* (2nd ed., pp. 95–121). Mahwah, NJ: Erlbaum.

Mahoney, M. J., & Cairns, R. D (1997). Do extracurricular activities protect against early school dropout? *Developmental Psychology, 33,* 241–253.

Masters, J. C., & Furman, W. (1981). Popularity, individual friendship selection, and specific peer interaction among children. *Developmental Psychology, 17,* 344–350.

McCartney, K., Burchinal, M., Clarke-Stewart, A., Bub, K.L., Owen, M.T., & Belsky, J. (2010). Testing a series of causal propositions relating time in child care to children's externalizing behavior. *Developmental Psychology, 46,* 1–17.

Medrich, E. A, Roizen, J., Rubin, V., & Buckley, S. (1982). *The serious business of growing up: A study of children's lives outside of school.* Berkeley: University of California Press.

Meehan, B. T., Hughes, J. N., & Cavell, T. A. (2003). Teacher–student relationships as compensatory resources for aggressive children. *Child Development, 74,* 1145–1157.

Mize, J., & Ladd, G. W. (1988). Predicting preschoolers' peer behavior and status from their interpersonal strategies: A comparison of verbal and enactive responses to hypothetical social dilemmas. *Developmental Psychology, 24,* 782–788.

Mize J., & Ladd, G. W. (1990). A cognitive-social learning approach to social skills training with low-status preschool children. *Developmental Psychology, 26,* 388–397.

Moore, S. G. (1967). Correlates of peer acceptance in nursery school children. In W. W. Hartup & N. L. Smothergill (Eds.), *The young child* (pp. 229–247). Washington, DC: National Association for the Education of Young Children.

Nansel, T. R., Overpeck, M., Pilla, R. S., Ruan, W. J., Simons-Morton, B., & Scheidt, P. (2001). Bullying behaviors among US youth. *Journal of the American Medical Association, 285,* 2094–2100.

National Institutes of Child Health and Human Development, Early Child Care Research Network (NICHHD, ECCRN). (2001). Child care and children's peer interactions at 24 and 26 months: The NICHD Study of Early Child Care. *Child Development, 72,* 1478–1500.

National Institutes of Child Health and Human Development, Early Child Care Research Network (NICHHD, ECCRN). (2003). Does amount of time spent in child care predict socioemotional adjustment during the transition to kindergarten? *Child Development, 74,* 976–1005.

National Institutes of Child Health and Human Development, Early Child Care Research Network (NICHHD, ECCRN). (2004). Are child developmental outcomes related to before- and after-school care arrangements? Results from the NICHD Study of Early Childhood. *Child Development, 75,* 280–295.

Nelson, L. J., Rubin, K. H., & Fox, N. A. (2005). Social withdrawal, observed peer acceptance, and the development of self-perceptions in children ages 4 to 7 years. *Early Childhood Research Quarterly, 20,* 185–200.

Newcomb, A. F., & Bagwell, C. L. (1995). Children's friendship relations: A meta-analytic review. *Psychological Bulletin, 117,* 306–347.

Newcomb, A. F., & Bukowski, W. M. (1983). Social impact and social preference as determinants of children's peer group status. *Developmental Psychology, 19,* 856–867.

O'Connor, R. D. (1969). Modification of social withdrawal through symbolic modeling. *Journal of Applied Behavior Analysis, 2,* 15–22.

O'Connor, R. D. (1972). Relative efficacy of modeling, shaping, and the combined procedures for modification of social withdrawal. *Journal of Abnormal Psychology, 79,* 327–334.

Oden, S., & Asher, S. R. (1977). Coaching children in social skills for friendship making. *Child Development, 48,* 495–506.

O'Donnell, L., & Stueve, A. (1983). Mothers as social agents: Structuring the community activities of school aged children. In H. Z. Lopata & J. H. Pleck (Eds.), *Research in the interweave of social roles: Families and jobs* (pp. 113–129). Greenwich, CT: JAI Press.

Olson, S. L., Sameroff, A. J., Kerr, D. C. R., Lopez, N. L., & Wellman, H. M. (2005). Developmental foundations of externalizing problems in young children: The role of effortful control. *Development and Psychopathology, 17,* 25–45.

Olweus, D. (1978). *Aggression in the schools: Bullies and whipping boys.* Washington, DC: Hemisphere.

Olweus, D. (1984). Aggressors and their victims: Bullying at school. In N. Frude & H. Gault (Eds.), *Disruptive behavior in schools* (pp. 57–76). New York: Wiley.

Olweus, D. (1993). Bullies on the playground: The role of victimization. In C. H. Hart (Ed.), *Children on playgrounds: Research perspectives and applications* (pp. 85–127). Albany: State University of New York Press.

Olweus, D. (2001). Peer victimization: A critical analysis of some important issues. In J. Juvonen & S. Graham (Eds.), *Peer harassment in school* (pp. 3–23). New York: Guilford.

Olweus, D. (1999). Sweden. In P. K. Smith, Y. Morita, J. Junger-Tas, D. Olweus, R. Catalano, & P. Slee (Eds.). *The nature of school bullying: A cross-national perspective.* New York: Routledge.

Paley, V. G. (1992). *You can't say you can't play.* Cambridge, MA: Harvard University Press.

Park, K. A., & Waters, E. (1989). Security of attachment and preschool friendships. *Child Development, 60,* 1076–1081.

Parke, R. D., & Ladd, G. W. (Eds.). (1992). *Family–peer relationships: Modes of linkage* (pp. 255–294). Hillsdale, NJ: Erlbaum.

Parke, R. D., MacDonald, K., Beitel, A., & Bhavnagri, N. (1988). The role of the family in the development of peer relationships. In R. Peters & R. J. McMahon (Eds.), *Social learning systems approaches to marriage and the family* (pp. 17–44). New York: Bruner/Mazel.

Parke, R. D., MacDonald, K., Burks, V. M., Carson, J., Bhavnagri, N., Barth, J. M., et al. (1989). Family and peer linkages: In search of linkages. In K. Kreppner & R. M. Lerner (Eds.), *Family systems and life span development* (pp. 65–92). Hillsdale, NJ: Erlbaum.

Parker, J. G. (1986). Becoming friends: Conversational skills for friendship formation in young children. In J. M. Gottman & J. G. Parker (Eds.), *Conversations of friends* (pp. 103–138). New York: Cambridge University Press.

Parker, J. G., & Asher, S. R. (1987). Peer relations and later personal adjustment: Are low-accepted children at risk? *Psychological Bulletin, 102,* 357–389.

Parker, J. G., & Asher, S. R. (1989, April). Peer relations and social adjustment: Are friendship and group acceptance distinct domains? In W. Bukowski (Chair), *Properties, processes, and effects of friendship relations during childhood and adolescence.* Symposium conducted at the biennial meeting of the Society for Research on Child Development, Kansas City, KS.

Parker, J. G., & Asher, S. R. (1993). Friendship and friendship quality in middle childhood: Links with peer group acceptance and feelings of loneliness and social dissatisfaction. *Developmental Psychology, 29,* 611–621.

Parker, J. G., & Gottman, J. M. (1989). Social and emotional development in a relational context: Friendship interaction from early childhood to adolescence. In T. J. Berndt & G. W. Ladd (Eds.), *Peer relationships in child development* (pp. 95–131). New York: Wiley.

Parker, J. G., & Seal, J. (1996). Forming, losing, renewing, and replacing friendships: Applying temporal parameters to the assessment of children's friendship experiences. *Child Development, 67,* 2248–2268.

Patterson, C. J., Vaden, N. A., & Kupersmidt, J. B. (1991). Family background, recent life events, and peer rejection during childhood. *Journal of Social and Personal Relationships, 8,* 347–362.

Patterson, G. R., Reid, J. B., & Dishion, T. J. (1992). *Antisocial boys.* Eugene, OR: Castalia.

Perren, S., & Alsaker, F. D. (2006). Social behavior and peer relationships of victims, bully-victims, and bullies in kindergarten. *Journal of Child Psychology and Psychiatry, 47,* 45–57.

Perry, D. G., Hodges, E. V., & Egan, S. (2001). Determinants of chronic victimization by peers: A review and new model of family influence. In J. Juvonen & S. Graham (Eds.), *Peer harassment in school: The plight of the vulnerable and victimized* (pp. 73–104). New York: Guilford.

Perry, D. G., Kusel, S. J., & Perry, L. C. (1988). Victims of peer aggression. *Developmental Psychology, 24,* 807–814.

Perry, K. E., & Weinstein, R. S. (1998). The social context of early schooling and children's school adjustment. *Educational Psychologist, 33,* 177–194.

Pettit, G. S., Bates, J. E., & Dodge, K. A. (1997). Supportive parenting, ecological context, and children's adjustment: A seven-year longitudinal study. *Child Development, 68,* 908–923.

Pettit, G. S., Bates, J. E., Dodge, K. A., & Meece, D. (1999). The impact of after school peer contact on early adolescent externalizing problems is moderated by parental monitoring, perceived neighborhood safety, and prior adjustment. *Child Development, 70,* 768–778.

Pettit, G. S., Brown, E. G., Mize, J., & Lindsey, E. (1998). Mothers' and father's socializing behaviors in three contexts: Links with children's peer competence. *Merrill-Palmer Quarterly, 44,* 173–193.

Pettit, G. S., Clawson, M., Dodge, K. A., & Bates, J. E. (1996). Stability and change in peer-rejected status: The role of child behavior, parenting, and family ecology. *Merrill-Palmer Quarterly, 42,* 267–294.

Pettit, G. S, & Harrist, A. W. (1993). Children's aggressive and socially unskilled playground behavior with peers: Origins in early family relations. In C. H. Hart (Ed.), *Children on playgrounds: Research perspective and applications* (pp. 240–270). Albany: State University of New York Press.

Pettit, G. S., Laird, R. D., Bates, J. E., & Dodge, K. A. (1997). Patterns of after school care in middle childhood: Risk factors and developmental outcomes. *Merrill-Palmer Quarterly, 43,* 515–538.

Phyfe-Perkins, E. (1980). Children's behavior in preschool settings: A review of research concerning the influence of physical environment. In L. G. Katz (Ed.), *Current topics in early childhood education* (Vol. 3, pp. 91–125). Norwood, NJ: Ablex.

Piaget, J. (1965). *The moral judgment of the child.* New York: Free Press.

Pianta, R. C., Hamre, B., & Stuhlman, M. (2003). Relationships between teachers and children. In W. M. Reynolds & G. E. Miller (Eds.), *Handbook of psychology: Educational psychology* (pp. 199–234). New York: Wiley.

Pianta, R. C., & Steinberg, M. (1992). Teacher–child relationships and the process of adjusting to school. *New Directions for Child Development, 57,* 61–80.

Pianta, R. C., Steinberg, M., & Rollins, K. (1995). The first two years of school: Teacher–child relationships and deflections in children's school adjustment. *Development and Psychopathology, 7,* 295–312.

Pierce, K. M., Bolt, D. M., & Vandell, D. L. (2010). Specific features of after-school program quality: Associations with children's functioning in middle childhood. *American Journal of Community Psychology, 45,* 381–393.

Pierce, K. A., & Cohen, R. (1995). Aggressors and their victims: Toward a contextual framework for understanding children's aggressor victim relationships. *Developmental Review, 15,* 292–310.

Posner, J. K., & Vandell, D. L. (1994). Low income children's after school care: Are there beneficial effects of after school programs? *Child Development, 65,* 440–456.

Poteat, G. M., Ironsmith, M., & Bullock, J. (1986). The classification of preschool children's sociometric status. *Early Childhood Research Quarterly, 1,* 349–360.

Poulin, F., Cillessen, A., Hubbard, J. A., Coie, J. D., Dodge, K. A., & Schwartz, D. (1997). Children's friends and behavioral similarity in two social contexts. *Social Development, 6,* 224–236.

Price, J. M., & Ladd, G. W. (1986). Assessment of children's friendships: Implications for social competence and social adjustment. In R. Prinz (Ed.), *Advances in behavioral assessment of children and families* (Vol. 2., pp. 121–149). Greenwich, CT: JAI Press.

Prodromidis, M., Lamb, M., Sternberg, K., Hwang, C., & Broberg, A. (1995). Aggression and noncompliance among Swedish children in center-based care, family day care, and home care. *International Journal of Behavioral Development, 18,* 43–62.

Putallaz, M. (1983). Predicting children's sociometric status from their behavior. *Child Development, 54,* 1417–1426.

Putallaz, M., & Gottman, J. M. (1981). An interactional model of children's entry into peer groups. *Child Development, 52,* 986–944.

Putallaz, M., & Wasserman, A. (1989). Children's naturalistic entry behavior and sociometric status: A developmental perspective. *Developmental Psychology, 25,* 297–305.

Reavis, R. D., Keane, S. P., & Calkins, S. D. (2010). Trajectories of peer victimization: The role of multiple relationships. *Merrill-Palmer Quarterly, 56,* 303–332.

Renshaw, P. D., & Asher, S. R. (1983). Children's goals and strategies for social interaction. *Merrill-Palmer Quarterly, 29,* 353–374.

Renshaw, P. D., & Brown, P. J. (1993). Loneliness in middle childhood: Concurrent and longitudinal predictors. *Child Development, 64,* 1271–1284.

Rigby, K. (1998). The relationship between reported health and involvement in bully/victim problems among male and female secondary schoolchildren. *Journal of Health Psychology, 3,* 465–476.

Rigby, K. (2001). Health consequences of bullying and its prevention in schools. In J. Juvonen & S. Graham (Eds.), *Peer harassment in school: The plight of the vulnerable and victimized* (pp. 310–331). New York: Guilford.

Ross, H. S., & Lollis, S. P. (1989). A social relations analysis of toddler peer relationships. *Child Development, 60,* 1082–1091.

Rothbart, M. K., Ahadi, S. A., Hersey, K. L., & Fisher, P. (2001). Investigations of temperament at three to seven years: The Children's Behavior Questionnaire. *Child Development, 72,* 1394–1408.

Rothbart, M. K., & Bates, J. E. (2006). Temperament. In W. Damon & N. Eisenberg (Eds.), *Handbook of child psychology: Social, emotional, and personality development* (6th ed., Vol. 3, pp. 99–166). New York: Wiley.

Rubenstein, J. L., & Howes, C. (1983). Social-emotional development of toddlers in day care: The role of peers and of individual differences. In S. Kilmer (Ed.), *Advances in early education and child care* (Vol. 3, pp. 13–45). Greenwich, CT: JAI Press

Rubin, K. H. (1977). Play behaviors of young children. *Young Children, 32,* 16–24.

Rubin, K. H. (1982). Nonsocial play in preschoolers: Necessary evil? *Child Development, 53,* 651–657.

Rubin, K. H., Burgess, K. B., & Hastings, P. D. (2002). Stability and social-behavioral consequences of toddlers' inhibited temperament and parenting behaviors. *Child Development, 73,* 483–495.

Rubin, K. H., Bukowski, W. M., & B. Laursen (2009). *Handbook of peer interactions, relationships, and groups.* New York: Guilford.

Rubin, K. H., Coplan, R. J., & Bowker, J. C. (2009). Social withdrawal in childhood. *Annual Review of Psychology, 60,* 141–171.

Rubin, K. H., Fein, G., & Vandenberg, B. (1983). Play. In E. M. Hetherington (Ed.) & P. H. Mussen (Series Editor), *Handbook of child psychology: Social development* (pp. 693–774). New York: Wiley.

Rubin, K. H., Lynch, D., Coplan, R., Rose-Krasnor, L., & Booth, C. L. (1994) Birds of a feather…": Behavioral concordances and preferential personal attraction in children. *Child Development, 65,* 1778–1785.

Rudasill, K. M., & Rimm-Kaufman, S. E. (2009). Teacher–child relationship quality: The roles of child temperament and teacher–child interactions. *Early Childhood Research Quarterly, 24,* 107–120.

Russell, A., Pettit, G. S., & Mize, J. (1998). Horizontal qualities in parent–child relationships: Parallels with and possible consequences for children's peer relationships. *Developmental Review, 18,* 313–352.

Rutter, M. (1979). Maternal deprivation, 1972–1978: New findings, new concepts, new approaches. *Child Development, 50,* 283–305.

Rutter, M. (1990). Commentary: Some focus and process considerations regarding effects of parental depression on children. *Developmental Psychology, 26,* 60–67.

Sanson, A. V., & Rothbart, M. K. (1995). Child temperament and parenting. In M. Bornstein (Ed.), *Handbook of parenting: Vol. 4. Applied and practical parenting* (pp. 299–321). New York: Erlbaum.

Savin-Williams, R. C., & Berndt, T. J. (1990). Friendship and peer relations. In S. S. Feldman & G. R. Elliott (Eds.), *At the threshold: The developing adolescent* (pp. 277–307). Cambridge, MA: Harvard University Press.

Schneider, B. H., Atkinson, L., & Tardif, C. (2001). Child–parent attachment and children's peer relations: A quantitative review. *Developmental Psychology, 37,* 86–100.

Schwartz, D. (2000). Subtypes of aggressors and victims in children's peer groups. *Journal of Abnormal Child Psychology, 28,* 181–192.

Schwartz, D., Dodge, K. A., Pettit, G. S., & Bates, J. E. (1997). The early socialization of aggressive victims of bullying. *Child Development, 68,* 665–675.

Schwartz, D., Dodge, K. A., Pettit, G. S., & Bates, J. E. (2000). Friendship as a moderating factor in the pathway between early harsh home environment and later victimization in the peer group. *Developmental Psychology, 36,* 646–662.

Schwartz, D., McFadyen-Ketchum, S. A., Dodge, K. A., Pettit, G. S., & Bates, J. E. (1998). Peer group victimization as a predictor of children's behavior problems at home and in school. *Development and Psychopathology, 10,* 87–99.

Schwartz, D., Proctor, L. J., & Chien, H. (2001). The aggressive victim of bullying. In J. Juvonen & S. Graham (Eds.), *Peer harassment in school: The plight of the vulnerable and victimized* (pp. 147–174). New York: Guilford.

Sears, R. R. (1975). Your ancients revisited. In E. M. Hetherington (Ed.), *Review of child development research* (Vol. 5, pp. 1–74). Chicago, IL: University of Chicago Press.

Sebanc, A. M. (2003). The friendship features of preschool children: Links with prosocial behavior and aggression. *Social Development, 12,* 249–268.

Segoe, M. (1939). Factors influencing the selection of associates. *Journal of Educational Research, 27,* 32–40.

Seligson, M., Gannett, E., & Cotlin, L. (1992). Before- and after-school care for elementary school children. In B. Spodek & O. N. Saracho (Eds.), *Issues in child care* (pp. 125–142). New York: Teacher's College Press.

Sharp, S. (1995) How much does bullying hurt? The effects of bullying on the personal well-being and educational progress of secondary aged students. *Educational and Child Psychology, 12,* 81–88.

Slee, P. T. (1994). Life in school used to be so good. *Youth Studies Australia, 1,* 20–23.

Slee, P. T. (1995). Bullying: Health concerns of Australian secondary school students. *International Journal of Adolescence and Youth, 5,* 215–224.

Smith, P. K., & Connolly, K. J. (1980). *The ecology of preschool behavior.* Cambridge, England: Cambridge University Press.

Smith, P. K., Pepler, D., & Rigby, K. (2004). *Bullying in schools: How successful can interventions be?* New York: Cambridge University Press.

Snyder, J., Brooker, M., Patrick, M. R., Snyder, A., Schrepferman, L., & Stoolmiller, M. (2003). Observed peer victimization during early elementary school: Continuity, growth, and relation to risk for child antisocial and depressive behavior. *Child Development, 74,* 1881–1898.

Spinrad T. L., Eisenberg N., Cumberland A., Fabes R. A., Valiente C., Shepard S. A., et al. (2006). Relation of emotion-related regulation to children's social competence: A longitudinal study. *Emotion, 6,* 498–510.

Stattin, H., & Kerr, M. (2000). Parental monitoring: A reinterpretation. *Child Development, 71,* 1072–1085.

Sullivan, H. S. (1953). *The interpersonal theory of psychiatry.* New York: Norton.

Thomas, A., & Chess, S. (1977). Temperament and development. Oxford, England: Brunner/Mazel.

Tout, K., de Haan, M., Campbell, E. K., Gunnar, M. R. (1998). Social behavior correlates of cortisol activity in child care: Gender differences and time-of-day effects. *Child Development, 69,* 1247–1262.

Troy, M., & Sroufe, L. A. (1987). Victimization among preschoolers: Role of attachment relationship history. *Journal of the American Academy of Child and Adolescent Psychiatry, 26,* 166–172.

Vandell, D. L. (2000). Parents, peer groups, and other socializing influences. *Developmental Psychology, 36,* 699–710.

Vandell, D. L. (2004). Early child care: The known and the unknown. *Merrill-Palmer Quarterly, 50,* 387–414.

Vandell, D. L., & Hembree, S. E. (1994). Peer social status and friendship: Independent contributors to children's social and academic adjustment. *Merrill-Palmer Quarterly, 40,* 461–477.

Vandell, D. L., & Mueller, E. C. (1980). Peer play and friendships during the first two years. In H. C. Foot, A. J. Chapman, & J. R. Smith (Eds.), *Friendship and social relations in children* (pp. 181–208). Chichester, England: Wiley.

Vandell, D. L., Pierce, K. M., & Dadisman, K. (2005). Out-of-school settings as a developmental context for children and youth. In R.V. Kail (Ed.), *Advances in child development and behavior* (Vol. 33, pp.43–77). Oxford, England: Elsevier.

Vaughn, B. E., & Langlois, J. H. (1983). Physical attractiveness as a correlate of peer status and social competence in preschool children. *Developmental Psychology, 19,* 561–567.

Vincze, M. (1971). The social contacts of infants and young children reared together. *Early Child Development and Care, 1,* 99–109.

Watamura, S. E., Donzella, B., Alwin, J., & Gunnar, M. R. (2003). Morning-to-afternoon increases in cortisol concentrations for infants and toddlers at child care: Age differences and behavioral correlates. *Child Development, 74,* 1006–1020.

Waters, E., Wippman, J., & Sroufe, L. A. (1979). Attachment, positive affect, and competence in the peer group: Two studies in construct validation. *Child Development, 50,* 821–829.

Williams, K., Chambers, M., Logan, S., & Robinson, D. (1996). Association of common health symptoms with bullying in primary school children. *British Medical Journal, 313,* 17–19.

Wilson, B. J. (2003). The role of attentional processes in children's prosocial behavior with peers: Attention shifting and emotion. *Development and Psychopathology, 15,* 313–329.

Wright, J. C., Giammarino, M., & Parad, H. W. (1986). Social status in small groups: Individual-group similarity and the social "misfit." *Journal of Personality and Social Psychology, 50,* 523–536.

Youngblade, L. M. (2003). Peer and teacher ratings of third and fourth grade children's social behavior as a function of early maternal employment. *Journal of Child Psychology and Psychiatry, 44,* 477–488.

Zarbatany, L., & Pepper, S. (1996). The role of the group in peer group entry. *Social Development, 5,* 251–260.

Zarbatany, L., Van Brunschot, M., Meadows, K., & Pepper, S. (1996). Effects of friendship and gender on peer group entry. *Child Development, 67,* 2287–2300.

4

The Emotional Basis of Learning and Development in Early Childhood Education

Susanne A. Denham, Katherine M. Zinsser, and Chavaughn A. Brown
George Mason University

Petey runs, darts, and jumps with a ball clenched tightly in his arms. He screams "ok" to an invitation to play, but is unable to restrain his desire to keep the ball and game as his own. He pulls the ball away from another boy, angrily shoving him and screaming insults. In free play, individual, small group, or whole-group activities, he is angry, often out of control, hitting and throwing objects.

Sean speaks hesitantly, often echoing others' communications, as if practicing. He is always the third, fourth, or last to attempt a task, never asserting ideas or desires. He is quiet, sometimes looking quite sad on the sidelines, seeking the comfort of his thumb. He seems overwhelmed and withdrawn.

Jeremy plays and interacts with peers fairly well; teachers note that he has difficulty permitting other children to lead activities or reject his ideas, and he is very upset when he makes a mistake.

The current educational climate, focusing as it does upon children's cognitive development, promotes early literacy and numeracy. Although these preacademic skills are immensely important, Petey, Sean, and Jeremy are not alone in needing us to focus on other domains of development. Their experiences illustrate that, in order for all young children to learn, and for their development as "whole" persons, emotional development requires equally careful nurturing. It is more important than ever to reflect upon what we know about children's emotional competence, how they deal with the ever-present emotions in their lives. Young children must learn to send and receive emotional messages, using their knowledge about emotions and their abilities to regulate emotions, so that they may successfully negotiate interpersonal exchanges, form relationships, and maintain curiosity and enthusiasm (Halberstadt, Denham, & Dunsmore, 2001; Saarni, 1999). Internal, intrapersonal processes, such as the child's temperament and language abilities, contribute to these components. Importantly, these aspects of emotional competence are also impacted by others' modeling of emotional expressiveness, reacting to children's emotions, and discussing and teaching about emotions.

Further, emotional competence is crucial not only in its own right, but for positive social outcomes. The components of emotional competence help to ensure effective social interactions built upon specific skills such as listening, cooperating, appropriate help seeking, joining interactions, and negotiating. The socially successful child is in a good position to thrive. Successful, independent interaction with age mates is a crucial predictor of later mental health and well-being, beginning during preschool, continuing during the grade school years when peer reputations solidify, and thereafter (Denham & Holt, 1993; Robins & Rutter, 1990).

Through its contributions to social competence and self-regulation, emotional competence also supports, both directly and indirectly, cognitive development, preacademic achievement, school readiness, and school adjustment (Blair, 2002; Greenberg & Snell, 1997). Children who enter kindergarten with more positive profiles of emotional and social competence have not only more success in developing positive attitudes about and successful early adjustment to school, but also have improved grades and achievement (Birch, Ladd, & Blecher-Sass, 1997; Ladd, Birch, & Buhs, 1999; Ladd, Kochenderfer, & Coleman, 1996). In particular, when children enter school with friends, are well liked, are able to make and sustain new friendships, and are able to initiate positive relationships with their teachers, *all of which are supported by emotional competence*, they also feel more positive about school, participate in school more, and achieve more than children who are not described this way. In contrast, children who are angry, and otherwise less emotionally competent, have more school adjustment problems, and are at risk for numerous problems, including school difficulties with academic tasks. Later on, they are more likely to drop out and persist in their antisocial behavior, such as delinquency and drug abuse (Gagnon, Craig, Tremblay, Zhou, & Vitaro, 1995; Kochenderfer & Ladd, 1996; Raver & Knitzer, 2002). In short, aspects of emotional competence, such as emotion knowledge and emotion regulatory abilities, often uniquely predict school success, even when other pertinent factors, including earlier school success, are already taken into account (see Denham, Brown, & Domitrovich, 2010, for a review). We now turn to a more detailed consideration of the general nature and specific manifestations of emotional competence during the early childhood timeframe.

What is Emotional Competence?

The social-emotional skills that preschoolers normally develop are quite impressive. Not everyone looks like Petey, Sean, or Jeremy. Consider the following example:

> Four-year-olds Darrell and Jessica are pretending Blue's Clues®. They have drawn a "map" and have pencils and pads ready to "write" the clues, even a magnifying glass. They are having fun! But then things get complicated, changing fast, as interaction often does. They are trying to decide what to hunt for to bring back to Circle Time. Jessica suddenly decides that she should be Blue, and that she doesn't want to hunt for clues at the bakery; she wants to go to the music store instead. Darrell shouts, "No way, you have to be Joe!" After a second he adds, with a smile, "Anyway, I wanted to do clues for doughnuts—they're your favorite, too!"
>
> Now Jimmy, who had been nearby, runs over, whining to join them. No way!! Darrell, still concentrating on Jessica's demands, doesn't want Jimmy to join them—he's too much of a baby. Almost simultaneously, Jessica hurts her hand with one of the pencils, and starts to cry. And Tomas, the class bully, approaches, laughing at four-year-olds making believe and crying.

This was much more than a simple playtime. Imagine the skills of emotional competence that are needed to successfully negotiate these interactions! Within a five-minute play period, a variety of emotional competencies are called for if the social interaction is to proceed successfully. For example, Darrell has to know how to handle Jessica's emotions and his own during their disagreement, react to Jimmy's whining without hurting his feelings, and "handle" Tomas safely. Darrell needs to learn how to express his emotions in socially appropriate ways, handle provocation without getting too mad or too scared, engage with others positively, and build emotional relationships. Taken together, these abilities are vital for how Darrell gets along with others, understands himself, and feels good in his world, with himself, and with others.

Many children Darrell and Jessica's age are learning to cope with their emotions and with the many difficulties that arise when dealing with other people. Specifically, emotionally competent young children begin to: (1) experience and purposefully express a broad variety of emotions, without incapacitating intensity or duration; (2) regulate their emotion whenever its experience is "too much" or "too little" for themselves, or when its expression is "too much" or "too little" to meet others' expectations; and (3) understand their own and others' emotions. These abilities are situated within a theoretical model of emotional competence.

A Model of Emotional Competence

It is important to view the development of emotional competence in terms of children's key emotional tasks. During the early childhood years, emotional competence skills are organized around developmental tasks of maintaining emotionally positive emotional engagement with the physical and social world, while managing emotional arousal in the context of social interaction and cognitive demands. These skills are not easy ones for children just entering the peer arena, and the new classroom context can tax children's ability to navigate successfully. Children need to sit still, attend, follow directions, approach group play, complete preacademic tasks, and get along with others, in ways that challenge their nascent abilities.

The components of emotional competence operate within these key developmental tasks (see Figure 4.1). We define the emotional competence construct, at the topmost level of the model, as *emotional effectiveness*, the functional capacity by which a child can reach his or her short- and long-term goals, during or after an emotion-eliciting encounter (Saarni, 1999).

Within this theoretical view, it also is necessary to decide what contexts to focus upon when evaluating evidence of a child's emotional competence (the next level of the model). Are we interested in knowing the child's view of success in meeting emotional competence goals, or the views of others? Differentiating the evaluators of a child's emotional competence is important; depending on the goal that the child holds, his or her view of the effectiveness of interaction could be quite different from those of others in the environment (Saarni, 2001). Sammy may think his bout of glee met the goal of having fun, but his teacher may be disgruntled because Sammy's raucous laughing and tumbling got the other boys "overexcited," too.

The bottom level of the model contains the specific emotional competencies to which we have already referred: (a) emotional experience and expression; (b) emotional regulation; and (c) emotion knowledge. As well, the depth dimension of the model in Figure 4.1 refers to important contextual/setting moderators of emotional competence (e.g., gender, culture, experiences in preschool or child care, to which we will return later). The skills of emotional competence seen in the bottommost level of Figure 4.1 are vividly played out in interactions and within relationships with others, in multiple social contexts (e.g., peer relationships, family, community activities, teacher relationships, preschool/childcare; Campos, Mumme, Kermoian, & Campos, 1994; Mashburn & Pianta, 2006). The emotional competence skills appropriate for any given situation can depend on social context—the very emotional expressiveness that rendered Sammy sought-after in peer interactions

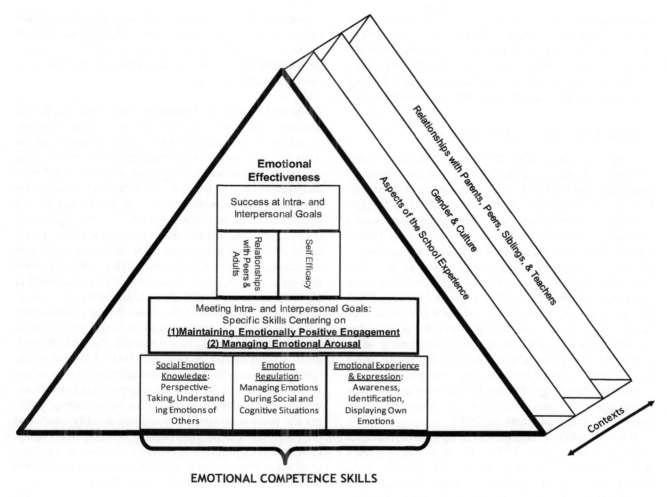

Emotional Effectiveness

Success at Intra- and Interpersonal Goals

Relationships with Peers & Adults

Self Efficacy

Meeting Intra- and Interpersonal Goals:
Specific Skills Centering on
(1)Maintaining Emotionally Positive Engagement
(2) Managing Emotional Arousal

Social Emotion Knowledge: Perspective-Taking, Understanding Emotions of Others

Emotion Regulation: Managing Emotions During Social and Cognitive Situations

Emotional Experience & Expression: Awareness, Identification, Displaying Own Emotions

Relationships with Parents, Peers, Siblings, & Teachers

Gender & Culture

Aspects of the School Experience

Contexts

EMOTIONAL COMPETENCE SKILLS

Figure 4.1

made it difficult for his teacher to convey important concepts to him. Cross-context flexibility in emotional competence skills becomes crucial as children mature.

Expression, experience, regulation, and knowledge of emotions affect interpersonal relations; conversely, interpersonal interactions guide development of these skills (Halberstadt et al., 2001). Emotions are inherently social and functional. Thus, although the components of emotional competence are often considered from an individual differences perspective, our model builds upon these social roots, informed by both social constructivist and functionalist theoretical perspectives. The social constructivist approach focuses on emotions as social products. The meaning of emotions and their expression vary markedly across social dimensions, such as socialization according to cultural values and norms (Saarni, 1998). For example, the value that certain cultures put on empathic emotions is not emphasized by others.

Further, many emotion theorists also take a functionalist view of expressiveness. Emotional expressiveness within a social setting is not only important information for oneself, but also for others because others' behaviors often constitute

antecedent conditions for one's own emotions, and vice versa. Most importantly, the expression of emotion signals whether the child or other people need to modify or continue their goal-directed behavior (Campos et al., 1994).

For example, if a girl experiences anger while playing at the puzzle activity table with another child, she may try to avoid the other child the next day, and even tell her mother "I don't want *her* to come to my birthday party." The experience of anger gave her important information that affects her subsequent behavior. Her anger also gives information to others that affects their subsequent behavior—witnesses to her anger may seek to avoid her until she calms down.

Based on these theoretical precepts, the major goals of this chapter are to fully describe: (a) the breadth and depth of what we know about the separate components of emotional competence—emotional experience and expressiveness, emotion knowledge, and emotion regulation—as they emerge for typically developing children through the preschool and primary periods; and (b) the research based on these facets' direct and indirect contributions to successful social development and school success. After each of these descriptions, we summarize the promotion of emotional competence by parents, teachers, and others, and consider the roles of gender, culture, and childcare/school experience in the socialization of emotional competence. Finally, the role of early childhood education in addressing each component of emotional competence is considered, along with ideas for future research and applied considerations.

Emotional Experience and Expressiveness

This aspect of emotional competence includes identifying, labeling, and expressing one's own emotions. Emotion-related areas of the brain are more mature than some cognitive areas during early childhood, and play a central role in children's awareness of their own emotional experiences and their expressions of emotions (Nelson, 1994). Hence, young children become aware of their own emotional experiences and expressiveness; current research suggests that they understand and can report upon emotional experience much more reliably than previously assumed (Durbin, 2010; Warren & Stifter, 2008). Along with such awareness, they begin to know how to use emotions to express nonverbal messages about a social situation or relationship (e.g., stamping feet or giving a hug). They also develop empathic involvement in others' emotions (e.g., patting a classmate who fell off the swings). Further, they appropriately display social and self-conscious emotions, such as guilt, pride, shame, and contempt (Denham, 1998).

But what affective message should be sent for successful interaction during early childhood? Children slowly learn which expressions of emotions facilitate specific goals. Jimmy learns that his whiny voice tones, downcast face, and slightly averted body posture are not associated with successful entry into play. Young children also learn the appropriate affective message that "works" in a particular setting or with a specific playmate. Jimmy learns that a calm smile is the better key to unlock the door to shared play with Darrell; on the other hand, if he needs to defend himself, an angry scowl may get Tomas to back off.

Awareness of emotions becomes more complex during early childhood. Young children begin to realize that one may feel a certain way "on the inside," but show a different outward demeanor (Denham, 1998). In particular, they learn that expressions of socially disapproved feelings may be controlled, in favor of more socially appropriate ones (Misailidi, 2006).

Thus, there are times when real affective messages are not appropriate. Some are relevant to the situation but not the context, and some irrelevant ones need to be masked. For example, disappointment and even rage at being reprimanded by a parent or teacher may be relevant when that adult has blocked the child's goal, but such anger with adults is usually imprudent to express. Anxiety when playing a new game is probably irrelevant to the goal of having fun, and needs to be suppressed. So, preschoolers learn that sometimes real affective messages are inappropriate, "false" messages must be managed, and one must keep in mind the constraints of both self-protective and prosocial display rules (Misailidi, 2006). For example, Darrell controlled his feelings of fear when Tomas approached, in favor of showing a neutral expression that masked his internal shakiness; this tactic kept him safe.

Emotional Expression, Emotional Experience, and School Success. Preschoolers' expression of specific emotions, especially their enduring patterns of expressiveness, relates to their overall success in interacting with peers (i.e., peer status) and to their teachers' evaluation of their friendliness and aggression. Children who show relatively more happy than angry emotions: (a) are rated higher by teachers on friendliness and assertiveness, and lower on aggressiveness and sadness; (b) respond more prosocially to peers' emotions; and (c) are seen as more likable by their peers (Denham, McKinley, Couchound, & Holt, 1990; Denham, Renwick, & Holt, 1991; Eisenberg, Fabes, Shephard et al., 1997; Rydell, Berlin, & Bohlin, 2003). Sadness or fear, whether observed in the classroom or in interaction with mother, is related to teacher ratings of withdrawal and internalizing difficulties (Denham, Renwick, & Holt, 1991; Rydell, Berlin, & Bohlin, 2003). Moreover, young children who respond to the emotional expressions of others by sharing positive affect or reacting prosocially to others' distress are more likely to succeed in the peer arena; teachers and peers alike view them as more socially competent than their more antisocial, "mean" counterparts. Finally, contextually appropriate expression of emotion (i.e., lack of mood swings, modulated emotional intensity) is related to school success (e.g., Shields et al., 2001).

Emotion Regulation

Emotion regulation includes monitoring feelings and modifying them when necessary, so that they aid rather than impede the ways in which the child is able to cope with varying situations, to meet intrapersonal, interpersonal, and cognitive goals (Gross & Thompson, 2007). When the intensity, duration, or other parameters of the experience and expression of emotion are "too much" or "too little" to meet the goals and expectations of the child or social partners, emotion regulation is needed (Cole, Martin, & Dennis, 2004; Denham, 1998; Saarni, 1999; Thompson, 1994). Emotions that may need to be regulated include those that are aversive or distressing and those that are positive but possibly overwhelming, as well as emotions that need to be amplified, for either intra- or interpersonally strategic reasons (e.g., crying to elicit help).

Attending preschool and kindergarten is a particularly important transition that taxes young children's emotion regulation skills; the increasing complexity of a young child's world requires that emotion regulation must be cultivated. Peer play is replete with conflict; unlike adults, peers are neither skilled at negotiation, nor at helping dysregulated friends. Moreover, the social cost of emotional dysregulation (e.g., angry outbursts or tantrums, uncontrolled crying) is high with both teachers and peers. At the same time, the challenges of classroom rules are hard to follow when a child is preoccupied with feelings. Initiating, maintaining, and negotiating play, earning acceptance, and succeeding at literacy and numeracy skills all require young children to "keep the emotional lid on" (Raver, Blackburn, & Bancroft, 1999).

To succeed at emotion regulation, several abilities are key (Halberstadt et al., 2001). One must experience clear rather than diffused feelings, to know what to regulate. One also can use emotions to facilitate communication and achieve a goal. For example, a falling boy feels mad at himself because others are watching, as well as feeling hurt. Maybe he can "use" his anger to motivate a quick, albeit hobbling recovery. In sum, children learn to retain or enhance those emotions that are relevant and helpful (e.g., showing happiness to get playmates), to attenuate those that are relevant but not helpful (e.g., minimizing anger that would get in the way of interacting with a peer or be inappropriate with a teacher), and to dampen those that are irrelevant (e.g., ignoring grumpiness when waking up). Moderating emotional intensity when it threatens to overwhelm, enhancing it when necessary to meet a goal, and shifting between emotion states help children to maintain genuine and satisfying relationships with others and pay attention to preacademic tasks.

How Does Emotion Regulation Develop? First, the experience of emotion (i.e., sensory input and physiological arousal) may need to be diminished or modulated. A child may modulate the emotional experience via self-soothing. Or, she may even alter the emotion being expressed; a child feeling anxious during group times at preschool may smile to convince herself and others that she is happy. Others may avoid situations, or try to change them, to avoid overarousal.

Perceptual and cognitive management of emotion is also possible; a child may relinquish a goal, choose a substitute goal, or think through new causal attributions, to help herself feel more comfortable in her world. For example, a preschooler who is angry about being punished may say to herself, "I didn't want that cookie anyway." Refocusing attention is a useful perceptual means of managing the emotional experience. When trying to join Jessica and Darrell, Jimmy may focus on the game's "props" rather than the two children whose higher social status makes him uncomfortable. Problem solving reasoning also can be particularly useful as a regulatory coping strategy. When Darrell becomes irritated with Jessica, he may suggest a compromise that makes them both feel better. Finally, children also *do* things to cope with the experience of emotion: fix the problem, look for support from adults, lash out aggressively, or cry even harder to vent emotion (Eisenberg, Fabes, Nyman, Bernzweig, & Pinuelas, 1994).

These strategies are not automatically available, however. Preschoolers often need external support to become skilled at such regulation; caregivers' support allows their strategies to be maximally effective. Adults assist them in cognitive coping strategies they will eventually use themselves (e.g., purposely redeploying attention). Adults also use emotion language to help children regulate emotion by identifying and construing their feelings (e.g., "this will hurt only a little"), and to process causal associations between events and emotions. Adults demonstrate behavioral coping strategies when structuring the environment to facilitate regulation (e.g., avoiding situations that will frighten a daughter), or problem-solving emotional situations.

Over time, preschoolers become more able to make their own independent emotion regulation attempts (Grolnick, Bridges, & Connell, 1996). With their increase in cognitive ability and control of both attention and emotionality, preschoolers' awareness of the need for, and their use of, emotion regulation strategies increases (von Salisch, 2008). Preschoolers begin to see the connections between their emotion regulation efforts and changes in their feelings, and become more flexible in choosing optimal ways of coping in specific contexts; they become increasingly aware of strategies to regulate their own emotions, and such understanding of regulatory strategies often predicts their usage (Cole, Dennis, Smith-Simon, & Cohen, 2009). Thus, they begin to use very specific coping strategies for regulation: problem solving, support seeking, distancing, internalizing, externalizing, distraction, reframing or redefining the problem, cognitive "blunting," and denial. Many such strategies are quite useful for emotion regulation; they are sequentially associated with decreased anger (Gilliom, Shaw, Beck, Schonberg, & Lukon, 2002). In short, preschoolers are slowly moving from reliance upon other-regulation of emotions to self-regulation of their feelings. Accordingly, the behavioral disorganization resulting from strong emotion decreases dramatically around the transition to school.

Emotion Regulation and School Success. Children's ability to regulate emotion is related to their classroom adjustment and academic achievement. Emotion regulation is a crucial ability for managing the demands inherent in interpersonal situations (von Salisch, 2008); it allows the young child to show more socially appropriate emotions (Kieras, Tobin, Graziano, & Rothbart, 2005). Further, specific emotion regulation strategies are related to specific social behaviors; for example, reliance on attention-shifting emotion regulation strategies is associated with low externalizing problems and high cooperation, whereas reliance on information gathering strategies is correlated with assertiveness (Gilliom et al., 2002). Not surprisingly, then, emotion regulation is related to having friends in preschool (Walden, Lemerise, & Smith, 1999) and teacher-rated social competence (Eisenberg , Fabes, Bernzweig et al., 1993; Eisenberg, Fabes, Shepard et al., 1997; Eisenberg, Gershoff et al., 2001; Eisenberg, Valiente et al., 2003). In contrast, toddlers' emotional dysregulation predicts externalizing at age four, even with earlier aggressiveness controlled (Rubin, Burgess, Dwyer, & Hastings, 2003). Dysregulation of both exuberant positive emotions and fear are, respectively, also related to preschoolers' externalizing and internalizing (Rydell et al., 2003). In sum, adults and peers see emotionally regulated children as functioning well. Inability to regulate emotions figures into the trajectory toward behavior difficulties at school entry and thereafter.

As already implied, emotion regulation and expressiveness often operate in concert. Children who experience intense negative emotions, *and* are unable to regulate their expressions of such emotion, are especially likely to suffer deficits in their social competence (Contreras, Kerns, Weimer, Gentzler, & Tomich, 2000; Hubbard & Coie, 1994). Specifically, young children who are most emotionally intense, and poorly regulate this intense emotion, show the most difficulty in maintaining positive social behavior and have more troubled relationships with peers (Eisenberg, Fabes, Guthrie et al., 1996; Eisenberg, Fabes, Murphy et al., 1995; Eisenberg, Fabes, Shepard et al., 1997; Murphy, Shepard, Eisenberg, Fabes, & Guthrie, 1999). Kindergarten teachers see children who showed a lot of anger, *and* did not regulate it constructively during preschool, as having problems with oppositionality two years later, at the end of kindergarten (Denham, Blair, DeMulder et al., 2003; Denham, Blair, Schmidt, & DeMulder, 2002). In contrast, good emotion regulation skills, which caring adults can teach, buffer emotionally negative children from peer problems (Eisenberg, Fabes, Guthrie et al., 1996; Eisenberg, Fabes, Murphy et al., 1995; Eisenberg, Fabes, Shepard et al., 1997; Murphy et al., 1999).

Children who have difficulties dealing with negative emotions may not have the personal resources to focus on learning, whereas those who can maintain a positive emotional tone might be able to remain positively engaged with classroom tasks. More specifically, Shields and colleagues (2001) assessed Head Start teachers' views of preschoolers' emotion regulation (their adaptive regulation, including their flexibility, equanimity) and the contextual appropriateness of their emotional expression. Emotion regulation evaluated early in the year predicted children's later school/classroom adjustment (i.e., preacademic progress, cooperation, and engagement in the classroom, creation of relationships with staff, and enjoyment of school), even with age, verbal ability, emotional ability, and emotion knowledge covaried—see also Graziano, Reavis, Keane, & Calkins (2007) for emotion regulation, as assessed by the same measure, contributing to kindergartners' school success/productivity and achievement, even with IQ controlled. Researchers have also observed preschoolers' emotion regulation in the classroom, and found that observed emotional dysregulation was negatively related to teachers' ratings of children's motivation to learn (Miller, Seifer, Stroud, Sheinkopf, & Dickstein, 2006).

Howse and colleagues (Howse, Calkins, Anastopoulos, Keane, & Shelton, 2003) also found that preschoolers' emotion regulation (assessed using the same rating scale as Shields and colleagues, but also including a series of frustration tasks) predicted kindergarten achievement; this effect was, however, mediated by the contribution of *behavioral* regulation. That is, emotionally regulated children were more able to focus their attention to stay on tasks and finish them, plan, and focus, which in turn predicted their kindergarten achievement. Similarly, Trentacosta and Izard (2007) also found that kindergartners' emotion regulation, measured as in Shields et al. (2001), predicted first graders' attentional regulation, which in turned predicted academic success, even with age, verbal ability, and early attentional regulation covaried. These results portray a trajectory of different aspects of regulation working together to contribute to academic success. Clearly, emotion regulation skills help facilitate both social and academic success in school settings.

Social Emotion Knowledge

Children are constantly attempting to understand their own and others' behavior, and emotions convey crucial interpersonal information that can guide interaction (Dodge, Laird, Lochman, Zelli, & Conduct Problems Research Group, 2002). Inability to interpret others' emotions can make the classroom a confusing, overwhelming place for children (Raver, Garner, & Smith-Donald, 2007). Emotion knowledge used in social encounters will be discussed from four angles: acquiring basic emotion knowledge, understanding complex causal parameters, learning display rules, and appreciating complex emotions. Following the discussion of how such "social emotion knowledge" is accomplished and its association with school success, we present an explanation of how lack of such knowledge can hamper interaction.

How Does Social Emotion Knowledge Develop? Once they are perceived, affective messages must be interpreted accurately. As with all levels of affective information processing, errors in interpretation can lead to both intrapersonal and social difficulties. Children need to be able to (a) label emotional expressions both verbally and nonverbally; (b) identify emotion-eliciting situations; and (c) infer the causes of emotion eliciting situations, and the consequences of specific emotions. Thus, preschoolers' abilities to verbally label and nonverbally recognize emotional expressions increase from ages two to five (Denham & Couchoud, 1990), with the first distinction learned between being happy and not being happy, feeling good versus feeling bad. Early recognition of happy expressions is greater than recognition of negative emotions, with an understanding of anger and fear slowly emerging from the "not happy/sad" emotion category.

However, simply understanding expressions of emotion is not always sufficient to comprehend one's own or others' emotions; situational cues can be very important, especially when expressions may be masked or dissembled.

Preschoolers' flexibility in interpreting emotional signals is increased by understanding the events that can elicit emotion, as well as accompanying expressions. For example, Jessica may note, "When we don't listen, our teacher feels bad," and adjust her behavior, even if her teacher's negative expressions are very muted.

As with expressions, preschoolers initially tend to have a better understanding of happy situations compared to negative ones (Fabes, Eisenberg, Nyman, & Michealieu, 1991). They gradually learn to differentiate among negative emotions; for example, realizing that one feels more sad than angry when getting a "time out" from one's preschool teacher. Children slowly separate angry situations from sad ones (Denham & Couchoud, 1990; Fabes, Eisenberg, Nyman et al., 1991); fear situations present the most difficulty (Widen & Russell, 2010). Preschoolers also increasingly use emotion language to describe emotional situations (e.g., reminiscing about family sadness when a pet died; Harris, 2008; Lagattuta & Wellman, 2002). In sum, young preschoolers' emotion categories are broad, often including peripheral concepts, especially for negative emotions; preschoolers' emotion concepts gradually narrow (Widen & Russell, 2008, 2010).

Young children go further than just recognizing the expressions and eliciting situations for discrete emotions. Using everyday experiences to create theories about the causes of happiness, sadness, and anger, older preschoolers cite causes for familiar emotions that are similar to ones given by adults (Fabes et al., 1991; Lagattuta & Wellman, 2002). If asked, Jessica could point out that her older brother gets mad because he doesn't want to go to school, but that Daddy is happy to go to work. Preschoolers also ascribe different causes to different emotions, building upon early understanding of more general emotional situations to create causal scenarios for specific persons' feelings (Denham & Zoller, 1991; Dunn & Hughes, 1998).

Through their increased social sensitivity and experience, older preschoolers also develop strategies for appraising others' emotions when available cues are less salient and consensual. Five-year-olds are more likely than three- and four-year-olds to focus their explanations of emotions on personal dispositions as opposed to goal states (e.g., "She had a bad day" instead of "She didn't want Billy to play with her"). For older preschoolers, knowing more abstract causes for emotion can be useful in actual interaction with friends (Fabes, Eisenberg, Nyman et al., 1991).

Sometimes one must also understand consequences of emotion. Young children already realize many such consequences; for example, Maddie knows that her mother will comfort her when she is upset. Clearly, knowing why an emotion is expressed (its cause), and its likely aftermath (its behavioral result in self or others), aids one in regulating behavior or emotion, and in reacting to others' emotions (Morgan, Izard, & King, 2010). In short, discerning consequences of emotion can help a child know what to do when experiencing or witnessing emotion.

Thus, preschoolers learn to distinguish the causes of emotions from their consequences (Denham, 1998; Russell, 1990); for example, fathers "dance" when they're happy, mothers "lay in their bed" when sad, and fathers "give spankings" when angry. What do people do as a consequence of someone else's emotions? Four- and five-year olds attribute plausible, nonrandom parental reactions to their own emotions (Denham, 1998), such as their parents' matching their own happiness; performing pragmatic action after sadness; punishing anger; and comforting or acting to alleviate the fear-eliciting stimulus. These findings suggest that preschoolers have solid conceptions of the consequences of some emotions for self and others.

Understanding Complex Causal Parameters. To more accurately interpret emotional information, data specific to a particular person in a particular situation may be needed. Although this aspect of emotion knowledge is very important, it can be quite difficult to acquire and use. In a series of thought-provoking inquiries, Gnepp and colleagues (e.g., Gnepp, 1989; Gnepp & Gould, 1985; Gnepp, McKee, & Domanic, 1987) described how children develop the ability to use various types of information to determine others' emotions; although this seminal series of reports has withstood the passage of time, a few more recent investigations have occurred (e.g., Lagattuta, 2007). Important elements of emotional information are whether (a) the situation is equivocal (i.e., could elicit more than one emotion), (b) there are conflicting cues in the person's expressive patterns and the situation, and (c) person-specific information is needed.

Regarding *equivocality*, different people feel different emotions during some emotion-eliciting events. One child is happy to encounter a large, friendly looking dog, panting and "smiling" with mouth open, but another child is terrified. More personal information is needed if we are to know how each person is feeling, and preschoolers are becoming aware of this need. They are beginning to recognize the inherent equivocality of some emotion situations, even if they cannot always identify it spontaneously. Ability to detect and use information about equivocal situations continues developing through early and middle childhood (Gnepp et al., 1987).

Even when a situation is not emotionally equivocal, it still may be hard to discern what a person is feeling. For example, the person experiencing the event may react *atypically;* there may be a conflict between situational and expressive knowledge. In one of Gnepp's (1989) stories, the protagonist smiled when seeing a spider dropping into the room on a strand of web. Most people wouldn't do that. However, interpreting a reaction as atypical requires a rather sophisticated decision, namely *resolving* conflicting expressive and situational cues to emotions rather than relying on one cue or the other. Young children do not perform such problem solving easily or well; they usually still prefer simple, script-based understanding of emotion.

Over time, however, older preschoolers can assess expressive and situational sources of emotional information separately and strategically, much as they come to utilize multiple sources of information in nonsocial cognitive tasks. One way they use to resolving conflicting emotion cues is attributing an idiosyncratic perspective. A child may say, "She is smiling because she likes shots." Such attribution of idiosyncrasy may be a precursor of more fully understanding the psychological causes of atypical reactions to emotion-eliciting situations (Gnepp, 1989).

If using complex information to attribute emotions to others is so difficult, what types of personal information are preschoolers able to use successfully in interpreting atypical emotions? First, they can use *unique normative information*, such as, "Sarah lives in Green Valley, where all people are friendly with tigers and play games with them all the time" (Gnepp, Klayman, & Trabasso, 1982). When asked how Sarah would feel, preschoolers used unique information about liking tigers to modify their responses to a normally unequivocal situation. Preschoolers are also becoming aware that cultural categories such as age and gender moderate emotions experienced in differing situations. For example, a boy might not be overjoyed to receive a doll as a gift.

Other *person-specific information* also is sometimes needed. Gnepp and colleagues (1982) provided stories in which characters' behavioral dispositions modified normally strong emotion–event associations. "Mark eats grass whenever he can.... Mother says they're having grass for dinner. How will Mark feel?" Older preschoolers were able to utilize such information, with responses reflecting the unique perspective of the character in the story. For example, Mark would be happy to eat grass, even though most preschoolers definitely would not. Overall, learning complex causal parameters about emotions is only emerging for preschoolers.

Learning Display Rules. It is tricky to interpret true *or* false emotional signals from others while interacting with them. One must be able to ignore false affective messages if to do so benefits one's goals, or to accept them as real if that is advantageous. One must also: (a) pick up real, relevant, helpful messages; (b) ignore real but irrelevant messages; and (c) somehow deal with real and relevant but not helpful messages. For example, perhaps Kristen's physiognomy, especially her droopy eyebrows and downturned lips, looks rather sad naturally; her playmates need to know this and not try to comfort her, or worse yet, avoid her. Darrell needs to ignore Tomas's low intensity glares as he makes an effort to play with him.

Prior to understanding the actual display rules that people use for minimizing, or substituting one emotion for another, and when they use them, young children understand the effort to completely hide, or mask, emotion. Masking emotions can be advantageous to young children as soon as they realize that they can pose expression voluntarily. It is immeasurably valuable in maintaining social relations to know when to show or not show emotions. To dissemble in this way does not require knowledge of display rules that are normative to a family or culture, but merely an understanding of the need to send a signal that differs from the emotion felt. The ability to, and knowledge of dissembling continues to develop through grade school (Gross & Harris, 1988).

Understanding of specific cultural or personal display rules, whether prosocial or self-protective, appears rudimentary during early childhood (Misailidi, 2006), even though children already modify expressiveness to fit such rules. Nonetheless, close to half the preschool children in the Gnepp and Hess (1986) study cited at least verbal, if not emotional, rules for regulating emotion (i.e., verbal masking: "I don't care that I lost this silly contest"). Importantly, investigators using developmentally appropriate methodological simplifications have found that even young children may begin to understand display rules as they begin to use them (Banerjee, 1997; Josephs, 1994), perhaps beginning with emotions subject to socialization pressure, such as anger (i.e., when children are urged not to show anger, they not only stop expressing the emotion, but also understand that there is a "not showing anger" rule; Feito, 1997).

It is not uncommon to experience "mixed emotions," as when three-year-old Maddie is somewhat amused at her baby brother's antics, lurching from his newly attained seated posture to grab her Dora™ backpack, but mostly annoyed when he tries to bite it. Because young children's expressiveness becomes more intricate within the preschool period, they begin to experience simultaneous emotions and ambivalence themselves, and thus begin to slowly understand them (Wintre, Polivy, & Murray, 1990; Wintre & Vallance, 1994). Wintre and colleagues found that preschoolers could report experiencing multiple same-valence, maximum intensity emotions. First graders could predict experiencing same-valence emotions of varying intensity. At age eight years and older, children could discuss multiple emotions of varying intensity and opposite valence. Clearly the process of acquiring such knowledge takes time.

However, asking questions via age-appropriate methodologies has revealed that some of these trajectories can be accelerated, with preschoolers understanding more about mixed emotions than previously assumed (Kestenbaum & Gelman, 1995; Peng, Johnson, Pollock, Glasspool, & Harris, 1992). For example, Kestenbaum used story characters with two heads, and young children more readily attributed two feelings to them than to more "normal" story characters. Across these studies, as with other complex aspects of emotion knowledge, we see that young children's ability to spontaneously recognize conflicting emotions, especially their own mixed emotions, is just emerging (Larson, Yen, & Fireman, 2007).

Appreciating Complex Emotions. Another accomplishment in the domain of emotion knowledge is understanding the more complex emotions, particularly sociomoral emotions such as guilt and shame, and also such self- and other-referent emotions as pride, embarrassment, and empathy. Because young children and their peers are beginning to express complex emotions, they have some understanding of them, but it is still quite limited, and the development of such understanding proceeds quite slowly. For example, Russell and Paris (1994) found that even four-year-olds understood the valence and arousal level associated with pride, gratitude, shame, worry, and jealousy, but they could not accurately discuss or explain evoking situations. Partial conceptualizations of these emotions seem to predominate.

Even older preschoolers are unable to accurately name the feelings of pride, guilt, or shame accompanying success, failure, and transgression—pride at a gymnastic feat or resisting temptation or guilt for stealing a few coins out of a parent's wallet—until at least age six (Arsenio & Lover, 1995; Berti, Garattoni, & Venturini, 2000). They tend to report simpler, noncomplex emotions, and make specific, important errors (e.g., saying that a transgressor would feel happy). Young children may not yet appreciate guilt, for example, because of their incomplete appreciation of the societal rules and obligations that evoke it (Harris, 2008).

In summary, young children acquire much emotion knowledge to assist them in social interactions with family and peers. However, many of the finer nuances of emotion knowledge are either emerging as they enter elementary school, or not yet within their repertoire at all.

Social Emotion Knowledge and School Success. Because personal experiences and social interactions or relationships are guided, even defined, by emotional transactions (Arsenio & Lemerise, 2001; Denham, 1998; Halberstadt et al., 2001; Saarni, 1999), emotion knowledge figures prominently in personal and social success. When one moves into the world of peers emotion knowledge is called for. For example, if a preschooler sees one peer bickering with another, and correctly deduces that the peer suddenly experiences sadness or fear, rather than intensified anger, she may comfort her friend rather than retreat or enter the fray. The youngster who understands emotions of others should interact more successfully when a friend gets angry with him or her, and can be more empathic with a peer who gets hurt on the playground. Hence, emotion knowledge supports young children's attempts to deal with and communicate about emotions experienced by self and others, and allows them to selectively attend to other aspects of social experiences (Denham, 1998). Accordingly, children who understand emotions are more prosocially responsive to their peers, and rated as more socially competent by both teachers and peers (Denham & Couchoud, 1991; Denham, McKinley et al., 1990; Roberts & Strayer, 1996; Smith, 2001).

More specifically, dyad members' emotion situation knowledge and child-friend emotion conversation are involved in conflict resolution, positive play, cooperative shared pretend, and successful communication (Brown, Donelan-McCall, & Dunn, 1996; Dunn, Brown, & Maguire, 1995; Dunn & Cutting, 1999; Dunn & Herrera, 1997). Preschoolers' understanding of emotion expressions and situations are also related to use of reasoned argument with,

and caregiving of, siblings (Dunn, Slomkowski, Donelan, & Herrera, 1995; Garner, Jones, & Miner, 1994). As well, preschoolers' spontaneous use of emotion language is related to higher quality peer interactions and greater peer acceptance (Fabes, Eisenberg, Hanish, & Spinrad, 2001; Garner & Estep, 2001). Further, young children's understanding of emotion situations is *negatively* related to nonconstructive anger during peer play (Garner & Estep, 2001). Finally, understanding mixed emotions in kindergarten is associated with understanding friends, as well as expecting teachers to react benignly to one's mistakes (Cutting & Dunn, 2002; Dunn, Cutting, & Fisher, 2002).

Increasingly, researchers are confirming a link between school success and young children's emotion knowledge. For example, Leerkes, Paradise, O'Brien, Calkins, and Lange (2008) showed that emotion knowledge was related to preschoolers' preacademic achievement (see also Garner & Waajid, 2008, for relations between low income preschooler's emotion knowledge and classroom adjustment and achievement). Shields et al. (2001) demonstrated that emotion knowledge at the beginning of the Head Start year uniquely predicted, as did emotion regulation, year-end school adjustment (i.e., behavioral regulation, preacademic ability, compliance/participation, ability to form relationships). Similarly, Izard and colleagues (2001) found that five-year-olds' emotion knowledge predicted age nine social and academic competence.

In addition to the direct effects of emotion knowledge on academic outcomes, it also plays the role of mediator. In a longitudinal study of Head Start children, emotion knowledge in preschool mediated the effect of verbal ability on academic competence in third grade; that is, children with higher verbal ability in Head Start had greater emotion knowledge, which predicted third grade academic competence (Izard, 2002a). These reports are exciting in aggregate, in that they add longitudinal and school success elements to the current arguments, and show more about *how* emotion knowledge can augment children's performance with peers (i.e., via reasoning about social encounters and choice of positive social behaviors).

Lack of Emotion Knowledge and Unsuccessful Social Interactions. Lack of emotion knowledge is associated with impairment in behavioral responses to playmates. For example, preschoolers with identified aggression and oppositionality or peer problems show specific deficits in understanding emotion expressions and situations, both concurrently and predictively (Denham, Blair et al., 2002; Denham, Caverly et al., 2002; Denham, Mason, Kochanoff, Neal, & Hamada, 2003; Hughes, Dunn, & White, 1998). Further, low income, predominantly African American first graders' difficulties in understanding emotional expressions were related to their problems with peers and social withdrawal, even when preschool verbal ability and self-control measures were partialled (Izard et al., 2001; Schultz, Izard, Ackerman, & Youngstrom, 2001; Smith, 2001).

Specific errors in emotion understanding made by young children may be pivotally related to risk for aggression problems. For example, Barth and Bastiani (1997) uncovered a subtle relation that may underlie aggressive children's social difficulties. They found an association between preschoolers' mistaken perceptions (overattributions) of peers' expressions as angry and negative social behavior. Such overattributions of anger, similar to the hostile attribution bias seen in older children, are also concurrently related to preschool aggression and peer rejection (Denham, McKinley et al., 1990; Schultz, Izard, & Ackerman, 2000). These results suggest that deficits in emotion knowledge are related to children's social and behavior problems preceding, and extending into, the primary grades. This link highlights the importance of boosting early emotion knowledge before school entry. Ascertaining these early social cognitive difficulties could make it easier to intervene with children before aggression becomes entrenched.

Connecting the Pieces of Emotional Competence

Finally, the interrelationships of all aspects of emotional competence must be underscored. Emotion knowledge plays an important role in children's expressive patterns and their ability to regulate emotion (Schultz et al., 2001). When a child knows, for example, that her playmate is delighted to have heaved the tricycle upright at last, she no longer is distressed herself, trying to figure out what to do with an angry friend. She can focus her attention on other aspects of the situation. Thus, due to the intricate synergy of emotion knowledge, emotional expressiveness, and emotion regulation, both deficits in emotion knowledge and underregulated expression of anger at age three to four predicted difficulties with teachers and peers in kindergarten (Denham, Caverly et al., 2002). Even more evidence is needed about the ways in which emotion expressiveness, knowledge, and regulation work together during this age range, so that early childhood educators can refine social-emotional curricula.

What Fuels the Development of Emotional Competence?

Both intrapersonal and interpersonal factors impact the developing competencies described here. First, intrapersonal contributors no doubt are important; abilities and attributes of the children themselves can either promote or hinder emotional competence. For example, some children are blessed with cognitive and language skills that allow them to better understand their social world, including the emotions within it, as well as to better communicate their own feelings, wishes, desires, and goals for social interactions and relationships (Cutting & Dunn, 1999). A preschooler who can reason more flexibly can probably also more readily perceive how another person might emotionally react to a situation in a different manner than he himself would—some people really are fearful of swimming pools,

even though they delight *me*. In a similar manner, children with greater verbal abilities can ask more pointed questions about their own and others' emotions (e.g., "Why is he crying?"), and understand the answers to these questions, giving them a special advantage in understanding and dealing with emotions. A preschooler with more advanced expressive language also can describe his own emotions more pointedly ("I don't *want* to go to bed! I am *mad*!"), not only allowing him to get his emotional point across, but also allowing others to communicate with him.

Similarly, children with different emotional dispositions (i.e., different temperaments) are particularly well- or ill-equipped to demonstrate emotional competence. An especially emotionally negative child, for example, will probably find she has a greater need for emotion regulation, even though it is at the same time harder for her to do so. Such a double bind taxes her abilities to "unhook" from an intense emotional experience (e.g., Eisenberg, Fabes, Bernzweig et al., 1993; Eisenberg, Fabes, Nyman et al., 1994; Eisenberg, Fabes, Shepard et al., 1997). Conversely, a child whose temperament predisposes him to flexibly focus attention on a comforting action, object, or thought, and shift attention from a distressing situation, is better able to regulate emotions, even intense ones.

Socialization of Emotional Competence

Children come to their preschool years with particular intrapersonal factors well in place. These intrapersonal factors are either foundations of or roadblocks to emotional and social competence. Caring adults are faced with such children on a daily basis. What differences do our efforts make? How do we foster these emotional and social competencies in children as they move into their school years? Much of the individual variation in the components of children's emotional competence derives from experiences within the family and preschool classroom (Denham, 1998; Hyson, 1994). Important adults (and children) in each child's life have crucial roles in the development of emotional competence.

Socialization of emotions is ubiquitous in children's everyday contact with parents, teachers, caregivers, and peers. All people who interact with children exhibit a variety of emotions which the children observe. Further, children's emotions often require some kind of reaction from their social partners, and intentionally instructing children about the world of emotions is considered by some adults to be an important area of teaching (Engle & McElwain, in press). Three mechanisms describe socialization of emotion: modeling emotional expressiveness, reacting to children's emotions, and teaching about emotion (Denham, 1998; Denham, Bassett, & Wyatt, 2010; Eisenberg, Cumberland, & Spinrad, 1998). Each can influence children's emotional expression, understanding, and regulation, as well as their social functioning.

Most of the extant research on the socialization of social

and emotional competence involves young children and their parents (e.g., Dunsmore & Karn, 2001). Of course, parents are not the only socializers of emotional competence. Others, including preschool teachers and daycare caregivers, siblings, and peers, are important from the preschool years on. In the following sections, results regarding young children's interactions with their parents are most often reported, because by far the most research exists on these socializers. However, it is likely that many of the influences identified likely hold true for other adults in preschoolers' lives, as well. Where there is specific information on teachers, siblings, and peers, it is highlighted.

Modeling Emotional Expressiveness. Children observe adults' emotions and incorporate their observations into their expressive behavior, often via affective contagion. They vicariously learn *how* to exhibit emotional expressions, and *which* to express *when* and in what context (Denham & Grout, 1993; Denham, Mitchell-Copeland, Strandberg, Auerbach, & Blair, 1997).

Parents' emotional displays also foster their children's emotion knowledge, by telling children about the emotional significance of differing events, which behaviors accompany differing emotions, and others' likely reactions. By modeling various emotions, moderately expressive parents give children information about the nature of happiness, sadness, anger, and fear—their expression, likely eliciting situations, and more personalized causes. Thus, adults' emotional expressiveness is associated with children's emotion knowledge, as well as their expressive patterns (Denham & Couchoud, 1990; Denham & Grout, 1993; Denham, Mitchell-Copeland et al., 1997; Denham, Zoller, & Couchoud, 1994; Liew et al., 2003).

A mostly positive emotional climate makes emotions more accessible to children, in terms of their own emotion regulation, emotion knowledge, and concomitant positive social behavior. Thus, when children have experience with clear but not overpowering parental emotions, they also may have more experience with empathic involvement with others' emotions (Martin, Clements, & Crnic, 2002; Valiente, 2004). Both middle- and low-income preschoolers' emotion regulation is facilitated by their mothers' appropriate expressiveness (Garner, Jones, & Miner, 1994). Parents whose expressiveness is quite limited impart little information about emotions.

Hence, clear and mostly positive emotional environments are associated with positive outcomes in young children's emotional expressiveness, emotion knowledge, emotion regulation, and positive social behavior. Much less research has clearly targeted the expressive modeling of teachers, despite the existence of observational ratings that can be used to capture the emotional environment in early childhood classrooms (e.g., Harms, Clifford, & Cryer, 1998). Denham, Grant, and Hamada (2002) have, however, found evidence that the socialization of emotion of both preschool teachers and mothers is important for development of children's emotion regulation; maternal expressiveness and teachers' attitudes about teaching about emotion were the most important predictors of emotion regulation.

Conversely, parental expressiveness can make it more difficult for young children to address issues of emotion altogether. In particular, exposure to negative emotions expressed by adults in their lives can be problematic for young children. Children whose mothers self-report more frequent anger and tension also are less prosocial, and less well liked than children of more positive mothers (Eisenberg, Gershoff et al., 2001; Eisenberg, Valiente et al., 2003; Garner & Spears, 2000). Although exposure to *well-modulated* negative emotion can be positively related to emotion knowledge, parents' frequent and intense negative emotions may disturb children, as well as discourage self-reflection, so that little is learned about emotions, other than how to express negativity (Denham, 1998). It is easy to imagine the confusion and pain of children relentlessly exposed to parents' negative emotions. In extreme cases, such as neglect and abuse, children make fewer, skewed distinctions among emotions; their emotion knowledge is impaired (Pollak, Cicchetti, Hornung, & Reed, 2000; Sullivan, Bennett, Carpenter, & Lewis, 2008).

As well, the trajectory from the aggressiveness of age two to the externalizing of problems at age four is clearest for toddlers who experience high levels of maternal negative expressiveness (Rubin et al., 2003). Emotionally negative preschool classroom environments also have been linked to displays of aggressive, disruptive peer behavior in second grade, especially for boys (Howes, 2000). Thus, it may be that exposure to higher levels of adult negativity overarouses the young child who cannot yet regulate emotions well, and represents a hostile-aggressive template for children to follow in their reactions to people and events.

In sum, with regard to modeling, exposure to parents' and others' broad but not overly negative emotions helps children learn about emotions and express similar profiles. In particular, whether in families or classrooms, adult negative emotion is deleterious to young children's emotion knowledge, profiles of expressiveness, emotion regulation, and social competence.

Contingent Reactions to Children's Emotions. Adults' contingent reactions to children's behaviors and emotional displays are also linked to young children's emotional competence. Contingent reactions include behavioral and emotional encouragement or discouragement of specific behaviors and emotions. More specifically, adults may punish children's experiences and expressions of emotions, or show a dismissive attitude toward the world of emotions, by ignoring the child's emotions in a well-meant effort to "make it better" (Denham, Renwick-DeBardi, & Hewes., 1994; Denham, Zoller et al., 1994). In emotion-evoking contexts, children who experience such adult reactions have more to be upset about—not only their emotion's elicitor, but also adults' reactions (Eisenberg,

Cumberland, & Spinrad, 1998; Eisenberg, Fabes, Shepard, Guthrie et al., 1999).

Positive reactions, such as tolerance or comfort, convey a very different message: that emotions are manageable, even useful (Gottman, Katz, & Hooven, 1997). Parents who are good "emotion coaches," at least in the United States, accept children's experiences of emotion and their expression of emotions that do not harm others; they empathize with and validate emotions. Emotional moments are seen as opportunities for intimacy (Denham & Kochanoff, 2003; Eisenberg, Fabes, & Murphy, 1996). As children develop emotion regulatory abilities, parents decrease the frequency, intensity, and nature of their reactions, slowly transferring responsibility for regulation to the child (Grolnick, Kurowski, McMenamy, Rivkin, & Bridges, 1998).

Thus, there is much more research on the ways in which parents respond to young children's emotions, as compared to very rare research on the reactions of teachers (see below), siblings, and age mates. The clearest take-home message is that adults' and older siblings' optimal emotional and behavioral responses to children's emotions are associated with young children's own emotional expressiveness, emotion knowledge, and empathic reactions to peers' and others' emotions (Denham & Kochanoff, 2003; Fabes, Leonard, Kupanoff, & Martin, 2001; Fabes, Poulin, Eisenberg, & Madden-Derdich, 2003; Strandberg-Sawyer et al., 2003). For example, when mothers do not react with their own distress or with punishment, but instead are supportive and accepting in response to children's negative emotions, children show less egoistic distress and more sympathetic concern to the distress of others. They have warm, empathic, nurturant guides to follow in responding to others' distress (Denham & Grout, 1993). Much more research is needed in this area, especially to better elucidate links between parental reactions to children's emotions and children's patterns of emotional expressiveness, and of other socializers.

Teaching about Emotions. This last aspect of emotion socialization is the most direct. What parents and other adults say, or intentionally convey through other means, may impact their children's emotion knowledge. Teaching about emotions often consists of explaining an emotion and its relation to an observed event or expression. It may also include directing the child's attention to salient emotional cues, helping children understand and manage their own responses, and segmenting social interactions into manageable emotional components (Denham & Auerbach, 1995). Adults who are aware of emotions, especially negative ones, and talk about them in a differentiated manner (e.g., clarifying, explaining, pointing out the child's responsibility for others' feelings, but not "preaching") assist their children in expressing, experiencing, identifying, and regulating their own emotions (Gottman et al., 1997). Dismissive adults may want to be helpful, but refrain from talking too much about children's emotions. Alternatively,

some adults actively punish children for showing or querying about emotions.

Teachers' and parents' tendencies to discuss emotions, if nested within a warm relationship, help children acquire all aspects of emotional competence (Harris, 2008). Discussing emotions provides children with reflective distance from feeling states themselves, and space in which to interpret and evaluate their feelings and to reflect upon causes and consequences (Mirabile, Scaramella, Sohr-Preston, & Robison, 2009). Thus, verbal give-and-take about emotional experience within the scaffolded context of chatting with parent or teacher helps the young child to formulate a coherent body of knowledge about emotional expressions, situations, and causes (Denham, Renwick-DeBardi et al., 1994; Denham, Zoller, & Couchoud 1994; Dunn, Brown, & Beardsall, 1991; Dunn, Brown, Slomkowski et al., 1991; Dunn, Slomkowski et al., 1995). Such conversations coach children to perceive the social consequences of their actions (e.g., "Johnny will be mad at you and not want to play with you, if you keep taking away his toys") and to empathize or consider another's viewpoint (e.g., "That hurt Toby's feelings—look, he feels sad"). When parents discuss and explain their own and others' emotions, their children show more empathic involvement with peers (Denham & Grout, 1992; Denham, Renwick-DeBardi & Hughes, 1994; Denham, Zoller, & Couchoud, 1994). The general trend of these findings also holds true for low-income, minority families (Garner, Jones, Gaddy, & Rennie, 1997). Associations between mothers' emotion language and preschoolers' emotion knowledge also are often independent of the child's linguistic ability.

In one study of children in childcare transitions (Dunn, 1994), preschoolers remembered both sadness and fear during these times, as well as the support given them by teachers and friends, to help them feel better. So, young children absorb not only the content, but also the form and quality of nonparental adults' teaching about emotion; how can this content, form, and quality be characterized? Two investigators (Ahn, 2005; Ahn & Stifter, 2006; Reimer, 1996) have found that teachers of toddlers and preschoolers socialize children's emotions differentially based on age, tailoring their reactions to children's emotions, and their teaching about emotions, to the developmental level of the children. In Ahn's studies, toddler teachers used physical comfort and distraction in response to children's negative emotions more often than did preschool teachers. Instead, preschool teachers helped children infer the causes of their negative emotions, and taught them constructive ways of expressing negative emotion. Teachers of older children were also less likely to match the positive or encourage positive emotion, and more likely to discourage such displays. Finally, this study demonstrated that teachers did not validate children's negative emotion very often—one of the major tenets of teaching about emotion.

Reimer (1996) also found that teachers respond to about half of preschool children's emotions, most often in service of socializing emotion regulation; verbal references to children's emotions constituted about one-half of their responses. These teacher verbalizations referred to causes and consequences of the child's emotion, which emotions were appropriate, and how to express emotions under various circumstances. Overall, these studies suggest that, to promote emotional competence, teacher/caregiver training should focus on validating children's emotions, while at the same time creating and sustaining adult–child emotion conversations.

Summary: How Adults Socialize Emotional Competence. In sum, there is a growing body of knowledge regarding the contributions of adults to young children's emotional and social competence. These elements will be useful in building adult roles in any successful social-emotional programming for young children. Furthermore, cultural values and variations require our attention because we must honor the unique perspectives of both adults and children. A generally positive picture emerges of the type of emotion teaching called "emotion coaching" (Gottman et al., 1997). Its elements will be useful not only in parenting, but also in building any successful social-emotional programming for young children. In terms of promoting emotional and social competence, teacher/caregiver training should include a focus on ways to assist early childhood educators in becoming good emotion coaches. Although it would follow that children in such classrooms would have a greater chance of becoming emotionally competent, the literature has not yet progressed to this point; much more research is clearly needed on how teachers of young children socialize emotional competence.

The Roles of Gender, Culture, and Classroom Experience

The aspects of emotional competence and their socialization already outlined here hold true in a general sense for all children and families. But as already noted, the ways in which emotional competence is expressed and the ways that it is taught may differ between girls and boys, mothers and fathers, across disparate cultures, and depending on varying contexts within the early childhood classroom any particular child attends. Thus, although a full treatment of these important matters is beyond the scope of this chapter, an outline may be sketched.

Gender of Child and Parent

It is important to acknowledge the role of gender in socialization of emotional competence (Brody & Hall, 2008). First, regarding modeling emotion, parents sometimes differ in the emotions that they express around their children. Garner and colleagues (Garner, Robertson, and Smith, 1997) have found that mothers reported showing more positive emotion (especially to daughters) and more

sadness around their preschool children, than fathers (see also Denham, Brown, & Domitrovitch, 2010). In Garner and colleagues' work, parents of sons, especially fathers, reported showing more anger. Fathers, however, made an additional contribution when they were positive, over and above the effect of mothers when they were positive, which Denham et al. saw as explaining the variance in children's own positivity during a challenging peer play session. As well, compared to mothers, fathers hold more punitive ideas about how they should react to children's emotions (Denham, Brown, & Domitrovitch, 2010).

Although not all findings converge, and fathers' emotion conversations are not as deeply studied as those of mothers, we know that mothers, more than fathers, value teaching their children about emotions (Denham, Brown, & Domitrovitch, 2010). Further, parents often talk more to their preschool-aged daughters about emotions, especially specific ones such as sadness; mothers and fathers also may differ in emotion talk to sons and daughters (Fivush, Berlin, Sales, Mennuti-Washburn, & Cassidy, 2003; Fivush, Brotman, Buckner, & Goodman, 2000). Mothers stress the interpersonal nature of emotions (Fivush, 1991; Flannagan & Perese, 1998), and fathers sometimes appear *not* to view family conversations as opportunities to discuss emotions (Chance & Fiese, 1999).

There seems to be more difference in mothers' and fathers' socialization of emotion than in their treatment of sons and daughters, but evidence for gender-specific contributions of parental socialization to emotional competence does exist (e.g., Engle & McElwain, in press). In Denham and colleagues (Denham, Mitchell-Copeland et al., 1997), girls' ability to regulate negative emotions was especially vulnerable to the detrimental effects of parental negative emotions and antisocial reactions to child emotions, and to the positive effects of their parents' own happiness relative to their anger. The greater salience of the family context for girls' behavior, and girls' greater sensitivity to parental influences, need to be studied more explicitly in the realm of emotional competence.

Other findings on how maternal and paternal socialization of emotion variously contribute to young children's emotional competence are complex, but it is clear that inclusion of paternal report and observations of fathers are important in fleshing out the entire picture of socialization of emotion during the preschool years. Studying only maternal socialization of emotion would yield an incomplete understanding of the socialization of young children's emotional competence. For example, at times maternal and paternal contributions to emotional competence seem to complement one another, as when mild maternal negativity along with paternal positive expressiveness predicted preschoolers' emotion knowledge (Denham, Brown, & Domitrovitch, 2010). Mothers' more frequent, gender-expected, negative expressiveness may be part of their "emotional gatekeeper" role in the family, with fathers acting as loving playmates. How these issues play out in the female-dominated world of early childhood education is an area lacking in research—how do boys fare in this environment, for example? Are girls still more susceptible to emotion socialization messages? The gendered world of emotion reminds us that attention to context is necessary to our fullest understanding of young children's emotional competence.

Culture

Similarly, when considering how cultures, both within and between nations, might differ in the socialization and expression of preschoolers' emotional competence, one might expect qualitative differences in the emotions modeled, reactions to emotions, and teaching about emotions. One might even expect subtle differences in how young children display emotional competence, and in its developmental course.

We use Japanese culture as an example to examine these principles, given its clear differences from Western culture and relative abundance of pertinent research (see also Denham, Mason et al., 2003). Regarding socialization of emotional expression, it is likely that emotions of friendliness, calmness, and connectedness would be most available for observation by Japanese children, given their culture's value on interdependence. In contrast, anger, regarded as an extremely negative disturbance of interdependence, would be modeled less frequently (Denham, Caal, Bassett, Benga, & Geangu, 2004; Markus & Kitayama, 1994).

Japanese parents' reactions to children's emotions sometimes also differ from those of U.S. parents (Kanaya, Nakamura, & Miyake, 1989). In general, U.S. parents see expression of emotions as legitimate and part of healthy self-assertion. In contrast, inhibitory self-regulation (e.g., obedience, cooperation, interacting empathically), and acquisition of good manners (control of impulses/desires, knowledge of what is permitted) are typical Japanese parenting goals (Ujiie, 1997). Thus, Japanese parents react most positively to children's suppression of emotion and demonstration of empathy; Zahn-Waxler, Friedman, Cole, Mizuta, and Hiruma (1996) note that Japanese mothers encouraged emotional expression less than their American counterparts.

Emerging research suggests that Japanese mothers also talk to their preschoolers about emotions (Clancy, 1999; Kojima, 2000; Sonoda & Muto, 1996). They use emotion language for similar reasons as American mothers—to instruct their children about emotional meanings, to negotiate, to explain the feelings of one sibling to another. What differs is the content of their conversations, which may focus more on behavior, and on aspects of emotion relevant for Japanese culture (Saarni, 1998; cf. Doan & Wang, 2010).

Given the differences between these two cultures, especially in emotions emphasized by socializers, differences in emotions expressed by children would be expected. For example, Japanese preschoolers show less anger and distress

in conflict situations than U.S. children, but do not differ in conflict *behaviors* (Zahn-Waxler et al., 1996). These differences fit the Japanese taboo on public expression of negative emotions (Nakamura, Buck, & Kenny, 1990).

In contrast, the trajectory of developing competent emotion knowledge seems similar for Japanese and Western children. For example, even two-year-olds use some emotion language, and by the end of the preschool period, their understanding of emotion language appropriate to their culture is acute. They begin to understand dissemblance of emotion (Matsuo, 1997; Sawada, 1997). Furthermore, the trajectory of emotion regulation from other-dependent toward independent is similar in Japanese and Western preschoolers (Kanamaru & Muto, 2004).

Thus, many important differences exist between the exemplar cultures in socialization of emotion and in early childhood emotional competence itself. However, it is important to point out that many aspects are very similar across cultures, including general appraisals of the origins of parental emotions, such as happiness, sadness, and anger resulting from enjoying time with children, loss, and child disobedience (Denham et al., 2003. Differences lie in the details, such as the type of loss or what constitutes disobedience. As with cultural competence required in other aspects of early childhood education, teachers need to consider the socialization messages pupils are absorbing at home, and how to integrate these emotional meanings in the classroom.

Classroom Experience

Although aspects of classroom experience (e.g., student–teacher relationships, classroom quality, class size, child: staff ratio, teacher turnover and stress, and curricular emphases) are good candidates for contextual moderators of both socialization of emotion and the development of emotional competence, far less research has been done in this area. The following constitutes the current state of knowledge.

Student–Teacher Relationships. The quality of children's relationships with their teachers may intervene between children's emotional competence skills and their ultimate academic success; for example, Graziano et al. (2007) found that the relation between emotion regulation and academic success was mediated by the closeness of the student–teacher relationship. Of course, the opposite direction of effect is also possible (i.e., from emotional competence to student–teacher relationship; Spritz, Sandberg, Maher, & Zajdel, 2010). In Garner and Waajid (2008), the association between teacher–child closeness and school adjustment was mediated by children's emotion knowledge. Given our statement that emotional competence influences social relationships and vice versa, the direction of effect may be insoluble without longitudinal research; however, we can say that student–teacher relationships are important correlates of young children's emotional competence. This area is ripe for further investigation.

Other Aspects of the Educational Experience. The only emotional competence research that could be found regarding classroom or childcare quality showed that high quality of care was related to children's positive emotional expressiveness (Hagekull & Bohlin, 1995). However, although no quantitative studies exist, several early childhood educators show a growing attunement to issues of emotional competence. For example, Jones (2008) makes concrete suggestions about how to use various group sizes and arrangements during the early childhood classroom day, ranging from one child helping with an errand to organizing a team to work on a joint task, so that emotional competence may be promoted. Ashiabi (2007) notes that curricula should make room for the social–emotional benefits of play; Lindsey and Colwell (2003) corroborated this notion, showing that experience with pretend play was associated with emotion knowledge, and, in girls, emotion regulation.

Application to the Early Childhood Classroom

The material covered in this chapter shows that *emotions matter* (Raver, 2002)—there is a clear association between emotional competence and both social and school success. The development of emotional competence improves children's abilities to cope with stressful situations, leads to improved brain development, and plays an integral role in learning through its role in facilitating attention and persistence (Blair, 2002). At the same time, the development of social competence, buttressed by emotional competence, enables children to form positive relationships and refrain from problem behavior. These competencies are inextricably intertwined, forming an important foundation for school success (Hawkins, Smith, & Catalano, 2004). We are also seeing more direct associations between emotional competence and school success (Denham, Brown, & Domitrovich, 2010).

Thus, the development of emotional competence should not be left to chance. This point is especially true for those at risk due to poverty, community violence, family stress, un- or underemployment, maltreatment, or family life changes (Peth-Pierce, 2000; Pianta & Nimetz, 1992). Young children with deficits in emotional competence may learn to act in increasingly antisocial ways, and become less accepted by both peers and teachers. They participate less, do worse in school, are considered hard to teach, and are provided with less instruction and positive feedback, even in preschool. Even the cognitive competencies of children showing negative behaviors are less likely to be recognized than those of more socially skilled age mates. As a final snub, peers don't want to work with such children; gradually, the emotionally and socially less competent children come to avoid school altogether (Raver & Knitzer, 2002).

Preschool and kindergarten teachers, as well as daycare providers, concur with these views, reporting that difficult behavior resulting from emotional and social competence deficits is their single greatest challenge (Arnold, McWilliams, & Arnold, 1998; Poulou, 2005; Rimm-Kaufman, Pianta, & Cox, 2000). There has, in fact, been a call for primary and secondary prevention programs targeted at preschoolers' emotional and social competence needs (Knitzer, 1993), to ensure their smooth transition to kindergarten and early school success, so they do not fall behind from the start. Along with averting problems, however, specific strengths need to be developed.

However, although early childhood educators may recognize the need to bolster students' emotional competence, their concern has historically often been implicit, rather than made explicit through specific interventions, or more informal but developmentally appropriate teaching practices (Denham, Lydick, Mitchell-Copeland, & Sawyer, 1996). At the same time, the public is demanding greater accountability for students' academic achievement, with increased emphasis on test scores and related standards. Early childhood educators often experience so much pressure to meet various standards that they do not have the time or energy to devote to anything else (Strain & Joseph, 2004). In addition, many educators are uncertain about how to address emotional and social competence issues most effectively (Zins, Weissberg, Wang, & Walberg, 2004). Thus, because of the crucial nature of early childhood social and emotional competences, and the considerable risk associated with their absence, early childhood educators need support so that they may give more attention to promoting emotional and social competence. Two sources of evidence-based support already exist: (1) the early childhood special education interventions literature (e.g., McEvoy & Yoder, 1993; though much material in this area refers to solely social, rather than emotional, competence); and (2) the Head Start Center for Social-Emotional Foundations to Early Learning (n.d.), which has a variety of information on teaching social-emotional skills.

In terms of specific prevention and intervention programming, attention to these areas during early childhood has blossomed in the past decade, due to their centrality for later well-being, mental health, and even learning and school success (Huffman, Mehlinger, & Kerivan, 2000; Peth-Pierce, 2000; Raver & Knitzer, 2002). More and more evidence-based prevention and intervention programming is being tested, found efficacious, and promoted in early childhood education (Denham & Burton, 1996, 2003; Domitrovich, Cortes, & Greenberg, 2007; Izard, 2002b; Izard et al., 2008; Joseph & Strain, 2003; Kramer, Caldarella, Christensen, & Shatzer, 2010; Webster-Stratton & Reid, 2003, 2004, 2007). Many programs are delivered universally to all children in specific classrooms (e.g., Domitrovich et al., 2007; Izard et al., 2008; Webster-Stratton & Reid, 2003); these vary in their emphasis on emotional expressiveness and utilization, emotion knowledge, and emotion regulation. Some feature work with parents, training parents on awareness, acceptance, and understanding of children's emotions and helping children to use words to describe how they feel (Havighurst, Wilson, Harley, Prior, & Kehoe, 2010), or using videotapes, and are intended to stimulate group discussion, role-plays, and problem solving, along with practice, rehearsal, and homework assignments (Webster-Stratton & Reid, 2007). Webster-Stratton's behaviorally based parenting programs are accompanied by universal and targeted classroom based programming (Webster-Stratton & Reid, 2003, 2004). Recent programming has also profitably incorporated literacy components with those on emotional competence (Bierman et al., 2008).

There also are clearly identified, evidence-based means for early childhood educators to more informally promote emotional competence (although at times reliant on the parental socialization of emotions literature; Hyson, 2002), which fit well with the material conveyed in this chapter: (1) modeling genuine, appropriate emotional responses; (2) helping children to understand their own and others' emotions; (3) supporting children's regulation of emotions; (4) recognizing and honoring children's expressive styles while promoting appropriate expressiveness; and (5) giving children many opportunities to experience the joys and to overcome the frustrations of new learning opportunities (see also Ashiabi, 2000; Nissen & Hawkins, 2010). Early childhood teachers and caregivers generally believe that children need physical affection and emotional closeness from teachers, that children learn about emotions from seeing how adults behave, and that children learn from adults how to express feelings acceptably (Hyson & Molinaro, 2001). They seem to quickly recognize the emotional competence needs of children in their care, when these are brought to their attention; for many it is like turning on a faucet of understanding. When emotional competence is highlighted, as in Hyson's suggestions, the appropriate handling of emotions in the classroom becomes a great concern to them, commensurate to their concerns about children's behavior.

However, early childhood educators still vary in their beliefs about their role in promoting young children's emotional competence—whether it is their role to actively teach about emotions at all, the importance of modeling emotional expressiveness and talking about children's feelings in the classroom, and how early young children can learn to control emotions. Some retain the notion that emotions are not the province of their work at all (Hyson & Lee, 1996). These differences in beliefs are associated with teacher training and culture, as well as their own relationship styles and emotional competence (Perry & Ball, 2008).

A clearer path to the promotion of young children's emotional competence by early childhood teachers is sorely needed. Early childhood education research indicates that teachers are likely to engage in many of the emotion socialization behaviors previously observed in parents, and to be important socializers of emotion. This assertion

derives from several circumstances (Pianta, 1999; Rabineau, 2005): (1) early childhood teachers spend significant amounts of time with children, performing most of the same emotion-laden caregiving tasks, and have been shown to be sources of emotional security to young children; (2) they are trained to deal with emotionally charged events and even have specific curricula training them and giving them supports to address emotional development of their charges. Although early childhood educators' emotional influence is less permanent than that of parents, and could be said to be "diluted" because of their need to attend to a group of children and assume an instructive role, many arguments point to teachers as socializers of emotional competence.

Thus, we see from a multitude of angles that research centering on preschoolers' emotional competence in the classroom is sorely needed; that is, its response to programming, whether and how it is specifically socialized by teachers and peers, and the contextual details that support its development. In particular, we need to extend the research on parents to the contributions made by early childhood teachers' modeling of emotions, reactions to children's emotions, and teaching about emotions. Further, over and above providing teachers with evidence-based tools to foster children's social and emotional development, we need to know how: (1) teachers' own emotional competence and beliefs about emotions vary, and why; (2) how classroom practices vary with teachers' emotion-related beliefs and emotional competence; (3) what kind of preservice and in-service experiences help teachers to attend to their own emotional competence, and cultivate positive attitudes toward an active role in socialization of emotion (Jennings & Greenberg, 2008).

With greater understanding of both teachers' mechanisms of emotion socialization, as well as maximization of teachers' own emotional competence, we could apply our knowledge to children's optimal emotional competence development within early childhood education. As well, there are several higher-order needs that early childhood educators and applied developmental psychologists may help to meet (Hyson, 2002):

- To increase policymakers' awareness of research linking emotional competence and later social and school success. One promising initiative was HR 4223, the Academic, Social, and Emotional Learning Act, new legislation introduced in December 2009, which authorizes the U.S. Department of Education to establish programs and allocate funds to:
- Establish a National Technical Assistance and Training Center for SEL
- Provide grants to support evidence-based SEL programming; and
- Conduct a national evaluation of school-based SEL programming (Collaborative for Academic, Social and Emotional Learning [CASEL], 2009).
- Advocate for resources for emotional competence and

social competence-focused assessment and programming

- See that early childhood standards, curricula, and assessment tools incorporate developmentally appropriate attention to emotional competence;
- Continue evaluating extant emotional competence programming for acceptability by families and teachers, treatment fidelity and maintenance, generalization and social validity of outcomes, and replication across investigators, early childhood education groups and settings, and across ethnic/racially diverse groups (Joseph & Strain, 2003).

Moving in these directions will help to ensure that our efforts in this area will be efficacious. Working together, we can make sure that Darrell continues from his early excellent footing in emotional and social competence, to successfully meet the challenges of learning to read, write, calculate, problem solve, and sustain more complex relationships with others. We can help Jimmy, Tomas, and even Jessica to find better ways to interact so that their well-regulated behaviors support their social, emotional, and academic pursuits throughout their lives.

References

Ahn, H. J. (2005). Teachers' discussions of emotion in child care centers. *Early Childhood Education Journal, 32*, 237–242. doi: 10.1007/s10643-004-1424-6

Ahn, H., & Stifter, C. (2006). Child care teachers' response to children's emotional expression. *Early Education and Development, 17*, 253–270. doi: 10.1207/s15566935eed1702_3

Arnold, D. H., McWilliams, L., & Arnold, E. H. (1998). Teacher discipline and child misbehavior in day care: Untangling causality with correlational data. *Developmental Psychology, 34*, 276–287. doi:10.1037/0012-1649.34.2.276

Arsenio, W., & Lemerise, E. A. (2001). Varieties of childhood bullying: Values, emotion processes and social competence. *Social Development, 10*, 57–74. doi:10.1111/1467-9507.00148

Arsenio, W., & Lover, A. (1995). Children's conceptions of sociomoral affect: Happy victimizers, mixed emotions and other expectancies. In M. K. D. Hart (Ed.), *Morality in everyday life: Developmental perspectives* (pp. 87–128). Cambridge, England: Cambridge University Press.

Ashiabi, G. S. (2000). Promoting the emotional development of preschoolers, *Early Childhood Education Journal, 28*, 79–84. doi: 10.1023/A:1009543203089

Ashiabi, G. S. (2007). Play in the preschool classroom: Its socioemotional significance and the teacher's role in play. *Early Childhood Education Journal, 35*, 199–207. doi:10.1007/s10643-007-0165-8

Banerjee, M. (1997). Hidden emotions: Preschoolers' knowledge of appearance-reality and emotion display rules. *Social Development, 15*, 107–132.

Barth, J. M., & Bastiani, A. (1997). A longitudinal study of emotional recognition and preschool children's social behavior. *Merrill-Palmer Quarterly, 43*, 107–128.

Berti, A. E., Garattoni, C., & Venturini, B. A. (2000). The understanding of sadness, guilt, and shame in 5-, 7-, and 9-year-old children. *Genetic, Social, and General Psychology Monographs, 126*, 293–318.

Bierman, K., Domitrovich, C., Nix, R., Gest, S., Welsh, J., Greenberg, … Gill, S. (2008). Promoting academic and social-emotional school readiness: The Head Start REDI program. *Child Development, 79*(6), 1802–1817. doi: 10.1111/j.1467-8624.2008.01227.x

Birch, S. H., Ladd, G. W., & Blecher-Sass, H. (1997). The teacher-child relationship and children's early school adjustment: Good-byes can build trust. *Journal of School Psychology, 35*, 61–79. doi:10.1016/S0022-4405(96)00029-5

Blair, C. (2002). School readiness: Integrating cognition and emotion in a neurobiological conceptualization of children's functioning at school entry. *American Psychologist, 57*, 111–127. doi:10.1037/0003-066X.57.2.111

Brody, L. R., & Hall, J. A. (2008). Gender and emotion in context. In M. Lewis & J. M. Haviland-Jones (Eds.), *Handbook of emotions* (3rd ed., 395–408). New York: Guilford.

Brown, J. R., Donelan-McCall, N., & Dunn, J. (1996). Why talk about mental states? The significance of children's conversations with friends, siblings, and mothers. *Child Development, 67*, 836–849. doi:10.2307/1131864

Campos, J. J., Mumme, D. L., Kermoian, R., & Campos, R. G. (1994). A functionalist perspective on the nature of emotion. *Monographs of the Society for Research in Child Development, 59*(2–3), 284–303. doi:10.2307/1166150

Chance, C., & Fiese, B. H. (1999). Gender-stereotyped lessons about emotion in family narratives. *Narrative Inquiry, 9*, 243–255.

Clancy, P. M. (1999). The socialization of affect in Japanese mother–child conversation. *Journal of Pragmatics, 31*, 1397–1421. doi: 10.1016/S0378-2166(98)00112-X

Cole, P. M., Dennis, T. A., Smith-Simon, K. E., Cohen, L. H. (2009). Preschoolers' emotion regulation strategy understanding: Relations with emotion socialization and child self-regulation. *Social Development, 18*, 324–352. doi: 10.1111/j.1467-9507.2008.00503.x

Cole, P. M., Martin, S. E., & Dennis, T. A. (2004). Emotion regulation as a scientific construct: Methodological challenges and directions for child development research. *Child Development, 75*, 317–333. doi: 10.1111/j.1467-8624.2004.00673.x

Collaborative for Academic, Social and Emotional Learning. (2009). SEL Act 2009. Press release. http://www.casel.org/news.php

Contreras, J. M., Kerns, K., Weimer, B. L., Gentzler, A. L., & Tomich, P. L. (2000). Emotion regulation as a mediator of associations between mother–child attachment and peer relationships in middle childhood. *Journal of Family Psychology, 14*, 111–124. doi:10.1037/0893-3200.14.1.111

Cutting, A. L., & Dunn, J. (1999). Theory of mind, emotion understanding, language, and family background: Individual differences and interrelations. *Child Development, 70*, 853–865. doi:10.1111/1467-8624.00061

Denham, S. A. (1998). *Emotional development in young children*. New York: Guilford.

Denham, S. A., & Auerbach, S. (1995). Mother–child dialogue about emotions. *Genetic, Social, and General Psychology Monographs, 121*, 311–338.

Denham, S. A., Bassett, H. H., & Wyatt, T. (2010). Gender differences in the socialization of preschoolers' emotional competence. In A. Kennedy Root & S. A. Denham (Eds.), *The role of parent and child gender in the socialization of emotional competence* (pp. 29–50; New Directions for Child and Adolescent Development). San Francisco, CA: Jossey-Bass.

Denham, S. A., Blair, K. A., DeMulder, E., Levitas, J., Sawyer, K. S., Auerbach-Major, S. T., … Quenan, P. (2003). Preschoolers' emotional competence: Pathway to mental health? *Child Development, 74*, 238–256. doi:10.1111/1467-8624.00533

Denham, S. A., Blair, K. A., Schmidt, M. S., & DeMulder, E. (2002). Compromised emotional competence: Seeds of violence sown early? *American Journal of Orthopsychiatry, 72*, 70–82. doi:10.1037/0002-9432.72.1.70

Denham, S. A., Brown, C. A., & Domitrovich, C. (2010). "Plays nice with others": Social-emotional learning and academic success [Special issue]. *Early Education and Development, 21*, 652–680. doi: 10.1080/10409289.2010.497450

Denham, S. A., & Burton, R. (1996). A social-emotional intervention for at-risk 4-year-olds. *Journal of School Psychology, 34*, 225–245. doi:10.1016/0022-4405(96)00013-1

Denham, S. A., & Burton, R. (2003). *Social and emotional prevention and intervention programming for preschoolers.* New York: Kluwer-Plenum.

Denham, S. A., Caal, S., Bassett, H. H., Benga, O., & Geangu, E. (2004). Listening to parents: Cultural variations in the meaning of emotions and emotion socialization. *CognitieCreierComportament, 8,* 321–350.

Denham, S. A., Caverly, S., Schmidt, M., Blair, K., DeMulder, E., Caal, S., … Mason, T. (2002). Preschool understanding of emotions: Contributions to classroom anger and aggression. *Journal of Child Psychology and Psychiatry, 43,* 901–916. doi:10.1111/1469-7610.00139

Denham, S. A., & Couchoud, E. A. (1990). Young preschoolers' understanding of emotion. *Child Study Journal, 20,* 171–192.

Denham, S. A., & Couchoud, E. A. (1991). Social-emotional predictors of preschoolers' responses to an adult's negative emotions. *Journal of Child Psychology and Psychiatry, 32,* 595–608. doi:10.1111/j.1469-7610.1991.tb00337.x

Denham, S. A., Grant, S., & Hamada, H. A. (2002, June). *"I have two 1st teachers": Mother and teacher socialization of preschoolers' emotional and social competence.* Paper presented at the 7th Head Start Research Conference, Washington, DC.

Denham, S. A., & Grout, L. (1992). Mothers' emotional expressiveness and coping: Topography and relations with preschoolers' social-emotional competence. *Genetic, Social, and General Psychology Monographs, 118,* 75–101.

Denham, S. A., & Grout, L. (1993). Socialization of emotion: Pathway to preschoolers' affect regulation. *Journal of Nonverbal Behavior, 17,* 215–227. doi: 10.1007/BF00986120

Denham, S. A., & Holt, R. W. (1993). Preschoolers' likability as cause or consequence of their social behavior. *Developmental Psychology, 29,* 271–275. doi:10.1037/0012-1649.29.2.271

Denham, S. A., & Kochanoff, A. T. (2003). Parental contributions to preschoolers' understanding of emotion. *Marriage & Family Review, 34*(3/4), 311–345. doi: 10.1300/J002v34n03_06

Denham, S. A., Lydick, S., Mitchell-Copeland, J., & Sawyer, K. (1996). Social-emotional assessment for atypical infants and preschoolers. In M. Lewis & M. E. Sullivan (Eds.), *Emotional development in atypical children* (pp. 227–271). Hillsdale, NJ: Erlbaum.

Denham, S. A., Mason, T., Kochanoff, A., Neal, K., & Hamada, H. (2003). Emotional development. In D. Cavalieri (Ed.), *International Encyclopedia of Marriage and Family Relationships* (2nd ed., pp. 419–426). New York: Macmillan.

Denham, S. A., McKinley, M., Couchoud, E. A., & Holt, R. (1990). Emotional and behavioral predictors of peer status in young preschoolers. *Child Development, 61,* 1145–1152. doi:10.2307/1130882

Denham, S. A., Mitchell-Copeland, J., Strandberg, K., Auerbach, S., & Blair, K. (1997). Parental contributions to preschoolers' emotional competence: Direct and indirect effects. *Motivation and Emotion, 27,* 65–86. doi:10.1023/A:1024426431247

Denham, S. A., Renwick, S., & Holt, R. (1991). Working and playing together: Prediction of preschool social-emotional competence from mother-child interaction. *Child Development, 62,* 242–249. doi:10.2307/1131000

Denham, S. A., Renwick-DeBardi, S., & Hewes, S. (1994). Affective communication between mothers and preschoolers: Relations with social-emotional competence. *Merrill-Palmer Quarterly, 40,* 488–508.

Denham, S. A., & Zoller, D. (1991). "When my hamster died, I cried": Preschoolers' attributions of the causes of emotions. *Journal of Genetic Psychology, 152,* 371–373.

Denham, S. A., Zoller, D., & Couchoud, E. A. (1994). Socialization of preschoolers' understanding of emotion. *Developmental Psychology, 30,* 928–936. doi:10.1037/0012-1649.30.6.928

Doan, S. N., & Wang, Q. (2010). Maternal discussions of mental states and behaviors: Relations to emotion situation knowledge in European American and immigrant Chinese children. *Child Development, 81,* 1490–1503. doi: 10.1111/j.1467-8624.2010.01487.x

Dodge, K. A., Laird, R., Lochman, J. E., Zelli, A., & Conduct Problems Prevention Research Group. (2002). Multidimensional latent-construct analysis of children's social information processing patters: Correlations with aggressive behavior problems. *Psychological Assessment, 14,* 60–73. doi:10.1037/1040-3590.14.1.60

Domitrovich. C. E., Cortes, R. C., & Greenberg, M. T. (2007). Improving young children's social and emotional competence: A randomized trial of the preschool "PATHS" curriculum. *The Journal of Primary Prevention, 28,* 67–91. doi:10.1007/s10935-007-0081-0

Dunn, J. (1994). Understanding others and the social world: Current issues in developmental research and their relation to preschool experiences and practice. *Journal of Applied Developmental Psychology, 15,* 571–583. doi:10.1016/0193-3973(94)90023-X

Dunn, J., Brown, J. R., & Beardsall, L. A. (1991). Family talk about emotions, and children's later understanding of others' emotions. *Developmental Psychology, 27,* 448–455. doi:10.1037/0012-1649.27.3.448

Dunn, J., Brown, J. R., & Maguire, M. (1995). The development of children's moral sensibility: Individual differences and emotion understanding. *Developmental Psychology, 31,* 649–659. doi:10.1037/0012-1649.31.4.649

Dunn, J., Brown, J. R., Slomkowski, C., Tesla, C., & Youngblade, L. (1991). Young children's understanding of other people's feelings and beliefs: Individual differences and their antecedents. *Child Development, 62,* 1352–1366. doi:10.2307/1130811

Dunn, J., & Cutting, A. L. (1999). Understanding others, and individual differences in friendship interactions in young children. *Social Development, 8,* 201–219. doi:10.1111/1467-9507.00091

Dunn, J., Cutting, A. L., & Fisher, N. (2002). Old friends, new friends: Predictors of children's perspective on their friends at school. *Child Development, 73*(2), 621–635. doi:10.1111/1467-9507.00091

Dunn, J., & Herrera, C. (1997). Conflict resolution with friends, siblings, and mothers: A developmental perspective. *Aggressive Behavior, 23,* 343–357. doi:10.1111/1467-9507.00091

Dunn, J., & Hughes, C. (1998). Young children's understanding of emotions within close relationships. *Cognition & Emotion, 12,* 171–190. doi:10.1080/026999398379709

Dunn, J., Slomkowski, C., Donelan, N., & Herrera, C. (1995). Conflict, understanding, and relationships: Developments and differences in the preschool years. *Early Education and Development, 6,* 303–316. doi:10.1207/s15566935eed0604_2

Dunsmore, J. C., & Karn, M. A. (2001). Mothers' beliefs about feelings and children's emotional understanding. *Early Education and Development, 12*(1), 117–138. doi: 10.1207/s15566935eed1201_7

Durbin, C. E. (2010). Validity of young children's self-reports of their emotion in response to structured laboratory tasks. *Emotion, 10,* 519–535. doi: 10.1037/a0019008

Eisenberg, N., Cumberland, A., & Spinrad, T. L. (1998). Parental socialization of emotion. *Psychological Inquiry, 9,* 241–273. doi:10.1207/s15327965pli0904_1

Eisenberg, N., Fabes, R. A., Bernzweig, J., Karbon, M., Poulin, R., & Hanish, L. (1993). The relations of emotionality and regulation to preschoolers' social skills and sociometric status. *Child Development, 64,* 1418–1438. doi:10.2307/1131543

Eisenberg, N., Fabes, R. A., Guthrie, I. K., Murphy, B. C., Maszk, P., Holmgren, R., … Sun, K. (1996). The relations of regulation and emotionality to problem behavior in elementary school children. *Development & Psychopathology, 8,* 141–162. doi: 10.1017/S095457940000701X

Eisenberg, N., Fabes, R. A., & Murphy, B. (1996). Parents' reactions to children's negative emotions: Relations to children's social competence and comforting behavior. *Child Development, 67*(5), 2227–2247. doi:10.2307/1131620

Eisenberg, N., Fabes, R. A., Murphy, B., Maszk, P., Smith, M., & Karbon, M. (1995). The role of emotionality and regulation in children's social functioning: A longitudinal study. *Child Development, 66,* 1360–1384. doi:10.2307/1131652

Eisenberg, N., Fabes, R. A., Nyman, M., Bernzweig, J., & Pinuelas, A. (1994). The relation of emotionality and regulation to preschoolers' anger-related reactions. *Child Development, 65,* 1352–1366. doi:10.2307/1131369

Eisenberg, N., Fabes, R. A., Shepard, S. A., Guthrie, I., Murphy, B. C., & Reiser, M. (1999). Parental reactions to children's negative emotions: Longitudinal relations to quality of children's social functioning. *Child Development, 70,* 513–534. doi:10.1111/1467-8624.00037

Eisenberg, N., Fabes, R. A., Shepard, S. A., Murphy, B. C., Guthrie, I. K., Jones, S., ... Maszk, P. (1997). Contemporaneous and longitudinal prediction of children's social functioning from regulation and emotionality. *Child Development, 68,* 642–664. doi:10.2307/1132116

Eisenberg, N., Gershoff, E. T., Fabes, R. A., Shepard, S. A., Cumberland, A., Losoya, S., ... Murphy, B. C. (2001). Mothers' emotional expressivity and children's behavior problems and social competence: Mediation through children's regulation. *Developmental Psychology, 37,* 475–490. doi:10.1037/0012-1649.37.4.475

Eisenberg, N., Valiente, C., Morris, A. S., Fabes, R. A., Cumberland, A., Reiser, M., ... Loysoya, S. (2003). Longitudinal relations among parental emotional expressivity, children's regulation, and quality of socioemotional function. *Developmental Psychology, 39*(1), 3–19. doi:10.1037/0012-1649.39.1.3

Engle, J. M., & McElwain, N. L. (in press). Parental reactions to toddlers' negative emotions and child negative emotionality as correlates of problem behavior at the age of three. *Social Development.* doi:10.1111/j.1467-9507.2010.00583.x

Fabes, R., Eisenberg, N., Hanish, L. D., & Spinrad, T. L. (2001). Preschoolers' spontaneous emotion vocabulary: Relations to likeability. *Early Education and Development, 12*(1), 11–28. doi:10.1207/s15566935eed1201_2

Fabes, R. A., Eisenberg, N., Nyman, M., & Michealieu, Q. (1991). Young children's appraisal of others spontaneous emotional reactions. *Developmental Psychology, 27,* 858–866. doi:10.1037/0012-1649.27.5.858

Fabes, R. A., Leonard, S. A., Kupanoff, K., & Martin, C. L. (2001). Parental coping with children's negative emotions: Relations with children's emotional and social responding. *Child Development, 72*(3), 907–920. doi:10.1111/1467-8624.00323

Fabes, R. A., Poulin, R. E., Eisenberg, N., & Madden-Derdich, D. A. (2003). The Coping with Children's Negative Emotions Scale (CCNES): Psychometric properties and relations with children's emotional competence. *Marriage & Family Review, 34*(3/4), 285–310. doi: 10.1300/J002v34n03_05

Feito, J. A. (1997). Children's beliefs about the social consequences of emotional expression. *Dissertation Abstracts International, 59*(03B), 1411.

Fivush, R. (1991). Gender and emotion in mother–child conversations about the past. *Journal of Narrative and Life History, 1,* 325–341.

Fivush, R., Berlin, L. J., Sales, J. M., Mennuti-Washburn, J., & Cassidy, J. (2003). Functions of parent–child reminiscing about emotionally negative events. *Memory, 11,* 179–192. doi: 10.1080/741938209

Fivush, R., Brotman, M. A., Buckner, J. P., & Goodman, S. H. (2000). Gender differences in parent–child emotion narratives. *Sex Roles, 42,* 233–253. doi: 10.1023/A:1007091207068

Flannagan, D., & Perese, S. (1998). Emotional references in mother–daughter and mother–son dyads' conversations about school. *Sex Roles, 39,* 353–367. doi: 10.1023/A:1018866908472

Gagnon, C., Craig, W. M., Tremblay, R. E., Zhou, R. M., & Vitaro, F. A. (1995). Kindergarten predictors of boys' stable behavior problems at the end of elementary school. *Journal of Abnormal Child Psychology, 23,* 751–766. doi:10.1007/BF01447475

Garner, P. W., & Estep, K. M. (2001). Emotional competence, emotion socialization, and young children's peer-related social competence. *Early Education and Development, 12*(1), 29–48. doi:10.1207/s15566935eed1201_3

Garner, P. W., Jones, D. C., Gaddy, G., & Rennie, K. (1997). Low income mothers' conversations about emotions and their children's emotional competence. *Social Development, 6,* 37–52. doi:10.1111/j.1467-9507.1997.tb00093.x

Garner, P. W., Jones, D. C., & Miner, J. L. (1994). Social competence among low-income preschoolers: Emotion socialization practices and social cognitive correlates. *Child Development, 65,* 622–637. doi:10.2307/1131405

Garner, P. W., Robertson, S., & Smith, G. (1997). Preschool children's emotional expressions with peers: The roles of gender and emotion socialization. *Sex Roles: A Journal of Research, 36,* 675–691. doi: 10.1023/A:1025601104859

Garner, P. W., & Spears, F. M. (2000). Emotion regulation in low-income preschoolers. *Social Development, 9,* 246–264. doi:10.1111/1467-9507.00122

Garner, P., & Waajid, B. (2008). The associations of emotion knowledge and teacher-child relationships to preschool children's school-related developmental competence. *Journal of Applied Developmental Psychology, 29*(2), 89–100. doi:10.1016/j.appdev.2007.12.001

Gilliom, M., Shaw, D. S., Beck, J. E., Schonberg, M. A., & Lukon, J. L. (2002). Anger regulation in disadvantaged preschool boys: Strategies, antecedents, and the development of self-control. *Developmental Psychology, 38*(2), 222–235. doi:10.1037/0012-1649.38.2.222

Gnepp, J. (1989). Personalized inferences of emotions and appraisals: Component processes and correlates. *Developmental Psychology, 25,* 277–288. doi:10.1037/0012-1649.25.2.277

Gnepp, J., & Gould, M. E. (1985). The development of personalized inferences: Understanding other people's emotional reactions in light of their prior experiences. *Child Development, 56,* 1455–1464. doi:10.2307/1130465

Gnepp, J., & Hess, D. L. (1986). Children's understanding of verbal and facial display rules. *Developmental Psychology, 22*(1), 103–108. doi:10.1037/0012-1649.22.1.103

Gnepp, J., Klayman, J., & Trabasso, T. (1982). A hierarchy of information sources for inferring emotional reactions. *Journal of Experimental Child Psychology, 33,* 111–123. doi:10.1016/0022-0965(82)90009-1

Gnepp, J., McKee, E., & Domanic, J. A. (1987). Children's use of situational information to infer emotion: Understanding emotionally equivocal situations. *Developmental Psychology, 23,* 114–123. doi:10.1037/0012-1649.23.1.114

Gottman, J. M., Katz, L. F., & Hooven, C. (1997). *Meta-emotion: How families communicate emotionally.* Mahwah, NJ: Erlbaum.

Graziano, P. A., Reavis, R. D., Keane, S. P., & Calkins, S. D. (2007). The role of emotion regulation in children's early academic success. Journal of School Psychology, 45(1), 3–19. doi:10.1016/j.jsp.2006.09.002

Greenberg, M. T., & Snell, J. L. (1997). Brain development and emotional development: The role of teaching in organizing the frontal lobe. In P. Salovey & D. J. Sluyter (Eds.), *Emotional development and emotional intelligence* (pp. 93–119). New York: Basic Books.

Grolnick, W. S., Bridges, L. J., & Connell, J. P. (1996). Emotion regulation in two-year-olds: Strategies and emotional expression in four contexts. *Child Development, 67,* 928–941. doi:10.2307/1131871

Grolnick, W. S., Kurowski, C. O., McMenamy, J. M., Rivkin, I., & Bridges, L. J. (1998). Mothers' strategies for regulating their toddlers' distress. *Infant Behavior & Development, 21*(3), 437–450. doi:10.1016/S0163-6383(98)90018-2

Gross, D., & Harris, P. (1988). Understanding false beliefs about emotion. *International Journal of Behavioral Development, 11,* 475–488.

Gross, J. J., & Thompson, R. A. (2007). Emotion regulation: Conceptual foundations. In J. J. Gross (Ed), *Handbook of emotion regulation* (pp. 3–24). New York: Guilford.

Hagekull, B., & Bohlin, G. (1995). Day care quality, family and child characteristics, and socioemotional development. *Early Childhood Research Quarterly, 10,* 505–526. doi: 10.1016/0885-2006(95)90019-5

Halberstadt, A. G., Denham, S. A., & Dunsmore, J. (2001). Affective social competence. *Social Development, 10,* 79–119. doi: 10.1111/1467-9507.00150

Harms, T., Clifford, R. M., & Cryer, D. (1998). *Early childhood environment rating scale-revised.* New York: Teachers College Press.

Harris, P. (2008). Children's understanding of emotions. In M. Lewis, J.

M. Haviland-Jones, & L. F. Barrett (Eds.), *Handbook of emotions* (pp. 320–331). New York: Guilford.

Havighurst, S. S., Wilson, K. R., Harley, A. E., Prior, M. R., & Kehoe, C. (2010).Tuning in to kids: Improving emotion socialization practices in parents of preschool children-findings from a community trial. *Journal of Child Psychology and Psychiatry, 51*, 1342–1350. doi: 10.1111/j.1469-7610.2010.02303.x

Hawkins, J. D., Smith, B. H., & Catalano, R. F. (2004). Social development and social and emotional learning: The Seattle Social Development Project. In J. E. Zins, R. P. Weissberg, M. C. Wang, & H. J. Walberg (Eds.), *Building school success on social and emotional learning: what does the research say?* (pp. 130–150), New York: Teachers College Press.

Head Start Center for Social-Emotional Foundations to Early Learning. (n.d.). Retrieved from http://www.vanderbilt.edu/csefel/

Howes, C. (2000). Social-emotional classroom climate in child care child–teacher relationships and children's second grade peer relations. *Social Development, 9*, 191–204. doi:10.1111/1467-9507.00119

Howse, R., Calkins, S., Anastopoulos, A., Keane, S., & Shelton, T. (2003). Regulatory contributors to children's kindergarten achievement. *Early Education and Development, 14*(1), 101–119. doi:10.1207/s15566935eed1401_7

Hubbard, J. A., & Coie, J. D. (1994). Emotional correlates of social competence in children's peer relationships. *Merrill-Palmer Quarterly, 40*, 1–20.

Huffman, L. C., Mehlinger, S. L., & Kerivan, A. S. (2000). Risk factors for academic and behavioral problems at the beginning of school. *Off to a good start: Research on the risk factors for early school problems and selected federal policies affecting children's social and emotional development and their readiness for school.* Chapel Hill: FPG Child Development Center, University of North Carolina.

Hughes, C., Dunn, J., & White, A. (1998). Trick or treat?: Uneven understanding of mind and emotion and executive dysfunction in hard-to-manage preschoolers. *Journal of Child Psychology and Psychiatry, 39*, 981–994. doi: 10.1111/1469-7610.00401

Hyson, M. (2002). Emotional development and school readiness. Professional development. *Young Children, 57*(6), 76–78.

Hyson, M. C. (1994). *The emotional development of young children: Building an emotion-centered curriculum.* New York: Teachers College Press.

Hyson, M. C., & Lee, K.-M. (1996). Assessing early childhood teachers' beliefs about emotions: Content, contexts, and implications for practice. *Early Education and Development, 7*, 59–78. doi: 10.1207/s15566935eed0701_5

Hyson, M. C., & Molinaro, J. (2001). Learning through feeling: Children's development, teachers' beliefs and relationships, and classroom practices. In S. L. Golbeck (Ed.), *Psychological perspectives on early childhood education: Reframing dilemmas in research and practice The Rutgers invitational symposium on education series* (pp. 107–130). Mahwah, NJ: Erlbaum.

Izard, C. E. (2002a). Emotion knowledge and emotion utilization facilitate school readiness. *SRCD Social Policy Report, 16*(3), 8.

Izard, C. E. (2002b). Translating emotion theory and research into preventive interventions. *Psychological Bulletin, 128*, 796–824. doi:10.1037/0033-2909.128.5.796

Izard, C. E., Fine, S., Schultz, D., Mostow, A., Ackerman, B., & Youngstrom, E. (2001). Emotions knowledge as a predictor of social behavior and academic competence in children at risk. *Psychological Science, 12*, 18–23. doi:10.1111/1467-9280.00304

Izard, C. E., King, K. A., Trentacosta, C. J., Morgan, J. K., Laurenceau, J., Krauthamer-Ewing, E. S., & Finlon, K. J. (2008). Accelerating the development of emotion competence in Head Start children: Effects on adaptive and maladaptive behavior. *Development and Psychopathology, 20*, 369–397. doi: 10.1017/S0954579408000175

Jennings, P. A., & Greenberg, M. T. (2009). The prosocial classroom: Teacher social and emotional competence in relation to student and classroom outcomes. *Review of Educational Research, 79*(1), 491–525. doi:10.3102/0034654308325693

Jones, N. P. (2008). 2, 4, or 6?: Grouping children to promote social and emotional development. *Young Children, 63*(3), 34–39.

Joseph, G. E., & Strain, P. S. (2003). Comprehensive evidence-based social-emotional curricula for young children: An analysis of efficacious adoption potential. *Topics in Early Childhood Special Education, 23*(2), 65–76. doi:10.1177/02711214030230020201

Josephs, I. (1994). Display rule behavior and understanding in preschool children. *Journal of Nonverbal Behavior, 18*, 301–326. doi:10.1007/BF02172291

Kanamaru, T., & Muto, T. (2004). Individual differences in emotional regulation of two-year old children during interactions with mothers. *Japanese Journal of Developmental Psychology, 15*, 183–194.

Kanaya, Y., Nakamura, C., & Miyake, K. (1989). Cross-cultural study of expressive behavior of mothers in response to their 5-month-old infants' different emotion expression. *Research and Clinical Center for Child Development, 11*, 25–31.

Kestenbaum, R., & Gelman, S. (1995). Preschool children's identification and understanding of mixed emotions. *Cognitive Development, 10*, 443–458. doi:10.1016/0885-2014(95)90006-3

Kieras, J. C., Tobin, R. M., Graziano, W. G., & Rothbart, M. K. (2005). You can't always get what you want: Effortful control and children's responses to undesirable gifts. *Psychological Science, 16*,391–396. doi: 10.1111/j.0956-7976.2005.01546.x

Knitzer, J. (1993). Children's mental health policy: Challenging the future. *Journal of Emotional and Behavioral Disorders, 1*, 8–16. doi: 10.1177/106342669300100104

Kochenderfer, B. J., & Ladd, G. W. (1996). Peer victimization: Cause or consequence of school maladjustment? *Child Development, 67*, 1305–1317. doi: 10.2307/1131701

Kojima, Y. (2000). Maternal regulation of sibling interactions in the preschool years: Observational study of Japanese families. *Child Development, 71*, 1640–1647.

Kramer, T. J., Calderella, P., Christenson, L., & Shatzer, R. H. (2010). Social and emotional learning in the kindergarten classroom: Evaluation of the Strong Start curriculum. *Early Childhood Education Journal, 37*, 303–309. doi: 10.1007/s10643-009-0354-8

Ladd, G. W., Birch, S. H., & Buhs, E. S. (1999). Children's social and scholastic lives in kindergarten: Related spheres of influence? *Child Development, 70*, 1373–1400. doi: 10.1111/1467-8624.00101

Ladd, G. W., Kochenderfer, B. J., & Coleman, C. C. (1996). Friendship quality as a predictor of young children's early school adjustment. *Child Development, 67*, 1103–1118. doi:10.2307/1131882

Lagattuta, K. (2007). Thinking about the future because of the past: Young children's knowledge about the causes of worry and preventative decisions. *Child Development, 78*(5), 1492–1509. doi: 10.1111/j.1467-8624.2007.01079.x

Lagattuta, K., & Wellman, H. (2002). Differences in early parent–child conversations about negative versus positive emotions: Implications for the development of psychological understanding. *Developmental Psychology, 38*(4), 564–580. doi: 10.1037/0012-1649.38.4.564

Larson, J., Yen, M., & Fireman, G. (2007). Children's understanding and experience of mixed emotions. *Psychological Science, 18*(2), 186–191. doi: 10.1111/j.1467-9280.2007.01870.x

Leerkes, E., Paradise, M., O'Brien, M., Calkins, S., & Lange, G. (2008). Emotion and cognition processes in preschool children. *Merrill-Palmer Quarterly, 54*(1), 102–124. doi:10.1353/mpq.2008.0009

Liew, J., Eisenberg, N., Losoya, S. H., Fabes, R. A., Guthrie, I. K., & Murphy, B. C. (2003). Children's physiological indices of empathy and their socioemotional adjustment: Does caregivers' expressivity matter? *Journal of Family Psychology, 17*(4), 584–597. doi: 10.1037/0893-3200.17.4.584

Lindsey, E. W., & Colwell, M. J. (2003). Preschoolers' emotional competence: Links to pretend and physical play. *Child Study Journal, 33*, 39–52.

Markus, H. R., & Kitayama, S. (1994). The cultural construction of self and emotion: Implications for social behavior. In S. Kitayama & H. R. Markus (Eds.), *Emotion and culture: Empirical studies of mutual influence* (pp. 89–130). Washington, DC: American Psychological Association.

Martin, S., Clements, M., & Crnic, K. (2002). Maternal emotions during mother–toddler interaction: Parenting in affective context. *Parenting, 2*(2), 105–126. doi: 10.1207/S15327922PAR0202_02

Mashburn, A. J., & Pianta, R. C. (2006). Social relationships and school readiness. *Early Education and Development, 17,* 151–176. doi: 10.1207/s15566935eed1701_7

Matsuo, K. (1997). Young children's comprehension of figurative language which describe emotions. *Japanese Journal of Developmental Psychology, 8,* 165–175.

McEvoy, M. A., & Yoder, P. (1993). *Interventions to promote social skills and emotional development: DEC recommended practices.* Pittsburgh, PA: DEC.

Miller, A. L., Seifer, R., Stroud, L., Sheinkopf, S. J., & Dickstein, S. (2006). Biobehavioral indices of emotion regulation relate to school attitudes, motivation, and behavior problems in a low-income preschool sample. *Annals of the New York Academy of Science, 1094,* 325–329. doi: 10.1196/annals.1376.043

Mirabile, S. P., Scaramella, L. V., Sohr-Preston, S. L., & Robison, S. D. (2009). Mothers' socialization of emotion regulation: The moderating role of children's negative emotional reactivity. *Child & Youth Care Forum, 38*(1), 19–37. doi: 10.1007/s10566-008-9063-5

Misailidi, P. (2006). Young children's display rule knowledge: Understanding the distinction between apparent and real emotions and the motives underlying the use of display rules. *Social Behavior and Personality, 34,* 1285–1296. doi: 10.2224/sbp.2006.34.10.1285

Morgan, J. K., Izard, C. E., & King, K. A. (2010). Construct validity of the Emotion Matching Task: Preliminary evidence for convergent and criterion validity of a new emotion knowledge measure for young children. *Social Development, 19,* 52–70. doi: 10.1111/j.1467-9507.2008.00529.x

Murphy, B. C., Shepard, S., Eisenberg, N., Fabes, R. A., & Guthrie, I. K. (1999). Contemporaneous and longitudinal relations of dispositional sympathy to emotionality, regulation, and social functioning. *Journal of Early Adolescence, 19,* 66–97. doi:10.1177/0272431699019001004

Nakamura, M., Buck, R., & Kenny, D. A. (1990). Relative contributions of expression behavior and contextual information to the judgment of the emotional state of another. *Journal of Personality and Social Psychology, 59,* 1032–1039. doi: 10.1037/0022-3514.59.5.1032

Nelson, C. A. (1994). Neural bases of infant temperament. In J. E. Bates & T. E. Wachs (Eds.), *Temperament: Individual differences at the interface of biology and behavior* (pp. 47–82). Washington, DC: American Psychological Association. doi: 10.1037/10149-002

Nissen, H., & Hawkins, C. J. (2010). Promoting emotional competence in the preschool classroom. *Childhood Education, 86,* 255–259.

Peng, M., Johnson, C. N., Pollock, J., Glasspool, R., & Harris, P. L. (1992). Training young children to acknowledge mixed emotions. *Cognition and Emotion, 6,* 387–401. doi:10.1080/02699939208409693

Perry, C., & Ball, I. (2008). Identifying the underlying dimensions of teachers' emotional intelligence. *Problems of Education in the 21st Century,* 789–798.

Peth-Pierce, R. (2000). *A good beginning: Sending America's children to school with the social and emotional competence they need to succeed.* Chapel Hill, NC: The Child Mental Health Foundations and Agencies Network.

Pianta, R. C. (1999). *Enhancing relationships between children and teachers.* Washington, DC: American Psychological Association.

Pianta, R. C., & Nimetz, S. L. (1992). Development of young children in stressful contexts: Theory, assessment, and prevention. In M. Gettinger, S. N. Elliott, & T. R. Kratochwill (Eds.), *Preschool and early childhood treatment directions* (pp. 151–185). Hillsdale, NJ: Erlbaum.

Pollak, S. D., Cicchetti, D., Hornung, K., & Reed, A. (2000). Recog-

nizing emotion in faces: Developmental effects of child abuse and neglect. *Developmental Psychology, 36,* 679–688. doi: 10.1037/0012-1649.36.5.679

Poulou, M. (2005) The prevention of emotional and behavioural difficulties in schools: Teachers' suggestions. *Educational Psychology in Practice, 21,* 37–52. doi: 10.1080/02667360500035181

Rabineau, K. M. (2005). Parent and teacher socialization of emotions and preschoolers' emotion regulation development. *Dissertation Abstracts International: Section B: The Sciences and Engineering,* 4301.

Raver, C. C. (2002). Emotions matter: Making the case for the role of young children's emotional development for early school readiness. *SRCD Social Policy Report, 16*(3), 3–18.

Raver, C. C., Blackburn, E. K., & Bancroft, M. (1999). Relations between effective emotional self-regulation, attentional control, and low-income preschoolers' social competence with peers. *Early Education and Development, 10,* 333–350. doi: 10.1207/s15566935eed1003_6

Raver, C. C., Garner, P. W., & Smith-Donald, R. (2007). The roles of emotion regulation and emotion knowledge for children's academic readiness: Are the links causal? In R. C. Pianta, M. J. Cox, & K. L. Snow (Eds.), *School readiness and the transition to kindergarten in the era of accountability,* (pp.121–147). Baltimore, MD: Brookes.

Raver, C. C., & Knitzer, J. (2002). *Ready to enter: What research tells policymakers about strategies to promote social and emotional school readiness among three- and four-year-olds.* New York: National Center for Children in Poverty.

Reimer, K. J. (1996). Emotion socialization and children's emotional expressiveness in the preschool context (emotional expression). *Dissertation Abstracts International, 57*(07A), 0010.

Rimm-Kaufman, S. E., Pianta, R. C., & Cox, M. J. (2000). Teachers' judgements of problems in the transition to kindergarten. *Early Childhood Research Quarterly, 15,* 147–166. doi: 10.1016/S0885-2006(00)00049-1

Roberts, W. R., & Strayer, J. A. (1996). Empathy, emotional expressiveness, and prosocial behavior. *Child Development, 67,* 449–470. doi: 10.2307/1131826

Robins, L. N., & Rutter, M. (1990). *Straight and devious pathways from childhood to adulthood.* Cambridge, UK: Cambridge University Press.

Rubin, K. H., Burgess, K. B., Dwyer, K. M., & Hastings, P. (2003). Predicting preschoolers' externalizing behaviors from toddler temperament, conflict, and maternal negativity. *Developmental Psychology, 39*(1), 164–176. doi: 10.1037/0012-1649.39.1.164

Russell, J. A. (1990). The preschooler's understanding of the causes and consequences of emotion. *Child Development, 61,* 1872–1881. doi: 10.2307/1130843

Russell, J. A., & Paris, F. A. (1994). Do children acquire concepts for complex emotions abruptly? *International Journal of Behavioral Development, 17*(2), 349–365. doi: 10.1177/016502549401700207

Rydell, A.-M., Berlin, L., & Bohlin, G. (2003). Emotionality, emotion regulation, and adaptation among 5- to 8-year-old children. *Emotion, 3*(1), 30–47. doi: 10.1037/1528-3542.3.1.30

Saarni, C. (1998). Issues of cultural meaningfulness in emotional development. *Developmental Psychology, 34,* 647–652. doi: 10.1037/0012-1649.34.4.647

Saarni, C. (1999). *Children's emotional competence.* New York: Guilford.

Saarni, C. (2001). Cognition, context, and goals: Significant components in social-emotional effectiveness. *Social Development, 10,* 125–129. doi: 10.1111/1467-9507.00152

Salisch, M. von. (2008). Themes in the development of emotion regulation in childhood and adolescence and a transactional model. In S. Kronast, C. von Scheve, S. Ismer, S. Jung, & M. Vandekerckhove (Eds.), *Regulating emotions: Social necessity and biological inheritance.* (pp. 146–167). Oxford, England: Blackwell.

Sawada, T. (1997). Development of children's understanding of emotional dissemblance in another person. *Japanese Journal of Educational Psychology, 45,* 50–59.

Schultz, D., Izard, C. E., & Ackerman, B. P. (2000). Children's anger attribution bias: Relations to family environment and social adjustment. *Social Development, 9*, 284–301. doi: 10.1111/1467-9507.00126

Schultz, D., Izard, C. E., Ackerman, B. P., & Youngstrom, E. A. (2001). Emotion knowledge in economically disadvantaged children: Self-regulatory antecedents and relations to social difficulties and withdrawal. *Development & Psychopathology, 13*, 53–67. doi: 10.1017/S0954579401001043

Shields, A., Dickstein, S., Seifer, R., Giusti, L., Magee, K. D., & Spritz, B. (2001). Emotional competence and early school adjustment: A study of preschoolers at risk. *Early Education and Development, 12*(1), 73–97. doi: 10.1207/s15566935eed1201_5

Smith, M. (2001). Social and emotional competencies: Contributions to young African-American children's peer acceptance. *Early Education and Development, 12*(1), 49–72. doi: 10.1207/s15566935eed1201_4

Sonoda, N., & Muto, T. (1996). References to internal states in mother-child interactions: Effect of different settings and maternal individual differences. *Japanese Journal of Developmental Psychology, 7*, 159–169.

Spritz, B. L., Sandberg, E. H., Maher, E., & Zajdel, R. T. (2010). Models of emotion skills and social competence in the Head Start classroom. *Early Education and Development, 21*, 495–516. doi: 10.1080/10409280902895097

Strain, P. S., & Joseph, G. E. (2004). Engaged supervision to support recommended practices for young children with challenging behavior. *Topics in Early Childhood Special Education, 24*, 39–50. doi: 10.1177/02711214040240010401

Strandberg-Sawyer, K., Denham, S. A., DeMulder, E., Blair, K., Auerbach-Major, S., & Levitas, J. (2003). The contribution of older siblings' reactions to emotions to preschoolers' emotional and social competence. *Marriage & Family Review, 34*(3/4), 183–212. doi: 10.1300/J002v34n03_01

Sullivan, M. W., Bennett, D.S., Carpenter, K., & Lewis, M. (2008). Emotion knowledge in young neglected children. *Child Maltreatment, 13*, 301–306. doi: 10.1177/1077559507313725

Thompson, R. A. (1994). Emotion regulation: A theme in search of definition. In N. A. Fox (Ed.), *The development of emotion regulation: Biological and behavioral considerations. Monographs of the Society for Research in Child Development*, Serial No. 240, 259 (242–243), 225–252.

Trentacosta, C., & Izard, C. (2007). Kindergarten children's emotion competence as a predictor of their academic competence in first grade. *Emotion, 7*(1), 77–88. doi: 10.1037/1528-3542.7.1.77

Ujiie, T. (1997). How do Japanese mothers treat children's negativism? *Journal of Applied Developmental Psychology, 18*, 467–483. doi: 10.1016/S0193-3973(97)90022-8

Valiente, C. (2004). The relations of mothers' negative expressivity to children's experience and expression of negative emotion. *Journal of Applied Developmental Psychology, 25*(2), 215–235. doi:10.1016/j.appdev.2004.02.006

Walden, T., Lemerise, E. A., & Smith, M. C. (1999). Friendship and popularity in preschool classrooms. *Early Education and Development, 10*, 351–371. doi: 10.1207/s15566935eed1003_7

Warren, H. K., & Stifter, C. A. (2008). Maternal emotion-related socialization and preschoolers' developing emotion self-awareness. *Social Development, 17*, 239–258. doi: 10.1111/j.1467-9507.2007.00423.x

Webster-Stratton, C., & Reid, M. J. (2003). Treating conduct problems and strengthening social and emotional competence in young children: The Dina Dinosaur Program. *Journal of Emotional and Behavioral Disorders, 2*, 130–143. doi: 10.1177/10634266030110030101

Webster-Stratton, C., & Reid, M. J. (2004). Strengthening social and emotional competence in young children—The foundation for early school readiness and success: Incredible Years classroom social skills and problem-solving curriculum. *Infants and Young Children, 17*, 96–113. doi: 10.1097/00001163-200404000-00002

Webster-Stratton, C., & Reid, M. J. (2007). Incredible Years parents and teachers training series: A Head Start partnership to promote social competence and prevent conduct problems. In P. Tolan, J. Szapocznik, & S. Sambrano Soledad (Eds.), *Preventing youth substance abuse: Science-based programs for children and adolescents* (pp. 67–88). Washington, DC: American Psychological Association. doi: 10.1037/11488-003

Widen, S. C., & Russell, J. A. (2008). Children acquire emotion categories gradually. *Cognitive Development, 23*, 291–312. doi: 10.1016/j.cogdev.2008.01.002

Widen, S. C., & Russell, J. A. (2010). Differentiation in preschooler's categories of emotion. *Emotion, 10*, 651–661. doi: 10.1037/a0019005

Wintre, M., Polivy, J., & Murray, M. A. (1990). Self-predictions of emotional response patterns: Age, sex, and situational determinants. *Child Development, 61*, 1124–1133. doi: 10.2307/1130880

Wintre, M., & Vallance, D. D. (1994). A developmental sequence in the comprehension of emotions: Multiple emotions, intensity and valence. *Developmental Psychology, 30*, 509–514. doi: 10.1037/0012-1649.30.4.509

Zahn-Waxler, C., Friedman, R. J., Cole, P. M., Mizuta, I., & Hiruma, N. (1996). Japanese and United States preschool children's responses to conflict and distress. *Child Development, 67*, 2462–2477. doi: 10.2307/1131634

Zins, J., Weissberg, R. P., Wang, M. C., & Walberg, H. J. (Eds.). (2004). *Building academic success on social and emotional learning: What does the research say?* New York: Teachers College Press.

5

Motor Development in Young Children

The Ohio State University

JOHN C. OZMUN
Indiana Wesleyan University

DAVID L. GALLAHUE
Indiana University

A group of preschoolers spills out into the playground run-ning and squealing with the joy of being outside. Two little girls hold hands and start skipping around the playground together while a couple of boys start throwing stones to-ward a tree. It seems like a typical day on the playground. We often assume that young children naturally learn these motor skills of childhood and that all children look alike in the patterns of movement they demonstrate; but this is not so. If we were to look carefully at this picture we might see one girl skipping with an easy, rhythmical pattern with her arms swinging in opposition to her legs. Meanwhile her friend keeps up by showing a one-sided step-hop pat-tern with the right knee and right arm coming up together and the left side just stepping, never hopping (she cannot skip). If we look across to the boys, one boy can throw his stones a considerable distance showing a sideways stance, arm–leg opposition, and arm windup and follow-through. In contrast, the other boy performs a "chop throw" by standing facing forward with both feet planted wide, and making a chopping motion with his dominant arm; his stone only goes a few feet in front of him. It is clear from this closer analysis that these children vary considerably in their motor development and movement competence. So how do young children learn motor skills? And what factors influence their motor development?

Definition of Motor Development

In its simplest form the term *development* refers to change in function over time. As such, development encompasses all change throughout the life span in the cognitive, affective, and motor domains of human behavior. Understanding the motor development of young children is of keen interest to parents and educators, as well as scholars, physicians, and therapists. *Motor development* may be defined as adaptive

change toward competence in motor behavior across the life span. Clark and Whitall (1989) define motor development as "the changes in motor behavior over the lifespan and the processes which underlie these changes" (p. 194). As such, motor development is studied both as a product and as a process. Knowledge of the *products* (i.e., the outcomes) and the *processes* (i.e., the underlying mechanisms) of changes in motor behavior over time provide us with information that is vital to understanding the individual, particularly during a time of rapid developmental change such as the period of early childhood.

In terms of "product," understanding the motor devel-opment of young children provides us with descriptive profiles of developmental change in the motor behavior of typically developing children, thereby providing us with information about the "what" of motor development. Namely: (a) What are the typical phases and stages of mo-tor development during early childhood? (b) What are the approximate age-periods associated with typical markers of motor behavior in young children? and (c) What do we know about predictable patterns of change in motor behav-ior that are typically seen in normally developing children as compared to those who may be either developmentally delayed, or developmentally advanced? In short, descriptive views of motor development equip us with a better under-standing, in general terms, of what lies ahead in terms of anticipated change and thus can inform instructional and curricula decisions. It is here we need to make an important distinction between *"age-dependent"* changes as opposed to *"age-related"* changes. Age-dependent changes suggest that all children of a certain age perform a motor skill in a specific way. However, age-related changes suggest that *some* children of the same age will show similar movement skills but others may vary both in the rate and sequence of development. That is, children raised in different ecological and cultural settings or children with disabilities may be significantly ahead or behind their age mates in terms of movement skill acquisition and physical development.

In terms of "process," understanding the motor development of young children helps us address the mechanisms that underlie developmental change. As such we gain information about the "how" and "why" of development. Namely: (a) How does change occur as it does? (b) Why is developmental change a nonlinear, self-organizing dynamic process? (c) How do heredity and the environment interact with the requirements of the motor task as one strives for greater motor control and movement competence? In short, better understanding the mechanisms that underlie motor development provides us with valuable information on why change occurs as it does in young children. By understanding the mechanisms of change we can be better equipped to intervene and assist children in developing age-appropriate motor skills. There are certain principles of motor development that can help guide us as we seek to understand both the *product* and *process* of motor development.

Principles of Motor Development

Motor development looks at the changes in motor behavior across the lifespan. It is important to remember that these changes do not occur just because we get older, they require accompanying experiences. The following principles are valuable as we consider changes in motor behavior:

- *Change is qualitatively different and sequential.* As children "develop" motorically one can see qualitatively different patterns of movement (Gallahue, Ozmun, & Goodway, 2012; Haywood & Getchell, 2009; Payne & Isaacs, 2008; Seefeldt, 1982). In the less developed child this pattern of movement may be crude and inefficient but in the more developed child it may be more mechanically efficient and able to be applied across multiple contexts (Payne & Isaacs, 2008). Let's think back to the opening throwing scenario. One boy used a stationary "chop throw" which was developmentally immature and had little utility, force, or distance. In comparison the more developed child used a contralateral pattern (opposition of hand to foot) in throwing and could achieve considerable force, distance, and accuracy. However, despite qualitatively different throwing patterns between the boys, the sequence of development for throwing will typically (but not always) be the same for both boys. It is the age and rate of development through the sequence that varies. We have identified many of these sequences of motor development and knowledge of these sequences is valuable in teaching the young child movement skills. These sequences will be discussed later in the chapter.
- *Change is cumulative and directional.* Developmental change is built on previous capabilities. Early behaviors serve as the building blocks for later emerging skills. In the early childhood years it is important that children

develop competency in a set of skills called fundamental motor skills (FMS) such as throwing, skipping, and catching (Gallahue, Ozmun, & Goodway, 2012). These FMS are built upon the reflexes, reactions, and rudimentary skills acquired in infancy. Development also gives direction to the change; that is, it is "going somewhere" toward some end goal that may either advance or decline the motor performance. Young children often "negotiate" a given movement task and that will result in a variety of movement responses to the task. More competent performers will frequently make a task harder for themselves whereas less competent performers may make it easier. Understanding the motivation behind children's selection of movement responses can be valuable when developing instructional activities to engage learners of all levels.

- *Change is multifactorial based upon the interaction between the learner, the environment, and the task.* Changes in motor development are influenced by interaction of factors from the learner, the environment, and the task (Newell, 1984, 1986). In the playground throwing example above, the task may have been to throw the stone as far as possible. The potential learner factors influencing the pattern of movement may be things like balance, strength, and the ability to demonstrate a *contralateral* (arm–leg opposition) pattern. In the more competent thrower the child has good balance, and good trunk and arm strength, with the ability to step with opposition; thus his movement was more sophisticated. In the less competent thrower, the child probably has poor balance and is incapable of arm–leg opposition thus choosing a front facing, wide-legged stance. He may also have poor arm and trunk strength thus utilizing a chopping motion with his arm. In both examples, the interaction of these factors resulted in the throwing pattern demonstrated by the children. However, if the throwing task was modified from one of distance to accuracy to a closer target, both children may choose a front facing stance with a chop throw as this pattern of movement is more functional to achieve the given task.
- *Change is variable between children.* This principle highlights the individuality in all learning. The sequence of progression through the developmental sequences is generally fairly consistent for most children. The rate, however, may vary considerably, depending on a combination of both environmental and biological factors (Malina, Bouchard, & Bar-Or, 2004). Whether a child reaches the proficient stage depends primarily on the ecological context of the environment including factors such as instruction, encouragement, and opportunities for practice, and biological factors such as perceptual-motor maturity and various anatomical and physiological considerations.

Overall, these principles offer insight into the products and processes of motor development. Three models of motor development also offer insight into the "what" of motor development and the sequential nature of the kinds of skills emerging during the early childhood period.

Models of Motor Development

Three models of motor development share commonalities in the emergence of motor skills across childhood, but each model offers a slightly unique perspective on this process.

Hourglass Model of Motor Development

Gallahue, Ozmun, & Goodway (2012) used an "hourglass" to describe the processes of motor development. The sands falling into the hourglass represent the development of motor skills and they are influenced by both heredity and environment. As the sands land in the bottom of the hourglass, they build the phases and stages of motor development across the lifespan. The *reflexive movement phase* starts prenatally and develops well into the first year of life. Primitive reflexes such as the Moro reflex, as well as postural reflexes such as the body righting reflex, are inhibited (disappear) on a universally predictable schedule in typically developing infants. In the next phase, the *rudimentary movement phase*, the infant develops a variety of basic movement patterns such as control of the head, neck, and trunk (body stability), controlled reaching, grasping, and releasing (object manipulation) and proficiency in creeping and crawling (purposeful locomotion).

During the early childhood and primary school years children can be seen in the *fundamental movement phase* of motor development. This is the period of time during which young children experiment and explore their movement potential in a variety of fundamental motor skills (FMS) that form the building blocks for the more complex movement skills at the fourth and final phase. Later in this chapter we will focus our discussion on FMS development during early childhood. In the final phase, *specialized movement skill phase*, more complex movement skills such as those in sports and games are refined and mastered. Variability in the rate and extent of skill acquisition is determined by a wide variety of environmental as well as biological factors.

Sequential Progression in the Achievement of Motor Proficiency

Seefeldt (1982) proposed one of the earliest models in motor development shaped like a pyramid. The progression through this model is very similar to the Hourglass approach above. In this four phase sequential approach, the "*Reflexes and Reactions*" of infancy are at the bottom of the pyramid and serve as the foundation for all future movement skills. Built upon this foundation the young child begins to develop "*Fundamental Motor Skills.*" including *locomotor* skills such as running and skipping and *manipulation* skills such as catching and throwing. The unique part to this model is

the notion of a "*Proficiency Barrier*" after FMS. Seefeldt suggested that the development of basic competence in FMS is a perquisite for future sports and games and FMS are the movement equivalent of the ABCs. That is, a child who cannot run and throw and catch with basic competency is unlikely to engage successfully in sports where these skills are needed. Seefeldt believed the development of basic FMS competence in early childhood years was necessary if the child were to move to higher levels of the pyramid and engage in sports, games, and dances with competency. Acquiring competency in FMS allows children to move through to the last two phases of the model, "*Transitional Skills*" (e.g., those that lead up to soccer, t-ball) and "*Specific Sports Skills and Dances*" of middle childhood and adolescence. Thus, this model highlights the importance of the early childhood years in developing the FMS movement competency necessary for lifelong participation in sports and other physical activities.

Mountain of Motor Development

Clark and Metcalfe (2002) developed one of the most recent models of motor development, a six-phase mountain of motor development model as a metaphorical way to understand the development of motor skills across the lifespan. Their model is based on the dynamical systems framework of multiply-developing systems that self-organize in nonlinear ways. Clark and Metcalfe proposed that progression up the mountain was specific to an individual's experiences and the constraints they experienced along the route. Similar to the Gallahue, Ozmun, and Goodway model, the first two phases of this model consisted of the "*Reflexive*" period and the "*Preadapted*" period; that is, reflexes and reactions shift to voluntary movements ending in the onset of independent walking and self-feeding behaviors. The third phase is the "*fundamental movement*" phase of the model. Like the other two models these FMS are considered key building blocks to later movement. Clark and Metcalfe referred to FMS as the "base camp" of the mountain that provides the basis for later "motor skillfulness" (p. 17). Further up the mountain children begin to apply FMS to "*Context Specific*" environments such as throwing, which becomes pitching in baseball; and ultimately with appropriate experiences, children may develop "*Skillfulness*" (the top of the mountain). Unlike other models, Clark and Metcalfe recognize that no individual becomes skillful across a broad variety of activities. For example a highly proficient gymnast may not be a good volleyball player. Thus, the mountain has different "peaks" (different sports or activities) with each peak being of a different height, reflecting the notion that individuals will have varying levels of skillfulness across different activities. The constraints operating on an individual drive progression up the mountain range and ultimately to a specific mountain peak. Age is not a primary factor in this model as progression is determined by these individual experiences, and not by how long an individual remains on

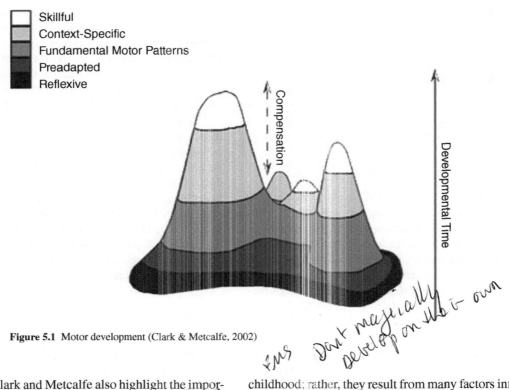

- ☐ Skillful
- ◻ Context-Specific
- ◼ Fundamental Motor Patterns
- ◼ Preadapted
- ◼ Reflexive

Figure 5.1 Motor development (Clark & Metcalfe, 2002)

FMS Don't magically develop on their own

the mountain. Clark and Metcalfe also highlight the importance of early childhood in developing a broad base of FMS by about age 7 years. If these skills are developed, children are well positioned from their "base camp" on the mountain of motor development to navigate many different mountain peaks (sports and physical activities) given sufficient and appropriate experiences (see Figure 5.1).

In conclusion, these three models highlight to the early childhood educator the importance of FMS development during the early childhood years and how FMS competence is critical to lifelong physical activity. But how do these FMS develop? And what can we do to promote motor competence in FMS? In the next part of the chapter we hope to answer some of these questions.

Acquisition of Fundamental Motor Skills

As children approach their second birthdays, marked changes can be observed in how they relate to their surroundings. By the end of the second year, most have mastered the rudimentary movement abilities of infancy. From here, children begin to develop and refine the FMS of early childhood and the specialized movement skills of later childhood and beyond. Two major categories of movement make up FMS. Specifically, *locomotor skills* propel or transfer the body through space or from one point to another (e.g., run, gallop, skip, hop, jump, slide) while *manipulation skills* focus on those skills in which a child manipulates an object with the hands, feet, or other body parts (e.g., catch, throw, kick, strike, dribble, and roll; Gallahue, Ozmun, & Goodway, 2012; Payne & Isaacs, 2008). However, these skills do not naturally "emerge" during early

childhood; rather, they result from many factors influencing the child's motor skill development (Newell, 1984, 1986). Therefore, movement experiences early in one's life play a substantial role in acquisition of FMS (Seefeldt, 1982; Stodden & Goodway, 2007; Stodden, et al., 2008).

Developmental Sequences of FMS

Historically, developmental sequences have been a common way for motor development researchers (e.g., Branta, Gallahue, Halverson, Haubenstricker, Langendorfer, Roberton, Seefeldt, Williams) to examine the emergence of FMS. A developmental sequence is a series of highly predictable movements that are qualitatively different from each other and hierarchically placed in order (Roberton, 1978). There are two kinds of developmental sequences: *interskill* and *intraskill* sequences. Interskill sequences are between skill sequences where motor development researchers have placed different skills in developmental order. For example, first we learn to stand, then walk, and then run. Intraskill sequences consist of "with-in" skill sequences. In the motor development literature this consists of describing common patterns of movement seen for a specific skill like catching; and then placing those patterns in a "developmental sequence" going from more crude and inefficient patterns of movement to more sophisticated and efficient patterns of movement (Roberton, 1978). It is valuable for the early childhood educator to understand both interskill and intraskill sequences.

A variety of different approaches to intraskill developmental sequences in FMS have been utilized in the literature. Gallahue and Ozmun (2006) presented a simple three-stage approach to FMS. This consists of classifying individuals at the "initial," "elementary," or "mature" stage of development. At the "initial" level the skill is just emerging and the child begins to develop some basic elements of the motor skill. By the "elementary" level children have begun to master key aspects of the skill and by the "mature" level they can perform the skills with mechanical efficiency and be able to apply the skill to a variety of different contexts. It is important to remember that children will vary in the age at which they progress through these stages of development.

The Total Body Approach to developmental sequences was developed by Seefeldt, Haubenstricker, Branta and colleagues (see Payne & Isaacs, 2008; Gallahue, Ozmun, & Goodway, 2012). This involves a description of how the body performs in each of the stages of development. The first stage of any sequence is immature and inefficient and the last stage of any skill is more advanced and mechanically efficient. Total body sequences range from a three-stage (skip, gallop), to four-stage (kick, strike, punt, run, jump, hop), or five-stage (throw, catch) sequences. For example, in the throwing example provided at the beginning of the chapter, two of the five stages were described. The immature boy demonstrated a stage 1 "chop throw" while the more advanced boy showed a stage 5 of throwing with windup and a contralateral pattern of movement.

The final approach to developmental sequences is the _segmental or component approach_. Researchers using the component method conceptualized sequences slightly differently by determining developmental sequences for various body segments within a skill (Langendorfer & Roberton, 2002). In this method, specific stage characteristics are determined for each body segment and those stages can be combined in various ways across the total body. In throwing, stages may be identified for each of five different body components: step (4 stages), trunk (3 stages), backswing (4 stages), humerus (3 stages), and forearm (3 stages). For example, the immature child in the scenario at the start of the chapter would be assigned a 1-1-1-1-1 rating. The component method provides rich detail in describing how specific body segments change over time and how one body segment may be linked to another one but can be more challenging to see in the real world of the gymnasium.

All of these different sequential approaches provide excellent information on skill patterns readily identified as children acquire and refine their motor skills. In some cases, such as in research and elite level sport, the component approach may be the best way to examine performance. However, for the early childhood educator, the total body approach may be more readily accessible and easily used to assess the motor skill development of children.

Summary of Total Body Developmental Sequences for Locomotor and Manipulation Skills

Table 5.1 provides a description of the developmental stages for five locomotor skills (run, gallop, skip, hop, jump) and

Table 5.2 for five manipulation skills (catch, throw, kick, punt, strike). While seemingly different, there are strong similarities between the Gallahue and Ozmun approach (initial, elementary, mature) and the total body approach. The "initial" stage of Gallahue and Ozmun's skills can be considered the first stage of the total body approach. The "elementary" stage can be thought of as those stages in the total body approach that are emerging and developing. For a three-stage sequence there will be one stage in the "elementary" level, but in a five-stage sequence there will be three stages in the "elementary" level. The "mature" stage of Gallahue and Ozmun can be correlated with the last stage in the total body approach. Tables 5.1 and 5.2 overlay both approaches. More detail and pictures surrounding these stages can be found in Payne and Isaacs (2008) and Gallahue, Ozmun, and Goodway (2012). Knowledge of these developmental sequences can assist early childhood educators in identifying the correct developmental level of the child, and knowing what will come next in the developmental sequence; thus being able to plan more effectively to move the child to the next level of development.

While developmental sequences provide useful information on skill development, two weaknesses need to be addressed. First, these linear models do not account for the varied performance we often see within a young child from trial to trial. Second, these models do not explain the processes underlying why children vary their performance. Dynamical systems research (Thelen, 1995) has expanded our understanding of motor development patterns and provides a conceptual framework with which to examine the underlying systems that affect pattern shifts. Initial review of developmental sequences as opposed to dynamical systems methods of research often concludes that the two approaches are antithetical to each other. However, we contend that much can be gained by combining the two approaches. Newell (1984, 1986) suggests that FMS emerge within a dynamic system consisting of a specific task, performed by a learner with given characteristics, in a particular environment. In this dynamic systems theory perspective, factors (subsystems) within the learner will influence motor skill development. For example, motivation, strength, and neurological development, are just a few of these many learner factors that may influence the performance. In addition, environmental considerations such as equipment used (e.g., size of the ball), previous experience, and instruction may influence motor development. Both of these two factors (learner and environment) are specific to the task being asked of the performer.

A dynamical systems approach suggests that FMS development occurs in a nonlinear manner. That means that pattern shifts are not thought of in linear terms such as immature to mature (stage 1 to 2 to 3); rather, shifts result in individuals performing in a variety of states commonly called _behavioral attractors_. Attractors are common forms of movement seen in specific situations and are typically comfortable ways of moving to which individuals gravitate

Table 5.1   Summary of Total Body Locomotor Developmental Sequences

Fundamental Motor Skill	Stage 1	Stage 2	Stage 3	Stage 4
Gallahue & Ozmun	Initial Stage	Elementary or Emerging Stages		Mature Stage
Run	*Run High Guard.* Arms – high guard at head height Flat-footed contact. Short Stride. Wide stride-shoulder width apart.	*Run Middle Guard* Arms – middle guard at trunk level. Vertical component still great. Legs near full extension.	*Heel-Toe Arms Extended* Arms -low guard. Arm opposition-elbows nearly extended. Heel-toe contact	*Pumping Arms* Heel-toe contact (sometimes toe-heel when sprinting). Arm-Leg opposition. High heel recovery Elbow flexion at 90 degrees.
Gallop	*Choppy Run-Gallop* Resembles rhythmically uneven run. Trail leg crosses in front of lead leg during airborne phase & remains in front at contact.	*Stiff Back Leg* Slow-moderate tempo, choppy rhythm. Trail leg is stiff. Hips often orientated sideways. Vertical component exaggerated.	*Smooth Rhythmical* Smooth, rhythmical pattern with moderate tempo. Feet remain close to ground. Hips oriented forward.	
Skip	*Broken Skip* Broken skip pattern or irregular rhythm. Slow, deliberate movement. Ineffective arm action.	*High Arms & Legs* Rhythmical skip pattern. Arms provide body lift. Excessive vertical component.	*Rhythmical Skip* Arm action reduced/hands below shoulders. Easy, rhythmical movement. Support foot near surface on hop.	
Hop	*Foot in Front* Non-support foot in front with thigh parallel to floor. Body erect. Hands shoulder height.	Foot by Support Leg Non-support knee flexed with knee in front and foot behind support leg. Slight body lean forward. Bilateral arm action.	*Foot Behind Support Leg* Non-support thigh vertical with free foot behind support leg, knee flexed. More body lean forward. Bilateral arm action.	*Pendular Free Leg* Non-support leg is bent and knee pumps forward & back in a pendular action. Forward body lean. Arm opposition with swing leg.
Long Jump	*Braking Arms* Arms act as "brakes" moving toward trunk on jump. Large vertical component. Legs not extended.	*Winging Arms* Arms act as "wings" to side of body. Vertical component still great. Legs near full extension.	*Arms Swing to Head* Arms move forward/elbows in front of trunk at take-off. Hands to head height. Take-off angle still above 45 degrees. Legs often fully extended.	*Full Body Extension* Complete arm and leg extension at take-off. Take-off near 45 degree angle. Thighs parallel to surface when feet contact for landing.

as they practice moving. For example, an early attractor in catching is to "hug" the ball with the arms (stage 2, see Table 5.2) before a child moves to a more complex attractor of catching the ball with the hands (stage 4). Shifts from one attractor to another may occur in any direction (more advanced or regressive) dependent upon all impinging factors that affect that skill. For example, if a child is tossed a large ball they may "hug" the ball into their arms. However, if tossed a bean bag they may hand catch. Strong attractors are ones that are so embedded that it is difficult to shift that person out of that state. Weak attractors are patterns of movement we may see occasionally, but they are not as stable or as strong attractors and can more readily be changed by environmental and learner constraints. We believe the total body stages in Table 5.1 and 5.2 reflect the most common and most strong *attractors*.

Reconceptualizing stages of developmental sequences into the notion of various attractors provides a better interpretation of what we see as we watch young children perform motor skills. This dynamic approach also supports the idea that teachers can manipulate environmental and task constraints to help move children into new attractors that are more beneficial to the demands of a specific task. Thus, under a dynamic systems paradigm, children choose

from an array of movement patterns (the developmental stages) to select the most appropriate pattern to achieve the task at hand. Our job as teachers is to assist children in developing a large array of movement patterns from which they can select. Therefore, it is important for practitioners to consider not only the task but other constraints, when identifying what pattern should be employed to execute a skill. Constraints can be used and manipulated to assist teachers in understanding the development of FMS and teaching FMS.

Instructional Application of Fundamental Motor Skills

Now that we have a better conceptual understanding of how FMS develop, it may be valuable to understand how the notion of developmental sequences and behavioral attractors can be used instructionally. Let us continue with the throwing as an example. Table 5.2 describes the five stages of throwing a ball starting with an inefficient "chop throw" (stage 1) and ending in a mechanically efficient throwing pattern with arm–leg opposition and windup and follow through (stage 5). From a dynamic systems perspective each of these five different patterns of throwing are movement options for a child assuming they can perform all five

Table 5.2   Summary of Total Body Manipulative Developmental Stages

Fundamental Motor Skill	Stage 1	Stage 2	Stage 3	Stage 4	S
Gallahue & Ozmun	**Initial Stage**	**Elementary or Merging States**			**Mature Sta...**
Throw	*Chop* Vertical wind-up of arm. "Chop" throwing pattern. Feet stationary. Front facing & no spinal rotation.	*Sling Shot* Horizontal wind-up. "Sling shot throw" with body oriented sideways. Block Rotation of trunk. Follow-through across body.	*Ipsilateral Step* High wind up of arm. Ipsilateral step. Little spinal rotation. Follow-through across body.	*Contralateral Step* High wind up of arm. Contralateral step. Little spinal rotation. Follow-through across body.	*Wind Up* Downward arc wind up of arm. Contralateral step. Segmented body rotation. Arm-Leg Follow-through.
Catch	*Delayed Reaction* Delayed arm action. Arms straight in front until ball contact, then scooping action to chest. Feet stationary. Head often turns to side.	*Hugging* Arms encircle ball as it approaches. Ball is "hugged" to chest. Feet are stationary or may take one step.	*Scooping* "To chest" catch. Arms "scoop" under ball to trap it to chest. Single step may be used to approach the ball.	*Hand Catch* Initial contact with ball is with hands only. Hand catch of balls tossed to trunk. Feet stationary or limited to one step. Would not catch a ball tossed to side of body.	*Move to Ball* Tracks flight of ball & moves body under ball. Catch with hands only. Fine adjustment of fingers to ball position as ball is caught.
Kick	*Stationary Push* Little/No leg wind up. Stationary position. Foot "pushes" ball. Step backward after kick (usually).	*Stationary Leg Swing* Leg wind-up to the rear. Stationary position. Opposition of arms and legs.	*Moving Approach* Moving approach to ball. Foot travels in a low arc. Arm/Leg opposition. Forward or sideward step on follow-through.	*Leap-Kick-Hop* Rapid approach. Backward trunk lean during wind-up. Leap before kick. Hop after kick.	
Punt	*Yoking-Push* No leg wind-up. Ball toss erratic. Body stationary. Push ball/step back.	*Stationary Leg* Swing Leg wind-up to the rear. Ball toss still erratic. Body stationary. Forceful kick attempt.	*Moving Approach* Preparatory step(s) to ball. Some arm/leg yoking. Ball is tossed or droped.	*Leap-Punt-Hop* Rapid approach to the ball. Controlled drop of ball. Leap before ball contact. Hop after ball contact.	

(this will not necessarily be true for younger children). If a child is asked to throw for distance and force they would most likely select stage 5 from the movement options if capable as this pattern of throwing is most mechanically efficient. However, if you placed a child 5 feet from a wall and asked him or her to hit it with a ball, they would most likely choose from stages 1 to 3 as little force is required to achieve the stated task, and arm–leg opposition (stages 4 or 5) is not necessary. Thus, one of the first things a teacher must understand is that the movement option selected by the child will be driven, in part, by the nature of the task given. When trying to promote a specific pattern of performance the teacher needs to carefully design tasks that will promote the desired movement outcome. For example, to promote a stage 5 throw you might hang a sheet with bells on it, put a sticker on the opposite foot and hand, place a child further from the target, and encourage them to "step and throw hard" and make the bells jingle loudly.

Teachers need to undergo a five-step process in developing movement activities for young children: (1) observe and evaluate the developmental level of the child—e.g., stage 2 catch "hugging"; (2) identify the desired performance (attractor) for the child to perform—e.g., stage 4, "catching with the hands"; (3) consider what learner factors might be influencing the child—e.g., poor fine motor control, inability to track the ball in flight, fear of being hit in the face by the ball; (4) consider how to manipulate aspects of the environment to promote hand catching— e.g., have a large, squishy ball, place the tosser close to the child, toss slowly, cue the child "hands out, reach for the ball"; and (5) watch the child perform the task and modify it to make it more difficult or easier based upon your observations.

As can be seen from the above example, understanding the emergence of FMS is very valuable to the early childhood teacher in being able to identify the pattern of the child's performance, identify what comes next in the developmental sequence, and develop engaging and developmentally appropriate learning experiences for the child. There are many good resources to assist the early childhood teacher in providing developmentally appropriate instructional activities including lesson ideas provided by the following professional organizations:

- National Association of Sport and Physical Education (http://www.aahperd.org/naspe/)
- Physical education website—PE Central (http://www.pecentral.org/)
- Head Start Body Start (http://www.aahperd.org/headstartbodystart/)

In summary, during the early childhood years the key element is to develop basic competency and efficient body mechanics in a wide variety of FMS (Stodden et al., 2008). The locomotor and manipulation patterns identified above in Tables 5.1 and 5.2 are examples of FMS movement abilities first mastered separately by the child. These basic skills are then gradually combined and enhanced in a variety of ways to become more complex and specialized movement skills that are used in daily living, recreational, and sport activities (Seefeldt & Haubenstricker, 1982; Stodden et al., 2008). Although most typically developing children have the potential to develop the most proficient stage in most FMS, it is critically important that they have ample opportunities for practice and quality instruction in a caring and nurturing environment. As such a developmentally based physical education program should be a central component of young children's early education. Children who are skillful movers have the basic FMS building blocks necessary for an active way of life that maximizes their individual potential in terms of physical fitness and regular participation in physical activity (Gallahue, 1982; Stodden, et al., 2008).

Gender Differences in Fundamental Motor Skills and Physical Activity

Like other academic skills, gender differences exist in FMS development with boys demonstrating superior skills to girls in some areas (Seefeldt & Haubenstricker, 1982; Thomas & French, 1985). Thomas and French (1985) completed a meta-analysis of the throwing literature suggesting that gender differences exist as early as 3 years of age, increase with age, and favor males. These gender trends are found in other manipulative skills such as striking and kicking (Seefeldt & Haubenstricker, 1982), and throwing (Garcia & Garcia, 2002; Halverson, Roberton, & Langendorfer, 1982; Langendorfer & Roberton, 2002). A number of studies have suggested that biological factors such as muscular strength, joint diameters, shoulder: hip ratio, and percent body fat may account for these gender differences (Thomas & French, 1985). Others suggest environmental sources such as practice opportunities and sociocultural factors (Payne & Isaacs, 2008; Williams, Haywood, & Painter, 1996). Williams et al. (1996) suggested that gender differences are present because boys practice these skills more than girls, which leads boys to be more proficient movers. Although information is limited on young children, Beunen and Thomis (2000) reported that from 3 to 6 years of age there are minimal sex differences in strength and that strength gradually increases from year to year. In contrast, others (Armstrong & Welsman, 2000; Blimke & Sale, 1998) reported sex-related differences in favor of boys as young as 3 years of age.

Certain skills seem to present a greater magnitude of gender difference than other skills; throwing is one of those skills. Haubenstricker, Branta, and Seefeldt (1983) conducted a wide-scale study on throwing and found that 60% of boys exhibited the most mature throwing patterns around age 5, while 60% of girls do not reach the same pattern until the age of 8.5 years. The study aligned with the earlier work from Halverson et al. (1982) and found that boys perform more efficient and sophisticated throwing behaviors at an earlier age. The differences between genders are also seen in catching, this time in favor of girls. Haubenstricker et al. (1983) found that in early childhood girls moved through the early stages of catching before boys (this is one of the few skills where girls are in advance of boys). Other sociocultural factors may contribute to the gender differences reported. Nelson, Thomas, and Nelson (1991) suggested that the presence of a male adult in the home environment significantly predicted FMS development of young children. Early work from East and Hensley (1985) found that the presence of an active father figure in a girl's life accounted for 25% of the variance in females' motor skill performance.

More recent data on the FMS of preschool children in Head Start found differential gender effects between locomotor and manipulative skills across ethnicity and region (Goodway, Robinson, & Crowe, 2010; Robinson & Goodway, 2009). Goodway and her colleagues have consistently found there were no gender differences in locomotor skills but boys had significantly better manipulation skills than did girls (Goodway & Branta, 2003; Goodway, Crowe, & Ward, 2003; Goodway, Robinson, & Crowe, 2010; Robinson & Goodway, 2009). It is not clear from the research literature why this is so, but for the past decade these findings have remained consistent across geographic region and ethnicity. Locomotor skills are considered to be more phylogenetic (based upon neurological/genetic factors) than manipulative skills. The opportunity to practice locomotor skills requires available space to run, gallop, and jump but does not require equipment. Thus, it may be that girls and boys had equal opportunities to engage in locomotor skills within their respective communities. In contrast, potential explanations as to gender differences in manipulation skills may be factors such as biological differences between gender, differential access to equipment, role models, and motivational factors. Anecdotal comments from Goodway's research with preschoolers suggest that boys typically come to the testing environment with a greater familiarity of the vocabulary and equipment associated with manipulation skill performance than girls, perhaps suggesting prior experience plays a role in these findings (Goodway, Robinson, & Crowe, 2010). Other alternative explanations for gender differences in FMS may be that girls tend to be driven by more social factors in the learning environment (e.g., pleasing the teacher, receiving verbal encouragement, and smiles); while boys are more motivated by competition and the product of the performance (Garcia, 1994; Garcia & Garcia, 2002).

Developmental Delay in Disadvantaged Preschoolers

Children whose families qualify for Head Start programs are identified as being at-risk for delay in demonstrating (or developing) the requisite academic and social skills for future educational success (IDEA, 2004). This is also true in the motor realm. Preschool children enrolled in Head Start programs demonstrate developmental delays in their FMS, the foundational skills necessary for engagement in lifelong physical activity (Goodway & Branta, 2003; Goodway, Crowe, & Ward, 2003; Goodway, Robinson, & Crowe, 2010; Hamilton, Goodway, & Haubenstricker, 1999; Robinson & Goodway, 2009). Typically, developmental delay is identified when a child is below the 25th percentile (Ulrich, 2000) or 30th percentile (Individuals with Disabilities Education Act [IDEA], 2004) for same-aged peers with children between the 25th and 75th percentile considered typically developing. Children with such developmental delays require intervention to remediate those skills (Goodway, Robinson, & Crowe, 2010; Ulrich, 2000).

A fairly large scale study of the FMS of 275 preschool children enrolled in Head Start found that preschoolers were between the 10th to 17th percentile for locomotor skills and around the 16th percentile for manipulative skills (Goodway, Robinson, & Crowe, 2010). A review of the frequency data revealed that overall, 85% of the African American Midwestern preschoolers were developmentally delayed in manipulative skills (92% of the girls and 78% of boys). For locomotor data, 88% of Midwestern participants were delayed (90% of girls and 87% of boys). Similar findings were true for Southwestern Hispanic participants with 84% of participants being delayed in manipulative development (95% of girls and 72% of boys) and 91% in locomotor skills (92% of girls and 89% of boys). From these data, clearly a sizeable number of preschool children in Head Start were delayed in manipulative and locomotor skill development. Similar to the findings for gender above, the patterns found in the current study have remained fairly consistent for both African American and Hispanic populations, across regions, cities within the same region, and time (Goodway & Branta, 2003; Goodway, Crowe, & Ward, 2003; Hamilton et al., 1999; Robinson & Goodway, 2009). Based on this evidence, young children served by Head Start require motor skill intervention to remediate the developmental delays found in FMS.

Further research should attempt to gain a better understanding of the underlying mechanisms influencing the FMS of these children if motor interventions are to be successful. There has been no empirical data to explain the underlying mechanisms accounting for these delays, but clearly constraints are operating that are consistent across populations. Perhaps one of the most consistent and powerful constraints is that the child is being reared in a financially impoverished environment. It has also been hypothesized that disadvantaged preschool children are exposed to a variety of other environmental constraints that influence their motor development negatively (Goodway & Branta, 2003; Goodway, Crowe, & Ward, 2003). For example, lack of safe places to play and be active in the community, limited activity role models (especially for females), lack of access to motor skill programs; thus, no instruction or feedback on their motor skills may all contribute to these delays (Branta & Goodway, 1996; Goodway & Smith, 2005). Biological factors that stem from infancy such as poor prenatal care, small for gestational age at birth, and prematurity could be other constraints influencing the children.

But why are developmental delays in FMS of particular long term concern for this population of children? The delays reported above suggest that these populations of young children do not demonstrate the requisite competency in FMS to be able to break through Seefeldt's (1982) hypothetical proficiency barrier discussed under the models section above. That is, delays in motor development are a limiting factor in supporting children's success in ongoing sport and physical activity behaviors. It is interesting to note the parallel between the FMS delays found with African American/Hispanic preschool children who live in urban centers and their adolescent counterparts (poor, urban, African American, Hispanic) who demonstrate low levels of physical activity and high levels of obesity during the adolescent years (Anderson & Butcher, 2006; U.S. Department of Health & Human Services [USDHHS], 1996). We have yet to understand the underlying mechanisms and implications of low motor competence in the early years but it may be such low competence tracks into the adolescent years resulting in these children dropping out of sport and physical activity because it is not enjoyable and they are successful (refer to Stodden et al., 2008; Stodden & Goodway, 2007 for further elaboration of these ideas).

Motor Skill Intervention in Disadvantaged Preschoolers

An emerging body of evidence has led to an examination of the influence of motor skill intervention on the FMS of disadvantaged preschool children. These studies show that when motorically delayed preschool children receive well designed motor skill instruction, they can remediate these delays in FMS (Connor-Kuntz & Dummer, 1996; Goodway & Branta, 2003; Goodway, Crowe, & Ward, 2003; Hamilton et al., 1999; Robinson & Goodway, 2009). These motor skill interventions have taken place over 8 to 12 weeks with 16 to 24 sessions in total. The majority have focused on manipulation skills although some have also included locomotor skills. A variety of instructional techniques have been utilized to deliver the motor skill interventions including: (1) *direct instruction* (Connor-Kuntz & Dummer, 1996; Goodway & Branta, 2003; Goodway, Crowe, & Ward, 2003); (2) *mastery motivational climate* (Martin, Rudisill, & Hastie, 2009; Robinson & Goodway, 2009;

Valentini & Rudisill, 2004a; 2004b), and (3) *parents as teachers* (Hamilton et al., 1999).

Direct instruction in motor skills involves a teacher-oriented approach to teaching motor skills where the teacher clearly describes and demonstrates the task to be performed and the children respond accordingly (Graham, Holt-Hale, & Parker, 2007). In this setting the children do not have any choices or preferences to select a task or activity and the teacher instructs each element of the lesson (Graham et al., 2007). An example of a direct instruction motor skill program is the Successful Instruction for Preschoolers (*SKIP*) program developed by Goodway and her colleagues (Goodway & Branta, 2003; Goodway, Crowe, & Ward, 2003; Goodway & Robinson, 2006). One 45-minute SKIP lesson might look like this: (1) all children perform a 10-minute warm-up to music or a simple game to promote instant activity and get the heart rate up; (2) children are divided into three groups and assigned to one of three skill-stations (e.g., kick, catch, or throw); (3) tasks at all stations are explained and demonstrated by the teacher; (4) children go to the first station and engage in 10 minutes of skill activity/development at that station, the teacher rotates around providing feedback and refining tasks to meet the children's needs; (5) children complete three, 10-minute rotations going to each station, and (6) at the end of the lesson the teacher gathers the children for the debrief and final feedback (Goodway & Branta, 2003; Goodway, Crowe, & Ward, 2003; Goodway & Robinson, 2006).

On the other hand, students in a mastery motivational climate approach have student-centered instruction in which they have high autonomy to complete tasks and activities based on their preferences (Valentini & Rudisill, 2004a, 2004b). Several levels of challenge are also incorporated into the instruction (Valentini, Rudisill, & Goodway, 1999). The mastery motivation climate is developed by manipulating six Task, Authority, Recognition Grouping, Evaluation, Time (TARGET) structures within the lesson. The rationale behind this mastery motivational approach is that the instructional climate promotes students' motivation to engage in tasks and regulate their own pace of learning. For further information on motor-based mastery motivational climate refer to Valentini, Rudisill, and Goodway (1999). A 45-minute lesson example of mastery motivational climate might involve the following elements: (1) the teacher sets up three skills stations (e.g. kick, catch, throw) and at each station there are three to five levels of a task that vary the difficulty of the task (e.g., in catching different size balls thrown from different distances); (2) children perform a large-group 10-minute warm-up to music or a simple game to promote instant activity and get the heart rate up; (3) tasks at all stations are explained and demonstrated by the teacher; (4) over the next 30 minutes children are free to go to any station, select any task, and work with any child while the teacher acts as a facilitator providing feedback, suggesting new tasks, and encouraging the children to attempt different levels of tasks most appropriate to the individual's

level; and (5) at the end of the lesson, the teacher gathers the children for the debrief and final feedback (Robinson & Goodway, 2009; Valentini & Rudisill, 2004a, 2004b; Valentini, Rudisill, & Goodway, 1999).

Parental involvement is another approach to deliver motor skill instruction (Hamilton et al., 1999). Parent assisted instruction utilizes "parents" (i.e., mother, father, or primary caregiver) as the primary instructors of their children. Parents undergo parent training to learn about motor skill development and ways in which to work with their child. A lead teacher develops the lesson plans (which are very similar to the direct instruction outlined above), and acts as a facilitator to parents who instruct their child. The lead teacher moves around the gymnasium and makes sure the parent–child dyad is performing the activities according to the lesson plan and may step in and model appropriate instruction for parents when necessary.

All the motor skill intervention approaches identified above have been successful in significantly impacting the FMS development of disadvantaged preschoolers. In all of these interventions maximum opportunities to respond were provided, and as much as possible children had their own piece of equipment and tasks that were individualized to their own developmental needs. Goodway and Branta (2003) reported that African American preschoolers in a compensatory preschool program in the motor intervention group significantly increased their locomotor skills from the 15th to 80th percentile ($p<.001$) and their manipulative skills from the 17th to the 80th percentile ($p<.001$) from pre- to posttest. In contrast, the comparison group consisting of children in the same compensatory preschool who received the regular preschool curricula made no significant change. Goodway, Crowe, and Ward (2003) showed similar findings with Hispanic preschoolers in the intervention group significantly improving their locomotor skills from the 7th to 50th percentile and their object control skills from the 11th to 60th percentile ($p < .001$). Again, no significant change occurred in the comparison group children who received the regular Head Start curriculum. The parent-taught motor skill intervention (Hamilton et al., 1999) resulted in manipulative skills improving from the 20th to the 67th percentile. In contrast, the control participants did not improve their manipulative skills. A recent study (Robinson & Goodway, 2009) compared mastery motivational climate intervention to direct instruction (low autonomy). The findings showed that both mastery and low autonomy interventions yielded significantly better manipulative skills as compared to the control group that participated in the regular Head Start program. However, there were no significant differences between the two intervention groups, which demonstrated that both direct instruction and mastery motivational approaches to motor skill instruction were equally effective. Some general conclusions may be drawn from the studies identified above: (1) preschool children who attend Head Start are delayed in their motor skills and need intervention; (2)

when provided with developmentally appropriate motor instruction in their Head Start programs these children can make significant and often large gains in their motor skills remediating their prior delays; and (3) the children in the control groups who received the typical Head Start curricula where physical activity opportunities were often nonfacilitated and play-based, resulted in no improvements to FMS development. The latter point is particularly important as it suggests that play-based approaches to promoting motor skills in preschools across the country are unlikely to yield any positive effects. That is, just providing children with opportunities to play on the playground (even with motor equipment such as balls and bats) does not change the children's motor development (National Association for Sport and Physical Education [NASPE], 2009). Like any other academic skill, if motor skills are to be improved the following must occur: (1) thoughtful planning of motor skill development; (2) selection of a variety of good tasks aligned with the developmental level of the children; (3) many opportunities to practice a wide range of skills with maximum opportunities to respond; (4) teacher facilitation and demonstration of skills; (5) individual feedback on performance; and (6) reward structures or other motivational techniques (NASPE, 2009). It is also helpful when children are allowed to make choices within the instructional environment, self-monitor, and engage in self-assessment. In other words, without this kind of facilitated approach to motor development, in many children motor skills will not naturally emerge. If young children do not develop the requisite FMS competence then we may be placing this vulnerable population of children at greater risk for physical inactivity later in life.

Physical Activity and Physical Activity Guidelines in Early Childhood

In line with findings on older children, there has been a significant rise in the obesity levels of young children (Anderson & Butcher, 2006). Correspondingly, scholars have begun to focus increasing attention on the physical activity levels of young children and the factors associated with physical activity (Pate, O'Neill, & Mitchell, 2010; Reilly, 2010; Trost, Ward, & Senso, 2010; Ward, Vaughn, McWilliams, & Hales, 2010). Accurately evaluating the physical activity of young children presents some unique challenges as some of the common movements of this age group (swinging, climbing, sliding, playing in the sand pit, etc.) are often not detectable by typical evaluation methods of assessment such as accelerometers (Pate et al., 2010). More recently progress has been made in developing specific measurement techniques for such young children and a review by Pate et al. provides a summary of these issues (Pate et al., 2010). But how much activity is recommended for children in early childhood?

In 2009 the National Association of Sport and Physical Education (NASPE) revised "Active Start," a set of national physical activity guidelines for children aged 0 to 5 years. Overall, NASPE recommend that:

> All children from birth to age 5 should engage in daily physical activity that promotes movement skillfulness and foundations of health-related fitness.

The guidelines are different for infants (0–1 years), toddlers (1–3 years), and preschoolers (3–5 years). In each age category five guidelines are identified dealing with structured activity, unstructured activity, development of motor skills, safe places to be active, and education of caregivers. The following are a summary of the five physical activity guidelines for preschoolers (NASPE, 2009). Preschoolers should:

- Accumulate at least 60 minutes of structured physical activity per day.
- Engage in at least 60 minutes and up to several hours of unstructured physical activity per day and should not be sedentary for more than 60 minutes at a time except when sleeping.
- Develop competence in fundamental motor skills that will serve as the building blocks for future motor skillfulness and physical activity.
- Have indoor and outdoor areas that meet or exceed recommended safety standards for performing large muscle activities.
- Have caregivers in charge of their health and well-being who understand the importance of physical activity and promote movement skills by providing opportunities for structured and unstructured physical activity.

It is not possible within the limits of this chapter to summarize in detail the literature on early childhood physical activity. However, three recent reviews of the literature capture the major findings in this area and will point the reader to other relevant readings.

Reilly (2010) conducted a review of objectively measured physical activity and sedentary behavior in 3- to 6-year-olds during the childcare day yielding 12 articles and 13 studies involving more than 96 different child cares and more than 1,900 children. He concluded that children in child care get low levels of moderate to vigorous physical activity (MVPA) and high levels of sedentary behaviors. Specifically, in 9 of the studies children received less than 60 minutes of MVPA in an 8-hour childcare day (Reilly, 2010). Reilly also suggested that across populations and settings common features in the childcare settings have acted as barriers to promoting physical activity. However, both within and between studies there was variability in physical activity levels and future studies should attempt to identify these modifiable features in the childcare environment that might promote higher levels of physical activity.

Ward and colleagues (2010) reviewed the literature (N = 19 articles) surrounding interventions for increasing physical activity in childcare settings. Eight physical activity intervention-based studies were found, eight with physical activity-related outcomes, five with motor skill outcomes, and two with multiple outcomes. The majority of intervention studies produced positive outcomes tied to increasing physical activity (Ward et al., 2010). Twelve of the studies used a formal curriculum to increase daily total physical activity, motor skill development, or some other activity related outcome. Interestingly, programs that were more successful in increasing physical activity provided more frequency and duration of structured physical activity. Despite this, in the studies with higher amounts of structured physical activity, the amount of physical activity was still below the NASPE "Active Start" (2009) recommendations for preschoolers. The authors suggested that early childhood educators and scholars need to examine the childcare day to look at the balance between structured physical activity and children's free play. Other recommendations were to consider the extent to which a focus on academic skills reduced the time to be active, the role of policy in promoting physical activity, and the issue of well-trained staff to implement physical activity programming. Overall, Ward et al. suggested "cautious optimism" in interpreting findings due to the early nature of this body of literature and research design limitations (e.g., nonrandom assignment) in the studies reviewed. They suggested that further research is necessary before strong conclusions can be drawn and policy developed.

Trost, Ward, and Senso (2010) summarized the literature on childcare policy and the environment on children's physical activity. Only seven studies were found. Trost et al. suggested that several factors may account for between center variability in physical activity. Higher staff education, staff training on physical activity, and staff behavior on the playground appear to be positively correlated with increased physical activity levels. Teachers who prompted children to be active and had less conversation with them were associated with more activity. The findings on the physical environment were equivocal. In some cases less children per square meter of space and open vegetated areas were tied to more activity, in other cases this was not the case. Interestingly, despite the large amount of money spent on fixed playground structures, these structures were not reported to be associated with increased levels of physical activity. However the presence of portable play equipment was tied to physical activity. Trost and colleagues emphasized the importance of children having access to outdoor playtime but suggested multiple outdoor breaks may be more effective than a single episode, even if it is extended in nature. As with the other reviews, the authors suggested this is a new science and methodological inadequacies and the small numbers of studies mean caution should be exerted in making conclusions in this area.

Getting an "Active Start" in the Early Childhood Years

We believe the early years are critical to the lifelong health and physical activity of this nation's children. The area of motor skills is so often misunderstood, with the common misconception being that if we let children out to play, basic motor skills will naturally develop during the early childhood years. In this chapter, we have reviewed theoretical and empirical support on the emergence of FMS, how FMS may not emerge in a timely sequence in some populations, and the variety of factors that affect motor skill development. In addition, we have reviewed the developmental sequences of FMS and their practical application, along with a summary of the physical activity levels of young children. We also hope that we have provided motivation to design facilitated motor skill programming to promote FMS competence during early childhood. We believe that one marker of a high quality early childhood program is one where children receive regular *structured* (facilitated) motor skill instruction along with many opportunities to engage in *unstructured* physical activity experiences throughout the day (NASPE, 2009). Also, that the teachers of this program are knowledgeable about motor skill development and become important role models to their children in this important and often ignored area of development. Most importantly, we believe that FMS development is too important to be left to chance if we are truly concerned about increasing young children's level of physical activity and giving all young children an "Active Start" to life.

References

Anderson, P. M., & Butcher, K. F. (2006). Childhood obesity: Trends and potential causes. *The Future of Children: Childhood Obesity, 16,* 19–45.

Armstrong, N., & Welsman, J.R. (2000). Development of aerobic fitness during childhood and adolescence. *Pediatric Exercise Science, 12,* 128–149.

Beunen, G., & Thomis, M. (2000). Muscular strength development in children and adolescents. *Pediatric Exercise Science, 12,* 174–197.

Blimkie, C. J. R., & Sale, D. G. (1998). Strength development and trainability during childhood. In E. Van Praagh (Ed.), *Pediatric anaerobic performance* (pp. 193–224). Champaign, IL: Human Kinetics.

Branta, C. F., & Goodway, J. D. (1996). Facilitating social skills in urban school children through physical education. *Peace & Conflict: Journal of Peace Psychology, 2,* 305–319.

Clark, J. E., & Metcalfe, J. S. (2002). The mountain of motor development: A metaphor. In J. E. Clark & J. H. Humphrey (Eds.), *Motor development: Research and review* (Vol. 2, pp. 62–95). Reston, VA: NASPE.

Clark, J. E., & Whitall, J. (1989). What is motor development: The lessons of history. *Quest, 41,* 183–202.

Conner-Kuntz, F., & Dummer, G. (1996). Teaching across the curriculum: Language-enriched physical education for preschool children. *Adapted Physical Activity Quarterly, 13,* 302–315.

East, W. B., & Hensley, L. D. (1985). The effects of selected sociocultural factors upon the overhand-throwing performance of prepubescent children. In J. E. Clark & J. H. Humphrey (Eds.), *Motor development: Current selected research:* (Vol. 1, pp. 115–128). Princeton, NJ: Princeton Book Company.

Gallahue, D. L. (1982). *Developmental movement experiences for children.* New York: Wiley.

Gallahue, D. L., Ozmun, J. C., & Goodway, J. D. (2012). *Understanding motor development: Infants, children, adolescent and adults* (7th ed.). Boston, MA: McGraw-Hill.

Garcia, C. (1994). Gender differences in young children's interaction when learning fundamental motor skills. *Research Quarterly for Exercise & Sport, 65,* 213–225.

Garcia, C., & Garcia, L. (2002). Examining developmental changes in throwing. In J. E. Clark & J. H. Humphrey (Eds.), *Motor development: Research and review* (Vol. 2, pp. 62–95). Reston, VA: NASPE.

Goodway, J. D., & Branta, C. F. (2003). Influence of a motor skill intervention on fundamental motor skill development of disadvantaged preschool children. *Research Quarterly for Exercise & Sport, 74*, 36–47.

Goodway, J. D., Crowe, H., & Ward, P. (2003). Effects of motor skill instruction on fundamental motor skill development. *Adapted Physical Activity Quarterly, 20*, 298–314.

Goodway J. D., & Robinson, L. E. (2006). *S*KIPing toward an active start: Promoting physical activity in preschoolers. *Beyond the Journal: Young Children, 61*, 1–6.

Goodway, J. D., Robinson, L. E., & Crowe, H. (2010). Developmental delays in fundamental motor skill development of ethnically diverse and disadvantaged preschoolers. *Research Quarterly for Exercise & Sport, 81*, 17–25.

Goodway, J. D., & Smith, D. W. (2005). Keeping all children healthy: Challenges to leading an active lifestyle for preschool children qualifying for at-risk programs. *Family & Community Health, 28*, 142–155.

Graham, G., Holt-Hale, S. A., & Parker, M. (2007). *Children moving: A reflective approach to teaching physical education* (5th ed.). Mountain View, CA: Mayfield.

Halverson, L. E., Roberton, M. A., & Langendorfer, S. (1982). Development of the overhand throw: Movement and ball velocity changes by seventh grade. *Research Quarterly for Exercise & Sport, 53*, 198–205.

Hamilton, M., Goodway, J. D., & Haubenstricker, J. (1999). Parent-assisted instruction in a motor skill program for at-risk preschool children. *Adapted Physical Activity Quarterly, 16*, 415–426.

Haubenstricker, J. L., Branta, C. F., & Seefeldt, V. D. (1983). *Standards of performance for throwing and catching.* Paper presented at the Annual Conference of the North American Society for Psychology of Sport and Physical Activity, Asilomar, CA.

Haywood, K. M., & Getchell, N. (2009). *Lifespan motor development* (5th ed.). Champaign, IL: Human Kinetics.

Individuals with Disabilities Education Act of 2004 (IDEA)—Part C and H. Pub. L. 108-446. 3. Dec. 2004. 118 Stat. 2647. Retrieved from http://idea.ed.gov

Langendorfer, S. J., & Roberton, M. A. (2002). Developmental profiles in overarm throwing: Searching for "attractors," "stages," and "constraints." In J. E. Clark & J. H. Humphrey (Eds.), *Motor development: Research and review* (Vol. 2, pp.1–25). Reston, VA: NASPE.

Malina, R. M., Bouchard, C. L., & Bar-Or, O. (2004). *Growth, maturation, and physical activity* (2nd ed.). Champaign, IL: Human Kinetics.

Martin, E. H., Rudisill, M. E., & Hastie, P., (2009). The effectiveness of a mastery motivational climate motor skill intervention in a naturalistic physical education setting. *Physical Education and Sport Pedagogy, 14*, 227–240.

National Association for Sport and Physical Education (NASPE). (2009). *Active start: A statement of physical activity guidelines for children birth to five years* (2nd ed.). Oxon Hill, MD: AAHPERD.

Nelson, J. D., Thomas, J. R., & Nelson, K. R. (1991). Longitudinal change in throwing performance: Gender differences. *Research Quarterly for Exercise & Sport, 62*, 105–108.

Newell, K. M. (1984). Physical constraints to development of motor skills. In J. Thomas (Ed.), Motor development during preschool and elementary years (pp. 105–120). Minneapolis, MN: Burgess.

Newell, K. M. (1986). Constraints on the development of coordination. In M. G. Wade & H. T. Whiting (Eds.), *Motor development in children: Aspects of coordination and control* (pp. 341–360). Dordrecht, the Netherlands: Nijhoff.

Pate, R. R., O'Neill, J. R., & Mitchell, J. (2010). Measurement of physical activity in preschool children. *Medicine & Science in Sports & Exercise, 42*, 508–512.

Payne, V. G., & Isaacs, L. D. (2008). *Human motor development: A lifespan approach* (7th ed.). Boston, MA: McGraw-Hill.

Reilly, J. J. (2010). Low levels of objectively measured physical activity in preschoolers in child care. *Medicine & Science in Sports & Exercise, 42*, 502–507.

Roberton, M. A. (1978). Stages in motor development. In M. V. Ridenour (Ed.), *Motor development: Issues and Applications* (pp. 63–81). Princeton, NJ: Princeton Book Company.

Roberton, M. A. (1982). Describing "stages" within and across motor tasks. In J. A. S. Kelso & J. E. Clark (Eds.), *The development of movement control and co-ordination* (pp. 294–307). New York: Wiley.

Robinson, L. E., & Goodway, J. D. (2009). Instructional climates in preschool children who are at risk. Part I: object control skill development. *Research Quarterly for Exercise & Sport, 80*, 533–542.

Seefeldt, V. (1982). The concepts of readiness applied to motor skill acquisition. In R. A. Magill, M. J. Ash, & F. L. Smoll (Eds.), *Children in sport* (pp. 31–37). Champaign, IL: Human Kinetics.

Seefeldt, V., & Haubenstricker, J. (1982). Patterns, phases, or stages: An analytic model for the study of developmental movement. In J. A. S. Kelso & J. E. Clark (Eds.), *The development of movement control and co-ordination* (pp. 309–318). New York: Wiley.

Stodden, D. F., & Goodway, J. D (2007). The dynamic association between motor skill development and physical activity. *Journal of Physical Education, Recreation and Dance, 78*, 33–49.

Stodden, D. F., Goodway, J. D., Langendorfer, S. J., Roberton, M. A., Rudisill, M. E, Garcia, C., & Garcia L. E. (2008). A developmental perspective on the role of motor skill competence in physical activity: An emergent relationship. *Quest, 60*, 290–306.

Thomas, J. R., & French, K. E. (1985). Gender differences across age in motor performance: A meta-analysis. *Psychological Bulletin, 98*, 260–282.

Thelen, E. (1995). Motor development: A new synthesis. *American Psychologist, 50*, 79–95.

Trost, S. G., Ward, D. S., & Senso, M. (2010). Effects of child care policy and environment on physical activity. *Medicine & Science in Sports & Exercise, 42*, 520–525.

Ulrich, D. (2000). *Test of Gross Motor Development-2*. Austin, TX: Pro-Ed.

U.S Department of Health and Human Services. (1996). *Physical activity and health: A report of the Surgeon General*. Atlanta, GA: Centers for Disease Control and Prevention.

Valentini, N. C., & Rudisill, M. E., (2004a). An inclusive mastery climate intervention and the motor skill development of children with and without disabilities. *Adapted Physical Activity Quarterly, 21*, 330–347.

Valentini, N. C., & Rudisill, M. E., (2004b). Motivational climate, motor skills development, and perceived competence: Two studies of developmental delayed kindergarten children. *Journal of Teaching Physical Education, 23*, 216–234.

Valentini, N. C., Rudisill, M., & Goodway, J. D. (1999). Incorporating a mastery climate into physical education: It's developmentally appropriate. *Journal of Physical Education Recreation and Dance, 7*, 28–32.

Williams, K., Haywood, K. M., & Painter, M. A. (1996). Environmental versus biological influences on the on gender differences in the overarm throw for force: Dominant and nondominant arm throws. *Women in Sport and Physical Activity, 5*, 29–48.

Ward, D. S., Vaughn, A., McWilliams, C., & Hales, D. (2010). Interventions for increasing physical activity at child care. *Medicine & Science in Sports & Exercise, 42*, 526–534.

6

The Development of Children's Creativity

MARK A. RUNCO AND NUR CAYIRDAG
University of Georgia

Creativity is very important for children and their development. Consider the creativity of preschoolers, as expressed in their spontaneous comments, songs, play, drawings, and dance. Gradually, the school-aged child's creativity is expressed in more deliberate activities that may lead to works of art or novel solutions to hassles and problems. Researchers are making great strides in formulating age-appropriate assessments of childhood creativity and understanding its development.

The creativity of young persons is not easy to assess. It is unlike the creativity of adults and not easy to put into the objective, scientific terms that are needed for assessment (Runco, 2007). The creativity of adults often leads to some product, such as a work of art, a solution to a problem, a new way of accomplishing something. Children's creativity, on the other hand, may not produce a tangible product or result. It may take the form of imaginative play, self-expression, or a new understanding of the world. We can compare the art of Lichtenstein with that of Warhol, but we cannot rely on norms to understand the creativity of children.

Creativity is critical to children's development in much the same way that variation is vital for societal progress and biological evolution. Children are creative when they pretend, for example, and when they express themselves in an uninhibited fashion. Play and the construction of meaning (which is necessary for self-expression) provide children with a grasp of what is possible. Because children do pretend and do express themselves in an uninhibited fashion, the range of possibilities is enormous. They can think about, explore, and act on both the realistic and the imaginary. In that sense, children have larger repertoires than adults. Children are more playful and less inhibited; they have fewer routines, make fewer assumptions, and are often more spontaneous than adults. Each of these allows children to think broadly, divergently, and imaginatively. As they grow older, however, they are socialized, which simply put means that they are taught which ideas and behaviors are appropriate, and which are not appropriate. In this light,

imaginative play and creative thinking provide the variations, and socialization is a kind of selection.

If children do not fully utilize their imaginations, explore possibilities, try new things, consider new actions, invent understandings, and experiment, they will not be able to discover who they are, what they are capable of, and what is acceptable in their family, school, peer-group, and culture. Parents and teachers should therefore both support children's imaginative play and experimentation, but also provide feedback, structure, and appropriate values. Parenting (and teaching, for that matter) is very much a matter of balance (Runco & Gaynor, 1993). If such balanced experiences are available to children, they can develop mature forms of creative talent, and perhaps become productive adults. At the very least children will maintain the capacity to express themselves with only optimal and healthful levels of inhibition. The child will also, through creative self-expression, recognize his or her own uniqueness. The range of options mentioned above will provide the creative child with possible solutions to problems, so he or she is likely to be good at solving problems, both those presented in school and those encountered in the natural environment (Runco, 2003). The creative child will be in position to avoid psychological disturbance and even illness—many psychological disorders can be connected to a lack of self-expression (Pennebaker, 1997). Children who receive balanced experiences, with opportunities to explore and experiment, as well as receive mature feedback, will be able to cope with and adapt to our ever-changing world. Creativity is an important part of development, and if encouraged, children will have a better chance to fulfill their potential and may be enabled to contribute in a meaningful fashion to society.

This chapter reviews the research on children's creativity. It identifies influences on children's creativity and defines it in a manner that allows adults to recognize it. We begin by reviewing two concepts (i.e., *stages* and *domains*) which describe the ways in which creative children may differ from one another. The creativity of preschool children, for instance, differs from that of school-aged children, which in turn differs from that of adolescents and adults. *Domains of creative performance* are explored next, for it is impossible to understand creativity without putting it into context. This is especially true on the individual level: A child who has creative potential in the musical domain may be quite dissimilar to the child who has creative potential in the mathematical, verbal, athletic, or some other domains.[1] These two concepts—stages and domains—are described first because very little about creativity applies across the board; almost everything else about creativity must be qualified by taking stage and domain into account. The remainder of this chapter explores "almost everything else," but in particular examines influences on creative potential and its fulfillment. Family and cultural context are, for instance, discussed in this chapter, for each is a significant influence on creativity and its development. The *implicit theories* held by parents and teachers are described after cultural context, and research on creativity and play, art, and divergent thinking are reviewed. Because it deemphasizes products and achievements, the theory of *personal creativity* is very useful when thinking about the creativity of children and is therefore described in some detail. This chapter concludes with a brief elaboration of the concept of optimization, which, as we will see, is the most general practical principle: Creativity flourishes when developmental experiences and conditions are optimal.

Stages

Creative talents and potentials express themselves in different ways at different ages. Evidence suggests that there are stages, for example, and that the creativity of a preschool child differs from that of a school-aged child or an adolescent (Gardner, 1982; Runco, 1999; Smith, Michael, & Hocevar, 1990; Torrance, 1968a). The most famous stage, or perhaps we should say the most infamous stage is probably the one that takes place in fourth grade, for a number of investigations have identified a fourth grade slump in original thinking (Raina, 1980; Runco, 1999; Torrance, 1968a). One explanation for the slump, when it occurs, emphasizes the environment. By fourth grade, children have experienced several years of formal education and have been expected to raise hands before speaking, sit in rows, and follow a precise daily schedule. This structure may be internalized such that, by fourth grade, there is a loss of initiative and original thought. Yet it seems that at least some of the slump is maturational and tied to biological changes. The nervous system may become increasingly sensitive to conventions at this stage, and, of course, conventional behavior is unlikely to be original. An increase in conventionality will lead directly to a decrease in originality. This perspective is consistent with reports of a literal stage in language (Gardner, 1982), a conventional stage of moral reasoning (Kohlberg, 1966), and the tendency of children

to adhere in a rigid fashion to rules when playing games (Runco & Charles, 1993). Smith and Carlsson (1982) suggested that there is a second slump (the first being the fourth grade) in preadolescence. Claxton, Pannells, and Rhoads (2005) examined the changes in the cognitive and affective components of creativity from fourth grade through beginning adolescence in ninth grade with a longitudinal study from 1998 to 2003. Total Test of Divergent Thinking and Divergent Feeling scores increased significantly from sixth grade to ninth grade, but there was no significant change when comparing fourth grade and sixth grade students. Total divergent thinking scores also increased from fourth grade to ninth grade. In originality factor, there was a decrease from fourth grade to sixth grade, but no significant changes from sixth grade to ninth grade. No significant changes were found in fluency and flexibility factors.

Conventionality is apparently quite relevant to children's artistic endeavors. Rosenblatt and Winner (1988), for instance, found that professional artists prefer the artwork of preschool children over that of older children, the reason being that the former were more spontaneous and self-expressive than the latter. Preschool children were described as *preconventional* because they did not produce art that was a clear representation of reality—a kind of conventional thinking—but instead drew from their own preferences and uninhibited feelings. The older children in this research (those in the middle and later grades of elementary school) had apparently entered the conventional stage and tried to produce art that was representational and realistic; the result being that their art was commonplace and judged to be uncreative.

The idea of preconventional artwork suggests that preschool-aged children can be creative. Their creativity is, however, different from that of older children, adolescents, and adults. Preschool children do not produce works of art or solutions to problems which help and assist other people; their creativity is typically authentic self-expression. This self-expression is typically original—after all, it is preconventional—and fitting, at least given the child's own situation. What is most important is that even though the things they do are not intended for wide audiences, young children do things which satisfy the two requirements of creativity: originality and usefulness. This is probably most apparent in studies of young children's play. Schmukler (1985), for instance, emphasized children's play and imagination as bases for later creative skill. As she put it,

> Play [is] an activity which is not obviously goal-directed, such as recreating and acting out what the child has observed. Imaginative play refers to the introduction by the child of settings, times, and characters which are not immediately present in the environment and, since it makes something out of nothing, can be seen as creative expression with important developmental implications. (p. 75)

Russ (1993; Russ & Fionelli, 2010), Ayman-Nolley (1992), Smolucha (1992a, 1992b), and Singer and Singer (in press) also tie the play of young children to creative potential. Garaigordobil (2006) assessed the effectiveness of a play program on creativity in 10- and 11-year-old children. The program consisted of 2-hour intervention sessions each week throughout the school year. Creativity was measured by the Torrance Test of Creative Thinking (TTCT) and evaluations of expert judgments. Results showed that the program increased participants' verbal and graphic-figural creativity. The program also improved creativity scores of participants who showed low levels of creativity before the program. Russ and Schaffer (2006) examined the relationship between divergent thinking and affect in play and concluded that affect in play is related to both originality and fluency. On the other hand, Moore and Russ (2008) studied the effects of a pretend play intervention on 45 first and second grade students. They found that pretend play did not contribute to creativity. Daugherty (1993) agreed that young children have creative potentials, but she felt these potentials were expressed in private speech. Matuga (2004) also saw creativity in the private speech of young children, as well as in their drawings.

Piaget's (1962) description of imaginative play as assimilatory implies a strong connection to creative potentials, and he too saw a kind of peak in imaginative behavior in preschool children. He described the imaginative play of young children as highly assimilatory, meaning that children's thinking tendencies allowed them to interpret objective experience in a personal and subjective fashion. No wonder children can play being superheroes, believing themselves to be Superman, Spiderman, or some other ultrastrong being, even though they are in actuality small and physically immature. They may not look like superheroes but that does not keep children from creating imaginary worlds where they are superheroes.

Imaginary companions can be a sign of creativity in the early years and also in adulthood (Hoff, 2005; Myers, 1979). According to Somers and Yawkey (1984) imaginary companions help children to discover new things, explore new materials, and use them in new situations. Also, the number of imaginary companions and detailed description of the imaginary companions' characteristics showed the creative potential. Hoff (2005) found that children with imaginary companions were significantly more creative than children without imaginary companions.

Dudek (1974) raised the possibility that children are not really creative. She described their original insights and behavior as accidental rather than creative. She felt that children sometimes do not know what is the correct or conventional thing to say or way to behave, and as a consequence they do the wrong thing. This may surprise adult onlookers, who then explain the child's mistakes as creative rather than accidental. Runco and Charles (1993) argued for the other extreme perspective and went so far as to suggest that young children are more creative than individuals at any other age. They described children as extremely playful and unfamiliar with routines. Children also do not make many, if any, assumptions, and they are not inhibited by social conventions. All of this may give them an edge and allow them to think and behave in a spontaneous and original fashion.

Runco and Charles (1997) additionally suggested that the fourth grade slump is only a potential loss and need not occur if parents and educators provide the opportunities, models, and reinforcement for continued self-expression and original behavior. At present, many children tend to slump, and the slump has been reported again and again for at least 30 years since Torrance (1968a) first identified it, but this does not indicate how things should or must be. Indeed, the fourth grade slump is far from universal. Torrance (1968a) found approximately 50 to 60% of the children in his sample experienced it.

The best way to view stages is as age-bounded potentials (Runco & Charles, 1993). Usually potentials imply the possibility of growth (Cohen, 1989; Kohlberg, 1987; Piaget, 1976), but apparently children also have the possible potential to experience a slump or two at particular ages. These drops may not occur; they are just possibilities, or potential slumps. In this light, they might be avoided. Just as experiences are necessary for an individual to fulfill his or her potential, so too can a slump probably be avoided with the right experiences. Suggestions for avoiding slumps and enhancing creativity are discussed below.

Before leaving the topic of preconventional thinking, something should be said about creative morality. This is germane in part because the original conception of conventional thinking developing in stages (i.e., preconventional, conventional, and postconventional) was an attempt at describing moral reasoning (Kohlberg, 1987). Rosenblatt and Winner (1982) later used the same stages to describe the development of artistic skills, and Runco and Charles (1997) even later applied it to divergent thinking. There is, however, an intriguing and important connection between creativity and morality, and indeed, a number of attempts have been made to encourage investments specifically in this area (Gruber, 1993, 1997; Runco, 1993). Gruber (1997) pointed specifically to the need to develop *creative altruism*. In his words:

> The term "altruism" implies some unsolved problem in the disposition of human resources: it also implies that there may be something that ought to be done, which if done will eliminate the discrepancy between the actual and desired state of affairs.... The self-chosen task of the creative altruist, to work to bring such a change about, necessarily involves an exchange with others. In this exchange, there is a donor with available assets and a recipient with an unmet need. No matter how such exchanges begin, in the ideal case the long range outcome will be to reduce or eliminate the discrepancy. Moreover, appropriate planning and action will require cooperation among all the participants, that is, both the donors and recipients. Only through such cooperation can the desired change be brought about; indeed, such cooperation is not only part of the solution process but often part of the goal. (Gruber, 1997, p. 466)

The need for creative morality and altruism is especially pressing now, with evolution occurring at such a rapid pace and ethical dilemmas being so numerous (McLaren, 1993). Everyone studying creative morality seems to feel that the solution is to encourage empathy, altruism, and integrity in the schools along with creative thinking. Haste (1993) detailed an educational program which would be of great value along these lines.

The connection between moral reasoning and creativity was explored by Runco (1993), who used the stages of conventional thought, mentioned above, and Gruber (1993, 1997). Runco concluded that parents and teachers need to target postconventional thought, for here the individual takes morals, laws, rules, traditional, and conventions into account, but he or she thinks for him- or herself. Gruber (1997) focused on the

> awareness of the possibility of something new, followed by the patient evolution of the understanding of the problem. Both [creativity and moral reasoning] require the translation of the inner life of desire and fantasy into forms of action in and upon the world. Both require prolonged, intentional search for adequate and harmonious solutions. Both require sensitivity to the impact of the innovation on some prospective audience or recipients. Especially in creative altruism, this takes the form of empathic awareness of the needs and feelings of the other. (p. 466)

Domain Differences

Domain differences have long been recognized in studies of creativity, though early on the focus was on creative adults with special skills in poetry, music, architecture, and so on (e.g., Patrick, 1935, 1937; MacKinnon, 1960). Many fascinating differences were uncovered by the Institute for Personality Assessment and Research in Berkeley, when creativity research was first becoming unambiguously scientific (Barron, 1969; Helson, 1999; MacKinnon, 1960). In 1983 Gardner identified seven clear-cut domains of talent and supported their independence with cognitive, psychometric, developmental, and neuropsychological evidence. The first seven domains were verbal-symbolic, mathematical-logical, musical, spatial, bodily-kinesthetic, intrapersonal, and interpersonal. Later he used the same criteria for domains and added "the naturalist." Gardner argued that each of these domains depended on particular core characteristics (e.g., symbols for the verbal domain), and on the nervous system. For Gardner, the domain-specific talents of prodigies and gifted children also depend on idiosyncratic developmental experiences.

This particular claim about idiosyncratic developmental experiences has been compellingly supported by the longitudinal work of Albert (1980, 1994). Longitudinal studies, like Albert's, are extremely useful for understanding development because they allow researchers to actually observe changes that occur as individuals age (also see Helson, 1999; Subotnik & Arnold, 1999; Plucker, 1999). Albert began his study 30 years ago with two groups of children, one exceptionally gifted in the sense of a high IQ score (all above 155), and one equally exceptionally gifted but with talents specifically in mathematics. His premise was that there are differences in the developmental backgrounds of individuals in different domains, and differences at different levels of talent. Albert's interest in developmental background led him to collect a huge amount of data from the families of the exceptionally gifted children. Various developmental experiences have been related to the creative talents of the children involved in the longitudinal research: Level of independence, for example, was associated with creative potential (Runco & Albert, 1985), as was achievement motivation that does not lead to conformity (Runco & Albert, 2005). As Gardner (1983) predicted, particular developmental experiences characterized children with talents in different domains. Albert and Runco found, for instance, that boys with exceptional talents in the mathematical domain had fathers who were more stereotypically masculine than other fathers.

Empirical demonstrations of domain differences have also been presented by Milgram (1990), Runco (1987), and Wallach and Wing (1969). Very significantly, Wallach and Wing not only discovered that original and creative thinking were predictive of achievement in specific extracurricular domains (e.g., leadership, art, music, mathematics); they also demonstrated that GPA and school performances were of limited validity. GPA and traditional intelligence was related only to academic achievements, while creative thinking seemed to contribute to performance in the natural environment. Along the same lines, Milgram (1990) proposed that extracurricular (leisure time) activities are important to consider because they reflect what a child is actually motivated to do. In school, the child may be responding to incentives and grades, but what happens when those are not available? The child may not behave in the same fashion. But if a child chooses to do something during his or her leisure time (e.g., write a poem), it is much more likely that this child will pursue that domain and continue working within it. This emphasis on leisure time activities can be used when there is a need to identify gifted and talented children—it allows reliable assessment (Milgram, 1990). It is also justified by the research showing that creative work is often intrinsically motivated (Amabile, 1990; Eisenberger & Shanock, 2003; MacKinnon, 1960). Renzulli (1978) proposed that intrinsic motivation ("task commitment"), creative potential, and traditional intelligence each be used to identify gifted children.

Most definitions of giftedness include IQ or general intellectual ability. The alternative is to recognize specific domains of talent which may be extricable from general ability. The recognition of domains would seem to be justified by cultural differences and by the biases and sometimes questionable validity of IQ tests (Gardner, 1983). For present purposes what may be most important is that it is feasible to define giftedness such that creativity is a prerequisite. This is precisely what Renzulli (1978) suggested. The curvilinear relationship between traditional intelligence and creativity test scores (Guilford, 1968; Runco & Albert, 1986), however, suggests that some creative children may have only a moderate level of tested intelligence. It may be best to recognize different kinds of giftedness, both in terms of the various domains, but also in terms of creative talents. A child may be creatively gifted, for example, with exceptional creative potential but only moderate levels of traditional intelligence, or academically gifted, with high levels of traditional intelligence but unexceptional creative talents. Such specificity in definitions would allow parents and teachers to best understand each individual child.

Writing is an important domain of creativity. However, some sorts of writing require more creativity than others. Kohanyi (2005) conducted a retrospective study on creative writers in comparison to journalists. Results indicated that love of imagination is a distinguishing factor for creative writers in their early ages. They had a keen interest in words and possessed a large vocabulary. Like journalists, they loved language while their relation to language was more about aesthetics of language such as prosody rather than syntax and multilingualism reported by journalists. They had learned to read before starting school. Both groups read excessively while creative writers often read fiction, which then triggered them to write in that genre. Onset of writing was earlier in creative writers, as early as 3 years old, than the journalists, who started after 9. More creative writers had imaginary companions than journalists, and they developed more complex fantasy worlds with them. More creative writers felt different from other kids than the journalists. Creative writers had a less happy childhood, stressful family environment, trauma, and stress which induced their creative works. Creative writers, however, had less trouble and conflict than did the journalists.

In a similar study about a different domain, Goldstein and Winner (2009) investigated the early predictors of acting talent with lawyers as comparison group. They found that actors' childhood memories include a deep involvement in imaginary and fictional worlds, and emotional and mental states. Like creative writers, they reported feeling different from others. They rebelled against their parents' advice about their careers. More actors than lawyers reported a boring school time but good memory for books and words. They were also superior to lawyers in mimicry in their childhood.

Tacher and Readdick (2006) pointed out an aggression correlate of creativity in the verbal domain. The results indicated that verbal fluency, verbal flexibility, and verbal originality from TTCT were highly correlated ($r > .42$) with verbal aggression as indicated by Teachers' Report Form. Also, verbal creativity was correlated with physical aggression and threats of aggression. Figural originality was correlated with the threats of aggression, too. Butcher and Niec (2005) also found that disruptive behaviors can explain creativity significantly as measured by divergent thinking tasks ($R^2=.06$) and caregivers reports ($R^2=.25$). However, further analyses indicated that affect regulation mediated the relationship between disruptive behaviors and creativity, and when it was controlled the relationship was not significant.

Bournelli, Makri, and Mylonas (2009) have studied the relationship between motor creativity and self-concept based on the belief that children can easily exhibit their creativity by their movements. Factor analysis results of the self-concept scale are noteworthy: Mother–child interaction was the strongest factor explaining self-concept. The intercorrelations among motor creativity tasks and self-concept factors indicated that mother–child interaction had the highest correlation with all three creativity tasks (above .30) whereas perceived scholastic competence had the lowest (around .20). Peer social acceptance and perceived physical competence were correlated in between. Canonical correlations among those two sets (three creativity tasks versus self-concept factors extracted) yielded one pair of canonical correlations, which led to the conclusion that higher levels in specific motor tasks (ball-wall and the parallel lines) are correlated with higher self-concept. In another study, Pagona and Costas (2008) implemented a physical education program to improve motor creativity as measured by the parallel lines test, the ball wall test, and the hoop test. In the ninth-year follow-up, performance of the third graders who attended teaching sessions was better in all three tasks than the control group with no such training. These findings indicated that motor creativity can be taught and improved and the influence of the training is retained for a considerable period of time.

Another interesting domain concerns mathematics. Since mathematics require a high level of convergent thinking, mathematical creativity represents a blend of both convergent and divergent thinking. Sak and Maker (2006) asked the participants to write original math problems as part of a larger assessment called DISCOVER. They were specifically interested in the way age and knowledge influences the performance in flexibility, originality, elaboration, and fluency. They analyzed the former three separately from fluency. The results indicated that knowledge is very critical for mathematical creativity. Higher levels of knowledge were associated with higher scores in the combination of flexibility, originality, and elaboration while the relationship was rather weak and stable for fluency. The influence of age had a very different pattern: It explained a great amount in the lower grades but after the third grade drastically declined for flexibility, originality, and elaboration. For fluency, however, the relationship increased with age. Those results are noteworthy because creativity in particular domains can require more knowledge and increased convergent thinking.

Which academic subjects are more interesting or motivating among creative students? Sarsani (2008) divided the students into three groups based on their scores on a creativity test as high, moderate, and low creatives. High creatives liked English (as a second language Indian population), science, and math classes, and disliked studying their own languages (Telagu and Hindi) and social studies. Low creatives also liked English but they also liked their native languages while disliking social studies, math, and sciences. When it came to occupations, members of the high creative group wanted to be a pilot, district collector, army officer, scientist, political leader, computer professional, technician, and subinspector of police more than did the low creative group. An interesting goal mentioned by the high creative group was to "maintain law and order" which is at odds with conventional understanding of creativity.

It is possible that other domains of creative performance exist, in addition to those proposed by Gardner (1983). Some of these may be subdomains, however, for someone who has a talent for poetry may not do much journalism or prose. It is one thing to write music, but something else to perform it. Of special importance is the idea that there is a domain which has been called "everyday creativity" (Runco & Richards, 1997). The basic idea here is that individuals may not be interested or talented in music, mathematics, the language arts, or any widely recognized domain, but that individual may be highly creative in the natural (everyday) environment. He or she may be creative when solving problems involving friends, pets, allowances, homework, or attire. Admittedly, the everyday domain of creative talent has not yet been verified with the same criteria and rigor used by Gardner (1983).

Family Background

The family thus plays a critical role in the development of children's creativity. Actually, it plays various critical roles. Parents are models for their children, for example, and provide *resources, values*, and *opportunities*. Discipline styles may also have some impact. The idea of balance, introduced above, may apply to discipline: It is likely that some autonomy is beneficial for children and allows them to learn to think for themselves; yet too much freedom and they may not learn to focus on a task until it is completed or put enough effort into traditional skills as they should. A bit more will be said below about autonomy. Turning to resources, creative children frequently have had *diverse experiences* (Schaefer, 1971). Experience very clearly plays a role in insightful problem solving, and insight is just as clearly frequently tied to creative thinking (Epstein, 1990). Sadly, resources may be influenced by socioeconomic status and the like, meaning that certain children have advantages and others disadvantages which are germane to creative potential.

In her discussion of "facilitating family environments," Schmukler (1985) emphasized children's play and imagination as bases for creative skill. She also suggested that a child's opportunities for play, and thus the development of creativity, are determined by the parents, and often mostly by the mother. This view is consistent with the Ayman-Nolley (1992) and Smolucha's (1992a, 1992b) ideas mentioned above. They too emphasized social interactions and play as influences on creative potentials.

Gute, Gute, Nakamura, and Csikszentmihalyi (2008) found a more complex family system in their qualitative study with nine creative people. According to them, an optimal family environment that brings differentiation is the one which not only establishes a consistent and cohesive psychological and social foundation, which provides integration, but also defies the excessive emotional control which may hinder independence.

Less intentional family influence is exerted by so-called *family structure*. This includes "sibsize" (number of siblings), age gap (interval between two siblings), and birth order (or ordinal position). Sibsize is very strongly related to traditional intelligence (Zajonc, 1976), but it is an inverse relationship: Larger families tend to have children with lower scholastic aptitude test (SAT) scores. Zajonc's explanation for this focuses on the intellectual climate of the home. Apparently, when there are few children, that climate can be quite stimulating intellectually. When there are more children, the climate of the home is not as likely to be intellectually stimulating. Very importantly, one small study suggests that what held true for SAT does not hold true for creative potential. Runco and Bahleda (1986) reported that larger families tended to have children with higher scores on a battery of divergent thinking tests. These tap a child's potential for solving problems in an original fashion (and are described in more detail later in this chapter). Perhaps large families provide children with more autonomy, which in turn allows them to develop independent and original thought. Recall here that autonomy and independence have been tied to creative potential in developmental, personality, and cognitive research (Albert & Runco, 1989). Family size was, however, related to creative potential in one relatively small investigation (with 240 children) and replications are certainly warranted.

Birth order and age gap are at least as important a variable as sibsize. Sulloway (1997), for instance, found that middle children are "born to rebel." Apparently many older children develop a need for achievement in traditional areas (like education), and although they may do well in school or other similar areas, their achievement motives take them only to conventional areas and thinking styles. Middle children tend to seek unique family niches and thereby avoid conflicts with the older, more mature sibling. If the older sibling tends to a conventional direction, the middle child goes in the opposite direction, namely, the unconventional one. Such unconventional behavior is easily tied to original thought; and Sulloway's data confirm that many rebels in the arts and sciences have indeed been middle children. A child's tendency toward unconventional thought and action might be mitigated by a large age gap. If the older sibling is much older, there is no need to work to find a unique niche. Age itself provides uniqueness. Hence with large gaps, there is less diversity and less likelihood of the middle child being unconventional.

Baer, Oldham, Hollingshead, and Jacobsohn (2005) have examined the influence of number of siblings on the relationship between birth order and creativity. They found that sibling age and sibsize moderate the relation between creativity and birth order. More specifically, firstborns with larger sibling groups tend to be more creative, as measured with eight problem-solving tasks, and are more creative when they have opposite sex siblings or those in a closer age group. This study indicated that sibling constellation should be taken into consideration in terms of its influence on birth order and creativity.

Aside from family planning, studies of family structure may not sound as though they are very useful. There are, however, a number of things parents can actually control. Runco (1991) suggested that families need to provide three things: *Opportunities* to practice creative thinking, *models* of creativity, and an *appreciation* of creative efforts. Clearly, parents who model and value creativity, are more likely to raise creative children than are other parents. Models may be the parents or siblings, or they may be *remote models* (i.e., creative people in books or in the media). The appreciation may take the form of rewards and reinforcers (Epstein, 1990), yet care must be taken here. This is because rewards and the like can actually undermine the intrinsic motivation that tends to support creative efforts. This is the *overjustification effect* (Amabile, 1990). If an individual enjoys something, but then receives rewards for doing it, he or she may forget that the task was at one point intrinsically interesting.

Independence and autonomy, mentioned above, should be explored further. It makes good theoretical sense that these would be related to creative potential; originality assumes a kind of independence. It assumes an independence from conventional ways of thinking, and independence from norms and sometimes expectations. Albert and Runco (1989) found support for the relationship between parental independence and creative thinking in three samples of children. One was nongifted, and the other two exceptionally gifted. The mothers of the children with exceptionally high IQs (all in excess of 150) reported the highest levels of independence, meaning that they allowed their children to do more things on their own at younger ages. The ratings of independence from the children (i.e., their expectations about what they could do on their own) and those from the mothers were both significantly correlated with divergent thinking test scores. This indicates that the children's expectations about autonomy, and the mothers' allowing independence in the home, were both predictive of the children's capacity for original thought. Weisberg and Springer (1961) also offered support for the relationship between creative potential and independence in the home.

Independence in the family environment is strongly tied to parenting style. Lim and Smith (2008) tested the relationship between two parenting styles, leniency and acceptance with a large group of students in South Korea (N=421). Using the structural equation model, they found that leniency was related to loneliness but not to creative personality while acceptance correlated with creative personality. It is important to note that teachers rated students' creativity, and loneliness and parenting styles were rated by the children.

It is possible that the relationship of independence and children's divergent thinking reflects *practice*, which is one reason children need opportunities to think for themselves in an original fashion. If children have numerous opportunities to solve problems on their own—opportunities to work independently and autonomously—they will be able to practice the requisite skills. The relationship between parental independence and divergent thinking could also reflect family values. These are communicated to children in various ways (e.g., parents' own actions suggest what they value), and families that value independent thinking will probably communicate in many ways the idea that autonomy is a respectable capacity. The same thing can be said about creativity per se; it is probably directly related to family values (Cheung, Lau, Chan, & Wu, 2003; Kwang, 2002). This takes us to cultural context, for many family values are determined by culture.

Cultural Context

Children's creativity depends a great deal on the family, and on the educational system, but it also depends on the wider cultural context. This was implied by the earlier discussion of domain differences. Certain domains are recognized in any one particular culture, and other domains ignored. Each culture defines the talents which will be encouraged. This is of course another way of describing the values found within a given culture, and those values in turn define what is appropriate and what is not. Earlier I referred to this as socialization. Domains in which a child expresses an interest may be judged as appropriate or inappropriate, as will particular behaviors and even ideas. This process is analogous to *sex-typing*, where cultural values proscribe what boys and girls are expected to do and what they are not supposed to do.

Cultural values are communicated to children within the family and, later, the school system, but they are also communicated via the media and other informal experiences. Most experimental research on the impact of the media on children's creativity has focused on the media themselves, not on the values broadcast by the media. TV, for example, may provide too much information to children (pictures, sounds, and so on) and not allow them to use their imaginations (Meline, 1976; & Runco & Pezdek, 1984). Additionally, the models available on TV programming are often quite stereotyped, and this in turn leaves little room for the individuality that is more conducive to creative behavior.

Sex typing is a good example of the socialization processes because it is both clearly related to culture and to creative potentials. Although the data are not overwhelming in this regard, by and large children and adolescents who exhibit high levels of *psychological androgeny* tend to perform in the most creative fashion (Baer, 1998; Harrington, 1990). Androgenous individuals have access to both stereotypically masculine and stereotypically feminine behaviors. They do not conform to expectations about sex roles and make choices based on what is expected of them based on their being a boy or a girl, but instead think for themselves and react in a spontaneous and personally meaningful fashion. Since they do not conform to stereotypes, they have a wide range of options available to them for solving problems. An androgenous boy will not think only of stereotypically masculine solutions to a problem, for example, and an androgenous girl will not think merely of stereotypically feminine solutions. Each will consider appropriate solutions regardless of, or at least deemphasizing stereotypes. It is really just another example of the unconventional capacities of creative persons, though it is also useful to view it from the other direction of effect as well, namely with androgeny as an influence on creative potential. Interestingly, androgenous individuals also tend to be psychologically healthy.

Much has been made of differences between Eastern and Western cultural values (e.g., Kwang, 2002), though, of course, this is a generalization. Not all Eastern cultures are identical, nor are Western cultures all the same. There is much variation and difference within each. Definitions of appropriateness may differ among the 50 U.S. states, to mention one example that is close to home, and of course most cultures are diverse with regard to socioeconomics, religion, and dialects. Yet there are commonalities. The most recognized and relevant include an appreciation of harmony and collaboration in the East, and independence and competition in the West.

Immediate Context

Contextual influences on creativity may be immediate and local. This was implied by the discussion of the family above, with resources and so on potentially influencing creativity and its development. Parallel influences may be exerted by the school environment (Dudek, Strobel, & Runco, 1994; Wallach & Kogan, 1965). Wallach and Kogan, for instance, found that a *permissive school environment* allowed children to think divergently and creatively. A test oriented environment, in contrast, seemed to inhibit creative thinking. Indeed, when school children were given divergent thinking exercises in the test oriented environment, only children who had done well on traditional academic tests performed at high levels. But when the same exercises were administered in the permissive environment (i.e., children were told that the exercises were games, not tests, that spelling did not matter, and that no grades would be given), many children who did not do well on traditional academic tests performed at very high levels. These children had outstanding creative potential which would have been overlooked if they had received either (a) tests of academic aptitude or (b) tests of creative potential administered in a structured environment. Dudek et al. also found the classroom and school environments to be significantly related to performance on tests of creative potential.

Hunter, Bedell, and Mumford's (2007) meta-analytic review of 42 articles on the relationship between creativity and different dimensions of climate provides important clues about the nature of good climate for creativity. They found that a large effect size for the characteristics of climates such as positive interpersonal exchange ($\Delta=.91$), intellectual stimulation ($\Delta=.88$), challenge ($\Delta=.85$); and a medium effect size for flexibility and risk-taking ($\Delta=.78$), top management support ($\Delta=.75$), positive supervisor relations ($\Delta=.73$), organizational integration ($\Delta=.62$), mission clarity ($\Delta=62$), participation ($\Delta=.61$), product emphasis ($\Delta=.59$), resources ($\Delta=.51$), and autonomy ($\Delta=.48$).

The physical environment may have some influence on creativity. Much has been made of this in the organizational literature and in the research on adults' creativity (Mace & Ward, 2002; McCoy & Evans, 2002), but no doubt many of the factors they identify could also influence children's creativity. McCoy and Evans suggested that five situational factors are related to creative performances: color (few cool colors), view of the natural environment, and complexity of visual detail, natural materials, and few artificial ones.

Importantly, all levels of context, from the cultural to the more specific immediate environment, include people. The home environment, for example, is often defined by parents, and the school environment is defined by educators. One way of examining this kind of influence is to study *implicit theories*. These are the assumptions and expectations held by people. They are implicit in the sense that they may not be articulated nor tested. In fact, it may be easiest to explain implicit theories by contrasting them with explicit theories; that is, those held by scientists and researchers. They are explicit in the sense that they are articulated and tested. Scientists may have a theory of creativity, but they must explore it and share it with colleagues; and to be scientific, they must extract hypotheses, make these known, and test them. Importantly, the implicit theories of various groups, including parents, teachers, children, artists, and scientists, seem to differ from each other.

Johnson, Runco, & Raina (2003) examined the implicit theories of parents and teachers in India and the United States. Interestingly, Johnson et al. obtained ratings of creativity, taking both indicative and contraindicative traits into account, and ratings of social desirability. The last of these was examined because frequently profiles of "the ideal child" (Singh, 1987; Torrance, 1963) emphasize conformity, punctuality, consideration, and other traits that have little to do with original or creative behavior. Johnson et al. confirmed that the parents and teachers in India and the United States recognized both indicative and contraindicative aspects of creativity. There were, then, traits which they felt supported creative efforts, and traits which inhibited it. In that light the implicit theories of the parents and teachers were consistent with explicit theories of creativity. Most parents and teachers in Johnson et al.'s study gave high social desirability ratings to the traits that were associated with creative talent. This was not true of all creative traits, but it was true of most of them. The adults in India differed from the U.S. adults in ratings of various "intellectual" and "attitudinal" traits, but surprisingly, there were negligible differences between the parents and teachers. This was a surprise because earlier work had found parents to value the intellectual aspects of creativity, and teachers to value the more social aspects (Runco, 1984, 1989). In another investigation Proctor and Burnett (2004) described the

> traits often exhibited by creative students and noted in the literature…are: asking "what if?" questions; being full of ideas; possessing high verbal fluency; being constructive and building and rebuilding; coping with several ideas at once; becoming irritated and bored by the routine and obvious; going beyond assigned tasks; enjoying telling about own discoveries or inventions; finding different ways of doing things; and finally, not minding if others think he or she is a little different. (p. 424)

Here again there is some overlap with explicit theories of children's creativity, especially in the unconventional behaviors suggested by "not minding what others think."

In many ways the implicit theories of parents and teachers are more important than explicit theories. This is because the former lead directly to expectations, and expectations in turn lead directly to action. If a teacher expects creative children to be trouble-making nonconformists, for example, that teacher will expect a creative child to disrupt the classroom. Expectations are powerful influences on development (Rosenthal, 1991). The example just given may not sit well, for it suggests that creative children are nonconformists, but research does suggest that what teachers think of "an ideal student" is very different from the traits usually associated with creative children. Ideal students are polite, punctual, and conventional. Creative children ask questions, follow their own interests, and can be unconventional.

To make matters more difficult for adults, creative children tend to think in an idiosyncratic fashion. As a matter of fact, all creative thinking may be difficult to follow (that of both children and adults). Creative insights are new and original, and thus by definition different and surprising. This tendency is compounded when we take a child's stage of development into account. As Elkind (1981) put it, children are "cognitive aliens." They all think differently from the way adults think. Practically speaking, then, a child may have a remarkably creative idea for a project or assignment, but since he or she is a cognitive alien, and because the insight is original, an educator may not grasp its significance or creativity. The educator may not even see its relevance. If educators are not careful, and open to surprises, they will overlook creative thinking by children.

They certainly cannot reward creative thinking if they are unable to recognize it.

Evidence suggests that both parents and teachers have difficulty recognizing creative ideas (Runco, Nobel, & Luptak, 1990; Westby & Dawson, 1995). This evidence is based on judgments by parents and teachers when they were asked to rate the originality or creativity of ideas actually generated by children who were given open-ended divergent thinking exercises. The children might have been asked to "name all of the things you can think of that move on wheels," for example, or "list as many uses as you can for a brick." Such exercises allow children to think for themselves and to generate original ideas (Guilford, 1968; Runco, 1999; Torrance, 1968b). The thinking that is captured by these exercises is predictive of creative activity and accomplishment in the natural environment (Milgram, 1990; Runco, 1991; Runco, Plucker, & Lim, 2001–2002) and, very significantly, is independent of the kind of convergent thinking that is required by IQ tests and most traditional academic exercises and tests (Guilford, 1968; Runco & Albert, 1986). In other words, this kind of original thinking will not be found if educators rely on traditional examinations. Fortunately, many such exercises are available (Plucker & Renzulli, 1999), and many programs have been designed specifically to encourage divergent thinking.

Divergent thinking tests are probably the most commonly used measure of the potential for creative thought. They by no means guarantee actual performance: They are estimates of potential. They are highly reliable, with moderate predictions to creative activity in the natural environment (Runco, 1987, 2003; Torrance, 1981). Of course divergent thinking is related in different ways to creative activities in various domains. Other useful measures have been developed, some of the most impressive focus on performance in the natural environment rather than performance on a paper-and-pencil test (Milgram, 1990). Portfolios have also been used as indicators of creative potential (Williams, 1991). Sadly, there is a discrepancy between research and practice: Hunsaker and Callahan (1995) studied the creativity measurement instruments that were used by 418 school districts as part of their identification procedures for gifted students. Their results indicated that districts often selected instruments for assessing creativity without first paying careful attention to the definition of the construct.

Personal Creativity

Earlier in this chapter I pointed out that children's creativity is unlike that of adults. In fact, the stages mentioned twice in this chapter suggest that creativity takes one form early in life, another form a bit later, and so on throughout life.[2] Adult creativity is usually defined in terms of actual performance. Adults invent things, solve problems, and produce art and innovations. This facilitates the study of adult creativity because there are products which can be counted, monitored, studied. We can be objective, and therefore scientific, about creative products. Children do not create these kinds of things. If they do produce something, it is unlikely to be original by adult norms. It is likely to be original only by the child's own standards. It is still original and useful, which is how creativity is usually defined, but not by adult norms.

It is useful to look to children's divergent thinking, as suggested above, but creativity is not merely a result of cognitive skill. This is probably why predictions of actual creative performance from divergent thinking are only moderate (Plucker & Renzulli, 1999; Runco, 1991). They only take cognitive skills into account. Creativity is more than cognition. The intrinsic and extrinsic theories reviewed above included intrinsic motivation, openness, curiosity, and autonomy, just to mention a few extracognitive tendencies which often play a role in children's creative efforts.

This takes us back to the topic noted briefly early in this chapter, namely concerning the possibility of protecting children from slumps and allowing them to maintain high levels of self-expression and creativity. Amabile (1990) suggested that children can be "immunized" such that they will stick with their intrinsic interests. This immunization involves role-playing and discussion of video models. Many other educational programs focus on tactics which facilitate creative thinking and creative problems solving. Some tactics are easy to communicate to children. Harrington (1975), for example, demonstrated that originality can be enhanced if students are told to "be creative," and various investigations have used this idea with school aged children. The key idea is to be explicit about how the children can find creative ideas. Not surprisingly, this technique is called "explicit instructions." With young children, in early elementary school, it may be best to be concrete and suggest that they "give ideas that no one else will think of." That provides children with a technique that allows them to find original ideas, and it communicates the notion that being different can be a good thing. Runco (1987) and Milgram and Feingold (1977) found various explicit instructions to be very effective, even in third and fourth grade school children (also see Smith, Michael, & Hocevar, 1990).

Elsewhere I suggested that the most important thing parents and teachers can do is allow a child to develop ego strength (Runco, 1996, 2003), which is a bit like self-confidence. It allows the child to stand up to pressures to conform and to believe in his or her own thinking and ideas. Very likely the fourth grade slump in creativity occurs because children become very sensitive to peer pressure and conventions at about that age. They may still have original ideas, but they may not be willing to share and explore them. They will share and explore them if they are confident and have developed optimal ego strength. They will even think before conforming to conventional expectations. On the other hand, the situation changes when the group is positive: Hunter et al. (2007) found that there is a medium effect size between positive peer group and creativity ($\Delta = .69$).

Ego strength is also not sufficient. In the theory of personal creativity, children must also have the potential to construct original interpretations of experience. This, however, is probably a nearly universal talent. It parallels what Piaget (1976) said about assimilation and is involved in every adaptation a child makes. In that light adults probably don't need to do much for this aspect of creativity. Instead, they need to insure that children have ego strength—and discretion.

If a child lacks discretion, but has the ability to produce original ideas and the ego strength to believe in them, he or she may go too far. The child may rely entirely on original ideas and pay no attention to the curriculum or to standard knowledge. Discretion will allow the child to recognize when to be original, and when to conform. If he or she is working on an art project, very likely there is room for originality. If he or she is asked who invented the light bulb, it would be best to give the conventional answer rather than making one up. Many schools encourage students to "make good choices," and that applies to creative talents.

Conclusions

Children's creativity is related to individual skills and talents, including ego-strength and divergent thinking skills. It is also related to various extrapersonal influences—the family, school, and culture each play a role in the fulfillment of creative potential. These extrapersonal influences may be interpersonal (e.g., parents and teachers), or they may involve the physical environment. Creative potentials seem to vary in different stages, and there are clear differences between various domains of activity. Admittedly, the generality and specificity of creative skills is a matter of ongoing debate (Baer, 1998; Plucker, 1998).

Throughout this chapter I have suggested that children's creative potentials are related to autonomy (and postconventionality or independence of thought) and self-expression. Autonomy is a part of divergent thinking, for example; the original ideas which are recorded with divergent thinking exercises and tests require an independence of thought. Original ideas are unique or at least unusual, and they are found by thinking for one's self. Self-expression is also a reflection of autonomy, and it is by definition manifest. This is in turn important because children are often not creative in the sense of being productive, and looking to their original and meaningful self-expressions may give us a behavioral indicator of talent. Note the implied definition of children's creativity: it is behavior which is original, spontaneous, and self-expressive. It may not result in a tangible product but is instead manifested in a process, again, the process of original self-expression. Definitions of creativity which focus on adults always include value, fit, or appropriateness, as well as originality (Runco, 1988; Runco & Charles, 1993), and this makes sense because original things can be worthless! A highly bizarre invention may be original, but useless, and is thus just novel but not creative. A definition of children's creativity must accept self-expression instead of normative appropriateness. Children are not creative in the same fashion as adults. They behave in a creative fashion, but they do not produce things which will sell or attract wide attention. They may act in a creative fashion, play in a creative fashion, and behave in a creative fashion, but they do not produce creative products.

Obviously there are implications for adults who work with (or simply parent and raise) children. Self-expression is easy to identify and easy to encourage. It is also important that individuals who have the opportunity to express themselves tend to maintain psychological health. Admittedly some creative adults have had psychological problems (most common is probably a mood or affective disorder; Richards, 1990), but many creative persons are remarkably healthy. Indeed, creativity is sometimes a part of the highest level of psychological health, namely self-actualization (Maslow, 1973; Rogers, 1970; Runco, 1994). Creative self-expression may also lead to physical health (Eisenman, 1990; Pennebaker, Kiecolt-Glaser, & Glaser, 1997). We should not worry that helping our children to be creative will lead them to ill health or disturbance. More likely, creative talents will work to a child's advantage on both behavioral and psychological levels.

Recall also the idea introduced early in this chapter about balance. The optimization implied by balance is also germane to health, divergent thinking, ego strength, and conventionality. Indeed, optimization and balance may apply very generally to all kinds of creativity (Runco & Gaynor, 1993). Simply put, if the child is capable of creative and original behavior but balances this with the capacity for conventional actions, he or she is likely to be adaptive and healthy. Ill health is often due to a lack of balance and adaptability, or a lack of discretion that leads the individual to be original when he or she should conform. Applied to divergent thinking, optimization would allow children to find original ideas and solutions, but also to think convergently when taking a multiple choice test or when working in an area when they should focus on what adults have deemed to be correct. Ego strength may help children "just say no," but children should also be open minded and listen to what others have to say. It may be good to be unconventional some of the time, for the sake of originality, but much of the time it is good to consider conventional wisdom and conventional rules. Children should be capable of balance such that they can fit in and support peer group and family, but they should maintain the potential for creative thought as well.

Notes

1. There is an interesting issue here, regarding domains of performance. Essentially the issue is, how many domains? On the one hand it is useful to have a long list. With a longer list of domains we are the most likely to recognize any one child's talents. On the other hand, too long a list and we sacrifice the concept of talent and idea of giftedness. As Runco (1994) asked, "is every child gifted?" That may not sound so bad, but then again giftedness becomes a meaningless category if every child has talent; and every child will have talent of some sort, if the list is long enough.

2. It may be relevant for adults working with children to recognize one tendency of adulthood, namely to become less flexible (Chown, 1961; Rubenson & Runco, 1995). This not only influences our own creative behavior, but since we are models for children, it can influence theirs as well. Perhaps most notable is that our tendency to rely more and more on routines and assumptions can make us rigid in the sense that we do not consider new ideas. This is a huge problem when working with children, for it means that we will have difficulty recognizing their original thinking if it is contrary to what we expected or have grown accustomed to.

References

Albert, R. S. (1980). Family position and the attainment of eminence: A study of special family positions and special family experiences. *Gifted Child Quarterly, 24,* 87–95.

Albert, R. S. (1994). The achievement of eminence: A longitudinal study of exceptionally gifted boys and their families. In R. F. Subotnik & K. D. Arnold (Eds.), *Beyond Terman: Contemporary longitudinal studies of giftedness and talent* (pp. 282–315). Norwood, NJ: Ablex.

Albert, R. S., & Runco, M. A. (1989). Independence and cognitive ability in gifted and exceptionally gifted boys. *Journal of Youth and Adolescence, 18,* 221–230.

Amabile, T. M. (1990). Within you, without you: Towards a social psychology of creativity, and beyond. In M. A. Runco & R. S. Albert (Eds.), *Theories of creativity* (pp. 61–91). Newbury Park, CA: Sage.

Ayman-Nolley, S. (1992). Vygotsky's perspective on the development of imagination and creativity. *Creativity Research Journal, 5,* 101–109.

Baer, J. (1998). *Gender differences in the effects of extrinsic motivation on creativity.* The *Journal of Creative Behavior, 32,* 18–37.

Baer, M., Oldham, G. R., Hollingshead, A. B., & Jacobsohn, G. C. (2005). Revisiting the birth order-creativity connection: the role of sibling constellation. *Creativity Research Journal, 17,* 67–77.

Barron, F. (1969). *Creative person and creative process.* New York: Holt, Rinehart & Winston.

Bournelli, P., Makri, A., & Mylonas, K. (2009). Motor creativity and self-concept. *Creativity Research Journal, 21*(1), 104–110.

Butcher, J. L., & Niec, L. N. (2005). Disruptive behaviors and creativity in childhood: the importance of affect regulation. *Creativity Research Journal, 17,* 181–193.

Cheung, P.C., Lau, S., Chan, D. W., & Wu, W. Y. (2003). Creative potential of school children in Hong Kong: Norms of the Wallach-Kogan creativity tests and their implications. *Creativity Research Journal, 16,* 69–78.

Chown, S. M. (1961). Age and the rigidities. *Journal of Gerontology, 16,* 353–362.

Claxton, A. F., Pannells, T. C., & Rhoads, P. A. (2005). Developmental trends in the creativity of school-age children. *Creativity Research Journal, 17,* 327–335.

Cohen, L. M. (1989). A continuum of adaptive creative behaviors. *Creativity Research Journal, 2,* 169–183.

Daugherty, M. (1993). Creativity and private speech: Developmental trends. *Creativity Research Journal, 6,* 287–296.

Dudek, S. Z. (1974). Creativity in young children: Attitude or ability? *Journal of Creative Behavior, 8,* 282–292.

Dudek, S. Z., Strobel, M., & Runco, M. A. (1994). Cumulative and proximal influences of the social environment on creative potential. *Journal of Genetic Psychology, 154,* 487–499.

Eisenberger, R., & Shanock, L. (2003). Rewards, Intrinsic Motivation, and Creativity: A Case Study of Conceptual and Methodological Isolation. *Creativity Research Journal, 15,* 121–130.

Eisenman, R. (1990). Creativity, preference for complexity, and physical and mental illness. *Creativity Research Journal, 3,* 231–236.

Elkind, D. (1981). *Children and adolescence.* New York: Oxford University Press.

Epstein, R. (1990). Generativity theory. In M. A. Runco & R. S. Albert (Eds.), *Theories of creativity* (pp.116–140). Newbury Park, CA: Sage.

Garaigordobil, M. (2006). Intervention in creativity with children aged 10 and 11 years: Impact of a play program on verbal and graphic figural creativity. *Creativity Research Journal, 18,* 329–345.

Gardner, H. (1982). *Art, mind, and brain: A cognitive approach to creativity.* New York: Basic Books.

Gardner, H. (1983). *Frames of mind.* New York: Basic Books.

Goldstein, T. R., & Winner, E. (2009). Living in alternative and inner worlds: Early signs of acting talent. *Creativity Research Journal, 21*(1), 117–124.

Gruber, H. E. (1993). Creativity in the moral domain: Ought implies can implies create. *Creativity Research Journal, 6,* 3–15.

Gruber, H. E. (1997). Creative altruism, cooperation, and world peace. In M. A. Runco & R. Richards (Eds.) *Eminent creativity, everyday creativity, and health* (pp. 463–479). Greenwich, CT: Ablex.

Guilford, J. P. (1968). *Creativity, intelligence, and their educational implications.* San Diego, CA: Robert Knapp/EDITS.

Gute, G., Gute, D. S., Nakamura, J., & Csikszentmihalyi, M. (2008). The early lives of highly creative persons: The influence of the complex family. *Creativity Research Journal, 20*(4), 343–357.

Harrington, D. M. (1975). Effects of explicit instructions to be creative on the psychological meaning of divergent test scores. *Journal of Personality, 43,* 434–454.

Harrington, D. M. (1990). The ecology of human creativity: A psychological perspective. In M. A. Runco & R. S. Albert (Eds.), Theories of creativity (pp. 143–169). London: Sage.

Haste, H. (1993). Moral creativity and education for citizenship. *Creativity Research Journal, 6,* 153–164.

Helson, R. (1999). Institute of Personality Assessment and Research. In M. A. Runco & S. Pritzker (Eds.), *Encyclopedia of creativity* (pp. 71–79). San Diego, CA: Elsevier.

Hoff, E. V. (2005). Imaginary companions, creativity and self-image in middle childhood. *Creativity Research Journal, 17,* 167–180.

Hunsaker, S. L., & Callahan, C. M. (1995). Creativity and giftedness: Published instrument uses and abuses. *Gifted Child Quarterly, 39,* 110–114.

Hunter, S. T., Bedell, K. E., & Mumford, M. D. (2007). Climate for creativity: A quantitative review. *Creativity Research Journal, 19,* 69–90.

Johnson, D., Runco, M. A., & Raina, M. K. (2003). Parents' and teachers' implicit theories of children's creativity: A cross-cultural perspective. *Creativity Research Journal, 14,* 427–438.

Kohanyi, A. (2005). Turning inward versus turning outward: A retrospective study of the childhoods of creative writers versus journalists. *Creativity Research Journal, 17,* 309–320.

Kohlberg, L. (1966). A cognitive-developmental analysis of childhood sex role concepts and attitudes. In E. E. Maccoby (Ed.), *The development of sex differences* (pp. 179–204). Palo Alto, CA: Stanford University Press.

Kohlberg, L. (1987). The development of moral judgment and moral action. In L. Kohlberg (Ed.), *Child psychology and childhood education: A cognitive developmental view.* New York: Longman.

Kwang, N. (2002). *Why Asians are less creative than Westerners.* Singapore: Prentice-Hall.

Lim, S., & Smith, J. (2008). The structural relationships of parenting style, creative personality, and loneliness. *Creativity Research Journal, 20*(4), 412–419.

Mace, M. A., & Ward, T. (2002). Modeling the creative process: A grounded theory analysis of creativity in the domain of art making. *Creativity Research Journal, 14,* 179–192.

MacKinnon, D. (1960). The highly effective individual. In R. S. Albert (Ed.), *Genius and eminence: A social psychology of creativity and exceptional achievement* (pp. 114–127). Oxford: Pergamon.

MacKinnon, D. (1965). Personality and the realization of creative potential. *American Psychologist, 20,* 273–281.

Maslow, A. H. (1973). Creativity in self-actualizing people. In A. Rothen-berg and C. R. Hausman (Eds.), *The creative question* (pp. 86–92). Durham, NC: Duke University Press.

Matuga, J. M. (2004). Situated creative activity: The drawings and private speech of young children. *Creativity Research Journal, 16*(2–3), 267–281.

McCoy, J. M., & Evans, G. W. (2002). The potential role of the physical environment on fostering creativity. *Creativity Research Journal, 14,* 409–426.

McLaren, R. B. (1993). The dark side of creativity. *Creativity Research Journal, 6,* 137-144.

Meline, C. W. (1976). Does the medium matter? *Journal of Communication, 26,* 81–89.

Milgram, R. M. (1990). Creativity: An idea whose time has come and gone? In M. A. Runco & R. S. Albert (Eds.), *Theories of creativity* (pp. 215–233). Newbury Park, CA: Sage.

Milgram, R. M., & Feingold, S. (1977). Concrete and verbal reinforcement in creative thinking of disadvantaged students. *Perceptual and Motor Skills, 45,* 675–678.

Moore, M., & Russ, S. W. (2008). Follow-up of a pretend play intervention: Effects on play, creativity, and emotional processes in children. *Creativity Research Journal, 20*(4), 427–436.

Myers, W. A. (1979) Imaginary companions in childhood and adult creativity. *Psychoanalytic Quarterly, 48,* 292–307.

Pagona, B., & Costas, M. (2008). The development of motor creativity in elementary school children and its retention. *Creativity Research Journal, 20*(1), 72–80.

Patrick, C. (1935). Creative thought in poets. *Archives of Psychology, 26,* 1-74.

Patrick, C. (1937). Creative thought in artists. *Journal of Psychology, 5,* 35-73.

Pennebaker, J. W. (1997). Writing about emotional experiences as a therapeutic process. *Psychological Science, 8,* 162–166.

Pennebaker, J. W., Kiecolt-Glaser, J. K., & Glaser, R. (1997). Disclosure of trauma and immune functioning: Health implications for psychotherapy. In M. A. Runco & R. Richards (Eds.), *Eminent creativity, everyday creativity, and health* (pp. 287–302). Norwood, NJ: Ablex.

Piaget, J. (1962). *Play, dreams and imitation in childhood.* New York: Basic Books.

Piaget, J. (1976). *To understand is to invent.* New York: Penguin.

Plucker, J. A. (1998). Beware of simple conclusions: The case for content generality of creativity. *Creativity Research Journal, 11,* 179–182.

Plucker, J. A. (1999). Is the proof in the pudding? Reanalyses of Torrance's (1958 to Present) longitudinal data. *Creativity Research Journal, 12,* 103-114.

Proctor, R. M. J., & Burnett, P. C. (2004). Measuring cognitive and dispositional characteristics of creativity in elementary students. *Creativity Research Journal, 16,* 421–429.

Plucker, J. A., & Renzulli, J. S. (1999). Psychometric approaches to the study of human creativity. In R. J. Sternberg (Ed.).*Handbook of creativity* (pp. 35–61). Cambridge, UK: Cambridge University Press.

Raina, T. N. (1980). Sex differences in creativity in India: A second look. *Journal of Creative Behavior, 14,* 218–221.

Renzulli, J. (1978). What makes giftedness? Re-examining a defintion. *Phi Delta Kappan, 60,* 180–184.

Richards, R. (1990). Everyday creativity, eminent creativity, and health: "Afterview" for CRJ special issues on creativity and health. *Creativity Research Journal, 3,* 300–326.

Rogers, C. (1970). Toward a theory of creativity. In: P. Vernon (Ed.). *Creativity: Selected readings* (pp. 137–151). Harmondsworth: Penguin Books.

Rosenblatt, E., & Winner, E. (1988). The art of children's drawings. *Journal of Aesthetic Education, 22,* 3–15.

Rosenthal, R. (1991). Teacher expectancy effects: A brief update 25 years after the Pygmalion experiment. *Journal of Research in Education, 1,* 3–12.

Rubenson, D. L., & Runco, M. A. (1995). The psychoeconomic view of creative work in groups and organizations. *Creativity and Innovation Management, 4,* 232–241.

Runco, M. A. (1984). Teachers' judgments of creativity and social validation of divergent thinking tests. *Perceptual and Motor Skills, 59,* 711–717.

Runco, M. A. (1987) The generality of creative performance in gifted and nongifted children. *Gifted Child Quarterly, 31,*121–125.

Runco, M. A. (1988). Creativity research: Originality, utility, and integration. *Creativity Research Journal, 1,* 1–7.

Runco, M. A. (1989). Parents' and teachers' ratings of the creativity of children. *Journal of Social Behavior and Personality, 4,* 73–83.

Runco, M. A. (Ed.). (1991). *Divergent thinking.* Norwood, NJ: Ablex.

Runco, M. A. (1993). Moral creativity: Intentional and unconventional. *Creativity Research Journal, 6,* 17–28.

Runco, M. A. (1994). Giftedness as critical creative thought. In N. Colangelo, S. Assouline, & D. L. Ambroson (Eds.), *Talent development: Proceedings from the 1993 Henry B. and Jocelyn Wallace national research symposium on talent development* (vol. 2, pp. 239–249). Dayton, OH: Ohio Psychology Press.

Runco, M. A. (1996). Personal creativity: Definition and developmental issues. *New Directions for Child Development, 72* (Summer), 3–30.

Runco, M. A. (1997). Is every child gifted? *Roeper Review, 19,* 220–224.

Runco, M. A. (1999). The forth-grade slump. In M. A. Runco & S.Pritzker (Eds.), *Encyclopedia of creativity* (pp. 743–744). San Diego, CA: Academic Press.

Runco, M. A. (2003). Education for creative potential. *Scandinavian Journal of Education, 47,* 317–324.

Runco, M. A. (2007). *Creativity: Theories and themes: Research, development and practice.* San Diego, CA: Academic Press.

Runco, M. A., & Albert, R. S. (1985). The reliability and validity of ideational originality in the divergent thinking of academically gifted and nongifted children. *Educational and Psychological Measurement, 45,* 483–501.

Runco, M. A., & Albert, R. S. (1986). The threshold hypothesis regarding creativity and intelligence: An empirical test with gifted and nongifted children. *Creative Child and Adult Quarterly, 11,* 212–218.

Runco, M. A., & Albert, R. S. (2005). Parents' personality and the creative potential of exceptionally gifted boys. *Creativity Research Journal, 17,* 355–368.

Runco, M. A., & Bahleda, M. D. (1986). Implicit theories of artistic, scientific, and everyday creativity. *Journal of Creative Behavior, 20,* 93–98.

Runco, M. A., & Charles, R. (1993). Judgments of originality and appropriateness as predictors of creativity. *Personality and Individual Differences, 15,* 537–546.

Runco, M. A., & Charles, R. (1997). Developmental trends in creativity. In M. A. Runco (Ed.), *Creativity research handbook* (vol. 1, pp. 113–150). Cresskill, NJ: Hampton Press.

Runco, M. A., & Gaynor J. L. R. (1993). Creativity as optimal development. In J. Brzezinski, S. DiNuovo, T. Marek, & T. Maruszewski (Eds.), *Creativity and consciousness: Philosophical and psychological dimensions* (pp. 395–412). Amsterdam, the Netherlands: Rodopi.

Runco, M. A., Noble, E. P., & Luptak, Y. (1990). Agreement between mothers and sons on ratings of creative activity. *Educational and Psychological Measurement, 50,* 673–680.

Runco, M. A., & Pezdek, K. (1984). The effect of radio and television on children's creativity. *Human Communications Research, 11,* 109–120.

Runco, M. A., Plucker, J. A. & Lim, W. (2000-2001). Development and psychometric integrity of a measure of ideational behavior. *Creativity Research Journal, 13,* 393–400.

Runco, M. A., & Richards, R. (Eds.). (1997). *Eminent creativity, everyday creativity, and health.* Norwood, NJ: Ablex.

Russ, S. (1993). *Affect and creativity: The role of affect and play in the creative process.* Hillsdale, NJ: Lawrence Erlbaum Associates.

Russ, S. W. & Fiorelli, J. A. (2010). Developmental approaches to creativity. In J. C. Kaufman & R. J. Sternberg (Eds.), *The Cambridge handbook of creativity* (pp. 233–249). New York: Cambridge University Press.

Russ, S. W., & Schafer, E. D. (2006). Affect in fantasy play, emotion and memories, and divergent thinking. *Creativity Research Journal, 18,* 347–354.

Sak, U., & Maker, C. J. (2006). Developmental variation in children's creative mathematical thinking as a function of schooling, age, and knowledge. *Creativity Research Journal, 18,* 279–291.

Sarsani, M. R. (2008). Do high and low creative children differ in their cognition and motivation? *Creativity Research Journal, 20(2),* 155–170.

Schaefer, C. E. (1971). *Manual for the biographical inventory of creativity.* San Diego, CA: Educational and Industrial Testing Services.

Schmukler, D. (1985). Foundations of creativity: The facilitating environment. In J. Freeman (Ed.), *The psychology of gifted children* (pp. 75–91). New York: Wiley.

Singer, J., & Singer D. (in press). In M. A. Runco (Ed.), *Creativity research handbook* (Vol. 3). Cresskill, NJ: Hampton Press.

Singh, R. P. (1987). Parental perception about creative children. *Creative Child and Adult Quarterly, 12,* 39–42.

Smith, G. J. W., & Carlsson, I. (1983). Creativity in early and middle school years. *International Journal of Behavioral Development, 6,* 167–195.

Smith, G. J. W., & Carlsson, I. (1985). Creativity in middle and late school years. *International Journal of Behavioral Development, 8,* 329–343.

Smith, K. L. R., Michael, W. B., & Hocevar, D. (1990). Performance on creativity measures with examination-taking instructions intended to induce high or low levels of test anxiety. *Creativity Research Journal, 3,* 265–280.

Smolucha, F. (1992a). A reconstruction of Vygotsky's theory of creativity. *Creativity Research Journal, 5,* 49–67.

Smolucha, F. (1992b). The relevance of Vygotsky's theory of creative imagination for contemporary research on play. *Creativity Research Journal, 5,* 69–76.

Somers, J. U., &Yawkey, T. D. (1984). Imaginary companions: Contributions of creative and intellectual abilities of young children. *Journal of Creative Behavior, 18,* 77–89.

Subotnik, R. F., & Arnold, K. D. (1999). Longitudinal studies. In M. A. Runco & S.Pritzker (Eds.), *Encyclopedia of creativity* (pp. 163–168). San Diego, CA: Academic Press.

Sulloway, T. (1997). *Born to rebel: Birth order, family dynamics, and creative lives.* New York: Vintage.

Tacher, E. L., & Readdick, C. A. (2006). The relation between aggression and creativity among second graders. *Creativity Research Journal, 18,* 261–267.

Torrance, E. P. (1968a). A longitudinal examination of the fourth-grade slump in creativity. *Gifted Child Quarterly, 12,* 195–199.

Torrance, E. P. (1968b). Finding hidden talents among disadvantaged children. *Gifted Child Quarterly, 12,* 131-137.

Torrance, E. P. (1981). Non-test ways of identifying the creatively gifted. In J. C. Gowan, J. Khatena, & E. P. Torrance (Eds.), *Creativity: Its educational implications* (2nd ed., pp. 165–170). Dubuque, IA: Kendall/Hunt.

Wallach, M. A., & Kogan, N. (1965). *Modes of thinking in young children.* New York: Holt, Rinehart & Winston.

Wallach, M. A., & Wing, C. (1969). *The talented student.* New York: Holt, Rinehart & Winston.

Weisberg, P.A., & Springer, K. J. (1961). Environmental factors in creative functioning. *Archives of General Psychiatry, 5,* 64–74.

Westby, E. L., & Dawson, V. L. (1995). Creativity: Asset or burden in the classroom? *Creativity Research Journal, 8,* 1–10.

Williams, F. E. (1991). *Creativity assessment packet: Test manual.* Austin, TX: Pro-Ed.

Zajonc, R.B. (1976). Family configuration and intelligence. *Science, 192,* 227–235.

Part II

**Early Childhood Educational
Curriculum and Instruction**

7

Rethinking Language Education in Early Childhood

Sociocultural Perspectives

JIM ANDERSON
University of British Columbia

LYNDSAY MOFFATT
University of Western Sydney

MARIANNE McTAVISH AND JON SHAPIRO
University of British Columbia

Over the past 20 years or so, there has been a continuing shift, or reconceptualization, in terms of how researchers and educators approach early childhood language learning. According to Kramsch (2002), researchers interested in language acquisition from the end of 1960s to the end of the 1970s tended to be informed by a psycholinguistic perspective. They were apt to use a conception of *learner as computer* as they attempted to understand how learners transformed language *input* into language *output*. In contrast, from the late 1970s onward, researchers working from a language socialization perspective have been more likely to see learners as apprentices who learn to use language through active participation in a variety of language communities (e.g., Heath, 1983). Increasingly, researchers concerned with children's language acquisition have focused not just on new individual children's develop language skills but more on the contexts and conditions in which children acquire language. In particular, researchers have begun to ask how social interaction and sociocultural contexts affect language use and development.[1] This shift in research and theory has also affected the kinds of places that researchers have chosen to investigate and the methods they choose to collect data. Whereas earlier studies tended to take place in laboratories in (ostensibly) controlled conditions and to rely on quantitative research methods, more recent studies have examined children's language development in more naturalistic settings such as homes, day cares, preschools, and primary classrooms, using a variety of qualitative and quantitative methods (e.g., Dickinson, Darrow, & Tinbu, 2008; Li, 2006; Wohlwend, 2009a). Gee (1989) and others refer to this shift as the *social turn* or the burgeoning interest among researchers and theorists in the social nature of language, literacy, and indeed of learning.

By exploring language development in a variety of contexts using diverse methods, researchers in early language acquisition have begun to document how sociocultural context plays a significant role in the ways in which children acquire language. This research and the popularization of the work of key theorists such as Bakhtin (1986), Bourdieu (1990), and Vygotsky (1978) have had a significant impact on the way that early childhood researchers now conceptualize learning. Although previously researchers and theorists tended to see learning as linked to individual children's mental strategies, or characteristics, more recent conceptualizations of learning have stressed the importance of children's social relations and social positions or their *interactional circumstances* (McDermott, 1993). Although some researchers continue to describe students' relationships to language learning that focus on individual personality traits, others have begun to see language acquisition as embedded in sociocultural interactions. In other words, these theorists have argued that what people learn and how much they learn depends less on their supposedly innate capabilities and more on who they interact with or the kinds of *discourses* (Gee, 1989) to which they are exposed. Thus, although some researchers continue to examine the role of individual characteristics such as motivation in language and literacy learning (e.g., Watkins & Coffey, 2004), others examine the role of social relations and power dynamics in early childhood language/literacy acquisition. As noted by Toohey (2000), until recently, relatively little research on children's language acquisition has considered how social relations among learners, or among learners and those who judge their performances, might affect judgments of cognition, social adjustment, or learning styles. (p. 7)

In this chapter, we explore some of the current research in

early childhood language education. Three questions provide a framework for the organization of this chapter: (1) How can we best understand children's language development? (2) How can educators assess language competence? and (3) How can educators support children's language learning?

Understanding Language Development

Variation in Language Learning and Teaching

Studies of young children's language development reveal that there is considerable variation in terms of the kinds of talk that children are exposed to and produce (e.g., Hart & Risley, 1995; Reese, Sparkes, & Leyva, 2010). For example, in a large-scale longitudinal study of a heterogeneous group of preschool children, Dickinson (2001) and his colleagues found considerable variation in terms of the kinds of language that children from different families heard and participated in. A particularly striking example was the wide variation in terms of the amount of parent and child nonimmediate talk during storybook reading sessions, in parent–child play, and at mealtimes. De Temple (2001) noted that nonimmediate talk "typically involves longer utterances and more explicit, complex language than does labeling or the yes-no questioning that constitutes much of immediate talk" (p. 39). Children in families where there is less nonimmediate talk tend to perform less well on language and literacy measures that are often used in kindergarten.

Researchers such as Hart and Risley (1995) and Snow, Tabors, and Dickinson (2001) have considered variability in children's language in terms of the amount of talk at home or the use of decontextualized or more abstract language. However, another line of research has examined language differences from a functional perspective (e.g., Halliday, 1973). Hasan (1989) and her colleagues looked at semantic variation in everyday talk of mothers and children from different social classes. Semantic variation "refers to the systematic variation in the meanings people select in similar contexts as a function of their social positioning" (Williams, 2005, p. 457) and is based on the theory of a *restricted* and *elaborated* codes espoused by Bernstein (1971). Put simply, because of the nature of the materiality of their work, members of the working class tend to use a *restricted* code because "there is no functional reason to elaborate meanings because they are so well known." That is, they do not provide explanations or elaborations because these are not needed; the meanings are obvious by the context. However, for people whose work is distanced from the material work of production, greater elaboration is called for. Hasan (1989) found that mother–child dyads from low autonomy (i.e., working class) homes engaged in significantly less elaboration than did dyads from high autonomy homes. Williams (1995), in his study that focused on shared book reading, found essentially the same patterns; there was more semantic variation in high autonomy homes than in low autonomy or working class homes.

Dickinson (2001) also examined the influence of the preschool classroom on children's language and literacy development. Teachers varied in the amount of support they provided for children's language development. Several teacher and classroom variables were identified as contributing to children's language development, including the provision of a well-defined, well-equipped writing area. As well, teachers in classrooms with a lower teacher:student ratio tended to provide more opportunity for children to engage in discussion. Furthermore, better educated teachers tended to support children's language development across contexts more so than did less well-educated teachers. These findings demonstrate the need to allocate adequate resources to early childhood education in the form of well-equipped classrooms, adequate staffing, and properly trained, well-paid teachers. But as Dickinson indicated, our society tends to place very little value on early childhood education and early childhood teachers.

Much of the research on children's language acquisition has tended to focus on the role of adults in supporting children. More recently, researchers have begun to examine the important role of siblings and peers in children's language development. For example, Gregory (2005), in her work with Bangladeshi families in East London, documented the important roles that siblings play in supporting each other's language and literacy development, especially as they play school at home. In their study with three Punjabi speaking families who were sharing a home, Mui and Anderson (2008) found that cousins, as well as siblings, played important roles at home in helping each other acquire and develop language and literacy through assisting with homework, playing word/board games, and participating in elaborate role playing episodes. Long (1998) investigated the role of peers in language learning. She documented her daughter's learning of Icelandic over an 8-month period, concluding that her daughter's out-of-school play was the most supportive context for language learning; in school, learning was more gradual and involved less experimentation and more hesitancy. Long posited that her daughter's language learning was an embodiment of Cole's (1996) notion of prolepsis, "a form of support that occurs as more experienced cultural members represent/project in language and behavior, the newcomer's potential future" (Long, 1998, p. 10). In a study involving 1,812 kindergarten children in public schools in the United States, Mashburne, Justice, Downer, and Pianta (2010) found that children's receptive (i.e., listening) and expressive (i.e., talking) language development benefited from their being in a class with peers with more advanced expressive language, a finding consistent with Long's case study.

Bilingual and Biliteracy Development

In an era of unprecedented movement of people and rapid technological advancements, interest in children's acquisition of a second or additional language has received considerable attention from researchers. For example, Parke, Drury, Kenner, and Robertson (2002), noting the relative dearth of research documenting young children's simultaneous acquisition of English and a low-status mother tongue, described four studies conducted in an inner-city area of England involving children, ages 4 through 7, whose first languages were Pahari, Gujarati, or Urdu. The specific contexts of each of the studies were as follows: talking at home, writing in a nursery school, retelling English texts, and participating in a school assembly. In the first study, the children appropriated the routines and discourse patterns from their nursery school into their play as they practiced English at home. The children also demonstrated that they were adept code switchers, reverting to Pahari to keep siblings engaged or to insure that they clearly understood instructions. In the second study, analysis of a 4-year-old child's writing in the nursery school revealed that her writing was a hybrid text that incorporated orthographic features of English and Gujarati. Gregory (2005) maintained that as educators, we must come to understand the importance of this hybridity as children blend new and old practices.

In the third study, three children (ages 5:6, 6:3, and 6:8) retold in English and in their first language (Pahari or Urdu), a text that had been read to them in English. Although the children heard the text in English only, their retellings in their first language revealed that they comprehended the text fully and accurately whereas their retellings in English were less detailed, less coherent, and less accurate (p. 214). The final study examined the effects of introducing culturally relevant practice in a school assembly. In reviewing the changes in the children's behavior, the author contrasted a group of primary school children's disengagement—indeed disruptive behavior—during a regular school assembly with their concentration and attention when a language support teacher explained an upcoming Muslim religious festival. The change in the children's engagement when the discursive and textual practices from their own community were employed was striking:

> After some clearly signalled rituals such as covering her head, she [the support teacher] explains in both Pahari and English that she is about to read one small fraction of the Qu'ran in preparation for Eid. Then she proceeds to read. The children fall silent. Fifteen minutes later, the whole school is still able to concentrate and listen including that very disruptive year 2 class. (Parke et al., 2002, p. 215)

Bauer (2000) documented the biliteracy and bilingual development of her daughter, Elena. In this longitudinal case study, she traced her daughter's emerging language and literacy development commencing when the child turned 2. Data collection included: "field notes, journals, audio and videotaped observations of Elena's participation in literacy routines" (p. 109), with a particular focus on the child's code switching during shared reading. Bauer found that code switching was reduced in highly patterned texts, that the child's code switching was influenced by the child's view

of the task, and that the code switching that occurred during the discussions of the text resembled that which occurred in talk outside of literacy events. As Bauer (2002) indicated, there will be considerable variation in children's language and literacy learning across contexts, an important point that educators and researchers need always to consider.

More recently, researchers have begun to question the notion that children acquire a second language simply by being immersed in it (e.g., Krashen, 1981). For example, Haworth et al. (2006) investigated young children's bilingual development in New Zealand. They concluded that contrary to the position of Krashen (1981) and others, teachers and caregivers play a key mediating role and children do not acquire another language by osmosis. Spycher (2009) also compared implicit versus explicit instruction in kindergarten children's learning science vocabulary and concepts. She found that both the children learning English as a second language and children who spoke only English benefited from the more explicit instruction, a finding consistent with research in vocabulary instruction with monolingual children (e.g., Beck & McKeown, 2007). Raising alarms about language instruction for young children in California where one in three come to school speaking a language other than English, Spycher (2009) stated that most English language learners are taught by teachers who do not speak their language and who are inadequately trained and are not provided with the resources and support to meet their students' needs.

Although researchers have developed a fairly thorough understanding of young children's second or additional language learning from a psycholinguistic perspective, they have also highlighted the complexity of the phenomenon, especially when social and cultural aspects are considered. For example, some teachers and parents still believe that their children's learning of English will be negatively affected if they speak their home language (e.g., Pacini-Ketchbaw & Armstong de Almedia, 2006). Some parents also believe that their children will be stereotyped and their learning will be negatively impacted in school if they speak a language other than English and they rename their children with English names in an attempt to hide their linguistic identity (Souto-Manning, 2007). In addition, as is pointed out elsewhere in this chapter, young children have agency and may resist using their first or home language, especially if they view the language of the school as having higher status.

Over the years, researchers have consistently shown that children's language and literacy learning are enhanced if they learn to read and write initially in their first language (e.g., Bialystok, 1997; Gunderson, 2004; Snow, Burns, & Griffin, 1998). Although being bilingual or multilingual in a globalized world is increasingly regarded as an asset, young children's bilingual and biliteracy development is often actively discouraged. For example, in California, Proposition 227 effectively eliminated bilingual education for young children who are expected to learn English from the beginning. Canada has developed official policies in support of bilingualism and multiculturalism. However, in their analysis of documents produced by government departments and agencies in Canada, Pacini-Ketchbaw and Armstong de Almedia (2006) concluded:

> In the pamphlets, it is assumed: (a) that young children and families are culturally, racially, as well as linguistically homogeneous; (b) that child development theories that emphasize universal aspects of development and child-centred activities are the best for all children regardless of background and abilities; (c) that all children are monolingual, normalising English as the most relevant way to communication for children. (p. 316)

Alas, in Canada, the privileging of English extends beyond discourse. For example, the Early Development Instrument (EDI) is widely administered and produces maps of community strengths and weaknesses in terms of early child development. This instrument consists of 100 items, completed by the kindergarten teacher for each child without the children being present. Li, D'Angiulli, and Kendal (2007) in a critical review, raised a number of important questions and issues about the EDI. One of their troubling conclusions follows:

> Despite evidence to the contrary, the overwhelming message conveyed by the findings of the EDI implementation is that English as a second language in the preschool years leads to poor outcomes in language, communication skills and social competence in later life (Hart et al., 2003). An unintended consequence of this understanding is that bilingual language development will be discouraged within families and the community, generally. Thus, the EDI may potentially stifle cultural and linguistic diversity. (p. 231)

Given the issues we later raise regarding the problems associated with teachers from one cultural or linguistic group judging the language ability of children from another group, the evaluation by Li et al. should cause educators and policy makers to interpret the results of the EDI carefully.

Language Revitalization

Of course, for some children, learning a second language may involve learning their ancestral language and interest in language reclamation or language revitalization is receiving increasing attention in early childhood education. For example, in New Zealand *language nests* provide young Maori children with immersion and support in their ancestral language (Robust, 2002). In Ireland, preschools are supporting young children in learning the Gaelic language (Mhathuma, 2008) and there is considerable interest in Canada in revitalizing Indigenous languages, which, despite a growing Aboriginal population, are in decline or faced with extinction. Indeed, despite the many challenges, interest in language revitalization is increasing internationally. Given that the early years are optimal for language learning, this phenomenon will undoubtedly be of increasing importance in language education in early childhood.

Children's Written Language: Sociocultural Perspectives

Until fairly recently, young children were not seen as capable of writing. Until the 1980s, children in kindergarten and first grade children typically spent considerable time copying from the chalkboard or in workbooks and worksheets (Dyson, 2010). However, the foundational work of Chomsky (1971) and Read (1975) documented how, from a young age, children were developing an understanding of the writing system and that their early attempts were systematic and logical. Interest in young children's writing proliferated in the 1980s as other researchers (e.g., Bissex, 1980; Ferreiro & Teberosky, 1982) expanded on this earlier work. Indeed, interest in young children's writing peaked in the 1980s as Donald Graves and his colleagues introduced writing process pedagogy into early literacy classrooms. Child centered and progressive, process writing proponents argued that children at a very young age could write and that they could also revise and edit their work, just as professional writers do (Graves, 1983). However, several criticisms of the writing process arose, including: (1) much of the writing was narrative and personal and children were not learning to write a range of genres necessary in an increasingly complex world (e.g., Cope & Kalantzis, 1993); (2) children wrote in their vernacular and were not learning standard forms or *the power codes* (Delpit, 1995); and (3) the pedagogy was rooted in individualist ideology, ignoring the social dimensions of young children's learning (Dyson, 2010).

In the 1990s, researchers began to focus more on the sociocultural dimensions of children's writing. For example, Chapman (1994) documented the range of genres that children in a first grade class produced during writers' workshop including, dialogue, labels, letters, lists, narratives and so on. Wollman-Bonilla (2001) investigated the role of Family Message Journals in a first grade class, identifying a range of genres that children and parents employed, as well as documenting the important role that parents played in children's writing development. And Dyson (1999) explored how young children appropriate popular culture and other aspects of their social worlds in their writing. She argued, "By ignoring children's media use, schools collaborate in solidifying and perpetuating societal divisions in cultural art forms and in children's orientations to each other and to school itself" (Dyson, 2000, p. 356).

Dyson, a leader in research in young children's writing reminds us that children operate in the official world of school and the world of their own social realities. Over the last several years, the official world of school has seen literacy practices constrained by an emphasis on highly prescriptive curricula and standardized testing. However, a growing body of research suggests the importance of a sociocultural lens in examining and supporting young children's writing development. For example, in referencing their case study of Jewel, a kindergarten student, Siegel, Kontovourki, Schmier, and Enriquez (2008) pointed out:

The school curriculum continues to treat literacy as mono-modal, monolinguistic, and monocultural and thus appears to have more in common with what children learned about literacy a generation ago than with the literacies needed for the world in which Jewel lives. (p. 97)

A consistent theme in much of the current research on children's writing in the last decade or so is the manner in which children appropriate the knowledge they bring from their world outside the classroom in their writing in school (e.g., Marsh, 2000). For example, Wohlwend (2009b) documented the literacy practices of 21 students in a kindergarten class in the United States as part of a 3-year ethnographic study. Drawing on identity theory and focusing on a group of children who incorporated Disney Princess dolls into their writing, Wohlwend described how children "wrote narratives in their books, drew storyboard images, and voiced scripts" in contrast to "the repetitive labeling of static images" (p. 76) found in kindergarten classrooms where scripted texts and teacher centered curriculum and pedagogy prevail. Of course, children's use of popular culture can be problematic, and indeed gendered and stereotypical language and characters are often found in children's writing, as was the case with Zoe who typically ended "her books and plays with weddings for happily-ever-after endings" (p. 79). Acknowledging the tension involved in encouraging children to draw upon semiotic resources including popular culture in their writing, Wohl-wend (2009b) proposed, "children are not cultural dupes at the mercy of global corporations or cultural geniuses who shrewdly access and expertly manipulate vast networks of gendered multi-media for their own purposes" (p. 79).

Currently in many Western nations, there is much emphasis in schools and early childhood classrooms on print knowledge in young children's early literacy learning (e.g., Dyson, 2010). However, Siegel et al. (2008) and others argue that as children engage in literacy at home and at school, they utilize a range of semiotic resources that include their background knowledge and experiences, oral language, dramatic play, role playing, and drawing. For example, Dyson's work clearly demonstrates how young children capitalize on their knowledge of popular culture, such as superheroes, as they write. Her work also reveals the importance of talk as children compose and make meaning. Myhill and Jones (2009) also investigated the importance of talk in rehearsing for, and contributing to, writing. They found that children in early years classrooms used talk to shape their writing prior to commencing to compose on screen. Interestingly, they concluded that talk was important both "as an individual rehearsal process and as an interactive shared process with peers" (p. 265). Researchers have also continued to examine the role of drawing in young children's writing. As Dyson (2008) pointed out, drawing has tended to be viewed as a prewriting or planning strategy, and not an inherent part of the composing process. Like Sigel et al, Dyson argued that we need to think of children's writing from a *design* perspective as in the following description:

For example, even when Mrs. Kay urged the children to stop drawing and to write, Tionna kept drawing *if* spatial information mattered in her story. One day she wrote about a vehicle accident she had been in the day before. In this piece, not only did the spatial positioning of her grandma's truck matter, but so did the color of the traffic lights facing her grandma's truck (green) and the offending car (red). In fact, producing this composition was the only time Tionna violated the rule against using crayons during writing time. (Dyson, 2008, p.133)

Knowledge about print is essential in young children's literacy development but we must recognize that children use other resources as they construct and represent meaning.

In Dyson's (2008) study, Tionna's decision to use crayons because color was essential to her drawing highlights another theme in current research—children's agency in their writing. Indeed, Dyson asserted that children like Tionna are much more than "apprentices waiting to slip into the slots of school writing"; instead, they are "complex social beings who negotiate the meanings of official school practices" (p. 123). In their observational study of 11 preschool children, Rowe and Neitzel (2010) identified four types of interests that were reflected in children's play: conceptual, procedural, creative, or social. They found that children's interests influenced their early literacy and play behavior. They reported, "As early as age 2 and 3, very young children in our study shaped writing and play events according to their personal interests" and concluded, "even the youngest children exert agency in the service of their own participation and learning" (p. 2010).

In terms of early writing then, researchers continue to document that children come to school with a range of resources that they call upon as they engage in making meaning through writing. Children utilize different modalities as they create meaning through writing, even in classrooms where teachers emphasize print as they implement scripted curriculum. Related to this, children exert agency in their writing both in terms of what they write about and the modes they employ in their writing. And finally, children are capable of using digital tools in their writing in ways that make sense to them.

Writing and Digital Resources. In the area of shared book reading, a body of research (e.g., Kim & Anderson, 2008; Korat & Or, 2010) is emerging in terms of young children's reading with digital texts. Much less research is evident with regards to children's writing in the context of digital literacy. However, Mavers (2007) documented one young child's use of e-mail as she communicated with her uncle. Mavers pointed out that in considering children's use of tools such as e-mail, it is important to recognize the affordances that they offer the child here and now, commenting, "this is not about an adult-in-waiting for the communicational landscape of the future" (p.172). McKenney and Voogt (2009) described a project called PictoPal that is designed to promote children's use of writing on computers but provided little evidence of how children actually engaged with the digital tools.

To summarize, young children's language development is social with significant others such as parents, siblings, peers, and caregivers and teachers playing supportive roles. Furthermore, there is considerable variation in children's language learning and social-contextual factors such as social class appear to play a role in these differences. Young children are adroit at learning additional languages, although political and ideological factors sometimes mitigate this learning. Young children's writing is now seen as one aspect of their meaning making as they draw upon semiotic resources such as talk, drawing, dramatization, and so forth to make meaning. Finally, although there are concerns about the role of screen media in young children's language and literacy development, critical reviews of the literature suggest that these tools can be facilitative, if utilized appropriately.

Assessing Language Learning

According to Wohlwend (2009a), language assessment is a contested site, where various theories, ideas, and discourses of language learning and assessment compete, overlap, and challenge each other. A central question in current research concerning language assessment is how best to assess children's language learning given the complexity of contemporary language communities and what we know about how children learn to speak, read, and write. Research conducted over the past 40 years suggests that adults and children have a wide variety of ways of using language (Ball, 2009; Bedore & Pena, 2008; Carter et al., 2005; Craig & Washington, 2002; Cross, De Vaney, & Jones, 2001; Heath, 1986; Johnston & Wong, 2002; Pena, 1997). However, educators and speech language pathologists continue to rely on limited ways of assessing what children know about language and how it is used. While educators and other professionals are often concerned with locating "struggling" language learners, research suggests that doing so is fraught with a vast range of challenges. The first challenge for anyone charged with assessing young children's language development is the question of what form of assessment should be used. While the use of standardized language tests has come under considerable scrutiny over the past few decades, these kinds of assessments continue to be used in many contexts. Although there may be some situations in which standardized language tests are useful (e.g., as baseline data; in projects of large-scale assessment), current literature reveals the limitations of these tools, particularly when they are used to make judgments and decisions about individual children in isolation from more ecologically valid data (Caesar & Kohler, 2009; Carter et al., 2005; Gutierrez-Clellen & Simon-Cereijido, 2009; National Association for the Education of Young Children [NAEYC], 2003; Thurman & McGrath, 2008). It is important for educators, researchers and speech-language pathologists to understand some of the limitations of such assessments and what kinds of alternative approaches are available. In the following section, we explore some of these limitations and suggest some alternative methods for gauging what children know about language and how it is used.

The Limits of Standardized Language Tests

One of the reasons why standardized tests offer limited information about young children's language abilities stems from the complexity of language itself. Dockrell (2001) argued that the variability in normal patterns of language development, and the difficulty of distinguishing between enduring problems and transient ones, makes it difficult to draw useful conclusions about young children's language abilities from their scores on standardized language assessments alone. These complexities are also compounded by how children acquire language and by the diversity of dialect and language experiences in the current multicultural and multilingual world. If, as it appears, what children learn is greatly determined by the environments they are born into, then it is important to ask what standardized language tests are actually able to assess. Can they evaluate young children's ability to use language, and whether they need remedial attention? Or, can they merely help to describe *how* children currently use language in comparison with mainstream, or hegemonic, sociocultural groups? Sociocultural perspectives of language learning suggest that standardized tests can only accomplish the latter.

From this point of view, typical standardized tests are of limited value as tools for evaluating what a child can do with language or whether a child needs extra language support. From this perspective, standardized language assessments can only describe a child's use of language in a very specific kind of interaction, and in comparison with a very specific population—the children originally used to "norm" the test. Thurman and McGrath (2008) argued that these assessments often bear little resemblance to children's natural environments, or everyday interactions, thus, they cannot provide much information about children's actual language skills.

Some educators have claimed that the widespread use of standardized tests may reinforce racist and classist ideas of children's language use. Extensive research has documented how issues of bias can affect language assessments (Craig & Washington, 2002; Cross et al., 2001; Eriks-Brophy, Quittenbaum, Anderson, & Nelson 2008; Pena, 1997; Restrepo & Silverman, 2001; Scheffner-Hammer, Pennock-Roman, Rzaasa, & Tomblin, 2002; Spinelli, 2008). Eriks-Brophy, Quittenbaum, Anderson, and Nelson (2008) identified several ways that the validity of a standardized norm-referenced test may be compromised, particularly when it is used with children from marginalized language groups. Some of the ways the validity of these assessments can be compromised are: through the referral source (or the person who first refers the child for assessment), through the examiner, through the test procedures and materials, and through the language in which the assessment is conducted.

Examiner Bias

Over the years, researchers have found that both preservice and in-service teachers (some of whom administer standardized tests), bring cultural expectations to assessment tasks. For example, Cross et al. (2001) found that preservice teachers held more favorable attitudes toward speakers from cultural groups similar to their own. In an examination of 111 preservice teachers at a small college in the United States, they concluded that future educators were willing to make a range of judgments about readers' intelligence, friendliness, consideration, education, trustworthiness, ambition, honesty, and social status based solely on the readers' dialects. Results indicated that White respondents had more favorable impressions of White readers and that Black respondents had more favorable impressions of Black readers. It would seem likely that such judgments would play out when these educators began teaching and assessing students' performances. Similarly, in a study of teachers' ratings of the future academic competence of 105 poor and working-class kindergarten students, Hauser-Cram, Sirin, and Stipek (2003) found that teachers rated students as less likely to succeed when they perceived a value difference between themselves and their students' families, regardless of their students' actual competencies.

Research also suggests that teachers from different cultural backgrounds may have different understandings of the role of talk and the value of talkativeness in children. For example, Eriks-Brophy et al. (2008) found that Inuit and non-Inuit teachers had diametrically opposed understandings of what makes a child "successful" or "unsuccessful" in school and what would make a child a good candidate for special education, or intervention. For the non-Inuit teachers, "vocal kids" were seen as successful in school. For the Inuit teacher, talking "too much" was seen as a potential sign of "learning problems" and "low intelligence." It is likely that these teachers would have very different ideas of which children should be referred for language assessment and intervention. According to Westby (2009), many European-American educators and parents view a verbal, assertive child who initiates conversation with adults to be intelligent and mature; adults from other cultures that stress interdependence, rather than independence, may see the same child as immature and egocentric.

The results of these studies suggest that preservice and practicing teachers would likely benefit from intensive discussions of the origins and legitimacy of different dialects, the value of diversity, and the consequences of linguistic judgments and assessments in the classroom. For example, Fogel and Ehri (2006) described how teachers can be taught some of the syntactic features of African American English (AAE) as a way of helping them to work with their students who are AAE speakers. Similarly, a group of educators in Australia participated in an Action Research project concerning the development of "bidialectical" teaching practices (Cahill & Collard, 2003). Recognizing that Aboriginal English was the first dialect of most Indigenous students in Australia, these educators worked together to find two-way practices that would support their students' language and literacy development.

Other Biases

Further possibilities of bias can be found in test procedures and materials. There can be bias in test items, a situational bias, and bias in directions and values. For example, measures of expressive and receptive vocabulary often include pictures of items that may not be familiar to children from different regions or from different cultural and linguistic groups. Situational bias and linguistic bias can be seen in the interactional routines implicit in the assessment process. As Heath (1986) and Ball (2009) argued, the manner in which much testing is conducted reflects a particular cultural orientation. In a typical test situation, the person conducting the test takes a child aside and proceeds to ask him or her to label decontextualized pictures or to answer "known information" questions. Ethnographic and sociolinguistic research demonstrates that some cultures are far more likely than others to engage in these kinds of "school like" interactions and routines with children in their day-to-day lives outside of testing situations. These differences in cultural questioning practices may result in children from different cultural backgrounds having very different answers to the same assessment task. As Pena (1997, p. 323) remarked, "rehearsing facts particularly in the contexts of a question-answer routine between adult and child is not emphasized in the same manner or frequency across cultural/linguistic groups." Thus, when asked to name pictures of objects that the adult examiner presumably knows, a child from a sociocultural group that does not engage in known-information question routines may provide a description instead of the one word "correct" answer. For example, when presented with a picture of a pumpkin, the child may exclaim "Halloween!"; when presented with a picture of an umbrella, she or he may say "You use it when it is raining" (Pena, 1997). While these answers may be considered "incorrect" by the test protocol, they reveal that the child has familiarity with the objects and can produce relevant language when prompted. Similarly, recent research suggests that children from some language communities may have a different orientation to the use of nouns and verbs. For example, Lunney-Borden (2009) suggests that Mi'kmaq, spoken in Indigenous communities in eastern Canada, is a verb based language, while English is a more noun based language. In this way, descriptions made by speakers of these languages are often quite different. Mi'kmaw students speaking in English tend to include motion and states of being in their descriptions (e.g., "it goes straight" instead of "it is straight"; "it can sit still" instead of "it is flat"). This use of language is perfectly correct. However, monolingual English speakers, or English speakers unfamiliar with Mi'kmaq, may hear such descriptions as deviating from their expectations. In recognizing these differences in language use, it becomes important to ask questions about whether some of the perceived problems in vocabulary/language acquisition may have more to do with children's experiences with language and examiners' culturally based expectations, than with children's actual language abilities.

As the work of Ball (2009), Cross et al. (2001), Eriks-Brophy et al. (2008), Hauser-Cram et al. (2003), and Pena (1997) exemplifies, adults who assess young children's language abilities need to have an understanding of cultural, linguistic, dialectal, and socioeconomic differences. This understanding is particularly important when educators and speech language pathologists attempt to assess the language skills of children who come from sociocultural, socioeconomic, linguistic, or dialect backgrounds different from their own (e.g., Murphy, 1995). Westby (2009) noted that there are a number of resources that can help educators and speech language pathologists learn about various languages. However, this understanding needs to be anchored in skilled dialogue with parents and caregivers, and cannot be merely an intellectual knowledge of a culture. Given that bilingual and bidialectical learners comprise the majority of many urban schools, whereas 85% of teachers in the United States, for example, are Euro-American, these issues will likely remain at the forefront of attempts to create equitable and effective schools in the coming decades.

Researchers who have examined the validity of standardized tests have noted that, ironically, many tend both to over- and to underrefer children from marginalized communities for remediation (Laing, 2003; Laing & Kamhi, 2003; Pena, Iglesias, & Lidz, 2001). While these issues are particularly salient in middle and late childhood, there is evidence that children from linguistic minorities are often underreferred for remediation in early childhood and are overreferred in middle childhood. As the use of standardized tests appears to be on the rise in early childhood settings, considering these issues in the context of young children will likely become more pressing in the decades to come. On one level, overreferral may not seem problematic. Many educators and speech language pathologists may feel that it is better to overrefer than to underrefer when children's learning is at stake. However, it is important to recognize the impact that such overreferrals can have on individual children and their families, as well as on teachers' conceptions of various communities. For example, in the past 35 years, it has been found that, in the United States, African American children, bilingual children, children from linguistic minorities, children from lower socioeconomic classes, Hispanic children, and Indigenous children tend to be identified as needing language intervention at a much higher rate than children from White, Anglophone, middle-class families (Carter et al., 2005; Pena, 1997; Pena, Iglesias, &

Lidz, 2001; Spinelli, 2008). As Laing and Kamhi (2003) and Ball (2009) suggested, these differences in levels of identification may have more to do with which community has created the tests and what the test makers think of as "normal" language use, than with children's actual abilities or capacity for learning language or for becoming literate. Cross et al. (2001) and Feiler and Webster (1999) argued that the uncritical acceptance of standardized tests perpetuates racist and classist conceptions of children from certain communities as deficient, while it constructs others (usually children from White, Anglo, middle-class communities) as *normal* or *advanced*.

As standardized language tests offer limited information and may reflect and reinforce racist and classist ideas of children's language abilities, there is good reason to question the efficacy of using such tests with young children. However, there is also a need to be able to identify children who appear to be experiencing language delay or who struggle with literacy so that we may offer them extra assistance. In response, educators and speech language pathologists have begun to develop alternative ways of assessing young children's language abilities.

Alternative Modes of Assessment

Although there have been some attempts to modify standardized tests to accommodate different communities' language use, educators, parents, and speech language pathologists have also advocated using other methods to assess whether children need additional language support (Laing & Kahmi, 2003). There is strong support amongst many professionals for evaluations of student language skills that incorporate a range of data gathered across a variety of contexts. Multiple measures and procedures should be used to help assess and diagnose any child. Such measures and procedures could include and are not limited to: observations, interviews with parents and caregivers, and informal language sampling.

In observing children, educators and researchers can note when and how a child uses language and to what ends. For example, does the child appear to have a sense of storytelling language or the language of nonfiction? Does the child engage in language play or play with letters or texts? If so, when does she or he engage in these activities and with whom? By identifying what the child is already doing, educators and researchers can gain a sense of the child's current competencies and possible areas for further investigation or where the child is struggling. As argued by Spinelli (2008), these kinds of observations should be made in as many contexts as possible including but not limited to: structured and unstructured school settings (e.g., story time and free play time), with peers, in the home, and in the community.

Educators can also assess whether a child needs language support through open communication with the child's primary caregivers. Parents or primary caregivers are as reliable as standardized tests in terms of recognizing whether a child is struggling and needs extra language assistance or whether she or he is developing normally. Plainly, encouraging and maintaining open communication with parents and primary caregivers requires active work on the part of the educator and how the educator attempts to build this rapport is significant. In particular, it is important to remember that some parents may have had negative experiences in schools themselves and that they may need a variety of positive interactions with an educator before they feel comfortable discussing their child's needs. Similarly, some parents may feel uncomfortable being asked to evaluate their children in this way. Therefore, educators may need to think carefully about why they are concerned with a particular child's language skills and how to create informal and formal opportunities for positive interaction with a child's primary caregivers. They may also have to make repeated attempts at dialogue. However, as these efforts will hopefully assist in building a positive rapport with parents/caregivers, they also may translate into making the preschool, day care, and primary classroom a more productive learning environment. In doing so, educators will not only be more capable of assessing whether a child needs additional language support, but also may be providing a better learning community.

As language learning is more complicated than merely acquiring new grammatical structures and learning new vocabulary, other methods of assessment have been advocated in an attempt to capture what children actually know about language and whether they are suffering from language impairment. Some researchers have advocated using narrative assessments or play-based assessments to help evaluate young children's language abilities (Boudreau, 2008; Dykeman, 2008; Pena et al., 2006; Riley & Burrell, 2007; Thurman & McGrath, 2008). Narrative and play based assessments have been seen as more useful than standardized tests because narratives contain more elaborated speech than typical labeling tasks. In a narrative assessment, the educator/speech language pathologist elicits a narrative from a child by asking him or her particular questions. In a play-based assessment, the assessor introduces a range of toys and makes observations of prompted and spontaneous play. However, once again, issues of sociocultural context and bias present themselves, as children from different sociocultural groups often experience different forms of narrative socialization and play socialization (Bliss & McCabe, 2008; Delpit, 1995; Gutierrez-Clellen, Pena, & Quinn, 1995; Lai, Lee, & Lee, 2010). In other words, there is no universal logic to storytelling or play. Different sociocultural groups tell stories and play in different ways.

Finally, the persistent difficulty of creating an unbiased language assessment has led some researchers to experiment with process oriented, or dynamic assessments, and processing-dependent, as contrasted with knowledge-dependent, measures (Lidz, 1995; Pena et al., 2006; Thurman & McGrath, 2008). Educators and researchers begin with a pretest to assess certain aspects of a child's language use and then spend time teaching the skill or vocabulary that

they are attempting to assess. Following this minilesson, the child is assessed again. In this way, dynamic assessment can help educators and speech language pathologists understand how a child incorporates new knowledge into his or her language use. Studies suggest that such process oriented evaluations can help to differentiate effectively between language differences and language disorders (Pena et al. 2006; Pena, Iglesias, & Lidz, 2001). Experiments using "processing-dependent" measures (measures that place more emphasis on processing abilities than on prior knowledge), such as "nonword repetitions" have also had similar results when used on children 6 years old and older (Campbell & Dollaghan, 1997; Laing & Kamhi, 2003). However, recent research suggests caution in using nonword repetition assessments with younger children as these kinds of tests may deliver too many "false-positives" when used with young children.

Given the need to make distinctions between children who suffer from language impairments and those who do not, and the complexity of doing so, process oriented or dynamic assessments and process dependent measures may be the most potentially useful forms of assessment for educators and researchers attempting to gauge young children's language abilities. However, it bears noting that while some educators and researchers are content to assess children in isolation from their sociocultural context, others assert that the assessment of any child attending a school, preschool, or day care should actually begin with a focus on evaluating that child's instructional program. This step is particularly relevant for bilingual or bidialectical children but it could also be incorporated into regular practice so that examiners begin to see children as members of social environments. The kinds of questions that an evaluator might ask when assessing a program include: (1) Is the student in a culturally responsive climate? (2) Is the classroom conducive to learning and a supportive learning environment? (3) Does the teacher have high expectations for all students? Further questions might also include: (4) Do local policies support the creation of a culturally responsive climate? (5) How does the local administration support teachers' ongoing professional development as language and literacy educators? (6) How does the local school board or preschool board support teachers in creating positive learning environments? (7) How do state or provincial laws assist, or block, teachers' attempts to create inclusive and culturally responsive classrooms?

Assessing young children's language learning is a complex task. While many educators, researchers, and speech language pathologists continue to use standardized tests to measure children's language abilities, a great many others have recognized significant drawbacks to using these tools. One of the most significant drawbacks of these tools is the way that they tend to pathologize the diverse language use of bilingual, minority, and working class children. As these tests are generally normed to middle class, monolingual English speaking children, they cannot capture the wide range of linguistic competencies that many other children have in their day-to-day interactions. Recognizing these drawbacks to standardized tests has led numerous educators and researchers to advocate for the use of more informal methods of assessment such as observation, parent interviews, dynamic or process-based assessment, narrative assessment, and play-based assessments. As populations around the world continue to migrate and diversify, educators and researchers will need to continue to adapt their methods of assessing language learning. Given the need to accommodate language diversity, educators and researchers will likely continue to experiment with a variety of language assessments in the years to come.

Facilitating Language Learning

Shared Book Reading

Shared book reading has become a prominent phenomenon in young children's language and literacy development. Defined broadly, shared book reading refers to an experience between an adult and a preschool-aged child or group of children in which the adult reads a text and may engage the child/children in some discussion of the story or of related ideas (Hindman, Connor, Jewkes, & Morrison, 2008; Van Kleeck, Gillam, Hamilton, & McGrath, 1997; What Works Clearing House, 2006). Shared book reading has its genesis in the foundational research of Clark (1976) and Durkin (1966) who reported a common feature of young, precocious readers was that a significant other had read to them. Despite the fact that researchers (e.g., Bissex, 1980; Taylor, 1983) later documented that children engage in a wide range of literacy activities as they become literate, shared book reading has become "the literacy event par excellence" (Pellegrini, 1991, p. 380) seen in many circles as "the way" into literacy (Russ et al., 2007); hence, it has been afforded a central place in early childhood and primary grade classrooms, as well as many intervention programs (Anderson, Anderson, Lynch, & Shapiro, 2003).

During the 1990s, two meta-analyses were conducted on the effects of shared book reading and children's language and literacy development. Scarborough and Dobrich (1994) and Bus, Van Ijzendoorn, and Pellegrini (1995) agreed that shared book reading accounted for about 8% of the variance in children's later language performance. However, these reports differed significantly in their views of the importance of their findings. Bus et al. concluded that shared book reading is a "necessary preparation" (p. 17) for language and literacy learning, whereas Scarborough and Dobrich argued these findings might indicate an overemphasis on shared book reading as an intervention strategy and may even be counterproductive for some children. Given these contradictory views, efforts by researchers to untangle the effects of shared book reading proliferate (Cunningham & Zibulsky, 2011; Roy-Charland, Saint-Aubin, & Evans, 2007).

Research on Shared Book Reading Styles

Previous research has demonstrated that parents have diverse ways of interacting with their children (Hart, 2000) and there can be differences in the ways parents or primary caregivers (De Temple & Tabors, 1995; Shapiro, Anderson, & Anderson, 1997), and teachers (Dickinson & Smith, 1994) read books to children. More recent research has shown how these interactions with children may enhance their early literacy development (e.g., Lynch, Anderson, Anderson, & Shapiro, 2008; Mansell, Evans, & Hamilton-Hulak, 2005).

Whitehurst et al. (1988) were the first to report the effects of an intervention program, known as *dialogic reading,* on children's vocabulary learning. This approach, involving reading *with* the child rather than *to* the child, includes a number of techniques for the parent or caregiver to encourage the child to talk about the text. Parents also provide informative feedback (including expansions and corrective modeling), according to the child's developing abilities. The hypothesis is that practice with feedback and scaffolded interaction accelerates young children's language development. Whitehurst and his colleagues concluded that variations in reading to young children can have appreciable effects on vocabulary development.

A series of replication studies followed, experimentally testing the relations between adult tutoring during shared book reading and children's linguistic development, using groups of different ages and socioeconomic status (e.g., Arnold, Lonigan, Whitehurst, & Epstein, 1994; Blom-Hoffman, O'Neil-Pirozzi, Cutting, & Bissinger, 2007; Chow, McBride-Chang, Cheung, & Chow, 2008; Lonigan & Whitehurst, 1998). In 2008, Mol, Bus, de Jong, and Smeets conducted a meta-analysis of 16 of these replication studies to determine which variables may moderate outcomes of the intervention. Results indicated that dialogic book sharing conversations between parent and child strengthens the effects of book reading. However, the correlation between the intervention and a compound of linguistic skills was moderate, explaining about 4% of the outcome measures in the set of 16 studies that included 626 children. When the analyses were restricted to studies that assessed expressive vocabulary, the relation became stronger explaining about 8% of the variance, suggesting that the quality of book reading is as important for language development as its frequency. Mol et al. (2008) also found that dialogic conversations were most effective for increasing children's vocabulary growth when the children were between the ages of 2 and 3 years. They also concluded that there were reduced effects for children who were 4 to 5 years old, suggesting that older children are developmentally more able to independently understand stories without much adult support. Further, children at risk for language and literacy impairments (those in families of low-income or reportedly low maternal education status) benefited less, showing minimum effect size (explaining 1% of the variance) in comparison to the effect size of groups not at risk (7%). This finding parallels the Matthew effect (Stanovich, 1986) in reading; that is, good readers read more and become better readers, poor readers read less and fall further behind. While a book reading intervention standardized on middle-class White or suburban samples may not be appropriate for families from diverse groups, this meta-analysis suggests that there may be a need to pursue research that investigates different or more fine-grained training techniques with parents, particularly those of at-risk children.

Shared Reading and the Role of Parents in Literacy Acquisition

In keeping with Mol et al.'s (2008) assertion that the quality of book reading is as important for language development as its frequency, researchers have investigated the role parents take in promoting their children's literacy acquisition during parent–child reading activities. In 2008, Sénéchal and Young conducted a meta-analysis of 16 experimental and quasi-experimental shared book reading intervention studies to determine the role of parent actions in K-3 children's literacy development, particularly early literacy behaviors such as knowledge of letter names and sounds, early decoding abilities, and phonological awareness. The studies were divided into three types of parent involvement interventions: the parent reading to the child; the parent listening to the child read to them; and the parent tutoring the child in specific literacy skills with particular activities. Sénéchal and Young's meta-analysis suggests that parents can assist their children in learning to read as demonstrated by the moderately large effect size (0.65) across the studies. In addition to this general effect, the researchers found that parents who were trained to tutor their children on a specific literacy skill were twice as effective in enhancing their child's literacy than simply listening to the child read and almost six times as effective as just reading to the child.

In their review, Sénéchal and Young argued that early literacy and oral language may differ in the way these skills are developed, and previous research has suggested (e.g., Sénéchal, LeFevre, Smith-Chant, & Colton, 2000) that these skills may be subject to different influences. If so, there may be indirect relations between book reading and reading achievement; therefore, training parents to read to their children may influence later reading comprehension (Hargrave & Senechal, 2000), may facilitate reading due to increases in literate discourse (Purcell-Gates, McIntyre, & Freppon, 1995), and may result in an increase in reading for pleasure (Sénéchal, 2006). The authors call for intervention research to address these possibilities. Further, Sénéchal and Young's review highlights the need to address which specific beginning reading skills would be most beneficial for parents to receive training in, what role parental corrective feedback may play in the tutoring session, and when best to begin parent tutoring in relation to specific skills instruction at school.

Contributions of Shared Book Reading to Language and Literacy Skills

To acquire literacy, children must first develop early language and emergent literacy skills, and then more advanced skills in phonological processing, letter–sound relationships or phonics, sight words, vocabulary, and comprehension (Evans & Shaw, 2008). In 2008, the National Early Literacy Panel (NELP) conducted a meta-analysis of 19 experimental studies with preschool and kindergarten in school or home contexts on the effects of shared book reading interventions on conventional literacy skills (decoding, reading comprehension, and spelling) and predictors of conventional literacy skills (e.g., oral language skills, phonological awareness, alphabetic knowledge). The meta-analysis included studies that had received independent scientific review, evaluated the effects of interventions, and were not included in earlier meta-analyses (i.e., Bus et al., 1995; Scarborough & Dobrich, 1994). The NELP report (2008) revealed that overall, the largest impact of shared book reading interventions was on oral language outcomes across variations—consistent with previous research (i.e., Bus et al., 1995; Sénéchal & Young, 2008)—and moderate effects on print knowledge. The report outlined that for reasons unknown, the impact of the shared book reading was largest for vocabulary outcomes than for more complex oral language outcomes such as grammar, narrative understanding, or listening comprehension. The panel also concluded, based on the studies analyzed, that shared book reading interventions are beneficial to both younger and older children, as well as those children who are deemed at-risk, and those who are not. The report suggests that shared book reading as an intervention should be made available for diverse groups of children.

Currently, there are too few studies evaluating emergent (e.g., phonological awareness and alphabetic knowledge) and conventional (e.g., decoding and comprehension) literacy outcomes in order to conduct a meta-analysis to determine if shared book reading improves these skills. However, more recent research is beginning to fill the gaps on how shared book reading may contribute to the development of these skills, for example, the fostering of oral language skills that provide important foundations for later reading comprehension. For example, Skarakis-Doyle and Dempsey (2008) examined the comprehension monitoring ability in a group of 37 typically developing and language-impaired 4-year-olds during a shared book reading session. They found the language-impaired children's comprehension of story vocabulary was not significantly poorer than typically developing children of the same age or matched language ability; however, the language impaired-children answered fewer comprehension questions and repaired fewer story violations than the other groups. The researchers concluded that comprehension of story-related vocabulary is not solely sufficient for children's comprehension monitoring performance.

In another study, Zucker, Justice, Piasta, and Kaderavek (2010) examined 25 preschool teachers use of literal and inferential questions during whole-class shared reading with 159 preschoolers using an informational text having a narrative structure. They found that when the preschool teachers used inferential questions to discuss the text, they effectively encouraged the preschool children to use language output for the tasks of inferencing and analysis.

These studies demonstrate that shared book reading research is moving beyond simple language acquisition to advance the notion that shared book reading may promote other emergent and conventional literacy skills. Some researchers also call for a focus on longitudinal studies from preschool to fourth grade to determine long-term effects of shared book reading interventions on language and comprehension (e.g., Schickedanz & McGee, 2010).

In conclusion, although shared book reading continues to be heavily promoted by educators as one of the most valuable opportunities for promoting literacy development (Stevens, Van Meyer, & Warcholak, 2010), it is somewhat surprising that shared book reading does not have a stronger research foundation to support many of the contentions made about its impact and importance. While there is fairly solid correlational evidence that shared book reading benefits oral language skills, and promising support for its contributions to comprehension, there are too few studies to substantively conclude that shared book reading contributes to emergent or conventional literacy skills. There is great need for research to explore some of the issues addressed in previous sections; for example, research involving at-risk children and families, and longitudinal studies that look at the effects of shared book reading beyond the preschool and kindergarten years. Likewise, as digital texts become more widely available, there will be a need to examine their use in different contexts. As further investigation continues to untangle the effects of the quality and the engagement of the shared reading experience, it is also necessary to deeply understand the social and cultural contexts of these events as they contribute to children's literacy.

Phonemic Awareness

Over the last several decades, the role of phonemic awareness in learning to read has garnered much attention (e.g., Adams, 1990; Ukrainetz, 2009). Phonemic awareness is the ability to detect and manipulate phonemes, the smallest unit of language. It is a part of phonological awareness, which includes the ability to detect and manipulate larger units of language such as words and syllables, as well as phonemes. Phillips, Clancy-Menchetti, and Lonigan (2008) indicate that phonological awareness is developmental with children first becoming aware of, and able to manipulate increasingly smaller units of sound (e.g., word awareness, syllable awareness, onset-rime awareness, and phonemic awareness). However, they caution that there is overlap in the development and for example, children will have some

awareness of syllables while they are at the word awareness stage.

Phonemic Awareness and Learning to Read and Write. Many researchers now regard phonemic awareness as "necessary but not sufficient for the development of reading ability" (Phillips & Torgeson, 2006, p 101) in *alphabetic languages.* That is, "phonemic awareness makes phonemic decoding and phonemic spelling understandable" (p. 102).

Because it is generally accepted that phonemic awareness facilitates learning to read English and other alphabetic scripts, it is now considered an important component of an early literacy curriculum and in early childhood education classrooms. For example, Phillips, Clancy-Menchetti, and Lonigan (2008) recommend that children in preschool receive 10 to 15 minutes a day of phonological instruction in what they call developmentally appropriate ways. They state:

> Tasks that assess or teach phonemic awareness can include identity tasks (e.g., rhyme oddity, first sound matching) synthesis tasks (e.g., syllable or phoneme blending) or analysis tasks (e.g., word or syllable segmenting or deleting, phoneme counting tasks). Blending tasks are typically easier to manage than analysis tasks and tasks that require production are more challenging than recognition tasks, Also, tasks supported by visual props or that use multiple choice items are simpler for children than those that require more memory or verbal production. (p. 5)

Issues in Phonemic Awareness and Language and Literacy Learning. Although as stated, most educators recognize the importance of phonemic awareness in learning to read an alphabetic language and there is a significant literature that suggests that young children can be taught phonemic or phonological awareness through instruction, there are concerns about the amount of attention afforded phonemic awareness in early childhood curriculum and in early childhood classes. For example, Storch and Whitehurst (2002) suggest that "the role of phonological skills has been overemphasized and other components of oral language such as semantic and syntactic ability play a key role in reading achievement" (p. 935). Furthermore, although there is research evidence that phonemic awareness does predict some aspects of reading such as word decoding or reading pseudo-words in kindergarten and first grade, the relationship with reading ability when children are in the elementary grades is much less robust.

For example, Storch and Whitehurst (2002) tracked 626 4-year-old children from eight Head Start programs. The children's language and literacy skills were assessed in the spring of Head Start, kindergarten, and first through sixth grades. An array of measures were used that the researchers divided into two domains: code related skills and oral language skills. They found "strong correlations between oral language skills and code related skills in very young children" (p. 942). Furthermore, there was a weak and nonsignificant relationship between oral language skills and reading ability in the early years. However, children's phonological skills did not predict their reading comprehension in the later elementary grades where other language skills such as vocabulary and semantic and syntactic knowledge come into play more prominently. Indeed, Storch and Whitehurst concluded, "there may be a danger in employing phonological processing skills to the extent that the role of other language skills is underestimated" (p.943). Further evidence of the importance of more global language ability beyond phonemic or phonological awareness is provided in a study by Spira, Bracken, and Fischel (2005). Tracking 146 students from Head Start programs, they found that about 30% of the children who experienced difficulty in beginning reading were able to make steady progress through the end of fourth grade. Spira et al concluded that it was the children's relatively strong oral language ability that contributed to their improved reading ability through the grades.

To reiterate, many educators now take the position that some level of phonemic awareness is facilitative of children's literacy development and that it can be accomplished in developmentally appropriate ways. For example, Regush, Anderson, and Lee (2002) reported on an action research project in which they implemented a 6-week long, play-based, phonemic awareness program in a kindergarten classroom in a suburban middle class area of Vancouver, Canada. Pre- and postmeasures showed significant gains in children's phonemic awareness over the 6 weeks. A control group of children of similar ability and demographics who were taught by the same teacher using essentially the same curriculum and instruction as in the intervention class but without the play based phonemic awareness instruction did not make similar gains. The authors concluded that this play-based program of about 18 hours duration not only enhanced children's phonemic awareness but also led to an increase in children's inclusion of literacy materials and events in their play routines as observations of a subset of the children revealed. The results of that study suggest that helping children acquire phonemic awareness can be achieved in a relatively short time span in a manner that fits with a play-based curriculum favored by many early childhood educators and primary-grade teachers. The relatively brief duration is consistent with the findings from the reviews of Ehri and Nunes (2002) and Ukrainetz (2009), who concluded that 10 to 20 hours of instruction in phonemic awareness is optimal.

In summary then, phonemic awareness is important to young children in learning to read and write an alphabetic language such as English and it can be taught in developmentally appropriate ways to young children relatively quickly. Phonemic or phonological skills predict early reading and writing ability, especially when the measures focus on word recognition or pseudo-word decoding. However, other oral language skills such as vocabulary and syntactic and semantic knowledge relate more strongly to children's reading comprehension in later elementary

school. And finally, there is some evidence that phonemic awareness is related to vocabulary size and is a correlate of more general language ability (e.g., Dickinson, Golinkoff, & Hirsch-Pasak, 2010).

Family Literacy Programs

In recognizing the importance of families and communities in children's language and literacy learning, a number of researchers and educators (e.g., Rodriguez-Brown, 2004) have attempted to create programs that tap into families as a resource for encouraging children's language development. For example, Anderson, Morrison, and Friedrich (2010) described the Parents as Literacy Supporters (PALS) project wherein they worked with immigrant and refugee families from five linguistic groups (Farsi, Karen [a language spoken in Myanmar], Mandarin, Punjabi, and Vietnamese) in Vancouver, British Columbia. The aim of the PALS program is to work with parents and significant others in supporting their young children's early literacy and language development in their first language *and* in English, in other words, promoting *additive* bilingual and biliteracy development. The program is designed for 3- to 5-year-olds and their parents or significant others in their lives. Families participate in 10 or more 2-hour sessions offered in their first language. The topics for the sessions, which were identified through focus group sessions with families and early childhood educators, include: learning to read; learning to write; literacy and technology (or as the families say, "computers"), and early mathematics. Sessions begin with the families sharing a meal together. The facilitator and the parents spend about one-half-hour discussing the topic (e.g., early writing) that is the focus of the session while the children go to their classroom(s). During this part of the session, parents are encouraged to share their own experiences with the topic at hand and their observations of their children's engagement in that particular aspect of early literacy. Parents, children, and facilitators then spend an hour in the classroom(s) at a number of literacy and learning centers, each containing a different activity reflecting the topic of the day. Sessions conclude with the parents and facilitators discussing what they have observed about the children's learning and possibilities for continuing, expanding, and reinforcing that learning at home and in the community. Parents are then presented with a bilingual book or other literacy materials.

To measure changes in children's literacy knowledge over the course of the PALS in the Immigrant Communities project, the researchers administered the Test of Early Reading Ability-2 (Reid, Hresko, & Hammill, 1989), a widely used standardized instrument that taps children's emerging knowledge of the alphabet, concepts of print and meaning. Pre and post comparisons of children's mean Normal Curve Equivalent scores on the Test of Early Reading Ability-2 in which the norming group serves as a control showed significant growth ($p=.05$) with an effect size of .71.

This finding is consistent with other studies and indeed there is converging evidence that family literacy can positively affect young children's language and literacy development. For example, in a quasi-experimental study involving nearly 200 families in an urban area in Canada,, Phillips, Hayden, and Norris (2006) found that young children who participated in the Learning Together: Read and Write with Your Child program made statistically significant gains in literacy achievement compared to children in the control group. Two metastudies (Brooks, Pahl, Pollard, & Rees, 2008; National Early Literacy Panel, 2008) also confirmed the efficacy of family literacy programs in supporting young children's learning.

Conclusion

Despite the advances in our understanding of language development over the last several decades, many practices still reflect outdated conceptions of language and language development. For example, "English-only" policies in schools in the United States persist, despite evidence that children's language and literacy learning are enhanced if they learn to read and write initially in their first language (Gunderson, 2004; Soderman & Oshio, 2008). Furthermore, large-scale initiatives such as the American No Child Left Behind Act (2002), with its very heavy emphasis on accountability using standardized tests, do not reflect current understanding of young children's language and literacy development nor the diversity inherent in society. We believe that an overarching principle guiding research in early childhood language education should be the recognition of the increasingly global and diverse nature of society. For example, in Vancouver, British Columbia, where we work, more than 50% of children speak a language other than English at home, more than 150 language groups are represented in the school aged population, and in some early childhood classrooms, children speak more than a dozen different languages. We have moral and ethical obligations (Cummins, 2002), as well as pragmatic reasons (Soderman & Oshio, 2008) to pay attention to the realities of an increasingly global and diverse community.

In terms of future research, we see the need for a number of different foci. First, more research with different social and cultural groups is needed. Many new immigrants come from societies where conceptions of childhood and of language and literacy development differ in radical and fundamental ways from the mainstream North American views (e.g., Anderson & Morrison, 2011; Rogoff, 2003). It is important that researchers document the literacy practices of children and families from different backgrounds so that early childhood educators can support and build on these. In light of the increasing linguistic diversity of North American society, more research is needed in terms of young children's early biliteracy and bilingual development. And finally, the emerging research on the role of popular culture (e.g., Dyson, 2010) and technology (e.g.,

Kim & Anderson, 2008) in children's language and literacy development needs to be continued.

Furthermore, new programs, curricula and assessments will need to be developed to match the ever-changing demographics of contemporary early childhood classrooms. Educators and researchers will need to develop new and innovative ways in which to assess what children know about language and how it is used that recognize the diversity of their students/subjects. Given that parents are often the most reliable sources of information on their children's development, and families are very significant in terms of children's language and literacy development, educators may find themselves developing new language and literacy assessments and programs that focus on families and communities. In doing so they may help to transform schools, day cares, and preschools from isolated institutions into vibrant and evolving centers of community input and learning (e.g., Moll, 1992).

Note

1. Readers interested in reading further about sociocultural theories of learning should consult: B. Rogoff (2003). *The cultural nature of human development.* New York: Oxford University Press.

References

Adams, M. (1990). *Thinking and learning about print.* Cambridge, MA: MIT Press.

Anderson, J., Anderson, A., Lynch, J., & Shapiro, J. (2003). Storybook reading in a multicultural society: Critical perspectives. In A. van Kleeck, S. A. Stahl, & E. Bauer (Ed.), *On reading books to children: Parents and teachers* (pp. 203–230). Mahwah, NJ: Erlbaum.

Anderson, J. & Morrison, F. (2011). Learning from/with immigrant and refugee families in a family literacy program. In A. Lazar & P. Schmidt (Eds.), *We can teach and we can learn: Achievement in culturally responsive literacy classrooms* (pp. 30–38). New York: Teachers College Press.

Anderson, J., Morrison, F. & Friedrich, N. (2010, June). *Working with immigrant and refugee families in a bi-lingual family literacy program: Findings, insights, and challenges from year one of a three year project.* Paper presented at the annual conference of the Canadian Society for the Study of Education, Montreal, PQ.

Arnold, D., Lonigan, C., Whitehurst, G., & Epstein, J. (1994). Accelerating language-development through picture book reading: Replication and extension to a videotape training form. *Journal of Educational Psychology, 86*(2), 235–243.

Bakhtin, M. (1986). *Speech genres and other late essays.* Austin: University of Texas Press.

Ball, J. (2009). Supporting young Indigenous children's language development in Canada: A review of research on needs and promising practices. *Canadian Modern Language Review, 66*(1), 19–47.

Bauer, E. B. (2000). Code-switching during shared reading and independent reading: Lessons learned from a preschooler. *Research in the Teaching of English, 35*, 1010–130.

Beck, I. L., & McKeown, M. G. (2007). Increasing young low-income children's oral vocabulary repertoires through rich and focused instruction. *Elementary School Journal, 107*(3), 251–271.

Bedore, L., & Pena, E. (2008). Assessment of bilingual children for identification of language impairment: Current findings and implications for practice. *International Journal of Bilingual Education and Bilingualism, 11*(1), 1–29.

Bernstein, B. (1971). *Class, codes and control: Theoretical studies toward a sociology of language (Vol. 1)*. London: Routledge & Kegan Paul.

Bialystok, E. (1997). Effects of bilingualism and biliteracy on children's emerging concepts of print. *Developmental Psychology, 33*, 429–440.

Bissex, G. (1980). *Gyns at wrk: A child learns to write and read*. Cambridge, MA: Harvard University Press.

Bliss, L., & McCabe, A. (2008). Personal narratives: Cultural differences and clinical implications. *Topics in Language Disorders, 28*(2), 162–177.

Blom-Hoffman, J., O'Neil-Pirozzi, T., Cutting, J., & Bissinger, E. (2007). Instructing parents to use dialogic reading strategies with preschool children: Impact of a video-based training program on caregiver reading behaviors and children's related verbalizations. *Journal of Applied School Psychology, 23*(1), 117–131.

Boudreau, D. (2008). Narrative abilities: Advances in research and implications for clinical practice. *Topics in Language Disorders, 28*(2), 99–114.

Bourdieu, P. (1990). *Reproduction in education, society and culture*. London: Sage.

Brooks, G., Pahl, K., Pollard, A., & Rees, F. (2008). *Effective and inclusive practices in family literacy, language and numeracy: A Review of programmes and practice in the UK and internationally*. Reading, Berks, England: CfBT Education Trust.

Bus, A., Van Ijezendorn, M., & Pellegrini, A. D. (1995). Joint book reading makes for success in learning to read: A meta-analysis on intergenerational transmission of literacy. *Review of Educational Research, 65*, 1–21.

Caesar, L., & Kohler, P. (2009). The state of school-based bilingual assessment: Actual practice versus recommended guidelines. *Language, Speech and Hearing Services in Schools, 38*, 190–200.

Cahill, R., & Collard, G. (2003). Deadly ways to learn … A yarn about some learning we did together. *Comparative Education, 39*(2), 211–219.

Campbell, T., & Dollaghan, C. (1997). Reducing bias in language assessment: Processing-dependent measures. *Journal of Speech, Language and Hearing Research, 40*, 519–525.

Carter, J., Lees, J., Murira, G., Gona, J., Neville, B., & Newton, C. (2005). Issues in the development of cross cultural assessments of speech and language assessments for children. *International Journal of Language and Communication Disorders, 40*(4), 385–401.

Chapman, M. (1994). The emergence of genres: Some findings from an examination of first grade writing. *Written Communication, 11*, 348–380.

Chomsky, C. (1971). Write first, read later. *Childhood Education, 47*(6), 296–299.

Chow, B. W.-Y., McBride-Chang, C., Cheung, H., & Chow, C. S.-L. (2008). Dialogic reading and morphology training in Chinese children: Effects on language and literacy. *Developmental Psychology, 44*(1), 233–244.

Clark, M. (1976). *Young fluent readers: What can they teach us?* London: Heinemann.

Cole, M. (1996). *Cultural psychology: A once and future discipline*. Cambridge, MA: Harvard University Press.

Cope, B., & Kalantzis, M. (Eds.). (1993). *The powers of literacy: A genre approach to teaching writing*. Pittsburgh, PA: University of Pittsburgh Press.

Craig, H., & Washington, J. (2002). Oral language expectations for African American preschoolers and kindergarteners. *American Journal of Speech-Language Pathology, 11*, 59–70.

Cross, J., De Vaney, T., & Jones, G. (2001). Pre-service teacher attitudes toward differing dialects. *Linguistics and Education, 12*, 211–227.

Cummins, J. (2002). Rights and responsibilities of educators of bilingual/bicultural children. In L. D. Soto (Ed.), *Making a difference in the lives of bilingual/bicultural children* (pp. 195–210). New York: Peter Lang.

Cunningham, A., & Zibulsky, J. (2011). Tell me a story: Examining the benefits of shared reading. In S. Neuman, D. Dickinson, & D. Aram (Eds.), *Handbook of early literacy research* (Vol. 3, pp. 396–411). New York: Guilford.

Delpit, L. (1995). *Other people's children: Cultural conflict in the classroom*. New York: The New Press.

De Temple, J. (2001). Parents and children reading books together. In D. Dickinson & P. Tabors (Eds.), *Beginning literacy with language* (pp. 31–52). Toronto: Brookes.

De Temple, J., & Tabors, P. (1995). Styles of interaction during a book reading task: Implications for literacy intervention with low-income families. In C. Kinzer (Ed.), *Perspectives on literacy research and practice: 44th yearbook of the National Reading Conference* (pp. 265–271). Chicago, IL: National Reading Conference.

Dickinson, D. (2001). Book reading in preschool classrooms. In D. Dickinson & P. Tabors (Eds.), *Beginning literacy with language* (pp. 175–204). Toronto: Brookes.

Dickinson, D., Darrow, C., & Tinbu, T. (2008). Patterns of teacher–child conversation in Head Start classrooms: Implications for an empirically grounded approach to professional development. *Early Education and Development, 19*(3), 396–429.

Dickinson, D., Golinkoff, R., Hirsch-Pasek, K. (2010). Speaking out for language: Why language is central to reading development. *Educational Researcher, 39*(4), 305–310.

Dickinson, D., & Smith, M. (1994). Long term effects of preschool teachers' book readings on low-income children's vocabulary and story comprehension. *Reading Research Quarterly, 29*, 105–122.

Dockrell, J. (2001). Assessing language skills in preschool children. *Child Psychology & Psychiatry Review, 6*, 74–85.

Durkin, D. (1966). *Children who read early*. New York: Teachers College Press.

Dykeman, B. (2008). Play-based neuropsychological assessment of toddlers. *Journal of Instructional Psychology, 35*(4), 405–408.

Dyson, A. H. (1999). Coach Bombay's kids learn to write: Children's appropriation of media material for school literacy. *Research in the Teaching of English, 33*, 366–402.

Dyson, A. H. (2000). On reframing children's words: The perils, promises and pleasures of writing children. *Research in the Teaching of English, 34*, 352–367.

Dyson, A. (2008). Staying in the (curricular) lines: Practices, constraints, and possibilities in early childhood writing. *Written Communication. 25*(1), 119–159.

Dyson, A. (2010). Opening curricular closets in regulated times: Finding pedagogical keys. *English Education, 42*(3), 307–319.

Ehri, L., & Nunes, S. (2002). The role of phonemic awareness in learning to read. In A. Farstrup & S. J. Samuels (Eds.), *What research has to say about reading instruction* (pp. 110–139). Newark, DE: International Reading Association.

Eriks-Brophy, A., Quittenbaum, J., Anderson, D., & Nelson, T. (2008). Part of the problem or part of the solution? Communication assessments of Aboriginal children residing in remote communities using videoconferencing. *Clinical Linguistics & Phonetics, 22*(8), 589–609.

Evans, M., & Shaw, D. (2008). Home grown for reading: Parental contributions to young children's emergent literacy and word recognition. *Canadian Psychology, 49*(2), 89–95.

Ferreiro, E., & Teberosky, A. (1982). *Literacy before schooling*. Exeter, NH: Heinemann.

Feiler, A., & Webster, A. (1999). Teacher predictions of young children's literacy success or failure. *Assessment in Education, 6*, 3, 341–356.

Fogel, H., & Ehri, L. (2006). Teaching African American English forms to Standard American English-speaking teachers. *Journal of Teacher Education, 57*(5), 464–480.

Gee, J. P. (1989). What is literacy? *Journal of Education, 171*, 18–25.

Graves, D. (1983). *Writing: Teachers and children at work*. Exeter, NH: Heinemann.

Gregory, E. (2005). Guiding lights: Siblings as literacy teachers in a multicultural society. In J. Anderson, M. Kendrick, T. Rogers, & S. Smythe (Eds.), *Portraits of literacy across families, communities and schools: Intersections and tensions* (pp. 21–40). Mahwah, NJ: Erlbaum.

Gunderson, L. (2004). The language, literacy, achievement and social consequences of English-only programs for immigrant students. *53rd*

Yearbook of the National Reading Conference (pp. 1–27). Oak Creek, WI: National Reading Conference.

Gutierrez-Clellen, V., Pena, E., & Quinn, R. (1995). Accommodating cultural differences in narrative style: A multicultural perspective. *Topics in Language Disorders, 15*(4), 54–67.

Gutierrez-Clellen, V., & Simon-Cereijido, P. (2009). Using language sampling in clinical assessments with bilingual children: Challenges and future directions. *Seminars in Speech & Language, 30*(4), 234–245.

Halliday, M. (1973). *Explorations in the functions of language*. London: Edward Arnold.

Hargrave, A., & Sénéchal, M. (2000). A book reading intervention with preschool children who have limited vocabularies: The benefits of regular reading and dialogic reading. *Early Childhood Research Quarterly, 15*, 75–90.

Hart, B. (2000). A natural history of early language experience. *Topics in Early Childhood Special Education, 20*(1), 28.

Hart, B., & Risley, T. R. (1995). *Meaningful differences in the everyday experiences of young American children*. Baltimore, MD: Brookes.

Hasan, R. (1989). Semantic variation and sociolinguistics. *Australian Journal of Linguistics, 9*, 221–275.

Hauser-Cram, P., Sirin, S., & Stipek, D. (2003). When teachers' and parents' values differ: Ratings of academic competence in children from low income families. *Journal of Educational Psychology, 95*, 813–820.

Haworth, P., Cullen, J., Simmons, H., Schimanski, L., McGarva, P., & Woodhead, E. (2006). The role of acquisition and learning in young children's bilingual development: A socio-cultural interpretation. *International Journal of Bilingual Education and Bilingualism, 9*(3), 295–309.

Heath, S. (1983). *Ways with words: Language, life and work in communities and classrooms*. New York: Cambridge University Press.

Heath, S. (1986). *Sociocultural contexts of language development*. Los Angeles: California State University.

Hindman, A. H., Connor, C. M., Jewkes, A. M., & Morrison, F. J. (2008). Untangling the effects of shared book reading: Multiple factors and their associations with preschool literacy outcomes. *Early Childhood Research Quarterly, 23*(3), 330–350.

Johnston, J., & Wong, A. (2002). Cultural differences in beliefs and practices concerning talk to children. *Journal of Speech, Language, and Hearing Research, 45*, 916–926.

Kim, J., & Anderson, J. (2008). Mother–child shared reading with print and digital texts. *Journal of Early Childhood Literacy, 8*(2), 213–245.

Korat, O., & Or, T. (2010). How new technology influences parent–child interaction: The case of e-book reading. *First Language, 30*(2), 139–154.

Kramsch, C. (2002). Introduction: "How can we tell the dancer from the dance." In C. Kramsch (Ed.), *Language acquisition and socialization: Ecological perspectives* (pp. 1–29). London: Continuum.

Krashen, S. (1981) *Second language acquisition and second language learning*. Oxford, England: Pergamon Press.

Lai, W.-F., Lee, Y.-J., & Lee, J. (2010). Visiting doctor's offices: A comparison of Korean and Taiwanese preschool children's narrative development. *Early Education & Development, 21*(3), 445–467.

Laing, S. (2003). Assessment of phonology in preschool African American vernacular English speakers using an alternate response mode. *American Journal of Speech-Language Pathology, 12*, 273–281.

Laing, S., & Kamhi, A. (2003). Alternative assessment of language and literacy in culturally diverse populations. *Language, Speech and Hearing Services in Schools, 34*, 44–55.

Li, G. (2006). Biliteracy and trilingual practices in the home context: Case studies of Chinese-Canadian students. *Journal of Early Childhood Literacy, 6*(3), 355–381.

Li, J., D'Angiulli, A., & Kendall, G. (2007). The Early Development Index and children from culturally and linguistically diverse backgrounds. *Early Years, 27*(3), 221–235.

Lidz, C. (1995). Dynamic assessment and the legacy of L. S. Vygotsky. *School Psychology International, 16*, 143–153.

Long, S. (1998). Learning to get along: Language acquisition and literacy development in a new cultural setting. *Research in the Teaching of English, 33*, 8–47.

Lonigan, C., & Whitehurst, G. (1998). Reflective efficacy of parent and teacher involvement in a shared-reading intervention for preschool children from low-income backgrounds. *Early Childhood Research Quarterly, 13*, 263–290.

Lunney-Borden, L. (2009). *The verbification of mathematics*. Paper presented at the 33rd Conference of the International Group for the Psychology of Mathematics Education, Thessaloniki, Greece.

Lynch, J., Anderson, J., Anderson, A., & Shapiro, J. (2008). Parents and preschool children interacting with storybooks: Children's early literacy achievement. *Reading Horizons, 48*(4), 227–242.

Mansell, J., Evans, M., & Hamilton-Hulak, L. (2005). Developmental changes in parents' use of miscue feedback during shared book reading. *Reading Research Quarterly, 40*(3), 294–317.

Mashburne, A., Justice, L., Downer, J., & Pianta, R. (2010). Peer effects on children's language acquisition during kindergarten. *Child Development, 80*(3), 686–702.

Marsh, J. (2000). "But I want to fly too!" Girls and superhero play in the infant classroom. *Gender and Education, 12*, 209–220.

Mavers, D. (2007). Semantic resourcefulness: A young child's email exchange as design. *Journal of Early Childhood Literacy, 7*(2), 155–176.

McDermott, R. (1993). The acquisition of a child by a learning disability. In S. Chaiklin (Ed.), *Understanding practice: Perspectives on activity and context* (pp. 269–305). Cambridge, England: Cambridge University Press.

McKenney, S., & Voogt, J. (2009). Designing technology for emergent literacy: The Pictopal initiative. *Computers and Education, 52*, 719–729.

Mhathuma, M. (2008). Supporting children's participation in second-language stories in an Irish pre-school. *Early Years, 28*(3), 299–309.

Mol, S. E., Bus, A. G., de Jong, M. T., & Smeets, D. J. H. (2008). Added value of dialogic parent–child book readings: A meta-analysis. *Early Education and Development, 19*(1), 7–26.

Moll, L. (1992). Bilingual classroom studies and community analysis: Some recent trends. *Educational Researcher, 21*, 20–24.

Mui, S., & Anderson, J. (2008). At home with the Johars: Another look at family literacy. *The Reading Teacher, 62*, 234–243.

Murphy, P. (1995). Sources of inequity: Understanding students' responses to assessment. *Assessment in Education: Principles, Policy & Practice, 2*, 249–271.

Myhill, D., & Jones, S. (2009). How talk becomes text: The concept of oral rehearsal in early years classrooms. *British Journal of Educational Studies, 57*(3), 265–284.

National Association for the Education of Young Children (NAEYC). (2003). *Early childhood curriculum, assessment and program evaluation* (Position statement). Washington, DC: Author.

National Early Literacy Panel. (2008) *Developing early literacy: Report of the National Early Literacy Panel*. Retrieved from www.nifl.gov/publications/pdf/NELPReport09.pdf

No Child Left Behind. (2002). PL. 107-110.

Pacini-Ketchbaw, V., & Armstong de Almedia, A. (2006). Language discourses and ideologies at the heart of early childhood education. *International Journal of Bilingual Education and Bilingualism, 9*(3), 310–341.

Parke, T., Drury, R., Kenner, C., & Robertson, L. (2002). Revealing invisible worlds: Connecting the mainstream with bilingual children's home and community learning. *Journal of Early Childhood Literacy, 2*, 195–220.

Pellegrini, A. (1991). A critique of the concept of at risk as applied to emergent literacy. *Language Arts, 68*, 380–385.

Pena, E. (1997). Task familiarity: Effects on the test performance of Puerto Rican and African American children. *Language, Speech and Hearing Services in Schools, 28*, 323–332.

Pena, E., Gillam, R., Malek, M., Ruiz-Felter, R., Resendiz, M., & Fiestas, C. (2006). Dynamic assessment of school-age children's narrative ability: An experimental investigation of classification accuracy. *Journal of Speech, Language, and Hearing Research, 49*, 1037–1057.

Pena, E., Iglesias, A., & Lidz, C. (2001). Reducing test bias through dynamic assessment of children's word learning ability. *American Journal of Speech-Language Pathology, 10*, 138–153.

Phillips, B., Clancy-Menchetti, J, & Lonigan, C. (2008). Successful phonological awareness instruction with preschool children: Lessons from the classroom. *Topics in Early Childhood Special Education, 28*(1), 3–17.

Phillips, B., & Torgeson, J. (2006). Phonemic awareness and learning to read. In D. Dickinson & S. Neuman (Eds.), *Handbook of early research* (Vol. 2, pp. 101–112). New York: Guilford.

Phillips, L., Hayden, R., & Norris, S. (2006) *Family literacy matters: A longitudinal parent–child literacy intervention study.* Calgary, AB, Canada: Detselig Press.

Purcell-Gates, V., McIntyre, & Freppon, P. (1995). Learning written storybook language in school: A comparison of low-SES children in skills-based and whole language classrooms. *American Educational Research Journal, 32*, 659–685.

Read, C. (1975). *Children's categorization of speech sounds.* Urbana, IL: National Council of Teachers of English.

Reese, E., Sparks, A., & Leyva, D. (2010). A review of parent intervention for preschool children's language and emergent literacy. *Journal of Early Childhood Literacy, 10*(1), 97–117.

Regush, N., Anderson, J., & Lee, E. (2002). Using play to support the development of kindergarten children's phonemic awareness. In P. Linder, M. B. Sampson, J. Duggan, & B. Brancatto (Eds.), *Celebrating the faces of literacy* (pp. 234–246). Commerce, TX: College Reading Association.

Reid, D., Hresko, W., & Hammill, D. (1989). *Test of Early Reading Ability-2.* Austin, TX: PRO-ED.

Restrepo, M. A., & Silverman, S. (2001). Validity of the Spanish preschool language scale 3 for use with bilingual children. *American Journal of Speech-Language Pathology, 10*, 382–393.

Riley, J., & Burrell, A. (2007). Assessing children's oral storytelling in their first year of school. *International Journal of Early Years Education, 15*(2), 181–196.

Robust, T. (2002, May). *Ko te reo te mauri o te mana Maori: The language is the life essence of Maori existence.* Paper presented at the Annual Conference on Stabilizing Indigenous Languages, Toronto.

Rodriguez-Brown, F. (2004). Project flame: A parent support family literacy model. In B. Wasik (Ed.), *Handbook of family literacy* (pp. 213–29). Mahwah, NJ: Erlbaum.

Rogoff, B. (2003). *The cultural nature of human development.* New York: Oxford University Press.

Roy-Charland, A., Saint-Aubin, J., & Evans, M. (2007). Eye movements in shared book reading with children from kindergarten to grade 4. *Reading and Writing: An Interdisciplinary Journal, 20*(9), 909–931.

Russ, S., Perez, V., Garro, N., Klass, P., Kuo, A., & Gershun, M. (2007). *Executive Summary.* Retrieved from www.healthychild.ucla.edu/ROR/Executive_Summary.pdf

Scarborough, H., & Dobrich, W. (1994). On the efficacy of reading to preschoolers. *Developmental Review, 14*, 245–302.

Scheffner-Hammer, C., Pennock-Roman, M., Rzaasa, S. & Tomblin, J. (2002). An analysis of the Test of Language Development-primary for test bias. *American Journal of Speech-Language Pathology, 11*(3), 274–284.

Schickedanz, J., & McGee, L. (2010). The NELP report on shared story reading interventions (Chapter 4): Extending the story. *Educational Researcher, 39*(4), 323–324.

Sénéchal, M. (2006). Testing the home literacy model: Parent involvement in kindergarten is differentially related to grade 4 reading comprehension, fluency, spelling, and reading for pleasure. *Scientific Studies of Reading, 10*, 59–87.

Sénéchal, M., LeFevre, J., Hudson, E., & Lawson, E. (1996). Knowledge of storybooks as a predictor of young children's vocabulary. *Journal of Educational Psychology, 88*, 520–536.

Sénéchal, M., LeFevre, J., Smith-Chant, B., & Colton, K. (2000). On refining theoretical models of emergent literacy: The role of empirical evidence. *School Psychology, 39*, 439–460.

Sénéchal, M., & Young, L. (2008). The effect of family literacy interventions on children's acquisition of reading from kindergarten to grade 3: A meta-analytic review. *Review of Educational Research, 78*(4), 880–907. doi: 10.3102/0034654308320319.

Shapiro, J., Anderson, J., & Anderson, A. (1997). Diversity in parental storybook reading. *Early Childhood Development and Care, 127*, 47–59.

Siegel, M., Kontovourki, S., Schmier, S., & Enriquez, G. (2008). Literacy in motion: A case study of a shape shifting kindergartener. *Language Arts, 86*(2), 89–98.

Skarakis-Doyle, E., & Dempsey, L. (2008). The detection and monitoring of comprehension errors by preschool children with and without language impairment. *Journal of Speech, Language, and Hearing Research, 51*, 1227–1243.

Snow, C., Burns, M., & Griffin, P. (1998). *Preventing reading difficulties in young children.* Washington, DC: National Academy Press.

Snow, C., Tabors, P., & Dickinson, D. (2001). Language development in preschool years. In D. Dickinson & P. Tabors (Ed.), *Beginning literacy with language* (pp. 1–26). Toronto: Brookes.

Soderman, A., & Oshio, T. (2008). The social and cultural contexts of second language acquisition in young children. *European Early Childhood Education Research Journal, 16*(3), 297–311.

Souto-Manning, M. (2007). Immigrant families and children (re)develop identities in a new context. *Early Childhood Education Journal, 34*(6), 399–405.

Spinelli, C. (2008). Addressing the issue of cultural and linguistic diversity and assessment: Informal evaluation measures for English language learners. *Reading & Writing Quarterly, 24*, 101–118.

Spira, E., Bracken, S., & Fischel, J. (2005). Predicting improvement after first grade reading difficulties: The effect of oral language, emergent literacy, and behaviour skills. *Developmental Psychology, 41* (1), 225–234.

Spycher, P. (2009). Learning academic language through science in two linguistically diverse kindergarten classes. *Elementary School Journal, 109*(4), 359–379.

Stanovich, K. (1986). Matthew effects in reading: Some consequences of individual differences in the acquisition of literacy. *Reading Research Quarterly, 21*, 360–407.

Stevens, R., Van Meyer, P., & Warcholak, N. (2010). The effects of explicitly teaching story structure to primary grade children. *Journal of Literacy Research, 42*(2), 159–198.

Storch, S., & Whitehurst, G. (2002). Oral language and code related precursors to reading: Evidence from a longitudinal structural modelling. *Developmental Psychology, 38*(6), 934–947.

Taylor, D. (1983). *Family literacy: Young children learning to read and write.* Exeter, NH: Heinemann.

Thurman, S., & McGrath, M. (2008). Environmentally based assessment practices viable alternatives to standardized assessment for assessing emergent literacy skills in young children. *Reading & Writing Quarterly, 24*, 7–24.

Toohey, K. (2000). *Learning English at school: Identity, social relations and classroom practice.* Clevedon, England: Multilingual Matters.

Ukrainetz, T. (2009). Phonemic awareness: How much is enough within a changing picture of reading instruction? *Topics in Language Disorder, 29*(4), 344–359.

Van Kleeck, A., Gillam, R., Hamilton, L., & McGrath, C. (1997). The relationship between middle-class parents' book-sharing discussion and their preschoolers' language development. *Journal of Speech, Language, and Hearing Research, 40*, 1261–1271.

Vygotsky, L. (1978). *Mind in society: The development of higher psychological processes.* Cambridge, MA: Harvard University Press.

Watkins, M., & Coffey, D. (2004). Reading motivation: Multidimensional and indeterminate. *Journal of Educational Psychology, 96*, 110–118.

Westby, C. (2009). Considerations in working successfully with culturally/linguistically diverse families in assessment and intervention of communication disorders. *Seminars in Speech and Language, 30*(4), 279–289.

What Works Clearing House. (2006). *WWC intervention report: Shared Reading*. Washington, DC: Institute of Education Sciences.

Whitehurst, G., Falco, F., Lonigan, C., Fischel, J., De Baryshe, B., Valdez- Menchaca, M., & Caufield, M. (1988). Accelerating language development through picture book reading. *Developmental Psychology, 24*, 552–559.

Williams, G. (1995). *Joint book reading and literacy pedagogy: A socio-semantic interpretation (*Unpublished doctoral dissertation). Macquarie University, Sydney.

Williams, G. (2005). Semantic variation. In R. Hasan, C. Matthieson, & J. Webster (Eds.), *Continuing discourse on language: A functional perspective* (pp. 457–480). London: Eqinox.

Wohlwend, K. (2009a). Damsels in discourse: Girls consuming and practicing identity texts. *Reading Research Quarterly, 44*(1), 57–83.

Wohlwend, K. (2009b). Dilemmas and discourses of learning to write: Assessment as a contested site. *Language Arts, 86*(5), 341–351.

Wollman-Bonilla, J. (2001). Family involvement in early writing instruction. *Journal of Early Childhood Literacy, 1*, 167–192.

Zucker, T., Justice, L., Piasta, S., & Kaderavek, J. (2010). Preschool teachers' literal and inferential questions and children's responses during whole-class shared reading. *Early Childhood Research Quarterly, 25*(1), 65–83.

8

Views and Issues in Children's Literature

Olivia N. Saracho
University of Maryland

During the last century, children's literature came to be valued and appreciated as an art form for children. Research supports that it provides young children with a foundation for later literary understanding and aesthetic development. Young children's aesthetic experiences assist them in all facets of their lives including their use of language. In addition children's literature has a significant effect on young children's intellectual and emotional experiences to their wider world (Kiefer, 2004). The purpose of this chapter is to review the scholarship on children's literature; discuss how children's play is reflected in classic literature; provide an historical perspective on the development of scholarship in children's literature; describe the different theories in children's literature, including the controversies; report research in children's literature from a literary perspective; and review the implications of children's literature in early childhood education.

Defining Children's Literature

There are many definitions of children's literature, each with its own values and beliefs; some definitions overlap while others contradict one another. An understanding and integration of these definitions can provide an understanding of the field.

The *Oxford English Reference Dictionary* defines "literature" as "writing which has claim to consideration on the ground of beauty of form and emotional effect" (cited in Pearsall & Trumble, 1996, p. 837). The standard definition of children's literature refers to those books that are purposely written for children "excluding works such as comic books, joke books, cartoon books, and nonfiction works that are not intended to be read from front to back, such as dictionaries, encyclopedias, and other reference material" (Anderson, 2010, p. 2), even if many adults enjoy them. For example, several classic books were originally intended for adults but are now read by children, such as Mark Twain's *Adventures of Huckleberry Finn* (1884/2008)

and Charles Dickens's *A Christmas Carol* (1843/2004). These books continue to be enjoyed by both children and adults, and indeed there are numerous books that are classified as being appropriate for both categories of readers.

If the term *children's literature* refers to books that are written specifically for young children, it goes beyond the categories of the (a) fairy and wonder tales; (b) nursery rhymes and songs; (c) dull books of etiquette, admonition, and moral persuasion; and (d) stories of school, childrens play, or far flung adventure. Children's literature is the complete large body of literature that children have embraced. It becomes *their* own personal literature because it belongs to children rather than parents, teachers, preachers, or even the authors. It is children who define children's literature. Throughout the years, they abide by their own set of rules based on their intuition. Most children have rejected nearly everything that was purposefully written for them but accepted literature that was not intended for them. Over time, their decision has been justified (Commager, 1969). According to Hunt (1991)

> There are "live" books and "dead" books, books which no longer concern their primary audience (and [which] concern no-one else except historians).... Concepts of childhood change so rapidly that there is a sense in which books no longer applicable to childhood must fall into a limbo in which they are the preserve of the bibliographer, since they are of no interest to the current...child.... The history of the children's book may be interesting to the adult, but not for the child, and it is this dichotomy which is central [to defining children's books]. (pp. 61–62)

Nodelman (1992) disagrees with Hunt (1991). He believes that if children are actually unrestricted, then ideology has less influence. Nevertheless, if ideology really builds subjectivity, then culture is influential, even in infancy, leading children to develop expected and predetermined attitudes in their selection of children's books from the different genres available to readers.

Genres in Children's Literature

Children's literature for young children incorporates numerous genres including ABC and counting books, nursery rhymes and poetry collections, picture storybooks, novels, and nonfiction. The acknowledged criteria for these books are that they offer children literary and artistic experiences; that is, they present their readers with meaningful information that is presented in a format that is aesthetically pleasing to the children. The Association of Library Service to Children (ALSC, 2007) has recommended this set of criteria in selecting children's books. These criteria are used for esteemed awards such as the Newbery and Caldecott Medals (ALSC, 2007). Additional genres (e.g., historical fiction and fantasy, literary criticism, child development) can be used in selecting and using books with children. The genres in the study by Saracho and Spodek (2010) are traditional, modern fantasy, realistic fiction, information books, and poetry. They use Norton and Norton (2011) to define these genres:

- *Traditional literature* is a genre that has been handed down from generation to generation by word of mouth. The stories were initially oral and later were written down, such as songs, stories, poems, and riddles from anonymous sources. Traditional literature has a variety of forms (e.g., myths, fables, epics, ballads, legends, folk rhymes, folktales, fairy tales, apprenticeship tales and hero tales, numskull tales, trickster tales, tall tales, cumulative tales and pourquoi tales). Several of these forms overlap.
- *Modern fantasy* is a genre that requires the imagination to go to the world of make-believe. Its known authors take their readers to a time and setting where the inconceivable becomes authentically real. This type of literature has stories with places, people, creatures, and events that could not exist, like animals talking. For example, science fiction is a form of modern fantasy; in other words, the events and situations it describes may not be possible at the present time but might be possible in the future.
- *Contemporary realistic fiction* is a genre where the story (including characters, setting, and plot) represents the author's perception of people's lives in the contemporary world. The characters may be very ordinary or exaggerated and the plots may be mundane or preposterous. The term *realistic* means that the story could have happened, although the story is not based on fact.
- *Information books* focus on factual material, which requires careful evaluation of the books' content. It consists of books on subjects (e.g., history, space, animals, plants, geography, how things work) that are used to expand students' knowledge about topics studied in the content areas.
- *Poetry* is a literary genre that provides enjoyment, helps readers appreciate language, and makes children become aware about themselves. According to Rumer Godden (1988), one of the foremost English language authors of the 20th century, "True poetry, even in its smallest shape, should have form, meter, rhythm bound into a whole with words that so match and express its subject they seem inevitable" (p. 310, cited in Saracho & Spodek, 2010, p. 405).

The International Reading Association (IRA) and the National Council of Teachers of English (NCTE) developed a set of 12 national standards in the English language arts. The second standard states, "students read a wide range of literature from many periods in many genres to build an understanding of the many dimensions (e.g. philosophical, ethical, aesthetic) of human experience" (IRA & NCTE, 1996, p. 21). Such a standard indicates that children's literature has the important purpose, "of ensuring that all students are knowledgeable and proficient users of language" (IRA & NCTE, 1996, p. vii). However, the enjoyment of literature should be integrated into children's daily lives and their education. In any valuable reading of literature, whether fiction or nonfiction, readers will encounter emotional relationships and personal enlightenments as well as intellectual challenges and relationships to the wider world (Kiefer, 2004). According to Card (2001), "one can make a good case for the idea that children are often the guardians of the truly great literature of the world, for in their love of story and unconcern for stylistic fads and literary tricks, children unerringly gravitate toward truth and power." Therefore, the most comprehensive definition of children's literature relates to books that children actually choose to read, such as distinguished works written by contemporary authors and also literary classics (Anderson, 2010). Most of the work of literary classic scholars reflects children's play, which is an important component in early childhood education.

Children's Play in Classic Literature

Educational experiences for young children need to be both developmentally appropriate and content productive. Their development exceeds a straightforward biological process. Bruner (1990) includes a cultural process: "Cultures characteristically devise 'prosthetic devices' that permit us to transcend 'raw' biological limits—for example, the limits on memory capacity or the limits on our auditory range" (p. 34). Vygotsky (1967) claims that individuals expand their developmental ability when they attain "cultural tools"; these tools include language and different ways of knowing. The scholarly disciplines and language are essential to help young children understand themselves and the world they live in. Children learn and achieve optimal development in society through developmentally appropriate experiences that are based on their play, but that also include the disciplines of formal knowledge (Saracho, 2012). Theories of play define its meaning in relation to individuals' experiences, how they make sense of the world, how play influences the way they learn and thus supports their development (Saracho & Spodek, 2003).

Children's Play and Literature

Children's literature reflects children at play. A play experience is intrinsically motivated (done for its own sake), freely chosen, pleasurable, spontaneous, flexible, and actively engaged in both physically and psychologically. Children's literature has original, spontaneous, and flexible qualities. It provides knowledge that children can use to hypothesize and test out in their play. For example, children can use fictional stories to learn to cooperate, to share, to delay gratification of their impulses, and to imagine themselves assuming the characters' roles. Children's literature, as in play, promotes children's social, emotional, physical, and intellectual development (Saracho, 2012).

Children's literature offers young children numerous opportunities to interpret, improvise, and pretend. They can develop their own scripts, engage in storytelling, and assume a variety of roles that build on themes, characters, or ideas within the literature. Children may use literature as a basis to create stories (Saracho, 2012). A children's literature perspective extends the view of the process for appreciating books where social contexts in the books become pressing venues that introduce young children to knowledge, practices, and their social world. A children's literature and play relationship becomes more striking because play helps young children explore and comprehend the interactions between these two realms of activity. This relationship is so astonishing and play is reflected in the classic authors' life and work.

Classical Literature

Classic works on children's literature began to appear in the early to mid- 16th century and continued to do so throughout the 20th century. For example, Samuel Taylor Coleridge (1772–1834), an English romantic, wrote extensively on the nature of children's fantasy. William Wordsworth (1770–1850), another English romantic, idealized the child's mind for its honesty. He joined Samuel Taylor Coleridge to introduce the Romantic Age in English literature with the 1798 joint publication of *Lyrical Ballads*, a collection of poems (1798/2007). One of William Wordsworth's poems for children was "Daffodils," which he wrote in 1804. He was magically mesmerized when he saw the daffodils waving in the breeze. Those who know this poem can imagine a great mass of daffodils as they recall at least the introductory lines.

The English poet and playwright William Shakespeare (1564–1616), has been considered the greatest writer in the English language and the world's preeminent dramatist. He created most of his known work between 1589 and 1613 (Chambers, 1930). Shakespeare works included fantasies, images, illusions, and the whole inner world of fairies, goblins, and spirits. However, few children appeared as characters in his plays. Nonetheless, Shakespeare's work indicates that he was exceptionally knowledgeable about children's imagination. The English Shakespearean scholar, James Orchard Halliwell-Phillipps (1820–1889), collected English nursery rhymes and fairy tales. In 1842 he published the first edition of *Nursery Rhymes of England* followed by *Nursery Rhymes and Nursery Tales*, which included the first printed edition of the *Three Little Pigs* (Ashliman, 2008). The three little pigs assume adult roles as they construct a house for themselves. Children learn about this story and act out the roles of the various characters (e.g., pigs, mother, wolf). These English authors concentrate on the children's fantasy and make-believe, which are important elements in children's pretend play. In addition, pretend play has been represented in numerous works of classic literature (Saracho, 2010).

Early authors and illustrators of children's books portray childhood play experiences. Children's play was actually represented in the literature until approximately the middle of the 19th century. Throughout the 20th century, many writers and most psychologists rejected the concept of children's make-believe play. Auden's (1965) chronicle describes noteworthy illustrations of the way a particular type of mother's intimacy may have had an impact on the imaginative power of one of the 20th century's greatest English poets. Auden (1965) states:

> When I was eight years old, she taught me the words and music of the love potion scene in "Tristan and Isolde" and we used to sing it together. (p. 166)

In addition, Auden observed that the novelist Evelyn Waugh's father played charades daily throughout his life (Singer, 1973). The Russian novelist, social reformer, and moral philosopher Count Leo Tolstoy (1828–1910) reminisced about his childhood experiences. His brother started games where all the players pretended to be "ant people." He wrote of the impact such experiences had on his own development. Tolstoy (1853/1964) also wrote about his later visions when he was locked up as a penalty for misbehaving, reporting in specific detail his terror of his tutor. These are shockingly perplexing accounts of a 9- or 10-year-old child's mind.

Denis Daudet (1713–1784), the French Encyclopedist, philosopher, and man of letters, created naturalistic portraits of middle-class family life in his plays. His work, *Le Livre de Mon Ami* (My Friend's Book), effectively describes the imaginary and detailed visions of children isolated in their room at night. Approximately a century later, Alphonse Daudet (1840–1897), the French novelist, wrote some stories for children, including "La Belle Nivernaise," the story of an old boat and its crew. French author Gustave Flaubert (1821–1880), described the dreams of Madame Bovary as a young girl in a convent when she made an effort to envision the saints' lives and her own future. This is an impressive example of how to understand children's behavior in solitude.

More than any author, the Scottish novelist, poet, and essayist Robert Louis Stevenson (1850–1894), romanticized children's fantasy and pretend play in several short poems and a number of his semiautobiographical compositions. On September 1878, he published in *Cornhill Magazine* (a Victorian magazine and literary journal named after Cornhill Street in London) an essay on childhood titled, "Child's Play" (Stevenson, 1878/1930), where he creates the thought of imaginative play. He believes that play is a process of transforming reality:

> In the child's world of dim sensation, play is all in all. "Making believe" is the gist of his whole life, and he cannot so much as take a walk except in character.... When my cousin and I took our porridge of a morning, we had a device to enliven the course of the meal. He ate his with sugar, and explained it to be a country continually buried under snow. I took mine with milk, and explained it to be a country suffering gradual inundation. You can imagine us exchanging bulletins; how here was an island still unsubmerged, here a valley not yet covered with snow; what inventions were made; how his population lived in cabins on perches and travelled on stilts, and how mine was always in boats; how the interest grew furious, as the last corner of safe ground was cut off on all sides and grew smaller every moment; and how in fine, the food was of altogether secondary importance, and might even have been nauseous, so long as we seasoned it with these dreams. (Stevenson, 1930, pp. 161–162)

In view of the fact that children are this way, Stevenson states,

> One thing, at least, comes very clearly out of these considerations; that whatever we are to expect at the hands of children, it should not be any peddling exactitude about matters of fact.... I think it less than decent. You do not consider how little the child sees, or how swift he is to weave what he has seen into bewildering fiction; and that he cares no more for what you call truth, than you for a gingerbread dragoon. (Stevenson, 1930, p. 163)

In addition, Stevenson's (1885/1998) children's book titled, *Where Go the Boats?: Play-Poems of Robert Louis Stevenson* justifies the pleasure in play. The enjoyment of childhood (both past and present) is communicated in his ageless verse when he portrays young children who are building a ship with chairs and pillows, working with blocks to build a city, playing with toys on a bedspread, or sailing a toy boat down the river to an indefinite destination. His poem, "Where Go the Boats?" characterizes the voyage of two toy boats that depart from the country and sail down a river that passes through a patchwork countryside and goes without difficulty beyond a large city where urban children discover them. To motivate joyfulness in the children's imagination, Grover (the illustrator) gives a graphic explanation of Stevenson's words and presents the poetry that children have benefited from for many generations

(Bromer, 1999). Children as young as age 5 enjoy these poems with great enthusiasm.

When Robert Louis Stevenson began writing his children's poems for his book, *A Child's Garden of Verses* (Stevenson, 1885/1999), he had previously recorded 10 of his thoughts about his own childhood and the nature of childhood. Stevenson's book has four poems from his 1885 edition of *A Child's Garden of Verses* that includes rhymes that are supposedly about playing. In the poem titled, "A Good Play," two boys construct a provisional indoor ship:

> But Tom fell out and hurt his knee,
> So there was no one left but me.

The illustration has a lonesome boy holding a slice of cake and picking up his fork. An aqua-green sheet intensifies a scarlet toy house, a purple bedpost stands alongside a hot-yellow wall (Publishers Weekly, 1998). In addition, in "A Good Play," two boys construct a sailboat on a set of traditional stairs with sofa pillows and chairs and "go a-sailing on the billows." In "Block City," the configuration of green trees on a purple overstuffed chair is replicated in a young girl's visualization of a mountain in her fantasy town by the sea; while in "The Land of Counterpane," a green bedspread is transformed into green hills (Bromer, 1999).

The focus of Stevenson's poems in *A Child's Garden of Verses* is on imaginative play in an original and perceptive mode. The poems commemorate the contentment that derives from the transformative power of creativity. Stevenson believed that childhood was a period of time for play, imagination, innocence, and fear. Children are not considered in terms of their everyday reality. Rather, imaginative play is seen as a fascinating and exquisite departure from the boredom in their lives. However, it should be understood that these are modern-day views of children and their real and imaginary worlds, which may have been inappropriate in 1879 (Rosen, 1995). Such forms of play may certainly have been present, but the adult world may well have neglected to actually become concerned with childhood experiences. For instance, Mark Twain's work indicates that sociodramatic play surfaced prior to the 19th century (Singer, 1973). His novels (e.g., *Huckleberry Finn*, *The Prince and the Pauper*) focused on his own fantasies that led to acting several adult roles (e.g. pirates, captains) in his imaginative play. He clearly acknowledged the significance of the role of adult models and storytelling in choosing and promoting children's pretend play.

A number of Twain's books and stories offer the initial, finest realistic narration of make-believe play in fiction. In *Huckleberry Finn* (1884/2009), Huck and his friends pretend to be pirates, river boat captains, and other characters. The final part of *Huckleberry Finn* consists of the complex farce into which Huck and Jim are persuaded. Twain narrates Huck's personal fantasies and play in eventually achieving his aspiration to become a pirate. In *The Prince and the Pauper*, Twain (1881/1996) recounts Tom's progress while participating in imaginative play with his peers with himself as the leader. In numerous situations, Twain also supports the point that adults' enthusiasm in storytelling influences children's play (Singer, 1973).

The above-mentioned authors manifest a cultural concept of children's play. In addition, they are responsive interpreters who communicate an observation of humankind that "rings true." Researchers can study authors from various eras. They can collect system observations that are as valid as the most excellent current ethnographies of the children's play. Such aspects of the popular culture offer valid evidence of childhood.

Children's Literature and Scholarship: An Historical Perspective

Children's literature developed slowly as a scholarly field to the extent that its literary works were still not accepted by many literary scholars, even in the 1980s. Until the 1980s and 1990s children's literature was initially acknowledged as an area of expertise in a number of university English departments; until that time it tended to be offered only in schools that had competent programs in education or in library schools. Anthologies of national literatures (e.g., *The Norton Anthology of American Literature*), even now, regularly neglect children's literature. They may include stories like *Little Women* or *The Adventures of Huckleberry Finn*, but as Clark (2003) points out these stories are no longer considered exclusively as children's literature. because the concept is usually perceived to be similar in the context of Great Books. If children's literature is accepted within literary history it is frequently considered as a genre in and of itself (Mickenberg & Vallone, 2011). The recently published *Cambridge History of the American Novel* (Cassuto, Eby, & Reiss, 2011), however, has a chapter devoted to children's novels written by Mickenberg (2011). In addition, several university faculty began to promote scholarship in the field having found a lack of serious scholarship about children's literature.

Professional Organizations and Journals

Francelia Butler, a faculty member at the University of Connecticut, advocated for academic recognition of children's literature as a scholarly field of study. However, her colleagues did not perceive children's literature to be a scholarly field of study, because it did not have (a) a scholarly journal, (b) a humanities-oriented professional organization, (c) a literature-oriented textbook, and (d) any recognition from either the Modern Language Association or the National Endowment for the Humanities (Chaston, 2002).

In 1972 Jon Stott, Francelia Butler, John Graham, Ben Brockman, and Anne Jordan met to formally establish a professional organization devoted to scholarly research in

children's literature (Stott, 1978), which became the Children's Literature Association. In 1975 the group initiated the writing of a constitution so that the organization would be able to hold elections and elect board members to integrate members' interests and attitudes. In 1976 the constitution was approved by the Board of Directors in Philadelphia (Stott, 1978). The Children's Literature Association held its first conference the following March after their first meeting. Until the spring of 1976, Anne Jordan assumed the responsibilities of Executive Secretary, organizing the conference and mailing out the organization's newsletter to approximately 200 members. The organization doubled its membership the next year (Chaston, 2002). In his 1978 presidential address, Stott (1978) stated:

> We are working in a relatively new field. There are certain basic classics which, I'm sure we'd all agree, merit serious study. But we still do not have a basic canon of works, something possessed by all other fields of literature. I think that the ChLA could provide an invaluable service to teachers and researchers alike by working to establish a canon. What are the major books and authors in the field, the ones we should all know well? The establishment of a basic list would serve as a basis for a relatively uniform curriculum in university courses, something lacking now. We know that if a student takes an American fiction course, he'll have read Hawthorne, Melville, Twain, James and so forth. What will a student who has taken children's literature have read?
>
> Related to the establishment of a canon, is the mapping out of the field of scholarship and criticism of children's literature. What has been done and, more important, what needs to be done? Also…the attempt to answer the question, "What is children's literature?" We all have ideas—and in the end, there may be thirteen different ways of looking at this particular blackbird. But, in the end, by making the attempt or attempts we will clarify our own views. (p. 10)

From 1973 until the present time, the Association has sponsored the annual Children's Literature Association Conference in the United States, Canada, and France. The Children's Literature Association (ChLA) has become a nonprofit association of scholars, critics, professors, students, librarians, teachers, and institutions devoted to the academic study of children's literature.

Toward the end of 1972, Adams (2000) raised a concern that the newly formed ChLA was "gaining local recognition in Michigan, but needed a journal to put it on a national footing" (p. 184). Butler succeeded in eradicating her colleagues' criticisms when in 1972 she founded a children's literature journal, *Children's Literature: The Great Excluded*, now known as *Children's Literature* (Adams, 2000). A letter to Francelia Butler resulted in another meeting on June 3, 1973 where it was decided that *Children's Literature* would become ChLA's official journal (Chaston, 2002)—later another journal was added, *Children's Literature Association Quarterly*. Thus, the organization came to sponsor two peer-reviewed journals.

Children's Literature is now published annually by both the Children's Literature Association and the Modern Language Association Division on Children's Literature. The journal publishes theoretically based articles that provide an understanding of major issues and criticism in children's literature. Articles go through blind reviews and numerous revisions before final publication.

In the meantime, scholars in the United Kingdom launched two scholarly journals, which contributed to the scholarship in children's literature. In January 1970, Nancy Chambers published the first issue of the British journal *Signal*, which, as Peter Hunt (1984–1985) points out assisted children's literature researchers in breaking down the barriers between academic disciplines. An additional journal, *Children's Literature in Education*, with both a British and American editorial board, was launched the following year.

For more than two decades, the publication of critical writing on children's literature has increased. In 1984 the first edition of *The Oxford Companion to Children's Literature* (Carpenter & Prichard, 1984/1999) was published and revised in 1999 adding to the scholarly emphasis of the children's literature movement. A sizable increase of academic interest in the history of children's literature has been profoundly revelatory about the complex and changing attitudes toward childhood through the centuries. Literary critics and social historians have become involved in assuring that the study of children's literature achieves its planned purpose (Fearn, 1985) of assisting researchers and scholars.

Scholars in Children's Literature

Within literary studies, the study of children's literature continued to gain a significant foothold in the 1970s. Numerous colleges and universities developed programs in children's literature study. These were housed in English departments, library schools, and schools of education. Foundational works published since the late 1970s have shaped the field in important ways, helping to define its forms and unique qualities, bringing theoretical perspectives to bear, creating essential historical reviews, highlighting the intersection between ideologies and politics, and opening the canon of 19th century literature (and other periods) to include works for children, and attending to the child reader/writer (Mickenberg & Vallone, 2011).

Scholarship in children's literature involves three discrete disciplines: (1) literary studies in English and language departments; (2) library and information science; and (3) education (Wolf, Coats, Enciso, & Jenkins, 2010). Traditionally, some intersection may surface between the topics studied or the methodologies that are used to conduct research in each of these fields. However, lately the focus on children's literature scholarship is (1) on the way scholars from across disciplines are collaborating and (2) on the way each field of study shares unique information and theories. One of the major obstacles in promoting the scholarship in children's literature is its theoretical framework.

Theories on Children's Literature

Early critics of young children's literature focus on exploring the way children read literature and on identifying developmentally appropriate books for children. Critics differ in experience, values, and philosophy; therefore, they frequently disagree about the most appropriate theory to use in the selection of and justification for the best books for children. Although most critics continue to be child-centered, children's literature as a discipline has flourished and incorporated different ways to conduct analyses in research studies. As a result, criticism in children's literature has become an academic discipline that extends its research into literary theory and cultural studies. Some of the theories that researchers claim are literary criticism, literary theory, critical theory, and narrative theory. Since these theories overlap and scholars who use the same theory have difficulty agreeing on its definition, they are defined below and discussed in the next section.

- *Literary criticism* is the analysis, appraisal, and interpretation of literature. Contemporary literary criticism usually depends on literary theory including its techniques and purposes for theoretical discourse. Both literary criticism and literary theory are similar, but literary critics are not considered to be theorists. Many use literary criticism and literary theory interchangeably. However, several critics disagree and distinguish between the two terms. They refer to literary criticism as a practical application of literary theory, because criticism is usually used with specific literary works; whereas literary theory is more rigorous, general, and abstract. Literary criticism studies are frequently published in essay or book forms. In contrast, literary theory critics publish their work in academic journals.
- *Literary theory* refers to the systematic study of literature and methodology used to analyze literature, although it also includes intellectual history, moral philosophy, social prophecy, and other interdisciplinary themes related to how individuals interpret meaning (Culler, 2007). Many scholars use critical theory but only use the word *theory* (Culler, 2011). As a result, the term *theory* has become a general term in scholarly research as researchers analyze different reading texts.
- *Critical theory* examines and critiques society and culture. It has two separate meanings, origins, and histories. One derives from sociology whereas the other derives from literary criticism. Therefore, the term *critical theory* has a very literal and general function. It is used to explain any theory that uses critique analysis.
- *Narrative theory*, for which many use the term *narratology*, refers to both the theory and the study of narrative and narrative structure, and how these affect the ways in which narrative is perceived. According to Culler (2001), narratology has numerous elements that are combined to acknowledge that narrative theory needs to distinguish between story and sequence of actions or events that are

developed as separate from their expression in discourse, including the discursive narration of events.

Literary Criticism

Recently theorists in several fields have analyzed the composition of texts in the broadest meaning of the word. As a result, history, identity, and reality indicate the authors' understanding of the ineffectiveness of a permanent meaning. This outcome has been both refused and accepted in children's literature criticism. Some critics reject it, because they mainly consider children's literature to be a practical and an easy means to help children relate subject and object using language and images for interpretation. In contrast, other critics view children's literature as a very appropriate opportunity to discuss basic concepts such as reality, children, and identity. Literary criticism in children's literature has offered a developing interest in the importance of integrating childhood studies into criticism of children's literature (Christensen, 2003). However, Hunt (1984–1985) quotes Seymour Chatman, an American film and literary critic and a former professor of rhetoric at the University of California, Berkeley.

> But theory is not criticism. Its purpose is not to offer new or enhanced readings of works, but precisely to "explain what we all do in the act of normal reading, with unconscious felicity." (Hunt, 1984–1985, p. 191)

According to Nodelman (1992), Hunt (1991) makes an ambitious effort to use "critical theory and practice to help readers to deal with children's literature, and children's literature to help readers to deal with literary theory" (Hunt, 1991, p. 5), which suggests that criticism may be the second kind where researchers use their own thoughts. Hunt (1991) examines a large body of theory to determine ways to challenge general beliefs about children and their reading, literature in common, and children's literature specifically. He assumes that literary texts have intrinsic value. For example, he believes that Shakespeare's work is intrinsically better, truer, more beautiful than Barbara Cartland's or Beatrix Potter's. Such belief lowers the status of scholarship in children's literature in comparison to adult masterpieces. In relation to children's literature, it dismisses those texts that children frequently enjoy most (Nodelman, 1992).

Critical Theory

Critical theory appears to be unrelated to children and books, although Alan Garner (1977) in his book *Granny Reardun* suggests that if high quality in children's literature is to be maintained, the field needs logical and thoughtful criticism/theory. In relation to children's literature studies, Anita Moss (1981) states that "If we believe…that children's literature occupies a place in the traditions of all literature, we owe it to ourselves to explore what is going on

in the field of literary criticism, even if we decide to reject it" (p. 25). Hunt (1984–1985) opposes this statement. He believes that children's literature should be accepted, because as in the past "new" criticism and new theories modify the individuals' patterns of thought and become the norm.

Children's literature continues to be ahead of the scope of most literary studies. Thacker (2000) debates the extent to which children's literature will continue the use of critical theory, given the lack of studies on specific and multiple texts for socially developed readers. The development of critical theory during the last few decades suggests that theory *requires* children's literature. Theorists need to explore and shift from a textual focus toward (a) the interchange between reader and text; (b) the social and political powers that arbitrate those interactions; (c) the role assumed by texts that are written mainly for children; and (d) the way reading is made accessible to children, within a net of discourses that both support and manage interactions with fictional texts (Thacker, 2000).

Narrative Theory

Narrative theory refers to any systematic process that examines narrative. Narrative is defined as the interpretation of a sequence of incidents where the analysts identify such incidents. Culler (2001) considers that narrative theory distinguishes between "story," a sequence of actions or events articulated as separate from their appearance in discourse and the discursive arrangement of the narration of incidents. Narrative theory can be used to analyze texts. Culler (2001) criticizes the narratologist Mieke Bal (1997), because he considers that she provides exaggerated and condescending versions in her narrative theory with an explicitness that is unusual among narrative theorists. Jonathan Culler (2001) provides her quote.

> The story consists of the set of events in their chronological order, their location, and their relations with the actors who case or undergo them." and more specifically, the events have temporal relations with one another. Each one is either anterior to, simultaneous with, or posterior to every other event. (pp. 190–191)

Narrative theory in this sense is a disappointment, because it is an obvious issue where the child-centered and book-centered critics of children's literature can come together. Both theoreticians and practitioners should be interested in the readers' fascination with narrative, the way storytellers narrate their story, the reason readers continue to turn the page, and the way readers identify critical elements in narratives (Hunt, 1990b).

But, most of all, children's books focus on narrative: in a sense they are about narrative. Recently narrative has developed a better relationship with both theory and criticism. Children's books have encountered repercussions from associating or identifying with narrative but have also flourished with its theory, especially since a foremost domain of critical theory has its origins in Propp's (1968) work on the morphology of folk tales; while scholars who use psychological and sociological criticism, like Bruno Bettelheim (1976) and Jack Zipes (1983), use these tales as fundamental models. Nevertheless an unavoidable relationship exists between children's literature and modern criticism.

In summation, theories in literary response are at the developmental stage and are remarkably comparable to the understanding of criticism. The history of the novel was established apart from precisely the "transferred story teller" to the classic realist text of the 19th century, and to the current self-conscious forms, corresponding to the emerging relationship between the child-reader and texts. Hunt (1984–1985) believes that children's books should be the first priority and after that theory and criticism. Like Fernando Savater (1982) in his skeptical *Childhood Regained*, Hunt (1984–1985) separates himself from those " misleading believers" who allow that children's writers "have interest as *symptoms* and that they permit readings somewhat more profound than the ones usually assigned to them by entranced adolescents" (p. 194). The study needs to continue to be relevant to the audience. Savater (1982) states:

> Let me make it clear, therefore, that I like these storytellers for the same reasons that children do; that is, because they tell wonderful yarns, and tell them well and I know no loftier reason than this to read a book. (p. xii)

Criticism has a more passive purpose than children's literature, which is to use stories to provide an understanding of the way events occur. Hunt (1984–1985) believes that story is the "primary act of mind." According to Barbara Hardy (1976), "Nature, not art, makes us all storytellers," even if the text is unnatural (p. vii). Text may be created using an untruthful method while criticism and theory use a systematic and rigorous process.

Theory Selection

The different theories overlap and contradict each other, which makes it difficult to select a particular theory in conducting research. For some time the theory of children's literature has been in a state of confusion. Still, numerous good and important works of literature have been written that overcome the challenges from critical theorists. The lack of agreement in satisfaction in this state of affairs due to theoretical confusion will not limit the critical theorists' productivity, but it can cause major restrictions and impose directions upon them. The origin of various confused beliefs, including the belief that there is, in some major literary research in children's literature is to be found in the theory of a genre (Hughes, 1978).

A theory of literature examines its nature and meaning, the quantity and attributes of literary genres, and the like. Theory tends to concentrate on political, philosophical, linguistic, and ethical issues concerning meaning, identity, power, and political effects of different discursive procedures. In a conversation with Jonathan Culler, Hughes stated that an obvious characteristic in theory is a discourse that may arise in another discipline and become relevant and provoke thought within the realm of literary studies. This makes theory hard to define because it is often not clear why certain works of sociology, historiography, or philosophy have come to count as "theory" and others have not. They still can come to count as theory, of course, when claims are made for their seminal importance (Brand, 2008).

In addition, theory is interdisciplinary, self-reflective, making an attempt to be independent in understanding its meaning as thought, and exploratory when it provides a framework to support or reject hypotheses in studies that can be used to generalize discourse. Theory suggests different methodologies in examining cultural phenomena and using the outcomes of studies to contribute to the generalization of a theory. Frameworks that other researchers discover to be intellectually beneficial in developing reconceptualizations are considered to be theory (Brand, 2008).

Theory and Practice

Theory in children's literature is a difficult and intimidating phenomenon. It attempts to justify apparent thoughts and focuses on a number of the undisclosed difficulties in children's literature. Many can use theories effectively when they presume that something is correct even if they are doubtful. For example, they take for granted their assumptions and assume to know (a) the way individuals read and the results of their reading, (b) that the children and adults have similar perceptions and responses to books, and (c) the way and reason that stories are successful. Theory may not precisely resolve any of such predicaments, but theory challenges the results in previously conducted studies in children's literature (Hunt, 1984–1985).

The struggle in overcoming opposition to children's literature scholarship influences within the academic focus is in the past. Today, the large quantity of books that merge children's books and literary theory indicates the efforts to bypass the "seriousness" gap. However, there is an additional lack of knowledge at the essence of the literary endeavor that must be dealt with if the importance of both the texts and readers of children's literature are to be acknowledged. Theorists examine the consequences of the wide range of distribution and the impact of sociocultural structures in responding to fiction. The interaction between readers and texts provides a perspective that includes a continuum of experience that begins in childhood. While critics of children's literature utilize theory to dispute the argument for children's literature, theoreticians in general appear to be slow in accepting the scholarship in children's literature, regardless of its relevance (Thacker, 2000).

A straightforward justification is the unacceptable definition, although it appears to embrace what has occurred since the 1960s such as literary authors' writings from outside the field of literary studies. In addition, the term *theory* itself suggests two different concepts: *theory of relativity* and simply *theory*. The *theory of relativity* consists of a predetermined set of propositions. In contrast, *theory* is the normal use of the word *theory*. In literary studies, theory is a way of thinking and writing whose restrictions are very difficult to define. An understandable description of theory is works that challenge and renew thinking in all disciplines. Studies that are based on theory have a greater influence than their basic discipline (Culler, 2011).

Young Children's Literary Theory

For more than a decade, theory related to readers of children's literature has been supported. For example, Peter Hunt (1990a, 1991, 1992) and Rod McGillis (1996) show that critics of children's literature use theoretical approaches from conventional academic disciplines to challenge the field. In several situations, these discourses seem to parallel the area of children's literary theory (Thacker, 2000).

The extent to which theorists disregard the young readers' initial texts is unforeseeable, especially since Terry Eagleton (1983), the most influential contemporary British literary critic and theorist, acknowledges that "all literature is inter textual" (p. 138), and depends on the identification of codes within a text obtained from prior reading experiences. This is a well-known concept in theories that profit from response. The multiplicity and subjectivity of meaning based on the receptiveness of response theory engages the reader as an active member within the text, giving authority to each individual reader to interact creatively with any text. Children, as readers, are usually overlooked and children's texts are disregarded. Knowledge of both is essential to understand the way readers assume this creative undertaking (Thacker, 2000).

Young Children as Social Readers

In discovering the way young children develop into social readers, researchers support their ability to actively interact as readers with the text. Although theorists have failed to recognize young children's early experience with texts, there have been several attempts to develop a theory. For example, Culler's (2007) literary theory proposes that readers understand a text and its interpretation. Readers actively engage in making sense of a text. Culler (2011) believes that readers detect frequent recurring components which readers spontaneously apply based on the differences in texts.

Roland Barthes (1975) believes the reader needs to be the creator of the text rather than the consumer. In *The Pleasure of the Text,* Barthes (1975) differentiates between two types of text: the text of "pleasure" and the text of "bliss." The text of pleasure is when the text corresponds to the readers' ex-

pectations and the traditional cultural customs. In contrast, the text of bliss ignores the readers' expectations. Instead it confuses the readers' historical, cultural, and psychological assumptions and challenges their understanding of language. Barthes (1975) refers to these texts as "readerly" text and "writerly" text. Readerly text adapts to the readers' predictions; therefore, readers become passive. The writerly text is when the authors accept the readers' intelligence and challenges the readers' suppositions by shifting from the traditional norm conventions. As a result, the writerly text challenges readers to develop new meanings. The focal point of the writerly text is to open up the text to its multiple interpretations (Cutajar, 2010).

While Barthes (1975) recognizes that the power of education and culture limits the openness in dynamic texts, he disregards the relationship between the basis of the pleasure in the text and the children's position within the process of meaning, which indicates a critical void in his theory. Initial interactions with the language of fiction that promote a self-awareness of "playing the fiction game" is more often delegated to the most highly developed literary readers, which disregards children as active or deconstructive readers. This perception is essential for reading fairy tales and indeed most of children's literature (Appleyard, 1994).

Rather than considering the relationship between literary sources and the meaning of the "fictional factor" in children's mental development, childhood is established as independent and deficient in relation to adult experiences. None of these theorists discuss young children's initial experiences with text, though interpretations based on literary principles and beliefs are learned during childhood. When young readers read a text, their initial experiences establish their role as active and authoritative readers (Thacker, 2000). Thacker (2000) declares that children are inadequate as readers of fiction. However, studies provide strong support for the view that children are able to be active and confident readers, but they need to be provided with opportunities (e.g., reading interactions) to test, modify, and refine their abilities. Thacker (2000) does not dispute the Piagetian (Piaget, 1970) theory on preserving the development of understanding and knowledge in both the world and text. However, she believes that developing readers will experience difficulty with texts. Thacker (2000) examines the extent to which reliance on this theory replaces the dominance of response and active involvement with narrative that is inherent during infancy. A relationship may exist between Bruner's (1986) persistent view that the world is structured in language, used in the social context of mother–child interactions, and the imaginative relationship with language that is inferred in Iser's (1980) explanation of "literary engagement."

A theory of reading fiction is needed to support the concept of continuity and its conditional social discourses. Theorists in children's literature need to offer a wide-ranging perspective of the readers' social achievements and the outcomes of the discourses that embrace fiction in the development of their response (Thacker, 2000).

Research from a Literary Perspective

Typically, children's literature scholars from literature departments in universities (e.g., English, German, Spanish) conduct literary analyses of books. These studies are considered literary criticism analyses and may focus on an author, a theme, an issue, a genre, a period, or a literary theory. The results of this type of research are typically published as books or articles in scholarly journals. The highly regarded research journals that publish literary studies in children's literature include *Children's Literature Association Quarterly, Children's Literature in Education, Children's Literature, The Lion and the Unicorn,* and *International Research in Children's Literature.* According to Immroth and McCook (2000), for a long time the field of library and information science has conducted studies in children's literature. For example, in 1992 the Trejo Foster Foundation (TFF) for Hispanic Library Education was officially established to provide Library Services for Youth of Hispanic Heritage. TFF sponsors biannual, educational institutes for leaders, practitioners, and students in the library and information fields to deliberate and advocate for issues, policies, and practices that influence scholarship in the Hispanic Latino communities and individuals. Sharing scholarship and research offers a forum to discuss issues and public policy that can promote the scholarship in children's literature.

Although only recently has this discipline begun to earn serious recognition within the academic membership, the critical study of young children's literature has a well-established history. In the past century, serious or meticulous inquiry was ignored in the history of children's literature; because children's books were not considered to be important enough for scholarly research while the descriptions of literary scholars—to a lesser degree historians—concerning the issues in their fields are very limited to be integrated in the research of children's books. Disappointingly, researchers, educators, and librarians in this area have usually neglected or continued to be unaware of research in history, literature, and sociology that could contribute to augment the quality of the moderately limited understanding about children's literature. There are a small number of well-designed, highly detailed, and thoroughly documented studies that can be used as a basis for scholarly research (Kelly, 1963). Such studies have motivated contemporary researchers to continue scholarly research in children's literature.

Researchers and scholars are conducting critical analysis of children's literature. This developing interest focuses on childhood and its studies and critical analysis has introduced the academic study of children's literature with new enthusiasm. It has also emphasized the stimulating and imaginative facets of scholarship in children's literature that have taken advantage of the knowledge of numerous scholars from different disciplines such as historians, sociologists, psychologists, media studies, political scientists, legal scholars, literary critics, education, and library professionals. Contemporary scholars analyze the children's texts and their culture to develop theoretically sophisticated, politically immersed, and historicized wide ranging frameworks that indicate that children's literature is a remarkably dynamic field in relation to scholarly research. The study of children's literature has attracted contemporary scholars in a range of fields and has acquired high academic status. For example, researchers in the field show that children may know more about children's literature than they do.

Children's literature has been an important interest to both its authors and individuals who support its enjoyment. Critics of children's books have differentiated between literature for children versus that for adults. Their focus has been on the children's needs as readers of literature, which allows the validity of the authors' perspective and important statements they wish to make. A critical scholarly concern has emerged concerning the themes and structure of children's books (Fearn, 1985).

The critical study of young children's literature has a well-established history. Scholarly works on children's literature began to appear in the early to mid-20th century in works such as F. J. Harvey's (1932) *Children's Books in England: Five Centuries of Social Life* and Paul Hazard's (1944) *Books, Children, and Men* (which were originally published in French). Such books sought to place children's literature within a larger cultural context (Mickenberg & Vallone, 2011).

Apparent from researchers' studies on children and their literature throughout the centuries is the intricacy of the relationship between children, their books, and society in general. Since the mid-18th century (John Newbery's era), the children's book trade has continued to be extremely well-informed about the market's views of childhood. The 18th century book trade provides evidence concerning the fluctuating status of childhood while its position in 20th century society can be measured from the books that are published and advocated in the 21st century (Fearn, 1985).

Conclusion

Literature offers children education and socialization that conveys society's goals, fears, expectations, and demands (Landt, 2006; Louie, 2006). It also assists children in understanding their society's obvious and hidden values and usually explains and provides a rationale for "appropriate" patterns of behavior and belief. Children's literature serves as a medium to teach children cultural values by introducing a wide range of diversity in a multicultural society. In a study of children's literature in early childhood education, Boutte, Hopkins, and Waklatsi (2008) show three standard themes: (1) early childhood education content and skills; (2) imagination, fantasy, or humor; and (3) dispositions, morals, or life lessons. The combination of these behaviors provides the children with profound and long remembered experiences.

Literature provides a context where children interact with a variety of literary genres that support their social development and assist them in generating alternative perspectives. When young children read or listen to a story, they develop relationships with the information that is transmitted (Saracho, 2012). In such situations, young children interact with each other to integrate, construct, and relate knowledge from the printed text (Vygotsky, 1978). Literature experiences that are spontaneous, pleasurable, enthusiastic, and enrich children's lives promote their understanding and appreciation of literature (Saracho, 2012). Thus, children's literature assumes an increasingly critical role in literacy programs and in the content areas. However, as a new century has begun, many (including teacher preparation programs, state and national standards) have failed to recognize the value of children's literature. One reason may be their lack of understanding of its meaning and purpose. They have overlooked the complexities that provide an understanding of children's literature. Many may find children's literature to be complex, because it is difficult to relate the genre to any cultural or academic category (Hunt, 2001). However, they need to know that ideas and concepts about children's literature are based on the history of children's literary theory and the theories themselves as well as that children's literature criticism is moving toward a much more interdisciplinary mode of interpretation (Gubar, 2002).

References

Adams, G. (2000). The Francelia Butler watershed: Then and now. *Children's Literature Association Quarterly, 25*(4), 181–190.

Anderson, N. (2010). *Elementary children's literature: Infancy through Age 13*, (3rd ed.). Boston: Allyn & Bacon.

Appleyard, J. A. (1994). *Becoming a reader: The experience of fiction from childhood to adulthood*. New York: Cambridge University Press.

Ashliman, D. L. (2008). Three little pigs and other folktales of Aarne-Thompson-Uther type 124. *Folklore and mythology electronic texts*. Pittsburgh, PA: University of Pittsburgh. Retrieved from http://www.pitt.edu/~dash/type0124.html

Association for Library Service to Children. (2007). *2007 notable children's books*. Retrieved from http://www.ala.org/ala/alsc/awardsscholarships/childrensnotable/notablecbooklist/currentnotable.htm

Auden, W. H. (April 3, 1965). As it seemed to us. *New Yorker*, 159–192.

Bal, M. (1997). *Narratology: Introduction to the theory of narrative*. Toronto: University of Toronto Press.

Barthes, R. (1975). *The pleasure of the text* (R Miller, trans.) New York: Hill & Wang.

Bettelheim, B. (1976). *The uses of enchantment*. New York: Knopf.

Boutte, G. S., Hopkins, R., & Waklatsi, T. (2008). Perspectives, voices, and worldviews in frequently read children's books. *Early Education and Development, 19*(6), 941–962.

Brand, D. (January 24, 2008). Why deconstruction still matters: A conversation with Jonathan Culler. *Cornell Chronicle*. Retrieved from http://www.news.cornell.edu/stories/Jan08/JonathanCuller.html

Bromer, S. (April, 1999). Review of *Where go the boats?: Play-poems of Robert Louis Stevenson. School Library Journal, 45*(4), 125.

Bruner, J. (1986). *Actual minds, possible worlds*. Cambridge, MA: Harvard University Press.

Bruner, J. (1990). *Acts of meaning*. Cambridge, MA: Harvard University Press

Card, O. S. (November 5, 2001). "Hogwarts": Uncle Orson reviews everything. Hatrack River Enterprises. Retrieved from http://www.hatrack.com/osc/reviews/everything/2001-11-05.shtml.

Carpenter, H., & Prichard, M. (1999). *The Oxford companion to children's literature*. New York: Oxford University Press (Original work published 1984)

Cassuto, L., Eby, C, V., & Reiss, B. (Eds.) (2011). *The Cambridge history of the American novel*. New York: Cambridge University Press.

Chambers, E. K. (1930). *William Shakespeare: A study of facts and problems* (Vols. 1 & 2). New York: Clarendon Press.

Chaston, J. D. (2002). From Kalamazoo to Timbuktu: ChLA at 30. *Children's Literature Association Quarterly, 27*(4), 178–182.

Christensen, N. (2003). Childhood revisited: On the relationship between childhood studies and children's literature. *Children's Literature Association Quarterly, 28*(4), 230–239.

Clark, B. L. (2003). *Kiddie lit: The cultural construction of children's literature in America*. Baltimore MD: Johns Hopkins University Press.

Commager, H. S. (1969). Introduction. In C. Meigs, A. T. Eaton, E. Nesbitt, & R. H. Viguers (Eds.), *A critical history of children's literature* (pp. xi–xix). New York: Macmillan.

Culler, J. (2001). *The pursuit of signs: Semiotics, literature, deconstruction*. New York: Routledge & Kegan Paul.

Culler, J. (2007). *On deconstruction: Theory and criticism after structuralism*. Ithaca, NY: Cornell University Press.

Culler, J. (2011). *Literary theory: A very short introduction*. New York: Oxford University Press.

Cutajar, M. (September 29, 2010). *Roland Barthes: The writerly text*. Retrieved from http://maureencutajar.suite101.com/roland-barthes-the-pleasure-of-the-text-a291322

Dickens, C. (2004/1843). *A Christmas carol*. New York: Simon & Schuster (Original work published 1843)

Eagleton, T. (1983). *Literary theory: An introduction*. Oxford, England: Blackwell.

Fearn, M. (Ed.). (1985). Introduction. In M. Fearn (Ed.), *Only the best is good enough*. (pp. 1–5). London: Rossendale.

Garner, A. (1977). *Granny Reardun*. New York: HarperCollins.

Godden, R. (1988, May–June). Shining Popocatapetl: Poetry for children. *The Horn Book*, 305–314.

Gubar, M. (2002). Revising the seduction paradigm: The case of Ewing's The Brownsies. *Children's Literature , 30*, 42–55).

Hardy , B. N. (1976). *Tellers and listeners: The narrative imagination*. New York: Athlone Press.

Harvey, F. J. (1932) *Children's books in England: Five centuries of social life*. Cambridge, England: Cambridge University Press in association with the British Library.

Hazard, P. (1944) *Books, children, and men*. Boston, MA: Horn Book.

Hughes, F. A. (1978). Children's literature: Theory and practice. *ELH English Literary History, 45*(3), 542–561.

Hunt, P. (1984–1985). Narrative theory and children's literature. *Children's Literature Association Quarterly, 9*(4), 191–194.

Hunt, P. (1990a). *Children's literature: The development of criticism*. New York: Routledge.

Hunt, P. (1990b). New directions in narrative theory. *Children's Literature Association Quarterly, 15*(2), 46–47.

Hunt, P. (1991). *Criticism, theory, and children's literature*. Oxford: Blackwell.

Hunt, P. (Ed.). (1992). *Literature for children: Contemporary criticism*. New York: Routledge.

Hunt, P. (2001). *Children's literature*. Malden, MA: Blackwell s.

Immroth, B. F., & McCook, K. P. (2000). *Library services to youth of Hispanic heritage*. Jefferson, NC: McFarland.

International Reading Association and the National Council of Teachers of English. (1996). *Standards for the English language arts*. Urbana, IL: National Council of Teachers of English.

Iser, W. (1980). *The act of reading: A theory of aesthetic response.* Baltimore, MD: Johns Hopkins University Press.

Kelly, R. G. (1963). American children's literature: An historiographical review. *American Literary Realism, 6,* 89–107.

Kiefer, B. Z. (2004). Children's literature and children's literacy: Preparing early literacy teachers to understand the aesthetic values of children's literature. In O. N. Saracho & B. Spodek (Eds.), *Contemporary perspectives on language policy and literacy instruction in early childhood education* (pp. 161–180). Greenwich, CT: Information Age.

Landt, S. M. (2006). Multicultural literature and young adolescents: A kaleidoscope of opportunity. *Journal of Adolescent & Adult Literacy, 49,* 690–697.

Louie, B. Y. (2006). Guiding principles for teaching multicultural literature. *Reading Teacher, 59,* 438–448.

McGillis, R. (1996). Literary theory column. *Children's Literature Association Quarterly, 21*(4), 199–200.

Mickenberg, J. L. (2011). Children's novels. In L. Cassuto, C. V. Eby, & B. Reiss (Eds.) *The Cambridge history of the American novel* (pp. 861–878).

Mickenberg, J. L., & Vallone, L.(2011). Introduction. In J. L. Mickenberg & L. Vallone (Eds.), *The Oxford handbook of children's literature* (pp. 3–21). New York: Oxford University Press.

Moss, A. (1981). Structuralism and its critics. *Children's Literature Association Quarterly, 6*(1), 24–29.

Nodelman, P. (1992). The second kind of criticism. *Children's Literature Association Quarterly, 17*(3), 37–39.

Norton, D., & Norton, S. E. (2011). *Through the eyes of a child: An introduction to children's literature.* Upper Saddle River, NJ: Merrill Prentice Hall.

Pearsall, J., & Trumble B. (Eds.). (1996) *The Oxford English reference dictionary.* Oxford, England: Oxford University Press.

Piaget, J. (1970). *Structuralism.* New York: Basic Books.

Propp, V. (1968). *The morphology of the folk tale.* Austin: University of Texas Press.

Publishers Weekly. (1998, November). Review of *Where go the boats?: Play-poems of Robert Louis Stevenson. Publishers Weekly, 245,* 82.

Rosen, M. (1995). Robert Louis Stevenson and children's play: The contexts of a *Child's garden of verses. Children's Literature in Education, 26*(1), 53–72.

Saracho, O. N. (2010). Children's play in the visual arts and literature. *Early Child Development and Care, 180*(7), 947–956.

Saracho, O. N. (2012). *An integrated play-based curriculum for young children.* New York: Routledge

Saracho, O. N., & Spodek, B. (2003). Understanding play and its theories.

In O. N., Saracho & B. Spodek (Eds.), *Contemporary perspectives on play in early childhood* (pp. 1–19). Greenwich, CT: Information Age.

Saracho, O. N., & Spodek, B. (2010). Families' selection of children's literature books. *Early Childhood Education Journal, 37*(5), 401–409.

Savater, F. (1982). *Childhood regained.* New York: Columbia University Press.

Singer, J. L. (1973). Theories of play and the origins of imagination. In J. L. Singer (Ed.), *The child's world of make-believe* (pp. 1–26). New York: Academic Press.

Stevenson, R. L. (1999). *A child's garden of verses* (rev. ed.). New York: Simon & Schuster. (Original work published 1885) Retrieved from http://www.childrensbooksonline.org/child_garden_verses/pages/02_cbv.htm

Stevenson, R. L. (Ed.). (1930). Child's play. In *Virginibus Puerisque and other papers, memories and portraits.* Karnataka India: Standard Book. Retrieved from http://robert-louis-stevenson.classic-literature.co.uk/virginibus-puerisque/

Stevenson, R. L. (1998). *Where go the boats?: Play-poems of Robert Louis Stevenson.* San Diego, CA: Browndeer Press, Harcourt Brace. (Original work published 1885)

Stott, J. (1978). Presidential address. *The Children's Literature Association Quarterly, 3*(1–2), 9–11.

Thacker, D. (2000). Disdain or ignorance? Literary theory and the absence of children's literature. *The Lion and the Unicorn, 24*(1), 1–17.

Tolstoy, L. (1964). *Childhood, boyhood, youth* (R. Edmonds, Trans.). New York: Penguin Classics. (Original work published 1852)

Twain, M. (1994). *The adventures of Tom Sawyer.* New York: Penguin. (Original work published 1876)

Twain, M. (2008). *Adventures of Huckleberry Finn.* New York: Penguin (Original work published 1884)

Twain, M. (2000). *The prince and the pauper.* New York: Dover. (Original work published 1881) Retrieved from http://www.mtwain.com/The_Prince_and_the_Pauper/index.html

Vygotsky, L. S. (1967). Play and its role in the mental development of the child. *Soviet Psychology, 12,* 62–76.

Vygotsky, L. S. (1978). *Mind in society.* Cambridge, MA: Harvard University Press.

Wolf, S., Coats, K., Enciso, P., & Jenkins, C. A. (2010). *Handbook of research in children's and young adult literature.* New York: Routledge.

Wordsworth, W., & Coleridge, S. (2007). *Lyrical ballads.* Grasmere, LA: The Wordsworth Museum & Art Gallery. (Original work published 1798 Retrieved from http://www.wordsworth.org.uk/history/index.asp?pageid=123

Zipes, J. (1983). *Fairy tales and the art of subversion.* New York: Wildman Press.

9

Early Literacy

Towards a Semiotic Approach

SUSAN E. HILL AND SUE NICHOLS
University of South Australia

The definition of early literacy has always been dependent on social views about the nature of mature literate competence. That is, a view of the future adult and how he or she will read, write, and communicate has reached down to shape the education system's approach to inculcating young children into literacy and, consequently, parents' understandings of how to prepare their children for literacy instruction. The National Council of Teachers of English (NCTE) has called for a redefinition of the requirements for literate citizenship: "Because technology has increased the intensity and complexity of literate environments, the twenty-first century demands that a literate person possess a wide range of abilities and competencies, many literacies" (NCTE, 2008).

Literacy is changing along with social and technological advances and so the definition of early literacy also needs to change to take into account new forms of literacy practice. In an earlier *Handbook* chapter, we argued:

> The ability to simultaneously coordinate multiple linguistic and non-linguistic elements is now understood as a quality of literate competence in all social actors. The meaning of "emergent literacy" is changing with the acknowledgement that what the child is "emerging" into is a complex world of signification. (Hill & Nichols, 2006, p. 156)

A continual retrospective and prospective re-visioning of literacy development is needed to deal with this dynamic situation. As we look forward to try and anticipate the skills children will need (and thus which we hope to assist them to develop), we also look back to reconsider whether concepts of literacy prevailing at earlier stages can be built on. This is leading to a reconsideration of the notion of emergent literacy.

Research into new literacies in early childhood is increasingly exploring how the electronic world is changing the way in which alphabetic literacy is used, and how it also places new demands on children as they become literate (Duke & Moses, 2004). More recently, studies investigating the impact of communication technologies on early literacy development have developed research methodologies for exploring these phenomena.

Perspectives on Early Literacy

Current perspectives on early literacy embody a diverse range of theories and practices and have at their core different values and beliefs about the nature of literacy, the process of literacy learning, how children are viewed, and different futures for young children's education. These theoretical orientations may be viewed on a historical continuum. However, owing to the additive nature of educational knowledge (old theories are rarely completely discarded as new entrants arrive) currently many theories seeking to explain children's acquisition of literacy simultaneously contest the field of knowledge. In this chapter we begin by briefly looking back on some familiar understandings of early literacy and consider the strengths and limitations of each for conceptualizing young children's literacy acquisition in these times. The work of Crawford (1995) is useful in summarizing and analyzing these separate positions and we have drawn on her work in the discussion below.

We then turn to our main focus, a comparatively new entrant to the field, the semiotic perspective, which we believe holds considerable promise to enrich theorizations of a changing view of literacy that encompasses developments in communication technologies and new textual practices. Selected research that examines aspects of literacy from this perspective is then reviewed, including studies on new literacies, multimodality, electronic literacies, and multibilinguality.

Developmentalism and the Concept of Emergent Literacy

From a developmental perspective, all children pass through a series of invariant stages that cannot be hurried

(Fleer, 2006). Maturation occurs as a result of a biological process of neural ripening, a little like ripening fruit or a blossoming. In the allied developmental readiness view of literacy, the key idea is that children must be *ready* before they can learn how to read. However, in tension with this, yet embraced by the developmentalist view, is the idea that nurturance can influence development by accelerating the rate at which children pass through stages (Nichols, 2002; Walkerdine, 1984). From a literacy perspective this means that children's readiness for formal literacy learning can be influenced by preparatory activities facilitated by a caring adult; for example, matching and letter recognition. This view is allied to the connectionist perspective where knowledge of some complex phenomenon (for example, reading) is achieved by first learning the pieces and then putting them together (Crawford, 1995). The developmental readiness and connectionist perspectives focus on elements or pieces which may be predictive of future literacy achievement. For example, learning the letters of the alphabet has been viewed as central to early literacy outcomes.

However, Paris (2005) points out that letter knowledge is "constrained" to a small set of knowledge that is mastered in relatively brief periods of development. In comparison, vocabulary knowledge is "unconstrained" and develops over the duration of learning. Prescriptions to teach "constrained" skills like letter knowledge usually only lead to temporary gains and only in skills aligned with the "constrained" skill. In addition Snow and Van Hemel (2008) write that various components or elements of oral language and literacy, such as phonological awareness, letter knowledge, and name writing are of obvious importance in their own right and arguments about their predictive relationship to each other or to later developmental outcomes are unnecessary.

The emergent perspective is influenced by cognitive and developmental psychology: literacy learning is not viewed as the acquisition of a series of reading skills but rather as a dynamic, ongoing process that begins long before children commence formalized schooling (Teale & Sulzby, 1986). The process of oral language is provided as a model for the development of print related literacy. Teachers immerse children in a print rich environment with real books and encourage them to write original texts. Children develop as readers and writers through immersion in print rich environments and from experiences with print that encourage engagement, experimentation, and risk taking. Invented spellings and approximations are accepted as part of the learner's ongoing process of making sense and gaining control over literacy. Developmentally appropriate practices guide both the curriculum and the structure of class activities. Formal direct instruction, particularly the teaching of isolated skills and worksheets, are seen as inappropriate for young children.

Defining the boundaries of the emergent stage, McGee and Purcell-Gates (1997) limit the period of emergent literacy from birth to when literacy independence at a conventional level is in evidence. They suggest that there are two time periods (0–5 and 5–independence). The sociocultural context for the first period is the home and community and perhaps preschool and religious school, and for the second period the formal school instructional context and the home and community. The transition from home to school settings is a central issue and continuity between these settings is seen as the ideal situation.

The Capable Communicator in Social Context

The social constructivist perspective views children as competent and capable users of oral and written language and argues that formal literacy education should build upon these competencies (Crawford, 1995). Children purposefully learn and make sense of the complex semiotic signs and symbols of their culture through social participation. The child's family context is understood in a broader sociocultural context of the community which makes particular kinds of communication practices important and provides opportunities for their practice (Guttierez & Rogoff, 2003; Wallace, 2008). From this perspective, the communication and text production activities of even very young children are reflective of their culture and are characterized by both purposefulness and intentionality (Trushell, 1998). The differences between the processes of young readers and more proficient language users are understood to be a matter of sophistication, practice, and experience, not a particular stage of psychological development. In the social constructivist perspective the early literacy curriculum builds on the cultural and social language and literacy experiences children have before formal schooling. A key challenge in bringing the sociocultural perspective of literacy into the contemporary context is the difficulty in drawing boundaries around sociocultural communities because global "flows" caused by transnational migration, media, and the Internet are increasingly creating mixed and hybrid linguistic and cultural practices and identities (Gutiérrez, 2011; Marsh, 2006).

Critical perspectives acknowledge that the power bases within different sociopolitical contexts are not equal ones and are concerned with change and social action (Gee, 2002; Siegal & Fernandez, 2000). This view contends that social practices, including literacy practices and literacy teaching practices, are set up to meet the interests and help maintain the privileged positions of those within the dominant culture (Orellana & D'warte, 2010). Critical perspectives claim that the interests of the dominant culture are accepted more readily and have more influence than any minority interests that may seek to disrupt the existing hierarchical power relationships. However, the complexity of the sociocultural world and the struggle within and between groups entails more than a simple model of social transmission. Gee (2002) writes of the importance of teachers finding associational "bridges" between a child's primary Discourse and the school-based language and literacy practices if schools are to resonate with the child's experiences of the world and initial sense of self. A child's primary Discourse with a big *D* is similar to an identity kit and includes "ways of talking, listening, writing, reading, acting, interacting, feeling, believing, valuing, and feeling (and using various objects, symbols, images, tools, and technologies) in the service of enacting meaningful socially situated identities and activities" (Gee, 2002, p. 35).

Semiotic Perspectives on Young Children's Use of Multimodal Signs and Symbols

We now move to the semiotic perspective which has been used by researchers and theorists seeking to understand how young children emerge as makers, inventors, and users of sign systems and symbols (Halliday, 1994; Labbo & Ryan, 2010). A semiotic perspective explores how individuals and groups use print to make meanings as well as how meanings are made and goals accomplished using other "semiotic resources" such as oral language, visual imagery, numerical symbols and music (Lemke, 1990). We concur with the New London Group (1996) prediction that children will be increasingly exposed to communication tools and situations that are multimodal rather than exclusively linguistic. In the 21st century young children are increasingly making meaning by drawing on multiple sign systems and multimedia symbol systems and these electronic symbol making systems may be best understood from a semiotic perspective (Labbo, 1996; Labbo & Ryan 2010). The dynamic changes in literacy and the complexity of texts that young children engage with requires educators to go beyond

what can be described and given value through the lens of traditional literacy (Hill, 2010). Early literacy within a social semiotic perspective considers different genres as socially constructed language practices, reflecting community norms and expectations. These norms are not static but change to reflect changing sociocultural needs and contexts (Purcell-Gates, Duke, & Martineau, 2007). Increasingly young children are drawing on multiple sign systems and multimedia symbols systems and even in technologically restricted classrooms, in pretend play, children create their own props to use as cell phones, iPods, and video games (Wohlwend, 2009). The semiotic approach does not replace older definitions of literacy. Rather, it is inclusive of, and adds to, both the traditional print-oriented and the more recent language-oriented communications model. Figure 9.1, below, illustrates this.

The inner circle represents the traditional print-oriented definition of literacy. Here there is an emphasis on encoding and decoding print. The middle circle of Figure 9.1 represents a language-oriented definition of literacy, which includes print but extends the range of representational resources to include oral language. Importantly, oral and written forms of language are different ways of knowing, and different oral language functions allow students to think and access knowledge in different ways (Halliday, 1975). Moving to the outer circle, literacy encompasses print and language plus a broader range of representational resources or modalities. For example in multimedia, print is combined with sound, movement, and visual imagery to create complex texts that require the "reader" to process in multiple modes simultaneously (Bearne, 2009).

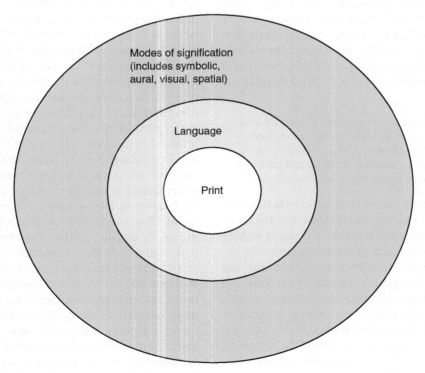

Figure 9.1 A semiotic model of literacy

Kress and Van Leeuwen (2001) developed a semiotic framework for the analysis of multimodal texts and communication practices which incorporate four "domains of practice" (p. 4): discourse, design, production and distribution/reproduction. An example of this approach applied at the level of a young child's literacy practices might be to consider how a child may design a text by drawing on elements from different domains such as media narratives, personal observations, as well as playground rituals and how this text may be distributed to audiences both immediate and distant using production technologies such as printing, texting, and uploading to the Internet. The concept of provenance is a central principle in this framework and refers to the sources of signs; so, in the example above, looking for the provenance of the signs used in a child's drawing may take us to a particular cartoon character and thus to the texts within which this character appears including TV programs, toys, clothing, as well as books.

Geosemiotics is a recent development in this field and is particularly concerned with how the dimension of the spatial context impacts on the production and reading of texts, broadly defined (Scollon & Scollon, 2001). Application of this approach to early literacy is a very recent development although it should be acknowledged that early ethnographic literacy researchers have long offered rich descriptions of the contexts of literacy events which can be read for insights into the importance of the spatial dimensions of context. Heath's (1983) landmark study of three contrasting communities did not just shed light on differences between the home-based pedagogies of middle-class and working-class families, and the former's greater alignment with school literacy practices. It also showed readers the importance of public spaces, such as the street or the front porch, for the performance of language practices, particularly those in which African American children participated. An example of a geosemiotic analysis of early literacy is Nichols (2011) study of children's activity spaces in libraries in which she argues that:

> the practicalities of how to get to a library by car, on foot or on the bus; the nature of the social invitation extended by a café; the sensory appeal of a curvilinear compared to an angular space; all are as salient as the librarian's choice of a book to present to an audience of young children.

A semiotic approach can be understood as building on earlier research from a sociocultural perspective. The use of a semiotic perspective extends the range of meaning-making resources that young children have access to and draw on. Semiotics makes the practices of design, production, and distribution as significant as the practices of decoding and interpretation to young children's literacy participation. Semiotics sensitizes educators to look for the provenance, or the source of the elements within texts produced by children, as well as texts provided for children. A semiotic framework in early childhood education enriches our analysis of the contexts of literacy by considering how discourse, design, production, and distribution/reproduction may impact on texts, their production, and their reception.

Electronic Literacies

New forms of electronic literacies designed for early childhood education are developing quickly and the research into young children's use of new technologies is also evolving quickly. Burnett (2010) reviewed the research from 2003 to 2009 focusing on young children's use of new technologies and found 698 relevant articles in the area. This contrasts with earlier reviews of literacy and technologies by Lankshear and Knobel (2003) where the authors found only a fraction of articles related to early childhood, new technologies, and literacy. In Lankshear and Knobel's (2003) review there was an overwhelming emphasis on using technology to promote abilities to handle conventional alphabetic print texts rather than to generate multimodal texts and to understand principles of multimodal meanings. In this section of the chapter we review research into electronic literacies exploring the recent themes of young children's home use of technology related to literacy; the use of multimodal technology to support reading; and importantly, young children's reading of e-books.

Several studies have focused on young children's use of technology in homes and communities and the disconnections between home and school use of electronic literacies. In a review of longitudinal studies into how very young children's communicative practices in the home are changing, due primarily to social change engendered by technology, Marsh (2006) noted that children played phonics games on computers, completed puzzles in comics, and played interactive games on satellite television. Parents across all of the reviewed studies reported on the development of a range of literacy skills, knowledge, and understanding that they felt had resulted from their children's engagement with a range of popular cultural and media texts. Language was a recurrent theme, with parents keen to point out the perceived effect of media on their children's linguistic repertoires, and some parents of bilingual children felt that their children had learned English from watching television. Anning (2003) in a longitudinal study of young children's drawing in the home, preschool, and school, writes that the communication systems such as television, videos, computer games, and the Internet are increasingly characterized by multimodality. Much of children's spontaneous play-based behaviors and related graphic representations before school reflect the multimodality of these communication systems. Mavers (2007) explored the e-mail exchanges between 6-year-old Kathleen and her uncle and highlighted the home based communication between family members engaging with electronic texts. In this study of e-mail communication, the choice of letter case, taps of the space bar, and punctuation marks were resources that enabled the 6-year-old to make meanings not so readily represented linguistically. Numerous studies provide strong evidence for young children's engagement at home with computer games, the Internet, and mobile phones (Marsh 2006; Pahl 2002). Labbo and Ryan (2010) suggest the time has come for children's e-literacies to be recognised as e-funds of knowledge and that the gaps between electronic literacy use in homes and communities needs to be addressed in early childhood settings.

Several research studies have explored the use of electronic multimedia technology to support reading development. Skouge, Rao, and Boisvert (2007) describe how audio, video, and digital photography can be used by educators to build literacy-rich contexts for children, in which stories that otherwise would go untold and unread can be made accessible to children and families. The authors state that educators and librarians may create audio books, make video book readings, and use the digital language experience approach to create texts to be used by children and their families. Multimedia adaptations of traditional storybooks have particular application for children with disabilities and forms of bilingual recorded books and book retellings can be created by educators for children and families with languages other than English. Hourcade, Parette, Boeckmann, and Blum (2010) researched the use of Microsoft PowerPoint for teaching word recognition and state that features such as animation color and sound are motivating for young children. Much of the research into using technology to enhance reading development is similar to earlier work using multimedia to enhance early book reading. For example, Hutinger and colleagues (1997) report on an early childhood literacy project that took place in 16 preschool classes involving preschoolers with mild to moderate disabilities working with graphics and story-making software. The study reported significant gains in communication and other early literacy behaviors as well as enhanced interpersonal interactions amongst learners.

Research into the reading of electronic books (Jong & Bus, 2003; Labbo & Kuhn, 2000) has focused on how electronic books combine multimedia to support early literacy development. Many e-books have been designed with read and play activities, text to speech and additional video formats displayed on e-book readers, iPod, iPad devices, or computers using e-book software programs. Korat and Shamir (2008) explored the effects of educational e-books on the literacy development of 149, 5- to 6-year-old kindergarteners in low and middle socioeconomic groups. Results revealed that knowledge of word meaning of children from both middle and low SES groups improved following the educational e-book activities. The children in the low SES group showed relatively greater improvement rates than did the children in the middle SES group. The children in the "Read with dictionary" and "Read and play" activity modes showed more improvement in their early literacy levels than did those in the "Read story only" mode. More advanced early readers benefited from the added tools and variety afforded by e-books (Weber & Cavanaugh, 2006).

Research into adult–child interactions with e-books has been investigated by Kim and Anderson (2008). This research compared mother–child interactions in three contexts: shared reading with a book in a traditional print format, with an e-book in a CD-ROM format, and with an e-book in a video clip format. The adult–child interactions involved mother–child interactions with 3-year-old and 7-year-old children and compared children's extratextual talk during the shared readings. The results indicated mother–child interactions differed in the contexts, with more complex talk evident with electronic texts. Children's extratextual talk differed depending on their ages, and the talk seemed to be context specific. Moody, Justice, and Cabell (2010) explored children's engagement with e-books versus traditional storybooks and found that e-storybooks afforded benefits to children's reading engagement and communicative participation. The authors found that both computerized and traditional storybooks can influence children's literacy and oral language; however, both book forms demand supportive interactions with an adult.

As e-books move from CD-ROM format to individual handheld Kindles and iPads, young children's responses to electronic books on e-readers has become a research focus. Larson (2010) explored the use of e-readers in a second grade classroom and found the children adjusted the font size, accessed the built-in dictionary to look up meanings of words, reviewed the phonetic spelling of words to help "sound out," text and also activated the text-to-speech feature to listen to words that they found difficult or to reread text passages. The children also made notes on the e-reader in response to the e-books and were able to use the e-reader to go online to search for additional information.

While electronic literacies in early childhood remains the focus of this section of the chapter, research into traditional forms of book reading continues to be important. Young children's multimodal responses to books have been the focus of a large body of research over several decades (Elster, 1994; Sulzby, 1985). More recent research has explored young children's multimodal responses to traditional picture books (Hassett & Curwood, 2009; Mol, Bus, and De Jong, 2009). However, Sulzby's (1985) early research remains seminal because it described early reading behaviors that developed from preschool image or picture-governed reading to print-governed reading. This earlier research revealed categories of early reading behaviors moving from nonnarrative to narrative language, from an oral-like to a written-like narrative register, and from picture-dominated to print-dominated reading. Similarly, Elster (1994) found that early readings of preschoolers were a sequence of reading and talk episodes. Children combined visual cues from pictures; they drew on their memories, experiences, and knowledge base, and on the social interactions with a listener long before beginning to attend to print. The features of the book being read, including the salience of the illustrations, predictable language patterns, and changing print formats influenced the strategies used by the early readers. The adult listeners were used as a resource as the preschool children moved from dialogue to monologue and from nonnarrative to narrative language.

Elster (1994) pointed out that early readers use multiple sources of information concurrently: pictures, print, social interaction, memory of teacher led discussions, attention to text language, and understanding of oral and written language conventions. Elster found through microanalysis of children's reading and talk about particular books, that these different sources of information were chosen and combined situationally by readers in response to the book, the child's memory, and social interaction.

Writing and Multimodal Meaning Making

The comment has been frequently made that writing has received less attention in early literacy research than has reading (Nixon & Topping, 2001). A strong body of work has been building over the last 10 years informed by sociocultural and semiotic theories that support a view of writing as a meaning-making practice undertaken in specific social contexts. For the purpose of this chapter, we concentrate on studies of early writing that focus on the significance of social context and on the place of writing within a complex repertoire of representational practices. This includes studies of the mark-making that is one of the first indicators of very young children's understanding of symbolic significance. Studies of early writing are contributing much to our understanding of the complex interrelationships between different representational practices and their contexts. These interrelationships have been explored in a range of studies.

Lancaster (2001) used video to look closely at a 2-year-old child making a Mother's Day card with her father. She identified the following meaning-making practices used by young Anna in this collaborative text production: oral language, gesture, gaze, and symbol making. For instance, the drawing of a zigzag mark, the finger pointing to the mark, the vocalizing "at's cat" [That's a cat] and the gaze towards her father all coordinate to signify "I have represented a cat with this mark. Please show that you recognise my meaning-making" (p. 141). Yang and Noel (2006) analyzed the drawings of 17, 4- to 5-year-old children and found that the development of children's functional literacy can be facilitated by encouraging them to use drawing as the starting point for name writing or letter reproduction. Adults can also use children's drawing as a "communicative act" to initiate "dialogue" between children and adults. Drawing can be viewed not only as a medium of representing meanings but also a tool for learning. Young children often explore diverse modes of graphic representations incorporating the semiotic representations embedded in the social-cultural environment. Adults can embrace children's diverse modes of symbolic representations by encouraging children's free exploration of all types of scribbles and placement patterns.

Dyson (2001) focused on 6-year-old children undertaking a classroom task, that of writing a factual report. Here also, the semiotic and sociocultural perspective enabled a rich description of the complex relationships of meaning-making involved in the production of a specific text, in this case a written report on the topic of Space. Dyson described one child, Noah, in the process of producing the text "Space Case says there was a space ship." (Space Case is a television adventure). The production of this text involved the coordination of writing, drawing, oral language, and symbolic sounds. Noah began by vocalizing each word in the text as he wrote it. However, halfway through the word *there*, he stopped writing and began drawing a space ship. At the same time he began to narrate a scene from a space adventure in a dramatic voice complete with sound effects. Noah's meaning making, his complete text, was multimodal and dynamic. It did not reside only in the piece of paper which held his marks.

Manipulation of objects, collaborative talk, and symbol production are interrelated elements in children's collaborative play as analyzed by Van Oers and Wardekker (1999). In the context of a junior school in the Netherlands, children aged between 4 and 6 played in the "shoe shop" area where they were provided with real shoes and blank, unlabeled boxes. The impetus to produce symbols came about at the point when the children realized that it was impossible for them to tell what kinds of shoes were in the boxes without opening the lids. They discussed how to mark the boxes and eventually come up with the symbols M (mama shoes), P (papa shoes), and K (*kinderen*—Dutch word for "children"). The shoes were sorted into their appropriately labeled boxes, the children then collaboratively produced a graphic representation of the piles of boxes, again using their symbols M, P, and K. The actual written linguistic text was limited to three letters and, from one perspective, tells us little about the children's competence. However, the production of linguistic symbols needed to be seen in the context of the full semiotic activity. The labeling of objects (the shoe boxes) was integrally related to the organizational task of sorting them into meaningful categories, and of making a visible recording of this organizational pattern.

Young children use a wide variety of materials in their representational practices, not all of them are conventional literacy materials such as paper and pencil. Pahl (2002, p. 146) uses the term *artefactual* to designate the practice of making texts out of objects. One example, from her ethnographic study of three boys at home and school, was of a child, Fatih, making a map out of beads on the carpet at home. This study brought to light the ephemeral and often invisible early literacy practices which are embedded in children's and families' activities. A few minutes before Fatih made the bead-map, he had been praying with the beads according to his family's religious practice, and shortly after its production the map was cleared away to make room for other activities. Pahl calls these ephemeral products "momentary texts" (p.160). This concept of the momentary text is particularly useful in thinking about literacy in the context of new technologies that enable children to rapidly create, destroy, and transform textual products.

Rich descriptions such as those discussed above have been a hallmark of early literacy research for decades.

However, they are assuming a different kind of significance in relation to current debates about the meaning of literacy, and of literacy acquisition, not just for young children but for all social actors. In the past, young children's use of a combination of linguistic and nonlinguistic resources for making meaning has been understood as a characteristic of an emergent stage prior to the achievement of literate competence. This view rested on a definition of literate competence as competence in the consumption and production of print (reading and writing).

Current redefinitions of what it means to be fully literate with new technology are changing the way we understand early writing and mark-making (Kress, Lankshear, & Noble, 2003; New London Group, 1996). The ability to simultaneously coordinate multiple linguistic and nonlinguistic elements has become understood as a quality of literate competence. Children's composition of complex multimodal texts goes beyond what can be described and given value through the lens of traditional print-based literacy.

Being Bilingual in a Changing World

We have argued that literacy, even when print language based, requires the mastery of multiple modes of representation and practices of communication. The picture becomes even more complex when we consider the multiple languages that are available within our communities. In countries with one official language, to be literate is understood in relation to that dominant language. Families with a different first language (L1) take on the official language as their second language (L2). Entry into the school system is often the point at which immersion in L2 begins. So at the same time as these "minority" children are encountering school literacy, many of them they are acquiring a second language and moving from monolinguality in L1 to bilinguality. We will be referring to English as the official language (and L2 for minority language speakers). Others argue that the forms of competence acquired by bi- and multilingual children challenge normative views of literacy development on which the concept of early literacy has been based (Orellana & D'warte, 2010).

When considering early literacy in situations where more than one language is in use it is useful to distinguish between different features of language. Some language features are specific to a particular language or group of languages, so in order to become fully competent in these languages one must acquire knowledge of and facility with these features. We present an example later in this section relating to acquisition of written Chinese. Other language features may cross linguistic boundaries. The concept of language register is useful here. Following Halliday, we define a language register as a "configuration of semantic resources that the member of a culture typically associates with a situation type" (1994, p. 26). What we have referred to as literate language is a register that can be expressed not only in English but in many languages.

A study of bilingual children's story retelling illustrates this point (Parke, Drury, Kenner, & Robertson, 2002). This study focused on three bilingual children aged between 5 and 7 whose L1 was either Pahari or Urdu and whose verbal competence in English was limited. The children were asked to listen to a story read to them in English and then to retell this story, first in English and then in their mother tongues. Their L1 retellings displayed significantly greater faithfulness to the original in language and narrative detail, were more coherent, and also more fluently delivered. Parke et al. (2002) noted that the children had "succeeded in internalizing the text-type" through listening to the original story. We would add that these children may well have brought to the task understandings of narrative structure acquired in home L1 contexts (for instance through an oral folktale tradition) which their L2 competence did not yet enable them to display. Whatever the explanation, young bilingual children's competence in the literate language register may well exceed their competence in English.

Another important language register that children acquire at school is the pedagogic register; that is, the pattern of language used in interactions around teaching and learning. For bilingual children, this represents an additional challenge at a time when they are just beginning to build L2 competence. As with literate language, children's understanding of pedagogic registers many not be visible, owing to their reticence in using their L2. This is demonstrated in a case study by Drury (reported in Parke et al., 2002). Samia, a 4-year-old girl whose first language is Pahari, attended a nursery school where there was a settled routine to facilitate children's learning. Every session, each child selected and planned an activity, indicating this by registering their name on a whiteboard. After carrying out the activity, they reported on their learning to the whole group. The pedagogic register here was characterized by self-regulatory and explanatory language on the part of children and facilitative language on the part of adults. Samia was observed to carry out the planning and the activities competently though with minimal interaction with peers or adults. At reporting time, she was extremely reticent, having only her limited L2 available for communication with the whole group.

At home, however, Samia played "nursery school" with her little brother. Here, she took on the teacher's facilitative language and encouraged her sibling to participate in the role of nursery student (that is, to take on what was her own role in real life). The play activity was conducted bilingually, as Samia switched between English and Pahari. What is interesting was her choice of language for different play elements. All the game activities and talk was conducted in English, while Samia's instructions as to how to play the game were given in Pahari. For instance, in the role of teacher, she said in English "you want paper" and "choose colour" while in the role of play fellow and sibling she says in Pahari (given here in English translation) "give it to big sister" (Parke et al., 2002, p. 204). From this we can see that Samia's understanding of the pedagogic register of her educational setting, and even her competence in L2 code, exceeds what may be visible to her teachers.

To investigate bilingual children's ability to make connections between languages and language practices from different domains in their lives, one study set up a series of peer-teaching activities (Kenner & Kress, 2003). Young children from three different L1 backgrounds (Arabic, Spanish, and Chinese) were first observed in home, school, and community settings. They were then invited to teach an English-speaking monolingual partner some of the basics of writing in the focus child's first language. In this way, researchers were able to discover children's understanding of pedagogic registers in literacy teaching and learning, as well as their competence in written language production.

One case focused on Selina, a Chinese background girl who attended a community school each Saturday morning. At this school, she learned to write characters by building up a sequence of strokes. Each page of her books was ruled into a grid and each character was written in the centre of a grid square. The learning routine consisted of teacher modeling with minimal explanation followed by sustained, silent writing of many repetitions of a single character. The researchers noted that many Western teachers "would not expect a five-year-old to be capable of such physical control over the act of writing" (Kenner & Kress, 2003, p. 186). Selina demonstrated her understanding of the pedagogic register of her L1 teaching when she acted as peer teacher. She demonstrated how to write the character and instructed her peer to "do it like this one." However, when her peer was unable to reproduce the character with sufficient accuracy, Selina showed that she had also grasped the pedagogic register of her mainstream educational setting. She increased her verbal feedback and suggested to her peer "pretend you're in Year 1 in Chinese school."

Kenner and Kress's study (2003) shows the advantage of taking a semiotic perspective to early literacy when considering the experiences of bilingual children for the reason that different language codes have different semiotic properties. The spatial arrangement of symbols on the field of the page is completely different in Arabic, for instance, than in English. Different perceptual and physical competencies are involved in producing and interpreting texts written using different language systems. Rather than seeing this as disadvantageous, new literacies will require a broader repertoire of representational practices: therefore bi- and multilingual children should be better positioned for multiliterate futures. This can only be the case, however, if their competencies are made visible within the mainstream and if the complexities of their double emergence into L1 and L2 literacy are understood.

Orellana and D'warte (2010) argue that bilingual children's special forms of competence should be recognized and capitalized on or they may even be lost as the children grow older. These researchers studied how bilingual children draw on their knowledge of home and dominant languages to interpret texts and communicate in ways responsive to the conditions of different social situations. Current teaching and assessment practices do not adequately value such linguistic flexibility and border crossing which, in conditions of increasing global flows of information and populations, may well become an element in mature literate competence. It is in recognizing this, that studies of bilingual literacy acquisition from a semiotic perspective challenge models of literacy development premised on a notion of mature literacy competence that was adequate for past times.

Summary

Much research into early literacy has been of a predictive nature to find discrete elements of literacy which may be a precursor or predictor for future development. In recent times, the field has been dominated by reports of scientifically based research studies providing evidence of which early literacy skills and abilities predict later literacy outcomes (Shanahan & Lonigan, 2010). The publication of the report of the National Early Literacy Panel (NELP, 2008) provides an extensive meta-analysis of approximately 300 studies examining which early literacy measures correlate with later literacy achievement. The report highlighted code-based skills which had moderate to large predictive relationships with later measures of literacy. Early literacy researchers have commented on the strengths and weaknesses of the NELP report and many view the report as narrow and reductive as it understates the importance of more global language competencies such as children's oral language and their conceptual and background knowledge (McGill-Franzen, 2010). From our perspective, a major issue is the changing meaning of mature literacy competence and the likelihood that today's children face futures of continually evolving new technologies for text production, new kinds of texts, and new practices of reading. While we continue to see print literacy as central, the ability to operate across multiple modalities, languages, and text types is becoming the hallmark of an effective literate citizen, making both the search for predictors and the drive to disaggregate literacy into components, of questionable relevance.

We believe that much is to be gained by defining literacy more broadly from a semiotic position to include linguistic and nonlinguistic forms of communication. Literacy is changing and children are increasingly exposed to communication tools and situations that are multimodal rather than exclusively linguistic. More research is required into children's knowledge of these multimodal electronic literacies and to do this it is necessary to broaden the base of what we know about early literacy to understand how children are making meaning with these new forms.

References

Anning, A. (2003). Pathways to the Graphicity Club: The crossroad of home and preschool. *Journal of Early Childhood Literacy, 3*(1), 5–35. Retrieved from EBSCO*host*

Bearne, E. (2009). Multimodality, literacy and texts: Developing a discourse. *Journal of Early Childhood Literacy, 9*(2), 156–187. doi: 10.1177/1468798409105585

Burnett, C. (2010). Technology and literacy in early childhood educational settings: A review of research *Journal of Early Childhood Literacy 10*(3), 247–270. doi: 10.1177/1468798410372154

Crawford, P. (1995). Early literacy: Emerging perspectives. *Journal of Research in Childhood Education, 10*(1), 71–86.

Duke, N., & Moses, A., (2004). Essay book review: On what crosses, and does not cross, our desks in early literacy. *Reading Research Quarterly, 39*(3), 360–366. doi: 10.1598/RRQ.39.3.11

Dyson, A. H. (2001). Where are the childhoods in childhood literacy?: An exploration in outer (school) space. *Journal of Early Childhood Literacy, 1*(1), 9–39. Retrieved from EBSCO*host*

Elster, C. (1994). Patterns within preschoolers' emergent readings. *Reading Research Quarterly, 29*(4), 402–418.

Fleer, M. (2006). The cultural construction of child development: Creating institutional and cultural intersubjectivity. *International Journal of Early Years Education, 14*(2), 127–140. doi: 10.1080/09669760600661294

Gee, J. (2002). A sociocultural perspective on early literacy development. In S. Neuman & D. Dickinson (Eds.), *Handbook of early literacy research* (pp. 40–42). Guildford: New York.

Gutiérrez, K., Bien, A., Selland, M., & Pierce, D. (2011). Polylingual and polycultural learning ecologies: Mediating academic literacies for dual language learners. *Journal of Early Childhood Literacy, 11*(2). 232–261. doi:10.1177/1468798411399273

Gutiérrez, K., & Rogoff, B. (2003). Cultural ways of learning: Individual traits or repertoires of practice. *Educational Researcher, 32*(5), 19–25. doi: 10.3102/0013189X032005019

Halliday, M. A. K. (1975). *Learning how to mean.* London: Arnold.

Halliday, M. A. K. (1994). Language as social semiotic. In J. Maybin (Ed.), *Language and literacy in social practice* (pp. 11–22). Clevedon, England: Multilingual Matters.

Hassett, D. D., & Curwood, J. (2009). Theories and practices of multimodal education: The instructional dynamics of picture books and primary classrooms. *The Reading Teacher, 63*(4), 270–282. doi: 10.1598/RT.63.4.2

Heath, S. B. (1983). *Ways with words: Language, life, and work in communities and classrooms.* New York: Cambridge University Press.

Hill, S. (2010). The millennium generation: Teacher-researchers exploring new forms of literacy. *Journal of Early Childhood Literacy, 10*(3), 314–340. doi: 10.1177/1468798410372820

Hill, S., & Nichols, S. (2006). Emergent literacy: Symbols at work. In B. Spodek & O. Saracho (Eds.), *Handbook of research on the education of young children* (2nd ed., pp. 153–65). Mahwah, NJ: Erlbaum.

Hourcade, J., Parette, H., Boeckmann, N., & Blum, C. (2010). Handy Manny and the emergent literacy technology toolkit. *Early Childhood Education Journal, 37*(6), 483–491. doi: 10.1007/s10643-010-0377-1

Hutinger, P., Bell, C., Beard, M., Bond, J., Johanson, J., & Terry, C. (1997). *Final report: The early childhood emergent literacy technology research study.* Macomb, IL: Western Illinois University. (ERIC Document Reproduction Service No. ED 418545)

Jong, M., & Bus, A. (2003). How well suited are electronic books to supporting literacy? *Journal of Early Childhood Literacy, 2*(3), 147–164. Retrieved from EBSCO*host*

Kenner, C., & Kress, G. (2003). The multisemiotic resources of biliterate children. *Journal of Early Childhood, 3*(2), 179–202. Retrieved from EBSCO*host*

Kim, J., & Anderson, J. (2008). Mother–child shared reading with print and digital texts. *Journal of Early Childhood Literacy, 8*(2), 213–245. doi: 10.1177/1468798409357387

Korat, O., & Shamir, A. (2008). The educational electronic book as a tool for supporting children's emergent literacy in low versus middle SES groups. *Computers & Education, 50*(1), 110–124. doi: 10.1016/j.compedu.2006.04.002

Kress, G., Lankshear, C., & Knobel, M. (2003). New technologies in early childhood literacy research: A review of research. *Journal of Early Childhood Literacy, 3*(1), 59–82. Retrieved from EBSCO*host*

Kress, G., & Van Leeuwen, T. (2001). *Multimodal discourse: The modes and media of contemporary communication.* London: Arnold.

Labbo, L. (1996). A semiotic analysis of young children's symbol making in a classroom computer center. *Reading Research Quarterly, 31*(4), 356–385. doi: 10.1598/RRQ.31.4.2

Labbo, L., & Kuhn, M. (2000). Weaving chains of affect and cognition: A young child's understanding of CD-ROM talking books. *Journal of Literacy Research, 32*(2), 187–210. doi: 10.1080/10862960009548073

Labbo, L., & Ryan, T. (2010). Traversing the "literacies" landscape: A semiotic perspective on early literacy acquisition and digital literacies instruction. In E. Baker (Ed.), *The new literacies: Multiple perspectives on research and practice.* (pp. 88–105). New York: Guilford.

Lancaster, L. (2001). Staring at the page: The functions of gaze in a young child's interpretation of symbolic forms. *Journal of Early Childhood Literacy, 1*(2), 131–152. Retrieved from EBSCO*host*

Lankshear, C., & Knobel, M. (2003). New technologies in early childhood literacy research: A review of research. *Journal of Early Childhood Literacy, 3*(1), 59–82. Retrieved from EBSCO*host*

Larson, L. C. (2010). Digital readers: The next chapter in e-book reading and response. *The Reading Teacher, 64*(1), 15–22. doi: 10.1598/RT.64.1.2

Lemke, J. (1990). *Talking science: Language, learning and values.* Norwood, NJ: Ablex.

Marsh, J. (2006). Global, local/public, private: Young children's engagement in digital literacy practices in the home. In K. Rowsell & J. Pahl (Eds.), *Travel notes from the new literacy studies.* (pp. 19–48). Clevedon, England: Multilingual Matters.

Mavers, D. (2007).Semiotic resourcefulness: A young child's email exchange as design. *Journal of Early Childhood Literacy, 7*(2), 155–176. doi: 10.1177/1468798407079285

McGee, L., & Purcell-Gates, V. (1997). Conversations: So what's going on in research in emergent literacy? *Reading Research Quarterly, 32*(3), 310–319. doi: 10.1598/RRQ.32.3.5

McGill-Franzen, A. (2010). Guest editor's introduction. *Educational Researcher, 39*(4), 275–278. doi: 10.3102/0013189X10370619

Mol, S. E., Bus, A. G., & De Jong, M. T. (2009). Interactive book reading in early education: A tool to stimulate print knowledge as well as oral language. *Review of Educational Research, 79*(2), 979–1007. doi: 10.3102/0034654309332561

Moody, A., Justice, L., & Cabell S. (2010). Electronic versus traditional storybooks: Relative influence on preschool children's engagement and communication. *Journal of Early Childhood Literacy, 10*(3), 294–313. doi: 10.1177/1468798410372162

National Council of Teachers of English. (2008). Retrieved from http://www.ncte.org/governance/literacies

National Early Literacy Panel. (2008). *Developing early literacy: A scientific synthesis of early literacy development and implications for intervention.* Washington, DC: National Institute for Literacy. Available at http://www.nifl.gov/earlychildhood/NELP/NELPreport.html

New London Group. (1996). A pedagogy of multiliteracies. *Harvard Educational Review, 60*(1), 66–92.

Nichols, S. (2002). Parents' construction of their children as gendered literate subjects: A critical discourse analysis. *Journal of Early Childhood Literacy, 2*(2), 123–144. Retrieved from EBSCO*host*

Nichols, S. (2011). Young children's literacy in the activity space of the library: A geo-semiotic investigation. *Journal of Early Childhood Literacy, 11*(2), 164–189

Nixon, J. G., & Topping, J. (2001). Emergent writing: The impact of structured peer interaction. *Educational Psychology, 21*(1), 41–56. doi: 10.1080/01443410020019821

Orellana, M., & D'warte, J. (2010). Recognizing different kinds of

"Head Starts." *Educational Researcher, 39*(4), 295–300. doi: 10.3102/0013189X10369829

Pahl, K. (2002). Ephemera, mess and miscellaneous piles: Texts and practices in families. *Journal of Early Childhood Literacy, 2*(2)145–166. Retrieved from EBSCO*host*

Paris, S. (2005). Reinterpreting the development of reading skills. *Reading Research Quarterly, 40*(2), 184–202. doi: 10.1598/RRQ.40.2.3

Parke, T., Drury, R., Kenner, C., & Robertson, L. H. (2002). Revealing invisible worlds: Connecting the mainstream with bilingual children's home and community learning. *Journal of Early Childhood Literacy, 2*(2), 195–220. Retrieved from EBSCO*host*

Purcell-Gates, V., Duke, N., & Martineau, J. (2007). Learning to read and write genre-specific text: Roles of authentic experience and explicit teaching. *Reading Research Quarterly, 42*(1), 8–45. doi: 10.1598/RRQ.42.1.1

Scollon, R., & Scollon, S.W. (2001). *Intercultural communication: A discourse approach.* (2nd ed.). Oxford, England: Basil Blackwell.

Shanahan, T., & Lonigan, C. J. (2010). The National Early Literacy Panel: A summary of the process and the report. *Educational Researcher, 39*(4), 279–285. doi: 10.3102/0013189X10369172

Siegal, M., & Fernandez, S. (2000). Critical approaches. In M. Kamil, P. Mosenthal, P. Pearson, & R. Barr (Eds.), *Handbook of reading research* (Vol. 3, pp. 141–151). Mahwah, NJ: Erlbaum.

Skouge, J., Rao, K., & Boisvert, P. (2007). Promoting early literacy for diverse learners using audio and video technology. *Early Childhood Education Journal, 35*(1), 5–11. doi: 10.1007/s10643-007-0170-y

Snow, C., & Van Hemel, S. (2008). *Early childhood assessment: Why, what and how.* Washington, DC: National Academies Press.

Sulzby, E. (1985). Children's emergent reading of favourite story books: A developmental study. *Reading Research Quarterly, 20*, 458–479.

Teale, W., & Sulzby, E. (1986). *Emergent literacy: Writing and reading.* Norwood, NJ: Ablex.

Trushell, J. (1998). Juliet makes her mark. *Reading, 32*(1), 29–32.

Van Oers, B., & Wardekker, W. (1999). On becoming an authentic learner: Semiotic activity in the early grades. *Journal of Curriculum Studies, 31*(2), 229–249.

Walkerdine, V. (1984). Developmental psychology and the child-centered pedagogy: The insertion of Piaget into early education. In W. H. J. Henriques, C. Urwin, C. Venn, & V. Walkerdine (Eds.), *Changing the subject: Psychology, social regulation and subjectivity* (pp. 153–202). London: Methuen.

Wallace, C. (2008). Literacy and identity: A view from the bridge in two multicultural London schools. *Journal of Language, Identity & Education, 7*(1), 61–80. doi: 10.1080/15348450701804722

Weber, C., & Cavanaugh, T. (2006). Promoting reading: Using ebooks with gifted and advanced readers. *Gifted Child Today, 29*(4), 56–63. doi: 10.4219/gct-2006-9

Wohlwend, K. (2009). Early adopters: Playing new literacies and pretending new technologies in print-centric classrooms. *Journal of Early Childhood Literacy, 9*(2) 117–140. doi: 10.1177/1468798409105583

Yang, H., & Noel, A. (2006). The developmental characteristics of four- and five-year-old pre-schoolers' drawing: An analysis of scribbles, placement patterns, emergent writing, and name writing in archived spontaneous drawing samples. *Journal of Early Childhood Literacy, 6*(2), 145–162. doi:10.1177/1468798406066442

10

The Education of Young Dual-Language Learners

An Overview

ROBERT RUEDA
University of Southern California

DAVID B. YADEN, JR.
University of Arizona

Introduction

The focus of this chapter is on the education of young, preschool-age, dual language learners in the area of literacy in particular. Our focus on this group is driven by the rapid demographic changes in American public schools, and the focus on literacy is driven by the strong relationship of early literacy to later academic outcomes. In an earlier version of this chapter (Rueda & Yaden, 2006), a comprehensive view of work prior to 2006 was provided; therefore, in this update we focus most heavily on research and developments since that time.

Some Caveats on Terminology

In this chapter, our use of the term *dual-language learner* (DLL) is purposeful as it denotes a child either learning two or more languages simultaneously or sequentially (cf. Ballantyne, Sanderman, & McLaughlin, 2008; National Head Start Training and Technical Assistance Resource Center [NHSTTARC], 2008). While there are a variety of terms which have been used to characterize students who fall in to this group, including *Limited English Proficient (LEP), English Learners (EL), linguistic minority students (LMS),* or *children who speak a language other than English (LOTE)*, just to name a few, these labels fail to capture the sense of language learning as a complex, developmental, and incremental process. Moreover, the standard terminology tends to define students along a single dimension, specifically proficiency in English, to the exclusion of the language environments they encounter outside of school and to the exclusion of their own daily language practices. Yet in immigrant families, an estimated 84% of individuals age 5 and older grow up in bilingual

environments and speak a language other than English (Pew Hispanic Center, 2009). Therefore, the term *dual-language learner* is more accurate in capturing the actual language environments and practices of students.

However, though we use the term *dual language learner* (DLL) throughout the review as preferable over others (e.g., LEP, EL) to describe children growing up in multilingual environments, we are, nevertheless, aware that this descriptor has its own limitations and ambiguities. Since the majority of the research on preschool- and school-age DLLs has been conducted with Spanish-speaking populations, it is easy, although misleading, to conflate the term with only that language group. While extant data and estimates from sources such as the National Clearinghouse for English Acquisition (NCELA, 2007), the National Center for Education Statistics (NCES, 2010), and the National Head Start Training and Technical Assistance Resource Center (NHSTTARC, 2008) do indicate that Spanish speakers constitute roughly 75% of the DLL population in K-12 public schooling and nearly 85% of the preschool DLLs in Early Head Start and Head Start, it should be noted that over the years Head Start has reported serving children speaking over 140 languages (NHSTTARC, 2008).

Nonetheless, despite the fact that 25% of the DLL school-age population speak languages other than Spanish (e.g., Asian/Pacific Islander languages, 12%; other Indo-European languages, 10%; and indigenous American Indian/Alaskan Native languages, 3%; Aud et al., 2010), explicit recommendations for research or instruction related to these other language groups, or even pertaining to the diversity of Spanish speakers, are hard to find in the research literature on DLLs (cf., for example, Ballantyne et al., 2008; Garcia &Wiese, 2009; Guiterrez, Zepeda, & Castro, 2010; Morrow, Rueda, & Lapp, 2009; NHSTTARC, 2008). Thus, in this review, we, too, will follow the example of Garcia and

Wiese (2009) who acknowledge the lack of research and discussion regarding DLLs speaking languages other than Spanish, and focus primarily upon the large-scale research efforts and recommendations for instruction related to the latter. However, we do not assume that the characteristics of immigrant Spanish speaking populations commonly cited, such as having lower incomes, less education, and less access to social and health services or the types of instructional interventions recommended apply equally to other immigrant or language groups and will attempt to avoid making such generalizations in our discussion.

Chapter Overview

In the remainder of the chapter, we examine recent work on young, preschool, DLL students mostly from homes where Spanish or a combination of Spanish and English are spoken. A central focus is on synthesizing recent national reports that have importance to this population. We begin by providing some recent data on characteristics of, and changes in the profiles of young children. In addition, while we are primarily examining studies with children under the age of 5 in this chapter, we have included some investigations of school-age children up to grade 3 since the outcomes from those grades are often reported in large-scale, national investigations of young children's literacy development after preschool. It is also the case, as pointed out by Ballantyne et al. (2008) that national data on the preschool DLL population is uneven and difficult to summarize since only 13 states disaggregate their reporting by ELL status and only five report assessment results for grades 1 and 2 (p. 8).

Therefore, a truly national database in terms of assessing the outcomes of preschool across the states or even kindergarten does not yet exist. While large-scale national studies such as the Early Childhood Longitudinal Study-Birth Cohort (ECLS-B, 2001), the Early Childhood Longitudinal Study-Kindergarten Cohort (ECLS-K, 1998, 2010), and the NICHD Study of Early Care and Youth Development (SECCYD, 2010) have provided researchers with nationally representative samples, these studies are descriptive only and cannot tease out *which* experiences in preschool will have *what* effect on a *particular* group of children speaking a *certain* language. Nonetheless, given the available evidence, in this review we attempt to draw a reasonable portrait of the status of young DLLs in the United States today.

A Demographic Overview of the Population

As in the previous two iterations of this chapter, demographics continue to be major factor to consider. In this section, we provide a brief look at the DLL population, starting first with the larger school aged population and then looking specifically at the early childhood subgroup.

The School-Age Population

Recent data suggest that DLL students comprise a growing percentage of the school age population. It is estimated that over 5.5 million—or 10% of all U.S. students—lack sufficient proficiency in English to engage academically without support. More notably for this review, the percentage of both Asian and Latino school age DLL students who speak English with difficulty is much higher, being 16% and 17%, respectively (Aud, Hussar et al., 2010). Further, in the decade between 1995 and 2005, the number of DLL students grew by 56% while the general school-age population in the country grew by just 2.6% (Batalova, Fix, & Murray, 2007). Using 1990 as a reference year, the number of DLL students has increased 150% (Goldenberg, 2008). Children who speak a language other than English now constitute over 20% of children ages 5 to 17 (Planty et al., 2009), and in the next decade DLL students are predicted to represent over 30% of all school children (Fix & Passel, 2003). Not surprisingly, Latino students make up the largest group in the United States that speaks a language other than English in the home, and 26% of the 6.9 million Latino public school students speak English with difficulty (Fry & Gonzales, 2008).

The DLL Early Childhood Population

There have been significant changes in the last two decades in the numbers of children participating in prekindergarten (Snyder & Dillow, 2010). Between 1985 and 2007, for example, enrollment in prekindergarten increased over 400% (from 0.2 to 1.1 million), while enrollment in other elementary grades (including kindergarten through grade 8 plus ungraded elementary programs) increased only 23% (from 26.9 to 33.1 million).

The Hispanic share of the nation's youngest children is considerably larger than their share of the population as a whole. For example, one analysis of the demographics of children in 2000 found that, among the 33.4 million children ages birth to 8 in the United States, 6.8 million were Hispanic—20% of the total. Moreover, the Hispanic share of the birth to 8 age group is projected to reach 26% as early as 2030 (Hernandez, 2006). In addition, the population of young children is more concentrated than the general population. In 2000, about four-fifths of young Hispanic children lived in just nine states: California, Texas, New York, Florida, Illinois, Arizona, New Jersey, Colorado, and New Mexico. Half were living in just two states: California and Texas (Hernandez, 2006). However, the growing number of young Hispanic children in other states was becoming evident as well. In 24 states, at least one in eight of the children in the birth to 8 age group were Hispanic. In 2004, babies born to Hispanic mothers accounted for at least 10% of the births in 27 states and the District of Columbia (Hamilton, Martin, Ventura, Sutton, & Menacker, 2005).

A majority of Latino children are either immigrants or

from families in which one or both parents are immigrants. A study of the birth to 8 population in 2000 found that 64% (4.4 million) of Hispanics were either immigrants themselves (first generation Americans) or the children of immigrants (second generation Americans). Only 36% (2.4 million) were children with two U.S.-born parents (third generation Americans). Nevertheless, this pattern varied considerably among Hispanic national origin groups. The split for Mexican Americans was 66% first or second generation and 34% third generation, while the split was 91% and 9% for those of South American heritage. Currently, among all immigrant families, regardless of their race or ethnicity, about 9 in 10 young children were born in the United States. Hispanics follow this pattern closely. About 88% of the 4.4 million first and second generation Hispanic children in the birth to 8 age group in 2000 were U.S.-born (National Task Force on Early Childhood Education for Hispanics, 2007a). This figure for the youngest children has undoubtedly increased in the last decade since, according to the U.S. Census in 2008, 91% of Latino children under the age of 18 were born in the United States (Mather & Foxen, 2010).

Academic Achievement

Early Literacy Abilities in Kindergarten

In general, the incidence of reading failure is high within low-income families, ethnic minority groups, and English language learners (National Task Force on Early Childhood Education for Hispanics, 2007b). Large-scale studies have shown that young children—those entering kindergarten and first grade—vary greatly in their attainment of the early precursor skills that provide the launching pad for later literacy learning (West, Denton, & Germino-Hausken, 2000; West, Denton, & Reaney, 2000). Table 10.1 presents data on students' reading skills at the start of kindergarten from the ECLS-K sample (Reardon & Galindo, 2006), and Table 10.2 presents the data by SES level and generation status.

Table 10.1 Percentage of Children Scoring[1] at or above Levels 1, 2, 3, and 4 in Reading at the Start of Kindergarten

Group	Level 1	Level 2	Level 3	Level 4
Third Generation White	73	34	20	4
All Hispanics	54	20	10	2
Mexican Descent	51	19	10	2
Cuban Descent	67	25	12	2
Puerto Rican Descent	62	26	14	2
Central American Descent	52	18	11	1
South American Descent	60	26	15	5

1 The ECLS-K Reading Proficiency Levels for K-5 include the following: Level 1: Recognition of letters; Level 2: Understanding beginning sounds of words; Level 3: Understanding ending sounds of words; Level 4: Sight recognition of words; Level 5: Comprehension of words in context; Level 6: Literal inference from words in text; Level 7: Extrapolating from text to derive meaning; Level 8: Evaluating and interpreting beyond text: Level 9: Evaluating nonfiction.
Source: Reardon, S.F., and Galindo, C. (2006). Patterns of Hispanic Students' Math and English Literacy Test Scores. Report to the National Task Force on Early Childhood Education for Hispanics. Tempe, AZ: Arizona State University.

Table 10.2 Percentage of Children Scoring at or above Levels 1, 2, 3, and 4 in Reading[1] at the Start of Kindergarten; Third Generation Whites and First, Second, and Third Generation Mexican Americans by SES Quintile

SES Quintile	Group	Level 1	Level 2	Level 3	Level 4
First (Low)	Hispanic	37	8	3	0
	White	48	13	6	0
Second	Hispanic	54	17	8	1
	White	60	20	10	1
Third	Hispanic	54	20	11	3
	White	69	29	16	3
Fourth	Hispanic	72	33	17	2
	White	80	38	21	3
Fifth (High)	Hispanic	73	41	25	5
	White	86	50	22	8

1 The ECLS-K Reading Proficiency Levels for K-5 include the following: Level 1: Recognition of letters; Level 2: Understanding beginning sounds of words; Level 3: Understanding ending sounds of words; Level 4: Sight recognition of words; Level 5: Comprehension of words in context; Level 6: Literal inference from words in text; Level 7: Extrapolating from text to derive meaning; Level 8: Evaluating and interpreting beyond text: Level 9: Evaluating nonfiction
Source: Reardon, S.F., and Galindo, C. (2006). Patterns of Hispanic Students' Math and English Literacy Test Scores. Report to the National Task Force on Early Childhood Education for Hispanics. Tempe, AZ: Arizona State University.

The DLL data do not include the 30% of Hispanic children in the ECLS-K sample that did not have oral English skills strong enough for them to take the English language reading readiness assessment as they entered kindergarten. Yet, even with 30% excluded, the data show that the remaining Hispanics lagged well behind third generation Whites in letter recognition, understanding beginning sounds of words, and understanding ending sounds, all key early literacy skills. They also lagged behind Whites in sight reading words, although few children from any group had that skill at the beginning of kindergarten. The strongest performing Hispanics at the start of kindergarten were children of South American origin, followed closely by youngsters of Cuban and Puerto Rican origin.

More recent analyses (Denton Flanagan & McPhee, 2009) of the ECLS-B data on reading scores for children born in 2001as they entered kindergarten for the first time is illustrative of differences among several key dimensions (see Table 10.3). In general, Latino students scored lower than all other groups with the exception of the much smaller American Indian/Alaskan Native group. In addition, results favored students who were from two-parent families, above the poverty threshold, and who had care either out of the home or by someone other than a family member or relative.

Figure 10.1 presents data from the same 2001 cohort in the areas of letter recognition and number and shape recognition. Overall, about a third (33%) of the 4-year-olds tested in 2005–2006 was proficient in letter recognition. Hispanic and American Indian/Alaska Native children had lower rates of proficiency (23% and 19%, respectively), while Asian children had a higher rate of proficiency (49%)

Robert Rueda and David B. Yaden, Jr.

Table 10.3 Average Early Reading Scale Scores for Children Born in 2001 as They Enter Kindergarten for the First Time, by Child and Family Characteristics: 2006–07 and 2007–08

Characteristic	Average early reading scale score
Total	43.9
Child's sex	
Male	43.0
Female	44.9
Child's race/ethnicity[1]	
White, non-Hispanic	46.4
Black, non-Hispanic	41.1
Hispanic	39.4
Asian, non-Hispanic	51.9
American Indian or Alaska Native, non-Hispanic	37.1
All other race/ethnicities, non-Hispanic	44.2
Family type[2]	
Two parent	45.2
Single parent	40.1
Other	38.9
Poverty status[3]	
At or above poverty threshold	46.0
Below poverty threshold	37.3
Primary home language[4]	
English	44.8
Non-English	40.4
Age at assessment	
Less than 5 years old	35.0
5 years old to 5½ years old	39.7
More than 5½ years old to 6 years old	45.8
More than 6 years old	50.4
Primary early care and education arrangement type the year prior to entering kindergarten[5]	
No nonparental early care and education	39.8
In nonparental early care and education	44.8
Center-based, non Head Start	47.2
Center-based, Head Start	40.3
Home-based, relative	39.5
Home-based, nonrelative	45.4
Multiple arrangement types	42.9

1 Black, non-Hispanic includes African American. Hispanic includes Latino. The category of all other non-Hispanic race/ethnicities includes Native Hawaiian/Other Pacific Islanders and children of two or more races.

2 Two parent includes biological mother and biological father, biological mother and other father, biological father and other mother, and two adoptive parents. Single parent refers to biological mother only, biological father only, and single adoptive parent. Other refers to related and/or unrelated guardians.

3 Poverty status is based on U.S. Census guidelines, which identify a dollar amount determined to meet a household's needs, given its size and composition. For example, in 2006, a family of four was considered to live below the poverty threshold if its income was less than $20,614. In 2007, a family of four was considered to live below the poverty threshold if its income was less than $21,203.

4 Primary home language was asked of the parent interview respondent.

5 Primary early care and education arrangement type the year prior to entering kindergarten is the setting in which the child spent the most hours outside of time with parents. If a child spent an equal amount of time in each of two or more arrangements, he or she is classified as being in multiple arrangement types. Center-based, non Head Start includes care and education in places such as early learning centers, nursery schools, and preschools. Center-based, Head Start includes care and education in centers identified as Head Start by the parent interview respondent. Home-based, relative includes care provided in either the child's home or in another private home by a relative of the child. Home-based, nonrelative includes care provided in either the child's home or in another private home by a person not related to the child.

Note: Estimates weighted by WKR0. The estimates pertain to children born in 2001 as they entered kindergarten for the first time; estimates exclude children who died or moved permanently abroad before kindergarten entry. The majority of children born in 2001 (about 75 percent) entered kindergarten in the 2006-07 school year; the other 25 percent entered kindergarten in the 2007-08 school year. Estimates in this table were produced by combining data collected in these two school years. The early reading assessment contained items measuring such skills as children's letter recognition, letter sound knowledge, recognition of simple words, phonological awareness, receptive and expressive vocabulary knowledge, and knowledge of print conventions. The reading scale score has a potential range of 0 to 85, with a standard deviation of 14.2. For more information on the reading assessment, see appendix A of this report.

Source: U.S. Department of Education, National Center for Education Statistics, Early Childhood Longitudinal Study, Birth Cohort (ECLS-B), Longitudinal 9-Month-Kindergarten 2007 Restricted-Use Data File.

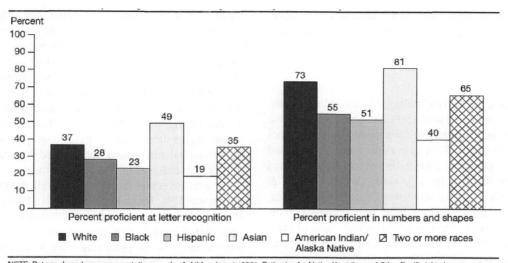

Figure 10.1 Percentage of children from the 2001 birth cohort who were proficient in letter and number and shape recognition at about 4 years old, by race/ethnicity: 2005–06. Adapted from Aud, S., Fox, M., and KewalRamani, A. (2010). *Status and Trends in the Education of Racial and Ethnic Groups* (NCES 2010-015). Washington, DC: U.S. Department of Education, National Center for Education Statistics. U.S. Government Printing Office.

than other groups. White children (37%) and children of two or more races (35%) had higher rates of proficiency than Black (28%), Hispanic (23%), and American Indian/Alaska Native (19%) children. In the area of recognizing numbers and shapes, about two-thirds (65%) of the 4-year-olds tested were proficient. American Indian/Alaska Native children had a lower rate of proficiency (40%) than Hispanic children (51%), Black children (55%), children of two or more races (65%), White children (73%), and Asian children (81%). Asian 4-year-olds had higher rates of proficiency than any other racial/ethnic group. No measurable differences were found between Hispanic and Black children.

The extensive recent analyses of achievement data by the National Task Force on Early Childhood Education for Hispanics (2007a, 2007b) as well as the other sources cited above show that on average Hispanic DLL students enter kindergarten with lower levels of school reading in reading and math than their White counterparts. Moreover, a high percentage of these students enter kindergarten with lower levels of oral proficiency in English. These differences are closely related to social class gaps between Latinos and White students. These gaps are evident even when the two groups are looked at within the same social class band. There are also differences within subgroups of Latinos based on country of origin; for example, South American and Cuban students tend to outperform Mexican and Central American students. These differences are consistent with the social class differences among the groups.

Language Status and Opportunity to Learn

It is important to keep in mind that language status does not occur in isolation from other factors which may have

an impact on school achievement such as SES, residence, and other "opportunity to learn" factors. First of all, large numbers of DLL students live in economically challenging situations. Nationwide, two-thirds of elementary DLL students lived in homes with incomes below 185% of the poverty level (Capps, Fix, Murray, Ost, Passel, & Herwantoro, 2005). This relationship is even more pronounced in areas such as California, which contains more than 30% of the nation's DLL population. Recent data indicated that 85% of the state's DLL students were eligible for free and reduced-price lunch, a commonly used measure of low income status (Legislative Analyst's Office, 2008).

Place of residence is another factor that is associate with DLL status. DLL students, for example, tend to be concentrated in urban areas. Sixty percent of the country's English learners live in 20 metropolitan areas, with the Los Angeles Unified School District and New York City Public School districts serving the largest number of English Learners of any districts in the nation (Swanson, 2009). The schools in those settings where these students attend are more likely, compared to non-DLL peers, to be larger, more urbanized, more racially and economically segregated, and with a teaching force that is less qualified and less stable (Gandara & Hopkins, 2010).

Finally, while it is often believed that language services and educational programs are more heavily geared toward DLL students that recently immigrated, an increasing number of DLL students are, in fact, second or third generation. Estimates put the presence of second or third generation English Learners in elementary schools at 76% (Goldenberg, 2008), and in middle and high schools at 57% (Batalova et al., 2007). As many have noted (Goldenberg & Coleman, 2010), DLL students constitute a very diverse population, ranging from those with several years of schooling and strong language proficiency in the native language to students with little formal schooling.

Language

As noted above, the Early Childhood Longitudinal Study, Kindergarten Class of 1998–1999 (ECLS-K), found that about 30% of the Hispanics in the national sample did not have strong enough oral English skills when they started kindergarten in the fall of 1998 to be given the test designed to assess their English literacy skills (West, Denton, & Germino-Hauskin, 2000). Moreover, because a large number of Hispanic children in immigrant families have parents with little formal education, as noted earlier, many of these youngsters' parents may have weak academic Spanish capabilities (Hernandez, 2006). Thus, a substantial percentage of Hispanic children may be starting kindergarten without either the English or Spanish literacy foundations needed to get off to a good start in school. These are among the lowest achieving Hispanics in the early elementary school years and, therefore, among those with the most urgent need for more and better early childhood education opportunities.

Early Child Care and Education

Effects of Child Care Arrangements on Achievement

There is some evidence that significant variation in child care arrangements for different groups of students exist (Aud, Fox, & KewalRamani, 2010) (see Table 10.4) and are potentially important to later outcomes because of the differing opportunities they offer with respect to factors such as language environments. As the figure illustrates, in 2005, 20% of all 4-year-olds stayed at home without any regular nonparental care, but for Hispanic 4-year-olds, the figure was 27%. This was 9 percentage points higher than Whites, 11 percentage points higher than Blacks, 10 percentage points higher than Asians, 7 percentage points higher than American Indians/Alaska Natives, and 9 percentage points higher than children of two or more races.

In terms of center-based care, overall, the rate of participation was 57%, but only 20% of Native Hawaiian or Other Pacific Islander 4-year-olds and 49% of Hispanic 4-year-olds participated in this type of care. These percentages were lower than the percentages for White, Black, Asian, and American Indian/Alaska Native 4-year-olds (which varied from 60 to 62%). These patterns were different in terms of care based at Head Start programs, the federal program for disadvantaged children. Thirty-one percent of American Indian/Alaska Native 4-year-olds and 25% of Black 4-year-olds were enrolled in Head Start, compared with 7% of Whites, 19% of Hispanics, 5% of Asians, and 5% of Native Hawaiians or Other Pacific Islanders. White (53%) and Asian (55%) 4-year-olds had the highest percentages of enrollment in center-based programs other than Head Start.

As indicated above, Latino preschoolers, for the most part, spend less time in center-based care and nonrelative care than do other ethnic/racial groups. One tentative con-

Table10.4   Percentage Distribution of Primary Type of Care Arrangements of Children from the 2001 Birth Cohort atAbout 4 Year sOld, byRace/Ethnicity: 2005–06

| Race/ethnicity | No regular nonparental arrangement | Home-based care | | Center-based care[1] | | | Multiple arrangements[2] |
		Relative care[3]	Non-relative care[4]	Total	Head Start	Other than Head Start	
Total	**20.0**	**13.1**	**7.6**	**57.5**	**12.7**	**44.8**	**1.9**
White	17.9	11.0	9.2	60.1	6.8	53.3	1.9
Black	16.0	13.9	4.3	62.4	25.4	37.1	3.3
Hispanic	27.2	15.9	6.2	49.4	18.6	30.9	1.2
Asian	17.5	16.0	3.4	60.7	5.5	55.3	2.3!
Native Hawaiian/ Pacific Islander	22.3!	45.0!	‡	19.9!	5.0!	14.91	‡
American Indian/ Alaska Native	20.0	14.0	5.3	59.6	31.1	28.5	1.11
Two or more races	17.8	17.5	8.9	53.9	12.2	41.7	1.8!

! Interpret data with caution.

‡ Reporting standards not met.

1 Care provided in places such as early learning centers, nursery schools, and preschools, including Head Start

2 Children who spent an equal amount of time in each of two or more arrangements.

3 Care provided in the child's home or in another private home by a relative (excluding parents).

4 Care provided in the child's home or in another private home by a person unrelated to the child.

Note: Primary type of care arrangement is the type of nonparental care in which the child spent the most hours. Data are based on a representative sample of children born in 2001. Detail may not sum to totals because of rounding and suppression of cells that do not meet standards.Race categories exclude persons of Hispanic ethnicity.

Source: U.S. Department of Education, National Center for Education Statistics, Early Childhood Longitudinal Study, Birth Cohort, Longitudinal 9-month-Preschool Restricted-Use Data File.

sideration of the implications of less time in nonrelative care during the preschool years may be found in a recent 15-year follow-up analysis of the cohort of children participating in the NICHD Early Child Care Study which began in 1991(see Vandell, Burchinal, Vandergrift, Belsky, & Steinberg, 2010). While the findings were not broken out by racial/ethnic group and the percentage of Latino children in the sample who could have been DLLs was small, the overall finding was that the effects of early child care *quality* on academic achievement were detectable 10 years after the children left child care, although *type* of care was not. However, the authors state, "It would seem misguided to conclude broadly that by mid-adolescence type of care no longer predicts children's development. It will be important to determine if center care effects on cognitive and social functioning reemerge in late adolescence or early adulthood" (p. 753). And since a general finding is that high quality child care prior to kindergarten benefits all children in general, particularly those from low-income families, one could speculate that the effects of such care might not accrue as quickly for young, immigrant Spanish/English DLLs as a result of less time spent in nonrelative care. But this is an empirical question which only further research can answer definitively.

Effects of Early Childhood Curriculum and Preschool Attendance on Achievement

The Preschool Curriculum Research Consortium (PCER). There has been some effort to look at the effects of specific types of curricula and programs on early childhood populations. An ambitious national effort was carried out by the Preschool Curriculum Evaluation Research Consortium (2008). In 2002, the Institute of Education Sciences (IES) formed the Preschool Curriculum Evaluation Research (PCER) initiative to conduct large scale evaluations of the most commonly used preschool curricula in preschool settings serving predominantly low-income children. The evaluation attempted to assess the impact of 14 distinct curricula on five student-level outcomes (reading, phonological awareness, language, mathematics, and behavior) and six classroom-level outcomes (classroom quality, teacher–child interaction, and four types of instruction) using a common set of measures with the cohort of children beginning preschool in the summer and fall of 2003. Twelve separate research teams, in a coordinated effort, implemented one or two curricula in preschool settings serving predominantly low-income children under an experimental design. For each team, preschools or classrooms were randomly assigned to the intervention curricula or control curricula and the children were followed from prekindergarten through kindergarten. Preschool programs taking part in the evaluation of the curricula included Head Start centers, private child care centers, and public prekindergarten programs in urban, rural, and suburban locations. The analyses included 2,911

children, 315 preschool classrooms, and 208 preschools. The sample was relatively diverse; One-third was White non-Hispanic, 43% were African American, and 16% were Hispanic.

As the study report notes, two of the 14 intervention curricula had impacts on the student-level outcomes for the prekindergarten year. *DLM Early Childhood Express supplemented with Open Court Reading Pre-K* positively affected reading, phonological awareness, and language. *Pre-K Mathematics supplemented with DLM Early Childhood Express Math software* curricula positively affected mathematics. In the kindergarten year, four of the curricula had impacts on the student-level outcomes, though three of these did not have impacts during the prekindergarten year. *DLM Early Childhood Express supplemented with Open Court Reading Pre-K* continued to have positive effects on reading, phonological awareness, and language in kindergarten as it did in prekindergarten. *Curiosity Corner*, which had no effects in prekindergarten, was found to positively affect reading in kindergarten. *Early Literacy and Learning Model (ELLM)*, which had no effects in prekindergarten, was found to positively affect language in kindergarten. And *Project Approach*, which had no effects in prekindergarten, was found to negatively affect behavior in kindergarten.

Unfortunately, despite the diversity of the participants in the study, results based on population subgroups were not provided, and all assessments were English-based. As Caswell and He (2008) have pointed out, however, studies like the PCER which have included diverse populations, including young DLLs, provide a substantial beginning point in determining the more specific effects of preschool curriculum on various types of learners; and, therefore secondary analyses of the results by subgroup should definitely be carried out.

First 5 LA. Another informative curricular evaluation was based in California and not national in scope, but is of interest because it was conducted using carefully selected bilingual measures in a variety of domains in a diverse urban environment (Los Angeles County). Hispanics are a particularly large segment of the population in California, and account for 59% of the population of children ages birth to 5 in Los Angeles County, the residents of which are diverse in language, race, ethnicity, and country of origin. Among the 10 million residents of the county, an estimated 224 languages are spoken, and approximately 156,000 4-year-old children live in the county as well. Of these 4-year-old children, almost two-thirds are Hispanic or Latino (61%), 18% are White, 9% are African American, 8% are Asian, and 4% are made up of other races/ethnicities.

About 44% of public school kindergarteners in the county were considered DLLs in 2004–2005 with Spanish being the most predominant non-English language. However, substantial numbers of DLLs speak Armenian, Korean, and Cantonese as well. In addition, approximately 60% of all public school students (K-12) receive free or reduced-price meals (Los Angeles County Chief Administrative Office, 2002).

In 1998, California voters passed Proposition 10, a voter initiative that levied a tax on tobacco products and earmarked the revenues to advance child and family development, health, education, and safety, from pregnancy until children enter kindergarten. A special state-level group known as the California Children and Families Commission, better known as First 5 California, was formed along with 58 county-level commissions. The largest of these commissions, based in Los Angeles County, is known as First 5 LA. The significant amount of funding was unprecedented, and led to First 5 LA's creation of the Los Angeles Universal Preschool (LAUP) Program. As part of this effort, in 2004 First 5 LA adopted a 10-year Universal Preschool Master Plan to increase the number of preschool slots in Los Angeles County and created LAUP to implement the plan. First 5 LA committed $580 million over five years to expand and improve existing preschool programs and build new facilities. The goal was to serve 4-year-olds throughout the county through center-based preschools and home-based family child care providers. As of 2006, LAUP had expended or committed funds to support 10,217 high-quality preschool spaces for 4-year-olds across Los Angeles County, with the goal to "have 70% of all 4-year-olds and their families in LA County actively participating in a LAUP program" by 2014 (LAUP, 2006). As of June 2008, LAUP was funding 201 preschool centers serving 6,210 4-year-olds (with another 1,397 children served by 123 family child care home providers) (LAUP 2008a).

In February 2007, First 5 LA contracted for an evaluation of the First 5 LA/LAUP Universal Preschool initiative. This evaluation study is of particular interest because the demographic characteristics of the area were deliberately taken into account. An initial pilot phase specifically examined the feasibility, reliability, and validity of selected measures with respect to their appropriateness for the culturally and linguistically diverse population of children served by LAUP programs. The study proper was conducted in the fall of 2007 and spring 2008 and examined the overall quality and implementation of LAUP programs in a pretest-posttest design. Among the variables examined were children's growth from fall to spring and the relationships between family characteristics and children's development over time. While the technical details of the report (Love et al., 2009) are more complex than can be adequately reviewed here, the highlights are informative. Among the selected findings were the following:

- On average, children's skills increased from fall to spring on most of the direct assessments, including teacher behavior rating scales, and parent behavior rating. Children showed some of their largest gains in letter knowledge, early writing, social cooperation, and executive functioning;
- Children performed better than the national mean in early

writing and problem behavior (that is, teachers rated them as displaying fewer problem behaviors);
- Children's performance was also better than the national mean in social cooperation, social interaction, social independence, and overall prosocial behavior but below the national mean in receptive and expressive English and Spanish vocabulary, attention, activity level, and sociability;
- Children's performance in the spring was related to how well they performed when they entered the program in the fall, with children who came into the program with higher performance levels also scoring higher in the spring;
- Not all children learned the same amount or at the same rate over the year. Although all groups of children progressed during the year, children who performed more poorly in the fall (that is, scored in the lowest quartile on a measure) learned as much or more during the year as the higher-performing (top quartile) children did, but were not performing sufficiently well in the spring to meet the national norms when they entered kindergarten. In fact, children in the lowest quartile in expressive vocabulary and social skills had lower mean scores in spring 2008 than children performing at the overall average had in fall 2007;
- Having more than three risk factors (out of the 10 we measured) was a consistent predictor of lower spring scores even after controlling for other factors (including the child's fall scores, age, language grouping, and number of days between fall and spring assessments);
- Membership in the Spanish-only or the Spanish-primarily language group was the most consistent, and often the strongest, predictor of spring scores even after controlling for fall scores, risk factors, and other child and family characteristics. For example, on the conceptually scored measure of expressive vocabulary, the difference between children in the English-language group and those in the Spanish-only group was approximately one-half a standard deviation;
- Most preschool classrooms include children whose developmental levels vary. LAUP classrooms differed in how much variation existed, and greater variation in children's expressive language skills when children entered the program in the fall was associated with higher spring scores in expressive language. This suggests that having children with a range of language skills in the classroom supports growth in language development and that in part children learn language from one another.

The study is particularly important in demonstrating that it is possible and feasible to adequately measure important developmental indicators for dual language learners.

The National Early Literacy Panel Report (NELP). The large numbers of DLL students at the elementary levels over the last decade has likely been a factor leading to the majority of research on bilingualism and second language learning focusing on the K-12 rather than the early childhood years (August & Shanahan, 2006). Even when early childhood has been the focus however, the trend has been to exclude DLL students from analyses. The National Early Literacy Panel Report (2008) is one such example. In 2002, the National Early Literacy Panel (NELP) was convened by the National Institute for Literacy, in consultation with the National Institute of Child Health and Human Development (NICHD), the U.S. Department of Education, the Head Start Bureau, and the U.S. Department of Health and Human Services. The Panel was commissioned to produce a report along the lines of the earlier National Reading Panel Report (NICHD, 2000) which had such a major influence on educational policy.

The specific charge to the NELP was to determine what instructional practices promote the development of children's early literacy skills. Toward that end, the panel posed four questions:

1. What are the skills and abilities of young children (birth through 5 years or kindergarten) that predict later reading, writing, or spelling outcomes?
2. Which instructional approaches or procedures contribute to gains in children's skills and abilities that are linked to later outcomes in reading, writing, or spelling?
3. What environments and settings are related to improvements in children's skills and abilities that are linked to later literacy outcomes?
4. What child characteristics are related to gains in children's skills and abilities that are linked to later literacy outcomes?

Eight thousand published articles were screened to determine their relevance to the research questions and their consistency with the panel's selection criteria. This led to the identification of approximately 500 research articles that were used in the meta-analyses. These meta-analyses summarized correlational data showing the relations among children's early abilities and later literacy development, and experimental data that showed the impact of various kinds of instruction on children's learning. Among the findings were that six early literacy skills (alphabet knowledge, phonological awareness, rapid automatic naming [RAN] of letters or digits, RAN of objects or colors, writing or writing one's name, and phonological memory) had moderate to large predictive relationships, for preschoolers and kindergartners, with later conventional literacy skills even with IQ and SES controlled. In addition, five other variables (concepts about print, print knowledge, reading readiness, oral language, and visual processing) had moderate relationships with at least one other later literacy achievement but in patterns that were more inconsistent.

In addition, with respect to interventions, code-focused programs, book sharing, programs for parents to use at home, and language-enhancement instruction were all found to improve children's oral language skills, but few interventions, with the exception of code-focused interventions, were found to improve conventional literacy skills or the precursor skills most related to later literacy growth.

While the NELP Report was highly informative, there have been a number of critiques work based on the narrowness of the work considered (Neuman, 2010), the narrowness of the definitions of the constructs used (Dail & Paine, 2010; Orellana & D'Warte, 2010), statistical issues (Paris & Luo, 2010), lack of sufficient attention to language (Dickinson, Golinkoff, & Hirsh-Pasek, 2010), and the narrowness of the instructional recommendations (Teale, Hoffman, & Paciga, 2010) among other factors. While a review of the entire report is beyond the scope of this chapter, the report does draw attention to the continuing and significant lack of work on important child characteristics. As the authors of the report admit:

> many substantive issues of great concern to educators and parents could not even be explored adequately because of limitations in the reporting of original studies. There are many theories, both naïve and scientific, suggesting the likelihood of individual differences in instructional effectiveness that demographic characteristics might mitigate. This meta-analysis evaluated whether such variables as race or SES mitigated or moderated the effectiveness of the various interventions. Unfortunately, it was all too rare that the original studies had provided sufficient data to allow for unambiguous conclusions to be drawn. (National Early Literacy Panel, 2008, p. x)

Summary. Of particular concern, related to the focus of this chapter, is the lack of attention to students who are dual language learners, not only in the NELP report, but in the general research literature. As Gutierrez et al. (2010) point out, the lack of attention to DLL students is illustrative of a larger problem in the literature on this age group in that while the Report did acknowledge the limitations related to empirical work on specific subpopulations of students, including DLL students, it nevertheless *did not exclude these groups from the instructional recommendations.* This led Gutierrez et al. (2010) to suggest that "there is insufficient empirical evidence to support generalizing NELP's findings to DLL populations, as they were not the focus of the meta-analysis" (p. 335) and to further recommend that "that the report not be used as a guide for making policy for this population of children" (p. 335).

Given the demographic portrait provided at the beginning of the chapter, this gap or failure of major studies of the preschool population such as the PCER and NELP represents a continuing and serious issue in the available research literature. We suspect that this lack of focus on the diversity of young DLL students may spring from several sources which may be scientific or intellectual, methodological as well as political. For example, the Head Start

Performance Standards (NHSTTARC, 2008) are very clear that instructional delivery, classroom interaction, and assessment instruments are to be tailored to the language and cultural group of the child. There are even recommendations that at least one member of the staff speak each language represented in the particular Head Start setting. However, the actual practice of this is far from being a reality since the vast majority of Head Start teachers speak and deliver the services of Head Start in English. Whether it is simply a matter of time and training for this goal to be reached, or the fact that the research or educational community has not yet discovered just how to manage a truly "culturally sensitive" curriculum is less clear.

In addition, no doubt the broad research questions which drive, for example, the national studies such as NELP or PCER divert attention away from focusing upon specific effects for specific language groups of children, despite the fact that large urban areas like Los Angeles County, as mentioned, are home to children speaking over 200 languages. In addition, large-scale studies of non-Spanish populations speaking Asian or other Indo-European languages are not common. This deficit may reflect a lack of both material and human resources to conduct this type of research, or point to the difficulty of gathering a sample size large enough to be representative and statistically viable. Alternatively, a more reactive political and financial reality may be at work which would render the motivation and funding for such a study impractical in our English-speaking educational system.

Conclusion

A study done in California by RAND researchers (Karoly & Bigelow, 2005) estimated that the potential benefits of a high-quality, one-year, voluntary preschool program, assuming a 70% participation rate, could generate $2.62 in benefits for every dollar spent. The study further estimated that for each annual cohort of 4-year-olds, the state would receive $2.7 billion in net benefits. Among the nonmonetary projected impact would be: (a) Nearly 14,000 fewer children ever retained in grade; (b) 9,100 fewer children using special education; (c) 10,000 fewer high-school dropouts; (d) 4,700 fewer children with a substantiated case of abuse or neglect; and (e) 7,300 fewer children with a juvenile arrest record. While this study focused on a single state, the results are eye-opening. They provide additional significance to the research which shows that high quality infant/toddler programs, prekindergarten (pre-K) programs, and kindergarten through third grade (K-3) education can contribute to meaningfully higher levels of school readiness and school achievement among low SES children, including low SES Hispanic DLLs.

However, gains produced by the most effective strategies to date have generally been modest and, therefore, have only been able to partially eliminate the readiness and achievement gaps between low SES children and their middle-class and high SES counterparts. In addition, little attention has been given to developing early childhood education strategies for improving outcomes for middle-class and high SES Hispanic children or those from other racial/ethnic groups (National Task Force on Early Childhood Education for Hispanics, 2007a). Although infant/toddler programs have demonstrated positive school readiness benefits for low SES children, they have been of limited size in the important area of language development. Thus, there is a pressing need to design, test, and evaluate new or modified infant/toddler strategies concerned with promoting greater language development for low SES children, including low SES DLL students.

We are in strong agreement with Gutierrez et al. (2010) that there are insufficient studies, especially on children from birth to age 4, which can be used as firm guidelines for policy, especially for DLL students. These students are often excluded from studies of early learning and there is less for policymakers to draw on than with other groups. As Gutierrez et al. (2010) note, these children often are subsumed under a broader "at-risk" category, making it difficult to understand underlying learning processes or to tease out relevant differences and factors. In addition, we believe that a promising area is to use more complex and more comprehensive techniques in order to better capture the varying influences that impact student outcomes (Fuller & Garcia Coll, 2010; Suarez-Orozco et al., 2010).

An especially needed area of research, given the fluid nature of population movements in the United States, is research on the role of early bilingualism and its influence on children's cognitive processing, including the cognitive benefits of bilingualism/biliteracy independent of the transfer issue, would be an important contribution (e.g., de Villiers, de Villiers, & Hobbs, 2009; Dickinson, McCabe, Clark-Chiarelli, & Wolf, 2004; Snow, 2006).

We concur with the recommendations of the National Task Force on Early Childhood Education for Hispanics (2007a) and see no reason why they could not be extended as appropriate to other language groups. These recommendations include the following:

- increasing access to high-quality early education for young, Latino children and preschoolers of other racial/ethnic groups who are DLLs;
- increasing the numbers of teachers and language-acquisition specialists who are proficient in both English, Spanish, and in other languages spoken by children entering preschool environments;
- increasing the capacity of center-based programs in Latino neighborhoods and where young DLLs of any language group are concentrated; and
- increasing efforts to design, test, and evaluate early childhood education strategies that can strengthen the language and literacy development of Latino or any group of young, dual-language learners.

References

Aud, S., Fox, M., & KewalRamani, A. (2010). *Status and trends in the education of racial and ethnic groups* (NCES 2010-015). Washington, DC: U.S. Department of Education, National Center for Education Statistics. Washington, DC: U.S. Government Printing Office.

Aud, S., Hussar, W., Planty, M., Snyder, T., Bianco, K., Fox, M., ... Drake, L. (2010). *The condition of education 2010* (NCES 2010-028). National Center for Education Statistics, Institute of Education Sciences, U.S. Department of Education. Washington, DC: Government Printing Office.

August, D., & Shanahan, T. (Eds.), *Developing literacy in second-language learners: Report of the National Literacy Panel on Language—Minority Children and Youth.* Mahwah, NJ: Erlbaum.

Batalova, J., Fix, M., & Murray, J. (2007). *The demography and literacy of adolescent English Language Learners.* Washington, DC: The Migration Policy Institute.

Capps, R., Fix, M. Murray, J., Ost, J. Passel, J., & Herwantoro. (2005). *The new demography of America's schools: Immigration and the No Child Left Behind Act.* Washington, DC: Urban Institute.

Caswell, L., & He, Y. (2008, October 21–22). *Appendix B.2: Approaches to promoting children's school readiness: A review of federally-funded research initiatives aimed at improving young children's language and literacy skills in early education and care settings.* A working paper prepared for a working meeting on recent school readiness research: Guiding the Synthesis of Early Childhood Research. Washington, DC: U.S. Department of Health and Human Services, Office of the Assistant Secretary for Planning and Evaluation (ASPE) and the Administration for Children and Families, Office of Planning, Research, and Evaluation (OPRE). Retrieved from http://aspe.hhs.gov/hsp/10/SchoolReadiness/apb2.shtml

Dail, A. R., & Payne, R. L. (2010). Recasting the role of family involvement in early literacy development: A response to the NELP Report. *Educational Researcher, 39,* 330–333. doi: 10.3102/0013189X10370207

Denton Flanagan, K., & McPhee, C. (2009). *The children born in 2001 at kindergarten entry: First findings from the kindergarten data collections of the Early Childhood Longitudinal Study, Birth Cohort (ECLS-B)* (NCES 2010-005). Washington, DC: National Center for Education Statistics, Institute of Education Sciences, U.S. Department of Education.

de Villiers, P., de Villiers, J. G., & Hobbs, K. (2009, April*). False belief reasoning in low-income bilingual preschoolers: Is there an effect of bilingualism?* Paper presented at the 2009 Biennial Meeting of the Society for Research in Child Development, Denver, Colorado.

Dickinson, D. K., Golinkoff, R. M., & Hirsh-Pasek, K. (2010). Speaking out for language: Why language is central to reading development. *Educational Researcher, 39,* 305–310. doi: 10.3102/0013189X10370204

Dickinson, D. K., McCabe, A., Clark-Chiarelli, N., & Wolf, N. (2004). Cross-language transfer of phonological awareness in low-income Spanish and English bilingual preschool children. *Applied Psycholinguistics, 25,* 323–347.

Dockterman, D. (2009). Statistical portrait of Hispanics in the United States, 2007. Washington, DC: Pew Hispanic Center.

Fix, M., & Passel, J. (2003). *U.S. immigration trends and implications for schools.* Washington, DC: Urban Institute.

Fry, R., & Gonzales, F. (2008). *One-in-five and growing fast: A profile of Hispanic public school students.* Washington, DC: Pew Hispanic Center.

Fuller, B., & Garcia Coll, C. (2010). Learning from Latinos: Contexts, families, and child development in motion. *Developmental Psychology, 46*(3), 559–565.

Gándara, P., & Hopkins, M. (2010). The changing linguistic landscape of the United States. In P. Gandara & M. Hopkins (Eds.), *English learners and restrictive language policies* (pp. 7–19). New York City: Teachers College Press.

Garcia, E. E., & Wiese, A. (2009). Policy related to issues of diversity and literacy: Implications for English learners. In L. Mandel, R. Rueda, &

D. Lapp (Eds.), *Handbook of research on literacy and diversity* (pp. 32–54). New York: Guilford.

Goldenberg, C. (2008). Teaching English language learners: What the research does and does not say. *American Educator, 32*(2), 8–23, 42–44.

Goldenberg, C., & Coleman, R. (2010). *Promoting academic achievement among English learners: A guide to the research.* Thousand Oaks, CA: Corwin.

Gutierrez, K. D., Zepeda, M., &. Castro, D. C. (2010). Advancing early literacy learning for all children: Implications of the NELP Report for dual-language learners. *Educational Researcher, 39,* 334–339. doi: 10.3102/0013189X10369831

Hamilton, B. E., Martin, J. S., Ventura, M. A., Sutton, P. D., & Menacker, F. (2005). Births: Preliminary data for 2004. *National Vital Statistics Reports, 54*(8), 1–18.

Hernandez, D. (2006). *Young Hispanic children in the U.S.: A demographic portrait based on census 2000* (Report to the National Task Force on Early Childhood Education for Hispanics). Tempe, AZ: Arizona State University.

Karoly, A. L., & Bigelow, J. H. (2005). *The economics of investing in universal preschool education in California* (Report MG-349-BF). Santa Monica, CA: RAND.

Legislative Analyst's Office. (2008). *Analysis of the 2007–08 Budget: English learners.* Sacramento, CA: Legislative Analysts Office.

Los Angeles County Chief Administrative Office, Service Integration Branch, Urban Research Section. (2002). *Estimates of race/ethnicity of Los Angeles County Children Ages 0–17, 2002.*

Love, J. M., Atkins-Burnett, S., Vogel, C., Aikens, N., Xue, Y., Mabutas, M., & Sprachman, S. (2009). *Los Angeles universal preschool programs, children served, and children's progress in the preschool year: Final report of the first 5 LA universal preschool child outcomes study.* Los Angeles, CA: First 5 LA.

Morrow, L. M., Rueda, R., & Lapp, D. (Eds.). (2009). *Handbook of research on literacy and diversity.* New York: Guilford.

Mather, M., & Foxen, P. (2010). *America's future: Latino child well-being in numbers and trends.* Washington, DC: National Council of La Raza.

National Center for Education Statistics (NCES). (2010). *Participation in education: Elementary/secondary education: Indicator five: Language minority school-age children.* Retrieved from http://nces.ed.gov/programs/coe/2010/section1/indicator05.asp

National Early Literacy Panel (NELP). (2008). *Developing early literacy: Report of the National Early Literacy Panel.* Washington, DC: National Institute for Literacy.

National Institute of Child Health and Human Development (NICHD). (2000). *Teaching children to read: An evidence-based assessment of the scientific research literature on reading and its implications for reading instruction.* (Report of the National Reading Panel; NIH Pub. No. 00–4769). Washington, DC: U.S. Government Printing Office.

National Task Force on Early Childhood Education for Hispanics. (2007a). *Expanding and improving early education for Hispanics: Main report.* Tempe, AZ: Author, Arizona State University.

National Task Force on Early Childhood Education for Hispanics. (2007b). *The school readiness and academic achievement in reading and mathematics of young Hispanic children in the United States.* Tempe, AZ: Author, Arizona State University.

Neuman, S. B. (2010). Lessons from my mother: Reflections on the National Early Literacy Panel Report. *Educational Researcher, 39,* 301–304. doi: 10.3102/0013189X10370475

Orellana, M. F., & D'warte, J. (2010). Recognizing different kinds of "Head Starts." *Educational Researcher, 39,* 295–300. doi: 10.3102/0013189X10369829

Paris, S. G., & Luo, S. W. (2010). Confounded statistical analyses hinder interpretation of the NELP Report. *Educational Researcher, 39,* 316–322. doi:10.3102/0013189X10369828

Planty, M., Hussar, W., Snyder, T., Kena, G., KewalRamani, A., Kemp, J., et al. (2009). *The condition of education 2009* (NCES 2009-081). Washington, DC: U.S. Department of Education, National Center for Education Statistics, Institute of Education Sciences.

Preschool Curriculum Evaluation Research Consortium. (2008). *Effects of preschool curriculum programs on school readiness* (NCER 2008-2009). Washington, DC: National Center for Education Research, Institute of Education Sciences, U.S. Department of Education. Washington, DC: U.S. Government Printing Office.

Reardon, S. F., & Galindo, C. (2006). *Patterns of Hispanic students' math and English literacy test scores* (Report to the National Task Force on Early Childhood Education for Hispanics). Tempe, AZ: Arizona State University.

Rueda, R., & Yaden, D. (2006). The literacy education of linguistically and culturally diverse young children: An overview of outcomes, assessment, and large-scale interventions. In B. Spodek & O.N. Saracho (Eds.), *Handbook of research on the education of young children* (2nd ed., pp. 167–186).Mahwah, NJ: Erlbaum.

Snow, C. E. (2006). Cross-cutting themes and future research directions. In D. August & T. Shanahan (Eds.), *Developing literacy in second-language learners* (Report of the National Literacy Panel on Language-Minority Children and Youth, pp. 631–652). Mahwah, NJ: Erlbaum.

Snyder, T. D., & Dillow, S. A. (2010). *Digest of education statistics 2009* (NCES 2010-013). National Center for Education Statistics, Institute of Education Sciences, U.S. Department of Education. Washington, DC: Government Printing Office.

Suarez-Orozco, C., Gaytan, F. X., Bang, H. J., Pakes, J., O'Connor, E., & Rhodes, J. (2010). Academic trajectories of newcomer immigrant youth. *Developmental Psychology, 46*(3), 602–618.

Swanson, C.B. (2009). *Perspectives on a population: English-language learners in American schools*. Bethesda, MD: Editorial Projects in Education.

Teale, W. H., Hoffman, J. L., & Paciga, K. A. (2010). Where Is NELP leading preschool literacy instruction? Potential positives and pitfalls. *Educational Researcher, 39*, 311–315. doi: 10.3102/0013189X10369830

Vandell, D. L., Burchinal, M., Vandergrift, N., Belsky, J., & Steinberg, L. (2010). Do effects of early childhood care extend to age 15 years? Results from the NICHD study of early child care and youth development. *Child Development, 81*, 737–756.

West, J., Denton, K., & Germino-Hausken, E. (2000). *America's kindergartners: Findings from the Early Childhood Longitudinal Study, kindergarten class of 1998–99, fall 1998*. Washington, DC: National Center for Education Statistics, U. S. Department of Education, Office of Educational Research and Improvement.

West, J., Denton, K., & Reaney, L. M. (2000). *The kindergarten year: Findings from the Early Childhood Longitudinal Study, kindergarten class of 1998–99*. Washington, DC: National Center for Education Statistics, U. S. Department of Education, Office of Educational Research and Improvement.

11

Mathematics for Early Childhood Education

CATHERINE SOPHIAN
University of Hawaii

There are now several preschool mathematics programs for which reliable evidence of effectiveness has been reported (e.g., Clements & Sarama, 2008; Gormley, Phillips, & Gayer, 2008; Klein, Starkey, Clements, Sarama, & Iyer, 2008). These programs represent the state of the art in early childhood mathematics, incorporating the best knowledge available today as to what young children need to learn about mathematics and how they can be supported in learning it. That knowledge, however, is still incomplete. Ongoing research in early childhood education (e.g., Anthony & Walshaw, 2009; Mulligan & Mitchelmore, 2009) and in developmental psychology (cf., Geary, 2006; Mix, 2010; Sophian, 2007) has the potential to further advance our knowledge about how young children think and learn about mathematics, and about how instruction can contribute to that thinking and learning.

My goal in this chapter is to review research on the development of mathematical knowledge in early childhood and to examine its implications for early childhood mathematics education. Following a brief examination of the evidence that children's early mathematical knowledge is an important predictor of school learning, I turn my attention to developmental research on the nature of young children's mathematical knowledge. That research has focused predominantly, although not entirely, on the development of numerical knowledge, and the material reviewed in this chapter will necessarily reflect that focus. However, a central theme in my review will be that children's understanding of numbers is inseparable from their understanding of relations between quantities, and an important limitation on that understanding in early childhood is that young children do not differentiate clearly among different quantitative dimensions. Understanding number thus is inseparable from understanding quantity more generally. In the concluding section of the chapter, I discuss the significance of this perspective on children's early quantitative knowledge not only for numeracy instruction but also for creating synergies between numeracy and other important components of early childhood mathematics.

The Impact of Early Childhood Mathematics Knowledge on Later Learning

There is now abundant evidence that children's early mathematical knowledge has an important influence on their subsequent learning. A particularly important set of findings supporting that conclusion comes from a meta-analysis of six longitudinal data sets carried out by Duncan et al. (2007). They found that children's mathematical knowledge at school entry was a stronger predictor both of mathematics achievement specifically, and of overall school achievement in middle childhood, than any other predictor examined, including measures of oral language and verbal abilities, reading skills, attention skills, social skills, and internalizing and externalizing problems.

Several subsequent studies have likewise found that children's early mathematical knowledge predicts subsequent learning. Jordan, Kaplan, Ramineni, and Locuniak (2009), for instance, found that kindergarten children's numerical competence predicted both their rate of growth in mathematics achievement between first and third grade and the level of mathematics achievement they attained by the end of third grade. Similarly, Krajewski and Schneider (2009) found that measures of quantitative knowledge collected in kindergarten predicted mathematical achievement in third grade; Jordan, Glutting, and Ramineni (2010) found that numerical and arithmetic knowledge at the beginning of first grade predicted mathematics achievement in first and third grade; De Smedt, Verschaffel, and Ghesquiere (2009) found that numerical comparison abilities at 6 years of age predicted performance on a general mathematics achievement test a year later; and Fuchs et al. (2010) found that measures of first graders' basic numerical cognition in the fall predicted the development of their arithmetic abilities over the course of the school year.

A persistent concern for both education and social policy more broadly is that socioeconomically disadvantaged children typically begin their schooling with substantially less mathematical knowledge than their middle-income peers (e.g., Jordan, Huttenlocher, & Levine, 1992; Jordan et al., 2006; Stipek & Ryan, 1997), and correspondingly are less successful in learning elementary school mathematics (Jordan et al., 2009). One factor contributing to early SES differences appears to be differences in how much and in what ways parents talk to their children about numbers. Levine, Suriyaham, Rowe, Huttenlocher, and Gunderson (2010) found that a measure of how much parents talked to their children about number when the children were between 14 and 30 months of age correlated positively with SES and also predicted children's numerical knowledge at 46 months. Socioeconomic differences have also been observed in the complexity of the numerical activities in which parents engage with their children (Saxe, Guberman, & Gearhart, 1987). Evidence that quality of early child care is a significant moderator of socioeconomic differences in middle childhood mathematics achievement (Dearing, McCartney, & Taylor, 2009) suggests that classroom activities can compensate for some of the limitations in the mathematical interactions characteristic of low-income children and their parents. Consistent with this idea, Klibanoff, Levine, Huttenlocher, Vasilyeva, and Hedges (2006) found that the extent to which preschool and day-care teachers engage in mathematics-related talk is significantly related to the amount of growth in children's mathematical knowledge over the course of the school year.

Mathematical Knowledge in Early Childhood

Notwithstanding the broad scope of the standards formulated by the National Council of Teachers of Mathematics (2000), the primary focus of developmental research on children's mathematical knowledge, including the research examining relations between early childhood knowledge and subsequent school learning, is still on what children know about number. An important impetus for that work came from Gelman and Gallistel's (1978) influential analysis of the systematicity of even very young children's counting. However, their work was itself a response to Piaget's (e.g., Piaget, 1952) view of numerical knowledge as inseparable from other kinds of quantitative knowledge and indeed from cognitive development as a whole. Although Piaget's theory is not widely accepted among developmental psychologists today, for two reasons it is useful to consider how his ideas shaped contemporary research. First, and most importantly for present purposes, his emphasis on children's understanding of relations between quantities remains vital to understanding the nature of early mathematical knowledge. More broadly, notwithstanding dissatisfaction with many particulars of his theory, his basic conception of knowledge

acquisition as an active and constructive process continues to inform both developmental psychology (see, e.g., Maynard, 2008; Overton, 2008) and mathematics education (see, e.g., Fuson, 2009; Kamii, 2000; Ojose, 2008).

Following a necessarily abbreviated summary of Piaget's ideas about children's early quantitative development and of subsequent research that critically evaluated his ideas, I turn my attention to the research on children's counting and numerical knowledge that grew out of challenges to Piaget's predominantly negative characterization of the young child's knowledge about quantities. A particularly important aspect of early numerical development, I will suggest, is the differentiation of number from other quantitative dimensions, and an important feature of number is its dependence on our choice of a unit.

I conclude this section of the chapter with a consideration of what is known about children's understanding of numerical relations between quantities. A fundamental distinction here is between additive relations and multiplicative relations, which provide the foundation for fundamentally different ways of using units to characterize how large one quantity is in comparison to another. Although multiplicative relations are intrinsically more complex than additive ones, young children are capable of reasoning both additively and multiplicatively about relations between quantities.

Young Children's Knowledge about Quantity

Piaget was primarily interested in a kind of knowledge that he termed "operative," knowledge that involves not just observing objects or events but mentally or physically transforming them in order to arrive at an understanding of relationships (Piaget, 1974). Thus, he emphasized the importance of being able to coordinate different ways of thinking about quantities, both for understanding quantitative relationships and for making sense of quantitative transformations such as rearranging a quantity or partitioning it into smaller quantities. This emphasis pervaded his thinking about the concepts of seriation, class inclusion, and conservation, which he viewed as the foundation for quantitative knowledge (Piaget, 1952; Inhelder & Piaget, 1964) but as developing only when children attain concrete-operational thought around 6 or 7 years of age.

Seriation consists of integrating information about variations in magnitude so as to form an ordered series. What makes this cognitively challenging is that judgments of less-than and greater-than must be coordinated, and items of intermediate magnitude must be placed appropriately in the series taking into account simultaneously that they are larger than some items and smaller than others. Young children are likely to form pairs composed of one short and one long item without coordinating those pairs with each other.

Class inclusion consists of comparing a part to the whole in which it is contained, and thus entails simultaneously thinking about the overall quantity as a whole and mentally decomposing it into parts so as to be able to compare one of those parts to the whole. Young children characteristically compare one part to another rather than comparing a part to the whole.

Conservation involves understanding that, as long as nothing is added or taken away, spatially rearranging a quantity does not change the overall quantity even though it changes characteristics such as the length of a row of items (when items are spread out) or the height of a column of liquid (when the liquid is poured from a wide container into a narrower one). To appreciate that quantity is conserved in the face of these salient changes, children must consider the compensatory relationship between them and other effects of the transformation (e.g., an increase in the distance between neighboring items; a decrease in the width of the column of liquid). Young children tend to focus on one salient change, such as an increase in the height of a column of liquid that has been poured into a narrow container, failing to coordinate it with the compensatory change that has taken place on another dimension, such as the width of the column, thus incorrectly concluding that the quantity is not conserved.

Piaget's predominantly negative conclusions about the quantitative understanding of children below 6 or 7 years of age were questioned by many subsequent investigators, who argued that young children's failures on Piaget's tasks stemmed from a misunderstanding of his questions and other sources of difficulty in his tasks rather than a lack of understanding of the quantitative concepts he had been investigating. Conservation was an especially frequent focus in research of this kind (although by no means the only one, cf., e.g., research on class inclusion; Markman, 1979; McGarrigle, Greaves, & Hughes, 1978). Conservation problems typically involve a three-part sequence in which the experimenter first asks a comparison question (e.g., "Does one row have more or are they the same?"), then deliberately makes a change, and then asks the child to make the same comparison again ("Now does one row have more or are they the same?"); and researchers conjectured that two aspects of this sequence might lead children astray. One concern was that the repetition of the comparison question (which is posed before the transformation and then again after it) could lead the child to think that the answer she or he gave initially was incorrect. A second concern was that the experimenter's deliberate transformation of the array between the two comparison questions might lead the child to believe that the experimenter wanted the child to change his or her answer. To test these ideas, some studies eliminated the initial comparison question (e.g., Neilson, Dockrell, & Mackenzie, 1983; Rose & Blank, 1974), while others changed the way the transformation was carried out, making it appear accidental rather than deliberate (e.g., Dockrell, Campbell, & Neilson, 1980; Hargreaves, Molloy, & Pratt, 1982; Light, Buckingham, & Robbins, 1979; McGarrigle & Donaldson, 1975; S. A. Miller, 1982; Siegal, Waters, & Dinwiddy, 1988). Both kinds of changes increased the frequency with which children gave conserving responses.

Siegal et al. (1988) obtained further support for the idea that children's misconstruals of the experimenter's expectations contribute to nonconservation responses by explicitly asking children to explain why a story character responded the way he or she did. In one of their studies, 69% of 4-, 5-, and 6-year-old children said the story character gave a nonconservation response "just to please the grown-up." In contrast, only 25% of the children explained a conservation response that way.

While these results support the idea that children's nonconservation responses stem at least in part from misinterpretations of the experimenter's intent, it does not follow that young children have a full understanding of conservation. Young children's reliance on social-interactional cues may be, in part, a reflection of their uncertainty about the effects of the conservation transformation. Because they are not sure what the correct response is, they look for cues as to the response the experimenter wants. Consistent with that idea, Neilson et al. (1983) found that repeating the comparison question increased the likelihood that children would change their responses after observing a conservation transformation, but it did not lead children to change their responses when the experimenter repeatedly asked about the relation between two quantities without altering them in any way.

A study by Light and Gilmour (1983) provides clear evidence that conserving responses to modified conservation problems are not necessarily indicative of mature knowledge. Light and Gilmour asked children to compare the areas of two fields, both before and after a transformation that involved rearranging the sections of fence that bordered the fields. Providing a rationale for rearranging the fence segments increased the likelihood that the children would say that the enclosed area was still the same after the transformation as before, even though in fact it was not (because area is not conserved, although perimeter is, when this type of transformation is performed). These results indicate that children's interpretations of the social context in which a problem is presented can lead them to make conserving responses (even when those are incorrect) as well as to make nonconserving ones. Thus, correct responses do not necessarily establish that they "really" do have the knowledge researchers are undertaking to examine, just as errors do not necessarily establish that they lack that knowledge.

The mixed findings obtained using different variations of the conservation problem have important instructional implications in that they remind us that children's knowledge can be tentative and fragile, defying absolute conclusions as to whether they do or do not "have" a target concept. While a 4- or 5-year-old may have a nascent idea of conservation, his or her knowledge is clearly quite different from that of an older child, who can hold to the conviction that quantity is not changed by a conservation transformation even in the face of social cues to the contrary such as the repetition of a comparison question and the deliberateness with which the transformation is performed. This insight has ramifications that extend far beyond the question of whether or not young children understand conservation, because many kinds of knowledge can vary in how tentative or firm they are, how readily they are accessed, and how easily disrupted; and those variations may have enormous consequences for children's ability to build on that knowledge as their mathematics learning advances. Accordingly, early childhood educators need to consider not only what children know but how well they know it.

The fragility of children's early conservation knowledge may be indicative of limitations on their grasp of the concept of quantity itself, in particular on their understanding of the distinction between different dimensions of quantity. Very often different quantitative dimensions covary: if two collections differ in number, then unless the items within the more numerous collection are smaller in size than those in the less numerous collection, the numerically greater one will also be greater in overall amount, and quite likely in spatial extent as well. Conservation problems, however, decouple different quantitative dimensions by transforming one dimension (such as length) while leaving another (such as number or volume) unchanged. Such transformations are bound to be confusing for children who do not differentiate clearly among different quantitative dimensions. Indeed, there is strong evidence that, on number conservation problems, children are heavily influenced by differences in the length of the rows of items to be compared (e.g., Bryant, 1972; Siegler, 1995). At the same time, on other kinds of problems, their judgments about nonnumerical quantitative dimensions can be inappropriately influenced by changes in number. In K. F. Miller's (1989) research, for example, 3- and 5-year-old children typically judged that two initially identical collections were no longer equal in aggregate amount after an item in one of the collections was cut in half (changing the number of items in the collection but not the total amount). Taken together, these results support the conclusion that an important limitation on young children's quantitative knowledge is that they do not differentiate clearly among different quantitative dimensions.

This perspective diverges from Piaget's in that it suggests that children's errors may not be symptomatic of profound limitations on their cognitive capabilities, but rather may reflect limitations on their experience with the relations among different quantitative dimensions, limitations that might be easily addressed through instruction. That idea is consistent with the finding that various forms of training can markedly improve children's conservation performance (cf., Field, 1987; Siegler, 1995).

Counting and Numerical Knowledge

Piaget's analysis of the importance of transformational knowledge, together with his findings indicating that children performed poorly on tasks assessing their understanding of such transformational concepts as class inclusion, seriation, and conservation, led him to dismiss children's

counting as a rote ability that had little significance for the acquisition of mathematical knowledge. In short, he reasoned that so long as a child does not understand the nature of quantity it is of little value for him or her to be able to recite the counting sequence or to arrive at the correct numerical value for a set of items. But for researchers seeking evidence that children might have more understanding of number than Piaget recognized, counting was of great interest as a numerical skill at which even young children showed some proficiency and within which nascent conceptual knowledge might be discernible. Two kinds of research were particularly important in reevaluating the conceptual significance of young children's counting abilities. First, careful study of how preschool children count, especially the influential work of Gelman and Gallistel (1978), showed that counting is by no means an entirely rote performance. But second, research examining how children adapt their counting to different goals—when they count, and what inferences they draw about relations between a quantity they have counted and other quantities—points to profound developmental changes in children's understanding of counting over the years of early childhood.

Gelman and Gallistel (1978) posited three principles that they considered essential to meaningful counting:

- the one-to-one principle, which holds that each item must be counted once and only once;
- the stable-order principle, which stipulates that the count words must be used in a fixed sequence (i.e., it is not acceptable to use the sequence "one, two, three…" in one count and "one, three, two…" in another); and
- the cardinality principle, which indicates that the last count word used is a representation of the cardinal value of the whole collection.

Gelman and Gallistel asked whether very young children's counts adhere to these principles, reasoning that if they do, their counting cannot be a rote activity. Indeed, they found that young children's counting is principled in these ways: they map successive counting terms one-to-one onto the objects they are counting; they use a stable sequence of counting terms (even if their sequence differs from the correct one); and they recognize that the last counting term used in a count has special significance as a representation of the total number of items. These regularities in children's early counting suggest that, even though young children would not be able to state the principles explicitly, at some level they have conceptual knowledge that shapes their counting efforts as they are learning to count.

Recent research shows that young children's numerical knowledge extends far beyond their counting range. Children who cannot yet count as high as 35, for example, still can generate estimates for larger collections that increase linearly with the numerical magnitude of the collection (Barth, Starr, & Sullivan, 2009). Thus, even children who are not yet skilled counters have some knowledge about the relative size of the quantities that are represented by numbers far beyond their counting range.

At the same time, their understanding of counting, even in relation to small sets, is limited in some noteworthy ways. Two-year-olds, if asked how many objects are in a set they have just counted, are likely to count the set again rather than to answer with the result of their previous count (Fuson, Pergament, Lyons, & Hall, 1985). By 3 or 3½ years of age, children are much more likely to give the result of the previous count in answer to the "how many" question (Fuson et al., 1985), but still they tend not to count when asked for a particular number of objects, instead grabbing a handful (Sophian, 1987; Wynn, 1990).

While counting is often studied—and practiced in early childhood classrooms—as though obtaining the numerical value of the set were a useful end in itself, what makes counting more than a rote symbolic activity is that we can use the results obtained by counting to compare different quantities. We count children before they get off the bus on a school trip and again after they have gotten back on board to make sure nobody is left behind; we count juice cartons to make sure we have one for each child. Even in counting transitory events, like the number of times a child claps her hands before catching a ball tossed in the air, we are often interested in making comparisons across occasions, for instance to see which child completes the most claps, or whether a given child was able to clap more times than she or he did previously.

As early as 3 years of age, children are able to use counting-based information to make inferences about relations among quantities. For instance, they successfully infer the number of objects in a hidden set based on information about its correspondence to a visible set if they are explicitly instructed to count the visible set (Sophian, Wood, & Vong, 1995). Yet, young children often fail to spontaneously engage in counting as a means of comparing quantities (Sophian, 1987; see also Michie, 1984; Muldoon, Lewis, & Francis, 2007; Saxe, 1977). Typically, if asked to compare two numerical quantities, they base their judgments on spatial cues such as differences in length or density. Four-year-olds' use of counting to compare sets can be increased, however, by providing feedback that helps them realize that it is a more reliable basis for identifying the more numerous set (Michie, 1984; Muldoon et al., 2007). The effectiveness of such feedback suggests that young preschoolers' limited use of counting is not due to a lack of understanding of counting as a source of information about relations between quantities, but rather reflects a lack of awareness of the fallibility of other ways of evaluating relations among quantities. Like young children's errors on conservation problems, then, the finding that young children often fail to count when asked to compare quantities may stem from limitations on their understanding of how numerical comparisons relate to, and potentially differ from, comparisons based on other quantitative dimensions.

An important feature of number, and correspondingly of counting, is that it depends not only on the physical properties of whatever we are enumerating but also on what we take as a unit. Consider, for example, the shoes depicted in Figure 11.1. We can enumerate them either as six shoes or as three pairs; and our conclusion about how their number compares to some other numerical quantity, say, four shoe boxes, will depend on which unit we choose. While preschool-aged children readily count individual objects, they perform poorly on problems that call for treating the parts of a connected object as separate items to be counted; for example, counting two parts that have been joined together to form an object as two pieces rather than one object, or treating several spatially discrete items as a single item to be counted; for example, counting the number of different types of objects in a collection rather than the number of individual objects (Shipley & Shepperson, 1990; Sophian & Kailihiwa, 1997). For example, Sophian and Kailihiwa (1997), using collections of toys composed of multiple exemplars of each of several different kinds of animals, found that 4- and 5-year-old children had no trouble counting individual animals of a particular type (e.g., rabbits) but did have trouble counting the number of different kinds of animals there were. When this type of question was posed, 4-year-olds still counted individual animals a majority of the time; and while the 5-year-olds were much more likely than the 4-year-olds to count all the animals of one kind together as a single family, fully 25% of them still counted individuals rather than families on a preponderance of the family-count trials.

Frydman and Bryant's (1988) research on children's partitioning of materials among different recipients produced converging evidence of limitations on children's understanding of units and of developmental changes in that understanding. Frydman and Bryant instructed children

Figure 11.1 Six shoes or three pairs

to give the same total number of blocks to two recipients, using blocks that were stuck together to form doubles or triples for one recipient and single blocks for the other recipient. Most of the 4-year-olds in their study treated each discrete piece as a unit, regardless of whether it was a single block or was composed of two or more blocks stuck together. Thus, they gave the same number of doubles or triples to the recipient who got those as they gave singles to the other recipient, so that the recipient of doubles or triples got far more blocks altogether than the recipient of singles. In contrast, most 5-year-olds were able to perform the task correctly. Recognizing that the relevant unit was a single block, for each double or triple allocated to one recipient they gave two or three single blocks to the other.

An understanding of numerical units is perhaps the most important single aspect of numerical knowledge that early childhood mathematics programs can help children to acquire. Most fundamentally, units are essential to understanding how abstract numerical symbols relate to concrete physical materials. Although we often speak of number as if it were a property of a collection, in fact we can arrive at a numerical value for a collection only when we have decided what counts as "one." Relatedly, an understanding of counting units is the foundation for understanding the relation between counting and measurement. In measuring continuous quantities like length, just as in enumerating discrete quantities, we arrive at a numerical value by first selecting a unit and then determining how many of those units are present in the material we are quantifying. Finally, a consideration of units provides an important link between additive and multiplicative ways of thinking about numerical relations. Counting is usually conceptualized additively, because if the unit is fixed, the numerical value obtained for a quantity increases or decreases in additive increments as the magnitude of the quantity itself is increased or decreased. However, if we keep the quantity fixed but change the size of the unit we use to enumerate it, we get proportional, and inverse, changes in the numerical value we obtain. Incorporating exploration of these kinds of relations in early counting activities, then, can familiarize children with kinds of numerical relations that will become important as their mathematics learning progresses.

Arithmetic and Numerical Relations among Quantities

Much of the power of numerical representations of quantity lies in the fact that they make it possible to use arithmetic operations to characterize relations among quantities. Without numerical representations, we can compare quantities spatially, for instance by placing two sticks side by side to see which is longer; however, if the quantities are unequal, without numbers we have no way to say how much longer one is than the other. Numerical representations, however, allow us to specify *how much greater* one quantity is than another. In fact, arithmetic offers two very different ways of specifying the relation between two quantities. We can specify that one stick is, for example, *two inches longer* than the other, or we can specify that one is *twice as long* as the other.

These alternative ways of describing how much longer one stick is than another correspond to two fundamentally different ways of thinking about the relation between two quantities, and correspondingly different ways of using units to represent that relation. In the first case, we are adopting a unit that is distinct from each of the quantities we are comparing, and using it to determine numerical values for each of the quantities and for the difference between them. In the second, we are taking the smaller of the two quantities as a unit and using that unit to obtain a numerical value for the larger quantity. The first approach depends on the notion of additive composition; as illustrated in the top portion of Figure 11.2, it conceptualizes the relation between two

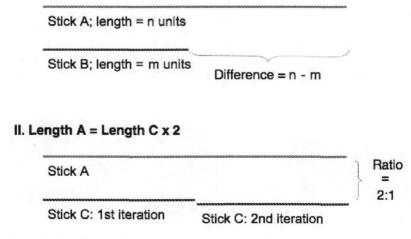

I. Length A = Length B + difference

Stick A; length = n units

Stick B; length = m units

Difference = n - m

II. Length A = Length C x 2

Stick A

Stick C: 1st iteration   Stick C: 2nd iteration

Ratio
=
2:1

Figure 11.2 Addictive and mulitplicative ways of numerically representing the relation between two lengths.

quantities as a difference (length A–length B). The second approach is multiplicative; as illustrated in the lower portion of Figure 11.2, it conceptualizes the relation between the two quantities as a ratio.

Multiplicative reasoning is intrinsically more complex than additive reasoning, since it is based on proportional relations (cf., Vergnaud, 1983). Nevertheless, there is evidence that young children are capable of reasoning both additively and multiplicatively about relations between quantities.

The development of additive thinking begins with the knowledge that adding something increases a quantity and taking something away decreases it. Even infants and toddlers show some understanding of these transformations in the way they search for hidden objects (Sophian & Adams, 1987; Starkey, 1992) and in their reactions to hiding and finding events they observe (e.g., McCrink & Wynn, 2004). Preschool children likewise show an understanding of the effects of additions and deletions on number. They can infer that something was added if they find more objects in a collection than there were before, and that something was removed if they find fewer objects than before (Gelman, 1972). Likewise, they know that the number of objects in a collection will increase if another object is added and decrease if one is removed (Sophian & Vong, 1995).

For many years, proportional reasoning was considered beyond the capabilities of young children. Piaget and Inhelder (1975) argued that because it involves reasoning about relations between relations, it entails formal-operational thought, which does not typically develop until 12 years of age or later. Many subsequent empirical studies, in addition to Piaget and Inhelder's own work, supported the view that proportional reasoning is a difficult and late-emerging developmental achievement (e.g., Lawton, 1993; Moore, Dixon, & Haines, 1991; cf., Behr, Harel, Post, & Lesh, 1992). Nevertheless, it is now clear that beginnings of multiplicative as well as additive reasoning can be identified even in early childhood.

McCrink and Spelke (2010) demonstrated knowledge of multiplicative relations in 5- to 7-year-old children who had not yet received any formal instruction in multiplication. After a series of training trials in which a specific multiplicative transformation such as doubling was applied to sets that initially contained 6, 10, or 14 items, the children were successful in identifying the numerical result of applying the same numerical transformation to sets of 4, 8, 12, or 16 items. McCrink and Spelke suggest that this multiplicative knowledge derives from the nature of children's intuitive representations of number.

Research on proportional reasoning, however, provides evidence that young children's sensitivity to ratio relations is not limited to numerical quantities. Sophian (2000) asked 4- and 5-year-old children to determine which of two small pictures of a birdlike figure matched a larger picture in the ratio of the size of the head to the size of the body. Children were successful in identifying proportional matches, even when the position of the head in relation to the body var-

ied between sample and test stimuli so that children could not identify the correct alternative on the basis of overall configuration.

Findings from Boyer, Levine, and Huttenlocher's (2008) research suggest that numerical representations of quantity may actually interfere with the detection of proportionality relations. Boyer et al. studied kindergarten through fourth grade children's proportional reasoning by asking them to identify which of two mixtures of juice and water, represented by columns composed of two differently colored segments that represented the amounts of juice and water in a particular mixture, matched a target proportion. On some problems, unit demarcations along the length of the columns made it possible to determine the numbers of units of water and juice comprising the target mixture and/or the response alternatives; while on other problems no such demarcations were present. Children at all grade levels did less well when both the target and the response stimuli were demarcated into units than when either or both were presented as continuous lengths. The kindergarten and first-grade children in the study, however, did not perform above chance even when the stimuli were not demarcated. Since Sophian's (2000) findings indicate that kindergartners are capable of proportional matching, it seems likely that the experimental procedure Boyer et al. used was not successful in communicating clearly to these children the need for a proportional match.

Inverse relations are a challenging aspect of proportionality for young children to understand. Sophian (2002) studied this aspect of children's mathematical knowledge using problems that involved thinking about how the size of objects affects how many of those objects fit in a given space. Given toy bears of different sizes and a toy bench, for instance, children were asked whether more of the smaller bears or more of the larger ones would fit on the bench. Initially, the children chose the larger bears more often than the smaller ones. Importantly, however, the children's thinking shifted when they were given the opportunity to observe what happened as progressively more of the smaller vs. larger bears were placed on identical benches. After just six training trials of that form (using a variety of different materials) children's performance improved markedly.

Similarly, Sophian, Garyantes, and Chang (1997) found that young children initially failed to appreciate the inverse nature of the relation between the number of recipients among whom a given quantity was to be shared, and the size of each recipient's share. In an initial experiment with 5-, 6- and 7-year-olds, all three age groups tended to expect that a greater number of recipients would result in larger, rather than smaller, shares for each. A subsequent experiment using a simplified procedure, however, elicited correct predictions from 7-year-olds although still not from 5-year-olds. Furthermore, the 5-year-olds improved after receiving a series of eight training trials in which they had the opportunity to observe what happened when two initially equal quantities were divided into different numbers of shares.

Children's difficulties with inverse relations may be a reflection of the same lack of differentiation in thinking about quantities that leads to errors on conservation problems. Just as young children do not consider the possibility that one quantity can be greater in spatial extent than another, but smaller numerically, they do not expect an increase in object size to result in a decrease in the number that fit in a given space or an increase in the number of recipients in a sharing situation to result in a decrease in the size of each share. Further, the success of training procedures like the one used by Sophian et al. (1997) in improving children's grasp of inverse relations suggests that, like their conservation knowledge, children's knowledge about inverse relations is highly responsive to experiences that illuminate the differences between different aspects of a quantitative situation. An important contribution that early childhood mathematics programs can make is to foster more differentiated thinking about quantity by presenting children with opportunities to discover the potential divergences as well as convergences among different quantitative dimensions.

Conclusions: Quantitative Relations and Early Childhood Mathematics Instruction

A core insight underlying Piaget's work on conservation and other quantitative concepts is that an understanding of number is inseparable from an understanding of quantitative relations. While several lines of research have challenged Piaget's analysis of the nature of the limitations on young children's quantitative reasoning, the recognition that an understanding of quantitative relations is vital to understanding number, and indeed mathematics more generally, remains valid and has important ramifications for early childhood mathematics instruction.

Most fundamentally, this perspective on numerical understanding suggests that a major goal of early childhood instruction in numeracy should be to help children to understand numbers as a tool for making quantitative comparisons. Several specific recommendations can be formulated based on this general insight and the specific research findings reviewed in the body of this chapter. First, children should be encouraged to use numbers to compare collections rather than just to assign numerical values to individual collections. Second, they should be encouraged to explore the relation between numerical comparisons and comparisons along other quantitative dimensions, such as the lengths of two rows of objects. Third, children should be helped to recognize that it is possible to use alternative numerical units and that different numerical values, and different conclusions about numerical relations, can result when different units are chosen. Exploration of the effects of using different units can, in turn, provide a foundation for introducing children to multiplicative relations.

An important consequence of basing numeracy instruction on quantitative comparisons is that it creates a synergy between numerical learning and other important forms of mathematical learning. The link to measurement is especially close, since measurement is fundamentally about the comparison of quantities. Learning to differentiate number from other quantitative dimensions can provide a foundation for grasping the distinction between units of length, area, volume, and weight. Further, the insight that numerical units are not determined by physical properties of a collection but chosen in accordance with our quantitative goals provides a foundation for understanding the measurement of continuous quantities, a process that entails partitioning a quantity into units that do not correspond to any physical demarcations. Likewise, learning about the ramifications of choosing different numerical units can help children appreciate the importance of using a constant unit in measuring; and exploring the effects of using different numerical units can provide a foundation for understanding how alternative units of measurement are related.

A focus on quantitative comparisons in the teaching of numeracy also bridges the gap between arithmetic and algebra. As Linchevski (1995) noted, it is possibly to think algebraically with numbers, and doing so involves interpreting arithmetic expressions as statements about equivalence relations rather than operations on quantities. Because algebraic reasoning depends heavily on the analysis of relationships between quantities (Kieran, 2006; Schmittau & Morris, 2004), treating numbers as tools for exploring relationships among quantities is highly conducive to the integration of algebra in early childhood mathematics.

A striking point of convergence in research on different aspects of children's early quantitative reasoning is that young children fail to appreciate the importance of differentiating among different aspects of quantity. It is not that they do not know that length, for instance, is different from number, but they do not understand that these quantitative dimensions can vary independently, and that some dimensions can even be inversely related. Early childhood instruction can help children gain that understanding, for instance by encouraging them to explore the effects on different quantitative dimensions of transformations like spreading out a collection of items or cutting the items into smaller pieces.

Number is a particularly powerful basis for quantitative comparison. It serves not only as a dimension along which we can compare discrete quantities but also, through measurement, as a tool for comparing continuous quantities. Even more important, it enables us to specify how much larger or smaller one quantity is than another. All of these uses of number depend on the notion of unit. Although children already have considerable experience with numerical quantities before they enter school, they need particular kinds of experiences to grasp the nature and importance of numerical units. Even preschool-aged children, with guidance, can explore the relations between different-sized units and a larger quantity (Sophian, 2002); and they can count materials using different counting units and observe how the numerical values they get change (Sophian, 2004). Through such activities, children can be familiarized with multiplicative as well as additive forms of numerical comparison.

In sum, developmental research on young children's mathematical knowledge calls attention to the importance of the ways they think about relationships between quantities; and an analysis of the available research findings from that perspective offers important insight for early childhood mathematics instruction. While developmental psychologists no longer agree with Piaget's characterization of young children as fundamentally lacking an understanding of quantity, the research does support the idea that their understanding of quantitative comparison, and correspondingly of number as a tool for quantitative comparison, is limited by a lack of clear differentiation between different quantitative dimensions and by a lack of understanding of numerical units. The good news for early childhood mathematics is that those limitations appear to be in large part a function of limited experience with the kinds of quantitative comparisons that can support a more differentiated understanding of quantity and an understanding of units. Early childhood instruction that provides these important forms of quantitative experience has the potential to markedly advance children's quantitative understanding and thus establish a strong foundation for further mathematics learning.

References

Anthony, G., & Walshaw, M. (2009). Mathematics education in the early years: Building bridges. *Contemporary Issues in Early Childhood, 10*, 107–121.

Barth, H., Starr, A., & Sullivan, J. (2009). Children's mappings of large number words to numerosities. *Cognitive Development, 24*, 248–264.

Behr, M. J., Harel, G., Post, T., & Lesh, R. (1992). Rational number, ratio, and proportion. In D. Grouws (Ed.), *Handbook of research on mathematics teaching and learning* (pp. 296–333). New York: Macmillan.

Boyer, T. W., Levine, S. C., & Huttenlocher, J. (2008). Development of proportional reasoning: Where young children go wrong. *Developmental Psychology, 44*, 1478–1490.

Bryant, P. E. (1972). The understanding of invariance by very young children. *Canadian Journal of Psychology, 26*, 78–96.

Clements, D. H., & Sarama, J. (2008). Experimental evaluation of the effects of a research-based preschool mathematics curriculum. *American Educational Research Journal, 45*, 443–494.

Dearing, E., McCartney, K., & Taylor, B. A. (2009). Does higher quality early child care promote low-income children's math and reading achievement in middle childhood? *Child Development, 80*, 1329–1349.

De Smedt, B., Verschaffel, L., & Ghesquiere, P. (2009). The predictive value of numerical magnitude comparison for individual differences in mathematics achievement. *Journal of Experimental Child Psychology, 103*, 469–479.

Dockrell, J., Campbell, R., & Neilson, I. (1980). Conservation accidents revisited. *International Journal of Behavioral Development, 3*, 423–439.

Duncan, G. J., Dowsett, C. J., Claessens, A., Magnuson, K., Huston, A. C., Klebanov, P.,…Japel, C. (2007). School readiness and later achievement. *Developmental Psychology, 43*, 1428–1446.

Field, D. (1987). A review of preschool conservation training: An analysis of analyses. *Developmental Review, 7*, 210–251.

Frydman, O., & Bryant, P. (1988). Sharing and the understanding of number equivalence by young children. *Cognitive Development, 3*, 323–339.

Fuchs, L. S., Geary, D. C., Compton, D. L., Fuchs, D., Hamlett, C. L., Seethaler, P. M., … Schatschneider, C. (2010). Do different types of

school mathematics development depend on different constellations of numerical versus general cognitive abilities? *Developmental Psychology, 46*, 1731–1746.

Fuson, K. (2009). Avoiding misinterpretations of Piaget and Vygotsky: Mathematical teaching without learning, learning without teaching, or helpful learning-path teaching? *Cognitive Development, 24*, 343–361.

Fuson, K. C., Pergament, G. G., Lyons, B. G., & Hall, J. W. (1985). Children's conformity to the cardinality rule as a function of set size and counting accuracy. *Child Development, 56*, 1429–1436.

Geary, D. C. (2006). Development of mathematical understanding. In W. Damon & R. M. Lerner (Series Eds.) & D. Kuhn & R. S. Siegler (Vol. Eds.), *Handbook of child psychology: Vol. 2. Cognition, perception, and language* (6th ed., pp. 777–810). New York: Wiley.

Gelman, R. (1972). Logical capacity of very young children: Number invariance rules. *Child Development, 43*, 75–90.

Gelman, R., & Gallistel, C. R. (1978). *The child's understanding of number*. Cambridge, MA: Harvard University Press.

Gormley, W. T., Phillips, D., & Gayer, T. (2008). Preschool programs can boost school readiness. *Science, 320*, 1723–1724.

Hargreaves, D. J., Molloy, C. G., & Pratt, A. R. (1982). Social factors in conservation. *British Journal of Psychology, 73*, 231–234. .

Inhelder, B., & Piaget, J. (1964). *The early growth of logic in the child: Classification and seriation*. New York: Harper & Row.

Jordan, N. C., Glutting, J., & Ramineni, C. (2010). The importance of number sense to mathematics achievement in first and third grades. *Learning and Individual Differences, 20*, 82–88.

Jordan, N. C., Huttenlocher, J., & Levine, S. C. (1992). Differential calculation abilities in young children from middle- and low-income families. *Developmental Psychology, 28*, 644–653.

Jordan, N. C., Kaplan, D., Olah, L. N., & Locuniak, M. N. (2006). Number sense growth in kindergarten: A longitudinal investigation of children at risk for mathematics difficulties. *Child Development, 77*, 153–175.

Jordan, N. C., Kaplan, D., Ramineni, C., & Locuniak, M. N. (2009). Early math matters: Kindergarten number competence and later mathematics outcomes. *Developmental Psychology, 45*, 850–867.

Kamii, C. (2000). *Young children reinvent arithmetic* (2nd ed.). New York: Teachers College Press.

Kieran, C. (2006). Research on the learning and teaching of algebra. In A. Gutierrez & P. Boero (Eds.), *Handbook of research on psychology of mathematics education: Past, present, and future* (pp.11–49). Rotterdam, the Netherlands: Sense.

Klein, A., Starkey, P., Clements, D., Sarama, J., & Iyer, R. (2008). Effects of a pre-kindergarten mathematics intervention: A randomized experiment. *Journal of Research on Educational Effectiveness, 1*, 155–178.

Klibanoff, R. S., Levine, S. C., Huttenlocher, J., Vasilyeva, M., & Hedges, L. V. (2006). Preschool children's mathematical knowledge: The effect of teacher "math talk." *Developmental Psychology, 42*, 59–69.

Krajewski, K., & Schneider, W. (2009). Exploring the impact of phonological awareness, visual-spatial working memory, and preschool quantity-number competencies on mathematics achievement in elementary school: Findings from a 3-year longitudinal study. *Journal of Experimental Child Psychology, 103*, 516–531.

Lawton, C. A. (1993). Contextual factors affecting errors in proportional reasoning. *Journal for Research in Mathematics Education, 24*, 460–466.

Levine, S. C., Suriyaham, L. W., Rowe, M. L., Huttenlocher, J., & Gunderson, E. A. (2010). What counts in the development of young children's number knowledge? *Developmental Psychology, 46*, 1309–1319.

Light, P. H., Buckingham, N., & Robbins, A. H. (1979). The conservation task as an interactional setting. *British Journal of Educational Psychology, 49*, 304–310.

Light, P. H., & Gilmour, A. (1983). Conservation or conversation? Contextual facilitation of inappropriate conservation judgments. *Journal of Experimental Child Psychology, 36*, 356–363.

Linchevski, L. (1995). Algebra with numbers and arithmetic with letters: A definition of pre-algebra. *Journal of Mathematical Behavior, 14*, 113–120.

Markman, E. M. (1979). Classes and collections: Conceptual organization and numerical abilities. *Cognitive Psychology, 11*, 395–411.

Maynard, A. E. (2008). What we thought we knew and how we came to know it: Four decades of cross-cultural research from a Piagetian point of view. *Human Development, 51*, 56–65.

McCrink, K., & Spelke, E. S. (2010). Core multiplication in childhood. *Cognition, 116*, 204–216.

McCrink, R., & Wynn, K. (2004). Large-number addition and subtraction by 9-month-old infants. *Psychological Science, 15*, 776–781.

McGarrigle, J., & Donaldson, M. (1974–1975). Conservation accidents. *Cognition, 3*, 341–350.

McGarrigle, J., Grieve, R., & Hughes, M. (1978). Interpreting inclusion: A contribution to the study of the child's cognitive and linguistic development. *Journal of Experimental Child Psychology, 26*, 528–550.

Michie, S. (1984). Why preschoolers are reluctant to count spontaneously. *British Journal of Developmental Psychology, 2*, 347–358.

Miller, K. F. (1989). Measurement as a tool for thought: The role of measuring procedures in children's understanding of quantitative invariance. *Developmental Psychology, 25*, 589–600.

Miller, S. A. (1982). On the generalizability of conservation: A comparison of different kinds of transformation. *British Journal of Psychology, 73*, 221–230.

Mix, K. S. (2010). Early numeracy: The transition from infancy to early childhood. In R. E. Trembley, R. G. Barr, R. DeV. Peters, & M. Boivin (Eds.), *Encyclopedia on early childhood development*. Montreal, Quebec: Centre of Excellence for Early Childhood Development. Retrieved from http://www.child- encyclopedia.com/documents/MixANGxp.pdf.

Moore, C. F., Dixon, J. A., & Haines, B. A. (1991). Components of understanding in proportional reasoning: A fuzzy set representation of developmental progressions. *Child Development, 62*, 441–459.

Muldoon, K. P., Lewis, C., & Francis, B. (2007). Using cardinality to compare quantities: The role of social-cognitive conflict in early numeracy. *Developmental Science, 10*, 694–711.

Mulligan, J., & Mitchelmore, M. (2009). Awareness of pattern and structure in early mathematical development. *Mathematics Education Research Journal, 21*, 33–49.

National Council of Teachers of Mathematics. (2000). *Principles and standards for school mathematics*. Retrieved from http://standards.nctm.org/document/chapter4/index.htm.

Neilson, I., Dockrell, J., & McKenzie, J. (1983). Does repetition of the question influence children's performance in conservation tasks? *British Journal of Developmental Psychology, 1*, 163–174.

Ojose, B. (2008). Applying Piaget's theory of cognitive development to mathematics instruction. *The Mathematics Educator, 18*, 26–30.

Overton, W. F. (2008). Embodiment from a relational perspective. In W. F. Overton & J. L. Newman (Eds.), *Developmental perspectives on embodiment and consciousness* (pp. 1–18). New York: Routledge.

Piaget, J. (1952). *The child's conception of number*. New York: Norton.

Piaget, J. (1974). *Biology and knowledge*. Chicago, IL: University of Chicago Press.

Piaget, J., & Inhelder, B. (1975). *The origin of the idea of chance in children*. New York: Norton.

Rose, S. A., & Blank, M. (1974). The potency of context in children's cognition: An illustration through conservation. *Child Development, 45*, 499–502.

Saxe, G. B. (1977). A developmental analysis of notational counting. *Child Development, 48*, 1512–1520.

Saxe, G. B., Guberman, S. R., & Gearhart, M. (1987). Social processes in early number development. *Monographs of the Society for Research in Child Development, 52*, serial no. 216.

Schmittau, J., & Morris, A. (2004). The development of algebra in the elementary mathematics curriculum of V. V. Davydov. *The Mathematics Educator, 8*, 60–87.

Shipley, E. F., & Shepperson, B. (1990). Countable entities: Developmental changes. *Cognition, 34*, 109–136.

Siegal, M., Waters, L. J., & Dinwiddy, L. S. (1988). Misleading children: Causal attributions for inconsistency under repeated questioning. *Journal of Experimental Child Psychology, 45*, 438–456.

Siegler, R. S. (1995). How does change occur: A microgenetic study of number conservation. *Cognitive Psychology, 28*, 225–273.

Sophian, C. (1987). Early developments in children's use of counting to solve quantitative problems. *Cognition and Instruction, 4*, 61–90.

Sophian, C. (2000). Perceptions of proportionality in young children: Matching spatial ratios. *Cognition, 75*, 145–170.

Sophian, C. (2002). Learning about what fits: Preschool children's reasoning about effects of object size. *Journal for Research in Mathematics Education, 33*, 290–302.

Sophian, C. (2004). Mathematics for the future: Developing a Head Start curriculum to support mathematics learning. *Early Childhood Research Quarterly, 19*, 59–81.

Sophian, C. (2007). *The origins of mathematical knowledge in childhood*. Mahwah, NJ: Erlbaum.

Sophian, C., & Adams, N. (1987). Infants' understanding of numerical transformations. *British Journal of Developmental Psychology, 5*, 257–264.

Sophian, C., Garyantes, D., & Chang, C. (1997). When three is less than two: Early developments in children's understanding of fractional quantities. *Developmental Psychology, 33*, 731–744.

Sophian, C., & Kailihiwa, C. (1998). Units of counting: Developmental changes. *Cognitive Development, 13*, 561–585.

Sophian, C., & Vong, K. I. (1995). The parts and wholes of arithmetic story problems: Developing knowledge in the preschool years. *Cognition and Instruction, 13*, 469–477.

Sophian, C., Wood, A., & Vong, K. I. (1995). Making numbers count: The early development of numerical inferences. *Developmental Psychology, 31*, 263–273.

Starkey, P. (1992). The early development of numerical reasoning. *Cognition, 43*, 93–126.

Stipek, D. J., & Ryan, R. H. (1997). Economically disadvantaged preschoolers: Ready to learn but further to go. *Developmental Psychology, 33*. 711–723.

Vergnaud, G. (1983). Multiplicative structures. In R. Lesh & M. Landau (Eds.), *Acquisition of mathematical concepts and processes* (pp. 127–174). New York: Academic Press.

Wynn, K. (1990). Children's understanding of counting. *Cognition, 36*, 155–193.

12

Science Education in the Early Years

LUCIA A. FRENCH AND SUZANNE D. WOODRING
University of Rochester

In her 1993 review for this *Handbook*, Howe noted a gap between the approaches to science education in preschool and the elementary grades: the elementary curriculum was based on a view of science as a body of facts to be mastered whereas preschool educators tended to adopt a Piagetian-inspired emphasis on independent exploration of the environment as a means for the child to construct knowledge. This gap has resolved such that there is a strong consensus among scholars that science education across all grade levels should involve students' active participation in conducting investigations, sharing ideas with peers, using specialized ways of talking and writing, and developing representations of phenomena. In other words, there has been a shift from a perspective that students need to "learn science in order to do science" to a perspective that they must "do science in order to learn science."

At the same time, with respect to science education at the early childhood level, there has been a reaction against assumptions based on the traditional interpretation of Piagetian theory that young children are unable to learn science because of cognitive limitations. Research commencing in the 1970s and continuing along various pathways since that time has shown that young children are much more cognitively capable than the traditional interpretations of Piagetian theory gave them credit for.

This chapter discusses young children's curiosity about and natural preparedness to learn about their everyday world, the form science education should take at the early childhood level, and ways of capitalizing on children's interest in learning about the everyday world as an authentic context for teaching vocabulary, early literacy, and mathematics. Ways of assessing young children's knowledge of science are also discussed as are the opportunities they are provided with during preschool and the primary grades to learn science. Materials available to support teachers in science education are described, including trade books and three preschool science curricula developed with support

from the National Science Foundation. Opportunities for parents and teachers to support children's participation in informal science learning and in citizen science activities are discussed. The efforts of a few scholars to introduce engineering into early childhood classrooms is described briefly, as are the differences and similarities between literature directed toward practitioners and scholars in early childhood science education.

A concluding section notes that very little science education takes place during the early childhood years, in large part because of the imperative teachers feel to teach literacy. There have been a number of small-scale implementations of science-based early childhood programs that have received positive responses from children, teachers, and parents, but at this point in time there is no mechanism for their large-scale dissemination and implementation. Recommendations are that state teacher certification requirements and teacher preparation programs be reformed to include courses on teaching science at the early childhood level, that professional development support teachers in learning to incorporate language, literacy, and mathematics into inquiry-based science activities, and that all adults take responsibility for introducing the children they care for to science inquiry and science content.

Some Background

There is widespread acknowledgment and concern that American students know less than students in other countries in the areas of science, technology, engineering, and mathematics (STEM; Program for International Student Assessment [PISA], 2010; Trends in International Mathematics and Science Study[TIMSS], 2007). In 2009, President Obama introduced a nationwide campaign, "Educate to Innovate," with the intent of moving American students, within 10 years, from the middle to the top in international comparisons in math and science; he reiterated the need for better science education in his 2011 State of the Union Address. The Educate to Innovate campaign involves partnerships among foundations, nonprofits, large companies, universities, and professional organizations representing scientists, engineers, and teachers. As part of this campaign, Time Warner Cable committed 80% of its corporate philanthropy to STEM, with a particular emphasis on after-school STEM activities; Discovery Communications committed to the creation of both a commercial-free educational block for children on the Science Channel and educational programming for 60,000 schools; and Sesame Workshop developed an "Early STEM Literacy Initiative," to include science and math in *Sesame Street*, a popular PBS television program for preschoolers.

The 1993 edition of this *Handbook* included a chapter on science education (Howe, 1993) but the more recent 2006 edition did not. Howe's (1993) chapter reviewed efforts to reform science education that took place in reaction to the Soviet launch of the Sputnik satellite in 1957. The launching of Sputnik surprised Americans and shook their confidence in the quality of their education; this prompted passage of the National Defense Education Act, which provided billions of dollars to the U.S. education system over a four-year period. A great deal has taken place in terms of science education since the 1993 review. However, it could be argued that these activities reflect developments in educational policies and in the philosophy underlying science education more than they reflect either an improvement in teaching science or an increase in the negligible amount of science education that takes place at the early childhood level (typically early childhood is defined as birth to age 8, with early childhood education extending from pre-K—1 or 2 years—through 2nd grade).

In response to the educational community's call for "standards" and "standards-based curriculum" in the 1990s, there was a thorough reconsideration and articulation of the goals and methods of science education across the K-12 years (American Association for the Advancement of Science, 1993; National Research Council, 1996). A parallel reform effort took place in Europe (Durant, 1993; European Commission, 1995; Millar & Osborne, 1998; Osborne, Simon, & Collins, 2003). More recently in the United States, the National Research Council convened a Committee on Science Learning that redefined what it means to be proficient in science and made recommendations for how to teach science (Duschl, Schweingruber, & Shouse, 2007; Michaels, Shouse, & Schweingruber, 2008). There is an increasing recognition of the role of informal science learning in complementing school-based science education and in creating a scientifically literate citizenry (AAAS, 1993). The National Science Foundation has an Informal Science Education program that funds research on learning science outside of school settings and the National Research Council has released two volumes that address informal science learning (Bell, Lewenstein, Shouse, & Feder, 2009; Finichel & Schweingruber, 2010).

As illustrated by the examples that follow, over the past 10 years there have been a variety of other indicators of ongoing interest in science education at the early childhood level. The National Science Foundation and the U.S. Department of Education have funded curriculum development and the creation of assessment tools in science at the early childhood level. The National Association for the Education of Young Children (NAEYC) has addressed the importance of science education in early childhood through special issues of both their practitioner-oriented journal (*Young Children*, September, 2002; reprinted as Koralek & Colker, 2003) and their researcher-oriented journal *Early Childhood Research Quarterly* (2004, *19*(1). The federally funded Head Start program for preschoolers living in poverty has included science knowledge, skills, and methods in their Child Outcomes Framework (Head Start Resource Center, n.d.). A number of states have established science standards at the early childhood level.[1] Science education at the early childhood level has been the topic of workshops sponsored by the American Association for the Advancement of Science (1999) and by the National Research Council (2005). An Office of Head Start Science Expert Meeting in 2009 served as preparation for creating professional development materials to assist Head Start staff in teaching science.[2] In May 2010, the Center for Early Education in Science, Technology, Engineering and Mathematics at the University of Northern Iowa sponsored a conference that focused on early childhood science education (Zan, 2010). Despite these recent developments, quality science activities are still not taking place in most preschools and elementary schools.

What is Science and How Should Science be Taught?

In order to adequately address science education at the early childhood level, it is necessary to briefly review the scholarship on science education more generally. This section offers broad definitions of science and compares the traditional practice of science education with the contemporary consensus among scholars for how science education should be implemented.

A relatively simple definition of science would describe it as a body of knowledge that provides the best available explanations of the natural world. A more complex definition would add a description of the activities by which this body of knowledge is generated. A yet more complex definition would add the social processes by which this body of knowledge achieves widespread acceptance and is subjected to continual challenge and refinement. From another perspective, science can be seen as the major cultural achievement of the past 300 years. It is both an approach to knowing and a body of knowledge that provides the foundation for the technology that makes contemporary everyday life possible in terms ranging from basic sanitation through manufacturing, farming, transportation, travel, financial transactions, health care, communication, and so forth. Even though the ordinary, everyday life of all but the most isolated groups of humans depends on the achievements of science, most Americans, even those considered to be well-educated, know little about science (AAAS/Pew Research Council, 2009).

Consistent criticism of science education by both students (e.g., Osborne & Collins, 2001) and scholars (e.g., Duschl et al., 2007) is twofold. First, science content is typically presented piecemeal with students not being exposed to the "big" or "important" ideas of science until they are in advanced courses. Second, science instruction typically relies on a discredited theory of learning based on transmission and memorization, with students rarely engaging in science discourse, open-ended investigations, or problem-based learning. The traditional view of (school) science as a body of facts to be taught/learned/assessed has resulted in curricula that provide broad coverage of "science facts" while failing to help students develop an appreciation of the social activities and consensus building that underlie the practice of science, an understanding of the central role of evidence in determining scientific knowledge, or the argumentation skills that allow comparison and resolution of different interpretations of that evidence (Kesidou & Roseman, 2002; Stern & Roseman, 2004). Traditional science instruction also focuses almost exclusively on basic science rather than attempting to engage students by contextualizing instruction (Rivet & Krajcik, 2008) around the technological innovations that have extensive impact on students' daily life (e.g., Hurd, 1998).

In her 1993 chapter for this handbook, Howe noted a gap between the approaches to science education in preschool and the elementary grades: the elementary curriculum was influenced by science educators who tended to view science as a body of facts to be mastered whereas preschool educators tended to adopt a Piagetian-inspired emphasis on independent exploration of the environment as a means for the child to construct knowledge. Howe suggested that this gap appeared to be diminishing at the time of her writing due to science educators' increasing acceptance of a constructivist view of learning.

The original publication of the *Benchmarks for Science Literacy* (AAAS, 1993/2009) in the same year as Howe's review supports her general conclusion regarding the direction of this trend, although with a general rather than a specifically Piagetian view of knowledge construction. Contemporary learning theory emphasizes that teaching/learning is not simply the verbal transmission of information (e.g., Bransford et al., 1999). Rather, people rely on their prior knowledge, their ongoing experiences, their goals, and linguistic input (oral or written) to actively construct knowledge. *Benchmarks for Science Literacy* emphasizes the importance in grades K through 12 of students' active engagement in investigations: learning by doing and discussing rather than learning simply by listening. This emphasis is again apparent in the *National Science Education Standards* published a few years later (National Research Council, 1996).

The emphasis on engaging in active investigations as a means of learning science was reiterated and expanded by the Committee on Science Learning convened by the National Research Council roughly a decade later. This committee produced two volumes. *Taking Science to School* (Duschl et al., 2007) describes current theory and research in the fields of learning sciences, child development, and science studies. *Ready, Set, Science* (Michaels et al., 2008) was written[3] to provide guidance for translating this research and theory into classroom practices.

Their deliberations and analysis of research led the Committee on Science Learning to take a science-as-practice perspective, which emphasizes that "conceptual understanding of natural systems is linked to the ability to develop explanations of phenomena and to carry out empirical investigations in order to develop or evaluate knowledge claims" (Duschl et al., 2007, p. 38). The science-as-practice perspective was developed in order to supplement and complement two prevailing views of science, science-as-theory-change and science-as-logical-reasoning (Lehrer & Schauble, 2006).

The science-as-practice perspective derives from observations of scientists carrying out scientific activities. From this perspective, science is a complex form of goal-directed human activity that includes not only theory development and reasoning but also social networks, specialized forms of discourse, the development of representations or models that make it possible to visualize and communicate phenomena, and so forth. From a science-as-practice perspective, learning science involves increasing ability to engage in the practices of science. *Taking Science to School* (Duschl et al., 2007) characterizes "doing science" as active participation in conducting investigations, sharing ideas with peers, using specialized ways of talking and writing, and developing representations of phenomena.

In characterizing science both as a body of knowledge and as engagement in active, evidence-based model building, the authors of this volume propose that science proficiency comprises four strands that should be seen as both learning goals for students and a broad framework for curriculum design:

1. Knowing, using, and interpreting scientific explanations of the natural world,
2. Generating and evaluating scientific evidence and explanations,
3. Understanding the nature and development of scientific knowledge, and
4. Participating productively in scientific practices and discourse.

Noting that knowledge and understanding develop in part through dialogue, Osborne (2007) suggests that the same processes that are central to dialogic interaction are central to science; these include describing, explaining, predicting, arguing, critiquing, explicating, and defining. In a similar vein, Duschl (2008) advocates a view of science education that engages learners in what he terms "conversations of inquiry" that move between evidence and explanations. The evidence–explanation continuum has three critical components: selecting/generating data to become evidence; using evidence to ascertain patterns and models; employing these models and patterns to propose explanations. Brown and Campione (1994) identify dialogue as the format within which novices acquire the discourse structure, goals, and belief systems of scientific practice.

In broad terms, these authors as well as many others emphasize the importance, in learning science, of students' active engagement in problem solving and in discourse with others (e.g., Bereiter, 1994; Brown, Metz, & Campione, 1996; Gee, 2005; Lemke, 1990; Peterson, 2009; Peterson & French, 2008). This emphasis can also be seen in Bruner's (1996) advice that "our instruction in science from the start to the finish should be mindful of the lively processes of science making, rather than being an account only of 'finished science' as represented in the textbook, in the handbook, and in the standard and often deadly 'demonstration experiment.'" (p. 127).

Can Young Children "Do Science"?

The shift over the past two decades in terms of how scholars in the field of science education conceptualize science and thus how they believe science should be taught can be summarized as movement from a belief that students must learn science in order to do science to a belief that students must do science in order to learn science. The view of science-as-practice and the constructivist view of learning place priority on the learners' active attempts—individually and during social interactions—to develop understanding and make meaning of their environment and experiences.

Changing the focus of science education from verbal transmission to active investigations and discourse opens much larger possibilities for science education during the early childhood years. "Doing science" fits the young child's reliance on personal experience as the foundation for learning. Preschool-aged children are learning language and learning from language, but they are not yet ready to learn exclusively or even primarily from language. That is, their cognitive and linguistic abilities are not yet adapted to creating new knowledge/mental representations on the basis of linguistic input only, as when older children and adults learn by listening to lectures (French, 1996; Nelson, 1991, 1996). Instead, preschoolers can use language to supplement and extend their prior knowledge and what they are learning through personal activity and experiences. They are also in the process of learning to use language for a variety of purposes suited to science investigations, such as describing, planning, explaining, and argumentation.

In the past, a major barrier to teaching science in early childhood has been a reliance on Piagetian theory as the primary framework for understanding children's development combined with a definition of science that involves

some combination of abstract principles and controlled experimentation with multiple variables. Metz (1995, 1997) argues that several faulty assumptions drawn from Piagetian theory have limited the quality of science education during the elementary grades, particularly in light of a primary principle of contemporary learning theory, that people learn best when they are actively pursuing a personally meaningful goal (e.g., Bransford, Brown, & Cocking, 1999). These faulty assumptions are that young children (1) are not capable of abstract thought, (2) do not have the cognitive abilities needed to develop explanations and make inferences, and (3) are unable to understand the purpose and results of controlled investigations/experiments. In line with these concerns, Metz points out that baseline levels of what children can or cannot do prior to any instruction cannot legitimately be taken as an indicator of what they would be capable of learning given an appropriate curriculum. She also argues against teaching science process skills in the absence of content and goals:

> The targeting of purportedly elementary science processes for the first years of school with a postponement of the integrated practice of goal-focused investigations until the higher grades results in decomposition and decontextualization in the teaching and learning of scientific inquiry. As a consequence young children engage in science activities such as observation and categorization apart from a rich goal structure or overriding purpose, a practice which is detrimental from cognitive, motivational, and epistemological perspectives. (Metz, 1997, p. 152)

Recent reviews of research in the learning sciences and in child development provide strong evidence that young children are much more capable of learning science than they have traditionally been given credit for (Duschl et al., 2007; Gelman, Brenneman, Macdonald & Román, 2010). For example, Metz (2004) documented that second grade children were able to conceptualize uncertainty—a key component of scientific inquiry—in investigations that they themselves had designed and implemented.

Some scholars in the field of child development have proposed that there are innate "learning mechanisms" that direct children's learning (e.g., Hatano & Inagaki, 2000) or that certain classes of infant knowledge can be described as early "theories" (e.g., Gelman, 1990; Gelman & Brenneman, 2004; Gelman et al., 2010; Gopnik & Schultz, 2004). Scholars who take the perspective that young children develop early theories believe that these theories function to organize past experience and generate new knowledge and that these theories are revised on an ongoing basis, being strengthened by supporting data or adapted to accommodate anomalous data. Other scholars, including Bruner (1996) do not attribute theories to young children, but instead believe that they organize their experience and knowledge in terms of narrative.

Regardless of whether young children's knowledge is better understood as early theories or as narratives, this knowledge is likely to include misconceptions. Some of these misconceptions are idiosyncratic and others are widely shared, if not universal, during the early childhood years. What reaction should science educators have toward young children's misconceptions? Some scholars, for example Lind (1999), consider these misconceptions to be an obstacle to science learning whereas others believe that they will self-correct as children have opportunities to learn science (e.g., Nguyen & Rosengren, 2004; Smith, diSessa, & Roschelle, 1994). Pea (1993) suggests that children's early knowledge is likely to be more piecemeal than the word *theory* conveys and, along with Bereiter (1994), argues that misconceptions provide an important starting point for learning and for concept change.

Claims of young children's cognitive limitations with respect to their ability to learn science have also been challenged by comparisons of experts and novices. Research has found that children with a great deal of specialized knowledge in areas as diverse as chess and dinosaurs can perform cognitive tasks (e.g., remembering, drawing inferences) at a higher level than adults who lack expert knowledge (e.g., Chi, 1978, 2006; Chi, Hutchinson, & Robin, 1989; Chi & Koeske, 1983). Although there are relatively few young chess masters, many, perhaps most children develop what Crowley and Jacobs (2002) refer to as "islands of expertise." These are domains in which a child develops an above average interest and level of knowledge. Crowley and Jacobs illustrate this construct using the example of a 24-month-old child who receives and repeatedly asks his parents to read aloud a book about a train; the parents respond to the child's apparent interest in trains by buying and engaging with the child in using toy trains, more books about trains, and videos about trains and by taking the child on excursions that involve visiting and viewing trains. Importantly from a developmental perspective, children's vocabulary, discourse skills (e.g., explanations, inferences), and process skills (e.g., classification, comparison) are considerably higher in their domain(s) of expertise than in other domains.

The central importance of social interaction to learning and development became widely accepted in the developmental and learning sciences starting in the late 1970s as scholars rediscovered the writings of the Russian psychologist Vygotsky, who died in 1934 (e.g., Brown & French, 1979; Bruner, 1985; Cole, 1996; Rogoff & Wertsch, 1984; Vygotsky, 1978; Wertsch, 1981, 1985). The gradual incorporation of a Vygotskian perspective into the theoretical foundations for early childhood education can be seen by comparing the three editions of the National Association for the Education of Young Children's guide *Developmentally Appropriate Practice in Early Childhood Programs* (Bredekamp, 1986; Bredekamp & Copple, 1997; Copple & Bredekamp, 2009). A common interpretation of Piagetian theory as it has been applied to early childhood education holds that children construct knowledge as a result of their independent exploration of the physical environment. Under this interpretation, which formed the theoretical foundation

for the first edition (Bredekamp, 1986), the adult has a relatively limited role that does not involve actively teaching the child content or supporting the child's reflection on and reasoning about her experiences. A Vygotskian perspective, emphasizing the importance of adult–child interaction and conversation in promoting development became more apparent in the second and third editions (Bredekamp & Copple, 1997; Copple & Bredekamp, 2009).

Bodrova and Leong (2003, 2006) and Berk and Winsler (1995) have written extensively about how to incorporate a Vygotskian perspective into the early childhood classroom. Within Vygotskian theory, in marked contrast to Piagetian theory, the adult is seen as having an essential and highly active role in supporting children's learning and development. The child learns by engaging in activities with the adult. In accord with Vygotsky's (1978) observation that development moves from interpersonal to intrapersonal, both physical (e.g., playing peek-a-boo, Bruner, 1983) and mental (Bodrova & Leong, 2006) activities that the child initially does with adult support later become activities that the child can do independently; adult–child conversation is a crucial component of this development (e.g., Wertsch, 1979).

"Doing Science" Builds on the Ordinary Learning and Development of Early Childhood

Any complete account of human development must take into consideration children's social and physical environments, their interactions with others, and their active cognitive role in representing, processing, and making meaning of their personal experiences (Nelson, 2007). Young children are inherently motivated to learn about the world they live in. The needs and abilities of humans to learn about their everyday world are as strong and as important to their survival as are their needs and abilities to learn language, to learn motor skills, and to engage socially. Parents and other adults mediate young children's opportunities to engage with the world and there are large differences in the nature of these opportunities across families, across socioeconomic groups within a culture, and across cultures and historical time. For example, currently in the United States some children go almost everywhere with their parents while other children spend most of their time in one or two locations (e.g., their own home and a daycare setting). Some children spend most of their time alone or with one family member while others are immersed in child care environments where they interact primarily with age mates. Some parents talk with their children a great deal about a variety of topics and other parents talk with their children much less and about a restricted range of topics (e.g., Hart & Risley, 1995, 1999). These variations in individual children's experiences are magnified across cultures and across history.

Despite the great variation in their experiences, virtually all children achieve similar basic developmental milestones in the first three years of life without any extraordinary or even deliberate attempts on the part of adults to instruct them. They learn to walk, to talk, and to engage socially with familiar and unfamiliar adults and children. They also develop knowledge of their everyday world that allows them to behave appropriately in a variety of situations and to understand, anticipate, and interpret the roles, objects, and temporal/causal structure associated with a variety of personally experienced events (e.g., French, 1985; French & Nelson, 1985; Nelson, 1986, 1996, 2007). Like learning to talk, this knowledge develops in the course of participating, with family members and others, in the ordinary activities of daily life.

Various interpretations of Piagetian theory notwithstanding, it is a relatively small step to move from saying that young children are innately prepared to learn about their everyday world to saying that they are emotionally and cognitively prepared to participate in science-as-practice and thus to embark on learning science. The same cognitive processes young children spontaneously use to develop an understanding of their everyday world will support science learning (Brewer & Samarapungavan, 1991; Gelman et al., 2010). Indeed, the skills that are often referred to as "science process skills" are basic cognitive abilities that are developing throughout the early childhood years. These include classification, sequencing, symbolic representation (words, drawings, graphs and charts, number), informal mathematics, understanding cause and effect and the vocabulary that expresses this relationship, understanding the nature of time and the words used to describe temporal relationships, observing, describing, explaining, and so forth.

Appropriate Science in Early Childhood Classrooms

Once it is agreed that children are capable of doing science during the early childhood years, the questions become whether it is important to introduce science and, if so, what sort of content and pedagogy are appropriate. For many years there has been a tension in the early childhood community regarding whether preschool and kindergarten should be primarily a time for social interaction and play or primarily a time for instruction. Over the past two decades, the emphasis has shifted to instruction, in large part because preschool programs are increasingly being funded by state and federal tax dollars with the goal of improving children's school readiness.

Instruction can take many forms, which vary in the extent to which they correspond with young children's cognitive strengths and limitations. Katz (2010) suggests that when making decisions about instruction it is essential to distinguish between academic and intellectual skills. She defines academic skills as those needed to acquire small discrete bits of disembedded information such as letter names and sound–letter correspondence. She defines intellectual skills as those that "address the life of the mind in its fullest sense, including a range of aesthetic and moral sensibilities.... [T]he concept of *intellectual* emphasizes

reasoning, hypothesizing, predicting, the quest for understanding and conjecturing as well as the development and analysis of ideas" (p. 3). She argues that current trends in early childhood education, with their heavy emphasis on decontextualized literacy and math skills, simultaneously reflect an overestimation of children's academic skills and an underestimation of their intellectual skills. She goes on to suggest that academic skills should be acquired in the service of intellectual pursuits:

> An appropriate curriculum in the early years is one that encourages and motivates children to seek mastery of basic academic skills, e.g., beginning writing skills, *in the service of their intellectual pursuits*. The children should be able to sense the purposefulness of their efforts to master a variety of academic skills (e.g. writing, counting, measuring, etc.) and to appreciate their usefulness and their various purposes. (p. 3)

Katz's perspective on the value of embedding academic skills in meaningful intellectual activities is fully in accord with contemporary learning theory as reflected in a number of publications (e.g., Bransford Baron et al., 2006; Bransford, Brown, & Cocking, 1999; Brown, 1994; Collins, 2006; Edelson & Reiser, 2006; Greeno, 2006; Herrington & Oliver, 2000; Krajcik & Blumenfeld, 2006).

There are any number of topics that could beneficially and productively be investigated in early childhood classrooms and that would provide a meaningful, goal-directed context within which teachers could deliberately embed instruction in language, literacy, and mathematics. Architecture, carpentry, gardening, and puppetry are all examples of meaningful, open-ended topics around which extensive projects and curricula could be built. Science has a privileged status among the possible content area topics for at least two reasons.

First, young children are biologically prepared and eager to learn about their everyday world. Indeed, they must learn about it in order to survive and thrive. This "ordinary" learning can easily be transformed into "science learning" by organizing children's encounters with everyday phenomena (a coherent and structured curriculum) and by adding language that provides children with vocabulary to express the concepts they are acquiring and that supports them in learning to observe, describe, predict, plan, and explain.

A second reason to focus on science in preschool is that it is rich with general content and provides children opportunities to learn vocabulary and to develop a rich knowledge base. Early childhood classrooms rarely provide substantive content that can help children build the type of rich knowledge base that is known to be important in terms of supporting later reading comprehension and higher-order reasoning skills (e.g., Hirsch, 2003; Neuman, 2001, 2006, 2010) and opportunities for this type of learning outside of the school setting are related to family income (e.g., Neuman & Celano, 2006; Viswanth & Finnegan, 1996).

What science content would be appropriate for young

children? The literature offers little guidance for addressing this question. Compared to math and literacy, there is little consensus as to what the content of science instruction at the early childhood level should be. Science is not structured according to foundational building blocks in the same way math and literacy are and the traditional division of science education into life sciences, earth sciences, and physical sciences provides a general framework but no details regarding what science content might be most meaningful to or useful for young children.

Kindergarten is the lower age limit discussed in the *Benchmarks for Science Literacy* (AAAS, 1993/2009), *National Science Education Standards* (National Research Council, 1996), and *Taking Science to School* (Duschl et al., 2007). However, it is easy to extrapolate implications for instruction and classroom activities downward to the pre-K level. While the details of using these benchmarks, standards, or strands as a foundation for learning goals and curriculum design must depend on students' age and background knowledge, there is nothing in the guidelines for K-2 that could be considered to deviate from developmentally appropriate practice for preschoolers. However, these guidelines also offer little in the way of concrete suggestions for content at the early childhood level.

Duschl (2008) suggests that science education across grade levels should address the most generative and core ideas of science, ideas that are "accessible to students in kindergarten and have the potential for sustained exploration across K-8" (p. 283), but he does not indicate what these core ideas might be. Gelman (1990; Gelman & Brenneman, 2004; Gelman et al., 2010) holds a neonativist perspective according to which young children are believed to be innately prepared to learn in some domains more easily than in others. *Preschool Pathways to Science* (Gelman et al., 2010) notes children's ability to engage in complex reasoning about the construct animate/inanimate. However, the authors' suggestions for topics to be investigated in preschool are not constrained to these privileged domains; instead they are extremely broad and include constructs such as "change" which the authors suggest could be investigated through consideration of "liquids and solids" or "seasons" or the "growth of plants and animals."

In the final section of a special issue of the *Early Childhood Research Quarterly* devoted to math and science, the editors write:

> Should the early study of science involve some form of biology or physics or psychology? Or does it matter? Perhaps what is most important is to inculcate the methods and values of scientific or critical thinking—the ability to make reasonable hypotheses and to use evidence honestly and systematically to evaluate them. (Ginsburg & Golbeck, 2004, p. 195)

This quote is somewhat dated in that it does not include the social and discourse components that are central to current views of science and science education (e.g., Duschl et al., 2007; Michaels et al., 2008). Nevertheless, the general point that it is the activity of *doing* science that is important rather than any particular content is well-taken.

Because learning about the everyday world is a major developmental task and developmental achievement of the early childhood years, our own view[4] is that science content for young children should focus on observable phenomena of their everyday life, phenomena that can be manipulated and investigated without specialized knowledge or tools (Bowman, Donovan & Burns, 2001; Conezio & French, 2002; French, 2004; French, Conezio, & Boynton, 2002; French & Peterson, 2009). The prior knowledge that children bring to science-oriented investigations of everyday phenomena supports both their deeper learning about these phenomena and their use and development of the inquiry and discourse skills associated with science investigations. In developing the ScienceStart!/LiteraSci curriculum, we selected only science topics and concepts that can be experienced in the immediate environment. This selection criterion eliminated some topics that are popular in early childhood classrooms such as those with no contemporary referents (e.g., dinosaurs), no local referents (e.g., oceans for children who live inland), and interesting mechanisms that are highly abstract and largely invisible (e.g., magnets). In addition to selecting topics based on observable phenomena of children's daily life, each day's lesson in the ScienceStart!/LiteraSci curriculum is structured according to a child-friendly, four-step version of the science cycle: reflect and ask, plan and predict, act and observe, report and reflect. These steps provide a predictable framework for doing science and support a variety of forms of science discourse.

Focusing on science during the early childhood years can have many benefits that reach beyond what is typically considered to be science knowledge. Children are highly engaged by inquiry-based science (e.g., S. Ellis, personal communication, February 2009; R. Gelman, personal communication, March 2004; K. Worth, personal communication, March 2004). Children's attentiveness and interest create a situation that can support many different forms of learning.

First, a focus on science supports children's acquisition of general content knowledge. This means that classmates will have a shared knowledge base that can support reasoning and discussion, that children will have less difficulty with reading comprehension (e.g., Hirsch, 2003), and that the knowledge gap that develops along socioeconomic lines (e.g., Neuman, 2006; Neuman & Celano, 2006) may be alleviated.

Second, a focus on science supports children's learning of mathematics, which is inherent in science-oriented investigations as children measure, quantify, classify, and compare objects. Such investigations provide an excellent and authentic context within which teachers can introduce and children can practice a variety of forms of mathematics and the vocabulary associated with sequencing and measurement of size, volume, and time.

Third, even though the need to teach literacy is the reason elementary teachers typically give for not teaching other subject matter, reading and writing have to be *about* something. Inquiry science provides an engaging context for the teacher to read aloud and talk about children's books related to a science investigation (e.g., Hapgood & Palincsar, 2007). Science investigations also provide an opportunity for the teacher to model writing as children make plans and predictions and for children to participate in writing as they dictate findings to the teacher, draw and write in journals, keep tallies during surveys, and participate in making classroom books about their investigations. Although letter names, sound–symbol correspondence (the alphabetic principle), and phonemic awareness can be taught in the absence of meaningful text, deliberate instruction in these domains can also be fully embedded within purposeful reading and writing activities.

Finally, language development is also a primary concern of early childhood educators. A focus on science provides children with the opportunity to acquire a great deal of "tier two" vocabulary (e.g., Beck, McKeown, & Kucan, 2002) and to participate in science conversations (Gallas, 1994, 1995), using discourse forms such as description, asking and answering questions, explaining, planning, and argumentation (Newton, 2002). Data from primarily low-income preschoolers who participated in classrooms where all activities were integrated around science investigations (ScienceStart! classrooms) showed that over the course of eight months, children made significant gains on standard scores on the Peabody Picture Vocabulary Test (French, 2004; French & Peterson, 2009), participated actively in science discourse (Cassata-Widera, Kato-Jones, Duckles, Conezio, & French, 2008; French & Peterson, 2009; Peterson, 2009; Peterson & French, 2008), and used science vocabulary such as transparent/translucent and primary / secondary color appropriately beyond the context in which the words were initially learned (including using them at home to the amazement of their parents).

Assessing Children and Classrooms

Some states have developed standards and benchmarks for science at the preschool level as has the federal Head Start program that provides pre-K education for 3- and 4-year-olds living in poverty. Only the Head Start guidelines will be provided here, as they are similar to published state standards and also applicable across the United States. The Head Start "Science Domain" is divided into two components, "Scientific Knowledge" and "Scientific Skills and Methods." These components are further specified as indicators, which are shown in Table 12.1.

Essentially, these federal Head Start indicators reflect developmental changes (begins to, develops increased ability to, develops growing awareness of, expands knowledge of and abilities to…) in children's content knowledge with respect to the natural world, their bodies, time, temperature, cause–effect relations, and change. According to these indicators, this knowledge can be seen in children's cognitive abilities to observe, describe, discuss, record, investigate, compare, generalize, and draw conclusions.

All of the interests and abilities mentioned in the Head Start indicators develop naturally and spontaneously during the preschool years as children participate in the activities of everyday life. It would be the rare, seriously disabled child whose development did not reflect the changes captured by these indicators. For this reason, it is of concern that analysis of a large, ethnically diverse database of Head Start children's performance on school readiness measures shows "that children end their pre-kindergarten year with science readiness scores significantly lower than readiness scores in all other measured domains" (Greenfield et al., 2009, p. 238).[5] The science scores were not only the lowest of the eight domains at the end of the year, but they also showed the smallest improvement over the course of the academic year. How could normally developing children fail to show improvement in the fundamental knowledge base and skills that characterize early childhood? Our interpretation of

Table 12.1   Head Start Child Outcomes Framework for the Domain "Science"

Indicators for Assessing Progress and Accomplishments of 3- to 5-Year-Olds	
Scientific Skills and Methods	**Scientific Knowledge**
Begins to use senses and a variety of tools and simple measuring devices to gather information, investigate materials and observe processes and relationships.	Expands knowledge of and abilities to observe, describe and discuss the natural world, materials, living things and natural processes.
Develops increased ability to observe and discuss common properties, differences and comparisons among objects and materials.	Expands knowledge of and respect for their body and the environment.
Begins to participate in simple investigations to test observations, discuss and draw conclusions and form generalizations.	Develops growing awareness of ideas and language related to attributes of time and temperature.
Develops growing abilities to collect, describe and record information through a variety of means, including discussion, drawings, maps and charts.	Shows increased awareness and beginning understanding of changes in materials and cause-effect relationships.
Begins to describe and discuss predictions, explanations and generalizations based on past experiences.	

these findings is that they result from a highly questionable approach to assessment/measurement.

Greenfield et al.'s (2009) sample (4,959 children) was assessed using the Galileo Scales for Head Start (Bergan et al., 2003). These scales contain 380 items (57 in the science domain) and the teacher responds "learned/not learned" for each item on an ongoing basis throughout the school year. To respond "learned" the teacher should have observed the child display the knowledge or skill covered by the item on three occasions. In each domain, skills to be evaluated cover a range of difficulty levels.

In science more so than in the other domains, many of the items require specific knowledge that would result from specific learning opportunities or that would be apparent to the teacher only under special circumstances (e.g., only if the teacher directly asked the child a specific question). For example, five items address children's ability to classify[6] physical phenomena—the easiest is "classifies objects by their state (e.g., liquid, solid, gas)" and the most difficult is "classifies objects based on whether or not they require electricity/battery." Seven items address children's predictions about living things. The easiest is "predicts what might come next in a life cycle sequence (e.g., seed to plant)," an intermediate is "predicts that human activity (e.g., building) may threaten animal habitat/survival," and the most difficult is "predicts that extreme weather (draught, freeze) will injure plants/wildlife."

Items such as these from the Galileo Scales are clearly within the realm of science and they will certainly distinguish children who "know more" from children who "know less." Nevertheless, the items lack face validity as indicators of children's growing understanding of the natural world. Partly this is because a positive evaluation ("learned") for the items depends heavily on both the teachers' opportunities to observe the child in an appropriate circumstance and on the child's opportunities for exposure to particular experiences or conversations. How can a teacher know if a child can classify on the basis of whether something is a liquid or a solid if she has never had a reason to ask him to do so? Yet, what is the likelihood that any 3- or 4-year-old would be unable to distinguish between liquids and solids? How would a child who has never had an opportunity to plant seeds know that they might grow? Children may be more familiar with seeds as "food" than as "immature plants." Another reason the items lack face validity is that they are simply developmentally inappropriate. How could a child who has been alive only 4 years make predictions about the long-term consequences of human activity or extreme weather without some extraordinary opportunities or unlikely conversations? And under what conditions would a teacher be able to determine—on three occasions—that the child could make such predictions?

An alternative means of using teachers' judgments to evaluate preschoolers' science knowledge and abilities is under development for the state of California, as part of the Desired Results Developmental Profile for preschool (California Department of Education, 2010). Instead of making a choice of learned/not learned, the teacher uses a four- or five-level scale that indicates increasing competence in a given area. Key concepts and competences are assessed rather than specific knowledge and each item is phrased in general terms with a variety of examples that illustrate the concept or competency being assessed.

There is a danger of interpreting data such as Greenfield et al.'s (2009) as reflecting a "crisis" in children's developing knowledge of science. Yet assessing and comparing individual children's science competencies is really beside the point until educators have made a commitment to provide children with opportunities to acquire and practice these competencies. To the extent that there is a "science crisis" at the early childhood level, it is a crisis caused by a lack of opportunities for children to learn science rather than their lack of ability to do so. At this point, it is more relevant to assess children's opportunities to learn science in early childhood settings than to assess what individual children might have picked up through idiosyncratic means (family conversations, a visit to a museum or park). It can be quite straightforward to monitor the extent to which classrooms and teachers provide opportunities for children to learn science content and to make use of and develop science processes and science discourse. As a first step, one might simply measure the amount of time devoted to science content.

For a more detailed view of science in the classroom, an instrument that was developed to assess implementation fidelity in classrooms using the ScienceStart!/LiteraSci Curriculum (Cassata-Widera, 2010) could be adapted for more general use. This instrument assesses the amount of time devoted to science in whole-group and small-group settings, the number of science inquiry events, children's attentiveness and contributions during science activities, the extent to which teacher-talk models and prompts inquiry, the extent to which child-talk reflects inquiry, and the relative amount of time the teacher takes on a collaborative, coexplorer role compared to a didactic role.

Materials, Locations, and Activities to Support Science Education at the Early Childhood Level

Science Curricula

Consideration of the science curriculum materials for the primary grades that are available from textbook publishers such as Foss, Delta, Harcourt Brace, and Pearson is beyond the scope of this review. Information about these materials can be found on the publishers' Web sites. In general, these materials are designed in accord with the current view that active investigations should be a major part of learning science. The publishers' Web sites include many supplementary materials to support teachers.

The National Science Foundation has funded the development of at least three curricular approaches to science education at the preschool level; these include projects directed by Karen Worth at the Educational Development Center, Rochel Gelman at UCLA/Rutgers, and Lucia French at the University of Rochester. Each of these curricula has been extensively field-tested and is being used in a number of locations. Each is inquiry-based and hands-on and each encourages long-term in-depth investigations in a single domain in order to support children in developing a rich knowledge base. Each is available commercially, though the formats are quite different from one another.

The Young Scientist Series (Chalufour & Worth, 2003, 2004, 2005) currently contains three activity guides that focus on nature, blocks, and water. Each volume includes a description of what science education should look like and why it is important and lists books and other media that can serve as appropriate supplements. The activities are designed as a cycle of open exploration of a topic, focused exploration of the same topic, and finally suggestions for extensions of the topic. The approach is play-based and generally more child-directed than adult-guided with only limited attention to integrating literacy and math activities into the science activities.

Preschool Pathways to Science (Gelman et al., 2010) is a book directed primarily toward early childhood teachers and students in teacher preparation courses. It explains the research base underlying the science curriculum that Gelman and her colleagues developed at an early childhood center located on the campus of UCLA and provides guidance for teachers who wish to develop and implement a similar approach to science education. Integrating instruction in literacy and mathematics into the science activities is encouraged.

ScienceStart!/LiteraSci (e.g., Bowman et al., 2001; Conezio & French, 2002; French, 2004; French, Conezio, & Boynton, 2002; French & Peterson, 2009) uses science inquiry as the core of a comprehensive, full-day program. The curriculum is divided into five coherent modules, each designed for in-depth study over a 6- to 12-week period. These modules are Measurement and Mapping, Properties of Matter, Color and Light, Neighborhood Habitat, and Movement and Machines. Daily lesson plans contain explicit guidance on integrating language, literacy, mathematics, art, music, small-group time, and outdoor play with the day's science topic.

Trade Books

Books on science topics offer teachers an immediate and easy way to integrate science, language development, and literacy. Twenty years ago there were few nonfiction books available for young children. Now there are hundreds, many of which offer an excellent introduction to science topics. For example, Delta offers a set of 12 big books on science topics such as "life in a pond" and "seeds" and Scholastic has an extensive *Rookie Read-About Science* series that introduces topics in physical science such as heat, sound, gravity, and color and science tools such as microscopes, balances, and thermometers.

Depending on the topic, many popular fiction books can also be used to support science investigations.[7] For example, if students were exploring the phenomenon of mixing primary colors to create secondary colors, the teacher might read and support children in talking about *Little Blue and Little Yellow* (Lionni, 1959), *White Rabbit's Color Book* (Baker, 1994), and *Mouse Paint* (Walsh, 1989). Children could then use these stories as background knowledge to make plans for mixing paints and to make predictions about what new colors they could create.

Informal Science Learning

Children spend only a fraction of their time in formal educational settings and a great deal of learning of all sorts takes place informally. There are many opportunities to learn science outside of school. Each child's experiences and informal knowledge is likely to be unique as the interests of parents and other family members typically mediate young children's access to and type of informal science experiences. Informal learning may range from independent exploration or reading, to a casual conversation with a parent, to a one-time visit to a museum, to participation in ongoing organized activities such as scouting or Saturday morning lessons, to attending the same summer camp over a number of years.

Many cities have zoos, science museums, and children's museums with science-oriented exhibits. These zoos and museums often offer classes for children of different ages and their gift shops are likely to sell science activities and books. There are a number of science- and nature-focused magazines for children including *Ranger Rick* and *National Geographic Kids*. Organizations such as National Geographic and the Audubon Society have science-focused Web sites with sections specifically for children or families that contain videos, stories, puzzles, and games.

Children's exposure to science themed television shows has been shown to support an increase in their amount of science talk (Penuel et al., 2010). There are several children's television programs that focus specifically on science, including *The Magic School Bus* (originally developed by PBS and now shown on NBC) and *Sid the Science Kid* (PBS) and other children's television programs that consistently address science, including *Sesame Street* and *Electric Company* (both PBS). In addition, there is a substantial amount of television programming on nature and science that is appropriate for, though not directly designed for children.

Families may also observe live feed from webcams that are maintained by others. Observing and talking about the same site over time can engage children's interest and support their learning about the natural world. For example, a number of webcams around the country show live footage of peregrine falcon and bald eagle nests. These webcams follow the birds from their annual arrival at the nest through mating, laying eggs, sitting on eggs, hatching and feeding of chicks, and the chicks' fledging and learning to fly. In some cases, blogs and other associated commentary provide additional information and create a virtual learning community. An Internet search for "wildlife cams" or "wildlife webcams" can locate live footage of a variety of sites around the world that attract wildlife. Live video of Earth is broadcast by NASA's webcam on the International Space Station. Many zoos have webcams inside enclosures.

Family activities such as preparing meals, baking cookies, hiking, biking, camping, or traveling all offer opportunities for science-related activities, conversations, and learning. Parents know that young children are fascinated by understanding how their bodies work and by watching the decomposition of leftover food, enthusiastically participate in activities such as planting and harvesting a garden, enjoy digging up and exploring the animal life in soil, and can observe and talk about the changes of matter that occur when ice melts or eggs cook. Family science practices often build on children's interests and can take many forms, from planned and structured activities to spontaneous "science moments" (e.g., Duckles, 2010).

Participation in Citizen Science Projects

The term *citizen scientist* refers to volunteers, of any age and any education level, who participate in science activities, often in collaboration with research scientists. An Internet search for citizen science projects identifies many sites. The mission statement of ScienceforCitizens (www. scienceforcitizens.net) lists four goals:

- Enable and encourage people to learn about, participate in, and contribute to science through both informal recreational activities and formal research efforts.
- Inspire greater appreciation and promote a better understanding of science and technology among the general public.
- Create a shared space where scientists can talk with citizens interested in working on or learning about their research projects.
- Satisfy the popular urge to tinker, build, and explore by making it simple and fun for people—singles, parents, grandparents, kids—to jump in and get their hands dirty with science.

At the most local level, a family may create a garden that attracts and supports birds, butterflies, and bees or students may work together to create a wildlife friendly schoolyard. Guidelines and lesson plans for these and many other local citizen scientist activities are available from the National Wildlife Federation (www.nwf.org), the Xerces Society (www.xerces.org), and other organizations that focus on the conservation of animals and habitats.

At a more organized level, individuals, families, or groups of students may make observations and report these to a research team that compiles input from many informants to monitor animal populations, study trends in population growth or decline, and so forth. Projects such as these provide important information to researchers, teach participants basic research skills, and foster the public's interest in conservation (Oberhauser & Prysby, 2008). Many of these organized projects can be accessed through www. citizenscience.org, www.ScienceforCitizens.net, and www. birds.cornell.edu/citscitoolkit.

One of the most enduring citizen science projects began on Christmas Day, 1900. At that time, many people showed their interest in birds by shooting and mounting them. An employee of the Audubon Society asked his friends to join him in counting, rather than shooting, birds. The Christmas Day Bird Count has taken place every year since 1900, with teams counting all the birds they can locate and identify within an assigned location. In 2010, 2,103 teams counted almost 61 million individual birds. Currently, scientists compare data from the Christmas Day Bird Count across years to study the relationship between climate change and migration patterns. Perhaps more appropriate for young children, the Audubon Society also sponsors an annual Great Backyard Bird Count and Cornell University's Lab of Ornithology sponsors an annual FeederWatch Project; each organization provides instructional materials for families and teachers. Other organizations invite and rely on citizen participation to record observations regarding amount of snowfall, whether bodies of water are covered in ice, the water quality of streams, and the occurrence of many species including toads, frogs, bats, and bumblebees.

The open-ended nature of learning from participation in citizen science projects can be illustrated by the Great Sunflower Project (www.greatsunflower.org). In recent years, widespread colony collapse of commercial honey bees used for pollination in large scale agriculture has raised concerns about the future availability of food. Very little is known about the many species of native bees and what they might contribute to large scale agriculture. The Great Sunflower Project has responded with a citizen science project to investigate the distribution and activity of wild bees across urban, suburban, and rural communities in the United States. Participants in this project plant a sunflower and then count and classify the bees that visit it within a given time period. Younger children participating in this project with their families or teachers can practice counting and classification skills, older children can learn about the role of pollination in plants' life cycle, and still older children can come to appreciate how humans depend on agriculture, which in turn depends on insect life.

Engineering Education in Early Childhood

An increased awareness of the importance of STEM subjects (e.g., America Competes Act, 2007) has led to an increased interest in introducing these topics at the early childhood level. Most early childhood teachers now devote considerable time to instruction in mathematics but there is virtually no attention to instruction in technology in early childhood. Engineering occupies a middle space, receiving some attention from scholars and practitioners, and mostly in ways that are not open to widespread dissemination.

Scholars suggest that children are naturally prepared and motivated to participate in activities that promote engineering learning and that teachers can nurture engineering dispositions (Brophy & Evangelou, 2007; Fleer, 1999, 2000; Habashi, Graziano, Evangelou, & Ngambeki,. 2009; Van Meeteren & Zan, 2010). Jeffers, Safferman, and Safferman (2004) note that "it has become clear to many educators that students must be introduced to engineering in the context of math and science at an early age" (p. 106). Equipment and materials found in most early childhood programs allow for implementing engineering activities if teachers are inclined to do so. For example, engineering interests can be encouraged through activities that require children to problem-solve and negotiate with peers while building with blocks (Van Meeteren & Zan, 2010) or exploring in the water table (Brophy & Evangelou, 2007).

Bagiati, Yoon, Evangelou, and Ngambeki (2010) report that under an assumption that early experiences strongly impact later experiences, "early childhood education is being examined as a starting point for reform in engineering education" (p. 2) and that there are a growing number of materials for formal or informal engineering activities being developed for the pre-K–3 level. However, when these same authors (Baguiati et al., 2010) did an extensive search for and review of engineering materials directed toward young children and available free through the Internet, they found virtually no high quality materials. They located seven Web sites with activities only and five Web sites with lesson plans and assessment tools; all 12 sites addressed some aspect of engineering but none included learning goals, coherent sets of activities, or reference to content area standards.

There have been several successful attempts to engage children in engineering activities through both in-school and out-of-school programs. With support from parents and college students, a member of the University of Oklahoma School of Industrial Engineering faculty established an informal after-school club to support young children in learning about engineering (Rhoads, Walden, & Winter, 2004). This program was designed to increase young children's exposure to engineering experiences without making teachers responsible for its implementation. The "Engineering is Elementary" program combines engineering topics and literacy initiatives (Brophy & Evangelou, 2007; Brophy, Klein, Portmore, & Rogers, 2008). The LEGO Engineering program (Wendell, Connolly, Wright, Jarvin, & Rogers, 2010), introduces students to science concepts while they are engaged in LEGO building projects. The students then use what they have learned to create LEGO structures that meet specific standards. LEGO Engineering is unique in its open-ended nature that allows students to make adjustments to their designs based on perceptions of what is working and what is not in order to find an appropriate solution (Brophy et al., 2008). Wendell et al. (2010) found that students' scores on pre- and posttest measures of science (material properties, animals, and machines) were higher for those students involved in the LEGO engineering curriculum than for students receiving more traditional science instruction.

At this point, the field has a number of successful "demonstration projects" showing that young children are engaged by engineering activities and that these activities promote development. However, as of now, there are very few curricular materials available for teachers interested in introducing engineering into their classrooms.

Publications in Science Education for Scholars and for Practitioners

There are two relatively distinct literatures in science education as scholars write for scholars and practitioners write for practitioners.[8] Researchers and practitioners alike recognize the importance of activities being meaningful and authentic. Both groups have focused on supporting science education in terms of both the quantity and the quality of children's exposure (Miller, 2010), have encouraged the integration of science and other content areas (Pratt & Pratt, 2004; Yager, 2004), and have emphasized the importance of inquiry in science education (Cullen, Akerson, & Hanson, 2010; Pratt & Pratt, 2004; Yager, 2004).

The research literature, directed toward other scholars, often emphasizes barriers to effective science teaching. The practitioner literature, however, is based on the assumption that teachers can teach science and are able to provide optimal learning opportunities with community oriented support. This difference very likely results from the scholars taking a broad view and attempting to account for why so little science education takes place in early childhood and the practitioners, a biased sample in terms of teachers who have successfully taught science, reflecting on their own practice.

The scholarly publications indicate that early childhood teachers are often not teaching science because they do not possess the content knowledge (Duschl et al., 2007; Miller, 2010; Saçkes, Trundle, Bell, & O'Connell, 2011; Yager, 2004); they are apprehensive about teaching science due to their own experiences in school (e.g., Abell, Appleton, & Hanuscin, 2010 use the term *science phobic,* p. 270); the emphasis on literacy does not allow time for science instruction (Greenfield et al., 2009), or they simply do not know how to implement inquiry science in their classrooms (Forbes & Davis, 2009). In contrast, the literature for practitioners rarely focuses on teacher deficits or constraints and provides suggestions for instruction and ways to get around obstacles that may impede effective science teaching.

Concluding Perspectives

Science Education Generally

The introduction to *Benchmarks for Science Literacy* (AAAS, 1993/2009) states:

> In a culture increasingly pervaded by science, mathematics, and technology, science literacy requires understandings and habits of mind that enable citizens to grasp what those enterprises are up to, to make some sense of how the natural and designed worlds work, to think critically and independently, to recognize and weigh alterative explanations of events and design trade-offs, and to deal sensibly with problems that involve evidence, numbers, patterns, logical arguments, and uncertainties. (p. xi)

Duschl (2008) identifies three overarching imperatives for science education: economic, democratic, and cultural. The economic imperative recognizes that science education is central to the goal of becoming and remaining competitive in the global marketplace. A typical response to the economic imperative has been to speak about how best to develop a "pipeline" that will lead to more college students majoring in science and going on to careers in science (Bhattacharjee, 2009; Russell & Atwater, 2005). However, in line with the democratic and cultural imperatives, Osborne (2007) argues that excellent science education is for everyone, not only for those who will have careers in science. He suggests that science educators need to change their focus from preparing future scientists who will eventually produce scientific knowledge to preparing future citizens who will be critical consumers of scientific knowledge. This broader focus will be of benefit even to future scientists because practicing scientists are so specialized that they are often uninformed about other areas of science.

Osborne (2007) suggests that explicitly adopting the goal of creating a scientifically literate citizenry should have the result of moving science education from the transmission/memorization of discrete facts to a focus on the major explanatory stories that the sciences offer, with an emphasis on conveying the key messages first and the details later. Osborne also suggests that explicitly adopting the goal of creating a scientifically literate citizenry should result in greater emphasis on science practice in the classroom, with students generating questions, collecting and interpreting evidence, engaging in evidence based argumentation, and so forth.

Scholars in the field of science education seem to have reached a consensus that, across all ages, authentic science learning and science proficiency involve active investigation of meaningful topics, the collection of evidence, and the use of language to exchange and evaluate observations, descriptions, predictions, conclusions, and explanations.

This consensus has, however, had little impact on classroom practice and student achievement across grade levels. Osborne (2007) writes that "the dominant form of science education that is common across the world rests on a set of values that have no merit" (p. 173), and Duschl et al. (2007) note that "after 15 years of focused standards-based reform, improvements in U.S. science education are modest at best" (p. 1).

Science Education at the Early Childhood Level

Visitors to child-oriented exhibits at science museums have very likely encountered crowds of highly enthusiastic and active children. Science-oriented magazines for children, such as *Ranger Rick* and *National Geographic Kids*, have survived in the marketplace for many years. However, young children have little exposure to science in school. How should we reconcile young children's high level of interest in science when it is made available either in the classroom or in informal learning environments with the minimal inclusion of science in early childhood education at the pre-K and primary levels? [9]

It is understandable that learning to read is a central goal of the early school years. But given what we know about the central roles of meaning-making and goal-directed activity in learning, why do teachers not more often capitalize on children's interest in learning about and understanding the natural world as a context within which children can practice and develop literacy skills? One reason is that teachers may simply not understand the importance of science education at the early childhood level or may not feel qualified to teach science. Early childhood teachers—particularly those who work at the pre-K level, but also those who are certified to teach at the K-6 level—are likely to have relatively weak science backgrounds themselves and relatively weak preparation in teaching science (e.g., California Council on Science and Technology, 2010; National Research Council, 2001).

Implications and Recommendations

We would like to end this chapter on an optimistic rather than pessimistic note. To that end, we have given considerable thought to what the impetus might possibly be for widespread implementation of developmentally appropriate, high-quality science education in early childhood classrooms. One of the most likely scenarios for widespread change is that science education will increase in the primary grades in response to atheoretical legislation such as the requirement of the No Child Left Behind Act that beginning in the 2007–2008 school year, all states assess children's science knowledge in the late elementary grades (the 3rd to 5th grade span). However, this type of impetus does not necessarily lead to developmentally appropriate and high-quality science education. In fact, it could be a cause for concern rather than optimism given the lack of teacher preparation in implementing the science-as-practice model of pedagogy (Forbes & Davis, 2009) and the lack of agreed upon measures for assessing what children learn when engaged in science-as-practice rather than in learning discrete facts.

Our work with more than a hundred individual teachers who have implemented the ScienceStart! Curriculum does give us cause for optimism at the microlevel. To varying degrees, but almost uniformly, these teachers have recognized the power of science to engage preschoolers' interest and the power of preschoolers to develop the inquiry skills, discourse skills, concepts, and vocabulary to participate in science practices (Cassata-Widera et al., 2008; Peterson & French, 2008). Science education at the early childhood level truly enhances school readiness, giving children the tools they need to move forward as active, self-regulated learners.

There are of course many early childhood classrooms where a great deal of student time is devoted to "doing science." This may occur because of the interests and skills of individual teachers, a principal's or superintendent's interest, or grant opportunities. While individual science-oriented programs appear to be engaging for children and attractive to parents, there is no effective mechanism to move toward expansion and widespread implementation of such programs.

With enough support/pressure from the federal government, it would be possible for the schools of education that prepare teachers to take a more proactive role in preparing early childhood teachers in science and for the states (which establish the requirements for teacher certification) to require that they do so. Teacher education programs need to place a great deal more emphasis on preparing early childhood teachers to teach science (National Research Council, 2001), and especially on ways to teach it as an integrative domain that gives purpose and meaning to developing language, literacy, and math skills and that provides a functional context within which to embed deliberate instruction in the academic components, such as alphabet knowledge, that are inherent in literacy learning (e.g., Katz, 2010).

Thoughtful integration of the literature based on empirical research and the literature directed toward practitioners could guide teacher preparation and professional development. Shakir-Costa and Haddad (2009) and Cullen, Akerson, and Hanson (2010) advocate the value of having teachers engage in action research around the inquiry process in their own classrooms. In action research, teachers act as researchers responsible for formulating hypotheses, collecting and analyzing data, and using their findings to propose ways to improve their own teaching. In Cullen et al.'s study, teachers were trained in how to implement action research in their classrooms, how to search for literature on their research topic, and how to interpret and think about the data collected and what the suggested implications for future practice might be. At the end of the process, the teachers provided insightful discussions about what they had learned about their classrooms, their students, and also their own teaching style from their experience with action research. They were also able to connect their personal process of data collection, analysis, and conclusion to the inquiry process experienced by a scientist.

Currently, the best recommendation we can make is that family members, teachers, principals, and superintendents take individual responsibility for supporting science learning for the children in their care. Superintendents and principals can provide leadership that welcomes inquiry-based science instruction in school. Teachers can develop their own science curriculum or purchase lesson plans/activity books. Parents and teachers can engage children in citizen science activities. Parents can make certain that their children have ample opportunities to learn science in informal settings—both in interaction with the family and in out-of-school/after-school programs.

Notes

1. State science standards for the elementary grades can be located using the Web site www.educationworld.com and some states also have posted pre-K science standards on their Web sites (e.g., Virginia Department of Education, 2007; Good Beginnings, *Hawaii Preschool Content Standards,* 2006; Arizona Department of Education, 2005).
2. These materials are online at http://eclkc.ohs.acf.hhs.gov/hslc/resources/cinema/Science%20Webcasts/ScienceWebcast.htm).
3. With financial support from the Merck Institute.
4. The first author has been involved in developing and implementing a preschool science curriculum since 1995; this has been known as "Preschool Curriculum for the 21st Century," "ScienceStart!" and "LiteraSci."
5. The other domains are language, literacy, creative arts, social and emotional development, approaches toward learning, motor skills, and physical health practices.
6. Although the skill of classification is never mentioned in the Head Start Science Indicators, 11 of 57 items (19%) on the Galileo Scales involve classification.
7. Lists of fiction and nonfiction books that can be used in conjunction with early childhood science lessons can be found at www.literasci.com. These are arranged by topic: measurement and mapping, color and light, properties of matter, neighborhood habitats, movement and machines.
8. This dichotomy does not capture the National Research Council's creation of practitioner oriented versions of their scholarly books *Learning Science in Informal Settings* and *Taking Science to School.*
9. The U.S. Department of Education (2010) estimates that in 2007 to 2008, children in grades 1 through 4 averaged 2.3 hours per week of science instruction, down from a high of 3 hours per week in 1992–1993. Exposure is undoubtedly much less for children in pre-K and kindergarten.

References

Abell, S. K., Appleton, K., & Hanuscin, D. L. (2010). *Designing and teaching the elementary science methods course.* New York: Routledge.

American Association for the Advancement of Science (AAAS). (1999). *Dialogue on early childhood science, mathematics, and technology education.* Washington, DC: Author.

American Association for the Advancement of Science (AAAS). (2009). *Benchmarks for science literacy.* Washington, DC: Author. (Original work published 1993)

American Association for the Advancement of Science (AAAS)/Pew Research Center. (2009, July 9). *Scientific achievements less prominent than a decade ago: Public praises science; Scientists fault public, media.* Press Release. Retrieved from http://people-press.org/files/legacy-pdf/528.pdf

America Competes Act. (2007). *National institute of standards and technology.* [Public Law 110-69]. Retrieved from http://www.nist.gov/mep/upload/PL110-69_8907.pdf

Arizona Department of Education. (2005). *Early learning standards.* Phoenix, AZ: Author. Retrieved from http://www.ade.az.gov/early-childhood/downloads/EarlyLearningStandards.pdf

Bagiati, A., Yoon, S. Y., Evangelou, D. & Ngambeki, I. (2010). Engineering curricula in early education: Describing the landscape of open resources. *Early Childhood Research & Practice, 12*(2). Retrieved from http://www.freepatentsonline.com/article/Early-Childhood-Research-Practice/248578497.html.

Baker, A. (1994). *White rabbit's color book.* Boston, MA: Kingfisher.

Beck, I. L., McKeown, M. G., & Kucan, L. (2002). *Bringing words to life: Robust vocabulary instruction.* New York: Guilford.

Bell, P., Lewenstein, B. V., Shouse, A., & Feder, M. (Eds.). (2009). *Learning science in informal environments: People, places, and pursuits.* Washington, DC: National Academies Press.

Bereiter, C. (1994). Implications of postmodernism for science, or, science as progressive discourse. *Educational Psychologist, 29*(1), 3–12.

Bergan, J., Bergan, J., Rattee, M, Feld, J. K., Smith, K., Cunningham, K., & Linne, K. (2003). *The Galileo system for electronic management of learning* (10th ed.). Tucson, AZ: Assessment Technology.

Berk, L. E, & Winsler, A. (1995). *Scaffolding children's learning: Vygotsky and early childhood education.* Washington, DC: National Association for the Education of Young Children.

Bhattacharjee, Y. (2009). Study finds science pipeline strong, but losing top students. *Science, 326*(5953), 654.

Bodrova, E., & Leong, D. J. (2003). Learning and development of preschool children from the Vygotskian perspective. In A. Kozulin, B. Gindis, V. S. Ageyev, & S. M. Miller (Eds.), *Vygotsky's educational theory in cultural context* (pp. 156–176). New York: Cambridge University Press.

Bodrova, E. & Leong, D. J. (2006). *Tools of the mind: The Vygotskian approach to early childhood education* (2nd ed.). Columbus, OH: Merrill/Prentice Hall.

Bowman, B. T., Donovan, M. S., & Burns, S. (Eds.). (2001). *Eager to learn: Educating our preschoolers.* Washington, DC: National Academies Press.

Bransford, J. D., Barron, B., Pea, R. D., Meltzoff, A., Kuhl, P., Bell, P.,.... Sabelli, N. H. (2006). Foundations and opportunities for an interdisciplinary science of learning. In R. K. Sawyer (Ed.), *The Cambridge handbook of the learning sciences* (pp. 19–34), New York, NY: Cambridge University Press.

Bransford, J. D., Brown, A. L., & Cocking, R. R. (1999). *How people learn.* Washington, DC: National Academies Press.

Bredekamp, S. (1986). *Developmentally appropriate practices in early childhood programs.* Washington, DC: National Association for the Education of Young Children.

Bredekamp, S., & Copple, C. (Eds.). (1997). *Developmentally appropriate practice in early childhood programs* (rev. ed.). Washington, DC: National Association for the Education of Young Children.

Brewer, W. F., & Samarapungavan, A. (1991). Children's theories vs. scientific theories: Differences in reasoning or differences in knowledge? In R. R. Hoffman & D. S. Palermo (Eds.), *Cognition and the symbolic process: Applied and ecological perspectives* (pp. 209–232). Hillsdale, NJ: Erlbaum.

Brophy, S., & Evangelou, D. (2007). *Precursors to engineering thinking.* Paper presented at the Annual Conference of the American Society of Engineering Education., Honolulu, HI. Retrieved from http://icee.usm.edu/icee/conferences/asee2007/papers/2926_PRECURSORS_TO_ENGINEERING_THINKING_PET_.pdf

Brophy, S., Klein, S., Portsmore, M., & Rogers, C. (2008). Advancing engineering education in p-12 classrooms. *Journal of Engineering Education, 97*(3), 369–387.

Brown, A. L. (1994). The advancement of learning. *Educational Researcher, 23*(8), 4–12.

Brown, A. L., & Campione, J. C. (1994). Guided discovery in a community of learners. In K. McGilly (Ed.), *Classroom lessons: Integrating cognitive theory and classroom practice* (pp. 229–270). Cambridge, England: Cambridge University Press.

Brown, A. L., & French, L. A. (1979). The zone of proximal development: Implications for intelligence testing in the year 2000. *Intelligence, 3*(3), 255–273.

Brown, A. L., Metz, K. E., & Campione, J. C. (1996). Social interaction and individual understanding in a community of learners: The influence of Piaget and Vygotsky. In A. Tryphon & J. Voneche (Eds.), *Piaget-Vygotsky: The social genesis of thought* (pp. 145–170). East Sussex, England: Psychology Press.

Bruner, J. (1983). *Child's talk: Learning to use language.* New York: Norton.

Bruner, J. (1985). Vygotsky: A historical and conceptual perspective. In J. Wertsch (Ed.), *Culture, communication and cognition: Vygotskian perspectives* (pp. 21–34). New York: Cambridge University Press.

Bruner, J. (1996). *The culture of education.* Cambridge, MA: Harvard University Press.

California Council on Science and Technology. (2010). *The preparation of elementary school teachers to teach science in California: Challenges and opportunities impacting teaching and learning science.* Sacramento, CA: Author. Retrieved from http://www.ccst.us/publications/2010/2010K-6.pdf

California Department of Education. (2010). *Desired results developmental portfolio preschool.* Sacramento, CA: Author. Retrieved from http://www.cde.ca.goav/sp/cd/ci/drdpforms.asp.

Cassata-Widera, A. E. (2010). *ScienceStart! Fidelity of implementation observation tool.* Nashville, TN: Vanderbilt University. (Unpublished instrument)

Cassata-Widera, A. E., Kato-Jones, Y., Duckles, J. M., Conezio, K., & French, L. A. (2008). Learning the language of science. *The International Journal of Learning, 15*(8) 141–152.

Chalufour, I., & Worth, K. (2003). *Discovering nature with young children.* St. Paul, MN: Redleaf.

Chalufour, I., & Worth, K. (2004). *Building structures with young children.* St. Paul, MN: Redleaf.

Chalufour, I., & Worth, K. (2005). *Exploring water with young children.* St. Paul, MN: Redleaf.

Chi, M. T. H. (1978). Knowledge structures and memory development. In R. Siegler (Ed.), *Children's thinking: What develops?* (pp. 73–96). Hillsdale, NJ: Erlbaum.

Chi, M. T. H. (2006). Two approaches to the study of experts' characteristics. In K. Ericsson, N. Charness, P. Feltovich, & R. Hoffman (Eds.), *The Cambridge handbook of expertise and expert performance* (pp. 21–30). New York: Cambridge University Press.

Chi, M. T. H., Hutchinson, J., & Robin, A. F. (1989). How inferences about novel domain-related concepts can be constrained by structured knowledge. *Merrill-Palmer Quarterly, 35*(1), 27–62.

Chi, M. T. H., & Koeske, R. D. (1983). Network representation of a child's dinosaur knowledge. *Developmental Psychology, 19*(1), 29–39.

Cole, M. (1996). *Cultural psychology: A once and future discipline.* Cambridge, MA: Harvard University Press.

Collins, A. (2006). Cognitive apprenticeship. In R. K. Sawyer (Ed.), *The Cambridge handbook of the learning sciences* (pp. 47–60). New York: Cambridge University Press.

Conezio, K., & French, L. (2002). Science in the preschool classroom: Capitalizing on children's fascination with the everyday world to foster language and literacy development. *Young Children, 57*(5), 12–18.

Copple, C., & Bredekamp, S. (Eds.). (2009). *Developmentally appropriate practice in early childhood programs serving children from birth through age 8.* (3rd ed.). Washington, DC: National Association for the Education of Young Children.

Crowley, K., & Jacobs, M. (2002). Building islands of expertise in everyday family activity. In G. Leinhardt, K. Crowley, & K. Knutson (Eds.), Learning conversations in museums (pp. 333–356). Mahwah, NJ: Erlbaum.

Cullen, T. A., Akerson, V. L., & Hanson, D. L. (2010). Using action research to engage K-6 teachers in nature of science inquiry as professional development. Journal of Science Teacher Education, 21(8), 971–972.

Duckles, J. (2010). Reconceptualizing active learning and science: Young children as active participants shaping family science practices. Paper presented at the Annual Meeting of the American Educational Research Association. Denver, CO.

Durant, J. (1993). What is scientific literacy? In J. Durant & J. Gregory (Eds.), Science and culture in Europe (pp. 129–138). London: Science Museum.

Duschl, R. A. (2008). Science education in three-part harmony: Balancing conceptual, epistemic and social learning goals. Review of Research in Education, 32(1), 268–291.

Duschl, R. A., Schweingruber, H. A., & Shouse, A. W. (Eds.). (2007). Taking science to school: Learning and teaching science in grades K-8. Washington, DC: National Academies Press.

Edelson, D. C., & Reiser, B. J. (2006). Making authentic practices accessible to learners: Design challenges and strategies. In R. K. Sawyer (Ed.), The Cambridge handbook of the learning sciences (pp. 335–354). New York: Cambridge University Press.

Engineering is Elementary. (2011). EiE: Engineering & technology lessons for children! Problem solving, inquiry, and innovation. Boston, MA: Museum of Science. Retrieved from: http://www.mos.org/eie/

European Commission. (1995). White paper on education and training: Teaching and learning towards the learning society. Luxembourg: Author. Retrieved from http://europa.eu/documents/comm/white_papers/pdf/com95_590_en.pdf

Finichel, M., & Schweingruber, H. A. (2010). Surrounded by science: Learning science in informal environments. Washington, DC: National Academies Press.

Fleer, M. (1999). Children's alternative views: Alternative to what? International Journal of Science Education, 21(2), 119–135.

Fleer, M. (2000). Working technologically: Investigations into how young children design and make during technology education. International Journal of Technology and Design Education, 10(1), 43–59.

Forbes, C. T., & Davis, E. A. (2010). Beginning elementary teachers' beliefs about the use of anchoring questions in science: A longitudinal study. Science Teacher Education, 94(2), 365–387.

French, L. A. (1985). Real-world knowledge as the basis for social and cognitive development. In J. B. Pryor & J. D. Day (Eds.), Social and developmental perspectives on social cognition (pp. 179–209). New York: Springer-Verlag.

French, L. A. (1996). "I told you all about it, so don't tell me you don't know": Two- year-olds and learning through language. Young Children, 51(2), 17–20.

French, L. A. (2004). Science as the hub of a coherent, integrated early childhood curriculum [Special issue]. Early Childhood Research Quarterly, 19(1), 138–149.

French, L. A., Conezio, K., & Boynton, M. (2002). Using science as the hub of an integrated early childhood curriculum: The ScienceStart! curriculum. In D. Rothenberg (Ed.), Issues in early childhood education: Curriculum, teacher education, and dissemination of information: Proceedings of the Lilian Katz symposium (pp. 303–312). Urbana, IL: ERIC-EECE.

French, L. A., & Nelson, K. (1985). Young children's understanding of relational terms: Some ifs, ors, and buts. New York: Springer-Verlag.

French, L. A. & Peterson, S. M. (2009). Learning language through preschool science. In C. Anderson, N. Scheuer, M. P. P. Echeverria, & E. Teubal (Eds.), Representational systems and practices as learning tools in different fields of knowledge (pp. 77–92). Rotterdam, the Netherlands: Sense.

Gallas, K. (1994). The languages of learning: How children talk, write, dance, draw, and sing their understanding of the world. New York: Teachers College Press.

Gallas, K. (1995). Talking their way into science: Hearing children's questions and theories, responding with curricula. New York: Teachers College Press.

Gee, J. P. (2005). Language in the science classroom: Academic social languages as the heart of school-based literacy. In R. K. Yerrick & W. M. Roth (Eds.), Establishing scientific classroom discourse communities: Multiple voices of teaching and learning research (pp. 19–38). Mahwah, NJ: Erlbaum.

Gelman, R. (1990). First principles organize attention to and learning about relevant data: Number and the animate-inanimate distinction as examples. Cognitive Science, 14(1), 79–106.

Gelman, R., & Brenneman, K. (2004). Science learning pathways for young children. Early Childhood Research Quarterly, 19(1), 150–158.

Gelman, R., Brenneman, K., Macdonald, G., & Román, M. (2010). Preschool pathways to science (PrePS): Facilitating scientific ways of thinking, talking, doing, and understanding. Baltimore, MD: Brookes.

Ginsburg, H. P., & Golbeck, S. L. (2004). Thoughts on the future of research on mathematics and science learning and education. Early Childhood Research Quarterly, 19(1), 190–200.

Good Beginnings. (2006). Hawaii preschool content standards (curriculum framework for programs for four-year-olds). Honolulu, HI: Author. Retrieved from http://www.goodbeginnings.org/images/uploads/Preschool_Standards_2006.pdf

Gopnik, A., & Schultz, L. (2004). Mechanisms of theory formation in young children. Trends in Cognitive Sciences, 8(1), 371–377.

Greenfield, D. B., Jirout, J., Dominguez, X., Greenberg, A., Maier, M., & Fuccillo, J. (2009). Science in the preschool program: A programmatic research agenda to improve school readiness. Early Education and Development, 20(2), 238–264.

Greeno, J. G. (2006). Learning in activity. In R. K. Sawyer (Ed.), The Cambridge handbook of the learning sciences (pp. 79–96). New York: Cambridge University Press.

Habashi, M. M., Graziano, W. G., Evangelou, D., & Ngambeki, I. (2009). Teacher influences on child interest in STEM careers. Proceedings of the Research in Engineering Education Symposium. Palm Cove, Queensland. Retrieved from http://rees2009.pbworks.com/f/rees2009_submission_100.pdf

Hapgood, S., & Palincsar, A. S. (2007). Where literacy and science intersect. Educational Leadership, 64(4), 56–60.

Hart, B., & Risley, T. R. (1995). Meaningful differences in the everyday experience of young American children. Baltimore, MD: Brookes.

Hart, B., & Risley, T. R. (1999). The social world of children learning to talk. Baltimore, MD: Brookes.

Hatano, G., & Inagaki, K. (2000). Domain-specific constraints of conceptual development. International Journal of Behavioral Development, 24(3), 267–275.

Head Start Resource Center. (n.d.). Head Start child outcomes framework.

Herrington, J., & Oliver, R. (2000). An instructional design framework for authentic learning environments. Educational Technology Research and Development, 48(3), 23–48.

Hirsch, E. D. (2003). Reading comprehension requires knowledge of words and the world. American Educator, 27(1), 10, 12–13, 16–22, 28–29, 44.

Howe, A. C. (1993). Science in early childhood education. In B. Spodek (Ed.), Handbook of research on the education of young children (pp. 225–235). New York: Macmillan.

Hurd, P. D. (1998). Scientific literacy: New minds for a changing world. Science Education, 82(3), 407–416.

Jeffers, A. T., Safferman, A. G., & Safferman, S. I. (2004). Understanding K-12 engineering outreach programs. Journal of Professional Issues in Engineering Education and Practice, 130(2), 95–108.

Katz, L. G. (2010, May 23–25). STEM in the early years. Paper presented at STEM in Early Education and Development, The Center for Early Education in Science, Technology, Engineering, and Mathematics at the University of Northern Iowa. Cedar Falls, Iowa.

Kesidou, S., & Roseman, J. E. (2002).How well do middle school science programs measure up? Findings from Project 2061's curriculum review. *Journal of Research in Science Teaching, 39*(6), 522–549.

Koralek, D., & Colker, L, (Eds.). (2003). *Spotlight on young children and science.* Washington, DC: National Association for the Education of Young Children.

Krajcik, J. S., & Blumenfeld, P. C. (2006). Project-based learning. In R. K. Sawyer (Ed.), *The Cambridge handbook of the learning sciences* (pp. 317–334), New York: Cambridge University Press.

Lehrer, R., & Schauble, L. (2006). Cultivating model-based reasoning in science education. In R. K. Sawyer (Ed.), *The Cambridge handbook of the learning sciences* (pp. 371–388). New York: Cambridge University Press.

Lemke, J. L. (1990). *Talking science: Language, learning, and values.* Norwood, NJ: Ablex.

Lind, K. K. (1999). *Science in early childhood: Developing and acquiring fundamental concepts and skills.* Paper presented at the Forum on Early Childhood Science, Mathematics, and Technology Education. Washington, DC: National Science Foundation. February 6–8, 1998. Retrieved from http://www.eric.ed.gov/PDFS/ED418777.pdf

Lionni, L. (1959). *Little blue and little yellow.* New York: Harper.

Metz, K. E. (1995). Reassessment of developmental constraints on children's science instruction. *Review of Educational Research, 65*(2), 93–127.

Metz, K. E. (1997). On the complex relation between cognitive development research and children's science curricula. *Review of Educational Research, 67*(1), 151–163.

Metz, K. E. (2004). Children's understanding of scientific inquiry: Their conceptualization of uncertainty in investigations of their own design. *Cognition and Instruction, 22*(2), 219–290.

Michaels, S., Shouse, A. W., & Schweingruber, H. A. (2008). *Ready, set, science! Putting research to work in K-8 science classrooms.* Washington, DC: National Academies Press.

Millar, R., & Osborne, J. F. (Eds.). (1998). *Beyond 2000: Science education for the future.* London: King's College London Press.

Miller, C. L. (2010). District leadership for science education: Using K-12 departments to support elementary science education under NCLB. *Science Educator, 19*(2), 22–30.

National Research Council. (1996). *National science education standards.* Washington, DC: National Academies Press.

National Research Council. (2001). *Educating teachers of science, mathematics, and technology: New practices for the new millennium.* Washington, DC: National Academies Press.

National Research Council. (2005). *Mathematical and scientific development in early childhood: A workshop summary.* Washington, DC: National Academies Press.

Nelson, K. (1986). *Event knowledge: Structure and function in development.* Hillsdale, NJ: Erlbaum.

Nelson, K. (1991). The matter of time: Interdependencies between language and thought in development. In S. A. Gelman & J. P. Byrnes (Eds.), *Perspectives on language and thought: Interrelations in development* (pp. 278–318). New York: Cambridge University Press.

Nelson, K. (1996). *Language in cognitive development: The emergence of the mediated mind.* New York: Cambridge University Press.

Nelson, K. (2007). *Young minds in social worlds.* Cambridge, MA: Harvard University Press.

Neuman, S. B. (2001). The role of knowledge in early literacy. *Reading Research Quarterly, 36*(4), 468–475.

Neuman, S. B. (2006). The knowledge gap: Implications for early education. In D. K. Dickinson & S. B. Neuman (Eds.), *Handbook of early literacy research* (Vol. 2, pp. 29–40). New York: Guilford.

Neuman, S. B. (2010). Lessons from my mother: Reflections on the National Early Literacy Panel report. *Educational Researcher, 39*(4), 301–304.

Neuman, S. B., & Celano, D. (2006). The knowledge gap: Implications of leveling the playing field for low-income and middle-income children. *Reading Research Quarterly, 41*(2), 176–201.

Newton, D. P. (2002). *Talking sense in science: Helping children understand through talk.* New York: Routledge.

Nguyen, S. P., & Rosengren, K. S. (2004). Parental reports of children's biological knowledge and misconceptions. *International Journal of Behavioral Development, 28*(5), 411–420.

Oberhauser, K. S., & Prysby, M. D. (2008). Citizen science: Creating a research army for conservation. *American Entomologist, 54*(2), 103–105.

Osborne, J. F. (2007). Science education for the twenty first century. *Eurasia Journal of Mathematics, Science & Technology Education, 3*(3), 173–184.

Osborne, J. F., & Collins, S. (2001). Pupils' views of the role and value of the science curriculum: A focus-group study. *International Journal of Science Education, 23*(5), 441–468.

Osborne, J. F., Simon, S., & Collins, S. (2003). Attitudes towards science: A review of the literature and its implications. *International Journal of Science Education, 25*(9), 1049–1079.

Pea, R. D. (1993). Learning scientific concepts through material and social activities: Conversational analysis meets conceptual change. *Educational Psychologist, 28*(3), 265–277.

Penuel, W. R., Bates, L., Pasnik, S., Townsend, E., Gallagher, L. P., Llorente, C., & Hupert, N. (2010). *The impact of a media-rich science curriculum on low-income preschoolers' science talk at home.* Paper presented at the 9th International Conference of the Learning Sciences, Chicago, IL. Retrieved from http://cct.edc.org/rtl/pdf/ICLS_RTL_Science_Paper_FINAL_for_CCT_Web.pdf

Peterson, S. M. (2009). Narrative and paradigmatic explanations in preschool science discourse. *Discourse Processes, 46*(4), 369–399.

Peterson, S. M., & French, L. A. (2008). Supporting young children's explanations through inquiry science in preschool. *Early Childhood Research Quarterly, 28*(3), 395–408.

Pratt, H., & Pratt, N. (2004). Integrating science and literacy instruction with a common goal of learning science content. In E. W. Saul (Ed.), *Crossing borders in literacy and science instruction: Perspectives on theory and practice* (pp. 395–405). Newark, DE: International Reading Association.

Program for International Student Assessment (PISA). (2010). *2009 results.* Retrieved from http://www.oecd.org/dataoecd/54/12/46643496.pdf

Rhoads, T. R., Walden, S. E., & Winter, B. A. (2004). Sooner elementary engineering and science—A model for after-school science clubs based on university and K-5 partnership. *Journal of STEM Education: Innovations and Research, 5*(3 & 4), 47–52.

Rivet, A. E., & Krajcik, J. S. (2008). Contextualizing instruction: Leveraging students' prior knowledge and experiences to foster understanding of middle school science. *Journal of Research in Science Teaching, 45*(1), 79–100.

Rogoff, B., & Wertsch, J. V. (Eds.). (1984). *Children's learning in the zone of proximal development* (New Directions for Child Development). San Francisco, CA: Jossey-Bass.

Russell, M. L., & Atwater, M. M. (2005). Traveling the road to success: A discourse on persistence throughout the science pipeline with African American students at a predominantly White institution. *Journal of Research in Science Teaching, 42*(6), 691–715.

Saçkes, M., Trundle, K. C., Bell, R. L., & O'Connell, A. A. (2011). The influence of early science experience in kindergarten on children's immediate and later science achievement: Evidence from the early childhood longitudinal study. *Journal of Research in Science Teaching, 48*(2), 217–235.

Shakir-Costa, K., & Haddad, L. (2009). Practitioner research success! *Science and Children, 46*(5), 25–27.

Smith, J., di Sessa, A., & Roschelle, J. (1993). Misconceptions reconceived: A constructivist analysis of knowledge in transition. *Journal of the Learning Sciences, 3*(2), 115–163.

Stern, L., & Roseman, J. E. (2004). Can middle-school science textbooks help students learn important ideas? Findings from Project 2061's curriculum evaluation study: Life science. *Journal of Research in Science Teaching, 41*(6), 538–568.

Trends in International Mathematics and Science Study (TIMSS). (2007). *2007 International mathematics report*. Chestnut Hill, MA: TIMSS & PIRLS International Study Center, Boston College. Retrieved from http://nces.ed.gov/timss/results07.asp

U.S. Department of Education. (2010). *Schools and staffing survey*. Retrieved from http://nces.ed.gov/surveys/sass/tables/sass0708_005_t1n.asp

Van Meeteren, B. D., & Zan, B. (2010, May 23–25). *Revealing the work of young engineers in early childhood education*. Paper presented at STEM in Early Education and Development: An invitational working conference on early childhood science education. The Center for Early Education in Science, Technology, Engineering, and Mathematics at the University of Northern Iowa. Cedar Falls, Iowa.

Virginia Department of Education. (2007). *Preschool curriculum review rubric and planning tool*. Richmond, VA: Author. Retrieved from http://www.doe.virginia.gov/instruction/early_childhood/preschool_initiative/preschool_rubric.pdf

Viswanath, K., & Finnegan, J. R. (1996). The knowledge gap hypothesis: Twenty-five years later. In B. Burleson (Ed.), *Communication yearbook 19* (pp. 187–227). Thousand Oaks, CA: Sage.

Vygotsky, L. S. (1978). *Mind in Society*. Cambridge, MA: Harvard University Press.

Walsh, E. S. (1989). *Mouse paint*. New York: Harcourt.

Wendell, K. B., Connolly, K. G., Wright, C. G., Jarvin, L., & Rogers, C. (2010). *Children learning science through engineering: An investigation of four engineering-design-based curriculum modules*. Poster presented at the International Conference of the Learning Sciences, Chicago, IL.

Wertsch, J. V. (1979). From social interaction to higher psychological processes. *Human Development, 22*(1), 1–22.

Wertsch, J. V. (1981). The concept of activity in Soviet psychology: An introduction. In J. V. Wertsch (Ed.), *The concept of activity in Soviet psychology*. Armonk, NY: M.E. Sharpe.

Wertsch, J. V. (1985). *Vygotsky and the social formation of mind*. Cambridge, MA: Harvard University Press.

Yager, R. E. (2004). Mind engagement: What is not typically accomplished in typical science instruction. In E. W. Saul (Ed.), *Crossing borders in literacy and science instruction: Perspectives on theory and practice* (pp. 408–419). Newark, DE: International Reading Association.

Zan, B. (2010, May 23–25). [Convener]. STEM in early education and development: An invitational working conference on early childhood science education. The Center for Early Education in Science, Technology, Engineering and Mathematics at the University of Northern Iowa. Cedar Falls, Iowa.

13

Techno-Tykes

Digital Technologies in Early Childhood

MARINA UMASCHI BERS AND ELIZABETH R. KAZAKOFF
Tufts University

During the last decade new technologies have been playing a major role in the lives of young children. The focus of this chapter is on how these new technologies are having a positive impact on children's learning and development and how young children, ages 2 to 7, are making use of those technologies in different contexts. While some researchers have written about the negative impact of new technologies in early childhood (see Cordes & Miller, 2000), this chapter focuses on the positive aspects. To that end, we explore the use of new technologies in early childhood through the Positive Technological Development (PTD) framework (Bers, 2006; Bers, 2010). PTD is a natural extension of the computer literacy and technological fluency movements that have influenced the world of education (Pearson, Greg, Young, & Thomas, 2002), but it adds psychosocial, civic, and ethical components to the cognitive ones, which have a strong presence in the disciplines that study human development (Bers, 2008).

PTD examines the developmental tasks of a child growing up in our digital era, and provides a model for developing and evaluating technology-rich youth programs. The explicit end goal of PTD programs is not to teach children to use technology to accomplish a task, as the computer literacy movement does; neither is it solely focused on helping young children to design and program their own meaningfully interactive projects, as those who seek technological fluency do (Bers, 2010). Rather, the goal is to mentor children in the positive uses of technology so they can have more fulfilling lives by making the world a better place (Bers, 2006).

New technologies are changing the developmental landscape for young people. The goal of this chapter is to inform and inspire educators, parents, and influential adults in children's lives to use technology with young children in developmentally appropriate ways.

New Technologies

We define new technologies as emerging digital tools that involve cutting-edge developments. New technologies in early childhood come in various forms and platforms such as computer-mediated software programs, video/audio learning instruments, robotic building kits, electronic toys, handheld and mobile devices, and sensors embedded in everyday objects. New technologies can engage a child playing by herself or can involve multiple children; they can be used as standalone devices, connected to the Internet, or integrated into classroom curriculum. New technologies make possible different kinds of learning opportunities, new ways for peer social interactions, and many possibilities for creativity, social, and cognitive development.

The history of technological devices has changed dramatically in the past 40 years, thanks to less expensive and more powerful batteries, LCDs, touch screens, and increased memory. Children now have access to cell phones, digital cameras, digital book readers, digital media players, and smart toys (Buckleitner, 2009). Current and future generations will grow up surrounded by these new technologies and others we have yet to imagine. Parents and teachers have a duty to raise and educate children to become digitally intelligent in addition to mastering the classic school subjects (Prensky, 2008 as cited in Buckleitner, 2009).

The children born in the 1990s are the first generation of children entering Piaget's stage of formal operations, described by the ability to think in a logical and abstract way (Piaget & Inhelder, 1969), with access to new technologies, such as smart phones and YouTube. They have their e-mail and social networking programs, such as MySpace, Facebook, and Twitter all in their pockets. The class of 2012 is the first group to come to cognitive maturity with the new digital technologies of today (Buckleitner, 2009). Young children are coming of age surrounded by new technologies that will be prominent forces in their lives (Berson & Berson, 2010). Research is needed to understand the impact of these new technologies on the development of children and how children are using and appropriating these tools in their own ways.

Young children learn in different ways from older children or adults. For example, children in Piaget's sensorimotor to preoperational stages may understand concrete concepts, but abstract ideas such as symbolic representations, are more difficult for them to grasp (Elkind, 1986; Piaget & Inhelder, 1969). New technologies have the potential to bridge these gaps. An iPhone, for example, allows for easy transition between multiple representations of a concept. A child can see a picture of an animal and the spelling of its name; while hearing the sound of the word and the sound the animal makes, all from the same device (Buckleitner, 2009).

Widespread Use of New Technologies

Children are exposed to new technologies before ever making it to their preschool classroom. Even if parents are not handing over their iPad, there are still digital technologies everywhere—from sinks that "know" where little hands are to the GPS in their parent's car. Due to the ubiquitous nature of new technologies, some parents have begun to revisit the American Academy of Pediatrics (1999) recommendation of no screen time at all before the age of 2 as they believe that their children will need to be digitally literate and computer savvy to succeed in the 21st century (Calvert, Rideout, & Woolard, 2005). According to a 2007 Kaiser Foundation study, 70% of parents of children younger than 2 years of age allow their children screen time (Vanderwater et al., 2007).

Whether children are formally introduced to new technologies through parents or just encounter them in their surroundings, they are a large part of young children's lives and, therefore, important to study. Currently, 75% of U.S. households have broadband Internet access (Pew Research, 2010a), 93% of children 6 to 9 live in a home with a cell phone (Sesame Workshop, 2007), 19% of children grades K-2 have access to a smartphone with Internet connectivity, 53% have access to a desktop computer, 31% to a laptop, and 32% to an mp3 player (Project Tomorrow, 2009). Twenty-seven percent of 5- to 6-year-olds use a computer, for an average of 50 minutes per day (Vanderwater et al., 2007).

A gap in computer access has developed, however, between African American and rural households and European American households. Only 56% of African American adults have broadband in the home and only 50% of rural households do so (Pew Research, 2010a). Increasingly, Internet connectivity for these groups, and people across the globe, comes in the form of mobile technologies (Shuler, 2009b. In 2010, 64% of African Americans accessed the Internet from their mobile phone, and cell phone ownership

among African Americans and Latinos is higher than among European Americans (87% vs. 80%; Pew Research, 2010b).

Cell phone use is quickly becoming ubiquitous. More than half the world's population owns a cell phone. Children under 12 are the fastest growing group of mobile technology users (Shuler, 2009a). Between 2005 and 2008, mobile device ownership among children ages 4 to 14 doubled (NPD Group, 2008). Cell phones are cheaper, easy to transport, and easier to repair than traditional computers, which has led to their rapid growth in countries outside the United States. Whereas Americans tend to own multiple devices, people in many other countries access the Internet exclusively by cellular devises (World Economic Forum, 2010).

With cell phones, come apps (mobile applications). Almost half of the 100 best-selling apps for smartphones (47%) in 2009 were designed for preschool and elementary aged children; by April 2009, there were already 21,000 app games for young children compared to just a couple hundred for Nintendo DS or Playstation PSP (Shuler, 2009b). Thirty-five percent of apps are aimed at preschool children and, of the top 25 apps, over half of those are designed for the preschool age group (Shuler, 2009a). The most popular areas are early literacy, foreign language, and math, costing between 99 cents and $2.99. The low cost of these apps and the widespread availability of mobile devices, make apps a key area of development for educational material in the coming years (Shuler, 2009a, 2009b).

Early childhood is a time when children learn about their world and how to interact with it socially, and now, digitally. Children spend almost as much time with digital technologies as they do learning in school, leading to an opportunity to leverage these technologies (Shuler, 2007). Thus, we should ask ourselves not only what kinds of technologies are young people using, how often, and in what context, but most importantly, what are young children doing with these technologies. Are they using them in a way that is consistent with developmentally appropriate practice? Are children being supported by these technologies so that they engage in the developmental tasks appropriate for their age?

Interactive Fears

Through the centuries, the invention of all new technologies has been associated with a consistent fear regarding the impact that new technology will have on children. This fear happened with the invention of books, movies, radio, and now the Internet and mobile devices. However, one of the differences between the old concerns and the new ones is the interactive nature of digital technologies (Wartella & Jennings, 2000).

In the digital world, children not only consume but can also create content and interact with others. The increased interactivity can yield a potential benefit but it can also be harmful. On the one hand, with digital media, it is harder to protect children from accessing negative advertising, violent, or sexual content. Unlike television, there is less control over the online content (Belvins & Anton, 2008). Young children who are not yet cognitively developed past the preoperational stage might have trouble differentiating between what is programming versus advertising and what is real versus make-believe, which can be troublesome when viewing digital media (Piaget & Inhelder, 1969; Troseth, 2003). Young children may also lack the vocabulary necessary for insightful, metacognitive, evaluative explanations of their own behavior and may lack the ability to communicate about the content they are exposed to or their reactions to the content (Fleer, 1999).

Early on, Elkind (1986) argued that technology could amplify a young child's limitations in thinking. For example, he suggested that even though young children who were exposed to the Logo programming language could learn the sequences necessary for creating a computer program, they did not have yet the cognitive capacity to understand the rotation of the computer cursor. This lack of fundamental basic understanding could then lead to distress.

In addition, arguments previously made about television are similar to arguments made today about the Internet. Some researchers believe that rapid access to information and dozens of links to click online may be limiting human abilities to read deeply and concentrate and that there are fundamental brain changes occurring when we read information online (Carr, 2010; Small & Vorgan, 2008; Wolf, 2007). In 1986, Elkind also proposed that the rapid introduction of concepts on screen (i.e., *Sesame Street*) could be contributing to children's attention difficulties. With each new technology, similar concerns persist.

The digital world also brings about some new concerns, particularly around mobile technologies. There are concerns regarding the impact on physical health, the difficulty in monitoring activity, the potential for distraction, and the complexity of using the keyboards for children whose fine motor skills have not yet fully developed. Eighty-five percent of teachers surveyed by the Sesame Workshop in 2008 believe cell phones have no place in schools. This response was consistent even among teachers in their early 20s, who had grown up with cell phones (Shuler, 2009a).

The primary concern surrounding new technologies and children relates to the free accessibility provided by tools such as the Internet. This accessibility might mean access to misinformation, pornographic and violent online content, advertising, and communication with potentially dangerous people. Concerns also persist around the computer as a means of isolation for children (Cordes & Miller, 2000) and a replacement for other activities (Bus & Neuman, 2009), particularly those involving physical activity.

Positive Use of Technology: The PTD Framework

From a theoretical perspective, PTD integrates ideas from the fields of computer-mediated communication, computer-supported collaborative learning, and constructionist learning through technology, with research in applied development science and positive youth development. PTD focuses on positive behaviors supported by the technology and how those behaviors can, in turn, promote positive development (Bers, 2010).

Research on PTD, a framework that guides the design of technologically rich educational programs for children and teenagers, has shown technologies that support positive development and engage youngsters in the following activities (Bers, 2006, 2010):

Content Creation

The most powerful way in which children can use new technologies is to create personally meaningful projects. In the same way that young children use paintbrushes and clay to make art projects, technologies provide a new medium, programming tools, to add interactivity to their creations. Although young children are not developmentally ready to engage with sophisticated programming tools, research has shown that, when presented with developmentally appropriate interfaces, children as young as 4 years old can use different technologies to make their own projects come alive (Bers, 2008; Bers et al., 2006; Bers & Horn, 2010; Johnson, 2003). Children are not merely consuming information technology; they take an active role in creating, manipulating, and disseminating information (Berson, 2003).

Through the process of content creation, children develop *competence* regarding 21st century skills such as digital literacy (Ba, Tally, & Tsikalas, 2002; Karlstrom, Cerratto-Pargman, & Knutsson, 2008; McMillan, 1996;). Twenty-first century literacy means connecting digital dots, across media, including areas yet to be developed (Jones-Kavalier & Flannigan, 2008), and gaining skills in areas beyond the traditional subjects of reading, writing, and arithmetic. Twenty-first century skills include literacies in media, information, and communication technologies; in global awareness and in finance, business, entrepreneurship, and civic engagement (Wang, Berson, Haruszewicz, Hartle, & Rosen, 2010).

Technologies that enable children to become programmers can be powerful tools for teaching old and new skills and concepts (Bers, 2008; Clements, 2002; Papert, 1980), especially those related to problem solving and early math skills. For example, a large scale study of children using the Logo programming language demonstrated that children in grades K–6 scored significantly higher on mathematics, reasoning, and problem-solving tests (Clements, Batista, & Sarama, 2001). In addition, children can learn skills beyond those directly related to technology. Kazakoff and Bers (2010) found that kindergarten aged children who participated in computer programming workshops showed statistically significant gains in sequencing skills. These skills are foundational not only to mathematics and programming, but also to early literacy.

In order to create content, children engage in a design process which, like the scientific method, invites them to problem-solve. The kinds of technologies that promote content creation tend to belong to the family of constructionist learning environments that offer children tools to construct open-ended projects (Resnick, 2006; Resnick, Bruckman, & Martin, 1996), such as programming languages for children, or hands-on materials and manipulatives, such as building blocks and robotic construction kits (Bers, 2008). These constructionist technologies are in contrast with those belonging to the family of computer-assisted instructional instruments that use a drill and practice approach (such as computer software that teaches numbers and vocabularies that are commonly used in early childhood). Some examples of drill and practice software are

Math Blaster ® (www.knowledgeadventure.com/
  mathblaster/),
Millie's Math House (Edmark, 2005)
Bailey's Book House (www.edmark.com).

There are very few tools explicitly designed for young children to create content in a constructionist way. Examples include

KidPix (http://www.mackiev.com/kid_pix.html)
Robotics construction kits such
Lego® WeDo® (http://www.legoeducation.us) and
  CHERP (http://ase.tufts.edu/DevTech/tangiblek/
  research/cherp.asp)
Logo (http://www.microworlds.com/solutions/mwju-
  nior.html)

In addition, simply using digital cameras and voice recorders can allow children to create their own movies, stories, and slide shows. Digital cameras and audio recorders can be used to help children go beyond their egocentric thinking, allowing them to hear and see their surroundings and the people and objects in their world (Ching, Wang, & Kedem, 2006). Children interact with these tools in their households and are familiar with their function. Research needs to be conducted in order to create a powerful curriculum for their use and further integration into classrooms.

Creativity

New technologies that integrate multimedia tools allow children to generate new ideas and express them in innovative ways. Information and communication technologies incite creativity (Berson & Berson, 2010). Despite worries that computers stifle creativity, research has found that when used well, computers actually can help creativity bloom (Clements & Sarama, 2003). When children are engaged in creating their own computer-based projects and, in the process, find themselves solving technical problems in creative ways, they start to develop a sense of confidence in their learning potential.

Thus, in early childhood the most promising technolo-gies are those that invite creativity and the exploration of different strategies as opposed to efficiency in problem solving. For example, when a 4-year-old uses KidPix to create a story and animates the characters with motion and music and then presents a slideshow to her parents, or when a 5-year-old uses the CHERP (Bers & Horn, 2010) robotic programming language to make animals that can dance and move around in search of food, technology is opening a door to creativity (Bers, 2008; Johnson, 2003).

By combining recyclables and traditional art materials with technological components, young children can take a robotic base and turn it into anything they want; from a monster truck to a kitty cat to a flower for an interactive garden (Bers, 2008; Bers, Ponte, Juelich, Vietra, & Schenker, 2002; Rusk, Resnick, Berg, & Pezalla-Granlund, 2008). Robots are not just creatures such as Wall-E and R2D2, robotics can be a creative play space for storytelling, self-expression, and cultural awareness. Basic computer programs, such as Microsoft Paint or PowerPoint afford children opportunities to draw and manipulate objects and pictures. Music software can provide children with a medium for creating their own music, beyond using sometimes limited and expensive musical instruments.

Computers can be programmed so they can be anything to anyone, taking on a "thousand forms" for a "thousand functions" and appeal to a "thousand tastes" (Papert, 1980). This is the power of digital technology as an educational and artistic tool.

Collaboration

Research has shown that computers might instigate new forms of collaboration among young children, such as helping and instructing behaviors, discussion, and cooperation (New & Cochran, 2007). Different types of technologies are specifically designed to promote social interaction among users and may be used in a context that facilitates positive peer interaction. Children engage more frequently at turn taking, cooperative play, and language use at a computer than when using puzzles and blocks (Genishi, McCollum, & Strand, 1985). Children also prefer to work in teams rather than individually when using computers. Furthermore, computers allow for collaboration via e-mail, electronic field trips, and video conferencing with other classrooms; social interactions that were previously not possible due to physical location (National Association for the Education of Young Children [NAEYC], 1996).

For young children who are in the developmental process of learning how to work with others, the design features of the technology might promote social and prosocial development. Classic developmental theorists such as Piaget (1928) and Vygotsky (1978) both discussed the influence of children on one another in furthering cognitive development. Early childhood is a time of egocentrism. Collaboration with other children while using technology may help to foster interactions between peers who would otherwise be focused on their own thoughts and might lead to a child engaging in partnerships that involve her or his zone of proximal development. For example, a child who is better skilled at using the mouse or browsing the Web might work together with a child who has had less exposure to the technology; a child who has used a digital camera at home might show another child which button to press, and children may show each other their favorite smartphone apps and instruct one another on initial play instructions. Research shows that there is more spontaneous peer teaching and helping at a computer screen than during other classroom activities (Clements & Nastasi, 1992).

New technologies also have the benefit of being smaller, from netbooks to iPhones. Computers no longer fill entire rooms! This size element enables a child to easily collaborate with others. A piece of technological equipment can be easily picked up and brought across the room to a friend, teacher, or parent. This also gives the child the opportunity to move her body; there is no need to just sit at a computer. Children can make their own songs and videos to dance to, or act out the actions of their robots. Children can carry the laptop to show off their work to anyone around them or they can climb onto dad's lap to explore an iPad app with him. The mobility of new technologies lends itself to interactions.

Communication

Although in some cases the term communication is defined as an "exchange of data and information," when thinking about new technologies and young children, here we focus on communication as meaning the mechanisms that promote a sense of connection between peers or with adults. Technologies that effectively facilitate social interaction also promote language and literacy development. Activities around technologies that support interactions among peers by encouraging peer learning, peer teaching, and cooperation inevitably become venues for language-rich exchanges. At the computer, for example, research has shown that children speak twice as many words per minute than at other nontechnology related play activities such as Play-Doh and building blocks (New & Cochran, 2007) and speak to their peers nine times more than when working on traditional puzzles (Muller & Perlmutter, 1985). With mobile devices, children and parents can turn any moment, such as waiting in a doctor's office, or waiting in line at the grocery store, into interactive learning times. There are thousands of apps, ones for creativity and drawing (Brushes, Scribble), fun and education (Wheels on the Bus, Cute Math, Animal Match), ones that are just for fun (iPlayPhone, TicTacToe), and traditional stories (Dr. Seuss) that parents and children can explore together.

With products such as Skype, children are able to communicate face-to-face with their grandparents and loved ones. This can potentially eliminate the problems that arise when children, having not yet grasped object permanence (Piaget, 1954), try to engage in non-face-to-face communication. With Wikis, Web site, Google groups, and dozens of photo sharing programs, children's work and pictures from the day can be posted online, on password protected pages, for parents to view; thus bringing the classroom to the parents and providing the parent and child with many specific discussion points beyond "What did you do in school today?"

While even standalone drill and practice computer software can help children read and strengthen their vocabulary recall, the impact of technology is greatest with regard to language development when it is also used to facilitate peer interactions rather than as a replacement for teachers or tutors (New & Cochran, 2007). Research shows that when children are using computers, they are more likely to ask other children for advice and help, even if an adult is present, thus increasing socialization (Wartella & Jennings, 2002). Even in situations where each child has an individual computer or other piece of digital equipment to work with, children still choose to form groups (Druin, 1998). Children learn from each other and build communication skills by sharing, discussing, and asking questions about the new technologies they are using. They begin to move past parallel play to engage with the technology and each other. In addition, as children begin to explore virtual worlds (ex. Panwapa, Club Penguin) they utilize conversational scripts to continue learning about conversational patterns and communicating with others—the parent sitting next to them and the child across the globe. The growing trend of virtual worlds specifically developed for children is also having an impact in early childhood (Beals & Bers, 2009).

Community Building.

Early childhood education involves working both with the child on an individual basis, and with the child as a participant in her different communities. This challenge is also present in the theories that inform the design of technologies. For example, the Computer Supported Collaborative Learning (CSCL) paradigm (Koshmann, 1996) shifts the process of cognition as residing within the head of one individual to the view that cognition is situated within a particular community of learning or practice (Lave & Wenger, 1991). Therefore, educational technologies designed within this paradigm take seriously the need to provide tools for community building and community scaffolding of learning. This is well-aligned with the PTD framework (Bers, 2006) used to organize the ideas in this section. New technologies should promote children, even in early childhood, to see themselves as making contributions to the learning environment and their community. For example, new programming environments, such as Scratch (scratch.mit.edu) have vibrant online communities of sharing, contribution, and collaboration (Resnick et al., 2009).

In the spirit of the Reggio Emilia approach started by the Municipal Infant-Toddler Centers and Preschools of Reggio Emilia in Italy after World War II, new technologies

[handwritten: learn morals via interaction stories]

[handwritten left margin: new logic]

can encourage children's projects to be shared with the community via an open house, demo day, or exhibitions (Rinaldi, 1998), as well as by posting them online. This provides authentic opportunities for children to share and celebrate the process and products of their learning with family, friends, and community members.

Digital technologies allow us to be connected to the world at the click of a button. The children of the 21st century can communicate and collaborate both with the person next to them and someone across the globe. Community building and collaboration within and across cultures is a skill for young children to begin developing early, as it will be essential in their futures (Wang et al., 2010). Panwapa (http://www.panwapa.org/) developed by Sesame Workshop is an example of an online network to connect young children across the globe and so that they can learn about a variety of cultures, including their own.

[handwritten left margin: cultural learning]

Choices of Conduct

From a moral development standpoint, early childhood is a time of egocentrism and an early development of perspective taking. It is around this time that children begin to understand the concept of fairness (Colby & Kohlberg, 1987). New technologies may support this process by providing children with the opportunity to experiment with "what if" questions and potential consequences, and to provoke examination of values and exploration of *character traits.* Most explorations of the moral and ethical domain though new technologies happen later on, when children are avid users of the Internet and might face cyberbullying (Li, 2006, 2007) and the temptations of piracy (Chiou, Huang, & Lee, 2005; Logsdon, Thompson, & Reid, 1994). However, it is never too early to being teaching and modeling appropriate cybersafety and "netiquette" to young children (Berson & Berson, 2004; Shea, 1994; Straker, Pollock, & Burgess-Limerick, 2006). Virtual communities designed for young children, such as

Panwapa (http://www.panwapa.org/) and
Disney's Club Penguin (http://www.clubpenguin.com/)

do have safety features built in, such as preset chat scripts. These begin to provide models for appropriate behavior. Web sites, such as Webkinz (http://www.webkinz.com/) provide an opportunity for children to learn about taking care of pets and also integrate a social networking component. In addition, Webkinz integrates a physical component (stuffed animal) with the virtual world. However, sites such as Webkinz have been criticized for promoting consumerism, consumptionism, and competition (Dellinger-Pate & Conforti, 2010).

While the Internet is a natural playground for exploring issues of character, other new technologies might also be used with this purpose. For example, in our work with robotics and kindergarten-aged children, special attention

is paid to helping children explore personal and moral values by placing them in situations that invite them to make a conscious choice of conduct (Bers, 2008). For example, most robotic programs give each group of children an already sorted kit with all the LEGO building pieces and other materials to build a robot. On our work on the TangibleK program we take a different approach. We sort all materials by types and placed them in bins in the center of the room (instead of giving an already sorted robotic kit to each child or group). Thus children learn how to take what they need without depleting the bins of the "most wanted" pieces, such as special sensors or the colorful LEGO minifigures. They also learn how to negotiate for what they need. Our TangibleK program, inspired by the PTD philosophy, focuses not only on learning about robotics but also on helping young children develop an inner compass to guide their actions in a just and responsible way (Bers, 2010).

Future Directions

Children are growing up surrounded by technology but little is known about what impact this has on their learning and development. The public discourse regarding new technologies tends to group them altogether and disregard the design affordances of each of them and what developmental tasks they are best matched at supporting and enhancing. Computer games do not necessarily impact a child in the same way as an iPhone app, a robotic toy kit, technologically enhanced book, or a programming environment. Each new technology must be independently researched. What may be true for a computer is not necessarily true for an iPad and vice versa. We must be careful not to assume that all screens are created equal.

Research indicates new technologies, such as cell phone apps, may have a positive impact on vocabulary and literacy skills in 3 to 7 year olds (Chiong & Shuler, 2010). Developmentally appropriate computer programming in early childhood has also shown a positive impact on sequencing skills (Kazakoff & Bers, 2010) and computer use has shown positive impact on cognitive abilities such as abstraction, problem solving, and structural knowledge (Clements & Sarama, 2002; Haugland, 1992; Wang & Ching, 2003). Bers's work has also explored how, when presented with a developmentally appropriate interface, such as a tangible programming environment, kindergarteners can understand powerful computational ideas such as sequencing, control flow, loops, and branches and develop sophisticated levels of computational thinking (Bers, 2008; Bers & Horn, 2010; Bers et al., 2002).

Research is mixed on the integration of technology into conventional storybooks (Bus & Newman, 2009). Commercially available products for young children, such as LeapFrog's Tag Reading System help to digitally scaffold young children's reading comprehension strategies and encourage engagement in reading by asking questions of the reader that reinforce the storyline and character development (Gray, Bulat, Jaynes, & Cunningham, 2009). Books embedded with technological and interactive components have also been found to be distracting when animations and interactive components are not part of the storyline. These distractions may negatively impact comprehension of the story (Labbo & Kuhn, 2000).

We are in dire need of additional research to be conducted on the impact of new technologies on learning, personal-social development, and attention in early childhood. There is a body of research on the impact of television on young children (see Moses, 2008; Thakkar, Garrison, & Christakis, 2006; Uchikoshi, 2009 for a review) but not much for the new technologies, especially in regard to early childhood or the differences between new technologies. There are many unanswered questions, such as: What impact are new technologies having on early childhood education? What will young children need to know in order to be digitally literate and successful in the 21st century and beyond? What do children know about the technological worlds around them? What are the long term implications of growing up in the digital age? How can we create developmentally appropriate curricula for studying new technologies, such as laptops, cell phones, video recorders, cameras, to name a few, in order to ensure children can navigate the digital world and adapt to future technologies yet to be invented? Or, perhaps more importantly, How do we adequately prepare our children to be the people who create the future of technology and compete in a global economy?

Conclusion

Our forefathers believed children could not learn to read before age 6 or 7 (Hall, Larson, & Marsh, 2003), and we must not make the same assumptions about digital literacy. Historically, from 1883 when the word *literacy* first appeared in the dictionary until the late 1970s/early 80s it was believed children could not learn to read until ages 6½ or 7. Eventually, psychologists began to realize that children were certainly learning about words, letters, and language earlier than the point when they entered formal school because they were growing up surrounded by print, newspapers, billboards, and books.

The same holds true for new technologies. Children are exposed to the digital world continuously; it is part of their environment just like billboards, newspapers, books, and magazines. The time has come to challenge historical assumptions of what is developmentally appropriate and start teaching young children the skills they need to know to understand the world around them, a world that is increasingly more digital every day.

Although some uses of new technologies have come into the early childhood classrooms, they have not necessarily produced the expected outcomes. Too quickly they are becoming "oversold and underused" (Cuban, 2001). While these tools have the potential to enhance learning, Papert (1987) reminds us of the dangers of falling into the tech-

nocentric fallacy, the assumption that technology by itself can produce changes. New tools are only one of the many elements of the social and cultural context in which learning takes place and it is naïve to expect to introduce a new element and observe change resulting in the entire system.

The technocentric fallacy has largely permeated the past and present of educational technology. For example, research has found that, despite the nationwide large investment in new equipment and wiring of public schools, most of the computers "end up being souped-up typewriters" used in unimaginative ways (Cuban, 2001).

Technology is such an integral part of a child's daily life that learning environments without it are out of touch with a child's reality (Berson & Berson, 2010). However, teachers are not well prepared to know how to effectively integrate technology into the curriculum, how to craft developmentally appropriate technology-rich programs, or how to rethink the curriculum in the light of new technologies. These problems are in part due to the technocentric approach that puts too much emphasis on the technology and very little on the conditions in which the technology will be used. Making it possible for educators and children to use computers expressively and in creative ways involves not just the deployment or development of new tools, but also a framework to provide social support for learning and new supporting structures at both the micro- and macrolevels of the educational system, thus, our choice to organize this chapter on the positive impact of new technologies on early childhood around the PTD framework.

References

American Academy of Pediatrics. (1999). Media education. *Pediatrics, 104*, 341–342.

Ba, H., Tally, W., & Tsikalas, K. (2002). Investigating children's emerging digital literacies. *The Journal of Technology, Learning, and Assessment, 1*(4), 1–48.

Beals, L., & Bers, M. U. (2009). A developmental lens for designing virtual worlds for children and youth. *The International Journal of Learning and Media, 1*(1), 51–65.

Belvins, J. L., & Anton, F. (2008). Muted voices in the legislative process: The role of scholarship in US Congressional efforts to protect children from internet pornography. *New Media Society, 10*(1), 115–137.

Bers, M. (2006). The role of new technologies to foster positive youth development. *Applied Developmental Science, 10*(4), 200–219.

Bers, M. U. (2008). *Blocks to robots: Learning with technology in the early childhood classroom.* New York: Teacher's College Press.

Bers, M. (2010) Beyond computer literacy: Supporting youth's positive development through technology. In *New directions for youth development: Theory, practice, and research* (pp. 13–23). San Francisco, CA: Jossey-Bass.

Bers, M. U., & Chau, C. (2006). Fostering civic engagement by building a virtual city. *Journal of Computer-Mediated Communication, 11*(3), article 4. Retrieved from http://jcmc.indiana.edu/vol11/issue3/bers.html

Bers, M., & Horn, M. (2010). Tangible programming in early childhood: Revisiting developmental assumptions through new technologies. In I. R. Berson & M. J. Berson (Eds.), *High-tech tots: Childhood in a digital world* (pp. 49–70). Greenwich, CT: Information Age.

Bers, M, Ponte I, Juelich, K, Viera, A., & Schenker, J. (2002). Teachers as designers: Integrating robotics into early childhood education. *Information Technology in Childhood Education, 1*, 123–145.

Bers, M., Rogers, C., Beals, L., Portsmore, M., Staszowski, K., Cejka, E, Barnett, M. (2006, June). *Early childhood robotics for learning.* Poster Session at the International Conference on the Learning Sciences. Bloomington, IN.

Berson, I. R. (2003). Making the connection between brain processing and cyberawareness: A developmental reality. *Proceedings of the Netsafe II: Society, Safety and the Internet Symposium,* Auckland, New Zealand.

Berson, M. J., & Berson, I. R. (2004). Developing thoughtful "cybercitizens." *Social Studies and the Young Learner, 16*(4), 5–8.

Berson, I. R., & Berson, M. J. (Eds.). (2010). *High-tech tots: Childhood in a digital world.* Charlotte, NC: Information Age.

Buckleitner, W. (2009). Pocket rockets: The past, present, and future of children's portable computing in mobile technology for children. In A. Druin (Ed.), *Designing for interacting and learning* (pp. 43–61). Burlington, MA: Elsevier.

Bus, A. G., & Neuman, S. B. (2009). *Multimedia and literacy development: Improving achievement for young learners.* New York: Routledge.

Calvert, S. L., Rideout, V. J., &Woolard, J. L. (2005). Age, ethnicity, and socioeconomic patterns in early computer use: A national survey. *American Behavioral Scientist, 48*(5), 590–607.

Carr, N. (2010). *The shallows: What the internet is doing to our brains.* New York: Norton.

Ching, C. C., Wang, X. C., & Kedem, Y. (2006). Digital photo journals in a K-1 classroom: A novel approach to addressing early childhood technology standards and recommendations. In S. Tettegah & R. Hunter (Eds.), *Technology: Issues in administration, policy, and applications in K-12 classrooms* (pp. 253–269). Oxford, England: Elsevier.

Chiong, C., & Shuler, C. (2010). *Learning: Is there an app for that?* New York: Joan Ganz Cooney Center at Sesame Workshop.

Chiou, J., Huang, C., & Lee, H. (2005). The antecedents of music piracy attitudes and intentions. *Journal of Business Ethics, 57*(2), 161–174.

Clements, D. H. (2002). Computers in early childhood mathematics. *Contemporary Issues in Early Childhood, 3*(2), 160–181.

Clements, D. H., Battista, M. T., & Sarama, J. (2001). Logo and geometry. *Journal for Research in Mathematics Education Monograph Series, 10.*

Clements, D. H., & Nastasi, B. K. (1992). Computers and early childhood education. In M. Gettinger, S. N. Elliott, & T. R. Kratochwill (Eds.) *Advances in school psychology: Preschool and early childhood treatment directions* (pp. 187–246). Hillsdale, NJ: Erlbaum.

Clements, D. H., & Sarama, J. (2002). The role of technology in early childhood learning. *Teaching Children Mathematics, 8,* 340–343.

Clements, D. H. & Sarama, J. (2003). Strip mining for gold: Research and policy in educational technology: A response to "Fool's Gold". *AACE Journal, 11*(1), 7–69.

Colby, A., & Kohlberg, L. (1987). *The measurement of moral judgment.* New York: Cambridge University Press.

Cordes, C., & Miller, E. (2000). *Fool's gold: A critical look at computers in childhood.* College Park, MD: Alliance for Childhood.

Cuban, L. (2001). *Oversold and underused: Computers in the classroom.* Cambridge, MA: Harvard University Press.

Dellinger-Pate, C., & Conforti, R.J. (2010). Webkinz as a consumerist discourse: A critical ideological analysis. In I. R. Berson & M. J. Berson (Eds.), *High-tech tots: Childhood in a digital world* (pp. 249–267). Charlotte, NC: Information Age.

Druin, A. (1998). *The design of children's technology.* San Francisco, CA: Morgan Kaufmann.

Edmark. (2005). Millie's Math House [computer software]. Redmond, WA.

Elkind, D. (1986). Formal education and early childhood education: An essential difference. *The Phi Delta Kappan, 67*(9), 631–636.

Fleer, M. (1999). The science of technology: Young children working technologically. *International Journal of Technology and Design Education, 9,* 269–291.

Genishi, C., McCollum, P., & Strand, E. B. (1985). Research currents: The interactional richness of children's computer use. *Language Arts, 62*(5), 526–532.

Gray, J. H., Bulat, J., Jaynes, C., & Cunningham, A. (2009). LeapFrog learning design: Playful approaches to literacy from LeapPad to the Tag Reading System. In A. Druin (Ed.), *Mobile technology for children* (pp. 171–194). Burlington, MA: Morgan Kaufmann.

Hall, N., Larson, J., & Marsh, J. (2003). *Handbook of early childhood literacy.* Thousand Oaks, CA: Sage.

Haugland, S. W. (1992). The effect of computer software on preschool children's developmental gains. *Journal of Computing in Childhood Education. 3*(1), 15–30.

Johnson, J. (2003). Children, robotics, and education. *Artificial Life and Robotics. 7*(1/2), 16–21.

Jones-Kavalier, B. R., & Flannigan, S. L. (2008). Connecting the digital dots: Literacy of the 21st century. *Teacher Librarian, 35*(3), 13–16.

Karlstrom, P., Cerratto-Pargman, T., & Knutsson, O. (2008). Literate tools or tools for literacy? *Digital Kompetanse, 3,* 97–112.

Kazakoff, E. & Bers, M. (2010). Computer programming in kindergarten: The role of sequencing, *ICERI2010 Proceedings,* 6086–6089.

Koshmann, T. (1996). *CSCL: Theory of practice of an emerging paradigm.* Mahwah, NJ: Erlbaum.

Labbo, L. D., & Kuhn, M. R. (2000). Weaving chains of affect and cognition: A young child's understanding of CD-ROM talking books. *Journal of Literacy Research, 32*(2), 187–210.

Lave, J., & Wenger, E. (1991). *Situated learning: Legitimate peripheral participation.* New York: Cambridge University Press.

Li, Q. (2006). Cyberbullying in schools: A research of gender differences. *School Psychology International, 27*(2), 157–170.

Li, Q. (2007). New bottle but old wine: A research on cyberbullying in schools. *Computers in Human Behavior, 23*(4), 1777–1791.

Logsdon, J. M., Thompson, J. K., & Reid, R. A. (1994). Software piracy: Is it related to level of moral judgment? *Journal of Business Ethics, 13*(11), 849–857.

McMillan, S. (1996). Literacy and computer literacy: Definitions and comparisons. *Computers in Education, 27(3/4),* 161–170

Moses, A. M. (2008). Impacts of television viewing on young children's literacy development in the USA: A review of the literature. *Journal of Early Childhood Literacy, 8*(1), 67–102.

Muller, A. A., & Perlmutter, M. (1985). Preschool children's problem-solving interactions at computers and jigsaw puzzles. *Journal of Applied Developmental Psychology, 6,* 173–186.

National Association for the Education of Young Children (NAEYC). (1996). *Technology and young children—Ages 3 through 8* (NAEYC Position Statement). Washington, DC: Author.

New, R. S., & Cochran, M. (Eds.). (2007). *Early childhood education: An international encyclopedia,* (Vol. 3). Westport, CT: Praeger.

NPD Group. (2008). *Kids and consumer electronics* (Vol. 4). Port Washington, NY: Author.

Papert, S (1980) *Mindstorms: Children, computers and powerful ideas.* New York: Basic Books.

Papert, S. (1987). Computer criticism vs. technocentric thinking. *Educational Researcher, 16*(1), 22–30.

Pearson, G., Young, A. T. (2002). *Technically speaking: Why all Americans need to know more about technology.* Washington, DC: National Academies Press.

Pew Research. (2010a). *66%—Broadband adoption slows.* Pew Research Center, the Databank. Retrieved from http://pewresearch.org/databank/dailynumber/?NumberID=1070.

Pew Research. (2010b). Mobile access 2010. Retrieved from http://pewinternet.org/Reports/2010/Mobile-Access-2010/Summary-of-Findings.aspx.

Piaget, J. (1923). *Judgment and reasoning in the child.* London: Routledge & Kegan Paul.

Piaget, J. (1954). *The construction of reality in the child.* New York: Basic Books.

Piaget, J., & Inhelder, B. (1969). *The psychology of the child.* New York: Basic Books.

Project Tomorrow. (2009). *Speak up data.* Retrieved from http://www.tomorrow.org/speakup/speakup_your_data.html.

Resnick, M. (2006). Computer as a paintbrush: Technology, play, and the creative society. In D. Singer, R. M. Golinkoff, & K. Hirsh-Pasek (Eds.), *Play = learning: How play motivates and enhances children's cognitive and social-emotional growth* (pp. 192–208). New York: Oxford University Press.

Resnick, M., Bruckman, A., & Martin, F. (1996) Pianos not stereos: Creating computational construction kits. *Interactions, 3*(6), 41–50.

Resnick, M., Maloney, J., Monroy-Hernandez, A., Rusk, N., Eastmond, E., Brennan, K...Kafai, Y. (2009). Scratch: Programming for all. *Communications of the ACM, 52*(11. 60–67.

Rinaldi, C. (1998). Projected curriculum constructed through documentation-Progettazione: An interview with Lella Gandini. In C. Edwards, L. Gandini, & G. Forman (Eds.), *The hundred languages of children: The Reggio Emilia approach—Advanced reflections* (2nd ed., pp. 113–126). Greenwich, CT: Ablex.

Rusk, N., Resnick, M., Berg, R., & Pezalla-Granlund, M. (2008). New pathways into robotics: Strategies for broadening participation. *Journal of Science Education and Technology, 17,* 59–69.

Sesame Workshop. (2007). *The media utilization study.* New York: Author.

Shea, V. (1994). *Netiquette.* San Francisco, CA: Albion Books.

Shuler, C. (2007). *D is for digital.* New York: Joan Ganz Cooney Center at Sesame Workshop.

Shuler, C. (2009a). *Pockets of potential: Using mobile technologies to promote children's learning,* New York: Joan Ganz Cooney Center at Sesame Workshop.

Shuler, C. (2009b). *iLearn: A content analysis of the iTunes app store's education section.* New York: Joan Ganz Cooney Center at Sesame Workshop.

Small, G., & Vorgan, G. (2008). *iBrain: Surviving technological alteration of the modern mind.* New York: HarperCollins.

Straker, L., Pollock, C., & Burgess-Limerick, R. (2006). Towards evidence-based guidelines for wise use of computers by children. *International Journal of Industrial Ergonomics, 36*(12), 1045–1053.

Thakkar, R. P., Garrison, M. M., & Christakis, D. A. (2006). A systematic review for the effects of television viewing by infants and preschoolers, *Pediatrics, 118,* 2025–2031.

Troseth, G. L. (2003). TV Guide: 2-year-olds learn to use video as a source of information. *Developmental Psychology, 39*(1), 140–150.

Uchikoshi, Y. (2009). Effects of television on language and literacy development, In A. G. Bus & S. B. Neuman (Eds.), *Multimedia and literacy development: Improving achievement for young learners* (pp. 182–195). New York: Routledge.

Vandewater, E. A., Rideout, V., Wartella, E. A., Huang, X., Lee, J. H., & Shim, M. (2007). Digital childhood: Electronic media and technology use among infants, toddlers, and preschoolers.*Pediatrics, 119*(5), e1006–e1015.

Vygotsky, L. S. (1978). *Mind in society: The development of higher psychological processes.* Cambridge, MA: Harvard University Press.

Wang, X. C., Berson, I. R., Jaruszewicz, C. Hartle, L., & Rosen, D. (2010). Young children's technology experiences in multiple contexts: Bronfenbrenner's ecological theory reconsidered. In I. R. Berson & M. J. Berson (Eds.), *High-tech tots: Childhood in a digital world* (pp. 23–48). Charlotte, NC: Information Age.

Wang, X. C., & Ching, C. C. (2003). Social construction of computer experience in a first-grade classroom: Social processes and mediating artifacts. *Early Education and Development, 14*(3), 335– 361.

Wartella, E., & Jennings, N. (2000). Children and computers: New technology—Old concerns. *Children and Computer Technology, 10*(2), 31–43.

Wolf, M. (2007). *Proust & the squid: The science and story of the reading brain.* New York: HarperCollins.

World Economic Forum (2010). *The global information technology report 2009–2010,* Retrieved from http://www.networkedreadiness.com/gitr/main/fullreport/index.html.

14

Social Competence Education in Early Childhood

A Sociocultural Perspective

STACY DEZUTTER AND MELISSA K. KELLY
Millsaps College

This chapter examines research on early childhood educational programs that aim to prepare children for participation in democratic society. We write from the perspective that the development of social competence is an essential component of early childhood education and that a full understanding of such education requires a research corpus that is multilayered and examines practices and contexts. Recent research is shedding new light on the importance of attending to children's social development in early childhood education, but the centrality of social competence education to early schooling is far from a new idea. Foundational thinkers such as Dewey, Froebel, and Montessori emphasized the importance of preparing young children to be competent participants in society (Saracho & Spodek, 2007) and Vygotsky emphasized that social competence is fundamental to all areas of child development (Hedegaard, 2007; Vygotsky, 1978).

We examine three of the most prominent approaches to social competence education in American formal schooling for children ages 3 to 8: social studies education, democratic classrooms, and social skills education. Social studies seeks to introduce children to ways of thinking related to the social science disciplines, ways of thinking that help us make meaning around the social lives of human beings and provide us with tools for effective engagement in a democratic society. In contrast to social studies, which attempts to prepare children for social participation by building their knowledge about society through formal instruction, democratic classrooms aim to develop children's competence for social participation by making the classroom a microcosm of democratic society, in which children are immersed in democratic ideals and practices. Social skills training, on the other hand, focuses on enhancing children's abilities to engage in successful interpersonal interactions and prosocial behavior, which form the foundations of effective societal participation.

Our interest in social competence education in early childhood arises from a sociocultural perspective on learning and child development. As sociocultural scholars, we are interested in the ways individual child development is impelled by participation in the social world, and we therefore see children's developing capacity for social participation as foundational to their ability to learn in school and other social contexts. In addition, as socioculturalists, we recognize that any instance of social competence education is necessarily situated within a particular cultural space and historical moment, and mediated by the intellectual tools and social institutions of the communities in which it occurs. Motivated by these intellectual commitments, we examine the research literature on social competence education in early childhood through a sociocultural lens, evaluating the research landscape by asking how well existing bodies of scholarship account for the socioculturally situated nature of social competence education in early childhood schooling.

The chapter begins with an articulation of the sociocultural framework we use to guide our exploration. We then describe the current research landscape for three approaches to social competence education, suggesting areas where that landscape might be enriched in order to fulfill the aims of a socioculturally informed research agenda. Next, we examine an overarching issue that emerges when early childhood social competence education research is viewed from a sociocultural perspective: the imperative to account for the role of context in children's learning. The chapter concludes by noting three emerging lines of study in early childhood social competence education that we find especially promising.

A Sociocultural Perspective on Social Learning in Early Childhood Education

Contemporary sociocultural theory finds its roots in the work of Vygotsky, Dewey, Boas, and others, and represents the convergence of several disciplines including cultural psychology, anthropology, and linguistics (Daniels, Wertsch, & Cole, 2007; Vasquez, 2008). While the sociocultural perspective encompasses many diverse voices, the field is unified around its effort to understand the "social formation of mind" (Daniels, 2008, p. 51). The central insight in sociocultural theory is that human thought is of social, rather than strictly individual, origin. Higher-order mental processes, including memory, attention, and reasoning, are understood to be mediated by cultural tools such as language, systems for counting, mnemonic strategies, modes of logic, and so on. Cultural tools are recognized to be social artifacts that have emerged over the history of a group, evolving in response to that group's activities, goals, and circumstances. Development occurs as children (and adults) encounter these tools through interaction in the social world, and appropriate them for their own use. Since thinking and learning are mediated by these tools, it is impossible to understand human mental functioning apart from its specific cultural and historical situation.

In education, the sociocultural perspective has been embraced as a robust theory for understanding the teaching-learning process, because it presents a model that locates learning in the interaction between teacher (or peer) and student. Sociocultural theory has been of particular use in light of current challenges related to the growing diversity of the student population, because it provides educators with a framework for understanding differences in the ways students think and engage in schooling without resorting to a "deficit" view (Rogoff, 2003). From the sociocultural perspective, children arriving at school from differing home cultures will bring with them different sets of cultural tools, and these may or may not be well-aligned with the particular set of tools associated with formal schooling. Sociocultural theory has also helped educators make sense of the educational enterprise more broadly: from the sociocultural perspective, formal schooling is but one of many possible ways that members of a culture arrange for younger members to learn to use the valued intellectual tools of that culture. Western schooling involves a set of intellectual practices that, far from being universal as once assumed, are the products of the history of a particular culture (Cole, 1998; Rogoff, 1990).

Sociocultural theory, then, has three basic implications for research on social competence education in early childhood. First, to the extent that children's abilities to function in the social world rely on higher mental processes such as attention, memory, and reasoning, that development is mediated by cultural tools, and therefore must be viewed as a process that is situated within specific sociocultural contexts. Second, because social interaction is the basis for all higher-order learning, the development of effective social functioning becomes central to all other forms of learning, and therefore is an imperative for early childhood education. And third, because formal schooling is only one context in which children learn, research on early childhood social competence education must account for interaction between learning in the school setting and learning in other social settings in which the child participates.

Sociocultural Theory as a Framework for Research

Sociocultural research is characterized by methodological diversity, drawing on techniques from its numerous constituent disciplines, including naturalistic observation, discourse analysis, and laboratory experiments. The sociocultural perspective holds that the individual and the social context are coconstitutive; each is involved in the formation of the other, and they are not analytically separable. This perspective, then, raises questions about how much we can learn from experimental and quasi-experimental research, which depends on the isolation of particular variables. From the sociocultural perspective, what is of interest is the complex interaction between individual thought and sociocultural context, and studying either of these as if they were separable from the other has notable limitations. Vygotsky (1978) famously used an analogy to water to explain this concern, pointing out that studying water in terms of hydrogen and oxygen separately would yield a very misleading picture of water as a phenomenon.

The sociocultural assertion that the individual and the social context are inseparable also raises issues regarding the proper unit of analysis. Rather than focusing on the individual as the entity of analytic interest, socioculturalists are apt to focus on interacting dyads or larger social groups, interactional episodes, or instances of "mediated [intellectual] action" (Daniels, 2008; Rogoff, 1990; Sawyer, 2005; Wertsch, 1998). Of course, as Sawyer (2005) points out, there is considerable disagreement with regard to the degree of analytic separability of individual from context, and most researchers implicitly admit some level of separability in their research designs. Regardless, there is vociferous agreement about the need to maintain at least some amount of analytic connection between the individual and the sociocultural context.

In our review, we do not aim to subject individual studies conducted from other perspectives to the demands of taking a sociocultural perspective. We do not, for example, reject experimental studies or studies that take the individual as the unit of analysis. We do, however, apply a sociocultural sensibility to critique the bodies of research that exist on social competence education in early childhood. We ask how well each body of work accounts for the interdependence of individual and context. To do this, we adapt an approach articulated by Rogoff (1995; Rogoff, Topping, Baker-Sennett, & Lacasa, 2002) who asserted that the ideal sociocultural research agenda would include three interdependent foci of analysis: the individual, the interpersonal, and the community/institutional. In a given study, various facets of a phenomenon can be placed in the foreground while the others remain in the background, but a full research agenda must attend in turn to each of the foci of analysis, as well as the interrelations between those foci. From this standpoint, studies that have been conducted from other perspectives can still be of value within a sociocultural framework. Thus, a body of research that is fully developed from a sociocultural perspective would include works from many perspectives that as a group address all three of the foci and their interdependence.

Using this sociocultural framework, this review explores the promise and shortfalls of three strands of research on social competence education in early childhood. Although much of the research we review is not conducted from a sociocultural perspective, our aim is to integrate these findings into a socioculturally informed view of the landscape. In particular, we emphasize that children develop in multiple contexts, and so research focusing on social competence education within a particular context (in this case, early childhood schooling) must maintain an awareness that children bring with them patterns of behavior, cultural tools, goals, and expectations from other contexts. Research on the efficacy and broader impact of social competence education, then, must address the participation of the individual in multiple contexts and the interactions between those contexts. At a bare minimum, the implications for classroom teaching and learning of a child's movement between classroom, family, and community should be addressed; the relationship between the social practices of the family and those at school should be given particular attention because the family has been the primary context for development for most children prior to starting school. In addition, we emphasize that research examining learning in school must be framed within a larger understanding of coconstitutive social, institutional, and cultural-historical processes.

Research on Social Studies in Early Childhood Education

Social studies is perhaps the most well-established form of education for participation in democratic society; its presence in American schools dates from the early 20th century. As a curricular field within early childhood education, social studies aims to introduce young children to the disciplinary knowledge and practices of the social sciences, so as to

> equip them with the knowledge and understanding of the past necessary for coping with the present and planning for the future, enable them to understand and participate effectively in their world, and explain their relationship to other people and to social, economic, and political institutions. (National Council for Social Studies [NCSS], 1988; see also Thornton, 2008)

The NCSS in its position statement, *Social Studies for Early Childhood and Elementary School Children: Preparing for the 21st Century,* emphasizes the importance of providing a foundation for social thought and civic participation, via social studies, in the early years of schooling, asserting,

> The social studies in the early childhood/elementary years are crucial if we expect the young people of this nation to become active, responsible citizens for maintaining the democratic values upon which this nation was established.

Unless children acquire the foundations of knowledge, attitudes, and skills in social studies in the important elementary years, it is unlikely that teachers in the junior and senior high schools will be successful in preparing effective citizens for the 21st century. (NCSS, 1988)

Early childhood social studies has traditionally focused on concepts from the fields of history, geography, civics, and economics, and more recently has expanded to include concepts from other social sciences such as sociology and anthropology. Social studies in early childhood is generally organized around social experiences that are familiar to young children, particularly those of the family, the school, the neighborhood, and the local community (Saracho & Spodek, 2007).

The Research Landscape

Unfortunately, despite the weighty aims of the discipline, research on social studies in early childhood—and on social studies in general—is sparse. In the *Handbook of Research in Social Studies Education* (2008), editors Levstik and Tyson lament what they characterize as a paltry research base, noting that social studies journals and general education journals contained very little social studies research between 1995 and 2007, the years covered by their review. Levstik and Tyson's disappointment is echoed by authors throughout the *Handbook,* including Brophy and Alleman in their chapter on early elementary social studies. Both Levstik and Tyson and Brophy and Alleman cautiously forecast an increase in social studies research, but our review of social studies journals from January 2007 to June 2010 offered no reason to believe there is or will be a marked upswing in social studies research. As was the case when the *Handbook* was written, nonempirical articles offering advocacy, recommendation, or simple description far outnumber articles presenting systematic research.

A prime reason for the lack of research attention to social studies, we suspect, is that social studies is often treated as a "second-rank subject" (Jantz & Seefelt, 1999, p. 160), taking a backseat to literacy and mathematics instruction. A 2007 NCES report confirms this for grades 1 through 4, finding that social studies receives an average of 2.5 hours of instruction per week, compared to 11.3 hours of literacy and 5.4 hours of math (Morton & Dalton, 2007). Levstik and Tyson note that the early grades are "the most fragile portion of the social studies curriculum" (2008, p. 7); social studies is often set aside in favor of literacy and mathematics. Indeed, scholars have bemoaned the marginalization of social studies for quite some time, although the problem seems to have intensified in the wake of No Child Left Behind and high stakes testing (Brophy & Alleman, 2008; Vogler & Virtue, 2007). As a consequence of this tenuous position within the curriculum, a great deal of academic writing on social studies is devoted to arguing for its existence.

Research that has been done on social studies in early childhood has focused on the individual level of analysis, examining the development of children's thinking in the areas of history, geography, and economics. Research in history has examined young children's conceptions of historical time and their tendency to interpret historical events in terms of simplified narrative structures (Barton, 2008). Research in geography has focused on children's development of map skills and their expanding understanding of nested relationships such as neighborhood, city, state, and nation (Segall & Helfenbein, 2008). In economics, research has examined young children's understandings of basic concepts such as shelter, work and income, and trade (Miller & Vanfossen, 2008).

What's Needed

Given the paucity of research on social studies in early childhood, there are quite a few areas where research is needed. To begin, it remains unclear how much and what quality of social studies instruction is actually occurring (Levstik, 2008). Research is needed to better understand the institutional status of social studies in early childhood education, particularly the ways in which teachers are (and are not) including social studies in their classrooms.

While social studies in early childhood education has not been a research priority because it has not been a curricular priority, we wonder if the converse is also true, if social studies is easily pushed from the curriculum because we lack a research-based argument for its inclusion. Research that empirically investigates the effects of early childhood social studies, including the effects on the academic lives of students and the effects on their functioning as members of a democratic society, is sorely needed. It is worth noting that we were unable to find a research base to support the NCSS's two claims regarding the importance of social studies in early childhood education: that it is necessary for the creation of "active, responsible citizens" and for laying the groundwork for junior and senior high school instruction (NCSS, 1988). The first claim is closely linked to the problem of transfer, a difficult issue for researchers, which we take up in our section on "Context Matters." The second claim is perhaps easier to address empirically, through longitudinal and cross-sectional studies of children who have had varying degrees and types of social studies instruction at varying points in their education. Of course, given the unevenness with which social studies occurs in early childhood education, it seems unlikely that early instruction is a make-or-break factor for later social studies learning, as the NCSS statement implies. However, there may be important ways in which early social studies instruction can provide children with valuable tools for later learning, and this possibility is worthy of investigation.

Several authors in the *Handbook of Research in Social Studies Education* call for greater research attention to the teaching-learning process (Barton, 2008; Hahn & Alviar-Martin, 2008; Levstik, 2008; Miller & Vanfossen, 2008). Existing research examines children's evolving conceptions of various social studies concepts, but it does not examine how these conceptions change in response to instruction (Barton, 2008). In addition, it does not attend to differences in how children think about social studies concepts as a result of varying out-of-school experiences. From the sociocultural perspective, such research is essential, in order to understand children's classroom learning as a function of interpersonal and cross-contextual processes.

The teaching-learning process has been a prime area of research conducted from a sociocultural perspective; however, little of this research has been done in early childhood social studies. Nonetheless, sociocultural research on teaching and learning in other disciplines can suggest fruitful avenues for the study of early childhood social studies. In particular, sociocultural research has attended to classroom learning through three distinct but related lenses, each of which highlights the interaction between individual and interpersonal or community/institutional processes: studies of classroom interaction, studies of the interaction between school and other contexts for learning, and studies of the classroom as a microculture. Studies of *classroom interaction* examine the interpersonal processes through which children encounter (or create) and then appropriate tools for thinking during conversation and other forms of interaction with teachers and peers. Classroom interaction studies offer fine-grained, detailed accounts of how children's thinking changes in response to various forms of instructional interaction (e.g., Atencio, 2004; Cassata-Widera, Kato-Jones, Duckles, Conezio, & French, 2008; Chang-Wells & Wells, 1993; Palinscar, Brown, & Campione, 1993). Classroom interaction research would be especially valuable for early childhood social studies, because it provides a rich understanding of the teaching-learning process and can lead to recommendations for pedagogy and for teacher preparation.

Research examining the *interaction between classroom practices and those found in other contexts in which the child participates* has also proven to be a robust source of insight for understanding classroom learning (e.g., Anderson & Gold, 2006; Aubrey, Bottle, & Godfrey, 2003; Gallimore & Goldenberg, 1993; Heath, 1983). For example, a now classic study by Heath (1983) revealed important ways in which literacy practices, especially the construction of narrative, vary among different socioeconomic and ethnic groups, which in turn leads to varied ways of engaging in narrative when children come to school. Research that considers the multiple communities and institutions through which children learn is especially important for understanding teaching and learning of social content. We return to this point in our section, "Context Matters."

Studies examining *the classroom as a microculture* look at the sociointellectual norms that guide conversation and intellectual behavior and therefore shape learning. In addition, such studies often consider the collective learning of the class as an entity (e.g., Cobb, 1999; Nolan, 2001; Roth & Bowen, 1995; Webb, Nemer, & Ing, 2001; Yackel & Cobb, 1996). Research on the microculture of early childhood social studies classrooms could reveal important ways in which classroom norms support or inhibit the development of desirable dispositions and forms of thinking for civic life. Such research would serve as a valuable link between social studies research and the approach we discuss next, the design of classroom participation structures to support the development of democratic thought and behavior.

Research on Democratic Classrooms

Social studies aims to prepare children for civic life by explicitly teaching particular knowledge and disciplinary thinking skills. Another popular approach for preparing children to be effective members of democratic society is the design of the classroom sociointellectual environment to foster democratic attitudes, behaviors, and skills. The "democratic classroom" is ubiquitous in classroom management textbooks (e.g., Charles, 2011; Edwards, 2008; Kohn, 2006; Nelsen, Lott, & Glenn, 2000) and web-based teacher resources (e.g., www.servicelearning.org, www.tolerance.org) and typically involves engaging children in the practices of democratic society such as deliberation and shared decision making through activities such as classroom meetings and voting. The democratic classroom model emphasizes the use of child-centered instructional methods that offer children opportunities to exercise choice and to take responsibility for their own learning. The idea of an active, choice-driven schooling experience as an antecedent for democratic participation dates back to Dewey (1899/1959) and has been a mainstay in conversations about civic education.

The Research Landscape

Although the democratic classroom is advocated as a promising approach at all levels of schooling, including early childhood (e.g., McLennan, 2009), there is very little research examining the processes and outcomes of this model, and almost none at the early childhood level.

There is a small amount of research on early childhood democratic classrooms implemented in developing democracies, and this research may be instructive in envisioning a research agenda for democratic classrooms in established democracies such as those in the United States and Canada. By far, the most popular manifestation worldwide of the "democratic classroom" approach is the Step-by-Step program. Step-by-Step is an early childhood program designed to promote the dispositions and thinking skills necessary for successful participation in a democratic society (Hansen, Kaufman, & Saifer, 2004). The program has been implemented in more than 5,000 classrooms in 30 countries throughout Asia, Africa, and Eastern Europe (Brady, Dickinson, Hirschler, Cross, & Green, 1998; Coughlin, 1996; Li, 2008). The central tenet of the program is that classrooms should be organized around principles aligned with democratic values, including self-efficacy and personal responsibility, choice, participation, shared control between teacher and students, and appreciation of differences and similarities (Hansen et al., 2004). The program emphasizes active, exploratory learning, and parent and community involvement with the school. We were unable to find any peer-reviewed studies of the efficacy of the Step-by-Step program; however, a program evaluation by USAID looked at Step-by-Step in four countries, comparing students to children in traditional kindergartens (Brady et al., 1998). On academic measures, Step-by-Step children performed at least as well and often much better than their peers in traditional programs. Evidence of the civic outcomes of the program is more elusive, however. Using classroom observations, the Brady evaluation determined that Step-by-Step classrooms do indeed provide ideal conditions for promoting democracy, but even as the study asserts the program's success in educating for democracy, it offers no evidence as to whether the program is actually succeeding in producing more democratically inclined children.

While the Brady et al. (1998) study leaves us with the questionable assumption that if the conditions in the classroom are right, children will learn to think and behave more democratically, another study, conducted by DeBaessa, Chesterfield, and Ramos (2002) addresses this question head on. Their study examines the Nueva Escuela Unitaria (NEU) model of schooling in Guatemala, which was developed as part of a peace agreement that committed Guatemala to developing a decentralized, participatory government. Much like Step-by-Step, NEU emphasizes active participatory learning and family involvement. DeBaessa et al. compared first and second graders' behaviors in classrooms in NEU with those in traditional Guatemalan schools on a number of measures of democratic behavior including turn-taking, expressing opinions, assisting others, and directing others (which was conceptualized as an indicator of leadership development). The study revealed that students in NEU schools engage in these behaviors much more than students in traditional schools do, and they do so in far more collaborative and egalitarian ways. The researchers attributed this difference to the use of small, student-led groups (rather than large or teacher-controlled groups), which gave NEU students many more opportunities to engage in the desired behaviors. The DeBaessa et al. study, then, suggests that when facilitative conditions are present, children will indeed behave in more democratically.

What's Needed

More research like the DeBaessa et al. (2002) study is needed to fully understand how particular participation structures and classroom norms lead children to develop ways of thinking and interacting that are considered desirable for a democratic society. Indeed, the DeBaessa et al. (2002) study provides a useful model for how behavior change at the classroom level (*classroom as a microculture*) might be analyzed. What's more, the DeBaessa study's findings support the compelling idea that classrooms can be organized in such a way as to promote the development of democratic behaviors, a finding we hope will spur more research on democratic classrooms, including research on the model's use in a wider range of settings.

That said, we remain somewhat skeptical about the efficacy of the democratic classroom model, at least with regard to its implementation in the United States. We are aware of the many aspects of American classrooms, like teacher responsibility for safety and content coverage, which simply cannot be democratic (cf. Raywid, 1987). While there are elements of the classroom that can certainly be designed around democratic values, ultimately, the classroom is a space in which the teacher rules the day. We therefore feel it will be important for researchers to address the question of whether certain circumstances of schooling actually undercut, rather than foster, the development of democratic competence among children, especially very young children.

We would also call for a more complex analysis of programs like NEU and Step-by-Step, in addition to research on the democratic classroom model as implemented in established democracies. Researchers would do well to document and analyze the influence of such programs across multiple contexts, in particular, examining changes in behavior in civic contexts and at home. After all, changing the way people participate in society is what these programs are intended to do. Whether they succeed will be difficult to address empirically, given the complexity of the matter—we return to this challenge in our discussion on context, below. As a starting point, however, longitudinal research that studies children who have and have not experienced such programs could reveal the effects of early childhood exposure to a democratic classroom on later civic thought and participation. In addition, because many such programs emphasize family and community involvement, important observations are likely to arise from studies that examine this process of bridging the school, family, and community contexts.

Research on Programs that Explicitly Teach Social Skills

At the most basic level, social competence involves facility with interpersonal interaction. Early childhood programs for developing the skills involved in successful interpersonal interaction have developed and expanded over the last 30 years. Basic social skills like listening, interacting prosocially with peers, and deciphering others' behaviors have recently become an especial focus for interventions for increasing the social participation of students with behavior problems. From a sociocultural perspective it is absolutely vital to understand and develop students' social skills because education itself is a deeply social process. If a student cannot listen, interprets the environment as inherently hostile, is easily distracted or stressed by the presence of peers, or is unaware of socially appropriate ways to interact with adult authority figures, any instruction in a classroom setting will be deeply flawed at best. When Asher and Renshaw (1981) found that socially rejected children could be trained to higher levels of social competence through fairly simple interventions they opened the door for new approaches to reducing the sequelae of peer rejection such as truancy, dropping out of school, depression, and delinquency. Social skills training is often focused on problem students and programs usually address developing intrapersonal skills like emotion regulation, interpersonal skills like social problem solving and prosocial behavior, and reducing problem behaviors. As Vygotsky would have predicted, intervention programs have been found to have the greatest efficacy when they engage multiple contexts for each child, in particular, peers, schools, and families (McConaughy, Kay, Welkowitz, Hewitt, & Fitzgerald, 2007; Sprague & Perkins, 2009; Webster-Stratton, Reid, & Stoolmiller, 2008).

Social skills as defined by measures like the Social Skills and Attitudes Scale (SSAS) generally cover two related areas: knowledge of self and interaction with others. Knowledge of self includes confidence and emotion regulation based on self-understanding and control skills; interaction with others includes appropriateness, basic manners, age appropriate communication skills, and conflict management (Richardson, Myran, & Tonelson, 2009). Researchers such as Raver and Zigler, as early as 1997, were calling for assessments of social skills abilities to be used along with academic assessments as outcome measures for Head Start programs. They did so because they recognized a connection between social and academic development. Once again, as Vygotsky would have predicted, it has become increasingly clear that the benefits of social skills interventions reach beyond lessening conflict in the classroom to impact academic and achievement test results as well (Ladd, 1990; Miller, Lane, & Wehby, 2005; Ray & Elliott, 2006; Wentzel, 1993).

The Research Landscape

Attempts to increase our understanding of the mechanisms underlying the success of social skills interventions have led to the development of cognitive models of aggression and social situations (Crick & Dodge, 1994,) new interventions (e.g., CASEL, 2003,), and attempts to be proactive about peer rejection by introducing social skills training into school curricula much earlier (e.g., Head Start Self-Determination Curriculum, Incredible Years, Connecting with Others, Second Step). While the early work in this area focused on adolescents and middle or high schools, research has indicated that even earlier training in social skills could be beneficial in reducing the numbers of students who are socially rejected by simply preventing it. Most of the research to date has focused on programs designed for children who are at risk for rejection by virtue of learning or other disabilities (Dodge & Mallard, 1992) or who are identified as at risk due to poverty or other demographic characteristics (Forness, Serna, Kavale, & Nielsen, 1998), or research has focused on intervention programs for children with behavior problems (McConaughy et al., 2007). Bearing out Vygotsky's original insight that learning and cognition are social, academic abilities are increased along with social competency; students who have gained skills that allow them to attend, to understand others, to ask for clarification, and to interact successfully with peers do better on academic performance tasks (Ladd, 1990; M. J. Miller et al., 2005; Ray & Elliott, 2006; Wentzel, 2003).

Because of the nature of intervention programs, much of the research on social skills interventions has necessarily focused on clinical populations and on first grade and older children (Durlak & Wells, 1997). Programs like The Incredible Years (Webster-Stratton et al., 2008,) Communication Lab (Dodge & Mallard, 1992), and First Step to Success (Sprague & Perkins, 2009) are implemented either with specific target children who have been identified as having serious difficulty with social skills, or with classrooms that include such children. Research seems to indicate that social skills interventions help both target and nontarget children to decrease undesirable behavior and increase prosocial behaviors (e.g., Sprague & Perkins, 2009), reducing their risk of academic failure related to difficult peer relationships (Feschbach & Feschbach, 1987) and increasing their ability to spend class time productively (Sharpe, Brown, & Crider, 1995) with some measurable impact on achievement scores (O'Neil, Welsh, Parke, Wang, & Strand, 1997).

What's Needed

We are encouraged by the research in this particular area, both in terms of its promise for more effective educational practices and in terms of the development of curricula that involve the multiple contexts of school, peers, and home. The program implementation that is being done in this field is often sensitive to and calls for the involvement of interventions on multiple planes, with peers, in class, and at home (McConaughy et al., 2007; Sprague & Perkins, 2009; Webster-Stratton et al., 2008), although as yet there is little research, beyond anecdotal parent reports, on behavior changes in a nonschool context. We also recognize that there is still a need for basic research on early educational programs rather than on later elementary and older children. For example, it is still unclear whether academic gains among nontarget children are due to better social competence on their own part, to better classroom environment due to improvement in target children, to some greater sensitivity to students elicited from teachers due to their involvement in an intervention program, or to some combination of all of these factors.

There is a significant need for more research on nonclinical populations. Longitudinal studies that compare classrooms where all children possess appropriate social skills to classrooms that include target children will more clearly illuminate the factors that lead to better social ability and to the mechanisms by which social ability influences academic abilities. As social skills programs become more widespread, there will also be a need for implementation assessment. For instance, what is the impact of teaching respect for peers in a classroom where the teacher or teacher's assistants do not address one's peers with respect? From a sociocultural perspective, a clear understanding of the ways that social skills training works or does not work requires observation of both the intentional and nonintentional socialization that is occurring in the classroom and at home.

A Note about Nonintentional Social Learning in Early Childhood Education

Of course, not all social learning in early childhood education comes about through deliberate curricular or pedagogical efforts. Sociocultural researchers have often emphasized the ways in which schooling experiences implicitly socialize children toward particular norms, values, and patterns of thought. For example, Rogoff and her colleagues have found a general effect of schooling to be a decrease in how well attention is paid to third-party instruction (Correa-Chavez & Rogoff, 2009). Research on nonintentional socialization within social competence education programs has yet to be done, but the nature of these programs makes them a particularly vital area for examining such contextual effects. Because so many of the social skills interventions actually involve changing the usual classroom mode of instruction by, for example, adding puppets or using sociodrama, these programs could be especially useful settings for examining how socialization differences affect the learning of particular material. Also, as mentioned above, it will be important to examine the mechanisms of nonintentional social learning with regard to democracy education. For example, if the teacher is teaching the importance of participating in a democracy by voting, yet spending the vast majority of the school day organizing the children's activities without their input, what do they learn about self-efficacy and their ability to be decision makers and participants? Even more than with math and literacy, the congruence and discontinuity between explicit aims of instruction and implicit socialization practices stand to impact the outcomes of social competence education. We highly recommend attention to nonintentional social learning within the research landscape of social competence education.

Context Matters

The sociocultural perspective views the individual, interpersonal, and cultural/institutional planes as coconstitutive; each is formative of the other. From this perspective, research on social learning must attend to the ways in which learning happens within a particular social, institutional, and cultural/historical context. In addition, it must attend to the fact that learners often move between multiple social contexts. In this section, we suggest several broad lines of research toward the aim of situating our understanding of young children's school-based social learning within and across contexts.

Comparative and Cross-National Research

Hahn and Alviar-Martin (2008) list several advantages to comparative and international research, among these that such studies allow for a sort of quasi-experimental research in which "[o]ne can see the effects of different policies and practices in a way that might not be possible within a single nation" and that "by stepping out of one's familiar surroundings and looking at social studies and citizenship education in different national settings one can view her or his own taken-for-granted assumptions with fresh eyes" (p. 82). These advantages would surely apply to lines of research on social competence education considered in this chapter.

At present, great opportunity exists for comparative and international studies of social competence education in early childhood education. In recent years, several countries have implemented social studies, civic education, or democratic education curricula where none existed before (e.g., Step-by-Step, NEU; see also Krogh, 2008). Studies of the implementation and effects of programs like these could provide interesting insights regarding the potential and challenges of deliberate curricular attempts to educate for democracy and civic participation. Comparative studies of programs with differing practices but similar aims might also be useful, because they would allow us to identify the specific processes by which such programs succeed or fail. As has been the case with examinations of newly established schooling (e.g., Maynard, 2004), research on newly implemented social education programs may shed light on programs with longer traditions, such as those in the United States and Canada that expose inherent assumptions and entrenched practices that need no longer be taken as givens in the presence of contrasting cases. In locations where implementation is partial, the opportunity exists to compare students with and without exposure to such programs on a variety of outcomes, and to compare the teaching-learning processes in these programs with those in more traditional models (e.g., DeBaessa et al., 2002).

Lifewide Research

One of the insights from sociocultural research on teaching and learning is that schools are not the sole contexts in which children learn. Research in math, science, and literacy has revealed that children learn to think in ways valued by these disciplines through participation in a wide range of nonschool activities, including "informal" educational contexts such as museums, extracurricular activities, clubs, and enrichment classes, as well as everyday activities within their families and communities, which are not explicitly instructional but nonetheless provide contexts for learning (Bransford et al., 2006; Hedegaard, 2009). Such research has proved a potent source of insight for school-based educators, because it allows us to work in tandem with, rather than against, the tools for thinking that children bring with them from other contexts in which they participate. Early childhood social studies and social skills education would certainly benefit from this sort of "lifewide" approach (Bransford et al., 2006).

Lifewide research has not yet been a substantial component of research on social competence education. Of the three bodies of research discussed in this chapter, only social skills research has made initial steps toward a lifewide perspective, by highlighting the importance of nonschool contexts and noting that the greatest efficacy in learning occurs when there is involvement of both teacher and family.

An example of how lifewide research can provide useful findings can be found in Hart and Atkins's (2002) study of adolescents. This ecological study of civic competence found that a lack of opportunity to participate in activities such as clubs and teams explained why urban youth lagged behind in civic knowledge and participation, compared to their suburban counterparts who had such opportunities. Although the Hart and Atkins study focused on teenagers, it reveals the importance of a lifewide understanding of civic education and raises questions about which experiences beyond schooling might be especially important for establishing a foundation for civic competence in young children. Research will need to delve deeper into the relationships between various contexts; for example, examining interactions between the forms of civic thought and participation children encounter in their families, religious communities, and elsewhere, and the forms being promoted at school. In all areas of social learning in early childhood, it will be important to investigate the ways children move between multiple contexts for learning, and how they negotiate points of discontinuity among the various contexts in which they participate.

The Problem of Transfer

Socioculturalists have critiqued schooling as an enterprise because it assumes the unproblematic transfer of skills and knowledge learned in one context to another, for example that students who learn to do math problems in school can then apply the same mathematical procedures in everyday situations—an assumption that has proven to be largely untrue (Packer, 2001). The question of transfer across contexts is one to which researchers in early childhood social competence education will need to attend. Often, the stated claims of social education programs involve outcomes beyond the classroom; for example, the democratic classroom or social studies as characterized by the NCSS. Indeed, most programs reviewed in this chapter aim to change the ways children participate in social life broadly defined, and especially in the activities and institutions of democratic society. Unfortunately, it is by no means clear that these programs do in fact have an impact beyond the classroom. There is some research on older children that suggests that participation in classrooms that bear certain characteristics associated with the democratic classroom model, such as an open environment for discussions and use of active learning pedagogies, fosters civic engagement as well as democratic thinking (Hahn & Alviar-Martin, 2008,) but this research does not include young children, and it is not clear what these findings mean for life beyond school. The social skills literature has not yet made a substantive examination of results outside of the classroom, although links have been made between social skills and academic achievement and it seems that, for older children, benefits of better social skills may include decreasing delinquency, truancy, and clinical diagnoses (Feshbach & Feshbach, 1987; Parker & Asher, 1987; Zsolnai, 2002). The social studies literature is largely silent on the issue of the discipline's impact beyond the K-12 classroom, which is unfortunate given its tenuous position within the curriculum.

The transfer problem presents researchers of early childhood social education with a considerable challenge. To demonstrate transfer, researchers must track learners' social thought or practices across contexts; but the relationship between contexts is likely to be complex, with multiple directions of influence. The issue is further complicated when education for civic participation is of interest, because young children have few immediate opportunities to participate in the forms of civic life for which such programs are meant to prepare them. Their participation is distant in time, and a great deal of further education will come in between. In our discussions above, we have called for longitudinal studies to test claims that early childhood social education has an effect on social competence later in life. At the same time, we acknowledge that research that treats early exposure to social education as an isolable variable runs the risk of missing the complex ways in which these programs interact with other opportunities for learning and the ways in which multiple factors interact to shape social and civic behavior. Thus, observational and qualitative studies, which can provide descriptions of process as well as outcome, will be important complements to quasi-experimental research. Indeed, it will be important not only to investigate *whether* social competence developed in school transfers to life beyond school, but *how* and *why,* and to understand what factors influence the degree and form of any transfer that occurs.

Investigating transfer is important to the extent that the rationale for social education programs includes the idea that the programs will have an impact beyond the classrooms where they occur. At the same time, we suspect that there is value to such programs within the classroom itself. For example, the inclusion of social studies content could be interesting and exciting, and therefore motivational, for young children. Social skills programs and democratic classrooms may help children be better members of the school community. The active learning component of demo-cratic classrooms has been shown to improve academic performance, as has training in social skills (DeBaessa et al. 2002; Hahn & Alviar-Martin, 2008; Ladd, 1990; M. J. Miller et al., 2005; Ray & Elliott, 2006; Wentzel, 2003). Thus, researchers would do well to investigate the benefits of social competence education that accrue within early childhood classrooms, in addition to examining how they affect children in their lives beyond the classroom.

Directions

In this section, we discuss three recently emerging lines of research that we believe to hold particular promise from the sociocultural perspective.

Tools of the Mind

Self-regulation is a key component in effective social participation (McKown, Gumbiner, Russo, & Lipton, 2009) and perhaps for this reason, self-regulation has been shown to be more strongly associated with school readiness than entering math and reading scores or IQ (Diamond, Barnett, Thomas, & Munro, 2007). Tools of the Mind is an early childhood curriculum that aims to develop children's self-regulation abilities in order to facilitate their success at learning in a social context, in particular, learning in school. The Tools of the Mind program was designed by Elena Bodrova and Deborah Leong, based on the Vygotskian insight that social learning is fundamental to children's academic and life success. As understood by Vygotsky and his colleagues, the development of self-regulation is not a matter of mere maturation but rather is learned through certain types of interactions within the social world. Much of the Tools of the Mind curriculum focuses on dramatic play; as Vygotsky noted, play is an excellent setting for the development of self-regulation because it requires children to exercise a great deal of constraint. In order to play together successfully, children must maintain certain agreed-upon conventions and behaviors appropriate for their roles and for the imaginary situation.

While the theoretical basis for Tools of the Mind is quite well developed (Bodrova & Leong, 2001, 2005,) there is not yet a substantial research base documenting the effects of the program. In an early evaluation conducted by the program's creators, Tools students performed better than matched peers in a conventional preschool on all measures in posttest. In Barnett et al.'s (2008) study, 274 children were randomly assigned to either the Tools curriculum or the district's existing literacy-focused curriculum. The most notable effects documented in this study were in the areas of social development, including teacher reports of the near elimination of behavior problems. While Tools also showed consistent positive effects on measures of cognitive development, these effects were small and often were not statistically significant. Diamond et al. (2007) looked specifically at the effects of Tools on measures of executive function (EF), which is considered to be a key component of self-regulation. Using a sample of 147 children who had been randomly assigned to either the Tools curriculum or the district's "balanced literacy" (dBL) curriculum, Diamond et al.'s study revealed that children in the Tools condition significantly outperformed children in the dBL condition on executive function tasks, and the more demanding the task, the greater the effect size.

Barnett et al. (2008) and Diamond et al. (2007) provide several suggestions for further research on Tools, including studies with greater statistical power and with measures taken later in implementation when academic effects may be more pronounced. In addition, longitudinal studies are needed to examine the long-term effects of participation in Tools on the academic and social success of children as they progress through school and enter the workforce.

Children as Creators of Their Social Environment

From a sociocultural perspective, any review of research on social competence education in early childhood would not be complete without attending to children as agents of their own social learning. Socioculturalists emphasize that children are active, agentic learners, who contribute to the creation of the social plane in which they encounter and learn to use the cultural tools that drive their development. Unfortunately, research on social education too often assumes a unidirectional process, from adult to child. However, recent research has begun to attend to children's role in creating the social environment in the classroom.

In a study investigating children's socialization into classroom computer practices, Wang and Ching (2003) found that the children created their own peer culture around computer use, a culture based on a collaborative participation structure that contrasted with the solitary approach advanced by the teacher. Lash (2008) looked at the ways in which children circumvent or modify classroom rules that limit their opportunities to engage in behaviors they enjoy and value, observing that children's peer culture both "works in concert and in opposition to the teacher's promoted classroom community" (p. 38). Hainnikainen's (2007) study similarly illustrates how children move between the official preschool culture and their own created culture, and how they negotiate and exploit the tensions between these two realms in order to advance their own social learning.

One implication of this line of research for educators is that an awareness of children's social agency allows that agency to be leveraged in explicit instructional efforts. For example, X. C. Wang and Ching (2003) suggest that teachers might discuss issues surrounding classroom rules and norms with children, making their own negotiation processes explicit, and thereby further engaging them in complex social thought. In addition to future research into the ways children themselves create the social climate and culture of their classrooms, researchers might examine

ways in which educators can incorporate this process into deliberate efforts to develop social competence.

Computer-Supported Collaborative Learning

In recent decades, interest in socioculturally informed uses of educational technology has burgeoned. In particular, computer-supported collaborative learning (CSCL), which explores the design and use of platforms for supporting content-based social interaction and collaborative knowledge generation, has emerged as a field with a vigorous and ever-expanding research base. CSCL has not attended extensively to early childhood education and has all but ignored social studies and social skills education. However, a few recent papers suggest that there is great potential for CSCL in these areas. F. Wang, Kinzie, McGuire, and Pan (2010) review recent literature that supports the possibility that CSCL can be used effectively for teaching scientific inquiry in early childhood education. In another recent paper, Ligorio and Van Veen (2006) describe an online virtual space in which students aged 9 to 14 from Dutch and Italian schools interacted to build a virtual world. Based on Wang et al.'s discussion, it seems likely that platforms of this type could be designed for younger children as well. Thus, we see CSCL as a potentially potent tool for developing social scientific thinking and for engaging students in conversations about cultural and national difference.

Conclusion

Research on social competence education in early childhood has been uneven and in some areas nonexistent; this leaves much work to be done. Perhaps most urgently, there is a need for research to justify the inclusion of social studies within the early childhood curriculum. By contrast, social skills education is already fairly well justified by research demonstrating its beneficial effects on academic performance. Indeed, we suspect that further research on all forms of social competence education will confirm Vygotsky's assertion that social and academic learning are intricately intertwined. Programs like Tools of the Mind will be especially valuable contexts for exploring this possibility.

Most of the research referenced in this chapter has been done at the individual level, with some work at the classroom level of analysis. From a sociocultural perspective, it is imperative that researchers looking at social education in early childhood strive to develop a more nuanced understanding of these planes of analysis, including much greater attention to the intrapersonal processes that drive social learning. In addition, from the sociocultural perspective, it is critical to situate our understanding of teaching and learning in social competence education within institutional and cultural/historical contexts, and to attend to children's movement across multiple contexts, especially the family.

In closing, we would like to predict that a denser research landscape will reveal early childhood social competence education to be far from a "second-rank subject." Just as competence in literacy transcends its boundaries and influences one's ability to self-educate and to participate as a learner in other areas, competence in the social realm may well be a necessity for mastering other academic subjects as well as for enjoying a rich and productive place in the social life of one's community.

References

Anderson, D. D., & Gold, E. (2006). Home to school: Numeracy practices and mathematical identities. *Mathematical Thinking & Learning, 8*(3), 261–286.

Asher, S. R., & Renshaw, P. D. (1981). Children without friends: Social knowledge and social-skill training. In S. R. Asher & J. M. Gottman (Eds.), *The development of children's friendships* (pp. 273–296). New York: Cambridge University Press.

Atencio, D. J. (2004). Structured autonomy or guided participation? Constructing interest and understanding in a lab activity. *Early Childhood Education Journal, 31*(4), 233–239.

Aubrey, C., Bottle, G., & Godfrey, R. (2003). Early mathematics in the home and out-of-home contexts. *International Journal of Early Years Education, 11*(2), 91–102.

Barnett, S.W., Jung, K., Yarosz, D. J., Thomas, J., Hornbeck, A., Stechuk, R., & Burns, S. (2008). Educational effects of the *Tools of the Mind* curriculum: A randomized trial. *Early Childhood Research Quarterly, 23*(3), 299–313.

Barton, K.C. (2008). Research on students' ideas about history. In L. S. Levstik & C. A. Tyson (Eds.), *Handbook of research in social studies education* (pp. 239–258). New York: Routledge.

Bodrova, E., & Leong, D.J. (2001). *Tools of the mind: A case study of implementing the Vygotskian approach in American early childhood and primary classrooms.* Geneva, Switzerland: International Bureau of Education.

Bodrova, E., & Leong, D. J. (2005). High quality pre-school programs: What would Vygotsky say? *Early Education in Development, 16*(4), 435–444.

Brady, J. P., Dickinson, D. K., Hirschler, J. A., Cross, T., & Green, L. C. (1998). *Evaluation of the Step-by-Step program: Executive summary.* Arlington, VA: U.S. Agency for International Development.

Bransford, J., Vye, N., Stevens, R., Kuhl, P., Schwartz, D., & Bell, P. (2006). Learning theories and education: Toward a decade of synergy. In P. Alexander & P. Winne (Eds.), *Handbook of educational psychology* (2nd ed., pp. 209–244). Mahwah, NJ: Erlbaum.

Brophy, J. & Alleman, J. (2008). Early elementary social studies. In L. S. Levstik & C. A. Tyson (Eds.), *Handbook of research in social studies education* (pp. 33–39). New York: Routledge.

CASEL (2003). *Safe and sound: An educational leader's guide to evidence-based social and emotional (SEL) learning programs.* Chicago, IL: CASEL. Retrieved from http://www.casel.org/downloads/Safe%20 and%20Sound/1A_Safe_&_Sound.pdf

Cassata-Widera, A., Kato-Jones, Y., Duckles, J. M., Conezio, K., & French, L. (2008). Learning the language of science. *The International Journal of Learning, 15*(8), 141–152.

Chang-Wells, G. M., & Wells, G. (1993). Dynamics of discourse: Literacy and the construction of knowledge. In E. A. Forman, N. Minick, & C. A. Stone (Eds.), *Contexts for learning: Sociocultural dynamics in children's development* (pp. 58–90). New York: Oxford University Press.

Charles, C. M. (2011). *Building classroom discipline* (10th ed.). Boston, MA: Pearson.

Cobb, P. (1999). Individual and collective mathematical development: The case of statistical data analysis. *Mathematical Thinking and Learning, 1*, 5–44.

Cole, Michael. (1998). *Cultural psychology: A once and future discipline.* Cambridge, MA: Harvard University Press.

Correa-Chavez, M., & Rogoff, B. (2009). Children's attention to interactions directed to others: Guatemalan Mayan and European American patterns. *Developmental Psychology, 45*(3), 630–641.

Coughlin, P. (1996). Child-centered early childhood education in Eastern Europe: The Step-by-Step approach. *Childhood Education, 72,* 337–340.

Crick, N. C., & Dodge, K. A., (1994). A review and reformulation of social information-processing mechanisms in children's social adjustment. *Psychological Bulletin, 115*(1), 74–101.

Daniels, H. (2008). *Vygotsky and research.* London: Routledge.

Daniels, H., Wertsch, J., & Cole, M. (Eds.). (2007). *The Cambridge companion to Vygotsky.* Cambridge, England: Cambridge University Press.

DeBaessa, Y., Chesterfield, R., & Ramos, T. (2002). Active learning and democratic behavior in Guatemalan primary schools. *Compare, 32*(2), 205–218.

Dewey, J. (1959). *Dewey on education: Selections* (M. S. Dworkin, Ed.). New York: Teachers College Press.

Diamond, A., Barnett, W. S., Thomas, J., & Munro, S. (2007). Preschool program improves cognitive control. *Science, 318,* 1387–1388.

Dodge, E. P., & Mallard, A R. (1992). Social skills training using a collaborative service delivery model. *Language, Speech, and Hearing Services in Schools, 23,* 130–135.

Durlak, J. A., & Wells, A. M. (1997). Primary prevention mental health programs for children and adolescents: A meta-analytic review. *American Journal of Community Psychology, 25*(2), 115–152.

Edwards, C. H. (2008). *Classroom discipline and management.* (5th ed.). Hoboken, NJ: Wiley.

Feshbach, N. D., & Feshbach, S., (1987). Affective processes and academic achievement. *Child Development, 58,* 1335–1347.

Forness, S., Serna, L., Kavale, K., & Nielsen, E. (1998). Mental health and head start: Teaching adaptive skills. *Education and Treatment of Children, 21*(3), 258.

Gallimore, R., & Goldenberg, C. (1993). Activity settings of early literacy: Home and school factors in children's emergent literacy. In E. A. Forman, N. Minick, & C. A. Stone (Eds.), *Contexts for learning: Sociocultural dynamics in children's development* (pp. 315–335). New York: Oxford University Press.

Hahn, C. L., & Alviar-Martin, T. (2008). International political socialization research. In L. S. Levstik & C. A. Tyson (Eds.), *Handbook of research in social studies education* (pp. 81–108). New York: Routledge.

Hainnikainen, M. (2007). Creating togetherness and building a preschool community of learners: The role of play and games. In T. Jambor & J. Van Gils (Eds.), *Several perspectives in children's play: Scientific reflections for practitioners* (pp. 147–160). Antwerp, Belgium: Garant.

Hansen, K., Kaufman, R. K., & Saifer, S. (2004). *Education and the culture of democracy: Early childhood practice.* Washington, DC: Children's Resources International.

Hart, D., & Atkins, R. (2002). Civic competence in urban youth. *Applied Developmental Science, 6*(4), 227–236.

Heath, S. B. (1983).*Ways with words: Language, life, and work in communities and classrooms.* New York: Cambridge University Press.

Hedegaard, M. (2007). The development of children's conceptual relation to the world, with a focus on concept formation in preschool children's activity. In H. Daniels, J. Wertsch, & M. Cole (Eds.), *The Cambridge companion to Vygotsky* (pp. 246–275). Cambridge, England: Cambridge University Press.

Hedegaard, M. (2009). Children's development from a cultural-historical approach: Children's activity in everyday local settings as foundation for their development. *Mind, Culture and Activity, 16*(1), 64–82.

Jantz, R. K., & Seefeldt, C. (1999). Early childhood social studies. In C. Seefeldt (Ed.), *The early childhood curriculum: Current findings in theory and practice* (3rd ed., pp. 160–181). New York: Teachers College Press.

Kohn, A. (2006). *Beyond discipline: From compliance to community.* Alexandria, VA: ASCD.

Krogh, S. (2008). Making Bosnia-Herzegovina safe for democracy. *Democracy and Education, 18*(1), 41–45.

Ladd, G. W. (1990). Having friends, keeping friends, making friends, and being liked by peers in the classroom: Predictors of children's early school adjustment? *Child Development, 61*, 1081–1100.

Lash, M. (2008). Classroom community and peer culture in kindergarten. *Early Childhood Education, 36*, 33–38.

Levstik, L. S. (2008). What happens in social studies classrooms? Research on K-12 social studies practice. In L. S. Levstik & C. A. Tyson (Eds.), *Handbook of research in social studies education* (pp. 50–64). New York: Routledge.

Levstik, L. S., & Tyson, C. A., (2008). Introduction. In L. S. Levstik & C. A. Tyson (Eds.), *Handbook of research in social studies education* (pp. 1–14). New York: Routledge.

Li, J. (2008). *Improving early childhood education in Central and Eastern Europe step by step*. Santa Monica, CA: Rand. Retrieved from http://www.rand.org/content/dam/rand/pubs/research_briefs/2008/RAND_RB9391.pdf

Ligorio, M. B., & Van Veen, K. (2006). Constructing a successful crossnational virtual learning environment in primary and secondary education. *AACE Journal, 14*(2), 103–128.

Maynard, A. E. (2004). Cultures of teaching in childhood: Formal schooling and Mayan sibling teaching at home. *Cognitive Development, 19*, 517–535.

McConaughy, S. H., Kay, P., Welkowitz, J. A., Hewitt, K., & Fitzgerald, M. D. (2007). *Collaborating with parents for early school success*. New York: Guilford.

McKown, C., Gumbiner, L. M., Russo, N. M., & Lipton, M. (2009). Socio-emotional learning skill, self-regulation, and social competence in typically developing and clinically-referred children. *Journal of Clinical Child and Adolescent Psychiatry, 38*(6), 858–871.

McLennan, D. M. P. (2009). Ten ways to create a more democratic classroom. *Young Children, 64*(4), 100–101.

Miller, M. J., Lane, K. L., & Wehby, J. (2005). Social skills for instruction for students with high incidence disabilities: A school-based intervention to address acquisition deficits. *Preventing School Failure, 49*, 27–40.

Miller, S. L., & Vanfossen, P. J. (2008). Recent research on the teaching and learning of pre-collegiate economics. In L. S. Levstik & C. A. Tyson (Eds.), *Handbook of research in social studies education* (pp. 284–306). New York: Routledge.

Morton, B. A. & Dalton, B. (2007). *Changes in instructional hours in four subjects by public school teachers of grades 1 through 4*. Washington DC: National Center for Education Statistics.

National Council for Social Studies (NCSS). (1988). *Social studies for early childhood and elementary school children: Preparing for the 21st century*. Retrieved from http://www.socialstudies.org/positions/elementary

Nelsen, J., Lott, L., Glenn, H. S. (2000). *Positive discipline in the classroom: Developing mutual respect, cooperation, and responsibility in your classroom*. New York: Three Rivers Press.

Nolan, S. B. (2001). Constructing literacy in the kindergarten: Task structure, collaboration, motivation. *Cognition and Instruction, 19*(1), 95–142.

O'Neil, R., Welsh, M., Parke, R., Wang, S., & Strand, C. (1997) A longitudinal assessment of the academic correlates of early peer acceptance and rejection. *Journal of Clinical Child Psychology, 26*(3) 290–303.

Packer, M. (2001). The problem of transfer, and the sociocultural critique of schooling. *Journal of the Learning Sciences, 10*(4), 493–514.

Palincsar, A. S., Brown, A. L., & Campione, J.C. (1993). First-grade dialogues for knowledge acquisition and use. In E. A. Forman, N. Minick, & C. A. Stone (Eds.), *Contexts for learning: Sociocultural dynamics in children's development* (pp. 43–57). New York: Oxford University Press.

Parker, J. G., & Asher, S. R. (1987). Peer relations and later personal adjustment: Are low-accepted children at risk? *Psychological Bulletin, 102*, 357–389.

Raver, C. C., & Zigler, E. F. (1997). Social competence: An untapped dimension in evaluating Head Start's success. *Early Childhood Research Quarterly, 12*(4), 363–385.

Ray, C. E., & Elliott, S. N. (2006). Social adjustment and academic achievement: A predictive model for students with diverse academic and behavior competencies. *School Psychology Review, 35*, 493–501.

Raywid, M. A. (1987). The democratic classroom: mistake or misnomer. *Theory into Practice, 26*, 480–489.

Richardson, R. T., Myran, S. P., & Tonelson, S. (2009). Teaching social and educational competence in early childhood. *International Journal of Special Education, 24*(3), 143–149.

Rogoff, B. (1990). *Apprenticeship in thinking: Cognitive development in social context*. New York: Oxford University press.

Rogoff, B. (1995). Observing sociocultural activity on three planes: participatory appropriation, guided participation, and apprenticeship. In J. V. Wertsch, P. D. Rio, & A. Alvarez (Eds.), *Sociocultural studies of mind* (pp. 139–164). Cambridge, England: Cambridge University Press.

Rogoff, B. (2003). *The cultural nature of human development*. New York: Oxford University Press.

Rogoff, B., Topping, K., Baker-Sennett, J., & Lacasa, P. (2002) Mutual contributions of individuals, partners, and institutions: Planning to remember in Girl Scout cookie sales. *Social Development, 11*(2), 266–289.

Roth, W. M., & Bowen, G. M. (1995). Knowing and interacting: A study of culture, practices, and resources in a grade 8 open-inquiry science classroom guided by a cognitive apprenticeship metaphor. *Cognition and Instruction, 13*, 73–128.

Saracho, O. N., & Spodek, B. (Eds.). (2007). Social learning as the basis for early childhood education. In O. N. Saracho & B. Spodek (Eds.), *Contemporary perspectives on social learning in early childhood education* (pp. 303– 310). Charlotte, NC: Information Age.

Sawyer, R. (2005). *Social emergence: Societies as complex systems*. New York: Cambridge University Press.

Segall, A. & Helfenbein, R.J. (2008). Research on K-12 geography education. In L. S. Levstik & C. A. Tyson (Eds.), *Handbook of research in social studies education* (pp. 259–283). New York: Routledge.

Sharpe, T., Brown, M., & Crider, K. (1995). The effects of a sportsmanship curriculum intervention on generalized positive social behavior of urban elementary school students. *Journal of Applied Behavior Analysis, 28*(4), 401–416.

Sprague, J., & Perkins, K. (2009). Direct and collateral effects of the first step to success program. *Journal of Positive Behavior Intervention, 11*(4), 208–221.

Thornton, S. J. (2008). Continuity and change in social studies curriculum. In L. S. Levstik & C. A. Tyson (Eds.), *Handbook of research in social studies education* (pp. 15–32). New York: Routledge.

Torney-Purta, J. (2002). The school's role in developing civic engagement: A study of adolescents in twenty-eight countries. *Applied Developmental Science, 6*(4), 203–212.

Vasquez, O. A. (2008). Cross national explorations of sociocultural research on learning. *Review of Research in Education, 30*, 33–64.

Vogler, K. E., & Virtue, D. (2007). "Just the facts, ma'am": Teaching social studies in the era of standards and high-stakes testing. *The Social Studies, 98*(2), 54–58.

Vygotsky, L. S. (1978). *Mind in society: The development of higher psychological processes* (M. Cole, V. John-Steiner, S. Scribner, & E. Souberman, Eds.). Cambridge, MA: Harvard University Press.

Wentzel, K. R. (2003). School adjustment. In W. Reynolds & G. Miller (Eds.), *Handbook of psychology: Vol. 7. Educational Psychology* (pp. 235–258). New York: Wiley.

Wang, X. C., & Ching, C. C, (2003). Social construction of computer experience in a first-grade classroom: Social processes and mediating artifacts. *Early Education and Development, 14*(3), 335–362.

Wang, F., Kinzie, M. B., McGuire, P. & Pan, E. (2010). Applying technology to inquiry-based learning in early childhood education. *Early Childhood Education, 37*, 381–389.

Webb, N. M., Nemer, K. M., & Ing, M. (2006). Small-group reflections:

Parallels between teacher discourse and student behavior in peer-directed groups. *Journal of the Learning Sciences, 15*(1), 63–119.

Webster-Stratton, C., Reid, M. J., & Stoolmiller, M. (2008). Preventing conduct problems and improving school readiness: Evaluation of the Incredible Years teacher and child training programs in high risk schools. *Journal of Child Psychology and Psychiatry, 49*(5), 471–488.

Wertsch, J. (1998). *Mind as action.* New York: Oxford University Press.

Yackel, E., & Cobb, P. (1996). Socio-mathematical norms, argumentation, and autonomy in mathematics. *Journal for Research in Mathematics Education, 27*, 458–477.

Zsolnai, A. (2002). Relationship between children's social competence, learning motivation and school achievement. *Educational Psychology, 22*(3), 317–329.

15

Repositioning the Visual Arts in Early Childhood Education

Continuing Reconsideration

CHRISTINE MARMÉ THOMPSON
The Pennsylvania State University

Five minutes remained before class was scheduled to begin, but Ming-Jen had already arrived at his Saturday morning art class. The opening routine was familiar and he moved through it without hesitation, retrieving his name tag and his sketchbook from the counter just inside the door, locating a carpet square close to a container brimming with markers, and settling on the floor to draw. He selected a spot close to a favorite student teacher, a young man seated in the midst of carpet squares, markers, and children, ready to watch and to respond to the children and their drawings. The atmosphere was industrious as children trailed in sleepily or bounded through the door with great exuberance, and, having been greeted by teachers and friends, settled quickly to their work.

Ming-Jen's first drawing of the morning, his warm-up, stood out among his more typical renditions of exotic creatures and landscapes. He drew a flower, a center surrounded by petals, each outlined and filled with a different markered color, placed symmetrically around the central perimeter. As unremarkable as it may be for a young child to draw a flower, there was something unusual about the way that this drawing was constructed. Like many of Ming-Jen's drawings—and unlike those of many young children who compose their drawings part-by-contiguous-part until objects are completed or spaces filled—this one was composed deliberately in such a way that room was reserved for parts not yet drawn, negative spaces left between stem and center to be filled later with petals.

As soon as this drawing was finished, Ming-Jen turned to a fresh page in his sketchbook, taking a moment to smooth the pages with the side of his hand. Grabbing a blue marker from the bin beside him, he drew a scalloped line across the two-page spread open before him. Just above this line in the middle of the left-hand page, he added a curving triangular shape. The student teacher just behind Ming-Jen noticed what he had done and intoned, "Uh-oh." Another child, sprawled on the floor three feet away, declared, "A shark's fin," in recognition of Ming-Jen's plan, executed silently with a faint smile on his lips. Clearly aware that he had attracted a growing and attentive audience, Ming-Jen drew the sweep of a whale's tail emerging from the waterline. A child looking on observed, "Well, he draws a lot," as if to reassure his companion that there *was* an explanation for the remarkable ability Ming-Jen was demonstrating before their eyes. Ming-Jen continued to add details beneath the waterline, and the student teacher next to him remarked, very quietly, "That's a wonderful picture." A small grin played with Ming-Jen's lips, but he drew on without comment, conscious of the spectators huddled around him, willing to keep them guessing as the drawing continued to materialize on the page. "Are you gonna color it?" one of the children asked, noticing that the scene so far had been drawn in a single color, with one marker flowing continuously across the page, describing one object, then another. "What's that?" Yujie inquired as Ming-Jen began a large form that straddled the central spiral bisecting his drawing surface: "A big starfish," she suggested, "or an octopus?" Again Ming-Jen failed to respond, drawing on with the undivided attention of three onlookers focused upon him. Finally, the page filled with flotsam and jetsam, his performance completed, Ming-Jen leaned back against the knee of the student teacher behind him, and shared a satisfied smile with the group.

In many respects, this was a small and ordinary incident of classroom life, readily recognizable as the type of fleeting interaction that occurs at drawing tables or art centers, as children gather to admire the skillful performance of one of their peers. And yet accounts of children drawing in the social space of early childhood classrooms are still relatively rare. Once, and not so very long ago, researchers concerned with children's art would have focused their attention exclusively on Ming-Jen himself, the solitary artist in dialogue with his work (Brooks, 2005; Dyson, 1989). The presence of others, their comments and questions, their critical or appreciative responses, would have been reduced to background noise or erased entirely from an account of this drawing being made (Atkinson, 2002; Matthews, 1999). As Pearson (2001) suggests, the act of drawing might have passed without remark, in favor of an analysis of the drawing itself, for children's artworks have often been granted greater significance than the work that produced them. Even when advice to teachers continued to insist upon the primacy of process over product, researchers focused attention exclusively on the residue of that process.

In recent years, educators concerned with the education of young children have devoted considerable energy to the serious critique of the research and theory upon which practice in early childhood art has been based. Stimulated by a renewed sense of responsibility for early childhood education, and more direct involvement with young children and their teachers, art educators in museums, schools, and universities have joined in questioning many of their shared assumptions about young children and their encounters with art. This reconceptualization draws upon sources previously overlooked or lightly used in the past, when developmental psychology structured thinking about young children and their art and radically child-centered approaches to early art education were widely accepted as exemplary practice. Almost 20 years ago, Jeffers (1993) reported that the art educators she surveyed emphasized developmental issues in the methods classes they offered to university students majoring in early childhood and elementary education, identifying development as one of three major concerns addressed in such courses. This finding was somewhat surprising in an era in which a discipline-based approach to art education prevailed, and, to an extent unprecedented in the history of North American art education, developmental issues vanished from ongoing conversations within and beyond that field.

This discipline-based perspective has evolved in the past decade, expanding toward a focus on visual culture, broadly defined (e.g., Duncum, 2003; Wilson, 2004), but leaving in its wake an enduring commitment among art educators to the study of images and objects in their aesthetic, critical, historical, social, and political contexts. There has also been a marked resurgence of interest in the art experience of contemporary children and adolescents, and in the development of curricular theory and instructional approaches that are responsive to that experience.

Jeffers's (1993) reading of the content of preservice education of teachers suggests that there has long been an arrhythmia in the field, a lack of syncopation between what beginning teachers are taught, and what researchers and theorists recommend (Richards, 2007). McArdle and Piscatelli (2002) suggest that early childhood art education is best viewed as a "palimpsest," where old and new ideas from multiple informing disciplines persist and coexist, even when they may be deeply incompatible. The devel-

opmental stage theories that served as the foundation of early art education throughout much of the 20th century are undeniably appealing to prospective teachers, providing a measure of predictability in a curricular area that many classroom teachers approach with considerable uncertainty and apprehension. Developmental stages supply a structure that is comprehensible and comprehensive, an approach to early art education that can be reproduced in any classroom, if children's experiences with art are structured in a particular way that accords well with the child-centered traditions of early childhood practice. At the same time, researchers and theorists who focus on early art education question the "hegemony of developmental psychology on our understanding of children" (Tarr, 2003, p. 7) and the traditional structure of universal stages with their tendency to "decontextualize child and children" (Tarr, 2003, p. 7).

Art education research, necessarily interdisciplinary in focus, has become increasingly attuned to larger cultural issues. A pervasive reconceptualization of the "image of the child" (Malaguzzi, 1995) can be seen in the emergence of the new sociology of childhood (James, Jenks, & Prout, 1998) and studies of children's culture (Dyson, 2003; Jenkins, 1998), and exemplified in the practice of preschool education in Reggio Emilia (New, 2007; Rinaldi, 2006). The most dramatic changes that have occurred in research on early childhood art and art education involve changes of perspective or theoretical orientation. Different forms and emphases have emerged as priorities in art education research as our understanding of young children and of the content and contexts of art education have continued to evolve.

Art education's relationship to early childhood practice is historically close and often beset by difficulty. Art educators seldom teach young children directly, although the establishment of preschool programs in public schools, and interest in the role of the *atelierista* (Vecchi, 1998) has changed this situation to some extent, in some communities. Indeed, many of the art educators who have worked most closely with young children, and who have written about those experiences, entered early childhood classrooms as researchers, often simultaneously working with those who are actually doing the teaching (e.g., Tarr, 1995; Taunton & Colbert, 2000; Thompson, 1999, 2002, 2003; Thompson & Bales, 1991). Art education in early childhood classrooms depends primarily on early childhood specialists (Baker, 1994), who sometimes rely on advice provided by art educators through publication or teaching. This means, among many other things, that art educators are often outside observers in the early childhood settings where their research takes place, and seldom in a position to submit their ideas directly to the test of practice. This may account for a tendency, apparent in research on children's art from the beginning of its history, to wrap descriptions of child art in prescriptions for practice, to offer educational advice extrapolated from psychological study (see, for example, Kellogg, 1970; Luquet, 1927/2001; Matthews,

2002). This advice was frequently motivated by a desire to preserve children's art in the most unadulterated state possible. Fortunately, this tendency seems to be muted as researchers enter classrooms with the intention of viewing children's art making and response as "social practice" in action (Pearson, 2001), and confront the urgency of formulating advice for teachers that is sound, practical, and clearly articulated.

As Wilson (1997) points out,

Child "art" is a product of the modernist era. To the modernist art educator and psychologist, artistic development was essentially a natural unfolding process that led to individual expression. This belief was not unlike the preferred modernist view of the artist as an individual with the obligation, perhaps the moral imperative, to develop a unique style of expression unconstrained by artistic convention. (p. 82)

But, Wilson continues, child art, like all art, is an "open concept" (Weitz, 1959, pp. 145–156), defined and redefined in response to changing conditions: "objects and events become child art when they are so interpreted" (Wilson, 1997, p. 81). The boundaries of art continually expand, as new media, new experiences, and new understandings become available. The emergence of photography projects for children (Ewald & Lightfoot, 2001) and video as a medium for telling stories in the classroom (Brooks, 2006; Grace & Tobin, 2002; McClure, 2009) are recent examples of approaches to art making that fundamentally alter the circumstances in which children experience themselves as artists. Wilson acknowledges that understanding child art inevitably requires interpretation, and that this phenomenon, historically and persistently of interest to so many different constituencies, cannot help but mean different things to different people: "When individuals with different sets of interests and values interpret children's objects differently, those objects are transformed into very different things, things that are sometimes works of art and sometimes not" (Wilson, 1997, p. 82). The world of art, the world of education, and the world of the child provide distinct perspectives on the same phenomenon, and each perspective, on its own, may well conceal as much as it reveals.

The attitudes we hold toward children's art and art experience are inevitably conditioned by prevailing cultural beliefs about art and childhood (Korzenik, 1981; Leeds, 1989; Wilson, 1997), beliefs that are shaped by things seen and discussions heard through the media, in our daily conversations with colleagues and service station attendants and our children's teachers, or in the more rarified conversations that occur in the "official" art worlds of galleries, museums, and critical reviews, and the equally heady realms of educational research and theory. At one time, in the middle of the 20th century, the lush easel paintings produced by preschool children were prized, both by artists who saw in them an enviable freedom of gesture and a complete indifference to the task of representing tangible objects and scenes, and by psychologists and educators who saw them as evidence of a healthy confidence and exuberant well-being. More recently, interest in the narrative dimensions of children's art emerged among artists and critics, coinciding with increased attention among educators to the role of drawing in the "prehistory" of writing (Vygotsky, 1962) and in the process of meaning making in which young children are constantly engaged (Wilson & Wilson, 1982/2009). These values, absorbed from our culture in the process of living, affect the kinds of experience teachers provide for children, and the interests researchers bring to the classrooms where these experiences are pursued. Neither childhood nor art is a simple or static concept, and neither of them is amenable to stable or enduring definition in a manner that will stand the test of time or transfer intact from one context to another. In the early years of the 21st century, the primary focus of research in early art education, defined in the broadest possible terms, is the process through which children learn to represent and to read the world by means of visual images. As it has been throughout its history, early childhood art remains an object of scholarly attention for psychologists, art educators, and early childhood specialists, artists, and art historians, and has an immediate practical interest for parents and teachers. These multiple perspectives, diverse as they often are, converge in three broad, overlapping categories—development, context, and curriculum (Bresler & Thompson, 2002)—that provide organization to the remainder of this discussion.

Development: Questioning Traditional Views

Can we think beyond the developmental stages in art that we have taken for granted for so long and that have implicitly limited the possibilities of experiences and materials that we have offered children? (Tarr, 2003, p. 8)

Although the developmentalist perspective has been subjected to repeated challenges over the past 20 years (Wilson & Wilson, 1982/2009; Wolf & Perry, 1988), the basic description of evolutionary patterns in children's drawings formulated in the first half of the 20th century retains a powerful presence in early childhood education. Textbooks published within the past decade for teachers who are preparing to work with young children continue to feature stages of artistic development originally described by Viktor Lowenfeld in the 1940s (Edwards, 1997; Schirrmacher, 1993), by Rhoda Kellogg in the 1960s (Schirrmacher, 1993), occasionally supplemented, though not supplanted, by more current research (Jalongo & Stamp, 1997). In many cases, these texts reflect the continuing influence of Piaget on thinking in the field (Atkinson, 2002), even as the recommendations for teaching that they offer suggest the need for adult structure (often overt structure) in art programs for young children. A more Vygotskian perspective is apparent in a text published more recently by Althouse, Johnson, and Mitchell (2003), who recognize the essential role that adults play in initiating, scaffolding, and responding to young children's earliest encounters with art, and in the work of Brooks (2003, 2005, 2009).

Cognitive psychologists continue to undertake studies related to children's art experiences, operating within an established consensus regarding the nature of age-related changes in children's drawings (e.g., Cox, 1992, 2005; Freeman & Cox, 1985; Lange-Kuettner & Thomas, 1995; Thomas & Silk, 1990). Reith (1997) observes persistent interest among his colleagues in children's passage from "intellectual" to "visual realism" (Luquet, 1927/2001). He notes that psychologists are particularly interested in the phenomena that seem to occur after age 5, when children display more concern with the inclusion of relevant details in their drawings, and, at 8 or 9, when children seem to develop a more acute (and critical) sense of what might be seen from a particular viewpoint (see also Korzenik, 1973–1974). The ongoing debate, Reith notes, concerns the explanations for these phenomena. Some psychologists stress the role of "knowledge about objects" (Reith, 1997, p. 61): "Drawings are believed to reflect the subject's mental representations and conceptual knowledge about the objects they draw. Drawings become more accurate and detailed as children's mental models of the world become more extensive and differentiated" (p. 61). As Reith points out, this belief about the relationship between drawing and cognition is firmly established, having served as the basis for the Draw-a-Man Test (Goodenough, 1926; D. B. Harris, 1963). Recent research tends to stress the negative impact of knowledge on drawing (Cox, 1989; Freeman & Janikoun, 1972), the extent to which what children *know* about an object prevents them from drawing what they *see*. A classic example of this tendency is seen when young children include details of an object that are hidden from their view, choosing to depict the canonical view in preference to one that is more accurate to the model, but less informative about the characteristic features of the object as the child knows them. Presented with the challenge of drawing a mug with its handle turned away from their view, for example, young children often include the unseen handle in the interest of clearly depicting a mug that, distinct from a drinking glass, depends upon this appendage (Cox, 1992).

Some psychologists who concentrate on this area of research challenge the proposition that the major questions surrounding child art have been satisfactorily answered. Golomb (1997) suggests that, "Despite much productive research in the domain of drawing, no clear consensus has been reached regarding the course of development, the nature of the progression, the validity of a stage conception, and the goals or end-states of graphic development" (p. 131). The possibility of continual generation of fresh perspectives on child art is seen in Matthews's (1999) reconsiderations of scribbling, in which he links early forms of motor behavior that are first mastered and then continued as playful manipulations, with markers in hand, but also in play with scarves and blocks and toy trucks and action

figures. At the same time, Matthews raises objections to the widely held assumption that scribbles are "prerepresentational" traces of motor activity caught on paper—gestural, pleasurable, nonreferential. Matthews stresses the basis of these early marks in children's effort to produce meaning:

> During the phase when infants are supposed to be mindlessly scribbling, they imbue their marking actions with profound expressive and representational intention.... For many children, these drawings are products of a systematic investigation, rather than haphazard actions, of the expressive and representational potential of visual media. (p. 19)

Matthews continues, contributing to the critique of the ways in which representation is defined in discussions of child art: "Early drawings lack meaning only if one assumes that drawing is necessarily the depiction of objects" (p. 20). He contends that children are also interested in the expression of movement and emotion:

> In the hands of a 1- or 2-year-old, drawing and painting become sensitive media, responsive to even minute fluctuations in the child's own feelings and in the ambient emotional temperature. When representational values appear in children's drawing these are unrecognizable to those who assume that visual representation is about recognizable pictures of recognizable things. Some early paintings and drawings are not pictures of things, but they are representations in a fuller sense, in that they record the child's process of attention to objects and event. (Matthews, 1999, pp. 20–21)

As Egan (1988, 1999; Egan & Ling, 2002) suggests, many "taken-for-granted truisms about children's thinking and learning" (1999, p. 86) continue to permeate educational thought, persisting, implicit and unquestioned, both in everyday discussions and teaching practice, and in research. Egan points, instead, to those things that young children do well, in some cases, more spontaneously and fluidly than they will at other periods of their lives, including the contemplation of philosophical questions (Matthews, 1980) and participation in the arts. Egan's recognition of the rich resources for thought and action young children demonstrate in artistic pursuits supports Howard Gardner's (1980) description of the late preschool years as a "golden age," a time in which children demonstrate intellectual and imaginative versatility. Egan and Ling conclude, "The basics of our cultural lives are the arts" (2002, p. 100), effectively inverting the fundamental teleologies underlying traditional understandings of what children are developing from, and toward.

In decades past, participating in a more general critique of the developmentalist perspective, researchers have raised the possibility that the conceptualization of human development that guides much educational discourse may begin with a fundamental understanding that is particularly detrimental to consideration of children's art or symbolic behaviors. As Gallas (1994) frames the question:

What if we were to assume that children came to school more, rather than less, able to communicate their thinking about the world? Why not assume that when the child enters school, he or she presents us with an enormous number of innate tools for acquiring knowledge and, rather than considering them to be "constraints" as Gardner (1991) suggests, consider them to be assets? (p. xv)

For much of the 20th century, a model of "natural development" prevailed in discussions of child art, describing an innate and universal process with children "located in one of several stages, which are internally consistent, formally logical and intellectually revealing" (Freedman, 1997, p. 95). These stages of artistic development, as outlined by Luquet (1927/2001), Costall (2001), Lowenfeld (1957), and others, were supported by psychobiological explanations. Based upon the "presupposition of innate ability" (Atkinson, 2002, p. 7), stage theory encouraged the belief that artistic competence unfolds predictably from within the individual child, given the most minimal encouragement. Landmarks along the path of artistic development were labeled differently and sometimes described in terms that varied, if only slightly, from one researcher to the next. Puzzling detours and derailments of the process in its later stages were noted. However, the journey's destination remained constant: Children were developing toward the capacity to draw realistically, to capture visual likeness on the drawing page, to create convincing two-dimensional versions of a three-dimensional world.

Two assumptions underlying the traditional model of artistic development, have come into question since the 1980s. Doubts initially raised by Wilson and Wilson (1982/2009), Wolf and Perry (1988), and others about two elements of developmental theory have been confirmed by subsequent research: (1) the idea that representational accuracy is the sole or universal endpoint of the process of artistic development, and (2) the belief that benign neglect was the most favorable ground in which this process would unfold.

Questioning the Standard of Realism

Although few researchers in art education overtly acknowledge their debt to Piaget, the research and theory of artistic development, from Lowenfeld to the present day, has emerged in dialogue with Piagetian assumptions (Atkinson, 2002; Brooks, 2003). Piaget rarely wrote directly about artistic development. In his occasional statements on the matter, Piaget admitted how puzzling he found children's drawings, in their defiance of the expected trajectory of skills developing toward increased refinement in middle childhood, and in their deviations from realistic representation.

The aspects of child art that provoked Piaget continue to puzzle researchers, leading to questions concerning both the validity of the original developmental descriptions, and their continued viability in contemporary culture (see, e.g., Kindler & Darras, 1997; Thompson, 2003; Walsh, 2002;

Wilson, 1997; Wilson & Wilson, 1977, 1982/2009; Wolf & Perry, 1988). These critiques frequently penetrate to the most basic assumptions of developmental theory. Kindler and Darras (1997), for example, point out that stage theories of artistic development define art too narrowly, focusing primarily on children's drawings, and excluding or ignoring large swaths of behavior that are considered artistic in contemporary practice, including many of the art works that children make for their own purposes and pleasure. They argue that stage theories of artistic development are too linear and monofocal to account for the multiple symbolic languages that children accumulate as they grow. They suggest instead that it is the distinctive "repertoires" (Wolf & Perry, 1988) that children acquire that allow them to choose between different styles of drawing as the occasion warrants (Bremner & Moore, 1984; Kindler, 1999).

Particularly problematic is the traditional emphasis on realistic representation as the single, desirable end-point of artistic development (Golomb, 1992/2004, 2002). This assumption is questionable from the standpoint of both Western and world art where expression and narrative frequently surpass realistic rendering as the primary concerns of visual representation. As psychologist Claire Golomb (1992/2004) remarks, in elevating photorealistic likeness to the pinnacle of artistic achievement, "we mistake a style valued by our culture for an intrinsic phase of human development" (p. 46).

Golomb (1997) suggests that young children fare badly in the face of "a hypothesized standard of realism," when their efforts to represent some aspect of their experience in the world, presumably intended to be realistic, are, almost inevitably, "declared…deficient" (p. 131). When research begins with this perspective on the nature of representation, deviations from reality are seen as evidence of conceptual immaturity. Golomb suggests that this notion has been adopted rather uncritically by Piagetians, neo-Piagetians, and the British school of researchers (i.e., Cox, 1992; Freeman, 1980; Freeman & Cox, 1985) who examine task demands and production deficits in children's drawings.

Yet these researchers have continued to examine issues of graphic representation in ways that acknowledge the complexity of factors contributing to that process. For example, Cox (1992, 1993, 1997; Freeman & Cox, 1985) offers a variation of the "production deficit hypothesis" (Golomb, 2002, p. 13) originally proposed by Freeman (1980; Freeman & Cox, 1985), a theory that looks to children's inexperience in drawing, rather than their conceptual deficits, to explain the problems they encounter when they attempt to compose a drawing. Attempting to explain why children's drawings of the same object may vary according to the task proposed to them, the intentions the child brings to the task, and the child's engagement in the process, Cox suggests that the child's internal mental model mediates between immediate perception, prior knowledge of the object, and the drawing currently appearing on the page. This conclusion is compatible with a theory of drawing developed by Wilson and Wilson (1977), which substitutes the notion that children develop and choose among multiple "drawing programs" for Lowenfeld's proposal that young children slowly develop and gradually modify schemas for each of the objects they draw and for the arrangement of those objects within the space of a drawing (Freedman, 1997, p. 101). Wilson and Wilson recognize the importance of small incremental changes in children's drawings, and the potential of simultaneously developing drawing programs, repertoires, and end-points (Wolf & Perry, 1988); however, Cox continues to regard the realistic vantage of the "view-centered" representation as the more advanced, and hence desirable, destination for children's drawing (Cooke, Griffin, & Cox, 1998).

Matthews (1999) raises the question, "What does it mean to talk about 'the way things really look'? What is the true shape of a cat or a cloud?" (p. 5). Influenced by the theoretical perspective of Arnheim, Golomb offers a perspective on children's artistic experience as a gradual process of differentiation, in which structures acquire greater fluidity, complexity, and detail as the intentions children bring to drawings change and the range of graphic strategies at their disposal expands. She adopts an inclusive definition of representation in order to acknowledge the centrality and the difficulty of the task children undertake in drawing and other symbolic activities: "Representation is a constructive mental activity; it is not a literal or exact imitation or copy of the object, although the perceiver may, at times, find a resemblance striking or even deceptive. Representation in this sense is a major biological, psychological, and cultural achievement" (Golomb, 2002, p. 5).

Atkinson (2002) ponders the extent to which the "natural attitude" (p. 34) toward representation is perpetuated and enforced through teaching practice at all educational levels. As he notes, this presumption creates a self-fulfilling prophecy in art education: "in valuing particular traditions of practice it attempts to reproduce them and thus perpetuate a particular cultural hegemony towards practice and understanding in art education" (p. 35).

Clearly this has been a significant period of unrest in terms of understanding children's artistic development. There seems to be an increasing allegiance to a "sociological perspective on development" (Freedman, 1997). There is an interest in retaining the sense that children's actions have "an internal structure and systematicity" (Matthews, 1999, p. 6), while acknowledging those factors in each child's environment and experience that may alter that internal structure and modify its systems of operation in ways that distinguish the artistry of a particular child (Thompson, 1999).

Sociocultural Perspectives: Development as Learning

Despite the caution they introduce about reliance on traditional stage theories of development, Kindler and Darras (1997) remark that existing descriptions of the earliest stages of children's art making, particularly the prerepresentational phase typically referred to as the "scribbling stage," seem to be relatively reliable. They note that stage theories tend to become increasingly unstable as children reach the middle school years and descend into the trough of the U-curve described by Gardner (1982) and others (Davis, 1997). At the same time, there is growing evidence that preschool art, even in these earliest moments, is culturally conditioned and socially influenced (Alland, 1983; Matthews, 1999). The most basic configurations of marks made on paper often reflect the prevailing aesthetic of a child's cultural surround. As Kindler and Darras (1997) observe, this recognition of the malleability of the artistic process renders reliance on stage theories problematic, since, "Stage theories are founded on a culture-free assumption and either neglect to consider the implications of the cultural and social context, or view any extraneous influences as detrimental to the natural, biologically defined process of development" (p. 19). The significance of sociocultural factors, recognized by many researchers engaged in cross-cultural study of children's drawings earlier in the 20th century (cf. Paget, 1932, for example), was downplayed by researchers intent on emphasizing the universality of child art (Kellogg, 1970; Golomb, 1992). However, as Kindler and Darras point out, those who are reluctant to admit exceptions to the rules of a universal language of child art are forced to minimize and discount obvious cultural and individual differences in children's drawings: "Even if one is willing to regard cultural and social factors as simply contributing to the variability within the general rule (Golomb, 1992), this variability needs to be acknowledged and addressed" (Kindler & Darras, 1997, p. 19). In a manner congruent with a more general post-Piagetian perspective (Inagaki, 1992), the existence and significance of these individual and cultural variations are increasingly recognized and addressed in art education research (Kindler, 1994; Thompson & Bales, 1991; Wilson & Wilson, 1977, 1982/2009, 1984, 1985).

Interest in social, cultural, and individual variations on the themes of artistic development has existed from the beginning of the study of child art. In the introduction to his translation of Luquet's *Le Dessin Enfantin* (1927/2001), Costall (2001) emphasizes Luquet's recognition that children make choices in the act of drawing: "The young child chooses intellectual realism.... Intellectual realism is not something the child 'undergoes' as a preliminary to visual realism. It reflects a 'reasonable' commitment to an alternative *ideal* of what a drawing should be" (pp. xvii–xviii), and persists as "a serious and enduring option" (p. xix) for image making throughout life. Following what Costall (2001) describes as an initial "frenzy for amassing vast collections of drawings, usually with the help of school teachers, but [with] the researchers seldom [having] anything to do with the children themselves"(pp. vii–viii), the study of child art has gravitated toward studies that are smaller in scale, often taking the form of longitudinal case studies, or, more recently, observations of classrooms and children working within them (e.g., Edens & Potter, 2004; Kendrick & McKay, 2004; Richards, 2009). There has been substantial interest at certain historical moments in children's responses to works of art and other visual phenomena, topics that have also been studied both through formal experimentation and informal methods of observation. Although traditional experimental designs are still employed, particularly in psychological approaches to the study of child art, qualitative approaches to research in early childhood art education have become increasingly prevalent.

Reconsidering the Art in Artistic Development

Zurmuehlen and Kantner (1995) demonstrate the ways in which general tendencies appear and are embodied in the work of individual children, sharing a more nuanced view of the process through which children acquire the rudiments of artistic practice. The authors illustrate the centrality of narrative in young children's art making, and the importance of repetition and "boundedness" in the transition from "doing" to "making," from exploratory play with materials and forms to intentional exploration of form and creation of meaning. In doing so, they emphasize the continuities of thought and practice that unite young children with mature artists, extending a strand of thought that envisions artistic development as a cumulative process rather than a series of radical reorganizations and displacements of the old by the new (Arnheim, 1969; Beittel, 1973; Gardner, 1973, 1980, 1982; Read, 1945; Schaefer-Simmern, 1948; Wilson & Wilson, 1982/2009; Winner, 1982; Wolf & Perry, 1988).

Researchers involved with Harvard's Project Zero, for example, point to the similarities between the works of young children and mature artists. Gardner (1980) refers to the ages between 5 and 7 as "the golden age of drawing," and the research team has devoted considerable attention to the apparent demise of artistry in middle to late childhood and its unreliable resurgence in adolescence. Even admitting clear differences between artists and children (Davis, 1997), the continuity of artistic practice has been an assumption of Project Zero since its inception in 1967, a basic premise of the "Symbol Systems Approach" (Davis, 1997, p. 46), grounded in the aesthetic theories of Nelson Goodman and Rudolph Arnheim, and the psychological work of Jean Piaget. Interested in young children's ready use of metaphor in words and images, Project Zero applied the same aesthetic criteria to the work of children and professional artists, investigating, for example, the existence of "repleteness" or exploitation of the potential of the medium, in the work of both groups. They began, too, with the belief that the production and the perception of images are equally important in the construction of symbolic meaning. As Davis (1997) explains,

> Through internal symbols or representations, the individual child or producer of art constructs a world view. Through external symbols or representations, the individual shares a world view. This happens when that construction of meaning is recognized or reconstructed by a receptive, equally active meaning-maker, the perceiver of art. (p. 48)

Among the most consistent findings of the research conducted by Project Zero is that the perception of the "aesthetic properties" in works of art seems to improve just as the ability to create aesthetically balanced and expressive images seems to decline, in middle childhood. Preschoolers' drawings are most likely to rival the expressiveness of adult art. As children approach middle childhood, the "flavorfulness" (Davis, 1997, p. 48) or visual richness of their art works appears to wane. Project Zero researchers attribute this phenomenon to the quest for photographic realism in drawing that children undertake between the ages of 8 and 11.

Davis (1997) reports a study involving a large and varied sample: 20 5-year-olds, 20 8-year-olds, 20 11-year-olds, 20 14-year-olds who considered themselves to be artists, 20 14-year-olds who did not think of themselves in this way, 20 nonartist adults and 20 professional artists. She asked each participant to draw the emotional states, "happy," "sad," and "angry," in any way they pleased The 420 drawings produced in response were judged on the following criteria: overall expression, balance, use of line and composition as appropriate to the emotion expressed. Davis found that it was the 5-year-olds and the 14-year-old artists whose works were judged to be closest to the work of professional artists: These groups of very young children and very highly motivated adolescents formed "the two high ends of the 'U'" (Davis, 1997, p. 53), both approximating the level of artistic accomplishment recognized as exemplary in contemporary American culture.

Artists were among the first groups to evince an interest in the aesthetic qualities and inventiveness of young children's images, as the 19th century turned to the 20th. Work by art historian Jonathon Fineberg (1997, 1998, 2006) documents the extent and longevity of this interest, and raises provocative questions about the cultural status of children's art, and the values it is assigned in differing historical periods.

Golomb (1974, 1997, 2002; Golomb & McCormick, 1995) has been persistent in her efforts to expand research attention to aspects of child art beyond drawings, traditionally the data of choice, since they are profusely available, easily stored and manipulated, and subject to comparison with many previous studies. Golomb's interest in doing so is not merely to acknowledge alternate media and forms of children's artistic practice, but to question basic assumptions about the stagelike progression of artistic development and the nature of the relationship between children's internal images and the representations they produce in clay, paint, or marker. Golomb's research in this area operationalizes a theoretical insight articulated, on separate occasions, by Arnheim (1954/1974) and Forman (1994), and embodied in the pedagogical strategies practiced in the preschools of

Reggio Emilia (Reggio Children & Project Zero, 2001); that is, the concept that each medium presents its own characteristic strengths and weaknesses, its own "affordances" (Forman, 1994, p. 42) that allow children to learn certain things about a topic that would be less readily evident in the terms of another medium.

Golomb and McCormick (1995) asked 109 children between the ages of 4 and 13 to model a series of eight objects in clay. These objects—a cup, a table, a man, a woman, a person bending down, a dog, a cow, and a turtle—were selected to vary in complexity, symmetry, and the technical difficulty of balancing a figure. Golomb and McCormick found that most children created three-dimensional forms in response to the tasks that were relatively simple in structure, symmetrical and balanced, especially in response to their request to model the cup and the table. Golomb (1997) noted that the work of the youngest participants in this study revealed "unsuspected competence": "Children seem to approach modeling with an incipiently three-dimensional conception that becomes gradually refined and differentiated, provided the child is exposed to this medium and experiments with various tasks and possibilities" (p. 139). The children encountered the same problems that more mature people with little experience working with clay encounter, "How to create a satisfying representation in a medium that puts a premium on balance, uprightness, and the modeling of multiple sides, all of which require great skill and patience" (Golomb, 1997, p. 140). For Golomb and others, this observation raises the question of whether principles governing child art might apply equally to beginners in a particular medium, regardless of age.

This, and other studies undertaken by Golomb and her associates, was designed to shed light on artistic development, highlighting the difference between constraints in children's approach to art making that are specific to art media with which they may have limited experience, and those constraints imposed by conceptual immaturity. As Golomb (2002) frames the question underlying these investigations, "Does a uniform concept override the properties of the medium, or does it respond selectively to its possibilities and constraints?" (p. 51). Extending a program of research that has been ongoing since the early 1970s, Golomb's recent research converges in a powerful critique of the conceptual deficit theory so often used to explain the apparent anomalies in child art. In a study by Gallo, Golomb, and Barroso (2003), for example, 45 children, ages 5, 7, and 9, were presented with three themes, and asked to represent each in three ways: in a drawing, with precut shapes on felt board, and on a wooden board with pieces provided. The researchers constructed these tasks to explore the conceptual deficit theory, particularly as expressed by Piaget and as countered by Arnheim. While Arnheim would predict change in the ways children represent an idea in each of the media provided, Piaget would predict uniformity, due to the dominance of a single mental model guiding the child's decisions. In this study, as well,

researchers found significant effects for age and medium, and ample support for Arnheim's theory that representational concepts are formed in response to the provisions of a particular medium. Children's work with felt board and three-dimensional wooden pieces demonstrated more sophisticated spatial understanding than was apparent in their drawings. The 5-year-olds were exceptionally enthusiastic about the opportunity to work out their concepts in three-dimensional media. The striking contrast the research team detected between two- and three-dimensional solutions suggests that children may achieve more sophisticated visual and conceptual solutions in response to "revisable tasks" (p. 20), in clay, collage, or construction, than they can produce in their capacity as "novices learning to draw" (Freeman, 1980).

An ambitious proposal formulated by Kindler and Darras (1997) strives to circumvent some of the difficulties inherent in traditional stage theories. They present this proposal as one that preserves the continuity of artistic practice from childhood through maturity, and respects the varieties of uses to which visual imagery may be put:

> [Theirs is] an attempt to conceptualize the development of pictorial representation in a way that does not rely on any particular definition of art.... [but] embraces a diversity of pictorial manifestations without implying value judgments on the artistic merit of any of them, allows for consideration of sociocultural variables, and is concerned with the process from its onset in early childhood and on through the adult years. (p. 19)

Kindler and Darras offer a semiotic model, based on the belief that all art is potentially communicative of "thoughts, ideas, emotions, values, states, understandings, or realities" (p. 19) that may be presented through the use of icons, indices, and symbols that constitute signs. Drawing upon the semiotic theory formulated by Peirce (1931–1935) and Vygotsky's perspective on development as a socially mediated process, their model describes artistic development in terms of three segments and five types of "iconicity," none of which are outgrown and discarded, all of which, once recognized, may be chosen as strategies at any time in life.

This emphasis on the way drawings function for children is equally central to the poststructuralist view of drawing practice offered by Atkinson (2002) who suggests:

> [D]rawing is a semiotic practice and when viewed as such this calls into question conventional understandings of visual representation as an attempt to represent or reproduce views of a prior reality. If drawing is concerned with signification rather than a conventional mimetic idea of representation, then any direct relation between representation and reality is fractured...as a semiotic practice, a drawing qua signifier relates not to a fixed external referent in the world which exists prior to the drawing, but to other signifiers which consist of other images and discourses in which we understand visual structures. (p. 15)

Context

In the context of childhood education the post-modern experience of being a kid represents a cultural earthquake. (Kincheloe, 1998, p. 172)

Much of the impetus for these changes in thinking about early art education derive from the unavoidable recognition of changes in the circumstances of young children's lives, which has, in many and complex ways, brought the education of young children back into the realm of art educators' responsibility. The opportunities for art educators and researchers to work directly with young children or with their teachers multiplied rapidly as increasing numbers of young children began to spend their days in the company of unrelated adults and peers, in preschools and day care settings. As a direct result, researchers concerned with early childhood art have begun to look at children in context, learning to draw and to make sense of images in classrooms and neighborhoods, with the help of other children and teachers as well as parents. The domesticated childhood, and the solitude of early artistic ventures, that were assumed in earlier studies, can no longer be considered the norm for young children in North America nor much of the world.

Young children's formal introductions to art experience frequently occur in contexts that are structured, social, and schoollike, making early art education an issue of equal importance to teachers and to parents. As art educators' contact with young children has increased, it has also become apparent that even the youngest among them bring prior aesthetic experiences and values to school, preferences developed through interactions with friends and family, established attachments to certain images and objects, and constant exposure to visual culture, including "art for children" (Bresler, 2002; Gibson & Mcallister, 2005; Lin & Thomas, 2002; Walsh, 2002).

With this recognition of the fluidity of demographic and sociological patterns has come an understanding that contemporary children and circumstances "no longer fit the existing explanations" (Graue & Walsh, 1998, p. 33). James, Jenks, and Prout (1998) note that the conceptions of childhood that inform educational thought and practice are subject to rapid and radical change within a culture, as they are to marked variations among cultures. Many of the assumptions we hold dear about young children, the conventional wisdom we exchange in daily conversations and professional discourse, do not withstand close scrutiny, as Jenkins (1998) observes: "Our grown-up fantasies of childhood as a simple space crumble when we recognize the complexity of forces shaping our children's lives and defining who they will be, how they will behave, and how they will understand their place in the world" (p. 4). As Duncum (2002) suggests, "children never were what they were" (p. 97). And child art, like childhood itself, is, was, and always will be, an interpreted phenomenon, a construction of adult understanding. Recognizing this, we are obliged to become conscious of the interests that accompany us when we watch

children making art, and to attempt to look more closely both at the child and the context in which he or she works: "If we are to understand child art we must look at what the child has represented and expressed, the conditions under which child art is made, and ourselves and others in the act of studying it" (Wilson, 1997, p. 83).

Among the most dramatic effects of this attention to the contexts of early art experience has been the recognition that much that was accepted as established knowledge about child art may no longer pertain to children's art when it is understood as a "social practice" (Pearson, 2001, p. 348). Previous research concentrated primarily upon analysis of the products or "artifactual residue" of the art making process, and often involved experimental procedures, designed quite deliberately to require children to grapple with problems that they would not attempt in their spontaneous drawings (e.g., Freeman & Janikoun, 1972; Willats, 1977). Matthews (1999) points out that, "Studies of children's art and drawing based solely upon experimental data always distort descriptions of development" (p. 3) for this reason. Matthews's own research relies heavily on naturalistic observational work, both with his own children at home and in classrooms in London and Singapore. He notes, however, that some experimental studies are useful in illuminating issues that are difficult to observe in naturalistic settings. Costall (2001) indicates that Luquet, working early in the 20th century, shared this conviction that direct observation was a far more appropriate and informative method for the study of children's art than formal experimentation.

Pearson, among others (Leeds, 1986; Thompson, 1997; Thompson & Bales, 1991), argues that children's reasons for making art can and should be distinguished from the products of that activity. Pearson acknowledges that the collection and analysis of children's drawings is an engrossing pursuit; that children's works, treated as archaeological artifacts, can and do yield intriguing information. Not only does analysis of drawings inform us about the construction of visual images, but, approached from a more postmodern perspective (e.g., Gamradt & Staples, 1994), it also promises insight into children's interests and concerns. As Pearson points out, however, children's drawings have typically been used in attempts to understand something that is not "children drawing," whether that is the nature of their experience at school or at home, or the ways in which they conceptualize and represent hierarchies of value or relationships among objects arrayed in space. Pearson's critique articulates a shift in thinking more profound, even, than the movement toward direct observation of drawing events, a trend that recognizes the thick layers of information that become available when researchers witness a drawing being made and the contextual influences that are enfolded in the final product. He points toward a movement beyond the consideration of children's drawings as developmental evidence, toward research that attempts to document the child's lived experience of making images, often within the mediated social space of a classroom or peer culture. The timeworn adage that advises teachers of young children to focus on the art process, rather than the product, applies to this more contextualized approach to research, with the qualification that the products of children's activity are frequently important as the documentation and embodiment of that process (Wilson & Thompson, 2007; Wright, 2003, 2005, 2007).

Pearson suggests further that traditional research, by insisting that drawing is a universal activity among young children, has failed to recognize the indisputable fact that some children, and many adults, do not draw. Pearson suggests that the reasons children choose to draw, or not to draw, are complex and heavily reliant on context:

> Whatever value drawing has for children is bound to the context in which it takes place, and as the context shifts so does the value. This is why drawing can be play activity, narrative activity, a measured strategy for social approval, or the equally measured pursuit of the inductively grasped competence appropriate to given representation systems. Drawing is also a strategy for coping with boredom, with isolation. It can be a retreat from violent social relations. It can be the means for pursuing a passionate interest in horses or trains which at the same time achieves some or all of the above ends. (pp. 357–358)

Pearson suggests that research on children drawing should move away from examinations of the documents that result from that process, toward the individual and situational factors that prompt children to make the choice to engage in that activity in the first place. Walsh (2002) cautions that children are unable to create "artistic selves" in the absence of opportunity, the availability of materials and models and the time to explore them, and the encouragement to do so. Pearson suggests that, when these conditions are in place, we may learn a great deal about the nature of art experience and its role in "good human functioning" (Arnheim, 1997, p. 11) by studying those children who do not take advantage of these opportunities as closely as those who do.

The concept that there are "varieties of visual experience" (Feldman, 1992) in which children participate is by no means new. Lark-Horovitz, Lewis, and Luca (1973) articulated subtle but significant differences in the content, form, and agency involved in spontaneous, voluntary, directed, and copied or to-be-completed works 30 years ago, and discussions of the characteristics and relative merits of school art and spontaneous children's art that begin with Wilson (1974) and Efland (1976, 1983), and continue today (Anderson & Milbrandt, 1998; Bresler, 1992, 1994, 2002; Hamblen, 2002). Contemporary research concentrates both on children's "directed" work, made in response to an adult request, usually with a topic specified, and their independent or "voluntary" drawings (Thompson, 1997). Research has identified clear differences between "spontaneous and scaffolded" (Boyatzis, 2000, p. 15) drawings, leading Boyatzis to recommend that both the actual developmental level

demonstrated in "spontaneous" drawings and the proximal developmental level attained in drawings made with instruction should be considered in evaluations of a child's developmental level: "perhaps artistic skill level ought to be conceived not only in terms of either the modal (functional) drawing level or the highest (optimal) level. Rather artistic skill may be better conceptualized as that range of symbolic flexibility between the two" (p. 15).

Several researchers are particularly concerned with children's choices, both habitual and occasional, and the manner in which choices of subject matter serve both as social and cultural capital, and in determining the trajectory of individual development. As Thunder-McGuire (1994) suggests, "Our preoccupation has been with individual works or performative acts, rather than a body of work," but different perspectives open when we consider the child's "sustained 'artistic serial'" (p. 51). The range of children's accomplishments and the idiosyncrasy and cultural specificity of the changes that occur in children's drawings have become significant preoccupations for researchers.

Drawing Together: Social Context and Child Art

> Researchers who study children's graphic symbolism stress the interaction between children and their own products.... In centers and classrooms, though, the dialogue between children and their papers can include other people, as children's skills as collaborative storytellers and players infuse their drawings. (Dyson, 1990, p. 54)

As early as 1979, Cocking and Copple noted that the "exposure to others" that occurs as children draw together expands children's conceptions of what is possible in drawing. For many years, partially due to the limited opportunities available to art educators to study young children in groups, the implications of this observation remained unexplored. Still operating under the deeply engrained cultural wisdom that defines artistic practice in general, and early artistic practice in particular, as highly individualized, unpredictable, and immune to influence, researchers frequently treated as extraneous any interactions that did occur in the classrooms they were studying. Matthews (1999) noted that: "Many accounts of the development of children's drawing seem to assume that some of the children's actions…are simply irrelevant to drawing proper" (p. 5). Now, as Boyatzis and Watson (2000) suggest, there is a growing tendency to see "social and symbolic processes" (p. 1) entwined in early artistic experiences.

There has been a movement toward adoption of a Vygotskian perspective in both art education practice and research in recent years, supplanting more clearly Piagetian approaches used in earlier research (Brooks, 2003, 2005, 2009; Newton & Kantner, 1997; Thompson & Bales, 1991) and teaching. As Atkinson (2002) points out, a still more radical poststructural perspective views both the nature and culture positions as discourses which create particular versions of the child: "From a post-structural perspective, the Piagetian or Vygotskian child is not to be viewed as a natural or social entity but as an ideological product of particular discourses in which the child is constructed accordingly" (p. 6). No matter what its prospects for longevity of influence may be, the Vygotskian perspective has been especially fruitful for art education research, particularly in regard to the attention it has drawn to peer learning as an almost inevitable, and desirable, fixture of classrooms in which children make art together (Zurmuehlen, 1990). Boyatzis and Albertini (2000) believe that peer influence reaches its maximum strength in middle childhood, when gender segregation, conformity, and criticality reach their peaks. However, the effects they describe are by no means absent from early childhood classrooms:

> [P]eer influence could occur through various means. Children's actual drawings—their themes, details, colors, or technical qualities—could function as models, offering children opportunities for observational learning. Observational learning has been posited as a crucial mechanism in children's learning in peer and collaborative contexts (for example, Botvin and Murray, 1975, Gauvain and Rogoff, 1989). Such learning would occur to the extent that children actually look at their peers' art, perhaps due to peers showing and displaying their work to others. In their conversations, children could share ideas and make explicit comparisons between each other's drawings and drawing techniques. Such exchanges would include many ability comparisons that could trigger artistic changes in children, particularly motivating then to improve their drawings to bring them more in line with local norms of style (that is, the themes, technical qualities, and meanings in their peers' drawings). (p. 33)

Many young children are inclined to accompany their actions with running commentaries that may be taken as conversational overtures, even when they are not intentionally addressed to another person (Anning & Ring, 2004; Mulcahy, 2002; Thompson, 2002; Thompson & Bales, 1991). When children draw in the presence of peers, such private speech is frequently mistaken as a form of address that elicits an answer from another child. Many of the resulting comments, which may or may not evolve into conversations, tend to be evaluative, with one child offering an (often unsolicited) evaluation of the other's work or of the thought that is impelling that work forward. Cunningham (1997) observed that 7-year-olds tend to offer positive comments in situations such as this, and these unsolicited evaluations often lead to revisions. Teachers may be squeamish about the sometimes brutal honesty of the critical comments children exchange. Boyatzis and Albertini (2000) suggest that there is more good than harm to be found in such exchanges which they consider a primary benefit of children drawing together in the social space of the classroom:

This image of artistic development as socially embedded is consistent with a Vygotskian model of development rather

than one that characterizes the child as a solitary graphic problem solver.... Children surely draw alone, make stylistic choices independently, and undergo endogenous symbolic development. But our observations...point toward the value of conceptualizing children's drawing and artistic development as occurring within sociocognitive contexts that may function as a zone of proximal development in which the interpsychological is internalized.... Surely children often draw alone, but even then they may benefit from hearing the internalized questions, evaluations, and suggestions of peers echoing from actual dyadic and group interaction. (pp. 45–46)

In line with contemporary reassessments of the developmental process in early art education, unprecedented attention has been paid to the necessity of adults and peers in structuring and supporting the process of learning to create and to respond to visual forms (Frisch, 2006; Kindler, 1995; Thompson, 1995, 1997, 2009; Zurmuehlen, 1990). In spite of this increased attention to the desirable influence of teachers and peers in the emergence of early childhood art, few studies have focused on the role of parents as children's first art teachers. Exceptions include studies by Knight (2009), Braswell (2001), and Yamagata (1997). Yamagata studied two parent–child dyads, drawing together at home, at one month intervals between the child's 24th and 30th months. He found that more representational drawings were produced in collaborative episodes than when the child drew alone or simply alongside the mother. He further noted that the intention to represent may emerge before the child develops the production skills needed to do so. Although mothers initially suggested more subjects for drawing more frequently than the children, the children took over this role as time passed. Braswell (2001) found similar patterns of guided participation and gradual exchange of roles in his study in which parents were asked to solicit both voluntary drawings and copies of complex forms from their young children.

Responding to Works of Art

Following a period of intense research activity on the issue of young children's responses to works of art (Kerlavage, 1995), relatively little research has been conducted on this issue in the past decade. A number of important theoretical and pedagogical texts have been published, though few of these explicitly address the aesthetic learning in young children (Danko McGhee, 2000, 2009, provides a notable exception), reflecting a movement away from assumptions grounded in formalist aesthetics and toward attention to more experiential, phenomenological, and cultural issues and methods of inquiry. The reciprocity between making and responding to images and objects created by others is by now firmly established as a principle of early art education, with aesthetic response, and historical and critical study of imagery, acknowledged as links to other areas of study within the curriculum. This dual interest in making and responding to works of art (and other elements of visual culture) has been a central tenet in the research on symbolic development conducted under the auspices of Harvard's Project Zero since the 1980s. A similar understanding was expressed in Parsons's (1988) identification of what he considered to be two primary issues in child art: (1) the significance of sociocultural influences on the process and content of art making; and (2) an interest in understanding of art in general and of particular works. Research by Harris (2000), Savva (2003), Savva and Trimis (2005), Trimis and Savva (2004), and others (see, for example, Xanthouthaki, Tickle, & Secules, 2003) signal a resurgence of interest in the topic.

Cross-Cultural Research: Questioning the Universality of Child Art

The long-established tradition of cross-cultural research in the study of children's art originated, and survived for many years, in an attempt to garner evidence of the universality of the impulse to make art, and of children's art as universal language, a political position adopted by many artists, philosophers, and educators following the World Wars (see, for example, Kellogg, 1970). Many early investigations, including the drawings collected by Harris (1963) in his refinement of the Draw-a-Man Test (Goodenough, 1926), were interpreted as support for the existence of a universal developmental process, stressing persistent structural similarities but not absolute likeness in drawings produced in distinct cultural environments. Earlier cross-cultural studies, many conducted by anthropologists such as Paget (1932), acknowledged local traditions within familiar characteristics, but emphasized the ubiquity of familiar graphic models and sequences. Golomb (2002) notes that, despite documentation of local variations across and even within cultures, "the dominant impression is of a universal graphic language clearly recognizable to the student of child art, a language whose basic grammar allows for variations on a common underlying structure" (p. 87). These commitments have sometimes proven difficult to forsake (Golomb, 1992; Kindler, 1997), but an awareness of the cultural specificity of educational supports and children's responses to them is strongly emphasized in recent research.

Golomb (2002) observes that recent cross-cultural studies vary radically in methodology, but often solicit drawings that are restricted to a single theme or a single trial. Most such studies are administered in group settings without attention to peer influence or the effects of prior instruction (Andersson, 1995; Court, 1994; Martlew & Connolly, 1996). In many cases, the studies are implicitly cross-cultural, insofar as the researchers enter a culture not their own, and inevitably interpret what they find there on the basis of what is known about child art, knowledge derived largely from studies in the West.

Most cross-cultural research focuses on art making, and drawing continues to predominate, despite observations by researchers such as Fortes (1981) who noted that Tallensi

children's favorite pastime was modeling small animals and figures to use as toys, and commented in passing on the strong three-dimensional understanding children displayed, even in the absence of relevant models in their culture. Newton and Kantner (1997) review cross-cultural studies in aesthetic response, describing studies (primarily from the 1970s and 1980s) that investigated children's perception of imagery from the perspectives of various research paradigms.

In the past decade, Kindler, Darras, and Kuo (2000) undertook an ambitious cross-cultural study of "the ways in which cultural contexts shape formation of knowledge about art in the early years" (p. 44). Choosing to focus on issues more inclusive than those tackled in many earlier studies of aesthetic response, this multilayered study examines children's conceptions of art; that is, how the term *art* is interpreted and understood by children in a variety of cultural contexts. The researchers share an interest in issues of globalization, and the effects of heritage and enculturation in the formation of social knowledge.

In structured interviews with 70 4- and 5-year-old children in Canada, France, and Taiwan, Kindler, Darras, and Kuo (2000) posed questions regarding the nature of art. They were particularly interested in speaking with diasporic or "transplanted" children in each culture: French Canadian and Chinese Canadian children. They asked three questions of each child interviewed: What is art? Does art have to be beautiful? Can nature make art or does art have to be made by a person? (p. 46). The results of these interviews confirm that understandings of art do not seem to be readily transplanted from one culture to another. Some traditional views of art and beauty seemed to be more persistent than others, and time spent in the new culture seemed to influence children's responses, as did the degree of assimilation cultivated by members of their community. The authors offer this study as confirmation of the fact that even very young children hold some preconceptions about art related to cultural and familial values. They recommend caution in assuming the "direct portability of cultural beliefs" (p. 52) in the design of multicultural art education, and emphasize the importance of considering both original and transplanted cultures as contexts.

In an earlier study, Kindler and Darras (1995) interviewed 80 children, ages 3 to 5, in Canada and France to explore their conceptions of the nature of drawing competencies and the ways in which they are achieved. The series of structured interviews they conducted confirmed the authors' prediction that children as young as 3 hold and can express beliefs about their own drawing ability and that of others, and that even very young children take note of the values enacted by those around them. Some differences in age and culture were detected: All Canadian kindergartners, for example, indicated that they were capable of drawing whatever they desired, while only 80% of their French peers expressed similarly unbridled confidence. More than half the children felt that all people know how to draw, and that generally drawing improves with age, though they acknowledged the importance of practice and teaching, and the role of significant others in support of drawing skills. Interestingly, children themselves did not experience the process of learning to draw as a natural unfolding: "the majority of children recognized the importance of socially mediated learning, valued imitative activities as a learning strategy, and did not regard development of drawing skills as a private process of biologically determined unfolding.... When asked how they learned how to draw, 69% of the French children and 40% of the Canadians reported that they learned from others" (Kindler & Darras, 1995, p. 92). Although few children thought of drawing as "an autonomous discovery" (Kindler & Darras, 1995, p. 92), this belief was somewhat more prevalent among Canadian children.

Asked the question, "Why do people draw?", half of the preschool subjects could not answer, and older children found the question more readily addressed in terms of personal enjoyment, a response offered by 60% of the children. As to the purposes of drawing, 64% of French children, 40% of Canadian kindergartners, and 30% of the Canadian preschoolers mentioned decoration or embellishment as primary purposes, with the production of gifts and surprises as a close second. Kindler and Darras observe, "The association between the giving and the beauty seems to be mediated very early to young children through routines that they observe in their immediate environment. Children's pictorial productions are judged by their parents and other family members as beautiful and consequently become desirable gifts" (p. 95). Finally, when asked whether it is important to learn how to draw, 80% of Canadian children but only 46% of French children responded affirmatively. These percentages parallel the responses to the question of whether children see their parents draw, an event that is witnessed with far greater frequency by Canadian children than by their French counterparts.

Chen (2001) studied Taiwanese young children and adolescents, comparing their responses to those obtained by Freeman and Sanger (1995) who constructed a "net of intentional relations" involving the Artist, Beholder, Picture, and World. Freeman and Sanger employed a questionnaire to measure the aesthetic understandings of 352 rural school children in the United Kingdom, the youngest in grade 3. Replicating this study in Taiwan, Chen found that, contrary to Freeman and Sanger's findings, young children in Taiwan tend to merge the roles of artist and beholder, assuming that they could infer intention from the works themselves, and that artists always work with beholders in mind.

Working within a research paradigm demonstrated by British psychologists including Norman Freeman and Maureen Cox (1985), Chun-Min Su (1995) studied American and Chinese children's ability to produce drawings of partially occluded figures, using a robber and policeman format to measure young children's ability to create the illusion of one-thing-hiding-behind-another when a meaningful motivation for doing so is presented. Su found,

among other things, that Chinese children were more likely than American children to erase their drawings and to emit other evidence of dissatisfaction with their response to the problem presented. She attributed this result, in part, to the demands of learning Chinese characters with the precision required to successfully write their own names.

Cox, Perera, and Fan (1999) compared drawings by 952 children between the ages of 6 and 13 in the United Kingdom and China. The researchers failed to detect any consistent cultural differences in the quality of the drawings, except for those produced by the 240 children in Beijing who attended weekend art school. These children's drawings were rated consistently higher by expert judges on criteria of style, composition, color, and depth. The authors invoked the results of this study in support of arguments for more structured and formal teaching in art. The exceptionally high and consistent aesthetic achievement of Chinese children's art was brought to the attention of Western educators through an article published by Ellen Winner (1989) and several exhibitions of art by Chinese children organized in England. The authors acknowledge the possibility that the quality of children's work may be attributed to the high status of art in Chinese culture, but they speculate that the way in which art is taught to children is equally significant. According to Winner (1989), Chinese art education at the elementary level focuses on technique and skill-building, with attention paid to copying schema from the blackboard, a practice antithetical to most (if not all) of the strictures that have surrounded art teaching in the West since at least the mid-20th century. In this study, children were all assigned the same topic, a scene described by the examiner, in order to compare children in three groups: in ordinary schools in the UK and in China and among children who chose to attend special art school. The resulting drawings were rated on a 5-point scale by two art advisers from the UK and one Chinese researcher familiar with children's drawings. Observation and videotapes of classrooms made during the collection of drawings suggest that Chinese art instruction is not as rigid or unidimensional as it is often characterized to be, nor are British instructions as laissez-faire as expected. But children's drawings displayed differences in style that made it easy for independent judges to guess the country of origin for each drawing.

Wilson (1997, 2002) examines the Japanese phenomenon of *manga,* both as a prime example of the collusion between children and commercial interests in the creation of national identity, and as a significant aspect of the process of learning to draw in a culture in which attractive and attainable graphic models are abundant—a process all children enact as they master the tools and symbols systems their particular culture provides (Vygotsky, 1978).

Gender as Social Mediation

Examinations of the influence of gender on the subject matter and style of children's drawings also boast a long tradition in visual arts research. Concern with the perpetuation of gender stereotypes through teaching (Collins & Sandell, 1996) and of the effects of gendered choices on children's drawings (Thompson, 1999; Tuman, 1999, 2000) represent recent trends in this inquiry.

In 1997, Duncum considered the subjects children choose to draw in their unsolicited drawings, a topic that has attracted sporadic bursts of attention throughout the history of the study of child art, beginning with Maitland's study of "what children draw to please themselves," published in 1895. Reviewing this literature, Duncum identified a striking consistency in the findings on thematic and subject matter preferences and gender differences: From the earliest studies (e.g., Ballard, 1913; Maitland, 1895; Munro, Lark-Horovitz, & Barnhart, 1942) to the most recent (Ivashevich, 2009; McClure, 2006a; Robertson, 1987; Thompson, 1999; Tuman, 1999, 2000), strong gender differences have been apparent. Girls tend to concentrate on scenes of ordinary life and autobiographical experience, while boys gravitate, quickly and noticeably, toward fantasy, historical fiction, combat, and strong action. Flannery and Watson (1995) found more aggressive themes in boys' drawings, and "argue that boys' drawing content reflects a socialized interest in fantasy and violence that extends beyond their everyday life experience, whereas girls' drawing content appears to be more realistic and tranquil and to relate to their everyday experience" (Tuman, 1999, p. 41).

Although exceptions certainly exist, these patterns appear to be remarkably robust, particularly among prolific "drawers" who tend to specialize in particular subjects or themes, most of which conform to gendered stereotypes. Duncum (1997) suggests that these motives are so firmly established that, "Boys and girls may draw what appears to be the same subject matter for a very different reason or purpose due to their gender socialization" (p. 111). As Tuman (2000) notes, "We have come to understand that the drawings of boys and girls reveal unique reflections of society through visual narratives of the world of personal experience" (p. 17).

While the conventional wisdom in art education once assumed that gender differences did not appear in children's drawings until they reached school age, Boyatzis and Albertini (2000) suggest that these distinctions are apparent long before clearly identifiable subject matter appears: "Gender differences in art emerge even earlier, in the preschool years, as boys' scribbles are rated as more masculine and girls' scribbles as more feminine by judges who are ignorant of the children's genders" (p. 31; see also Alland, 1983).

Other differences have been noted in more overtly representational drawings, in addition to the subject matter itself. There is growing evidence that the intentions children bring to their drawings, the subject matter they choose to practice and perfect, may influence the style of their work as profoundly as it determines the substance, as first suggested by Feinburg (1979) in her study of children's drawings of fighting and helping. As Tuman (1999) remarks, "favored

engendered content domains may foster favored tendencies in characteristics" (p. 41). Tuman expressed concern, however, that erroneous assertions have been made about the relative abilities of boys and girls through inadequate consideration of the themes children of each gender choose to draw. For example, Kerschensteiner (1905) concluded that boys' drawing ability surpassed that of girls on a measure of spatial relationships, but failed to take into account the relatively spacious subject matter that boys prefer and even require in order to stage the actions they tend to depict. Goodenough (1926) concluded that girls were superior to boys in their drawings of detailed human figures, a finding reaffirmed by later investigations in America, England, and Denmark (Cox, 1993; Harris, 1963; Koppitz, 1968; Mortensen, 1991), without probing deeply into the possible reasons for this phenomenon. Recent studies tend to turn away from questions of superiority or inferiority to examine more subtle issues of style and substance, manifesting particular interest in subject matter preferences.

In a study of 300 elementary students, in grades 1 through 5, Tuman (1999) investigated whether "gender differences in subject preference also call into play the manipulation of formal elements, which together with gendered context form a gender-related style" (p. 42). The children, primarily White and middle- to upper-middle class, listened to a narrative motivation designed to elicit stereotypical attitudes toward gender. The children were then asked to illustrate what they liked best in the story and to write a brief descriptive title for their finished art work. Tuman randomly selected 250 drawings for analysis in order to insure an equal number of boys and girls in the final sample. Tuman (1999) found that, "when presented with masculine and feminine content themes, boys and girls rarely incorporate subject matter choices outside predicted gendered content domains in their drawing" (p. 52). Her study did not replicate Kerschensteiner's findings of male superiority in spatial representation, but did raise concerns about the limitations imposed on the representational possibilities children of either gender are apt to explore, if they are allowed to persist in drawing within the stereotypical range. Tuman suggests that this may be particularly detrimental to girls, a concern shared by Thompson (1999) in her reflection on the choices of subject matter made by preschool and kindergarten children drawing in sketchbooks over a period of 12 years. The potential consequences of these choices for drawing development may well be profound, for the relative advantages of focusing upon imaginative scenarios that are continually evolving and available instead of relying upon personal experience to provide fodder for representation seem as evident as they are problematic (see, for example, Egan, 1988; Helm & Katz, 2001; Katz, 1998).

Curriculum

It would not be surprising to find that neither the operational curriculum nor instructional practices in early childhood art education have kept pace with the recommendations drawn from research and theory in recent years. What research would now suggest departs abruptly from the traditional wisdom long accepted as appropriate art education practice in early childhood settings. Art experiences are cherished by elementary and early childhood teachers as the last bastion of creative freedom in the schools (Bresler & Thompson, 2002), a freedom threatened by art educators' recent insistence that art is a process which must be structured and scaffolded if it is to satisfy children's expectations, much less fulfill its educational potential.

Katz (1998) remarked that one of the lessons she had learned from her many visits to the preschools of Reggio Emilia was that young children can use graphic languages--drawing, painting, collage, construction—"to record their ideas, observations, memories, and so forth...to explore understandings, to reconstruct previous ones, and to co-construct revisited understandings of the topics investigated" (p. 20). This understanding of "art as epistemology" (Gallas, 1994, p. 130), as a way of "enabling children to know what they know," allows us to recognize and employ art in the classroom as a "method for examining his[her] world as well as his[her] means of externalizing what he[she] was learning for others to share" (Gallas, 1994, p. 135). This interest in "drawing to learn" (Anning, 1999, p. 166), widespread in British schools and preschools, disrupts many strongly held beliefs about the young child as natural artist, and the role of the teacher in preserving that artistry untarnished by adult manipulation. It suggests not only that topics for drawings and painting can be assigned, but that experiences with art materials can, and perhaps should, be structured with both expressive and communicative purposes in mind. This approach to art as a symbolic language, the subject of considerable discussion in the waning decades of the last century, emphasizes the possibility of teachers helping children to develop facility in "the hundred languages" available to them (Malaguzzi, 1998, p. 3), to master an expanded range of the tools and symbol systems (Vygotsky, 1978) that are used in their culture.

Equally as influential as the accumulating consensus of research and theory in affecting this radical shift in thinking about the nature of curriculum and instruction in early childhood art has been the example of Reggio Emilia. Although serious and sustained research on the theory and practice of art education in the preschools of Reggio Emilia is accumulating slowly (e.g., Danko-McGhee & Slutsky, 2003; Vecchi, 2010; Wexler & Cardinal, 2009), the work routinely produced by the children who benefit from that practice demonstrates unequivocally the possibility of exceptional sophistication in teaching and learning, and the range of artistic expression that is possible for young children who are encouraged to explore challenging content through visual forms.

The influence of Reggio Emilia is extensive, the questions it raises for early art education are profound and challenging. Pitri (2003) observed a university-based preschool in order to document the conceptual problem solving that occurred during art activities. She found that some conceptual problems were teacher-generated, in situations in which the teacher asked children to plan and to make choices. Child-generated conceptual problems emerged in response to interpersonal or practical challenges; for example, in attempts to join an ongoing activity or negotiations about the sharing of art materials. Other problems were more substantive, "caused by children's representational or expressive challenges" (p. 20). Drawing upon previous research on the definition of problems during art activities, Pitri concluded that, "Problem finding is related to being receptive to ideas and responding to changes in the environment" (p. 21). She noted that this approach is exemplified in the practice of Reggio Emilia.

Tarr (2003) sees in the "image of the child" maintained in the theory and practice of Reggio Emilia an opportunity to question the image that guides curriculum development and instructional practice in North American early art education:

> What images of children do we hold when we plan curriculum that follows accepted practices of studio, criticism and art history? Do we plan a different delivery system where children individually recreate the art culture(s) they are in? When they have a discussion about a work of art, are they consuming culture or actively constructing understanding about the work that is unique to each child and to each group? Do we celebrate this construction, or do we try to replace it with cultural replication? (p. 10)

This discussion occurs, however, within earshot of continuing debates regarding the relative merits of "unfolding or teaching" (Gardner, 1976) in early art education. This debate may no longer rest upon the question of whether adults should influence child art, as it once did, but differences of opinion remain in regard to the nature and extent of that influence. Even this is a dramatic departure from the emphasis on "spontaneous self-instruction" (Froebel, cited in Kellogg, 1970, p. 62) that long characterized understandings of "best practices" in early art education.

Kindler (1995) states, "Adult intervention may not only be useful, but essential to children's artistic learning" (p. 11), and others readily agree (Boyatzis, 2000; Chapman, 1978; Davis & Gardner, 1993; Frisch, 2006; Golomb, 1992/2004; Reggio Children & Project Zero, 2001; Ring, 2006; Schulte, 2011; Thompson, 2009; Wilson, 2004, 2007). Even researchers long associated with traditional interpretations of the developmental process now advocate a more contextual approach to the understanding of art experience in childhood (Boyatzis, 2000)

Zimmerman and Zimmerman (2000, p. 87) point out that young children rely upon adults to make encounters with art possible, at the most basic level in which materials and occasions to use and discuss them are provided. As Daniel Walsh (2002) points out, children may never discover their "artistic selves" if they have no opportunity to do so, just as children growing up on the Plains may not discover propensities for water sports or marine biology. He argues that the possibility of developing "artistic selves" exists only in contexts which permit or encourage exploration of media and ideas, and that this possibility should be made available to all children. "The goal is not a society of artists, any more than a society of athletes or physicists, but a society of people with many well developed selves, one or more of which is artistic" (Walsh, 2002, p. 108).

Hamblen (2002) recognizes clear differences among the knowledge, values, and attitudes that are promoted in each context in which children encounter art. "School art" occupies ground distinct from the professional practices of artists and from the spontaneous art work of children and adults (Anderson & Milbrandt, 1998; Bresler, 1994, 1999, 2002; Efland, 1976; Greenberg, 1996; Smith, 1995; Wilson, 1974). Hamblen suggests that the informal learning that is characteristic of local contexts and traditional cultures typifies good early childhood practice, in that it is exploratory, concrete, experiential, and situated. She challenges art educators to preserve this approach to art making at all levels, valuing local contexts of art making even more than the professional art worlds as models for the majority of students.

With this recognition of the importance of adult influence and the scaffolding of early artistic learning has come a conviction that direct instruction of young children is not only possible but desirable, as an element within a curriculum that is constructed to preserve independent exploration. This balance between teacher direction and children's agency, between "voluntary" and "directed" work (Lark-Horovitz, Lewis, & Luca, 1973) has been achieved in a number of programs and projects documented in recent literature (Grace & Tobin, 2002; Tarr, 2003), most notably in the educational programs originating in Reggio Emilia. And yet the concept remains controversial, both among teachers for whom the concept of directing young children's work with art materials defies the doctrine they were taught and have come to accept, and among researchers, whose recommendations for teaching are more often appended as opinions than offered as corollaries of research (e.g., J. Matthews, 1999; Winner, 1989).

Several authors have pointed to the dangers inherent in these recommendations that teachers' involvement in early artistic learning increase. The difficulty of preserving children's choices, of reserving a space for the expression of ideas and experiences that matter most deeply to children, must be acknowledged (Tobin, 1995; Thompson, 2003). Writing about primary art education in the UK, Anning (1999) comments:

> Though the technicalities and styles of learning how to draw are left to serendipity, the content of drawings in schools is clearly prescribed by teachers. Children learn that their drawings in schools must reflect teachers' views of "childhood innocence"—nothing violent or unseemly—safe and sanitized portraits of "people who help us" or observational drawings of pot plants or stuffed animals in glass cases

borrowed from museums (Anning, 1995, 1997). In most primary classroom settings, as the children grapple with the conventions of "school art," their unofficial drawing about what really interests them goes underground. (p. 170)

The conflict of values that underlies the situation Anning describes has to do with teachers' understanding of art and of children, as well as their sense of what may be appropriate (or comfortable) to discuss in an educational context. It also suggests that, after decades of insisting upon its disciplinary status, art remains on the margins of educational thought and practice, conceived as something other than the sturdy fabric of education, a decorative element that may enhance the garment but is in no way essential to its function. Although researchers involved with child art have long insisted that art is far more tightly interwoven in the fabric of human learning than contemporary Western culture tends to admit, the complex sociocultural and historical reasons for the peripheral position of art in North American schools and preschools remain to be fully explicated, widely understood, and revised in action.

Egan and Ling (2002) draw on Vygotsky to formulate an argument for the centrality of art education in early childhood learning. Its current marginalization, they suggest, is based upon acceptance of "a set of basic educational ideas that are mistaken" (p. 93), those ideas about young children that are so often taken for granted in casual conversation, including the presumption that children are egocentric and easily distracted. They point to the ways in which these shared understandings pervade research and pedagogy, as well, citing in particular the tenacity of the belief that intellectual development follows a path much like biological development, climbing continually onward toward greater complexity and facility. Continued reliance upon these unquestioned assumptions results in "a devaluation of both the preschool child's state of knowing and the cognitive area of artistic expression" (Davis, 1997, p. 54). Egan and Ling propose instead that some important intellectual capacities reach their peak in the early years of life and decline thereafter, a possibility recognized by Piaget and others who have speculated on U-shaped developmental trajectories in children's drawing. Identifying those things that young children do more easily than they will at any other time in their lives, Egan and Ling refer specifically to the ability to think imaginatively.

Arnheim (1997) suggests that, "Child art, then, profits from being recognized as an inseparable aspect of good human functioning. No society can afford to ignore the fact that the capacity for behaving artistically is inherent in every human being and cannot be neglected without detriment to the individual and to society as a whole" (p. 11). There is a growing recognition of the arts as intrinsically interdisciplinary. Goldberg (1997) suggests the limitations of an art-for-arts-sake model, which emphasizes the disciplinary integrity of the subject at the expense of severing its ties to other aspects of children's learning: "Students can learn about the arts, learn with the arts, and learn through the arts.

The most familiar, most common, and least integrated experience students have with the arts is learning about them" (p. ix). Gallas (1994) suggests three ways to move the arts to a central position in the curriculum, by considering them as (1) methodologies for acquiring knowledge; (2) subjects of study; and (3) an array of expressive opportunities for communicating with others. She demonstrates these possibilities ably in her accounts of learning in her classrooms. Davis et al. (1993) note the need for more research documenting what many of those working in the schools observe on a daily basis, the positive impact of art learning on children's school experience: "the power of arts production to provide students with positive habits of learning from the realization of cultural roots and individual potential to the discipline of seeing a project through from beginning to end" (Davis, 1997, p. 54)

As Tarr (2003) acknowledges, these concepts regarding the depth of learning made possible when art is perceived as a form of inquiry are exemplified in the schools of Reggio Emilia:

> Experiences in visual expression are not add-ons or isolated activities but are a form of inquiry or way to investigate a theory, idea, or a problem, a way of clarifying understanding, the communication of an idea…Reggio educators present provocations to children that ask them to see situations from multiple perspectives, through the experiences they set up, and through the use of interpersonal encounters that challenge and support acceptance of diversity, flexibility, and creativity. … They provide situations where children translate ideas developed in one media [sic] to another, which helps clarify children's thinking about aspects of the problem not encountered in previous experience. (pp. 10–11)

Increasing interest in the role of the visual arts as components of "multiliteracies" or "visual literacies" (McArdle, 2008, p. 273; see also Duncum, 2004; Narey, 2009; New London Group, 1996; Ryan & Healy, 2008) build upon the recognition of art and visual culture as potent but underutilized languages in which young children may be particularly fluent. The wide "pictorial turn" occasioned by new modes of communication and information technologies in contemporary life, the acknowledged role of art making and visual imagery in early learning, and the intrinsic relationships among verbal, written, and graphic symbolic languages contribute to this growing interest in art as a form of learning. These developments may offer the arts a more central and integrated presence in early childhood education, but the possibility persists of relegating the visual to a supporting role in the transition to forms of literacy traditionally sanctioned by formal schooling.

Conclusion: Unanswered Questions and Emerging Issues

As this selective review of recent research in art education suggests, perennial questions remain unresolved, as new issues emerge. As in the past, these concerns reflect changes in art worlds and cultural life, as well as shifting perspectives on childhood and education.

One such issue, still largely unexamined in the research literature (but see Matthews, 1999; Matthews & Jessels, 1993a, 1993b), is the future of drawing and other traditional forms of artistic practice in an age of electronic media. As Atkinson (2002) poses the question, "The contemporary explosion of new forms of visual expression and visual production in a variety of media almost begs the question how is it possible to understand or theorise art practice today, what does this term mean?" (p. 13)

The problem Atkinson identifies has been considered also by teachers working in Reggio Emilia, where drawing to learn (and learning to draw) are integral to educational practice. As Vecchi (2001) notes:

> In comparison to the past, a great many images are available to children today, many of which come from TV—images that are beautiful or ugly, inventions that are intelligent, standard, or stereotyped. Having exposure to many images does not necessarily mean having the ability to draw better. Perhaps there is a greater distance between mental images and the level of graphic ability linked to biological age; children seem to find it harder than they did in the past to accept a graphic result so far removed from the representations of reality that they see and that contribute to constructing their imagery of the world. Equally, children find it hard to accept that better representational skills, and consequently greater satisfaction with their products, are gained by drawing more and accepting that they have to put themselves to the test again and again when drawing the same subject. (pp. 188–189)

Future research in early childhood art must address these issues of the nature of drawing and its evolution in an age in which imagery is arguably more ubiquitous and insistent than ever before, when the benefits of graphic representation as a means of inquiry have been documented and widely acknowledged. As Golomb (1992/2004) observes, "Clearly, drawings can provide multiple sources of satisfaction that are at once of an emotional, cognitive, and aesthetic order" (p. 162). It is possible to argue that the use of drawings, and sculpture and photography and other forms of graphic representation, should become central to North American educational practice, as means for "symbolic representation of thinking" (Gallas, 1994, p. xvi). It is necessary to recognize the fundamental restructuring of educational thought and practice that this attention to multiple languages for learning would entail. Carefully interpreted research documenting such theories in practice in preschools and elementary schools is necessary to support that proposition.

Closely related to this concern is the question of how early childhood education will, or should, be affected by the movement in art education toward the study of visual culture. In much the same way that young children were neither seen nor heard in discussions of the discipline-based proposals of the 1980s and 1990s, early childhood education has been represented in ongoing discussions of visual culture primarily in the form of theory and proposals for practice. In research conducted thus far, the entry of popular media culture into the classroom has been a dominant concern. Thompson (2003, 2006) traces changes in the subject matter of children's voluntary drawings as they are increasingly influenced by visual culture—especially media and peer culture—producing idiosyncratic developmental trajectories quite different from those that describe the kinds of drawings we recognize as child art classics. Grace and Tobin (2002) describe a classroom video production, in which the unofficial interests of children shift to center stage, and document the choices children make as they begin to consider the sensibilities of their audience. Recent studies by Matthews and Seow (2009) and McClure (2009) suggest that young children readily adopt digital media as means of expression, finding that these tools and processes expand their thinking in ways that mirror and supplement more traditional media and materials (Swann, 2005).

Interest in the application of digital technologies to research with young children is increasingly apparent, as researchers attempt to amplify children's role in the research process and the voices that are heard in research products (Pink, 2001; Richards, 2009; Thompson, 2009).

A growing convergence of interest in visual culture and cultural studies, particularly the area of children's culture, is apparent in work on the thematic and aesthetic choices of young children by Bhroin (2007), Eckhoff and Guberman (2006), McClure (2006b, 2007), Thompson (2006), Trafi (2008), and others.

At the end of this period devoted to reconsideration and reconceptualization of the assumptions that have guided educators and researchers concerned with art experience in the early childhood years, the time for focused research activity, addressing issues of development, context, and curriculum, has arrived. There is a clear consensus in this large and loosely organized field that traditional answers no longer tell us much about contemporary childhood; that art itself has changed in ways that must be reflected, even in the preschool classroom. There is a need for increasingly situated studies of children making art and interpreting visual images in the company of other children and adults, in the contexts where significant learning about art occurs, in classrooms and community-based programs, families, and neighborhoods.

References

Alland, A., Jr. (1983). *Playing with form: Children draw in six cultures.* New York: Columbia University Press.

Althouse, R., Johnson, M. H., & Mitchell, S. T. (2003). *The colors of learning: Integrating the visual arts into the early childhood curriculum.* New York: Teachers College Press; Washington, DC: National Association for the Education of Young Children.

Anderson, T. & Milbrandt, M. (1998). Authentic instruction in art: Why and how to dump the school art style. *Visual Arts Research, 24*(1), 13–20.

Andersson, S. B. (1995). Local conventions in children's drawings: A comparative study in three cultures. *Journal of Multicultural and Cross-Cultural Research in Art Education, 13,* 101–111.

Anning, A. (1999). Learning to draw and drawing to learn. *Journal of Art and Design Education, 18*(2), 163–172.

Anning, A. & Ring, K. (2004). *Making sense of children's drawings.* Maidenhead, England: Open University Press.

Arnheim, R. (1969). *Visual thinking.* Berkeley, CA: University of California Press.

Arnheim, R. (1974). *Art and visual perception.* Berkeley, CA: University of California Press. (Original work published 1954)

Arnheim, R. (1997). A look at a century of growth. In A. M. Kindler (Ed.), *Child development in art* (pp. 9–16). Reston, VA: National Art Education Association.

Atkinson, D. (2002). *Art in education: Identity and practice.* Boston, MA: Kluwer Academic Press.

Baker, D. (1994). Toward a sensible art education: Inquiring into the role of visual arts in early childhood education. *Visual Arts Research, 20*(2), 92–104.

Ballard, P. B. (1913). What children like to draw. *Journal of Experimental Pedagogy and Training College Record, 2,* 127–129.

Beittel, K. R. (1973). *Alternatives for art education research.* Dubuque, IA: Wm. C. Brown.

Bhroin, M. N. (2007). "A slice of life": The interrelationships among art, play and the "real" life of the young child. *International Journal of Education and the Arts, 8*(16). Retrieved from http://www.ijea.org/v8n16/.

Boyatzis, C. J. (2000). The artistic evolution of Mommy: A longitudinal case study of symbolic and social processes. In C. Boyatzis & M. W. Watson (Eds.), *Symbolic and social constraints on the development of children's artistic style* (pp. 5–30). San Francisco, CA: Jossey-Bass.

Boyatzis, C. J., & Albertini, G. (2000). A naturalistic observation of children drawing: Peer collaboration processes and influences in child art. In C. Boyatzis & M. W. Watson (Eds.), *Symbolic and social constraints on the development of children's artistic style* (pp. 31–48). San Francisco, CA: Jossey-Bass.

Boyatzis, C., & Watson, M. W. (Eds.). (2002). *Symbolic and social constraints on the development of children's artistic style.* San Francisco, CA: Jossey-Bass.

Braswell, G. (2001). Collaborative drawing during early mother–child interactions. *Visual Arts Research, 27*(2), 27–39.

Bremner, J. G., & Moore, S. (1984). Prior visual inspection and object naming: Two factors that enhance hidden feature inclusion in young children's drawings. *British Journal of Developmental Psychology, 2,* 371–376.

Bresler, L. (1992). Visual art in the primary grades: A portrait and analysis. *Early Childhood Research Quarterly, 7,* 397–414.

Bresler, L. (1994). Imitative, complementary and expansive: Three roles of visual arts curricula. *Studies in Art Education, 35*(2), 90–104.

Bresler, L. (1999). The hybridization and homogenization of school art: Institutional contexts for elementary art students. *Visual Arts Research, 25*(2), 25–37.

Bresler, L. (2002). School art as a hybrid genre: Institutional contexts for art curriculum. In L. Bresler & C. M. Thompson (Eds.), *The arts in children's lives: Context, culture, and curriculum* (pp. 169–183). Boston, MA: Kluwer Academic Press.

Bresler, L., & Thompson, C. M. (Eds.). (2002). *The arts in children's lives: Context, culture, and curriculum.* Boston, MA: Kluwer Academic Press.

Brooks, M. (2003). Drawing, thinking, meaning. Retrieved from http://www.lboro.ac.uk/departments/ac/tracey/thin/brooks.html/

Brooks, M. (2005). Drawing as a unique mental development tool for young children: Interpersonal and intrapersonal dialogues. *Contemporary Issues in Early Childhood, 6*(1), 8–91.

Brooks, M. (2006). Visual ethnography in the primary classroom. *Journal of Australian Research in Early Childhood Education, 13*(2), 67–80.

Brooks, M. (2009) What Vygotsky can teach us about young children's drawing. *International Art in Early Childhood Research Journal,* *1*(1). Retrieved from http://www.artinearlychildhood.org/artec/index.php?option=com_journals&Itemid=57&task=article&id=6

Chapman, L. (1978). *Approaches to art in education.* New York: Harcourt Brace Jovanovich.

Chen, J. C.-H. (2001). Aesthetic thinking of young children and adolescents. *Visual Arts Research, 27*(2), 47–56.

Chun-Min Su. (1995). A cross-cultural study of partial occlusion in children's drawings. In C. M. Thompson (Ed.), *The visual arts and early childhood learning* (pp. 91–94). Reston, VA: National Art Education Association.

Cocking, R. R., & Copple, C. E. (1979). Change through exposure to others: A study of children's verbalizations as they draw. In M. K. Poulsen & G. I. Lubin (Eds.), *Piagetian theory and its implications for the helping professions: Proceedings, Eighth Interdisciplinary Conference* (Vol. 2, pp. 124–132). University Park, CA: University of Southern California Press.

Collins, G., & Sandell, R. (1996). *Gender issues in art education: Content, context, and strategies.* Reston, VA: National Art Education Association.

Cooke, G., Griffin, D., & Cox, M. (1998). *Teaching young children to draw.* Bristol, PA: Falmer Press.

Costall, A. (2001). Introduction. In G-H. Luquet, *Children's drawings [Le dessin enfantin]* (A. Costall, Trans. & introduction, pp. vii–xxiv). New York: Free Association Books.

Court, E. (1994). Researching social influences in the drawings of rural Kenyan children. In D. Thistlewood, S. Paine, & E. Court (Eds.), *Drawing, art, and development* (pp. 219–260). London: Longmans.

Cox, M. (1992). *Children's drawings.* New York: Penguin Books.

Cox, M. (1993). *Children's drawings of the human figure.* Hove, England: Erlbaum.

Cox, M. (1997). *Drawings of people by the under-fives.* London: Falmer.

Cox, M. (2005). *The pictorial world of the child.* Cambridge, England: Cambridge University Press.

Cox, M. V. (1989). Knowledge and appearance in children's pictorial representation. *Educational Psychology, 9,* 15–25.

Cox, M., Perera, J., & Fan, X. (1999). Children's drawing in the UK and China. *Journal of Art & Design Education, 18*(2), 173–181.

Cunningham, A. (1997). Criteria and processes used by seven-year-old children in appraising art work of their peers. *Visual Arts Research, 23*(1), 41–48.

Danko-McGhee, K. (2000). *The aesthetic preferences of young children.* Lewistin, NY: E. Mellen Press.

Danko-McGhee, K. (2009). The environment as third teacher: Pre-service teacher's aesthetic transformation of an art learning environment for young children in a museum setting. *Art in Early Childhood Research Journal, 1*(1). Retrieved from http://www.artinearlychildhood.org/artec/index.php?option=com_journals&Itemid=57&task=article&id=1

Danko-McGhee, K., & Slutsky, R. (2003, July). Preparing early childhood teachers to use art in the classroom: Inspirations from Reggio Emilia. *Art Education, 60*(3), 12–18.

Danko-McGhee, K., & Slutsky, R. (2007). *The impact of early art experiences on literacy development.* Reston, VA: National Art Education Association.

Davis, J. (1997). The "U" and the wheel of "C": Development and devaluation of graphic symbolization and the cognitive approach at Harvard Project Zero. In A. M. Kindler (Ed.), *Child development in art* (pp. 45–58). Reston, VA: National Art Education Association.

Davis, J., & Gardner, H. (1993). The arts and early childhood education: A cognitive developmental portrait of the young child as artist. In B. Spodek (Ed.), *Handbook of research in early childhood education* (2nd ed., 191–206). New York: Macmillan.

Davis, J., Soep, E., Maira, S., Remba, N., Putnoi, D., Gardner, H., & Gonzalez-Pose, P. (1993). *Safe havens: Portraits of educational effectiveness in community art centers that focus on education.* Cambridge, MA: Project Co-Arts, Harvard Project Zero.

Duncum, P. (1984). How 35 children born between 1724 and 1900 learned to draw. *Studies in Art Education, 26*(2), 93–102.

Duncum, P. (1997). Subjects and themes in children's unsolicited drawings and gender socialization. In A. M. Kindler (Ed.), *Child development in art* (pp. 107–114). Reston, VA: National Art Education Association.

Duncum, P. (2002). Children never were what they were: Perspectives on childhood. In Y. Gaudelius & P. Speirs (Eds.), *Contemporary issues in art education* (pp. 97-106). Upper Saddle River, NJ: Prentice-Hall.

Duncum, P. (2003). Theorising everyday aesthetic experience with contemporary visual culture. *Visual Arts Research, 28*(2), 4–15.

Duncum, P. (2004). Visual culture isn't just visual: Multiliteracy, multimodality, and meaning. *Studies in Art Education, 45*(3), 252–264.

Dyson, A. H. (1989). *Multiple worlds of child writers: Friends learning to write.* New York: Teachers College Press.

Dyson, A. H. (1990). Symbol makers, symbol weavers: How children link play, pictures, and print. *Young Children, 42*(2), 50–57.

Dyson, A. H. (1997). *Writing superheroes: Contemporary childhood, popular culture, and classroom literacy.* New York: Teachers College Press.

Dyson, A. H. (2003). "Welcome to the jam": Popular culture, school literacy, and the making of childhoods. *Harvard Educational Review, 73*(3). Retrieved from http://www.edreview.org/harvard03/fa03/f03dyson/htm

Eckhoff, A., & Guberman, S. (2006). Daddy Daycare, Daffy Duck, and Salvador Dali: Popular culture and children's art viewing experience. *Art Education, 59*(5), 19–25.

Edens, K., & Potter, E. (2004). "Yes, it's a good picture": Preschoolers' evaluation of their pictures. *Arts and Learning Research Journal, 20*(1), 85–109.

Edwards, L. C. (1997). *The creative arts: A process approach for teachers and children* (2nd ed.). Upper Saddle River, NJ: Prentice-Hall.

Efland, A. D. (1983). School art and its social origin. *Studies in Art Education, 24,* 49–57.

Efland, A. D. (1976). School art style: A functional analysis. *Studies in Art Education, 17*(2), 37–44.

Egan, K. (1988). *Primary understanding: Education in early childhood.* New York: Routledge.

Egan, K. (1999). *Children's minds, talking rabbits, and clockwork oranges: Essays on education.* New York: Teachers College Press.

Egan, K., & Ling, M. (2002). We begin as poets: Conceptual tools and the arts in early childhood. In L. Bresler & C. M. Thompson (Eds.), *The arts in children's lives: Context, culture, and curriculum* (pp. 93–100). Boston, MA: Kluwer Academic Press.

Ewald, W. & Lightfoot, A. (2001). *I wanna take me a picture: Teaching photography and writing to children.* Boston, MA: Beacon Press.

Feinburg, S. (1979). The significance of what boys and girls choose to draw: Explorations of fighting and helping. In J. Loeb (Ed.), *Feminist collage: Educating women in the visual arts* (pp. 107–122). New York: Teachers College Press.

Feldman, E. B. (1992). *Varieties of visual experience.* Englewood Cliffs, NJ: Prentice Hall.

Fineberg, J. (1997). *The innocent eye: Children's art and the modern artist.* Princeton, NJ: Princeton University Press.

Fineberg, J. (Ed.). (1998). *Discovering child art: Essays on child art, primitivism, and modernism.* Princeton, NJ: Princeton University Press.

Fineberg, J. (2006). *When we were young: New perspectives on the art of the child.* Berkeley: University of California Press.

Flannery, K., & Watson, M. (1995). Sex differences and gender-role differences in children's drawings. *Studies in Art Education, 36*(2), 114–122.

Forman, G. (1994). Different media, different languages. In L. G. Katz & B. Cesarone (Eds.), *Reflections on the Reggio Emilia approach* (pp. 41–54). Urbana, IL: ERIC.

Fortes, M. (1981). Tallensi children's drawings. In B. Loyd & J. Gay (Eds.), *Universals of human thought* (pp. 46–70). Cambridge, England: Cambridge University Press.

Freeman, N. H. (1980). *Strategies of representation in young children.* London: Academic Press.

Freeman, N. H., & Cox, M. (1985). *Visual order.* London: Academic Press.

Freeman, N. H., & Janikoun, R. (1972). Intellectual realism in children's drawings of a familiar object with distinctive features. *Child Development, 43,* 1116–1121.

Freeman, N. H., & Sanger, D. (1995). Commonsense aesthetics of rural children. *Visual Arts Research, 21*(2), 1–10.

Freedman, K. (1997). Artistic development and curriculum: Sociocultural learning considerations. In A. M. Kindler (Ed.), *Child development in art* (pp. 95–106). Reston, VA: National Art Education Association.

Frisch, N. S. (2006). Drawing in preschools: A didactic experience. *International Journal of Art & Design Education, 25*(1), 74–85.

Gallas, K. (1994). *The languages of learning.* New York: Teachers College Press.

Gallo, F., Golomb, C., & Barroso, A. (2003). Compositional strategies in drawing: The effects of two- and three-dimensional media. *Visual Arts Research, 28*(1), 2–23.

Gamradt, J., & Staples, C. (1994). My school and me: Children's drawings in postmodern educational research and evaluation. *Visual Arts Research, 20*(1), 36–49.

Gardner, H. (1973). *The arts and human development.* New York: Wiley.

Gardner, H. (1976). Unfolding or teaching? On the optimal training of artistic skills. In E. W. Eisner (Ed.), *The arts, human development, and education* (pp. 5–18). Berkeley, CA: McCutchan.

Gardner, H. (1980). *Artful scribbles: The significance of children's drawings.* New York: Basic Books.

Gardner, H. (1982). *Art, mind, and brain.* New York: Basic Books.

Gibson, M., & Mcallister, N. (2005). BIG ART *small viewer:* A collaborative community project. *Contemporary Issues in Early Childhood, 6*(2), 204–208.

Goldberg, M. (1997). *Arts and learning.* New York: Longman.

Golomb, C. (1974). *Young children's sculpture and drawing: A study in representational development.* Cambridge, MA: Harvard University Press.

Golomb, C. (1997). Representational concepts in clay: The development of sculpture. In A. M. Kindler (Ed.), *Child development in art* (pp. 131–141). Reston, VA: National Art Education Association.

Golomb, C. (2002). *Child art in context: A cultural and comparative perspective.* Washington, DC: American Psychological Association.

Golomb, C. (2004). *The child's creation of a pictorial world* (2nd ed.). Berkeley: University of California Press. (Original work published 1992)

Golomb, C., & McCormick, M. (1995). Sculpture: The development of three-dimensional representation in clay. *Visual Arts Research, 21*(1), 35–50.

Goodenough, F. L. (1926). *Measurement of intelligence by drawing.* New York: Harcourt, Brace, & World.

Grace, D. J., & Tobin, J. (2002). Pleasure, creativity, and the carnivalesque in children's video production. In L. Bresler & C. M. Thompson (Eds.), *The arts in children's lives: Context, culture, and curriculum* (pp. 195–214). Boston, MA: Kluwer Academic Press.

Graue, M. E., & Walsh, D. J. (1998). *Studying children in context: Theories, methods and ethics.* Thousand Oaks, CA: Sage.

Greenberg, P. (1996). Time, money, and the new art education versus art and irrelevance. *Studies in Art Education, 37*(2), 115–116.

Hamblen, K. (2002). Children's contextual art knowledge: Local art and school art context comparisons. In L. Bresler & C. M. Thompson (Eds.), *The arts in children's lives: Context, culture, and curriculum* (pp. 15–27). Boston, MA: Kluwer Academic Press.

Harris, D. B. (1963). *Children's drawings as measures of intellectual maturity.* New York: Harcourt, Brace & World.

Harris, V. (2000). A unique pedagogical project contextualized within a children's art exhibition. *Contemporary Issues in Early Childhood, 1*(2), 185–199.

Helm, J. H., & Katz, L. (2001). *Young investigators: The project approach in the early years.* New York: Teachers College Press.

Inagaki, K. (1992). Piagetian and post-Piagetian conceptions of development and their implications for science education in early childhood. *Early Childhood Research Quarterly, 7,* 115–133.

Ivashevich, O. (2009). Children's drawing as a sociocultural practice: Remaking gender and popular culture. *Studies in Art Education, 51*(1), 50–63.

Jalongo, M. R., & Stamp, L. N. (1997). *The arts in children's lives: Aesthetic education in early childhood.* Needham Heights, MA: Allyn & Bacon.

James, A., Jenks, C. & Prout, A. (1998). *Theorizing childhood.* New York: Teachers College Press.

Jeffers, C. (1993). A survey of instructors of art methods classes for preservice elementary teachers. *Studies in Art Education, 34*(4), 233–243.

Jenkins, H. (1998). (Ed.). *The children's culture reader.* New York: New York University Press.

Katz, L. G. (1998). What can we learn from Reggio Emilia? In C. Edwards, L. Gandini, & G. Forman (Eds.), *The hundred languages of children: The Reggio Emilia approach—Advanced reflections* (2nd ed., pp. 27–45). Westport, CT: Ablex.

Kellogg, R. (1970). *Analyzing children's art.* Palo Alto, CA: Mayfield.

Kendrick, M., & McKay, R. (2004). Drawings as an alternative way of understanding young children's constructions of literacy. *Journal of Early Childhood Literacy, 4*(1), 109–127.

Kerlavage, M. (1995). A bunch of naked ladies and a tiger: Children's responses to adult works of art. In C. M. Thompson (Ed.), *The visual arts and early childhood learning* (pp. 56–62). Reston, VA: National Art Education Association.

Kerschensteiner, G. (1905). *Die Entwicklung der Zeichnerischen Begabung.* [The development of drawing talent]. Munich, Germany: Carl Greber.

Kincheloe, J. (1998). The new childhood: Home alone as a way of life. In H. Jenkins (Ed.), *The children's culture reader* (pp. 159–177). New York: New York University Press.

Kindler, A. M. (1994). Artistic learning in early childhood: A study of social interactions. *Canadian Review of Art Education, 21*(2), 91–106.

Kindler, A. M. (1995). Significance of adult input in early artistic development. In C. M. Thompson (Ed.), *The visual arts and early childhood learning* (pp. 10–14). Reston, VA: National Art Education Association.

Kindler, A. (Ed.). (1997). *Child development in art.* Reston, VA: National Art Education Association.

Kindler, A. M. (1999). "From endpoints to repertoires": A challenge to art education, *Studies in Art Education, 40*(4), 330–349.

Kindler, A. M., & Darras, B. (1995). Young children's understanding of the nature and acquisition of drawing skills: A cross-cultural study. *Journal of Multicultural and Cross-Cultural Research in Art Education, 13,* 85–100.

Kindler, A. M., & Darras, B. (1997). Map of artistic development. In A. M. Kindler (Ed.), *Child development in art* (pp. 17–44). Reston, VA: National Art Education Association.

Kindler, A., Darras. B., & Kuo, A. (2000). When a culture takes a trip: Evidence of heritage and enculturation in early conceptions of art. *Journal of Art & Design Education, 19*(1), 44–53.

Knight, L. M. (2009). Mother and child sharing through drawing: Intergenerational collaborative processes for making artworks, *International Art in Early Childhood Research Journal, 1*(1), 1–12.

Koppitz, E. (1968). *Psychological evaluation of children's human figure drawings.* New York: Grune & Stratton.

Korzenik, D. (1973–1974). Role-taking and children's drawings. *Studies in Art Education, 15*(3), 17–24.

Korzenik, D. (1981, September). Is children's work art? Some historical views. *Art Education,* 20–24.

Lange-Kuettner, C., & Thomas, G. V. (1995). *Drawing and looking.* New York: Harvester Wheatsheaf.

Lark-Horovitz, B., Lewis, H., & Luca, M. (1973). *Understanding children's art for better teaching* (2nd ed.). Columbus, OH: Charles E. Merrill.

Leeds, J. A. (1986). Teaching and the reasons for making art. *Art Education, 39*(7), 17–21.

Leeds, J. A. (1989). The history of attitudes toward child art. *Studies in Art Education, 30*(2), 93–103.

Lin, S. F., & Thomas, G. V. (2002). Development of understanding of popular graphic art: A study of everyday aesthetics in children, adolescents and young adults. *International Journal of Behavioral Development, 26*(3), 278–287.

Lowenfeld, V. (1957). *Creative and mental growth* (3rd ed.). New York: Macmillan.

Luquet, G-H. (1927/2001). *Children's drawings* (A. Costall, Trans. & intro). London: Free Association Books. (Original work published 1927 as *Le dessin enfantin*)

Maitland, L. M. (1895). What children draw to please themselves. *The Inland Educator, 1*, 77–81.

Malaguzzi, L. (1995, May). Your image of the child: Where teaching begins. *Child Care Information Exchange, 96*, 52–61.

Malaguzzi, L. (1998). No way. The hundred is there. In C. Edwards, L. Gandini, & G. Forman (Eds.), *The hundred languages of children: The Reggio Emilia approach—Advanced reflections* (p. 3). Westport, CT: Ablex.

Martlew, M., & Connolly, K. J. (1996). Human figure drawings by schooled and unschooled children in Papua New Guinea. *Child Development, 67*, 2743–2762.

Matthews, J. (2002). Infancy. In E. Eisner & M. Day (Eds.), *Handbook of research in art education* (pp. 253–298). Mahwah, NJ: Erlbaum.

Matthews, G. (1980). *Philosophy and the young child.* Cambridge, MA: Harvard University Press.

Matthews, J. (1999). *The art of childhood and adolescence: The construction of meaning.* Philadelphia, PA: Falmer Press.

Matthews, J., & Jessels, J. (1993). Very young children use electronic paint: The beginnings of drawing with traditional media and computer paintbox, *Visual Arts Research, 19*(1), 47–62.

Matthews, J., & Seow, P. (2009). Electronic paint: Understanding children's representation through their interactions with digital paint. In S. Herne, S. Cox, & R. Watts (Eds.), *Readings in primary art education* (pp. 269–286). Bristol, England: Intellect Books.

McArdle, F. (2008). Editorial. *Contemporary Issues in Early Childhood, 9*(4), 273–274.

McArdle, F., & Piscatelli, B. (2002). Early childhood art education: A palimpsest. *Australian Art Education, 25*(1), 11–15.

McClure, M. (2006a). Drawing on the toy: Contemporary perspectives on childhood by children. In P. Duncum (Ed.), *Visual culture in the art class: Case studies* (pp. 24–31). Reston, VA: National Art Education Association.

McClure, M. (2006b). Thank heaven for little girls: Girls' drawings as representations of self. *Visual Culture and Gender, 1*, 63–78.

McClure, M. (2007). Play as process: Choice, translation, reconfiguration, and the process of culture. *Visual Arts Research, 33*(65), 63–70.

McClure, M. (2009). Digital visual childhood: Little kids, video, and the blogosphere. In R. Sweeny (Ed.), *Inter/actions/inter/sections: Art education in a digital visual culture* (pp. 20–29). Reston, VA: National Art Education Association.

Mortenson, K. (1991). *Form and content in children's human figure drawings: Development, sex differences, and body experiences.* New York: New York University Press.

Mulcahy, C. (2002). Talking about art: Understanding children's perspectives. *Arts and Learning Research Journal, 18*(1), 19–35.

Munro, T., Lark-Horovitz, B., & Barnhart, E. N. (1942). Children's art abilities: Studies at the Cleveland Museum of Art. *Journal of Experimental Education, 11*(2), 97–155.

Narey, M. (Ed.). (2009). *Making meaning: Constructing multimodal perspectives of language, literacy, and learning through arts-based early childhood education.* New York: Springer.

New, R. (2007). Reggio Emilia as cultural activity: Theory in practice. *Theory into Practice, 46*(1), 5–13.

The New London Group (1996). A pedagogy of multiliteracies: Designing social futures. *Harvard Educational Review, 66*(1), 60–92.

Newton, C., & Kantner, L. (1997). Cross-cultural research in aesthetic development: A review. In A. M. Kindler (Ed.), *Child development in art* (pp. 165–182). Reston, VA: National Art Education Association.

Paget, G. W. (1932). Some drawings of men and women made by children of certain non-European races. *Journal of the Royal Anthropological Institute, 62*, 127–144.

Parsons, M. (1988). *How we understand art: A cognitive account of aesthetic development.* New York: Cambridge University Press.

Pearson, P. (2001) Towards a theory of children's drawing as social practice. *Studies in Art Education, 42*(4), 348–365.

Pink, S. (2001). *Doing visual ethnography: Image, media and representation in research.* London: Sage.

Pitri, E. (2003). Conceptual problem solving during artistic representation. *Art Education, 56*(4), 19–23.

Read, H. (1945). *Education through art.* New York: Pantheon.

Reggio Children & Project Zero (2001). *Making learning visible: Children as individual and group learners.* Reggio Emilia, Italy: Reggio Children.

Reith, E. (1997). Drawing development: The child's understanding of the dual reality of pictorial representations. In A. M. Kindler (Ed.), *Child development in art* (pp. 59–80). Reston, VA: National Art Education Association.

Richards, R. D. (2007). Outdated relics on hallowed ground: Unearthing attitudes and beliefs about young children's art. *Australian Journal of Early Childhood Education, 32*(4), 22–30.

Richards, R. D. (2009). Young visual ethnographers: Children's use of visual ethnography to record, share and extend their art experiences. *International Art in Early Childhood Research Journal, 1*(1). Retrieved from http://www.artinearlychildhood.org/artec//index. php?option=com_journals&Itemid=57&task=article&id=8

Rinaldi, C. (2006). *In dialogue with Reggio Emilia: Listening, researching and learning.* New York: Routledge.

Ring, K. (2006). Supporting young children drawing: Developing a role. *International Journal of Education through Art, 2*(3), 195–209.

Robertson, A. (1987). Development of Bruce's spontaneous drawings from six to sixteen. *Studies in Art Education, 29*(1), 37–51.

Ryan, M. E. & Healy, A. H. (2008). "Art"efacts of knowing: Multiliteracies and the arts. In A. H. Healy (Ed.), *Multiliteracies and diversity: New pedagogies for expanding landscapes* (pp. 82–101). South Melbourne, Australia: Oxford University Press.

Savva, A. (2003). Young pupils' responses to adult works of art. *Contemporary Issues in Early Childhood, 4*(3), 300–313.

Savva, A., & Trimis, E. (2005). Responses of young children to contemporary art exhibits: The role of artistic experiences. *International Journal of Education and the Arts, 6*(13). Retrieved from http://ijea.asu.edu/v6n13/

Schaefer-Simmern, H. (1948). *The unfolding of artistic activity.* Berkeley: University of California Press.

Schirrmacher, R. (1993). *Art and creative development for young children* (3rd ed.). Albany, NY: Delmar.

Schulte, C. M. (2011). Verbalization in children's drawing performances: Toward a metaphorical continuum of inscription, extension, and re-inscription. *Studies in Art Education, 53*(1), 20–34.

Smith, P. (1995). Commentary: Art and irrelevance. *Studies in Art Education, 36*(2), 123–125.

Su, C-M. (1995). A cross-cultural study of partial occlusion in children's drawings. In C. M. Thompson (Ed.), *The visual arts and early childhood learning* (pp. 91–94). Reston, VA: National Art Education Association.

Swann, A. (2005, July). The role of media and emerging representation in early childhood. *Art Education, 58*(3), 41–47

Tarr, P. (1995). Preschool children's socialization through art experiences. In C. M. Thompson (Ed.), *The visual arts and early childhood learning* (pp. 23–27). Reston, VA: National Art Education Association.

Tarr, P. (2003). Reflections on the image of the child: Reproducer or creator of culture. *Art Education, 56*(4), 6–11.

Taunton, M. & Colbert, C. (2000). Art in the early childhood classroom: Authentic experiences and extended dialogues. In N. J. Yelland (Ed.),

Promoting meaningful learning: Innovations in educating early child-hood professionals (pp. 67–76). Washington, DC: National Association for the Education of Young Children.

Thomas, G. V., & Silk, A. M. J. (1990). *An introduction to the psychology of children's drawings.* New York: New York University Press.

Thompson, C. M.(Ed.). (1995). *The visual arts and early childhood learning.* Reston, VA: National Art Education Association.

Thompson, C. M. (1999). Action, autobiography, and aesthetics in young children's self-initiated drawings. *Journal of Art & Design Education, 18*(2), 155–161.

Thompson, C. M. (2002). Drawing together: Peer influence in preschool-kindergarten art classes. In L. Bresler & C. M. Thompson (Eds.), *The arts in children's lives: Context, culture, and curriculum* (pp. 129–138). Boston, MA: Kluwer Academic Press.

Thompson, C. M. (1997). Transforming curriculum in the visual arts. In S. Bredekamp & T. Rosegrant (Eds.), *Reaching potentials: Transforming early childhood curriculum and assessment* (pp. 81–98). Washington, DC: National Association for the Education of Young Children.

Thompson, C. M. (2003). Kinderculture in the art classroom: Early childhood art and the mediation of culture. *Studies in Art Education, 44*(2), 135–146.

Thompson, C. M. (2006). The "ket aesthetic": Visual culture in childhood. In J. Fineberg (Ed.), *When we were young: New perspectives on the art of the child* (pp. 31–43). Berkeley: University of California Press.

Thompson, C. M. (2009). Mira! Looking, listening, and lingering in research with children. *Visual Arts Research, 35*(1), 24–34.

Thompson, C. & Bales, S. (1991). "Michael doesn't like my dinosaurs:" Conversations in a preschool art class. *Studies in Art Education, 33*(1), 43–55.

Thunder-McGuire, S. (1994). An inner critic in children's artists' book-making. *Visual Arts Research, 20*(2), 51–61.

Tobin, J. (1995, May). The irony of self-expression. *American Journal of Education, 103,* 233–258.

Trafi, L. (2008). A visual art education curriculum for early childhood teacher education: Re-constructing the family album. *Journal of Art and Design Education, 27*(1), 53–62.

Trimis, E., & Savva, A. (2004) The in-depth approach: Incorporating an art museum program into a preprimary classroom. *Art Education, 57*(6), 20–24/33–34.

Tuman, D. (1999). Gender style as form and content: An examination of gender stereotypes in the subject preference of children's drawing. *Studies in Art Education, 41*(1), 40–60.

Tuman, D. (2000). Defining differences: A historical overview of the research regarding the difference between the drawings of boys and girls. *The Journal of Gender Issues in Art and Education, 1,* 17–30.

Vecchi, V. (2001). The curiosity to understand. In Reggio Children & Project Zero (Eds.), *Making learning visible: Children as individual and group learners* (pp. 158–212). Reggio Emilia, Italy: Reggio Children.

Vecchi, V. (2010). *Art and creativity in Reggio Emilia: Exploring the role and potential of ateliers in early childhood education.* New York: Routledge.

Vecchi, V. (1998). The role of the *atelierista:* An interview with Lella Gandini. In C. Edwards, L. Gandini, & G. Forman (Eds.), *The hundred languages of children: The Reggio Emilia approach—Advanced reflections* (2nd ed., pp. 139–148). Westport, CT: Ablex.

Vygotsky, L. S. (1962). *Thought and language* (E. Hanfmann & G. Vakar, Trans. & Eds.). Cambridge, MA: Harvard University Press.

Vygotsky, L. S. (1978). *Mind in society.* Cambridge, MA: Harvard University Press.

Walsh, D. (2002). Constructing an artistic self: A cultural perspective. In L. Bresler & C. M. Thompson (Eds.), *The arts in children's lives: Context, culture, and curriculum* (pp. 101–111). Boston, MA: Kluwer Academic Press.

Weitz, M. (1959). The role of theory in aesthetics. In M. Weitz (Ed.), *Problems in aesthetics: An introductory book of readings* (pp. 145–159). New York: Macmillan.

Wexler, A. J., & Cardinal, R. (2009). *Art and disability: The social and political struggles facing education.* New York: Macmillan.

Willats, J. (1977). How children learn to draw realistic pictures. *Quarterly Journal of Experimental Psychology, 29,* 367–382.

Wilson, B. (1974). The superheroes of J. C. Holz. *Art Education, 27*(8), 2–9.

Wilson, B. (1997). Child art, multiple interpretations, and conflicts of interest. In A. M. Kindler (Ed.), *Child development in art* (pp. 81–94). Reston, VA: National Art Education Association.

Wilson, B. (2002). Becoming Japanese: Manga, children's drawings, and the construction of national character. In L. Bresler & C. M. Thompson (Eds.), *The arts in children's lives: Context, culture, and curriculum* (pp. 43–56). Boston, MA: Kluwer Academic Press.

Wilson, B. (2004). Child art after modernism: Visual culture and new narratives. In E. W. Eisner & M. D. Day (Eds.), *Handbook of research and policy in art education* (pp. 299–328). Mahwah, NJ: Erlbaum.

Wilson, B. (2007). Art, visual culture, and child/adult collaborative images: Recognizing the other-than. *Visual Arts Research, 33*(65), 6–20.

Wilson, B., & Thompson, C. M. (2007). Pedagogy and the visual culture of childhood and youth. *Visual Arts Research, 33*(65), 1–5.

Wilson, B., & Wilson, M. (1977). An iconoclastic view of the imagery sources in the drawings of young people. *Art Education,* 5–11.

Wilson, B., & Wilson, M. (1984). Children's drawings in Egypt: Cultural style acquisition as graphic development. *Visual Arts Research, 10*(1), 13–26.

Wilson, B., & Wilson, M. (1985). The artistic tower of Babel: Inextricable links between culture and graphic development. *Visual Arts Research, 11*(1), 90–104.

Wilson, B., & Wilson, M. (2009). *Teaching children to draw: A guide for parents and teachers.* Englewood Cliffs, NJ: Prentice-Hall. (Original work published 1982)

Winner, E. (1982). *Invented worlds.* Cambridge, MA: Harvard University Press.

Winner, E. (1989). How can Chinese children draw so well? *Journal of Aesthetic Education, 23*(1), 41–63.

Wolf, D. P., & Perry, M. D. (1988). From endpoint to repertoires: Some new conclusions about drawing development. *Journal of Aesthetic Education, 22*(1), 17–34.

Wright, S. (2005, September 15). Children's multi-modal meaning-making thru drawing and storytelling. *Teachers College Record.* Retrieved from http://www.tcrecord.org ID No.: 12175

Wright, S. (2007). Graphic-narrative play: Young children's authoring through drawing and telling. *International Journal of Education and the Arts, 8*(8). Retrieved from http://ijea.asu.edu/v8n8/

Wright, S. (2003) *The arts, young children and learning.* Boston, MA: Allyn & Bacon.

Xanthouthaki, M., Tickle, L., & Secules, V. (Eds.). (2003). *Researching visual arts ed in museums and galleries.* Dordrecht, the Netherlands: Kluwer.

Yamagata, K. (1997). Representational activity during mother–child interaction: The scribbling stage of drawing. *British Journal of Development, 15,* 355–366.

Zimmerman, E., & Zimmerman, L. (2000). Art education and early childhood education: The young child as creator and meaning maker within a community context. *Young Children,* 87–92.

Zurmuehlen, M. (1990). *Studio art: Praxis, symbol, presence.* Reston, VA: National Art Education Association.

Zurmuehlen, M., & Kantner, L. (1995). The narrative quality of young children's art. In C. M. Thompson (Ed.), *The visual arts and early childhood learning* (pp. 6–9). Reston, VA: National Art Education Association.

16

The Dance of Learning

KAREN KOHN BRADLEY
(ORIGINALLY WITH) MARY SZEGDA
University of Maryland College Park

In the life of a young child, every day is a new journey. The vehicle for the journey is movement. From the early morning bounce or slide out of bed, until the last crawl or rollover at night, every child negotiates his or her way along a pathway of body actions in space and time, with an ever-increasing and specific array of expressive and functional actions.

Movement may, in fact be considered the primary intelligence. It certainly precedes both vocal and verbal language development and is informed by and informs visual-spatial, auditory, and other sensory development. Touch response, tracking smells, auditory location, and visual attending are motor reactions to sensory inputs, and become movement patterns that then become expressive and functional. A child's evolving sense of self and her understanding of the world of objects are based on this feedback loop of reflexive, responsive, volitional, interactive, and expressive actions.

In this sense, the entire learning process may be seen as a form of "dancing"—as an increasingly conscious choosing to explore and interact with data that is based in rhythmic and spatial sequences of movements. Reflexive movement, which takes place in a lower aspect of the brain, provides information to the emotional and cognitive processing areas of the brain. The brain depends on the motor cortex and spinal column to provide information about sensations and interactions with the world outside the skin. It is this dance of inner and outer experiences, lower and higher processing centers, and functional and expressive actions that is the material of deep learning.

As the child develops, rhythm organizes and delineates the temporal aspects of expression and reception. From pat-a-cake to double-Dutch, from marching games to rap for kids, repetitive ever-more complex rhythmic structures bring children away from the passive entertainment world of television and some electronic games. Rhythm activates, focuses, and organizes them socially and interactively.

Ancient representations of children in art and other descriptions show clapping games and circle dances. More than 80 years ago, articles were written on how to use rhythms to help children organize for learning. Gerhardt (1973) describes rhythm as a "dynamic time-of-thought and time-of action relationship" (p. 51). Benari (1995) writes about the relationship of rhythmic awareness to breathing rhythms.

In many schools around the United States, dance education classes are called Rhythms. The expressive resultant phenomenon of temporally organized movement is valued, even when the art form of dance is not. In urban streets, in suburban basements, outside shopping malls, on playgrounds, wherever children gather, there are rhythmic games and boom box music. Children thereby demonstrate their need for organization and expression.

The author's evidence of the power of rhythm came in her son's fourth grade class. She was in the classroom for the day at the behest of the teacher, who was struggling with the group. The school was new, the children previously unknown to each other, and the atmosphere was chaotic most of the time. The day the author was there was also the day of the Stanford-9 tests (U.S. achievement tests administered annually in many public schools). All of the adults were in despair over the picture of such disorganized bodies (children) sitting at desks for two hours answering questions.

The fourth grade students began with growing and shrinking movements, based on breath rhythms and with the support of John Coltrane's version of "My Favorite Things," surely one of the most lush pieces of music ever recorded. They responded to the syncopated waltz rhythms immediately. The author and the students rolled down the spine and up the spine, stretched in all directions, and just got down with the music. After 20 minutes, the fourth graders sat at their desks, picked up their pencils, and began the test. One could have heard a pin drop.

Mastery of rhythm supports the kind of thinking/action interaction that reveals the complex nature of active learning. Therefore, the games of children worldwide make sense both as community building and as a set point for learning readiness. Warming up for learning, as in above example, allows for physical and mental organization, which is not the case for many children when asked to complete the more common lesson warm-up activity of answering questions from a book, or doing a sheet of math problems.

The development of the child can be thought of as both a continuing refinement of skills through practice and a construction of the nature of self and reality through interactions with the world of objects/people. If both of these processes are interactive and inform each other, it is but a small step to see how critical both functional and expressive movement are to the development of the cognitive, social, and kinesthetic life of the child.

Mihaly Csikszentmihaly (1990), in his book *Flow: The Psychology of Optimal Experience* addresses the feedback loop of active learning in regard to movement:

> Flow activities…have rules that require the learning of skills, they set up goals, they provide feedback, they make control possible….Because of the way they are constructed, they help participants and spectators achieve an ordered state of mind that is…enjoyable.(p.72)

Thus moving, however it forms and allows for encounters, is a priori to knowing. We do not know and then move; we move in order to know.

Components of Movement

Rhythm underlies one aspect of movement, the "how" or qualitative aspect of moving. Children move in space, using body parts and organizing them, with qualities such as degrees of attention, degrees of strength or resistance, degrees of hastening or lingering, and degrees of flowing through or holding back. These qualities modify actions of the body in space, and have been named *Effort* by the movement theorist

Rudolf Laban (1879–1958). Laban organized the analysis of movement into the components of Body (*what* is moving), Space (*where* it is moving), and Effort (*how* it is moving). Another category has been added to the Laban movement analysis (LMA) systematic analysis of human movement: Shape (*how* the body adjusts its shape in relationship to an external factor—such as an object or another person). (The Shape category was developed by Warren Lamb, with further work by Judith Kestenberg, which will be described later in this chapter.)

Laban's work found favor with physical educators and dance educators in Britain during and immediately following World War II (Preston-Dunlop, 2008, p. 230). Through the vocabulary that developed from Laban's theoretical framework, teachers encouraged children to discover how they could make up their own movement sentences: phrases of body parts moving in space, with rhythm and qualities, and in relationship to outside factors such as objects, partners, groups, or the space itself.

Marion North developed Laban's work further, utilizing the framework and map to observe children. In her studies (compiled in *Personality Assessment Through Movement*, 1975), she focused primarily on the *Effort* components, but she also made the point that it is the whole movement event that must be observed first (p. vi). North provides a clear overview of the Laban "map" for movement, and a number of examples of her own use of the vocabulary in assessing children from a movement analysis. Chapter 6 of her work is a comparative analysis of movements of deaf children using the *Effort* framework, classroom teachers' reports, and a personality test, the B scale, developed by a psychologist. There is a great deal of correlation between the movement analysis and the classroom teachers' reports; the B scale provides information regarding specific deficits in the child's makeup. What becomes apparent in her book is that there is a tremendous amount of information in a movement profile about how a child succeeds, while there is not much directive information in most personality tests. Both prescriptive and positive reinforcement responses are much more challenging in the case where such tests are the only source of diagnostic information.

Through the systematic observation of and exposure to movement experiences and movement interactions, children construct their own maps of the world of objects and beliefs. What is revealed when children create their own "dances" or phrases of expressive movement? We can see the very act of learning unfolding. We can see patterns of interaction with the fabric of the emerging self, and with the social/interpersonal field of possibilities. We also see applications of prior knowledge as the dancers make random movements meaningful. How exactly do they learn to move?

Children give rise to movement, voice, and mind from the simple and usually unconscious act of breathing. When the infant gasps, cries, coos, or sleeps, the body response to the rhythm and quality of the breath results in both voicing and movement.

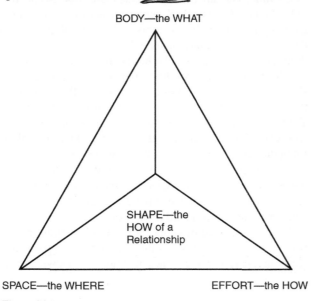

BODY—the WHAT

SHAPE—the HOW of a Relationship

SPACE—the WHERE   EFFORT—the HOW

Figure 16.1

Adults reflect, reinforce, and extend the expressions of infants by mirroring, bridging, accommodating, feeding, talking, singing, rocking, and playing with infants. It is in these interactions that the child begins to map his or her sense of the world of objects and the place of the self within that world.

Antonio Damasio (1999) wrote about how the self becomes conscious of itself. He describes two players, the organism and the object, in terms of the relationship between them. That relationship is a two-way street in which knowledge is constructed via the dynamic exchange between an organism and an object. The object in the relationship is causing a change in the organism (p. 133).

From such constructions of reality come beliefs, including beliefs about the nature of one's self. The child comes to see herself as competent, or clumsy, or delicate, or strong, depending, in part, on the responses of and interactions with the powerful adults in her life.

The role of mirror neurons in the construction of identity is just now (in 2011) beginning to be understood. To begin with, Gallese (2001) points out how critical action and interactions are in developing intentions, revealing desires, and constructing beliefs,

> far from being *exclusively* dependent upon mentalistic/linguistic abilities, the capacity for understanding others as intentional agents is deeply grounded in the *relational* nature of action. Action is relational, and the relation holds both between the agent and the object target of the action (see Gallese, 2000b), as between the agent of the action and his/her observer. (p.34)

Gallese (2001) points out later:

> One important aspect of the *self* is the result of the individual's mirroring in the social organization of the outer world. According to Mead, the only way to *objectify* us is to assume the other's perspective, like looking at our reflection in a mirror. Through the medium of intersubjective communication the consequences produced by our actions in the observed behaviour of others contribute to build our personal identity (see Mead, 1934). (p.44)

Therefore, the act of moving in response to others, whether in a parent–child interaction, a game, a dance class, or any of an endless number of such mind–body interfaces, produces transactions that help us to be more empathetic as well as identifiably ourselves.

The Kestenberg Movement Profile

The work of Dr. Judith Kestenberg, a protégé of Laban's and Anna Freud's, looks at how parent and infant interactions support and shape the development of the primary relationship on both the expressive and the social sides. The Kestenberg Movement Profile (KMP) allows the trained observer to note patterns of expressive and relational behavior through the degree of attunement in two categories.

The baby, Kestenberg proposed, enters the world with two primary regulatory systems that operate in the form of tension-flow and shape-flow. Tension-flow reflects the elasticity of effortful movement and affect-related expressivity. Shape-flow is the other side of tension-flow, and reflects the changing relational experience; how the organism relates to the structures around them (Sossin, n.d.).

An integral aspect within the KMP is attunement. Attunement occurs when two individuals share a common experience. It is essential in relational development and can occur on many levels. Tension-flow attunement is particularly powerful when engaging an infant in interaction. Rhythms shared lead to a sense of connection or synchrony—a phenomenon of groups that can build group cohesion and trust. Communication and understanding become more likely in environments in which two people attune, or "sync up."

Trust develops from patterns of mutual relatedness identifiable through shape-flow rhythms. A bonding process can happen as the result of attunement with in-utero shape-flow patterns. Since the shape-flow mode of self-attunement flows on breath rhythms, adults can, naturally or through training, attune breathing patterns to those of children and build up an atmosphere of mutuality and trust over time. The conscious attuning process is a technique used in Kestenberg's work both with infants in-utero and as a therapeutic technique with infants and young children.

Sossin notes that the KMP system is complex, possibly because it is based in both psychodynamic and movement analyses. Robert Prince (2006) describes Kestenberg's extensive psychodynamic training and describes favorable applications as predicted by respected peers of Dr. Kestenberg at the time of the development of the system. However, few educators or researchers are aware of the KMP.

Interrater reliability of the KMP is moderately high (Koch, 1997) to moderately low for a few aspects of the system. The fact that novice raters were more inconsistent than experienced raters places the KMP in a similar category to the Laban movement analysis system; that is, the building of consensus over time is a significant part of the training, and a factor in the degree of interrater reliability.

Research that has been completed using the KMP includes infant sleep pattern analysis (Lotan & Yirmiya, 2002), and as an assessment tool for identifying neglected children (Leirvag, 2001). In the Lotan study, 30 toddlers were videotaped as they fell asleep. Using the KMP, researchers determined that low intensity babies (babies whose movements were less "loaded" and expressed fewer qualities at the same time expressively and who fall more toward the free flow side of the spectrum) fell asleep more quickly than high intensity babies, and that the presence and length of presence of the parents in the room made a difference as well. Parents who spent more time in the room tended to have babies who kicked more, banged, and strained more (description of high intensity movement preferences), whereas parents who spent less time in the room tended to have lower intensity babies.

The movement variables were superior predictors of falling asleep time.

The implications of the research demonstrate that the KMP and movement analysis in general, can be important tools for unpacking behavior. Without the specificity and observability of such systems of analysis, parents and teachers may only speculate about the importance of their role in the development of the child.

Effort and Shape

The Kestenberg work looks at developmental stages in object relations and expressive movement threads. Laban movement analysis takes the analysis to the next stages developmentally, into the ways in which relationships to objects and personality are revealed through movement.

Effort is the category describing the qualitative expressive modifiers of action or the "how" of movement. As a child's personality develops, observable patterns of expressivity appear. One child may be "mild-mannered," while another is "intense." One is "strong-willed," another "light-hearted." The expressive components appear in recurring phrases of movement behavior that formulate a baseline. Children (as well as adults) are not limited to these characteristics. Everyone has a range. But certain patterns appear in specific contexts, and loved ones easily recognize the individual's patterns.

Effort observation is one way to track change and growth in a child's expressive range. A great deal of creative movement curricula that is utilized in schools includes development of a greater range of expressive actions, or a broadened palette of choices for personal expression.

Joan Russell (1965) describes Effort as "the attitude of the mover to the motion factors of weight, space, time, and flow" (p. 22). Sue Stinson (1988) uses the terms *space, time,* and *energy* to describe the expressive possibilities in creative movement. Her definition of these qualities is "factors that modify basic action" (p. 21). Whatever the specific definitions are of each factor, however, the changes in expressivity over time or in the moment are observable, and can be tracked.

Why is it desirable to develop the expressive range of children in movement? For one thing, exploration of a range of material is helpful in developing a sense of mastery. Such explorations allow children to understand that they have options. They can make choices about how they present themselves and can develop a degree of complexity of personality that is comfortable. Children who have an expressive range can accommodate to tasks more readily. It helps to have access to both quick and sustained time effort in most athletic endeavors, for example.

Children can also learn to observe the unique patterns in others and to appreciate the subtly different ways each of us negotiates our way through interactions, tasks, and creative endeavors. And a range of expressive choices supports innovative thinking that enables an individual to try a new idea just a little differently. The child can appreciate that another route may produce a new, and perhaps better destination.

Shape changes are modes of relating. While some children prefer to attend to self and will rock themselves to sleep and have lots of self-caretaking skills, others will relate to objects and loved ones through a bridging across the space and defining a boundary (a me–you relationship). Still others prefer to hug, mold, and shape around the "other" (an "us" relationship). Most children go through all three phases and utilize each as appropriate. But they have preferred modes that are a kind of default pattern; something to fall back on and rely on.

In movement learning situations, it is not common to find such different ways of relating to others addressed. Most of the literature describes shape as the making of a static shape, holding a position, much like a statue or sculpture. *Sculpture* is, in fact, a fairly common creative movement activity. Benzwie (1987) devotes 21 pages of her book to "Sculpting" activities, all of which direct children to be frozen, or still, or to hold a shape. But frozen shapes do not reveal a degree of relationship. It is only in the changing movement relationship that the preferred mode is revealed.

Consider the handshake and how much is conveyed within such a simple and often unconscious ritual. When one first encounters a friend, the mode of the handshake can tell a great deal about the relative status of the two participants, the mood of each, or the degree of intimacy between the two. If the clasp includes both self-care (shape-flow, as above in the KMP section) and shaping, the degree of intimacy is revealed and reinforced by the abilities of each to open up to his or her own flow of communication and to share equally in the encounter.

So, too, children interact with each other, recapitulating the relationship patterns they have developed with their parents and siblings. Children take care of themselves, connect to others, and share hugs based on many contextual cues, and on habit. Movement activities can reveal those patterns, but can also teach children to explore other choices as well. Mirroring games, follow-the-leader type games, and contact improvisation (where children can use a finger to follow a contact point through shared space and time with a partner), all lead to increased Shape choices.

Shape can be thought of as the container for Effort, just as the relationship of the child to others can be thought of as the container for the development of the self and one's personality. In movement terms, children adjust and accommodate to other movers and, within those adjustments, express who they are.

Space as Organizing

Rhythm is not the only organizer for movement. Children also organize by orienting in space.

> The newborn's … sense of space … is restricted to proprioceptive body experiences…. As the human being moves in a spatial surrounding, he gains awareness of the

all-encompassing quality of that space. Sounds, smells and sights exist in space relative to the front-back, top-bottom, and left-right of the body. (Gerhardt, 1973, pp.14–15)

Spatial differentiation is driven, of course, by gravity. If we did not have the pull toward the center of the earth, our movement and our construction of reality would be quite different, even with the same body part relationships. A great deal of early spatial orientation is built upon the establishment of equilibrium against and within the force of gravity.

From the midline and the subsequent patterns of laterality and verticality, children can develop a sense of the sagittal dimension, or front-back. The sagittal dimension allows for a sense of moving forward/moving back, both metaphorically and physically.

Rich vocabulary, such as laterality, verticality, directionality, pathways, reach space, and trace forms are all skills for mapping one's way through the world. The more options children have, the better the choices they can make. By the same token, simple experiences such as the defining of one's kinesphere (or personal space) can help children find a sense of "place" or home base.

Body as Kinesthetic Learning

The body itself is an organizational organism. Establishing a midline of the body is essential to any number of cognitive skills, not the least of which is reading. The vertical throughline of the body is a differentiation of right and left sides and in young infants is not yet established. But in the creeping pattern, which becomes the crawling pattern, each body half organizes to push and pull the baby forward and into locomotion. It is critical to the visual tracking that reading requires that a sense of midline exists, and that the child's eyes can track across the midline.

In American and other Western cultures, reading goes from left to right, crossing the midline of the body as the eyes track the letters and words. With children who have difficulty tracking, often we can also see a lack of midline organization. In one unpublished study this writer completed (Bradley, 1984), five dyslexic children were exposed to a set of whole body experiences (Bartenieff fundamentals) and Laban space exercises. Visual tracking across a midline improved significantly for those children who had experienced difficulty with it in the beginning.

Corso (1997; 1999a,b,c) completed a small study (28 students over 5 years) in which she correlated body organization (specifically, midline organizational abilities) with learning styles. Using writing and drawing activities, the 28 children's reading difficulties were revealed. Although this study is not a dance study per se, the indications that reading difficulties may correlate with midline organizational difficulties is worth exploring, and, potentially, remediating through movement.

It is the interaction of the bodily movement experiences connecting to the space at hand and modified by shape

and effort qualities that reveal exactly where each child's kinesthetic style lies. As such, movement speaks volumes about how each child maneuvers through and interacts with the world, and reveals potential, not just deficit.

As the dance/movement therapist and movement analyst, Suzi Tortora (2006) states:

A basic principle of the Ways of Seeing approach is that every individual creates a nonverbal movement style or profile composed of a unique combination of movement qualities that can be observed by a trained eye. These movement styles reveal aspects of the individual's experience with the surroundings ... early childhood development and early intervention/education are stressed for two reasons: 1) to highlight the significant role nonverbal communication plays in all levels of self-development established during the primary years and 2) to support the conviction that early intervention provides the strongest potential for change. (2006, p. 11)

Creative Movement

Once a child has established a sense of both regulation and choices within the body–space continuum, the possibility for true invention begins. Child's play is so often grounded in movement play: pretending to be a cloud or a princess, an animal or a cowboy. The child adapts his or her patterns to portray a role. Imagination, the inner construct of a reality wished for rather than directly experienced, comes from such explorations. And imagination may be the fast track to both empowerment and choices.

Creative movement is a divergent process. There are no right answers and the goals include a deepening of metaphoric and an enrichment of abstract material. As the child's imagination grows, the range of options also grows. We think of the child who daydreams as "not living up to her potential," but in fact, she may override her limits.

Gunilla Lindqvist (2001) addressed the relationship between play and dance in her study. She analyzed the dance experiences in five Swedish towns of children 6 to 8 years old. Lindqvist delineated two principles of early dance education; one based on the divergent approaches of Laban and the other a more imitative approach. Most of the Swedish students had positive responses to the first approach and saw the experience as play. A typical lesson included "circle time, warming up, practicing basic movements, steps and formations, improvisation, and reverence" (p. 47).

She went on to cite Laban's concerns that literary approaches to dance should be used sparingly for young children; that the movement itself is enough of a stimulus to help them make their own dances and tell their own stories. Lindqvist comes down firmly on the side of explorations and play as a source for dance in the early grades.

Sweden is not the only place where creative movement has been used to liberate the imagination in the classroom. Leong Lai Keun and Peggy Hunt (2009) described a program in Singapore in which 39 primary students (age 7) engaged in an exploration of coral reefs through movement.

The class met three times per week and the children were observed over five sessions. Although the authors (who were also the teachers) described a well-known tension between giving the children skills and allowing them to explore freely, the children did expand their access to both. And interestingly, the children also, without being directed, were able to construct dances that had a clear beginning, middle, and end.

Taking the notion of creative dance as liberation education even further, Sansom (2009) described the early childhood curriculum *Te Whāriki*, a program to reclaim the values and history of *Aotearoa* (New Zealand). The values behind this remarkable program are those of community-building and individual agency, channeling the Reggio Emilio approach and the Maori cultural ways. As Sansom described the program: "The four principles are empowerment (whakamana), holistic development (kotahitanga), family and community (whānau tangata), and relationships (ngā hononga) (Ministry of Education 1996)" (p. 165).

Creative movement is at the heart of the curriculum. But, as Sansom points out:

> For this kind of emergent dance to happen, children need to have access to the cultural capital to ensure their agency can be exercised. Not to honor the child in their creative endeavors in dance is negating the powerful and competent image of the child. (p. 171)

Movement is, therefore, in vivo practice of values and empowerment and creative movement is a vehicle for cognitive, social, emotional, and physical development. Sue Stinson (1988) has written extensively on the process of movement exploration. She points out that

> pre-school children think in concrete rather than abstract terms. For example, I might teach a class based on a theme of thunderstorms. With preschoolers I have no desire to teach the scientific explanation of thunderstorms: I prefer my own preschooler's explanation of the big black dragons in the sky that roar and breathe fire. I ask for and listen to their explanations and stories. However, merely directing children to "pretend to be a thundercloud or a big black dragon" yields little depth of movement … abstract movement concepts … "translate" the phenomenon into rich movement experiences. (p. 28)

Mastery over the realms of the imaginative and objective worlds gives children agency. From such an empowered stance, children find it easy to create whole pieces, stories, skits, drawings. Instead of becoming passive recipients of information, or mere translators of actions they have been shown, they are constructing knowledge, making art, and sharing their tales.

Dancing Children

Learning through dance is not the same thing as learning to dance. Every dance teacher has heard the story of Shirley Temple or Savion Glover, child prodigies who had full careers before the ages of 5 and 10 respectively. But the specificity of tap dancing, informed by the predilections of two talented children is not for every child. Yet, most young children love to dance, or at the very least relate to the role of the "dancer."

When the author's son was around 5, she signed him up for a dance class that was advertised as appropriate for boys and girls. He went to the first class and there was only one other boy there, who would not move. So the son sat with the other boy. The next week they returned, the son opened the door and quickly shut it again. He said, "I can't go in there. It's too pink!" And indeed it was. Every girl—and there were only girls in the room—was covered in pink, from the hair ribbons, through the tutus, and into beribboned pink slippers. They wanted to be dancers. The author's son just wanted to dance.

The act of dancing will continue to be overridden by the role of the dancer. Until we can, as a culture, transcend the role for the act, in Western education cultures, dancing will continue to be associated with gender. This is not as it should be, nor is it that way in other cultures. The act of dancing should not be precluded for any group or category of child. The functions of dance include technique (the execution of dance phrases), the style or form (ballet, modern, hip-hop, tap, etc.), choreography (or dance-making), and performance. Every child can benefit from any experiences within the field of dance, but to experience improvisation/creative movement, choreography, technique, and informal performance provides great benefits.

Still, there are questions that need to be raised about very young children studying technique, a particular dance form, or performing. Conventional wisdom holds that it is very difficult for the young child to maintain the level of motor control, nuanced expression, and sequences of steps or movements that are required for particular forms or styles. For the same reason that young children do not start training seriously for a competitive sport, the 2- to 5-year old needs exploratory and self-directed experiences first.

The dance recital in which costumed, made-up little girls twirl and glide and forget their steps is a well-known scenario. When a young child performs for family and friends, unconditional approval should ensue. Adding strangers, unreasonable expectations, flashbulbs, and video cameras has undone more than one budding ballerina.

Dance classes for 2- to 5-year-olds can and should be observed by parents, however. Such opportunities for feedback and audience can help a child learn in the moment, refining skills in the heightened context of demonstrating learning. Audience is a form of witnessing and giving approval, and a way of encouraging a child to learn more.

There are actually no studies of which the authors are aware that unpack the role of dance technique, style, or performance on the young child, including from other parts of the world. The "evidence" cited herein is anecdotal and part of an oral tradition within the field of dance education.

Cognitive Skills: Reading and Math, Problem-Solving

The construction of knowledge through movement is not a new discovery. An old Chinese saying says: "I hear and I forget, I see and I remember, I do and I understand." Piaget wrote "I think that human knowledge is essentially active" (2005, p. 9). And even though Howard Gardner (1983) identified eight intelligences, the bodily kinesthetic is, as pointed out in the beginning of this chapter, the first intelligence; the one from which the other areas derive.

The primacy of the bodily kinesthetic intelligence extends beyond the years of infancy. In the Chicago schools, the Whirlwind Basic Reading Through Dance program has amassed an impressive array of statistics that indicate support for such a notion (McMahon, Rose, & Parks, 2003). The program addresses basic reading skills, especially phoneme segmentation, rhythmic phrasing, and letter shapes.

In a study of 721 Chicago first graders, significant gains were found for the experimental group. The numbers were impressive, in part because the control group actually tested higher on the pretest. The students in the Whirlwind program advanced beyond them.

There are few literacy studies with the scope and rigor of the Whirlwind study. But anecdotal evidence and descriptive studies for the learning of math concepts, geography, science facts and processes, and other aspects of literacy through dance/movement do exist. The work of Anne Green Gilbert (personal communication, 2004) in the Seattle public schools has been lauded over the years, but not analyzed statistically. However, in 1977–1978, Gilbert did conduct a preliminary examination of 325 K-6 students who had been involved with her Dance and the Three R's programs. In a comparison of the 325 students with the test scores on the Metropolitan Achievement Tests that year, the students in her program averaged 13% higher than the rest of the District.

In the summary of the Whirlwind study, McMahon, Rose, and Parks (2003) conclude that "if reading instruction can focus more on visual and kinesthetic images and less on text-based information, children may be more likely to retain and recall the information they learn" (p.107).

The same is likely to hold true for concepts in math, science, social studies, and languages. Research needs to be done before we can know for certain, but the vast amount of evidence indicates that such an approach is likely to yield rich results.

In math, for example, computation is easily physicalized and externalized. So is calculation. Rhythm is metrical and can be divided into "sets" or phrases and quantified. Therefore, the oft-observed but never proven "Mozart Effect" (several U.S.-based researchers have claimed that listening to Mozart's music can increase intelligence, but the research is suspect; a quick web search can reveal both the claims and the disputing of the claims), may in fact be a phenomenon in which the complex rhythmic structures of Mozart's music affect the kinesthetic responses in the body in an organizing way. If that is so, the example of the students in the author's son's fourth grade class moving to Coltrane may be a similar phenomenon.

There is evidence that minority urban students would benefit greatly from approaches such as the Whirlwind and Gilbert programs. Park (1997a,b,c), White (1992), and Corso (1997) have all researched the role of race, body-level organization, and learning preferences in urban and suburban children. Park found that Asian American students in Los Angeles have a preference for kinesthetic learning. White found that African American students had preferences for auditory, tactile, and kinesthetic learning. These same students demonstrated a greater degree of success in field-dependent (relational) learning situations.

Early Childhood Standards

The National Dance Education Organization asked several members to develop *Standards for Dance in Early Childhood* (Faber et al., 2003), a guide for teachers, parents, and caregivers of young children. The standards are divided into outcomes for 2-, 3-, 4-, and 5-year-olds.

The structure of the standards is based on four categories that "provide a balance between creative freedom, that enhances individual expression and growth, and disciplined concentration that develops the proficient artist or capable, realistic adult." (p. 3). The categories: creating, performing, responding, and interconnecting, include content standards that remain constant across age groups and achievement standards that build on prior knowledge and increase in sophistication with each age group.

The standards are not designed to be a stand-alone curriculum for dance with young children, but can provide guidelines for what might be included in a rich program. Assessment rubrics are also included, so that the child's progress can be tracked. While the notion of developing standards for young children may seem strange to educators from other, less-competitive cultures, for Americans, defining dance education is not simple, as the author has attempted to demonstrate. Definitions and expectations are often based on culture and what the media has popularized. In a culture where even small children watch videos and cable television programs in which sexualized movement is common, where movements are shortened and edited into fractured moments, and where the all-pink ballet class is universal, clarifying appropriate material for the population of young children is a challenge. The standards help parents and early childhood educators understand a full range of components and experiences that are useful and appropriate.

Recommendations for Future Research

Comparisons of teacher-centered ("follow me") versus child-centered (exploratory) approaches for young children need to be made, especially as the two approaches affect the development of expressive choices and range. One finds assumptions that one approach is superior and the other inferior throughout the field of dance education practice. But one finds very little, if any, research comparing the two approaches in actual effects.

Unpacking the learning process in dance and movement is actually not difficult, because dance is a visual art form; the child's development of and within the material can be observed. With the vocabulary referred to above (i.e., Laban and Kestenberg), visible movement changes can be noted and learning patterns acknowledged. Such analysis requires time and expertise, but every dance and movement teacher already engages in such assessments informally, at least.

Next steps must include a concerted effort on the part of the dance education field to produce such research, but first, the administrators of educational institutions, policy groups, and legislative offices must understand the need for such studies. Funding, coordination, and resources are needed in order for such research to be meaningful and robust. The fact that serious examination of the process has not been sought, encouraged, or rewarded is regrettable, because so much of the learning process that is cognition is rendered visible as children move and solve challenges. With the emphasis on text-based testing in order to know if children are learning, the pressure on young children to produce language and text is extraordinary.

The quantitative research that has been done with young children typically requires the child to be able to complete some sort of pre- and posttest, usually text-based. Efforts are made to prove that the dependent variable is affected by the exposure to the independent variable. In the case of the Whirlwind study (McMahon et al., 2003), the independent variables (physicalizing letter shapes, moving sounds, blending sounds temporally and spatially) were designed to reflect and inform reading skills. The transfer was reinforced overtly. In the case of a dance program where the independent variables are neither so well delineated nor directly reinforced, any pre- or posttesting will be unlikely to reveal any effects. But that does not mean there are no effects. The effects simply may not be on the variable being tested.

There are other ways to unpack the dance learning process, including interviews, art-based responses such as collages and drawings, and scored rubrics. Interviews require, but may not account for, sophisticated verbal skills. Art-based responses require fine motor and visual-conceptual skills. Scored rubrics require the sophisticated eye of an observer, or observers, but, at least what is being observed is movement itself, not an application of movement to another response mode.

The challenge of assessment of learning in the arts, and in particular, dance is often presented as a negative; that is, as an area so subjective that appropriate assessment tools cannot be developed. That perception is accurate if text-based approaches and causal results are required in order for the type of learning that dance offers to be considered valid. However, if the teacher's eye is trained to see and track visible movement changes, learning can become transparent.

All around the world, dance teachers observe the style and details of how and how much their students are learning. Since dance is both preverbal and reflective of inner processes all that is necessary to assess its effects is an insightful observer. With appropriate support, analysis of content and process, comparisons with results and outcomes, dance education can take its rightful place as a potent, rich modality for young children to find their creative, interactive, rich way into the world.

Conclusion

The author unpacked the dance learning process using key studies to describe how dance components and creative movement processes fundamentally affect learning in every domain in the young child. The use of the fullest possible range of vocabulary for both content and assessment of learning was described, and a case made for understanding the neuroscience of movement as well as the language of dance. The research that has been published increasingly shows the value of dance for young children, especially because dance is empowering and helps to create community. Dance promotes shared values, engenders creative thinking, and actively engages children in learning about the world around them and inside their own body-minds. As a modality for the construction of intelligence, collaboration, and self-efficacy, dance is effective, but more studies must be done to demonstrate exactly how and what aspects of the dance experience are applicable.

To dance is to learn: in the moment, outside of the box, and on the feet. Dance fosters the young child to create and build a worldview that is resilient and joyful, and that is the right of every child.

References

Benari, N. (1995). *Inner rhythm.* Chur, Switzerland: Harwood Academic.

Benzwie, T. (1987). *A moving experience: Dance for lovers of children and the child within.* Tucson, AZ: Zephyr Press.

Bradley, K. (1984). *LMA and learning-disabled students: Laban/Bartenieff Institute of Movement Studies, New York.* (Unpublished certificate project)

Corso, M. (1997). *Children who desperately want to read but are not working at grade level: Using movement patterns as "windows" to discover why.* Paper presented at the Annual International Conference of the Association for Children's Education, Portland, Oregon. (ERIC Document Reproduction Service No. ED402549)

Corso, M. (1999a). Children who desperately want to read but are not working at grade level: Part II: The transverse midline. (ERIC Document Reproduction Service No. ED432733)

Corso, M. (1999b). Children who desperately want to read but are not working at grade level: Part III: The frontal midline. (ERIC Document Reproduction Service No. ED432751)

Corso, M. (1999c). Children who desperately want to read but are not working at grade level: Part IV: Crossing all midlines automatically. (ERIC Document Reproduction Service No. ED432752)

Csikszentmihaly, M. (1990). *Flow: The psychology of optimal experience.* New York: HarperCollins.

Damasio, A. (1999). *The feeling of what happens: Body and emotion in the making of consciousness.* New York: Harcourt.

Faber, R., Benzwie, T., Bradley, K., Bucek, L., Eliot, C., Gibb, S., et al. (2003). *Standards for dance in early childhood*. Bethesda MD: National Dance Education Organization.

Gallese, V. (2001). The "Shared Manifold" hypothesis: From mirror neurons to empathy. *Journal of Consciousness Studies, 8*(5–7), 33–50.

Gardner, H. (1983). *Frames of mind: The theory of multiple intelligences*. New York: Basic Books.

Gerhardt, L. (1973). *Moving and knowing: The young child orients himself in space*. Englewood Cliffs, NJ: Prentice Hall.

Gilbert, A. G. (1976). *Teaching the three r's through movement experience*. Minneapolis, MN: Burgess.

Keun, L., & P. Hunt. (2009). Use children as agents with creative dance: Singapore children's creative thinking and problem-solving responses as liberation education? *Research in Dance Education, 7*(1), 35–65.

Koch, S. (1997). *The Kestenberg movement profile* (Unpublished master's thesis). Allegheny University of Health Sciences, Philadelphia, PA.

Leirvag, L. M. (2001). *A proposed dance-movement therapy assessment to identify child neglect* (Unpublished master's thesis). Hahnemann University, Philadelphia, PA. Retrieved from http://www.livdans.org/livmarie.doc

Lindqvist, G. (2001). The relationship between play and dance. *Research in Dance Education, 2*(1), 41–52.

Lotan, N., & Yirmiya, N. (2002). Body movement, presence of parents, and the process of falling asleep in toddlers. *International Journal of Behavioral Development, 26*(1), 81–88

McMahon, S. D., Rose, D. S., & Parks, M. (2003). Basic reading through dance. *Evaluation Review, 27*(1/2), 104–125.

North, M. (1975). *Personality assessment through movement*. Boston, MA: Plays.

Park, C. C. (1997a). Learning style preferences of Asian-American (Chinese, Filipino, Korean, and Vietnamese) students in secondary schools. *Equity and Excellence in Education, 30*(2), 68–77.

Park, C. C. (1997b). Learning style preferences of Korean, Mexican-Armenian-American and Anglo students in secondary schools (Research brief). *National Association of Secondary School Principals Bulletin, 81*(585), 103–111.

Park, C. C. (1997c). Learning style preferences of Southeast Asian students. *Urban Education, 35*(3), 245–268.

Piaget, J. (2005). Genetic epistemology. *Childhood: Critical concepts in sociology*. New York: Routledge.

Preston-Dunlop, V. (2008) *Rudolf Laban: An extraordinary life*. Hightstown, NJ: Princeton Books.

Prince, R. (2006). Judith Kestenberg. Retrieved from Section Five: http://www.sectionfive.org/continuing_education/kestenberg/

Russell, J.(1965). *Creative dance in the primary school*. London: MacDonald & Evans.

Sansom, A. (2009). Mindful pedagogy in dance: Honoring the life of the child. *Research in Dance Education, 10* (3), 161–176.

Sossin, M. (n.d.). Toward understanding mutuality. American Psychological Association Web site: *Prevention, infant therapy and the treatment of adults section*. Retrieved from http:/www.sectionfive.org/kescomment.htm

Stinson, S. (1988) *Dance for young children: Finding the magic in movement*. Reston, VA: American Alliance for Health, Physical Education, Recreation, and Dance.

Stinson, S. (1986, May/June) Preschool dance curriculum: The process. *Journal of Physical Education, Recreation, and Dance, 57*, 27–28.

Tortora, S. (2006).*The dancing dialogue: Using the communicative power of movement with young children*. Baltimore, MD: Brookes.

White, S. E. (1992). Factors that contribute to learning differences among African American and Caucasian students. (ERIC Document Reproduction Services No. ED374177)

17

Musical Childhoods

A Survey of Contemporary Research

Susan Young
University of Exeter

In a baby-music group in Reykjavik, Iceland, a mother sings a traditional Icelandic lullaby she has just learned, soothing her slightly fractious young baby with gentle rocking. In a village compound in Bengland, Sub-Saharan Africa, a mixed-age group of young children playing together on the village compound tap gourd bowls and other found objects to make rhythmical percussion music to entertain two toddlers they are minding. In a well-equipped, college-based music room in New York, a group of 4-year-olds attending a private music class are highly engaged in finding their own spontaneous dance moves to a jazz song recording. In a small Welsh village, a 5-year-old girl spends after-school time in her bedroom with a karaoke video game singing High School Musical songs. Musical childhoods from birth to the first school years and their musical contexts are so various that the task of providing a balanced survey of research and scholarship across this field is daunting. The main development of the last decade has been considerable expansion into the many corners of early childhood musicality, from research into specific, tiny electrical impulses in the music-active brain of infants to consideration of broad cultural and political issues in diverse international contexts and how they impact on children's musical experiences. And between such extremes of scale and scope are complex interplays of social, material, technological, environmental, and cultural influences that constitute young children's musical experiences.

This chapter surveys contemporary research in early childhood music from birth to the age of 5 or 6 years old when in most "developed world" countries children first enter formal schooling. Theoretically the chapter aims to offer a broad overview from many different perspectives—psychology, neuroscience, sociology, education, ethnomusicology, anthropology, and childhood studies—and focuses mainly, but not exclusively, on the developments that have taken place since 2002. The disciplines of psychology and education have predominated in early childhood education but recently the dominance of these disciplines has loosened

to include multidisciplinary and varied theoretical perspectives. This probably, in broad terms, is the most important change in recent early childhood music education research and scholarship. This expansion into multidisciplinary perspectives reflects changes in how music and musical practices are being conceptualized and in how childhood and children's lives are being conceptualized. It also reflects contemporary social, cultural, and technological changes that are resulting in different patterns of family life, increased heterogeneity of communities (particularly in urban centers), and rapid changes in how music can be experienced through new technological innovations.

It is important to emphasize that it is children in the so-called developed world who have been the subjects of the research and recipients of the education activities under consideration in this chapter. Increased awareness of childhoods globally has resulted in greater sensitivity to the specific and culturally defined childhoods experienced by children in the developed world. Although in the field of early childhood education practitioners and researchers are becoming alert to these issues there is as yet little evidence of their influence in early childhood music education practice and research. However, in this chapter I include references to work from a wide range of sources, where it has been possible to do so, in order to diversify the view of musical childhoods and to start to dilute the dominance of Anglo-American research and academic writing.

In the last decade developments in early childhood music education activity have emerged in two broad directions. Previously research and practice had focused on the preschool years of 3 and 4 and on children's musical activity in educational contexts. But in recent years there has been increased interest in children from birth to 3, expanding early childhood music education research and practice to include this younger age phase. Research interest has focused on the musical abilities of babies and, to a lesser extent, toddlers. This is the first direction of development. The second direction has been into diverse contexts, beyond educational contexts to the wider variety of places in which young children are cared for and experience music, particularly the home. In the two paragraphs that follow I introduce these two directions, explaining why they have become areas of focus, before returning to them later as the chapter unfolds. However, these recent developments in early childhood music education research and practice clearly build on and add to what has gone before, but they do not supersede earlier work. Two early sections in the chapter will provide this background in some detail, with its main focus on models of musical development. The chapter then continues by introducing research in these two areas of development; the expansion into earlier age phases and the expansion into diverse contexts. A final section considers the relationship between research and practice and gives brief attention to the application of research in practice. Here too there is a look at the well-known approaches and methods in music education and their relationship with the main fields of early childhood music research.

As I have said, prior research and practice in early childhood music education had focused mainly on the preschool years of 3 and upwards and on educational contexts. One direction has moved downwards in age, to infants from birth to around 12 months of age and, to a lesser extent, continuing on through toddlerhood. Research in this new, younger age phase has burgeoned, mainly within the fields of music psychology and neuroscience (see Trainor & Zatorre, 2009 for a review), with a surge of interest in discovering how babies perceive and process the music they hear (Trehub, 2004, 2006, 2009). The research-based interest in babies and very young children is matched by increases in varied forms of early childhood musical provision for zero to 3-year-olds in day care, nursery, community settings, and private music classes (Young, 2003a). This increase reflects growing demands in developed countries for out-of-home care as family patterns change and more parents return to work. In addition, conceptions of upbringing have changed, with parenting and caring in the developed world no longer being concerned simply with providing physical care and comfort for the youngest children but concerned also with cognitive stimulation and entertainment (Lareau, 2003). Underlying this expansion of activity with babies and very young children, as Gruhn (2010) points out, are revised notions of infants and very young children from incompetent to competent.

The second direction has been to expand into wider contexts and to take much more account of the material, social, and cultural contexts within which young children's musical experiences take place. This reflects broad paradigmatic shifts away from the study of individual behavior in mainly education-derived activities toward taking much more account of context and studying how musical thinking and skills are acquired in diverse sociocultural and material environments. Strong influences from recent sociologically and anthropologically oriented activity in childhood studies (Kehily, 2004) has prompted research that is interested in

these broader contexts of childhood. Children's musical lives beyond the borders of educational institutions are becoming the focus of research, at home with families, in play spaces with peers, in community places, with a concern for activity that is everyday and its cultural variation. A small but growing field of ethnomusicology is interested in children's own cultural worlds (e.g., Koops, 2010; Kreutzer, 2001), not just in "far away" exotic places, but in keeping with recent trends in ethnomusicology, studying children's musical practices local to researchers (Campbell, 1998, 2006, 2007; Lew, 2005; Lum, 2009; Marsh, 2008). Very young children's music worlds will encompass people: parents, siblings, extended family, peers, caregivers, educators (both general and music specialist), community musicians, music therapists, music performers, and private instrumental teachers. Young children's music worlds will take place in a range of places: homes, family or village compound, day care, play-centers, community learning places such as libraries, arts centers, community performance spaces, private music classes, nurseries, and schools. Finally, there is the material and technological infrastructure: everyday domestic objects, toys and playthings, musical instruments, media-receiving technologies such as radio, TV, Internet-linked computers and phones. Researchers who are concerned to understand children's music within real-world contexts find themselves researching these intertwining, multifaceted situations. Having introduced the two areas of recent development, the chapter returns to look at the main areas of work from which these developments have emerged.

Models of Musical Development

Looking back to the 1960s through to the 1980s there was a surge of interest in child development and the early stages of learning, and a growing recognition that quality input in the early years might enhance the development of young children and provide a good foundation for later learning. There was interest in searching for a theory of chronological musical development, comparable to the general theories of development, most notably that of Piaget. Hargreaves's key text on musical development was published in 1986. In the same year two influential models of musical development were presented in journal articles; a general model of musical development by Swanwick and Tillman (1986; the Swanwick and Tillman spiral), and a model of singing development by Welch (1986; later revised in 1998). For a period of time interest in musical development gave form and direction to music education research and framed discussion around key conceptual ideas from psychology, such as concept formation, intuitive and formal learning, stages or phases of learning, and the interpretation of these conceptual ideas for and in music learning contexts. Swanwick (2001) provides a valuable review of this period of activity.

Swanwick and Tillman's (1986) "spiral of musical development" has received much attention, influencing early childhood curriculum models in some countries and so it deserves further explanation (e.g., Hentschke & Martinez, 2004; Ministry of Education and Culture, Cyprus, 2003). It consists of eight developmental modes spread through four levels of development spanning early through to late childhood/youth of which only the first two need concern us here. According to the model, at the first "mastery" level (0–4 years) children are in the "sensory mode." This mode is characterized by exploration of sounds. Children then enter the "manipulative" mode where they begin to demonstrate increasing control of musical materials, to be able to create a regular pulse, and to understand repetition of musical ideas. The second developmental level is "imitation" (4–9 years) which begins with the "personal" mode. For children in this mode, personal expressiveness is central, with hints of basic phrases and generally spontaneous musical ideas, although drawing heavily on the "vernacular" music into which they have been enculturated. In later publications Swanwick (2001) emphasizes, partly in response to criticisms of the model, that the levels are flexible in relation to age, that the spiral is circular and cumulative, and that the musical environment children experience will influence their movement through the levels.

Until very recently, theoretical writings on the topic of children's development were framed by certain taken-for-granted assumptions about childhoods (Burman, 2008). Although the research into musical development had been carried out with mainly middle-class children in developed world contexts acculturated to Western music, the descriptions have been presented as if widely applicable to all children, irrespective of class, race, gender, religion, ethnicity, physical ability, or family type. Even the most recent work on infant musicality from which universals of musical processing are being proposed is rooted in Western cultural practice and based on the responses of Western-encultured babies or children, using musical materials that conform to Western formal musical principles (Cross, 2009, p. 11). The sociology of childhood emphasizes the heterogeneity of childhood, contrasting this with psychology's tendency to homogenize (Burman, 2008; Kehily, 2004). Versions of children's musical competences and development derived from monocultural research with mainly White, Western middle-class children are no longer applicable—or indeed acceptable on grounds of social justice. Such postdevelopment perspectives are widespread in general early childhood educational theory (e.g., Wood, 2010) and although not yet widespread in early childhood music education practice, are just beginning to result in changes to research priorities and models of practice (e.g., Barrett, 2005a,b; Lum, 2008, 2009).

Mindful of these caveats concerning developmental models, the next sections look in more detail at areas of children's musical activity and what research has revealed in these domains. These sections continue to put in place the background to the two directions of recent development.

Understanding Children's Music-Making with Instruments

The Swanwick and Tillman model was based on analysis of data from a range of composition and improvisation tasks performed by a cohort of children aged 4 to 11 years who attended a London primary school. Subsequently, researchers such as Young (2000a, 2003b, 2008) and Gluschankof (2002) whose focus of interest has been early childhood music-making with instruments have pointed out that the "spiral" was based on limited data from the youngest children in the birth to 4 age phase and drawn from adult-prescribed tasks that channeled the children's musical responses in certain directions. The earliest spiral level was mostly based on speculation drawing on principles from Piagetian theory. A collection of studies of young children engaged in self-initiated and self-guided musical play reveals interesting interpretations of children's earliest musical explorations (Barrett, 1998a, 1998b; Céleste, Delalande, & Dumaurier, 1982; Cohen, 1980; Delalande & Cornara, 2010; Glover, 2000; Gluschankof, 2002; Pond, 1981; Young, 2000a). Young children's musical activity has often been characterized as a period of indeterminate sensorimotor activity that has little musical meaning and significance, a pre-stage of finding out what sounds can be produced, but other researchers have argued that analysis of their musical play reveals forms of structuring that imply intention and meaning (Sundin, 1998). The crucial difference is in the nature of the task—whether it is prescribed or more open-ended—and the method of analysis. If children's music-making is collected as aural recordings and then analyzed according to pitch and rhythm structures which are conventional to Western art music, then these generally are found to be lacking in children's music; hence analysis seems to support an interpretation of a random, exploratory phase. If, however, young children's music-making is studied as a form of multimodal behavior made up of many modes of engagement such as body movement, structured play with the sound-making objects, interaction with other children and adults and more, then forms of structuring and coherence do emerge. They emerge from a process of multimodal analysis.

Cohen (1980), for example, found that children's music is gesturally structured, arising from body movements organized as phrase-like gestures of direction toward a climax and closure. Young (2000b, 2003b) looked in more detail at children's spontaneous play with instruments and identified forms of organization not only arising from the child's body movement but also from the material and social environment, which reflects the paradigmatic shifts mentioned in the introduction. Children playing independently would find forms of organization from the structure of the instrument, striking the very top and bottom key of a xylophone and then swooshing the beater across the whole key bed, for example, and children playing with an adult play partner would find forms of organization from social interaction patterns; enjoying turn-taking or synchronizing their playing exactly with an adult. Young's study drew attention to the adult role; not as passive observer to the child but as active attender and play-partner, joining in with musical play on the children's terms (Young, 2003b).

Recent work led by Delalande (2010) provides more detailed accounts of music-making by 55 babies and very young children aged from 10 to 37 months who were attending daycare centers in North Italy. The accumulated body of data has been subject to various forms of analysis, some driven by theory, some by the more practice-oriented interests and priorities of the practitioner researchers. Delalande, as with Swanwick and Tillman, makes sense of his data through the lens of Piagetian theory, but his close reading of theory with empirical data is insightful, drawing attention to the processes of repetition and variation in even the youngest children's musical playing and their fascination with the sounds they produce. The instrument the children were given to play, a zither, is important to mention, for this instrument has affordances which are well suited to very young children's physical abilities and yet offers variety and interest.

Understanding children's music on their terms is part of a long-standing strand of research into children's music in which the Pillsbury Nursery studies stand as a historical landmark (Moorhead, Sandvik, & Wight, 1951/1978; Pond, 1981). Contemporary researchers in early childhood often refer back to this work because it represents a unique, longitudinal study of children's self-generated music play and its findings remain informative. It deserves attention, therefore, even though it sits well outside the last 10 years with which this chapter is mostly concerned. The Pillsbury Nursery, in California, was an experimental nursery established for the purpose of studying young children's innate musicality. Pond, a trained musician and composer, was appointed to observe, document, and analyze the children's self-initiated musical activity. The booklets giving notated examples of children's music-making and Pond's descriptions, collected from a wide age span of children over the extended life of the nursery remain an important source of insight (reissued as Moorhead & Pond, 1941/1978). The conceptions of children underlying the Pillsbury study are based on beliefs in children as possessing an innate musicality if offered a conducive environment where it could flourish. In the earliest, spontaneous activity of children, untrammeled by adults, Pond believed the sources of a pure, elemental music could be found. The Pillsbury study's child-centered, progressive conceptions of children continue in approaches to early childhood music today, although reframed by contemporary influences and images of children. In early childhood practice today the philosophy and approaches developed in the North Italian nurseries of Reggio Emilia offer a model of child-centered, democratic practice that is internationally emulated (e.g., Bancroft, Fawcett, & Hay, 2008; Bremmer & Huisingh, 2009). The pedagogy of Reggio Emilia emphasizes project work based on ideas

initiated by children and progresses through processes of problem solving, interaction, and collaborative meaning construction with adult educators.

In summarizing this group of studies that have focused on children's spontaneous music-making with instruments and sound-producing objects, collectively they propose that children's music-making should be studied as a complex process involving multimodal engagement and spatial, social, and material factors. The instruments themselves possess affordances that constrain and enable the children's playing in interaction with the child's movement vocabulary, which in turn is partly determined by maturation. Factors that impinge on the child's playing include how and where the instruments are positioned and the presence or not of other children or adults as observer/listeners or play-partners. Importance is given to the ways in which adults hear and respond to children's musical play, with expectations of its value and meaning for the children. Valuing musical play as "musical" on children's terms calls for definitions of music that are broad and generous. Some accounts of young children's music imply that it falls outside such definitions and is, therefore, a form of protomusic (e.g., Kratus, 1989, 1994). Adopting a competence-based view and taking the child's perspective, are all part of a general movement toward methodological innovations which attempt to treat children respectfully, not as the objects of research studies but as coparticipants (Kellett, 2010).

Understanding Children's Music with Voices

Music-making with voices, encompassing the first vocal explorations of babies, spontaneous forms of singing, and the singing performance of precomposed songs, is a strong and enduring strand of both research and practice in early childhood music (Imberty, 1996). The singing of songs is the mainstay of early childhood music education practice and plotting children's singing development has been an important focus. Hand-in-hand with the focus on children's processes of learning to sing has been discussion challenging familiar Western conceptions of singing ability as an innate capacity upon which learning can have little influence (e.g., Welch, 2006). The 1990s saw an important strand of writing in music psychology, strongly influenced by ethnomusicology, around the theme of musicality not as a genetic gift, but as a common human ability that all possess.

There are two major U.S. and UK studies that have drawn on developmental theories to propose models of singing development (Rutkowski, 1990, 1997; Welch, 1986, 1998; also Welch, Sergeant, & White, 1996). Both models are based on children's reproduction of songs in their first educational experiences when they enter preschool or elementary school around the age of 4 and upwards. They were evolved by their authors from considerable bodies of data, viewed and reviewed across periods of time. Rutkowski's nine-phase Singing Voice Development Measure (SVDM; Rutkowski, 1997; also Rutkowski & Miller, 2003) suggests that children move from speechlike chanting of the song text, to singing within a limited range ("speaking range singer") to the demonstration of an expanded vocal pitch range that is associated with the child's increased competency in vocal pitch matching. Both researchers have identified phases that form a possible developmental pathway, avoiding thereby the more rigid "age and stage" models of development. Welch's original model of 1986 was revised in 1998 following a substantial longitudinal study of children in their first years of schooling in London (4 years upwards). His revised model of Vocal Pitch-Matching Development (VPMD) suggests that the words of the song appear to be the initial center of interest rather than the melody, with singing often "chant like." This leads to a second phase in which there is growing awareness of the ability to change pitch and match it to a model. A third phase is characterized by mostly accurate melodic shape and intervals, but changes in tonality may occur to a final phase of almost complete accuracy of simple songs.

Welch raises many conditional factors in relation to his model. The nature of the song task is clearly a factor and complexity of words and melodies may challenge developing singers' capabilities. The longitudinal study led by Welch had also identified gender differences, with boys making less progress at singing complete songs over time than girls; this focus on gender difference, incidentally, is rare in early childhood music research. This difference may be attributed to gender stereotyping with singing perceived as being a more "feminine" activity. Welch also found an interesting contrast in the progress in learning to sing made by children attending two different schools. Better progress in one school was attributed to higher teacher expectations.

Stadler-Elmer (2000; Stadler Elmer & Elmer, 2000) based her research not only on children's reproduction of songs, as Welch and Rutkowski had done, but also on children's invention of new songs (either spontaneous songs or songs invented by request from the adult). She suggests that it is helpful to distinguish two different types of "singing rules": the invention of new songs by setting one's own rules, and the reproduction of songs by accepting given rules. Musical development as manifested in singing, Stadler Elmer proposes, may be best understood as a continuous process of simultaneous imitation and playful exploration. It is interesting to note her proposed simultaneity of imitation and exploration, in contrast to the Swanwick and Tillman spiral which separates these out as successive phases. As in many other accounts of children's musical development, she argues that this process is fostered by a musically stimulating environment that supports children's creative, playful engagement with music.

The importance of an environment which supports and enriches singing emerged from Yennari's set of case studies of under 4-year-olds (2010) who had received cochlear implants. She visited the children both at home and in their nursery. The opportunity to observe these young children singing in a range of situations, in particular as a sociable

family activity, resulted in a model of singing acquisition by Yennari which is multimodal and interpersonal. Her conclusions match the developments in understanding instrument playing that were described earlier in this chapter. Thus, young children's playing and singing are understood less as individual, abstracted activities defined by narrow musical parameters and more as context-bound, environmentally defined activities in which musical meaning derives from body movement and from emotionally positive interactions with others. In this respect, revised understandings of music as social, embodied practice primarily from ethnomusicology (Turino, 2008), social psychology, and music therapy are contributing to the theorizing of young children's musical activities.

Work in the last few years into children's singing has expanded in directions identified at the start of the chapter, with an increase in activity focusing on the years before preschool from birth through to 3 and in wider sociocultural contexts. With babies and younger children much attention has been given to emerging vocal activity both in the directions of language and music. This work in the field of psycholinguistics, music psychology, and increasingly, neuroscience, has provided ample information about children's first vocalizations and raised interesting questions concerning definitions of singing and speech, the confluence or divergence of music and language (Patel, 2009), whether infants can distinguish singing from speech, the functions of different vocal modes and their development. This area of interesting work has been enriched by studies into the interactive dimension of children with caregivers and understandings of the role that vocalization plays in these interactions, particularly to convey emotion and intention. A later section will return to these topics in more detail; for now we continue with a focus on singing.

Welch and Rutkowski's interest in singing development draws on work with children attending preschool and the first years of schooling, but Tafuri (2008) and Barrett (2010) have both carried out studies that reflect the contemporary expansion of contexts for early childhood music education by age and setting. Located in Bologna, Italy, Tafuri recruited mothers in the final trimester of pregnancy to commit to a longitudinal research project that would continue until the children reached school age. Parents and their children attended regular music sessions at which data were collected and they completed prestructured parent diaries that documented their children's musical activity outside the sessions. The work offers valuable longitudinal information that plots many dimensions of musical activity among a relatively large group, although singing was a focus. Interestingly the children in Tafuri's group acquired singing competences—in particular learning to sing in tune—at an age earlier than might have been formerly implied by research studies. This Tafuri attributes to the enriched musical environment of home and positive expectations on the part of parents; environment and expectations being key components once again.

Barrett (2010) similarly recruited 18 parent–child pairs (the children being between 18 and 54 months and attending music sessions and day care) to study song-making, of both invented and canonic song, in order to study the "extent, purpose and use" of song-making in the children's lives. Barrett's findings suggest that young children use song-making in varied contexts in their daily lives and for a range of purposes, reflecting their capacity to adopt and adapt the musical features of their environment in their music-making. Song-making, according to Barrett, provides a means "by which young children practice and elaborate on the musical forms of their cultural settings" (Barrett, 2010), a rich repertoire of activity that underpins musical development.

With the exception of Stadler Elmer and Barrett's studies, interest in children's spontaneous singing tends to have occupied a separate strand of research interest. The Pillsbury studies once again offer a booklet describing notated instances of children's self-made songs accompanied by Pond's commentary that remain a valuable source if they are read mindful of the conceptions of children and music that underlie them (Moorhead & Pond, 1941/1978). Björkvold's (1989) study and writing on young children's spontaneous song in Scandinavian nursery settings is also informative for its connections between song and play, and Davies's (1992) study of invented songs by 5- to 7-year-olds still stands out for its analysis of the musical features of children's self-made songs, building on Dowling's (1984) earlier work. Young (2002, 2003c) carried out an observational study of children between the ages of 2 and 3. From a synthesis of earlier studies combined with this new data she identified different forms of spontaneous singing. Again these forms were tied into multimodal and environmental factors, and, Young argued, required broad definitions of children's expressive vocal play that could encompass the variety she observed (Young, 2002). She identified singing that blended with the children's movements, with their concentrated play with objects, with dramatic, enactive play with toys, vocal play to represent vehicle and animal sounds in play with toys, and singing as part of dramatic play with peers and other adults. The observation, documenting, and analysis of children's vocal play and spontaneous singing by these various researchers connects with child-centered perspectives and interests in children's own cultural worlds. Both Young and Marsh have pointed out that little room is made for children's self-generated and expressive vocal music-making in pedagogical practice (Marsh, 2008; Marsh & Young, 2006; Young, 2006). They argue that careful listening and documenting of this activity reveals competences that traditional pedagogical approaches to young children's singing often pitch below and rarely connect with or build on (Marsh & Young, 2006).

Studies have not only examined the specifics of early vocalization in laboratory-based studies but also in wider contexts at home (Adachi, 2006; Addessi, 2009; Barrett, 2010; Street, 2006), between family members and as part of parenting practices (Custodero, 2006; Custodero & Johnson-Green, 2008; deVries, 2005), in music classes (Reynolds, 2006; Tafuri, 2008), in varied community and sociocultural contexts (Dzansi, 2004; Emberly, 2009; Gottlieb, 2004; Marsh, 2008), and among children who are musically exceptional (Hendricks & McPherson, 2010; Schraer-Joiner & Chen-Haftek, 2009; Stadler Elmer, 2010; Yennari, 2010) .

Some studies have explored cross-cultural comparisons (Rutkowski & Chen-Haftek, 2000) and sought to identify cultural variations in children's singing acquisition and to develop more localized, culturally sensitive understandings of young children's singing activity. For example, children speaking Cantonese, a tone language, achieve singing mastery earlier than English counterparts (Mang, 2006) which suggests that children's native language may affect how children use their voices in singing (Rutkowski & Trollinger, 2005). There are studies of young children's cultural worlds that adopt an ethnomusicological perspective (Campbell, 1998; Marsh, 2008), and a few instances of general anthropologies of childhood which include instances of musical activity (Lancy, 1996; Gottlieb, 2004). Work is also starting to explore the influence of media (Marsh, 2008; Vestad, 2010) and new technologies on children's singing activity (Bickford, in press; Young, 2007, 2009).

Understanding Children Moving and Listening to Music

A lead position in early childhood music education research has been taken by children's learning to be singers, reflecting its importance in early childhood music education practice, with music-making with instruments also receiving much attention. There are other areas of activity in music that have also received some attention, including listening to music (Sims, 1986) and movement to music (Metz, 1986; Sims, 1985). A similar pattern occurs with earlier studies focused mainly on preschoolers in educational settings, and later work focusing more on younger children (Gruhn, 2002; Kida & Adachi, 2008; Reynolds, 1995) and more diverse contexts (deVries, 2003), at home (Chen-Haftek, 2004), attending day care, or participating in baby/toddler music classes (Retra, 2010). In preparing this overview, it is noticeable that although the value of movement integrated with music is recognized in educational practice, there is surprisingly little recent research that focuses on this dimension. Similarly, there is little research that focuses on children's listening to recorded or live music. However, the studies of infant musicality, of which there has been considerable expansion in recent years, generally take a global and multimodal view of musical activity that includes embodied and aural engagement. The reduced focus on these dimensions in more recent work reflects a move away from music as separated out into different areas of activity, as might be defined by curriculum prescription, to a focus more on how young children behave and participate in musical activity.

In simple terms this represents a shift from a focus on musical and curriculum content to children's integrated musical behaviors (e.g., Gruhn, 2002).

Again, studies framed by ethnomusicological thinking challenge Western images of children's participation in music. Mans (2002) provides an interesting description and discussion of modes of participation among young Namibian children where they may be included on the fringes of community music and dance occasions and their encouragement to participate is seen as an important aspect of socialization (Mans, 2002). We should, however, be mindful not to reify the musical participations of "other" cultures but recognize them too as shifting in line with contemporary and glocalized (a composite term to encapsulate changes that are both global, yet locally inflected) political, social, cultural, and technological changes (Emberly, 2009; Lum, 2008). Emberly (2009), for example, describes the shift from community to education-based, global-media-influenced musical activity among the Venda of South Africa. Blacking's original ethnomusicological studies of children's music (in a collected, later edition 1995) had described community-music processes that have now been transformed by social and political changes in South Africa.

Having provided a broad background of research into the musical activity of young children we return to look in more detail at the two directions of expansion as introduced at the beginning of the chapter.

Recent New Directions: Birth to Three Years

Much of the research in this area has emanated from North American laboratories in which researchers have developed procedures which enable them to infer infant skills on the basis of responses to musical stimuli (Trehub, 2009). These studies have revealed many inferences about the detail of infants' listening skills; that they can detect very small pitch differences, for example, and aspects of the relationships between pitches in melodies (see Trehub, 2006 for a detailed review). They appear also to be very interested in pitch contour (Stalinski, Schellenberg, & Trehub, 2008). Some of these skills appear to be present from birth or just after (Parncutt, 2006) and although babies are enculturated prenatally into the music of their family and immediate community, researchers tentatively propose that these indicate innate skills for listening and processing music hard-wired into human biology (Trehub, 2009). Research has also revealed early rhythmic capabilities; that infants appear to be able to group series of aural sounds in meaningful chunks (Bergeson & Trehub, 2006), that they are sensitive to musical phrasing, can identify similarities in rhythmic patterns, and seem to be sensitive to the metrical structure of music (again, reviewed comprehensively in Trehub, 2009).

Neuroscience has contributed new brain imaging techniques that give access to observing the music-active brain and exploring the neural bases of music (Bella et al., 2009; Overy, Norton, Cronin, Winner, & Schlaug, 2005; Schlaug, 2009). The remarkable advances of the last decade are allowing researchers to identify which part of the brain is used for which type of mental activity, which may be dedicated to music processing or share functions, the relationships between music and language (Patel, 2009), and the complex interplay between what might be genetic and cultural experience. The findings from these studies are beginning to suggest that structural changes and neural connectivity occur in the brain in response to environmental music experience and that this is especially the case among very young children when the brain is in the process of maturation (Schlaug, 2009). It had been known that the brains of musicians differed in certain structural ways from those of nonmusicians, but whether these structural changes occurred as a consequence of musical learning, or not, was unclear. Hyde and colleagues (2009) report on a study carried out in Boston, Massachusetts in which 15 5- to 7-year-olds received keyboard lessons for an extended period of 15 months in comparison with a matching group who received general music activity classes. Imaging of the children's brains showed certain structural changes as a result of learning an instrument, even after such a relatively short time.

Studies that aim for scientific precision are reductionist: either music is separated into decontextualized aural stimuli to compare slight variations in pitch and rhythm, or behavior is studied as simple observable responses or even unconscious brain activity. The search for infant musical competences and the implications for human biological capacities that ensue is one important contributing dimension in our understanding of early childhood musicality and one that is drawing much attention. But it is important to position this dimension as just one strand in the dynamic interplay among biological, environmental, material, social, and cultural influences.

It is suggested that since the development of the musical brain is flexible and "plastic" in the earliest years, and infants have a wealth of proclivities for music, that particular attention needs to be paid to the type and quality of input (Hodges, 2006). It is also suggested there may be critical periods during which the foundations for certain forms of perceptual and cognitive ability might be laid. To give one example, Hannon and Trehub (2005) found that infants are enculturated to regular and fairly simple meters over the age of 12 months, but that prior to that time, they appear to be more flexibly attentive to metrical variation, suggesting, therefore, that intensive early experience might raise the ability to perceive varied meter in the longer term. At the same time, others urge caution in interpreting the findings from infant music psychology and neuroscience as a message to "hot-house" very young children. Contemporary models of parenting in developed countries are increasingly causing parents to feel pressure to ensure stimulating, high quality environments for their young children as an investment for future success, but which may, in themselves, have detrimental consequences.

One strand of interest in infant musicality has focused more on social development. While interest in adult–infant interaction has evolved since the 1970s (e.g., Brazelton & Tronick, 1980; Trevarthen, 1977), the realization of its musical qualities arose initially in work by the Papousek (1996), basing their study on their own experiences of parenting, and more recently by Trevarthen and Malloch (Malloch & Trevarthen, 2009; Trevarthen, 2002; Trevarthen & Malloch, 2002). Based on this work, Malloch proposed a theory of "communicative musicality" (Malloch, 2000). From the moment of birth, close observational studies of infants in interaction with their immediate caregivers, usually their mothers, have revealed their ability to make eye contact, to gaze at faces, to listen intently to vocalizations (Nakata & Trehub, 2004), and to make reciprocating gestures. As their vocal and movement abilities develop, these vocalizations and gestures increasingly convey meaning and intention. Careful analysis of video-recorded interactions has revealed the musical features and qualities that underpin successful infant–adult interactions: rhythmic synchronization, well-timed reciprocal contributions, expressively contoured pitch variations, and carefully graduated and matching dynamic qualities (Trevarthen, 2000). Moreover, interactions are sustained by a careful balance of repetition of the same to generate predictability and to support sharing, and the introduction of novelty to stimulate interest and to raise the emotional tenor (Shenfield, Trehub, & Nakata, 2003; Young, 2000a, 2005a). This fundamental characteristic of time-based interactions (Young, 2011) has been proposed as a generative source in improvisations (Young, 2003b) that might be played out on instruments (Young, 2005a), in singing-play (Yennari, 2010), and playful pedagogical approaches (Custodero, 2008). In one respect this understanding of sociable infant behavior connects and leads on from the studies that explore perceptual and processing skills in detail, demonstrating their function in enabling young children to engage and communicate with those immediately around them. What is also fascinating is that the findings emerging from brain studies begin to identify processes that enable anticipation in time, so essential to communicative musical participation (Trainor & Zatorre, 2009). These neural processes seem to entail encoding what has just gone, predicting what might just happen, and then adjusting if the prediction is not fulfilled.

Yet again the proviso of cultural variation should be raised. It is suggested that parents throughout the world interact with their babies and very young children with vocalizing and moving their bodies rhythmically (Dissanayake, 2000a; Trehub, 2004) both to soothe and animate—and that this fundamental behavior represents a universal musical parenting strategy (Dissanayake, 2000b). However, there are variations in style that seem to be culturally determined. Gratier (1999) studied a group of newly arrived immigrant mothers in Paris whose "communicative musicality" appeared to be disrupted by the change of cultural environment in comparison with longer term arrived and resident mothers. While, as another example, parents in the United States may adopt an animated style of interaction with their children, mothers from other cultural backgrounds, the Netherlands, for example, may prefer a style that aims to soothe and quiet their children (DeLoache & Gottlieb, 2000).

What also emerges from the studies of adult–infant interaction, connecting with wider theorizing from ethnomusicology and music psychology, is the apparent human ability to synchronize rhythmically with others; to entrain. This ability has some interesting pedagogical applications. Kirschner and Tomasello (2010), for example, carried out a series of studies with 4-year-olds from which they propose an association between rhythmically synchronized musical activity with improved social behavior.

Recent New Directions: Expanding Contexts

The interest in adult–infant interaction in integrated and everyday contexts has turned researchers' attention to young children's experiences of music in families and the domestic environment. Most family life is, by its very nature, secluded and private raising challenges of access for researchers and ethical anxieties around intrusion. There is, however, a small body of research accumulating, some based on interviews (Custodero, Britto, & Brooks-Gunn, 2003; Ilari, 2005; Kida & Adachi, 2008; Young, 2008b; Young & Street, 2006), questionnaire and telephone surveys (Custodero, Britto, & Xin, 2002; deVries, 2007, 2009), and self-report diaries with parents (Tafuri, 2008), and some carried out by parents as case studies of their children (e.g., Papousek, 1996; deVries, 2005). The Day in the Life study (Gillen & Cameron, 2010) employed an innovative method in which one complete day of home care for seven 2-year-old girls in diverse international locations was video-recorded. Review of the video-data revealed quantities of music and dance taking place in the "days." Portions of the video data were extracted from the whole, grouped according to similarity of content, and then analyzed from different theoretical perspectives (Young & Gillen, 2010). A number of incidents of musical parenting, for example, were selected in which parents sang, chanted, or rhymed with their daughters to soothe or enliven them, often at transitional points in the day. Examples of musical practices involving commercial media were extracted from the different "days." Disney videos, for example, cropped up in four days allowing for interpretation of how listening and watching was interwoven into family life, to entertain, to occupy, to introduce social messages, with added commentary on the use of commercial media items in young children's domestic musical environments (see also, Young, 2007).

This work on music in families is valuable in helping to fill a gap that exists between the infancy studies, mainly laboratory-based which extend up to approximately the age of 12 months, and research into children's musical activity in preschool settings around the age of 3 years. Beyond the age of 1 year, babies are "on the move" and less amenable to laboratory studies, and although attendance at day care for under 3-year-olds is increasing in recent years, a majority of children in many communities still spend their day at home.

Since the home is the place where contemporary musical practices increasingly involve children's commercial media, purchased toys, and other musical items, research into music in families links with an emerging thread of activity which is interested in children's everyday musical activity as influenced by media and commodity items such as musical toys (Young, 2007, 2008b). Young interviewed 45 4- to 11-year-olds about their musical activity at home and followed up six girls aged between 6 and 11 years who regularly sang with video-game karaoke sets at home. In a current project researchers have visited 7-year-olds at home to talk to them about their everyday musical activity and to collect information about resources for music available to the children in the homes (Young et al., 2010). The changing nature of music and musical practices in the home, particularly as a result of digital technologies and changing conceptions of home life for children as being a place for entertainment and education, are emerging from both the karaoke and study of 7-year-olds. Both studies suggest that research and pedagogical activity needs to take heed of the changing nature of digital and commodified musical childhoods (Bickford, in press; Buckingham, 2004; also Vestad, 2010).

In both studies, however, the children visited belong to the more affluent middle classes who have the financial resources available to provide these musical environments. Cultural circumstances of families, the extent, for example, to which music is valued in the community to which the family belongs—and how it is valued—will impinge on how music is provided for and the approaches to musical upbringing (Campbell, 2006). For example, interviews with devout Muslim mothers of preschool children living in four British cities revealed certain religious doctrines around music that in some cases restricted what music was heard in the home and what participation in music was permissible, with differential expectations for young girls in comparison with boys (Young & Street, 2009).

The Application of Research to Practice

Although certain points have arisen in the preceding sections which relate research to pedagogical practice, this next section looks at this area more specifically. The design of pedagogical approaches can be considerably assisted by information offered by early childhood music research in its many different theoretical orientations. Research in the field of early childhood music education studies the application in practice of findings from research into infant and early childhood musicality and the effectiveness of research-informed pedagogical designs and interventions. However, the pathway from research to practice is not always direct and smooth, with criticisms levied at both researchers and educators for failures relating to the oft-quoted practice–theory divide. There are instances of research findings being adopted over zealously and in skewed ways without critique (e.g., Rauscher & Hinton, 2006), and instances where practice proceeds without recourse to research findings that might result in improved outcomes for young children. A study by Addessi and Carugati (2009) on student teachers' socially constructed representations of children as musical, their conceptions of musicality, is a valuable reminder that beliefs and images of musical childhoods held by practitioners will profoundly influence how research information is received and implemented. If, for example, as mentioned earlier in relation to singing, educators hold strong beliefs of singing ability as innate and fixed, they are unlikely to be receptive to research findings around effective methods to support children's learning in terms of singing. It is not that unhelpful assumptions are held only by educators; researchers too may hold inflexible beliefs that shape their research priorities or hinder their ability to relate their work to applied, real-world pedagogical contexts.

Perhaps the greater rapprochement between research and practice still persists in the area of musical development, particularly where the maturation of physical skills is involved, such as those involved in learning to sing or learning to coordinate movements rhythmically to participate in musical experiences. Looking in more detail, for example, at singing, aspects such as pitch range, ideal tessitura in relation to the physical development of the voice, early melodic pitch patterns which are most amenable to immature voices are all directly applicable to practice (Rutkowski & Trollinger, 2005). Similarly, in movement, developing movement vocabulary related to maturing coordination skills, the physical size of young children in relationship to movement rhythmic capabilities are all important aspects that impinge on pedagogical strategy and the planning of musical experiences (Retra, 2010).

Concern for developmentally appropriate practice then leads to closer examination of pedagogical strategies. In learning to sing, for example, comparative benefits may be explored between immersion and part or whole song learning strategies (Persellin & Bateman, 2009), between separating melody and words or combining them (Tafuri, Ferrari, & Perri, 2009), and different measures for evaluating children's singing (Nardo, Kenney, & Persellin, 2010).

The influence on practice of the increasing quantity of scientific information from the studies of musical competences in infancy is potentially valuable, but to date, less apparent. The primary area of influence is seen broadly in general rationales and advocacies by educators, politicians, commercial music providers, and policymakers for whom messages of potential general cognitive gains accruing from participation in music are highly attractive and promise convincing arguments. The strong belief that an early start is a good start is not borne out by research as Trehub (2006) emphasizes. Her extensive experience of the field gives authority to her statements. To be precise, she writes, only the development of absolute pitch (the ability to identify the exact pitch of aural sounds) appears to be influenced by training before the age of 6 years and even this ability is of dubious advantage to musicians (Trehub, 2006, p. 43). The thoughtful application of findings from neuroscience to early childhood music pedagogy is only just beginning with the authorship of research reviews and interpretations for applications to practice being proposed (Flohr, 2010; Gruhn 2009; Gruhn & Rauscher, 2008). Flohr, in keeping with many authors (e.g., Rauscher & Hinton, 2006; Trehub, 2006) urges caution in the blind adoption of "neuromyths" (see also Schellenberg, 2008).

Research by educators has also focused on the application of theories of engagement and learning to early childhood music. There has, in recent years, been a broad trend to develop more relational, interactive models of practice inspired by readings of Vygotskian theory and concomitant interest in the role of the adult (e.g., Hsee & Rutkowski, 2006). Custodero, in a significant corpus (1998, 2002, 2005) has applied Csikszentmihaly's theory of flow to young children's participation in music classes, providing thereby a pedagogical model which balances the challenge and enjoyment of participation in educationally framed musical activities with skill level. Custodero places importance on the child's opportunities to "self-assign" in music sessions, and the supportive role of the adult (Custodero, 2005). Holgersen, adopting a European theoretical perspective of phenomenology (2002) studied children aged 1 to 5 taking part in a music group and identified movement and social interaction as key dimensions of the children's participation. While the methods, theoretical framing, and contexts for studies in this vein may vary, when viewed collectively with other similar contemporary work (reviewed in Young, 2008c) some commonalities emerge that characterize contemporary, theory-based approaches to pedagogy. These commonalities are: the contribution of embodied and play-based approaches to children's music learning and a conception of music learning therefore which is multimodal; and the important role of the adult not as didactic instructor, but as interactive and responsive to children's contributions in order to value and attempt to understand the musical intentions and meanings underlying their actions.

There are individual examples of the application of other principles and theories to early childhood music education. The principles of multicultural education have influenced project studies by Chen-Haftek (2007), cultural studies in the work of Barrett (2005a), and some interpretations of critical pedagogy in a project study by Young and Street (2009). Addessi and Pachet's work heralds important new developments in early childhood music education with a focus on the application of interactive music technology to early childhood pedagogical contexts (Addessi & Pachet, 2005a, 2005b).

Other researchers have taken a different angle, starting with a need to develop models of practice appropriate to a widening range of adults working with young children in music as the places and spaces for early childhood music expand; for example, with generalist early childhood practitioners, particularly in daycare settings (Suthers, 2004), music performers from orchestras or community groups (Hennessy, Lowson, McCullough, & Young, 2008; Smith, 2011) and with parents to develop music practice in the home (Cooper & Cardany, 2008; Dionyssiou, 2009). Suthers notes that need for research of this type has become more pressing in recent years as the range of provision for under-3s has increased and with the increase, a need to promote quality practice. She states that programs for children under 3 are notably different in content and approach from those for older children, requiring, therefore qualitatively different approaches to how music might be integrated. Her work in devising integrated musical activity in day care arrived at three dimensions: music as part of caregiving routines; music as play; and sociable music experiences (Suthers, 1998).

The need to expand models of practice so that they are appropriate to the cultural, social, and political climates within their own countries is also pressing for a group of researchers and educators working outside the dominant U.S. and North West European countries; for example, in developing countries such as Kenya (Andang'o & Mugo, 2007), Brazil (Ilari, 2007), in postcolonial locations such as Singapore (Lum, 2008), postcommunist countries such as Estonia (Kiilu, 2010), and post-apartheid South Africa (Woodward, 2007), and for researchers cognizant of the increasing diversity of communities within their own countries as a consequence of immigration (Gustafson, 2009; Young, 2008c).

Research in early childhood music education has a relatively short history when compared with a longer history of pedagogical approaches. These practice-based approaches, referred to usually by the name of their originator, as for example, Kodaly, Orff, Dalcroze, Gordon, and Suzuki (see Campbell & Scott-Kassner, 2009 for descriptions of these approaches) still assume a strong position in early childhood music education with practitioners adopting and then often identifying strongly with one approach. On account of this strong position, they cannot be ignored in this chapter, concerned as it is to give a current and representative overview of early childhood music and its research field. However, in respect of their relationship to research and scholarship the pedagogical approaches are problematic. They have crystallized into specific pedagogies often underpinned with sets of ideas that are accorded the status of theory but have usually emerged from consensual versions of what counts as good practice rather than empirical study. They represent philosophies and approaches born of particular times and places embodying broad assumptions and ideals concerning childhood and music and insights into the values of societies where they originated or have been adopted. These pedagogical approaches perpetuate and are perpetuated through canonized texts and authorized practices that discourage reflective, truly open-minded appraisal of their approaches and are rarely open or flexible to external influence or new information from research.

Conclusion

In this chapter I present my version of an up-to-date picture of research into the musical childhoods of very young children and relate these to educational practice. I have explained recent developments as expanding on two fronts—the birth to 3 phase, and into wider social and cultural contexts—and I hope conveyed some of the valuable and interesting extensions to our understanding and knowledge of young children's musicality. The work which has attracted the greatest attention in recent years has no doubt been the music psychology and neuroscientific investigations into infant musical capabilities and processing. I have, however, tried to keep in fair balance the interplay between biological, social, material, and cultural dimensions of young children's early musical experiences. The active exploration and expansion of our understandings of musical childhoods in real life domestic contexts, daycare centers, and in culturally diverse situations has received less attention, been subject to fewer citings and collective reviews, and is, perhaps by its very nature, more fragmented and diffuse. What is in operation here too is the difference in value accorded to mainly North American and Northwest European, expensive, scientific, technological research in abstract laboratory situations focusing on decontextualized musical events and isolated responses in comparison with research, usually poorly funded, in real world contexts involving small children and their carers, mainly women, in playful, embodied music, taking place in homes, nurseries, and increasingly in "other" cultures. Of this latter, every aspect is accorded lower status.

At this present time, with research expanding in these new directions, early childhood music educators, according to my perception, are experiencing difficulty in identifying a framework within which to accommodate and conceptualize contemporary work. The period of time when an interest in developmental models predominated may have represented a heyday when research and practice united around common themes and enterprises. I have proposed a notion of "musical childhoods" that draws strongly from childhood studies as a possible frame within which to theorize this new diversity of activity (Young, 2008c). "Musical childhoods" could accommodate multiperspectival and multidimensional activity within a postdevelopment perspective that would introduce thinking tools from critical theory to discuss and examine assumptions, methods, and strategies that underpin research and practice with more vigor than I suggest is currently the case.

Since I set out to offer a survey, there are omissions and gaps that should be mentioned. I have deliberately left out

a couple of small areas: children's emergent notations and drawings to music and their first formal instrumental lessons. Both areas involve children at the older end of early childhood and are relatively distinct and specific areas of activity. In terms of gaps, there is still a paucity of research for the toddler years between 12 months and preschool around the age of 3 years. There has been little attention to variations according to gender, ethnicity, religion, or class. And, at risk of repetition, there is a pressing need to extend the scope of research to non-Western musical domains and to engage in investigating musical learning in all its cultural diversity. While contemporary childhoods are changing dramatically as technological developments and fields such as literacy education are actively researching and theorizing these changes, there has been very little response from early childhood music education.

In offering a concluding summary, we may confidently say that adults and infants throughout the world interact by vocalizing and moving rhythmically in ways that are intrinsically musical and expressive. We know that infants and small children possess sophisticated aural perceptual skills; and we know that the brain is "prewired" for music and that musical experience seems to influence how brain connections form. Infants enculturated to Western music can parse the music they hear in ways that are conventional to that musical style. Very young children take great interest in sounds and how they are produced, and are motivated to explore them and make music in ways that have forms of coherence. Small children engage in spontaneous forms of musical play with their voices, creating expressive vocalizations and songs, with their bodies in rhythmic movement, with objects and instruments and increasingly sophisticated forms of technology available to them. Young children live in environments in which there are forms of musical engagement and participation for them, ranging from the highly designed and formal, to those in which children are peripheral participants and that they attend, imitate, and absorb from those musical environments. Finally we know that adults are highly motivated to try to understand young children's musical worlds and how best to engender and enhance their musical experiences.

References

Adachi, M. (2006, August). Japanese home environments and infants' spontaneous responses to music: An initial report. Paper presented at the 9th ICMPC, Bologna, Italy.

Addessi, A. R. (2009). The musical dimension of daily routines with under-four children during diaper change, bedtime and free-play. *Early Child Development and Care, 179*(6), 747–68.

Addessi, A. R., & Pachet, F. (2005a). Experiments with a musical machine: Musical style replication in 3/5 year old children. *British Journal of Music Education, 22*(1), 21–46.

Addessi, A. R., & Pachet, F. (2005b). Young children confronting the Continuator, an interactive reflective musical system [Special Issue 2005–2006]. *Musicae Scientiae*, 13–39.

Andang'o, E., & Mugo, J. (2007). Early childhood music education in Kenya: Between broad national policies and local issues. *Arts Education Policy Review, 109*(2), 45–53.

Bancroft, S., Fawcett, M., & Hay, P. (Eds.). (2008). *Researching children researching the world: 5X5X5=creativity.* Stoke-on-Trent, England: Trentham Books.

Barrett, M. (1998a). Researching children's compositional processes and products: Connections to music education practice? In B. Sundin, G. E. McPherson, & G. Folkestad (Eds.), *Children composing: Research in music education 1998* (Vol. 1, pp. 10–34). Lund, Sweden: Malmo Academy of Music, Lund University.

Barrett, M. (1998b). Children composing: A view of aesthetic decision-making. In B. Sundin, G. E. McPherson, & G. Folkestad (Eds.), *Children composing: Research in music education 1998* (Vol. 1, pp. 57–81) Lund, Sweden: Malmo Academy of Music, Lund University.

Barrett, M. (2005a). Musical communication and children's communities of musical practice. In D. Miell, R. Macdonald, & D. J. Hargreaves (Eds.), *Musical communication* (pp. 261–280). Oxford, England: Oxford University Press.

Barrett, M. (2005b). Representation, cognition and communication: Invented notation in children's musical communication. In D. Miell, R. Macdonald, & D. J. Hargreaves (Eds.), *Musical communication* (pp. 116–142). Oxford, England: Oxford University Press.

Barrett, M. (2010, August 23-27). Young children's song-making: An analysis of patterns of use and development. In S. M. Demorest, S. J. Morrison, & P. S. Campbell (Eds.), *Proceedings of the 11th International Conference on Music Perception and Cognition* (ICMPC) (p. 74). Seattle, WA.

Bella, S. D., Kraus, N., Overy, N., Pantev, C., Snyder, J. S., Tervaniemi, M., ... Schlaug, G. (2009). *The neurosciences and music: Vol. 3. Disorders and plasticity* (Annals of the New York Academy of Sciences). Boston, MA: Blackwell.

Bergeson, T. R., & Trehub, S. E. (2006). Infants' perception of rhythmic patterns. *Music Perception, 23,* 345–360.

Bickford, T. (in press) Tinkering and tethering: Children's MP3 players as material culture. In P. S. Campbell & T. Wiggins (Eds.), *The Oxford handbook of children's musical cultures.* Oxford, England: Oxford University Press

Björkvold, J. (1989). *The muse within: Creativity and communication, song and play from childhood through maturity* (W. H. Halverson, Trans.). New York: HarperCollins.

Blacking, J. (1995). *Venda children's songs: Study in ethnomusicological analysis.* Chicago, IL: University of Chicago Press.

Brazelton, T., & Tronick, E. (1980). Preverbal communication between mothers and infants. In D. R. Olson (Ed.), *The social foundations of language and thought* (pp. 299–315). New York: Norton.

Bremmer, M., & Huisingh, A. (2009). *Muziek is als Geluiden Heel Mooi Door Elkaar Gaan* [Music is when sounds come together nicely].Amsterdam, the Netherlands: Amsterdamse Hogeschool voor de Kunsten.

Buckingham, D. (2004). New media, new childhoods? Children's changing cultural environments in the age of digital technology. In M. J. Kehily (Ed.), *An introduction to childhood studies* (pp. 108–121). Maidenhead, England: Open University Press.

Burman, E. (2008). *Deconstructing developmental psychology* (2nd rev. ed.). London: Brunner-Routledge.

Campbell, P. S. (1998). *Songs in their heads: Music and its meaning in children's lives.* Oxford, England: Oxford University Press.

Campbell, P. S. (2006). Global practices. In G. McPherson (Ed.), *The child as musician: A handbook of musical development* (pp. 415–437). New York: Oxford University Press.

Campbell, P. S. (2007). Musical meaning in children's cultures. In L. Bresler (Ed.), *Inter-national handbook of research in arts education* (pp. 881–894). Dordrecht, the Netherlands: Springer.

Campbell, P. S., & Scott-Kassner, C. (2009). *Music in childhood: From preschool through the elementary grades* (3rd rev. ed.). New York: Thompson/Schirmer.

Céleste, B., Delalande, F., & Dumaurier, E. (1982). *L'enfant du sonore au musical* [The child of musical sound]. Paris: Buchet/Chastel.

Chen-Haftek, L. (2004). Music and movement from zero to three: A window to children's musicality. In L. Custodero (Ed.), *Proceedings of the 11th International Conference of the ISME Early Childhood Commission* (pp. 45–54). Barcelona, Spain: Escola Superior de Musica de Catalunya/New York: Harper & Row.

Chen-Haftek, L. (2007). Contextual analyses of children's responses to an integrated Chinese music and culture experience. *Music Education Research, 9*(3), 337–353.

Cohen, V. (1980). The emergence of musical gestures in kindergarten children (Unpublished doctoral dissertation). University of Illinois, Urbana.

Cooper S., & Cardany, A. B. (2008). Making connections: Promoting music making in the home through a preschool music program. *General Music Today, 22*(4), 18–23.

Cross, I. (2009). The nature of music and its evolution. In S. Hallam, I. Cross, & M. Thaut (Eds.), *Oxford handbook of music psychology* (pp. 3–13). Oxford, England: Oxford University Press.

Custodero, L. A. (1998). Observing flow in young people's music learning. *General Music Today, 12*(1), 21–27.

Custodero, L. A. (2002). Seeking challenge, finding skill: Flow experience in music education. *Arts Education and Policy Review, 103*(3), 3–9.

Custodero, L. A. (2005). Observable indicators of flow experience: A developmental perspective on musical engagement in young children from infancy to school age. *Music Education Research, 7*(2), 185–209

Custodero, L. A. (2006). Singing practices in 10 families with young children. *Journal of Research in Music Education, 54*(1), 37–56.

Custodero, L. A. (2008). Living jazz, learning jazz: Thoughts on a responsive pedagogy of early childhood music. *General Music Today, 22*(5), 24–29.

Custodero, L. A., Britto P. R., & Brooks-Gunn J. (2003). Musical lives: A collective portrait of American parents and their young children. *Applied Developmental Psychology, 24,* 553–572.

Custodero, L. A., Britto, P. R., & Xin, T. (2002). From Mozart to Motown, lullabies to love songs: A preliminary report on the Parents Use of Music with Infants Survey. *Journal of Zero-to-Three, 23*(1), 41–46.

Custodero, L. A., & Johnson-Green E. A. (2008). Caregiving in counterpoint: Reciprocal influences in the musical parenting of younger and older infants. *Early Child Development and Care, 178*(1), 15–39.

Davies, C. V. (1992). Listen to my song: A study of songs invented by children aged 5 to 7 years. *British Journal of Music Education, 9*(1), 19–48.

Delalande, F., & Cornara, S. (2010). Sound explorations from the ages of 10 to 37 months: The ontogenesis of musical conducts. *Music Education Research, 12*(3), 257–268.

DeLoache, J., & Gottlieb, A. (Eds.). (2000). *A world of babies: Imagined childcare guides for seven societies.* Cambridge, England: Cambridge University Press.

deVries, P. (2003). Preschooler response to pre-recorded music in three different situations. *Australian Journal of Early Childhood, 28*(2), 15–19.

deVries, P. (2005). Lessons from home: Scaffolding vocal improvisation and song acquisition with a 2-year-old. *Early Childhood Education Journal, 32*(5), 307–312.

deVries, P. (2007). The use of music CDs and DVDs in the home with the under-fives: What the parents say. *Australian Journal of Early Childhood, 32*(4), 18–21.

deVries, P. (2009). Music at home with the under fives: What is happening? *Early Child Development and Care, 179*(4), 395–405.

Dionyssiou, Z. (2009). Encouraging musical communication between babies and parents: Report of a case study from Corfu. In A. R. Addessi & S. Young (Eds.), *Proceedings of the European network of music educators and researchers of young children* (pp. 303–312). Bologna, Italy: Bononia University Press.

Dissanayake, E. (2000a). Antecedents of the temporal arts in early mother–infant interaction. In N. W. Wallin, B. Merker, & S. Brown (Eds.), *The origins of music* (pp. 389–410). Cambridge, MA: MIT Press.

Dissanayake, E. (2000b). *Art and intimacy: How the arts began.* Seattle: University of Washington Press.

Dowling, W. J. (1984). Development of musical schemata in children's spontaneous singing. In W. R. Crozier & A. J. Chapman (Eds.),

Advances in psychology: Cognitive processes in the perception of art (pp. 145–163). Amsterdam, the Netherlands: Elsevier Science.

Dzansi, M. (2004). Playground music pedagogy of Ghanaian children. *Research Studies in Music Education, 22*(1), 83–92.

Emberly, A. (2009). "Mandela went to China…and India too": Musical cultures of childhood in South Africa (Unpublished doctoral dissertation). University of Washington, Seattle.

Flohr, J. W. (2010). Best practices for young children's music education: Guidance from brain research. *General Music Today, 23*(2), 13–19.

Gillen, J., & Cameron, C. A. (Eds.). (2010). *International perspectives on early childhood research: A day in the life.* Basingstoke, England: Palgrave Macmillan.

Glover, J. (2000). Children composing 4–14. London: RoutledgeFalmer.

Gluschankof, C. (2002). The local musical style of kindergarten children: A description and analysis of its natural variables. *Music Education Research, 4*(1), 37–49.

Gordon, E. E. (2007). *Learning sequences in music: A contemporary music learning theory.* Chicago: GIA.

Gottlieb, A. (2004). *The afterlife is where we come from: The culture of infancy in West Africa.* Chicago, IL: University of Chicago Press.

Gratier, M. (1999). Expressions of belonging: The effect of acculturation on the rhythm and harmony of mother–infant vocal interaction [Special Issue 1999–2000]. *Musicae Scientiae*, 93–122.

Gruhn, W. (2002). Phases and stages in early music learning: A longitudinal study on the development of young children's musical potential. *Music Education Research, 4*(1), 51–71.

Gruhn, W. (2009). How can neuroscience affect the theoretical concept of and practical application to early childhood music learning? In A. R. Addessi & S. Young (Eds.), *Proceedings of the European network of music educators and researchers of young children* (pp. 211–220). Bologna, Italy: Bononia University Press.

Gruhn, W. (2010). Music learning in early childhood: A review of psychological, educational, and neuromusical research. In P. Webster & R. Colwell (Eds.), *Handbook of music learning.* Oxford, England: Oxford University Press.

Gruhn, W., & Rauscher, F. H. (Eds.). (2008). *Neurosciences in music pedagogy.* New York: Oxford University Press.

Gustafson, I. R. (2009). *Race and curriculum: Music in childhood education.* Basingstoke, England: Palgrave Macmillan.

Hannon, E. E., & Trehub, S. E. (2005). Tuning into musical rhythms: Infants learn more readily than adults. *Proceedings of the National Academy of Sciences USA, 102*, 12639–12643.

Hargreaves, D. J. (1986). *The developmental psychology of music.* New York: Cambridge University Press.

Hendricks, K., & McPherson, G. (2010). Early stages of musical development: Relationships between sensory integration dysfunction, parental influence, and musical disposition of a three-year-old "maestro." *International Journal of Music Education, 28*(1), 88–103:

Hennessy, S., Lowson, O., McCullough, E., & Young, S. (2008). Cluster programme evaluation: Final report. (Unpublished report available from the Association of British Orchestras, London)

Hentschke, L., & Martinez, I. (2004). Mapping music education research in Brazil and Argentina: The British impact. *Psychology of Music, 32*(3), 357–367.

Hodges, D. A. (2006). The musical brain. In G. McPherson (Ed.), *The child as musician: A handbook of musical development* (pp. 52–68). New York: Oxford University Press.

Holgersen, S-E. (2002). *Mening og Deltagelse. Iagttagelse af 1-5 årige børns deltagelse i musikundervisning. Ph.d.-afhandling.Danmarks Pædagogiske Universitet, København.* [Meaning and participation: Observation of 1- to 5-year-old children's participation in music teaching] (Unpublished doctoral dissertation). The Danish University of Education, Copenhagen.

Hsee, Y., & Rutkowski, J. (2006, July 9-14,). Early musical experience in touch with general human development: An investigation of Vygotsky's scaffolding in music lessons for preschoolers. In L. Suthers (Ed.), *Touched by musical discovery, disciplinary and cultural perspectives:*

Proceedings of the ISME early childhood music education commission seminar (pp. 112–120). Taiwan: Chinese Cultural University Taipei.

Hyde, K. L., Lerch, J., Norton, A., Forgeard, M., Winner, E., Evans, A. C., & Schlaug, G. (2009). Musical training shapes structural brain development. *The Journal of Neuroscience, 29*(10), 3019 –3025.

Ilari, B. (2005). On musical parenting of young children: Musical beliefs and behaviors of mothers and infants. *Early Childhood Development and Care, 175*(7/8), 647–660.

Ilari, B. (2007). Music and early childhood in the Tristes Tropiques: The Brazilian experience. *Arts Education Policy Review, 109*(2), 7–18.

Imberty, M. (1996). Linguistic and musical development in preschool and school-age children. In I. Deliège & J. Sloboda (Eds.), *Musical beginnings: Origins and development of musical competence* (pp. 191–213). New York: Oxford University Press.

Kehily, M. J. (2004). *An introduction to childhood studies.* Maidenhead, England: Open University Press.

Kellett, M. (2010). Rethinking children and research. London: Continuum.

Kida, I., & Adachi, M. (2008, August 25–29). The role of the musical environment at home in the infant's development—Part 2: Exploring effects of early musical experiences on the infant's physical and motor development during the first 2 years. In M. Adachi (Ed.), *Proceedings of the 10th International Conference on Music Perception and Cognition* (ICMPC 10), Sapporo, Japan.

Kiilu, K. (2010). The development of the concept of music education in Estonian kindergartens, 1905–2008: A historical–critical overview. (Unpublished research report, Department of Teacher Education, University of Helsinki, P.O. Box 9)

Kirschner, S., & Tomasello, M. (2010). Joint music making promotes prosocial behavior in 4-year-old children. *Evolution and Human Behavior, 31*(5), 354–364.

Koops, L. H. (2010). Learning in The Gambia ''Deñuy jàngal seen bopp'' (They teach themselves): Children's music. *Journal of Research in Music Education, 58*(1), 20–36.

Kratus, J. (1989). A time analysis of the compositional processes used by children ages 7 to 11. *Journal of Research in Music Education, 37*(1), 5–20.

Kratus, J. (1994). How do children compose? Teaching Music, 2(3), 38–39.

Kreutzer, N. J. (2001). Song acquisition among rural Shona-speaking Zimbabwean children from birth to 7 years. *Journal of Research in Music Education, 49*, 198–211.

Lancy, D. (1996). *Playing on the mother ground, cultural routines for children's development.* New York: Guilford.

Lareau, A. (2003). *Unequal childhoods: Class, race and family life.* Berkeley: University of California Press.

Lew, C.-T. (2005). The musical lives of young Malaysian children: In school and at home (Unpublished doctoral dissertation). University of Washington, Seattle.

Lum, C. H. (2008). Home musical environment of children in Singapore. On Globalization, Technology, and Media. *Journal of Research in Music Education, 56*(2), 101–117.

Lum, C. H. (2009). Musical memories: Snapshots of a Chinese family in Singapore [Special Issue]. *Early Child Development and Care, 179*(6), 707–716.

Malloch, S. (2000). Mothers and infants and communicative musicality [Special Issue, 1999–2000]. *Musicae Scientiae*, 29–57.

Malloch, S., & Trevarthen, C. (Eds.). (2009). *Communicative musicality. Exploring the basis of human companionship.* Oxford, England: Oxford University Press.

Mang, E. (2006). The effects of age, gender and language on children's singing competency. *British Journal of Music Education, 23*(2), 161–174.

Mans, M. (2002). Playing the music: Comparing children's song and dance in Namibian education. In L. Bresler & C. M. Thompson (Eds.), *The arts in children's lives: Context, culture and curriculum* (pp. 71–86). Dordrecht, the Netherlands: Kluwer Academic.

Marsh, K. (2008). *The musical playground: Global tradition and change in children's songs and games.* New York: Oxford University Press.

Marsh, K., & Young, S. (2006). *Musical play. In G. McPherson (Ed.), The child as musician: A handbook of musical development* (pp. 289–310). New York: Oxford University Press.

Metz, E. (1986). Movement as a musical response among pre-school children. *Dissertation Abstracts International, 47*(10A), 3691.

Ministry of Education and Culture, Nicosia, Cyprus (2003). *The primary music education curriculum of Cyprus.* Nicosia, Cyprus: Author.

Moorhead, G. E., & Pond, D. (1978a). *Pillsbury Foundation studies: Music of young children* (5th ed.). Santa Barbara, CA: Pillsbury Foundation for Advancement of Music Education. (Original work published 1941)

Moorhead, G. E., & Pond, D. (1978b). Music of young children. In G. E. Moorhead & D. Pond, *Pillsbury Foundation studies, music of young children: Vol. 1.* Chant. Santa Barbara, CA: Pillsbury Foundation for the Advancement of Music Education [Music Educators National Conference Historical Center, University of Maryland, USA]. (Original work published 1941)

Moorhead, G. E., Sandvik, F., & Wight, D. (1978). *Music of young children. In Music of young children: Pillsbury Foundation studies: Vol. 4. Free use of instruments for musical growth.* Santa Barbara, CA: Pillsbury Foundation for Advancement of Music Education. [MENC Historical Center, University of Maryland, USA]. (Original work published 1951)

Nakata, T., & Trehub, S. E. (2004). Infants' responsiveness to maternal speech and singing. *Infant Behavior & Development, 27,* 455–464.

Nardo, R., Kenney, S., & Persellin, D. (2010, July 26–30). Assessment tools in early childhood music. In B. Ilari, B. & C. Glunschankof (Eds.), *Proceedings of the 14th Early Childhood Music Education Seminar* (p. 89). Beijing, China.

Overy, K., Norton, A., Cronin, K., Winner, E., & Schlaug, G. (2005). Examining rhythm and melody processing in young children using fMRI. In G. Avanzini, L. Lopez, S. Koelsch, & M. Majno (Eds.), *The neurosciences and music: From perception to performance* (Vol. 1060, pp. 210–218). New York: Annals of the New York Academy of Sciences.

Papousek, H. (1996). Musicality in infancy research: Biological and cultural origins of early musicality. In I. Deliège & J. Sloboda (Eds.), *Musical beginnings* (pp. 37–55). Oxford, England: Oxford University Press.

Parncutt, R. (2006). Prenatal development. In G. E. McPherson (Ed.), *The child as musician: A handbook of musical development* (pp. 1–32). Oxford, England: Oxford University Press.

Patel, A. D. (2009). Music and the brain: Three links to language. In S. Hallam, I. Cross, & M. Thaut (Eds.), *Oxford handbook of music psychology* (pp. 208–216). Oxford, England: Oxford University Press.

Persellin, D. C., & Bateman, L. (2009). A comparative study on the effectiveness of two song-teaching methods: Holistic vs. phrase-by-phrase. *Early Child Development and Care, 179*(6), 799–780.

Pond, D. (1981). A composer's study of young children's innate musicality. *Bulletin: Council for Research in Music Education, 68,* 1–12.

Rauscher, F. H., & Hinton, S. C. (2006). The Mozart effect: Music listening is not music instruction. *Educational Psychologist, 43,* 233–238.

Retra, J. (2010). Music is movement: A study into developmental aspects of movement representation of musical activities among preschool children in a Dutch music education setting (Unpublished doctoral dissertation). University of Exeter, England.

Reynolds, A. M. (1995) An investigation of the movement responses performed by children 18 months to 3 years of age. *Dissertation Abstracts International, 56,* 1293 (University Microfilms No. AAC9527531).

Reynolds, A. M. (2006). Vocal interactions during informal early childhood music classes. *Bulletin of the Council for Research in Music Education, 168,* 1–16.

Rutkowski, J. (1990). The evaluation and measurement of children's singing voice development. *The Quarterly, 1*(1–2), 81–95.

Rutkowski, J. (1997). The nature of children's singing voices: Characteristics and assessment. In B. A. Roberts (Ed.), *The phenomenon of singing* (pp. 201–209). St John's, NF: Memorial University Press.

Rutkowski, J., & Chen-Haftek, L. (2000, July 10–14). The singing voice within every child: A cross-cultural comparison of first graders' use of singing voice. Paper presented at the Early Childhood Music Edu-

cation Commission of the International Society of Music Education, Kingston, Canada.

Rutkowski, J., & Miller, M. S. (2003). A longitudinal study of elementary children's acquisition of their singing voices. *Update: Applications of Research in Music Education, 22*(1), 5–14.

Rutkowski, J., & Trollinger, V. L. (2005). Experiences: Singing. In J. W. Flohr (Ed.), *The musical lives of young children* (pp. 78–97). Upper Saddle River, NJ: Prentice Hall.

Schellenberg, E. G. (2008). Exposure to music: The truth about the consequences. In G. McPherson (Ed.), *The child as musician: A handbook of musical development* (pp. 111–134). New York: Oxford University Press.

Schlaug, G. (2009). Music, musicians and brain plasticity. In S. Hallam, I. Cross, & M. Thaut (Eds.), *Oxford handbook of music psychology* (pp. 171–183). Oxford, England: Oxford University Press.

Schraer-Joiner, L. E., & Chen-Hafteck, L. (2009). The responses of preschoolers with cochlear implants to musical activities: A multiple case study. *Early Childhood Development and Care, 179*(6), 785–798.

Shenfield, T., Trehub, S. E., & Nakata, T. (2003). Maternal singing modulates infant arousal. *Psychology of Music, 31,* 365–375.

Sims, W. L. (1985). Young children's creative movement to music: Categories of movement, rhythmic characteristics, and reactions to changes. *Contributions to Music Education, 12,* 42–50.

Sims, W. L. (1986). The effect of high versus low teacher affect and passive versus active student activity during music listening on preschool children's attention, piece preference, time spent listening, and piece recognition. *Journal of Research in Music Education, 34,* 173–191.

Smith, T. F. (2011). Presenting chamber music to young children. General Music Today, 24(2), 9–16.

Stadler Elmer, S. (2000). *Spiel und Nachahmung: Über die Entwicklung der elementaren musikalischen Aktivitäten* [Play and imitation: The development of elementary musical activities]. Aarau, Switzerland: Nepomuk.

Stadler Elmer, S. (2010, August 23–27). An autistic boy's spontaneous singing and related emotional states. In S. M. Demorest, S. J. Morrison, & P. S. Campbell (Eds.), *Proceedings of the 11th International Conference on Music Perception and Cognition* (ICMPC) (p. 65). Seattle, WA.

Stadler Elmer, S., & Elmer, F.-J. (2000). A new method for analyzing and representing singing. *Psychology of Music, 28*(1), 23–42.

Stalinski, S. M., Schellenberg, E. G., & Trehub, S. E. (2008). Developmental changes in the perception on pitch contour: Distinguishing up from down. *The Journal of the Acoustical Society of America, 124,* 1759–1763.

Street. A. (2006). The role of singing within mother–infant interactions (Unpublished doctoral dissertation). University of Surrey, England.

Sundin, B. (1998). Musical creativity in the first six years. In B. Sundin, G. E. McPherson, & G. Folkestad (Eds.), *Children composing: Research in music education 1998* (Vol. 1, pp. 35–56). Lund, Sweden: Malmo Academy of Music, Lund University.

Suthers, L. (2004). Music experiences for toddlers in day care centres. *Australian Journal of Early Childhood, 29,* 45–50.

Swanwick, K., & Tillman, J. (1986). The sequence of musical development. *British Journal of Music Education, 3*(3), 305–339.

Swanwick, K. (2001). 2001 Conference keynote: Musical development theories revisited. *Music Education Research, 3*(2), 227–242.

Tafuri, J. (2008). *Infant musicality: New research for educators and parents* (SEMPRE Studies in the Psychology of Music). Aldershot, England: Ashgate.

Tafuri, J., Ferrari, L., & Perri, M. (2009). The influence on music development of singing to infants with/without words. In A. R. Addessi & S. Young (Eds.), *Proceedings of the 4th Conference of the European Network of Music Educators and Researchers of Young Children* (pp. 421–422). Bologna, Italy: Bononia University Press.

Trainor, L. J., & Zatorre, R. J. (2009). The neurobiological basis of musical expectations. In S. Hallam, I. Cross, & M. Thaut (Eds.), *Oxford handbook of music psychology* (pp. 171–183). Oxford, England: Oxford University Press.

Trehub, S. E. (2004). Music in infancy. In J. Flohr (Ed.), Musical lives of young children (pp. 24–29). Englewood Cliffs, NJ: Prentice Hall.

Trehub, S. E. (2006). Infants as musical connoisseurs. In G. E. McPherson (Ed.), The child as musician (pp. 33–50). Oxford, England: Oxford University Press.

Trehub, S. E. (2009). Music lessons from infants. In S. Hallam, I. Cross, & M. Thaut (Eds.), Oxford handbook of music psychology (pp. 229–234). Oxford, England: Oxford University Press.

Trevarthen, C. (1977). Descriptive analyses of infant communication behaviour. In H. R. Schaffer (Ed.), Studies in mother–infant interaction: The Loch Lomond symposium (pp. 227–270). London: Academic Press.

Trevarthen, C. (2000). Musicality and the intrinsic motive pulse: Evidence from human psychobiology and infant communication [Special issue 1999–2000]. Musicae Scientiae, 155–215.

Trevarthen, C. (2002). Origins of musical identity: Evidence from infancy for musical social awareness. In R. MacDonald, D. J. Hargreaves, & D. Miell (Eds.), Musical identities (pp. 21–38). Oxford, England: Oxford University Press.

Trevarthen, C., & Malloch, S. (2002). Musicality and music before three: Human vitality and invention shared with pride. Zero to Three, 23(1), 10–18.

Turino, T. (2008). Music as social life: The politics of participation. Chicago, IL: University of Chicago Press.

Vestad, I. L. (2010). To play a soundtrack: How children use recorded music in their everyday lives. Music Education Research, 12(3), 243–255.

Welch, G. F. (1986). A developmental view of children's singing. British Journal of Music Education, 3(3), 295–303.

Welch, G. F. (1998). Early childhood musical development. Research Studies in Music Education, 11, 27–41.

Welch, G. F. (2006). Singing and vocal development. In G. McPherson (Ed.), The child as musician: A handbook of musical development (pp. 311–329). New York: Oxford University Press.

Welch, G. F., Sergeant, D. C., & White, P. (1996). The singing competences of five-year-old developing singers. Bulletin of the Council for Research in Music Education, 127, 155–162.

White, P., Sergeant, D. C., & Welch, G. F. (1996). Some observations on the singing development of five-year-olds. Early Child Development and Care, 118, 27–34.

Wood, E. (2010). Reconceptualizing the play–pedagogy relationship: From control to complexity. In L. Brooker & S. Edwards (Eds.), Engaging play (pp. 15–27). Maidenhead, England: Open University Press.

Woodward, S. C. (2007). Nation building—One child at a time: Early childhood music education in South Africa. Arts Education Policy Review, 109(2), 43–53.

Yennari, M. (2010). First attempts at singing of young deaf children using cochlear implants: The song they move, the song they feel, the song they share. Music Education Research, 12(3), 281–298.

Young, S. (2000a). Young children's spontaneous instrumental music-making in nursery settings (Unpublished doctoral dissertation). University of Surrey, England.

Young, S. (2000b). The interpersonal dimension: A potential source of creativity for young children? [Special issue: 1999–2000]. Musicae Scientiae, 165–179.

Young, S. (2002). Young children's spontaneous vocalisations in free-play: Observations of two- to three-year-olds in a day-care setting. Bulletin of the Council for Research in Music Education, 152, 43–53

Young, S. (2003a). Music with the under fours. London: Routledge Falmer Press.

Young, S. (2003b). Time-space structuring in spontaneous play on educational percussion instruments among three- and four-year-olds. British Journal of Music Education, 20(1), 45–59.

Young, S. (2003c). Giocando con le Canzoni [Playing with songs]. Musica Domani, 127, 10–15. Trimestrale di cultura e pedagogia musicale, Societa Italiana per l'Educazione Musicale [Quarterly culture and music pedagogy, Italian Society for Music Education]. Turin, Italy: Stampatre.

Young, S. (2005a). Musical communication between adults and young children. In D. Miell, R. MacDonald, & D. Hargreaves (Eds.), Musical communication (pp. 281–299). Oxford, England: Oxford University Press.

Young, S. (2005b). Changing tune: Reconceptualising music with the under-threes. International Journal of Early Years Education, 13(3), 289–303.

Young, S. (2006). Seen but not heard: Young children's improvised singing. Contemporary Issues in Early Childhood, 7(3), 270–280.

Young, S. (2007). Digital technologies, young children and music education practice. In K. Smithrim & R. Upitis (Eds.), Listen to their voices (pp. 330–343). Waterloo, ONT: Canadian Music Educators' Association.

Young, S. (2008a). Collaboration between three- and four-year-olds in self-initiated play with instruments. International Journal of Educational Research. 47(1), 3–10.

Young, S. (2008b). Lullaby light shows: Everyday musical experience among under-two-year-olds. International Journal of Music Education, 26(1), 33–46.

Young, S. (2008c). Music 3–5. London: RoutledgeFalmer.

Young, S. (2009). Young girls singing with karaoke at home. In A. R. Addessi & S. Young (Eds.), Proceedings of the 4th Conference of the European Network of Music Educators and Researchers of Young Children (pp. 343–352). Bologna, Italy: Bononia University Press.

Young, S. (2011). Children's creativity with time, space and intensity: Foundations for the temporal arts. In D. Faulkner & E. Coates (Eds.), Exploring children's creative narratives (pp. 177–199). Abingdon, England: Routledge.

Young, S., & Gillen, J. (2010). Musicality. In J. Gillen & C. A. Cameron (Eds.), International perspectives on early childhood research: A day in the life (pp. 27–36). Basingstoke, England: Palgrave Macmillan.

Young, S., Pérez, J., Andango, E., Gluschankof, C., Holgersen, S-E., Ilari, B., ... Retra, J. (2010). MyPlace, MyMusic: An international study of musical experiences in the home among seven-year-olds. In B. Ilari (Ed.), Proceedings of the International Society of Music Education, Commission for Early Childhood Music Education (ECME) 14th ECME Seminar (pp. 61–65). Beijing Normal University Beijing, China.

Young, S., & Street, A. (2006). Music one to one: Final report. Retrieved from http://education.exeter.ac.uk/music-one2one/downloads.php

Young, S., & Street, A. (2009). Time to play: Developing interculturally sensitive approaches to music in children's centres serving predominantly Muslim communities. In A. R. Addessi & S. Young (Eds.), Proceedings of the 4th Conference of the European Network of Music Educators and Researchers of Young Children (pp. 61–70). Bologna, Italy: Bononia University Press.

18

Play in Early Childhood Education

James E. Johnson, Serap Sevimli-Celik, and Monirah Al-Mansour
The Pennsylvania State University

The Nature of Play

Play in early childhood education (ECE) is a very broad topic that continues to generate much discussion and debate. Slogans such as "play is the business of childhood" or "play is the child's way of learning" are still heard but they are becoming less convincing. Voicing slogans such as these often encourages those who are opposed to play in education to dismiss it on the grounds that the idea seems too broad and vague to be a valid and useful basis for teaching and learning. It doesn't help when ECE programs claiming to be play-centered lack a thoughtful rationale for their play policies and practices or when low-level, unchallenging activities called "play" abound in their indoor and outdoor environments. This threatens the place of play in the ECE by inviting misguided attacks on it and by encouraging educators to devalue play's importance as a context and medium for development during the early years (Zigler & Bishop-Josef, 2004).

Even though play in the history of ECE has been viewed favorably as a cornerstone of learning (e.g., Froebel, 1887/1896; Pestalozzi, 1894/1915; Piaget, 1970; Vygotsky, 1978), there have always been its critics who advocate for more structured and direct instruction. Recently, however, the debate has intensified in an educational context strongly influenced by early learning standards and assessment of academic attainments (Christie & Roskos, 2007). Greater concern exists that play in ECE is slipping away and that a vigorous response is now needed to protect its important role (Miller & Almon, 2009). Three ways to make such response are to employ contemporary scholarship to better explain: (a) the nature of play, (b) the importance of play, and (c) play pedagogy.

The Nature of Play

Various attempts have been made over the years to understand play and its role in ECE, and these have assumed great importance in efforts to improve play's status in the field and in the public eye. For example, DeVries (2001)

recommended that much of what children do in ECE classrooms should be called "work activities," which would include construction, exploring, investigating, problem-solving, and experimenting. Pretending and group games remain play forms. She recommended that teachers include in the curriculum high quality, intellectually challenging projects that stimulate social, emotional, moral, and intellectual development. Also for Elkind (2001), play is not the same as work in ECE. The confusion concerning play and work to some degree may be attributed to Maria Montessori (1912/1964, p. 53), who said that play is the child's work. Play is not work, nor is it the opposite of work.

Elkind sought to correct this misunderstanding by advancing the Piagetian view that play and work are complementary, two poles of an adaption process which requires both assimilation (play) and accommodation (work). Exploration and imitation, including exploratory play and imitative play, are more accommodative or stimulus-oriented. Play is more response-oriented, where personal meaning is more important than adjusting to external realty. Typically, a child's behaviors can be described as a mixture or a sequencing of "work" and "play," but the two states should not be lumped together or viewed as opposites. Play and work function together in serving the child in adapting to and learning from experiences. ECE activities for children have structure with degrees of play and work. Hardly ever would one label something that a child does as pure work or pure play.

Since ECE is concerned with the development of young children, a question to answer is how play can be a positive influence. To answer this question demands that play be appreciated as a complex and highly differentiated phenomenon. With its definition problematic, teachers and researchers often have used an additive model in which the following criteria are considered when judging whether play is occurring: (a) nonliterality, (b) positive affect, (c) process over product orientation, (d) intrinsic motivation, and (e) free choice. Applying these can help distinguish play from work,

265

routines, rituals, and play-related behaviors like exploration and imitation (Johnson, Christie, & Wardle, 2005).

Analysis of play is made on the basis of what is known about contexts, children's actions, and their inferred mental states. A useful distinction to make is between play frame or context (surrounding the play episode) and play script or text (within the play episode). The ECE teacher or researcher can keep separate metaplay negotiations or play disruptions (e.g., teacher intrusions or children's conflicts) which snap the play frame, from enactments occurring during play episodes. Observing and understanding play requires recognizing its multilayered qualities and synthesizing information about person, object, space, time, and situational factors.

Play enactments can be coded with respect to levels or forms exhibited. Many systems have been used in research and teaching. Prominent exemplars include Parten (1932) for level of social participation during play (e.g., solitary, parallel, associative, cooperative, onlooker, unoccupied); and for cognitive forms of play there are Piaget's (1962) sensorimotor, symbolic, and games with rules and Smilansky's (1968) functional, constructive, dramatic, and sociodramatic play. Cross-walking level of social play and type of cognitive play is common, having been first introduced by Rubin, Maioni, and Hornung (1976). In addition to classification, play behaviors of young children can be evaluated. As an early example, Smilansky (1968) used two criteria for crediting more mature sociodramatic play in relation to dramatic play: social interaction and verbal communication. Both dramatic play and sociodramatic play included role-play with respect to self and others, object and situation transformations, and persistence (at least 10 minutes). More recently, Bodrova (2008) discussed evaluating mature versus immature play using criteria such as: (a) ability to sustain a specific role by consistently engaging in actions, speech, and interactions that fit the character enacted; (b) ability to use substitute or pretend objects; (c) ability to follow rules associated with the make-believe scenario; and (d) ability to integrate many themes and ideas and sustain play over time spans of several days or weeks. Immature play is repetitive, dependent on concrete props, lacking in role enactment, including the presence of peer conflicts, not following implicit or explicit play rules, and simple or unelaborated content in play episodes of short duration. Schemes are used to score levels of other specific play forms, such as constructive block play (Forman, 1982).

Play evaluation is needed to gauge what children are doing so that teachers can then guide them toward more mature, developmentally enriching play. Descriptions of play need to retain action sequences and contextual information. Deliberate attention must be paid to children's goals, means for reaching them, and their understanding. With careful observations of play the teacher is better prepared for deciding on appropriate interventions (Johnson et al., 2005; Van Hoorn, Nourot, Scales, & Alward, 2010).

Importance of Play

The significance of play in ECE is recognized internationally and testimonies to its place in young children's development and well-being are based on considerable theoretical and empirical evidence as well as teacher lore and ideology (e.g., Dockett & Fleer, 1999; Johnson et al., 2005; Pellegrini, 2009; Wood & Attfield, 2005). Teachers' and parents' funds of knowledge about play and their skill in performing various adult roles to foster mature play are important factors in efforts to promote school readiness and continued learning in young children through providing them with effective play-based ECE curriculum and instruction. Teacher and parent beliefs about play and its importance have been studied over the years (e.g., Bennett, Wood, & Rogers, 1997; Fisher, Hirsh-Pasek, Golinkoff, & Gryfe, 2008; Kemple, 1996).

According to the neo-Vygotskian cultural-historical approach, as represented by Leont'ev (1981), pretend play is the "leading activity" in child development during the first five years (the most important activity psychologically but not the most common), but schoolwork is the leading activity for 5- to 10-year-old children (middle childhood). Hence, play and play pedagogy for the two age groups are similar but also fit differently into the child's development and learning over the range of years of ECE (birth to 8 years old). Contemporary research supports the importance of play during the early years in numerous areas of growth and development including: (a) self-regulation, social competence, and early academics; (b) physical well-being and fitness; and (c) problem-solving and creativity.

Self-Regulation, Social Competence, and Early Academics

Self-regulation is an executive function process of exercising control over one's emotions, cognitions, impulses, and actions. Mature play entails self-regulation in that it is purposeful and requires inhibition of inappropriate responses, the regulation of attention, and working memory in the service of organizing, sequencing, switching, and planning behaviors. Another component of self-regulation is theory of mind (e.g., perspective taking, emotional understanding). Vygotsky (1978) argues that play can help develop self-regulation when children create an imaginary situation, take on and act out roles, and follow rules implicit in the play scenario. Although mature role play has received a great deal of attention as a means of developing self-regulation (Bodrova, 2008), other play forms including games, constructive play, and physical play share this potential (Bodrova & Leong, 2007; Riley, San Juan, Klinkner, & Ramminger, 2008). Both social competence and early learning of academic content hinge upon the ability to be focused and maintain self-control, which themselves are strengthened by mature play.

Active experiencing found in good play stimulates the

maturation of executive function occurring in the prefrontal cortex of the brain (Diamond, Barnett, Thomas, & Munro, 2007). Play can foster a sense of control and self-regulation of one's own learning. During play children set their own challenges and determine their own attention and plans. These cognitive mechanisms can contribute to effortful, intentional use of imagination, creativity, and problem solving. Children create their own zone of proximal development and are self-scaffolded in play; during play children transcend the concrete here and now and use abstract thought and build symbolic competence (Vygotsky, 1978). Recent research has documented relations among play, self-regulation, and executive function in young children.

For example, Whitebread (2010) found that self-regulatory skills could be facilitated in 3- to 5-year old children through a variety of playful activities designed by 32 teachers in England. These activities included constructing a model, dressing a doll, and playing board and card games, either with peers or adults. Behaviors were rated as higher in metacognitive or self-regulatory quality when they happened in a social context characterized by extensive collaboration and talk. Analysis of 582 play episodes showed that adult questioning had a slight positive impact on what children could say about their own learning, but this greatly depressed children's self-regulation and motivation. Supporting play in educational settings to achieve self-regulation requires a mix of adult emotional support, children's initiation and feelings of control, cognitive challenges in the play activities, and private speech and collaborative talk to bring about learning and metacognitive awareness. In an important study, Diamond et al. (2007) tested 147 prekindergarteners in state funded programs and found that the Tools of the Mind curriculum, based on 40 activities that promoted executive functioning (including mature dramatic play), led to improved cognitive control at the end of the second year of the program on the Dots and Flanker tasks, Stroop-type measures of executive function (see Diamond et al., 2007 for task descriptions).

Social competence includes ability and willingness to engage in socially responsible behavior as well as in positive social play with peers. Both involve emotional regulation and perspective taking. Elias and Berk (2002) found that middle class 3- and 4-year-olds who engaged in more mature sociodramatic play were more cooperative during circle and clean-up times than were children with lower scores on the play measures, controlling for verbal ability and initial self-control scores. High impulse children as scored at the beginning of the school year, who engaged in complex sociodramatic play, improved the most in clean-up performance over the course of the year.

Peer interactions in open-ended play also benefit social skill learning, cooperation, and building confidence in dealing with other children. Broadhead, Howard, and Wood (2010) reported that when play is thematically driven by young children and they are able to follow their own in-

terests and plans there is more cooperation, rich language use, problem-solving, and reciprocity. Her Social Play Continuum tool is used by teachers and researchers to quantify but also locate and reflect upon peer play in the associative, social, highly social, and cooperative domains. Broadhead et al. also employed teacher-initiated and teacher-directed activities where children are shown that their play is valued. For example, if less mature social play is performed by older children, the teacher would wait until after the play is finished before engaging in discussions with them about it. This collaborative approach to play observation, intervention, and reflection aims to help teachers create a more harmonious classroom atmosphere where quality play can flourish. This sensitive child-centered approach to social play and building and respecting classroom community is similar to Rogers and Evans (2008) who used child focus groups to capture an insider's view of role-play. Child initiated and adult guided play aims to build self-regulation and social-emotional competence; mature play which is related to these two important attributes is viewed as a means to prepare children for academic achievement.

Play that strengthens self-regulation and increases social competence in young children helps them in attaining school readiness and subsequent classroom success. Play of this kind is important because it makes it more likely that children with this play background will be able to demonstrate social and emotional skills necessary for performing the student role. Taking turns, following directions, and other basics of school life depend on having these general skills. Play also is valuable during the preschool years for its benefits to emerging literacy and numeracy, and helping children do well in these high intensity academic areas (Hirsh-Pasek, Golinkoff, Berk, & Singer, 2009).

Research over past decades supports the importance of mature play for language and early learning (Christie, 2010; Roskos & Christie, 2004). Literacy rests on language and representational or symbolic competence in general. Play benefits these foundations as well as early literacy in the areas of alphabet knowledge, concepts about print, oral language, and comprehension, and phonological awareness. Roskos and Christie (2004) reviewed considerable research on the topic and concluded that play promotes literacy because play uses language and symbols and aids in children's making connections between oral and written media. As an example from many studies that could be mentioned, Dickinson and Tabors (2001) followed 74 low-income family 3-year olds over several years, and reported significant associations between children's talk during play and their later literacy scores. Note also that the play pedagogy techniques described later in this chapter, such as Paley's narrative approach, attest to and capitalize on the close affinity among play, stories, and literacy.

The play–math connection is a second critical area that has caught researchers' attention in recent years. Young children encounter many opportunities to acquire knowledge and develop math skills in their everyday activities, including their play. Ginsburg (2006) noted the potential for reading and book use to help children learn about perspectives, angles, covariation (e.g., the Three Bears and their bed sizes corresponding to their body sizes), numbers, and so forth. Block play invites considerable opportunities to develop spatial knowledge; play with small objects encourages counting, patterning, and grouping. Ginsberg's Everyday Math curriculum is developmentally appropriate with use of materials and physical actions, and balances play with more direct instruction. When teaching is not play per se, it can at least be playful.

Numerous other studies indicate support for the relation of play with emerging spatial and quantitative concepts in young children. Again, spontaneous child initiated play and adult guided play are shown to be valuable. Ness and Farenga (2007) cover a broad range of topics concerned with spatial concepts, including architecture. Gelman (2006) showed the motivating power of play; children learn and use math skills when they are embedded in a game more than when they are not. Ramani and Siegler (2008) showed that a relatively brief intervention with at risk preschoolers using the game "Chutes & Ladders" promoted their number line estimation ability, knowing the numerals, counting, and quantity. Worthington (2010) reported that during play young children invent math symbols and develop their imaginations and mathematical graphics, such as gestures to stand for the "take away" sign.

Physical Well-Being and Fitness

Play is an essential part of physical development and it helps to develop active and healthy bodies especially important in fighting against the obesity epidemic. According to a report from the Centers for Disease Control (CDC, 2009), obesity prevalence among low-income, preschool children has increased gradually from 12.4% in 1998 to 14.5% in 2003 and to 14.6% in 2008. In a longitudinal study, Taylor et al. (2009) described patterns of physical activity and inactivity of 3-, 4-, and 5-year-old children. They reported an increase in screen time and a decrease in physical activity, especially for 4- and 5-year-olds. Another recent study investigated physical activity of young children and playtime practices and policies in 96 childcare centers in North Carolina. The results of the study showed that few best practice guidelines were followed by a majority of the participating centers. Only 13.7% of childcare centers in North Carolina offered 120 minutes of active playtime during the school day (McWilliams et al., 2009).

Through play and exploration of the environment, children practice physical skills such as running, jumping, hopping, skipping, and galloping. By exploring and experimenting with the movement capabilities of their bodies, young children start to be aware of their personal spaces in relation to other persons' spaces; and children begin to gain more control over their bodies (Gallahue & Ozmun,

1998). Activities such as pulling, pushing, swinging, and hanging help children to develop their upper bodies; and their lower bodies develop through jumping, skipping, galloping, and hopping. These fundamental movement skills also improve children's body awareness (Sanders, 2002). Moreover, they have to be mastered before learning more complex specialized skills necessary for play relating to games, sports, and dance activities (Gallahue & Ozmun, 1998). For example, earlier appearing play that involves throwing and catching will contribute to later passing and shooting skills in basketball. Therefore, children exhibiting physical skills at an early age are more likely in the future to be active and participate in sports (Cliff, Okely, & McKeen, 2009).

Outdoor Play

The benefits of outdoor play on children's physical, cognitive, and social-emotional development is well known. Children who spend their time outdoors show superior gross motor skills, longer spans of concentration, and better language and collaborative skills (Fjortoft, 2001). According to Clements (2004), outdoor play helps children to develop a sense of community while enjoying sensory experiences with dirt, water, sand, and mud. Similarly, Rivkin (1995) highlighted the value of playing outdoors. She noted that when playing outdoors children experience "sensory qualities of the world" and can also experiment with "big behaviors" such as shouting, running, climbing, and jumping. Being outdoors also improves children's attention levels. For instances, Martensson et al. (2009) investigated the restorative potential of green outdoor environments for children in preschool settings. Results showed that having available areas surrounded with large trees, bushes, and hilly landscapes, reduced children's inattention. Besides nature, landscaping elements can add value to children's outdoor play. Greening the school grounds makes children more active and increases their play repertoires; green school grounds invite children to jump, climb, dig, and lift (Dyment & Bell, 2007).

Allowing for a variety of physical actions during outdoor play is important for promoting preschoolers' participation in moderate to vigorous physical activities. In their current research, Aarts, Wendel, Oers, Goor, and Schuit (2010) defined outdoor play as a "cheap and natural way for children to be physically active." They investigated the environmental determinants of outdoor play in children. Their results showed that to be physically active children needed adequate space, diverse play opportunities, and interaction with natural elements on the school grounds. They also found that children were more active when rules, policies, and supervision allowed for noncompetitive, open-ended play, and when opportunities were present to care for the garden and other green spaces (Aarts et al., 2010).

Creative Expression

Friedrich Froebel (1887/1896) emphasized play and its use of gifts (play materials) and occupations (activities). He believed that humans are essentially productive and creative, and that fulfillment comes through developing these elements in harmony with God and the world. As a result, Froebel sought to encourage the creation of educational environments that involved practical work and the direct use of materials. Through engaging with the world, understanding unfolds, hence the significance of play understood as a creative activity through which children become aware of their place in the world. Piaget (1962) and Vygotsky (1978) also viewed children as active explorers of their world. Play is therefore an important part of the process of constructing knowledge. It enables children to control what happens, and to use what they already know to further their understanding and development (Olsen & Sumsion, 2000).

Children learn best in an environment that permits discovery, curiosity, exploration, imagination, and play. Play is closely attached to the child's physical, social, emotional, and cognitive growth (Mayesky, 2009). Research suggests that children in their pretend play perform transformational operations that may be linked with creative thought (Mellou, 1995). The use of imagination in pretend play is a form of creativity according to several authors (Russ, 1993; Russ, Robins, & Christiano, 1999; Singer & Singer, 1990). In addition, constructive play is creative in that it can be open-ended play with multiple outcomes. Play expression varies and is more likely to approach being creative when conditions for it are free, spontaneous, and unstructured with many possible outcomes. Such play encourages creative thinking and sparks imagination (Ackermann, Gauntlrtt, & Weckstrom, 2009).

However, such an outcome is not automatic. Celebi-Oncu and Unluer (2010) examined creativity in children's play and use of play materials. Results showed that most of the children were not able to express creativity with different kinds of play materials; in their play children greatly preferred to use toys as play materials. In a second study Celebi-Oncu and Unluer (2010) found that most of the children were not able to use real objects creatively as play materials. Teachers have to encourage their students to play freely with different unstructured materials in different areas and situations. Play enables children to generate a range of creative behaviors in a low cost manner, especially after they have sampled the environment surrounding them; a range of creative behaviors that might be adaptive to their specific function (Pellegrini, Dupuis, & Smith, 2006).

Encouraging reusable, discarded, and open-ended materials brings the old-fashioned play back on track, which actually helps foster creativity with its components, such as playfulness, humor, curiosity, flexibility, and originality. It is fun without a set of specific goals or predetermined outcomes. As Almon (2003) exclaimed, working with open-ended materials is particularly effective as children attempt to solve problems. Open-ended materials encourage creative and divergent thinking. There is no right or wrong way to use these materials. Children can take risks and develop confidence. Each time they use these materials, they are creating something new.

Creative play does not require expensive and fancy materials to flourish. Research suggests that even in the poorest country in the world, children were capable of playing creatively despite their poverty. A study by Berinstein and Magalhaes (2009) aimed to gain an understanding of the essence of play experience for children in Zanzibar, the poorest country in the world. They found that play experience in Zanzibar had aspects of creativity and resourcefulness. What does this finding tell Western countries? Should this be an opportunity for rethinking play? Children are born with creative potential. They observe the world and react to it using their imagination. Simple material play can prop up their imagination and enhance their creative play from within. A great example of using reusable, discarded, and open-ended materials is REMIDA the creative recycling center in Reggio Emilia, Italy. Here discarded materials become resources and here unsold or rejected stock from shops is collected so that they can be reused for a different purpose. REMIDA is where you can make the most of waste materials, using them to create a new product that shows respect for the environment (Ferrari, 2005). When we consider the global economy today, REMIDA is a great way to foster creativity at a cost of next to nothing.

Reggio teaches that the best environment encourages a layered web of relationships to develop and grow (Cadwell, 1997). This web includes relations with things. Cobb (1998) states that "in childhood, the cognitive process is essentially poetic … it is a sensory integration of self and environment" (p. 89). Cobb emphasizes that children need to develop a relationship with materials from nature and those that are man-made, to shape small worlds of their own, and to enrich their imaginations.

In sum, a great deal of research supports the value of play for learning and development across different domains during the early years. An important challenge in ECE curriculum and instruction is to create appropriate and effective ways to harness play's potential in the design of programs and activities.

Play Pedagogy

Whether philosophically "at the center" or included peripherally in the curriculum (e.g., play opportunities in interest centers), play remains a common feature in programs for preschool children. The curricula of these programs vary a great deal and often are not a model curriculum such as HighScope, but are locally or regionally created ones. Policymakers responsible for these ECE programs often cite school readiness, meeting academic standards, and parent pressure as their reasons for reducing time for play, and play advocates have countered with information campaigns that are aimed to restore play in ECE programs. One way that play advocates have tried to do this is by making clear that ECE programs aim for mature and educational play, and not immature play. Implementation of specific play pedagogical techniques in ECE programs is another way, where play pedagogy refers to using methods to stimulate, monitor, and evaluate educational play in young children in ECE (Welen, 2005; Wood & Attfield, 2005).

The play and literacy movement is a prominent response to the negative trend of replacing play with teacher-led structured learning activities (Christie & Roskos, 2007). This movement seeks a blended curriculum in which more structured learning sessions (e.g., alphabet knowledge and letter sounds) are combined with related play sessions. These related activities for mature play typically include language and literacy-enhanced play props, such as phones and phone books, and pads and pencils for pretend writing which often involves invented spelling—an expression of phonemic awareness. Inscriptions, logos, signs, and other forms of environmental print are present that are thematically related to topics being taught or introduced elsewhere in the curriculum. For example, pretend play about a car repair garage would be linked to a storybook and art/drawing experiences about a mechanics shop, and even to drill and practice activities for learning vocabulary and basic concepts about machines, tools, and repair.

There is a continuum of play-literacy strategies that can be used. These range from low structure curriculum networking of play activities to content areas such as math and language and literacy for classrooms, to moderate structure such as play planning for small groups, to high structure child tutorials represented by the say-tell-do play vocabulary intervention of Burstein and Otto (Christie, 2010). Tiered activities and individualized teaching using play techniques are recommended in order to meet the needs and interests of all children.

An important issue is degree and type of adult involvement needed for quality child-governed play to occur (Johnson et al., 2005; Van Hoorn et al., 2010). Another issue, noted by Ugaste (2007), is the need to use and enrich actual experiences the children have had in the play so that the play contains a "personal" idea that is affect laden and motivating for the children. Play assistance in ECE, then, is much more than simply the teachers playing with the children or observing them play. An integrated approach is needed that combines: (a) providing children with real world experiences to set up motivation, a personal idea for play (a particular interest a child has), and knowledge about what is being played; (b) preparing the play environment with various props and materials; and (c) the teacher's role in scaffolding the play (Novosyolova et al., 1989). Methods teachers employ using the integrated approach include imaginative, sociodramatic, and thematic-fantasy play training procedures (e.g., Saltz & Johnson, 1974; Singer, 1973; and Smilanski, 1968), as well as other techniques related to learning and play that can serve classroom teachers.

One example is Vivian Paley's narrative approach mentioned earlier in this chapter. This method is becoming increasingly influential in ECE (McNamee, 2005; Wiltz & Fein, 1996). Paley's story-telling/story-acting methods are designed to generate social, multimodal literacy through play. Her techniques focus attention on promoting children's literacy-making behaviors that support the development of a classroom narrative culture (Groth & Darling, 2001; Nicolopoulou, 2002). Nicolopoulou, McDowell, and Brockmeyer (2006) have extended this method to include journal writing (scribbling to pictorial depictions to pseudo-writing using invented spelling) agreeing with Paley that fantasy play is the social glue that holds all the curricular components together and builds community.

A second example is Playworld developed in Finland by Lundqvist (1995) and currently used and researched by Hakkarainen (2007). Children and adults co-create a fantasy world based on fables and folk tales and children's literature. For an extended period of time, part of the classroom is turned into an imaginary world with teachers and children role-playing characters and commentators. Teachers scaffold the children in their creative behaviors and lead them from free play to more organized school activities involving academic subjects (Baumer, Ferholt, & Lecusay, 2005; Rainio, 2005). A related technique was used by Tyrrell (2001) in her first grade classroom in England. She successfully used fantasy figures to develop literacy in her students, sustaining over the entire school year an imaginative classroom environment in which literacy learning flourished and children's imaginations were extended and enriched.

A third example, workshop pedagogy developed by Arne Trageton, has been used in Norway for over 25 years and is used in many other countries (Trageton, 1994). Children in small groups work and play with concrete art and craft materials such as blocks, flexible materials, paper, clay, and rigid materials; their activities center around a common theme such as "our village." In social constructive play children make two- and three-dimensional representations of aspects of the theme, such as people, cars, shops, and houses. Children then dramatize what might happen in their constructed thematic environment. Next, based on the experiences the children have had so far doing the workshop activities, they are asked to make up a story related to their special theme about which they write narratives or draw pictures depending on their ability. Finally, the teacher can guide the group to do math around what they have made in the earlier stages of the workshop pedagogy that entailed work with concrete materials or based on their story narratives or play enactments. The teacher is a discussion facilitator during all the phases of the workshop pedagogy.

Trageton (2002) has advocated the use of computers so that children can publish books, classroom newspapers, and magazines in a collaborative manner, doing their reading and writing as purposeful pursuits assisted by technology. He has also had children with parents and teachers build hut villages on the school's outdoor playgrounds for socio-dramatic play to stimulate ideas for creative writing on the computers (Trageton, 2007).

A fourth example of play pedagogy from the United States is improvisational play intervention. With this procedure for educational play teachers and children create a playful and imaginative world together without employing pre-scripted material as is the case in Playworld (Lobman, 2003, 2006; Lobman & Lundquist, 2007). Lobman explored the use of improvisation as a cultural art form that can be used in the ECE classroom to enhance responsive teaching and teacher–child relations. In this method teacher–child interactions are viewed as an ensemble where teachers pick up on children's cues and find ways to encourage children, enhancing and extending their play activity, following principles of improvisation such as "Don't negate" and using "Yes and…" (see Lobman, 2003, 2006; Lobman & Lundquist, 2007). Mutual responsiveness and choice-making support and scaffold children, leading them to more successful play scenes and episodes from scratch so to speak because teachers are spontaneously using whatever materials are available at the time in the particular situation. Teachers are urged to create classroom environments and to allow for enough time to support spontaneous child–child narrative activity, but to be skillful partners themselves when they are needed to help children during improvisational play. This technique helps teachers learn how to play better with children. This is a worthy goal in itself, one often neglected in teacher education. More than just respecting and working with the play of children, teachers themselves, like all adults, should be playful (Csikszentmihalyi, 1990; Kerr & Apter, 1991; Lieberman, 1977; Terr, 1999). Improvisational play, like the Paley method, rests on a social and multiple symbol system view of literacy (Bearne, 2003).

Teachers are successful using play pedagogy when they know their children very well and have good relations with them, and have mastered play-based assessment and communication techniques.

Implications for ECE

In programs seeking to use play for learning, teachers intervene when immature play persists. Some children need a teacher to model or coach them if they are to learn how to engage in mature play. Hence, teacher education programs need to help teachers learn how to perform play facilitation strategies to improve children's play. No longer is it enough for an ECE teacher to simply respect playfulness in young children; they must also be playful themselves and master play facilitation techniques. Practice and exercises in remembering one's own past play can help teachers stay in touch with the child inside them. Teachers need to perform well all the various teacher play roles, such as stage manager, negotiator, scribe, coplayer, play tutor, play assessor, and communicator (Jones & Reynolds, 1992). Equally

important is for teachers to be able to judge when it is not necessary to intervene (Johnson et al., 2005).

An important issue is whether language learners or special needs children should have the same play opportunities as other children in an ECE program. Often children who are learning a language, who have underdeveloped skills and abilities, or who have special needs, are provided with more direction and structure than are other children. Consequently, they have less opportunity to play. Disparities in play opportunities like this should be kept to a minimum because all children need to play.

Immature play sometimes fulfills important affective or cognitive needs, such as catharsis or consolidation. While idiosyncratic, such play may be a child's response to a developmental or situational challenge. Patience and judgment on the part of the teacher is required. Although certainly social-emotional readiness (e.g., self-regulation) validates encouragement of mature play, less mature play at times should be accepted on the basis of its developmental clinical value. Teachers need to be prepared to be flexible when judging play and know how to respond appropriately to each specific situation.

Imagination and creativity are valued correlates or functions of play. In our concern with academic standards and school readiness we must not forget the importance of these budding traits in early childhood. While play is typically seen as a means to other ends, it should be valued as an end in itself. Going further, we can ask how literacy and early math and other learning activities can serve as a means to promote playfulness, imagination and creativity in children, including their skill in art, dance, and movement.

In addition, play also helps children develop resiliency and coping skills and can be an outlet for thinking about imagined futures and for spiritual growth. Play and child friendly programs such as Waldorf and Reggio should be kept in mind so that we remember the importance of play for imagination and spirituality, the creative impulse, and the "100 languages of childhood" (Edwards, Gandini, & Forman, 1993).

Stories and play are interwoven. The work of the late Greta Fein demonstrated the importance of seeing play as stories acted out, and how stories and play are important to who a child is, and is becoming, and who a child is in relation to a community of learners in an ECE setting (Goncu & Klein, 2001). Vivian Paley's books, and the narrative curriculum her work has spawned (Wiltz & Fein, 1996), extend and reinforce this perspective. Paley developed the story-telling/drama process. Young children are encouraged to go to the story table to tell the teacher an original story that the teacher writes down word for word echoing the story back to the child. Other children can listen and add to each other's stories. Afterwards during large-group time children take turns enacting together the different stories. The teacher reads the stories, picks children to be the characters, asks children if they remember their lines, and reminds them as needed. After the end of the story-acting the young thespians join hands and bow and the audience claps. A sense of community is thus created that involves children's shared thoughts and intimate feelings.

Group goals, then, not just individual child goals, should be part of the rationale for play (and stories) in the ECE programs, certainly ones serving heterogeneous groups of young children. Teachers must know different ways to do this. Extended time frames and the use of open-ended materials, such as blocks for complex constructive play, enables social commerce between minority and majority group children, even children who do not know each other's languages (Ong, 2005). Bringing children together and having them also share stories and play enactments promotes education that is multicultural and inclusive. Paley's narrative curriculum gives children voices, and a chance to relate to each other's lives outside the walls of the school; this can be a wonderful medium of expression, kindness, and sharing—crucial to schooling and development of the mind and the human spirit (McNamee, 2005).

What are our desired goals for children in ECE? School readiness is one important answer. Our answer must also include active learning, creativity, and physical and social competence. We want our children to be vibrant, to show vitality and exuberance. The doorways of play in the ECE curriculum lead to varied journeys in the world, as children construct their intrapsychic, interpersonal, physical realities. Play can foster imaginations, creativity, and problem-solving abilities to meet the challenges of an unknown future. And play which nourishes the deepest socioemotional needs can heal and fortify spiritually. Teachers need to appreciate the full array of play's potential value and provide for many possibilities.

Teacher education must cultivate the minds of new ECE practitioners so that their theories of practice will develop and be complex to match the realities they will face. These theories, for instance, will need to appreciate various play nuances, such as the value of mature play but also immature play. They will need to realize the need for curricular flexibility, or the blending of academic and play-based methods as seen in the U.S. play and literacy movement, to meet the needs and interests of children in a more comprehensive fashion. Moreover, both individual and group needs, of children and families, must be addressed.

Of the many topics concerning play and early education that deserve further study, especially recommended is to try to learn more about how variations in preservice and in-service instructional delivery and experiences differentially impact teachers' theoretical understanding, research knowledge, and procedural skills with respect to play and learning in young children. Future research can perhaps shed light on individual variability among teachers in their play understanding and practices, and how they acquire and develop expertise in this important area of early childhood education. Not only can such an agenda help inform teacher education and professional development opportunities, this program of research can eventually lead to better classrooms and play experiences for children.

References

Aarts, M. J., Wendel, V. W., Oers, H., Goor, I., & Schuit, A. J. (2010). Environmental determinants of outdoor play in children: A large-scale cross-sectional study. *American Journal of Preventive Medicine, 3,* 212–219.

Ackermann, E., Gauntlrtt, D., & Weckstrom, C. (2009). Defining systematic creativity: Explaining the nature of creativity and how the LEGO system of play relates to it. LEGO Group.

Almon, J. (2003). The vital role of play in early childhood education. In S. Olfman (Ed.), *All work and no play: How educational reforms are harming our preschoolers* (pp. 17–42). Westport, CT: Praeger.

Baumer, S., Ferholt, B., & Lecusay, R. (2005) Promoting narrative competence through adult–child joint pretense: Lessons from the Scandinavian educational practice of Playworld. *Cognitive Psychology, 20,* 576–590.

Bearne, E. (2003). Rethinking literacy: Communication, representation and text. *Reading literacy and language, 37*(3), 98–103.

Bennett, N., Wood, E., & Rogers, S. (1997). *Teaching through play: Reception teachers' theories and practice.* Buckingham, England: Open University Press.

Berinstein, S., & Magalhaes, L. (2009). *A study of the essence of play experience to children living in Zanzibar, Tanzania.* Retrieved from www.interscience.wiley.com

Bodrova, E. (2008). Make-believe play versus academic skills: A Vygotskian approach to today's dilemma of early childhood education. *European Early Childhood Education Research Journal, 16*(3), 357–369.

Bodrova, E., & Leong, D. (2007). *Tools of the mind* (2nd ed.). Upper Saddle River, NJ: Merrill/Pearson.

Broadhead, P., Howard, J., & Wood, E. (2010). *Play and learning in the early years.* Los Angeles, CA: Sage.

Cadwell, L. B. (1997). *Bringing Reggio Emilia home.* New York: Teachers College Press.

Celebi-Oncu, E., & Unluer, E. (2010). Preschool children's using of play materials creatively. *Procedia Social and Behavioral Sciences, 2,* 4457–4461. Retrieved from www.sciencedirect.com

Centers for Disease Control. (2009). Obesity prevalence among low-income, preschool-aged children—United States. *Morbidity and Mortality Weekly Report, 58,* 769–773.

Christie, J. (2010). *Integrating dramatic play into skills-based early literacy programs.* Paper presented at a meeting of the International Council for Children's Play, Lisbon, Portugal.

Christie, J., & Roskos, C. (2007). Play in an era of early childhood standards. In T. Jambor & J. Gils (Eds.), *Several perspectives on children's play: Scientific reflections for practitioners* (pp. 133–145). Philadelphia, PA: Garant.

Clements, R. (2004). An investigation of the status of outdoor play. *Contemporary Issues in Early Childhood, 5,* 68–80.

Cliff, D. P., Okely, A. D., & McKeen, K. (2009). Relationships between fundamental movement skills and objectively measured physical activity in preschool children. *Paediatric Exercise Science, 21,* 436–449

Cobb, E. (1998). *The ecology of imagination in childhood.* Putnam, CT: Spring.

Csikszentmihalyi, M. (1990). *Flow: The psychology of optimal experience.* New York: Harper & Row.

DeVries, R. (2001). Transforming the "play-oriented curriculum" and work in constructivist early education. In A. Goncu & E. Klein (Eds.), *Children in play, story, and school* (pp. 72–106). New York: Guilford.

Diamond, A., Barnett, S., Thomas, J., & Munro, S. (2007). Executive function can be improved in preschoolers by regular classroom teachers. *Science, 318,* 1387–1388.

Dickinson, D., & Tabors, P. (Eds.). (2001). *Beginning literacy with language: Young children learning at home and school.* Baltimore, MD: Brookes.

Dockett, S., & Fleer, M. (1999) *Play and pedagogy in early childhood: Bending the rules.* Brisbane, Australia: Harcourt Brace.

Dyment, J. E., & Bell, A. C. (2007). Grounds for movement: Green school grounds as sites for promoting physical activity. *Health Education Research, 23*, 952–962.

Edwards, C., Gandini, L., & Forman, G. (Eds.). (1993). *The one hundred languages of children: The Reggio Emilia approach to early childhood education.* Norwood, NJ: Ablex.

Elias, C. & Berk, L. (2002). Self-regulation in young children: Is there a role for sociodramatic play? *Early Childhood Research Quarterly, 17*, 216–238.

Elkind, D. (2001). The adaptive function of work and play. *Play, Policy, and Practice Connections, 6*, 6–7.

Ferrari, E. G. (2005). *Remida day: The creative recycling center Reggio children* AGAC Friends of Reggio Children Association Istituzione Scuole e Nidi d'Infanzia—Municipality of Reggio Emilia, Rolando Baldini, et al. Sergio Bagnacani,& Leslie Morrow (English version). Reggio Emilia, Italy: Reggio Children.

Fisher, K., Hirsh-Pasek, K., Golinkoff, R., & Gryfe, S. (2008). Conceptual split? Parents and experts' perceptions of play in the 21st century. *Journal of Applied Developmental Psychology, 29*, 305–316.

Fjortoft, I. (2001). The natural environment as a playground for children: The impact of outdoor play activities in pre-primary school children. *Early Childhood Education Journal, 29*, 111–117.

Forman, G. (1982). A search for the origins of equivalence concepts through a microanalysis of block play. In G. Forman (Ed.), *Action and thought: From sensorimotor schemes to symbolic operations* (pp. 97–136). New York: Academic.

Froebel, F. (1896). *The education of man* (W. N. Hailman, Trans.). New York: D. Appleton. (Original work published 1887)

Gallahue, D., & Ozmun, J. (1998). *Understanding motor development infants, children, adolescents, and adults.* New York: McGraw-Hill.

Gelman, R. (2006). Young natural-number arithmeticians. *Current Directions in Psychological Science, 15*, 193–197.

Ginsburg, H. (2006). Mathematical play and playful mathematics: A guide to early education. In D. Singer, R. Michnick Golinkoff, & K. Hirsh-Pasek (Eds.), *Play=learning: How play motivates and enhances children's cognitive and social-emotional growth* (pp. 145–165). New York: Oxford University Press.

Goncu, A., & Klein, E. (Eds.). (2001). *Children in play, story and school.* New York: Guilford.

Groth, L., & Darling, L. (2001). Playing "inside" stories. In A. Goncu & E. Klein (Eds.), *Children in play, story, and school* (pp. 220–237). New York: Guilford.

Hakkarainen, P. (2007). Do we really understand the worth of play? [Special issue on Vygotsky]. *Children in Europe: Exploring Issues, Celebrating Diversity.*, 19-20. Retrieved from www.childrenineurope.org

Hirsh-Pasek, K., Roberta, M. G., Berk, L. R., & Singer, D. (2009). *A mandate for playful learning in preschool.* New York: Oxford University Press.

Johnson, J., Christie, J., & Wardle, F. (2005). *Play, development, and early education.* Boston, MA: Allyn & Bacon.

Jones, E., & Reynolds, G. (1992). *The play's the thing: Teachers' roles in children's play.* New York: Teachers' College Press.

Kemple, K. (1996). Teachers' beliefs and reported practices concerning sociodramatic play. *Journal of Early Childhood Teacher Education, 17*(2), 19–31.

Kerr, J., & Apter, M. (Eds.). (1991). *Adult play.* Amsterdam, the Netherlands: Swets & Zeitlinger.

Leont'ev, A. (1981), *Activity, consciousness, and personality.* Englewood Cliffs, NJ: Prentice-Hall.

Lieberman, J. (1977). *Playfulness.* New York: Academic Press.

Lobman, C. (2003). The BUGS are coming! Improvisation and early childhood teaching. *Young Children, 58*, 18–23.

Lobman, C. (2006). Improvisation: An analytic tool for examining teacher child interactions in the early childhood classroom. *Early Childhood Research Quarterly, 24*, 455–470.

Lobman, C., & Lundquist, M. (2007). *Unscripted learning: Using improv activities across the K-8 curriculum.* New York: Teachers College Press.

Lundqvist, G. (1995*). The aesthetics of play: A didactic study of play and culture in preschools.* Uppsala, Sweden: Uppsala Studies in Education.

Martensson, F., Boldemann, C., Söderström, M., Blennow, M., Englund, J. E, & Grahn, P. (2009). Outdoor environmental assessment of attention promoting settings for preschool children. *Health Place, 15*, 1149–1157.

Mayesky, M. (2009). *Creative activity for young children* (9th ed.). New York: Cengage Learning.

McNamee, G. (2005). "The one who gathers children": The work of Vivian Gussin Paley and current debates about how we educate young children. *Journal of Early Childhood Teacher Education 25*, 275–296.

McWilliams, C., Ball, S. C., Benjamin, S. E., Hales, D., Vaughn, A., & Ward, D. S. (2009). Best-practice guidelines for physical activity at childcare. *Paediatrics, 124*, 1650–1659.

Mellou, E., (1995). Review of the relationship between dramatic play and creativity in young children. *Early Child Development and Care, 112*, 85–107.

Miller, E., & Almon, J. (2009). *Crisis in the kindergarten: Why children need to play in school.* College Park, MD: Alliance for Childhood.

Montessori, M. (1964). *The Montessori method.* New York: Schocken. (Original work published 1912)

Ness, D., & Farenga, S. J. (2007). *Knowledge under construction: The importance of play in developing children's special and geometric thinking.* Lanham, MD: Rowman & Littlefield.

Nicolopoulou, A. (2002). Peer-group culture and narrative development. In S. Blum-Kulka & C. Snow (Eds.), *Talking to adults: The contribution of multiparty discourse to language acquisition* (pp. 117–152). Mahwah, NJ: Erlbaum.

Nicolopoulou, A., McDowell, J., & Brockmeyer, C. (2006). Narrative play and emergent literacy: Storytelling and story-acting meet journal writing. In D. Singer, R. Michnick Golinkoff, & K. Hirsh-Pasek (Eds.), *Play=learning: How play motivates and enhances children's cognitive and social-emotional growth* (pp. 124–144) New York: Oxford University Press.

Novosyolova, S., Zvorygina, E., Ivankova, R., Kondratova, V., Saar, A., & Grinjaviciene, N. (1989). The integral method of play facilitation at the preschool age. In S. Novosyolova (Ed.), *Igra doshkol'nika* [Child's play at preschool age] (pp. 70–94xxx). Moscow, Russia: Pedaogika. (In Russian)

Olsen A. E., & Sumsion, J. (2000). *Early childhood teacher practices regarding the use of dramatic play in K-2 classrooms.* Paper presented at the Annual Conference of the Australian Association for Research in Education, Sydney, Institute of Early Childhood, Macquarie University.

Ong, N. (2005). *Cultural diversity in education.* Paper presented at "Block Building: Fostering Cognitive, Linguistic, and Social Competence Session," National Association for the Education of Young Children, Washington, DC.

Parten, M. (1932) Social participation among preschool children. *Journal of Abnormal and Social Psychology, 27*, 243–269.

Pellegrini, A. D. (2009). *The role of play in human development.* New York: Oxford University Press.

Pellegrini, A. D., Dupuis, D., & Smith, P. K., (October, 2006). *Play in evolution and development.* Retrieved from http://evolution.binghamton.edu/evos/wp-content/uploads/2008/11/Pellegrini01.pdf

Pestalozzi, J. (1915). *How Gertrude teaches her children* (L. Holland & F. C. Turner, Trans.). Syracuse, NY: C. W. Bardeen. (Original work published 1894)

Piaget, J. (1962). *Play, dreams and imitation in childhood.* New York: Norton.

Piaget, J. (1970). *The conditions of learning*. New York: Holt, Rinehart, & Winston.

Rainio, P. (2005). *Emergence of a playworld: The formation of subjects of learning in interaction between children and adults* (Working Paper 32). Helsinki, Finland: Center for Activity Theory and Developmental Work Research.

Ramani, G., & Siegler, R. (2008). Promoting broad and stable improvements in low-income children's numerical knowledge through playing board games. *Child Development, 79*(2), 375–394.

Riley, D., San Juan, R., Klinkner, J., & Ramminger, A. (2008). *Social and emotional development: Connecting science and practice in early childhood settings*. St. Paul, MN: Redleaf Press.

Rivkin, M. (1995). *The great outdoors: Restoring children's right to play outside*. Washington, DC: National Association for the Education of Young Children.

Rogers, S., & Evan, J. (2008). *Inside role-play in early childhood education: Researching young children's perspectives*. New York: Routledge.

Roskos, K., & Christie, J. (2004). Examining the play–literacy interface: A critical review and future directions. In E. F. Zigler, D, Singer, & S. Bishop-Josef (Eds.), *Children's play: Roots of reading* (pp. 95–123). Washington, DC: Zero to Three. .

Rubin, K., Maioni, T., & Hornung, M. (1976). Free play behaviors in middle- and lower- class children: Parten and Piaget revisited. *Child Development, 47*, 414–419.

Russ, S. (1993). *Affect and creativity: The role of affect and play in the creative process*. Hillsdale, NJ: Erlbaum.

Russ, S., Robins, A., & Christiano, B. (1999). Pretend play: longitudinal prediction of creativity and affect in fantasy in children. *Creativity Research Journal, 12*(2), 129–139.

Saltz, E., & Johnson, J. (1974). Training for thematic-fantasy play in culturally disadvantaged children: Preliminary results. *Journal of Educational Psychology, 66*, 623–630.

Sanders, S. (2002). *Active for life: Developmentally appropriate movement programs for young children*. Champaign, IL: Human Kinetics.

Singer, J. (1973). *The child's world of make-believe: Experimental studies of imaginative play*. New York: Academic Press.

Singer, J., & Singer, D. (1990). *The house of make-believe: Children's play and the developing imagination*. Cambridge, MA: Harvard University Press.

Smilansky, S. (1968). *The effects of socio-dramatic play on disadvantaged preschool children*. New York: Wiley.

Taylor, R. W., Murdoch, L. Carter, P., Gerrard, D. F., Williams, S. M., & Taylor, B. J. (2009). Longitudinal study of physical activity and inactivity in preschoolers: The FLAME study. *Medicine & Science in Sports & Exercise, 41*, 96–102.

Terr, L. (1999). *Beyond love and work: Why adults need to play*. New York: Touchstone.

Trageton, A. (1994). Workshop pedagogy-from concrete to abstract. *The Reading Teacher, 47*(4), 350.

Trageton, A. (2002). *Creative writing on computers and playful learning: Grade 1*. Paper presented at the Association for the Study of Play, annual meetings, Santa Fe, NM.

Trageton, A. (2007). Planning the playground: Hut building in grade 1 and 2. In T. Jambor & J. Van Gils (Eds.), *Several perspectives on children's play: Scientific reflections for practitioners—An initiative of ICCP in co-operation with IPA* (pp. 179–192). Antwerp-Apeldoom, the Netherlands: Garant.

Tyrrell, J. (2001). *The power of fantasy in early learning*. New York: Routledge Falmer.

Ugaste, A. (2007). The cultural-historical approach to play in the kindergarten context. In T. Jambor & J. Gils (Eds.), *Several perspectives on children's play: Scientific reflections for practitioners* (pp. 105–118). Philadelphia, PA: Garant.

Van Hoorn, J., Nourot, P. Scales, B., & Alward, K. (2010). *Play at the center of the curriculum* (5th ed.). Columbus, OH: Pearson Merrill Prentice Hall

Vygotsky, L. (1978). *Mind in society: The development of higher psychological processes*. Cambridge, MA: Harvard University Press.

Welen, T. (2005). Lekpedagogik (Play pedagogy): A review of research. *Play, Policy, & Practice Connections: Newsletter of the Play, Policy, & Practice Interest Forum of the National Association for the Education of Young Children, 9*(2),6–9.

Whitebread, D. (2010). Play, metacognition and self-regulation. In P. Broadhead, J. Howard, & E. Wood (Eds.), *Play and learning in the early years* (pp. 161–176). Los Angeles, CA: Sage.

Wiltz, N., & Fein, G. (1996, March). Evolution of a narrative curriculum: The contributions of Vivian Gussin Paley. *Young Children, 51*, 61–68.

Wood, E. & Attfield, J. (2005). *Play, learning and the early childhood curriculum* (2nd ed.). London: Paul Chapman.

Worthington, M. (2010). Play is a complex landscape: Imagination and symbolic meanings. In P. Broadhead, J. Howard, & E. Wood (Eds.), *Play and learning in the early years* (pp. 127–144). Los Angeles, CA: Sage.

Zigler, E., & Bishop-Josef, S. (2004). Play under siege: A historical overview. In E. Zigler, D. Singer, & S. Bishop-Josef (Eds.), *Children's play: The roots of reading* (pp. 1–14). Washington, DC: Zero to Three Press.

19

U.S. Early Childhood Multicultural Education

Francis Wardle
University of Phoenix School of Advanced Studies and Red Rocks Community College

Derman-Sparks and the ABC Taskforce's seminal book *The Anti-Bias Curriculum: Tools for Empowering Young Children*, was published in 1989. In 2010 the much-anticipated revised edition, *Anti-Bias Education for Young Children and Ourselves* by Derman-Sparks and Edwards was issued. Thus it is a fitting time to examine the state of early childhood multicultural education in the United States. According to the National Association for the Education of Young Children (NAEYC), early childhood education covers infants from birth through age 8. Children in this age group are served in a variety of settings, from family child care and nannies, to Head Start programs, community-based centers, and public school early childhood programs. In the field people who work with young children are variously called childcare providers, childcare workers, caregivers, teachers, and paraprofessionals (Neugebauer, 1999). In this chapter these names will be used interchangeably to describe people who work with children from birth to 8 years old.

Early Childhood Multicultural Education

The initial focus of early childhood multicultural education was on racial, gender, and disability inequalities. According to Pai and Adler (1997), the aims of multicultural education are,

> 1) The cultivation of an attitude of respect for and appreciation of the worth of cultural diversity; 2) the promotion of the belief in the intrinsic worth of each person and an abiding interest in the well-being of the larger society; 3) the development of multicultural competencies to function effectively in culturally varied settings, and 4) the facilitation of educational equity for all regardless of ethnicity, race, gender, age, or other exceptionalities. (pp. 121–122)

Nieto (2004) states that multicultural education is a process of comprehensive school reform and basic education for all students that challenges and rejects racism and other forms of discrimination in schools and society, and that accepts and affirms the pluralism that students, their communities, and teachers reflect. Because it uses critical pedagogy as its underlying philosophy, and focuses on knowledge, reflection, and action to produce social change, it promotes principles of social justice. And York (2003) believes multicultural education attempts to address educational inequalities that result from racism, by,

- Minimizing and healing damage to children's sense of self that results from racism;
- Minimizing the development of prejudice and increasing children's ability to function cross-culturally;
- Fostering children's identity and home language;
- Teaching children knowledge, attitudes, and skills that will help them fully function in society, which includes developing strong skills in basic academic subjects; and
- Teaching children to learn how to think critically, to recognize discrimination and injustice, and to work together to challenge injustice. (pp. 126–127)

The new edition of *Anti-Bias Curriculum for Young Children and Ourselves* (Derman-Sparks & Edwards, 2010) expands the coverage of the original edition to now include race/ethnicity, gender, language, economic class, family structure, differing abilities, sexual orientation, and multiracial children. According to this document, the goals of multicultural education today are,

1. Each child will demonstrate self-awareness, confidence, family pride, and positive social identities;
2. Each child will express comfort and joy with human diversity; accurate language for human differences; and deep, caring human connections;
3. Each child will increasingly recognize unfairness, have language to describe unfairness, and understand that unfairness hurts;

4. Each child will demonstrate empowerment and the skills to act, with others or alone, against prejudice, and/or discriminatory actions. (p. xiv)

The focus of the *Multicultural Principles* of Head Start (U.S. Department of Health and Human Services, 2010) is entirely on culture; for example, principle I states, "Every individual is rooted in culture" (p.11). This focus on culture then begs the question, what is culture? The American Psychological Association (2003) defines culture as belief systems and values that influence norms, practices, behaviors, psychological processes, and institutions. All individuals are cultural beings with cultural heritages. Culture is, however, fluid and dynamic, universal and specific. In the *Multicultural Principles* (U.S. Department of Health and Human Services, 2010) the view is added that each individual is positioned differently within a culture, depending on his or her own choices and experiences, a concept that is supported by West (2001).

According to Hall (1989, 1996) and Bhabha (1994), culture is in a process of continual change and negotiation. They reject the view of culture as a singular collective perspective shared by people of a common history and ancestry, and therefore reject the view that individuals from the same cultural group are the same. Ngo (2008) suggests that discourse in spoken and written language, both in popular and academic arenas, creates certain cultural and identity realities. For example, the discourse about Asian Americans presents a reality as a model minority. This view is then used to blame other groups (i.e., African American and Latino) for their lack of achievement. Further, this discourse makes invisible the struggle of groups such as the Lao and Hmong. Individual identity is thus a double movement: the history of discourse and the individual's response to this collective identity (Hall, 1996).

However, even with the concept of culture as the framework for diversity, and the understanding that cultures are dynamic and that each individual is uniquely situated within a culture or cultures, many multicultural educators view people as existing within large, static, clearly defined, self-contained homogenous groups. Ngo (2008) suggests this broad group approach actually reinforces stereotypes and the inaccurate common discourses. And, while the Head Start *Multicultural Principles* (2010) advises against this stereotypical view of identity, the document then asserts, "it is essential to learn accurate information about different groups of people (i.e. race, religion, gender)" (p. 27). And even Gonzalez-Mena (2008), who prides herself in not organizing her book by broad racial categories, uses these racialized group identifiers to discuss cultural, behavioral, and child-rearing differences. A single-group view of culture is particularly problematic for multiracial, transracially adopted, and third culture children, and new immigrants who have to negotiate a position within their own culture and the overall American culture (Fish, 2002; Ngo, 2008; West, 2001). Thus culture is all the things that

make each of us who we are: the prism through which we view the world (Bowman, 1994).

History of Multicultural Education

Multicultural education developed out of the history of this country and the role of education within that history. Schools reflect our history and our historical struggles (Pai & Adler, 1997). Thus it is important to briefly view the historical foundation of early childhood multicultural education. For a variety of obvious reasons, this discussion will be limited to a U.S. perspective; however, to be truly multicultural one must have a global perspective. The discussion begins with the historic 1954 Supreme Court decision. Certainly, there are other roots to the movement, but the history before this time is more about limiting the education of students from certain groups, rather than finding ways to enhance it, and efforts that did attempt to educate students from marginalized groups used extremely deficit approaches (Pai & Adler, 1987). In addition to the 1954 Supreme Court decision, *Brown v. Topeka Board of Education*, the Civil Rights movement, the War on Poverty, and the creation of Head Start and Title I programs, Individuals with Disabilities Education Act (IDEA), bilingual education, and the women's movement are all direct contributors to multiculturalism.

1954 Supreme Court Decision, Brown v. Topeka Board of Education

This seminal decision had, and continues to have, a tremendous impact on educational equity in schools and early childhood programs in the United States. It can truly be argued that this decision led to the Individuals with Disabilities Education Act (IDEA), Title IX, bilingual education, 504 of the Civil Rights Act, and other education policies and legal cases (Gargiulo, 2012). However, it must also be noted that it truly did not change schools until the Civil Rights legislation and the federal government's enforcement of the court decision. The decision continues to impact our understanding of the relationship between school integration and equity.

In 1975, the precursor to IDEA, the first of many laws addressing the educational rights of children with disabilities was passed. Today this law covers children 3 to 21 years of age; children from birth to 2 are served through a hodge-podge of state and federal agreements and local programs (Gargiulo, 2012). On the one hand IDEA has positively impacted multicultural education by actively addressing the needs of students with disabilities. However, its application in early childhood programs is not without controversy. For example, many believe the categorical nature of the law is destructive; further, it is well known that a disproportionate number of ethnic minorities and boys are labeled as being disabled (Gargiulo, 2012). It is also considered a deficit approach to diversity because it focuses on what children cannot do compared to other children (Gargiulo, 2012).

The 1974 Supreme Court case of *Lau v. Nichols* (Waugh & Koon, 1974) established the educational rights in our schools of children who do not speak English (Ovando, 2004). Thus non-English speaking students became part of multicultural education. However, since more than 400 non-English languages are spoken by students in U.S. schools (Kindler, 2002), many programs have struggled to serve this ever-increasing number of students who don't speak English as a first language. Serving the language needs of new immigrant children along with supporting Native American children's home languages in early childhood programs has proved to be extremely difficult (David et al., 2005).

Civil Rights Movement

The Civil Rights movement of the 1960s finally eliminated Jim Crow laws, and established legal equality in this country (Wardle & Cruz-Janzen, 2004). It also set in motion several trends that continue to have a powerful impact on multicultural education. Head Start was created in 1965, as was the Elementary and Secondary Education Act (ESEA; Title I), now known as No Child Left Behind (NCLB) (Wiles & Bondi, 2002). Further, the Civil Rights legislation required the U.S. Office of Management and Budget (OMB) to track expenditures of federal dollars according to the U.S. Census racial categories. This latter event has had a profound impact on multiculturalism, which has uncritically accepted the U.S. government-mandated approach to categorizing people, including new immigrants (Derman-Sparks & Edwards, 2010; Gonzalez-Mena, 2008).

Head Start is by far the largest U.S. government sponsored early childhood program (Wardle, 2009). Forty-eight states also have some form of state-funded preschool program, mostly targeted to children from low-income homes (Scott-Little, Kagan, & Frelow, 2006). Head Start was originally targeted for "culturally deprived" students; later changed to "culturally disadvantaged," and finally to "culturally different" (Pai & Adler, 1997). Baratz and Baratz (1970) argue that, "the entire notion of compensatory education was founded on the deficit view of minorities, which regarded cultural, linguistic, cognitive, and affective as well as behavioral differences as pathological conditions to be eliminated" (p. 34). Head Start and most state-funded programs target low-income students who are disproportionately minority (U.S. Department of Health and Human Services, 2008). Almost all state-funded preschool programs justify their existence with the argument that early intervention reduces school failure of "at risk" students (Scott-Little, Kagan, & Frelow, 2006).

Thus it can be argued that tax-supported early childhood programs are attempts to make all poor, minority, and disabled children match the standards of normally developing, middle-class children (Pai & Adler, 1997).

Tandem to the Civil Rights movement was the women's movement. Initially academics and political advocates led the movement; today it has influence throughout education, work, and politics. Curiously, however, its impact on the early childhood field has been somewhat contradictory. For example, while the early childhood field now enables women to work, attend college classes, and so forth, women who work in the field (97% of the early childhood workforce) receive atrocious wages and benefits (Neugebauer, 1999, 2004). Ironically, teachers at the famous childcare centers at the Kaiser shipbuilding facility during World War II, before the advent of the women's movement, received pay and benefits at the same level as the shipbuilding workers (Hurwitz, 1998). Further, for years the early childhood multicultural movement accepted the popular view that girls struggle in our programs (Copple, 2001; Derman-Sparks & the ABC Taskforce, 1989; Gonzalez-Mena, 2008). However, there is mounting evidence that boys struggle more than girls in early childhood programs (Berger, 2009; Gargiulo, 2012; Wardle, 1991).

Unique Aspects of Early Childhood Multicultural Education

The focus on this young age group for multicultural education poses some challenges different from K-12 and college multicultural education. This is significant, because the body of multicultural scholarship was developed for K-12 and higher education (Nieto, 2004). Some of the unique aspects of early childhood education that impact multicultural education include developmental levels, diverse sponsorship of early childhood programs, the almost total female culture of the field (Neugebauer, 1999), and the fact that many early childhood activities occur outside of traditional educational settings.

Developmental Levels

Most children in early childhood fall into Piaget's sensorimotor and preoperational stages, and Erikson's stages of trust vs. mistrust, autonomy vs. shame and doubt, and initiative vs. guilt (Berger, 2009). Children in the sensorimotor stage process information through the creation of sensorimotor schemas; in the preoperational stage, while able to represent ideas symbolically, they cannot think logically or rationally, as their thinking is controlled by centrism (one idea) and appearance (Ormrod, 2008). Further, they have not achieved conservation, and cannot understand the abstract identity of concepts. Therefore their understanding of diversity, be it gender, race/ethnicity, disability, and so on, is very simplistic, stereotypical, and usually wrong. Abstract concepts of justice, racism, discrimination, and power are beyond the simplistic thinking of preoperational children; the construct of group belonging—beyond grouping like physical characteristics—is also beyond their cognitive abilities (Aboud, 1987).

Erikson's first stage requires parents and caregivers to develop trust between the child and her world; in the second stage children need to experience a level of perceived freedom, and the third requires children to be encouraged to risk, experiment, try out new ideas, and make lots of mistakes (Berger, 2009). Thus parents and providers of children at this age need to support children's exploration, risk-taking, and experimentation, and understand that children's experimentations with complex constructs such as gender and race will at times be unsophisticated, and even unsettling to some adults.

Diversity of Providers

In the United States, most K-12 schools are public, and as such, they are subject to federal and state regulations and to local district governance. Early childhood programs are, on the other hand, sponsored by a variety of agencies, roughly divided into faith-based, not-for-profit, and private, for-profit programs. According to a report published by Exchange Every Day ("A Very Diverse Field," 2010), 47% of early childhood programs serving children under age 6 are independent centers (for-profit and nonprofit), 26% are religious-affiliated centers, 11% Head Start centers, 7% chain programs, 5% public school early childhood programs, and 4% employee-sponsored childcare centers. Faith-based programs come in a variety of different faiths, with the top four being the Roman Catholic Church, Southern Baptist Convention, United Methodist Church, and the Presbyterian Church (Neugebauer, 1999). Not-for-profit programs include local public schools, Head Start and state-funded programs, local agency programs, and campus programs; for-profit programs range from large international chains to stand-alone community programs, employee sponsored programs, and family day cares (Neugebauer, 1999).

Most faith-based programs abide by local licensing and health and safety standards, and teach a specific academic curriculum. While some of these programs are inclusive and do not require parents to belong to their faith, almost all teach the values and doctrines of their faith (Wardle, 2009). This poses several challenges to diversity and multicultural education. First, most of these programs are religiously and often racially homogenous; second, many faiths, such as Catholic, Baptist, and Muslim, are opposed to including gay, lesbian, and bisexual issues, and often have strict views regarding gender roles in the family and society (Bang, 2009; Luz, 2010).

As has been observed, Head Start and state-funded preschool programs are income-based (Scott-Little et al., 2006; Wardle, 2009). Head Start's racial breakdown is 31.3% African American, 35% White, and 32.9% Latino (U. S. Department of Health and Human Services, 2006). For-profit early childhood programs also tend to limit diversity. Most chain programs are located in middle-class neighborhoods, and employee-based programs serve well-paid employees (Neugebauer, 2004), providing a form of income segregation. Home-based child care and community centers serve specific neighborhoods, which, as we know, tend to be racially and economically segregated (Howard, 2007). Research also suggests that one factor parents use to select child care is a match between the program and the family's language and culture (Hofferth, 1989). Finally, many early childhood programs lack the training, financial resources, and community support needed to provide services to children with disabilities (Bradley & Kibera, 2006).

Female Culture of Early Childhood

As noted earlier, 97% of early childhood teachers are women; almost as many directors are also women (Neugebauer, 1999). Eighty-four percent of elementary schoolteachers are women, and most male teachers are to be found teaching grades 5 and 6 (Cunningham & Dorsey, 2004). Further, the early childhood field is well known for its abysmal pay and poor benefits (Neugebauer, 2004; Young, 2003). As Neugebauer (2004) suggests, "Needless to say…a price for working in the profession is low wages…. Suffice-it-to-say, that despite the growing awareness of the importance of the early years, the almost mandatory talk by politicians about the value of education, and the growing dependence of our economy on available child care…this recognition has not contributed to commensurate financial reward for those delivering the services" (p.16). There is, of course, nothing implicitly wrong with a field being dominated by women; in fact Feeney and Freeman (2002) see this as a definite advantage because of the caring, sacrificing nature of women. And, historically men have dominated many fields, and still do (Nieto, 2004).

Outside Traditional Education

One of the central differences between the early childhood field and K-12 education is that the former is closer to the culture, values, and beliefs of families and communities. This is because we address issues around the care and nurturing of infants and very young children, which cuts to the core of cultural child-rearing values, and brings programs into direct contact with deep, powerful cultural norms around child-rearing practices, feeding, discipline, views of child development, preacademic preparation, the value of play, and so on (Gonzalez-Mena, 2008). Further, most children in early childhood programs are at a developmental age where reason, content, and discrete academic information take second place to emotional, social, moral, and cognitive development, and brain-based development and learning (Berger, 2009; Ormrod, 2008; Schiller, 2010). This greatly impacts how young children learn about diversity and it is not so much about curricular content, materials, and learning activities.

Contemporary Influences on Multicultural Education

Over the last few years several events have greatly impacted early childhood multicultural education: (a) the Human Genome Project, (b) continued and increasing immigration, (c) multiracial children and their families, and (d) the federal legislation No Child Left Behind (NCLB).

The Human Genome Project

The Human Genome Project has produced radical advances in a variety of areas. From a multicultural perspective, it has forever challenged the largely accepted view that race is somehow biologically based (Fish, 2002). This breakthrough has resulted in a variety of alternative ways of understanding race, ethnicity, and culture. Many now view race and ethnicity as sociopolitical constructs (Derman-Sparks & Edwards, 2010; Nieto, 2004). It is also clear that the original construct of race, albeit first supported by religion, and then by science (Smedley, 2002), was a way to justify slavery and to create a hierarchy of power, discrimination, and influence. In the United States racial categories have become codified by the federal Office of Management and Budget (OMB), for use by the U.S. Census Bureau, and to assure equitable distribution of resources in federal programs, including schools and early childhood programs (Root, 1996). Many advocates and supporters of the current U.S. way of categorizing race believe that it is essential if we are to monitor the promises of the 1964 Civil Rights Act (Spencer, 2010).

One example of the sociopolitical nature of race and ethnicity is the creation of Hispanic as a category. In 1965, the U.S. Justice Department proposed to create a new racial category, Hispanic, which had not previously existed. However, after several false starts and opposition from influential Hispanics, the Hispanic ethnic category was created for the 2000 census, enabling Hispanics to have minority status without being identified with a lower-status racial group (Fernandez, 1996). Another example can be seen in the results of a DNA research study in Brazil (Alves-Silva et al., 2000), which focused on people who identified as European, Afro Brazilian, and Amerindian. The researchers then compared the DNA of these individuals with the DNA of homogenous racial groups. Results determined that individuals who identified only with a single racial group had some DNA from the other two racial groups. Another example is the view by many in the United States that anyone from Latin America, including Brazilians who speak Portuguese, is Latino (Hernandez & Lee, 2010), a label not even used in those countries (Fish, 2002).

In addition to the sociopolitical construction of race, many are challenging the simplistic notion of a single racial identity to describe the highly complex questions related to diverse populations (Wallace, 2004). "Researchers throughout the social sciences are progressively more critical of how identity constructs such as race, culture, ethnicity, and gender, reinscribe essentialist notions of human diversity" (Wallace, 2004, p. xv). They are interested in the ways identities are created and experienced within a variety of social and temporal contexts, and within ever-changing power hierarchies (Wallace, 2004).

Continued and Increased Immigration

In addition to the numbers of new immigrants, factors that have a profound impact on early childhood programs, include:

- There is an increased diversity of languages, from Eastern Europe and Russia and a variety of African countries with a multiplicity of languages, to children from Korea, Cambodia, and Vietnam. Kindler (2002) documents that over 400 different, non-English languages are spoken within our schools; David et al., state that 140 languages exist in Head Start (2005). Use of multiple non-English languages in a program challenges the notion of bilingual and bicultural programs, and places incredible pressure on these programs (U.S. Department of Health and Human Services, 2010). For many programs, providing curricula and testing documents and communication materials in each family's language is well-nigh impossible.
- There is an increased number of families with religious beliefs other than Christian (Lippy, 2004). This religious diversity challenges programs to address issues of food, prayer, and so on; it also challenges public programs to make sure they are not violating federal requirements regarding the separation of church and state (Lippy, 2004).
- There is increased diversity of non-Western child-rearing practices, gender roles for parents and children, and approaches to discipline (Gonzalez-Mena, 2008).
- There are diverse views of racial, tribal, and religious groups, and racism, prejudice, and discrimination. New immigrants bring to our programs their own cultural views of race, ethnicity, tribal affiliation, and prejudice that are very different from the views of contemporary American scholars and educators (Fish, 2002).

Multiracial Children

Educators are recognizing, if begrudgingly, both the increased number of multiracial children and their families in our programs, and their unique educational needs (Baxley, 2008; Cortes, 1999; Wallace, 2004). This recognition challenges early childhood programs in many ways. These challenges include:

- The view that racial and ethnic diversity means belonging to only a single racial or ethnic group; this forces multicultural educators to examine racial borders and to deconstruct the absolute and essentialist nature of race and ethnicity (Baxley, 2008; Pryce, 2001; Root, 1996; Wardle, 2010).

- The ways in which programs develop healthy identity in their children's minority heritage: For example, York (2003) provides several activities that are destructive to the healthy identity development of multiracial and transracially adopted children, because they require the child to match their own physical features with those of their parents, and ask them to select a single racial group for their identity. These children need activities that help them develop positive identities based on being mixed race and having parents who belong to different races. Programs now must honor and support each child's total racial identity (Baxley, 2008; Bowles, 1993; Wardle, 2007; West, 2001).
- The need for single-race staff working with multiracial and multiethnic children to examine their own biases and prejudices about mixed-heritage (Baxley, 2008).
- The need for programs to go beyond providing stereotypical tokens for each racial group for books, toys, pictures, miniature people, curricular content, and so on. For example, many education supply catalogs provide multicultural doll sets with one doll stereotypically matching each of the five U.S. Census racial groups; most multicultural children's book lists are ordered by single-race groupings, and child development and early childhood textbooks only list single-race groups in their indexes (Wardle, 2007). Fully embracing multiracial children and their families will require the deconstruction of these practices.

No Child Left Behind Federal Act

The No Child Left Behind (NCLB) federal act is an extension of the Elementary and Secondary Education Act of 1965, originally passed as part of President Johnson's War on Poverty. While NCLB is focused on K-12, it has had a major impact on early childhood education, which can be discussed under standards and closing the achievement gap.

Standards. All states that sponsor early childhood programs have developed and implemented standards (Scott-Little et al., 2006). While these standards are given different names, they all describe skills and concepts children should have mastered at a specific age (Gronlund, 2008). The implementation of NCLB has greatly increased the pressure on early childhood programs to focus on academics at the expense of the arts, social and emotional development, and physical education (Scott-Little et al., 2006), and many states are attempting to align their early childhood standards with their state's K-12 standards, as is Head Start (U. S. Department of Health and Human Services, 2008). Thus, public programs have shifted their curricular focus from social and emotional development, play, and the arts, to literacy, math, and science.

Private and nonprofit early childhood programs, including religious programs, are not beholden to these standards, but they have increased the academic nature of their curricula to prepare students (and appease parents) for successful kindergarten entry. The concomitant reduction of physical activities, the arts, and whole-child approaches in early childhood programs seems to negatively impact students who struggle with an overly academic approach (see the later discussion on boys).

Achievement Gap. The NCLB focuses on closing the achievement gap, and thus places the federal government squarely at the center of equity. Many view NCLB as a godsend, because it highlights the achievement gap between minorities (not Asians) and Whites (Bowman, 2006; Howard, 2007). Others, however, are not so sure, and believe the results of this focus negatively impacts minority and special needs students. One destructive result of NCLB is the creation of a nationwide focus on college entry. The great debates between Booker T. Washington and W. E. B. DuBois notwithstanding, it makes little sense to expect every child to attend college (DuBois, 2007).

This achievement-gap focus also creates a White vs. people of color dichotomy. As Gary Howard (2007), states, "low-income Haitian, Jamaican, Dominican, Latino and Black families from the city have moved into the community, and middle-class White families have, unfortunately but predictably, fled to private schools or other less diverse districts ..." (p. 21). Later, he claims that results of multicultural efforts in this same district have reduced the achievement gap. However, it would appear this result is partly due to reducing White and Asian competition. Thus one consequence of this focus on the gap between traditional minority groups and White and Asian students is to view White students (and their families) as the enemy. This anti-White (and to some extent, anti-male) view is evident in much of the early childhood multicultural literature (Derman-Sparks & Edwards, 2010; Gonzalez-Mena, 2008). However, one in five American children live in poverty, and many of these children are White—some living in homeless shelters, welfare hotels, and poor, substandard housing (National Center for Children in Poverty [NCCP], 2006). Thus this focus on closing the achievement gap does not seem to be a positive approach to addressing educational inequalities and maximizing educational outcomes for everyone.

Approaches to Multicultural Education

A critical challenge for multicultural education is to determine the most effective way to implement the multicultural goals. To this end, Sleeter and Grant (1999) have developed what they call the five approaches to race, class, and gender; further, the perspectives of postmodernism, critical pedagogy, social justice, and White privilege are used in this effort.

Five Approaches to Race, Class, and Gender

The five approaches to race, class, and gender (Sleeter & Grant, 1999), are summarized here, based on Ramsey (2006):

Teaching the Exceptional and the Culturally Different. This approach focuses on adapting curricula and learning approaches to meet the cultural needs of non-White students. It focuses on creating continuity between the home and school; however, it does not directly address discrimination and economic inequalities that impact academic success.

Human Relations. The intent of this approach is to enable students to interact positively with those who are different, to reduce prejudice, and for students to learn together with people from a variety of different backgrounds. It focuses on individual changes in attitudes and beliefs, especially of mainstream White students, but it ignores the issues of institutional biases, discrimination, and prejudice, also in educational programs.

Single-Group Studies. This approach focuses on a specific racial, ethnic, or national group, and changes the curricular content to present each group, to empower marginalized groups, and to educate mainstream White students. It can easily become both an isolated activity in learning, and focus on learning the differences between groups.

Multicultural Education. In this approach, children are exposed to a wide range of cultural and racial diversity (an extension of the single-group approach). The intent is to help children function effectively in diverse, multicultural groups, through the use of a variety of curricular materials, toys, books, and other diverse content. This tends to be a token and tourist approach that reinforces differences and group stereotypes, without developing a deeper understanding of cultural richness, values, and true diversity.

Education that Is Multicultural and Social Reconstructionist. In this approach several elements from the preceding approaches are included, but the focus is on the power relationships between groups—especially mainstream White versus marginalized groups. It stresses the societal and cultural issues that undergird discrimination and inequality—political, economic, social, and social justice. By challenging the very structure of society, it also challenges early childhood programs, schools, and universities. This latter approach is the preferred approach of the authors (Sleeter & Grant, 1999). However, it poses many challenges for the early childhood field, including the fact that the field in general is at the bottom of the economic hierarchy and is dominated by women (Derman-Sparks & Edwards, 2010). Further, one wonders the extent to which a 3-year-old can understand political, economic, and social justice perspectives of inequality.

Postmodernism

Postmodernism means after the modern era; the late 1960s is associated with the beginning of postmodernism (Grieshaber & Ryan, 2006). The modern view is that there is one truth, certainty, and universal assumption: a one size fits all approach to everything, including education. To the postmodernist, reason and objective knowledge are the norms, knowledge, and expectations of those in power: those in power determine knowledge (Pai & Adler, 1997) and reason and science come from social and historical power struggles (Giroux, 1993). At the center of postmodernism is a belief that all Western knowledge must be deconstructed and then reconstructed (Best & Kellner, 1991). It challenges the accepted epistemologies, giving hope to the marginalized, depressed, and disempowered; often addressing issues such as social justice and equity (Cannella & Bailey, 1999).

A basic belief of postmodernism is that our scholarship is biased from a Western White male perceptive. Thus a central focus of multicultural education from a postmodern perspective is to lessen White male privilege, and to replace it with positions and power that are reflective of minorities, women, the poor, and those with alternative sexual orientations. Postmodernism challenges traditional approaches to understanding children, child development, and early learning. According to Grieshaber (2001), "research is a cultural invention of the White Western (male) academic world, all research is political and represents a privileged position. Further, postmodernists deconstruct traditional early childhood theory, viewing it as a modernist view, created by White men about children in middle-class White, Western societies" (p. 136). Thus giants in our field—Dewey, Freud, Erikson, Skinner, Rousseau, Kohlberg, and others are roundly critiqued, particularly as they relate to understanding the developmental and educational needs of minority and poor children, female-headed households, and other nontraditional families.

Critical Pedagogy

Critical pedagogy encourages students to take risks and to critically question and seek their own answers to issues they are studying (Nieto, 2004). It acknowledges cultural and linguistic diversity, and requires students to critically analyze differing perspectives—challenging the orthodox, the official, and the dominant position, for a more accurate view—and usually one of marginalized groups. Critical pedagogy recognizes that all school-related decisions are political and reflect a certain political ideology, whether as regards curricula, tests, grouping of children, hidden curricula, hiring practices, and so on (Nieto, 2004). Students learn there are many ways to view reality and the content of the curriculum. For example, a study of Thanksgiving would provide a view from the perspective of the Wampanoag Indians and contemporary Native Americans (Nieto, 2004). Added to critical thinking is reflection—moving beyond discourse to actually taking action (Freire, 1970). With the Thanksgiving example, students might invite Indians from local nations at Thanksgiving to present their own unique viewpoints (Wardle, 2009). Much of critical pedagogy is to view historical and other events from the perspective of those impacted by these events: Native Americans in the westward expansion; Japanese, Germans, and Italians during World War II internments; and African Americans' struggle of resistance and rebellion during slavery and after. Sleeter (1996) argues that education must center on the conflicts in all people's experiences, with the primary goal of liberating people from oppression by challenging societal, economic, and political structures that maintain these inequalities.

Critical pedagogy also examines the realities behind some of the "truths" we teach: justice for all, equal treatment under the law, equal educational opportunity, and so on. It begins with the experiences and viewpoints of each student, and thus has its roots in Dewey (1997), but then expands the discussion beyond individual experiences, critically reflecting on multiple perspectives and divergent points of view (Nieto, 2004).

Social Justice

In teaching for social justice, teachers are responsible for raising the level of social awareness of their students and guiding the curriculum for social justice instruction (Lalas, 2007). It is a way of recognizing, respecting, and valuing differences in cultural beliefs, social norms, intellectual flexibility, and personal perspectives among students and their families, emphasizing equity, ethical values, justice, care, and respect (Marshall & Oliva, 2006). Further, many believe that teachers should assume an advocacy role as part of their work, paying specific attention to the social, political, and economic realities of their students and their families (Bemak & Chung, 2005). Darling-Hammond, French, and Garcia-Lopez (2002) stress that teachers need to examine their own worldviews and the sources of inequality and privilege, and Cochran-Smith (2004) adds that teachers must "struggle to unlearn racism itself," and help students develop thinking skills, process multiple perspectives, and learn to participate in a democratic society.

White Privilege

Since the publication of Peggy McIntosh's essay on White privilege (1989), White privilege and Whiteness studies have become popular throughout education (Leonardo, 2009). They focus on what it means to be White in America, especially the hidden privileges of being White, which shifts the focus away from studying ethnic minorities, to studying Whites as the creators and purveyors of racism and power hierarchies. Whiteness is viewed as the norm, the standard for universal human values by which all others are viewed and to which they are compared (Roediger, 1991). Rothenberg (2008) believes that we must identify and label White privilege and Whiteness before we can address it and determine the benefits we receive simply for being White.

White privilege is often invisible to those who benefit most from it. Many take such privileges for granted, such as being able to walk into a store and purchase something without being followed; never being asked in a class to "speak for your group," and being able to drive through a nice neighborhood without being followed by the police. Being White and wealthy brings with it more privileges; adding male to the equation adds even more. Gender, lack of wealth, and other disadvantages can mask White privilege. Thus White teachers must reflect on their own privileges and biases (Rothenberg, 2008). According to Rothenberg, (2008), "A society that distributes educational opportunities, housing, health care, food, even kindness, based on the color of people's skin and other arbitrary variables cannot guarantee the safety and security of its people" (2008, p. 4). One result of White privilege is that meritocracy is a myth, and democratic choice is not equally accessible to all. White privilege is institutionalized in America, including in schools and early childhood programs (Rothenberg, 2008).

Young Children's Understanding of Diversity

Since the creation of multicultural education, we have learned a great deal about diversity, children's development of racial and ethnic identity, the impact of racism and prejudice on development and learning, and the need for multicultural curricular materials. Below is a brief review of some of this body of knowledge. However, it must be pointed out that this knowledge is influenced by the various biases of researchers, theorists, and those who fund research (Ramsey, 2006). Further, research conducted at a typical campus early childhood program probably won't generalize to early childhood settings in rural Louisiana, urban St. Louis, or the Crow Indian Reservation in Montana. The review is organized under the headings of children and their identity development, parents' impact on early education, diversity of early childhood programs, preparation of teachers, and gender inequality.

Children and Their Identity Development

From birth to age 8 years, children are developing in a variety of ways. Socially and emotionally they are developing trust in the important people in their lives, and learning to feel secure within a family and community (Erikson, 1963). As they grow older they venture farther afield, and meet new and different people —people who are like them (physically and culturally), and people who are different. Cognitively, children this age try to understand and make sense of their world: how the world works and how they fit into it (Piaget, 1952). Two major tasks they begin to struggle with at this age are gender and race (Berger, 2009). Their understanding of gender and race are influenced both by biology and by social and cultural factors. To determine their gender, children look to role models—parents, teachers, symbolic models, and peers (Bandura, 1965). They try out the clothes of both genders, play with various gender-stereotypical toys, and talk about being a boy or a girl. Because children this age are in the sensorimotor and preoperational stages, they process most information through the way things appear.

This, of course, is also true of race and ethnicity—children are very interested in physical characteristics—how they are like others and different from them (Berger, 2009). Racial and ethnic identity development begins with being able to discriminate essentialist physical characteristics (hair color, skin color, eye shape, and so on) (Aboud, 1987). Thus, for children who have less distinctive physical characteristics, such as biracial children and some Hispanic and Native American children, this distinction is more difficult (Aboud, 1988). Transracially adopted minority children and biracial children in general also tend to struggle more. Other students are often confused by these children; biracial children report constant questioning of their race by adults and children (Baxley, 2008; Wardle & Cruz-Janzen, 2004). Finally, there is a body of work that suggests children not only pick friends who are like them, but also friends who are fun to be around: prosocial children have more friends; furthermore, children liked by adults are also liked by peers (Berger, 2009).

Racial Identity. Research on children's racial identity development and racial attitudes is confounded by the sociopolitical nature of race and how research is conducted. We do know that infants can discriminate light and dark stimuli (Berger, 2009). Furthermore, very young infants can process faces from a variety of different racial groups. However, between ages 3 and 9 months, they become more sensitive to faces from their own group, and less so to the faces of other groups. This is true of infants from all ethnic backgrounds, not just White infants (Kelly et al., 2007). However, this "narrowing of perception" does not occur with children whose early caregivers are from a variety of ethnic backgrounds (Kelly et al., 2007). Thus children are able to discriminate people with different physical characteristics as early as 6 months, and by 3- to 4 years old they can group people by some of these characteristics (Katz, 1976), much as they can other objects. They can also attach labels to groups (M. Goodman, 1952; Ramsey & Myers, 1990). As students move into the elementary grades, they add nonphysical cues to help group people (Alejandro-Wright, 1985). However, children have great difficulty when physical or other cues do not match stereotypical characteristics (Aboud, 1987; Wardle & Cruz-Jansen, 2004). This is not surprising, since adults have the same

problem (see the controversy surrounding the identity of mixed-race children [Baxley, 2008]).

As children's mental constructs mature, their view of racial and other group differences become more sophisticated. However, this is still difficult. For example, we now know that race is not always a permanent classification: an African American who travels to Brazil may be viewed as mixed-race on his arrival (Fish, 2002); some Americans who once accepted a single-race self-identity are now challenging this construct (Pryce, 2001; Wardle, 2011). However, during the late preschool and early elementary age, children's views of racial consistency, much like gender consistency, do develop (Aboud, 1987). The ability of children to discriminate race varies by type of activity and the mental constructs used to process this information (Bigler & Liben, 1993; Ramsey, 1991).

While some researchers suggest that negative racial attitudes consolidate with age, others believe that racial prejudice decreases as children develop the ability to empathize with others, recognize different perspectives, and use more sophisticated thought processes (Aboud, 1987; Aboud & Amato, 2001). Obviously racial attitudes are dramatically influenced by environmental factors: parents, communities, peers, schools, and the media (Cortes, 2000; Milner, 1983). In the United States, White children exhibit more same-race preferences than do African Americans (Aboud & Amato, 2001; Van Ausdale & Feagin, 2001); however, colorism exists, with African American children showing a preference for same-race peers with lighter skin. This preference for same-race peers with lighter skins is also true of children from other ethnic minority groups (Wardle & Cruz-Janzen, 2004).

Studies suggest preschool and elementary school children prefer same–race peers. This tends to consolidate as they grow older, and can become quite rigid during the identity-vs.-role-confusion period of adolescence (Patchen, 1982; Ramsey, 2006; Tatum, 1997). Many interracial parents discover that teachers, schools, and early childhood programs reinforce racial grouping, monoracial labels, and various other essentialist perspectives (Baxley, 2008; Wardle & Cruz-Janzen, 2004).

Income Disparity. Young children use physical characteristics to discriminate between things; thus physical indicators of wealth and poverty—cars, homes, clothes, gifts, number of toys, and so on—are recognized by children (Leahy, 1983). Also, at the preschool age children are learning to share and to play and work together. Thus they believe those who have more than others should share what they have. However, as they grow older and hear more messages about the value of hard work and the need to take personal responsibility, they begin to believe that poor people deserve to be poor (Leahy, 1990). For younger children, social indicators of wealth, such as education and type of employment, are not valid cues (Dittmar & Van Duuren, 1993). They do, however, begin to pick up cultural attitudes about wealth; for example, that rich people are happier and more likeable than poor people (Naimark, 1983; Ramsey, 1991). Thus, as children grow older they begin to struggle with a conflict between the idea that people get what they deserve, while also being taught about the democratic ideals of equity and fairness (Chafel, 1997).

Gender Identity. Gender identity theories explain how girls and boys develop a sense of gender identity within their cultural, racial, religious, family, and other contexts (Berger, 2009). Modeling by peers, parents, teachers, and symbolic models is instrumental in this process (Bandura, 1965), as are developmental levels of cognitive processing. A Piagetian perspective suggests preschool and young elementary school-age children create stereotypical schemas of what they think it means to belong to their gender, and then refine these schemas through social contacts with both genders. At the middle elementary age they become more sophisticated (Signorella, Bigler, & Liben, 1993).

Young children prefer same-sex peers; young children who engage in cross-gender behavior or who have cross-gender friends are often harassed both by adults and peers, and teachers often support and reinforce segregation through grouping—classes, teams, activities, and even chores. Children in same-sex groups had more stereotypical views about gender than those in more integrated settings (Bigler, 1995). Wardle (1991) determined that teachers in a Head Start program reinforced typical gender-based choices and behaviors.

Special Needs. Again, disabilities, as with other forms of diversity that can be observed by children, can be actively processed by them. Also, because of their limited experience and cognitive development (Berger, 2009), young children's reasoning about the causes of various disabilities is faulty, especially when they are in Piaget's preoperational stage. Unlike other forms of diversity, preschool children appear to be tolerant toward those with disabilities, but become less tolerant as they move through elementary school (De Grella & Green, 1984; J. E. Goodman, 1989). Children tend to be more accepting of physical disabilities, and less so of children with behavioral, cognitive, and language delays (Diamond, 1994). Children exposed to peers with disabilities become more accepting of differences (Favazza & Odom. 1997); they may also learn to treat them as equals, rather than pitying them and doing things for them (Kostelnik, Onaga, Rohde, & Whiren, 2002).

In summary, children's development of attitudes and behaviors toward gender, racial, socioeconomic, ability, language, and other differences is a complex interaction of developmental stages (Ormrod, 2008), educational environments, and the cultural contexts of family, community, racial groups, language, and so on. However, this knowledge is based on Western research conducted in Western countries. For example, in many non-Western countries, early child-

hood programs are segregated both by income and gender, do not include children with disabilities, and sometimes are segregated by race, tribal group, and religious affiliation (Wardle, 2009).

Parents' Impact on Early Education

According to Bronfenbrenner (1989), parents have a direct and immediate impact on a child's development. They not only provide the child with the basic needs of food and shelter, but also nurture them and introduce them to the values, expectations, and behaviors of their culture (Gonzalez-Mena, 2008). We know that every child's development and learning is embedded within a culture or cultures, and that parents are the first agents of these cultures (Bronfenbrenner, 1989).

Just as parents impact their children's values, patterns, and expectations, they also teach them what culture they are not—what Bruner calls a negative instance (Ormrod, 2008). Sometimes this exhibits itself in the process of creating a sense of family loyalty and cultural belonging—what Cross (1987) calls reference group orientation, and Erikson (1963) labels group belonging. Many believe this process is essential to protect minority children from the oppressive practices of mainstream society, and is a critical process for the development of the healthy self-image of minority children (Gonzalez-Mena, 2008; Tatum, 1997). However, there is a fine line between developing a sense of group loyalty and cultural pride, and in teaching children out-group antagonism, prejudice, and attitudes that can limit their personal and academic achievements (Pai & Adler, 1997).

Diversity of Early Childhood Programs

One thing that characterizes early childhood programs is their diversity (Neugebauer, 1999), another is that they tend to be more local than schools, and parents often find programs that match their family's cultural values. Finally, as has already been mentioned, the early childhood field is segregated by income, religious values, and even race and ethnicity. From a diversity point of view, family choice in early childhood options poses a double-edged sword. On the one hand programs can be, and often are, very responsive to a family's cultural needs and desires (Gonzalez-Mena, 2008), and diversity experts advise programs to create family-program cultural and linguistic consistency (Derman-Sparks & Edwards, 2010; Luz, 2010). On the other hand, because families have such a strong influence on programs, they often restrict the efforts of programs to be more culturally, linguistically, and religiously diverse (Neugebauer, 1999; Ramsey, 2006). With the increase of immigrants with religious and cultural values different from mainstream American values, issues such as gender equality and gender expectations are also being challenged (Bang, 2009; Luz, 2010).

Teacher Preparation

There is a great amount of material in the multicultural literature about teachers, describing them as White, middle-class individuals educated at White, middle-class institutions that teach a European American body of knowledge. As a result, these teachers are seen as being ill equipped to teach minority students (Gonzalez-Mena, 2008). However, this analysis is not quite so clear-cut in the early childhood field. Most teachers and caregivers of young children do not have four-year college degrees (Neugebauer, 2004). Also, state requirements for people caring for young children differ dramatically from state to state; the requirements to take classes beyond high school generally are fulfilled through classes provided by a state agency or community college. Additionally, because 97% of early childhood teachers are female, and because pay and benefits are so poor, a disproportionate percentage of childcare teachers and providers are women of color (Neugebauer, 1999). However, the content these teachers are taught about child development and learning, and program best practices and regulations they must follow, are based on White American and European theorists and researchers. The contention is that there is a mismatch between early childhood practices and the needs of minority children, which ultimately dooms these children to failure (Gonzalez-Mena, 2008).

Gender Inequality

As is detailed throughout the multicultural literature, gender is a central issue in equity discussions (Derman-Sparks, 1989; Ramsey, 2006). Researchers such as Sadker and Sadker (1994) have documented discrimination against girls in schools, especially in the areas of math and science. Title IX of the Civil Rights Act is designed to legally address gender inequality in education. However, the picture in early childhood is very different. Boys are clearly less successful as a group than girls in early childhood programs. More boys are placed in special education than girls (Gargiulo, 2012). Boys are four times as likely to be identified with a learning disability; AD/HD is diagnosed four to nine times more often in boys than girls (U.S. Department of Education, 2008); the risk of autism spectrum disorder is four times higher in boys than girls; and in general boys tend to be more at risk of exhibiting externalizing behavior disorders than girls (Gargiulo, 2012). Finally, children from minority groups are overrepresented in special education programs, especially African American and Latino boys (Gargiulo, 2012).

Recent advances in brain research enable us to make some gender comparisons. For example, according to Lenroot et al. (2007) and Sax (2007), the language center in a typical 5-year-old boy is similar to that of a typical 3-year-old girl; young girls tend to be more advanced in vocabulary, language, memory, perception, sustained attention, and self-control (Cornoyer, Solomon, & Trudel,

1998; Rothbart, 1989). This is particularly relevant given the current focus on early literacy development in schools. More boys than girls engage in rough and tumble play (Humphreys & Smith, 1984) and tend to be more aggressive than girls (Whiting & Edwards, 1988); boys are also more often disciplined and expelled (Skelton, 2001), while girls tend to be more advanced in emotional regulation and literacy development (Berger, 2009). Alloway and Gilbert believe that approaches to teaching literacy during the early ages marginalize boys (1997); Wardle (2004a) argues that early childhood programs constitute a female culture that is unable to provide the necessary goodness-of-fit to nurture optimal learning in boys.

Specific Research and Theoretical Articles

Because the early childhood field is so broad and multidimensional, it is difficult to decide what research should be examined from a multicultural perspective. I have selected research that covers some of the critical areas that impact young children's development and education. Parent involvement research is discussed because program–parent relationships are at the center of good early childhood practices; culture and identity are carefully discussed, due to the central nature of this issue on children's school success; I then review interesting studies on the impact of discipline approaches on the behavior of children, because of a growing body of literature that suggests normative approaches used in programs do not match the needs of children from diverse backgrounds. Social justice in early childhood programs is also reviewed, both because this is an emerging field, and because of the increasing number of low-income children in our programs; the impact of NCLB and standards on early childhood programs is addressed because its impact is so universal and pervasive. Finally, I examine research that addresses the impact on schools and early childhood programs of economic and other inequalities in society in general.

Parent Involvement and Underserved Families

In recent years parent involvement has been viewed as a central component of effective schools (Epstein & Sanders, 2002), and parent involvement has always been a central focus of Head Start (U.S. Health and Human Services, 2010). Hall and Taylor (2004) define parent involvement as: volunteering at school; communicating with teachers and other school personnel; assisting in academic activities at home; and attending school events, meetings of parent–teacher associations (PTA), and parent–teacher conferences. Head Start would add to this list, participation in classroom and center committees or the parent policy council; involvement in the program's self-assessment; being a bus aide; and volunteering on the playground or on fieldtrips (Wardle, 2009).

Research documents that for young children parent involvement in a child's program shows a positive association to academic and language skills, and improved school competence (Grolnick & Slowiaczek, 1994; Hill & Craft, 2003). However, parents with a higher income are more likely to be involved in their children's education, and parents with more education are more involved in their children's education (Hill & Taylor, 2004). Low-income parents face many barriers to involvement, including inflexible work schedules, transportation problems, and the need for babysitters for their younger children. However, if we want low-income and minority students to excel in early childhood programs, we must determine and implement approaches that are effective in improving parent involvement. According to Hill and Taylor (2004), parent involvement increases students' achievement through two mechanisms, (1) social capital and (2) social control. Social capital involves an increase in a parent's skills and information about how the school works, thus providing knowledge to help their child succeed. Social control is the confluence of ideas about achievement and behaviors between the home and school. When both are on the same page, achievement goes up (McNeal, 1999).

Teachers from cultural backgrounds different from their students are less likely to know their students and parents, and are also more likely to believe their students and families care less about education (Epstein & Dauber, 1991). Hill and Craft (2003) discovered a positive correlation between parents who volunteered at school and teachers' rating of students' academic skills and achievements. Self-perception also impacts parents' school involvement, with parents' confidence in their own intellectual abilities being the largest indicator of school involvement (Eccles & Harold, 1996). According to Hill and Taylor (2004), poverty has a particularly negative impact, due to stress, mental health, and parents' low self-perceptions. Poor parents often feel inadequate in their attempts to communicate with school personnel. Finally, parents' own experiences as students, both positive and negative, help shape their school involvement.

An early childhood program's context and policies regarding parent involvement have a tremendous impact. For example, because of the program's official position in regard to the support of parent involvement and a history of successful parent involvement, many local Head Start programs successfully involve parents in many activities to support their children's learning (Wardle, 2009). Teachers' encouragement and support of parent involvement is associated with an increase in parent confidence in both working with the school and in helping their children with school-related work at home (Epstein & Dauber, 1991). Schools that make an effort to involve parents in kindergarten transition activities have discovered these parents remain involved during their children's subsequent school years (LaParo, Kraft-Sayre, & Pianta, 2003).

Key Issues in Research   According to Hill and Taylor, parents' involvement in their children's education is complex, multidimensional, and comes in a vast array of forms. Research is beginning to examine all of the various forms that constitute parent involvement in early childhood programs and schools. However, this multidimensional understanding of parent involvement makes research difficult. There is no agreed-upon definition and no universal set of measures, thus making it difficult to compare findings across programs. Further, we have no way to measure the reciprocal relationship between variables; for example, how does the involvement of parents in the school increase parent support of school-related activities at home? And, who should be the object of these studies—parents, teachers, students, or administrators? Interestingly, one study shows that, while teachers', students', and parents' reports of school involvement were only moderately correlated with each other, each was highly related to student achievement (Hill & Taylor, 2004).

Almost all of the research to date is based on mothers. We have no research on father involvement. We don't know if the same factors, such as income and education, affect father involvement. We do know, however, that cultural factors are important (Bang, 2009). And, with the increased concern about the school failure of boys, especially minority boys (Gargiulo, 2012), we might hypothesize that one avenue for intervention is increased father involvement (Wardle, 2004b).

We have already discussed the research on the impact of teachers' perceptions of parent involvement on student performance. Epstein and Dauber (1991) also show that teachers tend to evaluate African American and low-income parents more negatively than White and middle-class parents; furthermore, teachers who don't support parent involvement in general tend to be most critical of African American and low-income parents.

A critically important question is how do we increase parent involvement with traditionally underserved and marginalized families? One suggestion is to increase the amount of information on parent-involvement best practices and research in college preparation programs (Hill & Taylor, 2004). However, according to Hill and Taylor (2004), we still face these challenges: (a) low income families are less likely to be involved with the schooling of their children, (b) minority parents are less likely to be involved in the education of their children, (c) schools in low-income, and often predominantly minority communities, are less likely to promote active parent involvement policies and activities, and (d) many teachers, practically White, middle-class teachers, tend to have negative opinions toward low-income and minority parents' commitment to education. As a result, students who would benefit most from active parent involvement in their schools and early childhood programs are less likely to actually have this involvement: It's the proverbial Catch-22.

According to Hill and Taylor (2004), this dilemma suggests that parent involvement programs that are successful with mainstream families may be ineffective in programs and school districts that serve high risk or disadvantaged communities; it is no longer appropriate for intervention programs to simply take ideas that work with the mainstream population and adapt them into programs for underserved and at-risk families. A new model needs to be created or maybe adapted from successful programs such as Head Start (Wardle 2009).

In her 2009 research, Bang addresses common issues that face new immigrants in their relationship with schools. She studied new parents of kindergarten students, and discovered that many schools and early childhood programs struggle to meet the needs of culturally and linguistically diverse families (S. Lee, 2005). While Bang's research looks at specific cultural and national groups (Pakistan, China, Korea), she generalizes her results to include all new immigrants who struggle with understanding the rules and expectations of American educational programs, regardless of their specific cultural, racial, or national backgrounds. This includes new, White immigrants from Eastern Europe and Western Russia (many of whom are Jewish). Bang (2009) developed a series of recommendations from her research:

- Families that are new to the United States do not understand how schools and early childhood programs function. They don't understand things like Back-to-School Night, fund-raiser book fairs, and Box Tops for Education. This lack of information can cause embarrassment and family stress, and eventually lack of involvement. These new families need concrete information about common practices.
- Families from other countries may be quiet and appear to be satisfied with everything going on in the program. However, they may be frustrated but believe that complaints might negatively impact their child. Some parents would rather move to another school than voice their concerns to staff. Thus it is critical to provide appropriate and direct communication tools. A suggestion box and an anonymous parent survey are two such ways to address this problem.
- Understand cultural roles of parents. Many cultures have different expectations for each gender regarding their children's education. For example, in Korea, Japan, and India, education of children is the mother's concern, as it is in the Middle Eastern countries. Men from these countries "feel awkward and embarrassed" to participate in school activities (Bang, 2009).
- Present parent meetings about how the education program works. Bang reports a Chinese father who punished his daughter for an "S" grade (satisfactory), because he assumed it was grade below an "F." Other families were frustrated when they received letters expressing concerns regarding their children, but did not know whom they should contact at the program. Thus, programs need to provide basic parent training about procedures, curricula, classroom management, and specific program policies such as student discipline and attendance.
- Offer English language classes. Lack of proficiency in English is a serious barrier to family involvement in a child's educational program (Lee, 2005). In her research, Bang discovered many families, while wanting to learn English, were disappointed and frustrated. Bang believes these programs should focus on conversational English and practical school-related dialogues.

In conclusion, teachers and administrators of early childhood programs working with new immigrant families, regardless of where they come from, their race, or language, need to understand what these new families need if they are to provide the best possible education opportunities for their children.

Culture and Identity

As has already been pointed out, two central issues in the early childhood multicultural literature are culture and identity. In this section studies are reviewed that add new insights to both of these complex concepts. While Ngo's (2008) study focuses on adolescence, the overall message is extremely relevant to issues of identity for young minority children and their families, including immigrants. Ngo (2008) begins the article by pointing out that much of the popular and academic literature presents the struggles of new immigrant children and their families to this country as opposing positions: differences between immigrant culture and U.S. culture; dualism of transitional vs. modern, rural vs. urban, first generation vs. second generation; cultural values that encourage underachieving at school vs. cultural values that encourage and support educational progress and achievement, and so on. She then states, "the cultural difference model for understanding immigrant experiences sets up binary oppositions between tradition and modernity, East and West, and First World and Third World, among others" (p. 5). She argues that this view is problematic for two reasons: (a) the focus on traditional cultural values presents something that is fixed and absolute, rather than a social process which finds meaning within social relationships, and (b) a binary approach creates a pecking order of good/bad, ours/theirs, culturally sensitive/insensitive, and so on.

Ngo (2008) argues that immigrant students' and their families' experiences are much more complex and ever-changing toward an in-between view of both culture and identity. The point is that immigrant students, along with other minorities, must struggle with representations and discourses, stereotypes if you will, about who they are, and their own individual experiences. One of the most common forms of dominant discourse is stereotypes and myths about different minority groups. For example, that all Asian immigrants are computer geniuses, good at math, passive, and martial arts experts (R. Lee, 1999), a view that results from lumping of individuals into generalized categories that ignore individual diversity and the diversity of various subgroups (Ngo, 2008).

In a study further investigating this issue of dominant discourse and personal identity, Ngo (2006) reports on students she studied in a proudly multiracial school. She reported that, while students were from several Asian groups, including Lao, Hmong, and Vietnamese, other students viewed them as either Asian or Chinese. According to Ngo (2008), this represents the erroneous but popular view that Cambodian, Chinese, East Indian, Filipino, Guamanian, Hawaiian, Hmong, Indonesian, Japanese, Korean, Laotian, Samoan, Taiwanese, and Vietnamese are all part of the same cultural group.

Identity development is a process fraught with tensions and disagreements. Individual immigrants must negotiate the in-between of culture and identity—expectations of others collide with an individual's own view of their identity (Hall, 1996). One student in this study was Lao and had many Hmong friends. Her parents and Lao friends believed she "wanted to be Hmong" because of her friends; her parents also worried that she would "turn out bad" (the stereotyped Lao view of the Hmong). This student struggled with her identity because her parents and Lao friends believed, (a) her speaking English would lead to her forgetting her Lao identity, and (b) having Hmong friends meant she was choosing to be Hmong. According to Ngo (2006), notions of immigrant experiences must move beyond an either-or paradigm toward an understanding of the in-between. Immigrant students are defining what it means to be a Lao American: they need to be empowered to express what it means to be Lao youth in American schools.

The either-or discussion of this study is relevant to early childhood multicultural education. Many early childhood multicultural documents present a variety of binary positions: mainstream White vs. minority, immigrant vs. American, girls vs. boys, English speaking vs. non-English speaking, individualist vs. communal values, competitive vs. collective behaviors, and so on (Gonzalez-Mena, 2008). But, according to Ngo (2008), we need to examine the in-between identity and culture negotiated both by immigrant families and their children, and by traditional American minority families and their children.

In the revised *Anti-Bias Education for Young Children and Ourselves* (Derman-Sparks & Edwards, 2010), Hernandez and Lee (2010) label all people from Latin America as Hispanic. However, more than 40 native languages are spoken in Latin America (Archive of the Indigenous Languages of Latin America, [AILLA], 2010), along with a variety of European languages, and each country's population includes a rich diversity of racial, ethnic, and cultural backgrounds. For example, the official government groups in Brazil include European (Spanish, Portuguese, German, Italian, Welsh, English, and so on), Asian/Japanese, Afro

Brazilian, Amerindian, Middle-Eastern, and mixed-race (IBGE/PNAD, 2008). Lumping this wonderful diversity into a large Hispanic or Latino category contradicts Ngo's (2008) point. Further, the tendency to view global racial diversity purely in terms of the U.S. Census categories should obviously be challenged.

Identity Development of Multiracial Children   Many multiracial children in our programs find themselves in the in-between place that Ngo (2008) talks about. While many educators still label these children with the single identity of their parent of color (Spencer, 2010; York, 2003), these students are struggling with their own understanding of who they are (Baxley, 2008; Root, 1996). Further, many teachers and peers misidentify them; single-race peers also accuse them of "wanting to be White, or Black or Latino, and so on." Some of this discourse is popular and academic, some based on ignorance. However, much of the multicultural literature supports this confusion and reinforces mainstream discourse at the expense of the child's own identity struggle (Derman-Sparks & Edward, 2010; Gonzalez-Mana, 2008; York, 2003). Clearly any binary concept of White vs. non-White is destructive for biracial children with one White parent and one parent of color (Wallace, 2004).

African American Children Need More Authoritarian Approaches

Janet Gonzalez-Mena (2008) writes, "My friend and training partner, Intisar Shareef, brings up the issue of authoritarianism and African American children. She says the gentle, unimpassioned, authoritative approaches of European-American teachers doesn't work with African American children who are used to authority looking, acting, and sounding different" (p. 19). This view is popular in multicultural texts. Wright (1998), however, counters this view, and states, "the conventional wisdom by many Blacks and Whites is that physical punishment is part of the Blacks' cultural heritage" and, "the legacy of slavery seems to be a major influence on the disciplinary methods of Blacks" (pp. 129–130), pointing out that slave owners used harsh physical punishment to control their slaves. Frequently beaten by their masters, adult slaves in turn beat their children. Over the years this legacy has been passed on from one generation to another. According to Wright (1998), unhealthy parenting practices rooted in those times have endured in too many Black families and are making life worse for Black children, while harming, not helping, their development.

In studying contextual differences in parenting behaviors, race and ethnicity in the United States have been studied as a moderator of the link between the use of physical discipline and children's adjustment (Polaha, Larzelere, Shapiro, & Pettit, 2004). A study conducted on 585 children from Knoxville, Tennessee, and Bloomington, Indiana, found that for European American children, physical discipline during the first five years was associated with higher levels of externalizing behavior problems, but not so for African American children (Deater-Deckard, Dodge, Bates, & Pettit, 1996). In an extension of this study, Lansford, Deater-Deckard, Dodge, Bates, and Pettit (2004) found that this early discipline along with punitive discipline during grades 6 to 8, related to higher levels of externalizing behaviors in grade 11 for European American adolescents, but lower levels of externalizing behaviors for African American adolescents. Others have reported similar racial-ethnic moderating effects (Gunnoe & Mariner, 1997). The common explanation for these differences is that physical discipline is more normative for African American families (Lansford et al., 2004).

In relation to physical discipline and young children, Lansford (2005) describes an experiment on the effects of physical discipline on children from six different countries. The impact of physical discipline on White children has received considerable research, with the general conclusion that physical discipline is associated with more child behavior problems such as aggression (Eron, Huesmann, & Zelli, 1991), delinquency (Farrington & Hawkins, 1991), and criminality (Gershoff, 2002). However, other studies suggest that these effects are not universal (Pinderhuges, Dodge, Bates, Petti & Zelli, 2000), and are influenced by various contexts.

This particular study sought to determine the specific relationship of cultural normativeness on the impact of physical punishment on children (Lansford, 2005). Six countries were selected: China, India, Italy, Kenya, the Philippines, and Thailand. Criteria used for the selection included individual versus collective orientation, religion, and legal issues, such as instances where parents' use of physical discipline had resulted in legal action against them. For this study, middle-class children from the dominant ethnic groups in each country were studied. Interviews of mothers were used to determine the normativeness of the use of physical discipline; two instruments were used to determine the impact of physical discipline on children (Achenbach, 1991).

The results showed the rank order of the use of physical punishment in countries, from lowest to highest, was Thailand, China, the Philippines, Italy, India, and Kenya. The study also found that more frequent use of physical discipline is less strongly associated with adverse child outcomes in contexts where there is a greater perception of the perceived normativeness of physical punishment. However, more frequently experiencing physical discipline was associated with more anxiety, regardless of whether the child perceived it as normative, and those children who perceived physical discipline as normative had higher levels of aggression, regardless of whether they actually experienced physical punishment. The findings support the hypothesis that mothers' use of physical discipline and child adjustment is moderated by the normativeness of physical discipline, while also showing some negative impacts of physical discipline on children, regardless of its normativeness.

It appears that these behaviors are also problematic when parents engage in them outside of their normative contexts; that is, when they immigrate to countries where physical discipline is less normative. The authors also suggest that, even when a practice is sanctioned by a cultural group, it does not necessarily mean that it is acceptable. Children have rights and parents have responsibilities. "There are times when it may be necessary to apply a global standard to protect children from serious long-term harm. Thus, it is important not to take an extreme position in [terms of] cultural relativism" (Lansford, 2005, p. 1242). The researchers also believe that children's cognitive interpretation of discipline events might be more important than parents' interpretation in determining how the event is related to children's adjustment.

Many child development specialists deeply believe that social context has a central impact on children's learning and development (Gonzalez-Mena, 2008; West, 2001). They subscribe to Bronfenbrenner's (1998) ecological systems theory. However, this view poses several major challenges for early childhood programs. The first challenge is for a program to be able to ascertain the cultural practices of a family. Not only does race/ethnicity not equal culture, but we also know that there is tremendous diversity within any large U.S. demographic group. For example, within the large Hispanic group there are long-time residents whose families were here before America became a country, people from Puerto Rico, and new immigrants from Mexico and Central and South America. Some are poor; some are not; some speak English, Spanish, Portuguese, French, and Native languages (AILLA, 2010), and so on. Then there is the dynamic nature of a family's culture (U.S. Department of Health and Human Services, 2010). Finally, a person's culture is greatly influenced by the extent to which she actively subscribes to its values and tenants (Luz, 2010; U.S. Department of Health and Human Services, 2010).

The most obvious solution to this dilemma is to respect parents' wishes (Gonzalez-Mena, 2008). However, we do not always do this. For example, Rodriquez (2008) admonishes teachers to inform parents about the value of supporting their child's home language, even if the parent believes it is more advantageous for their child to learn English as quickly as possible. Further, Rodriguez advises teachers to convince parents to use their home language at home, and involve their children in non-English-speaking activities in the community. In this case she believes it is more important for a program to educate parents regarding the value of supporting their home language than for the program to respond to the wishes of the parents. When conflicts like this arise, program staff should follow NAEYC (1999) guidelines in negotiating the best possible solution.

The second challenge has to do with how programs can become multicultural. It is generally agreed today that the United States is not a melting pot but a pluralistic society, and that our programs should reflect this pluralism (Derman-Sparks & Edwards, 2010; Gonzalez- Mena, 2008; Luz, 2010). Luz then suggests that early childhood programs should be bilingual and bicultural, reflecting immigrants' home language and culture, and the overall American culture; Rodriguez (2008) focuses on supporting a child's Spanish and English language and cultural development, while Gonzalez-Mena (2008) stresses the need for consistency between the child's home culture and the program.

But Kindler (2002) reports that 400 different languages are spoken in our schools; Howard (2007) describes a school district outside of New York City with Haitian, Jamaican, Dominican, Latino, and Black families; and David et al. (2005) document that, while Head Start used to serve primarily Spanish non-English-speaking children and their families, they now work with children and families who speak 140 different languages, with some individual Head Start programs struggling with 10 non-English languages. It is simply unrealistic to assume that most early childhood programs only serve families from two cultural and linguistic backgrounds.

Thus, when it comes to discipline, programs face a dilemma. And, as the authors also suggest (Lansford et al., 2005), even when a child's family comes from a culture where a more physical approach to discipline is normative, if the child sees that others are not using this approach (i.e., other families in the program) they may view it negatively.

Social Justice in Early Childhood Classrooms

Several researchers explore the research on social justice in early childhood classrooms. For example, Ryan and Grieshaber (2004) indicate that, while young children receive messages about power and privilege from home, classrooms play a significant role in this process. Hyland (2010) then reminds us that the U.S. population continues to become increasingly diverse with students from minority racial groups making up 50% of the U.S. school population by 2050. Ramani, Gilberson, Fox, and Provasnik (2007) document that today these students are still less successful than White and Asian students in our education programs. It is, therefore, essential that early childhood programs address these inequalities. Two separate approaches are then proposed to achieve equity: culturally relevant teaching and critical pedagogy (Hyland, 2010).

Culturally Relevant Teaching   Culturally relevant teaching is an approach to teaching that is culturally and politically relevant to a specific disenfranchised group (Ladson-Billings, 1994). Teachers use children's own personal stories and cultural knowledge as the heart of the curriculum and teachers learn the cultural norms and values of the racial, ethnic, or language groups they work with. In one study, teachers of second to fifth grade African American children integrated Afrocentric content into the curricula, and

also became allied with social justice issues in the African American community (Ladson-Billings, 1994). Ballenger (1999) conducted research on her own classroom practices. She worked with Haitian preschool children, and noted that White, European classroom management approaches, less authoritarian and more democratic, did not work with this population; over time she adopted the approach used by her Haitian colleagues, and her classroom management improved.

Many early childhood teachers attempt to include a variety of racial, gender, disability, and other material in their classrooms. However, the White mainstream materials and orientation still dominate, thus maintaining the norm. Dyson (2003) even suggests that relying on books as a curricular tool to teach literacy and other content, in and of itself is a White, middle-class value. Compton-Lilly (2006) worked with an African American student in teaching literacy, allowing him to use popular media images to structure his writing, and rap music to learn fluency through repetition. This approach successfully produced connections and overlap with the student's home culture and media culture, and with classroom activities and the literacy curriculum. These results show that careful observation and respect for a child's culture can create improved learning.

Critical Pedagogy   Critical pedagogy advocates teaching approaches and curricula aimed at examining power among marginalized groups compared to mainstream Whites (Hyland, 2010). It examines the way school practices create privilege and marginalize identities. Its goal is to teach learners how to take social action to address inequalities (Sleeter & McLaren, 1995). Research in this area focuses on teachers providing safe environments where children can discuss issues of justice and fairness. Marsh (1992) discusses how she worked in a kindergarten classroom to create social justice themes throughout the year, and how children became adept at talking about injustice related to immigrants, Native Americans, and other non-White cultures. They even engaged in actions to try to address what they perceived to be injustices in their school.

In looking at gender issues and critical pedagogy, two important concerns are, (1) how cultural messages assist children in developing their identities regarding gender and gender behaviors, and (2) how these messages can limit identity development (Hyland, 2010). Researchers have studied teachers who helped girls to become assertive and to challenge stereotypical behaviors and beliefs (Wilson-Keenan, Solsken, & Willett, 1999). They discovered that girls were more likely to challenge stereotypical gender behaviors when the teacher was present in the activitiy and less so when in peer groups.

As has already been discussed, we know that boys struggle in our programs (Hyland, 2010). Boys are more likely than girls to fall behind in literacy activities, have more discipline issues, and are more likely to be expelled (Skelton, 2001). Alloway and Gilbert (1997) believe that the content and approach to literacy in early childhood programs is feminized and causes conflict with boy's behaviors and their ideas of masculine identity. Compton-Lilly (2006) incorporated masculine literacy forms to encourage a boy's reading. She determined that the boy believed girls are smarter than boys, and that teachers like girls more than they like boys. Further, he saw girls as academically better; and said he would rather fight than excel academically in school. Using stereotypical masculine texts and subjects enabled the boy to match his own view of being a boy with doing well in school (Compton-Lilly, 2006). These results substantiate the general view that early childhood settings are female cultures with materials and activities that match up well with the needs of girls (Wardle, 2004a). However, Compton-Lilly's (2006) study shows that, when a deliberate attempt is made, even by female staff, to counter this approach, boys can achieve in literacy.

Hyland (2010) also recalls how her 2-year-old son liked to wear his hair and clothes in the fashion of his sisters. On one occasion when she dropped him off at his program attired this way, another parent criticized her, saying that her husband would never approve of this behavior. Clearly these and other messages convey the norm of heterosexuality, and can be damaging to children from gay and lesbian families (Clay, 2004). Teachers in early childhood settings must challenge homophobic remarks by children and staff (Surtees, 2005). Boldt (1996) recalls attempting to influence the discourse of children in her third grade classroom. For example, they insisted that girls and boys only wear certain clothes. To address this, she had them act out stories that challenged traditional gender assumptions. Ryan and Ochsner (1999) describe teachers asking children to rethink gender assumptions by challenging their logic. And Wardle (1991) suggested renaming the housekeeping area the dramatic play area, introducing stereotypical masculine props to this area and feminine props to the block area, and teachers challenging gender behaviors through modeling and the activity choices they provide.

Clearly young children need to be encouraged to develop a sense of justice, and teachers and programs need to provide educational opportunities where everyone can excel. However, many of these ideas seem to conflict with each other or with other approaches. As has already been stated, early childhood literature is filled with admonitions for teachers and programs to listen to the interests of parents and to adjust the curricula, teaching practices, and other approaches to meet the needs of these parents, especially when they challenge the program's normative practices (Derman-Sparks & Edwards, 2010; Gonzalez-Mena, 2008). However, these studies suggest that children develop many of their negative attitudes, values, and behaviors at home (Hyland, 2010). However, it is simply not correct to assume that all minority parents support social justice values and concepts, and all White parents do not. For example, many minority parents hold strong ideas that limit gender identity (Bang, 2009; Luz, 2010). To help sort out these apparent

conflicts, NAEYC's ethical guidelines should be consulted and applied (1996).

Marsh (1992) documents working with kindergarten children to engage them in activities to protest unjust behaviors. One wonders, however, how parents would respond to their children engaging in protests against perceived unfair behaviors at home (e.g., the physical punishment discussed earlier). And all parents know that their children believe some of their parents' behaviors and expectations are unjust. Finally, a major unjust issue in most early childhood programs is the fact that the pay for early childhood caregivers, almost all of whom are women, is so abysmal (Neugebauer, 2004; Young, 2003). It is therefore incumbent upon professional organizations such as NAEYC and anyone committed to multicultural education and equity to proactively advocate for improved salaries and benefits for individuals working with young children.

Dyson (2003) points out that not only are most curricula dominated by Eurocentric viewpoints, but that the very focus on literature and academics in our schools is a White, middle-class value. One of the central goals of early childhood programs is to prepare children for school success (Scott-Little et al., 2006), and with the advent of NCLB and the alignment of curricula to school learning standards, these mainstream American values have been solidified (Kagan, Carroll, Comer & Scott-Little, 2006). Whether we like it or not, if we want marginalized students to succeed in American schools, which is one of the goals of multicultural education, we must prepare them to be successful in these literacy standards. For example, on average a low-income child enters schools with an average vocabulary of 2,500 words; middle-class students with 10,000 words (Moats, 2001). Two possible approaches to these issues are increased and more effective parent involvement activities, tailored to the unique needs of minority and low-income families (Bang, 2009), and small class sizes in early childhood and early elementary programs (Krueger & Whitmore, 2001).

As has been documented throughout this chapter, one of the major areas of imbalance in the early childhood field is an almost total lack of men in the field (Neugebauer, 1999). Grieshaber and Ryan (2006) suggest that this concern has intensified over the last 30 years. One reason for this is because research has continually shown that both boys and girls need men in their lives to assist in their healthy gender development (Nelson, 2010). Grieshaber and Ryan (2006) believe this imbalance is largely due to the view held by many that men who choose to work with young children challenge society's view of what it means to be a man (and, thus also what it means to be a woman), and puts men in a no-win situation where they are presumed to be both homosexuals and pedophiles. They also believe that the feminized culture of the field and its low financial and social status, are major factors. Finally, they view society's unease regarding men in the field as symptoms of society's larger unease around child abuse, adults touching children, and pedophilia. Others believe that some women in the field are uncomfortable working with men, and see men involved in the field as a direct threat to their independence and control (Neugebauer, 1999; Wardle, 2004b).

Critical Literacy with Young Children   One in five children in the United States lives in poverty (National Center for Children in Poverty, 2006). Thus, many early childhood programs serve poor children and families. A critical literacy curriculum is an approach enabling teachers and students to explore socially significant issues, such as poverty (Chafel, Flint, Hammel, & Pomeroy, 2007). In this way they can process new understandings of the world and their place in it.

Chafel et al. (2007) describes four ministudies on the use of critical literacy with young children. In the first study the researcher implemented a critical literacy curriculum in an emergency shelter school, and determined that children should be encouraged to "express themselves and weave life experiences into their learning, while seriously addressing issues of social justice, equity, and diversity in developmentally appropriate language" (p. 74). In the second study, the book by DyAnne DiSalvo-Ryan, *Uncle Willie and the Soup Kitchen*, was read to 62 8-year olds in Midwestern public schools. The children then drew pictures and discussed their drawings. Results showed that books can be effectively used to engage children in conversations about poverty and to help them explore their understanding of poverty.

Another study (Hammel, 2003) of a K-2 grade mixed-age classroom also began with a book, *Teammates*, by P. Golenbock, which is about Jackie Robinson, who integrated major league baseball. The teacher then used other books, including the same book about soup kitchens, before progressing to involve the students in community service activities, including growing vegetables for a local soup kitchen. The researcher states, "Critical literacy has helped me and the children to reach beyond the four walls of the classroom into the arena of life" (Hammel, 2003, p. 77). Finally, the fourth study (Chafel et al., 2007), examined activities based on the book, *Tomas and the Library Lady*, by Pat Mora. The book is about growing up as the child of migrant workers. The study compared student engagement from 2000 and 2003. In 2000, the teacher asked children to respond to the book, and she reports that these responses were flat and somewhat superficial. In the 2003 example, the teacher made a conscious effort to bring children's lives and experiences into the discussion, helping them discuss their own personal experiences of poverty and being migrant workers. This resulted in more complex and substantive discussions by the students. Thus, in the 2003 example, the teacher shifted the conversation from text-driven discussions to student experience-driven discussions, building upon children's cultural resources and knowledge. Students discussed how their families used community assistance programs; they also learned to expand their thinking beyond their own personal world and into the community.

In summary, these four ministudies show how a literacy curriculum unfolds, beginning with the selection of a book, reading the book, and then discussing the content with young children, to moving to discussions driven by each child's personal experiences, and on to addressing children's concept of, and ability to think critically about, social issues such as poverty.

The Impact of NCLB on Student Achievement

As has already been mentioned, some educators view NCLB as a great advance in our commitment to equity education (Bowman, 2006), while others view it as a step backwards (Wardle & Cruz-Janzen, 2004). In her article, DuBois (2007) interviewed several experts to ascertain their view of the impact of NCLB on the achievements of minority children, low-income children, and children with disabilities.

Andrew Porter believes that NCLB is, "a beautiful thing," because it focuses our attention on the need for equality, opportunity, and accountability from schools. He also believes the shift from the process of teaching to content and output (proficiency) is positive. Porter favors school accountability, but also wants accountability from students and teachers. But he objects to what he considers a built-in failure in the goals of the act, which requires that by 2014, 100% of U.S. students will be 100% proficient. This is obviously unattainable. However, Stephen Elliot disagrees, arguing that disability advocates pushed for this 100% proficiency goal, believing it would guarantee that students with disabilities would receive the educational tools and services they need, rather than simply being pushed aside. While teachers complain that they are required to teach to the test, Stephen Elliot admonishes them by arguing that content standards should simply be used as a framework for their instruction (DuBois, 2007); however, according to DuBois (2007), "affluent children are receiving a better education than those who are struggling" (p. 16).

Porter and others have determined that the gap between preschoolers from middle-class families entering school versus those from impoverished families is huge, and as big as it will ever be while they are in school. This gap does not increase during the school year; however, it does increase during the summer, when children are out of school. This means that schools are being asked to fix family and societal problems that exist beyond the classroom (DuBois, 2007).

Advocates of students with disabilities also suggest that NCLB change its approach to assessment, using several short-term, less high-stakes formative assessments, two to three times a year. These assessments are more effective in helping teachers adjust the curriculum and instruction to meet the needs of struggling students. Further, Elliot argues that one of the major downsides of NCLB is the inability of states to manage all their data. One suggestion to address this problem is to create nationwide NCLB assessments—both their content and required proficiency levels (DuBois, 2007). Currently, all states implementing NCLB develop their own materials, standards, and assessments. Thus, the proposal is to create national content standards and national proficiency standards: a national curriculum, if you will.

NCLB promised an array of interventions for students attending failing schools. Many districts are not receiving the promised funding; and, while students are allowed to move to successful schools, this usually does not occur, because (a) schools that are successful do not want these students to drag down their scores, and (b) in some situations the entire school district is failing. Finally, poor and non-English-speaking parents find the move from the neighborhood school just too fraught with obstacles and barriers (DuBois, 2007). According to Donna Ford, one of the people interviewed by DuBois for this article, if we increase the rigor and quality of the curriculum a child experiences, either by improving the school or moving the child to a better school, low-income children will still fail unless they receive a great deal of support, not just to catch up but to keep up.

Finally, Porter suggests that improving the quality of our teachers can close the achievement gap. He argues that when a child has a good teacher every year, after 12 years the child should be caught up. However, according to Porter and Ford, the onus for having good teachers is on the universities that must prepare teachers with high expectations and who are well qualified.

Belfied (2009) demonstrates that quality preschool programs have a large impact on later school success, especially for minority and low-income students. The research also shows that quality preschool programs significantly reduce placement of children into special education classes (which are disproportionately minority and male), and reduce dropouts. Further, Krueger and Whitmore (2009) have analyzed the studies conducted on the Tennessee's Project STAR results, which show the tremendous academic benefit for small class size, especially for low income and minority children. These results also showed a reduction of the Black–White achievement gap at college entry of 60% by children who attended small K-3 classes.

The social justice approach calls for a dynamic interchange between teacher, learner, and classroom context, use of a variety of assessments to fairly monitor student progress, intellectual flexibility, and an approach that values personal perspectives and various dispositions among students (Lalas, 2007). A standardized approach to curricula, instruction, and assessment does none of these. Furthermore, the insistence by experts on a national curriculum and assessments appears to contradict many additional aspects of critical pedagogy and social justice (Lalas, 2007). Lalas also argues that a social justice view of education requires equitable allocation of resources. It is important to note that none of these experts complain about the financial and human resources dedicated to NCLB. Millions of dollars are spent developing standardized curricula and tests, and thousands of teachers' hours are used on preparing for and monitoring tests. Maybe a more equitable use of federal funds would be to assist local districts in their struggle

to fully implement the goals and requirements of IDEA (Gargiulo, 2012).

Inequalities Beyond the School

Rothstein (2008) argues that narrowing the achievement gap requires combining school reform with societal reforms that narrow socioeconomic inequalities in this country, He believes that poverty and its impact on children—poor health, increased school absenteeism, less adult attention from single parents, low birth weight, and fewer visits to libraries, museums, and zoos—has a significant impact on academic success. Boyd-Zaharias and Pate-Bain (2009) make similar claims. They state that, while they believe in good schools and good teachers, low academic achievement and dropping out of school are problems rooted in social and economic inequalities. And they believe the impact of these inequalities cannot be reversed simply through improved curricula, teaching practices, and other school reforms. Further, they believe that a focus solely on school improvement without the concomitant social and economic reforms will drive out the best teachers and administrators. Orfield (2008) suggests that simply engaging in educational reform while ignoring the need for fundamental changes in society is profoundly counterproductive.

The *Education that is Multicultural and Social Reconstructionist* view of education described by Sleeter and Grant (1999) argues that the central role of schools is to change society. And, as has been suggested throughout this chapter, a major multicultural goal for American education programs is for American society to become more equitable; that is, equity in terms of gender, race/ethnicity, culture, language, disability, income, and sexual orientation. But, as Rothstein (2008) states, many educators have been reluctant to address social and economic issues outside the school because this view appears to blame the victim, legitimizes racism, and seems to let the educational programs off the hook. Many also believe that, through education and hard work, any child can succeed in America, and thus our job is to make schools the best they can be (Howard, 2007; Rothstein, 2008).

Rothstein (2008), Howard (2007), Boyd-Zaharias and Pate-Bain (2009), and many others now suggest that multicultural educators should focus both on school reform and societal reform; that it is really not effective to do one without the other. To whit, Rothstein (2008) provides a few suggestions,

- Ensure pediatric and dental care for all students;
- Expand low-income housing subsidy programs;
- Provide mixed-income housing development in higher-income neighborhoods;
- Provide accessible, high quality child care for low income children;
- Increase the earned income tax credit, minimum wage, and collective bargaining rights;

- Fund quality after school programs;
- Require urban buses to use natural gas instead of diesel fuel; and
- Prohibit high-sulfur heating oil.

Additionally it is suggested here that people who work with young children and their families be provided with greatly enhanced salaries and benefits.

Conclusion

Because early childhood education in the United States covers the ages of birth through 8 years, and because children this age are cared for in a large variety of settings, research on early childhood multicultural education is very complex and challenging. Further, because so much of the education of young children occurs outside of an official educational curriculum, multicultural education must directly address a vast range of nonacademic factors: parents; discipline; economic, racial, cultural, religious and language diversity; a vast range of staff benefit issues; teacher selection and preparation, and so on. And, as we have discovered in this review, everything that impacts programs serving children has a political agenda and social justice perspective—nothing demonstrates this better than the way we choose to care for and educate young children in this country.

Most early childhood programs are staffed by women who receive extremely poor pay and benefits for their work; further, most teachers and caregivers are not required to earn a four-year college degree. Finally, while K-12 education is deemed to be a right for all American children, early childhood experiences are either funded by parents, or by taxpayers for low-income children and families "at risk" of school failure.

What is the best direction for new research in early childhood multicultural education? This, of course, depends on the multicultural education goals one focuses on. However, if NCLB and the subsequent standards approach adopted by most early childhood programs has produced anything positive, it is the understanding that outcomes are important. What outcomes do we expect from early childhood programs imbued with a multicultural perspective? Surely, the main outcome is for children who attend these programs, particularly underserved children, to excel in K-12 education.

Thus, we should go back to the famous Perry Preschool Research as a model, and compare a variety of program approaches. The Perry Preschool research was begun in the 1960s, and followed an experimental and control group of randomly assigned, low-income, primarily African American preschool children (Schweinhart et al., 2005). The experimental group attended a high-quality preschool program. These two groups have been followed to the present day, with the students being evaluated on a range of items, such as needing additional services in school, high school graduation, criminal activity, college graduation, in-come, and so on. Using a cost-benefit analysis, the research showed that, at age 40, every dollar invested in the quality program returned $17.07 in savings in social programs and increased taxes (Schweinhart et al., 2005).

Since Head Start was originally a demonstration program, maybe it could take the lead in comparing a variety of approaches. These comparisons must isolate the various variables discussed throughout this chapter to determine their effects on the academic success of marginalized students. Some of these comparisons might be, (1) different parent involvement models; (2) different approaches to multiple non-English languages in programs (not just two); (3) various approaches to working with parents over cultural conflicts, including discipline, gender roles, academic and religious content in the program, and so on; (4) enhanced training and benefits for staff; (5) programs where 50% of the staff are male; (6) programs where the staff match the cultural backgrounds of the parents; (7) programs that serve children with a range of disabilities without using a categorical, deficit approach, and so on. However, these programs must be similar enough to other programs serving diverse student populations that the results can be generalized. Surely, if we really want to reduce the achievement gap, and really want children from underserved groups to excel, we need to conduct extensive program comparisons to determine the approaches that actually work the best.

References

A very diverse field. (2010, December 7). *ExchangeEveryDay*. Retrieved from http://www exhangeeveryday@ccie.com

Aboud, F. E. (1987). The development of ethnic self-determination and attitudes. In J. Phinney & J. Rotheram (Eds.), *Children's ethnic solicitation, pluralism and development* (pp. 29–55). Newbury Park, CA: Sage.

Aboud, F. E. (1988). *Children and prejudice*. New York: Basil Blackwell.

Aboud, F. E., & Amato, M. (2001). Developmental and socialization influences on intergroup bias. In R. Brown & S. L. Gaerther (Eds.), *Blackwell handbook of social psychology: Intergroup processes* (pp. 65–85). Oxford, England: Blackwell.

Achenbach, T. M. (1991). *Integrative guide for the 1991 CBCL 14-18, YSR, and TRF profiles*. Burlington: Department of Psychology, University of Vermont.

Alejandro-Wright. N. M. (1985). The child's conception of racial classification: A socio-cognitive developmental model. In M. B. Spencer, G. K. Brookins, & W. R. Allen (Eds.), *Beginnings: The social and affective development of black children* (pp. 185–200). Hillsdale, NJ: Erlbaum.

Alloway, N., & Gilbert, P. (1997). Boys and literacy: Lessons from Australia. *Gender and Education, 9*(1) 49–60.

Alves-Silva, J., Santos, M. S., Guimaras, P. E. M., Ferreira, A. C. S., Bandelt, H. J., Pena, S. D. J. & Prado, V. M. (2000). The ancestry of Brazilian mtDNA lineages. *American Journal of Human Genetics, 67*, 444–461.

American Psychological Association. (2003). Guidelines on multicultural education, training, research, practice, and organizational change for psychologists. *American Psychologist, 58*(5), 377–402 .

Archive of the Indigenous Languages of Latin America (AILLA). (2010). *The indigenous languages of Latin America*. Retrieved from http://www.ailla.utexas.org/site/la_lang.html.

Ballenger, C. (1999). *Teaching other people's children: Literacy and learning in a bilingual classroom*. New York: Teachers College Press.

Bandura, A. (1965). Behavioral modification through modeling practices.

In L. Krasner & L. Ullman (Eds.), *Research on behavior modification* (pp. 310–340). New York: Holt, Rinehart & Winston.

Bang, Y. (2009). Helping all families participate in school life. *Young Children, 64*(6), 97–99.

Baratz, S. S., & Baratz, J. C. (1970). Early childhood intervention: The social science base of institutional racism. *Harvard Education Review, 40*(1), 29–50.

Baxley, T. R. (2008). Who are you? Biracial children in the classroom. *Childhood Education, 84,* 230–234.

Bemak, F., & Chung, R. (2005, February). Advocacy as a critical role for urban school counselors: Working toward equity and social justice. *ASCA Professional School Counseling, 8,* 196–202.

Belfield, C. R. (2007). The promise of early childhood education interventions. In C. R. Belfield & H. M. Levin (Eds.), *The price we pay: Economic and social consequences of inadequate education* (pp. 177–199). Washington, DC: Brookings Institution Press.

Berger, K. S. (2009). *The developing person: Through childhood and adolescence* (8th ed.). New York: Worth.

Best, S., & Kellner, D. (1991). *Postmodern theory: Critical interrogations.* London: Macmillan.

Bhabha, H. (1994). *The location of culture.* New York: Routledge.

Bigler, R. S. (1995). The role of classification skill in moderating environmental influences on children's gender stereotyping: A study of functional use of gender in the classroom. *Child Development, 66,* 1072–1087.

Bigler, R. S., & Liben, L. S. (1993). A cognitive-developmental approach to racial stereotyping and reconstructive memory in Euro-American children. *Child Development, 64,* 1507–1518.

Boldt, G. M. (1996). Sexist and heterosexist responses to gender bending in an elementary classroom. *Curriculum Inquiry, 26* (2), 113–131.

Bowles, D. D. (1993). Biracial identity: Children born to African American and White couples. *Clinical Social Work Journal, 21*(4), 417–428.

Bowman, B. (1994). The challenge of diversity. *Phi Beta Kappan, 76*(3), 21–225.

Bowman, B. (2006). Standards at the heart of educational equity. *Young Children, 61*(5), 42–48.

Boyd-Zaharias, J., & Pate-Bain, H. (2009, September). Class matters—In and out of school. Closing gaps requires attention of issues of race and poverty. *Phi Delta Kappan,* 40–44.

Bradley, J., & Kibera, P. (2006). Closing the gap. Culture and the promotion of inclusion in child care. *Young Children, 61*(1), 34–40.

Bronfenbrenner, U. (1989). Ecological systems theory. In R. Vasta (Ed.), *Annals of child development* (Vol. 6, pp. 187–251). Greenwich, CT: JAI Press.

Brown v. Board of Education of Topeka, 347 U.S. 483 (1954).

Cannella, G. S., & Bailey, C. (1999). Postmodern research in early childhood education. In. S. Reifel (Ed.), *Advances in early educational and day care* (Vol. 10, pp. 3–39). Greenwich, CT: JAI Press.

Chafel, J. A. (1997). Children's view of poverty: a review of research and implications for teaching. *The Educational Forum, 61,* 360–371.

Chafel, J. A., Flint, A. S., Hammel, J., & Pomeroy, K. H. (2007).Young children, social issues, and critical literacy: Stories of teachers and researchers. *Young Children, 62*(1), 73–81.

Clay, J. W. (2004). Creating safe, just places for children of lesbian and gay parents: The NAEYC Code of Ethics in action. *Young Children, 59*(6), 34–38.

Cochran-Smith, M. (2004). *Walking the road: Race, diversity, and social justice.* New York: Teachers College Press.

Compton-Lilly, C. (2006). Identity, childhood culture, and literacy learning: A case study. *Journal of Early Childhood Literacy, 6*(1) 57–76.

Copple, C. (2001). *A world of difference. Readings on teaching young children in a diverse sociality.* Washington, DC: National Association for the Education of Young Children.

Cornoyer, M., Solomon, C. R., & Trudel, M. (1998). I speak, then I expect: Language and self-control in young children and at home. *Canadian Journal of Behavioral Science, 30,* 69–81.

Cortes, C. E. (1999). Mixed-race children: Building bridges to new identities. *Reaching Today's Youths, 3*(2), 28–31.

Cortes, C. E. (2000). *The children are watching: How the media teach about diversity.* New York: Teacher's College Press.

Cross, W. (1987). A two-factor theory of black identity: Implications for the study of identity development in minority children. In J. S. Phinney & M. J. Rotheram (Eds.), *Children's ethnic socialization* (pp. 117–134). Newbury Park, CA: Sage,

Cunningham, B., & Dorsey, B. (2004). Out of sight but not out of mind: The harmful absence of men. *Child Care Information Exchange, 165,* 42–43.

Darling-Hammond, L., French, J., & Garcia-Lopez, S. (Eds.). (2002). *Learning to teach for social justice.* New York: Teachers College Press.

David, J., Onchonga, O., Drew, R., Grass, R., Stechuk, & Burns, S. M. (2005). Head Start embraces language diversity. *Young Children, 60*(6), 40–43.

Deater-Deckard, K., Dodge, K. A., Bates, J. E., & Pettit, G. S. (1996). Physical discipline among African American and European American mothers: Links to children's externalizing behaviors. *Developmental Psychology, 32,* 1065–1072.

DeGrella, I. H., & Green, V. P. (1984). Young children's attitudes toward orthopedic and sensory disabilities. *Education of the Visually Handicapped, 16*(1), 3–11.

Derman-Sparks, L., & the ABC Taskforce (1989). *The anti-bias curriculum: Tools for empowering young children.* Washington, DC: National Association for the Education of Young Children.

Derman-Sparks, L., & Edwards, J. O. (2010). *Anti-bias education for young children and ourselves.* Washington, DC: National Association for the Education of Young Children.

Dewey, J. (1897). *My pedagogic creed.* Washington, DC: The Progressive Educational Association,

Diamond, K. E. (1994). Evaluating preschool children's sensitivity to developmental differences in their peers. *Topics in Early Childhood Special Education, 14*(1), 49–62.

Dittmar, H., & Van Duuren, M. (1993, Spring). Human nature beliefs and perceptions of the economic world. *The Journal of Foundations of Organizational Research, 36,* 49–62.

DuBois, L. A. (2007, Summer). No child left behind. Who's accountable? *Peabody Reflector,* 14–20.

Dyson, A. H. (2003). *The brothers and sisters learn to write: Popular illiteracies in childhood and school cultures.* New York: Teachers College Press.

Eccles, J. S., & Harold, R. D. (1996). Family involvement in children's and adolescent's schooling. In A Booth & J. F. Dunn (Eds.), *Family-school links: How do they affect educational outcomes?* (pp. 3–34). Mahwah, NJ: Erlbaum.

Epstein, J. L., & Dauber, S. L. (1991). School programs and teacher practices of parent involvement in inner-city elementary and middle schools. *The Elementary School Journal, 91,* 289–305.

Epstein, J. L., & Sanders, M. G. (2002). Family, school, and community. In M. H. Bornstein (Ed.), *Handbook of parenting: Vol. 5. Practical issues in parenting* (pp. 407–437). Mahwah, NJ: Erlbaum.

Erikson, E. (1963). *Childhood and society* (2nd ed.) New York: W.W. Norton.

Eron, J. D., Huesmann, L. R., & Zelli, A. (1991). The role of parental variables in the learning of aggression. In D. Pepler & K. Rubin (Eds.), *The development and treatment of children's aggression* (pp. 169–188). Hillsdale, NJ: Erlbaum.

Farrington, D. P., & Hawkins, J. D. (1991). Predicting participation, early onset, and later persistence in officially recorded offending. *Criminal Behaviors and Mental Health, 1,* 1–33.

Favazza, P., & Odom, S. L. (1997). Promoting positive attitudes of kindergarten-age children toward people with disabilities. *Exceptional Children, 63,* 405–418.

Feeney, S., & Freeman, N. K. (2002, January). Early childhood education as an emerging profession: Ongoing conversations. *Child Care Information Exchange,* 38–41.

Fernandez, C. (1996). Government classification of multiracial/multiethnic people. In M. P. P. Root (Ed.), *The multiracial experience: Racial borders as the new frontier* (pp. 15–36*).* Thousand Oaks, CA: Sage.

Fish, J. M. (Ed.).(2002). *Race and intelligence: Separating science from myth*. Mahwah, NJ: Erlbaum.

Freire, P. (1970). *Pedagogy of the oppressed*. New York: Seabury Press

Gargiulo, R. (2012). *Special education in contemporary society*. Los Angeles, CA: Sage.

Gershoff, E. T. (2002). Corporal punishment by parents and associated child behaviors and experiences: A meta-analytic and theoretical review. *Psychological Bulletin, 128*, 539–579.

Giroux, H. A. (1993). *Border crossings: Cultural workers and the politics of education*. New York: Routledge.

Gonzalez-Mena, J. (2008). *Diversity in early care and education: Honoring differences* (5th ed.). New York: McGraw-Hill.

Goodman, J. E. (1989). Does retardation mean dumb? Children's perceptions of the nature, cause, and course of mental retardation. *The Journal of Special Education, 23*, 313–329.

Goodman, M. (1952). *Race awareness in young children*. Cambridge, MA: Addison-Wesley.

Grieshaber, S. (2001). Equity issues in research design. In G. MacNaughton, S. Rocco, & I. Siraj-Blatchford (Eds.), *Researching early childhood* (pp. 136–146). Crows Nest, Australia: Allen & Unwin.

Grieshaber, S., & Ryan, S. (2006). Beyond certainties: Postmodernism perspectives, research, and the education of young children. In B. Spodek & O. N. Saracho (Eds.), *Handbook of research on the education of young children* (2nd ed., pp. 533–553). Mahwah, NJ: Erlbaum.

Grolnick, W. S., & Slowiaczek, M. L. (1994). Parents' involvement in children's schooling: A multidimensional conceptualization and motivation model. *Child Development, 65*, 237–252.

Gronlund, G. (2008). Creative and thoughtful strategies for implementing learning standards. *Young Children, 63*(4), 10–13.

Gunnoe, M. L., & Mariner, C. L. (1997). Towards a developmental-contextual model of the effects of parental spanking on children's aggression. *Archives of Pediatrics and Adolescent Medicine, 151*, 768–775.

Hall, S. (1989). New ethnicities. In D. Morley & K. H. Chen (Eds.), *Stuart Hall: Critical dialogues in cultural studies* (pp. 441–449). London: Routledge.

Hall, S. (1996). Introduction: Who needs identity? In S. Hall & P. du Gay (Eds.), *Questions of cultural identity* (pp. 1–17). Thousand Oaks, CA: Sage.

Hammel, J. (2003). A critical literacy journey. *School Talk 8*(4), 3.

Hernandez, L. A., & Lee, L. (2010). Supporting new immigrant families and children. In L. Derman-Sparks & J. O. Edwards (Eds.), *Anti-bias education for young children and ourselves* (pp. 73–76) Washington, DC: NAEYC.

Hill, N. E., & Craft, S. A. (2003). Parent–school involvement and school performance: Mediated pathways among socioeconomically comparable African American and Euro-American families. *Journal of Educational Psychology, 95*, 74–83.

Hill, N. E., & Taylor, L. C. (2004). Parental school involvement and children's academic achievement. Pragmatic and issues. *Current Directions in Psychological Science, 13*(2), 161–164.

Hofferth, S. L. (1989). What is the demand for and supply of child care in the United States? *Young Children, 44*(5), 28–33.

Howard, G. (2007, March). As diversity grows, so must we. *Educational Leadership*, 16–22.

Humphreys, A., & Smith, P. (1984). Rough and tumble play in preschool and playground. In P. Smith (Ed.), *Play in animals and humans* (pp. 241–270). London: Blackwell.

Hurwitz, S. C. (1998). War nurseries—Lessons in quality. *Young children, 53*(3), 37–39.

Hyland, N. E. (2010). Social justice in early childhood classrooms. What the research tells us. *Young Children, 65*(1), 82–90.

Instituto Brasileiro de Geografic e Estatistica (IBGE) & Presginsa National por Amorstra de Domicilios (PNAD). (2008). *Populacao residente, por cor ou raca, situacao e sexo* [Resident population, by color or race, and gender situation]. Retrieved from www.ibge.gov.br/home.

Kagan, S. L. Carroll, J., Comer, J. P., & Scott-Little, C. (2006). Alignment: A missing link in early childhood transitions? *Young Children, 61*(5), 26–32.

Katz, P. A. (1976). The acquisition of racial attitudes in children. In P. A. Katz (Ed.), *Towards the elimination of racism* (pp. 125–154). New York: Pergamon.

Kelly, D.J., Quinn, P. C., Slater, A. M., Lee, K., Ge, L., & Pascalis, U. (2007, December), The other race effect develops during infancy: Evidence of perceptual narrowing. *Psychological Science, 8*(12), 1084–1089.

Kindler, A. L. (2002, May). *Survey of the state's limited English proficient students and available educational programs and services: 1999–2000 Summary report*. Washington, DC: U.S. Department of Education.

Kostelnik, M. J., Onaga, E., Rohde, B., & Whiren, A. (2002). *Children with special needs: Lessons for early childhood professionals*. New York: Teachers College Press.

Krueger, A. B., & Whitmore, D. M. (2001). Attending a small class in early grades in college-test taking and middle school test results: Evidence from Project STAR. *Economic Journal, 111*(468) 1–28.

Ladson-Billings, G. (1994). *The dreamkeepers: Successful teachers of African American children*. San Francisco, CA: Jossey-Bass.

Lalas, J. (2007, Spring). Teaching for social justice in multicultural urban schools: Conceptualization and classroom implementation. *Multicultural Education*, 17–21.

Lansford, J. E. (2005). Physical discipline and children's adjustments: Cultural normativeness as a moderator. *Child Development, 76*(6), 1234–1246.

Lansford, J. E., Deater-Deckard, K., Dodge, K. A., Bates, J. E., & Pettit, G. S. (2004). Ethnic differences in the link between physical discipline and later adolescent externalizing behaviors. *Journal of Child Physiology and Psychiatry, 45*, 801–812.

LaParo, K. M., Kraft-Sayre, M., & Pianta, R. C. (2003). Preschool-to-kindergarten transition activities: Involvement and satisfaction of families and teachers. *Journal of Research in Childhood Education, 17*(2), 147–158.

Lau v. Nichols. 414 US 563, 94 S. Ct. 786, 39 L. Ed. 2d—Supreme Court, 1974.

Leahy, R. (1983). The development of the conception of social class. In R. Leahy (Ed.), *The child's construction of inequality* (pp. 79–107). New York: Academic Press.

Leahy, R. (1990). The development of concepts of economic and social inequality. *New Direction for Child Development, 46*, 107–120.

Lee, R. (1999). *Orientals: Asian Americans in popular culture*. Philadelphia, PA: Temple University Press.

Lee, S. (2005). Selective parent participation: Structural and cultural factors that influence school participation among Korean parents. *Equity & Excellence in Education, 38*(4), 299–308.

Lenroot, R. K., Greenstein, D. K., Gogltay, N., Wallaces, G. L. Calsen, L. S., Blumenthal, J. D., ... Giedd, J. N. (2007). Sexual dimorphism of brain development trajectories during childhood and adolescences. *NeuroImage, 36*, 1065–1075.

Leonardo, Z. (2009). *Race, whiteness, and education*. New York: Routledge.

Lippy, C. H. (2004). Christian nation or pluralistic culture? Religion in American life. In J. A. Banks & C. A. M. Banks (Eds.), *In multicultural education: Issues and perspectives* (5th ed., pp. 110–132). Hoboken, NJ: Wiley.

Luz, C. (2010). Cultivating dispositions of cultural democracy. *Child Care Information Exchange, 32*(6), 58–60.

Marsh, M. (1992). Implementing anti-bias curriculum in the kindergarten classroom. In S. Kessler & B. B. Swadener (Eds.), *Reconceptualizing the early childhood curriculum: Beginning the dialogue* (pp. 267–288). New York: Teachers College Press.

Marshall, C., & Oliva, M. (2006). *Leadership for social justice: Making revolutions in education*. Boston, MA: Allyn & Bacon.

McIntosh, P. (1989). *White privilege and male privilege: A personal account of coming to see correspondence through work in women's studies* (Working paper 189). Wellesley College Center for Research on Women.

McNeal, R. B. (1999). Parent involvement as social capital: Differentiating effectiveness on science achievement, truancy, and dropping out. *Social Forces, 78,* 117–144.

Milner, D. (1983). *Children and race.* Beverly Hills, CA: Sage.

Moats, L. C. (2001). Overcoming the language gap. Invest generously in teacher professional development. *American Educator, 25*(2), 4–9.

Naimark, H. (1983). *Children's understandings of social class differences.* Paper presented at the biennial meeting of the Society for Research in Child Development, Detroit, MI.

National Association for the Education of Children (NAEYC). (1996). Position statement: Responding to linguistic and cultural diversity—Recommendations for effective early childhood education. *Young Children, 51*(2), 4–12.

National Association for the Education of Children (NAEYC). (1999). Using NAEYC's Code of Ethics to negotiate professional problems: How do we balance cultural diversity and our own values? *Young Children, 54*(5), 44–46.

National Center for Children in Poverty. (2006). *Basic facts about low-income children: Birth to age six.* Retrieved from www.nccp.org/pub_ycp06.html.

Nelson, B. G. (2010). From gender bias to gender equity in early childhood education staff. In L. Derman-Sparks & J. O. Edwards (Eds.), *Anti-bias education for young children and ourselves* (p. 100). Washington, DC: National Association for the Education of Young Children.

Neugebauer, R. (1999). *Inside child care: Trend 2000 report.* Redmond, WA: Child Care Information Exchange Press.

Neugebauer, R. (2004, July/August). Wages for early childhood professionals in North America: Results of an Exchange Insta-Poll. *Child Care Information Exchange,* 15–18.

Ngo, B. (2006). Learning from margins: Southeast and South Asian education in context. *Race, Ethnicity and Education, 9,* 51–65.

Ngo, B. (2008). Beyond "culture clash": Understanding of immigrant experiences. *Theory Into Practice, 47*(1), 4–11.

Nieto, S. (2004). *Affirming diversity: The sociopolitical context of multicultural education* (4th ed.). Boston, MA: Allyn & Bacon.

Orfield, G. (2008, Spring). *Race and schools: The need for action* (Visiting Scholars Series). Washington, DC: National Education Association.

Ormrod, J. E. (2008). *Human learning* (5th ed.). Upper Saddle River, NJ: Pearson.

Ovando, C. J. (2004). Language diversity in education. In J. A. Banks & C. A. M. Banks (Eds.), *Multicultural education: Issues and perspectives* (5th ed., pp. 289–313). Hoboken, NJ: Wiley.

Pai, Y., & Adler, S. A. (1997). *Cultural foundations of education* (2nd ed.). Upper Saddle River, NJ: Merrill.

Patchen, M. (1982). *Black-white contact in schools: Its social and academic effect.* West Lafayette, IN: Purdue University Press.

Piaget, J. (1952). *The origins of intelligence in children* (M. Cook, Trans.). New York: International Universities Press.

Pinderhuges, E. E., Dodge, K. A., Bates, J. E., Pettit, G. S., & Zelli, A. (2000). Discipline responses: Influences of parents' socioeconomic status, ethnicity, beliefs about parenting, stress, and cognitive-emotional processes. *Journal of Family Psychology, 14,* 380–400.

Polaha, J., Larzelere, R. E., Shapiro, S. K., & Petti, G. R. (2004). Physical discipline and child behavior problems: A study of ethnic group differences. *Parenting: Science and Practice, 4,* 339–360.

Pryce, D. D. (2001). Black Latina. In P. S. Rothenberg (Ed.), *Race, class, and gender in the United States: An integrated study* (5th ed., pp. 361–363). New York: Worth.

Ramani, A. K., Gilbertson, L., Fox, M. A., & Provasnik, S. (2007). *Status and trends in the education of racial and ethnic minorities.* Washington, DC: National Center for Educational Statistics. Retrieved from http://nces.ed.gov/pubs2007/minoritytrends

Ramsey, P. G. (1991). *Making friends in school: Promoting peer relationships in early childhood.* New York: Teachers College Press.

Ramsey, P. G. (2006). Early childhood multicultural education. In B.

Spodek & O. N. Saracho (Eds.), *Handbook of research on the education of young children* (2nd ed., pp. 279–3001). Mahwah, NJ: Erlbaum.

Ramsey, P. G., & Myers, L. C. (1990). Salience of race in young children's cognitive, affective and behavioral responses to social environments. *Journal of Applied Developmental Psychology, 11,* 49–67.

Rodriguez, M. V. (2008, Winter). How to support bilingualism in early childhood. *Texas Child Care Quarterly,* 24–29.

Roediger, D. (1991). *The wages of whiteness.* New York: Verso.

Root, M. P. P. (Ed.). (1996). *The multiracial experience: Racial border as the new frontier.* Thousand Oaks, CA: Sage.

Rothbart, M. K. (1989). Temperament and development. In G. A. Kohnstramm, J A. Bates, & M. K. Rothbart (Eds.), *Temperament in childhood* (pp. 59–73). New York: Wiley.

Rothenberg, P. S. (2008). *White privilege.* New York: Worth.

Rothstein, R. (2008, April). Whose problem is poverty? Its no cop-out to acknowledge the effects of socioeconomic disparities on student learning. Rather, it's a vital step to closing the achievement gap. *Educational Leadership,* 8–13.

Ryan, S., & Grieshaber, S. (2004). Research in review: It's more than just child development: Critical theories, research, and teaching young children. *Young Children, 59*(6), 44–52.

Ryan, S., & Ochsner, M. (1999) Traditional practices, new possibilities: Transforming dominant images of early childhood teachers. *Australian Journal of Early Childhood 24*(4), 14–20.

Sadker, D., & Sadker, M. (1994). *Dealing at fairness: How America's schools cheat girls.* New York: Scribner's.

Sax, L. (2007). The boy problem: Many boys think school is stupid and reading stinks. Is there a remedy? *School Literacy Journal, 53*(9), 40–43.

Schiller, P. (2010). Early brain development research review and update. *Child Care Information Exchange, 32*(6), 26–32.

Schweinhart, L. J., Montie, J., Xiang, Z., Barnett, W. S., Belfield, C. R., & Nores, M. (2005). *Lifetime effects: the High/Scope Perry Preschool Study through age 40.* Ypsilanti, MI: High/Scope Press.

Scott-Little, C. Kagan, S. L., & Frelow, (2006). State standards for children's learning: What do they mean for child care providers? *Child Care Information Exchange, 168,* 27–34.

Signorella, M. L., Bigler, R. S., & Liben, L. S. (1993). Developmental differences in children's gender schemata about others: A meta-analytic review. *Developmental Review, 13,* 147–183.

Skelton, C. (2001). *Schooling the boys: Masculinities and primary education: Educating boys, learning gender.* Buckingham, UK: Open University Press.

Sleeter, C. E. (1996). *Multicultural education as social activism.* Albany, NY: SUNY Press.

Sleeter, C. E., & Grant, C. A. (1999). *Making choices for multicultural education* (3rd ed.). Columbus, OH: Merrill.

Sleeter, C. E., & McLaren. (Eds.). (1995). *Multicultural education, critical pedagogy, and the politics of difference.* Albany, NY: SUNY Press.

Smedley, A. (2002). Science and the idea of race: A brief history. In J. M. Fish (Ed.), *Race and intelligence: Separating science for myth* (pp. 145–176). Mahwah, NJ: Erlbaum.

Spencer, R. (2010). Militant multiraciality: Rejecting race and rejecting the convenience of complicity. In J. O. Adekunle & H. V. Williams (Eds.), *Color struck: Essays on race and ethnicity in global perspective* (pp.155–172). New York: University Press of America.

Surtees, N. (2005). Teachers talk about and around sexuality in early childhood education: Deciphering an unwritten code. *Contemporary Issues in Early Childhood, 6*(1), 19–29.

Tatum, B., D. (1997). *Why are all the black kids sitting together in the cafeteria?* New York: Basic Books.

U.S. Department of Education. (2008). *Identifying and treating attention deficit hyperactivity disorders: A resource for schools and home.* Washington, DC: Author.

U.S. Department of Health and Human Services. (2010). *Revisiting and updating multicultural principles for Head Start programs serving children ages birth to five.* Washington, DC: Author.

U.S. Department of Health and Human Services, Administration for Children, Youth and Families, Head Start Bureau. (2006). Fiscal year 2005 fact sheet. Washington, DC: Author.

U.S. Department of Health and Human Services, Administration for Children and Families. (2008). *Head Start Act, amended.* Washington, DC: U. S. Government Printing Office.

Van Ausdale, D., & Feagin, J. R. (2001). *The first R: How children learn race and racism.* Lanham, MD: Rowman & Littlefield.

Wallace, K. R. (Ed.). (2004), *Working with multiracial students: Critical perspectives on research and practice.* Greenwich, CI. Information Age.

Wardle, F. (1991, May/June). Are we shortchanging boys? *Child Care Information Exchange*, 48–51.

Wardle, F. (2004a). The challenge of boys in our early childhood programs. *Early Childhood News, 16*(1), 16–21.

Wardle, F. (2004b). Men in early childhood: Fathers and teachers. *Early Childhood News, 16*(4), 34–42.

Wardle, F. (2007). Multiracial children in child development textbooks. *Early Childhood Education Journal, 35*(3), 253–259.

Wardle, F. (2009). *Approaches to early childhood and elementary education.* New York: Nova Science.

Wardle, F. (2010). The necessity of a multiracial category in a race conscious society. In J. O. Adekunle & H. V. Williams (Eds.), *Color struck: Essays on race and ethnicity in global perspective* (pp. 207–244). New York: University Press of America.

Wardle, F. (2011, March/April). Radical new directions for multicultural education. *Child Care Information Exchange* (Manuscript accepted for publication).

Wardle, F., & Cruz-Janzen, M. I. (2004). *Meeting the needs of multiethnic and multiracial children in schools.* Boston, MA: Allyn & Bacon.

Waugh, D., & Koon, B. (1974). *Breakthrough for bilingual education.* Washington, DC: U.S. Commission on Civil Rights.

West, M. (2001). Teaching the third culture child. *Young Children, 56*(5), 27–32.

Whiting, B., & Edwards, C. P. (1988). A cross-cultural analysis of sex differences in the behavior of children 3 through 11. In G. Handle (Ed.), *Childhood socialization* (pp. 281–297). New York, Aldine de Gruyter.

Wiles, J., & Bondi, J. (2002). *Curriculum development: A guide to practice* (6th ed.). Upper Saddle River, NJ: Prentice Hall.

Wilson-Keenan, J., Solsjen, J., & Willett, J (1999) "Only boys can jump high": Reconstructing gender relations in a first/second grade classroom. In B. Kamler (Ed.), *Constructing gender and differences: Critical perspectives on early childhood* (pp. 30–70). Creskill, NJ: Hampton Press.

Wright, M. A. (1998). *I'm chocolate, you're vanilla: Raising healthy black and biracial children in a race-conscious world: A guide for parents and teachers.* San Francisco, CA: Jossey-Bass.

York, S. (2003). *Roots and wings: Affirming culture in early childhood programs* (rev. ed.). St Paul, MN: Redleaf Press.

Young, B. (2003, July/August). The true cost of quality in early care and education programs. *Child Care Information Exchange*, 14–16.

Part III

Foundations of Early Childhood Educational Policy

20

Childhood Poverty

Implications for School Readiness and Early Childhood Education

REBECCA M. RYAN
Georgetown University

REBECCA C. FAUTH
National Children's Bureau (UK)

JEANNE BROOKS-GUNN
Teachers College, Columbia University

In 2009, over 1 in 5 children under age 6 in the United States were living below the official poverty threshold, which means that their before-tax income fell at or below a federally established threshold, which in 2009 was $17,285 for a single parent with two children (DeNavas-Walt, Proctor, & Smith, 2010). The number of all children living in poverty has increased by over 33% since 2000, with 3.8 million more children living in poverty today. Proportions are even higher for Black and Hispanic children, with 36% of Black children and 33% of Hispanic children living in poverty in 2009, compared to 12% of White children (DeNavas-Walt et al., 2010). Families living in "deep poverty," with incomes below 50% of the poverty threshold, represent 43% of the poverty population in the United States, indicating that many families with children subsist well below the actual poverty threshold, which is already quite modest. Children in poverty not only lack basic financial resources, but they also suffer hardships that often accompany poverty, such as inadequate food, clothing, housing, and health care (Haveman & Wolfe, 1994). Not surprisingly, these conditions have serious consequences for children's health and development.

Growing up in poverty can significantly impact a child's readiness to learn upon school entry. Early childhood, typically defined as birth to age 5, is a critical period for development. During this time, children are set on developmental trajectories that are mutable but become increasingly difficult to change (Carnegie Corporation, 1994; Knudsen, Heckman, Cameron, & Shonkoff, 2006). For this reason, young children are particularly vulnerable to the effects of poverty (Axinn, Duncan, & Thornton, 1997; Duncan, Ziol-Guest, & Kalil, 2010; Duncan, Yeung, Brooks-Gunn, & Smith, 1998). Differences between children living in

poor and nonpoor families, particularly in the cognitive domain, tend to appear around 24 months and are of equal or greater size by age 5 years. These early problems remain when children enter elementary school, where children living in poor families exhibit lower school achievement than children in nonpoor families (Duncan & Brooks-Gunn, 1997). The gap between children living in poor and nonpoor families often persists through middle and high school, where children living in poverty have higher rates of special education placement, grade retention, teenage pregnancy, and school dropout than their counterparts (Duncan, Yeung, Brooks-Gunn, & Smith, 1998; Votruba-Drzal, 2006). Not only are these early differences sustained into adolescence, but poverty experienced during the first 5 years is more harmful to children's development than poverty experienced in later childhood and adolescence (Duncan & Brooks-Gunn, 1997). For example, a recent study found that family income in the first 5 years of life, but not after, strongly predicted the level of earnings and hours worked in adulthood for children with annual family incomes below $25,000 (Duncan, Ziol-Guest, & Kalil, 2010). With 22% of young children growing up in poverty in this country (Wight & Chau, 2009), a percentage that exceeds rates for older children, early childhood poverty concerns all those involved in the field of early childhood education.

In this chapter, we examine the relationship between poverty and young children's development up to age 5, when most children leave early education programs and enter formal schooling (see below for an official definition of poverty). Most studies that explore the impacts of poverty on child development do so either by comparing the outcomes of children in poor versus nonpoor families or measuring the effects of family income on child outcomes and drawing conclusions from those estimates about the effects of poverty. We review both types of studies. First, we explore the complexities in measuring poverty and identifying its effects on young children. Second, we review findings from studies measuring direct associations between family income and children's cognitive and socioemotional outcomes during the first 5 years of life. Third, we consider the potential pathways through which poverty may influence child development. Here, two theories frame the discussion, one emphasizing the role of familial relationships and parenting (Conger & Elder, 1994; Elder & Caspi, 1988; McLoyd, 1990) and another stressing the impact of parental investments in resources for children (Becker, 1991; Mayer, 1997).

Finally, we consider the role of public policy in the lives of poor children. This section describes antipoverty programs that flow from the three major sources of government aid: direct cash assistance, such as Temporary Assistance for Needy Families (TANF); in-kind benefits, such as child care subsidies and food assistance; and early intervention programs for children and families, such as Head Start. We review what is known about how these programs impact the early outcomes of children reared in poor families as well as their parents. In conclusion, we analyze which types of programs may hold the most promise for enhancing the school readiness of children growing up in poverty.

Methodological Considerations in Studying Poverty

Children growing up in poverty are those in families with incomes at or below the poverty threshold, the official federal poverty measure in the U.S. This threshold, which was originally developed in 1959, is based on expected food expenditures for families of varying sizes and adjusted annually for the Consumer Price Index cost of living. In 2009, the poverty threshold for a single parent raising two children was an annual pretax income of $17,285 (DeNavas-Walt et al., 2010). The poverty threshold is mainly used for statistical purposes as it plainly demarcates families according to whether they are above or below the threshold.[1] To date, researchers have relied on the existing poverty threshold and its variants, including the number of years a family has lived in poverty, which reflects the *persistence* of family poverty, and the income-to-needs ratio (i.e., family income relative to their poverty threshold adjusted for family size), which gives an indication of the *depth* of poverty,[2] to assess associations between poverty and children's developmental outcomes (Duncan & Brooks-Gunn, 1997).

Many experts, however, have criticized the poverty threshold, claiming it underestimates the type and degree of expenditures families must outlay from month-to-month, ignores regional differences in living costs, and excludes alternative sources of income that were specifically designed for low-income families such as food stamps and housing subsidies (Citro & Michael, 1995). From 2011, a supplemental poverty measure (SPM) aimed at redressing many

of these criticisms will complement the existing threshold (U.S. Census Bureau, 2010). Specifically, the SPM will calibrate the threshold (to be adjusted geographically) based on the average expenditures of families living below the median income (but who are not poor), and will include it its calculation not only food costs, but also the costs of shelter, clothing, and utilities "plus a little more." Federal in-kind benefits (e.g., for food, shelter, clothing, and utilities) will be included in families' incomes and out-of-pocket medical expenses can be deducted from income calculations. Compared to the current measure, which is an *absolute* threshold (i.e., families are either living in poverty or not living in poverty depending on whether they fall above or below the threshold), the SPM is a *relative* threshold as a family's poverty status is calculated by comparing their resources relative to that of the average family (based on median family income). Thus, using the SPM, the rise and fall of median income can change a family's poverty status, even if the family's income is relatively stable over time. Researchers expect the U.S. poverty rate to increase under the SPM, revealing far more children living at the economic margins than the current poverty rate suggests.

Another methodological issue in studying the effects of poverty on child development is establishing that family income, and not factors associated with family income, is driving associations between poverty and child outcomes. Not only does poverty covary with other environmental disadvantages, such as dangerous neighborhoods and unsafe housing, that could negatively impact children irrespective of household income, but poor parents may differ from more affluent parents in terms of preferences, characteristics, and motivations in ways that simultaneously influence levels of family income and their allocation of resources to children (Mayer, 1997). Chief among these correlated factors are family characteristics such as low maternal education and single parenthood, which both relate to children's outcomes and to family poverty (Mayer, 1991). Indeed, some researchers have capitalized on this dependence by jointly exploring the links between combinations of childhood "risk factors," such as maternal education, family size, single parenthood, race/ethnicity, maternal mental health, and stressful life events, and children's outcomes, stressing that assessment of cumulative risk in children's lives is a better predictor of their outcomes than individual risks (Liaw & Brooks-Gunn, 1994; Sameroff, Seifer, Baldwin, & Baldwin, 1993).

While the cumulative risk approach is useful for showcasing the confluence of events in children's lives, the aim of the present chapter is to explore the independent effect of income poverty on young children's outcomes. Therefore, all studies reviewed here control for potentially confounding characteristics such as teenage parenthood, low maternal education, unemployment, single parenthood, and low child birth weight when estimating the effects of poverty on child outcomes. However, some confounding factors may be unmeasured, which means that what we want to label an "income effect" on children's outcomes may result from other family or environmental factors. Thus, we will also review studies that have attempted to remedy this problem using sophisticated analytic techniques such as "fixed effects" models that compare related children or use repeated observations of the same children over time (to control for unobserved family or child characteristics) or by taking advantage of changes in families' income resulting from exogenous (i.e., externally derived) conditions such as receipt of tax credits (e.g., Blau, 1999; Costello, Compton, Keeler, & Angold, 2003; Dahl & Lochner, 2009; Dearing, McCartney, & Taylor, 2006; Shea, 2000; Votruba-Drzal, 2006). Although we aim only to review studies where the effect of income on children's outcomes is isolated from other variables, it is probably impossible to statistically control for every potentially confounding variable.

Since the 1990s, researchers have had access to a number of large longitudinal studies of child development including the National Longitudinal Survey of Youth 1979 (NLSY79), the Infant Health and Development Program (IHDP), the Panel Study of Income Dynamics Child Development Supplement (PSID-CDS), the National Institute of Child Health and Human Development Study of Early Child Care and Youth Development (NICHD-SECCYD), and, more recently, the Early Childhood Longitudinal Study—Kindergarten Class of 1998–1999 (ECLS-K) and the Fragile Families and Child Wellbeing Study. Each of these studies includes large sample sizes (i.e., at least 700 children, but typically around 3,000), robust assessments of children's developmental outcomes over time, and detailed information on families' economic status and related characteristics including maternal education, maternal IQ, maternal mental health, family structure, and, in some instances, neighborhood residence (Brooks-Gunn, Berlin, & Fuligni, 2000). The studies reviewed below prioritize these studies rather than smaller-scale, nonrepresentative studies with limited outcome and economic data because the former offer more generalizable and rigorously controlled findings.

Associations between Poverty and Young Children's School Readiness

One of the main goals of early childhood education is to prepare young children for entry into kindergarten and elementary school. This preparedness, often referred to in policy contexts as school readiness, has been conceptualized in different ways since it gained acceptance in the United States in the 1920s (Kagan & Rigby, 2003; May & Campbell, 1981). All conceptualizations, however, maintain that school readiness involves not only children's cognitive skills upon school entry, but also the social, emotional, and physical domains of child development. From this holistic perspective, a child's ability to pay attention in class, form relationships with peers and teachers, and arrive at school in good health is as important to her early and later school success as her math and verbal skills. The following section

examines the extent to which growing up in poverty can compromise the cognitive and socioemotional aspects of children's development.

Cognitive Outcomes

Measures of cognitive development include children's IQ scores, premath, preliteracy, and verbal skills, and, for school-aged children, achievement. These domains are measured using full-scale intelligence tests, numeracy and problem solving assessments, expressive and receptive language assessments, and tests of learning ability, respectively. Across measures, negative associations between poverty and children's cognitive outcomes tend to emerge at 2 years of age, but generally not before (Klebanov, Brooks-Gunn, McCarton, & McCormick, 1998; Korenman & Miller, 1997; Smith, Brooks-Gunn, & Klebanov, 1997). Using data from (IHDP), a randomized intervention program for premature, low-birth-weight infants, Klebanov and colleagues (1998) tested the links between family poverty (defined as family income 150% of the poverty threshold or less) and children's IQ scores measured at ages 1, 2, and 3 years, and found that family risk factors associated with poverty, such as single parenthood and low maternal education had negative effects on IQ scores in the first year, while income itself did not. At 2 years of age, however, both family risk and income predicted lower scores. Averaging family income over the first 5 years of life, another study using the IHDP data found even larger associations between poverty status and age 2 IQ scores (Smith et al., 1997). Scholars debate why income effects only appear after infancy, while factors such as family risk level do impact early IQ scores. Some suggest that aspects of the early environment most affected by income, such as parent's ability to afford toys, books, and trips become important only at the onset of language (Klebanov et al., 1998). Alternatively, the measures used to assess infant IQ may not tap the domains of cognitive development most correlated with income, such as emergent verbal skills; thus differences between children living in poor and nonpoor families may be present but undetected (Brooks-Gunn, Leventhal, & Duncan, 1999).

It is clear, however, that negative associations between poverty and children's cognitive outcomes that emerge during toddlerhood tend to increase by 3 years of age and maintain or grow throughout early childhood. For instance, studies have shown that the income-related differences in children's IQ and vocabulary scores increased nearly 2 points from age 2 to 3 years (Klebanov et al., 1998). In other studies, variation in IQ, PPVT (a receptive language measure), and reading recognition scores by income remained stable over time with children living in nonpoor families scoring around 4 points or higher than children living in poor families at ages 2, 3, and 5 years (Duncan, Brooks-Gunn, & Klebanov, 1994; Smith et al., 1997). Taken together, results from these studies suggest that starting around the age of 2 years, children reared in poverty generally scored between 15% and 40% of a standard deviation lower on standardized cognitive assessments compared with their peers living in nonpoor families. To interpret the magnitude of these differences, consider that a typical IQ test has a mean of 100 and a standard deviation of 15 points. Young children in poor families thus score between 2.25 and 6 points lower than those in nonpoor families according to these studies; small but meaningful differences.

Although few dispute that poverty is negatively associated with children's cognitive development, researchers debate how large income associations really are with outcomes such as IQ and language development. Using more conservative estimation techniques than simply controlling for maternal education, age, and other family factors, such as controlling for maternal IQ and comparing children within families (e.g., Blau, 1999; Duncan, Yeung et al., 1998), some have found far smaller income effects on young children's cognitive outcomes than the 15% to 40% effect sizes reported above. Moreover, research has also found that the association between income and child outcomes is not as large as that of family background characteristics, such as maternal education (Blau, 1999; Klebanov, Brooks-Gunn, Chase-Lansdale, & Gordon, 1997; Mayer, 1997; Smith et al., 1997). Blau (1999), in particular, has suggested that income effects alone do not produce meaningful differences among children using analyses that include a rich set of control variables, such as maternal cognitive ability, and that compare the outcomes of cousins using the (NLSY79) data. Although there is debate about whether income or factors associated with it impact children's development most strongly, most studies using conservative estimation techniques, including Blau (1999), find that the average association between income and children's cognitive outcomes is small but significant.

Although the average effect of income may be small, studies that have compared income effects for low- and middle- income families have found that they are far larger for those at the lowest end of the income distribution. A recent study using data from the NICHD-SECCYD examined the differential impacts of income fluctuations and found that increases in income between 1 and 3 years of age were positively associated with cognitive outcomes measured at 3 years for children living in poor families only (Dearing, McCartney, & Taylor, 2001). Specifically, children living in poverty whose families experienced an increase in income-to-needs of at least 1 standard deviation above the mean scored on par with their nonpoor counterparts on all cognitive outcomes measured. A study using data from the PSID reported similar findings examining longer-term outcomes (Duncan, Ziol-Guest, & Kalil, 2010; Duncan, Yeung et al., 1998). Specifically, modest increases in income for families with incomes below $25,000 during the first 5 years of children's lives led to significant increases in hours worked and earnings in adulthood, effects not found for children in higher income families. Other studies that compared children's outcomes at different poverty levels

have found the largest cognitive deficits (in some studies 8 to 12 points) for young children living in deep poverty (i.e., 50% of the poverty threshold) (Korenman, Miller, & Sjaastad,1995; Smith, Brooks-Gunn, & Klebanov, 1997). Taken together, these findings indicate that income matters more at deeper levels of poverty, suggesting that the development of children living in poor families may be more sensitive to changes in income than development among children living in nonpoor families.

Socioemotional Outcomes

Young children's social or emotional development is typically measured using parent-report assessments of children's behavior, such as levels of friendliness, cooperation, and engagement as well as instances of temper tantrums, defiance, and aggression. According to existing research, a higher percentage of children living in poor families report emotional or behavioral problems than children living in nonpoor families from early childhood through their adolescence (Coiro, Zill, & Bloom, 1994; Pagani, Boulerice, & Tremblay, 1997). Typically, however, more modest income associations are found for children's socioemotional development when compared to the larger and more consistent associations with cognitive outcomes (see Blau, 1999 for an exception).[3] For example, while past research reported that increases in families' incomes were associated large increases in children's IQ scores, only small concomitant decreases in internalizing (e.g., withdrawal, depression) and externalizing (e.g., fighting, defiance) behavior problems were found (Dearing, McCartney, & Taylor, 2001; Duncan, Brooks-Gunn, & Klebanov, 1994). Stronger associations with behavioral outcomes are found when duration of poverty is considered. In the IHDP, 5-year-olds who lived in persistently poor families exhibited more internalizing and externalizing problems than children who experienced short-term poverty as well as those whose families had never been poor (Duncan, Brooks-Gunn, & Klebanov, 1994). Data from the NLSY79 revealed somewhat subtler trends: short-term poverty was related to externalizing problems and long-term poverty was associated with internalizing problems for 4- to 8-year-old children (McLeod & Shanahan, 1993, 1996). Although most of the behavioral effects are smaller and less significant than those for cognitive outcomes, there is still evidence that growing up in poverty is harmful to children's emotional as well as intellectual development.

As with cognitive outcomes, changes in family income have a much larger association with children's behavioral outcomes among children living in poor than nonpoor families. In a series of studies using data from the NICHD-SECCYD, Dearing, Taylor, and McCartney demonstrated that an increase in family income-to-needs is associated with improvements in children's behavior problems and prosocial skills either more strongly or only for children living in poor relative to nonpoor families (Dearing

McCartney, & Taylor, 2001; Taylor, Dearing, & McCartney, 2004). Most recently, they found that a $10,000 increase in family income among children living in never-poor families reduced externalizing behaviors by less than 1% of a standard deviation, or .10 points on a scale with a standard deviation of 10, whereas the same change produced a 15% of a standard deviation decrease in externalizing behaviors among children living in chronically poor families between age 2 and first grade, or 1.5 points on the same scale (Dearing, McCartney, & Taylor, 2006). These findings reveal how young children from the poorest families may be at a particular disadvantage upon entering school in terms of their ability to attend in class, regulate their behavior, and form relationships with peers and teachers.

The same factors correlated with income that could bias associations between family income and children's cognitive outcomes could bias associations between income and behavioral outcomes. Yet, studies using more conservative estimation techniques than controlling for family background variables have found small but significant income effects on children's behavior problems. For example, using models comparing siblings and cousins, Blau (1999) found significant associations between family income and internalizing and externalizing behavior problems that exceeded those for cognitive outcomes. Costello and colleagues (2003; Akee, Copeland, Keeler, Angold, & Costello, 2010) capitalized on the opening of a casino on a Native American reservation to assess the impact of income on children's psychiatric symptoms. They found that children in families who were lifted out of poverty by the casino opening, which granted a share of the profits to all reservation families, experienced a reduction in externalizing symptoms that put them on par with children living in nonpoor families; their internalizing symptoms, however, were unaffected by the income change. In the study described above, Dearing and colleagues (2006) examined the effect of changes in income on changes in children's behavioral outcomes, rather than comparing children's outcomes across family income levels, and found increases in income significantly reduced children's externalizing behaviors in poor families. Income did not, however, significantly reduce children's internalizing behavior problems. Taken together, these findings suggest that poverty affects internalizing and externalizing symptoms differently, with behaviors like aggression more sensitive to income fluctuations than symptoms like anxiety or depression.

Conclusion

In sum, there exists an abundance of research indicating that poverty experienced during the first 5 years of life can hinder child development in both cognitive and socioemotional domains. Although the effects of income poverty on children's cognitive and socioemotional outcomes may be small after other factors correlated with poverty are controlled, such as low maternal education, single or teenage parenthood, and low maternal intelligence, the preponderance of evidence suggests that the school readiness of young children living in poverty is lower than that of children not living in poverty, a gap which persists later in school. Moreover, the effect of poverty is much larger when poverty is deep (less than 50% of the poverty threshold), long-term, and present early in the child's life. This pattern also means, however, that increases in income can enhance the school readiness of children living in poor families much more than children in nonpoor families, significantly alleviating the effects of early poverty. Specifically, children who leave the poverty ranks during their first 3 years have been found to catch up with never poor children on cognitive tests and display significant reductions in externalizing (although not internalizing) behaviors by school entry. The next two sections describe processes through which poverty may influence these outcomes and the roles public policy can play in moderating that link.

Pathways through Which Poverty Impacts Young Children's School Readiness

The mechanisms or "pathways" through which poverty operates to influence child development are factors related to both income and to child outcomes that causally link the two. Pathways are distinct from correlates of poverty, such as low maternal education and single parenthood in that they imply a process by which income and child development are related: one that can help us to understand how poverty affects children's lives. Most pathways posited in the poverty literature can be grouped under two overarching theories.[4] The first focuses on the impact of poverty on relationships and interactions within families. In this view, exemplified by the "family stress model" (Conger & Elder, 1994; Elder, 1999), financial pressure or deprivation undermines parents' psychological and emotional resources, disrupting parenting styles, parent–child interactions, and child development as a result (Conger & Conger, 2000; Dodge, Pettit, & Bates, 1994). The second theory emphasizes the role of income in allowing parents to purchase materials, experiences, and services that foster children's skills and abilities. These goods and services include stimulating learning materials, nutritious food, safe living conditions, and quality child care. According to this perspective, children living in poverty have fewer opportunities to build their skills because their parents cannot afford to make the necessary time and money investments. This perspective, developed in the field of economics, is sometimes called the investment model (Haveman & Wolfe, 1994; Mayer, 1997). Figure 20.1 depicts the theoretical model linking both pathways to children's school readiness. The following section reviews processes implicated in both the family stress and investment models, identifying how these mechanisms affect different domains of child development and may operate in tandem to account for links between poverty and child development. Of course, because they may operate in tandem, the lines between the two models can blur; however, in the sections below, we aim to distinguish them and are explicit when studies have examined the two in combination.

The Family Stress Model

Economic stress includes poverty, unstable work, income loss, and unemployment. These conditions cause financial strain that frequently makes it necessary for families to cut back on consumption of goods and services, seek public assistance, live in undesirable and unsafe neighborhoods, or assume additional employment to make ends meet (Edin & Lein, 1997). According to the theory of family stress, these hardships can lead to emotional distress in parents, such as increased levels of depression and anxiety. In a 2006 study, Dearing and colleagues found that decreases in income were associated with increases in mothers' depressive symptoms and the probability of clinical depression, particularly for mothers initially living in poverty (Dearing, Taylor, & McCartney, 2006). Emotional instability can also trigger familial conflict. For example, using data from the PSID, Kalil and Wightman (2010) recently found that parental job loss, particularly when experienced by the father, was associated with increases in marital conflict and interpersonal violence.

These psychosocial stressors, in turn, can hinder a parent's ability to be supportive, sensitive, and consistent with children (McLoyd, 1990). The literature describing the importance of parenting to child development is too extensive to review here (see Bornstein, 1995, for a comprehensive review); however, parenting characterized by high levels of warmth, cognitive stimulation, and clear limit-setting has been consistently associated with favorable cognitive, emotional, and behavioral outcomes for children (Baumrind, 1966; Belsky, 1999; Berlin, Brady-Smith, & Brooks-Gunn, 2002; McLoyd, 1998). By contrast, parenting characterized by harsh, arbitrary discipline, or emotional detachment has been linked to the development of insecure infant–mother attachments, with possible long lasting effects on socio-emotional and cognitive outcomes (Shonkoff & Phillips, 2000). These associations—from financial strain, to parental depression and anxiety, to marital discord and disrupted parenting and finally to negative child outcomes—represent the crux of the family stress model (see Figure 20.1).

This theory is primarily used to explain how financial loss impacts child behavior (Conger, Rueter, & Conger, 2000). Research on financial loss is distinct from poverty studies in that it examines how declines in income alter family dynamics, rather than how persistent poverty shapes lives. In his classic work on the Great Depression, Elder (1999) found that parental emotional distress caused by income loss led to marital conflict and punitive parenting, particularly by fathers. However, researchers have extended the family stress model to explain the effects of poverty on child functioning. McLoyd (1990) hypothesizes that like income loss, living in poverty imposes extraordinary burdens on parents, such as struggling to afford basic food and clothing, living in low-quality housing conditions, and residing in unsafe neighborhoods. These burdens and the stress they cause adversely affect parent mental health and, subsequently, parenting practices. Specifically, maternal emotional distress and depression have been repeatedly

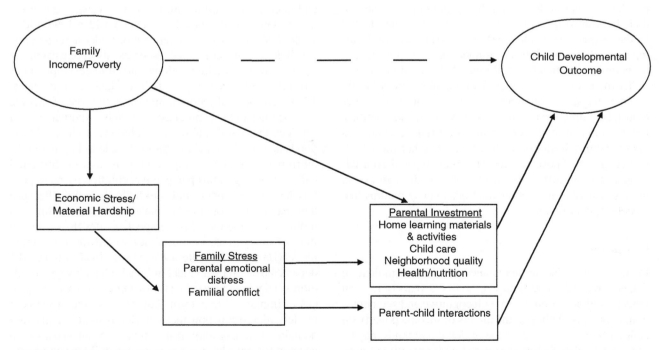

Figure 20.1 Theoretical model depicting pathways through which poverty impacts children's school readiness: the family stress model and the investment perspective.

(Maternal Stress)

associated with harsh discipline, low supportiveness, and parent emotional detachment, as well as higher conflict between parents and children (Petterson & Albers, 2001). Some studies suggest that the impact of this dynamic is more pronounced among disadvantaged families (Cicchetti & Toth, 1995; Petterson & Albers, 2001), with maternal depression and negative parenting practices exerting stronger influence over the developmental outcomes of children living in poor than nonpoor families.

While much research has examined this theory in relation to adolescents and older children (McLeod & Nonnemaker, 2000; Sampson & Laub, 1994), a growing literature has applied the family stress model to young children (Dodge, Pettit, & Bates, 1994; Duncan, Brooks-Gunn, & Klebanov, 1994; Gershoff, Aber, Raver, & Lennon, 2007; Jackson, Brooks-Gunn, Huang, & Glassman, 2000; Linver, Brooks-Gunn, & Kohen, 2002; McLeod & Shanahan, 1993; Yeung, Linver, & Brooks-Gunn, 2002). For example, Gershoff and colleagues (2007) have found that family income impacted young children's social and emotional competence (social skills, self-regulation, and internalizing and externalizing behavior), in part, because poverty elevated levels of material hardship (e.g., food security and housing stability) and levels of parenting stress, which, consequently, decreased parental warmth and cognitive stimulation. The study did not find similar links to children's cognitive outcomes. Other similar studies have also noted this distinction, finding that family stress either does not explain or explains far less of the income effect on cognitive than socioemotional development (Guo & Harris, 2000; Hanson, McLanahan, & Thomson, 1997; Jackson et al., 2000; Linver, Brooks-Gunn, & Kohen, 1999, 2002; Yeung et al., 2002). This finding suggests distinct pathways through which income impacts children's socioemotional and cognitive development, with socioemotional outcomes responding more strongly to family stress.

It is important to recognize that just as parental emotional distress and punitive parenting can disrupt early behavioral development, good parenting can buffer young children against the negative effects of growing up in poverty. Literature on economic stress and early child development contains much evidence that parenting behaviors characterized by warmth, supportiveness, and clear limit-setting can significantly reduce the risks associated with growing up in poverty (Apfel & Seitz, 1997; Cowen, Work, & Wyman, 1997; McLoyd, 1990; Werner & Smith, 1992). Factors that can help foster emotional health and positive parenting for low-income mothers include various forms of social support (Cowen, Wyman, Work, & Parker, 1990). Mothers who have stable emotional support, such as a confidant or some companionship, are less likely than mothers without social ties to report parenting anxiety or to parent in coercive and punitive ways (Crnic & Greenberg, 1987; McLoyd, 1997). Similarly, the availability of parenting support including other adults in the household to help with child care and household tasks has been shown to increase mothers' responsiveness and sensitivity to infants (Crockenberg, 1987). It is perhaps for this reason that recent research has linked higher levels of social support among low-income mothers to better behavioral and health outcomes among preschool-aged children (Leininger, Ryan, & Kalil, 2009; Ryan, Kalil, & Leininger, 2009). Although parents' resources somewhat determine the availability of social support, public policy initiatives such as social services, community-based programs, and early intervention can help to provide this kind of assistance (Shonkoff & Phillips, 2000). The role of early intervention programs in this regard are addressed in a later section.

The Investment Model

While the family stress model focuses on the links between economic deprivation and socioemotional environments in which children live, the investment model emphasizes the links between poverty and the resources available to children. It posits that without sufficient income, parents cannot buy the materials, experiences, and services that facilitate children's positive development. The theory attributes variation in cognitive and, to a lesser extent, behavioral outcomes between children living in poor and nonpoor families to this disparity in parental investments. Although the model stresses purchasing power, economists frame these investments in terms of both money (i.e., purchasing of goods and services) and time (i.e., providing stimulating experiences) (Becker, 1991). Extant research indeed suggests that poor parents have fewer money and time resources to invest in children (see McLanahan, 2004), not only because their earnings are low, but also because their work schedules are less flexible and more often nonstandard (Presser, 2003). Moreover, a disproportionate number of single parents shoulder both breadwinning and caregiving responsibilities, which limits time available for children (Kendig & Bianchi, 2008). In addition to poverty, the material hardship that so often accompanies it may also undermine parental investments. As parents struggling to make ends meet, they may not be able to purchase developmental supports for their children if it means foregoing necessary goods (Gershoff et al., 2007; Raver, Gershoff, & Aber, 2007). The following section explores some of these tensions, focusing on a selection of resources, activities, and environments that low-income parents provide to their young children and links between these investments and children's development.

Home Environment. Many aspects of the home environment are relevant to children's development including the availability of learning materials, parents' stimulation of children's learning, and the physical condition of the home (e.g., crowding, cleanliness). The most commonly used measure of the home learning environment is the Home Observation for Measurement of the Environment (HOME) (Caldwell & Bradley, 1984), which includes items assessing the availability of learning materials, such as the number of books, puzzles, and educational toys;[5] items gauging the physical conditions of the home, such as whether the home is cluttered, cramped, dirty, or unsafe; and parents' provision of out-of-home experiences for their children including visits to the library or zoo and extracurricular activities. Numerous studies have demonstrated links between low HOME scores and children's outcomes including developmental delay, growth stunting, poor school performance, and later IQ scores (Bradley & Corwyn, 2002; Garrett, Ng'andu, & Ferron, 1994).

Given that the HOME emphasizes aspects of the home environment that can be bought by parents (although they do not have to be), it should come as no surprise that HOME scores significantly vary according to families' income. A comprehensive descriptive study using the NLSY79 data revealed that children living in nonpoor families had greater access to stimulating materials in the home and were more likely to go on enriching trips (e.g., to a museum) than their counterparts living in poor families (Bradley, Corwyn, Pipes McAdoo, & Garcia Coll, 2001). Relative to children living in poor families, parents of children living in nonpoor families were twice as likely to read to their children several times a week; were more likely to teach their children letters, colors, shapes, and sizes; and had homes that were safer, cleaner, and less cluttered. A more recent study using the NICHD data examined the link between changes in both family income and home learning environments over the first 5 years of children's lives and found that the impact of family income on parents' ability to provide stimulating home environments was much stronger for parents at the low-end of income distribution than further up (Dearing & Taylor, 2007), suggesting increases in family income elevate the home environments of children living in poor families far more than their peers living in nonpoor families.

Several studies have also found that home environment quality accounts for a sizable proportion of the link between income and young children's outcomes, especially in the cognitive domain (Duncan, Brooks-Gunn, & Klebanov, 1994; Gershoff et al., 2007; Linver, Brooks-Gunn, & Kohen, 2002; Yeung, Linver, & Brooks-Gunn, 2002). One longitudinal study using NICHD data found that HOME scores mediated the unfavorable associations between shifts in family income over the first 3 years of children's lives and their school readiness, language development, and prosocial behavior (Dearing, McCartney, & Taylor 2001). Overall, HOME scores have been found to attenuate the associations between income and children's cognitive outcomes by up to one half (Bradley, 1995; Korenman, Miller, & Sjaastad, 1995). Children's early home learning environments may have long lasting influences on their development. One study reported that poor families' early involvement in their kindergarten children's education (i.e., reading to children, attending school meetings, communication with schools) was positively linked to children's later literacy performance in elementary school, particularly for children whose mothers had low educational attainment, suggesting that reading

to children and related activities can override the potentially deleterious combination of low-income and low maternal education on children's development (Dearing, McCartney, Weiss, Kreider, & Simpkins, 2004). Recent studies using the ECLS-K data have demonstrated that these relationships may be even more complex, reporting that the link between income and parents' provision of stimulating resources and activities is partly accounted for by families' perceptions of material hardship (Gershoff et al., 2007; Raver, Gershoff, & Aber, 2007).

The evidence is mixed on the links between home environment quality and children's behavioral outcomes, although several studies have reported significant associations comparable to those reported for children's cognitive outcomes (Dearing, McCartney, & Taylor, 2001; Linver, Brooks-Gunn, & Kohen, 2002; Yeung, Linver, & Brooks-Gunn, 2002). These associations may represent a joining of the family stress and investment models. That is, parents who experience high levels of depression and anxiety may be less likely than a parent with stable emotional health not only to interact positively with their children, but also to provide stimulating experiences. Figure 20.1 depicts this combination, as family stress not only predicts parenting behavior but also predicts parental investments. Supporting this theory, Yeung and colleagues (2002) found that HOME scores were associated with children's behavior problem scores via their influence on maternal emotional distress as well as parenting practices. In this way, the family stress and investment models may operate in tandem, with family stress impacting parents' ability and motivation to invest material and time resources in children's development (see Figure 20.1).

Neighborhoods. Although low-income parents face a limited set of choices about where to raise their children, the neighborhoods they choose to live in represent another investment that parents make in their children's development. It is in neighborhoods that young children receive child care, visit medical centers, attend school, and develop social relationships, all of which help shape children's developmental environments. The 1990s saw an explosion in research focusing on links between neighborhood characteristics including income or socioeconomic status (SES; i.e., percent poor, on public assistance, unemployed, professionals, college-educated, and female-headed households in a given geographic area) and children's outcomes, controlling for family-level income and other characteristics. For example, a series of studies by Brooks-Gunn and colleagues reported positive associations between neighborhood affluence and preschool-aged children's IQ and vocabulary scores (Brooks-Gunn. Duncan, Klebanov, & Sealand, 1993; Chase-Lansdale, Gordon, Brooks-Gunn, & Klebanov, 1997; Kohen, Brooks-Gunn, Leventhal, & Hertzman, 2002), and these associations persisted once children entered formal schooling (Chase-Lansdale et al., 1997; Duncan, Brooks-Gunn, & Klebanov, 1994). More nuanced analyses examining the timing and duration of residence in affluent neighborhoods reported that by the age of 5 years, children's IQ scores increased by 2.2 points for each year that they resided in an affluent neighborhood (Leventhal & Brooks-Gunn, 2001). Neighborhood characteristics, such as low average SES, high male unemployment, and low percentage of managerial or professional workers have also been unfavorably linked to young children's behavior (Brooks-Gunn et al., 1993; Chase-Lansdale et al., 1997; Duncan, Brooks-Gunn, & Klebanov, 1994).

Specific "neighborhood processes" such as social cohesion, disorder, and safety seem to underlie links between neighborhood characteristics and children's outcomes. Studies have found inverse associations between neighborhood cohesion and children's behavior problems (Curtis, Dooley, & Phipps, 2004), verbal ability (Kohen et al., 2002), and problem-solving skills (Caughy & O'Campo, 2006), and these links may be particularly strong among children living in neighborhoods with high levels of concentrated disadvantage (Caughy, Nettles, & O'Campo, 2008). Neighborhood disorder is also associated with young children's cognitive outcomes (Kohen et al., 2002) and their internalizing problems (Caughy, Nettles, & O'Campo, 2008). Neighborhood influences on parents' well-being represent another mechanism by which neighborhoods may indirectly influence children's development. A recent study found some support for this model, reporting a causal pathway from neighborhood disadvantage to low levels of neighborhood cohesion, to poor family functioning and maternal depression, to lower frequency of literacy activities and parenting inconsistency and harshness. These parenting behaviors, in turn, were linked to children's verbal ability and problem behavior at age 5 years (Kohen, Leventhal, Dahinten, & McIntosh, 2008).

Child Care. Along with aspects of the home environment and neighborhood, parents make investments in their children by placing them in nonmaternal child care and preschool programs. Although home environment and parenting quality are more powerful predictors of children's outcomes than child care characteristics (NICHD Early Child Care Research Network, 2003), most research suggests that experiences in child care do independently influence cognitive and socioemotional development. The size and direction of these associations are dependent on age of entry into care, time spent in child care, child care quality, and family income level.

Links between child care and unfavorable socioemotional outcomes such as aggression and noncompliance have been reported for children, primarily those who enter care in the first year of life and remain in full-time child care throughout early childhood (Baydar & Brooks-Gunn, 1991; NICHD Early Child Care Research Network, 2003). Evidence from NICHD reported a link between average number of hours young children spent in child care per week from the time they were infants and increased socioemotional adjustment problems as they transitioned into kindergarten after controlling for other child care characteristics including quality, as well as family background and maternal sensitivity (NICHD Early Child Care Research Network, 2003). The link between quantity and externalizing behaviors attenuated by the time the NICHD children were in sixth grade (Belsky et al., 2007); however, the most recent evidence reported significant associations between child care quantity and 15-year-olds' risk-taking and impulsive behaviors (Vandell et al., 2010). Similar work on maternal employment has found that full-time maternal employment before children reached 9 months was associated with poorer child cognitive outcomes by age 3 years for White children (Brooks-Gunn, Han, & Waldfogel, 2002). A more recent analysis found that the deleterious influence of early maternal employment on White children's cognitive scores remained at 4.5 years and first grade, but that these negative associations were attenuated by use of center-based child care and maternal sensitivity by age 4.5 years (Brooks-Gunn, Han, & Waldfogel, 2010). These findings suggest that hours in center-based child care may have different effects on behavioral and cognitive outcomes, leading to less optimal behavioral outcomes but better cognitive ones by school entry. In the same study, full-time maternal employment during the first year of children's lives was only associated with increased externalizing behavior problems at 4.5 years and first grade when mothers began work during the first 3 months of children's lives, and the use of center-based child care did not drive these unfavorable findings. The whole of these findings suggest that the links between early child care and children's outcomes are not simple, may vary by developmental domain, and need to take into account a range of factors that influence children's development.

A range of studies have also examined associations between child care quality and children's outcomes. In high-quality child care environments, children have access to a range of materials that stimulate emergent literacy, language development, logical reasoning, and social skills, and have caregivers who engage them in cognitively stimulating activities, initiate and respond to their verbalizations, and have frequent positive interactions with them that include smiling, touching, and holding, among many other socially and cognitively enhancing behaviors (Kisker & Maynard, 1991). Child care studies have shown with great consistency that utilization of high-quality (vs. low-quality) care predicts more favorable cognitive outcomes for children during their early years that continue well into the school age years (Belsky et al., 2007; Burchinal et al., 2000; Love, Harrison et al., 2003; NICHD Early Child Care Research Network, 2002). The most up-to-date NICHD findings reported positive associations between early child care quality and children's achievement in high school (Vandell et al., 2010). Determining the true "effects" of quality on children's outcomes is analytically challenging as it requires disentangling the obvious, but likely unmeasured, overlap between parental characteristics and choice of child care settings. One robust analysis of the NICHD data using a range models to overcome this problem reported that child care quality had a relatively modest, but reliable, impact on preschool children's cognitive and achievement scores (NICHD Early Child Care Research Network & Duncan, 2003). Recent research by Burchinal suggests this and other studies may find modest effects of child care quality on child outcomes because the effect of child care quality is nonlinear: that is, quality has a larger effect when it reaches a certain threshold of caregiver–child stimulation and sensitivity than it does throughout the quality continuum (Burchinal, Vandergrift, Pianta, & Mashburn, 2009). Thus, quality may need to be quite high—or improve by a substantial margin—to meaningfully enhance children's school readiness.

Studies have also examined links between child care and outcomes specifically for low-income children, yielding mixed results, with some reporting favorable associations between provider responsiveness and warmth and children's early literacy skills and social behavior (Loeb, Fuller, Kagan, & Carroll, 2004) and others finding small associations between child care quality and young children's behavior and no direct links to children's achievement (Votruba-Drzal, Coley, & Chase-Lansdale, 2004). However, studies that compared the effects of child care quality for higher versus lower income children tend to find that quality matters more for those with less (Pianta, Barnett, Burchinal, & Thornburg, 2009). For example, using data from NICHD, a study reported that high-quality child care impacted the school readiness of children in poverty far more than those above the poverty line such that it protected children living in poor families from the deleterious influence of poverty on school readiness (McCartney, Dearing, Taylor, & Bub, 2007). The same authors more recently reported that child care quality assessed through the preschool years moderated the association between family income-to-needs and children's achievement during middle childhood, in part, because early child care quality boosted the school readiness of preschoolers living in poor families (Dearing, McCartney, & Taylor, 2009).

Yet, while high-quality child care may serve as a protective factor for children living in poor families, low-quality child care may compound other risks. Studies not specifically addressing children living in poor families found that low-quality care, particularly if initiated within the first year, is unfavorably associated with a range of developmental outcomes (NICHD, 1997, 1998). A study using a low-income sample found that the combination of poor quality child care and understimulating home environments was linked to greater externalizing behaviors (Votruba-Drzal, Coley, & Chase-Lansdale, 2004). Thus, while high-quality child care can offer children much needed cognitive and socioemotional enrichment, low-quality child care may serve to further undermine the development of children living in poor families. Access to high-quality child care is particularly limited in low-income communities (Loeb et al., 2004), suggesting many children in low-income and poor families may be at-risk of this double jeopardy.

Child Health and Nutrition. Another type of parental investment important for children's well-being is the provision of medical care (including prenatal care), nutrition, and safe environments (Ross & Duff, 1982). Research has long documented an SES-health gradient, in which the most affluent members of society have significantly better health outcomes than the less affluent, particularly people who are living in poverty (Adler et al., 1994). Research has also found that, while stronger in adulthood, this gradient has its origins in childhood, particularly in terms of the onset and development of chronic conditions such as asthma, and is not explained by maternal education or availability of health insurance (Case, Lubotsky, & Paxson, 2002). Health problems and nutritional deficits are also more likely among children living in poor than nonpoor families and are an important pathway through which poverty affects children's cognitive and school-related outcomes. Past research suggests that the prevalence of health problems accounts for as much as 20% of the differential in IQ scores between preschool children living in poor than nonpoor families (Goldstein, 1990).

Disparities in child health outcomes by poverty status begin very early in life. Children living in poor families are more likely to be born with low birth weight than other children (Starfield et al. 1991), which is strongly related to a number of later difficulties including poorer development in math, motor and spatial skills, language, and memory, as well as increased likelihood of grade repetition and special education placements relative to normal birth-weight infants (Klebanov, Brooks-Gunn, & McCormick, 1994; McCormick, Brooks-Gunn, Workman-Daniels, Turner, & Peckham, 1992). Studies that have examined long-term outcomes of low birth-weight children have found that they are still at risk for adverse outcomes as adolescents and possibly into adulthood (Conley & Bennett, 2000).

Nutrition is a key influence on young children's health and well-being and something that parents can directly impact. Perhaps most relevant to poor families is the concept of food insecurity, which focuses on families' limited or uncertain ability to acquire nutritionally adequate and safe foods due to monetary constraints. Several studies have demonstrated that poverty and its correlates are predictors of food insecurity (Hernandez & Jacknowitz, 2009; Skalicky et al., 2006); immigrant status also seems to be important, with the risk of food insecurity particularly high in households headed by foreign-born mothers (Chilton et al., 2009; Kalil & Chen, 2008).

Although many recent studies have detected sizable links between food insecurity and young children's health (Chilton et al., 2009; Rose-Jacobs et al., 2008; Skalicky et al., 2006), few have examined links between food insecurity and young children's cognitive and socioemotional well-being. One study did find that food insecurity experienced in infancy was not linked to children's cognitive outcomes at 2 years of age, but that insecurity experienced at 2 years was significant (Hernandez & Jacknowitz, 2009). A review has summarized evidence suggesting that food insecurity experienced at school entry may have some longer lasting influences on children's mathematics and social outcomes in elementary school (Cook & Frank, 2008). Further research is needed to identify the relevant pathways of these associations.

Finally, parents invest in young children's health by avoiding residence in low-quality housing, which tends to elevate children's potential exposure to environmental toxins. Specifically, children living in poor families are four times as likely to experience elevated blood lead levels as their peers living in nonpoor families because of their heightened exposure to lead paint within the home prior to its ban in 1978 (Brody et al. 1994). Exposure to lead, even at relatively low levels, is associated with childhood problems in cognition, attention, aggression, impulse control, as well as growth and other physical impairments (Bellinger, 2004; Needleman, 1979, 1990; Needleman & Gatsonis, 1990; Needleman, Riess, Tobin, & Biesecker, 1996; Schwartz, 1994; Schwartz, Angle, & Pitcher, 1986; Schwartz & Otto, 1991). Childhood lead exposure can having lasting effects well into adulthood: one study found that early exposure was linked to decreased gray matter in certain areas of the adult brain affiliated with attention, executive functions, and decision making (Cecil et al., 2008). In addition to risk of lead poisoning, poor children have greater exposure to toxic environmental conditions resulting from residential proximity to waste incinerators or air pollution (Evans, 2001).

Conclusion

To understand the impacts of poverty on children's school readiness, one must consider the pathways through which poverty affects child development. Two broad theories characterize this literature, the family stress model and the investment model. Because the family stress model hinges on parenting and parent–child relationships, it is more closely related to child emotional and behavioral outcomes, although cognitive development is inextricably linked to these processes as well. The investment model implicates the monetary limitations poor parents face in raising their children. Regardless of parenting quality, children living in poor families are most likely to lack the materials, services, and resources at home, child care, and in their neighborhoods that children living in nonpoor families enjoy, and this disparity impacts their development. Although the quality of these environments relate more strongly to children's cognitive outcomes, children's socioemotional and physical health outcomes have also been linked to these investments. In the next section, we address how public policies can improve the quality of children's environments and alleviate family stress.

Policy Implications

Federal and state governments employ a range of social policy initiatives to alleviate poverty that have the potential improve family functioning, relieve material hardship, and enhance children's development. Overall, these antipoverty policies can be grouped into three overall types of programs (Currie, 2006): cash assistance to families, such as welfare and tax credits; in-kind benefit programs, such as child care subsidies and food assistance; and direct interventions with low-income children and their parents, such as Head Start. The former two program types increase families' economic resources and self-sufficiency, in doing so, can influence the pathways through which poverty impacts children, yet facilitating child development is not necessarily a stated goal of these programs. By contrast, the latter program type aims explicitly to alleviate poverty's impacts on children through child- and parent-focused services. The following section describes programs within each type that have documented impacts on family and child well-being. We conclude with an overview of strategies that hold the most promise for improving the school readiness of children growing up in poverty.

Cash Assistance Programs

Given the documented links between increases in family income and improved child cognitive and behavioral outcomes, programs that provide poor families with cash assistance offer the most direct route to ameliorating the effects of poverty on children's development. The most widespread cash assistance program is TANF, which in 1996 replaced the entitlement program Aid to Families with Dependent Children (AFDC) with time-limited, work-based assistance (Moffitt, 2003). Several pre-TANF welfare-to-work experiments illuminate the likely impacts of various TANF provisions including work mandates, income supplements, noncompliance sanctions, and time limits on family income as well as children's outcomes. Collectively, these studies suggest that work-oriented policies increase family income and decrease poverty rates (Schoeni & Blank, 2003), but that only programs that supplement parents' earnings with cash increase family income net of the decreases in welfare payments (Morris, Gennetian, & Duncan, 2005). Perhaps for this reason, a study of 13 welfare-to-work programs found that those providing earnings supplements increased children's cognitive test scores and achievement outcomes by approximately 7% of a standard deviation (Morris, Duncan, & Clark-Kaufman, 2005), whereas programs offering only work supports had no consistent effects. However, even the most comprehensive of these earning supplement programs produced only short-term impacts on young children's academic skills and test scores, with effects disappearing after the program ended (Huston et al., 2005).

Another way the federal government can impact family income is through refundable tax credits. For example, the

Earned Income Tax Credit (EITC), now the country's largest cash antipoverty program (Scholz, Moffitt, & Cowan, 2008), grants tax credits to low-income families based on their household composition and earnings. According to some estimates, EITC increases family income by over 20% for those living in poverty (Dahl & Lochner, 2009; Kim, 2001), while also encouraging parental employment. This increase in income, in turn, may enhance child outcomes, particularly in the cognitive domain. Indeed, Dahl and Lochner (2009) estimated that a $1,000 increase in family income derived from EITC produced a 6% increase in children's math and reading test scores with even larger effects for poor and minority families. However, as with the effects of welfare-based earning supplements, these improvements seem to fade out over time.

Taken together, these results suggest that programs work best if they raise family income rather than encourage parental employment alone. This finding should come as no surprise when one considers the direct effects of poverty on child development and the benefits associated with even small upward shifts in income, particularly for children living in deep and entrenched deprivation. These increases in income, however, must be substantial and long-lasting to effect long-term improvements to children's developmental outcomes, a finding that parallels the literature suggesting income changes must be substantial and permanent to meaningfully alter children's developmental trajectories (Blau, 1999). Combining parental employment with earnings supplements generous enough to lift and keep families out of poverty offers the most direct path to this goal (provided high-quality, affordable child care is readily available—see next section).

In-Kind Benefit Programs

Whereas cash assistance programs allow families to invest more material resources in children by increasing family income, in-kind benefit programs supply those investments directly to families. In her 2006 book, *The Invisible Safety Net*, Janet Currie posits that in-kind benefits such as child care subsidies and food assistance constitute the most essential, though largely invisible, part of the public welfare system. She argues that in-kind benefits often make up the difference between low-income families' household earnings and what it costs to buy family essentials like food, shelter, medical care, and child care. In Currie's words, these programs form "a broad-reaching and comprehensive net that especially protects young children in low-income families" (p. 3). Indeed, many of these programs, including child care subsidies, food stamps, and housing assistance have been shown to lessen material hardship and improve economic conditions in low-income families.

Nonetheless, very few in-kind benefit programs have been shown to favorably impact child outcomes. For example, child care subsidies may be crucial to low-income families' economic well-being, but the few studies that have

examined their impact on child outcomes do not suggest their receipt improves low-income children's school readiness (see below). Theoretically, subsides could indirectly improve child outcomes by promoting maternal employment and elevating family income, or by enabling families to purchase higher quality child care than they could otherwise afford, which would directly impact child outcomes. Using data from the 1999 National Survey of American Families, Blau and Tekin (2007) found that child care subsidies did increase employment among unwed mothers by as much as 33 percentage points. However, the few studies that have examined the effects of subsidies on children's child care quality have found that subsidy users choose lower quality child care environments than those provided by Head Start or public school-based preschools, but higher quality care than those in unsubsidized care (Ryan, Johnson, Rigby, & Brooks-Gunn, 2011). These mixed effects might explain why studies that examine the impact of subsidies on child outcomes find that impacts on cognitive, socioemotional, and health outcomes (e.g., obesity) are either neutral (Datta Gupta & Simonsen, 2010) or negative (Datta Gupta & Simonsen, 2010; Herbst & Tekin, 2008, 2009).

Another widespread type of in-kind benefit is food assistance. The two largest providers of food assistance to low-income families are the food stamp program, now called the Supplemental Nutrition Assistance Program (SNAP), and the Women, Infants, and Children (WIC) program. Whereas the effect of food stamps receipt on children's nutrition and health outcomes is unclear (see Currie, 2006 for a review), there is more consistent evidence that WIC receipt improves mothers' and children's nutritional intake, perhaps because WIC targets families with young children and requires families to purchase foods with nutritional value. A growing number of studies have linked WIC receipt with a range of health outcomes including lower rates of anemia, failure to thrive, low birth weight, and childhood obesity (Currie & Bitler, 2004; Kowalski-Jones & Duncan, 2002; Lee & Mackey-Bilaver, 2007). Each of these health outcomes, in turn, could impact children's cognitive and socioemotional skills upon school entry.

As we review above, research suggests that living in a low-income neighborhood may undermine children's cognitive or socioemotional development over and above the impact of family-level poverty. One of the ways the federal government aims to redress this effect is by providing families with housing vouchers or public housing that enable them to move to higher income areas. A program initiated by the U.S. Department of Housing and Urban Development called Moving to Opportunity (MTO) serves as a landmark evaluation of this approach. Because residents of housing projects were randomly assigned to move either to private housing in low-poverty areas, to private housing wherever they chose, or to remain in public housing, any effects can be attributed, causally, to the program, thus revealing the impacts of moving to low-poverty neighborhoods and residence in high-poverty neighborhoods. Although moving was associated with short-term cognitive benefits for certain subgroups of children (Ludwig, Ladd, & Duncan, 2001), there were either no effects or negative effects on cognitive and academic outcomes for children in the program group 5 years later (Leventhal, Fauth, & Brooks-Gunn, 2005). These findings cast doubt on the potential for housing assistance, at least assistance that encourages residential movement, to impact children's early outcomes.

Early Childhood Interventions

In contrast to cash and in-kind benefit programs that impact children indirectly by increasing families' economic resources, early intervention programs aim to facilitate favorable outcomes among low-income children through child-focused services (Brooks-Gunn, 2003). Early childhood intervention targets children in poor and low-income families before they enter elementary school, either starting prenatally with home health visits or from infancy or preschool. Although early intervention is a relatively broad term that encompasses a variety of tactics and programs, it typically involves center-based services that focus on children's development in both cognitive and socioemotional domains. Theory supporting these programs suggests that experiencing high-quality center care can mitigate the familial and environmental risks poor and low-income children face by providing opportunities for learning and socialization they may not receive at home. Some programs also aim to impact parents' emotional well-being or parenting behavior directly and, thus, child outcomes indirectly.

Model Programs. Much of the public support for early intervention is based on findings from studies of high-quality, intensive programs in which families were randomly assigned to receive services and children's development was assessed long-term even though these studies were conducted over 30 years ago, followed small samples of children, and evaluated far more expensive programs than those available in relatively large scale today. The best known of these model programs, the Perry Preschool and the Abecedarian Programs, produced substantial positive effects on a range of cognitive and socioemotional outcomes, as well as school achievement, job performance, and social behaviors long after the intervention ended (Campbell, Pungello, Miller-Johnson, Burchinal, & Ramey, 2001; Schweinhart et al., 2005). The two programs differed, however, in their effects on children's IQ scores. Children in both programs scored higher on IQ tests than control group children during early childhood; however, only children in Abecedarian's program group maintained that advantage through young adulthood. Perry's effects on children's IQ disappeared by age 10, a fade out effect reported for other intervention programs (see Currie & Thomas, 2000, for a critical assessment of Head Start fade out). It is possible that Abecedarian produced longer-lasting improvements in IQ because it began when children were infants, continued through age 8, and provided year-round, full-day center-based care, whereas Perry Preschool began at age 3, continued only through the preschool years, and provided part-year, half-day services (Knudsen et al., 2006). Nonetheless, children in the Perry program exhibited a range of other long-term benefits including higher high school graduation rates, better academic achievement, and higher earnings and home ownership in adulthood than control children (Schweinhart et al., 2005). The Abecedarian program also had long-term effects on social outcomes including higher college attendance rates, lower teenage pregnancy rates, and lower rates of smoking (Campbell et al., 2001). The apparent "noncognitive" benefits of intensive programs like Abecedarian and Perry have led researchers to argue that early intervention programs offer the most effective way to improve the outcomes of low-income children both from a developmental and an economic standpoint (Knudsen et al., 2006).

Early Intervention in the 21st Century. Abecedarian and Perry Preschool and more recent programs such as IHDP were small-scale, expensive interventions. For example, Abecedarian spent about $15,000 per year, per child (in 1999 dollars) for the first 5 years of the program and served fewer than 100 children (Currie, 2001). Although the total economic benefit of Abecedarian to society, in terms of the children's higher incomes, lower welfare dependency, and lower crime rates far exceeded program costs (Barnett & Masse, 2007), it would likely be politically infeasible for the government to fund such high-cost interventions for low-income children on a large scale. Thus, although model programs suggest what could be done to improve poor children's school readiness, existing publicly funded early education programs demonstrate what can be achieved for greater numbers of children in programs of more variable quality.

Head Start is the nation's largest and oldest early intervention program for young children in poverty today. A long history of nonexperimental studies on the effects of Head Start finds that it produces short-term gains in both test scores (Currie & Thomas, 1995; Zill et al., 1998) and socioemotional adjustment (Deming, 2009). Overall, these effects fade out during the school years, at least for cognitive outcomes (Currie & Thomas, 1995). However, this fade out may be largely attributable to the low-quality schools Head Start children typically attend rather than the program's ineffectiveness *per se* (Currie & Thomas, 2000). Moreover, studies have found that, like Perry Preschool, Head Start may benefit children in the long-term despite test score fade out by increasing children's likelihood of graduating high school and attending college and decreasing their likelihood of committing serious crimes and living in poverty as adults (Garces, Thomas, & Currie, 2002; Ludwig & Miller, 2007). From a policy perspective, these nonexperimental findings suggest that the developmental and social benefits of Head Start outweigh the costs, even if Head Start children score similarly to their peers on standardized tests.

In 2002, the first large-scale randomized evaluation of Head Start was initiated. In 2005, the study reported that Head Start had positive short-term impacts on children's language and literacy skills for both 3- and 4-year-olds, between 10 and 24% of a standard deviation depending on the outcome, but had no effect on math skills (U.S. Department of Health and Human Services, 2005). Three-year-olds in Head Start also had lower parent-reported behavior problems and hyperactivity by 13% and 18% of a standard deviation, respectively, although no socioemotional effects emerged for 4-year-olds. Despite these modest but significant short-term benefits, few differences remained by the end of first grade: Head Start children did significantly better on only one cognitive outcome per age group: the PPVT for 4-year-olds and the Woodcock-Johnson III test of Oral Comprehension for 3-year-olds (U.S. Department of Health and Human Services, 2005), while no clear pattern of benefits emerged for socioemotional outcomes. The national evaluation of Early Head Start, an analogous program for children from birth to 3 years, reported similar, albeit stronger, short-term impacts on children's cognitive and socioemotional outcomes at age 3, but few impacts lasted through age 5 (U.S. Department of Health and Human Services, 2006). In short, these experimental results resemble those from nonexperimental studies of Head Start in which children experience short-term cognitive and socioemotional benefits that reduce once children enter elementary school. The crucial question that remains is whether these children, if followed to adulthood, would nonetheless experience long-term benefits in terms of educational attainment and social adjustment, which the nonexperimental literature would predict.

A growing literature has examined the short-term effects of publicly funded prekindergarten (pre-K) programs on children's cognitive and socioemotional outcomes. Unlike Head Start, pre-K programs are available to all children, regardless of family income, and are thus often called "universal pre-K" programs to distinguish them from targeted interventions. Oklahoma's pre-K program, for example, has generated attention because it is based in the school system and reaches a higher percentage of 4-year-olds than other states' programs (Gormley, Phillips, & Gayer, 2008). Using a statistical technique that capitalizes on the birthday cutoff for pre-K enrollment, researchers determined that children who had spent a year in the program had better preliteracy, language, and premath skills than children entering kindergarten who had not attended pre-K by nearly a full standard deviation for some outcomes (Gormley et al., 2008). These effects are much larger than those reported for Head Start and for other state pre-K programs (Barnett, Lamy, & Jung, 2005), leaving some to question why certain universal pre-K programs might improve cognitive outcomes more than targeted interventions. One possibility is that pre-K programs, and Oklahoma's in particular, often require teachers to have B.A. degrees and early-childhood education certification. Pre-K curricula also emphasize academic skills, such as

recognizing letters and sounds more so than Head Start's (Gormley et al., 2008). Alternatively, the benefits of pre-K may be overestimated in nonexperimental studies, whereas the Head Start evaluation more accurately identified its program's effects (Duncan, Ludwig, & Magnuson, 2007). Whatever the explanation, a central challenge for the next generation of antipoverty policies will be to determine the relative merits of universal versus targeted early education programs and public school- or community-based initiatives.

Impacts on Parents. As we explained previously, parents' behavior with their children and their time and money investments can serve as important pathways mediating poverty effects on children's outcomes. Not only can early intervention programs moderate the deleterious impacts of early childhood disadvantage on children's outcomes, but these programs can also moderate poverty's impacts on parents, and children as a result. Benefits include improvements in mental health, parenting skills, and home environments.

A number of evaluations have reported treatment effects on maternal mental health, most notably levels of depression and anxiety (Barnard, Magyry, Booth, Mitchell, & Spieker, 1988; Booth, Mitchell, Barnard, & Spieker, 1989; Erickson, Korfmacher, & Egeland, 1992; Lyons-Ruth, Connell, Grunebaum, & Botein, 1990). Mothers whose low birth-weight children participated in the IHDP intervention reported lower emotional distress than nonintervention mothers 1 year into the program; findings were most pronounced for mothers experiencing large numbers of negative life events (Klebanov, Brooks-Gunn, & McCormick, 2001). Mothers of children who participated in the Early Head Start program did not differ from nonprogram families on assessments of their mental health, although parenting stress was lower among mothers in the treatment group compared with controls for families in home-based programs (Love et al., 2001). Home-visiting programs have had more success altering parenting behavior than they have with child outcomes, perhaps because these programs tend to be parent-focused. Home-based programs have been shown to enhance parental mental health as evidenced by the reduction of depressive affect and the increase in positive coping and provision of maternal support (see Brooks-Gunn, Berlin, & Fuligni, 2000).

By improving parent well-being, early intervention programs theoretically influence children's well-being indirectly. Supporting this theory, the most prominent impacts of early intervention programs on parents' outcomes are found for their interactions with their children. A number of studies have reported more positive parent–child interactions for dyads participating in interventions (Brooks-Gunn et al., 2000; Love et al., 2005). The Early Head Start evaluation, which videotaped in-home parent–child interactions, found program effects in terms of parents' increased supportiveness and decreased emotional detachment and harshness (Love et al., 2005). Most recently, the Head Start Impact

Study found that program parents used corporal punishment less often than control parents (U.S. Department of Health and Human Services, 2005).

Early intervention programs can also indirectly impact child outcomes by elevating the quality of the home environment. A review of early education impacts revealed that a number of home-based and mixed-approach interventions significantly improved HOME scores for participating families (Brooks-Gunn, Berlin, & Fuligni, 2000). Few studies include assessments of the home environment, however, making it difficult to generalize across all interventions. Data from the Early Head Start evaluation found that parents in the treatment group provided more language and learning experiences in the home including reading to their children daily compared with families in the control group (Love et al., 2005). The Head Start Impact Study reported similar findings in the short-term (U.S. Department of Health and Human Services, 2005), and effects on reading lasted through to the end of first grade for the youngest cohort (U.S. Department of Health and Human Services, 2010). As we reviewed above, providing a more stimulating home environment can enhance child cognitive, as well as socioemotional, development.

Most of the programs reviewed above that impact parent well-being, parenting practices, and home environment offer home-visiting services that directly target parents and the home environment in addition to center-based care for children (e.g., IHDP and EHS). Programs that exclusively offer home-visiting have also been found to improve domains of family functioning and child outcomes. Perhaps the most well-developed home visiting program in the United States is the Nurse Family-Partnership (NFP). NFP was developed in Elmira, New York to provide home visits to low-income, first-time mothers, beginning prenatally and continuing through the child's second birthday (Olds et al., 1997, 2002). Registered nurses work with mothers to encourage healthful behaviors during pregnancy, teach developmentally appropriate parenting skills, and improve the maternal life course by reducing the number of subsequent births and increasing the interval between pregnancies. Results of evaluations of the Elmira program indicate that NFP significantly reduced incidence of child abuse and neglect (Olds et al., 1997), and results of evaluations of subsequent programs in Memphis and Denver suggest the program also reduced levels of harsh maternal parenting (Olds et al., 2002) and increased levels of maternal sensitivity and responsiveness (Olds et al., 2004). In the Denver program only, program participants had higher HOME scores than the control group (Olds et al., 2002). Although the NFP showed positive effects on parent outcomes, findings across various home-visiting programs are decidedly mixed, with many showing few positive impacts on parents (see Howard & Brooks-Gunn, 2009 for a review of home-visiting programs and their effects on families and children).

Because effects of home-visiting programs on parenting are mixed and modest, their effects on child outcomes should be smaller still. Overall, few home-based programs find positive effects on children's development (Howard & Brooks-Gunn, 2009). However, there is some evidence that NFP enhanced children's cognitive outcomes, particularly among the most at-risk families (e.g., mothers with low social and psychological resources) (Olds et al., 2002; 2007), and that changes in children's outcomes were mediated by changes in parenting attitudes and behaviors. In a reanalysis of the Comprehensive Child Development Program evaluation, another home-visiting program, Burchinal, Lopez, and Brooks-Gunn found that children in the sites that provided more intensive home visiting services, versus less frequent home visits, had significant treatment effects on children's cognitive outcomes at ages 3 and 5 (Brooks-Gunn, Burchinal, & Lopez, 2002). Moreover, early intervention programs such as EHS and IHDP that offer *both* center- and home-based services, rather than home-visiting services alone, have demonstrated positive effects on child cognitive outcomes. In EHS particularly, some of the strongest effects on child outcomes were found in the programs providing both center- and home-based services rather than either home- or center-based alone (Love et al., 2005). These findings have been interpreted to mean that child cognitive functioning is unlikely to be altered without (intensive) high-quality child development center experience, but that the combination of center- and home-based services may provide optimal results.

Closing the School Readiness Gap: What Works

What does the foregoing research tell us about how to close the school readiness gap between children growing up in and out of poverty? Countless studies have demonstrated that, to varying degrees, poverty undermines children's school readiness across cognitive and socioemotional outcomes. However, strategies that seem like direct solutions do not produce the long-lasting benefits that basic research on children's development would predict. For example, programs to increase parental income or material resources produce either no meaningful effects on children's outcomes or only modest, short-term improvements. Research suggests that policies that change parents' economic resources substantially and over the long-term could facilitate long-lasting improvements in child well-being; however, few if any public programs can guarantee substantial, long-term changes in family income. Likewise, although research suggests that living in high-crime, high-poverty neighborhoods can negatively impact children's development, moving children out of such neighborhoods does not seem to improve their cognitive or socioemotional functioning with consistency. Thus, although gaps in children's school readiness may be partially attributable to poverty and disadvantaged environments, it does not appear that simply alleviating income poverty or removing children from an environment of concentrated poverty will close the school readiness gap.

Given existing research reviewed above, we believe that the most promising way to improve the school readiness of children in poverty would be to increase public investment in high-quality center-based early childhood education programs. Assuming we cannot feasibly offer intensive, expensive programs like Abecedarian or Perry Preschool to the vast majority of poor and low-income children, what features of those programs could we offer to the majority of children in poverty? Ideally services would begin during infancy by enrolling children in federal programs such as Early Head Start until they are 3-years-old. Children would then transition smoothly into state-sponsored preschool programs at age 4, either provided by a public school system, such as the Oklahoma UPK, or child-care centers and Head Start programs with similar standards and resources operated as part of state pre-K (Pianta et al., 2009). Most important, the care provided to children in the programs through the first 5 years should be of high quality. Indicators of high-quality include small classes with high teacher–pupil ratios, sensitive and stimulating caregiver–child interaction, and child-centered, developmentally sensitive materials and activities. Although a thorough analysis of possible approaches to enhancing and insuring access to high-quality early education is beyond the scope of this chapter, the question of quality improvement offers a rich and complex area of developmental and policy research (see Pianta et al., 2009).

Evidence from home-visiting and mixed-approach programs also suggests that the home environment should be a target for early intervention. The relative success of the NFP program indicates that an exclusive home-visiting program should begin during the prenatal period, offer intensive services, and focus on parenting practices and parent-child interactions. The success of the NFP also implies programs should employ highly trained professionals such as registered nurses rather than paraprofessionals, although this point is debated (see Howard & Brooks-Gunn, 2009). Additionally, findings from the EHS and IHDP studies, among others, suggest that the home-visiting approach could be successfully combined with center-based care for infants, toddlers, and preschoolers to yield the greatest benefits to children. It is difficult to say whether home visiting confers more benefits to disadvantaged families than more advantaged families because nearly all programs target poor and low-income families; however, even within disadvantaged target populations mothers with the fewest social and psychological resources seem to benefit the most from home-visiting services. This finding suggests that given current government budget limitations, the combination of high-quality early education with intensive home-visiting may be most effectively and feasibly targeted to the most disadvantaged families.

It is important to remember that even a set of comprehensive developmentally focused services such as those proposed above would not likely eliminate the school readiness gap between children in and out of poverty. A longer-term approach that extends through the elementary, middle, and high school years may help prevent some of the so-called fade out effects typically seen with early intervention programs and may continue closing the gap after school entry. However, it is clear that to narrow the school readiness gap to a meaningful degree, we need programs that are of the highest possible quality and intensity, begin at birth or before, and continue until children enter kindergarten ready to learn and succeed. It is possible that such a comprehensive set of services would also facilitate the success of welfare policies mandating work requirements, which could benefit child development indirectly. Although child care subsidies that are not tied to high-quality care do not seem to enhance child development, widely available high-quality early education could remove a barrier to consistent, full-time employment—one of the goals of welfare reform and a necessity for families to leave poverty—while also improving child well-being.

Although developmental trajectories are not fixed after children's first few years, early experiences are important for children's development and well-being. Without proper supports and interventions, many poor children will start off behind their nonpoor peers and will continue to lag behind over time. Through the kind of mindful support systems and targeted interventions outlined above, we can increase the odds of positive outcomes for children in poverty and begin to close that gap.

Notes

1. The poverty guidelines, which are a simplified version of the threshold, are also an official federal poverty measure, but are primarily used to determine financial eligibility for certain programs.
2. Families with incomes below 50% of the poverty threshold may be classified as living in "deep poverty."
3. Smaller effects of income on socioemotional outcomes could indicate that children's socioemotional development is less sensitive than their cognitive development to family income. However, this pattern could also stem from the use of parent report of early child behavior, which is less objective than cognitive assessments and, therefore, more vulnerable to bias and measurement error.
4. A third possible pathway stresses differences in the parenting practices and values of families across social class. For example, Hart and Risley (1995) compared the number of words parents of professional, working class, or welfare families spoke to young children and found that more parent–child speech among the professional families explained in part children's higher cognitive scores in this class. This study, and others like it (e.g., Lareau, 2003), do not isolate the effect of family income on child development from the effect of parental education or type of employment, so we do not review this literature. However, these studies reveal broad differences in the developmental environments of children from more and less affluent families that may help explain differences in school readiness.
5. The scale also taps parenting quality in terms of both teaching (e.g., how often parents read to the child or tell her stories) and emotional warmth (e.g., hugging and kissing, praising and responding to the child). In this way, the HOME scale measures factors associated with the family stress model, although its emphasis on materials and experiences for which parents spend time and money aligns it more closely with the investment model.

References

Adler, N E., Boyce, T., Chesney, M. A., Cohen, S., Folkman, S., Kahn, R. L., & Syme, S .L. (1994). Socioeconomic status and health. The challenge of the gradient. *The American Psychologist, 49*(1), 15–24.

Akee, K. Q., Copeland, W., Keeler, G., Angold, A., & Costello, J. (2010). Parents' incomes and children's outcomes: A quasi-experiment. *American Economic Journal: Applied Economics, 2*(1), 86–115.

Apfel, N., & Seitz, V. (1997). The firstborn sons of African American teenage mothers: Perspectives on risk and resilience. In S. S. Luthar, J. A. Burack, Ciccetti, D., & Weisz, J. R. (Eds.), *Developmental psychopathology: Perspectives on adjustment, risk, and disorder* (pp. 486–506). New York: Cambridge University Press.

Axinn, W., Duncan, G., & Thornton, A. (1997). The effects of parents' income, wealth and attitudes on children's completed schooling and self-esteem. In G. Duncan & J. Brooks-Gunn (Eds.), *Consequences of growing up poor* (pp. 518–540). New York: Russell Sage Foundation.

Barnard, K. E., Magyary, G. S., Booth, C. L., Mitchell, S. K., & Spieker, S. J. (1988). Prevention of parenting altercations for women with low social support. *Psychiatry, 51*, 248–253.

Barnett, W. S., Lamy, C., & Jung, K. (2005). *The effects of state prekindergarten programs on young children's school readiness in five states.* New Brunswick, NJ: National Institute for Early Education Research, Rutgers University. Retrieved from http://nieer.org/resources/research/multistate/fullreport.pdf

Barnett, W. S., & Masse, L. N. (2007). Early childhood program design and economic returns: Comparative benefit-cost analysis of the Abecedarian Program and policy implications. *Economics of Education Review, 26*(1), 113–125.

Baumrind, D. (1966). Effects of authoritative control on child behavior. *Child Development, 37*, 887–907.

Baydar, N., & Brooks-Gunn, J. (1991). Effects of maternal employment and child-care arrangements on preschoolers' cognitive and behavioral outcomes: Evidence from the Children of the National Longitudinal Survey of Youth. *Developmental Psychology, 27*(6), 932–945.

Becker, G. S. (1991). *A treatise on the family.* Cambridge, MA: Harvard University Press.

Bellinger, D. C. (2004). Lead. *Pediatrics, 113*(4), 1016–1022.

Belsky, J. (1999). Interactional and contextual determinants of attachment security. In J. Cassidy & P. Shaver (Eds.), *Handbook of attachment theory and research* (pp. 249–264). New York: Guilford.

Belsky, J., Vandell, D. L., Burchinal, M., Clarke-Stewart, K. A., McCartney, K., Owen, M. T., and the NICHD Early Child Care Research Network (2007). Are there long-term effects of early child care? *Child Development, 78*(2), 681–701.

Berlin, L. J., Brady-Smith, C., & Brooks-Gunn, J. (2002). Links between childbearing age and observed maternal behaviors with 14-month-olds in the Early Head Start Research and Evaluation Project. *Infant Mental Health Journal, 23*(1/2), 104–129.

Blau, D. M. (1999). The effect of income on child development. *Review of Economics and Statistics, 81*(2), 261–276.

Blau, D., & Tekin, E. (2007). The determinants and consequences of child care subsidies for single mothers in the USA. *Journal of Population Economics, 20,* 719–741.

Booth, C. L., Mitchell, S. K., Barnard, K. E., & Spieker, S. J. (1989). Development of maternal social skills in multiproblem families: Effects on the mother–child relationship. *Developmental Psychology, 25,* 403–412.

Bornstein, M. H. (Ed.). (1995). *Handbook of parenting.* Mahwah, NJ: Erlbaum.

Bradley, R. H. (1995). Environment and parenting. In M. H. Bornstein (Ed.), *Handbook of parenting: Vol. 2. Biology and ecology of parenting* (pp. 235–261). Mahwah, NJ: Erlbaum.

Bradley, R. H., & Corwyn, R. F. (2002). Socioeconomic status and child development. *Annual Review of Psychology, 53,* 371–399.

Bradley, R. H., Corwyn, R. F., McAdoo, H. P., & Garcia Coll, C. (2001). The home environments of children in the United States part I: Varia-

tions by age, ethnicity, and poverty status. *Child Development, 72*(6), 1844–1867.

Brody, D. J., Pirkle, J. L., Kramer, R. A., Flegel, K. M., Matte, T. D., Gunter, E. W., ... Paschal, D. C. (1994). Blood lead levels in the U.S. population: Phase 1 of the Third National Health and Nutrition Examination Survey (NHANES III, 1988–1991). *Journal of the American Medical Association, 272,* 277–283.

Brooks-Gunn, J. (2003). Do you believe in magic?: What we can expect from early childhood intervention programs. *Society for Research in Child Development Social Policy Report, 7*(1), 1–14.

Brooks-Gunn, J., Berlin, L. J., & Fuligni, A. S. (2000). Early childhood intervention programs: What about the family? In J. P. Shonkoff & S. J. Meisels (Eds.), *Handbook of early childhood intervention* (2nd ed., pp. 549–588). New York: Cambridge University Press.

Brooks-Gunn, J., Duncan, G. J., Klebanov, P., & Sealand, N. (1993). Do neighborhoods influence child and adolescent development? *American Journal of Sociology, 99,* 353–395.

Brooks-Gunn, J., Han, W. J., & Waldfogel, J. (2002). Maternal employment and child cognitive outcomes in the first three years of life: The NICHD Study of Early Child Care. *Child Development, 73*(4), 1052–1072.

Brooks-Gunn, J., Han, W. J., & Waldfogel, J. (2010). First-year maternal employment and child development in the first 7 years. *Monographs of the Society for Research in Child Development, Serial 296, 75*(2).

Brooks-Gunn, J., Leventhal, T., & Duncan, G. (1999). Why poverty matters for young children: Implications for policy. In J. D. Osofsky & H. E. Fitzgerald (Eds.), *WAIMH handbook of infant mental health: Vol.3. Parenting and child care* (pp. 92–131). New York: Wiley.

Burchinal, M. R., Roberts, J. E., Riggins, R., Jr., Zeisel, S. A., Neebe, E., & Bryant, D. (2000). Relating quality of center-based child care to early cognitive and language development longitudinally. *Child Development, 71*(2), 339–357.

Burchinal, M., Vandergrift, N., Pianta, R., & Mashburn, A. (2009). Threshold analysis of association between child care quality and child outcomes for low-income children in pre-kindergarten programs. *Early Childhood Research Quarterly, 25,* 166–176.

Caldwell, B. M., & Bradley, R. H. (1984). *Home observation for measurement of the environment.* Little Rock, AR: University of Arkansas.

Campbell, F. A., Pungello, E. P., Miller-Johnson, S., Burchinal, M., & Ramey, C. T. (2001). The development of cognitive and academic abilities: Growth curves from an early childhood educational experiment. *Developmental Psychology, 37,* 231–242.

Carnegie Corporation. (1994). *Starting points: Meeting the needs of our youngest children.* New York: Author.

Case, A., Lubotsky, D., & Paxson, C. (2002, February). *Economic status and health in childhood: The origins of the gradient.* Princeton, NJ: The Center for Health and Wellbeing, Princeton University.

Caughy, M. O. B., Nettles, S. M., & O'Campo, P. J. (2008). The effect of residential neighborhood on child behavior problems in first grade. *American Journal of Community Psychology, 42*(1–2), 39–50.

Caughy, M. O. B., & O'Campo, P. J. (2006). Neighborhood poverty, social capital, and the cognitive development of African American preschoolers. *American Journal of Community Psychology, 37*(1–2), 141–154.

Chase-Lansdale, P. L., Gordon, R. A., Brooks-Gunn, J., & Klebanov, P. (1997). Neighborhood and family influences on the intellectual and behavioral competence of preschool and early school-age children. In J. Brooks-Gunn, G. J. Duncan, & J. L. Aber (Eds.), *Neighborhood poverty: Vol. 1. Context and consequences for children* (pp. 79–118). New York: Russell Sage Foundation.

Cecil, K. M., Brubaker, C. J., Adler, C. M., Dietrich, K. N., Altaye, M., & Egelhoff, J. C..(2008). Decreased brain volume in adults with childhood lead exposure. *PLoS Medicine, 5*(5), 741–750.

Chilton, M., Black, M. M., Casey, P. H., Cook, J., Cutts, D., Jacobs, R. R., ... Frank, D. A. (2009). Food insecurity and risk of poor health among US-born children of immigrants. *American Journal of Public Health, 99*(3), 556–562.

Cicchetti, D., & Toth, S. L. (1995). Child maltreatment and attachment organization: Implications for intervention. In S. Goldberg, R. Muir,

& J. Kerr, (Eds.), *Attachment theory: Social, developmental, and clinical perspectives.*

Citro, C. F., & Michael, R. T. (Eds.). (1995). *Measuring poverty: A new approach.* Washington, DC: National Academy Press.

Coiro, M. J., Zill, N., & Bloom, B. (1994, December). *Health of our nation's children* (Vital Health and Statistics, Series 10, No.191). Hyattsville, MD: U.S. Department of Health and Human Services.

Conger, R. D., & Conger, K. J. (2000). Resilience in midwestern families: Selected findings from the first decade of a prospective longitudinal study. *Journal of Marriage & Family, 64*, 361–373.

Conger, R. D., & Elder, G. H. (1994). *Families in troubled times: Adapting to change in rural America.* New York: Aldine de Gruyter.

Conger, R. D., Patterson, G. R., & Ge, X. (1995). It takes two to replicate: A mediational model for the impact of parents' stress on adolescent adjustment. *Child Development, 66*, 80–97.

Conger, K. J., Rueter, M. A., & Conger, R. D. (2000). The role of economic pressure in the lives of parents and their adolescents: The Family Stress Model. In L. J. Crockett & R. K. Silbereisen (Eds.), *Negotiating adolescence in times of social change* (pp. 201–223). New York: Cambridge University Press.

Conley, D., & Bennett, N. G. (2000). Is biology destiny? Birth weight and life chances. *American Sociological Review, 65*, 458–467.

Cook, J. T. & Frank, D. A. (2008). Food insecurity, poverty, and human development in the United States. *Annals of the New York Academy of Sciences, 1136*, 193–209.

Costello, E. J., Compton, S. N., Keeler, G., & Angold, A. (2003). Relationships between poverty and psychopathology: A natural experiment. *Journal of the American Medical Association, 290*(15), 2023–2029.

Cowen, E. L., Work, W. C., & Wyman, P. A. (1997). The Rochester Child Resilience Project (RCRP): Facts found, lessons learned, future directions divined. In S. S. Luthar, J. A. Burack, J. Weisz, & D. Ciccetti (Eds.), *Developmental psychopathology: Perspectives on adjustment, risk, and disorder* (pp. 279–308). New York: Cambridge University Press.

Cowen, E. L., Wyman, P. A., Work, W. C., & Parker, G. R. (1990). The Rochester Child Resilience Project: Overview and summary of first year findings. *Development & Psychopathology, 2*(2), 193–212.

Crnic, K., & Greenberg, M. (1987). Maternal stress, social support, and coping: Influences on the early mother–infant relationship. In C. F. Z. Boukydis (Ed.), *Research on support for parents and infants in the postnatal period* (pp. 25–40). Norwood, NJ: Ablex.

Crockenberg, S. (1987). Predictors and correlates of anger toward and punitive control of toddlers by adolescent mothers. *Child Development, 58*(4), 964–975.

Currie, J. M. (2001). Early childhood education programs. *Journal of Economic Perspectives, 15*(2), 213–238.

Currie, J. M. (2006). *The invisible safety net: Protecting the nation's poor children and families.* Princeton, NJ: Princeton University Press.

Currie, J. M., & Bitler, M. (2004). Does WIC work? The effect of WIC on pregnancy and birth outcomes. *Journal of Policy Analysis and Management, 23*, 73–91.

Currie, J. M., & Thomas, D. (1995). Does Head Start make a difference? *The American Economic Review, 85*(3), 341–364.

Currie, J. M., & Thomas, D. (2000). School quality and the longer-term effects of Head Start. *Journal of Human Resources, 35*(4), 755–774.

Curtis, L., Dooley, M. & Phipps, S. (2004). Child well-being and neighbourhood quality: Evidence from the Canadian National Longitudinal Survey of Children and Youth. *Social Science and Medicine, 58*(10), 1917–1927.

Dahl, G. & Lochner, L. (2009). *The impact of family income on child achievement: Evidence from the Earned Income Tax Credit* (Working Paper No. 14599). Cambridge, MA: National Bureau of Economic Research. Retrieved from http://www.nber.org/papers/w14599.pdf.

Datta Gupta, N., & Simonson, M. (2010). Noncognitive child outcomes and universal high quality child care. *Journal of Public Economics, 94*, 30–43.

Dearing, E., McCartney, K., & Taylor, B. A. (2001). Change in family income-to-needs matters more for children with less. *Child Development, 72*(6), 1779–1793.

Dearing, E., McCartney, K., & Taylor, B. A. (2006). Within-child association between family income and externalizing and internalizing problems. *Developmental Psychology, 42*(2), 237–252.

Dearing, E., McCartney, K., & Taylor, B. (2009). Does higher quality early child care promote low income children's math and reading achievement in middle childhood? *Child Development, 80*, 1329–1349.

Dearing, E., McCartney, K., Weiss, H. B., Kreider, H., & Simpkins, S. (2004). The promotive effects of family educational involvement for low-income children's literacy. *Journal of School Psychology, 42*(6), 445–460.

Dearing, E., & Taylor, B. A. (2007). Home improvements: Within-family associations between income and the quality of children's home environments. *Journal of Applied Developmental Psychology, 28*(5-6), 427–444.

Dearing, E., Taylor, B. A., & McCartney, K. (2004). Implications of family income dynamics for women's depressive symptoms during the first 3 years after childbirth. *American Journal of Public Health, 94*(8), 1372–1377.

Deming, D. (2009). Early childhood intervention and life-cycle skill development: evidence from Head Start. *American Economic Journal: Applied Economics, 1*(3), 111–134.

DeNavas-Walt, C., Proctor, B. D., & Smith, J. C. (2010). *Current population reports, P60-238. Income, poverty, and health insurance coverage in the United States: 2009.* Washington, DC: U.S Census Bureau.

Dodge, K. H., Pettit, G. S., & Bates, J. E. (1994). Socialization mediators of the relation between socioeconomic status and child conduct problems. *Child Development, 65*, 649–665.

Duncan, G. J., & Brooks-Gunn, J. (Eds.). (1997). *Consequences of growing up poor.* New York: Russell Sage Foundation Press.

Duncan, G. J., & Brooks-Gunn, J. (2000). Family poverty, welfare reform, and child development. *Child Development, 71*(1), 188–196.

Duncan, G. J., Brooks-Gunn, J., & Klebanov, P. (1994). Economic deprivation and early-childhood development. *Child Development, 65*, 296–318.

Duncan, G. J., Ludwig, J., & Magnuson, K. A. (2007). Reducing poverty through preschool interventions. *Future of Children, 17*(2), 143–160.

Duncan, G. J., Yeung, W. J., Brooks-Gunn, J., & Smith, J. R. (1998). How much does childhood poverty affect the life chances of children? *American Sociological Review, 63*, 406–423.

Duncan, G. J., Ziol-Guest, K. M., Kalil, A. (2010). Early-childhood poverty and adult attainment, behavior, and health. *Child Development, 81*(1), 306–325.

Edin, K., & Lein, L. (1997). *Making ends meet: How single mothers survive welfare and low-wage work.* New York: Russell Sage Foundation.

Elder, G. H. (1999). *Children of the great depression: Social change in life experience.* Boulder, CO: Westview Press.

Elder, G. H., & Caspi, A. (1988). Economic stress in lives: Developmental perspectives. *Journal of Social Issues, 44*(4), 25–45.

Erickson, M. F., Korfmacher, J., & Egeland, B. R. (1992). Attachments past and present: Implications for therapeutic intervention with mother infant dyads. *Development and Psychopathology, 4*, 495–507.

Evans, G. W. (2001). Environmental stress and health. In A. Baum, T. A. Revenson, & J. E. Singer (Eds.), *Handbook of health psychology* (pp. 365–385). Mahwah, NJ: Erlbaum.

Garces, E., Duncan, T., & Currie, J. M. (2002). Longer term effects of Head Start. *American Economic Review, 92*(4), 999–1012.

Garrett, P., Ng'andu, N., & Ferron, J. (1994). Poverty experiences of young children and the quality of their home environments. *Child Development, 65*(2), 331–345.

Gershoff, E. T., Aber, J. L., Raver, C. C., & Lennon, M. C. (2007). Income is not enough: Incorporating material hardship into models of income associations with parenting and child development. *Child Development, 78*(1), 70–95.

Goldstein, N. (1990). *Explaining socioeconomic differences in children's cognitive test scores* (No. Working Paper no. H-90-1). Cambridge, MA:

Malcolm Weiner Center for Social Policy, John F. Kennedy School of Government, Harvard University.

Gormley, W. T., Phillips, D., & Gayer, T. (2008). Preschool programs can boost school readiness. *Science 320,* 1723–1724.

Guo, G., & Harris, K. M. (2000). The mechanisms mediating the effects of poverty on children's intellectual development. *Demography, 37,* 431–448.

Hanson, T. L., McLanahan, S., & Thomson, E. (1997). Economic resources, parental practices, and children's well-being. In G. J. Duncan & J. Brooks-Gunn (Eds.), *Consequences of growing up poor* (pp. 190–238). New York: Russell Sage Foundation.

Hart, B., & Risley, T.R. (1995). *Meaningful differences in the everyday experiences of young American children.* Baltimore, MD: Brookes.

Haveman, R., & Wolfe, B. (1994). *Succeeding generations: On the effects of investments in children.* New York: Russell Sage Foundation.

Herbst, C., & Tekin, E. (2008, November). *Child care subsidies and child development.* Paper presented at the annual meeting of the Association for Public Policy Analysis and Management. Los Angeles, CA.

Herbst, C., & Tekin, E. (2009). *Child care subsidies and child development* (Working paper 15007). Cambridge, MA: National Bureau of Economic Research.

Hernandez, D. C., & Jacknowitz, A. (2009). Transient, but not persistent adult food insecurity influences toddler development. *Journal of Nutrition, 139*(8), 1517–1524.

Howard, K., & Brooks-Gunn, J. (2009). The role of home-visiting programs in preventing child abuse and neglect. *Future of Children, 19*(2), 119–146.

Huston, A., Duncan, G., McLoyd, V., Crosby, D., Ripke, M., Weisner, T., & Eldred, C. (2005). Impacts on children of a policy to promote employment and reduce poverty for low-income parents: New Hope after five years. *Developmental Psychology, 41,* 902–918

Jackson, A. P., Brooks-Gunn, J., Huang, C.-C., & Glassman, M. (2000). Single mothers in low-wage jobs: Financial strain, parenting, and preschoolers' outcomes. *Child Development, 71*(5), 1409–1423.

Kagan, S. L., & Rigby, E. (2003, February). *Policy matters: Setting and measuring benchmarks for state policies.* Washington, DC: Center for the Study of Social Policy.

Kalil, A., & Chen, J. (2008). Family citizenship status and food insecurity among low-income children of immigrants. *New Directions in Child and Adolescent Development, 121,* 43–62.

Kalil, A., & Wightman, P. (July, 2010). *Parental job loss and family conflict* (Working Paper Series No. WP-10-07). Washington, DC: National Center for Family and Marriage Research.

Kendig, S., & Bianchi, S. M. (2008). Family structure differences in maternal time with children. *Journal of Marriage and Family, 70*(5), 1228–1240.

Kim, R. Y. (2001). The effects of the Earned Income Tax Credit on children's income and poverty: Who fares better? *Journal of Poverty, 5*(1), 1–22.

Klebanov, P. K., Brooks-Gunn, J., Chase-Lansdale, L., & Gordon, R. (1997). Are neighborhood effects on young children mediated by features of the home environment? In J. Brooks-Gunn, G. Duncan, & J. L. Aber (Eds.), *Neighborhood poverty: Context and consequences for children* (Vol. 1, pp. 119–145). New York: Russell Sage Foundation Press.

Klebanov, P. K., Brooks-Gunn, J., McCarton, C., & McCormick, M. C. (1998). The contribution of neighborhood and family income to developmental test scores over the first three years of life. *Child Development, 69,* 1420–1436.

Klebanov, P. K., Brooks-Gunn, J., & McCormick, M. C. (1994). School achievement and failure in very low birth weight children. *Journal of Developmental and Behavioral Pediatrics, 15,* 248–256.

Klebanov, P. K., Brooks-Gunn, J., & McCormick, M. C. (2001). Maternal coping strategies and emotional distress: Results of an early intervention program for low birth weight young children. *Developmental Psychology, 37*(5), 654–667.

Knudsen, E. I., Heckman, J., Cameron, J. L., & Shonkoff, J. P. (2006). Economic, neurobiological, and behavioral perspectives on building America's future workforce. *Proceedings of the National Academy of Sciences, 103*(27), 10155–10162.

Kohen, D., Brooks-Gunn, J., Leventhal, T., & Hertzman, C. (2002). Neighborhood income and physical and social disorder in Canada: Associations with young children's competencies. *Child Development, 73*(6), 1844–1860.

Kohen, D., Leventhal, T., Dahinten, S., & McIntosh, C. (2008). Neighborhood disadvantage: Pathways of effects for young children. *Child Development, 79*(1), 156–169.

Korenman, S., & Miller, J. E. (1997). Effects of long-term poverty on physical health of children in the National Longitudinal Survey of Youth. In G. J. Duncan & J. Brooks-Gunn (Eds.), *Consequences of growing up poor* (pp. 70–99). New York: Russell Sage Foundation.

Korenman, S., Miller, J. E., & Sjaastad, J. E. (1995). Long-term poverty and child development in the United States: Results from the NLSY. *Children and Youth Services Review, 17,* 127–155.

Kosker, E.. & Maynard, R. (1991). Quality. Cost, and parental choice of child care. In D. M. Blue (Ed.), *The Economics of Child Care* (pp. 127–144). New York: Russell Sage Foundation.

Kowalski-Jones, L. & Duncan, G. (2002). Effects of participation in the WIC program on birthweight: Evidence from the National Longitudinal Survey of Youth. *American Journal of Public Health, 92*(5), 799–804.

Lareau, A. (2003). *Unequal childhoods: Class, race and family life.* Berkeley, CA: University of California Press.

Lee, B. J., & Mackey-Bilaver, L. (2007). Effects of WIC and Food Stamp program participation on child outcomes. *Children and Youth Services Review, 29*(4), 501–517.

Leininger, L. J., Ryan, R. M., & Kalil, A. (2009). Low-income mothers' social support and children's injuries. *Social Science and Medicine, 68*(12), 2113–2121.

Leventhal, T., & Brooks-Gunn, J. (2001). Changing neighborhoods and child well-being: Understanding how children may be affected in the coming century. *Advances in Life Course Research, 6,* 263–301.

Leventhal, T., Fauth, R. C., & Brooks-Gunn, J. (2005). Neighborhood poverty and public policy: A 5-year follow-up of children's educational outcomes in the New York City Moving to Opportunity Demonstration. *Developmental Psychology, 41*(6), 933–952.

Liaw, F.-R., & Brooks-Gunn, J. (1994). Cumulative familial risks and low-birthweight children's cognitive and behavioral development. *Journal of Clinical Child Psychology, 23*(4), 360–372.

Linver, M. R., Brooks-Gunn, J., & Kohen, D. E. (1999). Parenting behavior and emotional health as mediators of family poverty effects upon young low-birthweight children's cognitive ability. *Annals of the New York Academy of Sciences, 896,* 376–378.

Linver, M. R., Brooks-Gunn, J., & Kohen, D. E. (2002). Family processes as pathways from income to young children's development. *Developmental Psychology, 38*(5), 719–734.

Loeb, S., Fuller, B., Kagan, S. L., & Carroll, B. (2004). Child care in poor communities: Early learning effects of type, quality, and stability. *Child Development, 75,* 47–65.

Love, J. M., Kisker, E. E., Ross, C. M., Schochet, P. Z., Brooks-Gunn, J., & Boller, K. (2001). *Building their futures: How Early Head Start programs are enhancing the lives of infants and toddlers in low-income families.* Washington, DC: U.S. Department of Health and Human Services.

Love, J. M., Harrison, L., Sagi-Schwartz, A., Van IJzendoorn, M. H., Ross, C., & Ungerer, J. A. (2003). Child care quality matters: How conclusions may vary with context. *Child Development, 74*(4), 1021–1033.

Love, J. M., Kisker, E. E., Ross, C., Raikes, H., Constantine, J., & Boller, K., ... (2005). The effectiveness of Early Head Start for 3-year-old children and their parents: Lessons for policy and programs. *Developmental Psychology, 41, 6,* 885–901.

Ludwig, J., Ladd, H., & Duncan, G. J. (2001). Urban poverty and educational outcomes. In W. G. Gale & J. R. Pack (Eds.), *Brookings–Wharton papers on urban affairs 2001* (pp. 147–201). Washington, DC: Brookings Institution Press.

Ludwig, J. & Miller, D. L. (2007). Does Head Start improve children's life chances? Evidence from a regression-discontinuity design. *Quarterly Journal of Economics, 122*(1), 159–208.

Lyons-Ruth, K., Connell, D. B., Grunebaum, H., & Botein, S. (1990). Infants at social risk: Maternal depression and family support services as mediators of infant development and security of attachment. *Child Development, 61*, 85–98.

May, C. R., & Campbell, R. M. (1981). Readiness for learning: Assumptions and realities. *Theory into Practice, 20*, 130–134.

Mayer, S. E. (1997). *What money can't buy: Family income and children's life chances.* Cambridge, MA: Harvard University Press.

McCartney, K., Dearing, E., Taylor, B. A., & Bub, K. L. (2007). Quality child care supports the achievement of low-income children: Direct and indirect pathways through caregiving and the home environment. *Journal of Applied Developmental Psychology, 28*(5–6), 411–426.

McCormick, M. C., Brooks-Gunn, J., Workman-Daniels, K., Turner, J., & Peckham, G. (1992). The health and developmental status of very low birth weight children at school age. *Journal of the American Medical Association, 267*, 2204–2208.

McLanahan S. S. (2004). Diverting destinies: How children are faring under the second demographic transition. *Demography, 41*, 607–627.

McLeod, J. D., & Nonnemaker, J. M. (2000). Poverty and child emotional and behavioral problems: Racial/ethnic differences in processes and effects. *Journal of Health and Social Behavior, 41*, 137–161.

McLeod, J. D., & Shanahan, M. J. (1993). Poverty, parenting, and children's mental health. *American Sociological Review, 58*, 351–366.

McLeod, J. D., & Shanahan, M. J. (1996). Trajectories of poverty and children's mental health. *Journal of Health and Social Behavior, 37*, 207–220.

McLoyd, V. C. (1990). The impact of economic hardship on black families and children: Psychological distress, parenting, and socioemotional development. *Child Development, 61*, 311–346.

McLoyd, V. C. (1997). The impact of poverty and low socioeconomic status on the socioemotional functioning of African-American children and adolescents: Mediating effects. In R. D. Taylor & M. C. Wang (Eds.), *Social and emotional adjustment and family relations in ethnic minority families* (pp. 7–34). Mahwah, NJ: Erlbaum.

McLoyd, V. C. (1998). Socioeconomic disadvantage and child development. *American Psychologist, 53*, 185–204.

Moffitt, R. (2003). The temporary assistance for needy families program. In R. Moffitt (Ed.), *Means-tested transfer programs in the United States* (pp. 291–364). Cambridge, MA: National Bureau of Economic Research.

Morris, P., Duncan, G., & Clark-Kaufman, E. (2005). Child well-being in an era of welfare reform: The sensitivity of transitions in development to policy change. *Developmental Psychology, 41*, 919–932.

Morris, P. A., Gennetian, L. A., & Duncan, G. J. (2005). Effects of welfare and employment policies on young children: New findings on policy experiments conducted in the early 1990s. *Social Policy Report Society for Research in Child Development, 19*(2), 3–17.

Needleman, H. L. (1979). Lead levels and children's psychologic performance. *New England Journal of Medicine, 301*(3), 163.

Needleman, H. L. (1990). The long-term effects of exposure to low doses of lead in childhood: An 11-year follow-up report. *New England Journal of Medicine, 322*(2), 83–88.

Needleman, H. L., & Gatsonis, C. A. (1990). Low-level lead exposure and the IQ of children: A meta-analysis of modern studies. *Journal of the American Medical Association, 263*(5), 673–678.

Needleman, H. L., Riess, J. A., Tobin, M. J., & Biesecker, G. E. (1996). Bone lead levels and delinquent behavior. *Journal of the American Medical Association, 275*(5), 363–369.

National Institute of Child Health and Development (NICHD), Early Child Care Research Network. (1997). The effects of infant child care on infant–mother attachment security: Results of the NICHD Study of Early Child Care. *Child Development, 68*(5), 860–879.

National Institute of Child Health and Development (NICHD), Early Child Care Research Network. (1998). Early child care and self-control, compliance, and problem behavior at 24 and 36 months. *Child Development, 69*, 1145–1170.

National Institute of Child Health and Development (NICHD), Early Child Care Research Network. (2002). Structure, process, outcome: Direct and indirect effects of caregiving quality on young children's development. *Psychological Science, 13*, 199–206.

National Institute of Child Health and Development (NICHD), Early Child Care Research Network & Duncan, G. J. (2003). Modeling the impacts of child care quality on children's preschool cognitive development. *Child Development, 74*(5), 1454–1475.

Olds, D. L., Eckenrode, J.; Henderson, C., Kkitzman, H., Powers, J., Cole, R., Sidora, K., Morris, P., Pettitt, L. M., & Luckey, D. (1997). Long term effects of home visitation on maternal life course and child abuse and neglect: Fifteen year follow up of a randomized trial. *JAMA, 278*(8), 637–643.

Olds, D., Kitzman, H., Cole, R., Robinson, J., Sidora, K., Luckey, D., Henderson, C., Hanks, C., Bondy, J., & Holmberg, J. (2004). *Pediatrics, 114*(6), 1550–1559.

Olds, D. L., Robinson, J., O'Brien, R., Luckey, D., Pettitt, L. M., Henderson, C., Ng, R. K. Sheff, K. L., Korfmacher, J., Hiatt, S., & Talmi, A. (2002). Home visiting by paraprofessionals and nurses: : A Randomized controlled trial. *Pediatrics, 110*(3), 486–496.

Pagani, L., Boulerice, B., & Tremblay, R. E. (1997). The influence of poverty on children's classroom placement and behavior problems. In G. J. Duncan & J. Brooks-Gunn (Eds.), *Consequences of growing up poor* (pp. 311–339). New York: Russell Sage Foundation.

Petterson, S. M., & Albers, A. B. (2001). Effects of poverty and maternal depression on early child development. *Child Development, 72*(6), 1794–1813.

Pianta, R. C., Barnett, W. S., Burchinal, M., & Thornburg, K. R. (2009). The effects of preschool education: What we know, how public policy is or is not aligned with the evidence base, and what we need to know. *Psychological Science in the Public Interest, 10*(2), 49–88.

Presser, H. B. (2003). *Working in a 24/7 economy: Challenges for American families.* New York: Russell Sage Foundation.

Raver, C. C., Gershoff, E. T., Aber, J. L. (2007). Testing equivalence of mediating models of income, parenting, and school readiness for white, black and Hispanic children in a national sample. *Child Development, 78*(1), 96–115.

Rose-Jacobs, R. Black, M. M., Casey, P. H., Cook, J. T., Cutts, D. B. … (2008). Household food insecurity: Associations with at-risk infant and toddler development. *Pediatrics, 121*(2), 65–72.

Ross, C. E., & Duff, R. S. (1982). Medical care, living conditions, and children's well-being. *Social Forces, 61*(2), 456–474.

Ryan, R. M., Johnson, A., Rigby, E., & Brooks-Gunn, J. (2011). The impact of child care subsidy use on child care quality. *Early Childhood Research Quarterly, 26*, 320–331.

Ryan R. M., Kalil, A., & Leininger, L. (2009). Low-income mothers' private safety nets and children's socioemotional well-being. *Journal of Marriage and Family, 71*(2), 278–297.

Sameroff, A. J., Seifer, R., Baldwin, A., & Baldwin, C. (1993). Stability of intelligence from preschool to adolescence: The influence of social and family risk factors. *Child Development, 64*(1), 80–97.

Sampson, R. J., & Laub, J. H. (1994). Urban poverty and the family context of delinquency: A new look at structure and process in a classic study. *Child Development, 65*, 523–540.

Schoeni, R. F., & Blank, R. M. (2003). *What has welfare reform accomplished? Impacts on welfare participation, employment, income, poverty, and family structure* (PSC Research Report No. 03-544). Ann Arbor, MI: Population Studies Center, University of Michigan.

Scholz, J. K., Moffitt, R., & Cowan, B. (2008, May 29–30). *Trends in income support.* Paper presented at the Institute for Research on Poverty at the University of Wisconsin–Madison conference, Changing Poverty.

Schwartz, J. (1994). Low level lead exposure and children's IQ: A meta-analysis and search for threshold. *Environmental Research, 65*, 42–55.

Schwartz, J., Angle, C. R., & Pitcher, H. (1986). Relationship between childhood blood lead levels and stature. *Pediatrics, 77,* 281–288.

Schwartz, J., & Otto, D. (1991). Lead and minor hearing impairment. *Archives of Environmental Health, 46,* 300–305.

Schweinhart, L. J., Montie, J., Xiang, Z., Barnett, W. S., Belfield, C. R., & Nores, M. (2005). *Lifetime effects: The High-Scope Perry preschool study through age 40.* Ypsilanti, MI: High Scope Foundation.

Shea, J. (2000). Does parents' money matter? *Journal of Public Economics, 77,* 155–184.

Shonkoff, J. P., & Phillips, D. A. (Eds.). (2000). *From neurons to neighborhoods: The science of early child development.* Washington, DC: National Academy of Sciences.

Skalicky, A., Meyers, A. F., Adams, W. G., Yang, Z., Cook, J. T., & Frank, D. A. (2006). Child food insecurity and iron deficiency anemia in low-income infants and toddlers in the United States. *Maternal and Child Health Journal, 10*(2), 177–185.

Smith, J. R., Brooks-Gunn, J., & Klebanov, P. (1997). Consequences of living in poverty for young children's cognitive and verbal ability and early school achievement. In G. J. Duncan & J. Brooks-Gunn (Eds.), *Consequences of growing up poor* (pp. 132–189). New York: Russell Sage Foundation.

Starfield, B., Shapiro, S., Weiss, J., Liang, K., Ra, K., Paige, D., & Wang, X. (1991). Race, Family income, and low birth weight. *American Journal of Epidemiology, 134*(10), 1167–1174.

Taylor, B. A., Dearing, E., & McCartney, K. (2004). Incomes and outcomes in early childhood. *Journal of Human Resources, 39,* 980–1007.

U.S. Census Bureau. (2010). *Observations from the Intragency Technical Working Group on Developing a Supplemental Poverty Measure.* Retrieved from http://www.census.gov/hhes/www/povmeas/SPM_TWGObservations.pdf

U.S. Department of Health and Human Services. (2005). *Head Start impact study: First year findings, May 2005.* Washington, DC: Administration for Children and Families, Office of Planning, Research and Evaluation. Retrieved from http://www.acf.hhs.gov/programs/opre/hs/impact_study/reports/first_yr_execsum/first_yr_execsum.pdf

U.S. Department of Health and Human Services. (2010, January). *Head Start impact study: Final report.* Washington, DC: Administration for Children and Families, Office of Planning, Research and Evaluation. Retrieved from http://www. acf.hhs.gov/programs/opre/hs/impact_study/

U.S. Deparatment of Health and Human Services. (2006). *Preliminary findings from the Early Head Start prekindergarten followup.* Washington, DC: Administration for Children and Families, Office of Planning, Research and Evaluation. Retrieved from http://www.acf.hhs.gov/programs/opre/ehs/ehs_resrch/reports/prekindergarten_followup/prekindergarten_followup.pdf

Vandell, D. L., Belsky, J., Burchinal, M., Steingerg, L., Vandergrift, N., & NICHD ECCRN. (2010). Do effects of early child care extend to age 15 years? Results from the NICHD Study of Early Child Care and Youth Development. *Child Development, 81*(3), 737–756.

Votruba-Drzal, E. (2006). Economic disparities in middle childhood: does income matter? *Developmental Psychology, 42*(6). 1154–1167.

Votruba-Drzal, E., Coley, R. L., & Chase-Lansdale, P. L. (2004). Child care and low-income children's development: Direct and moderated effects. *Child Development, 75,* 296–312.

Werner, E. E., & Smith, R. S. (1992). *Overcoming the odds: High risk children from birth to adulthood.* Ithaca, NY: Cornell University Press.

Wight, V. R., & Chau, M. (2009, November). Basic facts about low-income children: 2008 children under age 6. National Center for Children in Poverty, Mailman School of Public Health, Columbia University. Retrieved from http://nccp.org/publications/pdf/text_896.pdf.

Yeung, W. J., Linver, M., & Brooks-Gunn, J. (2002). How money matters for young children's development: Parental investment and family processes. *Child Development, 73*(6), 1861–1879.

Zill, N., Resnick, G., McKey, R. H., Clark, C., Connell, D., Swartz, K., O'Brien, R., & D'Elio, M. A. (1998, June). *Head Start program performance measures: Second progress report.* Washington, DC: Administration on Children, Youth, and Families, U.S. Department of Health and Human Services.

21

Effective Early Childhood Education Programs for Disadvantaged Children

A Systematic Review and Case Studies

BETTE CHAMBERS
University of York and Johns Hopkins University

OLI DE BOTTON
CfBT Education Trust

ALAN CHEUNG
Johns Hopkins University

ROBERT E. SLAVIN
Johns Hopkins University and University of York

The education of young children who are at risk for school failure due to poverty is widely recognized as an important factor in determining their future success in school and in life. Previous reviews of programs for disadvantaged children between the ages of 3 and 5, or before they begin kindergarten, demonstrate that early childhood education is a worthwhile investment (Barnett, Frede, Mosbasher, & Mohr, 1987; Reynolds, Temple, Robertson, & Mann, 2001). This chapter summarizes the findings of a current systematic review of studies that compared the research on different types of preschool programs (Chambers, Cheung, Slavin, Smith, & Lauranzano, 2010). Brief case studies provide snapshots of the highest rated programs to characterize the types of programs that the review found to be effective in promoting academic outcomes (de Botton, 2010).

While evaluations of Head Start and other early childhood programs in the United States and other countries have clearly shown positive effects of early education in comparison to no services, the important question before researchers and policy makers today is what *kind* of preschool program is most effective for young children. Which particular programs have positive outcomes and what elements of these programs contribute to their effectiveness? This chapter aims to provide guidance to educators selecting programs to implement in preschool settings, to policy makers deciding which programs to encourage early childhood educators to use, to developers creating preschool programs, and to researchers seeking up-to-date evidence on early childhood programs. It summarizes the evidence for the effectiveness of various preschool programs for young children who are at risk of school failure due to poverty. It reviews the quantitative research on the outcomes of early childhood programs provided in a group setting, applying consistent methodological standards to the research.

Previous Reviews

Most previous reviews of preschool programs have focused on the question of whether or not preschool attendance improves future school success for disadvantaged children, and mostly they conclude that it has done so (e.g., Camilli, Vargas, Ryan, & Barnett, 2009; Currie, 2000; Gilliam & Zigler, 2000; Gorey, 2001). Only a few, however, have made comparisons among different types of interventions (Barnett 1995; Chambers, Cheung, & Slavin, 2006; White, Taylor, & Moss, 1992). The meta-analytic review by White et al. (1992) concluded that early intervention benefited most children, but could not determine which types of interventions were most effective. Barnett (1995) reviewed 36 studies of preschool attendance, Head Start, child care, and home visiting programs. He concluded that early childhood interventions (compared to no preschool) generally have large short-term effects on intelligence measures and sizable effects on school achievement, grade retention, special education placement, and social adjustment. However, he was not able to compare alternative preschool programs. A review by Chambers et al. (2006) compared traditional, academic, and cognitive-developmental early childhood programs and found that academic programs generally produced better immediate and midterm cognitive outcomes. However, cognitive-developmental programs produced better long-term educational and social adjustment outcomes.

The National Early Literacy Panel's (2008) meta-analysis revealed that code-level instruction was correlated with higher levels of later literacy. This does not mean that we need to create first-grade level instruction in our preschools. It does mean creating developmentally appropriate activities that expose preschoolers to the alphabetic code, and to enhance their phonological and phonemic awareness.

In a meta-analysis of the effects of early childhood curricula on children's receptive and expressive vocabulary, Darrow (2009) evaluated 17 early childhood curricula and concluded that taken together, programs did not differ from their respective control groups on vocabulary development by the end of preschool, nor at the end of kindergarten. Nor could she determine the impacts of particular programs. Given the lack of specificity of most previous reviews in determining which specific programs are effective in preparing children for school and the number of studies conducted in the past decade, we conducted a systematic review of studies comparing different early childhood programs for children at risk of school failure due to poverty.

Current Approaches to Early Education

Recent research on cognitive development reinforces previous evidence that early education is crucial in preparing children for life (Bowman, Donovan, & Burns, 2001; Magnuson, Meyers, Ruhm, & Waldfogel, 2003). Based in part on this research and previous reviews, developers and national policy makers are establishing new early childhood programs and trying to improve the quality of the ones that exist. Most of these new programs take a cognitive-developmental perspective and combine elements of direct instruction for the whole class and small groups along with times when children individually choose activities. There is usually a focus on developing children's language and emergent literacy. Many recent studies have evaluated these new programs, and often the experimental programs from past studies (e.g., High/Scope, Creative Curriculum) are now the control condition in recent studies (Preschool Curriculum Evaluation Research, 2008). However, these two programs are implemented in more than 59% of Head Start classes despite there not being any evidence that they are more effective in preparing children for school than alternative approaches (Shanahan & Lonigan, 2010).

Preschool Curriculum Evaluation Research

In 2002, the Institute of Education Sciences (IES) initiated the Preschool Curriculum Evaluation Research (PCER) project to conduct efficacy evaluations of 14 preschool curricula. More than a third of the evaluations included in this review came from the PCER evaluations, so a summary of the project is presented here (for a detailed description of this project, see PCER, 2008). Twelve research teams implemented one or two curricula in preschool settings serving mostly low-income children under an experimental design. For each team, preschools were randomly assigned to the intervention curricula or control curricula and the children were followed from prekindergarten through kindergarten. IES contracted with two independent evaluators to assess the impact of each curriculum using a common set of measures with the cohort of children beginning preschool in the fall of 2003.

The PCER analyses included 2,911 children, 315 preschool classrooms, and 208 preschools. On average, the students were age 4.6 years at the time of the baseline data collection in the fall of 2003 and age 6.1 years at the time of the kindergarten follow-up in the spring of 2005. One-third of the children were White non-Hispanic, 43% were African American, and 16% were Hispanic. Child outcome measures were administered, assessing children's school readiness (reading, phonological awareness, language, mathematics, and behavior). For the eight outcome measures, administered at three separate points, a repeated measures spline model compared the treatment and control group means for the spring prekindergarten and spring kindergarten observations.

In the kindergarten year, four of the curricula had statistically significant impacts on the student-level outcomes. A combined program that included *DLM Early Childhood Express supplemented with Open Court Reading Pre-K* had positive effects on reading, phonological awareness, and language. *Curiosity Corner* was found to positively affect reading and *Early Literacy and Learning Model* positively affected language. *Project Approach* was found to negatively affect behavior in kindergarten.

All of the curricula that had positive effects had elements of teacher-directed activity, with a focus on language and literacy. None were open-ended programs that depended on teachers creating a program based on children's interests. In fact, the one program with negative effects was unstructured. Yet there remains considerable debate about what early childhood education programs should look like in practice. Specifically, there are two separate but interlinked questions that have stimulated debate: (a) What is the balance between a teacher-directed, academic approach that covers areas such as literacy and language acquisition, and a child-initiated, developmental approach that focuses on emotional and social well-being? (b)To what extent should activities be teacher directed or child initiated? Different philosophies have guided the development of different programs. In particular, there are two distinct approaches.

Teacher-Directed, Education Focused Approach

Practice in these programs is characterized by centralized development of the curriculum and explicit learning expectations and outcomes. These programs tend to focus on academic school readiness skills such as literacy and numeracy (Friendly, Doherty, & Beach, 2006) and teachers engage in some direct instruction. Assessment focuses on children's achievements in meeting prescribed learning expectations (E. Miller & Almon, 2009).

Child-Initiated, Developmental Approach

In contrast, child-initiated practices adopt a broad developmental framework, with curriculum decisions being made at a local level (OECD, 2006). These programs are driven by the interests of the children within the context of their families and immediate communities. The focus is on social–emotional goals, unstructured play, and interactivity with teachers and peers. In general, the programs have broad orientations, rather than prescribed outcomes. The acquisition of academic skills is perceived as a by-product rather than as the driver of children's experiences (Miller & Almon, 2009). The question addressed in this chapter is what types of programs promote the school readiness of children, particularly those living in poverty.

Methods

The review used an adapted form of best evidence synthesis (Slavin, 2008), used in reviewing literatures in which there are generally few studies evaluating each of many programs. Best evidence syntheses apply consistent, well-justified standards to identify unbiased, meaningful information from experimental studies, and pooling effect sizes across studies in substantively justified categories. This chapter summarizes the findings of the complete report, which can be found on the *Best Evidence Encyclopedia* Web site at www.bestevidence.org. Brief case studies of the programs with strong evidence of effectiveness follow the quantitative synthesis.

Search Procedures

Initially, the Centre for Reviews and Dissemination (CRD) at the University of York in the United Kingdom conducted a thorough search to locate all studies that compared alternative approaches to early childhood education from 1960 to the present. Thirty-two of the 38 qualifying studies were conducted after 2000 and only six before. Most studies prior to 2000 compared preschool attendance versus nonattendance, rather than comparing different programs.

Studies from all countries were included, as long as the studies were available in English. Study inclusion criteria included use of randomized or matched control groups, evidence of initial equality, and study duration of at least 12 weeks.

Studies included valid measures of language, literacy, phonological awareness, mathematical, and cognitive outcomes that were independent of the experimental treatments. We initially included social outcomes but there were not enough studies evaluating programs that used objective measures of these outcomes. Typically, social outcomes were assessed by teacher perceptions of children's social skills, rather than independent observations of children's behavior. Because the teachers were not blind to the treatment condition the children were in, and in fact had been responsible for implementing the program, we could not be sure that their assessments were unbiased.

The included studies compared children taught in classes using a given program or specified replicable practice to those using an alternative program or standard practices. The group setting could be prekindergarten or preschool classes in elementary schools, child-care centers, or Head Start centers. Any early childhood setting that offered a regularly scheduled educational program to a group of preschoolers was included.

Studies without control groups were excluded. Studies needed to have least two teachers and 25 individuals per condition in the analysis with no indications of initial inequality. A total of 38 studies evaluating 27 different programs met these criteria for outcomes assessed at the end of preschool or kindergarten.

Effect Sizes

In general, effect sizes were computed as the difference between experimental and control individual student posttests after adjustment for pretests and other covariates, divided by the unadjusted posttest control group standard deviation. The method is very similar to meta-analysis (Cooper, 1998; Lipsey & Wilson, 2001), adding an emphasis on narrative description of each study's contribution. See Slavin (2008) for an extended discussion and rationale for the procedures used in all of these reviews. Effect sizes were pooled across studies for each program. Effect sizes were broken down for measures of language, literacy, phonological awareness, mathematics, and cognition.

Importance of Lasting Effects

In studies of early childhood programs, children in innovative treatments are often taught skills not ordinarily introduced until the following year, in which case it is not surprising that they improve on measures administered at the end of preschool. For this reason it is particularly important to document outcomes at least through the end of kindergarten.

Program Rating Scale

The program outcomes were summarized using a modified version of a rating system that Slavin (2008) developed for the *Best Evidence Encyclopedia* to balance methodological quality, weighted mean effect sizes, sample sizes, and other factors. The categories of effectiveness are as follows.

Strong Evidence of Effectiveness. Programs in this category were evaluated in at least two studies, one of which was a large randomized or randomized quasi-experimental study, or multiple smaller studies, with a sample size-weighted effect size of at least +0.20, and a collective sample size across all studies of 250 children or 20 classes. The effects could be on any of the academic or cognitive outcomes, at the end of preschool or kindergarten.

Moderate Evidence of Effectiveness. Programs in this category were evaluated in at least one randomized or two matched studies of any qualifying design, with a collective sample size of 125 pupils or 10 classes, and a weighted mean effect size of at least +0.20 across all measures.

Limited Evidence of Effectiveness. Programs in this category had studies that met one of two conditions: either they met the criteria for "moderate evidence of effectiveness" except that the weighted mean effect size was +0.10 to +0.19 across all measures or the studies had a weighted mean effect size of at least +0.20, but did not qualify for "moderate evidence of effectiveness" due to insufficient numbers of studies or small sample sizes.

Insufficient Evidence of Effectiveness. Qualifying studies did not meet the criteria for "limited evidence of effectiveness."

No Qualifying Studies. Programs in this category did not have any qualifying studies.

Case Studies Methods

The qualitative aspect of this project aimed to explore in actual practice some of the programs which were highlighted as having strong evidence of effectiveness. In particular, we wanted to establish if there were any common themes and lessons learned for early childhood professionals and policy makers. We therefore conducted field visits to see programs in action and interview practitioners and program developers.

The second author contacted the developers or disseminators for each of the programs in the strong evidence category and conducted open-ended interviews to obtain an understanding of the structure of each program and the underlying philosophy. In most cases, the developer arranged for him to visit a setting that was implementing the program with a high level of fidelity. Often the contact accompanied the researcher on the site visit. Where possible, the researcher interviewed the teacher(s) implementing the program about their perceptions of it.

Results

Of the 27 programs evaluated, six showed strong evidence of effectiveness and five had moderate evidence of effec-

tiveness. Interestingly, averaging across all included studies of the interventions, there were small effects at the end of preschool for all outcomes: language (ES = +0.11), literacy (ES = +0.15), phonological awareness (ES = +0.15), mathematics (ES = +0.17), and cognition (ES = +0.13). Below are the individual programs that were rated as having strong, moderate, or limited evidence of effectiveness.

Program Ratings

The programs were rated as follows:

Strong Evidence of Effectiveness. Six early childhood programs produced strong evidence of effectiveness: *Curiosity Corner, Direct Instruction, ELLM, Interactive Book Reading, Let's Begin with the Letter People,* and *Ready Set Leap!* The effects for these programs were on language, literacy, or phonological awareness. For some of the studies meaningful effects were seen only at the end of preschool (*Direct Instruction and Interactive Book Reading*), and for others positive effects were apparent at the end of kindergarten (*Curiosity Corner, ELLM, and Ready Set Leap!*).

Moderate Evidence of Effectiveness. Five programs met the criteria for moderate evidence of effectiveness: *Breakthrough to Literacy, Bright Beginnings, PreK Mathematics plus DLM Express Software, DLM Express plus Open Court,* and *Project Approach.*

Limited Evidence of Effectiveness. Three programs met the criteria for limited evidence of effectiveness with weighted mean effect sizes between +0.10 and +0.19: *Doors to Discovery, Language Focus Curriculum, and Literacy Express.* Another three programs met the criteria for limited evidence of effectiveness with weak evidence for notable effects. Those programs were: *EMERGE, PATHS,* and *Sound Foundations.*

The remaining programs had insufficient evidence of effectiveness or no qualifying studies. A complete listing of all of the programs appears in the full report available at www.bestevidence.org. Table 21.1 presents the overall effect sizes for programs with strong, moderate, or limited evidence of effectiveness.

Case Studies Findings

The six programs with strong evidence of effectiveness, *Curiosity Corner, Direct Instruction, ELLM, Interactive Book Reading, Let's Begin with the Letter People,* and *Ready Set Leap!*, were the subject of the case study portion of the research.

Overview of Program Features. All the programs under review shared some key features, which practitioners and program developers considered crucial to success:

All six programs offered intensive support to achieve full

Table 21.1 Effects by Programme

Programme	End of PreK						End of K					
	Studies (N)	Lit	Lang	Phonol Aware	Math	Cog	Studies (N)	Lit	Lang	Phonol Aware	Math	Cog
Strong Evidence of Effectiveness												
Curiosity Corner	2	0.08	0.08	0.18	0.09	–	1	0.39	0.15	0.25	0.18	–
Direct Instruction	2	0.52	0.46	–	0.37	0.31	2	–	–	–	–	0.39
ELLM	2	0.19	0.16	0.18	–0.01	–	1	0.11	0.39	0.08	0.08	–
Interactive Book Reading	2	–0.33	0.86	–	–	–	0	–	–	–	–	–
Let's Begin with the Letter People	3	0.15	-0.01	0.24	0.09	–	1	–0.12	–0.06	-0.13	–0.09	–
Ready, Set, Leap!	2	0.14	0.06	–0.09	-0.04	–	1	0.24	–0.03	0.18	–0.02	–
Moderate Evidence of Effectiveness												
Breakthrough to Literacy	1	–	–	–	–	–	1	0.48	–	0.44	–	–
Bright Beginnings	1	0.31	0.11	-0.07	0.06	–	1	0.03	0.12	0.01	0.12	–
DLM with Open Court	1	0.55	0.40	0.32	0.26	–	1	0.49	0.47	0.38	0.23	–
Pre-K Mathematics plus DLM	1	0.11	0.17	0.04	0.33	–	1	0.19	0.10	–0.11	0.13	–
Project Approach	1	0.28	0.16	0.05	0.17	–	1	0.15	0.21	–0.17	0.24	–
Limited Evidence of Effectiveness												
Doors to Discovery	2	0.07	–0.05	0.15	0.00	–	1	–0.09	0.12	–0.09	-0.1	–
EMERGE	1	0.37	0.13	0.28	–	–	1	–	–	–	–	–
Language Focus Curriculum	1	0.17	0.02	0.20	0.12	–	1	0.06	-0.08	0.03	0.06	–
Literacy Express	1	0.17	0.07	0.14	–0.01	–	1	–0.01	0.13	0.08	–0.12	–
PATHS	1	–	–	–	–	0.16	0	–	–	–	–	–
Sound Foundations	1	0.43	–	–	–	–	1	0.21	–	–	–	–

and faithful implementation. Support was often provided by coaches, many of whom had worked with the program over a number of years and were either former practitioners themselves or linked to university faculties. Most coaches and teachers considered this level of support particularly important in light of the relatively low skill requirements to become an early childhood educator in most states. Support included training sessions before and during the school year, observations, and one-to-one coaching.

All Highly Rated Programs Provided a Planned Curriculum. Teacher support packages included suggested activities, lesson plans, and schemes of work which were linked to specific learning and developmental objectives. In all cases, except *Direction Instruction*, weekly or monthly themes guided activities, including class reading and structured play. Most also had assessment frameworks.

By Comparison to More Child-Initiated Approaches, All Highly Rated Programs Adopted Teacher-Directed Practices. Although most programs were designed to deliver a balance of teacher-directed and child-initiated actvities, practitioner input was often strongly encouraged. For example, in programs where children spent some time selecting activities themselves, choices remained linked to the topic of the day or the week, as determined by the program. Unstructured freeplay was not a defining feature of any of the programs.

All the Programs Highlighted that Their Design and Practice Had Been Informed by Academic Research and Most Even Underlined the Precise Links In Teaching Materials. One program, *ELLM* was directly managed from the University of North Florida, *Interactive Book Reading* orginated from research grants to John Hopkins University, and *Curiosity Corner* was created under a development grant to the Success for All Foundation (also associated with Johns Hopkins University).

All the Programs with Strong Evidence of Effectiveness Placed an Emphasis On Academic Skills Such as Sound, Letter, and Word Recognition to Prepare Children For Reading and Writing. However, practitioners used a variety of teaching methods to achieve this. Apart from *Direct Instruction*, practitioners used a combination of blended whole language (i.e., using oral language, books, and pictures to aid understanding and generate interest) with some distinct skill teaching (e.g., letter and sound repetition).

Program Categorization

The programs were categorized according to two important factors, the focus on academic content and the relative amount of teacher-directed versus child-initiated activity. As can be seen in Figure 21.1, compared to other early childhood programs, all of the highly rated programs could be characterized as employing predominantly teacher-directed practices with carefully planned, explicit curricula supported by direct practitioner input. However, some programs allow for more child-centered activities than others.

Also, on the continuum of the degree of academic focus, some programs placed a greater emphasis on academic skills such as language acquisition and literacy than others. However, all of the programs with strong evidence of effectiveness devoted considerable time and attention to teaching academic content.

The next section describes the programs that were found to have strong evidence of effectiveness, contrasting their key characteristics.

Direct Instruction. Direct Instruction (DI; Bereiter & Englemann, 1968; Salaway, 2008) is an explicitly teacher-led program designed to support at risk children with reading. Originally targeted at the kindergarten level, it has now been extended up and down the age range. The program is organized around a set of highly prescribed teaching strategies that involve small-group (maximum of 10 children) call and response, instant teacher correction of mistakes and repetition. DI does not include broader curriculum content or themes, but provides a set of specific instructions for teachers and children.

The program is carefully sequenced and children are tested at the beginning and throughout the year to assess where they should start and whether they should skip activities. Children are taught in groups with similar performance levels and do not move to the next set of lessons until they have mastered previous ones. National Institute for Direct Instruction (NFDI) coaches train and support practitioners of this program with data analysis and ongoing assessment and instructional practices.

Instruction begins with sound recognition (phonemic

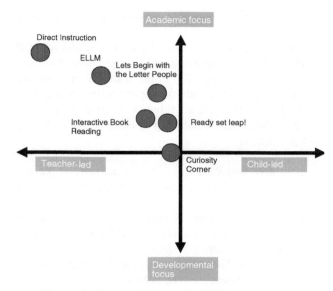

Figure 21.1 Categorization of the 6 Programs with Strong Evidence of Effectiveness.

awareness) then moves on to blending skills (i.e., bringing together sounds into whole words), and finally moves to word recognition and reading. Publicity for the program suggests that for high achieving children the journey from phonemic awareness to reading can take just six months during the kindergarten year. However, for 3- to 5-year-olds the program focuses mainly on phonemic awareness, with children progressing faster if they are ready.

The program is based on modeling, repetition, and constant consolidation. Only a small number of letters are introduced each week and the emphasis is on getting the basics right before moving on. DI promotes a style of learning that is teacher driven and wholly focused on academic outcomes. Developers of the program are adamant that if children are to be able to read, they need to be exposed in a highly structured way to sounds, letters, and words early and often. This is particularly important for children who may not have sufficient exposure to literacy at home.

Curiosity Corner. The program that perhaps provides the best contrast to DI is *Curiosity Corner,* which adopts a more child-centric approach, balancing teacher-directed and child-initiated activity. *Curiosity Corner* (CC; Chambers, 2009; Chambers, Cheung, Slavin, Smith & Lauranzano, 2010; PCER, 2008) is a comprehensive program that covers academic and social aspects of development. There are nine explicit domains which are covered in the thematic units: emotional-personal, interpersonal, language and literacy, cognitive, creative, mathematical, science, social studies, and physical. Weekly topical units touch on each of these domains and teachers map children's activities back to them.

Curiosity Corner uses a spiral curriculum with concepts and skills being repeated throughout the year. Unlike DI, where children do not progress with later lessons until early skills have been mastered, CC seeks to build knowledge through repeated exposure to concepts and practice using skills.

The thematic units contain detailed daily lessons built around children's literature and manipulative materials. Teachers receive intensive initial training and ongoing support and guidance about implementing cooperative learning activities and adapting instruction to meet the needs of the children. Each day consists of the following components:

> *Greetings and Readings.* The formal start of the day involves a daily message, often linked to the topic of the week.
>
> *Clues and Questions:* "Curiosity the Cat" is a puppet used by the teacher to introduce children to the current topic (e.g., nutrition, spring).
>
> *Rhyme Time:* The teacher leads children in rhymes and phonemic awareness activities.
>
> *Learning Labs:* This aspect of the day allows children to choose the activities they want to pursue. There is an "art lab," a "blocks lab," a "dramatic play lab," a "library and listening lab," a "sand lab," a "science lab," and a "writing lab."
>
> *Story Tree:* The teacher reads a story linked to the theme and encourages children to engage using interactive reading techniques.
>
> *Outside/ Gross Motor Play:* This aspect of the day promotes gross motor skills and physical exercise.
>
> *Question Reflection.* The day concludes with an activity that engages the children in synthesizing the concepts learned during the day or week.

Developers and practitioners considered that two key aspects were crucial to the success of the program: the highly structured nature of linked activities, and the supporting materials, which include not only highly detailed lesson plans and suggested classroom layouts but also matrices for assessing levels of implementation of the program. Teachers also considered that the structure of the program, which promotes social and academic skills in a rigorous way, was particularly beneficial for children who may not be well supported at home.

Ready Set Leap!   Ready Set Leap! (RSL; RMC, 2003; PCER 2008) also takes a more child-centered approach than DI, with a greater emphasis on individual active learning and multisensory activities. However, it too retains a clear focus on the role of the teacher, with provision for rigorous assessment procedures.

RSL emphasizes child-directed activities by promoting skill development through play and less formal activities. This is supported by technological components that foster self-regulated learning. More specifically, the technological components allow children to work individually or in groups to master early literacy skills such as letter recognition and sound awareness. The technological aspects both promote

child-centered, individualized learning, and also cater for classrooms where practitioners may not yet be ready to deliver detailed learning activities.

Despite this, there is still a considerable degree of teacher-directed activity in the program. Like *Curiosity Corner*, RSL is a comprehensive curriculum covering academic and developmental objectives. Consequently, there are planned schedules of work and suggested activities as well as instructions about how to support assessment of emergent academic skills. Teachers upload assessment results onto the *Ready Set Leap!* system and use data to analyze how children are progressing and to plan future learning experiences.

Interactive Book Reading.   *Interactive Book Reading* (IBR; Wasik & Bond, 2001; Wasik, Bond, & Hindman, 2006) is part of the Johns Hopkins Language and Literacy Project and is designed to promote early literacy through whole-class, interactive reading. IBR adapts dialogic reading techniques developed by Whitehurst and his colleagues (Whitehurst et al., 1994). Children engage in class reading and the teacher encourages interactivity by posing open and closed questions before, during, and after reading. The rationale behind the approach is to promote learning gains by enlivening the potentially passive activity of a teacher reading to the class. Specifically, IBR highlights three components:

> *Asking questions:* Before, during, and after reading the teacher asks children to reflect, predict, describe, react, recall, and reinforce. Questions span a range of levels, engaging higher and lower order thinking skills. Some questions are more analytical while others are based purely on recall.
>
> *Building vocabulary:* The teacher takes the opportunity during class reading, to define, recast, demonstrate, and point to particular words (in some cases using props). The teacher identifies key words beforehand and stops and discusses them during reading.
>
> *Making connections:* The teacher encourages thinking about themes, asking children to make connections between the text, their own lives, and the wider world.

Shared reading can be done in small groups, as well as with the whole class, and can be led by teaching assistants. IBR also highlights the need to use a wide range of books to engage all interests, including subjects that reflect the full diversity of children's backgrounds.

IBR focuses on engaging and contextualizing children's interests with stories and related group activities, delivering significant improvements in language development for learners. Practitioners and developers considered this approach in opposition to stand-alone techniques which place an emphasis on repetition and recall. Developers also considered that this approach was more beneficial to children in the long term since it generated a love of reading.

Let's Begin with the Letter People.   *Let's Begin with the Letter People* (LBLP; Assel, Landry, Swank, & Gunnewig, 2007; PCER 2008) also has a sharp focus on academic skill acquisition. However, as the name suggests, the program highlights letter and sound recognition as guiding learning aims, often independent of stories and books. The LBLP approach is designed to instil letter and sound recognition through repetition and direct teaching. Specifically, 26 letter puppets, each of which represents a letter of the alphabet, are used daily to engage children's interest. Teachers introduce five to six letter puppets for each six-week unit and letters are carefully sequenced to allow groups of sounds to be developed at the same time. Rhymes and songs that introduce the puppets and their associated letters are repeated by the whole class together. Children are also asked to identify the hidden letter that is stitched into every puppet. To complement these activities, LBLP has its own assessment system which judges whether children are developing letter and sound recognition skills.

LBLP focuses on other skills as well. After the specific letter-related activity, class reading and group work follow. During group work, some children take part in play (within a select number of choices) while the teacher works with a small group on emergent writing skills. Gross motor development and snack time are also built into the program.

Overall, LBLP is explicitly academic, extending children's formal learning down the age range. Practitioners commented that this was commensurate with increasing parental demand for high achievement, particularly in affluent areas where we observed LBLP in action. Program developers emphasize that the academic nature of the program helped to further professionalize and train the early learning workforce.

Early Language and Literacy Model.   *Early Language and Literacy Model* (ELLM; Cosgrove et al., 2006; PCER, 2008) is explicitly designed for children from low-income families, and is used in settings where children are deemed to be at risk of failure. Developers and practitioners considered that ELLM was successful because it was predominantly teacher-led, data rich, and innovative.

ELLM was developed in 1999 when the State of Florida introduced expected standards for all preschool children. The standards are age-specific, complement those for older children, and cover both academic and nonacademic areas (such as emotional and social well-being). The academic focus is perhaps more pronounced with accountability structures for settings linked to test scores on early reading, writing, and numeracy for 5-year-olds. Consequently, ELLM was initially designed to focus on emergent literacy, and this aspect remains the guiding principle for the program.

ELLM seeks to bridge the gap between what the state wants children to learn and what the system can deliver. It attempts to improve both literacy and preliteracy learning activities for young children from disadvantaged backgrounds while at the same time building the capacity of practitioners. Like other programs described above, ELLM offers curriculum guides, lesson plans, and practitioner support. Distinctive features of the program are as follows:

ELLM is literacy focused. The literacy-focused curriculum builds on children's cognitive development through literacy across the curriculum even while teaching in content areas. Children's acquisition of important cognitive and social-emotional development is facilitated through interactions with supportive teachers who encourage children's curiosity, persistence, and creativity.

ELLM maps all activities to state standards. For example, one prekindergarten (PK) standard for 3-year-olds is to "write for the following different purposes: labeling and story writing." ELLM provides activities and resources to achieve the standard. In this case the program suggests a teacher-led group activity following on from a class reading of the book *Why Write*? This level of mapping is crucial as Florida has a strict accountability regime which sees settings given the equivalent of a "notice to improve" if testing in kindergarten shows children have not met expected standards.

ELLM is rich in data. In order to meet accountability standards when children enter compulsory schooling, the program supports practitioners in student level observations. These observations provide detailed data about the skill levels of individual children. The Florida Institute of Education also provides sampling data from across the cohort. This support allows practitioners to reflect on the effects of their work.

ELLM insists on an intensive coaching model for practitioners. Program developers and setting principals highlighted the fact that entry requirements for early years practitioners were relatively low in Florida. Therefore, ELLM offers the services of University of Florida-based coaches to support, assess, and advise practitioners when implementing the program.

ELLM seeks to close the gap between theory and practice in a nuanced way. The team at the University is made up of academics and practitioners. The activities and objectives in the program are therefore both carefully linked to the evidence and also extensively road-tested in settings.

ELLM's network of settings, practitioners, and academics generates innovation. As a result of working closely with a small group of settings, developers are able to have constant and iterative conversations with front-line practitioners. Good practice is therefore shared quickly and often. There is also space for innovation. One example is the practice of giving children plastic bracelets as they go home that include questions for parents to ask them. Although developers eschew the label "direct instruction," they consider there is a considerable degree of teacher intervention, particularly around prereading, oral language, and sound and letter awareness. The program is underpinned by a desire to expose disadvantaged children to more words than they might otherwise get at home.

Discussion

This systematic review identified several early childhood programs with positive effects on important outcomes continuing to the end of kindergarten, suggesting that the preschool experience has impacts for at-risk children not limited to early exposure of academic content. The evidence supports the findings of the National Early Literacy Panel (2008), suggesting that programs with considerable academic focus and teacher direction are the most successful in promoting children's language and literacy. Additional longitudinal studies are needed to determine the long-term impacts of the current programs, beyond the end of kindergarten. There is evidence of long-term social and educational effects of some cognitive-developmental programs that were initially evaluated in the 1960s (L. B. Miller, & Bizzell, 1984; Reynolds et al., 2001; Schweinhart, Barnes, Weikart, Barnett, & Epstein, 1993). Perhaps some of the programs evaluated here will also stand the test of time.

The evidence from this review suggests that while a balance between teacher-directed and child-initiated activities and between focusing on academic and affective objectives is recommended, educators should consider implementing programs with some direct teaching of academic objectives to prepare preschoolers for success in kindergarten language and literacy skills. This may be particularly beneficial for children who do not have sufficient learning support and materials at home.

Beyond the curricular emphasis, another factor that differentiates programs is the degree of support that the teachers are provided in implementing the new curriculum. In most of the studies reported here, teachers received more support for implementation of the program than teachers typically receive when the program is implemented at scale. It usually takes ongoing support for teachers to learn to implement the innovative forms of instruction that new programs require. Researchers need to conduct research on educational programs as they are implemented at scale, without the additional support often provided in experimental studies. And program developers need to include significant ongoing professional development to ensure that fidelity of implementation occurs when their programs are implemented at scale.

While overall, the cognitive effects of all programs at the end of preschool were between +0.11 and +0. 17, some programs showed strong evidence of effectiveness. While there is a long way to go in determining exactly what constitutes the most effective forms of early childhood programs for improving the outcomes for children at risk due to poverty, the increasing number and quality of the studies on early childhood programs is heading the field in the right direction.

Limitations

There are several limitations of this review that need to be highlighted. First, the review includes only quantitative studies of academic outcomes of early childhood interventions. This is necessary to compare the effectiveness of different programs on a common scale. However, the case studies provide a richer description of the programs in action. The review does not report on experimenter-made measures of content taught in the experimental group but not the control group, although results on such measures may also be important. Also, the review does not include important social-emotional outcomes.

The review highlights replicable programs used in actual early childhood settings. This provides educators with useful information about the strength of evidence supporting various practical programs, but it does not include shorter, more theoretically driven studies that may also provide useful information.

Finally, the case studies are impressions of the programs' approaches based on brief visits to a small number of classes or interviews with the program developers. They may or may not represent typical implementations of the programs.

Conclusion

The findings of this review add to a growing body of evidence that early childhood programs can have an important impact on increasing the school readiness of young children. Yet the majority of programs have never been evaluated in a systematic way. There is a need for systematic, large-scale, longitudinal, preferably randomized evaluations of the effectiveness of preschool interventions in bringing children from high-risk environments to normative levels of academic achievement. However, this review identifies several promising approaches that could be used today to help children begin elementary school ready to succeed.

Acknowledgments

This research was funded by the CfBT Education Trust. However, any opinions expressed are those of the authors and do not necessarily represent CfBT positions or policies. Our appreciation goes to Dewi Smith, Diana Dugan, Susan Davis, Mary Lauranzano, and Michele Victor, who helped with locating and organizing the studies.

References

Assel, M., Landry, S., Swank, P., & Gunnewig, S. (2007). An evaluation of curriculum, setting, and mentoring on the performance of children enrolled in prekindergarten. *Reading and Writing, 20*(5), 463–494.

Barnett, W. S. (1995). Long-term effects of early childhood programs on cognitive and school outcomes. *The Future of Children, 5*(3), 25–50.

Barnett, W. S., Frede, E. C., Mosbasher, H., & Mohr, P. (1987). The efficacy of public preschool programs and the relationship of program quality to efficacy. *Educational Evaluation and Policy Analysis, 10*(1), 37–49.

Bereiter, C., & Engelmann, S. (1968). An academically oriented preschool for disadvantaged children: Results from the initial experimental group. In D. W. Brison & J. Hill (Eds.), Psychology and early childhood education (Monograph Series No. 4, pp. 17–36). Toronto: Ontario Institute for Studies in Education.

Bowman, B. T., Donovan, M. S., & Burns, M. (Eds.). (2001). *Eager to learn: Educating our preschoolers.* Washington, DC: National Research Council.

Camilli, G., Vargas, S., Ryan, S., & Barnett, S. (2010). Meta-analysis of the effects of early education interventions on cognitive and social development. *Teachers College Record, 112*(3). Retrieved from http://wwwtcrecord.org. ID Numbers: 15440.

Chambers, B. (2009). Curiosity Corner: Getting all children ready for school. *Early Childhood Services, 3*(3), 227–243.

Chambers, B., Cheung, A., & Slavin, R. E. (2006). Effective preschool programs for children at risk of school failure: A best-evidence synthesis. In B. Spodek & O. N. Saracho (Ed.), *Handbook of research on the education of young children* (3rd ed., pp. 347–360). New York: Erlbaum.

Chambers, B., Cheung, A., Slavin, R. E., Smith, D., & Lauranzano, M. (2010). *Effective early childhood programs: A best evidence synthesis.* Reading, England: CfBT Education Trust.

Cooper, H. (1998). *Synthesizing research* (3rd ed.). Thousand Oaks, CA: Sage.

Cosgrove, M., Fountain, C., Wehry, S., Wood, J., & Castren, K. (2006, April). *Randomized field trial of an early literacy curriculum and instructional support system.* Paper presented at the annual meeting of the American Educational Research Association, San Francisco, CA.

Currie, J. (2000). *Early childhood intervention programs: What do we know?* Chicago, IL: Joint Center for Poverty Research. Mahwah, NJ: Erlbaum.

Darrow, C. L. (2009, March*). Language and literacy effects of curriculum interventions for preschools serving economically disadvantaged children: A meta-analysis.* Paper presented at the annual meeting of the Society for Research on Educational Effectiveness, Alexandria, Virginia.

de Botton, O. (2010). *Effective early childhood education programs: Case studies.* Reading, England: CfBT Education Trust.

Friendly, M., Doherty, G., & Beach, J. (2006). *Quality by design: What do we know about quality in early learning and child care, and what do we think?* Toronto, Canada: Quality by design.

Gilliam, W. S., & Zigler, E. F. (2000). A critical meta-analysis of all evaluations of state funded preschool from 1977 to 1998: Implications for policy, service delivery and program evaluations. *Early Childhood Research Quarterly, 15,* 441–473.

Gorey, K. M. (2001). Early childhood education: A meta-analytic affirmation of the short- and long-term benefits of educational opportunity. *School Psychology Quarterly, 16,* 9–30.

Lipsey, M. W., & Wilson, D. B. (2001). *Practical meta-analysis.* Thousand Oaks, CA: Sage.

Magnuson, K., Meyers, M., Ruhm, C., & Waldfogel, J. (2003). *Inequality in preschool education and school readiness.* New York: Columbia University Press.

Miller, E., & Almon, J. (2009). *Crisis in the kindergarten: Why children need to play in school.* College Park, MD: Alliance for Childhood.

Miller, L. B., & Bizzell, R. P. (1984). Long-term effects of four preschool programs: Ninth- and tenth-grade results. *Child Development, 55,* 1570–1587.

National Early Literacy Panel. (2008). *Developing early literacy: Report of the National Early Literacy Panel.* Washington, DC: National Institute for Literacy.

OECD. (2006). *Starting strong II: Early childhood education and care.* Washington, DC: Author.

Preschool Curriculum Evaluation Research Consortium. (2008). *Effects of preschool curriculum programs on school readiness (NCER 2008-2009).* National Center for Education Research, Institute of Education Sciences, U.S. Department of Education. Washington, DC: U.S. Government Printing Office.

Reynolds, A. J., Temple, J. A., Robertson, D. L., & Mann, E. A. (2001). Long-term effects of an early childhood intervention on educational achievement and juvenile arrest: A 15-year follow-up of low-income children in public schools. *Journal of the American Medical Association, 285*(18), 2339–2346.

RMC. (2003). *The Literacy Center K-1 Las Vegas Project: A research study by RMC Research Corporation for LeapFrog SchoolHouse* (Final Report). Emeryville, CA: LeapFrog SchoolHouse.

Salaway, J. L. (2008). *Efficacy of a direct instruction approach to promote early learning* (Unpublished doctoral dissertation). Duquesne University, Pittsburgh, PA.

Schweinhart, L. J., Barnes, H. V., Weikart, D. P., Barnett, W. S., & Epstein, A. S. (1993). *Significant benefits: The High/Scope Perry Preschool study through age 27* (Monographs of the High/Scope Educational Research Foundation No. 10) Ypsilanti, MI: High/Scope Press.

Shanahan, T., & Lonigan, C. J. (2010). The National Early Literacy Panel: A summary of the process and the report. *Educational Researcher, 39,* 347.

Slavin, R. E. (2008). What works? Issues in synthesizing education program evaluations. *Educational Researcher, 37*(1), 5–14.

Wasik, B. A., & Bond, M. A. (2001). Beyond the pages of a book: Interactive book reading and language development in preschool classrooms. *Journal of Educational Psychology, 93*(2), 243–250.

Wasik, B. A., Bond, M. A., & Hindman, A. (2006). The effects of a language and literacy intervention on Head Start children and teachers. *Journal of Educational Psychology, 98*(1), 63–74.

White, K., Taylor, M., & Moss, V. (1992). Does research support claims about the benefits of involving parents in early intervention programs? *Review of Educational Research, 62,* 91–128.

Whitehurst, G. J., Epstein, J. N., Angell, A. C., Payne, A. C., Crone, D. A., & Fischel, J. E. (1994). Outcomes of an emergent literacy intervention in Head Start. *Journal of Educational Psychology, 86,* 542–555.

22

Educational Policy in the United States Regarding Bilinguals in Early Childhood Education

Eugene E. García
Arizona State University

Ann-Marie Wiese
WestEd, Center for Child and Family Studies

Introduction

Given that the population of children who enter school not speaking English has grown by 40% in the last decade (Garcia & Jensen, 2009), and that there continues to be no appreciable reduction in the achievement gap for these children as compared to their English-speaking monolingual peers (Gandara & Hopkins, 2010; Wiley, Lee, & Rumberger, 2009), educating children from bilingual families continues to be a major concern of educational systems throughout the United States. While the education of bilingual students[1] in the United States is a continuous story of underachievement, it need not be in the future. The current challenge is to improve academic outcomes, and as such, educational policy must focus both on providing equity and fostering excellence.

Historically, educational policy regarding bilingual students has been marked by a continuing tension between the ideologies of assimilation and multiculturalism (for a thorough discussion see García, Arias, Harris Murri, & Serna, 2010; Wiese & Garcia, 2001). Key policy "players" in the education of bilingual students have included the federal courts, the U.S. Congress, state related agencies, and state level initiatives. Still, while the education of these young children from age 5 (kindergarten) and age 10 (grade 3) has drawn significant policy attention, their *early* education (ages birth to 5) has not (García & Frede, 2010). In this chapter, we will describe the historical trends of both federal and state policy, and at the same time, we will focus on the emerging trend of restrictive language policies and the resulting responses (Gandara & Hopkins, 2010). We outline the major sections of this chapter below:

The historical role of federal courts in establishing legal rights of English learners, and recent trends that are undermining this legal right: This will include a discussion of landmark cases such as *Lau v. Nichols* (1974), *Castañeda v. Pickard* (1981), as well as more recent cases in areas outside of education, that have implications for educational policy as it relates to bilingual children.

The role of federal legislation in providing equal educational opportunity to English learners: A chronicle will be presented of The Bilingual Education Act of 1968 as part of the Elementary and Secondary Education Act, and its current counterpart, Title III of the No Child Left Behind (NLCB) Act of 2001. This section will also address the current reauthorization of No Child Left Behind.

The role of restrictive language policies in three states: California, Arizona, and Massachusetts all have restrictive language policies that set English as the language of instruction. In this section the authors will summarize these policies, and discuss their implications for the education of bilingual children.

The Federal Courts: Establishing Legal Rights

Lau v. Nichols: *Establishing Ground*

The 1974 U.S. Supreme Court decision of *Lau v. Nichols* is the landmark case that established language minority status as a claim for discrimination and indicated that limited English proficient students (LEP)[2] must be provided with support to access the curriculum:

> (T)here is no equality of treatment merely by providing students with English instruction. Students without the ability to understand English are effectively foreclosed from any meaningful discourse. Basic English skills are at the very core of what these public schools teach. Imposition of a requirement that, before a child can effectively participate in the education program he must already have acquired those basic skills is to make a mockery of public education. We know that those who do not understand English are certain to find their classroom experiences wholly incomprehensible and in no way meaningful. (p. 18)

This class action lawsuit was filed against the San Francisco Unified School District on March 25, 1970 and involved 12 Chinese students, including both immigrant and nonimmigrant children. In a 1967 school census, the district identified 2,456 LEP Chinese students. By 1970, the district had identified 2,856 such students. Of this number, more than half (1,790) received no special instruction, despite the fact that the district had initiated a pullout program in 1966, in response to parents' requests. In addition, over 2,600 of these students were taught by teachers who could not speak Chinese. The district maintained that it had made initial attempts to serve this population of students. The court's majority opinion overruled an appeals court that had ruled in favor of the district. Instead, the Court ruled in favor of the students and parents.

The opinion relied on statutory (legislative) grounds, and avoided any reference to constitutional determination, although plaintiffs had argued that the equal protection clause of the Fourteenth Amendment[3] of the U.S. Constitution was relevant to the case. The decision tied a student's right to special educational services to Title VI of the 1964 Civil Rights Act, which prohibits discrimination on the grounds of race, color, or national origin in programs or activities receiving federal financial assistance.[4] The plaintiffs did not request an explicit remedy, such as a bilingual or ESL program, and the court did not address this issue. Thus, *Lau* does not articulate that children must receive a *particular* educational service, but instead supports the mandate that districts take "affirmative steps to rectify the language deficiency in order to open its instructional program"—a mandate laid out in a May 25, 1970 Department of Health, Education, and Welfare memorandum. Avoidance on the part of the Supreme Court to specify a particular remedy has plagued efforts to identify primary language instruction as an essential component of instruction of bilingual students in subsequent federal litigation and legislation. After *Lau*, the domain of the language minority education lawsuits belonged almost exclusively to Latino bilingual litigants. Although some cases were litigated to ensure compliance with the *Lau* requirements of "affirmative steps," most subsequent cases involved issues left unanswered by *Lau*: Who are these students? What form of additional educational services must be provided?

In *Aspira of New York, Inc. v. Board of Education* (1975), a suit was brought by a community action group on behalf of all Hispanic children in the New York City schools. The plaintiff argued that these students could not successfully participate in an English schooling context because of their lack of English proficiency, but that they could successfully participate in a Spanish language curriculum (Roos, 1984). The U.S. district court hearing this case adopted a language dominance procedure to identify those students eligible for non-English, Spanish-language instructional programs.

The procedure called for parallel examinations to obtain language proficiency estimates on Spanish and English standardized achievement tests. All students scoring below the 20th percentile on an English language test were given the same (or a parallel) achievement test in Spanish. Students who scored higher on the Spanish achievement test and Spanish language proficiency test were to be placed in a Spanish-language program. These procedures assumed adequate reliability and validity for the language and achievement tests administered. Such an assumption was, and still is, highly questionable. However, the court argued that it acted in a "reasonable manner," admitting that in the absence of better assessment procedures it was forced to follow previous (*Lau*) precedents. A subsequent case, *Otero v. Mesa County School District No. 51* (1975), concluded that a clear relationship between low academic achievement and a lack of English proficiency must be clearly demonstrated before a court could mandate special instructional services. In essence the court refused to direct the school district in Colorado to implement bilingual education programs solely on the basis of low achievement exemplified by the non-English speaking students. While aforementioned cases established a requirement for eligibility regarding a special "action," the following section describes the court case which established a standard for "appropriate action" as required by *Lau*.

Castañeda v. Pickard: Articulating a Standard for "Appropriate Action"

In the key Fifth Circuit decision of *Castañeda v. Pickard* (1981), the court interpreted Section 1703(f) of the Equal Education Opportunity Act of (1974) as substantiating the holding of *Lau* that schools cannot ignore the special language needs of students. The Equal Educational Opportunities Act of 1974 (EEOA) extended Title VI of the Civil Rights Act of 1964 to all educational institutions, not just those receiving federal funding. Section 1703 (f) of the EEOA provides:

No state shall deny equal educational opportunities to an individual on account of his or her race, color, sex, or national origin by—the failure of an educational agency to take appropriate action to overcome language barriers that impede equal participation by its students in its instructional programs. (EEOA, 1974, §1703 (f))

The court then pondered whether the statutory requirement of the EEOA that districts take "appropriate action to overcome language barriers" should be further delineated. The plaintiffs urged on the court a construction of "appropriate action" that would necessitate programs that incorporated bilingual students' primary language. The court concluded, however, that Section 1703(f) did not embody a congressional mandate that any particular form of remedy be uniformly adopted. If Congress wished to intrude so extraordinarily on the local districts' traditional curricular discretion, it must speak more explicitly. This conclusion, the court argued, was buttressed by the congressional use of "appropriate action" in the statute, instead of "bilingual education" or any other educational terminology.

However, the court did conclude that Congress required districts to adopt an appropriate program, and that by creating a cause of action in federal court to enforce Section 1703(f) it left to federal judges the task of determining whether a given program was appropriate. While the court noted that Congress had not provided guidance in that statute or in its brief legislative history on what it intended by selecting "appropriateness" as the operative standard, it described a mode of analysis for a Section 1703(f) case:

1. The court will determine whether a district's program is "informed by an educational theory recognized as sound by some experts in the field or, at least, deemed a legitimate experimental strategy." The court explicitly declined to be an arbiter among competing theorists. The appropriate question is whether some justification exists, not the relative merits of competing alternatives.
2. The court will determine whether the district's programs and practices are reasonably calculated to implement effectively the educational theory adopted.
3. The court will determine whether the program, after operating long enough to be a legitimate trial, produces "results that indicate the language barriers are actually being overcome." A plan that is initially appropriate may have to be revised if expectations are not met or if the district's circumstances significantly change in such a way that the original plan is no longer sufficient. (p. 73)

As a result of *Castañeda*, it became legally possible to substantiate a violation of Section 1703(f), following from *Lau*, on three grounds: (a) The program which provides special language services to eligible language minority students is not based on sound educational theory; (b) the program is not implemented in an effective manner; or (c) the program, after a period of "reasonable implementation," does not produce results that substantiate language barriers are being overcome so as to eliminate achievement gaps between bilingual and monolingual English-speaking students. It is obvious that these criteria allow a local school district to continue to implement a program with some educational theoretical support for a "reasonable" time before it will make judgments upon its "positive" or "negative" effects.

Furthermore, in the *Castañeda* decision, the court again spoke, reluctantly but firmly, to the issue of program implementation. In particular, when a district adopts a particular educational theory, then the programs and practices must be afforded adequate resources and personnel. Implicit in these standards is the requirement that districts staff their programs with language minority education specialists, typically defined by state-approved credentials or professional course work (similar to criteria used to judge professional expertise in other areas of professional education). The *Keyes* court decision speaks directly to the issue of professionally competent personnel serving bilingual students.

The *Keyes v. School District No. 1, Denver, Colorado,* 1969 case was initiated in 1969 on behalf of minority children (African American and Latino) to desegregate the Denver public schools and to provide equal educational opportunities for all children. In granting the preliminary injunction the trial court found that during the previous decade the school board had willfully undertaken to maintain and intensify racial segregation. The Tenth District Court decision ordered a desegregation plan for a particular area of the schools in Denver, and then a Supreme Court decision in 1973 actually expanded the district court's jurisdiction making it applicable to the entire Denver public school system.

In 1974, during the development of a court-ordered desegregation plan, the Congress of Hispanic Educators (CHE) sought intervention on behalf of themselves as educators and on behalf of their own minor children who attended the Denver schools. The CHE sought to ensure that the desegregation plan include educational treatment of bilingual students to overcome the deficits created by numerous years of attendance in segregated and inferior schools. A sequence of additional proceedings and negotiations followed with final comprehensive court hearings commencing in May 1982.

In December 1983, Judge Richard Matsch issued a 31-page opinion applying the *Castañeda* standards. He found that Denver had failed to direct adequate resources to its language program, the question of teacher qualifications being a major concern. Moreover, this decision highlighted that the *Castañeda* standards applied to school districts nationwide. A few years later, the Seventh Circuit Court of Appeals, which includes Wisconsin, Illinois, and Indiana, ruled on the obligations of the states under the EEOA (*Gomez v. Illinois*, 1987). The Court applied the tripartite criteria established in *Castañeda* and extended to state education agencies, as well as to local education agencies, the obligation to ensure that the needs of the students of limited English proficiency be met. In doing so, the "*Castañeda* Standard" with deference to *Lau* has become the most visible legal articulation of educational rights for bilingual students in public schools.

In a more recent Supreme Court case, *Flores v. Arizona* (1999), a test of the *Castañeda* standards is underway at the district court level (Gandara & Hopkins, 2010). Specifically, the state of Arizona contends that the recent state "English only" policies regarding the treatment of ELL students up to the age of 10 combined with the accountability standards of federal educational policy meet the state's obligations to ELL students in their early schooling experiences (Mahoney, MacSwan, Haladyna, & Garcia, 2010). This case, when decided, has the potential of redefining educational rights for bilingual students at the national, state, and local level. We discuss the Arizona policy with regard to bilingual students later in this chapter.

A Summary: Rights of English Learners

The previous discussion highlighted the increasing number of court initiatives influencing the educational services for language minority students. The court opinions in particular have generated some understanding of a language minority pupil's legal standing as it relates to the educational treatment received. At the national level, this legal standing stems from court opinions specifically interpreting Section 1703(f) of the 1974 U.S. Equal Educational Opportunities Act. The courts have consistently refused to invoke a corollary to the Fourteenth Amendment to the U.S. Constitution with respect to educational treatment. Even so it is evident that litigation has increased (and is likely to continue) and has been an avenue of educational reform that has produced significant changes in educational programs for language minority students. However, like almost all litigation, it has been a long (range of 4–13 years in court prior to an operational decision) and often highly complicated and resource-consuming enterprise.

Federal Legislation: No Child Left Behind and the Demise of the Bilingual Education Act

As part of a larger 2001 reauthorization of the Elementary and Secondary Education Act of 1965, a measure known as No Child Left Behind (NCLB), the Bilingual Education Act was eliminated. Under provisions of this new reauthorization, specifically Title III: Language Instruction for Limited English Proficient and Immigrant Students, federal funds continue to support the education of bilingual students. However, Title III differs markedly from the initial enactment of Title VII: The Bilingual Education Act and any of its five subsequent reauthorizations.

The Bilingual Education Act, 1968–1988

Since its inception in 1968 through its final reauthorization in 1994, Title VII of ESEA: The Bilingual Education Act (BEA) stood as the primary federal legislative effort to provide equal educational opportunity to language minority students. The legislation was reauthorized on five occasions (1974, 1978, 1984, 1988, 1994). While the aim of the legislation was never one of establishing language policy, the role of language became a prominent marker as the legislation articulated the goals and nature of education for language minority students.

Like *Lau v. Nichols*, the initial Title VII legislation emanated from the Civil Rights Act of 1964 as part of the "war on poverty" legislation. The legislation was primarily a "crisis intervention," a political strategy to funnel poverty funds to the second largest minority group in the Southwest, Mexican Americans (Casanova, 1991; Garcia & Gonzalez, 1995). The BEA was intended as a remedial effort, aimed at meeting the educational needs of low-income bilingual children by addressing the children's "language deficiencies," and as such, responding to the call for equal educational opportunity (Navarro, 1990). No particular program of instruction was recommended; local educational agencies (LEAs) would receive financial assistance "to develop and

carry out new and imaginative...programs" (BEA, 1968, §702). Among the approved activities were the following programs: bilingual education, history and culture, early childhood education, and adult education for parents.

As a practical matter, all of the programs funded under the BEA in its early years featured native language instruction, despite the fact that the role of native language instruction was not specifically addressed until the 1974 reauthorization of the BEA. The 1974 reauthorization provided the following definition of bilingual education: "instruction given in, and study of, English, and, to the extent necessary to allow a child to progress effectively through the educational system, the native language" (§703(a)(4)(A)(i)).

The bilingual programs in Dade County, Florida founded to address the needs of the first wave of professional class Cuban immigrants influenced the decision to include native language instruction in the definition of bilingual education. This Cuban immigrant population saw themselves as temporary residents of the United States who would soon return to their country, and therefore, wanted to preserve their culture and language. Thus, the bilingual programs encouraged Spanish language maintenance and English language acquisition (Casanova, 1991). At the same time, the success of the programs gave encouragement to the idea of bilingual education as a method of instruction for students from disadvantaged backgrounds (Hakuta, 1986). Native language instruction could serve as a bridge to English language acquisition, by providing equal access to the curriculum until students were English proficient. While the BEA acknowledged the role native language could play in supporting a transition to English, it did not promote bilingual education as an enrichment program where the native language was maintained. These very programs were amongst those described in hearings on the 1968 law.

Other significant changes in terms of eligibility included the elimination of poverty as a requirement; the inclusion of Native American children as an eligible population; and a provision for English-speaking children to enroll in bilingual education programs to "acquire an understanding of the cultural heritage of the children of limited English-speaking ability" (§703 (a)(4)(B)).

Subsequent reauthorizations of the BEA shifted to focus on English acquisition as the primary goal of education for bilingual children. The 1978 reauthorization added language to the 1974 definition of bilingual education emphasizing the goal of English language proficiency. Encouraging native language maintenance might only foster children's allegiance to minority languages and culture, which should not be the responsibility of schools. Native language maintenance was the responsibility of families, churches, and other institutions outside the school (Casanova, 1991; Crawford, 1999). So, while bilingualism was still a laudable goal, the ultimate benefit of programs would be judged in terms of English language acquisition and subject matter learning (Birman & Ginsburg, 1983).

The 1984 reauthorization of the BEA targeted funds to

transitional bilingual education: 60% of Title VII funds were allocated to the various grant categories, and 75% of these funds were reserved for transitional bilingual education programs. Transitional bilingual education programs were specified as providing "structured English-language instruction, and, to the extent necessary to allow a child to achieve competence in the English language, instruction in the child's native language" (§703 (a)(4)(A)). So, the purpose of native language instruction was to support transition to English instruction. In contrast, developmental bilingual education programs were defined as providing "structured English-language instruction and instruction in a second language. Such programs shall be designed to help children achieve competence in English and a second language, while mastering subject matter skills" (§703 (a)(5)(A)). So, the goal of this program included native language and English language competence, yet no funding allocations were specified. The grant categories also included special alternative instructional programs (SAIPS) that did not require the use of native language and 4% of Title VII funds were allocated to SAIPS. These programs were created in recognition "that in some school districts establishment of bilingual education programs may be administratively impractical" (§702 (a)(7)).

While the 1984 grant categories remained the same for the 1988 reauthorization, 25% of direct funding for programs was designated specifically for SAIPS. Furthermore, the 1998 legislation included a three-year limit on an individual's participation: "No student may be enrolled in a bilingual program…for a period of more than 3 years" (§7021 (d)(3)(A)). The three-year limit runs contrary to the research literature which reports estimates of up to 10 years before children are fully proficient in English, including the academic uses of the language as compared to their native English-speaking peers (Collier, 1987; 1995; Hakuta, Goto Butler, & Witt, 2000; Mitchell, Destino, & Karam, 1997).

ESEA Reauthorizations of 1994 and 2001: From Bilingual Education to English Only

With regards to bilingual students, the 2001 reauthorization of the Elementary and Secondary Education Act marked a complete reversal from the reauthorization in 1994. Table 22.1 below provides a summary of key differences in how the 1994 and the 2001 reauthorizations of the ESEA address the education of LEP students.

As the summary of the legislation demonstrates, areas in which significant changes are evident include: purpose, program, allocation of funds, and accountability and assessment. Whereas the 1994 version of the Bilingual Education Act still included among its goals "developing the English skills and to the extent possible, the native-language skills" of LEP students, the new law focuses only on attaining "English proficiency." In fact, the word *bilingual* has been completely eliminated from the law and any government office affiliated with the law. A new federal office has been created to replace the Office of Bilingual Education and

Minority Languages Affairs (OBEMLA) and oversee the provisions of the new law. It is now the Office of English Language Acquisition, Language Enhancement, and Academic Achievement for Limited-English-Proficient Students (OELALEAALEPS or as it is commonly referred to, OELA). What was formerly known as the National Clearinghouse for Bilingual Education is now known as the National Clearinghouse for English Language Acquisition and Language Instruction Educational Programs.

Federal funds to serve bilingual students will no longer be federally administered via competitive grants designed to ensure equity and promote quality programs which served as guiding lights to the larger nation. Instead, resources will be allocated primarily through a state formula program for language instruction educational programs (LIEPs) that are "based on scientifically-based research" (U.S. Department of Education, 2002a). A LIEP is defined as "an instruction course in which LEP students are placed for the purpose of developing and attaining English proficiency, while meeting challenging State and academic content and student academic achievement standards; a LIEP may make use of both English and a child's native language to enable the child to develop and attain English proficiency" (U.S. Department of Education, 2003, p. 20). The formula grants are distributed to each state based on their enrollments of LEP and immigrant students.[5] Each state must then allocate 95% of the funds to individual local education agencies (LEAs). The argument for the formula grants claims that the previous system of competitive grants "benefited a small percentage of LEP students in relatively few schools" (U.S. Department of Education, n.d.). In fact, resources will be spread more thinly than before, between more states, more programs, and more students.

Finally, accountability provisions mandate annual assessment in English for any student who has attended school in the United States (excluding Puerto Rico) for three or more consecutive years and attainment of "annual measurable achievement objectives" (U.S. Department of Education, 2002a). States are required to hold subgrantees accountable for making adequately yearly progress (AYP).[6] Subgrantees must report every second fiscal year and include a description of the program as well as the progress made by children in learning English, meeting state standards, and attaining English proficiency. States report every second year to the Department of Education, and the Department of Education reports every second year to Congress. Subgrantees failing to meet AYP must develop an improvement plan with sanctions if they continue to fail for four years (U.S. Department of Education, 2002b). In fact, failure to meet AYP can eventually result in the loss of Title III funds.

Current Reauthorization of the Elementary and Secondary Education Act

The reauthorization of the U.S. Elementary and Secondary Education Act, known more prominently as the No Child

Table 22.1   Significant Differences in the 1994 and 2001 Reauthorizations of the ESEA

Issue	1994 Title VII: Bilingual Education Act	2001 Title III: Language Instruction, Limited English Proficient, and Immigrant Students
Eligible Populations	Limited English proficient students	Limited English proficient students
	Recent immigrants which: "have not been attending one or more schools in any one or more States for more than three full years." (§7501(7))	Immigrant children and youth: 3–21 years of age, not born in any state, "have not been attending one or more schools in any one or more states for more than 3 full academic years." §3301(6)
	Native Americans, Native Alaskans, Native Hawaiians, Native American Pacific Islanders	Native Americans, Native Alaskans, Native Hawaiians, Native American Pacific Islanders
Purpose	"(A) To help such children and youth develop proficiency in English, and to the extent possible, their native language; and (B) meet the same challenging State content standards and challenging State student performance standards expected of all children." (§7111(2))	"To help ensure that children who are limited English proficient, including immigrant children and youth, attain English proficiency, develop high levels of academic attainment in English, and meet the same challenging State academic content and student academic achievement standards as all children are expected to meet." (§3102(1))
	"The use of a child or youth's native language and culture in classroom instruction can—(A) promote self-esteem and contribute to academic achievement and learning English by limited English proficient children and youth." §7102(14))	Programs for Native Americans: "develop English proficiency and, to the extent possible, proficiency in their native language." §3211(2)
	The "unique status of Native American languages" and language enhancement.	
Programs	Competitive grants to local education agencies (schools, districts). State education agencies approve the grant application before submission but play no official role in the grant's implementation.	"To streamline language instruction educational programs into a program carried out through formula grants to State educational agencies and local educational agencies." (§3102(7))
	"Quality bilingual education programs enable children and youth to learn English and meet high academic standards including proficiency in more than one language." (§7102(9))	"To implement language instruction educational programs, based on scientifically-based research on teaching limited English proficient children." (§3102.(9))
	Priority is given to programs which "provide for development of bilingual proficiency both in English and another language for all participating students." (§7116 (i)(1))	
Allocation of Funds	Cap of 25% of funds for SAIPs, can be lifted if an applicant has demonstrated that developing and implementing a bilingual education program is not feasible.	95% of funds must be used for grants at the local level to teach LEP children; each state must spend this percentage to award formula subgrants to districts.
Accountability and Assessment	Local education agency (LEA) is the locus of control and is granted great flexibility on how to best serve students. LEA sets own goals and ways of assessing them.	To hold various educational agencies accountable for "increases in English proficiency and core academic content knowledge…by requiring—(A) demonstrated improvements in the English proficiency of limited English proficient students each fiscal year; and (B) adequate yearly progress" (§3102(8)).

Left Behind Act, is under consideration at the time of the writing of this chapter. As in previous reauthorizations, many issues will impact the education of young bilingual children. From a national policy perspective, there appears to be consensus around key inputs in early learning that maximize developmental and academic success in later years: literacy-rich environments, purposeful early childhood experiences to develop preliteracy skills, qualified staff in early childhood settings, and quality professional development to provide educators with the competencies to recognize cognitive assets and learning needs of children from birth to age 5 (Garcia & Frede, 2010). Current national policy proposals and draft legislation support comprehensive literacy programs, including a variety of state and local programs, that link learning from birth to prekindergarten years through grade 12. Pedagogically this approach has great merit but structural realities serve as major roadblocks.

Despite the movement toward what may seem like a con-

tinuum of education from birth to kindergarten and beyond, the systems that provide early education and school-age (K-12) public education remain uniquely distinct. The early childhood services and the public schools are governed by different statutes, rules, and regulations and are overseen by their respective state and federal agencies. Differing licensing authorities govern each segment and funding sources are distinct. Funding—particularly at the federal level—is authorized in different legislation and overseen by different agencies. While legislation may encourage coordination, the operational reality of administering federal programs calls for continuing operation within "silos," or in other words, independent of each other.

The child care services industry continues to respond to research calling for more early learning experiences and the market demand for such preacademic experiences. At the same time, an increasing number of public school systems are providing full day kindergarten and moving into supporting pre-K early learning for students who eventually will attend the public schools. Still, accountability for academic progress is the engine for ESEA, which is only strengthened in the legislative proposals and frameworks currently being considered in the nation's capital. Investing time and money from K-12 public education to coordinate and make stronger linkages to early learning is a challenge in these economic times and would require careful consideration as to how to help schools meet their accountability requirements.

At the same time, the following three key areas lend themselves to an exploration of the possibilities of coordination of policies and practices, (a) early and accurate identification of bilingual children, (b) strengthened human capital in early childhood education programs, and (c) enhanced coherence of program components.

Early and Accurate Identification of Bilingual Children. A significant percentage of children aged 0 to 5 years old come from homes where a language other than English is spoken, yet it is rare to find formal coordination between the 0- to 5-year-old service providers and the K-12 school districts regarding early identification of such students. A Home Language Survey is required for students entering K-12 (and pre-K, in some districts) but it seems to not be required in early learning programs. Depending upon the school district's policy, if a Home Language Survey indicates that the child may have limited proficiency in English, a formal assessment of English proficiency may be required. Concerns arise over testing students at such a young age as critics say such a test may likely be meaningless for such young children, whose development is in enormous flux.

To ensure appropriate instruction for young bilingual children, it is important to identify the language abilities and prior knowledge they bring to early childhood education settings, and in later years, to school. Sharing assessment information between the early childhood education providers and K-12 schools would prove helpful. SEAs could make funds available to LEAs and early childhood centers/providers to support coordination efforts to appropriately and accurately identify young bilingual children. The funding could support professional development, software purchase/redesign, data management activities, and valid screening efforts.

Strengthened Human Capital in Early Childhood Education Programs. Despite the high proportion of young bilinguals among the nation's birth to 5 populations there is no strategic effort to prepare, hire, and train individuals working in early childhood programs to acquire competencies to foster the language and literacy development of young bilingual children. Even in LEAs that have pre-K and kindergarten programs, there is often no coordination or targeted effort in hiring practices or in professional development that will build the required competencies for teaching literacy skills to children who are learning English as a second language.

In the absence of a national policy or program to support the development of relevant competencies and skills in the early learning community, the state education agencies (SEAs) could support such efforts at the local level. SEAs could make available funds to LEAs and early childhood centers/providers to collaborate on professional development efforts in this area. Given that school district resources for professional development resources are scarce, SEAs and the state agency responsible for the oversight of child care and early childhood centers would need to invest funds to support such coordinated professional development opportunities.

Enhanced Coherence of Programmatic Components. Public education K-12 systems typically lack coordination of the instructional program for English learners (ELs) between their early childhood programs and later grades. Oftentimes, staffing and program requirements vary and do not support English language acquisition in a coherent fashion. Some states (California, Texas, and New Mexico) have voluntary guidelines for preschool English learners. Some districts do recognize the language acquisition demands in early childhood program and have formally incorporated ESL into a pre-K and kindergarten instructional day. Other LEAs that support dual language programs are starting to build preliteracy skills in the native language and support the early stages of acquiring English during the preschool years and kindergarten.

Policy should encourage such programmatic coherence across fiscal entities, while allowing room for explicit instructional support for English language acquisition for bilingual children in early childhood programs. At the very least, this would also call for attention to oral language development in the home language, expanding children's vocabulary in both the home language and English, and engaging with families as partners. For LEAs that have pre-K and kindergarten they should better coordinate the instructional services for students as soon as they enter the school district.

In summary, federal policy—legislation and litigation—continues to emphasize the teaching and learning of English without emphasis on the development of academic bilingual competency for children who speak a language other than English. It is unclear whether this policy will "stay the course" as the proportion of bilinguals in the larger U.S. population increases significantly in coming years, despite the controversial nature of providing instruction in the home languages other than English. At the very least, Hakuta, Goto Butler, and Witt (2000) urge that a more sensible policy would "set aside the entire spectrum of the elementary grades as the realistic range within which English acquisition is accomplished, and (would plan) a balanced curriculum that pays attention not just to English, but to the full array of academic needs of students" (p. 14).

State Policy: Legislation and Initiatives

Overall, state policy regarding bilingual children can be characterized as follows:

1. Seventeen states implement instructional programs which allow or require instruction in a language other than English;
2. Fifteen states establish special qualifications for the certification of professional instructional staff;
3. Fifteen states provide school districts with supplementary funds to support educational programs;
4. Fifteen states mandate a cultural component; and
5. Eleven states require parental consent for enrollment of early grade students in bilingual education.

Eight states (Arizona, California, Colorado, Illinois, Indiana, Massachusetts, Rhode Island, and Texas) impose all of the above requirements concurrently.

"Restrictive Language" State Policies

Three state initiatives in California (1998), Arizona (2000), and Massachusetts (2002) illustrate state educational policy aimed at restricting the use of a language other than English in the delivery of educational services to bilingual children.[7] This chapter will generally discuss all three states, but then focus on Arizona to provide a more detailed account of one state. The general process by which such initiatives come before the public for a vote is similar in all three states. In essence, the initiative process allows citizens to place an issue of interest on the ballot for voter approval or rejection.[8] In California, the 1998 successful ballot initiative was titled "English Language in Public Schools," and along with the resulting changes to the state education code,

1. Requires all children be placed in "English language classrooms," and that English learners be educated through a prescribed methodology identified as "Structured English Immersion" or "Sheltered English Immersion."
2. Prescribes methodology that would be provided as a temporary transition period "not normally intended to exceed one year."

The law allows instruction in the child's native language only in situations in which a waiver is granted, done so in writing, and done so yearly by parents. A waiver can be granted so that a student can be enrolled in a bilingual education program under three circumstances:

(a) the child already knows English, "as measured by standardized tests of English vocabulary comprehension, reading and writing in which the child scores at or above the state average for his or her grade level or at or above the 5th grade average, whichever is lower";

(b) the "child is age 10 years or older" and such instruction is approved by the principal and the teacher; or
(c) the child has special needs and has been placed for a period of at least 30 days during that school year in an English language classroom and still the principal and teacher feel the child has special physical, emotional, psychological, or educational needs.

As it stands, this "restrictive language" policy allows native language instruction only through an exclusionary and complicated process for students that are identified as limited in their English language proficiency, and extends beyond current federal law which neither requires nor prohibits the use of native languages (Wiley et al., 2009). Moreover, teachers, administrators, and school board members can be held personally liable for fees and damages by the child's parents and guardians for using the native language when waivers have not been pursued or granted.

The Arizona and Massachusetts statutes, which passed in November of 2000 and 2002 respectively, are much like California's and require that all public school instruction be conducted in English. Like California, in Arizona and Massachusetts parents may still request a waiver of the requirements for children who already know English, are 10 years or older, or have special needs best suited to a different educational approach. However, the waiver provision becomes more restrictive in both states. Children who already know English are subject to an oral evaluation in addition to the written standardized measures. For children with special individual needs a written description of no less than 250 words documenting the special individual needs for the specific child must be provided and permanently added to the child's official school records. In addition, the special individual needs are more narrowly defined as physical or psychological only. The remainder of this section will focus on the how the policy in Arizona has played out since it became law in 2000.

Arizona's Extension of Restrictive Language Policies for Bilingual Children. Currently, it is estimated that there are 130,000 English learners (ELs) in public schools in Arizona (Mahoney et al., 2010), with 210 districts having reported EL enrollment in 2006 (Artiles, Klingner, Sullivan, & Fierros, 2010). This high number of ELs has brought a change in the demographics of public schools in the state, and a necessity to account for the educational experiences of these students, both linguistically and academically.

The current Structured English Immersion Model (SEI) was mandated in Arizona after the passage of Proposition 203 in 2000. The local flexibility that existed regarding the choice of program models for ELs ended (Mahoney, Haladyna, & MacSwan, 2009), and SEI was required to be used in school districts and charter schools in the state (Gandara et al., 2010). These regulations were made even more restrictive after the establishment of the Arizona English

Language Learners Task Force, which was responsible for the implementation of what is called the four-hour block (Mahoney et al., 2010). This four-hour block, which is regulated by the Arizona Revised Statutes 15-756.01, determines that ELs are required to receive English language development (ELD) services in an English-only immersion setting for a minimum of four hours per day for the first year in which they are classified as an EL (Gandara et al. 2010). The model is based on the assumption that ELs can achieve proficiency in English very quickly (usually within a year) in an English-only instructional environment (Mahoney, Haladyna, & MacSwan, 2009). Despite this one-year parameter, exiting from this mandated four-hour block is achievable only through the "mastery" of English at the student's grade level as measured by the state's English language test, the Arizona English Language and Literacy Assessment (AZELLA). The SEI also requires ELs to be grouped based on their English language proficiency, and each component has a predetermined number of minutes for language instruction (Gandara et al., 2010).

In fact, the most problematic definition in the Arizona law is the one for English Language Development (ELD) as it relates to how the teaching of English as a second language is to be organized. According to the definition, ELD focuses on phonology, morphology, syntax, lexicon, and semantics. This definition, with its focus on only "linguistic" features of the English development endeavor, completely disregards the cognitive infrastructure of second language development and teaching/development. No research exists that supports teaching young children English by having them practice isolated language parts for fixed periods of time, as suggested by the Arizona SEI policy: 60 minutes a day of grammar instruction; 60 minutes a day of vocabulary instruction, and so on (Krashen, Rolstad, & MacSwan, 2007). Indeed, in the *National Literacy Panel Report on Language-Minority Children and Youth*, August and Shanahan (2006) state that basic skills such as phonics and grammar should always be taught in context, and cognitive theories of bilingual development remind us that ignoring the cognitive and linguistic benefits of learning bilingually cannot be ignored in an instructional circumstance aimed at second language acquisition.

This type of prolonged segregation on a daily basis, coupled with the requirement to group students by language proficiency, and a specific time allocation of how English language development is to be taught, does not comprise a model associated with research in the field of second language acquisition and the cognitive infrastructure theories associated with bilingual development (August, Goldenberg, & Rueda, 2010). Present state policy has had negligible effects in overcoming the achievement gap for ELs, as shown by several studies (e.g., Losen, 2010; Rumberger & Tran, 2010).

Furthermore, the SEI model currently in place in Arizona disregards much of the literature related to the early education of bilingual students (Garcia & Frede, 2010). Gaining

academic proficiency in a second language usually requires more than one year of instruction (Cummins, 2000), and it necessarily involves the negotiation of meaning, contextualized instruction, comprehensible linguistic input, being pressed to communicate beyond one's level of proficiency for the purpose of communication, cognitive development, and, in schooling, access to academic concepts and content (Krashen et al., 2007; Ovando, Combs, & Collier, 2006). In addition, the current policies negate the cognitive, theoretical understanding and the empirically based findings that a bilingual child's language(s) development is interdependent with cognitive and linguistic intersections (Garcia, 2005). Language is not learned in isolation of cognitive and content learning experiences. There exists no scientifically based research to recommend the isolation of ELs for four hours a day into English language classes, where they are kept from participating in and benefiting from core content and cognitively rich instruction (August et al., 2010; Krashen et al., 2007). To progress in language learning, ELs need ample opportunities to interact with children who are beyond their level of proficiency, and to hear and participate in language and cognitive activities within educational content.

Increasing numbers of ELs are being placed in special education programs since the passing of the English-only policy in the state (Artiles et al., 2010), possibly as a compensating measure for the lack of appropriate language services directed at these students. Artiles and colleagues call attention to the danger of such an increase, hence many special education teachers are not adequately prepared to work with ELs.

Implementing a model that isolates ELs from mainstream students and classrooms for 80% of the school day also has severe social and cultural impacts on the lives of these students and their families. For one, ELs are silenced and marginalized in the greater school context, diminishing their sense of belonging to the educational environment (Nguyen & Stritikus, 2009), and consequently their chances of academic success. Also, no opportunity is given to these students to develop their heritage languages and heritage cultural knowledge, which are usually very strong factors for students' self-esteem, confidence, socialization, sense of identity and linguistic and academic achievement (Lee & Suarez, 2009).

Implications for Teacher Preparation. This problem becomes even more complex when teacher preparation is considered. Teachers of ELs need to know important issues specifically relevant to bilingual development: what to teach, how to teach it effectively, and how it will be assessed and monitored. However, teacher preparation in Arizona has been significantly reduced quantitatively and qualitatively since the establishment of restrictive policies in the state (de Jong, Arias, & Sanchez, 2010). De Jong and colleagues explain that quantitative effects of new teacher preparation practices established after Proposition 203 include the reduction of curricular requirements from 24 to 27 credits in English as a Second Language (ESL) and Bilingual Language Education (BLE) programs (between 360 and 405 hours) to 6 credits in the current SEI endorsement (90 hours). This new number accounts for approximately 10% of the preparation usually cited as needed to effectively serve these students. Moreover, data from 2006 to 2009 shows a decrease of 16% in the number of credentialed and certified bilingual instructors in the state (Arias, 2009).

From a qualitative perspective, de Jong et al. (2010) explain that most of the teacher preparation currently in place in the state of Arizona is focused on the knowledge of state policy related to SEI and the requirement that English as a second language instruction should focus on the linguistic domains of English instruction. Consequently, novice and experienced teachers have shown a lack of experience or knowledge related to some of the very effective practices in second language education, such as the integration of students' primary language in the classroom and the understanding of how language proficiency interacts with overall learning.

Denying ELs access to the core academic content within rich cognitively demanding educational circumstances while they are learning English denies these students the opportunity to receive the same educational experiences as students who are fully proficient in English (Gandara & Orfield, 2010; Losen, 2010), and thus violates their right to an education that respects their linguistic rights (Valdes, 2009). Moreover, it neglects some of the important understandings about second language acquisition, such as the necessity that students have to receive meaningful and understandable input and to practice academic language through cooperative learning. Finally, the SEI model currently in place restricts in-service and preservice teachers, as well as schools and districts, from being able to implement the best practices to enhance the linguistic and academic achievement of their EL students (de Jong et al., 2010).

Overall, the language regulations currently in place in Arizona are affecting the academic achievement and educational experiences of these students, as several studies have shown. Rumberger and Tran (2010), for instance, claim that states with restrictive policies usually present "larger achievement gaps than those without such policies" (p. 98), and that "state policies and school practices restricting the use of native-language instruction could limit the ability of states and schools to reduce the EL achievement gap" (p. 100). In a review of data from the National Assessment of Educational Progress (NAEP), Losen (2010) also asserts that English-only instruction has not been beneficial to ELs' reading and math attainment in Arizona. His data show that math scores for ELs in grades 4 and 8, during the period from 1998 to 2007, increased at first, but then declined, while the national average consistently improved. As for reading, fourth grade results in the same period also showed an initial increase followed by a subsequent decrease, which in this case brought scores down to their initial level, while in eighth grade there was an overall decline. These results

are especially important in that they show that SEI in this state is not meeting *Castañeda*'s third prong, which establishes that a program's success must be demonstrable after a trial period (a claim also made by Mahoney et al., 2010).

As mentioned earlier in this chapter, the state of Arizona presently justifies its policy within the construct of the *Flores v. Arizona* litigation. Much like the pending reauthorization of the No Child Left Behind Act, the adjudication for the *Flores v. Arizona* in the near future will do much to set precedent in litigation, and as such, influence federal and state policy. The practices engendered by these policies are likely to have substantive effects on the types of assessments, teachers, and educational programs and practices afforded to ELs, particularly in the early years of the educational experience.

Conclusion

This chapter has provided an overview of educational policy at the federal and state levels as it relates to bilingual children and students, and in particular the role of language in the articulation of those policies, which will continue at the forefront of future policy activity (Garcia & Frede, 2010). As the United States advances educational policy for students in an increasingly diversified population, the continued underachievement of bilingual children poses a particular challenge to educators and those among us who look to educational agencies for help in realizing the moral imperatives of equity and social justice. Wiley, Lee, and Rumberger (2010) remind us that many nation-states deal with issues of children entering early care and education settings, as well as public schools, not speaking the language of the schools. The United States is not a unique case. The United Nations has spoken directly to the rights of a minority group to its language by explicitly indicating,

> Prohibiting the use of the language of a group in daily discourse or in schools or the printing and circulation of publications in the language of the group falls within the agreed upon constraints regarding linguistic genocide. (United Nations, 1948)

In 1994, the United Nations Human Rights Committee spoke again to this international issue (United Nations, 1994). It is the most far-reaching human rights articulation of an international body addressing linguistic rights:

> In those states in which ethnic, religious or linguistic minorities exist, persons belonging to such minorities shall not be denied the right, in community with other members of their group, to enjoy their own culture, to profess and practice their own religion, or to use their own language.

Skutnabb-Kangas (2002) has summarized this UN position as: (a) protecting all individuals on the state's territory or under its jurisdiction such as immigrants and refugees irrespective of their legal status, (b) recognizing the existence of a linguistic right, and (c) imposing positive obligations on the State to protect that right. Under this interpretation, the United States might very well be in violation of the UN position. Still, throughout this chapter, several important conclusions regarding the responsibilities of educational agencies have been established. Using a question-and-answer format,

Table 22.2 sets out some of these responsibilities. These are adapted from Roos (1984) and Garcia (2005) and are still legally valid today. They represent a practical guide for understanding the legal status of bilingual students and the legal liability of the educational agencies that serve them, grounded in federal policy.

Table 22.2   Legal Rights of Bilingual Students and Legal Liabilities of Agencies that Serve Them

Question: Is there a legally acceptable procedure for identifying bilingual students in need of special instructional treatment?

Answer: Yes. The legal obligation is to identify all *school-age children* who have challenges speaking, understanding, reading, or writing English because of a home language background other than English. In order to do this, a two-phase approach is common and acceptable. First, the parents are asked, through a home language survey or on a registration form, whether a language other than English is spoken in the child's home. If the answer is affirmative, the second phase is triggered. In the second phase, students identified through the home language survey are given an oral language proficiency test and an assessment of their reading and writing skills.

Question: Once the students are identified, are there any minimal standards for the educational program provided to them?

Answer: Yes. First, a number of courts have recognized that special training is necessary to equip a teacher to provide meaningful assistance to English learners. The teacher (and it is clear that it must be a teacher, not an aide) must have training in second-language acquisition techniques in order to teach English as a second language. Second, the time spent on assisting these students must be sufficient to assure that they acquire English skills quickly enough to assure that their disadvantages in the English language classroom do not become a permanent educational disadvantage.

Question: Must students be provided with instruction in the student's native language as well as English?

Answer: At the present time, the federal obligation has not been construed to compel such a program. However, the federal mandate is not fully satisfied by an ESL program. The mandate requires English language help plus programs to assure that students not be substantively disadvantaged by any delay in learning English. To do this may require either (a) a bilingual program that keeps the students up in their course work while learning English or (b) a specially designed compensatory program to address the educational loss suffered by any delay in providing understandable substantive instruction. Finally, it is legally necessary to provide the material resources necessary for the instructional components. The program must be reasonably designed to succeed. Without adequate resources, this requirement cannot be met.

Question: What minimal standards must be met if a bilingual program is to be offered?

Answer: The heart of a basic bilingual program is a teacher who can speak the language of the students as well as address the students' limited English proficiency. Thus, a district offering a bilingual program must take affirmative steps to match teachers with these characteristics. These might include allocating teachers with language skills to bilingual classrooms, and affirmative recruitment of bilingual teachers. Additionally, it requires the district to establish a formal system to assess teachers to insure that they have the prerequisite skills. Finally, where there are insufficient teachers, there must be a system to insure that teachers with most (but not all) of the skills are in bilingual classrooms, that those teachers are on a track to obtain the necessary skills, and that bilingual aides are hired whenever the teacher lacks the necessary language skills.

Question: Must there be standards for removal of a student from a program? What might these be?

Answer: There must be definite standards. These generally mirror the standards for determining whether a student is in need of special language services in the first place. Thus, objective evidence that the student can compete with English-speaking peers without a lingering language disability is necessary.

Several common practices are unlawful. First, the establishment of an arbitrary cap on the amount of time a student can remain in a program fails to meet the requirement that all language minority students be assisted. Second, it is common to have programs terminate at a certain grade level, for example, sixth grade. While programs may change to accommodate different realities, it is unlawful to deny a student access to a program merely because of grade level.

Question: Must a district develop a design to monitor the success of its program?

Answer: Yes. The district is obligated to monitor the program and to make reasonable adjustments when the evidence suggests that the program is not successful. Monitoring is necessarily a two-part process. First, it is necessary to monitor the progress of students in the program to assure (a) that they are making reasonable progress toward learning and (b) that the program is providing the students with substantive instruction comparable to that given to English dominant students. Second, any assessment of the program must include a system to monitor the progress of students after they leave the program. The primary purpose of the program is to assure that the LEP students ultimately are able to compete on an equal footing with their English-speaking peers. This cannot be determined in the absence of such a post-reclassification monitoring system.

Question: May a district deny services to a student because there are few students in the district who speak her or his language?

Answer: No. The 1974 Equal Educational Opportunities Act and subsequent court decisions make it clear that every student is entitled to a program that is reasonably designed to overcome any handicaps occasioned by a language deficit. The number of students who speak a particular language may be considered to determine how to best address the student needs given human and fiscal resources available. Still, some form of special educational services must be provided.

Notes

1. Throughout various contexts such as research, litigation, legislation, and practice, a range of terms has been used to describe children who come to school with a primary language other than English. *Limited English proficient* (LEP) is the term most commonly found in legislation and litigation to refer to children whose primary language is a language other than English. *English language learner, bilingual learner, English learner* are terms more commonly found in the research literature and at times in educational settings. Further distinctions can be made based on ethnicity (Latino, Asian, etc.); primary language (Spanish, Mandarin, Vietnamese, etc.); nation of origin and other categories.

2. Ibid.

3. The Fourteenth Amendment was ratified on July 9, 1868 and "greatly expanded the protection of civil rights to all Americans and is cited in more litigation than any other amendment" (Library of Congress: Primary Documents in American History, n.d.) Section 1 of the Fourteenth Amendment states: "All persons born or naturalized in the United States, and subject to the jurisdiction thereof, are citizens of the United States and of the State wherein they reside. No State shall make or enforce any law which shall abridge the privileges or immunities of citizens of the United States; nor shall any State deprive any person of life, liberty, or property, without due process of law; nor deny to any person within its jurisdiction the equal protection of the laws" (U.S. Constitution).

4. The Equal Educational Opportunity Act of 1974 expanded the reach of Title VI of the Civil Rights Act of 1964 to all educational institutions not just those received federal assistance, but did not prescribe a specific remedy. It was an effort by the U.S. Congress to define what constitutes a denial of constitutionally guaranteed equal educational opportunity. See the following section, and Wiese & Garcia (2001), for further discussion.

5. Programs awarded funds under the 1994 reauthorization continue to be eligible.

6. As of February of 2004, for AYP calculations states can include in the LEP subgroup, students who have achieved English language proficiency to ensure they receive credit for improving English language proficiency from year to year (U.S. Department of Education, 2004).

7. A fourth state, Colorado, had a similar restrictive language policy which was defeated (Colorado, Amendment 31: English Language Education, 2002). For more information see: Escamilla, Shannon, Carlos, and Garcia (2003).

8. Additional information on the initiative process in each state can be found online: For California visit www.ss.ca.gov/elections_initiatives.htm; for Arizona visit www.azsos.gov; for Colorado visit www.sos.state.co.us/pubs/elections; and for Massachusetts visit www.sec.ma.us/ele.

References

Arias, B. (2009). Unpublished data based on Arizona Department of Education data. Arizona Revised Statutes, Title 15, Article 3.1, § 15-756.01 (2000).

Arizona, Proposition 203: English Language Education for Children in Public Schools (2000).

Artiles, A. J., Klingner, J. K., Sullivan, A., & Fierros, E. G. (2010). Shifting landscapes of professional practices: English learner special education placement in English-only states. In P. Gandara & M. Hopkins (Eds.), *Forbidden languages: English learners and restrictive language policies* (pp. 102–117). New York: Teachers College Press.

Aspira of New York v. Board of Education of the City of New York, 394 F. Supp. 1161 (1975).

August, D., Goldenberg, C., & Rueda, R. (2010). Restrictive state language policies: Are they scientifically based? In P. Gandara & M. Hopkins (Eds.), *Forbidden languages: English learners and restrictive language policies* (pp. 139–158). New York: Teachers College Press.

August, D., & Shanahan, T. (Eds.). (2006). *Developing literacy in second-language learners: Report of the National Literacy Panel on language-minority children and youth.* Mahwah, NJ: Erlbaum.

Bilingual Education Act, Pub. L. No. (90-247), 81 Stat. 816 (1968).

Bilingual Education Act, Pub. L. No. (93-380), 88 Stat. 503 (1974).

Bilingual Education Act, Pub. L. No. (95-561), 92 Stat. 2268 (1978).

Bilingual Education Act, Pub. L. No. (98-511), 98 Stat. 2370 (1984).

Bilingual Education Act, Pub. L. No. (100-297), 102 Stat. 279 (1988).

Bilingual Education Act, Pub L. No. (103-382), (1994).

Birman, B. F., & Ginsburg, A. L. (1983). Introduction: Addressing the needs of language minority children. In K. A. Baker & A. A. D. Kanter (Eds.), *Bilingual education: A reappraisal of federal policy* (pp. ix–xxi). Lexington, MA: D.C. Heath.

California, Proposition 227: English Language in Public Schools (1998).

Casanova, U. (1991). Bilingual education: Politics or pedagogy. In O. Garcia (Ed.), *Bilingual education* (Vol. 1, pp. 167–182). Amsterdam, the Netherlands: Benjamins.

Castañeda v. Pickard, 64b F.2d 989 (1981).

Civil Rights Act, Pub. L. No. (88-352), 78 Stat. (1964).

Collier, V. (1987). Age and rate of acquisition of second language for academic purposes. *TESOL Quarterly, 21*, 617–641.

Collier, V. P. (1995, Fall). Acquiring a second language for school. *Directions in Language and Education, 1*(4). Washington, DC: National Clearinghouse for English Language Acquisition (NCELA). Retrieved from http://1995_Acquiring-a-Second-Language-for-School_DLE4.pdf

Crawford, J. (1999). *Bilingual education: History, politics, theory, and practice.* (4th ed.). Los Angeles, CA: Bilingual Education Services.

Cummins, J. (2000). *Language, power and pedagogy: Bilingual children in the crossfire.* Clevedon, England: Multilingual Matters.

de Jong, E., Arias, M. B., & Sanchez, M. T. (2010). Undermining teacher competencies: Another look at the impact of restrictive language policies. In P. Gandara & M. Hopkins (Eds.), *Forbidden languages: English learners and restrictive language policies* (pp. 118–138). New York: Teachers College Press.

Elementary and Secondary Education Act, Title II, Pub. L. No. (89-10), 27 Stat. (1965).

Equal Educational Opportunities Act, Pub. L. No. (93-380), 88 Stat. 514 (1974).

Escamilla, K., Shannon, S., Carlos, S., & Garcia, J. (2003). Breaking the code: Colorado's defeat of the anti-bilingual education initiative (Amendment 31). *Bilingual Research Journal, 27*(3), 357–382.

Flores vs. Arizona, 48 F. Supp. 2d 937 (D. Ariz. 1999).

Gandara, P., & Hopkins, M. (2010). *Forbidden languages: English learners and restrictive language policies.* New York: Teachers College Press.

Gandara, P., Losen, D., August, D., Uriarte, M., Gomez, M. C., & Hopkins, M. (2010). Forbidden language: A brief history of U.S. language policy. In P. Gandara & M. Hopkins (Eds.), *Forbidden languages: English learners and restrictive language policies* (pp. 20–36). New York: Teachers College Press.

Gandara, P., & Orfield, G. (2010). Moving from failure to a new vision of language policy. In P. Gandara & M. Hopkins (Eds.), *Forbidden languages: English learners and restrictive language policies* (216–226). New York: Teachers College Press.

García, E. E. (2005). *Teaching and learning in two languages: Bilingualism and schooling in the United States.* New York: Teachers College Press.

Garcia, E., Arias, M. B., Harris Murri, N. J., & Serna, C. (2010). Developing responsive teachers: A challenge for a demographic reality. *Journal of Teacher Education, 61*(1-2), 132–142.

Garcia, E. E., & Frede, E. C. (2010). *Young English language learners.* New York: Teachers College Press.

Garcia, E. E., & Gonzalez, R. (1995). Issues in systemic reform for culturally and linguistically diverse students. *Teachers College Record, 96*(3), 418–431.

Garcia, E. E., & Jensen, B. T. (2009). Responding to changing demographics. *Educational Leadership*, *64*(6), 34–39.

Gomez v. Illinois State Board of Education, 811 F.2d 1030 (1987).

Hakuta, K. (1986). *Mirror of language: The debate on bilingualism*. New York: Basic Books.

Hakuta, K., Goto Butler, Y., & Witt, D. (2000). *How long does it take English learners to attain proficiency?* (Report 2000-1). University of California Linguistic Minority Research Institute Policy.

Keyes v. School Dist. No. 1. 303 F. Supp. 279 (1969).

Keyes v. School Dist. No. 1, Denver, Colorado, 413 U.S. 189 (1973).

Keyes v. School Dist. No. 1 (Keyes XIII), 576 F. Supp 1503 (1983).

Keyes v. Congress of Hispanic Educators (Keyes XIX), 902 F. Supp. 1274 (1995).

Krashen, S., Rolstad, K., & MacSwan, J. (2007). *Review of "Research summary and bibliography for structured English immersion programs" of the Arizona English Language Learners Task Force*. Takoma Park, MD: Institute for Language and Education Policy. Retrieved from http://bale. wiki.educ.msu.edu/file/view/Krashen_Rolstad_MacSwan_review. pdf/37126027/Krashen_Rolstad_MacSwan_review.pdf

Lau v. Nichols, 414 U.S. 563 (1974).

Lee, J. S., & Suarez, D. (2009). A synthesis of the roles of heritage language in the lives of children of immigrants: What educators need to know. In T. G. Wiley, J. S. Lee & R. W. Rumberger (Eds.), *The education of language minority immigrants in the United States* (pp. 136–171). Tonawanda, NY: Multilingual Matters.

Library of Congress: Primary documents in American history (n.d.). Retrieved from http://www.loc.gov/rr/program/bib/ ourdocs/14thamendment.html#American

Losen, D. (2010). Challenging limitations: The growing potential for overturning restrictive language policies and ensuring equal educational opportunity. In P. Gandara & M. Hopkins (Eds.), *Forbidden languages: English learners and restrictive language policies* (pp. 195–215). New York: Teachers College Press.

Mahoney, K., Haladyna, T., & MacSwan, J. (2009). The need for multiple measures in reclassification decisions: A validity study of the Stanford English language proficiency test. In T. G. Wiley, J. S. Lee, & R. W. Rumberger (Eds.), *The education of language minority immigrants in the United States* (pp. 240–262). Tonawanda, NY: Multilingual Matters.

Mahoney, K., MacSwan, J., Haladyna, T., & Garcia, D. (2010). Castañeda's third prong: Evaluating the achievement of Arizona's English learners under restrictive language policy. In P. Gandara & M. Hopkins (Eds.), *Forbidden languages: English learners and restrictive language policies* (pp. 50–64). New York: Teachers College Press.

Massachusetts, Question 2: English Language Education in Public Schools (2002).

Mitchell, D., Destino, T., & Karam, R. (1997). *Evaluation of English language development programs in the Santa Ana Unified School District: A report on data system reliability and statistical modelling of program impacts*. University of California, Riverside: California Educational Research Cooperative. Retrieved from http://cerc.ucr.edu/publications

Navarro, R. A. (1990). The problems of language, education, and society: Who decides? In E. E. Garcia & R. V. Padilla (Eds.), *Advances in bilingual education research* (pp. 289–313). Tucson: University of Arizona Press.

Nguyen, D. T., & Stritikus, T. (2009). Assimilation and resistance: How language and culture influence gender identity negotiation in first-generation Vietnamese immigrant youth. In T. G. Wiley, J. S. Lee, & R. W. Rumberger (Eds.), *The education of language minority immigrants in the United States* (pp. 172–201). Tonawanda, NY: Multilingual Matters.

No Child Left Behind, Congressional Record, Volume 147 (2001).

Otero v. Mesa County School District No. 51, (408 F. Supp. 162 (1975).

Ovando, C. J., Combs, M. C., & Collier, V. P. (2006). *Bilingual and ESL classrooms: Teaching in multicultural contexts* (4th ed). Boston, MA: McGraw-Hill.

Roos, P. (1984, July). *Legal guidelines for bilingual administrators*. Austin, TX: Society of Research in Child Development.

Rumberger, R. W., & Tran, L. (2010). State language policies, school language practices, and the English learner achievement gap. In P. Gandara & M. Hopkins (Eds.), *Forbidden languages: English learners and restrictive language policies* (pp. 86–101). New York: Teachers College Press.

Skutnabb-Kangas, T. (2002). American ambiguities and paranoias. *International Journal of the Sociology of Language*, *155/156*, 179–186.

United Nations. (1948). *The convention on the prevention and punishment of the crime of genocide*. New York: Author.

United Nations. (1994) *Convention on the prevention and punishment of the crime of genocide*, e794. New York: Author.

U.S. Department of Education. (2004). *Press release: Secretary Paige announces new policies to help English language learners*. Washington, DC: Author.

U.S. Department of Education, Office of Elementary and Secondary Education. (2002a). *Outline of programs and selected changes in the No Child Left Behind Act of 2001*. Washington, DC: Author.

U.S. Department of Education, Office of Elementary and Secondary Education. (2002b). *Outline of programs and selected changes in the No Child Left Behind Act of 2001*. Washington, DC: Author.

U.S. Department of Education. (n.d.) *Executive summary of the No Child Left Behind Act of 2001*. Retrieved from http://www.ed.gov/nclb/ overview/intro/execsumm.html

U.S. Department of Education, Office of English Language Acquisition, Language Enhancement, and Academic Achievement for Limited English Proficient Students. (2003). *Non-regulatory guidance on the Title III state formula grant program*. Washington, DC: Author.

Valdes, G. (2009). Commentary: Language, immigration and the quality of education: Moving toward a broader conversation. In T. G. Wiley, J. S. Lee , & R. W. Rumberger (Eds.), *The education of language minority immigrants in the United States*. Tonawanda, NY: Multilingual Matters.

Wiese, A., & Garcia, E. E. (2001). The bilingual education act: Language minority students and US federal educational policy. *International Journal of Bilingual Education and Bilingualism*, *4*(4), 229–248.

Wiley, T. G., Lee, J. S. & Rumberger, R. W. (2009). *The education of language minority immigrants in the United States*. Buffalo, NY: Multilingual Matters.

23

Young Children's Understanding of Disabilities

Implications for Attitude Development and Inclusive Education

SeonYeong Yu and Michaelene M. Ostrosky
University of Illinois at Urbana-Champaign

In the world of early childhood special education, services are provided along two oftentimes separate service delivery and funding streams that are designed to meet the needs of (a) infants and toddlers (birth to 3) and (b) preschool age children (ages 3–5). Preschool special education services are mandated (hence, required to be provided by states) while infant/toddler services are discretionary (Taylor, McGowan, & Linder, 2009). Inclusion of young children with disabilities in classrooms with typically developing peers has become a primary service option in early childhood special education (Odom, 2000). Data reveal that approximately half of all preschoolers with disabilities receive special education services in programs that include typically developing peers (U. S. Department of Education, 2004). Theoretical, empirical, and ethical rationales emphasize that children with disabilities should have opportunities to interact with their typically developing peers (Hestenes & Carroll, 2000, p. 229).

As children with disabilities are enrolled in settings with their typically developing peers, one challenge that teachers face is to create a classroom community whereby typically developing children understand and accept students with disabilities as peers and friends (Greenbaum, Varas, & Markel, 1980). In the early days of inclusion, the expression of positive attitudes toward children with disabilities was considered to be an indicator of success (McHale & Simeonsson, 1980; Siperstein & Chatillon, 1982; Westervelt, Brantley, & Ware, 1983; Westervelt & McKinney, 1980). Researchers identified positive attitude development as a benefit that typically developing children obtained from participating in inclusive programs (Okagaki, Diamond, Kontos, & Hestenes, 1998; Peck, Carlson, & Helmstetter, 1992). During that time, much of the research on the benefits of placing children with and without disabilities in the same environments focused on identifying existing negative attitudes of typically developing children toward their peers with disabilities and then intervening in an attempt

to modify these attitudes (Salend & Moe, 1983). Early efforts focused on providing teachers with information about disabilities so they could help typically developing children understand and accept their peers with disabilities (Greenbaum et al., 1980; Salend & Moe, 1983). Developing and implementing such programs was advocated, and methods such as these have been suggested to improve students' attitudes toward their peers with disabilities (Siperstein & Chatillon, 1982; Westervelt et al., 1983).

Researchers (Okagaki et al., 1998; Peck et al., 1992) have pointed out that the majority of empirical work in special education has focused on the outcomes of children with disabilities as a result of enrollment in inclusive programs with little research focusing on the benefits that typically developing children achieve as a result of participation in inclusive programs. However, typically developing children may learn about and show greater acceptance toward individuals with disabilities as a result of their experiences in inclusive settings (Diamond & Hestenes, 1994; Diamond, Hestenes, Carpenter, & Innes, 1997; Voeltz, 1980). Thus, understanding children's attitudes toward their classmates with disabilities is an important variable to consider when evaluating the experiences of typically developing children in inclusive classrooms (Diamond & Hestenes, 1994). Understanding typically developing children's ideas about what it means to have a disability and children's decisions to include or exclude a child with a disability in activities is critical in understanding the social environment within an inclusive classroom (Diamond, Hong, & Tu, 2008).

Moreover, positive attitude development is critical as social relationships develop between children with and without disabilities. Establishing social relationships with peers is a major developmental task in early childhood (Guralnick, 2001); positive peer relationships are associated with successful school adjustment as well as long-term social adjustment (Bush, Ladd, & Herald, 2006; Bagwell, Schmidt, Newcomb, & Bukowski, 2001).

depends on disabity (handwritten)

According to Odom, Zercher, Li, Marquart, Sandall, and Brown (2006), researchers have shown that social engagement and acceptance by peers during the early years appears to be a facilitator of social competence, while early social rejection is a strong predictor of poor outcomes in adulthood. Thus, it is reasonable to expect that children's peer relationships are enhanced when children with disabilities are accepted by, and have multiple opportunities to interact with, their typically developing peers (Diamond et al., 2008).

To date, researchers have studied how typically developing children perceive their peers' disabilities, assessment tools and techniques that can be used to measure children's attitudes, and programs that positively impact children's attitude development. However, much of the research has focused on older children with limited information about attitude development for young children, especially preschoolers or kindergarteners (Favazza & Odom, 1997; Stoneman, 1993). In particular, there is little research focusing on intervention programs that facilitate the development of positive attitudes of typically developing young children toward their peers with disabilities. Therefore, the purpose of this chapter is to describe what is known about the attitude development of typically developing young children toward their peers with disabilities, and critically review the research in this area. Suggestions for research conclude the chapter.

Young Children's Attitude Development

How children come to understand and interact with one another has been conceptualized as the process of attitude formation. A conceptual scheme developed by Triandis (1971) included three components of attitude formation: cognitive, affective, and behavioral aspects. In the case of young children's attitude formation toward their peers with disabilities, the cognitive component includes knowledge about disabilities and beliefs about their causes and consequences. Children's experiences with peers with disabilities may influence their understanding and beliefs about a disability and what they believe their peers with disabilities are able to do (Diamond et al., 1997). The affective component refers to emotional reactions that occur in response to peers with disabilities. For example, children with disabilities may elicit feelings of fear, anxiety, or pity from their typically developing peers. The behavioral component of attitude formation refers to a predisposition to act in a certain manner. Typically developing children may treat their peers with disabilities as helpless, or may assume such roles as assisting and directing peers with disabilities. Triandis cautioned, however, that there is not always a direct relationship between attitudes and behavior; attitudes are related to behaviors in complex ways.

Related to the conceptual scheme provided by Triandis (1971), Stoneman (1993) noted that two questions have been influential in guiding research on young children's

attitudes about disabilities: "Do children notice the presence of disabilities in other children?" and "Do children prefer to be with typically developing peers, rather than peers with disabilities?" The first question emphasizes the cognitive component of Triandis's conceptual scheme; being aware of someone's disability is a cognitive prerequisite to forming attitudes toward the person with a disability. Research focusing on Stoneman's second question emphasizes how children behave and interact with peers with disabilities. These two components are discussed next.

Cognitive Aspect

Related to the cognitive aspect of Triandis's conceptual model of attitude formation (1971), researchers have studied young children's awareness of a disability, their thoughts about peers with disabilities, and their understanding about the skill level of peers with disabilities. In one of the early studies to investigate young children's recognition of disabilities, Conant and Budoff (1983), interviewed 21 preschoolers (mean age=3.4 years) about specific types of disabilities (e.g., blindness, deafness, orthopedic disabilities, intellectual disabilities, psychological disturbance). With regard to each disability, the children were asked if they knew anyone with the disability, if they had ever seen a person with the disability, and if they knew the cause of the disability. Results showed that preschoolers were aware of sensory and orthopedic disabilities. However, they had difficulty understanding intellectual disabilities and were not aware of them until approximately 6.9 years of age.

In the 1990s, Diamond and her colleagues extended this research with a series of studies. In 1993, Diamond conducted a semistructured interview study with 28 typically developing 4-year-old children to examine how they viewed their peers with disabilities. She asked children to look at pictures of their classmates and then to identify any classmate who (a) did not walk or run the way the other children did, (b) did not talk as well as the other children, and (c) did not behave the way the other children did. Results revealed that the photos of all children with physical disabilities (e.g., cerebral palsy) and children with intellectual disabilities (e.g., Down syndrome) were selected in response to questions about classmates who did not walk or talk like other children. However, none of the children with mild to moderate speech and language delays were identified as having a disability. Two-thirds of participating children responded to a question about *why* their peers with disabilities could not walk or talk like the other students in the class. The most common answers suggested age as a reason for the child's difficulty walking or talking (e.g., "She is a baby"; "When she gets bigger she can walk like everybody else"). Some of the children referred to specific equipment (e.g., walker, hearing aid) or classroom placement (i.e., "He is in the other classroom.") as a reason for limited language and motor abilities. Another category

(handwritten marginal note): empa... impair

of explanations was related to accidents or other traumas (i.e., "He broke his leg"; "He can't talk because he got hit in the mouth").

Based on these results, Diamond (1993) discussed how young children organize and structure their knowledge about disabilities to reflect their attempts to assimilate a new phenomenon (disability) into already existing cognitive structures such as age, immaturity, or accident. Studies such as this one set the stage in suggesting that the early childhood years are a prime time to intervene on children's attitudes about disabilities as many of the preschoolers in Diamond's study were beginning to recognize and think about disabilities.

In a subsequent study, Diamond and Hestenes (1994) investigated typically developing preschoolers' understanding of their peers' hearing loss. These researchers interviewed 24 preschoolers in an inclusive preschool at the beginning of the year and again 3 months later. Thirteen children (mean age=48.2 months) were enrolled in a class that included a child with severe hearing loss, and 11 children (mean age=44.5 months) were enrolled in a class that included two children with disabilities but without hearing loss. At the beginning of the year, the majority of children in both classes reported that children could speak even if they could not hear. But 3 months later, the children in the class that included a child with hearing loss were significantly more likely than the other 11 children to believe that hearing loss impacted a child's ability to speak. The comments from children in the class, which included a peer with a hearing loss, indicated that they were aware that their peer used special equipment and was not able to hear even though some children had misperceptions about the equipment (i.e., "He can't hear if he doesn't have his headphones on" and "He has that thing on—you know, earphones—he's got music on his neck so he can't hear"). These findings suggested that interactions and observations during the school day impacted children's understanding of their peer's disability.

In a third study, Diamond and Hestenes (1996) explored preschoolers' perceptions of different disabilities and children's understanding of the strengths and skills of children with different disabilities. The researchers interviewed 46 preschoolers using photographs of unfamiliar children. The majority of children (75%) commented on the physical disabilities represented in the photographs. Also, some children (41%) commented on a child's visual impairment while only a few children (11%) mentioned hearing impairment as they looked at the photographs. None of the children commented on the physical characteristics of children with Down syndrome that were represented in photographs. The children rated the photograph of a child with a physical disability as having lower motor skills than the photographs of typically developing children or children with visual impairments, hearing impairments, or Down syndrome. The child with a hearing loss who was represented in a photograph received lower competency ratings for language skills than

did (photographs of) children with other disabilities or the typically developing child.

To investigate kindergarteners' understanding about, and attitudes toward, children with disabilities, Dyson (2005) interviewed 77 typically developing children in inclusive kindergarten classrooms in Canada. The participating children were asked six questions related to people with disabilities. In response to a question about understanding disabilities (i.e., "Tell me everything you know about a person who has a disability or special need"), 25% of the children mentioned physical disabilities and 16% described people with disabilities as ones who needed assistance and equipment. When asked if disabilities are contagious, 78% of the children replied, "No." Most participants (88%) responded that they thought people with disabilities were different from themselves, citing differences in appearance and abilities. In addition, 83% of the children reported that they liked people with disabilities because of their personality (e.g., "They are nice") or skills (e.g., "I can help them"). Most participants (91%) reported that they were not afraid of people with disabilities and half of the children reported that they had a friend with a disability. This study showed that overall, typically developing kindergarteners had positive attitudes toward individuals with disabilities.

In summary, it is clear that during the early childhood years, children begin to recognize their peers' differing abilities, understand the varying competencies of their peers, and identify things that might be difficult for a hypothetical peer with a disability. Research shows that young children are aware of some disabilities such as physical disabilities, hearing impairments, and visual impairments. Findings surrounding children's attitudes toward peers with specific disabilities, such as intellectual disabilities, are mixed. Conant and Budoff (1983) and Diamond and Hestenes (1996), for example, reported that young children do not consistently notice intellectual disabilities. However, these two teams of researchers used photographs of unfamiliar children or asked broad questions (i.e., "Do you know anyone who has a disability?") to investigate young children's understanding about intellectual disabilities. In contrast, Diamond (1993) demonstrated that when preschoolers were shown photographs of their classmates, the majority of them were aware of their peers' intellectual disabilities. Clearly, young children's understandings about disabilities and their attitudes toward their peers with disabilities are influenced by interactions with, and observations of, children with disabilities. Diamond and Huang (2005) stated that children's attitudes toward peers with disabilities are impacted by personal experience. It appears that the early childhood years are an ideal time to facilitate children's attitude development toward peers with disabilities. For researchers and educators alike, understanding attitude development is a critical step in designing interventions that encourage positive attitudes (Diamond, 1993) and promote a community of acceptance. Such positive attitudes can impact interactions with others throughout the life span.

Affective and Behavioral Aspects

Research on the affective and behavioral aspects of attitude formation discussed by Triandis (1971) has been conducted in two ways: investigating young children's stated willingness to play with peers with disabilities and examining the relationships between children's stated acceptance of, and their actual interactions with, peers with disabilities. For example, Diamond and Hestenes (1996) investigated 46 preschoolers' willingness to be friends with hypothetical peers with disabilities. Results showed that although the majority of the preschoolers (ages 3–6) were aware of the disabilities represented in the photographs, their willingness to be friends did not appear to be influenced by the hypothetical children's disabilities. Specifically, 69% of study participants reported that they would be friends with a child in a photograph who had a hearing loss, 71% reported that they would be friends with a child with a physical disability, Down syndrome, or a visual impairment, and 77% indicated that they would be friends with a child in a photograph who did not appear to have a disability (i.e., a "typically developing child"). Okagaki et al. (1998) also reported no differences in children's willingness to play with children of varying abilities as their study participants indicated that they were equally willing to play with hypothetical children with and without disabilities.

In addition to children's affective responses, several researchers have examined the relationship between young children's stated acceptance of peers with disabilities and their actual interactions with peers with disabilities (Diamond, 2001; Hestenes & Carroll, 2000; Okagaki et al., 1998). Okagaki et al. (1998) measured 36 typically developing preschoolers' (mean age = 55.2 months) social play with classmates with and without disabilities, using a 2 second look and 15 second record sweep method. The children were enrolled in three inclusive classrooms; 50 observations were recorded for each child during free play. The observers coded whether the target child was engaged in play behaviors with a peer (including social play and parallel play) and whether the child was playing with a typically developing peer or a peer with a disability. The researchers also interviewed the children to assess their social acceptance of hypothetical children with and without disabilities and their willingness to play with the hypothetical children. Results showed that children who expressed more willingness to play with hypothetical children with disabilities were more likely to interact with classmates with disabilities during free play.

Diamond (2001) also examined the relationships between children's ideas, emotional understanding, and social contact with classmates with disabilities by observing 45 typically developing preschoolers (mean age = 52.4 months) during free play. Children were observed during 10-minute intervals for no more than 3 hours each week over a 6-week period. Social contact was defined as verbal or physical exchanges or sustained visual regard, which indicated that the participants were aware of, and responsive to, each other. Diamond also interviewed participating children to assess their acceptance of hypothetical peers with disabilities and their emotional sensitivity to certain social situations. Results showed that children who interacted socially with classmates were more sensitive to the display of emotions and were more accepting of individuals with disabilities than were children who were observed playing only with typically developing peers.

Additionally, Hestenes and Carroll (2000) observed 29 typically developing preschoolers (mean age = 55.2 months) using a scan sampling technique. They selected one area of the classroom or playground to begin each observational session and then proceeded in a clockwise direction until the map was completed. During free play, observers watched each area (that contained at least one child) for 10 seconds and recorded the following information: children who were present, their level of play (e.g., solitary, cooperative), and whether or not a teacher was present. At least 43 observations were gathered on each child. The researchers also interviewed all children to assess their understanding of hypothetical children with disabilities and the children completed sociometric ratings on their classmates. Results revealed a relationship between children's preference to play with classmates with disabilities and their understanding of disabilities. Reporting contradictory results to previous research, Hestenes and Carroll found that neither understanding of disability nor playmate preference were related to children's social play in the classroom and on the playground. These researchers discussed the possible reasons for the inconsistent results from previous studies (i.e., Diamond 2001; Okagaki et al., 1998). One possible reason for the conflicting finding was that Hestenes and Carroll did not include parallel play as an observational category while Okagaki and colleagues merged parallel and social play. In addition, one of the two classrooms observed by Hestenes and Carroll only included children with disabilities during free play (about 3 hours per day) while Diamond (2001) and Okagaki et al. (1998) conducted their studies in inclusive classrooms.

With a focus on the behavioral aspects of attitude development, the majority of children in the studies just reviewed expressed a willingness to be friends with hypothetical children with disabilities (Diamond & Hestenes, 1996; Okagaki et al., 1998). Nonetheless, findings surrounding the relationships between children's attitudes and their actual behaviors toward peers with disabilities are mixed. Two research studies (Diamond, 2001; Okagaki et al., 1998) revealed that preschoolers who were more accepting of hypothetical peers with disabilities were more likely to play with their classmates with disabilities, while Hestenes and Carroll (2000) suggested that neither children's understanding of disability nor playmate preference was related to children's social play with their classmates with disabilities. However, noteworthy is the fact that there has been limited research on behavioral aspects of young children's attitudes toward peers with disabilities. In addition, Diamond's 2001 study is the only investigation that included an affective aspect (e.g., emotional sensitivity to social situations).

Theories of attitude development suggest that cognitive, affective, and behavioral characteristics interact in the development of attitudes toward individuals with disabilities (Stoneman, 1993; Triandis, 1971). However, attitudes can be formed as a result of one of these three processes alone (Diamond, 2001). Future research should include more emphasis on behavioral and affective aspects of attitude formation and an examination of how the three aspects (i.e., cognitive, affective, behavioral) are related to each other. The early childhood years are an important time period for studying the relationship between individual, familial, and environmental influences on children's cognitive, affective, and behavioral characteristics. Additional research should examine how these variables, alone or in combination, contribute to the development of positive attitudes toward individuals with disabilities.

Factors that Influence Attitude Development

An important topic in the area of attitude research is factors that influence the attitude development of typically developing young children toward their peers with disabilities. As inclusive education becomes more common practice, these factors should be studied with a critical eye toward identifying variables that are most likely to positively impact children's attitudes. Influential factors noted in the literature, and discussed next, include child characteristics such as gender, age, and disability as well as experiences that children have had in their home, school, or community environments.

Child Characteristics

Some research has shown that relationships exist between child characteristics (gender, age, and disability) and attitudes toward individuals with disabilities. In a study by Diamond and Hestenes (1996), when 35 preschoolers (age 3–6) were asked to respond to the question, "Could you be friends with her?" (a girl with a disability in each of five photographs), girls were significantly more likely than boys to respond that they could be friends with the girl with a disability in the photographs. This finding might support the idea that preschoolers prefer same-sex peers as playmates (Diamond, Le Furgy, & Blass, 1992; Maccoby, 1988). However, Diamond and Hestenes analyzed other dimensions (i.e., disability, age) that might influence playmate preference, and their results revealed that 50% of the child participants used gender as the salient dimension in sorting photographs, while 27% of their participants used disability, and 23% relied on age. Also, the majority of study participants responded that they could be friends with children with different disabilities (e.g., hearing loss, physical disabilities, Down syndrome, visual impairment).

These results show that young children do not automatically assume that a child whom they think has a disability should be avoided.

Diamond, Hong, and Tu (2008) also examined associations between age, gender, and children's decisions to include a peer with a physical disability in play. This research team found significant gender differences with girls (compared to boys) more likely to choose a child with a disability as a play partner. Age, however was not related to children's (mean age of participants = 52.9 months) choice of a play partner with a disability.

In a study by Tamm and Prellwitz (2001) in Sweden, results revealed that age influenced children's understanding of the cause of a disability. These researchers interviewed 48 children across three age groups (preschoolers, 8-year-olds, 10-year-olds). When children were asked "Why is this child sitting in a wheelchair?," 50% of the preschoolers suggested that the physical disability was a temporary condition resulting from an accident (e.g., broken leg) and 19% mentioned acquired, permanent disabilities (accidents leading to permanent disability). However, in the group of 10-year-olds, 12.5% of the children mentioned disabilities being temporary while 56.5% stated that the disabilities were acquired, permanent conditions. The researchers concluded that older children had a deeper understanding of the permanency of a disability.

Nowicki (2006) conducted a multivariate analysis of children's attitudes toward peers with disabilities in Canada. One hundred children between the ages of 4 and 10 participated in the study. Results showed that girls had more positive attitudes toward hypothetical peers with disabilities and younger children's attitudes were less positive than those of older children. Most of the participating children also preferred to play with hypothetical peers without disabilities or with physical disabilities over peers with intellectual disabilities.

When considering the impact of specific disabilities on children's attitudes, some researchers have reported that preschoolers with disabilities receive significantly lower sociometric ratings than their typically developing peers (Diamond et al., 1992; Odom et al., 2006). Also, Odom and his colleagues found that in a group of 80 children with disabilities (mean age = 3.9 years), approximately 28% were "well accepted" by peers in inclusive preschool classrooms. Among the participating children with disabilities, none of the children with autism-pervasive developmental delay, social-emotional, behavioral, or attention-deficit disorder were in the accepted group and relatively few children with speech delays or orthopedic impairments were in the rejected group.

In summary, several research studies have shown that girls have more positive attitudes than boys toward peers with disabilities. Results surrounding age are mixed with some research suggesting that age is not significantly related to children's choice of a play partner with a disability but that it may influence their attitudes or understanding about the cause of a disability. While preschoolers appear more aware of physical disabilities, visual impairments, and hearing impairments, the majority of children who participated in the above mentioned studies reported that they could be friends with peers who had different disabilities (e.g., physical disability, intellectual disability, visual or hearing impairment). However, two research studies (Nowicki, 2006; Odom et al., 2006) showed that children preferred to play with peers without disabilities or with physical disabilities compared to peers with intellectual disabilities, autism, or emotional or behavioral disorders. Children's attitudes appear to be associated with several factors such as gender, age, and type of disability yet these are complex associations. Thus, future research should investigate how type and severity of disability impact young children's understanding and acceptance of peers with disabilities.

Family Characteristics

Parents play an important role in their children's ideas about, and interactions with, peers (Diamond & Huang, 2005; Guralnick, 1999; Stoneman, 1993). For example, parents often decide when and under what circumstances their young children interact with other children. They also may directly influence children's peer relationships by modeling or teaching specific social skills (Finnie & Russell, 1988; MacDonald & Parke, 1984; McCollum & Ostrosky, 2008; Mize & Pettit, 1997). Additionally, children's ideas and attitudes about people with disabilities are influenced by the significant adults in their lives, especially caregivers and teachers (Innes & Diamond, 1999; Triandis, 1971). For example, the way parents answer their children's questions about people with disabilities is an important mechanism for transferring knowledge and values from parents to children (Stoneman, 1993).

Okagaki and her colleagues (1998) interviewed parents of 36 typically developing preschoolers (mean age = 55.2 months) to measure the parents' beliefs about socialization using separate mother and father questionnaires. Parents indicated what they would do if they were confronted with specific situations (i.e., A parent and a child are at a playground and a child with a physical disability is unable to join in the play with other children. The parent can either ask his or her child to do something with the child with disability, do nothing, or interact with the child with the disability by him- or herself.) The parents also completed a scale that focused on the ages they would teach their children each of six prosocial behaviors. Results showed that parents who were more likely to report that they would model involvement with children with disabilities had children who spent more time interacting with classmates with disabilities. Additionally, parents' expectations for their children's prosocial behaviors were positively related to their children's social play with peers with disabilities.

In another study on parental influence, Innes and Diamond (1999) examined the ways in which 40 mothers spoke with their preschoolers (mean age=56 months) about physical disabilities and Down syndrome, and the relationship between the mothers' comments, their children's ideas about disabilities, and children's interactions with classmates with disabilities. Results showed that the mothers and their children talked more about children with physical disabilities than about children with Down syndrome during a storytelling task. Also, the children who more frequently commented to their mothers about a child with a physical disability received higher scores on teachers' ratings of children's social interactions with classmates with disabilities. However, contrary to the researchers' expectations, mothers who made fewer comments about children with disabilities had children who received higher scores from teachers on ratings of social interactions with classmates with disabilities. One possible explanation for this last finding was that all participating children were enrolled in inclusive preschool programs therefore the parents and children had more opportunities to talk with each other about classmates with disabilities before they participated in the study. Thus, the conversations between mothers and their children during the study might have been reflective of earlier conversations. Another explanation provided by the authors was that mothers who encouraged their children to comment during the storytelling task might have provided more opportunities for their children to form their own ideas.

These limited studies on parental influence suggest that it is important to examine how adults talk with their children about people with disabilities. Bricker (1995) pointed out that positive attitudes toward peers with disabilities could be fostered and altered because children develop attitudes about people and events from their primary caregivers. Thus, parents and teachers need to be aware of the potential impact their words and behaviors have on the developing attitudes of young children (Innes & Diamond, 1999). The attitudes of the significant adults in a child's life can greatly impact his or her attitudes toward peers with disabilities.

School Characteristics

As described above, young children's ideas and attitudes are influenced by the values that important adults in their lives (e.g., parents and teachers) hold about experiences such as inclusion (Bricker, 1995). Lieber et al. (1998) suggested that teachers impact children's beliefs about inclusion in part by answering children's questions and by teaching them about individual differences, including disabilities. Teachers also manipulate classroom environments to provide children with exposure to various activities, model appropriate interactions, and facilitate peer interactions between children with and without disabilities (Guralnick, 2010; Hestenes & Carroll, 2000). Teachers also share their values and attitudes with their students through the content and affective tone of their responses, as well as the information they share about individuals with disabilities (Diamond & Huang, 2005; Innes & Diamond, 1999). Several researchers have suggested that a relationship exists between teachers' and students' attitudes toward individuals with disabilities (c.f., Goodman, 1990; Roberts & Lindsell, 1997).

Young children's ideas and attitudes about people with disabilities also are influenced by their overall school experiences (Innes & Diamond, 1999). One possible outcome of inclusive school experiences during the early childhood years is the acceptance of individuals with disabilities by typically developing children (Favazza & Odom, 1996). If typically developing children's experiences in inclusive classrooms are positive, those experiences will support the development of positive attitudes toward individuals with disabilities, both during preschool and in later years (Diamond, 2001). For example, Diamond and her colleagues (1997) found that children between the ages of 3 and 6 in inclusive classrooms gave higher social acceptance ratings for dolls with disabilities than did children from classes that did not include students with disabilities. Likewise, in a much earlier study Voeltz (1980) found that contact with schoolmates with severe disabilities was associated with more positive responses on her Acceptance Scale by children in second though seventh grade.

Diamond and Hestenes (1994) also showed that participation in inclusive classrooms helped children better understand disabilities. These researchers suggested that school experiences with a peer with a hearing impairment influenced typically developing preschoolers' understanding of hearing and hearing loss. In this study, children (mean age = 48.2 months) who had a deaf classmate were more likely to understand sign language than children without such a classroom experience. Also, the majority of children who had a deaf classmate understood the relationship between hearing and speaking.

In summary, certain child characteristics (e.g., gender, age, disability), family characteristics (beliefs about interacting with individuals with disabilities), and experiences across environments (e.g., home, school) have the potential to influence children's attitudes toward their peers with disabilities. However, what is missing from the empirical literature is a strong focus on strategies that parents and teachers can use to support children's positive attitude development toward peers with disabilities. Also, more research is needed to better understand how child, family, and school characteristics are related (Diamond & Huang, 2005; Hestenes & Carroll, 2000) in producing positive attitudes.

Intervention Programs to Support Positive Attitude Development

Participation in inclusive classrooms can provide many opportunities for young children to interact with peers with disabilities. However, simply being present in the same setting does not necessarily result in positive attitudes toward peers with disabilities. Including children with disabilities in inclusive classrooms is unlikely to spontaneously enhance interactions between children with and without disabilities

(Diamond & Tu, 2009). Numerous research studies have shown that children are more likely to play with typically developing peers than with peers with disabilities (Brown, Odom, Li, & Zercher, 1999; Diamond et al., 1992; Guralnick, Connor, Hammond, Gottman, & Kinnish, 1995; Odom et al., 2006). Thus, supporting social interactions by children with disabilities should be a goal of inclusion (Odom, 2002) and teachers need to help young children understand and accept peers with disabilities.

While intervention programs aimed at positive attitude development toward peers with disabilities are scarce, Cooper (2003) implemented two different interventions to promote preschoolers' understanding of, and positive attitudes toward peers, with physical disabilities. Fifty-five preschoolers (mean age = 52.7 months) were randomly assigned to one of two intervention groups or to a nonintervention group, during a 4-day period. One of the intervention programs provided participating children with opportunities to use a wheelchair to get around the school and then discuss their experiences using a wheelchair with classmates. The other intervention used children's books and videotapes to teach children about people with physical disabilities. Results showed that both intervention programs had significant effects on children's understanding of physical disabilities and on children's attitudes toward people with physical disabilities compared to children in the nonintervention group.

To promote kindergarteners' attitudes toward peers with disabilities, Favazza and Odom (1997) implemented an intervention package consisting of three components: indirect experiences (story time and class discussion about children with disabilities); direct experiences (structured cooperative play in a small group that included children with disabilities); and the child's primary social group (a home reading component using a book about children with disabilities). Forty-six typically developing kindergarteners participated in this study with 16 of the children assigned to a no-contact group. Fifteen children were assigned to a low-contact group during which the students saw children with disabilities in their schools, but they did not participate in any intervention. The other 15 students were randomly assigned to a high-contact group that included a 9-week intervention. Significantly positive differences in mean gains on the Acceptance Scale for Kindergartners (ASK-R; Favazza & Odom, 1996) from pretest to posttest were found for children in the high-contact group compared to children in the low-contact group and the no-contact group. These findings suggest that attitudes of young children can be altered by providing information about children with disabilities and by arranging social experiences between classmates with and without disabilities.

Similarly, Piercy and her colleagues (Piercy, Wilton, & Townsend, 2002) examined the effectiveness of cooperative-learning activities on young children's attitudes toward peers with disabilities in New Zealand. Forty-five typically developing children (ages 6 to 8) participated in one of two experimental groups (a cooperative-learning program or a social-contact program), or a control group (no program) for 10 weeks. Each group had 15 typically developing children. Children in both experimental groups participated in a 40-minute session with their peers with disabilities twice a week in the special education classroom where six boys with intellectual disabilities were served. In each cooperative-learning session, typically developing children worked in small groups of three to four children, including one child with intellectual disabilities. Cooperative learning activities included cutting and pasting magazine pictures for group posters, drawing or painting group murals, and producing short plays or mimes. Children in the social-contact group participated in activities that were similar to the cooperative-learning group, but they worked alongside the children with disabilities with no attempt made to incorporate cooperative learning strategies (e.g., working together, sharing things, helping each other). Results revealed that typically developing children in the cooperative-learning groups demonstrated significant increases in their acceptance of children with disabilities. The children with disabilities also showed increases in social interactions with typically developing peers in the cooperative-learning groups.

Surprisingly, compared to other aspects within the area of attitude research (i.e., children's attitudes toward peers with disabilities, measuring attitude development, influential factors), there are very few examples of intervention programs designed to promote young children's positive attitudes toward their peers with disabilities. Future research should focus on intervention programs that promote positive attitudes of young children.

Implications for Research and Practice

Many young children with disabilities spend large portions of each day in inclusive settings as they and their typically developing peers increasingly attend early childhood programs together as classmates. With the rise in the number of inclusive classrooms, the development of positive attitudes toward peers with disabilities has been considered an indicator of successful inclusion (McHale & Simeonsson, 1980; Westervelt & McKinney, 1980), a benefit that typically developing children can obtain from participating in inclusive classrooms (Diamond & Hestenes, 1994; Favazza & Odom, 1996; Okagaki et al., 1998), and a foundation from which to foster positive peer relationships between children with and without disabilities (Diamond et al., 2008).

Indeed, research has shown that typically developing children in inclusive preschool classrooms tend to have positive attitudes toward peers with disabilities (Diamond & Hestenes, 1996; Dyson, 2005; Okagaki et al., 1998; Tamm & Prellwitz, 2001). However, a number of studies have shown that in some inclusive classrooms children are more likely to play with typically developing peers than with peers with disabilities, and children with disabilities are less accepted by their peers compared to typically developing children (Diamond et al., 1992; Guralnick et al., 1995; Hestenes & Carroll, 2001; Odom et al., 2006). Research shows that preschoolers in inclusive classrooms are more likely to choose a typically developing peer rather than a child with disability as a play partner (Diamond et al., 2008). Diamond and Huang (2005) pointed out that such differences in children's peer interactions might depend on a child's disability (e.g., difficulties interacting with others) as well as on typically developing children's attitudes toward classmates with disabilities.

Based on these conflicting findings, researchers have emphasized that simply placing children with disabilities in inclusive classrooms is unlikely to result in enhanced interactions between children with and without disabilities (Diamond & Tu, 2009; Favazza, Phillipsen, & Kumaret, 2000). Inclusion alone is not sufficient to promote positive attitudes toward peers with disabilities. Thus, in an effort to support young children's positive attitudes toward peers with disabilities, researchers have examined the relationship between children's attitudes, child characteristics, and environment characteristics. Researchers also have investigated interventions designed to promote positive attitude development. However, most of the research has focused on older elementary age children (Favazza & Odom, 1996; Piercy et al., 2002). This has resulted in limited information on promoting young children's positive attitude development. Additional research on attitude interventions is needed, especially studies focusing on young children.

Given this need for research on attitude development, an important step is to identify high quality practices that are supported by (a) research, (b) experiences and values of stakeholders such as parents and practitioners, and (c) field validation (Smith, McLean, Sandall, Snyder, & Ramsey, 2007). In early childhood special education, as in other areas of education, the use of scientifically based or evidence-based practices (EBP) has taken center stage in the discussion of "high-quality" schooling. The focus on EBPs emerged from the medical field, with an emphasis on the importance of considering the research behind intervention strategies and instructional practices. The leading professional organization in early childhood special education, the Division for Early Childhood of the Council for Exceptional Children (DEC), has published *Recommended Practices: A Comprehensive Guide* (Sandall, Hemmeter, Smith, & McLean, 2007) to help professionals learn about research-based practices and strategies that lead to high quality services for young children with special needs.

Evidence-based practices that support positive attitude development can be used as a class-wide intervention in a response to intervention (RTI) framework. Although the application of RTI in early childhood special education is an emerging practice, RTI provides prevention and intervention approaches within an organized decision-making framework (Snyder, Wixson, Talapatra, & Roach, 2008). Moreover, the leading international organizations in early childhood education (National Association for the Education of Young Children [NAEYC]) and early childhood special education (DEC) have recommended practices highlighting social interaction as a critical component of early childhood practices (Bredekamp & Copple, 1997; Sandall et al., 2007). Such practices include the need to create environments that foster positive relationships among peers (Sandall et al., 2007). Research has shown that high quality physical and social environments impact children's development. In most states, early learning standards include social-emotional competencies (Scott-Little, Kagan, & Frelow, 2006), with most of the social emotional standards focusing on developing relationships and emotions, and interacting with adults and peers. These standards remind professionals that while our national policy agenda focuses on academic achievement, social and emotional development are important outcomes for society's youngest members. Research studies have shown that children who are well-liked in preschool remain well-liked as they grow, and those who are rejected by peers in preschool continue to be excluded when they are older (Denham & Holt, 1993). Thus, social behavior is relatively stable from preschool through the early elementary grades. Creating classroom environments (physical and social contexts) where children feel a part of the "community" is important. Children can feel connected as teachers read books that focus on social relationships and friendships, use guidance and problem solving strategies to address peer-related conflicts, and arrange cooperative learning activities to facilitate interaction (Kemple, 2004). Therefore, identifying and implementing class-wide practices for attitude development can help children acquire positive attitudes toward their peers with disabilities. Yet, administrators are challenged to provide teachers with the time, tools (i.e., coaching and mentoring in using a practice correctly), and resources (i.e., access to professional journals, involvement in research projects) necessary for them to gain the knowledge and skills needed to implement the evidence-based practices with fidelity.

Thus, research has shown that the early childhood years are a time when children begin to form attitudes about others; however, these attitudes are still malleable. During this time period adults can intervene in ways that assist children in seeing similarities between themselves and their peers, encourage discussions about similarities and differences, and support children in interacting with one another to foster relationships between children with and without disabilities in inclusive classrooms. The successful implementation of such intervention programs requires support from administrators, teachers, and parents (Favazza et al., 2000) so all stakeholders are aware of their contributions to children's attitude development.

Acknowledgment

This manuscript was made possible by grant number R324A080071 from the Institute of Educational Sciences, U.S. Department of Education. The contents are solely the responsibility of the authors and do not represent the official views or policies of the funding agenciy, nor does publication in any way constitute an endorsement by the funding agency.

References

Bagwell, C. L., Schimidt, M. E., Newcomb, A. F., & Bukowski, W. M. (2001, Spring). Friendship and peer rejection as predictors of adult adjustment. *New Directions for Child and Adolescent Development, 91*, 25–49.

Bredekamp, S., & Copple, C. (1997). *Developmentally appropriate practices in early childhood programs* (rev. ed.). Washington, DC: National Association for the Education of Young Children.

Bricker, D. D. (1995). The challenge of inclusion. *Journal of Early Intervention, 19*, 179–194.

Brown, W. H., Odom, S. L., Li, S., & Zercher, C. (1999). Ecobehavioral assessment in early childhood programs: A portrait of preschool inclusion. *Journal of Special Education, 33*, 138–153.

Bush, E. S., Ladd, G. W., & Herald, S. L. (2006). Peer exclusion and victimization: Processes that medicate the relation between peer group rejection and children's classroom engagement and achievement. *Journal of Education Psychology, 98*, 1–13.

Conant, S., & Budoff, M. (1983). Patterns of awareness in children's understanding of disabilities. *Mental Retardation, 21*, 119–125.

Cooper, D. G. (2003). *Promoting disability awareness in preschool* (Unpublished doctoral dissertation). Purdue University, West Lafayette, IN.

Denham, S. A., & Holt, R. W. (1993). Preschoolers' likability as cause or consequence of their social behavior. *Developmental Psychology, 29*, 271–275.

Diamond, K. E. (1993). Preschool children's concepts of disability in their peers. *Early Education and Development, 4*, 123–129.

Diamond, K. E. (2001). Relationships among young children's ideas, emotional understanding, and social contact with classmates with disabilities. *Topics in Early Childhood Special Education, 21*, 104–1113.

Diamond, K. E., & Hestenes, L. L. (1994). Preschool children's understanding of disability: Experiences leading to the elaboration of the concept of hearing loss. *Early Education and Development, 5*, 301–309.

Diamond, K. E., & Hestenes, L. L. (1996). Preschool children's conceptions of disabilities: The salience of disabilities in children's ideas about others. *Topics in Early Childhood Special Education, 16*, 458–471.

Diamond, K. E., Hestenes, L. L., Carpenter, E. S., & Innes, F. K. (1997). Relationships between enrollment in an inclusive class and preschool children's ideas about people with disabilities. *Topics in Early Childhood Special Education, 17*, 520–537.

Diamond, K. E., Hong, S., & Tu, H. (2008). Context influences preschool children's decisions to include a peer with a physical disability in play. *Exceptionality, 16*, 141–155.

Diamond, K. E., & Huang, H. (2005). Preschoolers' ideas about disabilities. *Infants and Young Children, 18*, 37–46.

Diamond, K. E., Le Furgy, W., & Blass, S. (1992). Attitudes of preschool children toward their peers with disabilities: A year-long intervention in integrated classrooms. *The Journal of Genetic Psychology, 152*, 215–221.

Diamond, K. E., & Tu, H. (2009). Relations between classroom context, physical disability and preschool children's inclusion decisions. *Journal of Applied Development Psychology, 30*, 75–81.

Dyson, L. L. (2005). Kindergarten children's understanding of and attitudes toward people with disabilities. *Topics in Early Childhood Special Education, 25*, 95–105.

Favazza, P. C., & Odom, S. L. (1996). Use of the acceptance scale to measure attitudes of kindergarten-age children. *Journal of Early Intervention, 20*, 232–249.

Favazza, P. C., & Odom, S. L. (1997). Promoting positive attitudes of kindergarten-age children toward people with disabilities. *Exceptional Children, 63*, 405–418.

Favazza, P. C., Phillipsen, L., & Kumar, P. (2000). Measuring and promoting acceptance of young children with disabilities. *Exceptional Children, 66,* 491–508.

Finnie, V., & Russell, A. (1988). Preschool children's social status and their mothers' behavior and knowledge in the supervisory role. *Developmental Psychology, 24,* 789–801.

Goodman, J. F. (1990). Variations in children's conceptualizations of mental retardation as a function of inquiry methods. *Journal of Child Psychology and Psychiatry, 31,* 935–948.

Greenbaum, J., Varas, M., & Markel, G. (1980). Using books about handicapped children. *The Reading Teacher, 33,* 416–419.

Guralnick, M. J. (1999). Family and child influences on the peer-related social competence of young children with developmental delays. *Mental Retardation and Developmental Disabilities, 5,* 21–29.

Guralnick, M. J. (2001). Social competence with peers and early childhood inclusion: Need for alternative approaches. In M. J. Guralnick (Ed.), *Early childhood inclusion: Focus on change* (pp. 481–502). Baltimore, MD: Brookes.

Guralnick, M. J. (2010). Early intervention approaches to enhance the peer-related social competence of young children with developmental delays. *Infants and Young Children, 23,* 73–83.

Guralnick, M. J., Connor, R. T., Hammond, M., Gottman, J. M., & Kinnish, K. (1995). Immediate effects of mainstreamed settings on the social interactions and social integration of preschool children. *American Journal on Mental Retardation, 100,* 359–377.

Hestenes, L. L., & Carroll, D. E. (2000). The play interactions of young children with and without disabilities: Individual and environmental influences. *Early Childhood Research Quarterly, 15,* 229–246.

Innes, F. K., & Diamond, K. E. (1999). Typically developing children's interactions with peers with disabilities: Relationships between mothers' comments and children's ideas about disabilities. *Topics in Early Childhood Special Education, 19,* 103–111.

Kemple, K. M. (2004). *Let's be friends: Peer competence and social inclusion in early childhood programs.* New York: Teachers College Press.

Lieber, J., Capell, K., Sandall, S. R., Wolfberg, P., Horn, E., & Beckman, P. (1998). Inclusive preschool programs: Teachers' beliefs and practice. *Early Childhood Research Quarterly, 13,* 87–106.

Maccoby, E. E. (1988). Gender as a social category. *Developmental Psychology, 55,* 755–765.

MacDonald, K., & Parke, R. D. (1984). Bridging the gap: Parent–child play interaction and peer interactive competence. *Child Development, 55,* 1265–1277.

McCollum, J. A., & Ostrosky, M. M. (2008). Family roles in young children's emerging peer-related social competence. In W. Brown, S. L. Odom, & S. R. McConnell (Eds.), *Social competence of young children* (pp. 31–60). Baltimore, MD: Brookes.

McHale, S. M., & Simeonsson, R. (1980). Effects of interaction on nonhandicaped children's attitudes toward autistic children. *American Journal of Mental Deficiency, 85,* 18–25.

Mize, J., & Pettit, G. S. (1997). Mothers' social coaching, mother–child relationship style, and children's peer competence: Is the medium the message? *Child Development, 68,* 312–332.

Nowicki, E. A. (2006). A cross-sectional multivariate analysis of children's attitudes towards disabilities. *Journal of Intellectual Disability Research, 50,* 335–348.

Odom, S. L. (2000). Preschool inclusion: What we know and where we go from here. *Topics in Early Childhood Special Education, 20*(1), 20–27.

Odom, S. L. (2002). Narrowing the question: Social integration and characteristics of children with disabilities in inclusive settings. *Early Childhood Research Quarterly, 17,* 167–170.

Odom, S. L., Zercher, C., Li, S., Marquart, J. M., Sandall, S., & Brown, W. H. (2006). Social acceptance and rejection of preschool children with disabilities: A mixed-method analysis. *Journal of Educational Psychology, 98,* 807–823.

Okagaki, L., Diamond, K. E., Kontos, S. J., & Hestenes, L. L. (1998). Correlates of young children's interactions with classmates with disabilities. *Early Childhood Research Quarterly, 13,* 67–86.

Peck, C. A., Carlson, P., & Helmstetter, E. (1992). Parent and teacher perceptions of outcomes for typically developing children enrolled in integrated early childhood programs: A statewide survey. *Journal of Early Intervention, 16,* 53–63.

Piercy, M., Wilton, K., & Townsend, M. (2002). Promoting the social acceptance of young children with moderate-severe intellectual disabilities using cooperative-learning techniques. *American Journal on Mental Retardation, 107,* 352–360.

Roberts, C. M., & Lindsell, J. S. (1997). Children's attitudes and behavioral intentions towards peers with disabilities. *International Journal of Disability, Development and Education, 44,* 133–145.

Salend, S. J., & Moe, L. (1983). Modifying nonhandicapped students' attitudes toward their handicapped peers through children's literature. *Journal for Special Educators, 19,* 22–28.

Sandall, S., Hemmeter, M. L., Smith, B. J., & McLean, M. E. (2007). *DEC recommended practices: A comprehensive guide for practical application.* Longmont, CO: Sopris West.

Scott-Little, C., Kagan, S. L., & Frelow, V. S. (2003). Creating the conditions for success with early learning standards: Results from a national study of state-level standards for children's learning prior to kindergarten. *Early Childhood Research and Practice, 5*(2). Retrieved from http://ecrp.uiuc.edu/v5n2/little.html

Siperstein, G. N., & Chatillon, A. C. (1982). Importance of perceived similarity in improving children's attitudes toward mentally retarded peers. *American Journal of Mental Deficiency, 86,* 453–458.

Smith, B., J., McLean, M. E., Sandall, S., Snyder, P., & Ramsey, A. B. (2007). DEC recommended practices: The procedures and evidence based used to establish them. In S. Sandall, M. L. Hemmeter, B. J. Smith, & M. E. McLean (Eds.), *DEC recommended practices: A comprehensive guide for practical application* (pp. 27–39). Longmont, CO: Sopris West.

Snyder, P. A., Wixson, C. S., Talapatra, D., & Roach, A. T. (2008). Assessment in early childhood: Instruction-focused strategies to support Response-to-Intervention frameworks. *Assessment for Effective Intervention, 34,* 25–34.

Stoneman, Y. (1993). The effects of attitude on preschool integration. In C. A. Peck, S. L. Odom, & D. D. Bricker (Eds.), *Integrating young children with disabilities into community programs.* Baltimore, MD: Brookes.

Tamm, M., & Prellwitz, M. (2001). "If I had a friend in a wheelchair": Children's thoughts on disabilities. *Child: Care, Health and Development, 27,* 223–240.

Taylor, J. M., McGowan, J., & Linder, T. (2009). *The program administrator's guide to early childhood special education.* Baltimore, MD: Brookes.

Triandis, H. (1971). *Attitudes and attitude change.* New York: Wiley.

U.S. Department of Education (2004). *Twenty-sixth annual report to Congress on the implementation of the Individuals with Disabilities Education Act.* Washington DC: Author. Retrieved from http://www.ed.gov/about/reports/annual/osep/2004/index.htm

Voeltz, L. M. (1980). Children's attitudes toward handicapped peers. *American Journal of Mental Deficiency, 84,* 455–464.

Westervelt, V. D., Brantley, J., & Ware, W. (1983). Changing children's attitudes toward physically handicapped peers: Effects of a film and teacher-led discussion. *Journal of Pediatric Psychology, 8,* 327–343.

Westervelt, V. D., & McKinney, J. D. (1980). Effects of a film on nonhandicapped children's attitudes toward handicapped children. *Exceptional Children, 46,* 294–296.

24

Child Care for Young Children

Kay Sanders
Whittier College

Carollee Howes
UCLA

This chapter marks the third edition of *Child Care for Young Children*. In the 2006 version, we organized the review around the major developments in the field since the first writing of this chapter on the state of child care research in the 1980s. Our central question with the 2006 version was *what has changed and what has stayed the same* since the first writing of this chapter? We found that a great deal had changed with the inclusion of ethnic and site diversity in research designs, and longitudinal or multisite studies beginning to be employed. However, important findings remained such as the importance of teacher–child relationships in the development and learning of children within child care contexts.

Today, early childhood is part of the national discourse. Research documenting the advances in neuroscience and the importance of the early years are advertised on television, reviewed by the popular press, and debated at informal gatherings. Major developments in policy initiatives also reflect the increased awareness of the importance of the early years. Quality Rating and Improvement Systems (QRIS) efforts are occurring across the United States. The concept of universal preschool is a national-level discussion with a few states actually creating such systems (Zigler, Gilliam, & Jones, 2006).

By these accounts, one would assume that child care support has arrived. Despite common knowledge regarding the importance of early experiences, child care in the United States is still highly variable in quality and quantity; with the ones who need it the most the least likely to receive it (Pianta et al., 2005). The dearth between the availability of high-quality care and the need for it will grow rather than diminish due to increases in immigration and population estimates for increasing numbers of children under 5 years of age (U.S. Census Bureau, 2009).

This edition will continue to ask what has changed and what has stayed the same in the field of evidence-based, child care research. Since the last publication of this chapter, the developments in research of child care for young

children have continued with nationally representative or multisite child care studies producing copious amounts of information on preschool-aged children's experiences in early education and the effects of early education on the school years and beyond. While much has changed, the importance of teacher–child interaction in terms of emotional and instructional support has not diminished. The focus on, and the definition of, quality, as well as the need to include ethnic and cultural diversity in study designs continue to be expanded.

In light of these conditions, this chapter will focus on the state of child care by discussing the research pertaining to child care and children's experiences in it. In the first section, we set the background by: defining child care, research-based definitions of high-quality, and alternative theoretical additions that scholars have proposed. The second section will discuss the major trends of selected, evidence-based research linking child care to childhood outcomes since 2003. While not all inclusive, to be considered for the second portion of the review, the study must have been published in a peer-reviewed journal, must include a quality measure and a link to childhood outcomes. Additionally, while there are interesting developments in child care research outside of the United States, this chapter limits studies to those that were conducted in the United States. We used quality as a criterion for selection because research consistently finds that the influence of child care on children's development stems, in large part, from the quality of that care. We did not include a criterion for the date of data collection because some publications are longitudinal findings from multistate research projects initially included in the earlier editions of this chapter (see Table 24.1). The third section will discuss an important policy movement that focuses on quality in child care: the Quality Rating and Improvement Systems (QRIS). While other initiatives, such as program accreditation by the National Association for the Education of Young Children (NAEYC) and director credentialing efforts are also occurring, the focus in the

Table 24.1 Multi-Site Studies With Focus on Child Care, Quality, Childhood Outcomes in Research Design

Name of Study	Principal Authors	Authors[1]	Data Collection Year Begin	Participants	Child Demographics	Scope of Study	Child Care Quality Structure	Child Care Quality Process	Foci of Published Studies	Child Outcomes
NCEDL Multi-State / SWEEP	Early Barbarin, Bryant, Burchinal, Chang, Clifford, Crawford, Weaver, Howes, Ritchie, Kraft-Sayre, Pianta, Barnett	Howes et al. '08; Early, et al. '10; Early, et al. '06; Barbarin, et al. '10; LoCasale-Crouch et al., '07, '08; Mashburn et al. '08; Burchinal et al., '08; Pianta, '05; Chang, '08; Clifford, '05	2001–02 Multi-State; 2003–04 SWEEP	705 classrooms approx. 2,900 pre-kindergarten children; their parents; teachers	35% White, 28% Latino, 22% African American, 3% Asian/Pacific Islander, 10% Multi-Racial, <1% Native American	2 data collection points 11 states	Teacher education, training; ratio; length of day	CLASS ECERS-R	Teacher-child relationships Contextual factors Transition practices Quality profiles Threshold effects	Academic skills Transition to K Social skills
ECLS-B[2]	U.S. Dept. of Education National Center for Education Statistics		2001	14,000 at birth; their parents; teachers; all types of care	54% White 14% Black 26% Latino 3% Asian Pac. Islander 4% Other	Longitudinal 4 waves (9 mo. - K)	Group size Teacher education & training	ECERS-R		Cognitive Social-emotional Physical
Welfare Children & Families: 3-City Study	Angel, Burton, Chase-Lansdale, Cherlin, Moffitt	Votruba-Drzal, 04	1999	2,400 households with children 0–4 or 10–14; their parents and teachers	All low income	3 waves (1999–2006)		ECERS-R, FDCERS, Arnett	Well being of children & families in post welfare reform era	Cognitive Social
Early Head Start (EHS) Research and Evaluation study	EHS Research Consortium	Whiteside-Mandell et al., 09 Helen et al. '06	1996	3001 children, families, providers All types of care	Head Start income eligible; 48% less than high school; 63% Latino or African American	Birth to Kindergarten, 17 sites	Ratio, group size, provider education, specialized training	ITERS, ECERS, caregiver sensitivity	Child resiliency Family conflict Aggression	Cognitive Language Social

Name of Study	Principal Authors	Authors[1]	Data Collection Year Begin	Participants	Child Demographics	Scope of Study	Child Care Quality Structure	Child Care Quality Process	Foci of Published Studies	Child Outcomes
NICHD Study of Early Child Care	NICHD-ECCRN	NICHD-ECCRN 04a, 04b, 05a, 05b, 06, 07, 08, 09; Belsky, 06; Tran & Weinraub, 06; Hirsh-Pasek & Burchinal, 06; Downer & Pianta, 06; Hynes & Habasevich-Brooks, 08; Dowsett et al., 08; Gordon et al., 08; Morrissey, 08, 09, 10; Pluess & Belsky, 09; Adi-Japha, Phina, '09; Vandell et al., '10; McCartney et al, '10; Burchinal et al., '10	1991	All types of care; 1,364 children, their parents & teachers	English speaking 78% White 11% African American; 6% Latino; greatest attrition nonwhite	Longitudinal 4 phases Birth through 15 years	Ratio, group size, provider education & training	ORCE	Child care effect size Attachment quality Child temperament Peer interactions Social behavior Adult sensitivity Child care attendance, timing, & continuity	Academic achievement School readiness Behavior problems Social status Social competences Language Cognition
FACES	Office Planning Research & Evaluation	(findings mainly technical reports) Quintero, '99; Hindman et al, 2010	1997	3,600 children 3–4 yrs. of age in 40 Head Start programs, their parents, and child care staff	Low-income 29% African American; 30% White; 28% Latino; 9% other	4 cohorts to-date: 1997, 2000, 2003, 2006 Embedded case study of longitudinal sample of 120 randomly selected families	Group size, ratios, teacher ed, training, major	ECERS Arnett	Evaluation of Head Start effectiveness Promotive factors to early school success	School readiness Social skills Behavior problems

Notes

1 Denotes only peer-reviewed publications.

2 ECLS-K is not included in this table since it does not have child care quality data but there are studies using ECLS-K data that address child care attendance and childhood outcomes in Kindergarten.

third section is on QRIS due to the emphasis the Office of Child Care has placed on these state-initiated movements at this time. The final section will conclude the chapter with future directions child care research may or should take.

Defining Child Care

Early education settings are varied. They include center-based, home-based, or family, friend, and neighbor care (FFN). Center-based organizations may operate through private, public, or individual ownership. These programs typically contain larger group sizes than home-based care and more than one classroom per setting. Center-based care can be further divided into prekindergarten (pre-K) or state preschool programs which tend to be publicly funded entities that focus on 4-year-old preparatory education for formal schooling in K-12. Center-based care may also include "child care," which can encompass children younger than age 4. Child care has been viewed by some as less educationally enriching than the pre-K or preschool program. This perception is false because all programs for young children have the potential to be stimulating places for young children. It is the authors' opinion that all settings that care for children can provide the high-quality care that is necessary for young children's development. Therefore, rather than perpetuate a false division, we use the term *child care* to incorporate all forms of early educational settings.

Unlike center-based care, home-based care (due to its location in someone's home) tends to contain small group sizes. Family, friend, and neighbor care (FFN) is informal and can fall under (but not always) unregulated care by a relative, neighbor, or licensed provider. When terms such as, *pre-K, family, friend,* and *neighbor,* or *center-based care* are used, it is to delineate that the research findings address a specific type of early education program.

High-Quality Child Care: What Is It?

Definitions of quality in child care are based upon theoretical orientations that incorporate an ecological framework (Bronfenbrenner, 1995). As such, conceptualizations of child care quality include distinct environmental dimensions that are assumed to influence each other in a bidirectional manner. The most common understanding of child care quality is that structural aspects and process features of the environment contribute to the levels of quality experienced within classrooms (Helburn & Howes, 1996). Structural indicators are those features that are regulated most easily: teachers' educational backgrounds, group size and adult to child ratios, as well as the number of bathrooms, or whether the room is an adequate size for children of a specific age, for example. Process features are those experiences that are proximal to the child. These features can include the type of instructional support provided, the emotional valence of a classroom, or the sensitivity provided to children by the teachers. Structural dimensions predict process

dimensions, not children's development. That is, there is a fit between a structure that supports good caregiving, and good caregiving enhances development. To test this conceptual framework, both structure and process dimensions of child care need to be measured but the measurement of process quality requires close observation and measuring instruments based on what developmental psychological research has defined as warm, sensitive, and stimulating (Howes & Sanders, 2005). Similarly, given that much of the research targets center-based care, it is unclear whether all types of care adhere to the structural-process framework. Early examinations of structural quality in home-based programs indicate that this framework applies to settings outside of center-based care (Burchinal, Howes, & Kontos, 2002; Clarke-Stewart, Vandell, Burchinal, O'Brien, & McCartney, 2002).

While research does support the framework in community-based programs (programs created and maintained by members of the community; Bowman, Donovan, & Burns, 2001), this definition of quality has come under scrutiny due to the fact that effect sizes incorporating measures of quality are relatively small (Blau, 2000). Additionally, structural quality measured in prekindergarten contexts is less consistent with previous findings in community-based programs. Teacher education, a heavily researched aspect of structural classroom quality, showed inconsistent relationships to classroom quality in pre-K programs (Early, Bryant et al., 2006). Teacher education also revealed null or contradictory evidence across seven studies that did not include only pre-K programs (Early, Maxwell et al., 2007). Similarly, ratios, program length, and location (three common standards included in state quality initiatives or licensing standards) were not predictive of higher quality or preacademic gains in childhood in pre-K programs (Howes et al., 2008). Perhaps connections between teacher education and childhood outcomes are part of a component of factors that include more directed and specific educational training toward teacher–child interaction (Early, Maxwell et al., 2007). Or, connections between teacher education and childhood outcomes need to include the incorporation of teacher beliefs regarding domain-specific learning in children, particularly for poor children (Brown, Molfese, & Molfese, 2008).

Accompanying these new findings in child care research is the introduction of new or rediscovered conceptualizations of child care quality. Two developments call for definitions of child care quality to incorporate multifaceted dimensions of quality or to contain multiple perspectives. Multifaceted quality definitions endorse the use of domain-focused quality measures, previously validated measures that assess quality broadly, and other measures that evaluate process quality (Dickinson, 2006). Measures that focus on domains of development or learning show promise by extending the definitions of child care quality. For example, instruction-specific indicators do predict academic outcomes positively (Brown et al., 2008). This is not surprising since domain-specific measures of quality are fine-grained elements conceptually linked to the instructional side of process quality.

The inclusion of such domain-specific measures may help to provide stronger linkages to childhood outcomes than current studies provide or establish links to outcomes, such as math readiness, that have been found to be underdeveloped in preschool instructional support (Howes et al., 2008). While these domain-specific additions to conceptions of quality show promise, there are limits to the implications of the findings. Many of these studies are limited due to the lack of comprehensive measurement within a domain and the strong emphasis on academically oriented outcomes that exclude the importance of social/emotional and culturally relevant indicators of child well-being (Forry, Vick, & Halle, 2009).

The multiple perspective position suggests that researcher-based definitions of quality endorse a "top-down" perspective that excludes important stakeholders who are part of the ecological environment of the developing child. Based on this perspective, quality can be defined from the child's, the researcher's, the society's, and the child care professional's experiences. The variety of perspectives allows the measurement of quality to incorporate each of these elements (Harrist, Thompson, & Norris, 2007; Sheridan, 2007). While these definitions broaden the understanding of child care quality, rigorous research that validates these conceptions beyond face validity is lacking. Furthermore, research that uses the multiple perspective framework lacks connections to childhood outcomes.

The multiple perspective framework does highlight that much goes into the placement of a child into child care. Parents choose child care for a variety of reasons and necessities (Hirshberg, Huang, & Fuller, 2005). Access to care is uneven across ethnic and income categories (Fuller, Kagan, Loeb, & Chang, 2004; LoCosale-Crouch, Mashburn, Downer, & Pianta, 2007). These disparities have to be considered when interpreting research findings from predominantly center-based community or pre-K contexts.

One theoretical development that has extended the child care framework is Rogoff's (2003) work pertaining to the relationship between culture and development. Rogoff interpreted culture as a dynamic interaction that is a "mutually constituting" (p. 51) process in which the individual is not viewed as nested or influenced by cultural processes but as a participant in the creation of cultural communities. Preschool experiences are embedded within the historical contexts of a cultural community. Human development cannot be disconnected from the contexts and histories of the communities in which that development occurs. As such, frameworks of quality should be sensitive to cultural communities.

It is important to note that sensitive and responsive teacher–child interactions are important to positive developmental outcomes for all ethnic groups (Burchinal & Cryer, 2003). Therefore, the centrality of positive emotional climates and constructive engagement in learning for all children cannot be understated. Rather, it appears that quality is embedded within the historical contexts of a community. Child care programs with deep connections to the community manifest those contexts and interpret child care practices with a perspective that is grounded in their shared history (Howes, 2010; Sanders, Deihl, & Kyler, 2007).

Research that incorporates cultural context into quality frameworks is scant and still in its infancy due to there being little knowledge as to the relevance of this work, and a small research base that lacks connections to childhood outcomes (Shivers, Sanders, Westbrook, & Najafi, 2010). A challenge for research in this area is to expand frameworks beyond racial and ethnic categories while not ignoring the historical centrality of race and ethnicity in the United States. This challenge is further complicated in that race and ethnicity can seldom be separated from social class (Lin & Harris, 2008). Studies that incorporate poverty also tend to have large samplings of children of color (West, Tarullo, Aikens, & Hulsey, 2008). Further efforts should be made to include samplings that decouple race/ethnicity and social class.

In summary, there is a strong research base that documents the importance of process quality. Warm, sensitive, and constructive interactions between teachers and children in child care are important to children's development. Features of structural quality do not have as consistent a research history as process quality. Present research findings support the assumption that some aspects of structural quality within community-based programs are needed to facilitate the interactions that are central to process quality. At this point, it is unclear whether these same elements of structural quality are central to quality within pre-K programs. It may be that future developments to the quality framework, such as domain-specific quality and cultural contexts to quality, can help to explain some of the variability still present in current models of quality on childhood outcomes.

The Effect of Child Care on Childhood Outcomes

The trend toward designing multisite, longitudinal studies that began in the 1990s has continued into the present century. There are many major, ongoing, multisite, multistate, longitudinally designed early childhood research projects that are documenting early childhood contexts and experiences and subsequent developmental outcomes (see Table 24.1). Two of these projects (National Center for Early Development and Learning [NCEDL] and National Institute for Child Health and Development [NICHD]) have provided substantial documentation regarding the effects of child care experiences on developmental outcomes. There is increased diversity in the types of programs that are included in research designs. As shown in Table 24.1, all forms of care have representation (while not all NICHD studies define it as such, the inclusion of father-care as part of the definition of nonmaternal care is problematic with the NICHD project).

The inclusion of non-White children in studies has continued to occur in child care research. However, there continues to be a problem with confounding ethnicity with social class in many studies. Additionally, examinations of what children are in which type of programs indicates that a reliance on center care research may under sample the expanding population of children from immigrant families. Research that examined child care usage among immigrant families found that these children tended to be placed in less formal arrangements of care than center-based care (Turney & Kao, 2009). However, these findings may be a matter of availability, as well as a masking of state-by-state differences (Santhiveeran, 2010).

Before focusing on the specific effects of child care, an important caveat to this body of research is that families influence children's development independent of child care (Early Child Care Research Network [ECCRN], 1998). Also, families influence children's development due to their selection of child care. Greater social advantage, such as education, income, stimulating home environments, large maternal vocabularies, and reduced authoritarian childrearing beliefs, contribute to enhanced cognitive, language, and social development across all ethnic groups (ECCRN, 1997; Johnson, Jaeger, Randolph, Cauce, & Ward, 2003; Pungello & Kurtz-Costes, 1999). Therefore, links between child care and childhood outcomes have to be interpreted within the context of these findings on families.

Child care can be viewed as operating within a constellation of factors that contribute to developmental pathways. This is particularly true when that care is of consistently high quality (Belsky et al., 2007). Parenting and quality of the family environment are the strongest and most consistent predictors of behavioral and cognitive/academic gains in children short and long term (Belsky et al., 2007; ECCRN, 2004a, 2005). However, sensitive caregiving from mother *and* teachers contribute to language and academic outcomes in first grade (Hirsh-Pasek & Burchinal, 2006). Cognitive stimulation across not only the home but also child care environments and first grade, contributes to higher math achievement in first grade children. Cognitive stimulation in home and child care significantly predicts higher reading achievement in first grade, particularly for low-income children (Crosnoe et al., 2010). Domain-specific quality within the child care context contributed to children's reading achievement in first grade (Downer & Pianta, 2006). Therefore, a high-quality child care environment in conjunction with a high-quality family environment supports positive academic gains during later school years.

Stability, Duration, and Type of Child Care

Family factors impact the variation of child care environments in substantial ways (ECCRN, 2004b; Morrissey, 2008), and variations in care bear upon the linkage between child care quality and childhood outcomes. Although research designs of child care assumed that children ex-perienced one level of care across a study period, recent research documents that this is a fallacy in many instances. Children experience multiple, concurrent arrangements in care (Morrissey, 2008; Tran & Weinraub, 2006); changing patterns of maternal and teacher sensitivity over time from infancy through the early years (Hirsh-Pasek & Burchinal, 2006); as well as variations in exposure to low versus high-quality care across the early years (Hynes & Habasevich-Brooks, 2008; Tran & Weinraub, 2006). Since quality measurements are connected typically to a teacher within a specific classroom, most research models do not account for within-center changes, such as the switching of staff from one hour or day to the next. Staff shifting occurs frequently within child care centers to meet ratio requirements (Zellman, Perlman, Le, & Setodji, 2008).

These variations in experiences while in child care are associated with children's functioning. For example Morrissey (2009) found that behavior problems in children were attributable to children experiencing multiple, concurrent arrangements in care. Rather than ignore the multitude of variation that occurs for children in child care, a useful approach may be to incorporate the parenting and child temperament goodness-of-fit model (Thomas & Chess, 1977) to measure these fluctuations in children's experiences alongside individual characteristics of the child (see De Schipper, Tavecchio, Van Ijzendoorn, & Van Zeijl, 2004 for an example of the goodness-of-fit model applied to child care in the Netherlands).

Understanding this variation in child care experiences for children is crucial because research on stress levels of children while in child care indicates that children experience higher stress levels in child care than when in home environments (Watamura, Kryzer, & Robertson, 2009). A certain amount of stress in a child care situation is to be expected and can be considered normative. However, child care quality makes a difference in terms of children's stress level ratings. Stress levels, as measured by daily cortisol levels in children, decrease during the day for children in high-quality, center-based care (Rappolt-Schlichtmann et al., 2009). Conversely, children in low-quality, center-based care experience an increase in diurnal cortisol levels (Dettling, Parker, Lane, Sebanc, & Gunnar, 2000). These changes in cortisol levels while in child care require further exploration because there are also indications that children experience increased cortisol levels while in high-quality child care (Watamura et al., 2009) and elevated cortisol levels in child care may contribute to an increase in the number of illnesses a child experiences while attending child care (Watamura, Coe, Laudenslager, & Robertson, 2010).

It may be that the overall quality levels of a classroom are not a close enough measure of a child's experiences in this instance. More discrete examinations of direct experiences of the child may be required. The amount of time a child engages in small versus large groupings or quality measures that focus on the direct experiences of individual children, such as the Modified Observational Record of the Caregiving Environment (Gunnar, Kryzer, Phillips, & Vandell, 2001), show promise in revealing significant differences in cortisol levels (Rappolt-Schlichtmann et al., 2009; Watamura et al., 2009).

Quality counts when children experience changes in their child care arrangements. Multiple arrangements within predominantly high-quality preschool contexts are less detrimental to childhood outcomes than multiple arrangements within predominantly low quality contexts (Tran & Weinraub, 2006). While children from all walks of life tend to experience varying levels of quality across contexts, low-income children are more likely to experience low-quality care across contexts than children who have never been poor (Hynes & Habasevich-Brooks, 2008).

The type of care and the hours spent in child care vary for individual children. An NICHD study found that large amounts of time spent in center-based care related significantly to higher (but nonclinical) levels of externalizing behavior problems (Belsky, 2006; ECCRN, 2004b). Significant differences in elevated behavior problems for children who experienced center care versus children who did not persisted into sixth grade (Belsky et al., 2007). A study of activities in pre-K programs found that much of children's time is spent in routines (Early, Iruka et al., 2010). Also, center-based programs are apt to have higher adult to child ratios and bigger peer groupings than other forms of care (Dowsett, Huston, Imes, & Genetian, 2008).

While centers do contain higher proportions of experiences that are not considered high quality, centers also tend to have teachers with higher levels of education specifically directed toward early childhood (Dowsett et al., 2008). Similar studies connecting quality and time spent in child care found consistent associations with cognitive and social-emotional gains (Loeb, Fuller, Kagan, & Carroll, 2004; Vortruba-Drzal, Coley, & Chase-Lansdale, 2004). The elevated behavior problems found in the NICHD sample may indicate that a certain amount of assertiveness and aggressiveness is needed for these young children to negotiate the larger peer groupings in center care efficiently and successfully. Nevertheless, negative findings related to child care led to concerns regarding the placement of young children in out-of-home care.

Contrary to the initial findings pertaining to behavior problems and time spent in child care, subsequent research identifies the need for quality measures, individual characteristics of the child, and sequencing in types of care to be included in designs on the effects of child care on children's outcomes. Further analysis of the NICHD data found that quality of a child care center and group size contribute to the relationship between externalizing behavior problems and time spent in child care programs (McCartney et al., 2010). Furthermore, in line with the ecological model which includes children as active participants in their development (Bronfenbrenner, 1995), children with difficult temperamental characteristics exhibited greater external-

izing behavior problems than children in higher quality care (Pluess & Belsky, 2009).

NICHD analyses pertaining to the sequencing in types of care as children age help unpack the conflicting findings connected to child care usage. Home-based care during the infant–toddler period and center care during the preschool period provide children with optimal opportunities to benefit from the increased emotional and social benefits of individualized child–adult interaction at the earliest years coupled with greater intellectual stimulation during the preschool years (Morrissey, 2010). Other research on NICHD data comparing out-of-home care to maternal care found that children who experienced child care had stronger relations between school readiness and parenting quality than those who experienced maternal care for the majority of time (Adi-Japha & Klein, 2009). It appears, therefore, that experiences in child care can contribute to positive childhood outcomes but the effects of child care must be interpreted in a manner that incorporates the complexities of a child's experiences.

Thresholds of Quality

Related to the issue of duration of care is the examination of thresholds of quality and corresponding effect sizes pertaining to child care quality and childhood outcomes. Child care does make "distinctive and independent contributions" to childhood outcomes thru the quality, quantity, and type of care (ECCRN, 2006, p. 111). An important policy question concerns where dollars should be placed to reap the greatest benefits to poor children. In other words, do the effects of quality level off at a certain point and if so, where?

There is limited support for the lack of ceiling effects as two studies address this question directly for poor children in child care. A threshold analysis of the NCEDL pre-K data found that high-quality classrooms, particularly the quality of instruction and teacher–child interaction, were crucial predictors of children's preacademic skills and social competence (Burchinal, Vandergrift, Pianta, & Mashburn, 2010). As such, high, rather than moderate or low quality levels of process quality, is most beneficial to children in poverty. This study also included a diverse sample in terms of ethnicity and the findings can be extended to include poor children across some main ethnic categories (African American, European American, Latino).

A smaller study, which tested the hypothesis that investment needs to be directed toward the improvement of low quality programs rather than improving programs with acceptable quality found that there were no ceiling effects in terms of effect sizes that linked high global quality programs to reduced social-emotional risk factors (Montes, Hightower, Brugger, & Moustafa, 2005). Therefore, there is tentative support that all programs can benefit from quality improvement, and based on the NCEDL study, all programs should be included in quality improvement efforts. While the outcomes included in each study are different, and the measures of quality assess different aspects of quality, both studies reinforce the need to improve childhood outcomes for children in poverty by providing high-quality, not just adequate quality child care.

Longitudinal Designs: Long-Term Effects

There is substantial documentation regarding the effects of child care in later years. Follow-up studies from multisite, longitudinal research projects find that higher quality care contributed to academic skills in elementary and high school (Vandell, Belsky, Burchinal, Steinberg, & Vandergrift, 2010). Children who experienced more positive peer experiences in child care continued to be successful in negotiating peer interactions in third grade (ECCRN, 2008). There were also less positive associations with child care in that increased time in child care was associated with weaker work habits and poorer social skills in third grade (ECCRN, 2005) and greater risk taking and impulsivity at 15 years of age (Vandell et al., 2010). Quality levels in child care tended to mitigate these negative effects, however. These longitudinal studies indicate that the experiences in child care during the early years carry through not only to elementary school but also into adolescence.

A continuing focus in child care research is the examination of longitudinal models with a specific focus on poor children (Burchinal, Howes et al., 2008; Burchinal, McCartney et al., 2011; Hindman, Skibbe, Miller, & Zimmerman, 2010; LoCasale-Crouch, Mashburn, Downer, & Pianta, 2008; Schweinhart, 2007). While kindergarten and first grade have been the years in which outcomes have been evaluated with many of these studies (Burchinal, Howes et al., 2008; Hindman et al., 2010; LoCasale-Crouch et al., 2008), there are longitudinal publications focusing on children in poverty that extend into elementary school (Burchinal et al., 2011) and even adulthood (Schweinhart, 2004).

Academic achievement or school readiness are a main focus with many of these studies. A meta-analysis confirms that educational outcomes are the largest longitudinal effect size for adolescent outcomes that are attributable to child care programs (Manning, Homel, & Smith, 2010). Some of the longitudinal findings reinforce earlier child care findings regarding the importance of process quality to children's academic and social skills for poor children. Children in pre-kindergarten programs who experienced stimulating and sensitive care, as well as constructive engagement in learning activities perform better in language, preacademic, and social skills at the end of the kindergarten year (Burchinal, Howes et al., 2008). Additionally, when there are direct transition to kindergarten practices between pre-K and kindergarten, children most at risk show stronger social competence and fewer behavior problems (LoCasale-Crouch et al., 2008). However, in a study using the Head Start FACES data, there were no relationships between quality (measured by the ECERS and Arnett scales) and subsequent academic or social skills at the end of first grade

(Hindman et al., 2010). Rather, child and family factors (early language and social skills) were the strongest predictors of children's school success in this study.

The discrepancies between these two studies may highlight differences between the state-administered pre-K versus Head Start programs. Due to the strict federal regulations of the environments in Head Start programs, global quality can be high when measured by the ECERS which emphasizes materials and the environment. Nationally, Head Start programs are quite high in terms of overall quality (FACES, 2000), and the sample in this study contained a majority of high scoring teachers on instructional quality. Therefore, the inconsistent finding in the Hindman et al. (2010) study may be due to these elevated levels of structural, global, and instructional quality within these programs.

While quality child care may make a difference in children's school success, poor children start pre-K programs with preacademic skills that are significantly lower than the national average (Hindman et al., 2010). Additionally, early differences in achievement between African American and White children persist into the school years (Burchinal, McCartney et al., 2011). This suggests that early intervention at preschool may be too late for the gap to be closed (Burchinal, McCartney et al., 2011).

It also suggests that stronger bridges between home and school may help to close the gaps between European American children and African American and Latino children. One study addresses how bridges between home and school may help or hinder childhood outcomes. This study examined how synchronous versus asynchronous belief systems between home and school predict school readiness in kindergarten (Barbarin, Downer, Odom, & Head, 2010). While there were ethnic differences in terms of the patterns of beliefs, the findings reveal that synchronous beliefs may be advantageous or not depending upon the type of belief systems that are parallel between home and school. Beliefs are one aspect of bridges between home and school, and it would be useful to understand how synchronous practices between home and school or cultural congruence at all levels contribute to childhood outcomes.

In summary, the multisite, longitudinal focus on the effects of child care has yielded useful information regarding the importance of high-quality experiences for young children. Engaged teachers who create warm, intellectually stimulating relationships with the children in their care make a difference to children's future development. However, the disparities between poor, ethnic minority children and the middle class are not easily addressed through child care interventions during the preschool years only.

Child Care Policy: Working Toward Quality Improvement

Quality rating and improvement systems (QRIS) are state-sponsored initiatives that aim to improve the quality of early education programs for young children. Similar to the health rating systems in parts of California, child care programs receive a ranking based on a standardized set of quality criteria. Parents tend not to use all information available to them when assessing the quality of a child care program (see Mocan, 2007 for a discussion on information asymmetry in the child care market). By providing a universal rating of child care quality, all individuals within a state will be provided with an equal level of information regarding the levels of care available for their children. The assumption is that public knowledge of the quality of a child care program will provide parents with valuable information that they can use to choose appropriate child care. Programs can benefit from quality ratings also when the system provides a ladder toward improvement. As of 2009, approximately 42 states have or are exploring, piloting, or locally operating QRIS (*Comparison of quality rating and improvement systems with Department of Defense standards for quality*, 2009).

Increasingly, QRIS are becoming high stakes. States are considering incentives or have linked the quality ratings already to subsidy rates or other initiatives that are connected to dollar figures (Zellman et al., 2008). Additionally, while QRIS are state-run initiatives, the federal funding entity for early education services in the United States, the Office of Child Care, has allocated $271 million to quality expansion activities through its Child Care and Development Fund (CCDF). Granted, not all of these monies are for QRIS but QRIS figure prominently in these efforts.

While, in principle, the idea of QRIS is good, and successful implementation of them could provide significant national-scale improvements in child care quality, the execution of these systems is difficult for a number of reasons. First, while the items included in most states' QRIS levels parallel research findings (teachers with training or group size, for example), the QRIS scoring systems lack validation and it is unclear that higher levels on a particular state's scoring rubric equate to increasingly better quality; or that QRIS appropriately gauges important aspects of quality related directly to childhood outcomes. Two reasons for the lack of certainty on such important elements are that states created these measures based on expert opinion rather than the protracted process of careful measurement construction. Second, states have different rating systems based on different state licensing standards. State licensing standards tend to be the starting point for most states' quality rating systems. A state with a strong tradition in supporting child care has licensing standards that are closer to good quality care than a state with limited funds or a weak history in child care support. As a result, a state with minimal licensing standards is starting the QRIS at a dangerously low level of quality. Improvements on the QRIS in these states may not even begin to meet the necessary improvements needed for positive childhood outcomes. These programs move up the QRIS ladder and score as being quite high when, in fact, they are still minimal in terms of research-based definitions of high quality.

Furthermore, what indicator or measure(s) should be used to validate the scale and each level within the quality rating systems? Many states rely on the Early Childhood Ratings Scales (Harms, Clifford, & Cryer, 1998; Harms, Cryer, & Clifford, 1990). It is unclear that an indicator of global quality validates a measure geared toward the improvement of quality. Furthermore, it appears that the ECERS measures structural quality predominantly (Cassidy et al., 2005). While structural quality provides a framework, the impact of quality to childhood outcomes resides within process quality which the ECERS does not assess fully.

Are other ranking systems such as accreditation by a National Association for the Education of Young Children (NAEYC) or director credentialing initiatives possible validation tools for QRIS systems? Accreditation, in particular, provides a universal and widely accepted assessment of child care standards from birth through 8. It is mainly child-focused and its efforts are on quality improvement also. It is uncertain that quality can or should be standardized across all types of care for children of all ages, however. Is there enough shared similarity to make QRIS across these systems of care valid? A study that compared state licensing regulations to NAEYC accreditation recommended against a one-size-fits-all approach toward quality improvement (Apple, 2006).

A second problem pertaining to the effectiveness of QRIS is the difficulty in getting high-quality child care to the most vulnerable children. Children who are poor benefit the most from high-quality child care (Pigott & Israel, 2005). However, there is a lack of high-quality care for poor children (Burchinal, Nelson, Carlson, & Brooks-Gunn, 2008; Pianta et al., 2005). QRIS are voluntary programs in many states, and it is not certain that these programs target children in poverty. There may not be a requirement in all states that programs that participate in QRIS serve children who are poor or that they maintain a substantial number of poor children in their programs. Instead, programs that opt to take part in QRIS may be programs that function well already and cater to middle-class families. Additionally, a large percentage of children in the United States have their children in family, friend, and neighbor (FFN) care (Smith, 2002) which represents a population of care that is largely unlicensed and unregulated. States have no means to include these programs into quality improvement systems. This results in the exclusion of a large population of children who could benefit from QRIS initiatives.

A third issue with QRIS is that state decision makers frequently push toward documented childhood outcomes related to these systems. However, it is unclear that the focus of QRIS program effectiveness should be on the childhood outcomes used most commonly in policy-related research (Elicker & Thornburg, 2010). It may be too soon to see change in childhood outcomes related to QRIS such as school readiness or academic achievement at this early stage, particularly when most states are struggling with the validation of those systems.

Similarly, there is some question as to what childhood outcomes are appropriate when the time is ripe for documenting children's progress. While academic school readiness indicators are frequently and justifiably a common childhood outcome in child care research, indicators pertaining to social and emotional school readiness may be more suitable (Hernandez, Denton, & Macartney, 2007; Johnson et al., 2003). Or, further consideration of indicators that are pertinent uniquely to children of color, a large percentage of America's poor, should be examined (Johnson et al., 2003). A review of QRIS systems found that few incorporate ratings pertaining to cultural and linguistic responsiveness (Bruner, Ray, Stover Wright, & Copeman, 2009).

In conclusion, while QRIS initiatives point the way toward needed improvements in child care quality, the first steps that have been taken in most states are truly first steps. The more difficult step will be for these initiatives to (a) validate their existing systems; (b) change what does not work; (c) continue to find ways to recruit and include programs that can benefit from quality improvement, and that target the children who make substantial gains in their development by experiencing high-quality programs.

Future Directions for Research and Policy

The Importance of Teacher Education

The research conducted on teacher education portrays a more complicated picture of teacher education since the last publication of this chapter. Teacher education, measured in various ways, demonstrates inconsistent relationships to quality. Rather than assume that teacher education is unimportant, which is hard to believe, the inconsistent findings may have more to do with the quality of teacher preparation and the complexity of influence that teachers bring to the child care environment. Education is but one of many features that may contribute to high-quality teaching. Instead of questioning the mandates of many states that require teachers to have a college education, further examination of teacher preparation programs and professional development should occur to ensure that teachers receive the training that is needed for high-quality care. The education of children has low social and economic value in U.S. society. Professionals in early childhood have even lower social and economic status than other education professionals. This translates into early childhood teachers receiving the lowest compensation within an already poorly compensated field. Some of the discrepancies found with this research may be indicative of this low status.

The Extent of Influence Child Care Has On Childhood Outcomes

As stated previously, family characteristics have the strongest effect on childhood outcomes. Children spend more time with family than they do with teachers and peers in child care. Therefore, it is not surprising that family characteristics are the strongest predictor of childhood outcomes. One can view the effect of child care on childhood outcomes as *added* value. The value-added effect of child care is greatest to childhood outcomes for children living in poverty. The value-added effect can also be examined in more detail by considering other factors that may contribute to the smaller effect sizes found in child care research. Three possibilities are discussed below.

First, most designs that deal with real life events are correlational rather than experimental. Therefore, the conclusions and impact of child care findings are diminished with correlational designs. Small effect sizes should challenge researchers to "think outside the box," and consider additions to established quality measures that may expand the impact of child care on childhood outcomes. Possible concepts to include are domain-focused measures, and an expansion of cultural models in child care research.

Second, we know about the effects of child care on some domains more so than on other domains. Academic achievement and related constructs, such as academic school readiness, are well documented. Often, research reports documenting school readiness have a strong emphasis on preacademic skills and less emphasis on social and emotional well-being. One reason for this is that indicators of academic school readiness are more developed than indicators of social and particularly emotional competence. Social and emotional competences include a variety of intra- and interpersonal aspects which are couched within the environment in which they are enacted. These domains have important connections to socioeconomic and cultural contexts (Denham, 2006). Current measures do not do an adequate job in capturing these complexities. There is a heavy reliance on teacher-reporting of behaviors and this format does not capture the nuances and complexities of emotional behaviors, in particular.

In terms of culturally relevant models for children of color, these models are not examined frequently in child care quality research. Models that are particularly pertinent to children of color may contribute to a deeper understanding of the processes at work during the later years and in terms of school readiness (Johnson et al., 2003; Shivers et al., 2010). Further research that measures home–school connections can contribute to the development of culturally relevant child care models for children of color. Or, work that focuses on childhood outcomes that are pertinent to ethnic minority children specifically (such as ethnic/racial awareness or racial/ethnic identity) will be a valued addition to research modeling the effects of child care.

Third, research does not go frequently enough to where the children are. A large population of young children is in informal child care arrangements (estimates indicate 9 million children in FFN care versus 5 million in center-type care; Smith 2002, as cited in Fuller et al., 2004). FFN care is more difficult to include in research studies than center care or even licensed family child care. There are practical reasons for the oversampling of center-type, preschool programs in child care research. This bias also limits the conclusions that can be drawn about child care quality overall when a substantial portion of the child care population is not included consistently. Given the unique environments of FFN care, can findings relating high-quality child care to positive childhood outcomes extend to this underresearched population? Most likely, the answer is not exactly because research demonstrates that the relationship between child care, quality, and childhood outcomes is multifaceted. Child care setting is a factor and findings that address center care need to be put into perspective with similar findings from family, friend, and neighbor care. Moving research on child care to where the children are becomes even more pressing given the projection estimates for children from immigrant families and research findings that ethnic groups within the immigrant population use informal care more than center care.

In summary, child care has modest effects on childhood outcomes over the long-term but this effect is most strong for the most at-risk children. While family characteristics are a major predictor of childhood outcomes across all domains, further work is needed to determine how less-examined factors, such as emotional development, and culturally relevant models of caring are part of, or are determined by, children's experiences across diverse child care contexts.

Culture, Immigration, Ethnicity

Child care research is just beginning to approach these important topics and examine how factors associated with culture impact child care research and concurrent or subsequent childhood outcomes. Ethnic markers, such as matching ethnicities between teachers and children in their classrooms, has yielded results predictive of attachment quality (Howes & Shivers, 2006) and also results that show inconsistent relationships to childhood outcomes (Burchinal & Cryer, 2003). While the inclusion of ethnic markers has gone beyond ethnicity as purely a control variable, attempting to include cultural conceptions outside of ethnicity is still rife with problems that are not solved at this point. Following are important questions for future research inclusive of ethnic minority children to consider in child care research.

How should culture be defined so that it is not static or reliant upon stereotypical classifications? Recent work found interesting results using a relationship-based mixed-method design (Howes, 2010). Researchers should consider not only ethnic matching but also the historical status of particular ethnic groups within research models. For example, research outside of the child care field documents how ethnic minority status adversely impacts social and psychological functioning for these individuals (Caughy, O'Campo, & Muntaner, 2004; Fischer & Holz, 2007; Ross & Turner, 2005; Thorne, 2005). Is there a similar pattern if these constructs are included in child care models during the early years and longitudinally?

How can sampling be accomplished to divide the all-too-common confound between ethnicity and class *and* also obtain large enough groups to accommodate the sophisticated designs that are needed? Given the overrepresentation of ethnic minority groups that are also poor in the U.S. population (Lin & Harris, 2008), this is a challenge for researchers who struggle with limited funding and limited time. It is much easier to contact the local Head Start and pre-K programs than discover the smaller, most likely private, community programs that middle and upper-income African American and Latino families may rely on. Despite these challenges, researchers must make greater attempts to flush out this confound by including ethnic minority samples from categories outside of poverty.

There are many questions but few answers from research at this point. Subsequent research during the coming years should provide guidance on these issues.

Conclusion

Research conducted since the last publication of this chapter further reinforces how important quality is to the effectiveness of child care to childhood outcomes, and how central high-quality interactions by teachers of young children are to these outcomes. The conundrum with child care is that programs directed toward poor children can be high-quality (such as Head Start), but research still documents the high proportions of poor children lacking access to high-quality care or the disproportionate numbers of poor children in programs with less than adequate quality. The introduction of quality initiatives presents an opportunity to address the disparities in the quality of child care if they are executed thoughtfully and inclusively. Recent legislative developments that are part of America's Healthy Future Act (2009), otherwise known as the health care reform act (S.176), may provide additional avenues to improve outcomes for the most at-risk children.

References

Adi-Japha, E., & Klein, P. (2009). Relations between parenting quality and cognitive performance of children experiencing varying amounts of childcare. *Child Development, 80*(3), 893–906.

Apple, P. (2006). A developmental approach to early childhood program quality improvement: The relation between state regulation and NAEYC accreditation. *Early Education & Development, 17*(4), 535–552.

Barbarin, O., Downer, J., Odom, E., & Head, D. (2010). Home–school differences in beliefs, support, and control during public pre-kindergarten and their link to children's kindergarten readiness. *Early Childhood Research Quarterly, 25*(3), 358–372.

Belsky, J. (2006). Early child care and early child development: Major findings of the NICHD study of early child care. *European Journal of Developmental Psychology, 3*(1), 95–110.

Belsky, J., Vandell, D., Burchinal, M., Clarke-Stewart, A., McCartney, K., Owen, M. (2007). Are there long-term effects of early child care? *Child Development, 78*(2), 681–701.

Blau, D. (2000). The production of quality in child-care centers: Another look. *Applied Developmental Science, 4*(3), 136–148.

Bowman, B. T., Donovan, M. S., & Burns, M. S. (Eds.). (2001). *Eager to learn: Educating our preschoolers*. Washington, DC: National Academy Press.

Bronfenbrenner, U. (1995). Developmental ecology through space and time: A future perspective. In P. Moen, G. Elder, & K. Luscher (Eds.), *Examining lives in context: Perspectives on the ecology of human development* (pp. 619–647). Washington, DC: American Psychological Association.

Brown, T., Molfese, V., & Molfese, P. (2008). Preschool student learning in literacy and mathematics: Impact of teacher experience, qualifications, and beliefs on an at-risk sample. *Journal of Education for Students Placed at Risk, 13*(1), 106–126.

Bruner, C., Ray, A., Stover Wright, M., & Copeman, A. (2009). Quality rating & improvement systems for a multi-ethnic society: BUILD initiative. Retrieved from: http://www.buildinitiative.org/files/QRIS%20for%20a%20Multi-Ethnic%20Society%20Policy%20Brief.pdf

Burchinal, M., & Cryer, D. (2003). Diversity, child care quality, and developmental outcomes. *Early Childhood Research Quarterly, 18*, 401–426.

Burchinal, M., Howes, C., & Kontos, S. (2002). Structural predictors of child care quality in child care homes. *Early Childhood Research Quarterly 17*, 87–105.

Burchinal, M., Howes, C., Pianta, R., Bryant, D., Early, D., Clifford, R., Barbarin, O. (2008). Predicting child outcomes at the end of kindergarten from the quality of pre-kindergarten teacher-child interactions and instruction. *Applied Developmental Science., 12*(3), 140–153.

Burchinal, M., McCartney, K., Steinberg, L., Crosnoe, R., Friedman, S., McLoyd, V. (2011). Examining the black-white achievement gap among low-income children using the NICHD study of early child care and youth development. *Child Development, 82*(5), 1404–1420.

Burchinal, M., Nelson, L., Carlson, M., & Brooks-Gunn, J. (2008). Neighborhood characteristics and child care type and quality. *Early Education and Development, 19*(5), 702–725.

Burchinal, M., Vandergrift, N., Pianta, R., & Mashburn, A. (2010). Threshold analysis of association between child care quality and child outcomes for low-income children in pre-kindergarten programs. *Early Childhood Research Quarterly, 25,* 166–176.

Cassidy, D., Hestenes, L., Hansen, J., Hegde, A., Shim, J., & Hestenes, S. (2005). Revisiting the two faces of child care quality: Structure and process. *Early Education & Development, 16*(4), 505–520.

Caughy, M., O'Campo, P., & Muntaner, C. (2004). Experiences of racism among African American parents and the mental health of their preschool-aged children. *American Journal of Public Health, 94*(12), 2118–2124.

Clarke-Stewart, A., Vandell, D., Burchinal, M., O'Brien, M., & McCartney, K. (2002). Do regulable features of child-care homes affect children's development? *Early Childhood Research Quarterly, 17,* 52–86.

Comparison of quality rating and improvement systems with Department of Defense standards for quality. (2009). (No. 724-0714). Arlington, VA: National Association of Child Care Resource and Referral Agencies.

Crosnoe, R., Leventhal, T., Wirth, R., Pierce, K., Pianta, R., & NICHD. (2010). Family socioeconomic status and consistent environmental stimulation in early childhood. *Child Development, 81*(3), 972–987.

Denham, S. (2006). Social-emotional competence as support for school readiness: What is it and how do we assess it? *Early Education and Development, 17*(1), 57–89.

De Schipper, J., Tavecchio, L., Van Ijzendoorn, M., & Van Zeijl, J. (2004). Goodness-of-fit in center day care: relations of temperament, stability, and quality of care with the child's adjustment. *Early Childhood Research Quarterly 19*, 257–272.

Dettling, A., Parker, S., Lane, S., Sebanc, A., & Gunnar, M. (2000). Quality of care and temperament determine changes in cortisol concentrations over the day for young children in child care. *Psychoneuroendocrinology, 25,*819–836.

Dickinson, D. (2006). Toward a toolkit approach to describing classroom quality. *Early Education & Development, 17*(1), 177–202.

Downer, J., & Pianta, R. (2006). Academic and cognitive functioning in first grade: Associations with earlier home and child care predictors and with concurrent home and classroom experiences. *School Psychology Review, 35*(1), 11–30.

Dowsett, C., Huston, A., Imes, A., & Genetian, L. (2008). Structural and process features in three types of child care for children from high and low income families. *Early Childhood Research Quarterly, 23*(1), 69–93.

Early, D., Bryant, D., Pianta, R., Clifford, R., Burchinal, M., Ritchie, S., … Barbarin, O. (2006). Are teachers' education, major, and credentials related to classroom quality and children's academic gains in pre-kindergarten? *Early Childhood Research Quarterly, 21*, 174–195.

Early, D., Iruka, I., Ritchie, S., Barbarin, O., Winn, D.-M., Crawford, G., … Pianta, R. (2010). How do pre-kindergarteners spend their time? Gender, ethnicity, and income as predictors of experiences in pre-kindergarten classrooms. *Early Childhood Research Quarterly, 25*(2), 177–193.

Early, D., Maxwell, K., Burchinal, M., Bender, R. H., Bryant, D., Cai, K., … Zill, N. (2007). Teachers' education, classroom quality, and young children's academic skills: Results from seven studies of preschool programs. *Child Development, 78*(2), 558–580.

Early Child Care Research Network (ECCRN). (1997). Familial factors association with characteristics of nonmaternal care for infants. *Journal of Marriage and Family, 59*, 389–408.

Early Child Care Research Network (ECCRN). (1998). Relations between family predictors and child oucomes: Are they weaker for children in child care? *Developmental Psychology, 34*, 1119–1128.

Early Child Care Research Network (ECCRN). (2004a). Multiple pathways to early academic achievement. *Harvard Educational Review, 74*(1), 1–28.

Early Child Care Research Network (ECCRN). (2004b). Type of child care and children's development at 54 months. *Early Childhood Research Quarterly, 19*(2), 203–230.

Early Child Care Research Network (ECCRN). (2005). Early child care and children's development in the primary grades: Follow-up results from the NICHD Study of Early Child Care. *American Educational Research Journal, 42*(3), 537–570.

Early Child Care Research Network (ECCRN). (2006). Child-care effect sizes for the NICHD Study of Early Child Care and Youth Development. *American Psychologist, 61*, 99–116.

Early Child Care Research Network (ECCRN). (2008). Social competence with peers in third grade: Associations with earlier peer experiences in child care. *Social Development, 17*(3), 419–453.

Elicker, J., & Thornburg, K. (2010). *Measuring child outcomes in evaluations of child care quality rating and improvement systems*. Washington, DC: Child Trends.

FACES. (2000). *FACES findings: New research on Head Start program quality and outcomes*. Washington, DC: United States Department of Health & Human Services.

Fischer, A., & Holz, K. B. (2007). Perceived discrimination and women's psychological distress: The roles of collective and personal self-esteem. *Journal of Counseling Psychology, 54*(2), 154–164.

Forry, N., Vick, J., & Halle, T. (2009). *Evaluating, developing, and enhancing domain-specific measures of child care quality*. Washington, DC: Child Trends.

Fuller, B., Kagan, S., Loeb, S., & Chang, Y.-W. (2004). Child care quality: Centers and home settings that serve poor families. *Early Childhood Research Quarterly, 19*(4), 505–527.

Gunnar, M., Kryzer, E. M., Phillips, D., & Vandell, D. (2001). *Modified observational ratings of the caregiving environment (M-ORCE)*. (Unpublished measure and manual)

Harms, T., Clifford, R. M., & Cryer, D. (1998). *Early childhood environment rating scale-revised edition*. New York: Teachers College Press.

Harms, T., Cryer, D., & Clifford, R. M. (1990). *Infant toddlers environment rating scale*. New York: Teachers College Press.

Harrist, A., Thompson, S., & Norris, D. (2007). Defining quality child care: Multiple stakeholder perspectives. *Early Education & Development, 18*(2), 305–336.

Helburn, S., & Howes, C. (1996). Child care cost and quality. *The Future of Children, 6*(2), 62–82.

Hernandez, D., Denton, N., & Macartney, S. (2007). Demographic trends and the transition years. In R. Pianta, M. Cox & K. Snow (Eds.), *School readiness and the transition to kindergarten in the era of accountability* (pp. 217–281). Baltimore, MD: Brookes.

Hindman, A., Skibbe, L., Miller, A., & Zimmerman, M. (2010). Ecological contexts and early learning: Contributions of child, family, and classroom factors during Head Start, to literacy and mathematics growth through first grade. *Early Childhood Research Quarterly, 25*(2), 235–250.

Hirshberg, D., Huang, D. S.-C., & Fuller, B. (2005). Which low-income parents select child-care? Family demand and neighborhood organizations. *Children and Youth Services Review, 27*(10), 1119–1148.

Hirsh-Pasek, K., & Burchinal, M. (2006). Mother and caregiver sensitivity over time: Predicting langauge and academic outcomes with variable and person-centered approaches. *Merrill-Palmer Quarterly, 52*(3), 449–485.

Howes, C. (2010). *Culture and child development in early childhood programs: Practices for quality education and care.* New York: Teachers College Press.

Howes, C., Burchinal, M., Pianta, R., Bryant, D., Early, D., Clifford, R., ... Barbarin, O. (2008). Ready to learn? Children's pre-academic achievement in pre-Kindergarten programs. *Early Childhood Research Quarterly, 23*, 27–50.

Howes, C., & Sanders, K. (2005). Child care for young children. In B. Spodek & O. Saracho (Eds.), *Handbook of research on the education of young children* (pp. 375–392). Mahwah, NJ: Erlbaum.

Howes, C., & Shivers, E. (2006). New child-caregiver attachment relationships: Entering child care when the caregiver is and is not an ethnic match. *Social Development, 15*, 343–360.

Hynes, K., & Habasevich-Brooks, T. (2008). The ups and downs of child care: Variations in child care quality and exposure across the early years. *Early Childhood Research Quarterly, 23*(4), 559–574.

Johnson, D., Jaeger, E., Randolph, S., Cauce, A. M., & Ward, J. (2003). Studying the effects of early child care experiences on the development of children of color in the United States: Toward a more inclusive research agenda. *Child Development, 74*(5), 1227–1244.

Lin, A. C., & Harris, D. R. (Eds.). (2008). *The colors of poverty: Why racial and ethnic disparities persist.* New York: Russell Sage Foundation.

LoCasale-Crouch, J., Mashburn, A., Downer, J., & Pianta, R. (2008). Pre-kindergarten teachers' use of transition practices and children's adjustment to kindergarten. *Early Childhood Research Quarterly, 23*(1), 124–139.

LoCosale-Crouch, J., Konold, T., Pianta, R., Howes, C., Burchinal, M., Bryant, D., ... Barbarin, O. (2007). Observed classroom quality profiles in state-funded pre-kindergarten programs and associations with teacher, program, and classroom characteristics. *Early Childhood Research Quarterly, 22*, 3–17.

Loeb, S., Fuller, B., Kagan, S., & Carrol, B. (2004). Child care in poor communities: Early learning effects of type, quality, and stability. *Child Development, 75*(1), 47–65.

Manning, M., Homel, R., & Smith, C. (2010). A meta-analysis of the effects of early developmental prevention programs in at-risk populations on non-health outcomes in adolescence. *Children and Youth Services Review, 32*(4), 506–519.

McCartney, K., Burchinal, M., Clarke-Stewart, A., Bub, K., Owen, M., Belsky, J. (2010). Testing a series of causal propositions relating time in child care to children's externalizing behavior. *Developmental Psychology, 46*(1).

Mocan, N. (2007). Can consumers detect lemons? An empirical analysis of information asymmetry in the market for child care. *Journal of Popular Economics, 20*, 743–780.

Montes, G., Hightower, A. D., Brugger, L., & Moustafa, E. (2005).

Quality child care and socio-emotional risk factors: No evidence of diminishing returns for urban children. *Early Childhood Research Quarterly 20*, 361–372.

Morrissey, T. (2008). Familial factors associated with the use of multiple child-care arrangements. *Journal of Marriage and Family, 70*(2), 549–563.

Morrissey, T. (2009). Multiple child-care arrangements and young children's behavioral outcomes. *Child Development, 80*(1), 59–76.

Morrissey, T. (2010). Sequence of child care type and child development: what role does peer exposure play? *Early Childhood Research Quarterly, 25*(1), 33–50.

Pianta, R., Howes, C., Burchinal, M., Bryant, D., Clifford, R., Early, D., ... Barbarin, O. (2005). Features of pre-kindergarten programs, classrooms, and teachers: Do they predict observed classroom quality and child-teacher interactions? *Applied Developmental Science, 9*(3), 144–159.

Pigott, T. D., & Israel, M. S. (2005). Head Start children's transition to kindergarten: Evidence from the early childhood longitudinal study. *Journal of Early Childhood Research, 3*(1), 77–104.

Pluess, M., & Belsky, J. (2009). Differential susceptibility to rearing experience: The case of childcare. *Journal of Child Psychology and Psychiatry, 50*(4), 396–404.

Pungello, L., & Kurtz-Costes, B. (1999). Why and how working women choose child care: A review with a focus on infancy. *Developmental Review, 19*, 31–96.

Rappolt-Schlichtmann, G., Willet, J., Ayoub, C., Lindsley, R., Hulette, A., & Fischer, K. (2009). Poverty, relationship conflict, and the regulation of cortisol in small and large group contexts at child care. *Mind, Brain, and Education, 3*(3), 131–142.

Rogoff, B. (2003). *The cultural nature of human development.* Oxford, England: Oxford University Press.

Ross, S., & Turner, M. (2005). Housing discrimination in metropolitan America: Explaining changes between 1989 and 2000. [empirical]. *Social Problems, 52*(2), 152–180.

Sanders, K., Deihl, A., & Kyler, A. (2007). D.A.P. in the 'hood: Perceptions of child care practices by African American child care directors caring for children of color. *Early Childhood Research Quarterly, 22*, 394–406.

Santhiveeran, J. (2010). Who uses formal, early child care in California? A comparative study of children from immigrant and nonimmigrant families. *Child and Adolescent Social Work Journal, 27*(2), 151–160.

Schweinhart, L. (2004). *The High / Scope Perry Preschool study through age 40: Summary, conclusions, and frequently asked questions.* Ypsilanti, MI: High/Scope Educational Research Foundation.

Schweinhart, L. (2007). Crime prevention by the High/Scope Perry Preschool Program [Special Issue on early intervention]. *Victims and Offenders, 2*(2), 141–160.

Sheridan, S. (2007). Dimensions of pedagogical quality in preschool. *International Journal of Early Years Education, 15*(2), 197–217.

Shivers, E., Sanders, K., Westbrook, T. P., & Najafi, B. (2010). Measuring culturally responsive early care and education. In M. Zaslow & K. Tout (Eds.), *Measuring quality in early childhood settings.* Baltimore, MD: Brookes.

Smith, A. (2002). *Who's minding the children? Child care arrangements, spring 1997.* Current Population Reports, P70-86. Washington, DC: United States Census Bureau.

Thomas, A., & Chess, S. (1977). *Temperament and development.* New York: Brunner/Mazel.

Thorne, B. (2005). Unpacking school lunchtime: Structure, practice, and the negotiation of differences. In C. Cooper, C. Garcia-Coll, T. Bartko, H. Davis, & C. Chatman (Eds.), *Developmental pathways through middle childhood: Rethinking contexts and diversity as resources* (pp. 63–88). Mahwah, NJ: Erlbaum.

Tran, H., & Weinraub, M. (2006). Child care effects in context: Quality, stability, and multiplicity in nonmaternal child care arrangements during the first 15 months of life. *Developmental Psychology, 42*(3), 566–582.

Turney, K., & Kao, G. (2009). Pre-kindergarten child care and behavioral outcomes among children of immigrants. *Early Childhood Research Quarterly, 24*(4), 432–444.

U.S. Census Bureau. (2009). *Projected change in population size by race and Hispanic origin for the United States: 2000–2050* [Data file].Retrieved from http://www.census.gov/population/www/projections/2009lnmsSumTabs.html

Vandell, D., Belsky, J., Burchinal, M., Steinberg, L., & Vandergrift, N. (2010). Do effects of early child care extend to age 15 years? Results from the NICHD study of early child care and youth development. *Child Development, 81*(3), 737–756.

Vortruba-Drzal, E., Coley, R., & Chase-Lansdale, L. (2004). Child care and low-income children's development: Direct and moderated effects. *Child Development, 75*(1), 296–312.

Watamura, S., Coe, C., Laudenslager, M., & Robertson, S. (2010). Child care setting affects salivary cortisol and antibody secretion in young children. *Psychoneuroendocrinology 35*, 1156–1166.

Watamura, S., Kryzer, E. M., & Robertson, S. (2009). Cortisol patterns at home and child care: Afternoon differences and evening recovery in children attending very high quality full-day center-based child care. *Journal of Applied Developmental Psychology 30*, 475–485.

West, J., Tarullo, L., Aikens, N., & Hulsey, L. (2008). *Study design and data tables for FACES 2006 baseline report*. Washington, DC: Office of Planning Research and Evaluation, Administration for Children, Youth, and Families.

Zellman, G., Perlman, M., Le, V.-N., & Setodji, C. (2008). *Assessing the validity of the Qualistar Early Learning Quality Rating and Improvement System as a tool for improving child-care quality*. Los Angeles, CA: Rand.

Zigler, E., Gilliam, W., & Jones, S. (2006). *A vision for universal preschool education*. New York: Cambridge University Press.

25

Family Context in Early Childhood

Connecting Beliefs, Practices, and Ecologies

Barbara H. Fiese
University of Illinois at Urbana-Champaign

All children are raised in some form of family. But families take different forms in terms of number of adults in the household, contact with extended kin, and sheer size of the group. Families differ in the beliefs that they hold about trustworthiness of relationships and in their daily practices and routines. Families live in neighborhoods that reflect available resources for healthy foods, physical activity, social support, and quality of education. This chapter describes how families are dynamic systems with shared practices and beliefs that contribute to child well-being and preparedness to learn. These practices and beliefs are embedded in a socioeconomic context that includes cultural influences as well as neighborhood context. Thus, an ecological model (Bronfenbrenner & Morris, 1998) is proposed to situate the family in a larger developmental context.

In some cases, and at some times, families function in such a way that children's growth is fostered and there is optimal development. In other cases, however, individual and socioeconomic forces compromise the family's ability to provide a supportive environment for their children. Examples are provided of the effects of cumulative risk under high-risk child-raising conditions such as poverty or parental psychopathology that may derail positive family process and make children vulnerable to behavioral and learning problems. There is reason for optimism, however, as protective factors may promote positive development through responsive parent–child interactions and structured home environments.

Family life is often marked by transitions: Marriage, the birth of a child, going to school, leaving home, marriage of children, becoming grandparents are just a few of the transitions that members experience as part of normative changes (Walsh, 2003). Several transitions are apparent during early childhood; gaining autonomy through learning to walk, asserting opinions in learning to talk, and being poised to learn when transitioning from home to school. An important transition where characteristics of the child, family, social institutions, and culture transact is the transition to formal school. The family plays an important role in easing these transitions by establishing partnerships with childcare providers and school personnel. However, this transition is moderated by available resources in the community and the cultural context in which education is provided. The third section of the chapter discusses family partnerships with early care providers and educators and transition to kindergarten as important settings for early learning. Further, the section highlights the importance of establishing partnerships between early care settings in light of increasing diversity in family life.

Family Ecologies

Ecological Models

Ecological models (Bronfenbrenner & Morris, 1998) propose that development is the result of multiple levels of influence including those that are most proximal to the child's experience (parent–child interactions) and those that are more distal (cultural values and practices) (See Figure 25.1). At the core is the child herself, possessing her own temperament, style of engaging with others, and personality. The family context includes structural aspects of the family such as number of adults in the household, marital status, and number of people residing in the household. Variations in numbers of adults in the household and stability in marital status have been found to be related to cognitive, social, and emotional outcomes for children (Amato, 2005). However, these outcomes are likely to be moderated by family economic status and neighborhood resources.

The family context also includes social interaction features such as parenting style, family belief systems, family routines and rituals, and contact with extended kin. Over the past two decades, there has been consistent support for the importance of sensitive and responsive parent–child

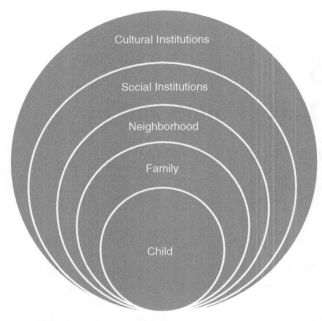

Figure 25.1 Ecological models

interaction in supporting healthy outcomes for children and youth (Cox & Paley, 1997). From an ecological systems perspective, parent–child interaction patterns are seen as embedded in the larger social system and sensitive to current strains in the marital relationship, economic conditions, and regulated by cultural norms. In turn, families and their routine and ritual practices are considered to be influenced by generational traditions and cultural context.

The neighborhood level is important for child development because it provides not only the geography where children live but also is the broader economic context that houses businesses and institutions such as childcare sites, schools, and places of worship (Leventhal & Brooks-Gunn, 2000). Neighborhoods may influence the effects of family processes on child outcomes through relational support, collective self-efficacy, and tangible resources related to positive development. For example, children raised in more affluent neighborhoods are consistently better prepared to enter kindergarten (Chase-Landsdale & Gordon, 1996) and have better access to quality child care than children raised in lower income neighborhoods (Burchinal, Nelson, Carlson, & Brooks-Gunn, 2008). Support for institutions such as child care, schools, and social support programs can also influence child outcomes through family processes. For example, providing balanced nutrition during the early childhood years is essential for optimal brain development. However, for some families limited economic resources may restrict their ability to adequately feed their children and thus they rely on federally supported programs such as the Supplemental Nutrition Assistance Program (SNAP) or the Women, Infants, and Children (WIC) program administered by the U.S. Department of Agriculture (USDA). Most distal to the child's experience are cultural institutions. Certainly, cultural values and traditions affect

child development through family practices and beliefs. For example, immigrant families are less likely to enroll their children in center based child care than nonimmigrant families (Brandon, 2004) and children from Latino families are less likely to receive out of home care prior to entering kindergarten (Buysse, Castro, West, & Skinner, 2005). While an ecological approach provides an appreciation of the complexity of child development, in and of itself it does not allude to the process by which individual children develop well or poorly in particular contexts. In order to understand the mechanisms linking different ecologies to child outcome it is important to consider how risk may operate across contexts and how different processes may mediate or moderate the effects of risk.

Cumulative Risk

Ecological models emphasize the complexity in child development. To take into account this complexity it is important to recognize that a child's current state is rarely the result of a single factor, but instead is the result of multiple factors that accumulate over time. In terms of the family context this means that family functioning at any point in time will be the result of several factors including the child's current state, family of origin factors such as mental health history of the parents and grandparents, current economic conditions, and cumulative history of family stability. Take for example the effects of family instability on children's social and emotional development. Children have the opportunity to thrive when there is stability in their lives including predictable routines, regular schedules, and a safe place to call home. When a family moves there is the chance that friendships are lost, there is a transition to a new school, and routines are disrupted. Household moves are often the result of a relationship breakup by the mother (Adam & Chase-Landsdale, 2002). Thus family instability also indicates a change in relationships in the family and potential for increased levels of family conflict. Family instability has been defined as number of residential moves, relationship disruptions, and job loss. This index of family instability was related to teacher and parent report of children's behavior problems (Ackerman, Kogos, Youngstrom, Schoff, & Izard, 1999). However, the effects were moderated by child temperament in that children with more difficult temperaments were more susceptible to family instability and this was expressed through higher levels of internalizing behavior problems. Children who experience family instability earlier in life and over longer periods of time were at the greatest risk for internalizing problems (Ackerman, Brown, & Izard, 2004). However, the likelihood for externalizing behavior and academic problems were just as great if the child had recently experienced family instability.

Examining environmental risk factors such as family instability provides some insight into the cumulative indexes that may predict child outcomes at any given point in time. Although providing guidance in terms of identifying potential risk factors, it does not provide direction as to the process by which behavior is changed and the role that family organizational and belief systems may operate in promoting health and well-being in children. In order to specify the processes by which families affect child outcome it is important to provide a model of how behavior changes over time.

Transactions in Development

The transactional model as proposed by Sameroff and colleagues (Sameroff, 2010; Sameroff & Fiese, 2000) emphasizes the mutual effects between parent and caregiver, embedded and regulated by cultural codes. In this model, child outcome is neither predictable by the state of the child alone nor the environment in which he or she is being raised. Rather, it is a result of a series of transactions that evolve over time with the child responding to and altering the environment. Thus, to be able to predict how families influence children one must also ask how children influence families.

Let us take a very simple example of parents telling bedtime stories to their children and its connection to early literacy skills (Beals, 2001). Consider a situation where there are birth complications and the caregiver has recently moved due to a breakup with the child's father. Once the caregiver brings the infant home from the hospital there may be residues of worry and anxiety about the child's health, anger about the father leaving her and the child at a time of great need, and concern about how to pay for continued care. The worry and concern may lead to inconsistent parenting patterns such that at times the child is responded to sensitively and at other times the caregiver's preoccupations with paying the bills, lost relationship, and adjusting to a new baby leave her irritable and inconsistent in her parenting style. In an attempt to get the caregiver's attention, the child may develop some behaviors that can be interpreted as indicative of a difficult temperament (e.g., whining, difficulty in soothing, persistence). When bedtime arrives the caregiver may be exhausted by strained interactions throughout the day and prefer to leave the child with a bottle rather than reading a story. Over time, the child is not exposed to joint book reading and family routines are carried out in a perfunctory way rather than as an op-

portunity to set aside time to be together. When the child arrives at school he or she is ill-equipped to read and may not meet normative expectations for language development. The process is outlined in Figure 25.2.

What was the cause of this outcome? Did the mother's reasonable worry about a potentially medically vulnerable child lead to poor language skills? Did the recent breakup with the child's father and being a single parent cement the child's future in terms of school problems? Did the child's difficult temperament cause him or her not to read? Did the disruption of bedtime routines directly result in delays in language development? From a transactional perspective, poor literacy skills are not the result of any one factor but develop over time through a series of exchanges between child and caregiver in a given environment. For early childhood educators, the significance of this model resides both in understanding dynamic change processes as well as opportunities for intervention. If child outcome is the product of multiple influences then there are multiple avenues for implementing change. In this case, it may be possible to redefine the relationship between caregiver and child through interaction coaching and encouraging responsive parenting styles (McDonough, 2000). It may also be possible to educate caregivers about the significance of joint book reading and create a bedtime routine that involves caregiver and child.

The transactional model also highlights the importance of how parent–child interactions become part of parent belief systems that regulate child behavior over time. In order to better-elucidate this process, it is important to consider how families, as a group, regulate behavior and how children contribute to family process.

Family Practices and Representations

In light of the discussion about developmental ecologies and transactions, it is important to consider the essential tasks of the family and how families organize themselves as a group to fulfill the daily responsibilities of raising healthy children. At the heart of family life is the creation and maintenance of flourishing relationships. Relationships undergo change when they are formed through marriage, transition through time as children age, and interact with an

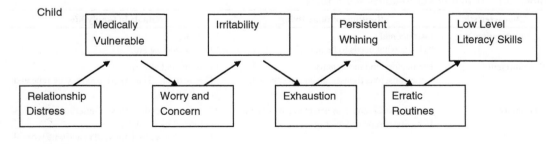

Figure 25.2 Transactions in development model

increasing number of people outside of the family, and in the process roles are renegotiated (Cowan & Cowan, 2003). The timeless backdrop to family life is keeping relationships alive and the need to adapt to the developmental, life-course, and individual needs of family members.

From a systems perspective, healthy families are created when communication is clear and direct, routines are in place, affect is responded to in a developmentally responsive manner, problems are solved to promote health and well-being for all family members, and there are clear boundaries between the older and younger generation (N. B. Epstein, Ryan, Bishop, Miller, & Keitner, 2003; Parke, 2004). These qualities are often expressed through the family's daily routine practices and the beliefs that they hold as expressed in narratives and family stories.

Reiss (1989) has made the distinction between the practicing and representing family. Family practices are directly observable patterns of interaction that serve to stabilize family life through their predictability and repetitiveness over time. These interactions tend to be fairly consistent but are often altered when the child undergoes a developmental transition. For example, warmth and responsiveness may be detectable during infancy by parent and child maintaining close physical proximity and back and forth eye contact. Once the child is a toddler, however, interaction patterns shift to encourage autonomy and a smile across the room replaces direct physical contact. During the preschool years, interactions through language and the expression of support and reinforcement shifts from physical to verbal displays.

Family representations, on the other hand, are detected indirectly and refer to the belief systems that families create that in turn regulate behavior. Internal working models of relationships develop within the context of the family and guide individual behavior over time (Stevenson-Hinde, 1990). In contrast to family practices that are reportable and observable, family representations must be detected indirectly and rely on interpretations of personal events (Fiese & Sameroff, 1999). Family practices and representations are embedded in transactional process whereby family practices become the subject of representations, which in turn affect how family members interact with each other. Two aspects of family life capture these processes,

both of which have practicing and representing elements. Family routines and stories are provided as illustrations of the practicing and representing family and their influences during early childhood.

Family Routines and Rituals

A distinction can be made between routines of daily living and rituals in family life that parallel aspects of the practicing and representing family (Fiese & Spagnola, 2007). Routines and rituals can be considered in terms of how they are communicated, time commitment, and continuity. In the case of routines, communication tends to be fairly instrumental with a focus on "this is what needs to be done." Routines typically involve a momentary commitment with little thought being given to the activity once it is completed. Routines tend to be repeated over time in a similar manner. Rituals, on the other hand, are communicated through symbols and convey "this is who we are" as a group. There is an emotional commitment to rituals and they often evoke strong affect. Once the activity is over, there is a tendency to replay it in memory with particular attention to feelings of belonging and connection with others. Rituals provide continuity over time and are frequently passed down across generations. When routines are disrupted, it is a hassle. When rituals are disrupted, there is a threat to group identity. The distinguishing features are outlined in Table 25.1.

Routines are most closely associated with family practices and can be part of daily and weekly activities such as mealtime, bedtime, and getting ready for school. Rituals can also occur in these settings if there is a symbolic and emotional investment in the activity and may also extend to settings such as annual celebrations (e.g., birthdays) and religious observances. During the child-raising years, maintaining routines and rituals is one way in which family tasks are carried out (Fiese, 2006). Indeed, there is reason to believe that the practice of family routines is sensitive to developmental transitions within the family. Families of infants are less likely to report the establishment of routines around mealtime, weekends, and special celebrations than parents of children of preschool age (Fiese, Hooker, Kotary, & Schwagler, 1993). However, once routines are

Table 25.1 Definitions of Routines and Rituals

Characteristic	Routines of daily living	Rituals in family life
Communication	Instrumental "This is what needs to be done."	Symbolic "This is who we are."
Commitment	Perfunctory and momentary Little conscious thought given after the act.	Enduring and affective "This is right." The experience may be repeated in memory.
Continuity	Directly observable and detectable by outsiders. Behavior is repeated over time.	Meaning extends across Generations and is interpreted by insiders. "This is what we look forward to and who we will continue to be across generations."

Reprinted from Fiese, et al., 2002. A review of 50 years of research in naturally occurring family routines and rituals: Cause for celebration? *Journal of Family Psychology*, 16, 381-390.

established, mothers of infants feel more confident in their capacity to parent (Sprunger, Boyce, & Gaines, 1985).

Early child care routines, such as feeding, provide structure for social interaction. When the infant cries, the caregiver responds and there is the opportunity to interact through eye contact, vocalizations, and physical contact. Beginning in infancy, feeding routines have the opportunity to become somewhat regularly scheduled. There is some evidence to suggest that on-demand feeding routines reinforce the infant's wake-sleep cycle and promote healthier nighttime sleep habits (Hellbrugge, Lange, Rutenfranz, & Stehr, 1964). Thus, predictability in two early routines (feeding and sleeping) can become intertwined and set the stage for healthy outcomes.

During the preschool and early school years, predictability of mealtime and bedtime routines are also associated with more optimal child outcomes. For example, low frequency of family mealtimes for children in kindergarten is associated with greater risk for obesity, particularly if meals are accompanied by television viewing (Gable, Chang, & Krull, 2007). How families interact during mealtimes is also associated with child mental health outcomes. Families who provide clear and direct communication, are responsive to the child's affect, and provide structure to the meal itself, are less likely to have children with problematic behaviors (Dickstein, St. Andre, Sameroff, Seifer, & Schiller, 1999; Fiese & Marjinsky, 1999).

Similarly, the establishment of regular bedtime routines during preschool and early childhood years is associated with better outcomes for young children. Preschool children who experience both regular mealtimes and bedtimes in their families are less likely to develop obesity (Andersen & Whitaker, 2010). During the preschool years, less sleep at night is related to increased odds for developing problematic behaviors, particularly externalizing problems (Lavigne et al., 1999). However, consistent with the ecological approach, the effects of mealtime and bedtime routines on child outcomes may not be direct but are also influenced by sociodemographic context.

Regularity of bedtimes and mealtimes varies by socioeconomic context. The likelihood that children between 4 and 35 months will have the same bedtime and mealtime every day varies by family income in one report using a national database. Less than 50% of the low income households reported having the same bedtime and mealtime for their young children in comparison to 70% of the higher income families (Child Trends, 2003). Further, the type of bedtime routines that families practice with their young varies by racial and ethnic background. White families are more likely to provide comfort objects or read to their child than non-White non-Latino families (Milan, Snow, & Belay, 2007). African American families are more likely to use bathing as part of a bedtime routine. Latino families are most likely to provide a bottle to their child as part of a bedtime routine.

The routines of daily living begin to shape children's behavior and expectations very early on. Infants and toddlers learn to sooth themselves during bedtime routines, expand their vocabulary during playtime routines, and become part of the social group during family mealtimes. What may appear on the surface to be mundane daily activities in fact form the child's early learning playground. The daily routines of early childhood prepare the child for more formalized learning on several levels. The repetition of routine activities may reinforce newly learned skills. The predictability of routines may aid in regulating behavior, providing a guide for what is acceptable and what is not. Routines that are flexible encourage children to become more active participants in family life, which in turn may lead to feelings of competence when approaching new and novel tasks. It is also likely that families who create organized households through regular routines also set the stage for optimal early literacy skills. For example, children's early literacy skills are associated with not only a parent's beliefs about the importance of developing such skills but also daily home routines such as dinnertime and sharing in family homework time (Serpell, Sonnenschein, Baker, & Ganapathy, 2002). Thus, families create a social environment where mundane activities are planned ahead, genuine interest in the day's events are communicated, and the repetitiveness of these events provides a sense of belongingness that can promote health and well-being for the child.

Daily routines will also be regulated by cultural expectations. For example, Caribbean immigrant families expect young children (prekindergarten and kindergarten age) to have homework and will organize approximately 5 hours per week in the family's routine to attend to the child's homework (Roopnarine, Bynoe, & Singh, 2004). Less frequent, but equally important in developing a sense of personal identity are cultural celebrations that remind family members of their origins and often involve opportunities for storytelling and cementing relationships through the preparation of different ethnic dishes (Falicov, 2003).

To summarize, routines are directly observable and provide predictability and order to family life. During early childhood, families are faced with the task of creating schedules around feeding, sleeping, and increasingly over time activities to connect the child to other institutions such as schools. There is the potential for these family based practices to set the stage for the child's responsiveness to structure and order in the classroom. Children who have experienced regular routines in the home may have expectations for environmental orderliness that eases their transition to school where key educational tasks are embedded in structured and sequenced activities (Norton, 1993). Early childhood educators have the opportunity to partner with families to encourage regular routines in the home. One important example is preparation for the transition to kindergarten. Early childhood educators can play a pivotal role in preparing the child not only for her new role in more formal learning environments but also assisting parents in what to expect. For example, in a survey of parents anticipating their child's transition to kindergarten there was a consistent lack of knowledge about what to expect about their child's daily routines in kindergarten and lack of preparedness at home (Wildenger, McIntyre, Fiese, & Ecker, 2008). Most parents anticipated that their children would need to go to bed close to an hour earlier, wake up 30 minutes earlier, and that mealtimes would need to be adjusted. However, the summer prior to entry into kindergarten no changes had been made. Early childhood educators have the opportunity to partner with parents to identify new schedules and plan for changes at home.

Whereas the routines of daily living may prepare children to respond to order, rituals in family life reflect the affective and emotional climate of relationships. Children who are raised in homes where collective gatherings are deliberately planned, eagerly anticipated, and hold symbolic significance are likely to feel that they belong to a valued group and in turn create a stronger sense of self (Fiese, 2006).

There is preliminary evidence to suggest that families that maintain meaningful family rituals across the transition from kindergarten to elementary school have children who perform better academically. In a longitudinal study of 70 families who were originally interviewed when their child was 4 and then again when their child was 9 years of age we found different patterns of family ritual stability. For some families, the meaning associated with family rituals remained relatively high over the five-year period, for others it remained relatively low. There were some families where the affective component declined over time. It was this latter group where children experienced the most difficulty in the early school years and performed less well on tests of academic achievement (Fiese, 2002). We speculate that in instances where meaningful rituals are disrupted there are likely to be other stresses within the family. Children may be keenly aware of changes in routines and ritual involvement. Whereas young children may not be able to articulate the amount of stress present in the family environment they certainly notice when eagerly anticipated events are cancelled or altered in a significant way. Rituals may signify to the child the relative health of family relationships. Thus, children who feel emotionally connected to their families may be less likely to develop internalizing and externalizing symptoms that can affect engaging in classroom activities (Brody & Flor, 1997; Fiese, 2000).

Family routines and rituals are one way to access family practices and representations relevant to early child development. Whereas these practices and beliefs may provide templates for regular patterned interactions on a daily basis, families also face the task of dealing with events that may be out of the ordinary and are cause for comment. In these instances, it is helpful to consider how family stories may be part of the practicing and representing family.

Family Stories

Family stories can be rich accounts of how the family makes sense of its social world, expressions of rules of conduct, and beliefs about the trustworthiness of relationships. When families are called up to recount a personal experience they set an interpretive frame that reflects how individuals understand events, how family members work together (or not), and expectations for reward or disappointment when interacting with others. It is possible to distinguish between the *act* of storytelling and the *content* of family tales. The act is closely linked to the practicing family and includes how parents and children engage each other in recounting personal experiences. The content, or coherence, of family narratives reflects beliefs and holds messages for conduct. We discuss each aspect in turn.

There are notable developmental and individual differences associated with the act of storytelling during early childhood. Parents report telling stories about their own growing up experiences, from infancy throughout the preschool years, and they report doing so with increasing regularity and as a family event (Fiese, Hooker, Kotary, Schwagler, & Rimmer, 1995). Children as young as 3 years of age will actively engage in conversations with their parents about personal experiences that later remain as autobiographical memories (Hudson, 2002). Parents assist children in the process of talking about past personal events in a scaffolding process, providing support for elaboration of details and reflection on how to behave. There are important individual differences in these interactions that have significant connections to the child's language development and later literacy skills. Simply put, some parents encourage their children to elaborate on past events with particular attention to how the child felt, how others responded, and connections across time and setting. Other parents, however, focus on just getting the facts and tend to repeat details rather than elaborate. These stylistic differences are related to the child's socioemotional development as well the development of literacy skills. For example, children raised in households where daily events are discussed in an elaborative narrative style tend to have children who are more securely attached (Fivush & Vasudeva, 2002; Laible, 2004). Further, elaborative styles are also associated with the development of early literacy skills (Reese, 1995).

The content of family stories, in contrast to the act, revolves around themes associated with socialization and trustworthiness of relationships. Through routine talk about trips to the park, personal transgressions when growing up, and lessons learned during challenging times families create a scrapbook of experiences that serve to represent family identity and provide roadmaps for behavior (Pratt & Fiese, 2004).

There is a developmental course to, and individual differences in, the thematic content of these stories. During early childhood, many of these tales include metaphors for how to behave. Many of the personal accounts and reminiscences between parent and child during the early school years focus around such themes as "How did you feel?" and "What would you do next time?" (Fivush & Fromhoff, 1988). These exchanges provide opportunities for parents to reinforce expectations for conduct as well as opportunities for the child to bring his or her own concerns and dilemmas to the conversation.

Interestingly, the types of stories told to boys and girls may differ in their emphasis on emotion versus practical advice. Boys are more likely to hear stories that involve elements of striving for success and how things work (Fiese & Bickham, 2004), whereas girls are more likely to hear stories that include themes of personal relationships and emotional significance (Fivush, Bohanke, Robertson, & Duke, 2004).

Family narratives also depict the trustworthiness of relationships and provide guidance in terms of how family members are to behave when they are together as a group. Families that recount personal experiences as times for establishing rewarding relationships and expect that others can be trusted are more likely to create social environments that are responsive to the child's emotions and reduce the likelihood that problematic behaviors will develop in early childhood (Fiese & Spangola, 2007; Warren, Emde, & Sroufe, 2000).

Variations in thematic content and elaborative style are a reflection of the cultural context of family narratives. Cultures differ in the degree to which there is value placed on the role of the individual and independence in contrast to maintaining social relationships in the interest of the group. These closely held values can be seen in the ways in which parents engage children in narratives across cultures. European American families tend to support conversations with their children about the self (Q. Wang, 2004). Spanish speaking immigrant mothers, however, tend focus on social skills and good behavior (Melzi, 2000).

Although family stories can be sources of entertainment, we are interested in them as markers of family functioning and illustrative of how personal meaning is transmitted across generations. There is a transactional process evident between the act of storytelling and the beliefs that are created over time. Children who engage in elaborative storytelling and reminiscence during preschool years are exposed to narratives rich in vocabulary and explanation. As an act, the child develops narrative competence that is associated with emerging literacy skills. The ways in which relationships are depicted in these stories provide a template for relationship expectations and guide behavior. Children who are exposed to personal accounts that depict social relationships as sources of support and reward are more likely to view others as trustworthy and may ultimately become more socially competent. No doubt educators can detect differences in children who come to school with a story to tell that revolves around excitement about learning and engaging in new experiences in contrast to children who are wary to share family secrets and shy away from interacting with others.

One way that early childhood educators may directly partner with parents to affect the transactional process is to create a partnership in the promotion of joint book reading and storytelling. Storybook reading can be most effective when it is an active process that fully engages the child. Families that incorporate reading aloud as part of their regular routines promote early literacy skills even when controlling for social address (Serpell et al., 2002). Reading aloud practices in early childhood settings that involve repetition of the story, active engagement of the children through physical prompts, are culturally relevant and involve dramatic play (Gillanders & Castro, 2011) can be reinforced in the home through lending libraries between home and school and tip sheets for parents distributed by early care centers. It is also possible to take advantage of new technologies such as PhotoVoice whereby families create scrapbooks and stories about important events in their lives (C. C. Wang & Pies, 2004). Working together with early childhood providers, it is possible for families to create stories of events such as the upcoming transition to kindergarten that reinforce positive interactions and have the potential for building literacy skills. An important feature of these storytelling tasks is not only the opportunities for building language skills but also the cementing of close personal relationships and building expectations for success. For further discussion on planning interventions based on the transactional model see Fiese & Wamboldt (2001; Sameroff & Fiese (2000).

Integrating Family Practices and Representations

From a transactional perspective, both the practicing and representing family code behavior across time and affect one another. Repetitive family practices come to have meaning over time and become the subject of representations. Representations, in turn, affect how the family interacts. We return to bedtime stories to illustrate this process. Consider a situation where parents have been brought up in the tradition of telling bedtime stories. Around the time that the child begins to talk, the parents implement a routine where they settle the child to sleep with a story. Initially, the stories may be short and take the form of nursery tales. As the child begins to expect the routine event, they may ask for particular stories, some of which may be experiences that the parent had when he or she was a child. These stories are told over and over again in an interactional context where the child is exposed not only to the content of the event but is a conversational partner. If the parent recounts tales of personal success or connectedness with others the child creates images of relationships as rewarding and sources of support in times of need. As the child begins to tell her or his own stories at bedtime, parents and child have the opportunity to problem solve about personal challenges that may encourage feelings of competence. At the point that the child transitions to school, he or she is a competent narrator paving the way for early literacy skills and socially ready to engage with others. We represent this process in Figure 25.2.

To summarize, family effects on child development are multiply determined and evolve over time. The child contributes to this process through his or her own personal style and experiences that are part of family life. Through repetitive interaction patterns and reinforcement of beliefs family identity is created. These interactions and beliefs serve to stabilize family life, ease transitions, and regulate child behavior. When there are environmental risks, however, different aspects of family functioning can be compromised making the child vulnerable to developing behavioral and learning problems. We now turn to two risk factors, poverty and parental psychopathology, and examine the potential for family practices and representations to protect children from the known risks associated with these conditions.

Family Risk and Protective Factors

We have emphasized the multiply determined nature of family process in relation to child development. Family process is not a unidimensional variable but one that operates in the realm of behavior and beliefs that are subject to stresses and conditions in the environment. Risk conditions do not operate in isolation either and are likely to cluster together and have cumulative rather than singular effects (Sameroff, 1995). Poverty has an overwhelming effect on child development (Evans, 2004). This section is dedicated to a discussion of the effects of poverty on family processes, with particular attention to neighborhood poverty and the potential for environmental chaos to act as a mediating factor.

Poverty and the Family

For the past decade, there has been an upward trend in the number of children living in poverty. Between 2000 and 2008, there was a 21% increase in the number of children living in families with income below the federal poverty level. Approximately 14 million children in the United States lived in poverty in the first decade of the 21st century (Wight, Chau, & Aratani, 2010). What are the consequences of living in poverty for young children and what role does the family play in potentially protecting children from the harmful effects of poverty?

First, young children living in poverty often experience food insecurity. That is, they do not have adequate sources of food at all times or a variety of nutritious foods. Food insecurity is a household problem that affects the entire family. In a recent survey of food insecure households with children, 52% reported that at times they could not afford to feed their children balanced meals and 25% reported that at times their children were not eating enough because the family could not afford enough food (Nord, 2003). The consequences of inadequate sources of, and poor quality food in, early childhood include a compromised immune system with preschool children having more colds (Alaimo, Olson, Frongillo, & Briefel, 2001), poorer health overall (Cook, et al., 2004), performing less well in kindergarten

(Winicki & Jemison, 2003), and being at increased risk for internalizing and externalizing behavior problems (Slopen, Fitzmaurice, Williams, & Gilman, 2010).

How might the overlapping conditions of poverty and household food insecurity affect family processes known to affect child development? First, families who rely on supplemental food assistance programs to adequately feed their children spend more time shopping for and preparing food and less time eating together than higher income families (Andrews & Hamrick, 2009). Lower income families experience more of a burden in carrying out daily routines (Fiese, Winter, & Botti, 2011; Roy, Tubbs, & Burton, 2004). This burden is often expressed through feelings of not being able to sufficiently balance caregiving tasks with added demands on time needed for transportation, finding child care, and oftentimes working more than one job (Roy et al., 2004). Further, parents with fewer economic resources also experience more stress in parenting, engaging in either harsh or nonresponsive parenting styles (Evans, 2004).

Children raised in poverty are often ill-equipped to make the transition from home to school (Rimm-Kaufmann, Pianta, & Cox, 2000). By the time they reach school age, children raised in low-income or poverty conditions are more likely than middle- or upper-middle-class children to experience multiple stressors in their immediate environment; overcrowding, poor quality of housing, and neighborhood violence, to name a few (Evans, 2004). Factors such as these have been linked to greater psychological distress in both urban and rural children (G.J. Duncan & Brooks-Gunn, 1997; Evans & English, 2002) and arguably have a negative impact on children's ability to explore new learning experiences and develop intellectually. Children who are more challenged psychologically by experiencing multiple stressors are in a less positive position to acquire new skills.

There are anecdotal examples of children who have succeeded despite any one of these stressors. One may call to mind a child who has thrived in school despite a background of poverty. If this child "made it," why can't another? Despite similarities in one or a few risk factors, it is important to consider that is not the presence of any particular stressor or a specific combination of risk factors that is uniquely detrimental for children. Rather, it is the cumulative value of any combination of them (Sameroff, 2010; Sameroff & MacKenzie, 2003). Sameroff and colleagues have demonstrated that when parental education, employment status, parental psychopathology, parent–child interaction patterns, child temperament, and neighborhood conditions are considered simultaneously child intelligence levels can be predicted both concurrently and prospectively (Guttman, Sameroff, & Cole, 2003). What is of interest for our discussion is that neither a single risk variable or even clusters of risk predicted child performance. Multiple risk factors acting in concert predict less optimal outcomes. For this reason, it is not possible to devise a simple formula identifying exactly which factors determine a negative outcome. Thus, it is not sufficient to state that being raised in poverty leads to poor outcomes for children. Rather, it is essential to consider which aspects of poverty, when, for whom, and under what conditions lead to compromised functioning. We consider how neighborhood factors, parental psychopathology, and family process may contribute to child outcome in these high-risk conditions.

Neighborhood Factors.   Families live in neighborhoods, and neighborhood factors, particularly high concentrations of poverty within relatively small geographic areas, have been associated with poorer child performance on measures of mental health, verbal ability, IQ scores, and school achievement (Leventhal & Brooks-Gunn, 2000; Leventhal & Newman, 2010). Findings such as these are not exclusive to children in urban neighborhoods. Low-income and poverty status in children and families living in rural communities have been identified as a risk factor as well (Evans, 2004).

Neighborhoods vary in terms of the social capital that is made available to families. This capital ranges from the physical and built environment that includes locations for learning such as libraries, cultural enrichment such as performance centers, and places for physical activity such as parks and recreation facilities. Lower income neighborhoods are typically less well-resourced in terms of technologies that promote learning (Evans, 2004) and parks for physical activity (Gordon-Larsen, Nelson, Page, & Popkin, 2006). For young children, this means decreased opportunities to interact in environments that have up-to-date computing equipment similar to what will be used in schools. Further, lack of access to parks and recreation facilities places the child at risk for developing unhealthy weight and its associated health consequences.

Social capital in neighborhoods also includes the availability of social support and relationships with neighbors. Poorer neighborhoods are also characterized by poor lighting, poorly maintained streets and sidewalks, and high rates of unoccupied buildings (Evans, 2004). Opportunities to form relationships with neighbors and develop sources of support can be compromised when there is a need to keep doors locked and transience is common. Faced with increasing rates of violence, families may feel powerless in protecting their children from gangs and illegal activities (Brooks-Gunn, 1997). What may be considered adaptive and supportive behavior in middle-class neighborhoods may actually place children at greater risk in poorer neighborhoods. For example, maintaining distance from some neighbors and sacrificing employment to be able to monitor children's behavior more closely may be adaptive for some high-risk families (Burton & Jarrett, 2000).

There are several differences in early literacy skills and the home environments of children raised in poverty compared to those who are not. In a large study of nearly 30,000 children and their families using NLSY data files, Bradley and colleagues (Bradley, Corwyn, McAdoo, &

Coll, 2001) employed the HOME inventory to assess different aspects of children's experiences in their homes, targeting specific comparisons between nonpoor and poor families, further broken down by race/ethnicity, comparing poor and nonpoor European American, African American, and Latino American families. For European American, African American, and Latino American families, it was observed that nonpoor parents were more likely to spontaneously speak to their children (excluding scolding) than poor parents. In addition, it was found that regardless of racial/ethnic group, poor families were more likely to have no books in the household and that regardless of race/ethnicity, poor parents were more likely than nonpoor parents to endorse that they never read to their children or only read to them a few times per year.

Poverty status had a greater impact on the availability of learning materials than did ethnicity. Generally, poor children were much less likely to have three or more children's books during infancy and early childhood than were nonpoor children. In addition, poor children were less likely to visit enriching places and events in the community. These differences were found across all ethnic groups and all age groups. During infancy and childhood, and across all racial/ethnic groups, nonpoor mothers were twice as likely as were poor mothers to read to their children three or more times per week.

The results of the Bradley and colleagues study suggest that children raised in poorer environments are less likely to be exposed to routine book reading and that their verbal environment, overall, may be relatively impoverished. However, it is possible to affect literacy skills and qualities of the home environment related to the child's preparedness to learn.

Recall the role that elaborative reminiscing and family storytelling may play in creating a sense of family identity and socializing children. Reese and colleagues have developed an intervention for families participating in Head Start that encourages elaborative reminiscing as part of a program to promote early literacy skills (Reese, Leywa, Sparks, & Grolnick, 2010). Mothers of children enrolled in Head Start were visited in their home and trained in either a dialogic (question/answer) joint book reading style or in elaborative reminiscing. The elaborative reminiscing group was encouraged to discuss past events with their children on a daily basis and then elaborate with their children through open ended questions and increasing their child's participation. At the end of the school year, children who had been exposed to the elaborative reminiscing practices in the home scored higher on an expressive vocabulary test, had better story comprehension, and produced narratives of higher quality than children exposed to the dialogic joint book reading intervention. This preliminary study suggests that home based interventions that promote family storytelling about routine events may have a positive effect on early literacy skills for children raised in low income environments.

Chaos in Low Income Environments

Consistent with the ecological model, the effects of poverty on child development can be seen as part of the cumulative effect of exposure to adverse events in the neighborhood and family, and compromised social capital. However, a focus on the risk factors alone does not indicate the process by which poverty may affect the promotive factors known to positively affect child development. From a family systems perspective, it is particularly important to identify how families respond to and potentially counteract the harmful effects of high risk environments in order to protect children and promote health and well-being. One framework that allows for an examination of process level factors and the intersection of family and neighborhood factors is an examination of family chaos.

Bronfenbrenner and Evans (2000) have offered a perspective on chaos in family life describing it as "frenetic activity, lack of structure, unpredictability in everyday activities, [and] high levels of ambient stimulation" (p. 21). There are several characteristics that are shared by chaotic environments, whether at home, in neighborhoods, or in schools. There is a high level of background noise, physical crowding, schedules are disrupted and plans have to be changed at the last minute, time is perceived to be out of one's control, and conversations are often interrupted (Bradley, 2004; Evans, Gonnella, Marcynyszyn, Gentile, & Salpekar, 2005; Fiese & Winter, 2010). Living in chaotic environments involves not only the disruption of daily activities but also the felt experience of an uncontrollable environment.

For families living in poverty, juggling time is an ever present occupation. For parents with limited economic resources, daily routines of feeding, grooming, dropping off children to multiple care providers, is more than just hectic, report Roy and colleagues (Roy et al., 2004). There is a sense that time is out of control and daily routines are driven by those outside the family such as bus drivers, bosses, and a carillon of childcare providers.

Chaotic living conditions including high levels of background noise (e.g., the constant presence of television) and family instability (changes in residence and partners) affect young children's health and preparedness to learn. In a small pilot study of children enrolled in Head Start it was found that children who lived in more chaotic households got less sleep and evidenced a sense of learned helplessness toward learning (E. D. Brown & Low, 2008). Longitudinal studies also suggest that environmental chaos (noise, crowding, foot traffic) and home chaos (lack of routines, confusion) mediate the relation between poverty and child socioemotional development (Evans, et al., 2005).

In addition to creating feelings of learned helplessness, chaotic environments may also disrupt positive parenting practices. High levels of home chaos have been found to be related to higher levels of negative parenting and lower levels of positive parenting (Coldwell, Pike, & Dunn, 2006; Dumas, Nissley et al., 2005). Further, parents in chaotic households are less likely to positively respond to their child's emotions, and that in turn is related to behavior problems (Valiente, Lemery-Chalfant, & Reiser, 2007).

Neighborhoods can also be characterized by relative degrees of chaos: Housing density, physical disorder, instability of residents, neighborhood level routines (e.g., rhythm of daily life in terms of the number of residents leaving for work at the same time), and supervision and monitoring of children in the neighborhood (Brooks-Gunn, Johnson, & Leventhal, 2010). Unfortunately, the empirical base indicating the cumulative effects of neighborhood chaos factors on child development is scant. There is evidence to suggest, however, that living in noisy neighborhoods (e.g., those close to airports) increases risk for reading problems and lowers academic performance (Evans, 2006). Perhaps the strongest evidence linking neighborhood chaos and child outcomes is the role of neighborhood monitoring of children's activities and collective efficacy. When family members feel that they can trust their neighbors and have a sense that there is collective support in the neighborhood in contrast to chaotic and unpredictable relationships with neighbors, then there is typically more monitoring of child and adolescent behavior. This type of collective monitoring is most closely associated with rates of violence in the neighborhood (Leventhal & Brooks-Gunn, 2000). Although most commonly studied in families with adolescents, neighborhood peer relationships in the preschool years are also important, and aggressive behaviors can be modeled from neighborhood peers as young as 3 years of age (Leventhal & Brooks-Gunn, 2000).

A Resiliency Framework for Early Childhood Educators

Whereas an examination of environmental chaos points to the multiple layers of influence on child development and an appreciation of the ecological foundations of early learning, it provides little direction in terms of active solutions for families in their daily lives. In order to more fully appreciate how families face daily challenges so that their children may thrive, a family resiliency framework is warranted. Researchers have identified a set of family level characteristics that promote resiliency and increase the likelihood that children will be able to face and overcome adversity (Black & Lobo, 2008; Luthar, Cicchetti, & Becker, 2000; Masten, 2001; Patterson, 2002). In general, families that are able to set aside time to be together, interact in a warm and supportive manner, communicate their thoughts and feelings in a direct manner, create regular and meaningful routines and rituals, and are flexible during normative and nonnormative transitions are more likely to protect their children from the harmful effects of risk. We have already discussed the important role of family routines in promoting health development for children. As a process for promoting resiliency, it is important to point out how routines and rituals that include supportive and positive forms of communication are more likely to be associated with positive outcomes for children (Dickstein, Seifer et al., 1998; Fiese, Winter, & Botti, 2011).

Consistent with the resiliency framework that has identified core elements at the family level that may serve as resources for children under high risk conditions, there are parallel processes in early childhood settings that may serve similar functions. Yates and colleagues have proposed that (Yates, Egeland, & Sroufe, 2003) early childhood education and care settings are provision resources that may moderate the effects of family level adversity. Applying principles of developmental theory and evidence supporting the central role of attachment relationships during the early years, qualities of the early care and education environment can serve as a resource for resilience. Indeed, Hall and colleagues have demonstrated in a random sample of over 2,000 preschool age children, the moderating effects of teacher–child relationships on cognitive development in the context of family risk (e.g., low levels of maternal education, unemployment, number of nonparental caregivers; Hall et al., 2009).

Considering the strong influence of regular routines in family life, the power of strong relationships, and the importance of stability for young children there are several opportunities where early childhood educators can serve as resources for families. Efforts to provide parents with educational materials about the importance of regular routines, information about how to overcome barriers to implementing routines, reinforcing regular storytelling, and providing connections between activities at home and school appear to be warranted. Early childhood educators are uniquely poised to take their knowledge of the importance of building quality relationships to build these important parenting skills.

Summary

Household poverty places a major challenge in raising children prepared to learn. However, poverty is more than just a lack of economic resources. It affects nearly every aspect of daily living from place of residence, allocation of time, and creation of routines. Household poverty increases the risk that children will be raised in chaotic environments that include high levels of ambient noise, residential crowding, low levels of collective efficacy in neighborhoods, disruption of family routines such as mealtime and bedtime, and promotion of feelings of learned helplessness.

There is cause for optimism, however. A resiliency framework suggests that family level processes that include a cohesive family unit, regular routines, and open communication can protect children from risk. Further, the quality of the preschool environment may further buffer children from adversity. Figure 25.3 outlines those factors that may protect children from chaotic environments and those that will likely increase risk. A review of risk and

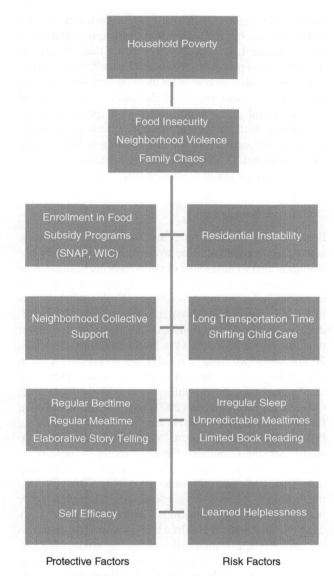

Figure 25.3 Possible factors to protect children in chaotic environments or increase their risk

resilience also points to the important role of connecting schools with families.

Connecting Schools with the Changing Face of Families

A child's early success in school will rely in part on how well connected the family is to the school and how aware of school practices. Families who form active partnerships with early childhood settings and in the early elementary school years have a positive impact on child outcomes (J. L. Epstein & Sanders, 2002). The research on promoting family–school partnerships is relatively extensive and consistent in supporting more parental involvement in the early school years (Arnold, Zeljo, Doctoroff, & Ortiz, 2008; J. L. Epstein & Sanders, 2002; Reynolds, 1992). However, there is some indication that for some parents more involvement may be due to calls from schools as a result of their children's disruptive behaviors (Pomerantz, Moorman, & Litwack, 2007). Rather than detail the mechanisms of parent involvement and connecting schools and families, this section is focused on how the changing face of families may present challenges to early childhood educators and offers some solutions to promote better engagement with families. In particular, this section focuses on the increasing number of children being raised in single parent households and ways to involve fathers more in early childhood education.

Diversity in Family Life

Family living arrangements are becoming increasingly complex, which affects the availability of resources for young children. The number of children being born to single parents has risen from 5% in 1960 to approximately 40% at the beginning of the 21st century (Kreider, 2007). This increase is due, primarily, to the increasing number of children being raised in households where cohabitation rather than marriage characterizes the family structure (Bumpass, 2000). About two-fifths of all children spend some time in a cohabiting family. This is important because cohabitation results in relationship instability for children. For example, Osborne and McLanahan (2007) have identified different forms of unmarried households to include cohabiting, households where there were "visiting" or dating relationships, and single mothers. Children living in these types of households experienced different levels of relationship transitions such that 30% of single parent, 20% of "visiting," and 10% of cohabiting households experienced three or more relationship transitions between birth and 3 years of age. In contrast, for children born in married households the rate of relationship transitions was approximately 2%.

The effects of relationship instability on early child development may be both direct and indirect. Relationship instability may indirectly affect child cognitive and social development by compromising parenting skills. Mothers who experience multiple relationship transitions during the early child raising years are more likely to experience stress and feel ill-equipped to meet the demands of parenting (S. L. Brown, 2010). This stress and ambiguity in relationship status may affect the child's sense of security. Single parents may also spend less time with their children (Sandberg & Hofferth, 2001), a known resource to protect children from adversity. Most notable is that the effects of relationship instability and transitions are most profound during the early childhood years. Young children are more sensitive to changes in relationships, the effects of residential moves, and economic hardships than during middle childhood (G. J. Duncan, Brooks-Gunn, Yeung, & Smith, 1998; Shonkoff & Phillips, 2000). The consequences of early relationship disruptions and instability include poorer health, problematic behaviors, and poorer peer relationships (S. L. Brown, 2010; Cavanagh & Huston, 2008).

The solution, however, does not appear to be promoting marriage at any cost (S. L. Brown, 2010). The essential ingredients associated with outcomes during early childhood appear to be the quality of relationships and provision of resources. In this regard, there are several opportunities for early childhood educators to form positive partnerships with parents who may have the sole responsibility for raising their children. Parent involvement in early care and education has proven to predict later academic achievement and school competence above and beyond the influence of family background (Miedel & Reynolds, 1999; Reynolds, 2000). The key elements to promoting family involvement appear to be establishing a partnership of shared responsibility for the child's learning, involvement in early care and education activities, and establishing quality relationships between parents and educators (Weiss, Lopez, & Rosenberg, 2010). Common activities that would promote early learning in the home and school could be shared book reading and encouraging parents to attend meals and snacks in schools. This reinforcement of parallel activities in home and early care settings has the potential to benefit the child as well as model and reinforce self-efficacy for the parent.

Involving Fathers in Early Childhood Education

Although there has been an increasing appreciation of the important role that fathers play in child development (Parke, 2004), fathers have not always been included in systematic ways in family–school partnership programs. This is somewhat surprising given the evidence that when fathers are involved in the educational process their children do better in school (National Center for Education Statistics [NCES], 1998). An innovative program has been developed by McBride and colleagues to promote father involvement in a prekindergarten program that serves children at risk for later school failure (McBride, Rane, & Bae, 2001). Involving fathers is set as a priority in the pre-K program, but by intervening directly with teachers, rather than with fathers. In-service sessions with teachers were conducted to provide information about the positive benefits of father involvement and set goals for father involvement. Activities were identified that would encourage father involvement such as bowling nights with children. After the 26-week program, the treatment group had significantly more family involvement overall with, and more father involvement than families served by a control group where teacher behavior was not altered.

McBride offers general principles of program development for early childhood educators that can promote more father involvement (McBride, Dyer, & Rane, 2008):

1. Develop a clear rationale. If an early childhood program desires to involve fathers more in its programming it is important to clearly articulate the benefits of father involvement. This will be likely to include a deeper understanding of the family ecology including sociode-

mographic factors within the family and the role of the father in the family.

2. Acknowledge resistance. Not all teachers will embrace initiatives that focus on fathers. This may be particularly true when fathers are seen as "absent" partners and there is a question of directing limited resources to resistant players.

3. Clearly specify targets. This advice holds true for any program development. However, when launching a new initiative to promote father engagement it is important to clearly specify who in the family may be playing the role of the father. This may not be the biological father but may be an uncle or other male figure.

4. Do not reinvent the wheel. Educators should consider whether volunteer programs designed for mothers or other community members may fit well with initiatives to encourage father involvement.

5. Help women become facilitators. It is unlikely that early childhood programs will be fully staffed with enough men to launch such an effort. Identifying women in the organization who can provide outreach and facilitate program development is important.

6. Involve mothers in developing the initiative. It is important to keep mothers involved in program development. Mothers are often the gatekeepers for access to their children (McBride, Schoppe-Sullivan, & Ho, 2005) and can make or break initiatives involving fathers if they feel that the mother's role is not also acknowledged.

7. Continue to meet mothers' needs. Consistent with the role of gatekeeper it is important to keep mothers involved for a whole family approach.

8. Create a father/male friendly environment. Create a space for fathers including their own bulletin board, make sure there are adequate facilities for men, and tailor activities for men.

9. Acknowledge diversity. As has been noted in this chapter, family structures can change. It is important to keep track of the changes in family structure and whether changes in residence also mean changes in partnership.

10. Proceed slowly. Start slow in building father initiatives and do not get discouraged if it takes a while for the initiative to gain speed.

11. Provide training and support services. Seek out experts in your community on the benefits of father involvement and have them provide in-service sessions for staff members.

12. Evaluate and revise efforts. Programming should be an ongoing and evolving practice that takes into account successes as well as barriers to implementation.

Involving the whole family, including fathers, into early childhood programs has the potential to benefit children in several ways. There are opportunities for an enriched learning environment through added verbal stimulation as well as physical play. There is also the added benefit that fathers can provide support for mothers and become more fully engaged in the daily life of the child. Although it may take added effort to include fathers systematically in early childhood programs, they too are part of the child's future.

Integrating Family Context and Early Childhood Education: Summary and Conclusions

Families are complex and dynamic systems. Families practice regular routines that organize daily life and can provide a sense of order and predictability for young children. Over time, families create beliefs about relationships based, in part, on repetitive interactions occurring in routine settings such as mealtime, bedtime, and preparing for school. Child functioning at any given point in time is the result of a series of transactions between parenting practices and beliefs about relationships. Children may be placed at risk for less than optimal outcomes when they are raised in chaotic environments. For early childhood educators, the take home message is that families come to create definitions of who they are as a group. This family identity will shape how the child responds to classroom structure, his or her preparedness to engage in educational activities, and potentially in academic success. There are multiple ways in which families create their identity. For some families, there are high expectations for child success and daily life is organized around supporting enriching activities. For other families, protecting children from harm is a priority and family level efforts must be directed toward keeping the family safe. In either case, families typically work hard to insure optimal development for their children given the context in which they live.

There are four lessons to consider when linking families and early childhood educators. First, it may be beneficial to capitalize on routines as a way to connect families and educators. Setting aside regular times to review newly learned skills at home and perhaps creating family night activities that support learning can become part of routine communications between parents and early childhood educators. Parents should be assured that what appears as a mundane task may afford opportunities for learning. Routine conversations at the dinner table, counting the silverware when putting away the dishes, learning about bacteria when taking a walk to the pond, are examples where daily practices are rich learning opportunities. Indeed, folding learning into these routine interactions will likely result in more sustained interest than presenting children with additional drill sheets during homework time.

Second, storytelling provides a rich opportunity to develop early literacy skills, problem solve, and gain valuable insight to the world of children. These stories need not be complicated, or even revealing of family secrets. Rather they can set the stage for linking personal events experienced in home and school.

Third, families are diverse. With the changing nature of family structure, it is important to remember that a child's family is not necessarily restricted to a mother or father. Extended family members, neighbors, and kinship ties outside the local area can be sources of support. Each family will create its own unique routines and have its own stories to tell that can aid educators in better understanding the children under their charge. It is also important to include fathers or prominent male figures in early childhood programs.

Fourth, by their very nature families change. Not only are there changes in membership through births, deaths, and dissolution of relationships, but there are also developmental changes that foster the child's growth. By being sensitive to the ways in which families negotiate transitions between developmental stages as well as prepare their children to transition from home to school settings, educators may become a valuable resource for families during these vulnerable periods.

Families and early childhood educators bear the responsibility of preparing future generations to become productive citizens and lifelong learners. Recognizing the complexity of family life is not an impossible challenge but one worthy of respect. Being aware of the potential chaos in a child's family life and creating opportunities for calm, organized, and meaningful exchanges between home and school places, early childhood educators play an important role in the health and well-being of all children.

Acknowledgments

Preparation of this chapter was supported, in part, by grants from the National Institute of Mental Health (MH51771), National Institute of Child Health and Human Development (HD057447), and the U.S. Department of Agriculture (Hatch 793-328). Address all correspondence: to Barbara H. Fiese, PhD, The Family Resiliency Center, 1016B Doris Kelley Christopher Hall, MC-081, 904 W. Nevada, Urbana, IL, 61801, bhfiese@illinois.edu.

References

Ackerman, B. P., Brown, E. D., & Izard, C. E. (2004). The relations between persistent poverty and contextual risk and children's behavior in elementary school. *Developmental Psychology, 40*, 367–377.

Ackerman, B. P., Kogos, J., Youngstrom, E., Schoff, K., & Izard, C. (1999). Family instability and the problem behaviors of children from economically disadvantaged families. *Developmental Psychology, 35*, 258–268.

Adam, E. K., & Chase-Landsdale, P. L. (2002). Home sweet home(s): Parental separations, residential moves and adjustment in low-income adolescent girls. *Developmental Psychology, 38*, 792–805.

Alaimo, K., Olson, C. M., Frongillo, E. A., & Briefel, R. R. (2001). Food insufficiency, family income, and health in US preschool and school-aged children. *American Journal of Public Health, 91*, 781–786.

Amato, P. R. (2005). The impact of family formation change on the cognitive, social, and emotional well-being of the next generation. *Future of Children, 15*, 75–96.

Andersen, S. E., & Whitaker, R. C. (2010). Household routines and obesity in US preschool-aged children. *Pediatrics, 125*(3), 420–428.

Andrews, M., & Hamrick, K. (2009). *Shopping for, preparing, and eating food: Where does the time go?* Retrieved from http://www.ers.usda.gov/AmberWaves/December09/Findings/ShoppingFood.htm.

Arnold, D. H., Zeljo, A., Doctoroff, G. L., & Ortiz, C. (2008). Parent involvement in preschool: Predictors and the relation of involvement to preliteracy development. *School Psychology Review, 37*, 74–90.

Beals, D. E. (2001). Eating and reading: Links between family conversations with preschoolers and later language and literacy. In D. K. Dickinson & P. O. Tabors (Eds.), *Beginning literacy with language: Young children at home and school* (pp. 75–92). Baltimore, MD: Brookes.

Black, K., & Lobo, M. (2008). A conceptual review of family resilience factors. *Journal of Family Nursing, 14*, 33–55.

Bradley, R. H. (2004). Chaos, culture, and covariance structures: A dynamic systems view of children's experiences at home. *Parenting: Science and Practice, 4*, 243–257.

Bradley, R. H., Corwyn, R. F., McAdoo, H. P., & Coll, C. G. (2001). The home environments of children in the United States. Part I: Variations by age, ethnicity, and poverty status. *Child Development, 72*, 1844–1867.

Brandon, P. D. (2004). The child care arrangements of preschool-age children in immigrant families in the United States. *International Migration, 49*(42), 65–87.

Brody, G. H., & Flor, D. L. (1997). Maternal psychological functioning, family processes, and child adjustment in rural, single-parent, African American families. *Developmental Psychology, 33*, 1000–1011.

Bronfenbrenner, U., & Evans, G. W. (2000). Developmental science in the 21st century: Emerging questions, theoretical models, research designs, and empirical findings. *Social Development, 9*, 115–125.

Bronfenbrenner, U., & Morris, P. A. (1998). The ecology of developmental processes. In W. Damon & R. M. Lerner (Eds.), *Handbook of child psychology* (pp. 993–1028). Hoboken, NJ: Wiley.

Brooks-Gunn, J. (1997). Neighborhood poverty. In G. D. J. Brooks-Gunn, & L. Aber (Eds.), *Neighborhood Poverty: Context and consequences for children* (pp. 279–298). New York: Russell Sage Foundation.

Brooks-Gunn, J., Johnson, A. D., & Leventhal, T. (2010). Disorder, turbulence, and resources in children's homes and neighborhoods. In G. W. Evans & T. D. Wachs (Eds.), *Chaos and its influence on children's development: An ecological perspective* (pp. 155–170). Washington, DC: American Psychological Association.

Brown, E. D., & Low, C. M. (2008). Chaotic living conditions and sleep problems associated with children's responses to academic challenges. *Journal of Family Psychology, 22*, 920–923.

Brown, S. L. (2010). Marriage and child well-being: Research and policy perspectives. *Journal of Marriage and Family, 72*, 1059–1077.

Bumpass, L. L. H. (2000). Trends in cohabitation and implications for children's family contexts in the United States. *Population Studies, 54*, 29–41.

Burchinal, M., Nelson, L., Carlson, M., & Brooks-Gunn, J. (2008). Neighborhood characteristics and child care type and quality. *Early Education and Development, 19*, 702–725.

Burton, L. M., & Jarrett, R. L. (2000). In the mix, yet on the margins: The place of families in urban neighborhood and child development research. *Journal of Marriage and Family, 62*, 1114–1135.

Buysse, V., Castro, D. C., West, T., & Skinner, M. (2005). Addressing the needs of Latino children: A national survey of state administrators of early childhood programs. *Early Childhood Research Quarterly, 20*, 146–163.

Cavanagh, S. E., & Huston, A. C. (2008). The timing of family instability and children's social development. *Journal of Marriage and Family, 70*, 1258–1269.

Chase-Landsdale, P. L., & Gordon, R. A. (1996). Economic hardship and the development of five- and six-year-olds: Neighborhoods and regional perspectives. *Child Development, 67*, 3338–3367.

Child Trends, C. (2003). Regular bedtime and mealtime. Retrieved from http://www.childtrendsdatabank.org/archivepgs/91.htm

Coldwell, J., Pike, A., & Dunn, J. (2006). Household chaos-links with parenting and child behaviour. *Journal of Child Psychology and Psychiatry, 47*, 1116–1122.

Cook, J. T., Frank, D. A., Berkowitz, C., Black, M. M., Casey, P. H., Cutts, D. B., et al. (2004). Food insecurity is associated with adverse health outcomes among human infants and toddlers. *Journal of Nutrition, 134*, 1432–1438.

Cowan, P. A., & Cowan, C. P. (Eds.). (2003). *Normative family transitions, normal family processes, and healthy child development* (3rd ed.). New York: Guilford.

Cox, M., & Paley, B. (1997). Families as systems. *Annual Review of Psychology, 48*, 243–267.

Dickstein, S., Seifer, R., Hayden, L. C., Schiller, M., Sameroff, A. J., Keitner, G. I., et al. (1998). Levels of family assessment: II. Impact of maternal psychopathology on family functioning. *Journal of Family Psychology, 12*, 23–40.

Dickstein, S., St. Andre, M., Sameroff, A. J., Seifer, R., & Schiller, M. (1999). Maternal depression, family functioning, and child outcomes: A narrative assessment. In B. H. Fiese, A. J. Sameroff, H. D. Grotevant, F. S. Wamboldt, S. Dickstein, & D. L. Fravel (Eds.), *The stories that families tell: Narrative coherence, narrative interaction, and relationship beliefs. Monographs of the Society for Research in Child Development, 64*(2), Serial No. 257, 84–104).

Dumas, J. E., Nissley, J., Nordstrom, A., Smith, E. P., Prinz, R. J., & Levine, D. W. (2005). Home chaos: Sociodemographic, parenting, interactional, and child correlates. *Journal of Clinical Child and Adolescent Psychology, 34*, 93–104.

Duncan, G. J., & Brooks-Gunn, J. (1997). *Consequences of growing up poor.* New York: Russell Sage Foundation.

Duncan, G. J., Brooks-Gunn, J., Yeung, W. J., & Smith, J. R. (1998). How much does childhood poverty affect the lives of children? *American Sociological Review, 63*, 406–423.

Epstein, J. L., & Sanders, M. G. (2002). Family, school, and community partnershps. In M. H. Bornstein (Ed.), *Handbook of Parenting* (Vol. 5, pp. 407–437). Mahwah, NJ: Erlbaum.

Epstein, N. B., Ryan, C. E., Bishop, D. S., Miller, I. W., & Keitner, G. I. (2003). The McMaster model: A view of healthy family functioning. In F. Walsh (Ed.), *Normal family processes* (3rd ed., pp. 581–607). New York: Guilford.

Evans, G. W. (2004). The environment of childhood poverty. *American Psychologist, 59*, 77–92.

Evans, G. W. (2006). Child development and the physical environment. *Annual Review of Psychology, 57*, 423–451.

Evans, G. W., & English, K. (2002). The environment of poverty: Multiple stressor exposure, psychophysiological stress, and socioemotional adjustment. *Child Development, 73*, 1238–1248.

Evans, G. W., Gonnella, C., Marcynyszyn, L. A., Gentile, L., & Salpekar, N. (2005). The role of chaos and poverty and children's socioemotional adjustment. *Psychological Science, 16*, 560–565.

Falicov, C. J. (2003). Immigrant family processes. In F. Walsh (Ed.), *Normal Family Processes* (3rd ed., pp. 280–300). New York: Guilford.

Fiese, B. H. (2000). Family matters: A systems view of family effects on children's cognitive health. In R. J. Sternberg & E. L. Grigorenko (Eds.), *Environmental effects on cognitive abilities* (pp. 39–57). Mahwah, NJ: Erlbaum.

Fiese, B. H. (2002). Routines of daily living and rituals in family life: A glimpse at stability and change during the early school years. *Zero to Three, 22*, 10–13.

Fiese, B. H. (2006). *Family routines and rituals.* New Haven, CT: Yale University Press.

Fiese, B. H., & Bickham, N. L. (2004). Pincurling grandpa's hair in the comfy chair: Parents' stories of growing up and potential links to socialization in the preschool years. In M. W. Pratt & B. H. Fiese (Eds.), *Family stories across time and generations* (pp. 259–277). Mahwah, NJ: Erlbaum.

Fiese, B. H., Hooker, K. A., Kotary, L., & Schwagler, J. (1993). Family rituals in the early stages of parenthood. *Journal of Marriage and the Family, 55*(3), 633–642.

Fiese, B. H., Hooker, K. A., Kotary, L., Schwagler, J., & Rimmer, M. (1995). Family stories in the early stages of parenthood. *Journal of Marriage and the Family, 57*(3), 763–770.

Fiese, B. H., & Marjinsky, K. A. T. (1999). Dinnertime stories: Connecting relationship beliefs and child behavior. In B. H. Fiese, A. J. Sameroff, H. D. Grotevant, F. S. Wamboldt, S. Dickstein, & D. Fravel (Eds.), *The stories that families tell: Narrative coherence, narrative interaction, and relationship beliefs. Monographs of the Society for Research in Child Development, 64*(2), Serial No. 257, 52–68).

Fiese, B. H., & Sameroff, A. J. (1999). The family narrative consortium: A multidimensional approach to narratives. In B. H. Fiese, A. J. Sameroff, H. D. Grotevant, F. S. Wamboldt, S. Dickstein, & D. L. Fravel (Eds.), *The stories that families tell: Narrative coherence, narrative interaction, and relationship beliefs. Monographs of the Society for Research in Child Development, 64*(2, Serial No. 257,. 1–36).

Fiese, B. H., & Spangola, M. (2007). The interior life of the family: Looking from the inside out and outside in. In A. S. Masten (Ed.), *Multilevel dynamics in developmental psychopathology: Pathways to the future.* (pp. 119–150). Mahwah, NJ: Erlbaum.

Fiese, B. H., & Wamboldt, F. S. (2001). Family routines, rituals, and asthma management: A proposal for family based strategies to increase treatment adherence. *Families, Systems, and Health, 18*, 405–418.

Fiese, B. H., & Winter, M. A. (2010). Family dynamics of chaos and its relation to children's socio-emotional wellbeing. . In G. W. Evans & T. D. Wachs (Eds.), *Chaos and children's development: Levels of analysis and mechanisms* (pp. 49–66). Washington DC: American Psychological Association Press.

Fiese, B. H., Winter, M. A., & Botti, J. C. (2011). The ABC's of family mealtimes: Observational lessons for promoting healthy outcomes for children with persistent asthma. *Child Development, 82*, 133–145.

Fivush, R., Bohanke, J., Robertson, R., & Duke, M. (2004). Family narratives and the development of children's emotional well-being. In M. W. Pratt & B. H. Fiese (Eds.), *Family narratives across time and generations* (pp. 55–76). Mahwah, NJ: Erlbaum.

Fivush, R., & Fromhoff, F. A. (1988). Style and structure in mother–child conversations about the past. *Discourse Processes, 11*, 337–355.

Fivush, R., & Vasudeva, A. (2002). Remembering to relate: Socioemotional correlates of mother–child reminiscing. *Journal of Cognition and Development, 3*, 73–90.

Gable, S., Chang, Y., & Krull, J. L. (2007). Television watching and frequency of family meals are predictive of overweight onset and persistence in a national sample of school-age children. *Journal of the American Dietetic Association, 107*, 53–61.

Gillanders, C., & Castro, D. C. (2011). Storybook reading for young dual language learners. *Young Children, 66*(1), 91–93.

Gordon-Larsen, P., Nelson, M., Page, P., & Popkin, B. M. (2006). Inequality in the built environment underlies key health disparities in physical activity and obesity. *Pediatrics, 117*, 417–424.

Guttman, L. M., Sameroff, A. J., & Cole, R. (2003). Academic growth curve trajectories from 1st to 12th grade: Effects of multiple social risk factors and perschool child factors. *Developmental Psychology, 39*, 777–790.

Hall, J., Sylva, K., Melhuish, E., Sammons, P., Siraj-Blatchford, I., & Taggart, B. (2009). The role of pre-school quality in promoting resilience in the cognitive development of young children. *Oxford Review of Education, 35*, 331–352.

Hellbrugge, T., Lange, J. E., Rutenfranz, J., & Stehr, K. (1964). Circadian periodicity of physiological functions in different stages of infancy and childhood. *Annals of the New York Academy of Science, 117*, 361–373.

Hudson, J. A. (2002). Do you know what we're going to do this summer? Mothers' talk to preschool children about future events. *Journal of Cognitive Development, 3*, 49–71.

Kreider, R. M. (2007). *Living arrangements of children:2004. Current populations report.* Washington DC: U. S. Census Bureau.

Laible, D. (2004). Mother–child discourse in two contexts: Links with child temperament, attachment security, and socioemotional competence. *Developmental Psychology, 40*, 979–992.

Lavigne, J. V., Arend, R., Rosenblum, D., Smith, A., Weissbluth, M., Binns, H., et al. (1999). Sleep and behavior problems among preschoolers. *Journal of Developmental and Behavioral Pediatrics, 20*, 164–169.

Leventhal, T., & Brooks-Gunn, J. (2000). The neighborhoods they live in: The effects of neighborhood residence on child and adolescent outcomes. *Psychological Bulletin, 126*, 309–337.

Leventhal, T., & Newman, S. (2010). Housing and child development. *Children and Youth Services Review, 32*, 1165–1174.

Luthar, S. S., Cicchetti, D., & Becker, B. (2000). The construct of resilience: A critical evaluation and guidelines for future work. *Child Development, 71*, 543–562.

Masten, A. S. (2001). Ordinary magic: Resilience processes in development. *American Psychologist, 56*, 227–238.

McBride, B. A., Dyer, W. J., & Rane, T. R. (2008). Family partnerships in early childhood programs: Don't forget fathers/men. In M. M. Cornish (Ed.), *Promising practices for partnering with families in the early years* (pp. 41–57). Charlotte, NC: Information Age.

McBride, B. A., Rane, T. R., & Bae, J. (2001). Intervening with teachers to encourage father/male involvement in early childhood programs. *Early Childhood Research Quarterly, 16*, 77–93.

McBride, B. A., Schoppe-Sullivan, S. J., & Ho, M. (2005). The mediating role of fathers' school involvement on student achievement. *Journal of Applied Developmental Psychology, 26*, 201–216.

McDonough, S. C. (2000). Interaction guidance: An approach for difficult to engage families. In C. H. Zeenah (Ed.), *Handbook of infant mental health* (pp. 485–493). New York: Guilford.

Melzi, G. (2000). Cultural variations in the construction of personal narratives: Central American and European American mothers' elicitation styles. *Discourse Processes, 30*, 153–177.

Miedel, W. T., & Reynolds, A. J. (1999). Parent involvement in early intervention for disadvantaged children: Does it matter? *Journal of School Psychology, 37*, 379–402.

Milan, S., Snow, S., & Belay, S. (2007). The context of preschool children's sleep: Racial/Ethnic differences in sleep locations, routines, and concerns. *Journal of Family Psychology, 21*, 20–28.

National Center for Education Statistics (NCES). (1998). Students do better when their fathers are involved in school. Retrieved from http://www/nces.ed.gov/pubs98/98121.html

Nord, M. (2003). *Food insecurity in households with children.* Retrieved from http://www.ers.usda.gov/publications/fanrr34/fanrr34-13/.

Norton, D. (1993). Diversity, early socialization, and temporal development: The dual perspective revisited. *Social Work, 38*, 82–90.

Osborne, C., & McClanahan, S. (2007). Partnership instability and child well-being. *Journal of Marriage and Family, 69*, 1065–1083.

Parke, R. D. (2004). Development in the family. *Annual Review of Psychology, 55*, 365–399.

Patterson, J. M. (2002). Understanding family resilience. *Journal of Clinical Psychology, 7*, 233–246.

Pomerantz, E. M., Moorman, E. A., & Litwack, S. D. (2007). The how, whom, and why of parents' involvement in children's academic lives: More is not always better. *Review of Educational Research, 77*, 373–410.

Pratt, M. W., & Fiese, B. H. (2004). Families, stories and the life course: An ecological context. In M. W. Pratt & B. H. Fiese (Eds.), *Family stories across time and generations* (pp. 1–26). Mahwah, NJ: Erlbaum.

Reese, E. (1995). Predicting children's literacy from mother–child conversations. *Cognitive Development, 10*, 381–405.

Reese, E., Leywa, D., Sparks, A., & Grolnick, W. (2010). Maternal elaborative reminiscing increases low-income children's narrative skills relative to dialogic reading. *Early Education and Development, 21*, 318–342.

Reiss, D. (1989). The practicing and representing family. In A. J. Sameroff & R. Emde (Eds.), *Relationship disturbances in early childhood* (pp. 191–220). New York: Basic Books.

Reynolds, A. J. (1992). Comparing measures of parental involvement and their effects on academic achievement. *Early Childhood Research Quarterly,, 7*, 441–462.

Reynolds, A. J. (2000). *Success in early intervention: The Chicago Child–Parent Centers.* Lincoln: University of Nebraska Press.

Rimm-Kaufmann, S. E., Pianta, R. C., & Cox, M. J. (2000). Teachers' judgments of problems in the transition to kindergarten. *Early Childhood Research Quarterly,, 15*, 147–166.

Roopnarine, J., Bynoe, P. F., & Singh, R. (2004). Factors tied to the schooling of children of English-speaking and Caribbean immigrants in the United States. In U. P. Gielen & J. Roopnarine (Eds.), *Childhood and adolescence: Cross-cultural perspectives and applications* (pp. 319–349). Westport, CT: Praeger.

Roy, K. M., Tubbs, C. Y., & Burton, L. M. (2004). Don't have no time: Daily rhythms and the organization of time for low-income families. *Family Relations, 53*, 168–178.

Sameroff, A. J. (1995). General systems theories and developmental psychopathology. In D. Cicchetti & D. Cohen (Eds.), *Handbook of developmental psychopathology* (Vol. 1, pp. 659–695). New York: Wiley.

Sameroff, A. J. (2010). A unified theory of development: A dialectic integration of nature and nurture. *Child Development, 81*, 6–22.

Sameroff, A. J., & Fiese, B. H. (2000). Transactional regulation: The developmental ecology of early intervention. In S. J. Meisels & J. P. Shonkoff (Eds.), *Early intervention: A handbook of theory, practice, and analysis.* (pp. 3–19). New York: Cambridge University Press.

Sameroff, A. J., & MacKenzie, M. J. (2003). Research strategies for capturing transactional models of development: The limits of the possible. *Development and Psychopathology, 15*, 613–640.

Sandberg, J. F., & Hofferth, S. L. (2001). Changes in children's time with parents: United States, 1981–1997. *Demography, 38*, 423–436.

Serpell, R., Sonnenschein, S., Baker, L., & Ganapathy, H. (2002). Intimate culture of families in the early socialization of literacy. *Journal of Family Psychology, 16*, 391–405.

Shonkoff, J. P., & Phillips, D. A. (2000). *From neurons to neighborhoods: The science of early childhood development.* Washington DC: National Academies Press.

Slopen, N., Fitzmaurice, G., Williams, D. R., & Gilman, S. E. (2010). Poverty, food insecurity, and the behavior for childhood internalizing and externalizing disorders. *Journal of the American Academy of Child and Adolescent Psychiatry, 49*, 444–452.

Sprunger, L. W., Boyce, W. T., & Gaines, J. A. (1985). Family–infant congruence: Routines and rhythmicity in family adaptations to a young infant. *Child Development, 56*, 564–572.

Stevenson-Hinde, J. (1990). Attachment within family systems—An overview. *Infant Mental Health Journal, 11*, 218–227.

Valiente, C., Lemery-Chalfant, K., & Reiser, M. (2007). Pathways to problem behaviors: Chaotic homes, parent and child effortful control, and parenting. *Social Development, 16*, 249–267.

Walsh, F. (2003). *Normal family processes* (3rd. ed.). New York: Guilford.

Wang, C. C., & Pies, C. A. (2004). Family, maternal, and child health through photovoice. *Matern Child Health Journal, 8*(2), 95–102.

Wang, Q. (2004). The cultural context of parent–child reminiscing: A functional analysis. In M. W. Pratt & B. H. Fiese (Eds.), *Family stories and the life course: Across time and generations* (pp. 279–301). Mahwah, NJ: Erlbaum.

Warren, S., Emde, R., & Sroufe, L. A. (2000). Internal representations: Predicting anxiety from children's play narratives. *Journal of American Academy of Child and Adolescent Psychiatry, 39*, 100–107.

Weiss, H. M., Lopez, E., & Rosenberg, H. (2010). *Beyond random acts: Family, school, and community engagement as an integral part of education reform.* Cambridge, MA: Harvard Family Research Project.

Wight, V. R., Chau, M., & Aratani, Y. (2010). Who are America's poor children? Retrieved from http://nccp.org/publications/pub_912.html

Wildenger, L. H., McIntyre, L. L., Fiese, B. H., & Eckert, T. L. (2008). Children's daily routines during kindergarten transition. *Early Childhood Education Journal, 36*, 69–74..

Winicki, J., & Jemison, K. (2003). Food security and hunger in the kindergarten classroom: Its effect on learning and growth. *Contemporary Economic Policy, 21*, 145–157.

Yates, T. M., Egeland, B., & Sroufe, L. A. (2003). Rethinking resilience: A developmental process perspective. In S. S. Luthar (Ed.), *Resilience and vulnerability: Adaptation in the context of childhood adversity.* (pp. 243–265). Cambridge, England: Cambridge University Press.

26

Promising Approaches to Professional Development for Early Childhood Educators

Douglas R. Powell, Karen E. Diamond, and Mary K. Cockburn
Purdue University

Currently there is considerable interest in professional development (PD) for in-service teachers as a tool for strengthening the impact of early childhood classrooms on children's learning and development. PD is a central feature of recent policy and programmatic initiatives aimed at improving the effects of programs for young children across a range of early childhood sectors, including child care, state-supported prekindergarten, and Head Start (Martinez-Beck & Zaslow, 2006). The view of PD as the pathway to better student outcomes is not limited to the early childhood period. Increasingly, education reform is synonymous with teachers' professional development (Sykes, 1996).

The press for expansion of PD is accompanied by an emerging conceptualization of effective PD that emphasizes intensive and sustained opportunities for teacher learning, content focused on what teachers are expected to teach and on the realities of a teacher's classroom and larger context, and modes of participation that facilitate active learning and collaborative relationships with PD staff or teacher colleagues (e.g., Garet, Porter, Desimone, Birman, & Yoon, 2001; Hawley & Valli, 1998; Wayne, Yoon, Zhu, Cronen, & Garet, 2008). These emphases in PD reflect a growing recognition of how adults, including teachers, learn new knowledge and skills through opportunities that are presented through their own practice and interactions with content experts over an extended period of time (Bransford, Brown, & Cocking, 1999). In current views of best practices in PD, a one-time workshop as a sole source of support to teachers is "out" and longer-term work with teachers is "in" (e.g., Goldenberg & Gallimore, 1991).

Research has not kept pace with the growth of PD (Desimone, 2009) and thus the extant literature on PD lacks concrete guidance on basic and cost-sensitive PD parameters such as intensity and length (Wayne et al., 2008). Currently a search is underway for the outcomes of specific PD strategies. For example, evidence from a descriptive study suggests that a two-day workshop may help teachers implement prescribed lessons of a structured language and literacy curriculum with a high level of *procedural* fidelity (e.g., all prescribed materials for a lesson are available and easily accessible) but not necessarily at a high level of instructional quality (Justice, Mashburn, Hamre, & Pianta, 2008). At the same time, researchers are examining effects of programs at the upper end of the PD intensity continuum such as comprehensive interventions that combine coursework, individualized work with teachers in their classrooms, and the use of student progress monitoring tools (Landry, Anthony, Swank, & Monesque-Bailey, 2009).

This chapter examines three promising approaches to PD with early childhood educators. We describe professional learning communities, including "communities of practice" models, that have been employed to improve the quality of instruction and learning in early childhood classrooms. Collaborative group work with teachers and other experts is a core feature of this approach to PD. We also describe programs in which content experts (e.g., early literacy specialists) provide individualized supports to teachers in the context of their classrooms. The term *coaching* is increasingly used to describe this strategy of PD, although some programs refer to individualized work with teachers as "consultation" or "mentoring." Lastly, we consider technological innovations aimed at improving the efficiency and accessibility of PD. Attention is given to recent advances in the uses of technology in PD, specifically technologically mediated forms of individualized work with teachers.

Each of the PD approaches examined in this chapter embraces the emerging conceptualization of PD briefly characterized above. Common across program designs is regular and active engagement of an ongoing PD activity for a semester or year, for example. Another shared premise across PD approaches is that conventional forms of PD, especially one-time workshops or coursework, are limited in their ability to promote significant change in teachers' actions in their classrooms. A closer look suggests that each of the broad approaches to PD considered in this chapter adheres to a distinctive theory of change, however.

In coaching, feedback from a content expert on a teacher's implementation of a new teaching practice in his or her classroom is among the presumed drivers of instructional change. The hypothesized active ingredients of a professional learning community, however, are collaborative group work with colleagues on the development of lessons or activities and collective sharing of reflections on their uses in group participants' classrooms.

Regardless of format, there are important differences in the uses of PD vis-à-vis the targeted content and method of instruction. Specifically, some initiatives aimed at improving the quality of early childhood classrooms employ PD as a means of supporting teachers in the implementation of a new curriculum or supplementary curriculum resources (e.g., Bierman et al., 2008). Other instructional improvement efforts use PD to promote teachers' adoption of effective research-based instructional strategies within the context of a classroom's existing curriculum (e.g., Powell, Diamond, Burchinal, & Koehler, 2010). PD also may be used as a forum for teachers to generate lessons or activities, as noted earlier. Interventions that offer both new PD and curriculum resources leave important questions unanswered about the relative contribution to student outcomes of the PD approach and new curriculum unless the PD and curriculum components are systematically varied to provide distinctive intervention conditions.

Professional Learning Communities

A professional learning community in the field of education typically consists of a small group of educators and other stakeholders who meet regularly to work collaboratively on instructional or curriculum changes aimed at improving student learning (Vescio, Ross, & Adams, 2008). Mutually supportive reflection on participants' descriptions of efforts to implement new or revised teaching practices is often a core element of a group's efforts. Several examples of using a professional learning community to improve student outcomes in early childhood education are described below.

The Teacher Study Group (TSG) program is a form of learning community that, in a study by Gersten and colleagues, focused on a specific domain of evidence-based instruction and involved teachers from the same grade in the same school (Gersten, Dimino, Jayanthi, Kim, & Santoro, 2010). In this investigation, the TSG model was implemented with first grade teachers in three different school districts in an effort to improve reading comprehension and vocabulary instruction. The goal was to enhance the existing curriculum by strengthening teachers' use of research-based instruction in the targeted content. The approach called for teachers to meet twice monthly in small groups, ranging from three to eight participants across schools, for 75-minute sessions for a total of 16 sessions. The first eight sessions focused on vocabulary instruction, based on the work of Beck, McKeown, and Kucan (2002), and the subsequent eight sessions addressed strategies for

teaching reading comprehension, using a set of research readings. Each of the group sessions employed a common format in which teachers (a) reported on their experiences in implementing a lesson they planned collaboratively at the previous session; (b) discussed instructional concepts in the reading assigned for the session; (c) reviewed and discussed possible modifications of a forthcoming lessons in the school district's core reading program; and (d) worked in pairs or as a whole group to plan a lesson that built on the targeted research principle.

In a study with preschool teachers, three levels of a learning community were established to support teachers' implementation of a comprehensive early childhood curriculum developed and examined by Fantuzzo, Gadsden, and McDermott (2011). The curriculum, known as the Evidence-Based Program for the Integration of Curricula (EPIC), seeks to promote skills in mathematics, language, literacy, and approaches to learning. The learning community levels included the classroom teaching team (lead teacher and assistant), a small group comprised of five to six teaching teams and a mentor teacher who had experiences implementing the EPIC curriculum, and a large group comprised of all teaching teams plus the Head Start program's educational coordinator. The implementation plan called for each teaching team to meet weekly to review children's progress and plan for curriculum implementation in the upcoming week, the small group to meet monthly to reflect on a previous EPIC unit and prepare for a new curriculum unit, and the large group to meet quarterly to discuss implementation issues, share best practices, and review outcomes. The educational coordinator received in-depth training in the EPIC curriculum and visited each classroom to provide instructional support. The EPIC learning community model, based on principles of distributed leadership (Spillane, 2006), was designed to foster reciprocal teaching and learning relationships among educators who had different levels of expertise and experience with the EPIC curriculum.

Research on outcomes of the learning community model of PD is often limited to teachers' reports of their experiences in learning communities. Independent observations of instructional practices, assessments of student learning, and use of experimental designs are uncommon in this line of investigation (Vescio et al., 2008). Fortunately, effects of the TSG model and EPIC curriculum were examined recently in separate random assignment studies. The TSG model was investigated with a sample of 81 first grade teachers and their students in three large urban school districts in three states. Results pointed to positive effects of the TSG model on teachers' reading comprehension and vocabulary instruction and on teachers' knowledge of vocabulary instruction. There were marginally significant effects on students' oral vocabulary (Gersten et al., 2010). A study of the EPIC curriculum in 70 Head Start classrooms in a large urban area found positive effects on children's mathematics and listening comprehension skills (Fantuzzo et al., 2011). As noted earlier, it is not possible to determine the unique contributions of a PD model when it is coupled with a new curriculum.

The Gersten et al. (2010) and Fantuzzo et al. (2011) models of professional learning communities both focused on instructional practices informed by conventional modes of research. Their respective models differ from a "communities of practice" model in which a knowledge base on best practices is developed from teachers' collective experiences and collaborative actions with researchers (Buysse, Sparkman, & Wesley, 2003; Wesley & Buysse, 2006). For example, Perry and colleagues describe a community of practice PD effort in which teachers and researchers jointly developed early literacy activities and assessments (Perry, Walton, & Calder, 1999). In a variant of this model, a PD program aimed at improving the language and literacy outcomes of Latino dual language learners included community of practice meetings for teachers to create lessons around a commonly agreed upon goal within a scientifically based content framework (Buysse, Castro, & Peisner-Feinberg, 2010). In addition to creating lessons, community of practice meetings were used to provide feedback and reflection on teachers' implementation of lessons and generate a product for dissemination to other teachers. The PD program also included institutes and individual consultation with teachers. A random assignment study of the PD program, known as Nuestros Niños, found significant improvements in the quality of teachers' literacy and language instruction and gains in children's phonological awareness skills in their primary language.

Coaching

The format of coaching and similar forms of classroom-based work with a teacher or teaching team is highly conducive to individualizing the presentation of information on evidence-based practices and feedback on a teacher's efforts to implement recommended instruction (Powell & Diamond, 2011). Typically, coaching is offered as part of a multicomponent PD program that includes introductory (e.g., Powell et al., 2010) or concurrent (e.g., Raver et al., 2008) workshops, an ongoing course (e.g., Neuman & Wright, 2010), or web resources (Pianta, Mashburn, Downer, Hamre, & Justice, 2008; Powell et al., 2010) aimed at providing information on evidence-based practices related to the content of the PD. In some PD programs, coaches demonstrate or model the targeted practice in a teacher's classroom (Wasik, Bond, & Hindman, 2006).

It is common for a coach or mentor to observe a teacher in her or his classroom and then meet individually with the teacher to provide and discuss feedback on the observation. (See a later section of this chapter for a description of technologically mediated approaches to conducting observations and providing feedback.) Usually feedback includes two basic types of information that is aligned with the PD program's content: an identification of appropriately

implemented practices and recommendations for practice improvements. One PD program refers to these two forms of feedback as "glows" and "grows," respectively (Landry et al., 2009, p. 452). To help teachers reflect on their practices, some programs provide a teacher with records of his or her actions in the classroom via videotapes of the teacher's behaviors (Hamre, LoCasale-Crouch, & Pianta, 2008) or transcripts of audiotaped teacher interactions with children (Dickinson, Watson, & Farran, 2008).

The ExCELL program offered to Head Start teachers is illustrative of combining coaching with other forms of PD support to teachers (Wasik, 2010; Wasik & Hindman, 2011). ExCELL is a comprehensive PD model designed to train teachers to implement evidence-based practices that promote children's literacy and language development. The PD content is organized into five modules (e.g., interactive book reading, alphabet knowledge) that are the basis of three-hour group training sessions conducted monthly. In each group training session, a conceptual rationale for recommended practices is presented and specific teaching strategies are described and modeled by coaches. Teachers also have opportunities to test the strategies during group activities. A three-hour coaching session is offered weekly to each teacher. Each session includes observation and documentation of teaching practices related to targeted outcomes (e.g., emphasis on letters). In the week that follows a group training session, the coach models with children in each teacher's classroom the instructional strategies that were presented during the training. The teacher observes the coach's modeling by using an observation checklist that highlights key teaching behaviors. In addition to providing additional exposure to targeted instructional practices, a goal of the modeling is to demonstrate how the recommended practices can be used with children in the teacher's classroom. The teacher is given about one week to practice the targeted instruction prior to the coach observing the teacher implement the strategy in her classroom. The observation checklist used by the teacher to assess the coach's modeling of the practice is also used by the coach to observe the teacher's implementation of the practice. The coach's completed checklist is used as a discussion springboard at a conference with the teacher immediately following the observation. Coach feedback includes positive aspects of the teacher's actions and recommendations for improvement. Videotaping of the teacher's implementation of practices emphasized in ExCELL also occurs frequently as an additional tool to facilitate coach and teacher discussion of the teacher's practice. In addition to the monthly group training and weekly coaching sessions, teachers receive theme guides, suggested daily lesson plans, and a variety of classroom materials such as books and picture/word cards of targeted vocabulary.

There is a limited yet growing research literature on effects of coaching-based PD programs. A quasi-experimental study by Neuman and Cunningham (2009) found that center- and family-based child care providers' participation in a three-credit, 15-week course plus weekly coaching was associated with significant improvements in providers' language and literacy practices. Coursework alone had negligible effects on instructional quality. The lack of positive outcomes of the 15-week course is in contrast with findings from another quasi-experimental study that found a positive impact of a four-credit course, offered as two three-day intensive sessions, on classroom supports for early literacy (Dickinson & Caswell, 2007). The latter PD program, conducted with Head Start teachers, also provided training to teachers' on-site supervisors in how to support teachers' implementation of new practices. A subsequent study by Neuman and Wright (2010) sought to disentangle the three-credit course and coaching and provide an equal amount of support for both coaching and coursework PD conditions (i.e., three hours weekly across 10 weeks). At the end of the PD program, classrooms of teachers who participated in coaching only, compared to classrooms of teachers who participated in a course only, had higher quality book and writing areas plus literacy environments overall but not higher quality teaching strategies.

A handful of studies have employed experimental designs to examine effects of coaching-based PD for early childhood educators on children's outcomes. The pattern of results from this small number of investigations points to positive effects on children's learning (Bierman et al., 2008; Powell et al., 2010; Wasik et al., 2006). Results of an outcome study of the ExCELL program described above indicated that children in PD classrooms made significant gains in their vocabulary knowledge, for example (Wasik, 2010; Wasik & Hindman, 2011). The PD programs examined in these studies involved features related to the content of what was taught (e.g., scripted curriculum activities) in addition to coaching that prevent conclusions about the unique effects of coaching with teachers on child outcomes. A recent study that systematically examined effects of individualized coaching with elementary school teachers did not find positive effects on student learning. In an experimental design involving second grade teachers in six school districts, neither a teacher institute series that began in the summer and continued through most of the school year nor a PD condition that involved the teacher institute series plus in-school coaching led to improvements in students' reading outcomes. Both PD conditions led to improvements in teachers' knowledge of scientifically based reading instruction compared to the control group, and also in one of the instructional practices targeted by the PD (Garet et al., 2008).

Technological Innovations

Advances in computer and video technology extend opportunities for PD designed to enhance teachers' instruction and students' learning. In this chapter, our focus is on the use of technology for in-service PD that has the goal of enhancing teachers' use of effective instructional practices

with children in their classrooms. Although not the focus of this chapter, we want to acknowledge that technologies have been used in supporting teachers outside of in-service PD efforts, including the implementation of individualized instruction (Connor, Morrison, Fishman, Schatschneider, & Underwood, 2007; Landry et al., 2009) and the provision of video-based resources for preservice teachers (Barton & Wolery, 2008).

Technology holds great promise for extending the reach of PD, particularly to schools and teachers in rural and other geographically remote communities where PD opportunities are limited. Teachers have used technology for web-based learning, including accessing online courses and webinars, for a number of years (Amendum, Vernon-Feagans, & Ginsberg, 2011). Only recently, however, has there been sufficient development of web-based technologies that they have been used to provide teachers with individualized support and feedback integrated into their daily work teaching children in their classrooms, replacing traditional face-to-face real-time mentoring (Gentry, Denton, & Kurz, 2008).

Currently, computer-based technology is being used to provide PD through a variety of means, including web conferencing (Amendum et al., 2011), electronic mail (Hemmeter, Snyder, Kinder, & Artman, 2011), webcams in classrooms (Pianta et al., 2008), and software that links a mentor/coach's feedback to videotaped segments of teachers' instruction (linked teaching-feedback; Powell et al., 2010). In each of these different approaches, a goal is to provide teachers with information about what they do well and areas for growth. In some of these approaches, technology is used to link teacher and mentor concurrently (e.g., webcams, web conferencing) while others use technology to provide feedback asynchronously (communications between teacher and mentor occur outside of real-time through e-mail or linked teaching-feedback, for example). Advantages of mentoring experiences that occur asynchronously include more flexibility in scheduling and multiple opportunities for teachers to review feedback (Powell et al., 2010). In their research synthesis, Gentry and her colleagues (2008) found that teachers had generally favorable self-reported attitudes toward technologically mediated mentoring experiences such as these.

We noted earlier the different uses of PD in relation to implementation of a new curriculum or targeted instructional practices. Technologically mediated mentoring or coaching has been used to support teachers' implementation of a specific curriculum and lessons (e.g., MyTeachingPartner Language and Literacy Curriculum; Pianta et al., 2008) as well as to support teachers' use of effective instructional strategies that are independent of a specific curriculum (e.g., Amendum et al., 2011; Hemmeter et al., 2011; Powell et al., 2010).

In a recent PD intervention, Amendum and his colleagues used a webcam along with web-conferencing to observe and support individual teachers. The intervention focused on teachers' implementation of Targeted Reading Strategies (TRI), a Tier 2 intervention within a Response-to-Intervention framework for kindergarten and first-grade students who were struggling to read. This intervention was independent of the reading curriculum used in the classroom. Literacy coaches located at a distance provided real-time coaching for the teacher to support her implementation of these strategies. Coaching feedback was provided either during the TRI lesson, immediately following the lesson, or both, depending on the teacher's preferences; debriefing after the observation was included, if time permitted. Coaching "visits" via webcam occurred weekly and then biweekly as teachers implemented TRI strategies; additional web-conferencing included weekly "grade-level meetings about individual children's reading performance" as well as occasional PD sessions. Thus, this PD intervention used technology for "real-time" mentoring through individual webcam consultations along with group web-conferencing. The quality and frequency of teachers' implementation of TRI were assessed on a regular basis (as indicators of fidelity of implementation). Results suggested that kindergarten teachers implemented intervention strategies with higher fidelity than did first-grade teachers (Vernon-Feagans et al., 2010) and that there were significant effects of the intervention on kindergarten children's learning but not on the performance of first-graders.

Hemmeter and her colleagues (2011) have examined the impact of feedback delivered by e-mail on preschool teachers' use of descriptive praise for children's positive behaviors during group instruction, a strategy designed to increase children's engagement and decrease challenging behaviors. Initial training was provided to teachers face-to-face and focused on the use of, and rationale for using, descriptive praise. Following the initial training, trainers (coaches) observed circle time activities in the classroom two to three times per week and sent teachers e-mail feedback on their use of descriptive praise statements. Each e-mail feedback message included an embedded link, directing a teacher to view a trainer/coach-selected video clip of a teacher using descriptive praise statements in a similar preschool context. Teachers replied to the e-mail feedback to indicate that it had been received, but there was no way to determine the care with which feedback was reviewed. Unlike the TRI intervention described previously, trainers/coaches were physically present as teachers implemented the intervention but feedback was provided electronically, after the coach's observation. Advantages of providing feedback to teachers by e-mail included the opportunity for teachers to review feedback at a convenient time (i.e., feedback to the teacher did not disrupt the classroom routine) and to include links to real-life video examples of other teachers implementing practices with which they were struggling. In this multiple probe, single-subject study, training and feedback were associated with increases in teachers' use of descriptive praise. A classroom-wide measure revealed that children's challenging behaviors

decreased somewhat, but inconsistently, across the four classrooms included in the study.

Powell and his colleagues (2010) used individualized web-mediated feedback as part of a literacy-focused PD intervention with Head Start teachers. They used a randomized control-trial design to compare the effectiveness of two different approaches to providing PD (face-to-face or technologically mediated coaching). In the technologically mediated PD intervention, teachers videotaped their own instruction, sent the tape to their coach and received feedback on a CD that they could review on their laptop computer. The coaching feedback included comments paired with specific segments of their videotaped practice, along with links to video exemplars of other teachers implementing similar instructional approaches. There were significant effects of the literacy-focused PD intervention on the broad classroom environment and on teachers' instruction of letters and sounds, along with significant effects on children's knowledge of letters and sounds. Importantly, there were no consistent differences in outcomes for either teachers or children across the two intervention approaches (Powell et al., 2010). The results of this study are particularly important in suggesting that benefits to technologically mediated PD interventions may be similar to those in which the same intervention content is provided in face-to-face interaction.

Video libraries of effective instruction have been used in several recent studies of coaching interventions (cf., Hemmeter et al., 2011; Pianta et al., 2008; Powell et al., 2010). One form of a video library is a case-based hypermedia resource that provides teachers with video examples of evidence-based practices (cases) along with descriptive information that highlights specific aspects of instruction. Advantages of a case-based hypermedia resource include providing teachers with direct access to information related to specific teaching practices, along with opportunities to focus on specific instructional approaches that may be particularly challenging (Koehler, 2002). Powell, Diamond, and Koehler (2009) found that teachers in their intervention were most likely to use the hypermedia resource in the late afternoon and in the evening, suggesting that one of the advantages of this tool is that it can be used at a time most convenient for the teacher. Results of research by Pianta et al. (2008) suggest that providing teachers with access to video exemplars only, without coaching support, leads to quite modest improvements in teachers' instruction; individualized coaching feedback appears to add value to that provided by models or exemplars of evidence-based instruction.

Variations in PD Implementation and Engagement

Similar to the uses of curricula and other educational interventions, it is unusual for all components of a PD program to be implemented and engaged as intended. PD content areas may receive differential levels of emphasis (Powell, Steed, & Diamond, 2010), for example, and assigned readings may not be pursued in advance of a program session (Gersten et al., 2010). Available evidence points to considerable between-teacher variation in the amount of participation in PD programs, even when involvement is voluntary. In the Raver et al. (2008) program to improve teachers' emotionally supportive classroom practices, approximately 37% of teachers participated in less than half of five Saturday trainings. Forty-nine of 173 teachers (28%) involved in the MTP study did not submit even one videotape of their teaching during each of three time periods across the school year (Pianta et al., 2008). Twelve percent of teachers in the technologically mediated coaching condition of the Powell, Diamond, Burchinal et al. (2010) study submitted fewer than six of the seven videotapes specified in the one-semester coaching protocol.

Several researchers have investigated teacher characteristics as predictors of participation in a PD program. Downer and colleagues found that older teachers were more likely to spend more time engaged with a MTP consultant and web resources than younger teachers. Teachers with more pre-K teaching experience spent less time with MTP's web-based resources (Downer, Locasale-Crouch, Hamre, & Pianta, 2009). In contrast, Domitrovich and colleagues found that teachers' professional characteristics (e.g., training, experience) did not predict teachers' engagement in the coaching relationship or use of strategies emphasized in the REDI curriculum. However, coaches' ratings (three items) of teachers' openness to consultation uniquely predicted coaches' ratings of teachers' implementation of four dimensions of teaching strategies targeted by the intervention (language richness, social-emotional support, behavior management, and sensitivity-responsiveness). This association was stronger for lead teachers than for assistant teachers (Domitrovich, Gest, Gill, Jones, & DeRousie, 2009). Teachers may not fully engage a PD program when the teaching practice recommended by the program is viewed as out of reach or inconsistent with current approaches (Powell & Diamond, 2011). For example, Dickinson and colleagues describe a teacher who was minimally engaged in a language-focused PD program presumably because the PD program's request that she initiate interactions with children during center time was at odds with her "preferred habit of standing back and observing children, and interacting only when problems arose" (Dickinson et al., 2008, p. 145).

Growing interest in the use of innovative technologies to provide PD raises questions about whether lack of teacher familiarity with the use of technology creates a challenge for technologically mediated PD efforts. Kao and Tsai (2009) examined Taiwanese elementary school teachers' beliefs about web-learning and PD in an effort to understand how technology-related beliefs might influence teachers' response to a PD intervention. They found associations between teachers' positive beliefs about web-based learning in general and their attitudes toward web-based PD.

The knowledge and skills of PD program staff may con-tribute to variations in the fidelity of program implementation and teacher engagement. A study of the Partnerships for Inclusion program, in which assessments of the quality of an early childhood program were the basis of on-site consultation with early childhood program staff regarding improvement strategies, found that implementation of the program model differed widely by consultants. Some consultants found it difficult to use ratings of early childhood program quality to guide the development of individualized PD goals or activities (Bryant et al., 2009). In the Downer et al. (2009) study of the MyTeachingPartner (MTP) program, teachers' number of videotape submissions and average amount of conference time with their consultant varied across the program's six consultants. These findings may be confounded by school district because most teachers in a given school district were assigned to the same consultant.

There appear to be differences in the capacities of school districts and other organizational sponsors of early childhood education to implement a PD model with fidelity. For example, school district schedules and teacher release time policies in some schools led to 30-minute TSG sessions during teacher planning periods across multiple days whereas other school districts were able to provide a full 75-minute TSG meeting twice a month as specified in the program model. The shorter, more frequent sessions made it difficult to cover the full lesson. Also, the TSG model was implemented with a lower level of fidelity in school districts that did not use a core reading series. Specifically, teacher collaboration in lesson planning, a core component of the TSG model, was hindered when teachers lacked a common lesson. Further, TSG facilitators differed by school district in their skills in keeping the TSG sessions on track (e.g., preventing the session from being used by teachers to vent their frustrations).

Future Directions

Advances in the use of PD to improve the outcomes of early childhood programs require empirical evidence from well-designed studies of effects of varying approaches to PD. Random assignment studies and meta-analyses that compare outcomes of different PD methods, such as teacher study groups versus expert coaching with individual teachers, are especially needed. Research also is needed on thresholds of PD intensity and duration that yield meaningful change in children's learning. Nuanced understandings of how PD intensity and duration interact with teacher variables (e.g., initial quality of instruction) and other attributes of a PD program (e.g., complexity and novelty of the PD content) to produce improvements in teachers' instruction and student outcome gains may be particularly helpful in informing the design of future PD efforts. Findings of studies that disentangle features of comprehensive instructional improvement initiatives are essential to making prudent decisions about the active ingredients of educational reform efforts that include PD. More may not necessarily mean better.

The processes of teacher change warrant careful investigation (Sheridan, Edwards, Marvin, & Knoche, 2009). Little is known about mediators of improvements in teachers' instruction. For example, it is not clear whether and how teachers' increased knowledge of a content area leads to improvements in quality of instruction, and whether relations are linear. The prevailing assumption of many PD programs about the role of improved self-efficacy as a foundation of significant change in teachers' practices needs empirical attention, too (Tschannen-Moran & McMaster, 2009).

Another needed line of research pertains to conditions that support or impede the implementation of PD. Our review of promising PD programs revealed some possible influences that warrant further investigation. The existence of a common curriculum appeared to be a factor in facilitating the work of teacher study groups (Gersten et al., 2010). Findings of other research also suggest that the lack of a core curriculum weakens the effects of teacher training (Fukkink & Lont, 2007). Our review also noted that organizational capacity to promote change in core practices may moderate the implementation and effects of PD programs. There is some evidence that effects of mentoring varied by the organizational auspice of an early childhood program (e.g., Head Start, Title 1; Assel, Landry, Swank, & Gunnewig, 2007). The credentials and resourcefulness of PD staff seem obvious contributors to PD effects but, with few exceptions (e.g., Downer et al., 2009), PD outcome studies rarely examine staff variables. Because most PD studies lack an adequate sample of PD staff for analyses of outcomes by staff characteristics, research that analyzes pooled data from different PD studies may be a productive way to better understand staff contributions to PD outcomes.

The early childhood field's corpus of scientific knowledge about what works in supporting high-quality teaching is promising. Researchers have identified approaches to PD that are based on conceptually coherent frameworks and experimental evidence of effectiveness. To build on this impressive progress, researchers need to replicate outcome studies in diverse settings and conduct investigations that inform efforts to take effective PD approaches to scale. This requires attention to the conditions under which PD takes hold and contributes to significant and sustained improvements in teacher practices and children's outcomes. Without this line of research, we run the risk of wasting teacher time and other resources on PD approaches that yield little or no benefit. With well-developed programs of research on PD, the field has a great opportunity to move closer to realizing the promise of early childhood education as a foundation of school success.

References

Amendum, S. J., Vernon-Feagans, L., & Ginsberg, M. C. (2011). The effectiveness of a technologically-facilitated classroom-based early reading intervention: The Targeted Reading Intervention. *The Elementary School Journal, 112,* 107–131.

Assel, M. A., Landry, S. H., Swank, P. R., & Gunnewig, S. (2007). An evaluation of curriculum, setting, and mentoring on the performance of children enrolled in pre-kindergarten. *Reading and Writing, 20,* 463–494.

Barton, E. E., & Wolery, M. (2007). Evaluation of e-mail feedback on the verbal behaviors of pre-service teachers. *Journal of Early Intervention, 30,* 55–72.

Beck, I. L., McKeown, M. G., & Kucan, L. (2002). *Bringing words to life: Robust vocabulary instruction.* New York: Guilford.

Bierman, K. L., Domitrovich, C. E., Nix, R. L., Gest, S. D., Welsh, J. A, Greenberg, M. T....Gill, S. (2008). Promoting academic and social-emotional school readiness: The Head Start REDI Program. *Child Development, 79,* 1802–1817.

Bransford, J. D., Brown, A. L., & Cocking, R. R. (Eds.) (1999). *How people learn: Brain, mind, experience, and school.* Washington, DC: National Academy Press.

Bryant, D., Wesley, P., Burchinal, P. Sideris, J., Taylor, K., Fenson, C.,... Iruka, I. (2009). *The QUINCE-PFI study: An evaluation of a promising model for child care provider training.* Chapel Hill, NC: Frank Porter Graham Child Development Institute, University of North Carolina.

Buysse, V., Castro, D. C., & Peisner-Feinberg, E. (2010). Effects of a professional development program on classroom practices and outcomes for Latino dual language learners. *Early Childhood Research Quarterly, 25,* 194–206.

Buysse, V., Sparkman, K. L., & Wesley, P. W. (2003). Communities of practice: Connecting what we know with what we do. *Exceptional Children, 69,* 263–275.

Connor, C. M., Morrison, F. J., Fishman, B. J., Schatschneider, C., & Underwood, P. (2007). The early years: Algorithm-guided individualized reading instruction. *Science, 315,* 464–465.

Desimone, L. M. (2009). Improving impact studies of teachers' professional development: Toward better conceptualizations and measures. *Educational Researcher, 38,* 181–199.

Dickinson, D. K., & Caswell, L. (2007). Building support for language and early literacy in preschool classrooms through in-service professional development: Effects of the Literacy Environment Enrichment Program (LEEP). *Early Childhood Research Quarterly, 22,* 243–260.

Dickinson, D. K., Watson, B. G., & Farran, D. C. (2008). It's in the details: Approaches to describing and improving preschool classrooms. In L. M. Justice & C. Vukelich (Eds.), *Achieving excellence in preschool literacy instruction* (pp. 136–161). New York: Guilford.

Domitrovich, C. E., Gest, S. D., Gill, S., Jones, D., & DeRousie, R. S. (2009). Individual factors associated with PD training outcomes of the Head Start REDI program. *Early Education and Development, 20,* 402–430.

Downer, J. T., Locasale-Crouch, J., Hamre, B., & Pianta, R. (2009). Teacher characteristics associated with responsiveness and exposure to consultation and online PD resources. *Early Education and Development, 20,* 431–455.

Fantuzzo, J. W., Gadsden, V. L., & McDermott, P. A. (2011). An integrated curriculum to improve mathematics, language, and literacy for Head Start children. *American Educational Research Journal, 48,* 763–793.

Fukkink, R. G., & Lont, A. (2007). Does training matter? A meta-analysis and review of caregiver training studies. *Early Childhood Research Quarterly, 22,* 294–311.

Garet, M., Porter, A., Desimone, L., Birman, B., & Yoon, K. S. (2001). What makes professional development effective? Results from a national sample of teachers. *American Educational Research Journal, 38,* 915–945.

Garet, M. S., Cronen, S., Eaton, M., Kurki, A., Ludwig, M., Jones, W.,... Silverberg, M. (2008). *The impact of two professional development interventions on early reading instruction and achievement* (NCEE 2008-4038). Washington, DC: U.S. Department of Education, Institute of Education Sciences.

Gentry, L. B., Denton, C. A., & Kurtz, T. (2008). Technologically-based mentoring provided to teachers: A synthesis of the literature. *Journal of Technology and Teacher Education, 16,* 339–373.

Gersten, R., Dimino, J., Jayanthi, M., Kim, J. S., & Santoro, L. E. (2010).

Teacher study group: Impact of the professional development model on reading instruction and student outcomes in first grade classrooms. *American Educational Research Journal, 47*, 694–739.

Goldenberg, C., & Gallimore, R. (1991). Changing teaching takes more than a one-shot workshop. *Educational Leadership, 49*, 69–72.

Hamre, B. K., LoCasale-Crouch, J., & Pianta, R. C. (2008). Formative assessment of classrooms: Using classroom observations to improve implementation quality. In L. M. Justice & C. Vukelich (Eds.), *Achieving excellence in preschool literacy instruction* (pp. 102–119). New York: Guilford.

Hawley, W. D., & Valli, L. (1998). The essentials of effective professional development: A new consensus. In L. S. Darling Hammond & G. Sykes (Eds.), *The heart of the matter: Teaching as a learning profession* (pp. 86–124). San Francisco, CA: Jossey-Bass.

Hemmeter, M. L., Snyder, P., Kinder, K., & Artman, K. (2011). Impact of performance feedback delivered via electronic mail on preschool teachers' use of descriptive praise. *Early Childhood Research Quarterly, 26*, 96–109.

Justice, L. M., Mashburn, A. J., Hamre, B. K., & Pianta, R. C. (2008). Quality of language and literacy instruction in preschool classrooms serving at-risk pupils. *Early Childhood Research Quarterly, 23*, 51–68.

Kao, C., & Tsai, C. (2009). Teachers' attitudes towards web-based professional development, with relation to Internet self-efficacy and beliefs about web-based learning. *Computers and Education, 53*, 66–73.

Koehler, M. J. (2002). Designing case-based hypermedia for developing understanding of children's mathematical reasoning. *Cognition and Instruction, 20*, 151–195.

Landry, S. H., Anthony, J. L., Swank, P. R., & Monesque-Bailey, P. (2009). Effectiveness of comprehensive professional development for teachers of at-risk preschoolers. *Journal of Educational Psychology, 101*, 448–465.

Martinez-Beck, I., & Zaslow, M. (2006). The context for critical issues in early childhood professional development. In M. Zaslow & I. Martinez-Beck (Eds.), *Critical issues in early childhood professional development* (pp. 1–16). Baltimore, MD: Brookes.

Neuman, S. B., & Cunningham, L. (2009). The impact of professional development and coaching on early language and literacy instructional practices. *American Educational Research Journal, 46*, 532–566.

Neuman, S. B., & Wright, T. S. (2010). Promoting language and literacy development for early childhood educators: A mixed-methods study of coursework and coaching. *The Elementary School Journal, 111*, 63–86.

Perry, N. E., Walton, C., & Calder, K. (1999). Teachers developing assessments of early literacy: A community of practice project. *Teacher Education and Special Education, 22*, 218–233.

Pianta, R. C., Mashburn, A. J., Downer, J. T., Hamre, B. K., & Justice, L. (2008). Effects of web-mediated professional development resources on teacher-child interactions in pre-kindergarten classrooms. *Early Childhood Research Quarterly, 23*, 431–451.

Powell, D. R., & Diamond, K. E. (2011). Improving the outcomes of coaching-based professional development interventions. In S. B. Neuman & D. K. Dickinson (Eds.), *Handbook of early literacy research* (Vol. 3, pp. 295–307). New York: Guilford.

Powell, D. R., Diamond, K. E., Burchinal, M. R., & Koehler, M. J. (2010). Effects of an early literacy professional development intervention on Head Start teachers and children. *Journal of Educational Psychology, 102*, 299–312.

Powell, D. R., Diamond, K. E., & Koehler, M. J. (2009). Use of a case-based hypermedia resource in an early literacy coaching intervention with pre-kindergarten teachers. *Topics in Early Childhood Special Education, 29*, 239–249.

Powell, D. R., Steed, E. A., & Diamond, K. E. (2010). Dimensions of literacy coaching with Head Start teachers. *Topics in Early Childhood Special Education, 30*, 148–161.

Raver, C. C., Jones, S. M., Li-Grining, C. P., Metzger, M., Champion, K. M., & Sardin, L. (2008). Improving preschool classroom processes: Preliminary findings from a randomized trial implemented in Head Start settings. *Early Childhood Research Quarterly, 23*, 10–26.

Sheridan S. M., Edwards, C. P., Marvin, C. A., & Knoche, L. L. (2009). Professional development in early childhood programs: Process issues and research needs. *Early Education and Development, 20*, 377–401.

Spillane, J. P. (2006). *Distributed leadership.* San Francisco, CA: Jossey-Bass.

Sykes, G. (1996). Reform of and as professional development. *Phi Delta Kappan, 77*, 465–489.

Tschannen-Moran, M., & McMaster, P. (2009). Sources of self-efficacy: Four professional development formats and their relationship to self-efficacy and implementation of a new teaching strategy. *The Elementary School Journal, 110*, 228–245.

Vernon-Feagans, L., Gallagher, K., Ginsberg, M., Amendum, S., Kainz, K., Rose, J., & Burchinal, M. (2010). A diagnostic teaching intervention for classroom teachers: Helping struggling readers in early elementary school. *Learning Disabilities Research and Practice, 25*, 183–193.

Vescio, V., Ross, D., & Adams, A. (2008). A review of research on the impact of professional learning communities on teaching practice and student learning. *Teaching and Teacher Education, 24*, 80–91.

Wasik, B. A. (2010). What teachers can do to promote preschoolers' vocabulary development: Strategies from an effective language and literacy professional development coaching model. *The Reading Teacher, 63*, 621–633.

Wasik, B. A., Bond, M. A., & Hindman, A. (2006). The effects of a language and literacy intervention on Head Start children and teachers. *Journal of Educational Psychology, 98*, 63–74.

Wasik, B. A., & Hindman, A. H. (2011). Identifying critical components of an effective preschool language and literacy coaching intervention. In S. B. Neuman & D. K. Dickinson (Eds.), *Handbook of early literacy research* (Vol. 3, pp. 322–336). New York: Guilford.

Wayne, A. J., Yoon, K. S., Zhu, P., Cronen, S., & Garet, M. S. (2008). Experimenting with teacher professional development: Motives and methods. *Educational Researcher, 37*, 469–479.

Wesley, P. W., & Buysse, V. (2006). Building the evidence base through communities of practice. In V. Buysse & P. W. Wesley (Eds.), *Evidence-based practice in the early childhood field* (pp. 161–194). Washington, DC: Zero to Three Press.

27

Lifting Preschool Quality

Nurturing Effective Teachers

BRUCE FULLER AND REBECCA ANGUIANO
University of California, Berkeley

JOHN W. GASKO
University of Texas, Houston

Parents and government now spend over $48 billion each year on early childhood services, which involves a robust array of local organizations that continue to expand (Marketdata Enterprises, 2005). Two-thirds of the nation's 4-year-olds now attend a preschool center, up from just one-sixth in the 1950s.[1] A half-century of research shows that preschool organizations, when offering vibrant, high-quality programs, yield strong and sustained benefits for children from low-income families.[2]

Yet the quality of preschools remains uneven. Even mediocre programs, of course, allow millions of parents to enter the labor force, which serves to lift household income. But these programs often fail to appreciably boost children's early learning. After tracking children through Head Start, the massive program serving low-income families, and into elementary school, federal evaluators found slight lasting benefits for children (Puma et al., 2010). Nor have researchers been able to detect consistent benefits for middle-class children who are enrolled in typical preschool centers, even after attending for two years (Loeb, Bridges, Bassok, Fuller, & Rumberger, 2007; Magnuson, Ruhm, & Waldfogel, 2007). Until consistent results across wider swaths of children are seen, proposals that lift their health, social skills, and early school achievement, other priorities may eclipse public concern for young children.

We know that preschools pack a stiffer punch when they display stronger quality (Loeb, Fuller, Kagan, & Carrol, 2004; Love et al., 2007; Peisner-Feinberg et al., 2001). But how can we best improve preschool quality? How is the science of early intervention illuminating the surest ways for lifting children's early learning? How can government and early educators elevate quality across diverse public and private programs, serving an equally colorful range of families?

This chapter informs these questions, first detailing the preschool quality problem, then reviewing the emerging research that identifies effective ways of raising quality and results for children. Empirical dead-ends are examined as well. We dig into four specific topics:

- Recent studies show that more intense *regulation* by state governments—especially mandating higher credentials for preschool teachers—yields few developmental benefits for children.
- Stronger gains for children stem from sensitive and demanding *relationships* between teachers and children, and by organizing *learning tasks* that invoke rich language and build preliteracy skills.
- New *classroom interventions*—assessing teaching practices, building stronger skills, and tracking children's progress—show promising results.
- *Taking these models to scale*—nurturing stronger classroom practices and offering mentoring and feedback to teachers—is unfolding in a handful of states. Early lessons can inform leaders in others states and Washington policy makers.

Uneven Preschool Quality

Preschool enrollments climbed dramatically over the past half-century as millions of women moved into the labor force and government invested heavily in early childhood programs. In 1970 just 28% of the nation's 4-year-olds were attending a preschool center; only 12% of 3-year-olds were enrolled. These percentages climbed to 68% among 4-year-olds by 2005, and 41% for 3-year-olds (Fuller, 2007). More work remains to equalize family access to preschool programs, especially in providing affordable access for Latino children from low-income families.

Yet as enrollments and public spending have climbed it

is not surprising that worries would arise over the quality and benefits of preschool organizations. From the scientific world the news has been mixed. A four-state study in the 1990s, which received widespread media attention, found that two-thirds of all preschools reflected poor to mediocre quality (Helburn, 1995). This inference stemmed from a single quality-assessment tool, although the team also found uneven education levels among classroom staff. Subsequent work revealed that quality lagged in blue-collar and middle-class suburbs, where preschools depended on parent fees, didn't qualify for public support, and therefore could only afford poorly educated teachers (Fuller, Raudenbush, Wei, & Holloway, 1993).

Two specific quality gaps were revealed in more recent studies. First, the average preschool serving children from middle-class families was found to yield tepid benefits at best. One careful investigation—mounted by the National Institute of Child Health and Human Development (NICHD)—tracked children from birth through a variety of child care and preschool settings. The sample of 1,364 children was drawn mostly from middle-class families (as poorer families left the sample at higher rates). The NICHD team (Duncan et al., 2003) found that attending a preschool center at age 3 or 4 was associated with a modest gain in cognitive growth, net a variety of prior family background factors (about 0.27 of a standard deviation, *SD*; Figure 27.1). But by third grade this benefit had largely disappeared. Drawing on contemporary data sets (provided by the federal government's Early Childhood Longitudinal Study), two independent teams have found similarly disappointing short-term effects for middle-class children who attend preschool (Bassok, 2010; Loeb et al., 2007; Magnuson et al., 2007). Short-term benefits do appear but dissipate soon after children enter elementary school.

The second quality worry is preschool's disappointing returns for many poor children. Washington now spends $8 billion each year to enroll almost 1 million children in local Head Start centers. Rigorous studies in the 1990s showed modest yet lasting effects for Head Start graduates (e.g., Currie & Thomas, 1999). But the latest federal evaluation, released in 2010, found small and inconsistent benefits as children moved into elementary school, after randomly assigning youngsters to Head Start or a control group (Puma et al., 2010). The research team tracked nearly 5,000 children, ages 3 and 4, through Head Start centers and into elementary school. After one or two years in these programs, Head Start children displayed significantly higher levels of cognitive development and positive social behaviors. But few benefits lasted past first grade, compared with children in the control group. The findings were blurred because about one-fourth of children in the control group ended up in a non-Head Start preschool or other form of nonparental care.

Regulating Quality: A Useful but Insufficient First Step

State policy makers, aiming to lift preschool quality, typically rely on rules, seeking to regulate organizational or "structural" features of preschools. When it comes to K-12 education government holds schools accountable for raising student performance, going well beyond the regulation of inputs or simple features of the organization. Beyond periodic evaluations, as with Head Start, preschools are not gauged by their efficacy in lifting kids' developmental outcomes. From a political viewpoint, the intensity of regulation as exercised by state capitals has become the currency by which advocacy groups define their own influence as they earnestly try to elevate quality: reducing preschool class size or boosting teacher credentials comes to be seen as a policy win.

Certain regulated proxies of quality may contribute indirectly to gains in children's growth. Learning gains have been detected, for instance, among young children attending classrooms with lower ratios of kids per adult. These richer staffing ratios are related to more frequent exposure to adult language and greater responsiveness by teachers

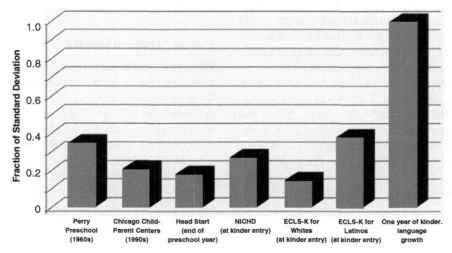

Figure 27.1 Quality worries: Uneven cognition gains when children attend Pre-K programs.

(Blanchford, Goldstein, Martin, & Brown, 2002; Burchinal, Roberts, Nabors, & Bryant, 1996; Phillips, Voran, Kisker, Howes, & Whitebook, 1994).

We also know that in the absence of minimal regulatory standards preschool quality can sink quite low, minimizing benefits for children.[3] Several studies have demonstrated that better educated teachers and more carefully organized learning activities tend to be situated in states that regulate more aggressively (Helburn, 1995; Loeb et al., 2004). But these findings remain inconsistent or show weak relationships, and often fail to take into account possible selection bias.[4]

Andrew Mashburn et al. (2008) at the University of Virginia directed a study that examined the extent to which 671 preschool classrooms complied with nine regulatory standards endorsed by the National Institute for Early Education Research (e.g., maximum class size, teacher credential levels).[5] Regulatory indicators were not associated with stronger developmental outcomes among 2,439 4-year-olds. One exception was that when teachers received specialized training in child development, including at community colleges, on average their preschoolers' displayed discernibly steeper growth.

Some preschool advocates push policy makers to mandate that all preschool teachers obtain a bachelor's degree, and the Congress has moved in this direction, hoping to lift the quality of Head Start. But evidence remains weak that this regulatory mandate pays off for children. The most exhaustive study to date was led by Diane Early and colleagues (2007), who analyzed data from seven independent studies, each including near-identical measures of teacher education levels. The statistical analysis was similar across data sets, and stringent controls were used to take into account the prior attributes of children and teachers. Five of the seven original studies drew on nationally representative data.

Early's team detected few associations between teacher credentials, including holding a bachelor's degree, with the quality of care provided in the classroom. Data from two of the seven studies found that holding a four-year degree was predictive of stronger teaching practices; but analysis of the remaining five data sets found no or negative effects. And, most important, measured benefits for children were no more promising. When estimating children's early language or math proficiencies, the majority of studies found no significant effect from being in a classroom with a teacher with a bachelor's degree. Other studies confirm Early's findings, including a quasi-experimental study tracking twins, just one of whom experienced Head Start (methodologically taking into account confounding factors that might drive both selection of preschool and child outcomes; Currie & Neidel, 2007).

The Quality Nexus: Teachers Who Nurture Relationships, Organize Learning Activities

Recent work inside preschool classrooms illuminates a telling nexus—a pair of interwoven, human-scale practices that lift children's development. First, the encouragement, feedback, and steady emotional support offered by preschool teachers are predictive of various positive outcomes for children. But attention to youngsters' social-emotional growth alone does not necessarily advance development in cognitive and preliteracy domains. This nexus of effective practices must also include well-structured learning tasks and child–teacher interactions that challenge kids cognitively (Hamre & Pianta, 2005; Mashburn & Pianta, 2006). Quality preschools aim to advance young children's competencies as active learners within complex social environments, like classrooms or households. Learning and cognitive facilitation by adults is facilitated by close, respectful, and encouraging relationships with adults and with the child's peers. So, for example, when a preschool teacher sensitively mediates a dispute between two 4-year-olds, nudging them to reason about the problem and weigh possible remedies, a trusting relationship acts to advance cognitive and linguistic skills (Fuller, Kagan, Loeb, & Chang, 2004);[6] that is, sound relationships are intertwined with early learning, a postulate long understood by fine preschool teachers.

We emphasize that this nexus of emotional support and instructional organization is nested within cultural and linguistic boundaries. Children's acquired norms for being assertive, vocal, and independent in preschool classrooms may stem from a particular upbringing, defined by the class and cultural heritage of the family. The child's pursuit of competence—learning to fit into a social setting and acquiring requisite cognitive and linguistic skills—is situated in culturally set roles and expected behaviors, internalized long before the child enters preschool. So, as interventions are crafted to advance this nexus between emotional support and instructional organization, they must be adapted to cultural and linguistic norms.[7]

Promising Teacher Development Models: Building from Theory

Moving from this nexus between social development and instructional organization, we next review two models that show promise in lifting the quality of preschool classrooms. One, developed by Robert Pianta and University of Virginia colleagues, is based from the closeness and trust inherent in motivating child–teacher relationships, then builds from this cornerstone to how teachers can better organize learning tasks (Pianta, 2010). The second model, built by Susan Landry and her University of Texas, Houston team, starts with effective ways of sparking children's oral language and preliteracy skills, while nurturing stronger social relationships (Landry, Anthony, Swank, & Monseque-Bailey, 2009).

Each model builds from earlier work that emphasizes how artful teaching practices can advance the child's feeling of belonging and motivation to learn, along with presenting cognitively challenging activities, in specific ways:

- Sensitive teachers listen carefully to children, encourage more precise language, and reason through problems together. This builds trust and offers cognitive challenges, scaffolding-up from what the child already knows.
- Teachers can model warm and respectful relationships. When this spills over to peer relations, children are more likely to converse and learn from one another, and display fewer social conflicts. This, in turn, allows the child to engage in learning tasks with greater self-regulation and less dependence upon adult direction.
- When children experience teachers as responsive and cognitively demanding, youngsters are more motivated to engage new cognitive challenges and novel peer relations.
- Language, new knowledge, and imaginative ideas travel more readily across stronger social ties. Put another way: rich and colorful materials will do little to facilitate cognitive growth unless animated by stimulating and supportive interaction between children and teachers.

Developmental scientists continue to extend and improve measures to better describe and gauge variation in these classroom dynamics and developmental benefits for children (Figure 27.2).

At the same time, the richness of social relationships does not guarantee that teachers effectively organize learning tasks inside their preschool classrooms. Research by Hamre and Pianta (2007) shows that many preschool teachers are quite proficient in offering emotional support and attending to children's social skills, but their classrooms are unevenly organized in terms of challenging, cognitively stimulating tasks. It is this balance, at the nexus of social nurturing and challenging tasks, that is key to advancing children's early learning (see also, Burchinal, Vandergrift, Pianta, & Mashburn, 2009).

The new science on preschool quality finds that the emotional support of young children, often displayed by teachers, is necessary but insufficient to advance children's growth in the cognitive domain, especially when it comes

Preschool staff work from their beliefs and daily experiences to judge what makes for a caring and effective teacher. Researchers advance this conversation by describing child-adult interactions and ways of organizing learning tasks that predict steeper growth curves for young children. Progress has been made over the past quarter-century in specifying, observing, and measuring these elements of efficacious preschool teachers.

- *Arnett Caregiver Interaction Scale.* Psychologist Jeff Arnett, back in the 1980s, built an instrument for observing the interaction between caregivers and young children, including 26 different scales. This boils-down to four discernable facets of quality interactions: warm and responsive behavior by the teacher or caregiver to the child's utterances; harsh or punitive discipline of misbehavior; the adult's or child's detachment from one another; and the extent to which the adult permits the child to engage in a variety of behaviors, even when disengaged from learning tasks. Scholars using the Arnett measure also find that it taps into the extent to which teachers explain misbehavior or reason with the child to resolve problems, inviting complex language.

- *Child-Caregiver Observation System.* This tool takes snapshots of preschool settings every five minutes to assess the activity and social actors with whom the child is engaged, learning materials involved, and the caregiver's verbal interaction with the child. Developed by scientists at Mathematica Policy Research, Inc., this tool can track the life of activities over several hours, and children's changing level of engagement. It has revealed that many children in a significant number of Preschool programs wander about, not engaged over time in any activity.

- *Observational Record of the Caregiving Environment* (ORCE) was initially designed to focus on the quality and content of child-adult interactions in Preschool and home-based child care. It records behaviors and global ratings of the social environment at regular time intervals. For preschool teachers, this includes observation of the adult's expression of affection and warmth, responsiveness to the child, avoidance of intrusive or restrictive discipline behaviors. Additional measures now include the teacher's attention to literacy skills and the quality of instructional materials.

- *Classroom Assessment Scoring System (CLASS).* Integrating concepts and scales from the earlier observational measures, the CLASS gauges the preschool classroom's social-emotional climate, facets of child-teacher interactions, and the management of learning activities, focusing on language and preliteracy skills. This tool records the extent to which teachers offer responsive and encouraging interactions with kids, the overall management of classroom activities and engagement levels, and the attention to language and preliteracy skills through well-structured tasks.

- *Early Childhood Environment Rating Scale (ECERS).* An industry standard, the ECERS is now employed in several states to assess the quality of preschool classrooms. It emphasizes the nature of physical space, types of activities provided, and the supply of learning materials. The second dimension often identified by researchers relates to the quality of child-adult interactions. Results from several students now demonstrate that these social-interaction subscales predict developmental gains, not necessarily the supply of learning materials.

Sources: Fuller, Kagan, Loeb, & Chang (2004), Mashburn & Pianta (2006), Pianta (2003).

Figure 27.2 Seeing and measuring teacher practices that lift early learning

to oral language and preliteracy skills. One reason that preschool programs continue to show few benefits for some children may stem from the disproportionate attention paid to emotional support by teachers, accompanied by little attention to instructional practices. Several dimensions of classroom management and learning tasks are predictive of early learning:

• Classroom tasks that manifest clear learning goals, managed carefully to ensure that children understand how they are expected to participate.
• Close and sensitive monitoring by the teacher, with steady feedback, to help children feel confident in completing organized learning tasks.
• Structuring tasks that involve rich oral language, scaffolding-up from children's linguistic skills and connecting oral language to written symbols.

Time spent on such challenging and enjoyable learning tasks—rather than watching videos or television, or roaming about unengaged—is predictive of children's cognitive growth. This is perhaps obvious, but several studies reveal sizable shares of time in which children are not involved in any particular task for a sustained period. And again, we know much about how to observe effective social relations and classroom organization (Figure 27.2).

As this empirical work illuminates how attention to social relationships interacts with the organization of learning tasks, how do we enrich teachers' agility in bringing this nexus to life inside their classrooms? This is the question to which we next turn.

Local Models to Enrich Teaching Practices in Preschool Classrooms

The past half-century of research has gone far in detailing what invigorating preschool classrooms look like. The recent advances in theory and evidence, centering on the synergy between social relationships and learning activities, now inform discrete models of teacher development. We next turn to a pair of programs that aim to improve teaching practices and the ways in which learning activities are structured.

Classroom Assessment Scoring System (CLASS)

Pianta (2010) and colleagues made a pivotal discovery as they observed teachers in 671 preschool classrooms spread across 11 states. They found that most teachers and aides were sensitive and responsive, working to boost their children's confidence and social skills. The extent to which teachers displayed this support did help to predict developmental outcomes during the preschool years. The problem, however, was that teachers' parallel skills in organizing rich and challenging learning tasks—especially in the area of language and literacy—remained weak overall.

Pianta's team observed many children, across large numbers of classrooms, who were sitting quietly or waiting for the next task. These weaknesses in classroom organization, in turn, slowed children's cognitive growth (see similar findings, Burchinal et al., 2008).

To remedy this imbalance, Pianta has built a teacher-development program that is showing promising results for preschool teachers and children. It starts with a classroom assessment tool, the CLASS. Pianta's group works with preschool staff to first use the CLASS to gauge the extent to which they (a) create a warm and encouraging climate in the classroom, showing sensitivity to kids and offering emotional support, (b) organize clear routines and structures in which children expect to engage in learning tasks, and (c) offer rich language and preliteracy skills, providing children with clear feedback on their performance. Pianta's theory of action is that effective socialization and academic learning stems from rich interactions between children and adults, and among peers. These social relations should be emotionally supportive and facilitate cognitive challenges related to language *and* preliteracy skills.

The CLASS program also involves videotaping classrooms and facilitating supportive discussions with fellow teachers and a live mentor. These are the first steps in a teacher development process called My Teaching Partner (MTP). This includes a library of videotaped classrooms in which teachers show exemplary proficiency in emotional support or classroom organization. Pianta's team is currently studying the comparative effects of mentoring with a live master teacher rather than relying on video clips to acquire effective forms of interaction with chilren and stronger ways to organize instructional tasks.

The CLASS model includes a new curriculum that focuses on development primarily in the language and literacy domain, again within the context of strengthening social relationships. This innovative curriculum is paired with preschool PATHS (Promoting Alternative Thinking Strategies). Still, the core theory accents the importance of emotional support and instructional management derived from strong child–teacher interactions in boosting early learning, rather than reliance on the use of codified curricular materials per se. And gauging change in social relations takes preschool staff back to the CLASS assessment tool, yielding feedback on their progress in improving practices.

Peer-reviewed studies of the CLASS model have recently been published gauging its effects on improved teaching practices and steeper developmental growth for children. When carefully implemented, the CLASS intervention, including the core elements of My Teaching Partner, appears to improve the observed sensitivity and responsiveness of preschool teachers. Gains also have been observed in the richness of language that teachers deploy in the classroom. Work remains to be done on estimating the magnitude of these benefits and whether the degree of change is sufficient to lift children's cognitive and social development.

Findings are clear that the forms of classroom interaction and instructional organization gauged by the CLASS are predictive of developmental outcomes for kids at modest levels of magnitude, after taking into account their family background.

Texas Early Education Model (TEEM)

The second teacher-training strategy, which is also showing encouraging results, stems from a differing theory of action. The designers of CLASS start with the question, what forms of interaction inside preschool classrooms will yield more robust early learning in terms of social and preliteracy skills. The architects of TEEM instead focus directly on curriculum, greater direct instruction through innovative activities, and the acquisition of preliteracy and math skills.

Susan Landry, the pediatric researcher who led the design of TEEM, emphasizes, "An alarming number of American preschool children lack sufficient language and literacy skills to succeed in kindergarten" (Assel, Landry, Swank, & Gunnewig, 2006, p. 450). To address this gap, preschool teachers must rethink their *role and pedagogical priorities*, according to the Houston-based TEEM designers. "One belief that can interfere with teachers making use of professional development is the long standing belief that children need to construct their own knowledge through self-directed discovery and … the teacher's role is supporting that discovery" (Landry et al., 2009). Nurturing children's own curiosity is not necessarily in conflict with the tighter organization of classroom activities that foster cognitive growth, according to these designers.

The TEEM intervention, which is similar to elements of CLASS, shows preschool teachers how they can "provide explicit information about vocabulary, number concepts, and letters in a more intentional approach." Landry and colleagues then build from core principles regarding *how adults learn*, including preschool teachers. This leads to a teacher-development model that (a) situates learning in authentic contexts where teachers are working daily, (b) creates situations where the teachers can learn and practice new methods side-by-side with their colleagues, and (c) develops stronger practices over a stretch of time, in contrast to sporadic in-service training. Strong mentoring with onsite trainers and via web clips helps to animate these principles inside classrooms.

The TEEM model begins with an intensive two-day training period, called CIRCLE, then moves to a web-based illustration of teaching practices dubbed eCIRCLE. This involves nine courses, conducted with fellow teachers and the demonstration of best practices by expert mentors, which cover classroom management, responsive teaching behaviors, and how to create learning activities based on the local preschool's own curricular materials. A TEEM mentor helps teachers move through the web-based material, practice in small groups, and implement new behaviors and learning activities for children in their classrooms.

TEEM requires school- and community-based preschool staff to work together and utilize state approved curricular guidelines, focusing in Texas on children's oral language, phonological awareness, knowledge of print materials, number and math concepts. TEEM also provides classroom-based school readiness and classroom management kits that gives teachers hands-on manipulatives to guide instructional activities.

On the social-development side, TEEM mentors encourage teachers to work with children on self-regulation and cooperation with peers, allowing them to engage rich learning tasks, along with getting kids to talk about their emotions and conflicts when they arise. Similar to CLASS, the TEEM designers see children's social-emotional vitality as interwoven with their capacity to engage instructional activities. And TEEM mentors demonstrate how these learning activities can be implemented with children in "a purposeful, planful, and playful way."

TEEM affiliates provide regular feedback to teachers; both how children are progressing and how well teachers are implementing pedagogical innovations. Teachers periodically assess children's progress through use of a hand-held device or laptop, noting levels of phonological awareness, letter knowledge, word recognition, prewriting skills, math, and social behaviors. These data are uploaded to a central database, and locally tailored reports go back to each teacher on children's progress over time. Mentors and teachers then work closely together to adjust instructional approaches and activities based on the needs of individual children. In addition, TEEM provides a tool for observing teachers and offering feedback on implementation of best practices and nurturing interactions with children, called the Teacher Behavior Rating Scale (TBRS). Participation in TEEM is linked to how Texas certifies and promotes preschool teachers as well.

Peer-reviewed evaluations of the TEEM model have begun to appear in the scientific literature—showing promising benefits for teachers and children. One study randomly assigned 220 preschool teachers to this teacher-development program or to a control group. Those participating in TEEM displayed moderate to strong changes in pedagogical practices, including greater attention to well-organized activities in book reading, phonological awareness, written expression, and children's use of print materials. Lesson planning was more carefully done by TEEM-assigned teachers, and compared with the control group they displayed greater responsiveness to children (Landry et al., 2009). Teacher effects were stronger when a second clinical trial compared the combination of web-based training, progress monitoring, and direct mentoring versus experiencing just one method.

TEEM researchers have detected significant effects on children's preliteracy skills, including letter recognition, oral vocabulary, and phonological awareness, assessed in English or Spanish. Effect sizes were variable in magnitude, ranging from 0.16 to 0.84 *SD*, depending on the outcome measure and whether children were with TEEM teachers for one or two years. The preliteracy skill scores of kindergartners climbed about 1.0 *SD* on average, so the benefits of TEEM training have been moderate to large in clinical trials.[7]

Going Statewide: Lifting Teachers across Diverse Preschools

These promising results from two training and mentoring programs offer a pivotal first step. But can such efforts be taken to scale, implemented across variegated networks of preschool organizations without sacrificing their integrity and thinning-out effects? The TEEM model continues to be implemented statewide in Texas, and the CLASS tools are currently being applied in a statewide effort in Georgia. We turn now to the issue of how preschool programs vary, and how this organizational kaleidoscope holds implications for taking these models to scale.

Organizational Variability

The first source of local variation, into which teacher-development models are dropped, pertains to the type of organized setting which young children enter. Let us take the case of Texas and the range of child care and preschool settings that are supported via parent fees or government aid. Figure 27.3 displays the count of organizations, including remunerated home-based settings, which populate the field. The high bar dominates the graph, indicating that over 200,000 children are being served in public-school preschool settings. Well over 60,000 young children are being served in Head Start centers, and approximately 130,000 children are being served in federally subsidized child care centers and home-based settings. As teacher training models are introduced, these vast organizational differences must be taken into account.

Philosophy, Networks, Resources

The various types of preschool programs manifest differing beliefs about what practices best nurture children's early learning. For decades many early educators, being versed in "developmentally appropriate practices," emphasized how young children learn through play. Adherents to this philosophical frame, reinforced by professional associations, at times discounted preliteracy activities and structured learning activities. At the same time, the rise of standards-based accountability in the schools lent strength to those who advocated more direct instruction with young children—at times failing to ask how the motivation and movement of young children may differ from that of school-age youngsters.

Diverse preschools are linked to differing funding streams and networks that advance competing philosophies and teaching practices, whether it is to encourage imaginary play or phonemic awareness. But this nexus between emotional support and instructional organization helps to bridge these differing perspectives. In this light, the dual-pronged agenda for preschool classrooms—nurturing support and better organized learning tasks—helps to bridge the old philosophical divide.

Demographic Diversity

Many early educators are quite familiar with the rising diversity of the families served by preschool programs. Today, just over one-fifth of children under 18 years of age are Latino; this will grow to 27% in the coming decade. English is not the home language of over two-fifths of all California families. One-third of all Texans speak Spanish or another language other than English at home. Just beneath this linguistic diversity lie a variety of social norms and cognitive requirements that vary among families. We know, for instance, that Latino children arrive at kindergarten with cooperative skills that rival their (economically) better-off White peers. But Latino children are less familiar with children's books than White children, and have a more

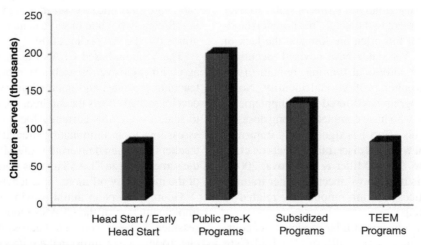

Figure 27.3 Colorful spectrum of Texas Pre-K Programs

restricted vocabulary and weaker cognitive agility within classroom settings (Galindo & Fuller, 2010).[8]

Young children learn quite early about how they should behave, seeking to become competent members of their immediate social groups, including within the family, classrooms, and among peers. Several studies have found that Latino children are more likely to abide by their parents' authority, are less often invited to reason about problems, and frequently put others' interests ahead of their own (for review, Fuller & García Coll, 2010). This may go against the methodology of mainstream developmentalists who encourage children to become more "autonomous," or to constantly verbalize and ask lots of questions inside preschool classrooms. We are not arguing that one cultural pattern is better than the other. But these findings do illustrate how the nurturing of social skills and classroom motivation would likely be more effective if teachers could carefully take into account such cultural differences. Put another way: it's difficult to see how preschool teachers could effectively offer emotional support, or set useful social rules for class activities, without first understanding the norms of interaction that children bring from home.

Similarly, preschool teachers may define the quality of social interaction differently, stemming from their particular linguistic or cultural heritage. Alison Wishard and Carollee Howes followed a multiethnic array of preschool teachers over time and concluded that "practices, more than (structural indicators of) quality, appear to be deeply embedded within value and belief systems that are rooted in ethnicity, community, and social class" (Wishard, Shriver, Howes, & Richie, 2003. p. 67).This team found that African American preschool teachers, on average, favored more direct instructional methods and the acquisition of oral language proficiency in English, compared with White teachers. The former also included greater curricular content from the Black community, while less frequent reference to cultural heritage was made by White teachers.

Weak Incentives, Uneven Commitments

Preschool programs vary greatly in terms of staff turnover and long-term commitment to the field. This is understandable given salaries that too often are low and the lack of advancement options. Yet states have devised incentives for teachers to pursue additional training, remain in the field, and build a stronger professional identity. North Carolina's TEACH program has offered wage supplements for preschool teachers who have completed strong doses of in-service training. This effort has significantly improved teaching practices, but with less discernible effects on child outcomes (Child Care, 2004; Miller & Bogatova, 2009). The policy question is how do we incent teacher training and classroom practices that are empirically related to children's early learning?

Several states now advance similar models to encourage professional advancement. California's Child Care Retention Incentive Program provides wage supplements to preschool teachers and aides who enroll in two- or four-year colleges, provided that they stay in the early-childhood field. A study tracked 2,783 participants and found significant positive effects in lowering staff turnover and (slowly) completing college-level courses (Bridges, Fuller, Huang, & Hamre, 2011). It remains unknown whether competencies are acquired that advance child development.

Promising teacher-development models, such as CLASS and TEEM, fit well within statewide incentive efforts. Rather than creating new in-service training outside preschool settings or relying on community colleges, these models provide mentorship and training within classrooms (in context), and supplement the training with helpful assessment tools for ongoing reflection and improvement. At the same time, if linked to wage or professional-growth incentives, more programs and teachers are likely to engage with comprehensive models like CLASS and TEEM.

TEEM's architects mindfully tested core elements, then initially (in 2003) ramped-up modestly in 11 diverse Texas communities. They articulated a clear strategy for "going to scale" while guarding against any erosion in the quality of teaching and professional development activities. "The current intervention includes a highly specified framework... without scripting the program and flexibility that allows administrators' and teachers' input into implementation," writes Susan Landry (Assel et al., 2006, p. 463). This strategy explicitly takes into account what's known about local implementation that's relevant and motivating across widely varying preschool settings and the families they serve.

After seven years of small-scale testing of the TEEM model through clinical trials, the Children's Learning Institute at the University of Texas Medical School at Houston has now scaled-up, taking the program across the state. The *Texas School Ready!* project, the second rendition of the TEEM model, has been implemented in more than 3,000 classrooms across 38 communities, including school- and community-based preschools and federal Head Start centers. Central to the Texas strategy is to form collaborative partnerships among various local programs. All types of early care and education settings are valued, and the model is sufficiently flexible to serve center and home-based programs (Gasko & Waxley, 2009).

The Virginia-based CLASS team began over a decade ago with extensive research inside preschools, identifying teaching practices and interaction styles that yield robust developmental effects for children. So, it's natural that going-to-scale for CLASS currently focuses more on classroom assessment tools, illuminating strengths and weaknesses for teachers, and then delivering professional development. At the same time, the CLASS team is studying which elements of the model pay off more for teachers and children.

Georgia offers an initial proving ground for statewide implementation of the CLASS model. The classroom assessment is being conducted across 4,000-plus preschool classrooms, a new thrust in the state's quality improvement effort. Georgia's early childhood agency has utilized other observation tools, aiming to better focus professional development activities. But the CLASS holds great appeal, given its emphasis on child–teacher interaction and the instructional organization of classrooms. Georgia's universal preschool program now serves over 84,000 children statewide, comparable in scope with the Texas initiative.

Sticking to Guiding Principles, Sharpening the State's Role

These recent lines of research illuminate the nexus between children's relationships and instructional organization, and test teacher-development models. This work also yields new insights into how we frame the problem of preschool quality and then elevate the effectiveness of teachers. The basic architecture builds from core foundations:

- The benefits of preschool for children remain constrained by uneven levels of quality.
- Tightening state regulation of structural elements of preschool organizations does not necessarily alter the social organization of life and instruction inside classrooms.
- No "silver bullets" exist. No single change in regulatory policy or practice will lift classroom quality. Multiple fronts are required to improve the organizational structure of preschools and the motivating life of classrooms.
- Improving child–teacher relationships and enriching learning activities yield the most promising benefits for children, advancing cognitive and social development.
- New models of teacher development—focusing on candid assessment of practices, attention to relationships and instruction, and ongoing mentoring—can effectively be taken to a statewide scale.
- Steady research and development further advances the effectiveness of these promising models for preschool teacher development.

We have seen how two states, Georgia and Texas, are moving from these empirical findings to build statewide strategies for lifting quality. Success depends upon building strong partnerships among local early-childhood leaders and the diverse array of organizations serving young children.

At the same time, the policy conversation should move beyond simply pushing for stricter state regulation. Minimal health and safety standards are essential for children's well-being, and states in the South continue to manifest weak regulatory standards. Yet we should not expect incremental changes in staffing ratios or broad (and expensive) mandates for higher teacher credentials to yield discernible gains for young children. The evidence simply doesn't show such benefits. In some ways, advocates and policy makers must go further, recognizing that progress depends upon elevating the skills of teachers to enrich relationships and the organization of instruction inside classrooms.

In short, preschools would benefit from a more surgical role for state governments. Yes, policy leaders must demonstrate a commitment to lifting the quality of early education if all young children are to become ready for school and socially adept to thrive inside classrooms. But state leaders and the advocates who nudge them should understand that old regulatory levers will only go so far in creating more robust classroom settings. Teacher-development models like CLASS and TEEM, when implemented carefully statewide, can yield stronger gains for young children in social development, oral language, and preliteracy skills. This requires state leaders to invest in quality-building strategies on the ground, inside preschool classrooms, not simply ratcheting up regulation from afar.

Parents and taxpayers invest heavily in the development of young children. President Obama and a bipartisan array of governors currently support even stronger public investment. But the benefits felt by many young children attending preschool remain limited by uneven quality. The rich policy discussion over preschool should not impoverish local strategies. Instead, we can build from the new science on quality, focusing on how we nurture caring and effective teachers and in turn lift the young children that they serve.

Acknowledgments

We thank Diane Early, Robert Pianta, and Guadalupe Peréz for their careful guidance and reviews of earlier drafts. Our work is supported by the Texas Workforce Commission in partnership with the Texas Education Agency and Berkeley's Institute of Human Development.

Notes

1. Alternative estimates of national enrollment levels appear in Fuller (2007).
2. Studies have been conducted in varying locations, at differing points in time, and with regional or national samples. Recent findings stem from Barnett, Lamy, and Chang (2005), Gormley Jr., Gayer, Phillips, and Brittany Dawson (2005), Karoly, Kilburn, and Cannon (2005), and Reynolds, Temple, Robertson, and Mann (2002).
3. When low-income mothers were nudged into jobs under Florida's welfare reform Susanna Loeb and colleagues discovered low quality inside preschools, some staffed by recent high school graduates (Loeb et al., 2004).
4. These kinds of associations could be explained by confounding factors. For instance, one study found that preschool teachers are better educated and earn more in states that spend more per child on preschool. But after taking into account state preschool spending levels, regulatory intensity exerted no additional benefits on teacher quality (Fuller et al., 2004).
5. David Blau (2007) also found little relationship between the intensity of state regulations and center-level quality, after taking other state attributes into account.
6. One study found that preschool teachers vary greatly in their propensity to invite children's verbalization, reasoning with the children, and encouraging productive work in group activities—practices that predict children's growth curves (Fuller et al., 2004).
7. Some benefits regarding teacher practices and classroom organization were stronger after one or two years of involvement with TEEM. However, these estimates may be somewhat inflated, given that

teachers, but not children, were randomly assigned to the treatment conditions. Family background controls were not included in estimation models, which may lead to understating home effects, although each child's pretest score was taken into account.

8. For a review of how cultural and linguistic differences among groups may condition young children's cognitive and social development see Fuller and García Coll (2010).

References

Assel, M., Landry, S., Swank, P., & Gunnewig, S. (2006). An evaluation of curriculum, setting, and mentoring on the performance of children enrolled in preschool kindergarten. *Reading and Writing, 20*, 463–494.

Barnett, S., Lamy, C., & Chang, K. (2005). *The effects of state prekindergarten programs on young children's school readiness in five states.* Trenton, NJ: National Institute for Early Education Research, Rutgers University.

Bassok, D. (2010). Do Black and Hispanic children benefit more from preschool? Understanding differences in preschool effects across racial groups. *Child Development, 81*, 1828–1845.

Blanchford, P., Goldstein, C., Martin, C., & Brown, W. (2002). A study of class size effects in English school reception classes. *British Educational Research Journal, 28*, 169–185.

Blau, D. (2007). Unintended consequences of child care regulations. *Labour Economics, 14*, 513–538.

Bridges, M. Fuller, B., Huang, D. S., & Hamre, B. K. (2011). Strengthening the early childhood workforce: How wage incentives may boost training and job stability. *Early Education & Development, 22*(6), 1009–1029.

Burchinal, M., Roberts, J., Nabors, L., & Bryant, D. (1996). Quality of center child care and infant and language development. *Child Development, 67*, 606–620.

Burchinal, M., Howes C., Pianta, R., Bryant, D., Early, D., & Clifford, R. (2008). Predicting child outcomes at the end of kindergarten from the quality preschool kindergarten teacher–child interactions and instruction. *Applied Developmental Science, 12*, 140–153.

Burchinal, M., Vandergrift, N., Pianta, R., & Mashburn, A. (2009). Threshold analysis of association between child care quality and child outcomes for low-income children in prekindergarten programs. *Early Childhood Research Quarterly, 25*, 166–176.

Child Care Services Association and Frank Porter Graham Child Development Institute. (2004). *Working in child care in North Carolina: Workforce survey, 2003.* Durham, NC: Author.

Currie, J., & Neidel, M. (2007). Getting inside the black box of Head Start quality: What matters and what doesn't. *Economics of Education Review, 26*, 83–99.

Currie, J., & Thomas, D. (1999). Does Head Start help Hispanic children? *Journal of Public Economics, 74*, 235–262.

Early, D. et al. (2007). Teachers' education, classroom quality, and young children's academic skills: Results from seven studies of preschool programs. *Child Development, 78*, 558–580.

Fuller, B. (2007). *Standardized childhood: The political and cultural struggle over early education.* Palo Alto, CA: Stanford University Press.

Fuller, B., & García Coll, C. (2010). Learning from Latinos: Contexts, families, and child development in motion. *Developmental Psychology, 46*, 559–565.

Fuller, B., Kagan, S., Loeb, S., & Chang, Y. (2004). Child care quality: Centers and home settings that serve poor families. *Early Childhood Research Quarterly, 19*, 505–527.

Fuller, B., Loeb, S., Strath, A., & Carrol, B. (2004). State formation of the child care sector: Family demand and policy action. *Sociology of Education, 77*, 337–358.

Fuller, B., Raudenbush, S., Wei, L., & Holloway, S. (1993). Can government raise child care quality? The influence of family demand, poverty, and policy. *Educational Evaluation and Policy Analysis, 15*, 255–278.

Galindo, C., & Fuller, B. (2010). The social competence of Latino kindergartners and growth in mathematical understanding. *Developmental Psychology, 46*, 579–592.

Gasko, J., & Waxley, T. (2009). *The Texas School Ready Project: Strategic approach.* Houston: Children's Learning Institute, University of Texas Health Science Center.

Gormley Jr., W., Gayer, T., Phillips, D., & Brittany Dawson, B. (2005). The effects of universal preschool on cognitive development. *Developmental Psychology, 41*, 872–884.

Hamre, B., & Pianta, R. (2005). Can instructional and emotional support in the first-grade classroom make a difference for children at risk of school failure? *Child Development, 76*, 949–967.

Helburn, S. (1995). *Cost, quality and child outcomes in child care centers: Technical report.* Denver: University of Colorado, Department of Economics.

Karoly, L., Kilburn, R., & Cannon, J. (2005). *Early childhood interventions: Proven results, future promise.* Santa Monica, CA: RAND.

Landry, S., Anthony, J., Swank, P., & Monseque-Bailey, P. (2009). Effectiveness of comprehensive professional development for teachers of at-risk preschoolers. *Journal of Educational Psychology, 101*, 448–465.

Loeb, S., Bridges, M., Bassok, D., Fuller, B., & Rumberger, R. (2007). How much is too much? The influence of preschool centers on children's early social and cognitive development. *Economics of Education Review, 26*, 52–66.

Loeb, S., Fuller, B., Kagan, S., & Carrol, B. (2004). Child care in poor communities: Early learning effects of type, quality, and stability. *Child Development, 75*, 47–66.

Love, J., Harrison, L., Sagi-Schwartz, A., Van IJzendoorn, M., Ross, C., Ungerer, J., & Chazan-Cohen, R. (2007). Child care quality matters: How conclusions may vary with context. *Child Development, 74*, 1021–1033.

Magnuson, K., Ruhm, M., & Waldfogel, J. (2007). Does prekindergarten improve school preparation and performance? *Economics of Education Review, 26*, 33–51.

Marketdata Enterprises (2005). *U.S. child day care services: An industry analysis.* Tampa, FL: Marketdata Enterprises.

Mashburn, A. et al. (2008). Measures of classroom quality in prekindergarten and children's development of academic, language, and social skills. *Child Development, 79*, 732–749.

Mashburn, A., & Pianta, R. (2006). Social relationships and school readiness. *Early Education and Development, 17*, 151–176.

Miller, J., & Bogatova, T. (2009). Quality improvements in the early care and education workforce: Outcomes and impact of the T.E.A.C.H. Early Childhood Project. *Evaluation and Program Planning, 32*, 257–277.

Peisner-Feinberg, E., Burchinal, M., Clifford, R., Culkin, M., Howes, C., Kagan, S., & Yazejian, N. (2001). The relation of preschool child-care quality to children's cognitive and social developmental trajectories through second grade. *Child Development, 72*, 1534–1553.

Phillips, D., Voran, M., Kisker, E., Howes, C., & Whitebook, M. (1994). Child care for children in poverty. *Child Development, 65*, 472–492.

Pianta, R. (2010, May 4). *Quality and impacts of preschool: Observing and improving teacher–child interactions.* Presentation at the Texas Early Learning Institute Conference, Austin.

Puma, M. et al. (2010). *Head Start impact study: Final report.* Washington, DC: U.S. Department of Health and Human Services.

Reynolds, A., Temple, J., Robertson, D., & Mann, E. (2002). Age 21 cost-benefit analysis of the Title I Chicago Child-Parent Centers. *Educational Evaluation and Policy Analysis, 24*, 267–303.

Shonkoff, J. P., & Phillips, D. A. (Eds.). (2000). *From neurons to neighborhoods: The science of early childhood development.* Washington, DC: National Academy Press.

Wishard, A., Shivers, E., Howes, C., Ritchie, S. (2003). Child care programs and teacher practices: Associations with quality and children's experiences. *Early Childhood Research Quarterly, 18*, 65–103.

28

Early Childhood Education Programs in the Public Schools

Jason T. Hustedt
University of Delaware

Dale J. Epstein
University of North Carolina at Chapel Hill

W. Steven Barnett
Rutgers University

Preschool program enrollment rates of 3- and 4-year-olds have increased dramatically since the mid-1960s, and most children now enter kindergarten having already participated in some type of early education program (Barnett & Yarosz, 2007). States have become increasingly interested in developing and financing prekindergarten education programs (pre-K), helping to fuel this growth, particularly during the past two decades (Barnett, Epstein, Friedman, Sansanelli, & Hustedt, 2009; Mitchell, 2001). Although state pre-K initiatives take a variety of different forms across the United States, they share a number of common features (Barnett, Epstein et al., 2009). First and foremost, they are funded and administered by state government, following specified state regulations. They focus primarily on education for 3- and 4-year-olds, rather than parent education or workforce development. These initiatives are not designed primarily to serve children with disabilities or to offer child care, though coordination with state special education and, to a lesser extent, child care systems is an important component of pre-K initiatives. State pre-K initiatives offer group-based learning experiences to children at least two days per week, and are always voluntary for parents. By fall 2008, state pre-K initiatives had enrolled more than 1.2 million children across 38 U.S. states. Total public spending on these initiatives topped $5.7 billion, including a commitment of $5.0 billion in state funds.

This chapter provides an overview of early childhood education programs in public schools, with a particular focus on the state-funded pre-K initiatives that drive publicly funded pre-K education. We begin with a discussion of the research base and of the effectiveness of public preschool programs. Next, we describe the current status of access, quality standards, and spending in state-funded pre-K. Our review of state pre-K initiatives is supported by data

from the seventh in a series of intensive annual surveys of state pre-K conducted by the National Institute for Early Education Research (Barnett, Epstein et al., 2009). We conclude with a discussion of policy issues related to the administration of public school-based early childhood education programs.

Impacts of Pre-K Programs in the Public Schools

Typical goals of preschool education programs, including state pre-K initiatives, include improving language and early literacy skills to build foundations for reading and writing success, as well as developing knowledge and skills that relate to math, science, and the physical and social world. Also important is the development of attitudes, habits, dispositions, and social skills. Many studies have found that preschool education programs can produce substantive gains in child development and that these can persist well into the school years. Two randomized trials of preschool programs in the public schools that date back to the 1960s are especially informative, even though the programs studied differ in the scale and depth of services compared to larger-scale state pre-K initiatives offered today (Barnett, 2008).

The first of these studies is the well-known High/Scope Perry Preschool study (Schweinhart et al., 2005). Most children participated in the Perry Preschool program for two years, beginning at age 3, but some had only one year beginning at age 4. Although similar in many ways to today's part-day state pre-K programs, the teacher to child ratio was much more intensive—1:6 or 7. The initial effects of this intervention on children's language and cognitive abilities were very impressive, about 0.90 standard deviations. Though effects on IQ were not persistent, there were persistent effects in literacy and math, as well as other positive outcomes such as better teacher-reported classroom and personal behavior, fewer special education placements, and higher high school graduation rates (Berrueta-Clement, Schweinhart, Barnett, Epstein, & Weikart, 1984; Schweinhart, Barnes, & Weikart, 1993).

The second study was conducted by the Institute for Developmental Studies (IDS; Deutsch, Deutsch, Jordan, & Grallow, 1983; Deutsch, Taleporos, & Victor, 1974; Jordan, Grallow, Deutsch, & Deutsch, 1985). In the IDS study, 402 children were randomly assigned to a one-year public pre-K program beginning at age 4, or to a control group. Classes of 17 children were staffed by one teacher and one aide. By the end of the pre-K year, estimated effects on measures of cognitive and language abilities were more than 0.40 standard deviations. An estimated effect of 0.20 standard deviations in these areas remained evident at least through third grade. Later follow-ups suffered from severe attrition, limiting their usefulness.

An early methodologically rigorous study of public school preschool focusing on a larger-scale initiative also dates back to the 1960s—the Chicago Parent Child Center (CPC) study (Reynolds, 2000). CPC programs operate within Chicago's public school system, and study participants attended half-day preschool programs for two years starting at age 3 or one year starting at age 4. There were also kindergarten and elementary school follow-on components for the CPC participants in this study. Classes of 18 children were staffed by a certified teacher and a teacher assistant; parent outreach and support were also provided. Initial effects of the CPC program by kindergarten varied by type of measure, but were in the range of 0.35 to 0.77 standard deviations (with effects of 0.20 to 0.65 standard deviations for a single year of attendance). Long-term positive impacts of the CPC program include higher test scores through middle school, increased high school graduation rates, and reduced rates of arrests and special education placements. These findings from the CPC study are especially important because they essentially replicate the findings of the Perry Preschool study in the context of a more broadly available, and somewhat less intensive, public preschool initiative (Barnett, 2008).

Recent Evidence

Many other studies provide evidence relevant to the impact of preschool education programs (see Barnett, 2008; Camilli, Vargas, Ryan, & Barnett, 2010). However, relatively few have evaluated the effects of state preschool programs and many of the studies that do exist suffer from methodological weaknesses (Gilliam & Zigler, 2000, 2004). Recently, Gormley and colleagues (Gormley, Gayer, Phillips, & Dawson, 2005; Gormley, Phillips, & Gayer, 2008) have conducted rigorous research on the state pre-K classrooms in the city of Tulsa, Oklahoma. These studies applied a regression-discontinuity approach to address the problem of selection bias, and found effects on literacy and math achievement of 0.36 to 0.99 standard deviations. Effects were only modestly smaller for children who did not qualify for free or reduced-price school lunches than for those who did. Researchers at the National Institute for Early Education Research have taken a similar approach to estimate the initial effects of state-funded pre-K on children's cognitive abilities in eight states (Barnett, Howes, & Jung, 2008; Hustedt, Barnett, Jung, & Goetze, 2009; Hustedt, Barnett, Jung, & Thomas, 2007; Wong, Cook, Barnett, & Jung, 2008). Average effect sizes across these eight states at kindergarten entry were 0.23 for cognitive and language ability, 0.31 for mathematics, and 0.79 for print awareness.

Effectiveness

Educational effectiveness is key to any critical discussion of early childhood education programs, regardless of the settings in which they occur. A main goal of these types of programs is to contribute to children's learning and development so that they begin kindergarten ready to succeed. While there is not an exact "input formula" that guarantees educational effectiveness for all children who participate in publicly funded preschool programs, research has shown that certain features are linked to substantial gains in preschoolers' learning and development. Four main features seem especially important (Barnett & Ackerman, in press; Frede, 1998), and our later discussion of quality expands upon these characteristics of effective programs. First, early childhood teachers should be well-educated, and well-paid. A bachelor's degree sets the minimum standard for teacher education in public school settings beginning in kindergarten. It is reasonable to expect that preschool teachers in public settings should have similar levels of educational attainment and be paid salaries comparable to those of kindergarten teachers. By having comparable salaries, programs are able to hire and retain more qualified teachers. Direct and indirect links have been found between levels of teacher compensation, program effectiveness, and child outcomes as compensation is related to education levels, morale, and workforce stability (Barnett, 2003b; Whitebook, Gomby, Bell, Sakai, & Kipnis, 2009). Second, teaching and instruction should be intentional, using a well-planned curriculum that helps children understand how to be successful in a school setting. Neither the field nor the government, at either the state or federal level, specifies one curriculum model as better than others for young children. However, when selecting a curriculum, pre-K initiatives should be mindful about the children they serve, the experience levels of their teachers, and the community and school settings (Frede & Ackerman, 2006). Third, class sizes and teacher to child ratios in preschool education programs should be structured to allow children to work in small groups or individually with teachers. Finally, teachers need strong mentoring and supervision to guide their instruction and interactions with students.

Of course, early childhood education programs vary tremendously in the degree to which they are able to consistently offer the features and capacities described above. *Professional capacity* is a term that refers to the skills and knowledge held by both individuals and their organizations (Johnson & Thomas, 2004). Simply put, public schools, private child care providers, and Head Start may each have different capacities to offer educationally effective early education programs that provide the greatest benefits to children. Each type of program stands to make valuable contributions to a broader system of publicly funded preschool education (Barnett & Ackerman, in press).

Important capacities of private childcare centers include wide availability and substantial amounts of physical space, staff who have made a commitment to meeting the needs of young children and whose cultural backgrounds more likely reflect those of their students, and schedules that meet the needs of working parents. Weaknesses of private child care centers may include low levels of emphasis on formal education or training for teachers and directors, low teacher salaries, and large class sizes (Ackerman, 2006; Barnett, Epstein et al., 2009). Head Start's strengths include the greater resources it receives as a product of federal funding, a growing emphasis on hiring teachers with bachelor's degrees, small class sizes, consistent program standards that apply to all sites nationwide, and the ability to provide comprehensive family support services. However, even Head Start teachers with bachelor's degrees receive much lower salaries than their public school counterparts, and the emphasis on comprehensive services may dilute the educational emphasis of programs (Barnett & Ackerman, in press).

Public school settings offer a number of strengths that can help facilitate the delivery of educationally effective state pre-K initiatives. They offer substantial organizational capacity, stricter educational standards for teachers that focus on bachelor's degrees and certification, and higher salaries. They are also experienced in aligning instruction to statewide standards (Council of Chief State School Officers and National Governors Association, n.d.). Further, public schools already serve large numbers of preschoolers with disabilities each year and can more easily integrate these children into regular education program when also serving children who do not have special needs or educational difficulties. Some drawbacks of public schools as sites for pre-K programs include teachers whose cultural backgrounds are less likely to reflect those of their students, potential obligations to make sacrifices in the interest of a larger system that is not focused specifically on early childhood (Barnett & Ackerman, in press), and a lack of capacity to respond quickly and inexpensively to needs for new facilities (Sussman & Gillman, 2007).

While public schools, private child care facilities, and Head Start each offer capacities that can be used to benefit publicly funded pre-K programs, there are also drawbacks associated with each type of program that could hinder the progress and effectiveness of state pre-K initiatives offered exclusively in a single program. Further, the early childhood sector currently lacks the level of financial backing that would be needed to fully implement effective, large-scale, programs without utilizing the resources of multiple types of settings. Barnett and Ackerman (in press) propose instead that public schools be used as the centerpiece of a larger system linking together early childhood programs from different types of settings. This type of mixed delivery model is already being used in states such as New Jersey, and can take advantage of strengths across different types of settings, including well-qualified teaching staff and wide availability to offer parents a higher level of choice in public pre-K providers.

Access

By the 2008-2009 school year, 1,216,077 children were enrolled in state-funded pre-K education programs. These initiatives were available in 38 U.S. states, and some states offered multiple distinct pre-K initiatives aimed at different groups of children. The vast majority of the children enrolled in state pre-K were 4-year-olds—representing 25% of all 4-year-olds in the country—but 4% of the nation's 3-year-olds were also enrolled. Overall enrollment figures in state pre-K continued a trend of annual increases dating back to at least the 2001-2002 school year, when we began collecting this type of data (Barnett, Epstein et al., 2009).

Current Enrollment Levels and Eligibility Criteria

Age is the primary eligibility criterion for state pre-K initiatives, and all state pre-K programs offer enrollment to 4-year-olds who will be eligible for kindergarten the following year. Oklahoma was the state that served the greatest percentage of its 4-year-old population during 2008-2009, with 71% of all 4-year-olds in the state enrolled. Other states serving more than half of their 4-year-olds included Florida (67%), Georgia (53%), Vermont (53%), and West Virginia (51%). Twenty-five of the 38 states with pre-K initiatives also offered enrollment to 3-year-olds, though always to a lesser degree than they offered enrollment to 4-year-olds. States that enrolled the greatest percentages of 3-year-olds were Illinois (21%), Vermont (17%), New Jersey (17%), and Kentucky (10%). All of the other states served fewer than 10% of their 3-year-olds in state pre-K (Barnett, Epstein, et al., 2009). Table 28.1 provides state-by-state enrollment information for each state offering a pre-K initiative.

In determining eligibility to publicly funded early childhood programs, most states also use factors other than the child's age. Family income limits are most common, as states set maximum income levels to target programs to the most financially disadvantaged. In at least 26 of the 38 states with pre-K initiatives, state income limits are used to determine eligibility for at least some subset of

Table 28.1 Access to State-Funded Pre-K Programs in 2008–2009

State	Total Number of Children Enrolled, Fall 2008 (All Ages)	Percentage of 4-Year-Olds Enrolled in State Pre-K	Percentage of 3-Year-Olds Enrolled in State Pre-K	Percentage of Children in Public Schools (Estimated)	Percentage of Children in Private Settings (Estimated)
Alabama	3,384	6%	0%	46%	54%
Arizona	5,447	5%	0%	93%	7%
Arkansas	20,476	44%	6%	60%	40%
California	97,948	13%	5%	75%	25%
Colorado	18,475	20%	6%	66%	34%
Connecticut	8,865	11%	8%	28%	72%
Delaware	843	7%	0%	46%	54%
Florida	147,762	67%	0%	13%	87%
Georgia	78,310	53%	0%	43%	57%
Illinois	95,123	29%	21%	100%	0%
Iowa	11,831	29%	1%	54%	46%
Kansas	8,247	21%	0%	91%	9%
Kentucky	21,485	28%	10%	100%	0%
Louisiana	19,720	32%	0%	93%	7%
Maine	2,731	19%	0%	96%	4%
Maryland	26,821	35%	1%	93%	7%
Massachusetts	10,797	11%	3%	36%	64%
Michigan	24,091	19%	0%	81%	19%
Minnesota	2,069	2%	1%	0%	100%
Missouri	4,568	4%	2%	87%	13%
Nebraska	2,723	7%	3%	70%	30%
Nevada	1,123	2%	1%	97%	3%
New Jersey	49,091	27%	17%	46%	54%
New Mexico	4,745	17%	0%	50%	50%
New York	102,282	43%	0%	47%	53%
North Carolina	31,485	25%	0%	48%	52%
Ohio	21,963	8%	5%	37%	63%
Oklahoma	36,042	71%	0%	88%	12%
Oregon	6,472	8%	5%	31%	69%
Pennsylvania	31,509	16%	5%	61%	39%
South Carolina	24,866	38%	4%	98%	2%
Tennessee	18,364	22%	1%	86%	14%
Texas	200,529	45%	5%	100%	0%
Vermont	4,658	53%	17%	93%	7%
Virginia	14,585	14%	0%	100%	0%
Washington	8,120	7%	2%	59%	41%
West Virginia	13,135	51%	9%	45%	55%
Wisconsin	35,392	48%	1%	96%	4%
National Total/Average	**1,216,077**	**25%**	**4%**	**67%**	**33%**

Note. Data are derived from Barnett, Epsten, et al. (2009). Twelve states are omitted because they did not offer state pre-K during the 2008-2009 school year. They are Alaska, Hawaii, Idaho, Indiana, Mississippi, Montana, New Hampshire, North Dakota, Rhode Island, South Dakota, Utah, and Wyoming.

the enrolled children (Barnett, Epstein et al., 2009). Some states use other risk factors to determine pre-K eligibility as well, such as low levels of parent education, disability or developmental delay, and having non-English-speaking family members (Barnett, Friedman, Hustedt, & Stevenson Boyd, 2009). A smaller but growing group of states has begun offering universally available pre-K programs that are intended (now or in the future) to be available to all 4-year-olds statewide—including Florida, Georgia, Illinois, Iowa, New York, Oklahoma, and West Virginia. Illinois is the only state that has committed to providing a universally available state pre-K program for 3-year-olds.

State Pre-K Programs in Public School Settings

Although state pre-K initiatives are all publicly financed, and are controlled and administered at the state level, states frequently partner with private organizations to operate state pre-K programs. This takes advantage of existing early childhood facilities and staff, as well as the ability of the private sector to grow quickly. Each of the 38 states with a pre-K initiative allows both public schools and private providers to receive state pre-K funds (Hustedt & Barnett, in press). The types of private agencies involved (e.g., Head Start, private child care providers, faith-based agencies) and the degree to which private agencies participate varies from state to state. However, the majority of participants in these initiatives do attend classrooms located in public schools.

We estimate that 67% of all children enrolled in state pre-K during the 2008-2009 school year were served in public school settings. As recently as the 2003-2004 school year, 76% of all state pre-K enrollees attended classrooms in the public schools. This decrease reflects a national trend toward growing enrollment levels in private settings as state pre-K programs become more widely available across the United States. For example, in 2002 West Virginia's pre-K initiative served all enrolled children at public school sites (Barnett, Hustedt, Robin, & Schulman, 2004), but by 2008 this initiative had grown considerably, and more than half of the children were enrolled in private settings. These changes come in the context of a 10-year phase-in process toward making pre-K available to all 4-year-olds in West Virginia by the 2012–2013 school year (Cavalluzzo, Clinton, Holian, Marr, & Taylor, 2009).

Table 28.1 provides state-by-state estimates of percentages of children who participated in public school-based state pre-K programs and percentages of children who attended programs based in private settings, during the 2008-2009 school year. Some states, including Texas, Virginia, and Kentucky, offer state pre-K programs that are heavily based in the public schools but may also be provided in a much more limited manner in non-public-school settings such as Head Start (Barnett, Epstein et al., 2009). These states are not able to provide enrollment breakdowns by type of school setting and for the current purposes we estimate that in such cases all pre-K children are enrolled in public schools. Using less conservative estimates in which we assume that 10% of state pre-K children in these states are enrolled in private settings has little impact on the national average. As a result, the best current estimate is that about two-thirds of children attending state pre-K programs are served directly in the public schools.

While some states distinguish between the standards that apply to public school pre-K programs and those offered in private settings, others make no such distinction and may even consider private settings an extension of the public schools. Oklahoma is a case in point. It allows public schools to collaborate with private providers by placing public school teachers in collaborative programs at community-based sites, including Head Start centers. Children in these sites are enrolled in the local public school system and receive the services offered by that public school system. Also, teacher salaries in collaborative settings must be equivalent to salaries in public schools. More than 4,100 of the approximately 36,000 children enrolled in Oklahoma's state pre-K initiative are served in these innovative collaborative programs (Barnett, Epstein et al., 2009).

Other Public Programs: Special Education and Local Preschool Initiatives

Special education programs are another important component of access to early childhood education initiatives in the public schools. During the 2008-2009 school year, more than 400,000 children received publicly funded special education services at ages 3 and 4, though some of these children received those services through state pre-K programs and are included in the state pre-K enrollment counts reported previously (Barnett, Epstein et al., 2009; Data Accountability Center, 2009). Special education programs are funded through a combination of federal, state, and local sources. There is great variability from state to state in percentages of children served, likely because states do not use identical sets of eligibility guidelines (Hustedt & Barnett, in press). Overall, we estimate that 3% of the nation's 4-year-olds and 3% of the nation's 3-year-olds receive special education services in addition to those already counted as part of state pre-K programs (Barnett, Epstein et al., 2009). A few states, most notably Kentucky and Wyoming (which does not offer a state pre-K program), have preschool special education programs that are much larger than the national average in terms of the percentage of the population served; they appear to serve a substantial number of children at risk of developmental delay.

Another component of access to publicly funded early childhood programs involves programs that are designed and administered at the local level, including local programs that make use of Title I and other federal funding streams. It is difficult to estimate the number of children enrolled in locally developed programs because such programs are not required to report their preschool enrollment to state or federal agencies.

Quality Standards

Research on early childhood educational programs has found links to quality regarding positive effects on children's development, academic success, and other outcomes that yield economic benefits to society. In establishing and expanding early childhood programs, decisions have to be made about program standards that will facilitate the provision of high quality learning environments to all children.

However, often the standards that may lead to the highest quality environments are also the most costly to implement, such as teacher qualifications and teacher to child ratios. Other quality standards such as having comprehensive early learning standards, providing meals, and conducting health screenings are less costly to provide.

Early childhood programs in public schools vary greatly in their policies regarding quality standards. The National Institute for Early Education Research conducts an annual survey that tracks 10 quality standards. These 10 standards and the benchmarks for "adequate" performance on each are presented in Table 28.2 (Barnett, Epstein et al., 2009). It is important to note that these quality standards and benchmarks are not judged to be of equal importance nor are the areas of focus all-inclusive. However, each of these standards is judged to contribute to the educational effectiveness of an early childhood program.

Teacher Qualifications in State Pre-K Programs

While findings may not be conclusive, there is a considerable body of research indicating that children whose lead teachers have bachelor's degrees and specializations in pre-K education have better academic outcomes (Barnett, 2003a; Burchinal, Cryer, Clifford, & Howes, 2002). Some researchers suggest that the evidence indicates teacher qualifications do not strongly contribute to preschool student learning, for a variety of reasons (Early et al., 2005; Mashburn et al., 2008). Others emphasize that only programs employing highly educated, well-paid teachers have been found to produce very large gains for students on broad measures of learning and development in randomized trails (Barnett, in press). Furthermore, continued teacher professional development is crucial for success in the classroom. In order to require these high levels of teacher qualifications in public early childhood programs, states typically need to offer supports and incentives, such as higher salaries, scholarships, and mentors to encourage teachers to obtain the necessary degrees. This often is costly and states vary in the emphasis they place on teacher training and degrees as evidenced in current policies for public pre-K programs.

While most state-funded early education programs have policies requiring pre-K specialization and professional development, many states still do not require teachers to have bachelor's degrees. Out of the 51 distinct state-funded pre-K initiatives offered in 38 states during the 2008-2009 school year, only 26 initiatives required all lead teachers to have a bachelor's degree while 44 required specialization in early childhood. This difference reflects the fact that many states not requiring a bachelor's degree do require a child development associate (CDA) credential, which is a specialization in early childhood. While approximately half of all state-funded initiatives require lead teachers to have bachelor's degrees, only 15 of the 51 state pre-K initiatives require all teachers to be paid on the public school salary scale. Another 21 initiatives require teachers to be paid on a public school scale if they are in a public setting, but not if they are located in a nonpublic setting. Similar to requiring specialization in early childhood, 42 state pre-K initiatives required at least 15 hours per year of professional development.

Though public early childhood programs continue to increase the quality requirements for lead teachers, very few programs have strict educational requirements for assistant teachers. Similar to research supporting the need for high quality lead teachers, findings indicate that there is a relationship between assistant teachers' qualifications and their effectiveness in the classroom (Barnett, 2003a; Bowman, Donovan, & Burns, 2001; Burchinal et al., 2002). During the 2008-2009 school year, only 14 state-funded prekindergarten initiatives required assistant teachers to have at least a CDA or equivalent. This is an increase of only three initiatives since the 2001-2002 school year, indicating virtually no progress being made in this area.

Teacher Qualifications in Public School Pre-K Settings

When examining state-funded pre-K programs, in general policies and program standards apply equally to all types of auspices in which the program is located. However, in some states there are key differences in educational requirements for teachers depending on location. Twelve states have

Table 28.2 Quality Standard Benchmarks

Early Childhood Program Policy Early learning standards	Quality Standard Benchmark Comprehensive
Teacher degree	At least a BA
Teacher specialized training	Specializing in pre-K
Assistant teacher degree	CDA or equivalent
Teacher in-service	At least 15 hours/year
Maximum class size	20 or lower
Staff-child ratio	1:10 or better
Screening/referral and support services	Vision, hearing, health; at least one support service
Meals	At least 1/day
Monitoring	Site visits

Note. Benchmarks are derived from Barnett, Epstein et al. (2009).

pre-K initiatives with different educational requirements for lead teachers in public settings compared to teachers in nonpublic settings. Although each state requirement differs slightly, all 12 require lead teachers in public school to have a bachelor's degree, whereas for nonpublic settings degree requirements range from none to an associate's degree (AA) or CDA. Ten of these 12 initiatives also have different certification requirements for lead teachers based on whether they work in public or nonpublic settings. On the other hand, 28 states have initiatives that apply the same degree requirements to lead teachers in both public and nonpublic settings, though some require a minimum of an AA for all teachers and others require a BA for all. In three of these states (Alabama, Michigan, and Ohio), while the degree requirements are the same, certification requirements differ by program location. Lastly, there are a few state-funded pre-K initiatives that currently operate only in public school settings, all of which require lead teachers to have bachelor's degrees: the Kansas At-Risk program, Louisiana's 8(g) program, Pennsylvania's K4 and School-Based Pre-K program, and South Carolina's 4K program.

For assistant teachers, almost all state-funded pre-K initiatives require the same educational requirements regardless of program location. Only five states have initiatives where there are distinct differences: Kentucky, Massachusetts, New York, Vermont, and Virginia. In addition, only New Mexico and New York have different assistant teacher specialized training requirements for teachers in public and nonpublic schools.

Other Program Standards in State Pre-K

In addition to teacher qualifications, it is important to understand what other standards are in place to determine the quality of a program. As of the 2008-2009 school year, all but four state pre-K initiatives had comprehensive early learning standards. Of the four that did not have early learning standards, one of them, California, had already developed early learning standards, but they were not expected to be implemented until the 2010-2011 school year (Barnett, Epstein et al., 2009). Early learning standards provide a framework for programs to ensure that all areas of children's learning and development are covered in the classrooms. Comprehensive early learning standards should cover all areas as identified by the National Educational Goals Panel (1991): children's physical well-being and motor development, social/emotional development, approaches toward learning, language development, and cognition and general knowledge. Moreover, some state-funded pre-K initiatives have state-approved comprehensive curriculum requirements for their programs, although only 14 out of 38 states have this type of mandate. These states allow programs to select their curriculum from a prespecified list, such as Creative Curriculum, HighScope, and Tools of the Mind.

Other aspects of program structure such as class size and staff-to-child ratios are important determinants of program effectiveness. Research suggests that young children perform better in classrooms with fewer students and low staff-to-child ratios, especially disadvantaged children (Barnett, 1998; Bowman et al.; 2001; Frede, 1998). Smaller classes with more adults present allow for more teacher–child interactions and individualized attention, resulting in both short-term and long-term academic and social–emotional gains. It is recommended that to enhance program quality and in turn effectiveness, early childhood programs should have a maximum class size of 20, with at least two adults in the classroom, creating a 1:10 staff-to-child ratio or lower. For the 2008-2009 school year, 45 out of 51 state-funded pre-K initiatives met both of these benchmarks. Texas and Pennsylvania's K4 program continued to be the only state-funded pre-K initiatives not to set limits on maximum class size and staff-to-child ratios. While Florida, Maine, Ohio, and Wisconsin's 4K programs do set limits, they do not meet the recommendations of 20 or fewer children and a 1:10 staff-to-child ratio.

Good nutrition and health are directly related to brain development and learning (Shonkoff & Phillips, 2000). Moreover, early detection of health, vision, and hearing problems can prevent or ameliorate later developmental and learning issues. It is recommended that early education programs serve at least one meal a day, and that meals follow U.S. Department of Agriculture Child and Adult Care Food Program nutritional guidelines. However, less than half (21 of 51) the state-funded pre-K initiatives in the United States require at least one meal a day. More state pre-K initiatives (32 of 51) require screenings and referrals for at least vision, hearing, and health for children enrolled in those initiatives.

Lastly, while it is important to have policies in place regarding quality standards, it is critical to conduct monitoring activities aimed at ensuring that programs are correctly and successfully implementing these standards. Unfortunately, unless programs are held accountable, not all of them will take the necessary steps to create high-quality learning environments for young children. The majority of pre-K initiatives (40 of 51) conduct site visits along with other monitoring activities to ensure that all programs are meeting the required quality standards. However, 11 initiatives still do not have such statewide provisions in place to hold programs accountable for meeting the minimum required standards.

Over the last decade, public early childhood initiatives have worked to increase levels of quality in their classrooms through implementing new policies. However, as noted above, some states are making more progress and reaching their goals faster than others. It is important that all public programs provide the necessary resources to create high-quality learning environments for young children so that all children have a chance to reach their potential.

Resources

The amount of resources a state allocates to pre-K affects the accessibility of the program (including availability as well as the types of services provided), and the quality standards that can be put in place. Without sufficient funding, a program can lack the ability to implement required quality standards or may subvert quality by making unwise trade-offs, which in turn may have an impact on children's learning and development. Or, a program may require high standards but lack sufficient resources to serve more than a small percentage of children in the state.

State Investments for Pre-K Programs

State government investments in pre-K are substantial, totaling more than $5 billion across the 38 states that offered pre-K initiatives during the 2008–2009 school year. While spending on pre-K by public education has consistently climbed over the last decade, 2008-2009 marked a slowdown in the growth rate compared to previous years. Also, while there has been a national trend toward increased spending, there are marked differences in spending patterns between individual states (Barnett, Epstein et al., 2009).

Individual state spending on pre-K ranges from under $5 million to over $760 million (Barnett, Epstein et al., 2009). In order to accurately understand a state's investment in pre-K, accessibility and enrollment levels must also be considered. For example, Texas spends over $760 million for its state pre-K initiative, while New Jersey spends over $550 million. However, because Texas is a much larger state and enrolls a much higher percentage of its 4-year-olds, the picture is quite different when looking at per child spending. Texas spends $3,790 per child, while New Jersey spends $11,205 per child. Therefore, when comparing state-allocated resources in public programs, it is useful to look at funding amounts per child enrolled, as well.

Additional Resources Used in Pre-K

In addition to state-allocated resources, most state pre-K programs employ other sources of funding such as federal and local funds. These funding streams can substantially increase the total amount of funding for a public program and, when available, can be used as a better gauge to determine total funding levels for a program. When states were asked to report all sources of funding, including federal and local dollars, the nationwide total rose to over $5.7 billion. For example, in Maryland per-child state spending is $3,765; but when all reported resources are added, the total jumps to $8,304, as there are significant required local funds that contribute to the program. However, states often lack a complete accounting of dollars spent at the local level, including funds raised by local public schools and federal Title I dollars allocated to state pre-K initiatives at the local level. This makes it difficult to compare spending across all the states.

In Table 28.3 information is provided on total state spending and state spending per child enrolled, ranked by per-child state spending amounts. Additionally, data on per-child spending including all reported resources are provided for states that are able to report additional federal and local funds used in their pre-K programs. When identical dollar amounts are listed for both state per-child spending and all reported per-child spending, this means that a state either does not use additional resources for its program or is unable to report the additional amounts from federal and local sources.

While the majority of states are continuing to invest in their public pre-K programs during the current economic downturn, commitments of resources toward pre-K have declined as states struggle to deal with budget deficits. When taking inflation into account, per-child spending for pre-K decreased slightly during the 2008–2009 school year. Preliminary indications are that this situation worsened in 2010. States must continue to make pre-K programs a priority by investing scarce resources in programs that ensure better outcomes for young children.

Conclusions and Policy Issues

Publicly funded pre-K in general, and state pre-K initiatives in particular, have expanded significantly over the past two decades. However, there is tremendous variation from state to state with respect to availability, quality, and spending. While some states, such as Oklahoma, have model programs that succeed in combining wide availability, high standards for quality, and adequate funding, these states are the exception (Barnett, Epstein et al., 2009). Therefore, it would be highly constructive if the federal government had a program that incentivized states to move in this direction. Current federal policy relies on Head Start to provide a quality program for children in poverty and the Child Care and Development Fund to support largely custodial child care. Increased financial support from the federal government would allow states to reach a higher level of consistency in the public early childhood programs that are offered. These additional funds could help ensure that all states are able to reach the threshold of quality that is needed for an effective early childhood education, especially for states that lag behind.

Even in the absence of increased financial support, there are steps that the federal government could take during the economic downturn to promote a better integrated system of early childhood education in the United States. One recommended step involves reducing the regulatory burden on Head Start programs in order to permit greater alignment and collaboration between state pre-K programs and Head Start providers. Another recommendation involves assisting the states in merging child care funds with state pre-K funds so as to raise the quality of services provided

Table 28.3 State and All Reported Spending in State Pre-K (2009 Dollars)

State	Resource rank based on state spending	Total state spending	State spending per child	All reported spending per child*
New Jersey	1	$550,081,566	$11,205	$11,205
Minnesota	2	$20,678,000	$9,994	$9,994
Connecticut	3	$72,194,403	$8,144	$10,303
Oregon	4	$51,906,604	$8,020	$8,020
Ohio	5	$151,642,502	$6,904	$6,904
Washington	6	$55,942,961	$6,890	$6,890
Delaware	7	$5,727,800	$6,795	$6,795
Massachusetts	8	$64,719,994	$5,994	$5,994
Pennsylvania	9	$179,944,302	$5,711	$5,711
Arkansas	10	$111,000,000	$5,421	$8,399
North Carolina	11	$170,471,908	$5,414	$7,713
Louisiana	12	$104,539,103	$5,301	$5,403
West Virginia	13	$69,147,853	$5,264	$8,743
Alabama	14	$17,374,590	$5,134	$5,134
Tennessee	15	$83,000,000	$4,520	$5,763
Michigan	16	$103,250,000	$4,286	$4,286
Georgia	17	$331,542,255	$4,234	$4,239
Oklahoma	18	$147,185,345	$4,084	$7,853
Virginia	19	$58,679,197	$4,023	$6,284
Texas	20	$760,059,287	$3,790	$3,790
Maryland	21	$100,974,791	$3,765	$8,304
California	22	$360,594,045	$3,681	$3,681
New York	23	$375,176,216	$3,668	$3,668
Kentucky	24	$75,127,700	$3,497	$4,941
Vermont	25	$16,150,120	$3,467	$3,467
Illinois	26	$327,024,460	$3,438	$3,438
New Mexico	27	$15,920,660	$3,355	$3,355
Wisconsin	28	$112,212,500	$3,171	$4,725
Iowa	29	$36,257,604	$3,065	$4,054
Kansas	30	$24,952,460	$3,026	$3,026
Nevada	31	$3,338,875	$2,973	$2,973
Missouri	32	$13,156,901	$2,880	$2,880
Nebraska	33	$7,684,420	$2,822	$5,184
Florida	34	$361,764,938	$2,448	$2,448
Arizona	35	$12,239,918	$2,247	$2,247
Colorado	36	$41,321,362	$2,237	$3,572
South Carolina	37	$40,596,640	$1,633	$3,409
Maine	38	$4,115,453	$1,507	$2,901

Note. Data are derived from Barnett, Epstein et al. (2009). Twelve states are not ranked because they did not offer state pre-K during the 2008-2009 school year. They are Alaska, Hawaii, Idaho, Indiana, Mississippi, Montana, New Hampshire, North Dakota, Rhode Island, South Dakota, Utah, and Wyoming.
* Not all states were able to report funding from federal and local sources, but funding from these sources is included in calculations when data are available.

while minimizing unnecessary duplication of services. Both recommended steps should help to maximize efficient use of the state and federal early childhood systems that are already in place.

As publicly funded pre-K programs continue to expand, and as the federal government becomes more involved, there are several key questions that must be addressed.

First, how will collaboration and coordination be handled across existing public programs that currently have distinct missions—including special education, Head Start, child care, and state pre-K? This is part of the mission of the early learning councils that are required in each state through the most recent Head Start reauthorization. It is crucial that public schools fully participate in this process. State-funded .

pre-K programs have the potential to serve as a hub for services across different types of auspices. Second, how will publicly funded early childhood programs fit into the new educational policy promoted by the Obama administration through its Race to the Top initiative that began providing new federal funds to state public school systems in 2010? And finally, what lessons will be learned and adapted by K-12 public education systems, based on the approach taken by pre-K in creating public–private partnerships? Because public early education programs employ a diverse delivery approach, newly coordinated state and federal early childhood systems stand to benefit from the best strengths and capacities of each type of setting. In turn, K-12 education systems can learn from this type of collaboration to better serve the needs of public school children.

Author Note

This work was made possible through the support of the Pew Charitable Trusts. However, any opinions expressed here are those of the authors, and do not necessarily reflect those of the Trusts.

References

Ackerman, D. J. (2006). The costs of being a child care teacher: Revisiting the problem of low wages. *Educational Policy, 20*, 85–112. doi: 10.1177/0895904805285283.

Barnett, W. S. (1998). Long-term effects on cognitive development and school success. In W. S. Barnett & S. S. Boocock (Eds.),*Early care and education for children in poverty: Promises, programs, and long-term results* (pp.11–44). Albany, NY: SUNY Press.

Barnett, W. S. (2003a). Better teachers, better preschools: Student achievement linked to teacher qualifications [policy brief]. *Preschool Policy Matters, 2*, 1–12. New Brunswick, NJ: National Institute for Early Education Research.

Barnett, W. S. (2003b). Low wages=low quality: Solving the real preschool teacher crisis [policy brief]. *Preschool Policy Matters, 3*, 1–8. New Brunswick, NJ: National Institute for Early Education Research.

Barnett, W. S. (2008). *Preschool education and its lasting effects: Research and policy implications.* Boulder, CO & Tempe, AZ: Education and the Public Interest Center, University of Colorado & Education Policy Research Unit, Arizona State University.

Barnett, W. S. (in press). Minimum requirements for preschool teacher educational qualifications. In E. Zigler, W. S. Barnett, & W. Gilliam (Eds.), *Current debates and issues in prekindergarten education.* Baltimore, MD: Brookes.

Barnett, W. S., & Ackerman, D. J. (in press). Public schools as the hub of a mixed delivery system of early care and education. In E. Zigler, W. S. Barnett, & W. Gilliam (Eds.), *Current debates and issues in prekindergarten education.* Baltimore, MD: Brookes.

Barnett, W. S., Epstein, D. J., Friedman, A. H., Sansanelli, R. A., & Hustedt, J. T. (2009). *The state of preschool 2009: State preschool yearbook.* New Brunswick, NJ: National Institute for Early Education Research, Rutgers University.

Barnett, W. S., Friedman, A. H., Hustedt, J. T., & Stevenson Boyd, J. (2009). An overview of prekindergarten policy in the United States: Program governance, eligibility, standards, and finance. In R. C. Pianta & C. Howes (Eds.), *The promise of pre-K* (pp. 3–30). Baltimore, MD: Brookes.

Barnett, W. S., Howes, C., & Jung, K. (2008). *California's state pre-K program: Quality and effects on children's learning* (Working paper).

New Brunswick, NJ: National Institute for Early Education Research, Rutgers University.

Barnett, W. S., Hustedt, J. T., Robin, K. B., & Schulman, K. L. (2004). *The state of preschool: 2004 state preschool yearbook.* New Brunswick, NJ: National Institute for Early Education Research, Rutgers University.

Barnett, W. S., & Yarosz, D. J. (2007). *Who goes to preschool and why does it matter?* (Preschool Policy Brief, 15). New Brunswick, NJ: National Institute for Early Education Research, Rutgers University.

Berrueta-Clement, J. R., Schweinhart, L. J., Barnett, W. S., Epstein, A. S., & Weikart, D. P. (1984). *Changed lives: The effects of the Perry Preschool Program on youths through age 19.* Ypsilanti, MI: High/Scope Press.

Bowman, B. T., Donovan, M. S., & Burns, M.S. (Eds.). (2001). *Eager to learn: Educating our preschoolers.* Washington, DC: National Academy Press.

Burchinal, M. R., Cryer, D., Clifford, R. M., & Howes, C. (2002). Caregiver training and classroom quality in child care centers. *Applied Developmental Science, 6*, 2–11. doi: 10.1207/S1532480XADS0601_01.

Camilli, G., Vargas, S., Ryan, S., & Barnett, W. S. (2010). Meta-analysis of the effects of early education interventions on cognitive and social development. *Teachers College Record, 112*(3), 579–620.

Cavalluzzo, L., Clinton, Y., Holian, L., Marr, L., & Taylor, L. (2009). West Virginia's progress toward universal prekindergarten (Issues & Answers Report, REL 2009–No. 070). Washington, DC: U.S. Department of Education, Institute of Education Sciences, National Center for Education Evaluation and Regional Assistance, Regional Educational Laboratory Appalachia.

Council of Chief State School Officers and National Governors Association. (n.d.). *Common core state standards initiative.* Retrieved from http://www.corestandards.org/.

Data Accountability Center. (2009). Individuals with Disabilities Education Act (IDEA). Data: Part B Child Count 2008. Retrieved from https://www.ideadata.org/PartBChildCount.asp.

Deutsch, M., Deutsch, C. P., Jordan, T. J., & Grallow, R. (1983). The IDS program: An experiment in early and sustained enrichment. In Consortium for Longitudinal Studies (Eds.), *As the twig is bent: Lasting effects of preschool programs* (pp. 377–410). Hillsdale, NJ: Erlbaum.

Deutsch, M., Taleporos, E., & Victor, J. (1974). A brief synopsis of an initial enrichment program in early childhood. In S. Ryan (Ed.), *A report on longitudinal evaluations of preschool programs: Vol.1. Longitudinal evaluations* (pp. 49–60). Washington, DC: Office of Child Development, U.S. Department of Health, Education, and Welfare.

Early, D., Barbarin, O., Bryant, D., Burchinal, M., Chang, F., Clifford, R., … Barnett, W. S. (2005). *Prekindergarten in eleven states: NCEDL's multi state study of pre-kindergarten and study of state wide early education programs* (SWEEP) (NCEDL Working Paper). Chapel Hill, NC: National Center for Early Development & Learning.

Frede, E. C. (1998). Preschool program quality in programs for children in poverty. In W. S. Barnett & S. S. Bocock (Eds.), *Early care and education for children in poverty* (pp. 77–98). Albany, NY: SUNY Press.

Frede, E.., & Ackerman, D.J. (2006). *Curriculum decision-making: Dimensions to consider.* New Brunswick, NJ: National Institute for Early Education Research, Rutgers University.

Gilliam W. S., & Zigler, E. F. (2000). A critical meta-analysis of all evaluations of state-funded preschool from 1977 to 1998: Implications for policy, service delivery and program evaluation. *Early Childhood Research Quarterly, 15*, 441–473 doi:10.1016/S0885-2006(01)00073-4 .

Gilliam, W. S., & Zigler, E. F. (2004). *State efforts to evaluate the effects of prekindergarten: 1977 to 2003.* New Haven, CT: Yale University Child Study Center.

Gormley, W. T., Jr., Gayer, T., Phillips, D., & Dawson, B. (2005). The effects of universal pre-K on cognitive development. *Developmental Psychology, 41*, 872–884. doi: 10.1037/0012-1649.41.6.872.

Gormley, W. T., Jr., Phillips, D., & Gayer, T. (2008). Preschool programs can boost school readiness. *Science, 320*, 1723–1724. doi: 10.1037/0012-1649.41.6.872.

Hustedt, J. T., & Barnett, W. S. (in press). Private providers in state pre-K: Vital partners. *Young Children*.

Hustedt, J. T., Barnett, W. S., Jung, K., & Goetze, L. D. (2009). *The New Mexico PreK Evaluation: Results from the initial four years of a new state preschool initiative: Final report*. New Brunswick, NJ: National Institute for Early Education Research, Rutgers University.

Hustedt, J. T., Barnett, W. S., Jung, K., & Thomas, J. (2007). *The effects of the Arkansas Better Chance Program on young children's school readiness*. New Brunswick, NJ: National Institute for Early Education Research, Rutgers University.

Johnson, H., & Thomas, A. (2004). Professional capacity and organizational change as measures of educational effectiveness: Assessing the impact of postgraduate education in development policy and management. *Compare: A Journal of Comparative Education, 34*, 301–314. doi: 10.1080/0305792042000257149 .

Jordan, T. J., Grallow, R., Deutsch, M., & Deutsch, C. P. (1985). Long-term effects of early enrichment: A 20-year perspective on persistence and change. *American Journal of Community Psychology, 13*(4), 393–415. doi: 10.1007/BF00911216 .

Mashburn, A. J., Pianta, R. C., Hamre, B. K., Downer, J. T., Barbarin, O. A., Bryant, D.,...Howes, C. (2008). Measures of classroom quality in prekindergarten and children's development of academic, language, and social skills. *Child Development, 79*(3), 732–749. doi: 10.1111/j.1467-8624.2008.01154.x .

Mitchell, A. W. (2001). *Education for all young children: The role of states and the federal government in promoting prekindergarten and kindergarten* (FCD Working Paper). New York: Foundation for Child Development.

National Educational Goals Panel. (1991). *The Goal 1 Technical Planning Subgroup report on school readiness*. Washington, DC: Author.

Reynolds, A. J. (2000). *Success in early intervention: The Chicago child-parent centers*. Lincoln: University of Nebraska Press.

Schweinhart, L. J., Barnes, H. V., & Weikart, D. P. (1993). *Significant benefits: The High/Scope Perry Preschool Study through age 27*. Ypsilanti, MI: High/Scope Press.

Schweinhart, L. J., Montie, J., Xiang, Z., Barnett, W. S., Belfield, C. R., & Nores, M. (2005). *Lifetime effects: The High/Scope Perry Preschool Study through age 40* (Monographs of the High/Scope Educational Research Foundation, 14). Ypsilanti, MI: High/Scope Press.

Shonkoff, J. P., & Phillips, D. A. (Eds.). (2000). *From neurons to neighborhoods: The science of early childhood development*. Washington, DC: National Academy Press.

Sussman, C., & Gillman, A. (2007). Building early childhood facilities: What states can do to create supply and promote quality. *Preschool Policy Brief, 14*. New Brunswick, NJ: National Institute for Early Education Research, Rutgers University.

Wong, V. C., Cook, T. D., Barnett, W. S., & Jung, K. (2008). An effectiveness-based evaluation of five state prekindergarten programs. *Journal of Policy Analysis and Management, 27*(1), 122–154. doi: 10.1002/pam.20310.

Whitebook, M., Gomby, D., Bellm, D., Sakai, L., & Kipnis, F. (2009). *Preparing teachers of young children: The current state of knowledge, and a blueprint for the future: Part I. Teacher preparation and professional development in grades K-12 and in early care and education: Differences and similarities, and implications for research*. Berkeley, CA: Center for the Study of Child Care Employment, Institute for Research on Labor and Employment, University of California at Berkeley.

29

Assessing Children's Learning in Early Childhood Education Settings

Dominic F. Gullo
Drexel University

Understanding the role that assessment plays in early childhood education is a complex process. In the field of early childhood there are diverse contexts in which children learn and develop as well as a multiplicity of reasons for assessing them. The early childhood education focus of this chapter will be on prekindergarten through third grade, as issues related to assessment during infancy and the toddler years bring with them special considerations that are beyond the scope of this chapter.

The significance and importance of assessment in early childhood education has never been as integral to the accountability of the field as it is today. With the passing of P.L. 107–110 (No Child Left Behind Act, 2001), assessment of children's learning is in the forefront of the minds of school administrators, teachers, caregivers, policy makers, and parents. According to the U.S. Department of Education (2002), the passing of the No Child Left Behind Act, would result in "the creation of assessments in each state that measure what children know and learn in reading and math.... Student progress and achievement will be measured according to tests that will be given to every child, every year."

According to the National Association for the Education of Young Children (NAEYC, 2003), ongoing assessment of children's learning in early childhood education should occur primarily to determine children's curricular needs. The early childhood curriculum should be modified to match the strengths and needs of each child based on the information gleaned from the assessment data. In a report, the Committee on Developmental Outcomes and Assessments for Young Children (Snow & Van Hemel, 2008), stated: "Well-planned and effective assessment can inform teaching and program improvement, and contribute to better outcomes for children" (p. 12). The Committee goes on to suggest that current practices in assessing young children do not generally reflect all that we know about how to do early childhood assessments well. Assessments can only be effective if they are designed well, are effectively

implemented, are systematic, and are used appropriately. The National Early Childhood Assessment Resource Group identified four appropriate uses of assessment, which include: supporting children's learning and development; identifying children who are in need of health or social services; examining trends and evaluating programs; and for monitoring student, teacher, and school accountability (Shepard, Kagan, Lynn, & Wurtz, 1998).

In this chapter, the assessment of individual children will be the primary emphasis as other chapters in this volume will discuss program evaluation and accountability. Four areas related to early childhood assessment will be examined. First, the research addressing general assessment issues in early childhood education will be discussed, including criticisms related to the use of norm-referenced assessment. In the second section, the focus will be on authentic assessment as a means to respond to the criticisms previously mentioned. In the third and fourth sections of this chapter, assessment concerns related to special populations of children will be examined. Specifically, the focus will be on the examination of the research and issues related to young children who are culturally and linguistically different as well as on children who have been identified as having special educational needs.

General Assessment Issues in Early Childhood Education

When one thinks of assessment, one often thinks of the paper and pencil tests that were pervasive in one's own schooling. While this type of assessment practice may provide valid information about older children's learning, these methods are often problematic when assessing younger children's current academic performance status or progress (Gullo, 2005, 2006b; Snow & Van Hemel, 2008; Wortham; 2008). According to Gullo, the problem stems from the mismatch between the young child's developmental capabilities and the performance expected on various paper and pencil assessment formats, as well as the mismatch between the content and strategies assessed and the content and strategies emphasized in the early childhood curriculum.

Snow and Hemel (2008) suggest that early childhood assessment should be "purposeful." As such, early education professionals should determine why assessments are done, what is the specific purpose of doing the assessment, and is the assessment being used optimal for meeting that purpose? To engage in early childhood assessment practices that are not "purposeful" runs the risk of providing information that is not useful, and may even be harmful to the child being assessed, resulting from inappropriate educational decision making.

In its policy statement, the National Association for Education of Young Children (NAEYC) states that early childhood assessment practices should reflect and take into account children's level of developmental capabilities and performance (2003). Early childhood professionals agree that the developmental characteristics of young children may affect assessment outcomes, as their behavioral capabilities often don't match what is required of them by the assessment procedures (Gullo, 2005, 2006b; Kallemeyn & DeStefano, 2009, 2010a, 2010b; Meisels, 1987, 2006; NAEYC, 2003, 2004). These include developmental limitations in areas such as language, cognitive, and physical responses (Espinosa, 2005; Gullo, 2005; Lin, 2010; NAEYC, 2005; Wortham; 2008), motivational differences (Gullo, 2005), children's perceptions of their performance (Flavell & Hartman, 2004), and their ability to generalize knowledge from one context to another (Gullo, 2005; Meisels, 1993).

With regard to the curriculum, the process of assessment should be consistent with the manner in which the curriculum is viewed by the early childhood education profession (Meisels, 1992; National Commission on Testing and Public Policy, 1990; Snow & Hemel, 2008). Two implications are advised related to the relationship between curriculum and assessment. First, children should be assessed within the context of the classroom as they are engaged in meaningful curriculum activities. Second, the primary purpose of assessment is to inform practice (Downer, Booren, Lima, Luckner, & Pianta, 2010; Hallam, Grisham-Brown, Gao, & Brookshire, 2007; Roach, McGrath, Wixson, & Talapatra, 2010; Thurman & McGrath, 2008). Assessment findings should suggest to teachers how the curriculum is working for individual children (Buldu, 2010; Gullo, 2006b; Hallam et al., 2007).

Given the relationship between the child's development and assessment and between curriculum practice and assessment, conventional paper and pencil or norm-referenced assessment procedures are contraindicated as the singular means of assessing children within the early childhood age span. The results of these types of assessments often do not yield the kinds of information that will inform practice and are oftentimes unreliable due to the developmental capabilities of the child during the early years. Therefore, the results from these assessments should be used in conjunc-

tion with performance-based assessments conducted within the learning environment. As long as one is aware of the limitations of norm-referenced assessment, their results can be used in proper perspective. Some of the limitations of norm-referenced assessments are discussed below.

Standardized Test Administration

As has been discussed previously, children in the early childhood classroom represent vast differences in developmental levels, approaches to learning, and individual needs. Due to the design nature of norm-referenced assessments, one must strictly adhere to the instructions for test administration. The same procedures are utilized for all children and there is little room for modification of those procedures to meet the needs or learning styles of individual or specific groups of children (Gullo, 2005; Mindes, 2003; Thurman & McGrath, 2008; Wortham, 2008). This has direct implications for assessing children with special needs (Macy & Bagnato, 2010; Pierce, Summer, & O'deKirk, 2009), and for children who are cultural or linguistic minorities or come from homes of economic poverty (Espinosa, 2005). Espinosa and Lopez (2007) warn that many assessments used with the latter groups of children are merely direct interpretations of English language assessments and as such do not take into account the linguistic or cultural relevance of the assessment. Further discussion of these issues will be addressed later.

Prior Learning Experiences Are Not Reflected

Norm-referenced assessments do not reflect how test performance is affected by prior experiences. In addition, they do not take into account how children actually learn the material that is being assessed (Buldu, 2010; Meisels, 2006; Meyers, Pfeffer, & Erlbaum, 1985; NAEYC, 2003). Many norm-referenced assessments do not match the goals and objectives of the curriculum that is being taught in the classroom. In these instances, curriculum goals and objectives are inadequately represented in test items.

Bias

One should be cognizant of the composition of the sample on which the norm-referenced assessment was standardized. "Children's backgrounds have a profound influence on their knowledge, vocabulary, and skills" (McAfee & Leong, 2002, p. 19): Often assessments are biased against children of different cultural or linguistic backgrounds (Espinosa, 2005; Gullo, 2005; McLean, 1998, 2000; Meisels, 2006; Mindes, 2003; Neisworth & Bagnato, 1996), as well as biased against children with developmental delays or special needs (Cohen & Spenciner, 2003). One of the greatest challenges that early childhood educators face today is the ability to identify appropriate assessment instruments and procedures that are bias free. Valencia and Suzuki (2001) argue for a judicious use of a variety of assessments and strategies.

Influence on the Curriculum

Norm-referenced assessments do not reflect curriculum sensitivity (Gullo, 2005; Mindes, 2003; Thurman, 2008; Wortham, 2008). Many published norm-referenced assessments do not take into account contemporary approaches to curriculum and instruction in early childhood education. They are often based on skill development approaches alone and reflect a theoretical perspective that is more behavioral than one that reflects multiple theoretical approaches. They assess specific skills or knowledge learned rather than assessing the process of learning. This oftentimes leads to teachers teaching to the test, thus the norm-referenced assessment has the effect of narrowing the curriculum. This is of particular concern given the passing of No Child Left Behind (U.S. Department of Education, 2002). Additionally, norm-referenced assessments may not reflect the characteristics of individual children such as motivation, level of cognitive or language development, or educational settings (Gullo, 2006b; Meisels, 2006).

In light of the criticisms of norm-referenced assessments, what is suggested are alternative means of assessing children's learning within the context of the early childhood curriculum as a complement to mandated norm-referenced test that may be used. Together, these two forms of assessment can provide information that reflects both product (what was learned) and process (children's learning strategies).

In the following section, the research related to authentic assessment will be discussed. Authentic assessment will be defined along with the evidence for its efficacy as being a valid measure of student performance. In addition, the research related to various types of authentic assessment is discussed.

Authentic Assessment

According to the North Central Regional Educational Laboratory (NCREL; 2003), alternative assessment is defined as "any form of assessment that requires students to produce a response rather than select from a list of possible responses … [alternative assessment] measures more complex learning goals that … [support] the instruction needed to help students achieve these goals" (2003). "Both researchers and practitioners are challenging the use of traditional norm-referenced assessment measures and recognize informal, authentic assessment procedures to be practical and useful in assessing literacy skill development and instructional needs in students of all ages, abilities, and cultures" (Spinelli, 2008, p. 1).

When considering alternative forms of assessment, there are a number of principles that should be kept in mind when making assessment decisions. First, alternative assessment practices should be developmentally appropriate and capitalize on the actual work taking place in the classroom. Assessing children within a meaningful context is important for both curriculum considerations (Copple & Bredekamp, 2009; Gullo, 1992, 2006b; Thurman & McGrath, 2008) as well as in considering appropriate alternative assessment practices and strategies (Freeman & Brown, 2008; Gullo, 2005; Hills, 1993; Wortham, 2008). In addition, alternative assessment practices should reflect and take into account the cultural and linguistic backgrounds of children Since most assessment as well as curriculum practices tend to reflect the social, cultural, and economic interests of political bureaucracies (O'Malley, 2009), it is imperative the cultural traditions of children be present in engaging in assessment practices that are embedded within the teaching-learning process.

Second, alternative assessment practices should enhance both the teacher's and the child's involvement in the process of assessment (Brown, 2008; Gullo, 2005; Seitz & Bartholomew, 2008). Both teachers and children should be actively involved in the assessment process. This will inform both the teacher and the learner in ways that should ultimately enhance both instruction and learning. According to Cohen and Spenciner (1994), the role of the teacher changes when alternative assessment procedures are used. The teacher has a direct influence on the assessment process, and assessment and curriculum are linked. When there is a close relationship between curriculum content, instructional strategies, and assessment, the goals for instruction, views of teaching, and theories of how children learn and develop are articulated and aligned (Herman, Aschbacher, & Winters (1992).

Third, alternative assessment practices should be informative to others, such as parents and school administrators, as well as teachers (Allen, 2007; Seitz & Bartholomew, 2008). The information obtained from alternative assessment practices should provide a clear and concrete basis for presenting information about the child's progress (Gullo, 2005).

Fourth, alternative assessment practices should provide a close match between the assessment and curriculum goals. When schools make decisions about assessment with little regard as to how the assessment fits curriculum goals and objectives, they run the risk of collecting information about the child that will have little relevance to curriculum planning and modification (Bergan & Field, 1993; Gullo, 2005; Thurman & McGrath, 2008). A greater risk ensues when curriculum decisions are made based on assessment information that has little relevance to curriculum content or instructional strategies (Meisels, 1989, 2006; Meisels & Atkins-Burnett, 2004).

Mindes (2003) suggests that there are reasons why professionals in early childhood education should consider alternative assessment strategies in lieu of, or in addition to, using only norm-referenced measures. Often, there is little overlap between what is measured in norm-referenced assessments and what actually goes on in the classroom with children. The purpose of these assessments is to contrast the relative performance of one child to other children of similar age or grade characteristics. Norm-referenced assessments do not assess the manner in which a child changes over time, developmentally or academically. In other words, it is difficult to compare the child to him- or herself during the course of the year, using norm-referenced assessments as they do not measure the process of learning. The results of norm-referenced assessments are not very useful in helping early childhood teachers individualize instruction. This is important in that developmental levels vary widely among children in early childhood classrooms. In addition, because children with special needs are often mainstreamed into the regular classroom, the need for individualization is paramount (Macy & Bagnato, 2010)

Three approaches to alternative assessment will be described and discussed below. In addition, research examining the efficacy of each of these approaches will be presented. The three approaches that will be discussed include: curriculum-based assessment; play-based assessment; and dynamic assessment. These alternative assessment approaches share some common traits, but at the same time, are unique in their specific approach to assessing children in the context of the classroom. In addition, while there may be similarities in the ways in which teachers use the data collected from these approaches, there are also some distinct differences. It should be noted that these approaches to alternative assessment represent categories into which various assessment strategies and specific assessments fall.

There are other forms of alternative assessment approaches used in early childhood education classrooms, such as task analysis and responsive assessment. However, those that are the focus of this chapter are those that are most widely used in typical early childhood classroom settings and have theoretical cores that are consistent with early childhood practice.

Curriculum Based Assessment

Curriculum-based assessment describes a wide-ranging approach for alternative assessment that directly links the assessment process to the curriculum content and instructional strategies used within the early childhood classroom (Cohen & Spenciner, 1994). According to Bergen (1997), assessing a child within the learning context is extremely useful and informative. Thurman and McGrath (2008) refer to this as "ecological validity." Ecological validity is critical in assessing young children, according to Thurman and McGrath in that it argues for using environmentally based assessment as well as having an understanding of the individual child's ecology. Specifically, assessing a child within the learning context makes it possible to assess the child and context variables that may affect the learning capacity and the demonstration of learning for that child (Bergen & Mosley-Howard, 1994; Macy & Bagnato, 2010; Thurman & McGrath, 2008). This proves useful for cur-

riculum planning and modification. With young children, it may be observed that learning within a specific context may be different from day to day, and all of these factors must be taken into account when assessing the child's learning.

One specific application, albeit a comprehensive application of curriculum-based assessment, is the Work Sampling System (Meisels, Jablon, Dichtelmiller, Dorfman, & Mardsen, 2001). This system is a standards-based approach and can be modified to meet all state and local needs, including requirements for children with special educational needs. The Work Sampling System is comprised of three distinct components: developmental checklists, developmental portfolios, and a summary report. According to Wortham (2001), the Work Sampling System is based on a philosophy that the assessment of children's learning within the context of the curriculum is fitting, in that this approach:

- Documents the child's daily activity
- Reflects an individualized approach to assessment
- Integrates assessment with curriculum and instruction
- Assesses many elements of learning
- Allows teachers to learn how children reconstruct knowledge through interacting with materials and peers. (p. 252)

Research has demonstrated that the use of curriculum-based assessment is effective in a number of ways in early childhood classrooms. One of the primary findings is that curriculum-based assessment, when applied appropriately, leads to educators being able to amend and align their instruction to meet the individual needs of students in their classrooms (Deno, Fuchs, Marston, & Shin, 2001; Meisels, Bickel, Nicholson, Xue, & Atkins-Burnett, 2001; Phillips, Fuchs, & Fuchs, 1994; VanDerHeyden, Witt, Naquin, & Noell, 2001). The result of this is that curriculum-based assessment improves teaching practice.

Play Based Assessment

It is often said that play is at the heart of the early childhood curriculum, especially for children at the younger age-ranges. Play, for young children, is voluntary and intrinsically motivating. When teachers systematically observe children at play, they can gain valuable insights into developmental and academic competencies.

According to Mindes (2003), it is the teacher as assessor role that makes this approach to assessment work. As the assessor, the early childhood educator makes numerous decisions during the assessment process. One of the easiest ways for early childhood educators to begin assessing children utilizing a play-based approach is to make a list of the critical skills and applications of knowledge and use this list by matching it to the curriculum goals and objectives (Van Hoorn, Nourot, Scales, & Alward, 1999).

Assessing children's knowledge and skills using play-based assessment procedures is not an entirely new phenomenon. Teachers have long been observing children during play and making decisions about the child based on those observations. Much of the development and research on play-based assessment, however, has been done on young children with special needs. One specific approach to play-based assessment is "Transdisciplinary Play-Based Assessment" (Linder, 2008). In this approach teams are created in order to develop an accurate and dynamic picture of the child. Using play as a medium, children's performance is assessed through observation in the areas of cognitive, social, emotional, speech and language, and communication skills. Teams are often comprised of teachers, specialists, as well as parents.

Regarding the research on the usefulness of play-based assessment, Bricker, Pretti-Frontczak, and McComas (1998), suggest making a chart with specific behavioral categories to use with young children who have special needs. They also suggest that this approach be integrated into the planned curriculum activities which are designed to meet the individual goals for the child. The information from this particular type of approach can then be used for further intervention, curriculum modification, and individualized planning.

Calhoon (1997) studied young children with language delays in order to determine the effectiveness of a play-based assessment approach in analyzing children's language capabilities. The author concluded that a play-based assessment approach provided a much broader picture of children's linguistic capabilities as compared to other assessment approaches. In addition, it was found that the play-based approach also yielded more helpful information than other more traditional approaches in planning curricular modifications and interventions. In a similar study, Farmer-Dougan and Kaszuba (1999) compared a play-based assessment model to standardized assessment of cognition and social skills in preschool children. The authors found that the findings gleaned from the play-based assessment accurately reflected the children's level of cognitive and social functioning.

It has also been shown that the play context may affect the assessment outcome. Malone (1994) conducted a study with preschool children having cognitive delays. The children in the study were observed at home during independent play and at school during group free play. It was found that the children's assessed developmental age was more predictive of the behaviors during the independent play episodes at home than in the group free play episodes at school. The author suggests that these findings highlight the need to consider that the variations in behavior may be associated with the specific play context.

Finally, Myers (1996) conducted a study to ascertain the relative efficacy of play-based assessment as compared to other forms of assessment. In this study, preschool children who were referred for special education were randomly assigned to either a multidisciplinary, standardized assessment or a play-based assessment group. The results of the study found that play-based assessments took less time to complete and had a high congruence with other forms of developmental ratings. In addition, the play-based assessment group also resulted in more favorable parent and staff perceptions and provided more useful reports.

Dynamic Assessment

Dynamic assessment is a form of alternative assessment that can be combined with other forms of assessments. In this type of assessment, the learner is directly engaged in the learning process by using mediated learning experiences, which are the foci of dynamic assessment (Cohen & Spenciner, 1994).

This approach utilizes a test-intervene-retest design. A mediated learning experience can be described as an interaction that takes place between the assessor and the child. The assessor mediates the environment to the child through appropriate framing, selecting, focusing, and feeding back to the child the experiences that the child is having. The purpose in doing this is to produce in the child appropriate learning systems and routines. Actual curriculum activities comprise the assessment tasks that are presented to the child. Thus, the approach combines both assessment and teaching. Dynamic assessment is a procedure that was designed by Reuven Feuerstein (1979, 1980), and based upon the theoretical work of Vygotsky (1978, 1986).

According to Mindes (2003), the dynamic assessment approach is particularly useful for early childhood teachers who are interested in linking classroom instruction to specific learner outcomes. Mindes states that "the approach links test results to task analysis to teaching to individualization of instruction. It is an opportunity for making the learning process apparent to those children who may need special assistance in linking thinking to academic requirements…" (p. 159).

A number of studies have been conducted examining the efficacy of dynamic assessment as compared to other forms of assessment or the ways in which it added to the information yielded from different assessment systems. In one study Jacobs (2001) found that by incorporating dynamic assessment components to a computerized preschool language-screening test, the computerized assessment was enhanced and continued investigation of its validity was possible.

In another study (Bolig & Day, 1993), it was found that dynamic assessment could be used to respond to the criticism of traditional intelligence tests. The researchers found that dynamic assessment could be used to identify children's learning ability, to determine how or what to teach to children, to assess giftedness in culturally diverse children and children who come from homes of economic poverty. In addition, they found that through the use of dynamic assessment, individual differences could be controlled and different domains of giftedness could be identified and explored.

In one study, examining the effects of dynamic assessment on content specific material, Jitendra and Kameenui (1993) found that children at different levels of mathematical performance could be identified. In their study of third graders, they found that dynamic assessment indicated important and significant differences between novices and experts in their ability to use specific mathematical strategies for solving problems.

In another study, Spector (1992) found that dynamic assessment was able to measure phonemic awareness to predict progress in beginning reading. This study, conducted with kindergarteners, supported the utility of the developed measures and was able to demonstrate the applicability of the principles of dynamic assessment to the measurement in kindergarten-aged children.

There have also been studies utilizing dynamic assessment procedures that were conducted with young children with special needs and those whose native language was not English. Findings from these studies have implications for both teachers and children. Lin (2010) found that among kindergarten children who were learning English as a second language, dynamic assessment provided a context within the assessment process from which program decisions could be made. Lin found that because of the nature of dynamic assessment procedures, which included interpersonal interaction, information could be gleaned about children that could otherwise not be determined from more traditional assessments.

In another study, Petersen (2010) used dynamic assessment to estimate reading difficulties among Hispanic children. He used it as a predictive measure, assessing children in kindergarten and then again in first grade in the areas of English and Spanish phonemic awareness, decoding strategies, and fluency. He found that static measures of reading proficiency did not account for the unique variance in children's reading behaviors other than for letter identification. He concluded that dynamic assessment procedures were more sensitive to the process features of reading performance than were static measures. Hasson and Botting (2010) found similar results in a study with language impaired children. They felt that dynamic assessment was sensitive to the differentiated amounts of change in children's language following mediated language training.

A Word About Portfolios

Portfolios are not, in and of themselves, a form of alternative assessment, but they play an important role in assessing young children's learning. Venn (2000) defines a portfolio as "a systematic collection of student work and related material that depicts a student's activities, accomplishments, and achievements in one or more school subjects. The collection should include evidence of student reflection and self-evaluation, guidelines for selecting the portfolio contents, and criteria for judging the quality of the work (p. 530).

According to Sewell, Marczak, and Horn (2003), the use of portfolios is widely utilized in early childhood educational settings as a means for examining and measuring children's progress. This is accomplished by documenting the learning process as it occurs naturally within the classroom context. The use of portfolios as a method to organize various forms of assessment and document children's learning is based on the principle that children should demonstrate what they know and what they do (Cole, Ryan, & Kick, 1995). Demonstrating what they know and what they can do can be contrasted with *telling* what they know, the latter being more typical in formal forms of assessments such as teacher-made tests or standardized tests.

Sewell et al. (2003) cite instances in which portfolio use was most useful and instances in which this approach may not be particularly useful. The extent to which portfolios are useful for documenting student performance and making educational decisions based on this documentation will depend on how one plans to use the information as well as the characteristics of the programs that the children attend.

Research has shown that using portfolios is effective and useful in a number of ways. Benson and Smith (1998), in an in-depth qualitative study found that first grade teachers who utilized a portfolio approach to document student performance realized a number of benefits. The study demonstrated that teachers:

- Found portfolios were beneficial as a means of communicating more effectively with children's families about the kinds of progress their child was making in the class. This finding was also demonstrated in a study with kindergarten teachers (Diffily & Fleege, 1994) who found portfolios helpful in reporting children's progress to parents.
- Viewed portfolios as an effective tool to motivate, encourage, and instruct children in their classrooms in the skills of self-assessment; and
- Saw portfolios as a mechanism to monitor and improve on their own instructional skills and curriculum modification.

In another study with teachers of exceptional learners, Shaklee and Viechnicki (1995) found that using portfolios was an effective model for assessing children as exceptional learners, as well as assessing their ability to use, generate, and pursue knowledge. They also noted that the use of portfolios was efficacious in terms of credibility, transferability, dependability, and confirmability.

A stated goal of alternative assessment procedures as discussed and described in this chapter is to be sensitive to individual differences in children. A parallel to this is that any alternative assessment approach used should also be sensitive to the unique characteristics of the curriculum that is being implemented in the classroom. There should be a link among the curriculum content, teaching strategies, and assessment procedures. As described, one of the advantages of using an alternative assessment approach is that it doesn't disrupt the process of curriculum implementation, and in fact reflects the goals of the curriculum. The many developmental and learning activity areas in the early childhood classroom afford teachers countless opportunities to engage in the assessment of children within contexts that are meaningful and diverse.

While much of the research on alternative forms of assessment and the use of portfolios found that teachers viewed the information gathered as useful and informative, there are also cautions to consider. In most situations, alternative forms of assessment should not be considered as a substitute for formal standardized assessment, but rather as another piece to the puzzle, a part of the picture representing the whole child. The information gathered during alternative assessment procedures is only as good as the quality of the contexts in which children are assessed, or the quality of the artifacts collected. Alternative assessments are time consuming and challenging to evaluate. Many times the content of the information collected will vary widely among students. Much of the research on alternative forms of assessments consists of documentations of success within individual settings. More research needs to be conducted in which different forms of assessment are compared in order to determine comparability and their ability to provide useful information for making educational decisions.

Assessing Special Populations of Children

The children who are now in early childhood programs differ in some respects from those who were in these classrooms 20 years ago. The number of children who come from culturally or linguistically different backgrounds has increased dramatically (Espinosa & Lopez, 2007). The National Center for Education Statistics (2002) reports that Whites (non-Hispanic) comprise 63.5% of public school enrollment, with Blacks (non-Hispanic) accounting for 17%, Hispanics for 14.4%, Asian/Pacific Islanders for 3.9%, and American Indian/Alaskan Natives for 1.2%. Hernandez (2004) projects that between 2020 and 2030, more than half of all children in the United States will be from minority groups. This increase in the numbers of children who are culturally or linguistically diverse brings with it assessment challenges. At the forefront of these assessment challenges is identifying children who are in need of special education services. For example, according to Espinosa (2005), there is an underlying dilemma for educators who must distinguish the difference between a language disorder and a language difference. The number of children who come from culturally or linguistically different backgrounds who are referred for special education services are higher than what would be expected for the general population, particularly in the area of speech and language (Espinosa & Lopez, 2007).

In general, the number of young children who have been identified as having special educational needs and who are included in regular classrooms has also increased.

This is primarily due to the changes in laws and changes in our ability to identify children who have special needs at earlier ages. The increase in these numbers also brings with it challenges for early childhood teachers and other professionals. At the vanguard of these challenges is the use of assessment to inform curriculum and teaching. In the next section, we will examine special issues related to assessment with culturally or linguistically different children and children with special educational needs.

Assessing Children with Culturally and Linguistically Different Backgrounds

"Children's backgrounds have a profound influence on their knowledge, vocabulary, and skills" (McAfee & Leong, 2002, p. 19): While this quote certainly applies to all children, it is of special significance for children who come from culturally or linguistically different backgrounds. Assessment procedures for this population of children need to be different. Assessments that are not biased by the linguistic or cultural diversity of the child need to be used in order to obtain valid and reliable results. Careful selection of assessment instruments and procedures is necessary (Espinosa, 2005; McLean, 1998, 2005).

When making decisions about assessing children with linguistically different backgrounds, Espinosa and Lopez (2007) indicate that it is important to distinguish between different types of assessments. Within the classroom, early childhood professionals use a variety of assessment strategies to assess young learners in order to guide and improve curriculum and instruction. These strategies often include nonstandardized authentic assessment strategies such as observation notes, work samples, check lists, and rating scales. Issues and concerns related to these types of assessment strategies have been discussed earlier and apply here as well.

A different type of assessment should be considered when the focus is on measuring academic performance or progress, school readiness, or different developmental domains, such as level of language proficiency or cognitive functioning (Espinosa & Lopez, 2007). When these are the foci, more formal or standardized assessments are used, such as norm-referenced or criterion-referenced assessments. Formal or standardized assessments have special issues and concerns when assessing children from culturally or linguistically different backgrounds. These issues and concerns will be the focus of this section.

One of the primary questions to ask is whether assessments have built-in safeguards to insure that the instruments or procedures are sensitive to cultural and linguistic diversity? Is it possible to distinguish the difference between the influence of cultural and linguistic diversity on the child's development and learning and the presence of a learning difficulty or developmental delay (Espinosa & Lopez, 2007; McLean, 2000)? The Division of Early Childhood of the Council for Exceptional Children recommends the following when assessing children who come from backgrounds that are culturally or linguistically diverse (reported in McLean, 2000):

- Prior to assessment, appropriate early childhood professionals should gather information in order to determine whether a child should be referred for special education screening or whether a child's development and behavior can be explained by language or cultural differences.
- Appropriate procedures should be followed to determine which language should be used in assessing the child. The assessor should also understand the impact of second language learning on the child's development and performance in early childhood school settings.
- Appropriate assessment strategies should be tailored to the individual child and family when culturally appropriate and nonbiased instruments cannot be identified. (pp. 2–3)

The Early Childhood Research Institute for Culturally and Linguistically Appropriate Services (CLAS) developed a set of guidelines for selecting assessments to be used with culturally and linguistically diverse backgrounds (McLean, 2000). Assessments that are most appropriate are those that address the elements of the CLAS guidelines.

1. **Scoring procedures.** When assessments have scoring or rating scales, it should be noted which types of cultural or linguistic groups of children were included in the development of these scales. In addition, it should be noted whether there are separate scoring or normative scales for specific linguistic or cultural groups. Appropriate assessments are those that were developed involving different linguistic and cultural groups and that have separate scoring scales.
2. **Incorporation of information from specific culture into the assessment procedures.** If an assessment indicates that it is appropriate for particular cultural or linguistic groups, it should be noted as to whether information about parenting practices and child development that is typical for the specific cultural group is taken into account in the design and implementation of the assessment. This should be clearly stated in the assessment manual for implementation and interpretation procedures.
3. **Modification of the assessment.** Suggestions for modifying the assessment for this population of children should be clearly stated in the examiner's manual. Children who come from culturally or linguistically different backgrounds do not necessarily behave or respond in the same manner to assessment questions. These differences in behaviors may result in erroneous results if modifications are not suggested.
4. **Interpretation of the findings.** Specific procedures for interpreting the findings of assessments for children who represent culturally or linguistically diverse back-

grounds should also be clearly stated in the examiner's manual. These procedures for interpretation should reflect the above stated guidelines.

As Espinosa asserts (2005), "Children's linguistic and cultural differences as well as differences in their learning needs and abilities must be considered throughout all phases of child assessments" (p. 849). This is true whether the assessments are authentic and conducted within the learning environment or are formal, more standardized types of assessments.

Assessing Children with Special Needs

As stated previously in this section, the numbers of children in early childhood classrooms and settings who are identified as having special education needs is increasing. This is primarily due to changes in federal legislation. These increases have played an important role in changing the landscape of assessment practices in early childhood education. While many of the assessment principles previously discussed also apply to children with special needs, there are some differences resulting from mandated guidelines for the identification and planning for children identified as having special educational needs, particularly when using formal norm-referenced or criterion-referenced assessments.

In identifying children who are in need of special education services, the assessment practices used should be valid for all young children as well as appropriate for supporting instruction and learning (Kagan, Scott-Little, & Clifford, 2003). Assessment practices should also serve to plan programs for children who have been identified as having special education needs and to monitor the intervention process (Neisworth & Bagnato, 2005). It should be recognized that as with all children, each child identified as having special needs along with his or her family is unique (Division of Early Childhood, 2007). Therefore, the process of implementing assessment systems should be family centered and team-based as well as individualized and developmentally appropriate.

Critical Attributes of High-Quality Assessments

In its position statement on *Promoting Positive Outcomes for Children with Disabilities* (2007), the Division for Early Childhood of the Council for Exceptional Children describes three critical attributes to consider when choosing assessments to be used with young children identified as having special needs. Information from these assessments should be used to guide the decision-making process of families and professional team members.

First, *assessment measures have utility and are used for specific purposes* p. 12). These include screening, diagnosis, program eligibility, instructional planning, placement, monitoring progress, and program evaluation (Wolery, Strain, & Bailey, 1992). It should be recognized that one assessment tool cannot achieve all of these assessment purposes. Therefore a multimodal assessment approach should be used in which different types of assessments are used to respond to different assessment purposes (McCormick & Nellis, 2004; Roid & Sampers, 2004). To achieve this, information from authentic assessments should be considered in combination with information from formal standardized assessments to make programming decisions.

Second, *assessment tools are authentic* (p. 14). A multimodal approach to assessment relies heavily on authentic assessments that document children's performance within functional academic and family contexts (Losardo & Notari-Syverson, 2001; Neisworth & Bagnato, 2004). The advantages and concerns related to using authentic assessments has been discussed elsewhere in this chapter. Using authentic assessment in conjunction with more formal assessment measures has been found to authenticate the strengths and needs of young children with disabilities in inclusive settings (Cook, 2004). Cook found that using an authentic assessment approach in conjunction with a criterion-referenced assessment for accountability, but administered within a classroom context, supported early childhood professionals in meeting national standards. This ecological approach to assessing young special needs children recognizes the importance of understanding that the various contexts in which children live and learn are interwoven and affect behavior and academic performance.

Third, *assessment tools have good psychometric qualities* (p. 15). The importance of an assessment tool having good psychometric qualities is of general concern within the field of early childhood education and has additional significance when assessing young children who have been identified as having special needs. Scores obtained from many early childhood measures tend to be unstable (Bailey, 2004) due to the fact that children at this age grow and develop at rapid and unpredictable rates. This is of special concern for young special needs children in that although they also experience growth and developmental spurts, these spurts tend to be more unpredictable and therefore create more instability in measurement scores. Many early childhood assessment measures also lack predictive validity. That is, test results are often not related to future academic performance or later development. When choosing assessment measures, early childhood professionals should look for instruments with evidence of good predictive validity. According to the DEC (2007), when assessing young children identified as having special needs, the assessment team must "select tools that best reveal the child's skills and abilities while minimizing the impact of disability on the results" (p. 15).

Assessment Concerns

The assessment process is helpful in identifying young children who have special needs as well as for their educational planning. There are, however, concerns related to

this process (Division for Early Childhood of the Council for Exceptional Children , 2002, 2007; NAEYC, 2003). Specifically, three concerns have been expressed:

1. There exists the potential that labeling children too early as having special needs will be detrimental for those children and their ability to reach their potential.
2. There is a lack of adequate assessments for young children that are both valid and reliable measures of their learning potential and developmental status.
3. There is the belief that some of the categories used to describe a young child's disability, which are also used to describe the special needs of older children, may not be appropriate where young children are concerned. Consequently, states are permitted to use the term *developmental delay* when referring children between the ages of 3 and 9, so that these children can receive special education services without being labeled.

Early childhood professionals need to be particularly aware of the issues surrounding assessment and the identification of children with special needs. They are often the first individuals who see these children in settings that may indicate that these children are in need of special services.

Conclusions

What should be evident from the information, ideas, and research presented in this chapter is that assessment in early childhood education should ideally flow out of, if not become integrated within, curriculum and instructional practices. Assessment should serve the teacher's needs as well as the learner's by being sensitive to the individual manner in which children learn and develop and the manner in which each child negotiates the challenges of curriculum requirements. In addition, assessment should be sensitive to the cultural and linguistic diversity of the children in early childhood programs today. Assessment should also be the driving force for modification of the curriculum in order to meet children's individual needs.

A stated goal of assessment as described in this chapter is to be sensitive to individual differences in children. A parallel to this is that assessment should be thought of as a system, and as such, should also be sensitive to the unique characteristics of the curriculum that is being implemented in the classroom. There should be a link between the curriculum content, teaching strategies, and assessment procedures. One of the advantages in using an assessment system approach is that it shouldn't disrupt the process of curriculum implementation, and, in fact, reflects the goals of the curriculum. The many developmental and learning activity areas in the early childhood classroom afford teachers countless opportunities to engage in the assessment of children within contexts that are meaningful and diverse.

At the beginning of this chapter it was stated that, "understanding the role that assessment plays in early childhood education is a complex process." Early childhood professionals need to increase their understanding of the nature and use of the various forms of assessment and how these different assessment forms can impact the teaching-learning process.

School and teacher education reform efforts should concentrate on assuring that various forms of assessment are used to insure that students' developmental and learning needs are being met. Expanded research and efforts need to be focused on enhancing the quality of assessment instruments and practices aimed at improving instruction, positively influencing children's developmental and academic performance, informing teacher accountability, and program quality. School districts should provide opportunities for in-service teachers to continually improve their assessment skills through professional development. Teacher education programs should increase the opportunities that preservice teachers have for learning about various forms of assessment and how to use assessment information to improve learning opportunities for children. Specific and more specialized coursework is called for, in conjunction with opportunities to use the knowledge and skills acquired in these courses through clinical and field experiences in early childhood settings.

Through all of these efforts, the use of assessments in early childhood will continue to improve. If early childhood assessments improve, children's learning will improve, teacher performance will improve, and early childhood services and programs will improve.

References

Allen, S. F. (2007). Assessing the development of young children in child care: A survey of formal assessment practice in one state. *Early Childhood Education Journal, 34*(6), 455–465.

Bailey, D. B. (2004). Tests and test development. In M. Mclean, M. Wolery, & D. B. Bailey (Eds.), *Assessing infants and preschoolers with special needs* (3rd ed., pp. 22–44). Upper Saddle River, NJ: Pearson.

Benson, T. R., & Smith, L. J. (1998). Portfolios in first grade: Four teachers learn to use alternative assessment. *Early Childhood Education, 25*(3), 173–180.

Bergan, J., & Field, J. K. (1993). Developmental assessment: New directions. *Young Children, 48*(5), 41–47.

Bergen, D. (Ed.). (1994). *Assessment methods for infants and toddlers: Transdisciplinary team approaches.* New York: Teachers College Press.

Bergen, D. (1997). Using observational techniques for evaluating young children's learning. In O. Saracho & B. Spodek (Eds.), *Issues in early childhood educational assessment and evaluation* (pp. 108–128). New York: Teachers College Press.

Bergen, D., & Mosley-Howard, S. (1994). Assessment methods for culturally diverse young children. In D. Bergen (Ed.), *Assessment methods for infants and toddlers: Transdisciplinary team approaches* (pp. 190–206). New York: Teachers College Press.

Bolig, E. E., & Day, J. D. (1993). Dynamic assessment and giftedness: The promise of assessing training responsiveness. *Roeper Review, 16*(2), 110–113.

Brown, W. (2008). Young children assess their learning: The power of the quick check strategy. *Young Children, 63*(6), 14–20.

Bricker, D., Pretti-Frontczak, K., & McComas, N. (1998). *An activity-based approach to early intervention.* Baltimore, MD: Brookes.

Buldu, M. (2010). Making learning visible in kindergarten classrooms: Pedagogical documentation as a formative assessment technique. *Teaching and Teacher Education, 26,* 1439–1449.

Calhoon, J. M. (1997). Comparison of assessment results between a formal standardized measure and a play-based format. *Infant-Toddler Intervention: The Transdisciplinary Journal, 7*(3), 201–204.

Cohen, L. G., & Spenciner, L. J. (1994). *Assessment of young children.* New York: Longman.

Cohen, L. G., & Spenciner, L. J. (2003). *Assessment of children and youth with special needs.* White Plains, NY: Longman.

Cole, D. J., Ryan, C. W., & Kick, F. (1995). *Portfolios across the curriculum and beyond.* Thousand Oaks, CA: Corwin Press.

Copple, C., & Bredekamp, S. (Eds.). (2009). *Developmentally appropriate practice in early childhood programs* (3rd ed.). Washington, DC: National Association for the Education of Young Children.

Decker, C. A., & Decker, J. R. (1990). *Planning and administering early childhood programs.* Columbus, OH: Merrill.

Deno, S. L., Fuchs, L. S., Marston, D., & Shin, J. (2001). Using curriculum-based measurement to establish growth standards for students with learning disabilities. *School Psychology Review, 30*(4), 507–524.

Diffily, D., & Fleege, P. O. (1994). The power of portfolios for communicating with families. *Dimensions of Early Childhood, 22*(2), 40–41.

Division for Early Childhood (DEC). (2002). *Developmental delay as an eligibility category* (DEC Position Paper). Missoula, MT: Council for Exceptional Children.

Division for Early Childhood (DEC). (2007). *Promoting positive outcomes for children with disabilities: Recommendations for curriculum, assessment, and program evaluation* (DEC Position Paper). Missoula, MT: Author.

Downer, J. T., Booren, L. M., Lima, O. K., Luckner, A. E., & Pianta, R. C. (2010). The individualized classroom assessment scoring system: Preliminary reliability and validity of a system for observing preschoolers' competence in classroom interactions. *Early Childhood Research Quarterly, 25*(1), 1–16.

Espinosa, L. M. (2005). Curriculum and assessment considerations for young children from culturally, linguistically, and economically diverse backgrounds. *Psychology in the Schools, 42*(8), 837–853.

Espinosa, L. M., & Lopez, M. L. (2007). *Assessment considerations for young English language learners across different levels of accountability.* (Position statement prepared for The National Early Childhood Accountability Task Force and First 5). Los Angeles, CA: Author.

Farmer-Dougan, V., & Kaszuba, T. (1999). Reliability and validity of play-based observations: Relationship between the PLAY Behaviour Observation System and the standardized measures of cognitive and social skills. *Educational Psychology: An International Journal of Experimental Educational Psychology, 19*(4), 429–440.

Feurestein, R. (1979). *Dynamic assessment of retarded performers.* Baltimore, MD: University Park Press.

Feurestein, R. (1980). *Instrumental enrichment.* Baltimore, MD: University Park Press.

Flavell, J., & Hartman, B. (2004). Research in review: What children know about mental experiences. *Young Children, 59*(4), 102–109.

Freeman, N., & Brown, M. (2008). An authentic approach to assessing pre-kindergarten programs: Redefining readiness. *Childhood Education, 84*(5), 267–274.

Galagan, J. E. (1985). Psychoeducational testing: Turn out the lights, the party's over. *Exceptional Children, 52*(3), 288–299.

Gullo, D. F. (1992). *Understanding appropriate teaching in early childhood education: Curriculum, implementation, evaluation.* Washington, DC: National Education Association.

Gullo, D. F. (2005). *Understanding assessment and evaluation in early childhood education* (2nd ed.). New York: Teachers College Press.

Gullo, D. F. (Ed.). (2006a). *K Today: Teaching and learning in the kindergarten year.* Washington, DC: NAEYC.

Gullo, D. F. (2006b): Assessment in kindergarten: Using assessment to inform decisions about promoting children's learning. In D. F. Gullo (Ed.), *K today: Teaching and learning in the kindergarten* year (pp. 138–147). Washington, DC: NAEYC.

Hallam, R., Grisham-Brown, J., Gao, X., & Brookshire, R. (2007, Fall). The effects of outcomes-driven authentic assessment on classroom quality. *Early Childhood Research and Practice, 9*(2). Retrieved from: http://ecrp.uiuc.edu/v9n2/hallam.html.

Hasson, N., & Botting, N. (2010). Dynamic assessment of children with language impairments: A pilot study. *Child Language Teaching and Therapy, 26*(3), 249–272.

Herman, J. L., Aschbacher, P. R., & Winters, L. (1992). *A practical guide to alternative assessment.* Alexandria, VA: Association for Supervision and Curriculum Development.

Hernandez, D. (2004, September). *Children in newcomer families.* Paper presented at the annual meeting of the Early Childhood Funders, San Francisco.

Hills, T.. (1993). Assessment in context: Teachers and children at work. *Young Children, 48* (5), 20–28.

Jacobs, E. L. (2001). The effects of dynamic assessment components to a computerized preschool language screening test. *Communication Disorders Quarterly, 22*(4), 217–226.

Jitendra, A. K., & Kameenui, E. J. (1993). An exploratory study of dynamic assessment involving two instructional strategies on experts' and novices' performance in solving part-whole mathematical word problems. *Diagnostique, 18*(4), 305–325

Kagan, S. L., Scott-Little, C., & Clifford, R. M. (2003). Assessing young children: What policy makers need to know and do. In C. Scott-Little, S. L. Kagan, & R. M. Clifford (Eds.), *Assessing the state of state assessments: Perspectives on assessing young children* (pp. 5–11). Greensboro, NC: SERVE.

Kallemeyn, L. M., & DeStefano, L. (2009). The (limited) use of local-level assessment system: A case study of the Head Start National Reporting System and ongoing child assessments in a local program. *Early Childhood Research Quarterly, 24*(2), 157–174.

Kallemeyn, L. M., & DeStefano, L. (2010a). Lessons learned about perceived purposes of the Head Start National Reporting System at the local program level. *NHSA Dialog: A Research-to-Practice Journal for the Early Intervention Field, 13*(1), 46–52.

Kallemeyn, L. M., & DeStefano, L. (2010b). Perceived purposes of the Head Start National Reporting System at the local program level: A case study. *NHSA Dialog: A Research-to-Practice Journal for the Early Intervention Field, 13*(1), 21–41.

Lin, Z. (2010). Interactive dynamic assessment with children learning EFL in kindergarten. *Early Childhood Education Journal, 37,* 279–287.

Linder, T. (2008). *Transdisciplinary play-based assessment* (2nd ed.). Baltimore, MD: Brookes.

Losardo, A., & Notari-Syverson, A. (2001). *Alternative approaches to assessing young children.* Baltimore, MD: Brookes.

Macy, M., & Bagnato, S. J. (2010). Keeping it "R-E-A-L" with authentic assessment. *NHSA Dialog: A Research-to-Practice Journal for the Early Intervention Field, 13*(1), 1–20.

Malone, D. M. (1994). Contextual variation of correspondences among measures of play and developmental level of preschool children. *Journal of Early Intervention, 18*(2), 199–215.

McAfee, O., & Leong, D. J. (2002). *Assessing and guiding young children's development and learning* (3rd ed.).Boston, MA: Allyn & Bacon.

McCormick, K., & Nellis, L. (2004). Assessing cognitive development. In M. McLean, M. Wollery, & D. B. Bailey (Eds.), *Assessing infants and preschoolers with special needs* (3rd Ed.), 256–300. Upper Saddle River, NJ: Pearson.

McLean, M. (1998). Assessing children for whom English is a second language. *Young Exceptional Children, 1*(3), 20–25.

McLean, M. (2000). *Conducting child assessments* (CLAS Technical report No. 2.). Champaign, IL: University of Illinois at Urbana-Champaign, Early Childhood Research Institute on Culturally and Linguistically Appropriate Services.

McLean, M. (2005). Conducting child assessments. In S. Fowler, R. Santos, & R. Corso (Eds.), *Appropriate screening, assessment, and family information gathering* (pp. 23–31). Longmont, CO: Sopris West.

Meisels, S. J. (1987). Uses and abuses of developmental screening and school readiness testing. *Young Children, 42*(4–6), 68–73.

Meisels, S. J. (1989). High stakes testing in kindergarten. *Educational Leadership, 46*(7), 16–22.

Meisels, S. J. (1992). *The work sampling system: An overview.* Ann Arbor: University of Michigan.

Meisels, S. J. (1993). Remaking classroom assessment with the work sampling system. *Young Children, 48*(5), 34–40.

Meisels, S. J. (2006). *Accountability in early childhood: No easy answers* (Occasional Paper). Chicago, IL: Erikson Institute.

Meisels, S. J., & Atkins-Burnett, S. (2004). The Head Start National Reporting System. *Young Children, 59*(1), 64–66.

Meisels, S. J., Bickel, D. D., Nicholson, J., Xue, Y., & Atkins-Burnett, S. (2001). Trusting teachers' judgments: A validity study of curriculum-embedded performance assessment in kindergarten–grade 3. *American Educational Research Journal, 38*(1), 73–95.

Meisels, S. J., Jablon, F. R., Dichtelmiller, M. L. Dorfman, A. B., & Marsden, D. B. (2001). *The work sampling system* (4th ed.). New York: Pearson Early Learning.

Meyers, J., Pfeffer, J., & Erlbaum, V. (1985). Process assessment: A model for broadening assessment. *Journal of Special Education, 18*(2), 1–84.

Mindes, G. (2003). *Assessing young children.* Upper Saddle River, NJ: Merrill Prentice Hall.

Myers, C.L. (1996). Play-based assessment in early childhood special education: An examination of social validity. *Topics in Early Childhood Special Education, 16*(1),102–126.

National Association for the Education of Young Children (NAEYC). (2003). *Early childhood curriculum, assessment, and program evaluation: Building an effective, accountable system in programs for children birth through age 8* (Position Statement). Washington, DC: Author.

National Association for the Education of Young Children (NAEYC). (2004). Early education experts highlight concerns about new nationwide test of four-year-olds in Head Start. Retrieved from http://www.naeyc.org/about/releases/20040226.asp.

National Association for the Education of Young Children (NAEYC). (2005). *Screening and assessment of young English-language learners* (Position Statement). Washington, DC: Author.

National Center for Educational Statistics. (2002). *Digest of educational statistics: 2001* (NCES 2002–031). Washington, DC: U.S. Department of Education, Office of Educational Research and Improvement.

National Commission on Testing and Public Policy. (1990). *From gatekeeper to gateway: Transforming testing in America.* Chestnut Hill, MA: Author.

Neisworth, J., & Bagnato, S. (1996). Assessment. In S. Odom & M. McLean (Eds.), *Early intervention/early childhood special education: Recommended practices.* Austin, TX: Pro-Ed.

Neisworth, J., & Bagnato, S. (2004). The mismeasure of young children. *Infants and Young Children, 17*(3), 198–212.

Neisworth, J., & Bagnato, S. (2005). DEC recommended practices: Assessment. In S. Sandall, M. L. Hemmeter, B. Smith, & M. McLean (Eds.), *DEC recommended practices: A comprehensive guide for practical application* (pp. 45–69). Missoula, MT: DEC.

North Central Regional Educational Laboratory. (2003). Student assessment. Retrieved from www.ncrel.org/sdrs/areas/issues/methods/assment/as7stud.htm.

O'Malley, M. P. (2009). Pedagogies of absence: Education beyond an ethos of standardization. *Childhood Education, 85*(4), 250–252.

Petersen, D. B. (2010). Using static and dynamic measures to estimate reading difficulty for Hispanic children. *All Graduate Theses and Dissertations, Paper 540.* http://digitalcommons.usu.edu/etd/540

Phillips, N. B., Fuchs, L. S., Fuchs, D. (1994). Effects of class wide curriculum-based measurement and peer tutoring: A collaborative researcher-practitioner interview study. *Journal of Learning Disabilities, 27*(7). 420–434.

Pierce, P. L., Summer, G., & O'deKirk, M. (2009). The bridge: An authentic literacy assessment strategy for individualizing and informing practice with young children with disabilities. *Young Exceptional Children, 12*(3), 2–14.

Roach, A. T., McGrath, D., Wixson, C., & Talapatra, D. (2010). Aligning an early childhood assessment to state kindergarten content standards: Application of a nationally recognized alignment framework. *Educational Measurement: Issues and Practices, 29*(1), 25–37.

Roid, G., & Sampers, J. (2004). *Merrill-Palmer-R: Scales of development manual*. Chicago, IL: Stoelting.

Saracho, O., & Spodek, B. (Eds.).(1997). *Issues in early childhood educational assessment and evaluation*. New York: Teachers College Press.

Seitz, H., & Bartholomew, C. (2008). Powerful portfolios for young children. *Early Childhood Education Journal, 36*(1), 63–68.

Sewell, M., Marczak, M., & Horn, M. (2003). The use of portfolio assessment in evaluation. Retrieved from http://ag.arizona.edu/fcr/fs/cyfar/Portfo~3htm.

Shaklee, B. D., Barbour, N. E., Ambrose, R., & Hansford, S. J. (1997). *Designing and using portfolios*. Boston, MA: Allyn & Bacon.

Shaklee, B. D., & Viechnicki, K. J. (1995). A qualitative approach to portfolios: The early assessment for exceptional children. *Journal for the Education of the Gifted, 18*(2), 156–170.

Shepard, L., Kagan, S. L., Lynn, S., & Wurtz, E. (1998). *Principles and recommendations for early childhood assessments*. Washington, DC: National Goals Panel.

Snow, C. E., & Van Hemel, S. B. (Eds.). (2008). *Early childhood assessment: Why, what and how*. Washington, DC: The National Academies Press.

Spector, J. E. (1992). Predicting progress in beginning reading: Dynamic assessment of phonemic awareness. *Journal of Educational Psychology, 84*(3), 553–563.

Spinelli, C. G. (2008). The benefits, uses, and practical application of informal assessment procedures. *Reading and Writing Quarterly, 24*(1), 1–6.

Thurman, S. K., & McGrath, M. C. (2008). Environmentally based assessment practices: Viable alternatives to standardized assessment for assessing emergent literacy skills in young children. *Reading and Writing Quarterly, 24*(1), 7–24.

U.S. Department of Education. (2002). Inside No Child Left Behind. Retrieved from www.ed.gov/offices/OESE/esea/factsheet.html.

Valencial, R. R., & Suzuki, L. A. (2001). *Intelligence testing and minority students: Foundations, performance factors, and assessment*. Thousand Oaks, CA: Sage.

VanDerHeyden, A. M., Witt, J. C., Naquin, G., & Noell, G. (2001). The reliability and validity of curriculum-based measurement readiness probes for kindergarten students. *School Psychology Review, 79*, 59–65.

Van Hoorn, J., Nourot, P., Scales, B., & Alward, K. (1999). *Play at the center of the curriculum*. Upper Saddle, NJ: Merrill Prentice Hall.

Venn, J. J. (2000). *Assessing students with special needs* (2nd ed.). Upper Saddle River, NJ: Merrill.

Vygotsky, L. (1978). *Mind and society: The development of higher psychological processes* (M. Cole, V. John-Steiner, S. Scribner, & E. Souberman, Eds.). Cambridge, MA: Harvard University Press.

Vygotsky, L. (1986). *Thought and language* (A. Kosulin, Trans.). Cambridge, MA: Harvard University Press.

Wolery, M., Strain, P., & Bailey, D. (1992). Reaching potentials of children with special needs. In S. Bredekamp & T. Rosegrant, (Eds.), *Reaching potentials: Appropriate curriculum and assessment for young children* (Vol. 1, 92–112). Washington, DC: NAEYC.

Wortham, S. C. (2001). *Tests and measurements in early childhood education*. Columbus, OH: Merrill.

Wortham, S. C. (2008). *Assessment in early childhood education* (5th ed.). Upper Saddle River, NJ: Pearson.

30

Evaluating the Quality of Early Childhood Education Programs

DALE C. FARRAN AND KERRY G. HOFER
Peabody Research Institute, Vanderbilt University

In 2008, 67% of the 4-year-old children in the United States were enrolled in some form of early childhood education center-based program (Planty et al., 2008), and the number continues to rise. Today's preschoolers will soon begin their formal schooling years. In another 15 years, most of those children will be entering the country's work force. The extension of public education into the prekindergarten years makes early childhood settings the first introduction for many children to the world of more formal learning and to doing so in a group setting. These early experiences are critical for establishing learning and dispositional patterns that may affect children's interactions with classrooms for years to come. Over the years, however, no clear or coherent focus has emerged for the purpose of early childhood education; that is, whether there should be different purposes in caring for or educating young children than there are for older children.

Historically, the purpose of caring for young children was to allow impoverished mothers to work: "Day care was founded, therefore, as a necessary social service to alleviate the child care problems of parents who had to work and to prevent young children from wandering the street" (Scarr & Weinberg, 1986, p. 1141). By the 1970s, it was no longer just immigrants, seamen, or other parents, both of whom were working and one of whom had a job distant from home, whose families needed care; mothers were entering the labor force to preserve their families' middle level incomes and consequently needed care for their children. Concurrently with this surge of mothers entering the labor force was a growing concern for the quality of the alternative care the children received. Scarr and Weinberg described this history in detail through the mid-1980s. They reported that in 1980 a group of professionals from different agencies and universities developed and proposed a national set of standards for child care that would cover educational aspects as well as the health and safety issues states were ordinarily concerned with. These standards were never adopted, and since then

there has not been a uniform, agreed upon set of standards for the care of children before formal schooling. While all states have regulations concerning health and safety, and these sometimes also include educational requirements for teachers and regulations about teacher to child ratios and group size, about half the states have developed their own more comprehensive quality standards. In July 2010, the National Association for the Education of Young Children (NAEYC) reported that 24 states had *statewide* quality rating and improvement systems (NAEYC, 2010).

Another role for programs for young children prior to formal school entry has been as compensatory education, beginning with Head Start in 1965 (Farran, 2007; Scarr & Weinberg, 1986) and continuing with the 1987 amendment to the Elementary and Secondary Education Act that allowed Title I funds to be used for whole school program improvement, ushering in the creation of Title I funded prekindergarten classes in many school districts (Ewing & Matthews, 2005). Neither Head Start nor Title I was intended to be full day care; the usual hours of care for each have been public school hours or less and do not cover the before- or after-school care needed by working families. Although some programs provide these services as an option, many do not. Recently, there has been an increase in the number of children served in states that either provide state funds for early intervention prekindergarten programs or that coordinate sources of funding for these programs at the state level. In 2009, 38 states funded preschools and enrolled over 1 million 4-year-olds (Barnett, Epstein, Friedman, Sansanelli, & Hustedt, 2009); this is not much more than the number of states that provided such funds in 1998 (Mitchell, Ripple, & Chanana, 1998), but those states with programs enrolled more children each year (until 2010). These state-funded programs are primarily intended as compensatory for children from poor families; 32 of the states have income requirements for enrollment.

Given the different missions of community child care

and compensatory preschools, it has been difficult to find a common quality measure that was suitable for both types of programs. The importance of aligning quality measures with the purposes a program is to achieve is explored in the next section.

Definitions of Quality by Programmatic Purpose

Caring Purpose

The purpose of community child care programs is to care for children whose parents work. The concerns related to this purpose revolve around ensuring safe and appropriate environments for children who are young and vulnerable and therefore dependent on adults to create their environments. Moreover, when other adults, outside of "kith and kin," are responsible for children, they may be unknown to the parents, at least initially. Thus, regulatory agencies become involved. Child care centers are supposed to be licensed to meet health and safety regulations and are inspected by those agencies.[1] In addition, increasingly since the mid- to late 1990s, child care programs across the country have been evaluated for their quality, using standardized rating forms administered in various ways, but most often during a visit from the day care division of state departments of human services. Scores presented as indications of the quality of a program are often made publicly available to parents in order to aid them in the selection of their child's preschool placement. Indiana's *Paths to Quality* is a good example of a quality rating system; run by the Indiana Family and Social Services Administration, its Web site allows parents to find ratings of child care centers they are considering (http://www.in.gov/fssa/2554.htm).

These quality scores are also used by the policy world in decisions about program funding and child care reform. Currently many states assess child care quality to determine the amount of money that is awarded to preschool programs in state support for the care of children from low income families. This process effectively ties a program's score to, among other things, the salaries of the program's staff. This type of real consequence in the use of a quality measure lends urgency to a determination of the validity of such measures.

Education Purpose

scores ←↑ funding

Starting from quite a different point and perspective, programs whose primary purpose is compensatory education may be very separate from programs for which caring is primary. Head Start programs do not typically provide full-day or year-round care, and are therefore not good sources of care for working parents,[2] but most Head Start programs are licensed and reviewed in ways similar to child care in their respective states. Prekindergarten programs funded by Title I or by state funds, on the other hand, are often located in public school buildings or connected to local education

agencies (LEAs); this connection, for example, is required for programs receiving state funding in Tennessee. Historically these programs have been resistant to coming under the supervision of the departments of health and human services and day care regulations.

In order to create a standard for evaluating these types of state-funded programs, the National Institute for Early Education Research (NIEER) developed a set of 10 Benchmarks on which states are graded each year. None of the Benchmarks requires actual observations of the classrooms. Instead they deal with regulatory issues such as the adoption of early learning standards in the state, the requirement that lead teachers in each classroom have a bachelor's degree, the condition that assistants have a child development associates (CDA) degree or equivalent, as well as issues of staff to child ratios and group size. NIEER gathers the data related to the Benchmarks each year and issues a yearbook giving state by state evaluations (Barnett et al., 2009).

Outcomes Related to Differences in Programmatic Goals

Measures of quality logically should be related to the types of outcomes desired. While it might be the case that a universal measure of quality could encompass the outcomes intended by both types of programs described above, it is unlikely. In the general literature, quality is described in terms relating to excellence, value, conformance to specifications, or meeting customer expectations (Reeves & Bednar, 1994). Since the expectations for these two types of programs are quite different, it has been difficult to find a single measure to capture the quality of both. It is important to note that this paper is focused on the expectations of two types of early childhood programs in the United States; other countries have different expectations about young children's development, have different programmatic structures, and therefore different quality standards.

For the caring mission, the emphasis has been more on *preventing* the presumed deleterious consequences of poor quality care. By assuring that child care environments are safe, organized, material-rich, and filled with positive teacher–child interactions, children should develop typically. The types of outcomes often examined as a function of *poor* quality care are socioemotional in nature (to be discussed in detail later). This perspective has been influential on the types of quality measures developed for these environments. Group care for young children in the United States is stressful, as studies by Gunnar and her colleagues have shown (Gunnar, Tout, de Haan, Pierce, & Stansbury, 1997; Watamura, Kryzer, & Robertson, 2009). The evidence is that children evinced greater stress as the day progressed even in high quality child care centers, though quality was found to ameliorate the effect.

For the education mission, much greater clarity would be expected for the definition of outcomes to be obtained. In the United States these programs were specifically established to prevent school failure for children from poor families. Determining which proximal outcomes at the end of pre-K will be associated with long-term school success is therefore important. One source of useful guidance is the analysis of data from six major longitudinal studies from the United States, Canada, and Great Britain (Duncan et al., 2007), findings confirmed by analyses from additional longitudinal studies (Hooper, Roberts, Sideris, Burchinal, & Zeisel, 2010). Gains in reading (or language and literacy at pre-K) during the pre-K and kindergarten years were found to be associated with better performance in reading at grades 3 to 5, a finding consistent with other longitudinal studies of reading (Schatschneider, Carlson, Francis, Foorman, & Fletcher, 2002). Also, early measures of children's math skills predicted later reading and math skills. Indeed, early measures of math were somewhat more predictive of later reading achievement than were early measures of reading skills. Finally, Duncan et al. found measures of cognitive self-regulation (distinguished from emotional regulation and social skills) to be a significant correlate of later achievement. Cognitive self-regulation consists of effortful control of attention, task persistence, sustaining attention, and inhibition of impulses.

Both Duncan et al. and Hooper et al. concluded that the best skills to effect in these prekindergarten programs are those related to math, reading, and attention, in that order. Knowing these should be the desired outcomes for education-focused prekindergarten programs provides a lens through which to judge measures of quality; the utility of a quality measure for these classrooms should be judged by its association with gains for children in these three areas.

Caring Mission: Measurements and Consequences of Quality Measures

There are a number of instruments designed to assess general quality in early child care environments, and several of these instruments have been shown to measure similar aspects of the classroom. These instruments differ in their concentration either on the classroom environment as a whole, including physical characteristics, or on instruction and interactions alone. Though each has a different focus, many of the instruments are consistently used in the assessment of early childhood classrooms both domestically and internationally. One instrument designed to assess quality is the Early Childhood Environment Rating Scale (ECERS; Harms & Clifford, 1980), which is perhaps the most widely used measure used to evaluate program quality (Sakai et al., 2003).

Because of its extensive use, the ECERS has become an anchor scale for other instruments. Many research studies using other instruments to assess quality correlate those instruments with the ECERS. Scores from the ECERS have been correlated with the Classroom Assessment Scoring System (CLASS; LaParo & Pianta, 2003) and the Emerging Academics Snapshot (Ritchie, Howes, Kraft-Sayre, &

Weiser, 2002) in reports from the National Center for Early Development and Learning's Multi-State Pre-Kindergarten Study (LaParo, Pianta, & Stuhlman, 2004; Pianta et al., 2005). Additionally, the ECERS has been correlated with the Caregiver Interaction Scale (CIS; Arnett, 1989), the Early Childhood Observation Form (ECOF; Stipek, Daniels, Galuzzo, & Milburn, 1992), and the Adult Involvement Scale (AIS; Howes & Stewart, 1987). Researchers have also found correlations between the ECERS and the Assessment Profile for Early Childhood Programs (Abbott-Shim & Sibley, 1987), a similar measure examining the quality of the classroom setting (Phillips, Mekos, Scarr, McCartney, & Abbott-Shim, 2000; Scarr, Eisenberg, & Deater-Deckard, 1994). Although some of these instruments relate more strongly to the ECERS than others, researchers have found statistically significant correlations between the ECERS (total score or subscale scores) and all of the above-mentioned measures (total score or subscale scores), some as high as $r = .91$.

Socioemotional Outcomes

It is difficult to address socioemotional development in relation to quality during the preschool years. Measures of socioemotional development are usually obtained through adult ratings, provided either by teachers or parents, each of which has its problems as will be described in this section. The better studies in this area use individuals not associated with the quality of the child care program to obtain the teacher ratings when children are in kindergarten or beyond. Positive findings from these sorts of studies would go a long way to validate the use of a measure like the ECERS for programs whose mission is in the care domain. There have been a number of such studies, and the findings are mixed.

Two studies followed children into elementary school whose preschools had been rated previously with the ECERS. In a study from the United Kingdom, Sylva et al. (2006) found ECERS scores to be related to first grade teacher ratings of children's cooperation and conformity. Higher scores on the ECERS total score as well as the Interaction scale in particular were associated with more positive social outcomes later. On the other hand, Peisner-Feinberg et al. (2001), using a composite score of quality that included the ECERS total, found no relationship between quality and second grade teachers' ratings of children's social competence. Both of these studies were focused on a heterogeneous population of children in community child care programs. It is conceivable that the quality of child care might be more important for children who come from high risk circumstances as the following studies examined.

The Three-City Study has followed a large sample of children from low-income families whose mothers were required to return to work following welfare reform in 1996 (Loeb, Fuller, Kagan, & Carrol, 2004; Votruba-Drzal, Coley, & Chase-Lansdale, 2004; Votruba-Drzal, Coley, Maldonado-Carreño, Li-Grining, & Chase-Lansdale, 2010).

The child care arrangements of the children were documented; child care centers were observed; and a quality score was determined from a combination of the ECERS and the Caregiver Interaction Scale (CIS). The initial study examined socioemotional competency in the children as preschoolers from ratings given by their mothers. Higher CIS scores were associated with fewer ratings of social problems by the mothers, while the ECERS total score was not (possibly because the ECERS scores in the three cities differed significantly from each other) (Loeb et al., 2004). In the same study, Votruba-Drzal et al. (2010) found an interaction between reports of problem behaviors, the ECERS total score, and time in care—the more hours a day children were in low quality care, the higher their externalizing scores. The importance of global child care quality emerged (that includes the teacher–child relationship) when they followed the children into middle grades: "The most consistent results from this analysis highlight the importance of quality of care in the reduction of problem behaviors" (Votruba-Drzal et al., 2010, p. 1469). The ability of high quality child care to reduce the later emergence of behavioral problems in children of poor families was particularly apparent for boys and for African Americans.

Thus it appears that a global quality rating like the EC-ERS, perhaps best in combination with a more in-depth measure of the teacher's interaction style with children, is associated with the kinds of outcomes with which care-mission programs are most concerned—the long-term social and emotional outcomes of early care. While child care quality appears in some studies to be an important factor for all children, the studies reviewed indicated that quality of early care rated generally and globally was especially important for males and African Americans from low income families. Assuming that programs with a mission of caring for young children should be most concerned with social and emotional long-term outcomes, the ECERS and other more focused interaction measures appear to document aspects of quality related to the purpose of the programs.

Academic and Cognitive Outcomes

The predictive utility of these global measures has been less successful in predicting cognitive outcomes for children. While one could argue that it was not the intention of programs with a caring mission to effect change in academic outcomes, measures like the ECERS have been used for just this sort of investigation. A primary difficulty with much of this research for determining the usefulness of this quality measure to track academic outcomes is the fact that many of the studies did not use pre and post measures and could not assess *gain across time* in relation to quality. As would be expected, there is a strong relationship between child care quality scores and children's skill levels, given that parents are the ones who choose and must pay for the programs. Parents with higher incomes and more education have many more choices and the freedom to choose higher

quality programs; their children are also likely to be better prepared for school. A few studies have examined change over time and related the amount of change in children's skills to measures of child care quality.

For example, in a longitudinal study exploring the effects of preschool, Sylva et al. (2006) examined 26 preschools in England for the relationship between child care environmental quality and children's development. She and her colleagues used both the ECERS and the ECERS-Extension (ECERS-E; Sylva, Siraj-Blatchford, & Taggart, 2003). The ECERS-E was developed as a supplement to the ECERS. Developers of the extension argued that the ECERS did not devote enough attention to the cognitive and pedagogical demands of the classroom necessary for children's intellectual and social development (Sylva et al., 2006). Three of the ECERS-E's four subscales refer to a specific academic environment (literacy, science, and math), and the fourth subscale examines the emphasis on diversity within the classroom.

On average, participating programs scored in the adequate to good range on the ECERS and in the adequate range on the ECERS-E. Children were assessed for their cognitive skills and language knowledge at age 3 and again at age 5 using the British Ability scales. At age 5, children were also given a test of letter recognition and phonological awareness. After controlling for age, pretest scores, and child and family background variables, quality as measured by the ECERS-E (both total and subscale scores) was significantly predictive of children's posttest scores on the prereading, general math concepts, and nonverbal reasoning skills assessed at age 5. Effect sizes, however, were fairly small, ranging from .11 to .17, indicating that the average difference in child scores due to increases in classroom quality was less than one fifth of a standard deviation. To illustrate what this effect size means from data in this study, the effect of average total ECERS-E scores on children's gains across the year in prereading skills was reported as approximately .17. The authors reported a raw grand mean and standard deviation for this outcome as 21.57 and 12.67, respectively, indicating fairly strong variability in this outcome across classrooms. An effect size of .17 indicates that differences in the prereading gains based on classroom quality (measured by the Extension of the ECERS) were likely around 2.15 points. However, the article authors did not explicitly state their results this way and, as such, it is difficult to interpret their original effect sizes—suffice it to say, they were modest. For the other outcomes measured, ECERS-E quality scores did not predict gains in spatial awareness or language.

On the other hand, the more commonly used quality measure, the total ECERS quality score, was not significantly related to gains in any of the child academic outcomes at age 5, although one of the subscales, Interaction, was related to gains in children's general math concepts scores at age 5 (with an effect size of .199).

Two studies of academic outcomes in connection to

global child care quality have results that seem both conflicting and hard to resolve, one reporting a significant effect on math outcomes but not reading outcomes, and the other reporting exactly the opposite. As part of a large-scale study of center-based child care and longitudinal child outcomes, the Cost, Quality, and Child Outcomes in Child Care Centers Study, researchers assessed program quality and child outcomes in child care, kindergarten, and second grade (Peisner-Feinberg et al., 2001). Preschool quality was measured with a combination of instruments, the ECERS, CIS, ECOF, and AIS, and the scores were combined through a principal components analysis to yield one composite quality index for each classroom. Children's receptive vocabulary, letter-word knowledge, and premath abilities were assessed in kindergarten and second grade. The quality of children's elementary school classrooms in kindergarten and second grade was also rated. Hierarchical regression analyses revealed that, when maternal education, ethnicity, gender, age, quality in kindergarten and second grade, and teacher–child relationship measures were included in the model, only math outcomes were significantly predicted by preschool quality, a similar finding to that of Sylva et al. (2006). Children from child care environments of higher quality tended to have higher math outcomes in second grade. Researchers did not find a predictive relationship between child care quality and vocabulary or letter-word outcomes.

In contrast to the findings of Peisner-Feinberg et al. (2001), a similar study examining the effects of child care experiences through sixth grade did not find a relationship between quality and math outcomes (Belsky et al., 2007). This study was part of the National Institute of Child Health and Human Development Study of Early Child Care and Youth Development that began in the 1990s and examined the effect of child care on longitudinal outcomes, following children from birth through sixth grade. Researchers observed the quality of child care that children experienced at 6, 15, 24, 36, and 54 months of age using the ORCE, a measure of the quality of the caregiver–target child interactions. During the formal elementary years, researchers used the COS to measure quality in first through fifth grade classrooms that included target children.

Both the ORCE and the COS differ from the ECERS and other global classroom measures in that each focuses on the individual target children and the environment around those children. Children's outcomes were assessed in preschool, first, third, and fifth grade, with either a letter-word knowledge task or general reading task (based on age), an applied problems mathematics assessment, and an assessment of expressive vocabulary knowledge. Controlling for child and family demographic measures, the only fifth-grade outcome that was significantly predicted by child care quality was expressive vocabulary. Children who experienced higher quality child care had slightly higher expressive vocabulary scores in fifth grade. This relationship was not found for the reading measure or the math measure; reading scores

were predicted by previous child care quality through kindergarten but not beyond.

Upon first glance, it seems confusing, especially for determining a good quality measure for child care, that two large longitudinal studies of child care quality and academic outcomes could report such contradictory findings. However, the two studies and the British study of Sylva and her colleagues share one common characteristic; none was experimental. Rather, all studies tracked children through their early years, measuring characteristics of their home and care experiences as they transitioned to and progressed through school. All three of these studies are important; child care is not an experience that lends itself easily to random assignment. When random assignment and group design are not utilized, however, differences in study groups, both before and after attrition, and differences in the experiences of those participants in study classrooms can be quite great. Descriptive studies of this type have been more common than experimental ones in the area of child care because in early childhood research it is really impossible to experiment with variations in the quality of care young children receive. This is not the case for programs with an education mission, as the next section will demonstrate.

Education Mission: Measurements and Consequences of Quality Measures

There are both more measures and more types of measures associated with assessing the quality of programs whose mission is compensatory education than there were with child care. The ECERS, however, has been used extensively to measure the quality of educationally oriented programs, especially those connected with Head Start, even though its roots are in child care. We have mentioned the efforts in England to develop a supplement to the ECERS that is focused specifically on the academic environment, the ECERS-E. Sylva and other international researchers are the only ones so far to have done much work with that measure, though it appears promising. The Early Language and Literacy Classroom Observation (ELLCO; Smith, Dickinson, Sangeorge, & Anastasopoulos, 2003) is a recent development that has an ECERS type format for its ratings together with a checklist for particular environmental features associated with literacy instruction. So far, it appears to have been used primarily for professional development, as an aid to help teachers set up their prekindergarten classrooms to focus on literacy skills. An instrument rapidly increasing in use is the Classroom Assessment Scoring System (CLASS; Pianta, La Paro, & Hamre, 2008). This rating system is structured differently from the ECERS; observers watch interactions within the classroom for a period of time, usually 20 to 30 minutes and then give 1 to 7 ratings on nine scales grouped into two or three dimensions. CLASS ratings can also be done from videotapes. In either case, total observation time can range from 2 hours to all day; in some studies observers visited the classrooms twice and averaged the ratings across the days. As with the ECERS, the focus of the observation is on the classroom as a whole, and the CLASS is focused particularly on the behavior of the teacher.

Other systems focus on individual children in the classroom. A picture of the classroom as a whole can be determined by aggregating scores from the individual children; alternatively, analyses are conducted with children's scores nested within classrooms. Three such measures are of note. The first is the Emerging Academics Snapshot (Ritchie et al., 2002), sometimes just referred to as *Snapshot*, the second is an eco-behavioral system developed by Kontos and Keyes (1999), and the third is a measure developed by Farran and colleagues specifically for use in prekindergarten classrooms, the Child Observation in Preschool (COP; Farran, & Son-Yarbrough, 2001; Farran, Son-Yarbrough, Silveri, & Culp, 1993).[3] Although not much research has been done linking child focused systems for examining quality with those focused on the teacher/whole classroom, they appear to be measuring different and independent attributes of quality in the classroom.

In the following sections, we will examine the effects of variations in quality as measured by one or more of these systems on the outcomes Duncan et al. (2007) and Hooper et al. (2010) demonstrated are important for prekindergarten programs focused on compensatory education: literacy/language, math, and attention. First, however, we will present information on attempts to link the NIEER Benchmarks to outcomes. These structural features related to regulations are quite different from attempts to capture within-classroom variability in quality. Structural characteristics have featured prominently in requirements for programs with a child care mission, though we did not review their effects in that section. These features are very important for programs with a compensatory education mission because they are key components of the NIEER Benchmarks being used as the guidelines for states establishing prekindergarten programs for children from low income families and because they have recently been questioned in several large studies.

Structural Quality and Outcomes

The most ambitious and comprehensive study of the relationship between structural characteristics and child outcomes can be found in the National Center for Early Development and Learning's Multi-State Study of Pre-Kindergarten (Multi-State) and the State-Wide Early Education Programs Study (SWEEP; Mashburn et al., 2008). These large studies have been rich sources of information about the effects of prekindergarten studies and will be referred to again in this chapter.

Although the NIEER Benchmarks are intended to rate overall state policies across 10 dimensions, Mashburn et al. created individual measures for the 671 classrooms included in the study. Because these are state-funded prekindergarten programs, many of the Benchmarks were met by 70% or more of the programs; for example, most tended to have teachers with bachelor's degrees, to have class sizes of 20 or under, and to have student–teacher ratios of 10:1. They served meals and provided family supports (though the latter is not always specified in detail). They were somewhat less likely to use a comprehensive curriculum, offer health services, or require their assistant teachers to have a CDA. It is important to list these details because it is variation in the latter three that is likely to carry the weight of prediction for outcomes, given the smaller amount of variation in the other Benchmarks.

Associations between gains in language, literacy, and math measures and the Benchmarks, collectively and individually, were examined. The total NIEER Benchmark score was related to none of the outcomes. Similarly none of the individual Benchmarks predicted gains on the outcomes with the exception of a negative relationship between serving meals and gains in receptive vocabulary, likely a function of the fact that programs serving poorer families are required to serve meals.

The relationship between teacher credentials and child outcomes has been the focus of intense study over the past few years. The same Multi-State study provided more detailed data on teacher preparation (years of teaching, highest degree earned, whether the teacher had a bachelor's degree or licensure) and found no effects on children's gains in language and literacy for any of the teacher preparation measures (Early et al., 2006). The only outcome for which teachers' education had a positive effect was a small one on math skills. Exploring the issue of teacher credentialing further and in samples with much greater variation in teachers' educational status is the recent analysis of data from seven major studies, the majority of which involved prekindergarten or Head Start programs (Early et al., 2007). The overwhelming conclusion across these seven studies is that neither the presence or absence of a bachelor's degree, having a teaching license, or majoring in early childhood education was related to children's gains on either language/literacy or math measures.

The surprising lack of relationship between structural measures of quality, especially teacher credentials, requires careful reflection. A belief in the importance of both structural characteristics and teacher credentials has been strong at least since the publication of *Children at the Center* (Roupp, Travers, Glantz, & Coelen, 1979); the requirement that teachers have a bachelor's degree is the primary recommendation of the National Research Council's 2001 report on preschool education. One possible explanation for the lack of relationship is two pronged: Children are not making a great deal of gain in these prekindergarten programs, especially in the areas of language and mathematics (Howes et al., 2008; U.S. Department of Health and Human Services, 2010), and teachers are not observed delivering very high quality instruction in their classrooms (e.g., Justice, Mashburn, Hamre, & Pianta, 2008). It appears that having a bachelor's degree is not sufficient to prepare teachers to be effective in classrooms where the purpose is to work specifically with children whose school entry skills are low. Teaching young children who are developmentally quite different from each other has many challenges (see Farran, 2005); working with children who are enrolling in formal education for the first time and who are there because they do not possess school entry skills is the most formidable challenge of all. It is not clear where teachers would have been expected to learn these unusual, multidimensional instructional skills, nor has there been sufficient research to determine if these skills could be obtained through professional development activities.

Language and Literacy Outcomes and Prekindergarten Quality

Data available from several longitudinal studies of prekindergarten quality have found small and mixed effects for quality on language and literacy gains over the prekindergarten year. The most common measure of language is the Peabody Picture Vocabulary Test (PPVT), a measure of receptive vocabulary, although the Multi-State Study and SWEEP also used the Oral Expression scale from the Oral and Written Language Scale (OWLS). Gains in the PPVT and OWLS were analyzed in relation to the ECERS total score and to the two CLASS dimensions: Emotional Support and Instructional Support. The findings are presented in several publications from this major study (e.g., Howes et al., 2008; Mashburn et al., 2008). None of the three quality measures predicted gains on the PPVT; the PPVT is a complex measure of language, focusing not just on nouns (names of things) but also on verbs, adjectives, and adverbs. The total score on the ECERS was associated with gains in expressive language measured by OWLS, but the effects were modest. ECERS total scores and the two CLASS dimensions were also examined for their effects on gains in literacy skills (e.g., letter naming, rhyming, print awareness; Guo, Piasta, Justice, & Kaderavek, 2010; Howes et al., 2008). There were similar, small effects (d = .06 and .07) on these outcomes. Overall, it appears that the gains were small in these programs, although there was classroom variation in how much children gained. However, it appears that the summary ratings from ECERS or CLASS are accounting for very little of the variation in children's developmental outcomes.

The CLASS observations have been explored in a different way. Rather than using summary scores (a variable analysis), LoCasale-Crouch created profiles of teachers from scores on the CLASS dimensions and item scores within each dimension (LoCasale-Couch et al., 2007). Profile 1 was labeled the "highest quality"—the teachers in this cluster had the highest CLASS scores on Emotional Support; these classrooms also had the highest ECERS scores. The profile with the lowest CLASS scores across all the dimensions was Profile 5. Profile 5 also had the lowest ECERS scores, included the most Head Start classrooms,

and enrolled the highest proportion of poor and minority children.

In a follow-up study, Curby and colleagues examined the fall and spring academic gains for children who were taught by teachers in each of the profiles (Curby et al., 2009). Children taught by Profile 2 teachers made substantially greater gains on the PPVT, the language measure, than children taught by teachers in Profile 5, with an effect size of d=.21. Teachers in Profile 2 were not as warm or emotionally supportive as teachers in Profile 1, but they had the highest scores on the CLASS item, Concept Development, of any of the profile clusters. Concept Development is one of the items scored under Instructional Support on the CLASS. No data on early literacy assessments were presented as outcomes even though these two reports are focused on findings from the Multi-State Study and SWEEP.

In sum, examining the quality of prekindergarten programs for its effects on language/literacy outcomes leads to the conclusion that there is a lot of work to do to find an instrument that will capture important differences among these classrooms that relate to child gain. Curby et al. (2009) report substantial classroom variance in the outcomes studied, but it appears that little of that variance is related to current measures of quality.

An alternative potential measure of quality and its relation to language and literacy involves focusing on child rather than teacher behavior. Most of the research in this area is descriptive, and few studies have tried to link summaries of child behavior to prekindergarten child outcomes. The Multi-State Study and SWEEP collected Snapshot, CLASS, and ECERS data from the same classrooms in which they assessed children's behaviors. These large studies only focused on four children per classroom; children were observed from the beginning of class to naptime on two different days. Chien et al. (2010) used Snapshot data to create profiles of children's time use across the day. Profile 1 was characterized as the "free play" profile and included 51% of the children; these children spent less time in preacademic activities than children in any of the other three profiles. Profile 2, constituting only 9% of the children observed, was labeled "individual instruction." Profile 2 children spent more time on activities like worksheets or computers, activities that involved individual work. Profile 3 (27%) spent more time in whole- and small-group instruction, while the 13% of the children in Profile 4 spent their time in scaffolded instruction.

These profiles of experience in prekindergarten classrooms were associated with gains in language and literacy measures in surprising ways. There were no differences in language outcomes among the four profiles for more complex measures of language like the PPVT and OWLS. On letter naming and writing legibly, children in Profile 2 made significantly more gains than children who had experiences associated with the other profiles. What is important is that the Profile 2 children from poor families made the most gains of any group including nonpoor children in the other profiles. While these effects are very small (*d*=. 04), the idea that we might capture the quality of a prekindergarten classroom by examining the profile of experiences children have during the day is intriguing. Of interest also is the fact that classroom environmental characteristics associated with this profile were not captured by the ECERS scores. In fact, the highest ECERS scores were found in classrooms characterized by Profile 1, which contained children who showed less growth in all measures compared to children in the other profiles.

In sum, efforts to link existing quality measures with gains in complex language skills have been unproductive for the most part. Children do not make much gain in these measures, and the gains they do make seem to be either unrelated or very modestly related to the currently extensively used quality measures of prekindergarten environments. The Snapshot approach appears promising, but it, too, only showed relationships to gains on the more concrete measures of literacy such as learning the names of letters and writing one's name.

Mathematics Skills and Prekindergarten Quality

Despite the fact that Duncan et al. (2007) and Hooper et al. (2010) listed mathematics skills as the first set of skills important to effect in prekindergarten programs (followed by reading and attention), much less attention has been paid to what facilitates the development of skills in this area for young children from poor environments. In fact, unlike language and literacy, one primary test of skill development dominates the research that has been done in early mathematics, the Woodcock Johnson III Applied Problems Subscale. Several of the studies already reviewed also included Applied Problems as a child measure; no study examined growth in mathematics skills in depth or as the sole focus of the study.

Growth in mathematics was predicted at about the same small magnitude of effect and by many of the same quality measures as the literacy measures. Ratings on the CLASS Instructional Support subscale predicted gains in Applied Problems (Mashburn et al., 2008), and, it follows, that children who had teachers in Profile 2, the profile with the highest Concept Development scores, made more gains in mathematics. The effect size of 0.19 on Applied Problems between children who had Profile 2 teachers and those whose teachers were Profile 5 is one of the largest obtained in this set of studies. Finally, children who displayed the Individual Instruction profile (Profile 2) also showed more gains in math as well as the literacy measures.

Another investigation of child behavior in prekindergarten and Head Start classrooms used the Child Observation in Preschool (COP) to measure such child behaviors as verbalizations, engagement, and time spent with various materials (Hofer, Cummings, & Farran, 2012). The COP is organized so that researchers can examine contingent probabilities, one of which involves children verbalizing while engaged in a math activity. In this large study of an early mathematics curriculum enacted in prekindergarten and Head Start classrooms, talking while engaged in math was relatively rare, but significantly associated with gains in mathematics across the prekindergarten year.

In sum, relatively less is known about the relationship between quality measures and mathematics development for children in prekindergarten classrooms. Promising areas for further study involve the complexity of teacher instruction, time to practice mathematics skills in individual work, and the encouragement of child verbalization when engaged with math tasks. It does seem as if these three areas could be straightforwardly incorporated into a measure of quality that includes the importance of mathematics gains among its foci.

Attention Skills and Prekindergarten Quality

The quality of prekindergarten classrooms associated with gains in attention has been characterized by neglect. Attention is a positive child behavior that belongs in a cluster of behaviors often called "learning dispositions" (Katz, 1999). One of the great difficulties in studying this important area is the lack of validated measures, especially any which are not based on teacher ratings. Teacher ratings of learning dispositions taken during the prekindergarten year are difficult to use as an outcome measure against which to investigate the effects of quality. This is especially the case if teachers are aware of the focus on dispositions and would like their children to make improvements. One of the few studies to focus on attention is the Dominguez, Vitiello, Maier, and Greenfield (2010) study of 275 children in 29 Head Start classrooms. Teachers rated children's "learning behaviors" three times over the prekindergarten year. Their classrooms were observed with the CLASS once during the year.

There was considerable variation among the classrooms in the rate of change in learning behaviors portrayed by the teachers. Organization was the only CLASS item related to these ratings, accounting for 1% of the variation in the rates of change in learning behavior. The lack of relationship between classroom quality measures and ratings of learning behaviors led the researchers to conclude that "additional classroom-level predictors should be examined" (p. 42).

Social competencies and problem behaviors have more often been investigated, although these are not the behaviors so far shown to have long term significance for school achievement. Social competence and problem behaviors are not measures of attention; in fact, Duncan et al. (2007) separated social skills ratings from attention ratings and found that social ratings accounted for very little of the variation in children's school achievement while, as already noted, early measures of attention were significant and independent predictors. The large multistate studies of the National Center for Early Development and Learning included measures of social competence and problem behaviors in the children, with ratings provided both by the prekindergarten teachers and, for a substantial number of children, their kindergarten teachers. During the prekindergarten year, changes in teacher ratings of children's social skills were predicted to a small degree by CLASS ratings of Emotional Support in the classroom (Mashburn et al., 2008); at the end of kindergarten the quality of children's prekindergarten experiences as captured by CLASS had little to no effect on teacher ratings (Curby et al., 2009). In fact, the strongest predictor of social skills was being female, and for having problem behaviors, being a member of a minority group.

The awareness of the importance of attention or learning dispositions is relatively recent, and little research has so far been published to investigate the quality of classrooms that might facilitate its development. But one can imagine that very different aspects of the environment could be involved in helping children learn to focus, persist, and pay attention than would be involved in learning other skills. Clever and careful thinking will be required.

Issues in Measuring Quality for Both the Care and Education Missions

The Use of Observer Ratings

The primary measures of the quality of child care and prekindergarten classrooms rely on observer ratings. For the following reasons the use of ratings may, in fact, contribute to the fact that quality has been such an ephemeral construct.

First, ratings require a judgment, and judgments have a subjective component. It is exceptionally difficult for raters to adopt enough of a shared perspective to insure that they are all rating the same qualities of teacher behaviors and classroom organization. Because of the difficulty of agreement, many studies reviewed in this chapter count as "agreement" when raters come within one point of each other. This tendency effectively reduces the scale metric; one rater's score of 3, for example, on CLASS and ECERS, could be rated as a 2 or a 4 and be counted as an agreement. But scores of 2 and 4 on both instruments are assumed to have quite different meanings.

Compounding the problem with the way agreement is determined is the fact that in many studies reliability is only established during the training phase using videotapes provided by the scale developers. This practice has at least two flaws: first, training reliability should always be followed up by field reliability across the length of the data collection period to check for observer drift especially in subjective ratings, and second, reliability should always be established in the type of setting in which data will be collected. A videotape is not the same stimulus as a live classroom; if observers are going to collect data in live classrooms, classrooms must be the places where reliability is obtained.

Second, rating scales begin with the assumption that qualities of classrooms can be described on continua from poor to exemplary along prespecified dimensions. Because

not enough empirical work has determined which particular behaviors of teachers and aspects of classroom organization are related to child outcomes of interest, rating scales have emerged from ideological beliefs in the importance of particular qualities. The ECERS reflects a perspective that the materials in the classroom, the ways they are organized, and the amount of time children are allowed to explore them freely are critical quality features. The empirical work required to determine which aspects of organization, which and how many types of materials, and how to facilitate children's focus during free play has not occurred. CLASS proceeds from a perspective that the emotional atmosphere of a classroom and the teachers' interactions with children are the critical quality features. The point is not to call these ideological perspectives into question but to demonstrate that these are *beliefs* and not empirically determined measures of quality demonstrated to link to the outcomes of interest to the programs. Curby et al. (2009) concluded their investigation of quality in prekindergarten classes by remarking, "Given their [prekindergarten programs] explicit intention of changing students' school readiness and performance trajectories, it is important to identify classroom practices that promote student learning and, thus could serve as a target for intervention" (p. 364) and, one might add, could serve as the basis for the development of a quality rating scale.

Child Perspective versus a Teacher/Classroom Perspective

Most of the current measures of quality focus on the classroom as a whole; in effect, investigating the classroom from the "top down." A "bottom up" or child perspective might provide a very different picture of classroom quality (e.g., Powell, Burchinal, File, & Kontos, 2008). Examining only what the teacher does can be misleading because it does not provide the observer with information about what children are actually receiving. Hofer (2006) conducted a small study of word learning by children during storybook reading. She supplemented pre and post assessments of the children's knowledge of words in the teacher-read stories with observations of child attention during whole group story reading (using the COP). Only the few children who had been rated as attentive during the storybook reading actually learned any of the words. On a measure of the quality of storybook reading, the teachers would have been rated highly. They read the stories well, called attention to the new words, and offered definitions. From a top-down perspective, they performed well, but from the children's perspective the lessons were mostly ineffective.

The national evaluation of Early Reading First (ERF) is a good example of the problems in taking a teacher-only perspective (Jackson et. al., 2007). Teachers in classrooms funded by ERF were observed and rated on literacy practices that would seem to reflect the types of instruction that should lead to strong literacy growth in children. The rating scales used were the ECERS and the Teacher Behavior Rating Scale (TBRS; Landry, Crawford, Gunnewig, & Swank, 2004). Teachers in ERF-funded classrooms were rated significantly higher on both ECERS and TBRS than prekindergarten teachers in nonfunded classrooms. Despite these large and significant differences in teacher behaviors, no differences were found in child outcomes between those children who had been in ERF classrooms and those who had not. Observing how the children were actually reacting to the increased literacy instruction would have been an informative supplement to these global quality ratings of teacher practices.

A global rating of the classroom by definition blurs individual differences among the children and assumes that the impact of the practices studied will be uniform. The *quality* of a prekindergarten classroom must be concerned with its connection to the needs of the children, even when those needs are quite varied. It may be possible to design a quality measure for early childhood that combines both a classroom and a child perspective, but to date, researchers seem to focus pretty exclusively on one or the other.

Conclusion

Finding a measure that can evaluate the quality of early childhood education has been complicated by the very different histories and missions of programs in this field. The caring mission involves a heterogeneous group of children and families. Children are cared for by adults other than their families away from their homes for large portions of the day. The original measures of quality developed to assess these environments helped to bring attention to the needs of young children and made states aware of their responsibilities to do more than just make sure these locations were healthy and safe. These quality measures have not, however, transferred effectively to programs with a compensatory education mission. For those programs, the clear implication of their mission is that children's academic outcomes must be improved. According to current wisdom, the academic outcomes most important for later school success are math, reading (language/literacy), and attention, and the small number of these skills provides a clear starting point for the development of measures that would be related to growth in these areas. None of the quality measures currently in the field have shown much capacity for identifying classrooms that are more effective in helping children learn those skills. We argue that the first step in developing an effective measure of classroom quality has got to be empirical investigations of the behaviors of teachers and children demonstrated to be linked to gains in those three skill areas.

Hughes (2010) has asserted that, "The identification of specific classroom transactions or processes that predict the growth in skills that enable children to make a successful transition to kindergarten and first grade is critical to realizing the promise of preschool education" (p.48). Only

observational measures that describe specific behaviors (of teachers and children) and examine those behaviors in relation to child growth will be useful in the identification of these important classroom transactions.

Notes

1. Unregulated child care programs exist in all states, as a type of underground economy, and may avoid even the basic licensing requirements.
2. While some Head Start programs arrange full day options for working parents, they are not required to by law. The most recent Head Start Program Standards to be found online (http://edocket.access.gpo.gov/cfr_2007/octqtr/45cfr1306.32.htm) list the following as the hours of care:

    (b) Center-based program option requirements. (1) Classes must operate for four or five days per week or some combination of four and five days per week. (2) Classes must operate for a minimum of three and one-half to a maximum of six hours per day with four hours being optimal." Moreover, programs do not operate year round: "Programs that operate for four days per week must provide at least 128 days per year of planned class operations. Programs that operate for five days per week must provide at least 160 days per year of planned class operations.

3. While the M-ORCE and its originator the ORCE are focused on individual children in the classroom, they have been used almost exclusively in studies of child care and will not be reviewed in this section.

References

Abbott-Shim, M., & Sibley, A. (1987). *Assessment profile for early childhood programs: Pre-school, infant and school age.* Atlanta, GA: Quality Assist.

Arnett, J. (1989). Caregivers in day-care centers: Does training matter? *Journal of Applied Developmental Psychology, 10,* 541–442.

Barnett, W. S., Epstein, D., Friedman, A., Sansanelli, R., & Hustedt, J. (2009). *The state of preschool 2009: State preschool yearbook.* Rutgers, NJ: National Institute for Early Education Research, Rutgers Graduate School of Education.

Belsky, J., Vandell, D. L., Burchinal, M., Clarke-Stewart, K. A., McCartney, K., & Owen, M. T. (2007, March/April). Are there long-term effects of child care? *Child Development, 78*(2), 681–701.

Chien, N., Howes, C., Burchinal, M., Pianta, R., Ritchie, S., Bryant, D., …Barbarin, O. (2010). Children's classroom engagement and school readiness gains in prekindergarten. *Child Development, 81,* 1534–1549.

Curby, T., LoCasale-Crouch, J., Konold, T., Pianta, R., Howes, C., Burchinal, M., …Barbarin, O. (2009). The relations of observed pre-k classroom quality profiles to children's achievement and social competence. *Early Education and Development, 20,* 346–372.

Dominguez, X., Vitiello, V., Maier, M., & Greenfield, D. (2010). A longitudinal examination of young children's learning behavior: Child-level and classroom-level predictors of change throughout the preschool year. *School Psychology Review, 39,* 29–47.

Duncan, G. J., Dowsett, C. J., Claessens, A., Magnuson, K., Huston, A. C., Klebanov, P., & Japel, C. (2007). School readiness and later achievement. *Developmental Psychology, 43*(6), 1428–1446.

Early, D., Bryant, D., Pianta, R., Clifford, R., Burchinal, M., Ritchie, S.,…Barbarin, O. (2006). Are teachers' education, major, and credentials related to classroom quality and children's gains in pre-kindergarten? *Early Childhood Research Quarterly, 21,* 174–195.

Early, D., Maxwell, K., Burchinal, M., Alva, S., Bender, R., Bryant, D.,…Zill, N. (2007). Teachers' education, classroom quality, and young children's academic skills: Results from seven studies of preschool programs. *Child Development, 78*, 558–580.

Ewing, D., & Matthews, H. (2005). *The potential of Title I for high quality preschool*. Washington, DC: The Center for Law and Social Policy.

Farran, D. C. (2005). Developing and implementing preventive intervention programs for children at risk: Poverty as a case in point. In M. Guralnik (Ed.), *A developmental systems approach to early intervention: National and international perspectives* (pp. 267–304). Baltimore, MD: Brookes.

Farran, D. C. (2007). Is education the way out of poverty? A reflection on the 40th anniversary of Head Start (with commentaries by James King and Bernard L. Charles). *Monographs of the Center for Research on Children's Development & Learning*, 3 (50 pages; ISBN: 0-9727709-2-5).

Farran, D. C., & Son-Yarbrough, W. (2001). Title I funded preschools as a developmental context for children's play and verbal behaviors. *Early Childhood Research Quarterly, 16*, 245–262.

Farran, D. C., Son-Yarbrough, W., Silveri, B., & Culp, A. (1993). Measuring the environment in public school preschools for disadvantaged children: What is developmentally appropriate? In S. Reifel (Ed.), *Advances in early education and day care* (pp. 75–93). Greenwich CT: JAI Press.

Gunnar, M. R., Tout, K., de Haan, M., Pierce, S., & Stansbury, K. (1997). Temperament, social competence, and adrenocortical activity in preschoolers. *Developmental Psychobiology, 31*, 65–85.

Guo, Y., Piasta, S., Justice, L., & Kaderavek, J. (2010). Relations among preschool teachers' self-efficacy, classroom quality, and children's language and literacy gains. *Teaching and Teacher Education, 26*, 1094–1103.

Harms, T., & Clifford, R. M. (1980). *The Early Childhood Environment Rating Scale*. New York: Teachers College Press.

Hofer, K. G. (2006, October). *Attention and vocabulary learning from shared book reading*. Poster session presented at Vanderbilt University's First Year Research Project Presentations, Department of Teaching and Learning, Nashville, TN.

Hofer, K. G., Cummings, T. C., & Farran, D. C. (2012). *Preparing prekindergarteners with math readiness skills: The effect of children's talk, focus, and engagement on math achievement*. Manuscript submitted for publication.

Hooper, S., Roberts, J., Sideris, J., Burchinal, M., & Zeisel, S. (2010). Longitudinal predictors of reading and math trajectories through middle school for African American versus Caucasian students across two samples. *Developmental Psychology, 46*, 1019–1029.

Howes, C., Burchinal, M., Pianta, R., Bryant, D., Early, D., Clifford, R., & Barbarin, O. (2008). Ready to learn? Children's re-academic achievement in pre-kindergarten programs. *Early Childhood Research Quarterly, 23*, 27–50.

Howes, C., & Stewart, P. (1987). Child's play with adults, toys, and peers: An examination of family and child care influences. *Developmental Psychology, 23*, 423–430.

Hughes, J. (2010). Identifying quality in preschool education: Progress and challenge. *School Psychology Review, 39*, 48–53.

Jackson, R., McCoy, A., Pistorino, C., Wilkinson, A., Burghardt, J., Clark, M., ...Swank, P. (2007). *National evaluation of Early Reading First: Final report*. U.S. Department of Education, Institute of Education Sciences, Washington, DC: U.S. Government Printing Office.

Justice, L., Mashburn, A., Hamre, B., & Pianta, R. (2008). Quality of language and literacy instruction in preschool classrooms serving at-risk pupils. *Early Childhood Research Quarterly, 23*, 51–68.

Katz, L. (1999). Another look at what young children should be learning. ERIC Digest, EDO-PS-99-5. Retrieved from ERIC database (ED430735).

Kontos, S., & Keyes, L. (1999). An ecobehavioral analysis of early childhood classrooms. *Early Childhood Research Quarterly, 14*, 35–50.

Landry, S., Crawford, A., Gunnewig, S., & Swank, P. (2004). *Teacher Behavior Rating Scale (TBRS)*. Houston, TX: Center for Improving the Readiness of Children for Learning and Education, unpublished research instrument.

LaParo, K. M., & Pianta, R. C. (2003). *CLASS: Classroom assessment scoring system*. Charlottesville: University of Virginia.

LaParo, K. M., Pianta, R. C., & Stuhlman, M. (2004, May). The classroom assessment scoring system: Findings from the prekindergarten year. *The Elementary School Journal, 104*(5), 409–426.

LoCasale-Crouch, J., Konold, T., Pianta, R., Howes, C., Burchinal, M., Bryant, D....Barbarin, O. (2007). Observed classroom quality profiles in state-funded pre-kindergarten programs and associations with teacher, program, and classroom characteristics. *Early Childhood Research Quarterly, 22*, 3–17.

Loeb, S., Fuller, B., Kagan, S., & Carrol, B. (2004). Child care in poor communities: Early learning effects of type, quality, and stability. *Child Development, 75*, 47–65.

Mashburn, A., Pianta, R., Hamre, B., Downer, J., Barbarin, O., Bryant, D.,...Howes, C. (2008). Measures of classroom quality in prekindergarten and children's development of academic, language, and social skills. *Child Development, 79*, 732–749.

Mitchell, A., Ripple, C., & Chanana, N. (1998). *Prekindergarten programs funded by the states: Essential elements for policy makers*. New York: Families and Work Institute.

National Association for the Education of Young Children (NAEYC). (2010, July). *Quality rating and improvement systems (QRIS) and the National Association for the Education of Young Children (NAEYC) accreditation*. NAECY Public Policy Fact Sheet. Washington, DC: Author.

National Research Council, Commission on Behavioral and Social Sciences and Education (2001). *Eager to learn: Educating our preschoolers*. (Committee on Early Childhood Pedagogy, B. T. Bowman, M. S. Donovan, & M. S. Burns, Eds.). Washington, DC: National Academy Press.

Peisner-Feinberg, E. S., Burchinal, M. R., Clifford, R. M., Culkin, M. L., Howes, C., Kagan, S. L., & Yazejian, N. (2001). The relation of preschool child-care quality to children's cognitive and social developmental trajectories through second grade. *Child Development, 72*(5), 1534–1553.

Phillips, D., Mekos, D., Scarr, S., McCartney, K., & Abbott-Shim, M. (2000). Within and beyond the classroom door: Assessing quality in child care centers. *Early Childhood Research Quarterly, 15*(4), 475–496.

Pianta, R., Howes, C., Burchinal, M., Bryant, D., Clifford, R., Early, D., Barbarin, O. (2005). Features of pre-kindergarten programs, classrooms, and teachers: Do they predict observed classroom quality and child-teacher interactions? *Applied Developmental Science, 9*(3), 144–159.

Pianta, R.C., La Paro, K., & Hamre, B. (2008). Classroom Assessment Scoring System. Baltimore, MD: Brookes.

Planty, M., Hussar, W., Snyder, T., Provasnik, S., Kena, G., Dinkes, R., ... Kemp, J. (2008). *The condition of education 2008* (NCES 2008-031). Washington, DC: National Center for Education Statistics, Institute of Education Sciences, U.S. Department of Education.

Powell, D., Burchinal, M., File, N., & Kontos, S. (2008). An eco-behavioral analysis of children's engagement in urban public school preschool classrooms. *Early Childhood Research Quarterly, 23*, 108–123.

Reeves, C. A., & Bednar, D. A. (1994, July). Defining quality: Alternatives and implications. *Academy of Management Review, 19*(3), 419–445.

Ritchie, S., Howes, C., Kraft-Sayre, M., & Weiser, B. (2002). *Emerging academics snapshot*. Los Angeles: University of California, Los Angeles.

Roupp, R., Travers, J., Glantz, F., & Coelen, C. 1979. *Children at the center: Final results of the national day care study*. Cambridge, MA: Abt Books.

Sakai, L. M., Whitebook, M., Wishard, A., & Howes, C. (2003). Evaluating the Early Childhood Environment Rating Scale (ECERS): Assessing differences between the first and revised edition. *Early Childhood Research Quarterly, 18*, 427–445.

Scarr, S., Eisenberg, M., & Deater-Deckard, K. (1994). Measurement of quality in child care centers. *Early Childhood Research Quarterly, 9*(2), 131–151.

Scarr, S., & Weinberg, R. (1986). The early childhood enterprise: Care and education of the young. *American Psychologist, 41,* 1140–1146.

Schatschneider, C., Carlson, C., Francis, D., Foorman, B., & Fletcher, J. (2002). Relationship of rapid automized naming and phonological awareness in early reading development: Implications for the double-deficit hypothesis. *Journal of Learning Disabilities, 35,* 245–256.

Smith, M., Dickinson, D., Sangeorge, A., & Anastasopoulos, L. (2003). Early language and literacy environment classroom observation (Research ed.). Baltimore, MD: Brookes.

Stipek, D., Daniels, D. Galuzzo, D., & Milburn, S. (1992). Characterizing early childhood education programs for poor and middle-class children. *Early Childhood Research Quarterly, 7,* 1–19.

Sylva, K., Siraj-Blatchford, I., & Taggart, B. (2003). *Assessing quality in the early years: Early Childhood Environment Rating Scale-Extension (ECERS-E): Four curricular subscales.* Stoke-on-Trent, England: Trentham.

Sylva, K., Siraj-Blatchford, I., Taggart, B., Sammons, P., Melhuish, E., Elliot, K., Totsika, V. (2006). Capturing quality in early childhood through environmental rating scales. *Early Childhood Research Quarterly, 21*(1), 76–92.

U.S. Department of Health and Human Services, Administration for Children and Families (2010, January). *Head Start impact study: Final report.* Washington, DC: Author.

Votruba-Drzal, E., Coley, R., Maldonado-Carreño, C., Li-Grining, C., & Chase-Lansdale, P. (2010). Child care and the development of behavior problems in economically disadvantaged children in middle childhood. *Child Development, 81,* 1460–1474.

Votruba-Drzal, E., Coley, R., & Chase-Lansdale, L. (2004). Child care and low-income children's development: Direct and moderated effects. *Child Development, 75,* 296–312.

Watamura, S. E., Kryzer, E. M., & Robertson, S.S. (2009). Cortisol patterns at home and child care: Afternoon differences and evening recovery in children attending very high quality full-day center-based child care. *Journal of Applied Developmental Psychology, 30*(4), 475–485.

About the Contributors

Monirah A. Al-Mansour is a Ph.D. Candidate in Early Childhood Education at The Pennsylvania State University in University Park. She received her Master's degree in Early Childhood Special Education at George Washington University. Her research interests are open-ended play as a vehicle for creative expression for young children, the use of recycled items and reusable resources to enhance creativity, and also children's play in nature.

Jim Anderson is a professor in the Department of Language and Literacy Education at the University of British Columbia where he teaches and conducts research in early literacy and family literacy. He worked for 15 years as a classroom teacher, reading specialist, school principal, language arts consultant, and assistant superintendent of education prior to joining UBC. He recently completed an intergenerational literacy project with immigrant and refugee families and is completing another bilingual family literacy project with new Canadian families.

Rebecca Anguiano is a doctoral candidate in School Psychology at the University of California, Berkeley. She helps edit the journal, *Human Development*. Her research interests include bilingual education, Latino parent involvement, and acculturation in Mexican immigrant families.

W. Steven Barnett is a Board of Governors Professor and Co-Director of the National Institute for Early Education Research (NIEER) at Rutgers University. His research includes studies of the economics of early care and education including costs and benefits, the long-term effects of preschool programs on children's learning and development, and the distribution of educational opportunities. Dr. Barnett earned his Ph.D. in economics at the University of Michigan. He has authored or co-authored over 160 publications including 14 books. Research interests include the economics of human development and practical policies for translating research findings into effective public investments. His best known works include: reviews of the research on long-term effects; benefit-cost analyses of the Perry Preschool and Abecedarian programs; randomized trials comparing alternative approaches to educating children including length of day, mono-lingual versus dual-language immersion, and the Tools of the Mind curriculum; and, the series of *State Preschool Yearbooks* providing annual state-by-state analyses of progress in public pre-K.

Marina Umaschi Bers is an associate professor at the Eliot-Pearson Department of Child Development and an adjunct professor in the Computer Science Department at Tufts University. She is the head of the interdisciplinary Developmental Technologies (DevTech) Research Group. Professor Bers earned her Ph.D. from the MIT Media Lab and received the Presidential Early Career Award for Scientist and Engineers (PECASE), the highest honor given by the U.S. government to promising and groundbreaking investigators who are starting their independent careers.

Karen Kohn Bradley is Associate Professor of Dance and Director of Graduate Studies in Theatre, Dance and Performance Studies in the new School of Theatre, Dance, and Performance Studies at the University of Maryland, College Park. She is the Government Affairs Director of the Board of the National Dance Education Organization, is on the Board of Directors of the Laban/Bartenieff Institute of Movement Studies where she is also Director of Research. Ms. Bradley reviewed the dance studies and wrote the essay on dance for the Arts Education Partnership's Critical Links: Learning in the Arts and Student Academic and Social Development. She was a chair of research for the National Dance Education Organization's Research in Dance Education project, and she has written several articles on dance education research. Bradley is a Certified Movement Analyst in Laban Movement Analysis and has worked in dance therapy, with learning disabled children, and in arts education research and policy. She has also worked as a classroom teacher, dance/movement therapist, massage and bodywork practitioner, and theatre choreographer, applying her training in LMA and related modalities to all.

Jeanne Brooks-Gunn, Ph.D. is the Virginia and Leonard Marx Professor of Child Development and Education at Teachers College and the College of Physicians and Surgeons at Columbia University and she directs the National Center for Children and Families (www.policyforchildren.org). She is interested in factors that contribute to both positive and negative outcomes across childhood, adolescence, and adulthood, with a particular focus on key social and biological transitions over the life course. She designs and evaluates intervention programs for children and parents (Early Head Start, Infant Health and Development Program, Head Start Quality Program). Other large-scale longitudinal studies include the Fragile Families and Child Well-being Study and the Project on Human Development in Chicago Neighborhoods (co-PI of both). She is the author of 4 books and more than 350 publications. She has been elected into the Institute of Medicine of the National Academies and she has received life-time achievement awards from the Society for Research in Child Development, American Academy of Political and Social Science, the American Psychological Society, American Psychological Association and Society for Research on Adolescence.

Nur Cayirdag received her M.A. degree in counseling psychology and givted and creative education. She is a Ph.D. candidate in counseling psychology. Her most recent article appears in the revised edition of the *Encyclopedia of Creativity*. She co-authored the book chapter "Quantitative Research on Creativity" published in the *Researching Creative Learning: Methods and Approaches* (edited by. Pat Thomson and Julian Sefton-Green). She is a member of the American Counseling Association, American Psychological Association, and National Association for Gifted Children.

Chavaughn A. Brown received her M.A. in School Psychology and Ph.D. in Applied Devleopmental Psychology from George Mason University. Her doctoral dissertation focused on the role of social-emotional competence in children's academic functioning. She currently serves as the Assessment and Evaluation Manager at AppleTree Institute for Education Innovation in Washington, DC.

Bette Chambers received a Ph.D. in Educational Psychology in 1990 from McGill University in Montreal, Quebec. She taught and researched early childhood education at Concordia University in Montreal for many years and then developed and evaluated early childhood programs at the Success for All Foundation in Baltimore, MD. She is currently Director of the Institute for Effective Education at the University of York. Professor Chambers develops and evaluates effective practices in early childhood and literacy education and promotes the use of evidence-based practices. She has authored or co-authored numerous articles, books, and practical guides for teachers, including *Let's Cooperate* and *Two Million Children: Success for All.*

Alan Cheung is an Associate Professor in the Center for Research and Reform in Education at Johns Hopkins University. His research areas include bilingual education, school reform, early childhood education, and research reviews. Dr. Cheung has authored and co-authored numerous articles and book chapters on school reform, technology infusion in literacy, and early childhood education.

Mary K. Cockburn is a Ph.D. candidate in the Department of Human Development and Family Studies at Purdue Uni-

versity. Her research interests focus on the quality of teachers' language and at-risk children's literary and language skills, and technological innovations in early childhood educator professional development programs.

Oli de Botton has wide ranging experience in education, both as a practitioner and a researcher. Before joining CfBT Education Trust, Oli was an English teacher and senior manager at a challenging London secondary school. He is a graduate of the Fast Track program for excellent teachers and was also a member of inaugural *Teach First* cohort for top graduates. Since leaving the classroom Oli has worked on a number of high profile evaluations for the UK government and has conducted research on behalf of several departments. He co-founded School 21, an academy in London, UK.

Susanne A. Denham is an applied developmental psychologist and professor of psychology at George Mason University. Her research focuses on the role of emotional competence in children's social and academic functioning. Denham's program on social-emotional assessment for school readiness is currently funded by the National Institute for Child Health and Human Development. As well, her work on the intra- and interpersonal contributors to children's forgiveness, and her longitudinal investigation on the development of emotional competence, are ongoing. She is the author of two books, *Emotional Development in Young Children* and, with Dr. Rosemary Burton, *Social and Emotional Prevention and Intervention Programming for Preschoolers,* and numerous scholarly articles. Having served as a member of numerous editorial boards, Denham is currently the editor of *Early Education and Development.* Denham received a M.A. from The Johns Hopkins University and a Ph.D. from the University of Maryland, Baltimore County.

Stacy DeZutter teaches methods of instruction and educational psychology at Millsaps College. She received her Ph.D. from Washington University in St. Louis, where she specialized in sociocultural perspectives on teaching and learning. DeZutter's recent research examines the social formation of teacher cognition and identity. She has also published on the sociocultural processes of literacy development in early childhood and on distributed creativity, a theory of group collaborative creation. Because her scholarship requires the coordination of individual and social planes of analysis, DeZutter's work includes innovation in research methodology, such as the development of a method for documenting cultural models (cognitive structures shared by members of a group) and the articulation of an advanced form of interaction analysis that allows the study of creative emergence within groups. Prior to earning her Ph.D., DeZutter taught drama, music, art, and media to grades PreK4 through 8.

Karen E. Diamond is Professor of Developmental Studies in the Department of Human Development and Family Studies at Purdue University. She is past Editor of the *Early Childhood Research Quarterly*. Her research focuses on classroom interventions to improve outcomes for preschool children from lower-income families and for children with disabilities.

Dale J. Epstein is an Investigator at Frank Porter Graham Child Development Institute at the University of North Carolina at Chapel Hill. She previously servesd as the coordinator of the *State Preschool Yearbook* for the National Institute for Early Education Research (NIEER) at Rutgers University, an annual report on pre-K policies across the United States. Her work focuses on early childhood policies at the state and national levels as well as professional development and evidence-based practices. Her research interests include parental involvement and early childhood education, especially among low-income and minority children and families. Her previous work includes research on early childhood initiatives in Kentucky and Arkansas. Dr. Epstein holds a Ph.D. in human development with specializations in early childhood education and developmental science from the University of Maryland.

Dale C. Farran was appointed in the fall of 1996 as a Professor in the Departments of Teaching and Learning, and Psychology and Human Development in Peabody College at Vanderbilt University; since 2009, she is also the Senior Associate Director of the Peabody Research Institute. Until July 2001, she served as Director of the Susan Gray School for Children, the largest early intervention program in Tennessee. Prior to coming to Peabody, she was a professor in the department of Human Development and Family Studies at the University of North Carolina at Greensboro where she also was chair from 1987 to 1995. Dr. Farran has been involved in research and intervention for high-risk children and youth for all of her professional career. She has conducted research at the Frank Porter Graham Child Development Center in Chapel Hill, NC and the Kamehameha Schools Early Education Project in Hawaii. Dr. Farran is the editor of two books both dealing with risk and poverty, the author of more than 80 journal articles and book chapters, and a regular presenter at national conferences. Her recent research emphasis is on evaluating the effectiveness of alternative preschool curricula for preparing children from low-income families to transition successfully to school. She has been Co-PI of a *Preschool Curriculum Evaluation Research* project, of a project to evaluate an Early Reading First county wide program in TN, and of two projects associated with a math scale up project being conducted in Tennessee, New York, and Massachusetts. Currently she is directing an evaluation of the *Tools of the Mind* curriculum and co-directing an evaluation of the State of Tennessee's Prekindergarten program.

Rebecca C. Fauth received her Ph.D. in Developmental Psychology from Columbia University in 2005. She currently resides in London, England where she serves as Principal Research Officer at the United Kingdom's National Children's Bureau (NCB). NCB is the leading UK charity to advocate on behalf of children, young people, and families, and those who work with them. For the NCF, Dr. Fauth leads program evaluations and synthesizes existing research knowledge in ways that inform programs to benefit children and families who are socioeconomically or otherwise at-risk.

Barbara H. Fiese is Professor of Human Development and Family Studies; Pampered Chef, Ltd. Endowed Chair in Family Resiliency; and director of the Family Resiliency Center at the University of Illinois at Urbana-Champaign. Dr. Fiese's research focuses on family level factors that promote health and well being in children at risk due to physical illness and/or poor child raising conditions. Her current research focuses on how family routines may promote healthy outcomes including reducing risk for childhood obesity and increasing medical adherence for children with asthma. She is an Associate Editor of the *Journal of Family Psychology* and serves on the editorial boards of *Family Process, Health Psychology*, and the *Journal of Pediatric Psychology*.

Lucia A. French, Ph.D. (University of Illinois, 1980) is a developmental psychologist on the faculty of the Margaret Warner Graduate School of Education and Human Development, University of Rochester. She has been a Spencer Fellow and a Fulbright Scholar. Her basic research has been at the intersection of language development and cognitive development; her applied research has focused on designing preschool curriculum that supports school readiness, particularly in the areas of language development and conceptual development. Since 1995, she has been involved in creating, evaluating, and refining an integrated preschool curriculum that supports children in exploring their everyday world (ScienceStart!/LiteraSci).

Bruce Fuller, professor of education and public policy, University of California, Berkeley, studies the interplay between policy makers and pluralistic families and children. His current effort, *Public Projects, Tribal Ties*, examines inventive local organizations that nurture richer relationships between practitioners and clients. Fuller is author of *Standardized Childhood* (Stanford University Press), *Inside Charter Schools* (Harvard University Press), and *Government Confronts Culture* (Taylor & Francis).

David L. Gallahue is Professor and Dean Emeritus of the School of Health, Physical Education, and Recreation (HPER) at Indiana University. He is active in the study of the applied aspects of the motor development and movement skill learning of young children and youth in physical activity and sport settings, and is the author of numerous textbooks, book chapters, and journal articles. His work has been translated into Chinese, Greek, Japanese, Portuguese, and Spanish.

Dr. Gallahue has been a visiting professor, guest lecturer and keynote speaker on over 300 occasions at universities and professional conferences in 23 countries. He is a Past-president of the National Association for Sport and Physical Education, a Past-chair of the Council on Physical Education for Children, and the Motor Development Academy. He is an elected member of the NASPE Hall-of-Fame, the American Academy of Kinesiology and the North American Society for HPER.SD. He also received the Healthy American Fitness Award in recognition of his work with young children. Dr. Gallahue has served as a consultant to numerous school districts as well as the California Department of Education on the development of *Preschool Learning Foundations in the Physical Development of Young Children*. Dr. Gallahue has been recognized nationally and internationally for scholarship and leadership focused on young children, and has received *Honorary Professorships* at Beijing Sport University and Chengdu Sport University, both in China.

Eugene E. García is presently Vice President for Education Partnerships at Arizona State University. He was Dean of the Mary Lou Fulton College of Education from 2002–2006. He joined ASU from the University of California, Berkeley where he was Dean of The Graduate School of Education. From 2004–2008 he chaired the National Task Force on Early Education for Hispanics funded by the Foundation for Child Development and four additional foundations. His most recent book is *Teaching and Learning in Two Languages: Bilingualism and Schooling in the United States* (2005).

John W. Gasko is the Director of Statewide Initiatives for the Children's Learning Institute at the University of Texas at Houston Health Science Center and serves as the Chair of Governor Rick Perry's Texas Early Learning Council. He is currently leading the development of Texas' first integrated early childhood health and education data system.

Jacqueline D. Goodway, Ph.D. is a faculty member in the area of motor development and elementary physical education in the School of Physical Activity and Educational Services at The Ohio State University. Dr. Goodway's research agenda focuses on issues associated with the promotion of motor skill development and physical activity in young children who are economically disadvantaged. She has published 34 peer-reviewed articles, over 50 published abstracts, 3 book chapters, and over 100 international and national presentations in this area. Dr. Goodway has received the Lolas E. Halverson Young Investigator award from the Motor Development Academy of the National As-

sociation of Sport and Physical Education (NASPE) and the Mabel Lee Award from the American Alliance of Health, Physical Education, Recreation and Dance (AAHPERD). Dr. Goodway is a Fellow of the Research Consortium of AAHPERD. Dr. Goodway has also served on national committees for NASPE and recently chaired the writing of the *"Active Start"* national physical activity guidelines for the 0- to 5-year-old age group. She has also served as a consultant on the development of Nickelodeon Fit, a Wii video game to promote physical activity for preschoolers. Dr. Goodway actively works to promote physical activity for young children in underserved communities.

Dominic F. Gullo is a professor of early childhood education at Drexel University in Philadelphia. His specializations within early childhood include assessment, curriculum development, and early language and cognitive development. Dom serves on numerous national boards, and is a former member of the Governing Board of the National Association for the Education of Young Children. He is the author of five books, two early childhood curricula, over 75 research-based publications and numerous book chapters. His research interests include studying the relative and long-range effects of full-day kindergarten and prekindergarten on children's achievement and social adaptation to school routine, particularly among at-risk and high-risk children. He has also completed writing the second edition of his book, *Understanding Assessment and Evaluation in Early Childhood Education* and is the Editor of the recent NAEYC publication *K-Today: Teaching and Learning in the Kindergarten Year*. He has presented his work both nationally and internationally.

Before becoming a professor, Dom taught for 5 years in the public schools at the prekindergarten and kindergarten levels and as a speech and language pathologist. He was also a teacher in the Head Start program. At the university level, he has taught courses in child development, assessment, language development and early literacy, curriculum, home, school, community relations, and research methods. He often serves as a consultant to school districts around the country in early childhood education, language and literacy, and assessment.

Susan E. Hill is an Associate Professor at the University of South Australia. She teaches courses on early literacy and early childhood curriculum. Her research interests are oral language and reading development, children's literature (new and old forms) and literacy pedagogy in early childhood. She is the author of a number of books, research articles and teacher-researcher reports on effective early childhood practices and new literacies. Relevant publications include: *Developing Early Literacy: Assessment and Teaching, Building Literacy Before School*, and *Mapping Multiliteracies: Children in the New Millennium*.

Kerry G. Hofer is a Research Associate at the Peabody Research Institute at Vanderbilt University. Hofer received her Ph.D. in Development, Learning, and Diversity from the Department of Teaching and Learning at Vanderbilt with a concentration on research methodology. She was supported in her doctoral program by the Institute of Educational Sciences (IES)/Experimental Education Research Training Program (ExpERT) predoctoral fellow training grant, a program focusing on developing the knowledge and skills necessary to conduct rigorous randomized trials in educational field settings. Following completion of her master's degree at the University of Tennessee at Chattanooga in Research Psychology, Hofer served as the Project Manager for a $1.2 million federal ECEPD grant that provided low-income childcare providers with professional development designed to foster children's language, literacy, and social skills. Her dissertation research took an in-depth look at the currently most widely-used measure of quality in early childcare environments. Currently, Hofer is working on several large-scale federally-funded grant projects, primarily focusing on analytic techniques. Current projects include the Tennessee State Pre-K Evaluation and Improving Language and Literacy Outcomes for Preschool Children at Highest Risk for Reading Problems. The majority of her research involves evaluations of early educational programs and practices.

Carollee Howes, Ph.D. is a Professor of Education (Psychological Studies in Education Division) at UCLA and has been the Principal Investigator on the National Child Care Staffing Study, The Family and Relative Care Study, the Cost Quality and Outcomes Study, and the Then and Now Study. She is Advisor to the current National Study of Child Care in Low Income Families and the National Head Start Families and Children Experiences and Random Assignment Studies. She also serves as a member of the Steering Committee of the National Consortium for the Evaluation of Early Head Start and as Principal Investigator and core leadership council member of the National Center for Development and Learning in Early Childhood. Dr. Howes' research focuses on children's experiences in child care, their concurrent and long-term outcomes from child care experiences, and efforts to improve child care quality. She has been active in public policy for children and families in the county, state, and nation.

Jason T. Hustedt is an Assistant Professor in the Department of Human Development and Family Studies at the University of Delaware. His work focuses on the impacts of state-funded pre-K initiatives on young children, federal and state early childhood policy, and preschoolers' and toddlers' interactions with their parents and peers. Dr. Hustedt recently completed a large-scale, multi-year evaluation of the statewide pre-K program in New Mexico. His previous work also includes evaluations of state early childhood initiatives in Arkansas and Rhode Island. He is

an expert on state pre-K policy across the United States, and was involved in developing and managing the *State Preschool Yearbook*, a report on pre-K policies in all 50 states issued annually by the National Institute for Early Education Research (NIEER) at Rutgers University. Dr. Hustedt has a Ph.D. in Developmental Psychology from Cornell University, with an emphasis in social and cognitive development. He also served as a Graduate Head Start Research Scholar and completed a postdoctoral fellowship in urban education at the University of Pennsylvania's Graduate School of Education.

James E. Johnson is Professor-In-Charge of Early Childhood Education at The Pennsylvania State University-University Park. He received a Ph.D. from Wayne State University in Life-Span Developmental Psychology in 1974, and was a Post-Doctoral Fellow at Educational Testing Service in Princeton, New Jersey and a former faculty member at the University of Wisconsin-Madison before joining Penn State in 1983. Past President of The Association for the Study of Play, he currently is Series Editor for their publication *Play & Culture Studies* and is a USA representative on the Scientific Committee of the International Council for Children's Play.

Elizabeth R. Kazakoff is a Ph.D. student in the DevTech Lab at the Eliot-Pearson Department of Child Development at Tufts University. She earned her B.S. in Psychology from Rensselaer Polytechnic Institute and her M.Ed. from Cambridge College.

Melissa K. Kelly teaches cognitive and developmental psychology at Millsaps College. She received her Ph.D. from the University of Illinois at Urbana-Champaign where her work focused on similarities and differences between mainland China and the United States. She was an NIMH training grant post-doctoral fellow at the University of California, Santa Cruz and focused on using census data to help define between-school economic, linguistic and ethnic differences in California. Her research focuses on the impact of task demands and social context on child development and learning.

Gary W. Ladd is the Cowden Distinguished Professor of Family and Human Development at Arizona State University. Previously, he was a Professor at Purdue University and the University of Illinois at Urbana-Champaign, and a Fellow at the Center for Advanced Studies in the Behavioral Sciences at Stanford. Ladd was Associate Editor for the scientific journals *Child Development* and the *Journal of Social and Personal Relationships*, and currently is Editor of *Merrill-Palmer Quarterly*. He is Director of the Pathways Project, a long-term study of children from kindergarten through high school. Ladd has published books, empirical studies, theoretical articles, and reviews of research on children's social development, and is interested in how socialization experiences with peers, parents, and teachers influence children's early psychological and school adjustment. His recent publications include *Children's Peer Relationships and Social Competence: A Century of Progress* (Yale University Press).

Marianne McTavish, Ph.D., is an Instructor in Emergent and Early Literacy in the Department of Language and Literacy Education at the University of British Columbia. She teaches courses in early childhood, language, and literacy in the teacher education and graduate programs. She taught K-3 and special education classes for 25 years prior to joining the faculty at UBC. Her research interests include the information literacy practices of young children in school and out-of-school contexts

Lyndsay Moffatt earned her Ph.D. in Literacy Education from the University of British Columbia. She is a full time Researcher Teacher Educator, and Lecturer in K-6 Literacy Curriculum and Pedagogy at the University of Western Sydney, Australia. Her current research interests include critical approaches to literacy education, discourse analysis, sociology of education, seeing research interviews as social interaction, and early childhood literacy curricula. She is currently involved in a multi-site examination of literacy curricula in full day Kindergarten classrooms.

Sue Nichols is a literacy researcher and teacher educator at the University of South Australia whose work crosses formal and informal sites of learning. Her research is published in the journals *Literacy, The Journal of Early Childhood Literacy, The Australian Journal of Language* and *Literacy and Early Years,* among others.

Michaelene M. Ostrosky is a Goldstick Family Scholar and Head of the Department of Special Education at the University of Illinois. Her research interests include: attitudes toward children with disabilities, social communication interventions, social emotional competence, and challenging behavior. She is especially interested in intervention strategies that help young children be successful as they interact socially and physically with the materials, adults, and peers within classroom and home settings.

John C. Ozmun is a Professor in the Division of Health and Human Performance at Indiana Wesleyan University. He received his doctorate from Indiana University with major areas in motor development and adapted physical education. Dr. Ozmun is active in the study of early childhood motor development and physical fitness. He is the co-author of the textbook Understanding Motor Development: Infants, Children, Adolescents, Adults, and has authored or co-authored several book chapters and journal articles. He has made numerous scholarly presentations in the area of early childhood motor development at the national and international levels.

Douglas R. Powell is Distinguished Professor in Purdue University's Department of Human Development and Family Studies. His research focuses on interventions to improve young children's school readiness, including effects of professional development on early childhood educators working in low-income communities.

Robert Rueda is the Stephen H. Crocker Professor of Education at the Rossier School of Education at the University of Southern California, with a courtesy appointment in Psychology. His research focuses on motivational and sociocultural processes in teaching and learning, with a particular focus on reading and literacy.

Mark A. Runco earned a Ph.D. in Cognitive Psychology from the Claremont Graduate School. His dissertation was on divergent thinking and he has studied creativity ever since. He founded the Creativity Research Journal over 20 years ago and remains Editor in Chief. He is currently the E. Paul Torrance Professor of Creative Studies at the University of Georgia, Athens. He is a Fellow and Past President of the American Psychological Association's Division 10 (Psychology, Art, and Creativity) and was Director of the Torrance Creativity Center at UGA from 2008 to 2010. His textbook on creativity, from 2007, has been translated into half a dozen languages, and he is co-editor of the *Encyclopedia of Creativity*.

Rebecca M. Ryan joined the Department of Psychology at Georgetown University in the Fall of 2009 after completing a Post-Doctoral Fellowship at the University of Chicago's Harris School of Public Policy Studies, a position she held since earning a Ph.D. in Developmental Psychology from Columbia University. Her research explores the implications of the recent rise in nonmarital childbirth for young children's well-being as well as the relationship between parenting and children's development more generally. Both strains of research explore two fundamental influences on children's early environments: the quality of parent-child interactions and parents' ability to invest time and money in children's environments. Her broad aim is to link developmental psychology to child and family policy in an effort to enrich both fields.

Kay Sanders is an Associate Professor of Child Development in the Department of Education & Child Development at Whittier College. Before her academic career, Dr. Sanders was a teacher of young children and a program director of child care programs for low-income families. This past work with young children who were recent immigrants, and / or members of language, ethnic, and racial minority groups is the driving force behind her work as a researcher. Her research focuses on child care experiences associated with culture, race and ethnicity; children's present and future development as a result of those experiences; and community-based practices that are connected with child care quality. She is a 2009 research fellow of the National Center for Research on Early Childhood Education, and a Principal Investigator of Exploring Child Care Cultural Congruency: Predictors and Pathways to Social and Emotional Outcomes in Kindergarten, Secondary Analyses of Data on Child Care, Department of Health and Human Services, Office of Planning, Research, and Evaluation.

Olivia N. Saracho is Professor of Education in the Department of Teaching, Learning, Policy and Leadership at the University of Maryland. She taught Head Start, preschool, kindergarten, and elementary classes. Her current research and writing is in the field of early childhood education. She has conducted research and written numerous articles on children's play and emergent literacy. She is the author of *An Integrated Play-based Curriculum for Young Children* (Routledge/Taylor & Francis). She has also edited books on children's play such as *Contemporary Perspectives on Play in Early Childhood Education* (Information Age Publishers) and *Multiple Perspectives on Play in Early Childhood Education* (State University of New York Press). She has also presented at national and international conferences in that areas of language, literacy, and play in early childhood education.

Casey M. Sechler is a doctoral student in Family and Human Development at Arizona State University. Her research interests include children's social and scholastic competence, particularly how social influences shape children's attitudes and behaviors regarding academic engagement and motivation.

Kelvin L. Seifert is professor of educational psychology at the University of Manitoba, Winnipeg, Canada. He earned a B.A. from Swarthmore College in 1967 and a Ph.D. from the University of Michigan in 1973, in a combined program in education and psychology. He has published numerous research articles on gender development of children, the professional development of early childhood teachers, and most recently on the development of effective strategies of blended learning. He is the author of five university textbooks about educational psychology and child development (four in print format, one in open-access online format). Currently he serves as co-editor of the online *Canadian Journal of Educational Administration and Policy*.

Serap Sevimli-Celik is a Ph.D. student and research assistant in Early Childhood Education at Pensylvania State University in University Park. She received her Master of Science degree in Physical Education and Sports Department. Her research interests are movement as active play and children's outdoor play environments.

Jon Shapiro is a Professor in the Department of Language and Literacy Education at the University of British Colum-

bia. His research interests lie in the areas of early reading and affective dimensions of literacy acquisition.

Robert E. Slavin is currently Director of the Center for Research and Reform in Education at Johns Hopkins University, part-time Professor at the Institute for Effective Education at the University of York (England), and Chairman of the Success for All Foundation. He received his B.A. in Psychology from Reed College in 1972, and his Ph.D. in Social Relations in 1975 from Johns Hopkins University. Dr. Slavin has authored or co-authored more than 300 articles and book chapters on such topics as cooperative learning, comprehensive school reform, ability grouping, school and classroom organization, desegregation, mainstreaming, research review, and evidence-based reform. Dr. Slavin is the author or co-author of 24 books, including *Educational Psychology: Theory into Practice* (Allyn & Bacon, 1986, 1988, 1991, 1994, 1997, 2000, 2003, 2006, 2009), *Cooperative Learning: Theory, Research, and Practice* (Allyn & Bacon, 1990, 1995), *Show Me the Evidence: Proven and Promising Programs for America's Schools* (Corwin, 1998), *Effective Programs for Latino Students* (Erlbaum, 2000), *Educational Research in the Age of Accountability* (Allyn & Bacon, 2007), and *Two Million Children: Success for All* (Corwin, 2009). He received the American Educational Research Association's Raymond B. Cattell Early Career Award for Programmatic Research in 1986, the Palmer O. Johnson award for the best article in an AERA journal in 1988, the Charles A. Dana award in 1994, the James Bryant Conant Award from the Education Commission of the States in 1998, the Outstanding Leadership in Education Award from the Horace Mann League in 1999, the Distinguished Services Award from the Council of Chief State School Officers in 2000, the AERA Review of Research Award in 2009, the Palmer O. Johnson Award for the best article in an AERA journal in 2008, and was appointed as a Member of the National Academy of Education in 2009 and an AERA Fellow in 2010.

Catherine Sophian is a Professor of Psychology at the University of Hawaii at Manoa. Her research is primarily concerned with the development of mathematical concepts in early childhood. She is the author of the 2007 book, *The Origins of Mathematical Knowledge in Childhood*, and co-author, with Barbara J. Dougherty, Alfinio Flores, and Everett Louis, of the NCTM volume, *Developing Essential Understanding of Number and Numeration for Teaching Mathematics in Pre-K-2*.

Bernard Spodek is Professor Emeritus of Early Childhood Education at the University of Illinois. He began his career in 1952 as an early childhood teacher in the New York City area. In 1962 he received his doctorate from Teachers College, Columbia University. In 1961, the year before graduation, he joined the University of Wisconsin-

Milwaukee. In 1965, he joined the University of Illinois where he conducted research in teacher education, curriculum, and other areas in early childhood education. His research and scholarly interests continued to be in the areas of curriculum, teaching, and teacher education in early childhood education. For several years, he was a member of the Bureau of Educational Research at the University of Illinois. From 1976 1978, he was President of the National Association for the Education of Young Children and from 2000 to 2008, he was President of the Pacific Early Childhood Education Research Association. During the 1983–1984 academic year, he served as Chair of the Early Childhood and Child Development Special Interest Group of the American Educational Research Association. Bernard Spodek was co-editor with Olivia N. Saracho of the *Yearbook in Early Childhood Education* Series (Teachers College Press). Between 2001 to 2010, he was co-editor of the *Contemporary Perspectives in Early Childhood Education* series (Information Age Publishers).

Christine Marmé Thompson is a professor in the School of Visual Arts at The Pennsylvania State University. Professor Thompson earned her Ph.D. in art education at The University of Iowa in 1985, and taught at the University of Illinois at Urbana-Champaign from 1985–2001. Her research focuses on issues of children's culture and art learning, with an emphasis on the dialogues that surround drawing events in early childhood settings. Professor Thompson's writings have appeared in national and international journals in art and early childhood education, and in numerous edited collections, and she has presented keynote addresses on art in early childhood in Taiwan, Korea, Finland, and the United States. She is co-editor, with Liora Bresler, of *The Arts in Children's Lives: Context, Culture, and Curriculum* (2002), published by Kluwer Academic Press, and editor of *The Visual Arts and Early Childhood Learning* (1995), published by the National Art Education Association (NAEA). She currently serves as co-editor of *The International Journal of Education and the Arts*, and as book review editor for *Visual Arts Research*. Dr. Thompson was president of the Seminar for Research in Art Education from 2003–2005, and Early Childhood Art Educators from 2008-2010. A member of the Council for Policy Studies in Art Education, Professor Thompson received the Mary Rouse Award (1995) and the June King Mc Fee Award (2005) from the Women's Caucus of NAEA, and the Marilyn Zurmuehlen Award (1994) from the Seminar for Research in Art Education.

Francis Wardle was raised on a small farm in Shropshire, England. He came to the United States with his family when he was 16 years old. Dr. Wardle has a B.S. from The Pennsylvania State University (Art Education), a M.S. from the University of Wisconsin (Cultural Foundations of Education), and a Ph.D. from the University of Kansas (Curriculum and Instruction, with a minor in Human Development and Family Life). He has taught elementary school in Taos, New Mexico, and Kansas City, Missouri; worked for Head Start as an educational manager, director, and national program evaluator; and was the National Education Director for Children's World Learning Centers. Presently, he teaches for Red Rocks Community College (Denver) and the University of Phoenix School of Advanced Studies (online), and writes for a variety of national and international books and journals. He is a member of the Colorado/Minas Gerais (Brazil) chapter of Partners of the Americas, a board member of Partners International, and a founding board member of Educacao do Instituto Estrela do Mar (Maceio, Alagoas, Brazil).

Ann-Marie Wiese is a Senior Research Associate with WestEd's Center for Child and Family Studies (CCFS). Ann-Marie Wiese focuses on issues related to the education of young dual language learners. Wiese has contributed to the development of preschool foundations in English language development and an accompanying curriculum framework. Prior to joining WestEd, she was an Assistant Professor of Education at the University of California at Santa Cruz, where she taught courses on first and second language acquisition, teaching methods for English language development, and bilingual literacy development and instruction. In 2007, she participated in a working group called by the National Task Force for Hispanics in Early Childhood Education.

Suzanne D. Woodring is a doctoral student at the Margaret Warner Graduate School of Education and Human Development, University of Rochester. Her research focuses on cognition in early childhood including knowledge transfer and other areas of mental functioning. She is also interested in the development and evaluation of learning curricula and environments designed to promote optimal learning experiences for young children.

David B. Yaden, Jr. is Professor of Language, Reading and Culture in the College of Education at the University of Arizona, and Director of the Center for Policy and Research on Children's Early Education and Development (PROCEED). He is also Co-Principal Investigator of the First Things First External Evaluation, an early childhood research consortium evaluating Arizona's early childhood initiative, First Things First. His research specializations include developmental issues in early childhood education, the acquisition of literacy and biliteracy in alphabetic and non-alphabetic scripts, family literacy, theories of reading disability, and the application developmental science methodologies to the acquisition of reading and writing.

Susan Young is senior lecturer in early childhood studies and music education at the University of Exeter. She is also senior research fellow at the Centre for International Research in Learning and Creativity in Education (CIRCLE), University of Roehampton, London and Associate of the Centre for Research in Early Childhood, Birmingham. She combines university lecturing with a range of freelance research, evaluation, and consultancy specializing in early years arts, music, and education. She originally trained as a pianist at the Royal College of Music London and spent her early career teaching music in secondary and primary schools and in a range of early years settings before gaining a Ph.D. in early childhood music from the University of Surrey. She has published widely in professional and academic journals and is frequently invited to present at conferences, both nationally and internationally. She has written several books, including *Music with the Under Fours* and *Music 3-5*. One of the founder members, she is now Chair of the European early childhood music network: MERYC.

SeonYeong Yu is an Assistant Professor in the Department of Teacher Education and Curriculum Studies at the University of Massachusetts Amherst. She was an early childhood special education teacher in Korea before starting her doctoral program in Special Education at the University of Illinois at Urbana-Champaign. Her research interests include young children's friendships and positive attitude development toward peers with disabilities.

Katherine M. Zinsser is a doctoral student in the applied developmental psychology program at George Mason University and serves as the Project Manager in Dr. Susanne Denham's Child Development Lab. She graduated from Smith College in Northampton, Massachusetts in 2005 and completed her M.A. at George Mason in 2010. Before coming to George Mason, Katherine worked with adolescents in a wilderness-based therapy program in Utah and has conducted research on juvenile justice substance abuse treatment programs. Her research focuses on contexts of emotional development and the social emotional antecedents to risky behavior choices by adolescents.

Index